BUSINESS ORGANIZATIONS IN A PLANNING CONTEXT

CASES, MATERIALS AND STUDY PROBLEMS

■ ■ ■

By

Dwight Drake
University of Washington School of Law

AMERICAN CASEBOOK SERIES®

WEST.

Mat #41409850

© 2013 LEG, Inc. d/b/a West Academic Publishing

610 Opperman Drive
St. Paul, MN 55123
1-800-313-9378

Printed in the United States of America

ISBN: 978-0-314-28735-9

To the wonderful souls who motivate me every day –
Audrey, B, Dene, Der, Jar, Jen, Julia, Justin, Kath, Laura,
Lauren, Lucy, Mark, Natalie, and Olivia

PREFACE

This book was written for an introductory corporations/business organizations course. I teach such a course to about 90 law students each year. For most students, this course is their first significant introduction to business law. For some students, this is the only course dealing with business organizations that they will take during their law school training. My overriding objective in this course is to expose the students to a broad range of fundamental entity, business, and planning concepts that I believe all lawyers should know something about. Plus, the subject matter is ideal for focusing on legal planning challenges and promoting the development of analytical, writing, teamwork and presentation skills.

I identified the following eight objectives when I set out to write this book for the course:

1. To ensure that the book's planning focus promotes the study of core corporate concepts, leading cases (e.g., *Aronson, Blasius, Van Gorkom, Caremark, Borak, TSC Industries, Cady Roberts, Weinberger, Unocal, Revlon,* etc.), and their progenies.

2. To illustrate the dynamics of corporate and business law by focusing on contemporary challenges and developments. Examples include the ever-evolving social, political, and charitable influence of large corporations; Sarbanes, Dodd-Frank, the JOBS Act of 2012; new say-on-pay challenges; the latest shareholder proposal trends; the dot.com boom, the fiscal crisis, and related corporate roles; *Citizens United* and its impact; director nomination developments; round two of advance notice bylaws; and more.

3. To offer mini case study problems throughout the book that provide a mechanism for teamwork and writing exercises and enable students to daily analyze and apply the substance of what they are reading to specific fact situations. There are 66 such case study problems in the book.

4. To include comprehensive discussions on a wide range of important planning challenges: choice-of entity, buy-sell agreements, employee protections, co-owner operational deal solutions, ethical challenges, shareholder debt, securities law exemptions, structuring business sales, director protections, oppression avoidance, corporate transition planning, controlling shareholder risks, hostile takeover bids, executive compensation, risk management, and more.

5. To provide practical, understandable discussions on core business literacy topics: reading financial statements; fundamental financial concepts (e.g., operating ratios, going concern value, leverage, etc.), business entity taxation, capital formation challenges, going public realties, bonds, mutual funds, drafting key organizational documents, business valuation techniques, and more.

6. To sequence topics in the book to strengthen the learning process. For example, an in-depth discussion of director fiduciary duties is helped if students have first studied the derivative litigation materials, which in turn is helped if students have preliminarily studied the basics of the business judgment rule. Similarly, a choice-of-entity planning discussion is helped if it follows the study of the structural basics of partnerships, LLCs and corporations and core business entity tax concepts. There are various sequencing links throughout the book.

7. To keep the book's core reading materials at about 900 pages and to include sufficient court opinions and statutory materials to eliminate the need for supplementary materials. With this subject matter, onerous daily reading assignments end up hurting the learning process for many students. This objective of the book required careful editing and an ongoing effort to be succinct in every discussion.

8. To support the book with a teacher's manual that provides answers to the case study problems, recaps court opinions, and explains how the book is used to develop analytical, writing, presentation, and teamwork skills in a large class. There is also a companion website that provides sample exam questions and a PowerPoint slide library that can help in providing students answers to the case study problems.

A key theme throughout the book is the importance of smart planning. During my decades of practice, I was continually amazed at how frequently a graduate had studied a body of business law without gaining any insights into the strategic challenges that business owners face on a regular basis. These graduates had never been exposed to basic business concepts and the planning process that drives the development of successful businesses.

I thank those who made direct contributes to this effort (each of whom is identified before his or her written words), the Seattle firm of Foster Pepper PLLC for use of the six forms included in Chapter 17, attorney Michael Heatherly for his proofreading help, and my wonderful assistant Ilse Allison.

Above all, I want to acknowledge a vitally important group that made this effort possible. It is those business owners and executives who I had the privilege of serving for many years. These clients did much more than just give me a means to earn a living and practice my craft. They taught me. They inspired me. The happiest, most energetic, most interesting, most effective, most fun-to-be-with people I have ever known are those who build businesses. Many of them experience the ongoing joy of self-discovery and improvement and, through example and words, inspire all in their midst. I will be forever grateful for the opportunity that I had to play in their league for many years.

DWIGHT DRAKE
Fall City, Washington
March 2013

SUMMARY OF CONTENTS

———

TABLE OF CONTENTS

———

Table of Cases

BUSINESS ORGANIZATIONS IN A PLANNING CONTEXT

CASES, MATERIALS AND STUDY PROBLEMS

CHAPTER 1

AGENCY: RISKS AND PLANNING CHALLENGES

A. SCOPE OF VICARIOUS LIABILITY

Nearly every business is dependent upon imperfect, fallible human resources. In order to carry out the mission of the enterprise and advance its profit-seeking activities, a company needs to hire employees to act for the business. The law exacts a price for this privilege. Perhaps it is more accurate to say that it extracts a responsibility. In general, the company is responsible and liable for those acts of its employees that are carried out within the scope of their employment. This is a true vicarious liability. It is one of the broadest forms of vicarious, third-party liability in the law. Planning requires an understanding of the scope of this exposure.

WARE v. TIMMONS
954 So.2d 545 (Ala. 2006)

SEE, Justice

William P. Ware, D.O., an anesthesiologist; Lil Hayes, a certified registered nurse anesthetist ("CRNA"); and Anesthesiology & Pain Medicine of Montgomery, P.C., appeal the trial court's judgment entered on a jury verdict in favor of Johnnie Timmons, as the administratrix of the estate of her daughter, Brandi Timmons, deceased. We reverse and remand.

On December 23, 1998, 17-year-old Brandi Timmons underwent elective surgery to correct an overbite. Approximately 15 minutes after that surgery was completed, CRNA Lil Hayes ("Nurse Hayes") decided to remove the breathing tube that was used to counteract the effects of anesthetization. An anesthesiologist was summoned over the hospital speaker system to monitor the removal of the tube, and Dr. Ware arrived to watch Nurse Hayes remove Brandi's breathing tube. Brandi was then disconnected from the equipment that monitored her vital signs and was moved to the postanesthesia care unit ("PACU").

Minutes after she was reconnected to monitoring equipment in the PACU, Brandi went into cardiac arrest. Tests later revealed that Brandi's brain had suffered irreversible damage caused by events that occurred during her recovery from anesthesia. Brandi later died as a result of the brain damage.

Johnnie Timmons, on behalf of her daughter's estate, sued Nurse Hayes; Dr. Ware; and Anesthesiology & Pain Medicine of Montgomery, P.C., Nurse Hayes and Dr. Ware's employer at the time of Brandi's surgery, alleging medical malpractice and wrongful death. Timmons alleged that the treatment Nurse Hayes provided to Brandi during her postoperative recovery fell below the applicable standard of care. Invoking the doctrine of respondeat superior, Timmons alleged that both Dr. Ware, as Nurse Hayes's supervising anesthesiologist, and Anesthesiology & Pain Medicine of Montgomery, P.C., as Nurse Hayes's employer, were vicariously liable for Nurse Hayes's conduct.

At trial, the defense objected to Timmons's claim that Dr. Ware could be held vicariously liable for Nurse Hayes's conduct, arguing that Nurse Hayes was an employee of Anesthesiology & Pain Medicine of Montgomery, P.C., not of Dr. Ware individually. The trial court overruled the objection and gave the jury the following instruction:

"I charge you-as it relates to agency and vicarious liability, I charge you the issue of agency in this case is not in dispute. Both the physician [Dr. Ware] and the CRNA [Nurse Hayes] were at all times working within the line and scope of their employment with Anesthesiology & Pain Medicine of Montgomery, P.C.

"Therefore, I charge you if you should return a verdict in favor of the plaintiff and against either Dr. Ware or Nurse Hayes, that necessarily requires that you also return a verdict in favor of the plaintiff against Anesthesiology & Pain Medicine of Montgomery, P.C., as well.

"The Court charges you further that the responsibility of Dr. Ware for the acts and omissions of Nurse Hayes is likewise not in dispute. Therefore, should you return a verdict in favor of the plaintiff and against [Nurse] Hayes, you must necessarily also return a verdict against Dr. Ware as well."

The jury returned a verdict against Nurse Hayes, Dr. Ware, and Anesthesiology & Pain Medicine of Montgomery, P.C. The trial court, entering a judgment on the jury's verdict, awarded Timmons $13.7 million in damages. Dr. Ware, Nurse Hayes, and Anesthesiology & Pain Medicine of Montgomery, P.C., appeal.

The trial court instructed the jury that based on the doctrine of respondeat superior Dr. Ware is liable as a matter of law for Nurse Hayes's tortious acts. Under that doctrine, a master shall be civilly liable for the tortious acts of his servant. The dispositive issue on this appeal is whether, as Dr. Ware argues, the trial court erred in instructing the jury as to his vicarious liability for the acts of Nurse Hayes.

Dr. Ware asserts that Timmons conceded at trial that Dr. Ware and Nurse Hayes were co-employees; therefore, Dr. Ware argues, he could not be held vicariously liable for Nurse Hayes's conduct under the doctrine of respondeat superior. Timmons argues, however, that she introduced uncontroverted evidence showing that Dr. Ware, as the supervising anesthesiologist, had a reserved right of control over Nurse Hayes's acts and omissions, which, she argues, entitled the trial court to charge the jury that Dr. Ware was vicariously liable for Nurse Hayes's conduct. Thus, we must first resolve the dispute between the parties concerning the appropriate standard for determining the applicability of the doctrine of respondeat superior to the relationship between Dr. Ware and Nurse Hayes.

A trial court's ruling on a question of law carries no presumption of correctness. Accordingly, this Court reviews de novo the trial court's conclusion as to the appropriate standard for determining whether a master-servant relationship exists.

"To recover against a defendant under the theory of respondeat superior, it is necessary for the plaintiff to establish the status of employer and employee-master and servant." *Hendley v. Springhill Mem'l Hosp.*, 575 So.2d 547, 550 (Ala.1990). We have previously stated that "[p]roof of a master and servant relationship is tested by the degree of control the alleged master retains over the alleged servant." *Gossett v. Twin County Cable T.V., Inc.*, 594 So.2d 635, 639 (Ala.1992). Thus, Timmons argues that Dr. Ware, as the supervising anesthesiologist, had a reserved right of control over Nurse Hayes's acts and omissions and is consequently liable under the doctrine of respondeat superior. The right-of-control test is pertinent to whether there is a master-servant relationship, but it is dispositive only when the question is the limited one of whether an alleged servant is in fact a servant or, instead, an independent contractor:

> "The test for determining whether a person is an agent or employee of another, rather than an independent contractor with that other person, is whether that other person has reserved the right of control over the means and method by which the person's work will be performed."
> *Martin v. Goodies Distrib.*, 695 So.2d 1175, 1177 (Ala.1997)

Dr. Ware does not assert that Nurse Hayes was an independent contractor, nor does he otherwise challenge Nurse Hayes's classification as a servant under the doctrine of respondeat superior. Instead, Dr. Ware questions the trial court's jury instruction that he was Nurse Hayes's master. He argues that he cannot be vicariously liable for the acts or omissions of Nurse Hayes because she was an employee of Anesthesiology & Pain Medicine of Montgomery, P.C., not of Dr. Ware individually.

We premise our opinion on Dr. Ware's argument to this Court on appeal that Dr. Ware could not be vicariously liable for the acts of an employee of Anesthesiology & Pain Medicine of Montgomery, P.C., simply because he was her supervisor. The dissent asserts that Dr. Ware and Nurse Hayes's "relationship as co-employees is incidental, and totally irrelevant, to their specific relationship at issue in this case of supervising anesthesiologist and supervised CRNA." However, the co-employee relationship simply cannot be irrelevant when, as the trial court instructed, "[b]oth the physician [Dr. Ware] and the CRNA [Nurse Hayes] were at all times working within the line and scope of their employment with Anesthesiology & Pain Medicine of Montgomery, P.C.," and that, for that reason, Anesthesiology & Pain Medicine of Montgomery, P.C., is vicariously liable for Nurse Hayes's actions. The only issue before this Court is the propriety of the trial court's instruction to the jury. In reviewing a trial court's jury instruction for reversible error, this Court is required to "look to the entirety of the trial court's charge." Consequently, the co-employee relationship between Nurse Hayes and Dr. Ware established by the first part of the trial court's instruction-which Timmons submitted to the trial court-is an integral part of any later analysis of Dr. Ware's vicarious liability.

The right-of-control test, by itself, "cannot provide a meaningful answer" to the question whether Dr. Ware was Nurse Hayes's master. In Hendrix v. Frisco Builders, Inc., we stated: "He is master who has the supreme choice, control and direction of the servant and whose will the servant represents in the ultimate result and in all its details." Thus, " [t]he general rule is that to constitute the relationship between master and servant for the purpose of fixing liability on the former for the acts of the latter under the doctrine of respondeat superior, it is indispensable that the right to select the person claimed to be a servant should exist. "

Because a master-servant relationship must be consensual, to qualify as a master, one must have the power to select the alleged servant. This requirement of consent derives not from the direct test for imposing vicarious liability, but from the elements necessary to form the agency relationship upon which the application of the doctrine of respondeat superior is founded. "As a reminder to the bench and bar of the analytical underpinnings involved in this analysis, we note that a master-servant relationship is a subgroup of principal-agent relationships; a master is a subspecies of principal and a servant is a subspecies of agent." Thus, "[t]he rules applicable generally to principal and agent as to the creation of the relation, delegability and capacity of the parties apply to master and servant." *Restatement (Second) of Agency* § 25 (1958).

Thus, the trial court's instruction on Dr. Ware's liability, submitted to the trial court by Timmons, is not error if the facts in the record demonstrate that the only rational conclusion to be drawn from the evidence is that Dr. Ware both had the reserved right to control Nurse Hayes's actions and also had entered into a consensual relationship with Nurse Hayes for the performance of Brandi's surgery.

Although the evidence introduced at trial amply supports the premise that Dr. Ware had the right of control over Nurse Hayes's actions, it does not support the premise that Dr. Ware, in his individual capacity, chose Nurse Hayes for Brandi's surgery. To the contrary, the evidence indicates that the right of selection of a CRNA to assist Dr. Ware resided in Anesthesiology & Pain Medicine of Montgomery, P.C...

The *Restatement (Second) of Agency* expressly rejects the idea that co-employees are vicariously liable for one another's torts:

> "The agent of a disclosed or partially disclosed principal is not subject to liability for the conduct of other agents unless he is at fault in appointing, supervising, or cooperating with them."

The trial court's decision to charge the jury that Dr. Ware was vicariously liable for Nurse Hayes's conduct apparently was based on the belief that a reserved right of control was the only factor Timmons needed to prove to establish that Dr. Ware was Nurse Hayes's master. Timmons reinforces that conclusion when she argues in support of the trial court's instruction that "Dr. Ware, as the supervising or directing anesthesiologist, necessarily must be liable in respondeat superior for the [CRNA] he is directing." However, if Dr. Ware merely controlled Nurse Hayes's acts in his capacity as a co-employee of Nurse Hayes, and as her supervisor, he is not by virtue of that relationship vicariously liable under the doctrine of respondeat superior.

Although we have concluded that Dr. Ware is not vicariously liable for Nurse Hayes's conduct based on his supervisory status alone, that determination does not end our inquiry. We may affirm the trial court's judgment if it is correct for any reason. Timmons argues that two additional facts support the trial court's decision to instruct the jury on vicarious liability as to Dr. Ware: (1) Dr. Ware's status as a professional practicing in a professional corporation, and (2) Dr. Ware's status as a primary shareholder in Anesthesiology & Pain Medicine of Montgomery, P.C.

Section 10-4-390(a), Ala.Code 1975, provides:

> "Every individual who renders professional services as an employee of a domestic or professional corporation shall be liable for any negligent or wrongful act or omission in which he personally participates to the same extent as if he rendered such services as a sole practitioner."

At trial, Dr. Ware described himself as practicing medicine at Anesthesiology & Pain Medicine of Montgomery, P.C., a professional corporation. Timmons argues that because Dr. Ware participated in Brandi's surgery, he is vicariously liable under § 10-4-390, Ala.Code 1975, for Nurse Hayes's conduct to the same extent that he would have been had he supervised Nurse Hayes as a sole practitioner. Thus, Timmons argues, the statute-in abrogation of the common-law doctrine of respondeat superior-imposes on supervisors who are professionals practicing in a professional corporation vicarious liability for the conduct of their subordinates.

By its text, § 10-4-390(a), Ala.Code 1975, imposes on Dr. Ware direct liability only for his own negligence, wrongful acts, or omissions. It states that the professional "shall be liable for any negligent or wrongful act or omission in which he personally participates." Dr. Ware's status as a physician practicing in a professional corporation does not supply a basis for affirming the trial court's judgment on the basis that it did not err in instructing the jury that Dr. Ware is vicariously liable for Nurse Hayes's conduct.

Dr. Ware described himself as a partner in Anesthesiology & Pain Medicine of Montgomery, P.C. Timmons argues that Dr. Ware's status as a shareholder in a professional corporation subjects him to vicarious liability for Nurse Hayes's conduct. However, § 10-4-390(b), Ala.Code 1975, states:

> "The personal liability of a shareholder, employee, director or officer of a domestic professional corporation ... shall be no greater in any respect than that of a shareholder, employee, director or officer of a corporation organized under the Alabama Business Corporation Act."

This Court recognizes that the common-law doctrine of respondeat superior governs the vicarious liability of corporations organized under the Alabama Business Corporation Act. Thus, § 10-4-390(b) does not impose vicarious liability where the doctrine of respondeat superior would not do so. Accordingly, Dr. Ware's testimony regarding his status as a shareholder of Anesthesiology & Pain Medicine of Montgomery, P.C., does not permit the conclusion that he is vicariously liable for Nurse Hayes's acts and omissions. The jury instruction therefore cannot be held to be proper on this basis.

Giving the jury instruction that Dr. Ware is vicariously liable for Nurse Hayes's conduct was reversible error. Absent evidence showing that Dr. Ware had the ability, in his individual capacity, to select and to dismiss Nurse Hayes, not only was Timmons not entitled to the jury instruction given by the trial court, but also, as a matter of law, the jury was not entitled to hold Dr. Ware liable based on Nurse Hayes's conduct. Thus, the trial court's erroneous instruction prejudiced Dr. Ware by affecting his substantial rights.

REVERSED AND REMANDED.

HARWOOD, Justice (dissenting)

I dissent. The majority reverses the trial court's judgment on the basis that Johnnie Timmons, the plaintiff, failed to establish that the defendant William P. Ware, D.O., "had a right of selection" with respect to the services of a certified registered nurse anesthetist ("CRNA"), Lil Hayes ("Nurse Hayes"), also a defendant below.

Concerning the right of control, and in otherwise undertaking to state, with purported completeness, the appropriate test for determining whether a servant in the general employ of one party has become, for the time being, the servant of another as special master, this Court has had the following to say:

> He is master who has the supreme choice, control, and direction of the servant and whose will the servant represents in the ultimate result and in all its details. The ultimate test in determining whether an employee has become a loaned servant is a determination of whose work the employee was doing and under whose control he was doing it. It is the reserved right of control, rather than the actual exercise of control, that furnishes the true test of the relationship. 'Power to control determines responsibility.' Martin v. Anniston Foundry Co., 259 Ala. [633,] 637, 68 So.2d [323,] 328 [(1953)]."

The evidence is overwhelmingly clear to the fact that Dr. Ware had "the supreme choice, control, and direction" of Nurse Hayes and it was his will she represented "in the ultimate results and in all of its details."

The fact that Dr. Ware and Nurse Hayes had separate responsibilities is of no consequence because, as previously discussed, he had authoritative control over all of her activities and thus was "responsible" for Nurse Hayes's "responsibilities." Likewise, the fact that many of the standard-of-care criticisms of Nurse Hayes by Timmons's expert related to "care, treatment, and judgments" by her at a point when Dr. Ware was not physically present is irrelevant because, as also earlier noted, Nurse Hayes was required by statute at all times to be functioning under Dr. Ware's direction and he was to be "immediately available." Defendants simply have not established cognizable reversible error by their argument in their principal appellate brief concerning the loaned-servant issue.

Timmons has been clear at all times, both before the trial court and this Court, in distinguishing between the relationship Dr. Ware and Nurse Hayes had as co-employees of the professional corporation and their relationship as supervising anesthesiologist and supervised CRNA. The two relationships are separate and independent. For purposes of analysis, Nurse Hayes could just as well have been the employee of another anesthesiology group or could have been working as a freelance CRNA, without any connection with the professional corporation, simply being assigned to work under Dr. Ware's direction on the occasion in question.

The majority opinion ignores the critical distinction between the relationship actually at issue in this case-that of directing anesthesiologist and directed CRNA, on the one hand, and the separate relationship of Dr. Ware and Nurse Hayes as co-employees of the professional corporation, on the other. Their relationship as co-employees is incidental, and totally irrelevant, to their specific relationship at issue in this case of supervising anesthesiologist and supervised CRNA. Dr. Ware's right of control over Nurse Hayes did not arise out of their relationship as co-employees and was not delegated to him by the professional corporation; it arose out of their separate and independent relationship as supervising anesthesiologist and supervised CRNA.

Accordingly, my analysis in this dissent has no implications for conventional intracompany supervisor/subordinate relationships, or the usual "chain of command" flow of responsibilities in a business or corporate setting. I focus solely on the singular and unique relationship and interaction between a paired anesthesiologist and CRNA, based on the dynamics peculiar to that relationship. Obviously, no corporate entity, whether a professional corporation or otherwise, can presume to practice medicine or interfere with the relationship between caregiver and patient. The professional corporation could not direct or supervise Nurse Hayes in the care she provided Brandi. Only Dr. Ware, *as* directing anesthesiologist, had that "right of control."

GALLANT INS. CO. v. ISAAC
732 N.E.2d 1262 (Ind.App.,2000)

RILEY, Judge

Plaintiff-Appellant, Gallant Insurance Company (Gallant), appeals from the trial court's grant of summary judgment in favor of Defendants-Appellees, Christina Isaac (Isaac) and Loretta Davis (Davis) (hereinafter referred to collectively as "Insured"), on its complaint for declaratory judgment regarding its insurance coverage of Isaac's accident.

Thompson-Harris is an independent insurance agent. Its authority includes the power to bind Gallant on new insurance policies, as well as interim policy endorsement such as adding a new driver, or changing and adding a vehicle insured under a policy. Although no written agreement describes the relation between Gallant and Thompson-Harris, the Record indicates Gallant became bound to provide insurance coverage at the time and date on which Thompson-Harris faxed or called the required information to Gallant's producing agent, and premiums were paid to Thompson-Harris.

On June 2, 1994, Gallant issued automobile insurance coverage on Isaac's 1986 Pontiac Fiero through its independent agent, Thompson-Harris. Thompson-Harris provided Isaac with a printed quote for liability insurance coverage, by Gallant only. That same day, Isaac decided to apply for coverage with Gallant through Thompson-Harris. Isaac signed a pre-application checklist as the "applicant" and the insurance agent counter-signed the same document as "agent." The printed application form, which had been filled out by the agent, showed that Isaac's coverage was bound as of 2:06 p.m. on June 2, 1994 until December 2, 1994.

The policy issued by Gallant had "CONDITIONS" regarding "Policy Period" and "Premium." With regard to "CHANGES" made to its conditions, the policy states that an agent shall not waive or change any part of the policy, except by endorsement issued to form a part of the policy, which is signed by a duly authorized representative of the company. The policy also stated that the written policy embodied all agreements existing between the insured, the company and all agents relating to the insurance.

On the last day of her insurance coverage, Isaac traded her 1986 Pontiac Fiero for a 1988 Pontiac Grand Prix. To obtain the newly purchased car, the financing bank required Isaac to obtain full coverage on it. That same day, Isaac contacted Thompson-Harris to notify it that she was purchasing the new car, and to discuss enhancing the existing insurance policy to meet bank requirements. Isaac told a Thompson-Harris employee that she must obtain "full insurance coverage" as a condition to receiving a loan. She also told the employee at Thompson-Harris that her current coverage expires on December 3, 1994, the next day.

In response, the Thompson-Harris employee informed Isaac that because their agency was about to close for the weekend, she would immediately "bind" coverage on the 1988 Grand Prix. They decided that Isaac would come in to Thompson-Harris on Monday, December 5, 1994, to complete the paperwork and pay the down payment on the premium. The employee also informed Isaac that the new coverage on her Pontiac Grand Prix would include the same coverage existing from her Pontiac Fiero, along with additional coverage to comply with conditions set by the bank.

The next day, on December 3, 1994, a different employee completed the "Personal Policy Change Request." This form deleted the 1987 Pontiac Fiero from Isaac's Policy and replaced it with the 1988 Pontiac Grand Prix. It also added additional coverage to the policy as well as additional loss payee/lienholder. The Personal Policy Change Request listed the "Agency" and "Producer" as Thompson-Harris, and stated that the "effective date of change" was December 3, 1994. Towards the bottom of the form, the Thompson-Harris employee typed "[s]he will be in at 9:00 a.m. Monday, 12/5/94, to [sic] down [sic] on renewal. What is [sic] new rate? Thanks." This form, which requested the listed changes, was faxed to Insurance Brokers of Indiana, Inc., on December 3, 1994.

On December 4, 1994, while driving her Pontiac Grand Prix, Isaac collided with another car in which Davis was a passenger. The next day, as planned, Isaac went to Thompson-Harris and paid $133.00 down payment on the new insurance policy. She also reported the accident. Thompson-Harris completed an "Indiana Operator's Vehicle Crash Report," which notified the State Police that Isaac had insurance coverage at the time of the accident, on December, 4, 1994. Thompson-Harris completed that form on behalf of Gallant. Later, on or about December 22, 1994, Gallant renewed Isaac's insurance policy, with an effective period of December 6, 1994 to June 6, 1995.

Soon afterwards, Gallant brought its complaint for declaratory judgment regarding its insurance coverage of Isaac's accident. It sought a judgment that stated Gallant was not liable for any losses incurred because the policy was not in force.

Gallant contends that Isaac's insurance coverage had lapsed at the time Isaac's accident occurred because the policy renewal premium was not paid as dictated in the policy. It is undisputed that Thompson-Harris is Gallant's independent insurance agent. However, Gallant insists that Thompson-Harris had no authority to renew the insurance policy or orally contract in a manner contrary to what the policy states without the approval of Gallant's producing agent, Insurance Brokers of Indiana, Inc. We disagree.

Gallant argues that Thompson-Harris had no actual or apparent authority to renew the insurance policy or orally contract to do so. Specifically, Gallant contends that it, as a principal, did not manifest any act toward Thompson-Harris or Isaac, whether directly or indirectly, that may have granted such authority. However, because we find that neither an actual nor apparent authority theory applies to the particular facts of this case, we instead address *sua sponte* Thompson-Harris's authority to act as Gallant's agent under an inherent authority theory.

Inherent agency power indicates the power of an agent that is derived not from authority, apparent or estoppel, but from the agency relation itself. This inherent authority theory exists for the protection of persons harmed by or dealing with a principal's servant or agent.

Inherent authority exists to hold an agent's principal liable when the acts in question (1) usually accompany or are incidental to transactions which the agent is authorized to conduct, even though they are forbidden by the principal; (2) the third party believes that the agent is authorized to do them; (3) and that third party has no notice that the agent is not so authorized.

In the case at bar, Thompson-Harris's renewal of Isaac's insurance policy constitutes an act which usually accompanies or is incidental to insurance transactions that it is authorized to conduct. Examining Gallant and Thompson-Harris's agency relation reveals that, as an agent, Thompson-Harris *was authorized to bind Gallant* on new insurance policies, as well as interim policy endorsements, such as changing and adding new drivers, or changing or adding the vehicle insured.

Next, a court looks to the *agent's* direct and indirect manifestations and determines whether the third party could have reasonably believed that the agent had authority to conduct the act in question. Here, Isaac could have reasonably believed that Thompson-Harris had authority to orally bind coverage. Isaac's past dealings were all through Thompson-Harris, whether involving payment of premiums, changing or including a driver, or requesting a new estimate. Direct communication between Gallant and Isaac never occurred. Thus, it was reasonable for Isaac to take at face value Thompson-Harris's communication that coverage was bound, and that she could come in at the end of the weekend to pay for the policy renewal.

In the case at bar, Isaac lacked notice that Thompson-Harris did not have authority to verbally bind coverage. The Record fails to indicate whether Isaac was aware that Thompson-Harris had limited authority. It does not mention whether Isaac knew of expressed limitations about the authority of Thompson-Harris to bind insurance coverage without actual payment. Therefore, we find Isaac did not have notice that Thompson-Harris was not authorized to verbally bind coverage, without payment.

Gallant and Isaac are two innocent parties who have suffered due to Thompson-Harris's betrayal of trust. Thompson-Harris was not authorized to verbally bind coverage without first receiving payment. Gallant, however, is the business enterprise better situated to "bear the burden of the losses created by the mistakes" of Thompson-Harris's overzealousness. Such liability may stimulate Gallant's watchfulness in selecting and supervising its agents, as well as taking affirmative acts to avoid mishaps as we witnessed here. As such, we conclude that the Record supports the trial court's findings that Isaac's insurance policy was in full force and effect on December 3, 1994, because Thompson-Harris had the inherent authority to bind coverage by Gallant verbally.

Affirmed.

B. PROTECTING AN ENTERPRISE FROM ACTS OF ITS EMPLOYEES

CASE PROBLEM 1-1

Brand Insurances Services ("Brand") is a large, professional insurance agency. Its target customers include successful business owners, professionals, and executives. It has a 260-person sales force, all of whom are employees of Brand. Its top performing salesperson, by a huge margin, is Luke Jones. Luke's annual volume typically exceeds that of Brand's next two highest producers.

Luke's success is attributable to three factors. First, he is a workaholic in the truest sense. Second, he loves entertaining clients and referral sources, and he spends a large portion of his high income on expensive parties and exotic weekend trips that, in the words of Brand's senior management, "often push the limits." Beyond the ever-flowing booze, rumors of drugs and adult thrills abound.

The third element of Luke's success is his determination to not let a client's lawyer get in the way of his sales efforts. Luke is well-schooled in the legal documents that are often needed to implement the insurance and related planning that he designs for his clients: wills, trusts, employment agreements, buy-sell agreements, and the like. He believes that lawyer involvement adds nothing substantive to the effort, delays the process, triggers mindless, negative dialogue, and balloons upfront costs for the client. To keep a client's lawyer out of the process, Luke champions self-help legal services, helps clients use such services, and offers his own slate of stock "fill-in-the-blank" forms. And when a lawyer is needed to prepare a document, Luke steers his clients to his buddy Joe Marsh, a lawyer who dutifully follows Luke's orders, quickly delivers the requested documents with no hassles, and charges the client an insignificant fee.

Brand's management cherishes the business that Luke delivers, but is concerned about Brand's potential liability exposure for Luke's "extreme entertaining activities" and his "proactive lawyer management practices." They are concerned about the risks of personal injury or accident, a client receiving substandard legal documents or poor legal advice, or a claim (heaven forbid) that Luke is involved in the unauthorized practice of law.

Brand management has asked for your advice on steps that Brand might take to limit its exposure for Luke's activities.

· Ten Steps to Consider

Can a business protect itself from liabilities that may be created by its employees? Too often the temptation simply is to toss up one's hands and conclude that, since the responsibility exists, there is nothing that can be done about it. This is a mistake. Steps can be taken to mitigate the exposure.

The company's vicarious liability can become a reality in a countless number of ways. In most instances, the liability surfaces because an employee has committed one of four wrongs. The first and perhaps most pervasive wrong occurs when the employee exceeds his or her authority in making a deal on behalf of the company, or goes beyond that authority in representing the interests of the company. The employee, justified or not, assumes too much authority and ends up making a deal, a commitment, a warranty, or a representation of some type that the company doesn't like.

The second wrong occurs when the employee, in the process of carrying out his or her duties, negligently or recklessly injures another party. It may be an injury to the other party's person, property, reputation, career or existing contractual rights. Some third party ends up injured, and the company ends up exposed because an employee negligently or recklessly caused the injury while acting on behalf of the business.

The third wrong is where an employee ignores or violates a black letter law that has been established for the good of all. For example, the employee refuses to hire someone on the basis of his or her sex, or fires someone on account of age. The employee fixes prices with a competitor. The employee ignores basic environmental regulations. The employee sexually harasses a co-worker. Whatever the event, when this condition exists, usually some combination of greed, bigotry and ignorance is at the root of the problem.

The fourth wrong is the worst and the rarest. It's intentional misconduct that, in some cases, may rise to the level of criminal conduct. Fraud is probably the most common example. But there are many others: bribery, extortion, embezzlement, malicious slander, insider trading, unlawful disposal of hazardous waste and a host of others. These are the most ugly employee circumstances that business owners dread having to deal with. Fortunately, many business owners never experience this dark side.

There are specific steps that a business owner can take to reduce or mitigate the scope of the liability that may be created by employees. These are reviewed below with no effort made to analyze the fine points of the law relating to masters and servants and principals and agents, or the limits of the vicarious liability *respondeat superior* doctrine. The focus here is on third-party liability exposure, not actions or complaints that may come from employees. Not all of the steps reviewed will be applicable to every business.

Step No. 1—Define the Scope

The whole concept of employer vicarious liability turns on the scope of the employee's authority or employment. If an employee injures another outside the scope of his or her employment – say by frolicking on off-hours – there generally is no employer liability. But if the employee is within the scope of his or her duties, the liability will pass to the employer. Therefore, it is advisable for a business owner to define the scope of the employment for each employee. If an executive is given authority to negotiate contracts on behalf of the business owner, clearly define the limits of that authority. If an employee is authorized to perform certain tasks on behalf of the business owner, define those tasks as specifically as possible. The vicarious liability of the employer extends only to the extent the employee is within the scope of his or her employment. Absent some definition of the scope, the business owner's exposure is increased.

The obvious question is: How is the scope defined? In many businesses, the best way to define the scope of employment is through carefully prepared job descriptions. Each job description spells out the employee's duties, limitations on the employee's authority and responsibilities, and matters that are outside the scope of the employment.

Often, it is impractical to fashion a specific job description for every employee. In such situations, a description for classes of employees may be necessary, certain prohibitions may be included in the employee manual, and a reasonable effort should be made to craft a specific job description for each key executive employee whose primary responsibility is to interface with outsiders on behalf of the company. The description does not need to be elaborate, but it should delineate the scope of the contractual authority of the executive and the scope of the executive's responsibilities and duties. In many cases, it will be included in a written employment agreement.

This task of defining the scope requires an effort up front, but this effort can mitigate the potential liability of the business owner in two important ways. First, if the scope of the employee's authority and activities is clearly defined at the outset, the possibility of the employee wandering beyond that scope and causing problems is reduced. The employee knows where he or she stands. The excuse "I didn't know" is gone. Second, if a problem is created because the employee did exceed the scope of his or her authority or responsibility, then the business owner, if required to defend against the liability claim, is in a much better position to establish that the employee was outside the scope of his or her responsibilities. The owner can point to a business record that was created before the incident to prove the limits of the employee's authority.

Step No. 2—Mind the Memos and Emails

Whenever a business dispute ripens, lawyers go for the evidence. Often the best available evidence is file memoranda and emails that were prepared at the time the event took place. These documents can be killers or savers, depending entirely on how they are drafted. Key employees, particularly high-ranking executives, should be instructed on the appropriate preparation and retention of file memoranda and email documents. Each memorandum should be prepared with a view that it may be scrutinized carefully in the future. Facts should be stated accurately and succinctly. Suspicions or innuendos should be deleted or at least clearly characterized as such. Inflammatory statements or rationales that are designed to make a competitive co-worker look bad if a problem arises down the road should be strongly discouraged.

Key employees should be specifically instructed against preparing documents that are designed only to protect themselves by pointing fingers at other people in the organization. If a written record needs to be prepared that may be damaging down the road, consider putting it in a confidential communication to a company lawyer. This may keep the record out of the hands of an adverse party in a future dispute or lawsuit because of the attorney-client privilege.

All written records are not bad. Quite the contrary. Executives should be instructed to carefully document the substance, time, and place of key statements made by others that may be helpful in a potential dispute down the road. Often outside parties make admissions or statements that they later deny having made when the dispute surfaces. A good executive will develop an ear for these types of statements, and will make a contemporaneous record of them in the form of a file memorandum. This type of information can be invaluable when the dispute materializes.

Step No. 3—Repudiate Fast

If an employee creates a problem by going beyond the scope of his or her authority, the business owner should act fast in determining whether steps are going to be taken to repudiate the actions of the employee. The emphasis here is on speed. Delay and equivocation may result in approval or ratification of the unauthorized act. If, for example, a particular executive makes an offer that is outside the scope of his or her authority, fast action may enable the company to revoke the offer before it is accepted and ripens into a contract. If the offer has already been accepted and presents a serious problem, the company immediately should consider the advisability of disclaiming the entire contract on the grounds that the executive did not have the authority to make the deal. In many cases, the best course of action will be to honor the bad contract even though it is distasteful to do so. But in some situations, the contract may be so bad that it is worth blowing the whistle and trying to find an exit.

The key is to move quickly before the other party has relied on it to its detriment. Too many business owners assume that they can't do anything in this situation—that there is no out. If it is clear that the employee exceeded his or her authority, moving quickly may create an opportunity to undo the damage.

In certain extreme instances, it may be necessary to fire the irresponsible employee to appropriately evidence the business owner's repudiation of the employee's actions. This may be necessary in situations where the employee has been totally irresponsible, has been compromised by a conflict of interest, or has acted in bad faith. Expulsion also may be required if the employee has demonstrated a pattern of unauthorized conduct that is likely to continue. By acting swiftly and decisively, the business owner may cut off any exposure to future acts and may create a basis for disclaiming some responsibility for prior acts, on the grounds that the employee was clearly acting outside the scope of his or her authority. If the owner ducks the situation and does nothing, the owner may get tagged for past acts and also future acts, on the ground that the future acts, although perhaps extreme, were being done with the knowledge and the consent of the owner.

Step No. 4—Watch the Titles

In business, titles go a long way in defining the scope of a particular employee's authority. Many business owners are careless with their titles. Why not have a group of vice presidents? They figure titles are cheap, so they can be generous with them. The result is that many employees end up over-titled. This can present two problems from a liability perspective.

First, the over-titled employee may focus on the title and start acting in a way that the owner never intended. An employee who has an over-inflated image of his or her importance and role in the business can be dangerous. The employee has a concept of what authority and discretion comes with the title of executive vice president, even though the business owner had no intention of giving the employee the real authority and control that an executive vice president title would suggest.

Second, it is common practice in the business world to rely on the title of an individual in assessing the scope of that individual's authority. By giving the title, the business owner may be presumed to have given the authority. It may be difficult or practically impossible for the owner to disclaim the authority on the theory that company never intended to give the broad-based authority that the title suggested.

Step No. 5—Customize the Insurance

A customized insurance program can be valuable in protecting the interests of a closely held business from the risks posed by its employees. The key is to have an insurance program that covers specific risks of the business. It is a mistake to assume that all risks can be insured against. But many can. What is needed is a quality insurance person who understands the business, the nature of the risks involved, and the best available products in the marketplace. Insurance policies can be deceiving. There is no effective substitute for an insurance professional who is thoroughly familiar with the exceptions and limitations of the various policy options.

Step No. 6—Check the Pedigrees

Before hiring an employee, check out his or her background – carefully. Some employees are trouble wherever they go. They can't play by the rules. They are always looking for shortcuts. Over-reacting, overstating, and risk-taking are compulsions. Sooner or later, they end up creating a problem for the business owner. Often it is hard to get a handle on this factor. Whenever possible, prior employers (listed or not as personal references) should be contacted.

These background checks can be critical in some situations, particularly where an employee is regularly exposed to members of the public. Some employers have found themselves facing a charge of "negligent hiring" made by a injured third party. The charge is that the employer should have checked and determined that the particular employee posed an undue risk because of a social, mental or physical disorder. For example, there have been cases based on prior records for assault, sexual misconduct, theft and perjury. Obviously there are limits on how far any business owner can go in checking out a prospective employee. The lesson is to be sensitive to the company's needs, to watch for danger signs in the hiring process, and to do that amount of checking that is reasonable and practical under the circumstances.

Step No. 7—Spread the Word

When the business owner delineates the authority and the scope of activities of the company's employees, the word needs to be spread – not only to the employees impacted, but also to those who are responsible for supervising and monitoring the activities of the employees. Hidden, undisclosed limitations will not be effective.

In certain instances, it may even be necessary to contact parties outside the business and inform them of limitations that have been placed on certain employees. It may be necessary to specifically warn prospective customers that employees and agents of the company have no authority to make any verbal representations or warranties outside of those that are specifically provided in writing by the company. In preliminary contract negotiations, it may be necessary to advise the other side that the company's negotiators do not have the authority to bind the company to any specified set of terms and conditions, and that another layer of review and approval exists. In some situations, it will be necessary to advise third parties that all activities of employees outside the normal working hours are not the responsibility of the company. Spreading the word when necessary can be very helpful. It helps define the limits of the authority, reminds the employee of those limits, and puts third parties on notice.

Step No. 8—Repeatedly Emphasize the Six "Big Nevers"

It is helpful to periodically emphasize to all employees the "Six Big Nevers." They are six things that generally should never be done. The goal is to ensure that no employee can plead ignorance on one of these.

1. Never talk or even joke about the possibility of hiring, firing or promoting on the basis of race, sex, age, national origin, sexual orientation, disability or religion. A dumb comment, although intended to be innocent or fun-loving, may boomerang down the road to create a liability problem if some employee feels that he or she has been unlawfully discriminated against. Sensitivity is the name of the game on this issue.

2. Never discuss or attempt to resolve a conflict with the other side's lawyer. Many lawyers develop a knack for getting others to make admissions that will embarrass them when the dispute ripens. It is generally a good idea to advise all employees that when the other side brings in a lawyer, you bring in yours.

3. Never encourage another party to breach a contract. This one recognizes that there is a difference between healthy competition in attempting to secure a contract and new business, and openly encouraging another party to breach an existing contract with a third party. If A encourages B to breach a contract with C, C may have a direct liability claim against A for interfering with its contractual relationships. Many successful people have a hard time determining where selling ends and interference with contractual relationships begins. In some situations, the distinction is a bright light that is simply ignored. This can result in undue liability exposure.

4. Never sign what you do not fully understand. This may sound axiomatic, but the truth is that many business executives sign agreements that they do not fully understand or that they have not carefully reviewed. Each employee should be instructed against the fear of appearing ignorant for not understanding the implication of a particular document. The lesson is to seek out appropriate counsel and advice on what the document actually says.

5. Never discuss with a competitor or a prospective competitor any matter involving prices, existing or potential market divisions, or existing or potential actions or plans to not do business with (boycott) a third party. The Sherman Act is always lurking. Lawyers love it. An aggrieved party can recover treble damages and attorney fees.

6. Never ignorantly look the other way. Many business owners have an employee who routinely breaks the rules, but who gets results. It is tempting sometimes to look the other way, take the risk of the liability exposure, and enjoy the benefits. What is important is not to be ignorant in assessing the magnitude of the risks. Look hard at the stakes before assessing the odds. There are some two-percent risks that should never be taken because the consequences of the

risks are so utterly severe that they could mean an end to the business. Other 50 percent risks can be taken all day because the consequence of the risk materializing is not severe in light of the potential benefits to be obtained. What is required is an intelligent risk analysis. It requires a case-by-case review. No pat formula will work in all cases. Looking the other way can be dangerous, particularly if it is done ignorantly.

Step No. 9—Education

Employees need to be educated. Do not assume that they know or appreciate basic laws or that they are sensitive to the risks that they may create for the business owner. Some areas of potential liability may require special education, such as price-fixing risks, hazardous waste disposal risks, employment discrimination, sexual harassment, and the like. Other areas of potential liability require one basic reminder: stay within your authority and be careful.

Some employees may need to be periodically reminded of their own personal liability if they wrongfully create a liability for the company. Many figure that since it's the company's problem, it sure can't be their problem also. This is faulty thinking. If an employee creates a problem, that employee will be in the middle of it all and, in many cases, will personally be responsible for any resulting liability.

Step No. 10—Reduce Turnover

In many respects, this last step is the most important. A stable, seasoned workforce is much safer than one that experiences high turnover rates. Plus, it's more efficient and productive. For many companies, a prerequisite to success is the ability to attract, retain and motivate quality employees.

Many factors can impact employee dissatisfaction and turnover rates. Some, such as the nature of the work or opportunities for career advancement, may be beyond the control of the owners of the business. But other critical factors, including the company's interest in the well-being of its employees, its vision for the future, and its willingness to embrace its employees as valued teammates, not expendable commodities, are completely within the control of management. There are many important steps that management can take in setting policy and operating day-to-day to bind and motivate employees.

Absent effective management, a workforce can quickly develop a destructive go-through-the-motions mindset that guarantees inefficiencies and waste and increases the potential of employee actions that create liability exposures for the company. Smart management can benefit everyone in an organization and reduce liability risks. The rewards for employees go far beyond any additional compensation they might net. The despair of complacency and an obsession to give only the minimum can soon disappear. Definable, measurable stakes in the effort can trigger an expanded purpose, a growing desire to excel and be careful, and an ongoing push to elevate the performance of the entire group. Everything seems faster, including the clock. A healthy sense of urgency, for the sake of efficiency, keeps everyone energized and focused. What some may regard as mundane, even demeaning, often becomes challenging and rewarding – sometimes even exciting.

Sound impossible? It happens every day in companies that, out of a desire to grow and protect their businesses, take positive actions to reward, incent, and cherish their employees by smartly tapping into the best the human spirit has to offer.

Three Myths

There are three myths that often permeate a discussion about a company's liability for the acts of its employees. These myths can provide a false sense of security and divert attention from the real issues.

Myth 1: If I make my employees independent contractors, I won't be liable for their actions. Some business owners believe that if they make all of their employees independent contractors, they can escape liability for the employees' activities. While it is true that a business owner may have less responsibility for true independent contractors (such as outside accountants and lawyers), the answer is not to make all employees independent contractors. Titles alone won't do the job. If a person is designated as an independent contractor, but the business owner retains the right to control and supervise that person's conduct, the liability will be just as great as it would have been had the person been called an "employee."

Myth 2: If one of my employees does something wrong and I immediately fire that employee, I am off the hook. This is a gross over-generalization. As discussed above, there may be extreme circumstances where an employee needs to be terminated in order to protect the business against future problems. But there is no assurance that, by terminating the employee, the business owner will be able to absolve the business of responsibility for prior acts committed by that employee. In addition, this myth can precipitate an over-reaction that results in an employee being needlessly terminated. In many situations, the employer can reasonably take the position that the employee was outside the scope of his or her authority without firing the employee, particularly if the employee has no history of creating such problems.

Myth 3: If I didn't know about it, I'm not responsible for it. Some business owners mistakenly assume that if they can just demonstrate their own ignorance of the matter, they are home free. It is natural for many to assume that they can't be liable for something that they did not know anything about. It's a true myth. As a general proposition, ignorance is no defense.

C. AGENCY LAW NUTS AND BOLTS

CASE PROBLEM 1-2

Instruction: Study the following excerpts from the *Restatement (Third) of Agency* as necessary to answer the following questions.

Facts: Jane knows food and is a party animal. After much thought and analysis, she quit her job a year ago and started a catering business. Her targeted clients are high-income couples who want the best when they throw a party. Jane started her business with $50,000, all of which was used to buy a van and essential equipment items. Assume (1) that, at the time Jane started her business, she formed a corporation, Golden Touch Catering, Inc. ("GTC") and has conducted all her business through GTC; (2) that she has always been the sole shareholder, director, president and chief executive officer (CEO) of GTC; and (3) that, from the outset, GTC has had only one other full-time employee, George, who has had the title "Event Coordinator."

Questions 1-3: (Consider each question separately)

1. Jane negotiates a contract with Micro Inc. ("Micro") to cater 14 product launch events. Who are the parties to the contract if Micro knows that Jane was acting in her capacity as CEO of GTC? Is Jane personally liable under the contract?

2. How would your answers in question 1 change if Micro had no knowledge of GTC and, therefore, assumed Jane was acting as an individual?

3. How would your answers in question 1 change if Micro knew Jane was acting on behalf of another party, but did not know the identity of the other party?

Extended Facts: Assume Jane is not the one who sourced and negotiated the Micro agreement. Jane has always told George that he may discuss potential business with a prospective or existing client, but that he may never make any commitment on behalf of GTC without first having all the details approved by Jane. Assume that Micro's VP of advertising, Doug, and George are neighbors. Doug approached George with the idea of GTC catering the 14 product launch events for Micro. After advising Doug that he was a VP of GTC, George discussed all the details with Doug and instantly committed to do the events without any consultation with Jane. George believed that this was premium corporate business that would excite Jane and demonstrate his ability to take on greater sales responsibilities. Plus, he did not want to tell his neighbor that he had to first seek Jane's permission before committing GTC. Upon learning of the agreement that George made with Micro, Jane immediately fired George.

Questions 4-9:

4. Does GTC or Jane have any liability under the agreement that George entered into with Micro? Does George have any liability to Micro, assuming Doug at all times knew that George was acting on behalf of GTC and not in his personal capacity? Does George have any liability to GTC?

5. How would your answers to question 4 change if Jane had given Doug the authority to commit GTC to single-event agreements but not multi-event deals?

6. How would your answers to question 4 change if, before approaching George, Doug had called Jane, as CEO of GTC, to ask "whether it was

appropriate to discuss some potential catering business with his neighbor George" and Jane had simply responded by saying "By all means"?

7.   How would your answers to question 4 change if, after firing George, Jane said nothing to Micro until the night before the first event and at that time disclaimed any responsibility on the theory that George had no authority to commit GTC?

8.   How would your answers to question 4 change if, after firing George, Jane determined that the agreement with Micro was an "awesome deal" and called Doug to confirm all the logistical details?

9.   How would your answers to question 4 change if, prior to Jane's call to Doug, Doug learned of George's firing through the neighborhood grapevine and immediately hired another firm to cater the 14 product launch events? Would Micro have any liability under the GTC agreement negotiated by George?

More Facts: Assume George (still employed by GTC) attends a party at the local country club where George discusses, among many other things, the great services provided by GTC. George gets smashed, attempts to drive home drunk, and negligently causes an accident that seriously injures Sue.

Questions 10-13:

10. Is Jane or GTC liable to Sue for George's negligence? Is George liable to Sue, Jane or GTC?

11. How would your answers to question 10 change if GTC had catered the country club event and George had attended the event to "make sure everything was going OK"?

12. How would your answers to question 11 change if Jane, aware of George's tendency to hit the bottle in the evening, had instructed George to never attend any evening events catered by GTC and George had no official responsibility for the event GTC catered at the country club?

13. Assume the accident and Sue's injuries were caused by the negligence of GTC's lawyer as he was driving to a meeting where the terms of GTC's contract with Micro were to be negotiated. Is GTC or Jane liable to Sue for the lawyer's negligence?

Excerpts from *Restatement (Third) of Agency*

§ 1.01 Agency Defined

Agency is the fiduciary relationship that arises when one person (a "principal") manifests assent to another person (an "agent") that the agent shall act on the principal's behalf and subject to the principal's control, and the agent manifests assent or otherwise consents so to act.

§ 1.03 Manifestation

A person manifests assent or intention through written or spoken words or other conduct.

§ 1.04 Terminology

(1) *Coagents.* Coagents have agency relationships with the same principal. A coagent may be appointed by the principal or by another agent actually or apparently authorized by the principal to do so.

(2) *Disclosed, undisclosed, and unidentified principals.*

(a) *Disclosed principal.* A principal is disclosed if, when an agent and a third party interact, the third party has notice that the agent is acting for a principal and has notice of the principal's identity.

(b) *Undisclosed principal.* A principal is undisclosed if, when an agent and a third party interact, the third party has no notice that the agent is acting for a principal.

(c) *Unidentified principal.* A principal is unidentified if, when an agent and a third party interact, the third party has notice that the agent is acting for a principal but does not have notice of the principal's identity.

(3) *Gratuitous agent.* A gratuitous agent acts without a right to compensation.

(4) *Notice.* A person has notice of a fact if the person knows the fact, has reason to know the fact, has received an effective notification of the fact, or should know the fact to fulfill a duty owed to another person. Notice of a fact that an agent knows or has reason to know is imputed to the principal as stated in §§ 5.03 and 5.04. A notification given to or by an agent is effective as notice to or by the principal as stated in § 5.02.

(5) *Person.* A person is (a) an individual; (b) an organization or association that has legal capacity to possess rights and incur obligations; (c) a government, political subdivision, or instrumentality or entity created by government; or (d) any other entity that has legal capacity to possess rights and incur obligations.

(7) *Power of attorney.* A power of attorney is an instrument that states an agent's authority.

(8) *Subagent.* A subagent is a person appointed by an agent to perform functions that the agent has consented to perform on behalf of the agent's principal and for whose conduct the appointing agent is responsible to the principal.

§ 2.01 Actual Authority

An agent acts with actual authority when, at the time of taking action that has legal consequences for the principal, the agent reasonably believes, in accordance with the principal's manifestations to the agent, that the principal wishes the agent so to act.

§ 2.02 Scope of Actual Authority

(1) An agent has actual authority to take action designated or implied in the principal's manifestations to the agent and acts necessary or incidental to achieving the principal's objectives, as the agent reasonably understands the

principal's manifestations and objectives when the agent determines how to act.

(2) An agent's interpretation of the principal's manifestations is reasonable if it reflects any meaning known by the agent to be ascribed by the principal and, in the absence of any meaning known to the agent, as a reasonable person in the agent's position would interpret the manifestations in light of the context, including circumstances of which the agent has notice and the agent's fiduciary duty to the principal.

(3) An agent's understanding of the principal's objectives is reasonable if it accords with the principal's manifestations and the inferences that a reasonable person in the agent's position would draw from the circumstances creating the agency.

§ 2.03 Apparent Authority

Apparent authority is the power held by an agent or other actor to affect a principal's legal relations with third parties when a third party reasonably believes the actor has authority to act on behalf of the principal and that belief is traceable to the principal's manifestations.

§ 2.04 Respondeat Superior

An employer is subject to liability for torts committed by employees while acting within the scope of their employment.

§ 2.05 Estoppel to Deny Existence of Agency Relationship

A person who has not made a manifestation that an actor has authority as an agent and who is not otherwise liable as a party to a transaction purportedly done by the actor on that person's account is subject to liability to a third party who justifiably is induced to make a detrimental change in position because the transaction is believed to be on the person's account, if

(1) the person intentionally or carelessly caused such belief, or

(2) having notice of such belief and that it might induce others to change their positions, the person did not take reasonable steps to notify them of the facts.

§ 2.06 Liability of Undisclosed Principal

(1) An undisclosed principal is subject to liability to a third party who is justifiably induced to make a detrimental change in position by an agent acting on the principal's behalf and without actual authority if the principal, having notice of the agent's conduct and that it might induce others to change their positions, did not take reasonable steps to notify them of the facts.

(2) An undisclosed principal may not rely on instructions given an agent that qualify or reduce the agent's authority to less than the authority a third party would reasonably believe the agent to have under the same circumstances if the principal had been disclosed.

§ 2.07 Restitution of Benefit

If a principal is unjustly enriched at the expense of another person by the action of an agent or a person who appears to be an agent, the principal is subject to a claim for restitution by that person.

§ 3.01 Creation of Actual Authority

Actual authority, as defined in § 2.01, is created by a principal's manifestation to an agent that, as reasonably understood by the agent, expresses the principal's assent that the agent take action on the principal's behalf.

§ 3.03 Creation of Apparent Authority

Apparent authority, as defined in § 2.03, is created by a person's manifestation that another has authority to act with legal consequences for the person who makes the manifestation, when a third party reasonably believes the actor to be authorized and the belief is traceable to the manifestation.

§ 3.04 Capacity to Act as Principal

(1) An individual has capacity to act as principal in a relationship of agency as defined in § 1.01 if, at the time the agent takes action, the individual would have capacity if acting in person.

(2) The law applicable to a person that is not an individual governs whether the person has capacity to be a principal in a relationship of agency as defined in § 1.01, as well as the effect of the person's lack or loss of capacity on those who interact with it.

(3) If performance of an act is not delegable, its performance by an agent does not constitute performance by the principal.

§ 3.05 Capacity to Act as Agent

Any person may ordinarily be empowered to act so as to affect the legal relations of another. The actor's capacity governs the extent to which, by so acting, the actor becomes subject to duties and liabilities to the person whose legal relations are affected or to third parties.

§ 3.06 Termination of Actual Authority--In General

An agent's actual authority may be terminated by:

(1) the agent's death, cessation of existence, or suspension of powers as stated in § 3.07(1) and (3); or

(2) the principal's death, cessation of existence, or suspension of powers as stated in § 3.07(2) and (4); or

(3) the principal's loss of capacity, as stated in § 3.08(1) and (3); or

(4) an agreement between the agent and the principal or the occurrence of circumstances on the basis of which the agent should reasonably conclude that the principal no longer would assent to the agent's taking action on the principal's behalf, as stated in § 3.09; or

(5) a manifestation of revocation by the principal to the agent, or of renunciation by the agent to the principal, as stated in § 3.10(1); or

(6) the occurrence of circumstances specified by statute.

§ 3.07 Death, Cessation of Existence, and Suspension of Powers

(1) The death of an individual agent terminates the agent's actual authority.

(2) The death of an individual principal terminates the agent's actual authority. The termination is effective only when the agent has notice of the principal's death. The termination is also effective as against a third party with whom the agent deals when the third party has notice of the principal's death.

(3) When an agent that is not an individual ceases to exist or commences a process that will lead to cessation of existence or when its powers are suspended, the agent's actual authority terminates except as provided by law.

(4) When a principal that is not an individual ceases to exist or commences a process that will lead to cessation of its existence or when its powers are suspended, the agent's actual authority terminates except as provided by law.

§ 3.08 Loss of Capacity

(1) An individual principal's loss of capacity to do an act terminates the agent's actual authority to do the act. The termination is effective only when the agent has notice that the principal's loss of capacity is permanent or that the principal has been adjudicated to lack capacity. The termination is also effective as against a third party with whom the agent deals when the third party has notice that the principal's loss of capacity is permanent or that the principal has been adjudicated to lack capacity.

(2) A written instrument may make an agent's actual authority effective upon a principal's loss of capacity, or confer it irrevocably regardless of such loss.

(3) If a principal that is not an individual loses capacity to do an act, its agent's actual authority to do the act is terminated.

§ 3.09 Termination by Agreement or by Occurrence of Changed Circumstances

An agent's actual authority terminates (1) as agreed by the agent and the principal, subject to the provisions of § 3.10; or (2) upon the occurrence of circumstances on the basis of which the agent should reasonably conclude that the principal no longer would assent to the agent's taking action on the principal's behalf.

§ 3.10 Manifestation Terminating Actual Authority

(1) Notwithstanding any agreement between principal and agent, an agent's actual authority terminates if the agent renounces it by a manifestation to the principal or if the principal revokes the agent's actual authority by a manifestation to the agent. A revocation or a renunciation is effective when the other party has notice of it.

(2) A principal's manifestation of revocation is, unless otherwise agreed, ineffective to terminate a power given as security or to terminate a proxy to vote

securities or other membership or ownership interests that is made irrevocable in compliance with applicable legislation. See §§ 3.12-3.13.

§ 3.11 Termination of Apparent Authority

(1) The termination of actual authority does not by itself end any apparent authority held by an agent.

(2) Apparent authority ends when it is no longer reasonable for the third party with whom an agent deals to believe that the agent continues to act with actual authority.

§ 3.15 Subagency

(1) A subagent is a person appointed by an agent to perform functions that the agent has consented to perform on behalf of the agent's principal and for whose conduct the appointing agent is responsible to the principal. The relationships between a subagent and the appointing agent and between the subagent and the appointing agent's principal are relationships of agency as stated in § 1.01.

(2) An agent may appoint a subagent only if the agent has actual or apparent authority to do so.

§ 3.16 Agent for Coprincipals

Two or more persons may as coprincipals appoint an agent to act for them in the same transaction or matter.

§ 4.01 Ratification Defined

(1) Ratification is the affirmance of a prior act done by another, whereby the act is given effect as if done by an agent acting with actual authority.

(2) A person ratifies an act by

(a) manifesting assent that the act shall affect the person's legal relations, or

(b) conduct that justifies a reasonable assumption that the person so consents.

(3) Ratification does not occur unless

(a) the act is ratifiable as stated in § 4.03,

(b) the person ratifying has capacity as stated in § 4.04,

(c) the ratification is timely as stated in § 4.05, and

(d) the ratification encompasses the act in its entirety as stated in § 4.07.

§ 4.02 Effect of Ratification

(1) Subject to the exceptions stated in subsection (2), ratification retroactively creates the effects of actual authority.

(2) Ratification is not effective:

(a) in favor of a person who causes it by misrepresentation or other conduct that would make a contract voidable;

(b) in favor of an agent against a principal when the principal ratifies to avoid a loss; or

(c) to diminish the rights or other interests of persons, not parties to the transaction, that were acquired in the subject matter prior to the ratification.

§ 4.03 Acts That May Be Ratified

A person may ratify an act if the actor acted or purported to act as an agent on the person's behalf.

§ 4.04 Capacity to Ratify

(1) A person may ratify an act if

(a) the person existed at the time of the act, and

(b) the person had capacity as defined in § 3.04 at the time of ratifying the act.

(2) At a later time, a principal may avoid a ratification made earlier when the principal lacked capacity as defined in § 3.04.

§ 4.05 Timing of Ratification

A ratification of a transaction is not effective unless it precedes the occurrence of circumstances that would cause the ratification to have adverse and inequitable effects on the rights of third parties. These circumstances include:

(1) any manifestation of intention to withdraw from the transaction made by the third party;

(2) any material change in circumstances that would make it inequitable to bind the third party, unless the third party chooses to be bound; and

(3) a specific time that determines whether a third party is deprived of a right or subjected to a liability.

§ 4.06 Knowledge Requisite to Ratification

A person is not bound by a ratification made without knowledge of material facts involved in the original act when the person was unaware of such lack of knowledge.

§ 4.07 No Partial Ratification

A ratification is not effective unless it encompasses the entirety of an act, contract, or other single transaction.

§ 4.08 Estoppel to Deny Ratification

If a person makes a manifestation that the person has ratified another's act and the manifestation, as reasonably understood by a third party, induces the third party to make a detrimental change in position, the person may be estopped to deny the ratification.

§ 5.01 Notifications and Notice--In General

(1) A notification is a manifestation that is made in the form required by agreement among parties or by applicable law, or in a reasonable manner in the absence of an agreement or an applicable law, with the intention of affecting the legal rights and duties of the notifier in relation to rights and duties of persons to whom the notification is given...

§ 5.02 Notification Given by or to an Agent

(1) A notification given to an agent is effective as notice to the principal if the agent has actual or apparent authority to receive the notification, unless the person who gives the notification knows or has reason to know that the agent is acting adversely to the principal as stated in § 5.04.

(2) A notification given by an agent is effective as notification given by the principal if the agent has actual or apparent authority to give the notification, unless the person who receives the notification knows or has reason to know that the agent is acting adversely to the principal as stated in § 5.04.

§ 5.03 Imputation of Notice of Fact To Principal

For purposes of determining a principal's legal relations with a third party, notice of a fact that an agent knows or has reason to know is imputed to the principal if knowledge of the fact is material to the agent's duties to the principal, unless the agent

(a) acts adversely to the principal as stated in § 5.04, or

(b) is subject to a duty to another not to disclose the fact to the principal.

§ 5.04 An Agent Who Acts Adversely to a Principal

For purposes of determining a principal's legal relations with a third party, notice of a fact that an agent knows or has reason to know is not imputed to the principal if the agent acts adversely to the principal in a transaction or matter, intending to act solely for the agent's own purposes or those of another person. Nevertheless, notice is imputed

(a) when necessary to protect the rights of a third party who dealt with the principal in good faith; or

(b) when the principal has ratified or knowingly retained a benefit from the agent's action.

A third party who deals with a principal through an agent, knowing or having reason to know that the agent acts adversely to the principal, does not deal in good faith for this purpose.

§ 6.01 Agent for Disclosed Principal

When an agent acting with actual or apparent authority makes a contract on behalf of a disclosed principal,

(1) the principal and the third party are parties to the contract; and

(2) the agent is not a party to the contract unless the agent and third party

agree otherwise.

§ 6.02 Agent for Unidentified Principal

When an agent acting with actual or apparent authority makes a contract on behalf of an unidentified principal,

(1) the principal and the third party are parties to the contract; and

(2) the agent is a party to the contract unless the agent and the third party agree otherwise.

§ 6.03 Agent for Undisclosed Principal

When an agent acting with actual authority makes a contract on behalf of an undisclosed principal,

(1) unless excluded by the contract, the principal is a party to the contract;

(2) the agent and the third party are parties to the contract; and

(3) the principal, if a party to the contract, and the third party have the same rights, liabilities, and defenses against each other as if the principal made the contract personally, subject to §§ 6.05-6.09.

§ 6.04 Principal Does Not Exist or Lacks Capacity

Unless the third party agrees otherwise, a person who makes a contract with a third party purportedly as an agent on behalf of a principal becomes a party to the contract if the purported agent knows or has reason to know that the purported principal does not exist or lacks capacity to be a party to a contract.

§ 6.05 Contract That is Unauthorized in Part or That Combines Orders of Several Principals

(1) If an agent makes a contract with a third party that differs from the contract that the agent had actual or apparent authority to make only in an amount or by the inclusion or exclusion of a separable part, the principal is subject to liability to the third party to the extent of the contract that the agent had actual or apparent authority to make if

(a) the third party seasonably makes a manifestation to the principal of willingness to be bound; and

(b) the principal has not changed position in reasonable reliance on the belief that no contract bound the principal and the third party…

§ 6.09 Effect of Judgment Against Agent or Principal

When an agent has made a contract with a third party on behalf of a principal, unless the contract provides otherwise,

(1) the liability, if any, of the principal or the agent to the third party is not discharged if the third party obtains a judgment against the other; and

(2) the liability, if any, of the principal or the agent to the third party is discharged to the extent a judgment against the other is satisfied.

§ 6.10 Agent's Implied Warranty of Authority

A person who purports to make a contract, representation, or conveyance to or with a third party on behalf of another person, lacking power to bind that person, gives an implied warranty of authority to the third party and is subject to liability to the third party for damages for loss caused by breach of that warranty, including loss of the benefit expected from performance by the principal, unless

(1) the principal or purported principal ratifies the act as stated in § 4.01; or

(2) the person who purports to make the contract, representation, or conveyance gives notice to the third party that no warranty of authority is given; or

(3) the third party knows that the person who purports to make the contract, representation, or conveyance acts without actual authority.

§ 6.11 Agent's Representations

(1) When an agent for a disclosed or unidentified principal makes a false representation about the agent's authority to a third party, the principal is not subject to liability unless the agent acted with actual or apparent authority in making the representation and the third party does not have notice that the agent's representation is false.

(2) A representation by an agent made incident to a contract or conveyance is attributed to a disclosed or unidentified principal as if the principal made the representation directly when the agent had actual or apparent authority to make the contract or conveyance unless the third party knew or had reason to know that the representation was untrue or that the agent acted without actual authority in making it.

(3) A representation by an agent made incident to a contract or conveyance is attributed to an undisclosed principal as if the principal made the representation directly when

(a) the agent acted with actual authority in making the representation, or

(b) the agent acted without actual authority in making the representation but had actual authority to make true representations about the same matter.

The agent's representation is not attributed to the principal when the third party knew or had reason to know it was untrue.

(4) When an agent who makes a contract or conveyance on behalf of an undisclosed principal falsely represents to the third party that the agent does not act on behalf of a principal, the third party may avoid the contract or conveyance if the principal or agent had notice that the third party would not have dealt with the principal.

§ 7.01 Agent's Liability to Third Party

An agent is subject to liability to a third party harmed by the agent's tortious conduct. Unless an applicable statute provides otherwise, an actor remains subject to liability although the actor acts as an agent or an employee, with actual or apparent authority, or within the scope of employment.

§ 7.02 Duty to Principal; Duty To Third Party

An agent's breach of a duty owed to the principal is not an independent basis for the agent's tort liability to a third party. An agent is subject to tort liability to a third party harmed by the agent's conduct only when the agent's conduct breaches a duty that the agent owes to the third party.

§ 7.03 Principal's Liability--In General

(1) A principal is subject to direct liability to a third party harmed by an agent's conduct when

(a) as stated in § 7.04, the agent acts with actual authority or the principal ratifies the agent's conduct and

(i) the agent's conduct is tortious, or

(ii) the agent's conduct, if that of the principal, would subject the principal to tort liability; or

(b) as stated in § 7.05, the principal is negligent in selecting, supervising, or otherwise controlling the agent; or

(c) as stated in § 7.06, the principal delegates performance of a duty to use care to protect other persons or their property to an agent who fails to perform the duty.

(2) A principal is subject to vicarious liability to a third party harmed by an agent's conduct when

(a) as stated in § 7.07, the agent is an employee who commits a tort while acting within the scope of employment; or

(b) as stated in § 7.08, the agent commits a tort when acting with apparent authority in dealing with a third party on or purportedly on behalf of the principal.

§ 7.04 Agent Acts with Actual Authority

A principal is subject to liability to a third party harmed by an agent's conduct when the agent's conduct is within the scope of the agent's actual authority or ratified by the principal; and

(1) the agent's conduct is tortious, or

(2) the agent's conduct, if that of the principal, would subject the principal to tort liability.

§ 7.05 Principal's Negligence in Conducting Activity Through Agent; Principal's Special Relationship with Another Person

(1) A principal who conducts an activity through an agent is subject to liability for harm to a third party caused by the agent's conduct if the harm was caused by the principal's negligence in selecting, training, retaining, supervising, or otherwise controlling the agent.

(2) When a principal has a special relationship with another person, the principal owes that person a duty of reasonable care with regard to risks arising out of the relationship, including the risk that agents of the principal will harm the person with whom the principal has such a special relationship.

§ 7.06 Failure in Performance of Principal's Duty of Protection

A principal required by contract or otherwise by law to protect another cannot avoid liability by delegating performance of the duty, whether or not the delegate is an agent.

§ 7.07 Employee Acting Within Scope of Employment

(1) An employer is subject to vicarious liability for a tort committed by its employee acting within the scope of employment.

(2) An employee acts within the scope of employment when performing work assigned by the employer or engaging in a course of conduct subject to the employer's control. An employee's act is not within the scope of employment when it occurs within an independent course of conduct not intended by the employee to serve any purpose of the employer.

(3) For purposes of this section,

(a) an employee is an agent whose principal controls or has the right to control the manner and means of the agent's performance of work, and

(b) the fact that work is performed gratuitously does not relieve a principal of liability.

§ 7.08 Agent Acts with Apparent Authority

A principal is subject to vicarious liability for a tort committed by an agent in dealing or communicating with a third party on or purportedly on behalf of the principal when actions taken by the agent with apparent authority constitute the tort or enable the agent to conceal its commission.

§ 8.01 General Fiduciary Principle

An agent has a fiduciary duty to act loyally for the principal's benefit in all matters connected with the agency relationship.

§ 8.02 Material Benefit Arising out of Position

An agent has a duty not to acquire a material benefit from a third party in connection with transactions conducted or other actions taken on behalf of the principal or otherwise through the agent's use of the agent's position.

§ 8.03 Acting as or on Behalf of an Adverse Party

An agent has a duty not to deal with the principal as or on behalf of an adverse party in a transaction connected with the agency relationship.

§ 8.04 Competition

Throughout the duration of an agency relationship, an agent has a duty to refrain from competing with the principal and from taking action on behalf of or otherwise assisting the principal's competitors. During that time, an agent may take action, not otherwise wrongful, to prepare for competition following termination of the agency relationship.

§ 8.07 Duty Created By Contract

An agent has a duty to act in accordance with the express and implied terms of any contract between the agent and the principal.

§ 8.08 Duties of Care, Competence, and Diligence

Subject to any agreement with the principal, an agent has a duty to the principal to act with the care, competence, and diligence normally exercised by agents in similar circumstances. Special skills or knowledge possessed by an agent are circumstances to be taken into account in determining whether the agent acted with due care and diligence. If an agent claims to possess special skills or knowledge, the agent has a duty to the principal to act with the care, competence, and diligence normally exercised by agents with such skills or knowledge.

§ 8.09 Duty to Act Only within Scope of Actual Authority and to Comply with Principal's Lawful Instructions

(1) An agent has a duty to take action only within the scope of the agent's actual authority.

(2) An agent has a duty to comply with all lawful instructions received from the principal and persons designated by the principal concerning the agent's actions on behalf of the principal.

§ 8.10 Duty of Good Conduct

An agent has a duty, within the scope of the agency relationship, to act reasonably and to refrain from conduct that is likely to damage the principal's enterprise.

§ 8.11 Duty to Provide Information

An agent has a duty to use reasonable effort to provide the principal with facts that the agent knows, has reason to know, or should know when

(1) subject to any manifestation by the principal, the agent knows or has reason to know that the principal would wish to have the facts or the facts are material to the agent's duties to the principal; and

(2) the facts can be provided to the principal without violating a superior duty owed by the agent to another person.

§ 8.13 Duty Created by Contract

A principal has a duty to act in accordance with the express and implied terms of any contract between the principal and the agent.

§ 8.14 Duty to Indemnify

A principal has a duty to indemnify an agent

(1) in accordance with the terms of any contract between them; and

(2) unless otherwise agreed,

(a) when the agent makes a payment

(i) within the scope of the agent's actual authority, or

(ii) that is beneficial to the principal, unless the agent acts officiously in making the payment; or

(b) when the agent suffers a loss that fairly should be borne by the principal in light of their relationship.

§ 8.15 Principal's Duty to Deal Fairly and In Good Faith

A principal has a duty to deal with the agent fairly and in good faith, including a duty to provide the agent with information about risks of physical harm or pecuniary loss that the principal knows, has reason to know, or should know are present in the agent's work but unknown to the agent.

D. CORPORATE AGENCY CHALLENGES

MENARD, INC. v. DAGE-MTI, INC.
726 N.E.2d 1206 (Ind. 2000)

SULLIVAN, Justice.

Menard, Inc., offered to purchase 30 acres of land from Dage-MTI, Inc., for $1,450,000. Arthur Sterling, Dage's president, accepted the offer in a written agreement in which he represented that he had the requisite authority to bind Dage to the sale. The Dage board of directors did not approve and refused to complete the transaction. We hold that as president, Sterling possessed the inherent authority to bind Dage in these circumstances.

Dage-MTI, Inc., is a closely held Indiana corporation which manufactures specialized electronics equipment. At all times relevant to this appeal, Dage was governed by a six-member board of directors ("Board"), consisting of Ronald and Lynn Kerrigan, Louis Piccolo (a financial consultant retained by Ronald Kerrigan), Arthur and Marie Sterling, and William Conners. In addition to being a Board member, Arthur Sterling ("Sterling") had served as president of Dage for at least 20 years at the time of the trial on this matter.*1209 Of the six directors, only Arthur and Marie Sterling resided in Indiana.

For many years, Sterling operated Dage without significant input from or oversight by the Board. Over the course of the summer and early fall of 1993, however, Kerrigan took steps to subject Dage management to Board control. Kerrigan hired New York-based financial consultant and future Board member Piccolo to assess the company's performance. Kerrigan also retained New York attorney Gerald Gorinsky to represent his interests concerning Dage.

In late October of 1993, the Dage shareholders met in New Jersey to discuss an offer by Sterling to purchase the Kerrigans' shares of Dage. During the course of the meeting, Sterling first informed other directors that Menard, Inc., had expressed interest in purchasing a 30-acre parcel of land owned by Dage and located in the Michigan City area. Menard is a Wisconsin corporation that owns and operates home improvement stores in the Midwestern region of the United States.

On October 30, 1993, Menard forwarded a formal offer to Sterling pertaining to the purchase of 10.5 acres of the 30-acre parcel. Upon receipt of the offer, Sterling did not contact Menard to discuss the terms and conditions of the offer. Instead, on or about November 4, 1993, he forwarded the offer to all the Dage directors with a cover note acknowledging that Board approval was required to accept or reject the offer. Ultimately, this offer was rejected: Kerrigan, Piccolo, and Gorinsky determined that the offer should be rejected due to the collective effect of certain sections of the purchase agreement submitted by Menard, as well as co-development obligations that the offer imposed on Dage. This rejection was communicated to Sterling, and although he viewed the offer to purchase favorably, he let the offer lapse. Later, he informed Menard's agent, Gary Litvin, that members of Dage's Board objected to various provisions of the offer.

On November 30, 1993, Sterling called Kerrigan and informed him that Menard would make a second offer for the entire 30-acre parcel. Sterling presented a two-part proposed resolution ("consent resolution") to the Board: the first part authorized Sterling to "offer and purchase" another parcel located immediately to the north of the 30-acre parcel and referred to as the "Simon property"; the second part authorized Sterling to "offer and sell" the 30-acre parcel. Sterling, Kerrigan, Piccolo, and Gorinsky discussed the offer and Sterling was told to change the "offer and sell" provision to "to offer for sale." He was also instructed that he could purchase the Simon property on behalf of Dage, but could only "offer" the 30-acre parcel to Menard at a particular price. Additionally, Sterling was told that in soliciting offers for the 30-acre parcel, he was not to negotiate the terms of a sale. Gorinsky reminded Sterling that any offer from Menard would require Board review and acceptance, and he instructed Sterling to forward any offer to the Board for approval or rejection.

Finally, Sterling was told that if Menard submitted an agreement with the same objectionable provisions as the first offer, it would be rejected. Sterling agreed to follow the instructions of the Board "as long as I don't have to pay for" Gorinsky's and Piccolo's services in reviewing the offer. Based upon the discussion, Sterling drafted a new resolution, which stated that he was authorized "to take such actions as are necessary to offer for sale our 30 acre parcel ... for a price not less than $1,200,000."

On December 6, 1993, Sterling informed Piccolo that Menard had agreed to make another offer. Piccolo reminded Sterling of his obligation to secure Board approval of the offer. Menard forwarded a second proposed purchase agreement to Sterling. This agreement contained the same provisions that the Board found objectionable in the first proposed agreement. However, this offer differed in that it was for the purchase of the entire 30-acre parcel for $1,450,000.

During a week-long series of discussions beginning December 14, 1993, and unknown to any other member of the Dage Board, Sterling negotiated several minor changes in the Menard agreement and then signed the revised offer on behalf of Dage. Menard also signed, accepting the offer. Under Paragraph 5(c)(I) of the agreement, Sterling, as president of Dage, represented as follows: "The persons signing this Agreement on behalf of the Seller are duly authorized to do so and their signatures bind the Seller in accordance with the terms of this Agreement." No one at Dage had informed Menard that Sterling's authority with respect to the sale of the 30-acre parcel was limited to only the solicitation of offers.

Upon learning of the signed agreement with Menard, the Board instructed Sterling to extricate Dage from the agreement. Later, the Board hired counsel to inform Menard of its intent to question the agreement's enforceability. However, it was not until March 29, 1994, that Dage first gave notice to Menard of this intent.

Menard ultimately filed suit to require Dage to specifically perform the agreement and to secure the payment of damages. Menard initially filed a motion for partial summary judgment, which was denied. Following a bench trial, the trial court ruled in favor of Dage. The Court of Appeals affirmed, finding that Sterling did not have the express or apparent authority to bind the corporation in this land transaction.

Two main classifications of authority are generally recognized: "actual authority" and "apparent authority." Actual authority is created "by written or spoken words or other conduct of the principal which, reasonably interpreted, causes the agent to believe that the principal desires him so to act on the principal's account." Apparent authority refers to a third party's reasonable belief that the principal has authorized the acts of its agent, it arises from the principal's indirect or direct manifestations to a third party and not from the representations or acts of the agent.

On occasion, Indiana has taken an expansive view of apparent authority, including within the discussion the concept of "inherent agency power." See *Koval v. Simon Telelect, Inc.,* 693 N.E.2d 1299, 1301 (Ind.1998) "Inherent agency power is a term used ... to indicate the power of an agent which is derived not from authority, apparent authority or estoppel, but solely from the agency relation and exists for the protection of persons harmed by or dealing with a servant or other agent." *Koval,* 693 N.E.2d at 1304. This " 'status based' ... [form of] vicarious liability rests upon certain important social and commercial policies," primarily that the " 'business enterprise should bear the burden of the losses created by the mistakes or overzealousness of its agents [because such liability] stimulates the watchfulness of the employer in selecting and supervising the agents." *In re Atlantic Fin. Management, Inc.,* 784 F.2d 29, 32 (1st Cir.1986). And while "representations of the principal to the third party are central for defining apparent authority," the concept of inherent authority differs and "originates from the customary authority of a person in the particular type of agency relationship so that no representations beyond the fact of the existence of the agency need be shown." *Cange v. Stotler & Co.,* 826 F.2d 581, 591 (7th Cir.1987)

We find the concept of inherent authority - rather than actual or apparent authority - controls our analysis in this case. Menard did not negotiate and ultimately contract with a lower-tiered employee or a prototypical "general" or "special" agent, with respect to whom actual or apparent authority might be at issue.

Our determination that the inherent agency concept controls our analysis does not end the inquiry, however. The Restatement (Second) of Agency § 161 provides that an agent's inherent authority subjects his principal to liability for acts done on his account which (1) usually accompany or are incidental to transactions which the agent is authorized to conduct if, although they are forbidden by the principal, (2) the other party reasonably believes that the agent is authorized to do them and (3) has no notice that he is not so authorized.

In this case, the Board positioned its corporate president, Sterling, to "conduct a series of transactions" with Menard concerning the sale of Dage real estate. Distilled to its basics, we find that Sterling had inherent authority here if: (1) first, Sterling acted within the usual and ordinary scope of his authority as president; (2) second, Menard reasonably believed that Sterling was authorized to contract for the sale and purchase of Dage real estate; and (3) third, Menard had no notice that Sterling was not authorized to sell the 30-acre parcel without Board approval.

As to whether Sterling acted within the usual and ordinary scope of his authority as president, the trial court found that Sterling, a director and substantial shareholder of Dage, had served as Dage's president from its inception; had managed the affairs of Dage for an extended period of time with little or no Board oversight; and had purchased real estate for Dage without Board approval. Thus, the court concluded that "Sterling was not performing an act that was appropriate in the ordinary course of Dage's business."

Given that the trial court found that Sterling, as president of the company since its inception, had managed its affairs for an extended period of time with little or no Board oversight and, in particular, had purchased real estate for Dage in the past without Board approval, we conclude that Sterling's actions at issue here were acts that "usually accompany or are incidental to transactions which [he was] authorized to conduct."

Next, we must determine whether Menard reasonably believed that Sterling was authorized to contract for the sale and purchase of Dage real estate. While Sterling's apparent authority to bind Dage was "vitiated" by Menard's knowledge that the sale of Dage real estate required Board approval, this information did not defeat Sterling's inherent authority as Dage president to bind the corporation in a "setting" where he was the sole negotiator.

Because the inherent agency theory "originates from the customary authority of a person in the particular type of agency relationship," we look to the agent's indirect or direct manifestations to determine whether Menard could have "reasonably believe[d]" that Sterling was authorized to contract for the sale and purchase of Dage real estate. And considering that the "agent" in this case is a general officer of the corporation (as opposed to an "appointed general agent" or "company general manager"), we find that Menard "should not be required to scrutinize too carefully the mandates of [this] permanent ... agent[ ] ... who [did] no more than what is usually done by [a corporate president]."

Here, the facts establish that Menard reasonably believed that Sterling was authorized to contract for the sale and purchase of Dage real estate. We find it reasonable that Menard did not question the corporate president's statement that he had "authority from his Board of Directors to proceed" with the land transaction. We also find it reasonable for Menard not to scrutinize Sterling's personal "acknowledge[ment] that he signed the agreement for the purchase and sale of the real estate by authority of Dage's board of directors." We believe this especially to be the case where (1) Sterling himself was a member of the Board, (2) the agreement contained an express representation that "[t]he persons signing this Agreement on behalf of the Seller are duly authorized to do so and their signatures bind the Seller in accordance with the terms of this Agreement," and (3) Menard was aware that Dage's corporate counsel, Patrick Donoghue, was involved in the review of the terms of the agreement.

Finally, we consider whether Menard had notice that Sterling was not authorized to sell the 30-acre parcel without Board approval. The record does not indicate that Menard was aware of the existence of the consent resolution, much less that it limited Sterling's authority as president.

It is true, as the Court of Appeals noted, that Menard was advised early in the transaction that Sterling had to go to the Board to obtain approval. This knowledge would have vitiated the apparent authority of a lower-tiered employee or a prototypical general or special agent. But we do not find it sufficient notice that Sterling, an officer with inherent authority, was not authorized to bind Dage at the closing.

In Koval, this Court said: "if one of two innocent parties must suffer due to a betrayal of trust-either the principal or the third party-the loss should fall on the party who is most at fault. Because the principal puts the agent in a position of trust, the principal should bear the loss." *Koval*, 693 N.E.2d at 1304. That maxim has particular resonance here. The record fails to reveal a single affirmative act that Dage took to inform Menard of Sterling's limited authority with respect to the 30-acre parcel, and the Board did not notify Menard that Sterling had acted without its authority until 104 days after it learned of Sterling's action. By this time, Sterling had taken additional steps to close the transaction. Dage's failure to act should not now form the basis of relief, penalizing Menard and depriving it of its bargain.

SHEPARD, Chief Justice, dissenting.

I think today's decision will leave most corporate lawyers wondering what the law actually is. A board of directors authorizes the president to sell some real estate but requires that the sale be submitted to the board for approval or disapproval. The president understands that he must submit any sale to the board. He tells the potential buyer that he must submit it. The buyer knows that its offer must be submitted to the board after the president signs the sales agreement. The agreement is in fact submitted to the board and disapproved. Our Court holds that the agreement is binding anyway.

The majority calls this "an expansive view of apparent authority." Facially, this seems like an understatement. On the other hand, the Court embarks upon its discussion of "inherent authority," which it rightfully describes as a specie of apparent authority, after endorsing the conclusions of the trial court and Court of Appeals that the corporation's president did not possess apparent authority to sell the land without board approval.

In the end, it is difficult to know how lawyers will advise their clients after today's decision. Where all parties to a corporate transaction understand that board approval is required and that it may or may not be forthcoming, the black letter law cited in today's opinion points toward a conclusion that the buyer's offer was not accepted by the seller.

While I agree with the general legal principles laid out by the majority, those principles seem undercut by the resolution of this case.

CASE PROBLEM 1-3

Linda Walsh is the president and CEO of Wharton Inc. ("Wharton"). She is also its largest shareholder, owning 28 percent of Wharton's outstanding stock. The balance of the stock is owned by 14 individuals. Wharton has a seven-member board of directors that includes Linda, three other officers of Wharton, and three outside directors, all of whom own stock in Wharton. Two of the outside directors, Peter and Debbie, despise Linda for personal reasons that have nothing to do with Linda's superb performance as Wharton's CEO.

Two days ago Linda learned that Wayne, a *bona fide* star sales VP for a competitor, was looking to make a move. Linda instantly jumped on a plane and went after Wayne. They cut a deal last night that would make Wayne the new Executive VP of Wharton in charge of sales, provide Wayne with a five-year no-cut contract, pay Wayne a base salary of $300,000 a year, and provide Wayne with a bonus package that could potentially triple his base pay.

Linda must contractually wrap the deal with Wayne immediately if she has any hope of getting him. Another competitor is knocking at his door, ready to offer even more. Linda has the inside track because Wayne likes the way Linda has built Wharton and how she treats her employees.

Linda's challenge to move fast is complicated by the fact that she needs approval of Wharton's board of directors to hire Wayne as a new officer of the company with such a lucrative pay package. She has discussed the matter by phone with the three board members who are officers of Wharton, and they all rubber stamped her desire to get the deal done. Linda fears, for good reason, that Peter and Debbie would likely object or, at a minimum, make a fuss that would drag the process out and end up killing the deal. The only other director is attending the funeral of a deceased grandchild in Germany and cannot be disturbed.

Linda needs advice as to how to proceed. She knows that a deal conditioned on board approval would not be acceptable to Wayne. He would end up talking to competitors. Linda's desire is to just go ahead and sign a contract with Wayne so that the deal is done and Wayne can announce his switch and make the move. Then Linda, in due course, would call a meeting of the board and have the board approve her actions. She thinks that she has four votes in the bag.

Is this an advisable course for Linda? What other options does Linda have? Assume Wharton is incorporated in a state that has the Model Business Corporation Act and that the following MBCA provisions are applicable.

MBCA § 8.20. MEETINGS

(a) The board of directors may hold regular or special meetings in or out of this state.

(b) Unless the articles of incorporation or bylaws provide otherwise, the board of directors may permit any or all directors to participate in a regular or special meeting by, or conduct the meeting through the use of, any means of communication by which all directors participating may simultaneously hear each other during the meeting. A director participating in a meeting by this means is deemed to be present in person at the meeting.

MBCA § 8.21. ACTION WITHOUT MEETING

(a) Except to the extent that the articles of incorporation or bylaws require that action by the board of directors be taken at a meeting, action required or permitted by this Act to be taken by the board of directors may be tak38cn without a meeting if each director signs a consent describing the action to be taken and delivers it to the corporation.

MBCA § 8.22. NOTICE OF MEETING

(b) Unless the articles of incorporation or bylaws provide for a longer or shorter period, special meetings of the board of directors must be preceded by at least two days' notice of the date, time, and place of the meeting. The notice need not describe the purpose of the special meeting unless required by the articles of incorporation or bylaws.

MBCA § 8.23. WAIVER OF NOTICE

(a) A director may waive any notice required by this Act, the articles of incorporation, or bylaws before or after the date and time stated in the notice. Except as provided by subsection (b), the waiver must be in writing, signed by the director entitled to the notice, and filed with the minutes or corporate records.

(b) A director's attendance at or participation in a meeting waives any required notice to him of the meeting unless the director at the beginning of the meeting (or promptly upon his arrival) objects to holding the meeting or transacting business at the meeting and does not thereafter vote for or assent to action taken at the meeting.

MBCA § 8.40(b). OFFICERS

(b) The board of directors may elect individuals to fill one or more offices of the corporation. An officer may appoint one or more officers if authorized by the bylaws or the board of directors.

MBCA § 8.41. FUNCTIONS OF OFFICERS

Each officer has the authority and shall perform the functions set forth in the bylaws or, to the extent consistent with the bylaws, the functions prescribed by the board of directors or by direction of an officer authorized by the board of directors to prescribe the duties of other officers.

MBCA § 8.42. STANDARDS OF CONDUCT FOR OFFICERS

(a) An officer, when performing in such capacity, shall act:

(1) in good faith;

(2) with the care that a person in a like position would reasonably exercise under similar circumstances; and

(3) in a manner the officer reasonably believes to be in the best interests of the corporation.

CHAPTER 2

PARTNERSHIP AND LLC BASICS

A. THE CHALLENGE

A lawyer needs to know the basics of partnerships (there are four types) and limited liability companies. These entities are essential planning tools for many successful businesses and families. Although LLCs continue to grow in popularity, a partnership option still emerges as the preferred candidate in many choice-of-entity analyses. An extended choice-of-entity planning discussion is provided in section B. of Chapter 5.

The statutory schemes for the various entity types are an essential starting point. Since 1914, uniform acts have been developed as needed to help states enact comprehensive acts dealing with partnerships and LLCs. Although states typically modify select uniform act provisions during the legislative process, this ongoing uniform act effort has had a powerful impact in promoting consistency between the states.

The following section of this chapter summarizes the latest uniform act provisions for LLCs and the various types of partnerships. The hope is that this summary discussion, coupled with Case Problems 2-1 through 2-4, will help students understand the core legal underpinnings of the various entity types and the primary differences between them.

Sections C though G of this chapter present court opinions, commentary, and case problems dealing with entity formation challenges, third party claims, fiduciary duties, authority and management disputes, and dissolution challenges. These sections illustrate, in the context of partnerships and LLCs, the types of legal challenges that often surface when parties join together to form and operate a business. Beyond enriching a student's understanding of partnerships and LLCs, these sections are designed to provide a foundation for more extensive corporate-based discussions in later chapters that address many of the same issues: defective organizations; pre-formation transactions; the value of organizational document customization; owner and manager personal liabilities; piercing-the-veil claims; derivative action obstacles; director and officer fiduciary duties; the value and limits of exculpatory provisions; allocations of authority between owners and managers; and more.

Section H of this chapter focuses on the all-important operating agreement between the partners or LLC members. With limited exceptions, this document can establish the entire deal between the parties and preempt all statutory default rules. The smart customization of this document is the primary planning challenge during the organizational process. From the lawyer's perspective, it requires an understanding of core legal principles, the ability to help parties identify and prioritize operational issues of concern, and careful attention to detail. The ignorant use of forms can be dangerous. That said, this section illustrates this planning challenge by discussing the purposes and options of key provisions of the LLC operating agreement form that is included in Chapter 17.

Family partnerships and LLCs are the subject of the final section of this chapter, partly in recognition of the fact that most businesses in the U.S. are dominated by a single family.[1] As illustrated in the discussion, partnerships and LLCs often are used to accomplish niche objectives as part of an overall business and family plan to protect and transition wealth.

B. ENTITY STATUTORY PROVISIONS

1. PARTNERSHIPS

The partnership is the oldest form of business entity between multiple parties. Its history predates corporations and business trusts. And it is the historical foundation for all the "limiteds": limited partnership, limited liability partnership, limited liability limited partnership, and limited liability company. Partnership statutes have been around for over 2,000 years, being tracked to King Khammurabi of Babylon.[2]

A partnership is formed when there is "an association of two or more persons to carry on as co-owners a business for profit…, whether or not the persons intend to form a partnership."[3] Two distinct theories have been forever advanced to explain the nature of a partnership: an "entity" theory that focuses on a partnership being separate and apart from its owners, and an "aggregate" theory that views a partnership as an amalgamation of owner rights and interests and deemphasizes the separateness of the entity.

Focusing on the underpinnings and reach of these theories does little to advance one's understanding of partnership law because both theories are evidenced in state statutory schemes. The reason is that all states, except Louisiana, have based their partnership statutes on the Uniform Partnership Act ("UPA"), first published in 1914. The latest version, known as the Revised Uniform Partnership Act ("RUPA"), was released in 1997 and has been adopted by 37 states. While the RUPA favors the entity theory, evidence of the aggregate theory shows up throughout the RUPA in issues dealing with owners' liability for a partnership's debts, the impact of an owner's disassociation from a partnership,

---

1. Some estimate that nearly 80 percent of U.S. businesses are family-dominated. See, generally, R. Duman, "Family Firms Are Different," Entrepreneurship Theory and Practice, 1992, pp. 13–21; and M. F. R. Kets de Vries, "The Dynamics of Family Controlled Firms: The Good News and the Bad News," Organizational Dynamics, 1993, pp. 59–71; W. G. Dyer, Cultural Change in Family Firms, Jossey-Bass, San Francisco, 1986; and P. L. Rosenblatt, M. R. Anderson and P. Johnson, The Family in Business, Jossey-Bass, San Francisco, 1985; Arthur Anderson/Mass Mutual, American Family Business Survey, 2002.

2. 1 Reed Rowley, Rowley on Partnership 2 (2d ed. 1960)

3. RUPA § 202(a).

and more.

Following Case Problem 2-1 is a recap of the key provisions of the RUPA that have been adopted in most states.

CASE PROBLEM 2-1

Son developed a unique internet marketing strategy (the "Strategy") that could be worth millions. He asked Dad to "invest" $50,000 to "get the business going." Dad transferred the $50,000 to Son, and Son insisted that Dad sign a document that simply stated, "I will run the whole show, but we are now partners in the OuterNet Company partnership." As to this venture:

1. Does Dad have any property rights in Strategy?

2. How will the profits of the enterprise be allocated between Dad and Son?

3. Will Dad bear the first $50,000 of losses?

4. Does Dad have the power to bind the enterprise to contracts with third parties? Does Son?

5. What duties do Dad and Son owe each other?

6. What would be the capital accounts of Dad and Son if the partnership loses the $50,000 and then shuts down after six months because future marketing prospects look hopeless and the entity has no assets? At the time of the shut down, would Dad or Son have a financial obligation to the partnership?

7. Would Dad have any personal liability exposure if Son borrowed $150,000 in the name of OuterNet Company from a local bank, the bank had no knowledge of Dad's involvement, and Dad did not know of the loan?

a. The Partnership Agreement

A core feature of state partnership statutes is that they exalt the agreement between the partners as the primary governing source for the entity. With limited exceptions (all important), the agreement will preempt state statutory provisions, which kick in only when the partnership agreement does not address a specific issue.[4] This puts a huge premium on the development of a smart partnership agreement during the planning process. Typically, a partnership agreement may not:[5]

• Vary the statutory rights of the partnership or a partner to file a statement with the secretary of state or other designated state agency to define or limit the rights of individuals to deal with partnership real estate or take other actions on behalf of the partnership.

• Unreasonably restrict a partner's right of access to books and records.

• Eliminate a partner's duty of loyalty, but, if not manifestly unreasonable, the partnership agreement may identify specific types or categories of activities that do not violate the duty of loyalty, and the partnership agreement may provide

---

4. RUPA § 103(a).
5. RUPA § 103(b).

that all of the partners or a number or percentage specified in the partnership agreement may authorize or ratify, after full disclosure of all material facts, a specific act or transaction that otherwise would violate the duty of loyalty.

- Unreasonably reduce a partner's duty of care.

- Eliminate a partner's obligation of good faith and fair dealing, but the partnership agreement may prescribe the standards by which the performance of the obligation is to be measured, if the standards are not manifestly unreasonable.

- Vary the power of a partner to dissociate as a partner, except the partnership agreement may require that a notice to dissociate be in writing.

- Vary the right of a court to expel a partner who (1) has engaged in wrongful conduct that adversely and materially affects the partnership's business, (2) has willfully and persistently committed a material breach of the partnership agreement or a duty owned to the partnership or other partners, or (3) has engaged in conduct that makes it not reasonably practicable to carry on the partnership's business.[6]

- Vary the requirement to wind up the partnership's business if (1) continuation of all or substantially all of the partnership's business is unlawful, (2) a partner seeks a judicial determination that the economic purpose of the partnership is unreasonably frustrated, a partner has engaged in conduct that makes it not reasonably practicable to carry on the partnership's business, or it is not reasonably practicable to carry on the partnership's business in accordance with the partnership agreement, or (3) a transferee of a partner's interest seeks a judicial determination that the partnership's term or undertaking has expired or that the partnership's term was at will.[7]

- Vary the manner in which the state's law is applicable to a limited liability partnership.

- Restrict rights of third parties.

b. Property Rights

Property acquired by a partnership is property of the partnership, not property co-owned by the individual partners.[8] A partner does not have an interest in partnership property that can be transferred, either voluntarily or involuntarily.[9] Property is presumed to be partnership property if purchased with partnership assets, even if not acquired in the name of the partnership.[10] Property acquired in the name of a partner, without use of partnership funds and a reference that the partner is acting on behalf of the partnership, is presumed to be separate property of the partner.[11]

c. Agency Authority

---

6. RUPA §§ 103(b)(7), 601(5).
7. RUPA §§ 103(b)(8), 801(4)(5)(6).
8. RUPA §§ 203, 501.
9. RUPA § 501.
10. RUPA § 204(c).
11. RUPA § 204(d).

Each partner is an agent of the partnership with authority to bind the partnership in the ordinary course of the partnership's business or business of the kind carried out by the partnership, unless the partner had no authority to act for the partnership and the third person with whom the partner dealt knew or had reason to know that the partner had no such authority.[12] A partnership may file a statement (good for five years) with the secretary of state (or, in the case of real estate, with the county recorder) that states the authority, or limitations on the authority, of specific partners to enter into transactions on behalf of the partnership. Such grant of authority is conclusive in favor of a third party who gives value in reliance of the statement.[13] A person named in any such statement may file a written denial of the person's authority or status as a partner.[14]

d. Liabilities.

Partner-Created Liabilities. A partnership is liable for any actionable loss or injury caused by a partner while acting within the ordinary course of the partnership's business or within the partner's authority.[15] Similarly, a partnership is liable if a partner, while acting in the course of the partnership's business or within the scope of authority, misapplies money or property that the partner receives or causes the partnership to receive from a third party.[16]

Entity Obligations. Partners are jointly and severally liable for all obligations of the partnership unless otherwise agreed to by the claimant or provided by law. Exceptions apply for a newly admitted partner's responsibility for pre-admission obligations and (as described below) for the partners of a limited liability partnership.[17]

Purported Partner Liabilities. A person who, through word or action, purports to be a partner or consents to being represented by another as a partner is liable as a partner to any third party who relies on any such representation. If the purported partner representation is made in a public announcement, liability may attach even if the purported partner had no knowledge of the specific claimant. Personal liability under this purported liability rule is not triggered simply because a person is incorrectly named in a statement of partnership authority.[18]

e. Rights Between Partners. Unless the partnership provides otherwise, the following provisions apply to the partners:

Capital Accounts. Each partner's capital account is increased by the amount of money and the value of any property (net of liabilities) contributed to the partnership and the partner's share of any partnership profits. Each partner's capital account is decreased by the amount of money and the value of any property (net of liabilities) distributed to the partner and the partner's share of

---

12. RUPA § 301.
13. RUPA § 303.
14. RUPA § 304.
15. RUPA § 305(a).
16. RUPA § 305(b).
17. RUPA § 306.
18. RUPA § 308.

any partnership losses.[19]

Profits and Losses. Partnership profits and losses are allocated equally among the partners.[20]

Partner Advances. A partnership is obligated to indemnify a partner for payments made and liabilities incurred in the ordinary course of business or to preserve the partnership's business or property. Any such payment constitutes a loan to the partnership that accrues interest.[21]

Excessive Contributions. A partnership is obligated to reimburse a partner for any contribution to the partnership that exceeds the partner's contribution obligation. Any such excessive contribution constitutes a loan to the partnership that accrues interest.[22]

Management Rights. Each partner has an equal right to manage and conduct the partnership's business.[23]

Use of Property. A partner may use or possess partnership property only on behalf of the partnership.[24]

Partner Compensation. A partner is not entitled to any compensation for services rendered to the partnership, except for reasonable compensation for services rendered in winding up the affairs of the partnership.[25]

New Partners. A person may become a partner only with the consent of all existing partners.[26]

Dispute Resolution. A majority of the partners may resolve any dispute that involves a matter within the ordinary course of the partnership's business. A matter outside the ordinary course or any amendment to the partnership agreement requires the unanimous consent of the partners.[27]

In-Kind Distributions. No partner has a right to receive, and may not be required to accept, a distribution in kind of partnership property.[28]

Records Inspection Access. A partner and the partner's agents and attorneys has access to the books and records of the partnership, which the partnership is obligated to maintain and keep at the partnership's chief executive office. The same rights extend to former partners and the legal representatives of a deceased and disabled partner. The partnership may impose reasonable charges for the costs (both labor and materials) of document copies.[29]

Duty of Loyalty. A partner's duty of loyalty to the partnership and other partners is limited to (1) accounting and holding as trustee any property, profit or

---

19. RUPA § 401(a).
20. RUPA § 401(b).
21. RUPA § 401(c).
22. RUPA § 401(d).
23. RUPA § 401(f).
24. RUPA § 401(g).
25. RUPA § 401(h).
26. RUPA § 401(i).
27. RUPA § 401(j).
28. RUPA § 402.
29. RUPA § 403.

benefit derived by the partner in the conduct or winding up of the partnership's business or from the use of partnership property, including the appropriation of partnership opportunity, (2) refraining from dealing with the partnership as, on behalf of, a person having an interest adverse to partnership, and (3) refraining from competing with the partnership.[30] A partner does not violate this duty or any other duty merely because the partner's conduct furthers the partner's own interests, nor is a partner prohibited from loaning money to a partnership or transacting other business with a partnership.[31]

Duty of Care. A partner's duty of care to the partnership and the other partners is limited to refraining from engaging in grossly negligent or reckless conduct, intentional misconduct, or a known violation of law.[32]

Duty of Good Faith. A partner is required to discharge duties to the partnership and other partners and exercise any rights in a manner that reflects good faith and fair dealing.[33]

Enforcement Actions. A partnership may maintain an action against a partner for violation of the partnership agreement or a violation of a duty owned to the partnership. A partner may maintain an action against the partnership or other partners for legal and equitable relief to enforce rights under the partnership agreement or state law and to enforce other interests of the partner.[34]

Partner's Transferable Interest. The only transferable interest of a partner is the partner's share of profits and losses and the right to receive distributions. This interest is personal property.[35] A partner's transfer of such interest (1) is permissible, (2) does not itself cause a dissolution or winding up of the partnership, (3) does not entitle the transferee to participate in the management or conduct of the partnership's business, to require access to information about partnership transactions, or to inspect or copy partnership books and records, and (4) entitles the transferee only to distributions and net dissolution amounts that otherwise would have been paid to the transferor partner and to seek a judicial determination that it is equitable to wind up the partnership's business.[36]

Partner's Third Party Debts. The creditor of a partner may seek a judicial charging order that constitutes a lien on the partner's transferable interest in the partnership. The court may appoint a receiver and enter other orders to enforce the charging order and may order a foreclosure of the interest. The acquirer at any such foreclosure sale receives only the rights of a transferee. Statutes usually specifically provide that this is the "exclusive remedy" of a partner's judgment creditor who seeks to satisfy a claim out of the partner's interest in the partnership.[37]

f. Partner's Termination (Dissociation).

---

30. RUPA § 404(b).
31. RUPA § 404(e),(f).
32. RUPA § 404(c).
33. RUPA § 404(d).
34. RUPA § 405.
35. RUPA § 502.
36. RUPA § 503.
37. RUPA § 504.

At Will Termination. A partner may dissociate from a partnership by notice expressing a will to withdraw as a partner. When the partnership is at will, such a withdrawal will trigger a dissolution and winding up of the partnership.[38] A partnership is at will when the partners have not agreed to remain partners until the expiration of a definite term or the completion of a particular undertaking.[39]

Other Triggers. Statutes typically provide that a partner's interest also may be terminated by the:

1) Occurrence of a dissociation event specified in the partnership agreement;

2) Expulsion of a partner pursuant to the partnership agreement;

3) Unanimous vote of the other partners if (a) it is unlawful to carry on business with the partner, (b) there has been a transfer of substantially all of a partner's interest in the partnership, (c) the partner is a corporation that has filed a certificate of dissolution or has had its charter revoked or its right to conduct business suspended, or (4) the partner is a partnership that has been dissolved;

4) A judicial determination of expulsion due to the partner's wrongful conduct, willful and persistent breach of the partnership agreement or duties owed, or conduct that makes it not reasonably practical to carry on the business with the partner;

5) Partner becoming a debtor in bankruptcy, executing an assignment for the benefit of creditors, or having a trustee, receiver or liquidator appointed to handle the partner's property;

6) Partner dying, having a guardian or conservator appointed to handle the partner's property, or being judicially determined to be incapable of performing the partner's duties under the partnership agreement;

7) Transfer of the partner's interest in the partnership by a trustee or a personal representative of an estate holding the partnership interest; and

8) Termination of any partner who is not an individual, partnership, corporation, trust, or estate.[40]

Purchase of Interest. Typically, a partner's dissociation does not force a dissolution and winding up of the partnership unless the dissociation is due to the death of a partner or one of the triggers described in items (5) through (8) above and over half of the partners approve a winding up of the partnership. Absent such circumstances, the interest of the departing partner is purchased for a price equal to the greater of the liquidation value of the partner's interest or the value based on a sale of the business as a going concern. State statutes usually specify the procedures for establishing the value.[41]

Dissociated Partner's Liabilities. A dissociated partner remains liable: (1) to the partnership and other partners for any damages or losses resulting from a

---

38. RUPA §§ 601(1), 801(1).
39. RUPA § 101(8).
40. RUPA § 601.
41. RUPA §§ 603, 701.

withdrawal that violated the partnership agreement or actions taken by the dissociated partner after the dissociation; and (2) to third parties for joint and several exposure obligations and liabilities arising prior to the dissociation. The dissociated partner's exposure on such a pre-dissociation obligation may be eliminated by agreement with the creditor and the other partners or by a material change in the terms of the obligation with the creditor having notice of the dissociation. Continued use of a dissociated partner's name in the partnership's name does not expose the dissociated partner to obligations of the partnership incurred after the dissociation.[42]

Third Party Protection. The partnership may be liable to third parties who reasonably believed that a dissociated partner was still a partner for actions taken by the dissociated partner within two years of the dissociation, provided the partnership may cut off this exposure 90 days after filing a notice of dissociation with the secretary of state.[43]

g. Dissolution and Winding Up

Triggering Events. A partnership is dissolved, and its business must be wound up when (1) a partner gives notice to withdraw in an at will partnership; (2) a majority of partners approve winding up when a partner dies or dissociates for one of the reasons described in items (5) though (8) above; (3) the partners all agree to a winding up of the business; (4) the partnership's specified term or undertaking has expired or been completed; (5) a dissolution event specified in the partnership agreement occurs; (6) an event (not curable in 90 days) occurs that makes it unlawful to carry on substantially all of the partnership's business; (7) on application of a partner, a court determines that the economic purpose of the partnership is unreasonably frustrated, a partner has engaged in conduct that makes it not reasonably practicable to carry on the partnership's business, or it is not reasonably practicable to carry on the partnership's business in accordance with the partnership agreement, or (8) on application of the transferee of a partner's interest, a court determines that it would be equitable to windup the affairs of the partnership.[44]

Winding Up. A partnership continues after dissolution only for purposes of winding up the business. At any time after dissolution, the partners may unanimously agree to terminate the winding up and resume the partnership's business activities.[45] Any partner who has not wrongfully dissociated from the partnership may participate in the winding up, subject to a court's power to order judicial supervision of the winding up. A person winding up a partnership may seek to preserve the business as a going concern for a reasonable time, prosecute and defend actions, settle and close the partnership's business, dispose of assets, pay liabilities, resolve disputes, bind the partnership for acts taken in connection with the winding up, and make distributions to partners.[46]

Statement of Dissolution. Any partner who has not dissociated may file a

---

42. RUPA §§ 702, 703.
43. RUPA §§ 702(a), 704.
44. RUPA § 801.
45. RUPA § 802.
46. RUPA § 803.

statement of dissolution which is deemed to give any third party notice of the dissolution and limitation on the partners' authority 90 days after filing.[47]

Account Settlement and Deficit Restoration Obligations. Proceeds from the winding up must first be used to discharge obligations to creditors. Remaining proceeds are distributed to the partners in accordance with the respective positive balances in their capital accounts. Any partner who has a negative capital account balance must make a contribution to the partnership in an amount equal to the negative balance. If such partner fails to restore the negative balance, any amount needed by the partnership to pay partnership debts as a result of such failure must be paid by the other partners in proportion to their loss sharing percentages, and such other partners may seek to recover such additional contributions from the defaulting partner. Any partnership obligations that surface after the settlement of all partner accounts must be paid by the partners making additional contributions in proportion to their loss allocation percentages.[48]

h. Choice of Law

State statutes typically provide that the laws of the jurisdiction where the partnership maintains its chief executive office will govern relationships among the partners and between the partners and the partnership.[49]

CASE PROBLEM 2-2

Jake and Luke formed a general partnership to sell a special yacht that would be designed and built in Italy. Jake's sole obligation was to provide the start-up capital of $125,000. He spent the balance of his time teaching law school.

Luke was the driving force behind the effort. He lined up a design and manufacturing firm in Italy, developed super-slick marketing materials, and started hustling customers for pre-orders. He ultimately collected $1.4 million in "advances" from nine customers located in seven different states. Luke regularly advised Jake that Jake's investment and the pre-order advances provided all the capital that was required to launch the business. He would exclaim, "Once the yachts start arriving, we will be gold."

Last month, Luke's wife and young daughter died in a tragic automobile accident. Devastated, Luke left the country and absconded with roughly $1.3 million, having spent only $225,000 on advances to the Italian company and marketing related expenses. The yacht venture instantly collapsed.

The nine customers soon learned of Luke's departure. They are claiming that Jake must repay them the amount of their advances, plus interest. If they are right, Jake will be forced into bankruptcy.

Is Jake personally liable to the nine customers? Would he be personally liable if Jake and Luke had formed a limited liability company? How about a

---

47. RUPA § 805.
48. RUPA § 806.
49. RUPA § 706(a).

limited partnership, with Luke as the general partner and Jake as the limited partner? How about a limited liability partnership?

2. LIMITED LIABILITY PARTNERSHIPS

A limited liability partnership ("LLP") is a partnership that has filed a statement of qualification (sometimes called an "application") with the state's secretary of state and that does not have a similar statement in effect in another jurisdiction.[50] The terms and conditions on which a partnership becomes an LLP must be approved by a vote necessary to amend the partnership agreement, but if the partnership agreement contains provisions that expressly consider obligations to contribute to the partnership, it must be approved by the vote necessary to amend such provisions.[51]

a. Qualification Statement. The statement of qualification usually must state the name of the partnership, the location of a registered office, the address of its principal office; and a statement that the partnership elects to be an LLP.[52] Some states require that the qualification statement also include the number of partners and a brief statement of the business in which the partnership engages. Typically, a majority of the partners, or one or more authorized partners, must execute documents submitted to the secretary of state. The LLP's registration is effective immediately after the date the application is filed, or at such later date specified in the application.[53]

b. Name. The name of an LLP must end with the words "Registered Limited Liability Partnership," "limited liability partnership" or the abbreviation "R.L.L.P.," "RLLP," "L.L.P.," or "LLP."[54]

c. Annual Report. An LLP must file an annual report with the secretary of state and pay an annual fee. The annual report must update the contact information for the LLP's chief executive office and registered agent.[55] Some states also require updated information on the number of partners currently in the partnership and whether there are any material changes in the information contained in the partnership's qualification statement.

d. Liability of Partners. A partner of an LLP is not personally liable for an obligation of the partnership incurred while the partnership is an LLP, whether arising in contract, tort, or otherwise, by reason of being a partner. This limited liability exists even if the partnership agreement contained inconsistent provisions before making the election to become an LLP.[56] This is the big advantage of an LLP over a general partnership.

e. Applicable Law. State statutes typically provide that the law under which a foreign LLP is formed governs relations among the partners and between

---

50. RUPA § 101(5).
51. RUPA § 1001(b).
52. RUPA § 1001(c).
53. RUPA § 1001(e).
54. RUPA § 1002.
55. RUPA § 1003.
56. RUPA § 306(c).

the partners and the partnership, and the liability of partners for obligations of the partnership.[57] States require a foreign LLP to file a statement of foreign qualification before transacting business in the state and typically provide that such a statement does not authorize a foreign LLP to engage in any business or exercise any power that a partnership in the state could not engage in or exercise as an LLP.[58] Absent the filing of such statement, a foreign LLP usually cannot maintain an action or proceeding in the state.[59]

f. Professional Service Providers. LLPs are often used by providers of professional services. Licensed partners of a professional provider LLP may be liable under state law for the partnership's debts if the partnership fails to maintain professional insurance coverage required by state law.

3. LIMITED PARTNERSHIPS

A limited partnership is an entity that has one or more general partners ("GP") and one or more limited partners ("LP") and is formed under a state's limited partnership act.[60] GPs have the authority to manage and conduct the business of the partnership and are personally liable for the debts and obligations of the partnership.[61] LPs typically are investors who have limited or minimal control over daily business decisions and operations of the partnership and have no personal liability for the obligations of the partnership beyond their capital contributions to the partnership.[62] If properly organized and managed, the limited partnership form of business organization allows persons to contribute capital to a business enterprise and share in its profits and losses without having liability exposure to the creditors of the business.

Limited partnerships did not exist at common law; they are creatures of state statutory law. The Uniform Limited Partnership Act ("ULPA"), with origins dating back to 1916 and most recently revised in 2001, has served as the basic framework for limited partnership statutes in 49 states. The 2001 version of the ULPA differs from prior versions in two significant respects. First, it no longer "links" its provisions to the Uniform Partnership Act. It is a "stand-alone" act that is considerably longer than the prior versions. Second, its revisions are targeted at those situations where a limited partnership is often the preferred entity form – sophisticated, manager-entrenched commercial deals whose participants commit for the long term and family limited partnerships used for estate planning purposes. The management powers of the GPs are increased; the management role and exit rights of LPs are decreased.

Although the 2001 version is not linked to the Revised Uniform Partnership Act, many state limited partnership acts remain linked to their versions of the Uniform Partnership Act. State adoption of the 2001 stand-alone version proceeds slowly.

---

57. RUPA § 1101(a).
58. RUPA §§ 1101(c), 1102.
59. RUPA § 1103(a).
60. ULPA §102(11) (2001).
61. ULPA §§ 402, 404 (2001).
62. ULPA §§ 302, 303 (2001).

CASE PROBLEM 2-3

Assume Son and Dad in Case Problem 2-1 form a limited partnership in a state that has adopted the Uniform Limited Partnership Act (2001), with Son as the general partner and Dad as the limited partner.

1. Does Dad have any property rights in Strategy?

2. How will distributions be allocated to Son and Dad if there is no specific agreement between the parties?

3. Would there be limits on the amount of distributions to Son and Dad?

4. Does Dad have the power to bind the enterprise to contracts with third parties? Does Son?

5. What duties do Dad and Son owe each other?

6. Would Dad have any personal liability exposure if Son borrowed $150,000 in the name of OuterNet Company from a local bank, the bank had no knowledge of Dad's involvement, and Dad did not know of the loan?

a. Entity Characteristics

A limited partnership is an entity distinct from its partners and may be organized for any lawful purpose and for a perpetual duration.[63] It has the power to do all things necessary and convenient to carry on its business, including the power to sue, be sued and defend in its own name.[64] The partnership agreement governs the operation of the entity, but, as in the case of a general partnership, there is a list of statutory provisions that cannot be changed by agreement. In most states, such list is substantively identical (or nearly so) to the list applicable to a general partnership,[65] as are the provisions relating to when a person will be deemed to have constructive notice of a fact regarding a limited partnership.[66] The name of the entity must contain the phrase "limited partnership," "L.P.," or "LP."[67]

b. Formation

A limited partnership is formed by filing a certificate of limited partnership with the state's secretary of state. At a minimum, state statutes require the certificate to state: the name of the limited partnership; the street and address of the entity's initial designated office; and the name, street and mailing address of each general partner and the entity's initial registered agent for service of process.[68] A limited partnership is actually formed when the secretary of state files the certificate.[69] Limited partnerships typically are required to file annual reports with the state's secretary of state.

---

63. ULPA § 104 (2001).
64. ULPA § 105 (2001).
65. ULPA § 110 (2001).
66. ULPA § 103 (2001).
67. ULPA § 108(b) (2001).
68. ULPA § 201 (2001).
69. ULPA § 201(c) (2001).

c. Rights and Liabilities of GPs and LPs

Agency and Management Authority. An LP has no power to act for or bind the entity.[70] A GP is an agent of the limited partnership with full authority to manage and conduct the affairs of the limited partnership and bind the entity.[71] Each GP has equal management rights, and any matter relating to the entity's activities may be exclusively decided by the GP or, if there is more than one GP, by a majority of the GPs.[72] A GP has the same reimbursement rights for advances and excessive contributions as a partner of a general partnership.[73] Absent a provision in the partnership agreement, a GP is not entitled to any remuneration for services rendered to the partnership.[74]

Liability for Entity Obligations. GPs are jointly and severally liable for the obligations of a limited partnership.[75] LPs have no personal liability for the entity's obligation.[76]

Fiduciary Obligations. A GP has the same duties of loyalty, care, good faith and fair dealing as a partner of a general partnership.[77] An LP has no fiduciary duties to the limited partnership or the other partners, but does have a good faith and fair dealing requirement in exercising rights under the limited partnership agreement.[78]

Dual Capacity Partner. A person may be both a GP and an LP and have the rights, duties and liabilities of each of those capacities.[79]

Information and Inspection Rights. An LP typically has an unlimited right to inspect and copy select core documents (specified by statute) during normal business hours, at an office designated by the entity, and on limited advance notice (normally 10 days). Other LP document requests relating to the activities or financial condition of the entity require a written request that must state a purpose reasonably related to the partnership, describe with particularity the information sought, and demonstrate that the information sought is related to the purpose. The GPs then decide whether to honor the request and may impose restrictions on the use of the information and charge the requesting LP any cost (labor and materials) incurred in connection with the request.[80] A GP has much broader information and inspection rights, being entitled to receive all information and documents reasonably required for the exercise of the GP's management rights and authority.[81]

Contributions. A partner's contribution may consist of tangible and intangible property, including promissory notes, services performed, and services

---

70. ULPA § 302 (2001).
71. ULPA § 402 (2001).
72. ULPA § 406(a) (2001).
73. ULPA § 406(c),(d),(e) (2001).
74. ULPA § 406(f) (2001).
75. ULPA § 404 (2001).
76. ULPA § 303 (2001).
77. ULPA § 408 (2001).
78. ULPA § 305 (2001).
79. ULPA § 113 (2001).
80. ULPA § 304 (2001).
81. ULPA § 407 (2001).

to be performed. A partner's contribution obligation is not excused by death, disability, or other inability to perform and may be compromised only be the consent of all partners. Any creditor who extends credit in reliance on a contribution obligation of a partner, with no notice that the obligation has been compromised, may enforce the original obligation.[82]

Distributions. Absent a contrary provision in the limited partnership agreement (which usually exists), distributions by a limited partnership are allocated among partners on the basis of the relative value of their contributions to the entity.[83] This default rule is significantly different from the corresponding default rule for general partnerships. A partner has no right to a distribution before the dissolution and winding up of the entity, nor does a partner have the right to demand or receive a distribution in any form other than cash. A limited partnership may elect to make a distribution of an asset in kind so long as each partner receives a proportionate share of the asset based on the partner's share of distributions. A partner who is entitled to receive a distribution under the partnership agreement has the rights of a creditor, subject to offset rights of the partnership for any amounts owed by the partner to the partnership. A limited partnership is prohibited from making a distribution in violation of the partnership agreement.[84]

Transferee Rights and Charging Orders. A state's limited partnership statutory provisions dealing with the "personal property" nature of a partner's interest, the rights to transfer a partnership interest, the rights of a transferee of a partnership interest, and the rights of a partner's creditors to obtain and foreclose on a charging order are usually substantially identical to the corresponding statutory provisions for general partnerships.[85] The personal representative of a deceased limited partner may exercise the rights of a transferee or the rights of an existing limited partner, as applicable.[86]

d. Prohibited Distributions

Statutory Limitations. A limited partnership usually is prohibited from making a distribution if, after the distribution, (1) the entity is unable to pay its debts as they become due in the ordinary course of business or (2) the entity's total assets have a value that is less than the sum of the entity's total liabilities plus the amount of any superior preferable distributions that would be due to other partners if the entity was dissolved and wound up. In applying this limitation, the limited partnership may value its assets based on financial statements prepared in accordance with accounting principles that are reasonable in the circumstances or on a fair valuation of the assets. Any indebtedness issued by a limited partnership to partners as part of a distribution is not considered a liability for purposes of the limitation calculation if, and only if, any payments of principal or interest on such indebtedness are to be made only if they would be permissible distributions at the time made.[87]

---

82. ULPA §§ 501, 502 (2001).
83. ULPA § 503 (2001).
84. ULPA §§ 504 through 507 (2001).
85. ULPA §§ 701 through 703 (2001).
86. ULPA § 704 (2001).
87. ULPA § 508 (2001).

Related Partner Liabilities. A GP who consents to a distribution that exceeds the statutory limitations on distributions is personally liable to the limited partnership for any excess distribution if it is established that the GP violated a duty of loyalty, care, good faith or fair dealing to the entity. Any partner or transferee who knowingly receives a distribution in excess of the statutory limits is personally liability to the entity for the amount of such excess.[88]

e. Partner Termination (Dissociation)

Limited Partners. Limited partners generally have no power to dissociate from a limited partnership prior to the termination of the limited partnership unless they are granted specific termination rights in the limited partnership agreement.[89] State limited partnership statutes that specify the circumstances in which a limited partner's interest may be terminated usually are substantively identical to the corresponding provisions for terminating a partner's interest in a general partnership.[90] The dissociation of a limited partner's interest terminates the rights of the dissociated partner, but does not terminate the entity, the dissociated partner's duties of good faith and fair dealing, or any obligation that the dissociated partner owes to the partnership or the other partners.[91]

General Partners. A GP may choose to dissociate from a limited partnership at any time, rightfully or wrongfully, by expressed will.[92] State limited partnership statutes that specify the circumstances in which a GP's interest may be terminated usually are substantively identical to the corresponding provisions for terminating a partner's interest in a general partnership.[93] A GP's dissociation is wrongful only if it violates the partnership agreement or, unless the agreement provides otherwise, it occurs before the partnership terminates and the dissociation is due to a voluntary withdrawal, a judicial expulsion, a bankruptcy of the GP, or the GP ceasing to exist as an entity.[94] A GP who wrongfully dissociates is liable to the limited partnership for any damages caused by the dissociation. The dissociation of a GP's interest terminates all managing rights, ongoing duties of loyalty and care, and (with very limited exceptions) the dissociated GP's liability for partnership obligations incurred after the dissociation. A dissociated GP remains personally liable for partnership obligations incurred prior to the dissociation unless the dissociated partner's exposure for a pre-dissociation obligation is eliminated by agreement with the creditor and the other partners or by a material change in the terms of the obligation with the creditor having notice of the dissociation.[95]

f. Dissolution and Winding Up

Triggering Events. Statutory provisions generally provide that a limited partnership must be dissolved and wound up on: (1) the occurrence of a

---

88. ULPA § 509 (2001).
89. ULPA § 601(a) (2001).
90. ULPA § 601(b) (2001).
91. ULPA § 602 (2001).
92. ULPA § 604(a) (2001).
93. ULPA § 603 (2001).
94. ULPA § 604(b) (2001).
95. ULPA § 607 (2001).

dissolution event specified in the partnership agreement; (2) the consent of all the GPs and LPs who own a majority of the distribution rights; (3) the dissociation of a GP with at least one remaining GP, and LPs who own a majority of distribution rights consent to the dissolution; (4) the dissociation of a GP with no remaining GP, unless within 90 days a GP is admitted and LPs who own a majority of distribution rights consent to continue business activities; (5) 90 days after the dissociation of the last LP, unless a new LP is admitted during such period; (6) a declaration of dissolution by the state's secretary of state for failure to file an annual report or pay required fees; or (7) by order of a court based on a determination that it is not reasonably practicable to carry on the activities of the limited partnership in accordance with the partnership agreement.[96]

Impacts. The statutory impacts of winding up a limited partnership are very similar to those of a general partnership with the clarification that if the entity does not have a GP, LPs who own a majority of the distribution rights may appoint a person to wind up and dissolve the entity. A GP who causes a limited partnership to incur inappropriate obligations during a winding up is liable to the limited partnership for such obligations.[97]

g. Litigation Rights

Some state statutes specifically authorize a partner of a limited partnership to bring a direct action against the partnership or other partners for legal or equitable relief to enforce the partner's rights under the partnership agreement or applicable law. The partner must plead and prove an actual or threatened injury to the partner, not the partnership. A right to an accounting upon a dissolution and winding up does not revive a claim barred by law.[98] Such statutes also usually permit a limited partner to maintain a derivative action on behalf of the limited partnership only if (1) the partner first makes a demand on GP's to bring the action or pleads with particularity why such a demand would be futile and (2) any recovery from the litigation is paid to the limited partnership. If such a derivative action is successful, the court may award a reimbursement of the plaintiff's attorney fees and costs from the recovery.[99]

4. LIMITED LIABILITY LIMITED PARTNERSHIPS

The limited liability limited partnership ("LLLP") is to a limited partnership what an LLP is to a general partnership. Its role is to eliminate the personal liability exposure that general partners have for the obligations of a limited partnership. It's a relatively new entity form that has been adopted in roughly half the states.

The LLLP statutory provisions are additions to each state's version of the Uniform Limited Partnership Act that mirror the LLP additions to the state's version of the Uniform Partnership Act. They include statutory requirements to elect LLLP status in the limited partnership's filed certificate[100] and use of a

---

96. ULPA §§ 801, 802 (2001).
97. ULPA §§ 803 through 805 (2001).
98. ULPA § 1001 (2001).
99. ULPA §§ 1002 through 1004 (2001).
100. ULPA § 201(a)(4) (2001).

name that includes the phrase "limited liability limited partnership," "LLLP," or "L.L.L.P."[101]

With LLLP status, a general partner is not personally liable for an obligation of the limited partnership incurred while the partnership is an LLLP, whether arising in contract, tort, or otherwise. This limited liability exists even if the partnership agreement contained inconsistent provisions before making the election to become an LLLP.[102]

5. LIMITED LIABILITY COMPANIES

CASE PROBLEM 2-4

Assume Son and Dad in Case Problem 2-1 form a limited liability company in a state that has adopted the Revised Uniform Limited Liability Company Act. How would you answer questions 1 through 6 of Case Problem 2-3 if the LLC is a member-managed LLC? How would your answers change if the LLC is a manager-managed LLC with Son as the manager?

a. LLC Characteristics

The limited liability company ("LLC") has emerged as the most popular form of non-corporate entity. It offers limited liability protection for the LLC's members and the flexibility of having an entity that is managed by designated managers or by the members generally. The framework for state LLC laws is the Uniform Limited Liability Company Act, originally adopted in 1995 and most recently amended in 2006.

A limited liability company is an entity distinct from its members and may be organized for any lawful purpose and for a perpetual duration.[103] It has the power to do all things necessary and convenient to carry on its business, including the power to sue, be sued and defend in its own name.[104] The LLC operating agreement governs: the relations among the members as members and between the members and the limited liability company; the rights and duties of a person in the capacity of manager; the activities of the company and the conduct of those activities; and the means and conditions for amending the operating agreement.[105]

As in the case of a partnership or limited partnership, there is a list of statutory provisions that cannot be changed by agreement. In most states, such list is similar in many respects to the list applicable to partnerships.[106] The name of the entity must contain the phrase "limited liability company," "limited company," "L.L.C.," "LLC," "L.C.," or "LC." The word "limited" may be abbreviated as "Ltd," and "company" may be abbreviated as "Co."[107]

---

101. ULPA § 108(c) (2001).
102. ULPA § 404(c)(2001).
103. RULLCA § 104
104. RULLCA § 105
105. RULLCA § 110(a).
106. RULLCA § 110(c).
107. RULLCA § 108(a).

b. Formation

A limited liability company is formed by one or more organizers filing a certificate of organization with the state's secretary of state. At a minimum, state statutes require the certificate to state: the name of the LLC; the street and address of the entity's initial designated office; the name, street and mailing address of the LLC's initial registered agent for service of process; and a statement that the LLC has no members if there are no members at time of filing.[108] If the LLC certificate states there are no members at time of filing, the certificate will lapse and be void if, within 90 days of filing, a follow-up filing is not made confirming that the LLC has at least one member.[109] An LLC is actually formed when the secretary of state files the certificate and the LLC has at least one member.[110] LLCs typically are required to file annual reports with the state's secretary of state.

c. Operating Agreement Limiting Provisions

State statutes often provide that, if not manifestly unreasonable, an LLC's operating agreement may:[111]

1. Restrict or eliminate a member's duty of loyalty.

2. Identify specific types or categories of activities that do not violate the duty of loyalty.

3. Alter the duty of care, except to authorize intentional misconduct or a known violation of law.

4. Alter any other fiduciary duty, including eliminating particular aspects of that duty.

5. Prescribe the standards by which to measure the performance of the obligations of good faith and fair dealing.

6. Specify the method by which a specific act or transaction that would otherwise violate the duty of loyalty may be authorized or ratified by one or more disinterested and independent persons after full disclosure of all material facts.

7. Eliminate or limit any fiduciary duty that would have pertained to a responsibility that a member has been relieved of under the LLC operating agreement.

8. Alter or eliminate any indemnification rights of a member or manager.

9. Eliminate or limit a member or manager's liability to the LLC and members for money damages, except for a breach of the duty of loyalty, a financial benefit received by a member or manager to which the member or manager is not entitled, a breach of a duty for unauthorized distributions, intentional infliction of harm on the company or a member, or an intentional violation of criminal law.

---

108. RULLCA § 201(b).
109. RULLCA § 201(e)(1).
110. RULLCA § 201(d)(1).
111. RULLCA § 110.

d. Agency and Management Authority

A member is not an agent of an LLC by reason of being a member.[112] An LLC is deemed to be a member-managed LLC unless the operating agreement expressly provides that it will be "manager-managed" or includes words of similar import.[113]

Member-Managed LLC. In a member-managed LLC: the management and conduct of the company are vested in the members; each member has equal rights in the management and conduct of the company's activities; any difference arising among members as to a matter in the ordinary course of the activities of the LLC may be decided by a majority of the members; an act outside the ordinary course of the activities of the LLC may be undertaken only with the consent of all members; and the operating agreement may be amended only with the consent of all members.[114]

Manager-Managed LLC. In a manager-managed LLC: any matter relating to the activities of the company is decided exclusively by the managers unless a statute specifically provides otherwise; each manager has equal rights in the management and conduct of the activities of the LLC; and a difference arising among managers as to a matter in the ordinary course of the activities of the LLC may be decided by a majority of the managers. Also, consent of all members is required to: sell or otherwise dispose of all, or substantially all, of the company's property; approve a merger, conversion, or domestication; undertake any other act outside the ordinary course of the company's activities; and amend the operating agreement.[115]

Manager Selection and Removal. A manager may be chosen at any time by the consent of a majority of the members and remains a manager until a successor has been chosen, unless the manager at an earlier time resigns, is removed, or dies, or, in the case of a manager that is not an individual, ceases to exist. A manager may be removed at any time by the consent of a majority of the members without notice or cause.[116] A person need not be a member to be a manager, but the dissociation of a member who is also a manager removes the person as a manager. If a person who is both a manager and a member ceases to be a manager, that cessation does not by itself dissociate the person as a member.[117] A person who wrongfully causes dissolution of the company loses the right to participate in management as a member and a manager.[118]

Written Consent. An action requiring the consent of members may be taken without a meeting by use of a written consent. A member may appoint a proxy or other agent to consent or otherwise act for the member.[119]

---

112. RULLCA § 301(a).
113. RULLCA § 407(a).
114. RULLCA § 407(b).
115. RULLCA § 407(c).
116. RULLCA § 407(c)(5).
117. RULLCA § 407(c)(6).
118. RULLCA § 407(e).
119. RULLCA § 407(d).

Compensation. A member is not entitled to remuneration for services performed for a member-managed LLC, except for reasonable compensation for services rendered in winding up the activities of the company.[120]

Indemnification. An LLC must reimburse for any payment made and indemnify for any debt, obligation, or other liability incurred by a member of a member-managed company or the manager of a manager-managed company in the course of the member's or manager's activities on behalf of the LLC unless the action involved a violation of a fiduciary duty or a prohibited distribution.[121]

Insurance. A limited liability company may purchase and maintain insurance on behalf of a member or manager of the LLC against liability asserted against or incurred by the member or manager.[122]

Statement of Authority. An LLC may file a statement (good for five years) with the secretary of state (or, in the case of real estate, with the county recorder) which states the authority, or limitations on the authority, of specific persons to enter into transactions on behalf of the LLC. Such grant of authority is conclusive in favor of a third party who gives value in reliance of the statement.[123] A person named in any such statement may file a written denial of the person's authority.[124]

e. LLC Member Rights and Duties

Liability for Entity Obligations. LLC members have no personal liability for the entity's obligation, whether arising in contract, tort or otherwise. The failure of an LLC to observe any particular formalities relating to the exercise of its powers or management of its activities is not a ground for imposing liability on the members or managers for the debts, obligations, or other liabilities of the LLC.[125]

Fiduciary Obligations in Member-Managed LLC. A member of a member-managed LLC owes to the LLC and other members a duty of loyalty to: account to the LLC and to hold as trustee for it any property, profit, or benefit derived by the member in the conduct or winding up of the company's activities; refrain from dealing with the LLC as or on behalf of a person having an interest adverse to the company (subject to a defense of fairness to the LLC); and refrain from competing with the LLC. All members may authorize or ratify, after full disclosure of all material facts, a specific act or transaction that otherwise would violate this duty of loyalty. Such member also has a contractual obligation of good faith and fair dealing and, subject to the business judgment rule, has a duty of care to act with the care that a person in a like position would reasonably exercise under similar circumstances and in a manner the member reasonably believes to be in the best interests of the LLC. In discharging this duty, a member may rely in good faith upon opinions, reports, statements, or other information provided by another person that the member reasonably believes is a competent

---

120. RULLCA § 407(f).
121. RULLCA § 408(a).
122. RULLCA § 408(b).
123. RULLCA § 302.
124. RULLCA § 303.
125. RULLCA § 304.

and reliable source for the information.[126]

Fiduciary Duties in Manager-Managed LLC. In a manager-managed LLC, members do not have any fiduciary duties to the LLC by reason of being a member, but do have a contractual obligation of good faith and fair dealing. Managers have the fiduciary duties of loyalty and care described above, along with a contractual obligation of good faith and fair dealing. Any approval or ratification of an act that violates the duty of loyalty requires the approval of all members.[127]

Information and Inspection Rights. In a member-managed LLC, a member typically has unlimited document inspection rights relating to the LLC's activities and financial condition. In a manager-managed LLC, such rights are reserved to the managers, and members must submit an inspection request that states a purpose material to the member's interests in the LLC, describes with particularity the information sought, and demonstrates that the information sought is related to the purpose. The LLC may then decide whether to honor the request, impose restrictions on the use of the information, and charge the requesting member the costs (labor and materials) incurred in connection with the request.[128]

Contributions. An LLC member's contribution may consist of tangible and intangible property, including promissory notes, services performed, and services to be performed. A member's contribution obligation is not excused by death, disability, or other inability to perform and may be compromised only by the consent of all members. Any creditor who extends credit in reliance on a contribution obligation of a member, with no notice that the obligation has been compromised, may enforce the original obligation.[129]

Distributions. Absent a contrary provision in the LLC operating agreement (which usually exists), distributions by an LLC prior to a dissolution and winding up must be in equal shares among the members. A member has no right to a distribution before the dissolution and winding up of the entity, nor does a member have the right to demand or receive a distribution in any form other than money. An LLC may elect to make a distribution of an asset in kind so long as each member receives a proportionate share of the asset based on the member's share of distributions. A member who is entitled to receive a distribution under the operating agreement has the rights of a creditor.[130]

Transferee Rights and Charging Orders. A state's LLC statutory provisions dealing with the "personal property" nature of a member's LLC interest, the rights to transfer an LLC interest, the rights of a transferee of an LLC interest, and the rights of an LLC member's creditors to obtain and foreclose on a charging order are usually substantially identical to the corresponding statutory provisions for partnerships. The personal representative of a deceased member may exercise the rights of a transferee or the rights of an existing member, as

---

126. RULLCA § 409(a)-(f).
127. RULLCA § 409(g).
128. RULLCA § 410.
129. RULLCA §§ 402, 403.
130. RULLCA §§ 404. RULLCA § 406.

applicable.[131]

f. Prohibited Distributions

Statutory Limitations. An LLC usually is prohibited from making a distribution if, after the distribution, (1) the entity in unable to pay its debts as they become due in the ordinary course of business or (2) the entity's total assets have a value that is less than the sum of the entity's total liabilities plus the amount of any superior preferable distributions that would be due to other partners if the entity was dissolved and wound up. In applying this limitation, the LLC may value its assets based on financial statements prepared in accordance with accounting principles that are reasonable in the circumstances or on a fair valuation of the assets. Any indebtedness issued by an LLC to members as part of a distribution is not considered a liability for purposes of the limitation calculation if, and only if, any payments of principal or interest on such indebtedness are to be made only if they would be permissible distributions at the time made.[132]

Related Member and Manager Liabilities. A member of a member-managed LLC or a manager of a manager-managed LLC who consents to a distribution that exceeds the statutory limitations on distributions is personally liable to the LLC for any excess distribution if it is established that the member or manager violated a duty of loyalty, care, good faith or fair dealing to the entity. A person who knowingly receives a distribution in excess of the statutory limits is personally liable to the entity for the amount of such excess.[133]

g. Member Dissociation

Dissociation Rights. A member may choose to dissociate from an LLC at any time, rightfully or wrongfully, by expressed will. State LLC statutes that specify the circumstances in which a member's interest may be terminated usually are very similar to the corresponding provisions for terminating a partner's interest in a general partnership. A member's dissociation is wrongful only if it violates the LLC agreement or, unless the agreement provides otherwise, it occurs before the LLC terminates and the dissociation is due to a voluntary withdrawal, a judicial expulsion, a bankruptcy of the member, or the member being dissolved or terminated. A member who wrongfully dissociates is liable to the LLC and to other members for any damages caused by the dissociation.[134]

Dissociation Impacts. The dissociation of a member interest terminates all managing rights, and, if the LLC is member-managed, all ongoing duties of loyalty and care end with regard to matters arising after the dissociation.[135]

h. Dissolution and Winding Up

Triggering Events. Statutory provisions generally provide that an LLC

---

131. RULLCA §§ 501 through 504.
132. RULLCA § 405.
133. RULLCA § 406.
134. RULLCA §§ 601, 602.
135. RULLCA § 603.

must be dissolved and wound up on: (1) the occurrence of a dissolution event specified in the LLC operating agreement; (2) the consent of all the members; (3) the passage of 90 days during which the LLC has no members; and (4) the entry of a court order dissolving the LLC on grounds that the LLC's activities are illegal or cannot be carried on in a reasonably practicable manner in accordance with the partnership agreement or that the managers or members in control have acted illegally or fraudulently or in an oppressive manner that has directly harmed the member initiating the proceeding.[136]

Winding Up. A dissolved LLC continues after dissolution only for the purpose of winding up. In winding up its activities, an LLC must discharge its debts and obligations, settle and close the LLC's activities, and marshal and distribute the assets of the LLC. It may deliver to the secretary of state a statement of dissolution, preserve the LLC's activities and property as a going concern for a reasonable time, prosecute and defend actions and proceedings, transfer the LLC's property, settle disputes by mediation or arbitration, file a statement of termination stating that the LLC is terminated, and take all other action necessary or appropriate to wind up the LLC. If a dissolved LLC has no members, the legal representative of the last person to have been a member may wind up the activities of the company.[137]

Notices Barring Claims. A dissolved LLC may notify its known creditors of the dissolution, specifying the required information and mailing address for a claim, stating the deadline for receipt of the claim (not less than 120 days after receipt of the notice date), and indicating that a claim will be barred if not received by the deadline. A claim against an LLC is barred if the notice is given and the claim is not received by the specified deadline. A timely received claim will be barred if the LLC rejects the claim and the claimant does not commence an action within 90 days of being notified of the rejection and the 90 day deadline for commencing an action.[138] In addition, a dissolved LLC may publish notice of its dissolution and request persons having claims against the LLC to present the claims in accordance with the notice, stating that a claim against the LLC will be barred if an enforcement action is not taken within five years to enforce the claim. If the notice is published in accordance with the statutory requirements, an unenforced claim not previously barred will be barred after such five-year period.[139]

Enforcement of Claims. A claim that has not been barred may be enforced against a dissolved LLC to the extent of its undistributed assets and, if assets of the LLC have been distributed after dissolution, against a member or transferee, but a person's total liability for such claims may not exceed the total amount of assets distributed to the person after dissolution.[140]

Final Distributions. After discharging its obligations to creditors, a dissolved LLC must first distribute any surplus proportionately to persons

---

136. RULLCA § 701.
137. RULLCA § 702.
138. RULLCA § 703.
139. RULLCA § 704.
140. RULLCA § 704(d).

owning a transferable interest based on the amount of their respective unreturned contributions and then distribute any remaining surplus in equal shares among members and dissociated members. All distributions must be paid in money.[141]

i. Litigation Rights

State statutes usually authorize a member of an LLC to bring a direct action against the LLC or other members for legal or equitable relief to enforce the partner's rights under the operating agreement or applicable law. The member must plead and prove an actual or threatened injury to the member, not just the LLC.[142]

Such statutes also typically permit a member to maintain a derivative action on behalf of the LLC if (1) the member first makes a demand on the manager in a manager-managed LLC, or the other members in a member-managed LLC to bring the action or pleads with particularity why such a demand would be futile and (2) any recovery from the litigation is paid to the LLC. If such a derivative action is successful, the court may award a reimbursement of the plaintiff's attorney fees and costs from the recovery.[143] Some statutes specifically authorize an LLC to appoint a special litigation committee made up of independent, disinterested persons (who may be members) to represent the interests of the LLC in a derivative proceeding.[144]

j. Mergers

State statutes generally authorize the merger of an LLC with another LLC, a partnership, a limited partnership, or a corporation, domestic or foreign.[145] Usually such merger statutes are patterned after the state's corporate merger statutes.

Documents and Process. A plan of merger must be approved by the members. The plan of merger usually sets forth the name of each party to the merger and the name of the surviving entity, the terms and conditions of the merger, the manner and basis of converting interests in each merging entity into the surviving entity or into cash or other property, and any required amendment's to the surviving entity's organizational documents.[146] Absent specific provisions in the governing LLC agreement, the plan must be approved by all members of the LLC.[147] Following approval of the plan of merger, the surviving entity files the articles of merger with the appropriate secretary of state offices. The articles of merger set forth, among other things: the plan of merger; the date the merge is effective; a statement that the merger was approved by each party to the merger as required by its governing statute; and any other information required by the governing statute of any party to the merger.[148]

Effect of Merger. Following the filing of the articles of merger, all entities

---

141. RULLCA § 708.
142. RULLCA § 901.
143. RULLCA §§ 902-904, 906.
144. RULLCA § 905.
145. RULLCA § 1002.
146. RULLCA § 1002(b).
147. RULLCA § 1002.
148. RULLCA § 1004.

that were parties to the merger, other than the surviving entity, cease to exist. Title to all property previously owned by each merged entity vests in the surviving entity, and the surviving entity is responsible for all liabilities of all other entities in the merger. If there is a legal proceeding pending against any party to the merger, it may either be continued as if the merger did not occur or the surviving entity may be substituted as the party in the proceeding. The governing instrument of the surviving entity (whether a certificate of formation, a certificate of limited partnership, or articles of incorporation) is deemed amended to the extent provided in the plan of merger.[149]

C. ENTITY FORMATION CHALLENGES

1. UNDEFINED, UNDOCUMENTED PARTNERSHIPS

CASE PROBLEM 2-5

There are three components to a golf club; the grip, the shaft, and the head. Tool Swing Inc. ("Tool"), owned by Pete Mack, is a specialty manufacturer of clubs. Many around Pete consider him "rich."

Duke, Pete's neighbor, is a struggling scientist. Pete describes Duke as "a materials nut who has never swung a golf club but who has developed the perfect plastic composite for a golf grip." Pete claims that Duke's grip produces a "feel" unlike anything on the market, weighs "virtually nothing," and has a natural "tackiness" that assures no slippage in rain or in the toughest competition.

Pete calls Duke's discovery the "Ghost Grip". With Duke's permission, Pete has tested the "Ghost Grip" with 30 top professionals. All of the professionals enthusiastically endorsed the grip on the spot and requested permission to use it on their clubs.

Pete provided Duke $62,000 to cover third-party expenses incurred in developing the Ghost Grip. Pete also paid an additional $24,000 to test the grip with industry experts and professionals. Duke has always provided Pete with an accounting for all sums spent and has regularly asked Pete about documenting the money advances. Pete would always respond by saying, "Let's not get tangled up in paperwork now. Once this thing is perfected, I will take it to the moon, and we will both make a killing."

Pete and Duke never signed any document or discussed the specifics of their relationship.

Last Monday, Duke visited Pete's home and delivered Pete a check for $92,000. The memo on the check read, "Loan repayment in full, plus interest at a rate of 12% per annum." Duke thanked Pete and explained that he had just sold all rights in the Ghost Grip to Nike for $7.8 million. Pete went berserk and mutilated the check in a rage.

Was a partnership created between Duke and Pete? What additional facts

---

149. RULLCA § 1005.

might help in making a determination? If a partnership was created, what are Pete's rights?

HOLMES v. LERNER
88 Cal.Rptr.2d 130 (Cal.App. 1999)

MARCHIANO, J.

This case involves an <u>oral partnership agreement to start a cosmetics company known as "Urban Decay.</u>" Patricia Holmes prevailed on her claim that Sandra Kruger Lerner breached her partnership agreement and that David Soward interfered with the Holmes-Lerner contract, resulting in Holmes's ouster from the business. Lerner and Soward appeal from the judgment finding them liable to Holmes for compensatory and punitive damages of over $1 million. Holmes appeals from the portion of the judgment imposing joint and several liability for the award of compensatory damages, and the court's order granting a nonsuit on various causes of action against Soward.

Sandra Lerner is a successful entrepreneur and an experienced business person. By the time of trial in this matter, Lerner was extremely wealthy. Patricia Holmes met Lerner in late 1993, when Lerner visited Holmes's horse training facility to arrange for training and boarding of two horses that Lerner was importing from England.

On July 31, 1995, the two women returned from England and stayed at Lerner's West Hollywood condominium while they waited for the horses to clear quarantine. While sitting at the kitchen table, they discussed nail polish, and colors. Len Bosack, Lerner's husband, was in and out of the room during the conversations. For approximately an hour and a half, Lerner and Holmes worked with the colors in a nail kit to try to create a different shade of purple. Holmes then said that she wanted to call the purple color she had made "Plague." Holmes had been reading about 16th-century England, and how people with the plague developed purple sores, and she thought the color looked like the plague sores. Lerner and Holmes discussed the fact that the names they were creating had an urban theme, and tried to think of other names to fit the theme. Len Bosack walked into the kitchen at that point, heard the conversation about the urban theme, and said "What about decay?" The two women liked the idea, and decided that "Urban Decay" was a good name for their concept.

Lerner said to Holmes: "This seems like a good [thing], it's something that we both like, and isn't out there. Do you think we should start a company?" Holmes responded: "Yes, I think it's a great idea." Lerner told Holmes that they would have to do market research and determine how to have the polishes produced, and that there were many things they would have to do. Lerner said: "We will hire people to work for us. We will do everything we can to get the company going, and then we'll be creative, and other people will do the work, so we'll have time to continue riding the horses." Holmes agreed that they would do those things. They did not separate out which tasks each of them would do, but planned to do it all together.

Although neither of the two women had any experience in the cosmetics business, they began work on their idea immediately. In early August, they met with a graphic artist, Andrea Kelly, and discussed putting together a logo and future advertising work for Urban Decay.

Prior to the first scheduled August meeting, Holmes told Lerner she was concerned about financing the venture. Lerner told her not to worry about it because Lerner thought they could convince Soward that the nail polish business would be a good investment. She told Holmes that Soward took care of Lerner's investment money. Holmes and Lerner discussed their plans for the company, and agreed that they would attempt to build it up and then sell it. Lerner and Holmes discussed the need to visit chemical companies and hire people to handle the daily operations of the company. However, the creative aspect, ideas, inspiration, and impetus for the company came from Holmes and Lerner.

On January 11, 1996, Lerner and Holmes met at a coffee shop. Holmes explained that she wanted "something in writing" and an explanation of her interest and position in the company. Lerner responded that a start-up business is "like a freight train ... you can either run and catch up, and get on, and take a piece of this company and make it your own, or get out of the way." As a result of this conversation, Holmes decided to double her efforts on behalf of Urban Decay. Because she was most comfortable working at the warehouse, she focused on that aspect of the business. Holmes was reimbursed for mileage, but received no pay for her work.

During January and February, Urban Decay was launching its new nail polish product. Publicity included press releases, brochures, and newspaper interviews with Lerner. An early press release stated: "The idea for Urban Decay was born after Lerner and her horse trainer, Pat Holmes, were sitting around in the English countryside." Lerner approved the press release. In February of 1996, an article was printed in the San Francisco Examiner containing the following quotes from Lerner. "Since we couldn't find good nail polish, in cool colors there must be a business opportunity here. Pat had the original idea. Urban Decay was my spin." The Examiner reporter testified at trial that the quote attributed to Lerner was accurate. Lerner was also interviewed in April by CNN. In that interview she told the story of herself and Holmes looking for unusual colors, mixing their own colors at the kitchen table, and that "we came up with the colors, and it just sort of suggested the urban thing."

Lerner had always notified Holmes whenever there was a board meeting, and she sent Holmes an agenda for the February 20, 1996 meeting. Lerner also sent a memo stating that she thought they should have an "operations meeting" with the warehouse supervisor first. Lerner's memo continued: "and then have a regular board meeting, including [Zomnir], me, David, and Pat, and no one else." Holmes understood that the regular board meeting would be for the purpose of discussing general Urban Decay business. At the operations meeting, Holmes made a presentation regarding the warehouse operations. The financial report showed $205,000 in revenues and $431,000 in expenses. The "directors" thought this early sales figure was "terrific." Soward handed out an organizational chart, which showed Lerner, with the title "CEO" at the top; Soward, as "President" beneath her; and Zomnir, as "COO" beneath Soward. Holmes asked "Where am

I?" Lerner responded by pointing to the top of the chart and telling Holmes that she was a director, and was at the top of the chart, above all the other names.

In March of 1996, Holmes received a document from Soward offering her a 1 percent ownership interest in Urban Decay. Soward explained that Urban Decay had been formed as a limited liability company, which was owned by its members. For the first time, Holmes realized that Lerner and Soward had produced an organizational document that did not include her, and she was now being asked to become a minor partner. When she studied the document, she discovered that it referred to an exhibit A, which was purported to show the distribution of ownership interests in Urban Decay. Soward had given Zomnir a copy of exhibit A when he offered her an ownership interest in Urban Decay. However, when Holmes asked Soward for a copy of exhibit A, he told her it did not exist. By this time, Holmes was planning to consult an attorney about the document.

Despite the deterioration of her friendship with Lerner, and her strained relationship with Soward, Holmes continued to attend the scheduled board meetings, hoping that her differences with Lerner could be resolved. She also continued to work at the warehouse on various administrative projects and on direct mail order sales. As late as the April board meeting, Holmes was still actively engaged in Urban Decay business. She made a presentation on a direct mail project she had been asked to undertake. As a result of Holmes's attendance at a sales presentation when she referred to herself as a cofounder of Urban Decay, Lerner instructed Zomnir to draft a dress code and an official history of Urban Decay. Lerner told Zomnir that it was a "real error in judgment" to allow Holmes to attend the sales presentation because she did not project the appropriate image. The official history, proposed in the memo, omitted any reference to Holmes. Finally, matters deteriorated to the point that Soward told Holmes not to attend the July board meeting because she was no longer welcome at Urban Decay.

On August 27, 1996, Holmes filed a complaint against Lerner and Soward, alleging 10 causes of action, including breach of an oral contract, intentional interference with contractual relations, fraud, breach of fiduciary duty, and constructive fraud. Holmes eventually dismissed some of her claims and the court dismissed others. At the trial, cosmetics industry expert Gabriella Zuckerman testified that Urban Decay was not just a fad. In her opinion, Urban Decay had discovered and capitalized on a trend that was just beginning. She reviewed projected sales figures of $19.9 million in 1997, going up to $52 million in 2003, and found them definitely obtainable. Arthur Clark, Holmes's expert at valuing start-up businesses, valued Urban Decay under different risk scenarios. In Clark's opinion, the value of Urban Decay to a potential buyer was between $4,672,000 and $6,270,000. Lerner's expert, who had never valued a cosmetics company, testified that Urban Decay had $2.7 million in sales in 1996. He estimated the value of Urban Decay as approximately $2 million, but concluded that it was not marketable.

Lerner and Soward claimed that Holmes was never a director, officer, or even an employee of Urban Decay. According to Lerner, she was just being nice to Holmes by letting her be present during Urban Decay business. Lerner denied Holmes had any role in creating the colors, names, or concepts for Urban Decay. When Holmes asked Lerner about her assets and liabilities in Urban Decay, Lerner thought she was asking for a job. She explained her statements to the press regarding Urban Decay being Holmes's idea as misquotes or the product of her stress.

The jury found in favor of Holmes on every cause of action. The jury assessed $480,000 in damages against Lerner, and $320,000 against Soward. Following presentation of evidence as to net worth, the jury awarded punitive damages of $500,000 against Lerner and $130,000 against Soward. In the judgment, the court declined to add the two amounts together, but stated that the verdict of $320,000 was against Lerner and Soward, jointly and severally, and that the additional $160,000 verdict was against Lerner individually. Lerner and Soward moved for a judgment notwithstanding the verdict, which was denied on December 16, 1997.

Lerner and Soward argue that there was no partnership agreement as a matter of law, that the evidence was insufficient to support the fraud judgment against Lerner, that damages were incorrectly calculated, that the evidence does not support the judgment against Soward and that the judgment for punitive damages must be reversed. In the consolidated appeal, Holmes argues that the trial court erred in granting a nonsuit on various causes of action and in awarding a lesser amount of damages than was reflected in the jury verdict.

Holmes testified that she and Lerner did not discuss sharing profits of the business during the July 31, "kitchen table" conversation. Throughout the case, Lerner and Soward have contended that without an agreement to share profits, there can be no partnership.

The UPA provides for the situation in which the partners have not expressly stated an agreement regarding sharing of profits. Former section 15018 provided in relevant part: "The rights and duties of the partners in relation to the partnership shall be determined, subject to any agreement between them, by the following rules: (a) Each partner shall ... share equally in the profits and surplus remaining after all liabilities, including those to partners, are satisfied." This provision states, subject to an agreement between the parties, partners "shall" share equally in the profits. Lerner and Soward argue that using former section 15018 to supply a missing term regarding profit sharing ignores the provision of former section 15007, subdivision (2). That section, headed "rules for determining existence of partnership," provided that mere joint ownership of common property "does not of itself establish a partnership, whether such co-owners do or do not share any profits made by the use of the property." Lerner and Soward are mistaken. The definition in former section 15006 provides that the association with the intent to carry on a business for profit is the essential requirement for a partnership. Following that definition does not transform mere joint ownership into the essence of a partnership.

The trial court in this case refused to add additional elements to the statutory definition and properly instructed the jury in the language of former section

15006. We agree with the trial court's interpretation of the law. The actual sharing of profits (with exceptions which do not apply here) is prima facie evidence, which is to be considered, in light of any other evidence, when determining if a partnership exists. In this case, there were no profits to share at the time Holmes was expelled from the business, so the evidentiary provision of former section 15007, subdivision (4) is not applicable. According to former section 15006, parties who expressly agree to associate as co-owners with the intent to carry on a business for profit, have established a partnership. Once the elements of that definition are established, other provisions of the UPA and the conduct of the parties supply the details of the agreement. Certainly implicit in the Holmes-Lerner agreement to operate Urban Decay together was an understanding to share in profits and losses as any business owners would. The evidence supported the jury's implicit finding that Holmes birthed an idea which was incubated jointly by Lerner and Holmes, from which they intended to profit once it was fully matured in their company.

Lerner and Soward argue that the agreement between Lerner and Holmes was too indefinite to be enforced. The cases they rely on do not support the argument. For example, in *Weddington Productions, Inc.* v. *Flick* (1998) 60 Cal.App.4th 793 [71 Cal.Rptr.2d 265], the court reversed an order enforcing a settlement agreement imposed by a mediator against the will of one of the parties. The issue was the lack of a meeting of the minds as to settlement. The court described the degree of certainty that is necessary to enforce a contract. "The parties' outward manifestations must show that the parties all agreed upon the same thing in the same sense. If there is no evidence establishing a manifestation of assent to the 'same thing' by both parties, then there is no mutual consent to contract and no contract formation." 60 Cal.App.4th at p. 811.) "The terms of a contract are reasonably certain if they provide a basis for determining the existence of a breach and for giving an appropriate remedy." *Ibid.* The evidence produced at trial in this case supplied the requisite degree of certainty described in *Weddington*.

The agreement between Holmes and Lerner was to take Holmes's idea and reduce it to concrete form. They decided to do it together, to form a company, to hire employees, and to engage in the entire process together. The agreement here, as presented to the jury, was that Holmes and Lerner would start a cosmetics company based on the unusual colors developed by Holmes, identified by the urban theme and the exotic names. The agreement is evidenced by Lerner's statements: "We will do ... everything," "[i]t's going to be our baby, and we're going to work on it together." Their agreement is reflected in Lerner's words: "We will hire people to work for us." "We will do ... everything we can to get the company going, and then we'll be creative, and other people will do the work, so we'll have time to continue riding the horses." The additional terms were filled in as the two women immediately began work on the multitude of details necessary to bring their idea to fruition. The fact that Holmes worked for almost a year, without expectation of pay, is further confirmation of the agreement. Lerner and Soward never objected to her work, her participation in board meetings and decision making, or her exercise of authority over the retail warehouse operation. Holmes was not seeking specific enforcement of a single vague term of the agreement. She was frozen out of the business altogether, and her agreement with Lerner was completely renounced. The agreement that was made and the subsequent acts of the parties supply sufficient certainty to determine the existence of a breach and a remedy.

Non-Partnership Arrangements

A "partnership" will be deemed to exist when there is association of two or more persons who carry on a business as co-owners for profit, whether or not they intend to form a partnership. Property co-ownership alone doesn't meet the definition. Thus, a joint tenancy, tenancy in common, tenancy by the entireties, joint property, or common property arrangement generally is not deemed a partnership even if the co-owners share profits made by the use of the property. Similarly, an arrangement to share gross returns, even when the sharing parties have a joint or common interest in the property that generates the returns, doesn't rise to the level of a partnership. Under the Revised Uniform Partnership Act, a person who receives a share of the profits from a business is presumed to be a partner, but not if the profits are received in payment:

- of a debt by installments or otherwise.

- for services as an independent contractor or of wages or other compensation to an employee.

- of rent.

- of an annuity or other retirement or health benefit to a beneficiary, representative, or designee of a deceased or retired partner.

- of interest or other charge on a loan, even if the amount of payment varies with the profits of the business.

- for the sale of the goodwill of a business or other property by installments or otherwise.

2. DE FACTO ORGANIZATION DOCTRINE

IN RE HAUSMAN
858 N.Y.S.2d 330 (N.Y.A.D. 2008)

WILLIAM F. MASTRO, J.P.

In a probate proceeding in which the executor petitioned to determine the validity of a deed executed by the decedent, Lena Hausman, the appeal is from an order of the Surrogate's Court, Kings County (Seddio, S.), dated May 11, 2007, which granted the petition to the extent of deeming the deed to be valid.

ORDERED that the order is reversed, on the law, with costs, the petition is denied, and the deed is deemed invalid.

On October 16, 2000, the late Lena Hausman (hereinafter the decedent) executed a will dividing her residuary estate between her son George Hausman (hereinafter George), her daughter Susan Ruth Bersani (hereinafter Susan), and seven of her grandchildren. At the time she executed her will, the decedent was the owner of real property located at 1373 56th Street in Brooklyn. Almost one year later, on October 4, 2001, George Hausman (hereinafter George) executed articles of organization to form 1373 Realty Co. LLC (hereinafter the LLC) for the purpose of owning, operating, and managing the real property. On the same day, George and Susan also signed an operating agreement, which provided that they were to be the sole members of the LLC. On November 2, 2001, the decedent executed a deed transferring ownership of the real property to the LLC. However, the LLC's articles of organization were not filed with the Department of State until November 16, 2001, two weeks after the conveyance. Thus, it is undisputed that the property was purportedly transferred to the LLC before the LLC came into legal existence.

Following the decedent's death, a dispute arose among George, Susan, and the seven grandchildren over whether the deed transferring the real property to the LLC prior to its legal formation was valid. George, in his capacity as executor of the decedent's estate, thereafter filed a petition asking the Surrogate's Court to make a legal determination as to the validity of the deed and its transfer. Based upon the undisputed facts set forth in the petition, the Surrogate's Court concluded that the deed was valid because the LLC was a de facto entity on the date the conveyance was made. We disagree.

As a general rule, a purported entity which is not yet in legal existence cannot take title to real property (*see Kiamesha Dev. Corp. v. Guild Props.*, 151 N.E.2d 214). However, New York has recognized that an unincorporated entity can take title or acquire rights by contract if it is a de facto corporation (*see Kiamesha Dev. Corp. v. Guild Props.*, 151 N.E.2d 214), and we agree with the Surrogate's finding that the de facto corporation doctrine is equally applicable to limited liability companies. However, to establish that an entity is a de facto corporation or limited liability company, there must be a showing that a colorable attempt was made to comply with the statutes governing incorporation or organization prior to the purported acceptance of the deed. Here, while it is undisputed that George executed the LLC's articles of organization on October 4, 2001, there is no evidence that an attempt to file the articles of organization was made prior to the execution of the deed on November 2, 2001. In the absence of a colorable attempt to comply with the statute governing the organization of limited liability companies by filing, we cannot find that the LLC was a de facto entity capably of taking title on the date the deed was executed. *Stone v. Jetmar Props., LLC*, 733 N.W.2d 480 (Minn.App. 2007). Accordingly, the decedent's purported conveyance of the real property was void.

De facto Corporation and Corporation-By-Estoppel Doctrines

These two, closely-related doctrines often surface in the same dispute. As the *Hausman* case illustrates, the de facto corporation doctrine recognizes the existence of a corporation when a colorable, but defective, attempt is made to comply with the state's statutory organizational requirements. As explained in section C of Chapter 6, this doctrine has been rejected by many states. The corporation-by-estoppel doctrine is applied in situations where it would be inequitable to allow a party to deny the existence of a corporation. As illustrated by the opinion in the 2007 case of *Stone v. Jetmar* (cited in Hausman and set forth in Chapter 6), this doctrine may be recognized in a state that has rejected the de facto corporation doctrine and will be applied to a non-corporate entity.

3. PRE-FORMATION TRANSACTIONS

CASE PROBLEM 2-6

Assume in Case Problem 2-2 that Luke entered into the nine pre-sale yacht contracts before meeting Jake. Luke was the named seller on the contracts. When Luke met Jake, they formed a member-managed limited liability company before Luke's tragedy and departure. Luke transferred the contracts to the LLC. Jake has now determined that the "best strategy to clean up the mess" is to complete the yachts and enforce the contracts. Can the LLC enforce the contracts? What additional facts would you like to have in answering this question?

LAKE STATE FEDERAL CREDIT UNION v. TRETSVEN
2008 WL 2732111 (Minn.App. 2008)

SCHELLHAS, Judge.

Appellant challenges the district court's ruling depriving him of rights to property against which he extended a mortgage. Because we hold that (1) as an individual, appellant has no standing to appeal the district court's ruling; and (2) appellant's claim to rights in the property fails because the alleged mortgagee was an unregistered limited liability company, we affirm.

On October 24, 2004, Defendant Richard Tretsven entered into a purchase agreement for a 160-acre parcel of property near Moose Lake, Minnesota. Later in December, Tretsven applied to respondent Lake State Federal Credit Union (Lake State) for a $148,000 purchase-money mortgage. Lake State agreed to finance the purchase and to allow Agility Title, Inc. (Agility), to handle the closing. Tretsven disclosed that he was an employee of Agility and wanted to use Agility to close on his purchase because, as an employee, he could receive a discount on the closing costs. Lake State then approved a $148,000 purchase-money mortgage to Tretsven. At this time, the president of Agility was Amanda M. Mahn, who apparently later became Tretsven's wife.

Tretsven was the sole signor of the mortgage note and mortgage running in favor of Lake State. Immediately after the closing, Agility provided Lake State copies of the executed warranty deed, settlement statement, promissory note, and mortgage, each document listing only Tretsven as purchaser, borrower, and grantee. Agility promised Lake State that it would immediately record the warranty deed and mortgage, but it failed to do so.

Sometime after the closing, Mahn's name was added to the original warranty deed as an additional grantee. Mahn's typewritten name is not aligned with, and is typed in a different font from, the other text in the warranty deed. On February 11, 2005, using the altered warranty deed, Mahn purported to grant a mortgage on the property to Hunter Financial, LLC. At that time, the sole shareholder of Hunter Financial was appellant Kenneth D. Woodard, and Hunter Financial was not registered with the Minnesota Secretary of State as a limited liability company (LLC); it was not registered as an LLC until September 13, 2005. Neither the mortgage note nor the mortgage allegedly granted to Hunter Financial, LLC, contains any mention of Woodard. Only Mahn signed the mortgage note and mortgage; Tretsven signed neither document. Woodard allegedly wired $57,000 in mortgage financing to Mahn on February 11, 2005 and recorded the warranty deed in the Carlton County Recorder's Office on March 1, 2005. At that time, Lake State's mortgage had not yet been recorded.

Tretsven failed to make the August, September, October, and November 2005 mortgage payments to Lake State. Thereafter, Lake State discovered that Agility had not recorded the original warranty deed, that the warranty deed had been altered, and that the altered warranty deed had allegedly been used to obtain mortgage financing from Hunter Financial. On December 5, 2005, Lake State commenced a foreclosure action against the property, notified all other lienholders, including Hunter Financial, and joined them as defendants. Lake State obtained summary judgment against Hunter Financial, the district court determining that the alleged mortgage given by Mahn to Hunter Financial was "void, having been obtained as the result of fraud," and ordering that the property be foreclosed and the proceeds from the foreclosure sale awarded to Lake State with any surplus sale proceeds paid into district court. This appeal followed.

Respondent argues that Woodard does not have standing to bring this appeal. "Whether a party has standing is a question of law that appellate courts review de novo." *In re Horton,* 668 N.W.2d 208, 212 (Minn.App.2003). Woodard was not a party to the original case; Hunter Financial, LLC, was the named defendant in the district court action and appeared pro se. This appeal is brought by Woodard, individually and pro se, not by Hunter Financial. Woodard's standing to participate in the district court proceedings was not raised in that court because he was not a party. Here, we address Woodard's standing to pursue this appeal because "the question of standing cannot be waived and may be raised at anytime." *Id.*

Standing is essential to a court's exercise of jurisdiction. A party may acquire standing either by suffering an injury-in-fact or through a legislative act granting standing. The fact that a party is not named in the original action does not necessarily deprive that party of standing to appeal a decision as to that action. "[T]he general rule is that a person may appeal from a judgment that adversely affects his or her rights, even if the person was not a party to the proceeding below." *In re Marriage of Sammons,* 642 N.W.2d 450, 456 (Minn.App.2002).

Lake State argues that Woodard does not have standing to appeal because he was simply a member, albeit the sole member, of the LLC named in the original action. Woodard argues that he is the proper party to this case because he personally issued the funds for the mortgage from his own account before Hunter Financial was registered. Although Woodard did not register Hunter Financial as an LLC until months after Mahn allegedly granted Hunter Financial a mortgage, the record is clear that the mortgagee in the mortgage allegedly granted by Mahn is Hunter Financial, not Woodard. And, the record does not establish whether Woodard transferred or assigned any of his interests to Hunter Financial after he registered the LLC and Woodard did not raise the question of mortgage ownership in the district court. As a general rule, we will not consider issues that were not argued and considered in the district court.

Minnesota Statutes, section 322B.88, provides that "a member of a limited liability company is not a proper party to a proceeding by or against a limited liability company," unless (1) the proceeding involves "member's right against, or liability to, the limited liability company"; or (2) "the proceeding involves a claim of personal liability or responsibility of that member and that claim has some basis other than the member's status as a member." Minn.Stat. § 322B.88 (2006). Because the case before us involves neither exception, we conclude that Woodard, as an individual, lacks standing as an individual to pursue this appeal.

Because Woodard's right to bring this appeal is precluded by Minn.Stat. § 322B.88, we need not consider the question of whether Woodard or his LLC had any legitimate rights in the foreclosed property. But because the parties may attempt to resolve this question with additional litigation, we find it in the interests of justice to address it here.

Woodard argues that the district court erred in determining, as a matter of law, that Hunter Financial had no interest in the property. Woodard bases much of his argument on his assertion that as a bona-fide purchaser under the Minnesota Recording Act, his interest in the property is superior to Lake State's interest. The Minnesota Recording Act provides that "[e]very conveyance of real estate ... [that is not] recorded shall be void as against any subsequent purchaser in good faith ... as against any attachment levied thereon ... of record prior to the recording of such conveyance." Minn.Stat. § 507.34 (2006). Woodard argues that he recorded Hunter Financial's mortgage against the property before Lake State recorded its mortgage and with no notice of Lake State's mortgage interest in the property. Thus, Woodard argues that he is a bona-fide purchaser with superior rights to the property.

But even assuming that Hunter Financial was a bona-fide purchaser under the Recording Act, neither Woodard nor Hunter Financial can claim any interest in the property because Hunter Financial was not a registered LLC when the mortgage was issued in Hunter Financial's name. *See Stone,* 733 N.W.2d at 486 (holding that deeds cannot be delivered to nonexistent entities, whether the entities are natural or legal, and that a deed conveying property to an unregistered LLC was void). The *Stone* court reasoned that because the LLC was a nonexistent entity, it could not accept delivery of the deed. *Id.* Although *Stone* concerned delivery requirements for deeds, a mortgage must also be delivered to a mortgagee to be valid. *Lee v. Fletcher,* 46 Minn. 49, 51, 48 N.W. 456, 457 (1891); *see also Tomlinson v. Kandiyohi County Bank,* 162 Minn. 230, 234, 202 N.W. 494, 496 (1925) ("It is elementary that delivery is essential to the validity of a deed or mortgage.").

The fact that Woodard registered Hunter Financial with the secretary of state after Mahn granted it the mortgage does not affect our analysis. In *Stone,* although the LLC was registered a year after the deed was delivered to one of its members, this court explicitly refused to recognize the LLC as a de facto entity. 733 N.W.2d at 487. "Allowing a form of future interest to vest in unorganized entities would be inconsistent with our public policy of encouraging legal organization." *Id.* We extend this conclusion to the case now before us and hold that because Hunter Financial was registered after the mortgage was granted to it, the mortgage allegedly conveying a property interest to it was void. We hold that neither Woodard nor Hunter Financial has any rights to the property. *See id.* (affirming a district court's finding that a deed conveying property to an unregistered LLC was void and awarding title to the property to the previous owner). We need not address the validity of the warranty deed nor Woodard's or Hunter Financial's alleged status as bona-fide purchasers. Similarly, we need not address what impact, if any, the voidness of the mortgage has on the debt associated with that mortgage. Affirmed.

The Power of Adoption and Ratification

The *Tretsven* case illustrates the dangers of pre-entity formation challenges that involve recorded real estate documents. The danger levels often drop in transactions that do involve recorded documents when the powers of adoption and ratification kick in. For example, In *02 Development, LLC v. 607 South Park, LLC,* 71 Cal.Rptr.3d 608 (Cal. App. 2 Dist. 2008), the court held that a limited liability company, the named buyer in a real estate purchase agreement, could enforce its rights under the agreement even though the LLC had not been formed at the time of the agreement. Referencing corporate law, the court stated:

> It is hornbook law that a corporation can enforce preincorporation contracts made in its behalf, as long as the corporation "has adopted the contract or otherwise succeeded to it." (1A Fletcher Cyclopedia of the Law of Private Corporations (2002 rev. vol.), § 214, pp. 448–450 ["Adoption or ratification may be express or implied. Indeed, one means of adopting a preincorporation contract is the corporation's institution of an action on it"].) California law does not deviate from that well-established norm. 607 South Park does not argue that limited liability companies should be treated differently from corporations in this respect, and we are aware of no authority that would support such a position. 607 South Park's first ground for its summary judgment motion—that there is no enforceable contract between 607 South Park and 02 Development because 02 Development did not exist when the assignment agreement was executed—therefore fails as a matter of law.

> 607 South Park's principal contention to the contrary is that a nonexistent business entity cannot be a party to a contract. The contention is true but irrelevant. When the assignment agreement was executed, 02 Development did not exist, so it was not then a party to the agreement. But once 02 Development came into existence, it could

enforce any pre-organization contract made in its behalf, such as the assignment agreement, if it adopted or ratified it.

D. THIRD PARTY CLAIMS

1. OWNER TORT EXPOSURES

HAIRE v. BONELLI
870 N.Y.S.2d 591 (N.Y.A.D. 2008)

KANE, J.

Defendant Robert Bonelli Jr. brought an assault rifle to defendant Hudson Valley Mall and began shooting indiscriminately. Of the nearly 60 rounds he fired, one hit plaintiff in the leg, injuring him severely. Plaintiff commenced this action against numerous individuals and entities associated with the mall (hereinafter collectively referred to as defendants) and Bonelli. As against defendants, plaintiff alleged causes of action sounding in negligence, gross negligence, public and private nuisance, common-law fraud and violations of General Business Law §§ 349 and 350. Defendants moved to dismiss the amended complaint. Supreme Court dismissed all causes of action against defendant PCK Development Company, and everything but the negligence cause of action against the remaining moving defendants.

Supreme Court correctly determined that plaintiff stated a negligence cause of action against the owners, operators and managers of the mall. Property owners and their agents have a duty to maintain the premises in a reasonably safe condition, which includes taking "minimal precautions to protect members of the public from the reasonably foreseeable criminal acts of third persons" (*Leyva v. Riverbay Corp.,* 620 N.Y.S.2d 333 [1994]. Plaintiff sufficiently alleged that inadequate security and warning and evacuation plans were in place to observe, detect or deter Bonelli or prevent him from injuring people in the mall.

Here, an attorney who is general counsel to one defendant provided information, from his own personal knowledge and his review of attached documents, regarding the corporate structure and relationships of the various defendants.

Plaintiff alleged that the individual defendants are officers or members of the defendant corporations or limited liability companies and participated in the commission of a tort in furtherance of company business or to benefit the business, namely reducing or eliminating mall security to maximize profits. These allegations, if proven, would be a sufficient basis to hold those individuals personally liable (*see Rothstein v. Equity Ventures, LLC,* 299 A.D.2d 472, 474, 750 N.Y.S.2d 625 [2002]. At this early stage of the action, and given defendants' failure to adequately explain the positions of the individual defendants and their roles in the business entities—let alone their roles in business decisions concerning mall security—we must accept the allegations as true. Thus, those individuals were not entitled to dismissal.

Failing to Perform and Fraud

Generally no personal liability will attach to a member of an LLC who fails to perform a contractual obligation on behalf of the LLC, even if the failure is the member's fault. In *American Realty Trust Inc. v. Matisse Capital Partners LLC*, 91 Fed.Appx. 904 (5th Cir. 2003), the court held that two individuals (Bagley and Takacs) were not personally liable for failing to provide adequate consulting services pursuant to a contract they signed on behalf of their LLC. The court stated;

> We believe that the district court was correct to reject the jury's verdict to the extent that the jury found that Bagley and Takacs individually, as opposed to Matisse Partners, LLC, had breached the Consulting Contract. The Consulting Contract states that it was "executed ... by and between MATISSE PARTNERS, LLC, a Colorado limited liability company" and the ART corporations. It was signed on Matisse's behalf by Takacs in his capacity as Matisse's managing director. It is of course true that a business entity can act only through its officers, employees, and other agents. If Matisse breached the contract, it would therefore necessarily be by virtue of acts taken by Bagley or Takacs. But that truism does *not* mean that any breach of the Consulting Contract, which breach could only happen through those two individuals' actions, creates individual liability on Bagley and Takacs. To so hold would ignore the fact that Matisse's principals were doing business as an LLC.

However, when the actions of the members acting on behalf of the LLC in a contractual context rise to the level of fraud, personal liability attaches. See, for example, *LJ Charter, L.L.C. v. Air America Jet Charter, Inc.*, 2009 WL 4794242 (Tex. App. 2009); Restatement (Third) of Agency § 7.01.

2. PIERCING THE VEIL

D.R. HORTON INC. - NEW JERSEY v. DYNASTAR DEVELOPMENT, L.L.C.
2005 WL 1939778 (N.J. Super. L. 2005)

OSTRER, J.

This lawsuit arises out of the construction of a planned residential retirement community on over 400 acres in West Windsor Township. Known as the Bear Creek Planned Development, the project was intended to satisfy part of the township's Mt. Laurel affordable housing obligation. The single-family development was ultimately named the Village Grande at Bear Creek. The townhome development was eventually called the Hamlet at Bear Creek.

Critical to the lawsuit is a contract dated April 26, 1996, entitled "PRRC Project Cooperation Agreement" ("PRRC Agreement"). In particular, the PRRC Agreement provided a formula for the parties to share the costs of improvements like roads, water line and sewer line extensions, which would be located outside each developer's respective property, but which would benefit that property. The PRRC Agreement stated that it was binding on the parties as well as their successors and assigns.

Lehigh Corp. on the CRRC side agreed to convey its interests in the project to Esplanade L.L.C., then a newly formed New Jersey limited liability company located in Covington, Louisiana, under an agreement made February 20, 1998 ("Lehigh-Esplanade Agreement")...Although Esplanade L.L.C. lacked capital initially, and depended on Dynastar to finance its operations, it ultimately secured financing through the EDA for the initial stage of the project. On the other hand, the plaintiff was on notice that Esplanade L.L.C. lacked sufficient capital to complete other stages. Thus, plaintiff should have been aware that it might not have had sufficient capital to complete the initial stage if overruns, delays, or other setbacks were experienced.

Esplanade L.L.C. breached the PRRC Agreement and failed to reimburse Horton NJ for various offsite improvements that benefited its property... Based on the findings of fact, applied to the conclusions of law discussed below, only Esplanade L.L.C. is liable for breaching the PRRC Agreement. The breach consists of not paying for off-site improvements, delaying completion of affordable housing units, and failing to complete on-site improvements. Horton NJ may not pierce Esplanade L.L.C.'s veil and assign liability to its members Borne and Dynastar, or to Borne's related entity, Evangeline... Simply put, in this case, no party other than Esplanade L.L.C. was bound contractually to Horton NJ. The defendants on the contract claims, Dynastar and Evangeline, contracted directly neither with Horton NJ nor SGS Adult L.L.C.

The court rejects plaintiff's claim that Esplanade L.L.C.'s "corporate veil" should be pierced, so that Borne, or Dynastar may be held liable. Under the facts of this case, equity does not require permitting plaintiff to pierce Esplanade L.L.C.'s veil and assign liability for its breach of contract to Borne or to any of his related entities. In reaching this conclusion, the court concludes that the issue of piercing the veil in this case is governed by New Jersey law, even though Dynastar and Evangeline are Louisiana business entities. The court also concludes that the plaintiff need prove its case for piercing the corporate veil by clear and convincing evidence. Nonetheless, even under a preponderance of evidence standard, the court is not persuaded that an injustice would be done by maintaining limited liability, given the court's conclusion that Borne's alleged misuse of the limited liability company form did not proximately caused plaintiff harm. Even if not an essential element of a veil piercing claim, causation necessarily must be a factor in the court's analysis of this claim for equitable relief. The court also concludes that the traditional factors for piercing the veil of a corporation must be modified in a case involving a limited liability company, to account for the special characteristics of that business entity. Applying that test, the court concludes that Esplanade L.L.C.'s veil need not be pierced, to avoid injustice, or to remedy fraud.

The apparent weight of authority agrees that veil-piercing analysis is governed by the law of the state of formation. Although the court has found no New Jersey case directly on point, the Supreme Court has in another context adopted Restatement (Second) of Conflicts of Laws § 307, which states that the law of the state of incorporation governs shareholders' liability. That may suggest a similar adoption of the incorporating state's law to a veil piercing claim.

An apparent minority of courts has suggested that the state with the most significant contacts would govern a veil-piercing dispute. Ultimately, the court need not resolve this issue, inasmuch as it concludes that the entity whose veil must be pierced as a threshold matter, Esplanade L.L.C., was both formed under New Jersey law, and maintained its most significant contacts here, and New Jersey certainly has the interest in this case to apply its veil-piercing law.

As discussed below, in order to obtain equity's aid in avoiding a duly executed contract, plaintiff needs to prove its claim by clear and convincing evidence. The court has found no New Jersey court decision that expressly addresses the standard of proof in veil-piercing claims. However, the court finds that this standard of proof is consistent with binding precedent establishing the same standard of proof in equitable and legal fraud claims. It is consistent with the public policy underlying that higher standard of proof in cases in which a party seeks to avoid a written contract. It is also supported by the public policy for limited liability for business entities, at least as it relates to contractual claims by voluntary creditors. Lastly, it is consistent with what this court finds is the better reasoned view of other courts.

Although limited liability is a statutory creation, the Legislature has not prescribed the standard of proof for piercing the veil. Indeed, piercing the veil is an equitable remedy, in derogation of the statute limiting liability. Thus, it is incumbent on this court to determine what our State's Supreme Court would deem the appropriate standard.

In choosing the standard of proof, the court must be mindful of the impact of a standard of proof in any proceeding. The preponderance standard imposes the risk of loss evenly between the two parties. In criminal cases, the defendant's liberty interest is so weighty that the beyond-a-reasonable-doubt standard of proof is designed to avoid as much as possible the risk of an erroneous judgment of conviction, even if means a guilty defendant may go free. The clear-and-convincing standard falls somewhere between the two extremes. Our Supreme Court has defined "clear and convincing" to mean evidence "so clear, direct and weighty and convincing as to enable either to come to a clear conviction, without hesitancy, of the truth of the precise facts in issue." In re Seaman, 133 N.J. 67, 74, 627 A.2d 106 (1993).

Applying these considerations, the court concludes that a fact-finder should have a higher degree of confidence in a claim to pierce the veil on a private contract claim. The heightened standard apparently has its roots in equity and the desire to demand higher proof before setting aside written contracts.

The court concludes that the traditional standard for piercing a corporation's veil must be modified to accommodate the special characteristics of a limited liability company.

The Supreme Court described the standard for piercing a corporation's veil in State Dep't of Environ. Prot. v. Ventron Corp., 94 N.J. 473, 500, 468 A.2d 150 (1983). A corporation is a separate entity from its shareholders.. One of the primary reasons for incorporation is to insulate shareholders from the liabilities of the corporate enterprise. Except in cases of fraud, injustice, or the like, courts will not pierce a corporate veil.

The Supreme Court established a two-part test to determine if the business entity has been used to defeat the ends of justice. First, the plaintiff must prove that the subsidiary was a mere instrumentality or alter ego of its owner. That is, that the parent or owner so dominated the subsidiary that it had no separate existence but "was merely a conduit for the parent." Id. at 500-01, 468 A.2d 150. Second, the plaintiff must prove that the parent or owner has abused the business form to perpetrate a fraud, injustice, or otherwise circumvent the law. "Even in the presence of dominance and control, liability will be imposed only where the parent has abused the privilege of incorporation by using the subsidiary to perpetrate a fraud or injustice, or otherwise to circumvent the law." State Dep't of Environ. Prot. v. Ventron Corp., supra, 94 N.J. at 501, 468 A.2d 150.

The first part of the test-pertaining to dominance and control-has been evidenced by facts that demonstrate the parent company's or owner's exercise of dominion and control over the subsidiary. In such instances, a subsidiary can properly be deemed an "alter ego" or "mere instrumentality" of the parent such that the entities operate as one. This requires proof of the complete domination and control of both the entity's policy and business practices. The alter ego or mere instrumentality factor is generally employed where two corporations or companies are realistically controlled as one entity because of common owners, officers, directors, members or lack of observance of corporate formalities between the two organizations. This test measures the separateness between the management of the corporation and its owners.

The second prong of the test-abuse of the privilege of incorporation consisting of fraud, injustice or circumvention of law-has been evidenced by facts that demonstrate some form of misrepresentation, deceit, undercapitalization, or other form of injustice. In determining whether a plaintiff has satisfied the second prong of the Ventron test, New Jersey courts have considered whether the defendant's use or misuse of the business entity's form caused harm. Several states hold that proof of injury or loss is an express prerequisite for veil-piercing. Including causation assures a proper balance between fulfilling the policy goals of limited liability, established by statute, and the policy goals of the veil-piercing doctrine, established in equity, to avoid injustice. Limited liability is said to promote investment, and allocate risk to more efficient risk-bearers.

Thus, to override a private bargain, the courts generally demand a showing of fraud, misrepresentation, or some violation of the express or implicit bargain of the parties.

[F]or close corporations, piercing the corporate veil is strongly rooted in the bargain setting. Because the market-related reasons for limited liability are absent in close corporations and corporate groups, the most important justification for limited liability is permitting parties in a consensual relationship to use the corporate form to allocate the risks of the transaction and the enterprise. Thus the presumption of limited liability is strongest when the outside party adversely affected by the corporation's limited assets was aware of the corporation's separate existence at the time of the transaction. Conversely, courts will disregard limited liability for the same reasons that other bargains are not respected by courts. For example, misrepresentation is one of the most frequent factors listed by courts when they pierce the veil.

Absent the element of causation, a creditor would be granted a better bargain than it made for itself, simply because of the fortuity that the debtor, say, inadvertently commingled assets, ignored corporate formalities, or dominated the corporation. "Accordingly, absent very compelling equitable circumstances, courts should not rewrite contracts or disturb the allocation of risk the parties have themselves established." 1 Fletcher Cyc. Of Private Corp. § 41.85 (2004).

While this court has found no New Jersey case expressly stating that proof of causation is an essential element of a veil-piercing claim, neither has the court found a case expressly stating that causation is irrelevant.

This court has found no New Jersey case in which the court has expressly addressed whether the corporate veil-piercing doctrine should be applied without change to a limited liability company. Therefore, this court must consider whether it should modify the Ventron two-part test in view of a limited liability company's special attributes. The court concludes that an adjustment is appropriate. Lesser weight should be afforded the element of domination and control and adherence to corporate formalities, because the statute authorizing limited liability companies expressly authorizes managers and members to operate the firm.

New Jersey's limited liability statute does not apply corporate veil-piercing doctrine to limited liability companies. Rather, it appears to endorse the evolution of court-made rules. These in turn may address this business form's special attributes.

Although the limited liability of an L.L.C. is identical to a corporation's, the L.L.C. is significantly different...New Jersey enacted the Limited Liability Company Act ("N.J.Act") to enable members and managers of a Limited Liability Company "to take advantage of both the limited liability afforded to shareholders and directors of corporations and the pass through tax advantages available to partnerships." Senate Commerce Committee Statement, S. 890 (June 14, 1993), republished at N.J.S.A. § 42:2B-1.

New Jersey's Limited Liability Company statute is distinct from its corporate counterpart. The statute expressly authorizes L.L.C. managers to engage in financial transactions with the company, including lending and borrowing money, and assuming obligations of the company. N.J.S.A § 42:2B-9. As will be discussed below, this is significant, when considering the "dominion and control" factor under Ventron.

Other states' statutes variously treat corporate veil-piercing doctrine. Some states expressly adopt the corporate veil-piercing doctrine and others expressly reject it, at least in part. For example, the statutes of Colorado and Minnesota apply corporate veil-piercing common law to L.L.C.'s in their jurisdictions. On the other hand, some states have expressly distinguished L.L.C.s from corporations, dispensing with the corporate formalities factor in a veil-piercing analysis involving a limited liability company.

Most states, however, do not explicitly and specifically address the issue of corporate veil-piercing doctrine by statute, and instead their laws only generally address member liability to third parties. See e.g., 6 Del.Code Ann. § 18-303 (Supp.1994) (stating that "no member or manager of a limited liability company shall be obligated personally for any ... debt, obligation or liability of the limited liability company solely by reason of being a member or acting as a manager."); Fla. Stat. Ann. § 608.436 (West 1996) (same).

Although the N.J. Act does not expressly address veil-piercing, an argument can be made the Legislature implicitly intended that courts not mechanically apply corporate veil-piercing law to limited liability companies. The original, introduced version of the limited liability legislation provided that case law on piercing the corporate veil would apply to a limited liability company. However, the Senate Committee Substitute that was ultimately passed and signed into law omitted that provision. See S. 890(SCS), 205th Leg. (1993), enacted as L. 1993, c. 210.

Indeed, rather than expressly address veil piercing doctrine, the Legislature apparently endorsed the continued evolution of the common law. "In any case not provided for in this act, the rules of law and equity, including the law merchant, shall govern." N.J.S.A. § 42:2B-67. This provision begs the question, what is the rule of law and equity on veil-piercing of a limited liability company. Apparently, it is for the courts to decide, grounded in the principles of equity, but mindful of the Legislature's expressed and implicit goals in creating this business form.

As discussed below, persuasive authorities indicate that corporate veil-piercing doctrine should not be mechanically applied to cases involving limited liability companies. In particular, a court should view in a different light the factors of adherence to corporate formalities, and scrutiny of owners' dominion and control.

Certainly, one may find cases in which courts have presumed that a plaintiff may pierce the veil of an L.L.C. just as it may pierce the veil of a corporation. However, courts that have expressly considered the differences between the two business forms have concluded that veil-piercing doctrine should be molded to accommodate the differences. In answering a certified question whether the veil-piercing remedy were available against a limited liability company, the Wyoming Supreme Court answered in the affirmative, but recognized that the applicable factors would differ from those applied to a corporate veil-piercing-in particular, adherence to corporate formalities should not weigh as much. The court also left for another day the identification of other differences.

Many commentators agree with the general principle that veil-piercing law for limited liability companies should be tailored to address that business form's special characteristics. As noted by the Wyoming Supreme Court, adherence to formalities is one factor that should weigh differently in the case of a limited liability company. First, a small-business owner's failure to adhere to formalities may simply reflect disregard of formalities "irrelevant to their actual operation", and lack of funds to hire lawyers and others to keep track of statutory obligations. None of that may evidence misuse of the statute. Second, "LLC's have relatively few statutorily mandated formalities and have a considerable amount of freedom and flexibility as to the management structure of the entity." This informality, encouraged by statute, should not then be a basis to avoid statutory limited liability.

Reliance on dominance and control of the L.L.C. form also conflicts with the underlying policy of flexibility within the L.L.C. statute. LLC's are more often than not managed by the LLC members. In addition, generally speaking, members are normally authorized agents and/or managers of LLC's for the purpose of conducting its affairs. As such, it could be argued that the later ego factor is usually satisfied for LLC's. As one commentator noted, given the statutory authorization of flexible LLC management structures, domination of LLC management by members of the LLC, absent other equitable issues, would appear to be an 'inappropriate' factor for the courts to use to pierce the veil to the detriment of the interest holders. Thus, application of the alter ego factor to LLC's will often lead to 'illogical' results.

Undercapitalization is another factor that should be weighed carefully in the L.L.C. context, particularly involving a start-up. One court, addressing facts similar to those in this case, affirmed the trial court's refusal to pierce a limited liability company's veil. Advanced Telephone Systems, Inc. v. Com-Net Prof. Mobile Radio, LLC, 846 A.2d 1264, 1280-81 (Pa.Sup.Ct.2004). The court found no injustice in maintaining limited liability where the plaintiff knew it was dealing with a limited liability company that initially had no assets, but would only acquire those assets when a certain contract was entered and financing obtained; when that contract fell through the L.L.C. was undercapitalized. Ibid. Commentators agree that a limited liability company's undercapitalization-albeit still a highly relevant factor-should be considered in light of the circumstances. See D. Cohen, supra, 51 Okla. L.Rev. at 491 (suggesting that courts inquire whether the entity was formed with explicit intent of engaging in risky transactions and being undercapitalized given the risks, and then concluding that such facts would be evidence of unconscionable behavior toward involuntary creditors, but not toward voluntary creditors "unless the LLC's purpose was obscured or misrepresented.").

In sum, out-of-state authority and commentators agree that the veil-piercing formula for limited liability companies should be molded to account for that business form's special attributes. As the Wyoming Supreme Court aptly suggested Kaycee Land and Livestock v. Flahive, supra, the particular standard should be developed over time, as courts address concrete cases. It is not for this court, solely on the facts presented to it in this case, to formulate a generally-applicable standard. It is sufficient for this court to conclude that in this case, Borne's failure to scrupulously identify the entity through which he was acting, his dominion and control of Esplanade L.L.C., and the entity's undercapitalization should not loom as large as it might were the entity a corporation.

As noted above, under the Ventron two-part test, Horton NJ must prove that (1) Esplanade L.L.C. was a mere instrumentality or alter ego of Borne; and (2) Borne abused the business form to perpetrate a fraud, injustice, or otherwise circumvent the law. Particularly given the lesser weight assigned to the formalities, and dominion-and-control factors, Horton NJ has failed to prove the first prong. Moreover, the court finds no injustice or circumvention of law, notwithstanding that Esplanade L.L.C. ultimately lacked sufficient capital to fulfill its obligations.

To prove the first prong of the Ventron test, Horton NJ relies on Borne's control of Esplanade L.L.C., and his failure to distinguish it from his Dynastar. As discussed above, there is no doubt that Borne failed to correct misimpressions of the entities' respective roles. He maintained control over all his entities, and used a central office, common employees, and common telephone lines. However, the separate entities served different functions. Borne did not intend to mislead. When entering formal contracts or obtaining payment, as opposed to informal correspondence, Borne was more careful to identify the correct entity. Finally, Borne's failure to correct Schoor's and Rothman's confusion did not cause Horton NJ to act to its detriment. Horton NJ would have made the same investments in off-site improvements even if Borne made it clear that Dynastar was performing services for Esplanade L.L.C., and Esplanade L.L.C. was the single purpose entity that owned the land.

Particularly given the lesser weight assigned to the formalities and dominion-and-control factors in an L.L.C. veil-piercing case, the court does not find that Borne's behavior justifies piercing Esplanade L.L.C.'s veil. Borne was a small-business owner. His lack of attention to detail-his misuse of stationery, for example-was not uncharacteristic of entrepreneurs and other L.L.C. owners. His operational efficiencies-in maintaining a central office for his various entities-was understandable. It presumably would have made little business sense for him to rent separate space, hire separate office-workers, and acquire separate phone lines for each of his related entities. To penalize him for rational economic behavior would be inconsistent with the business-promotion goals of the Limited Liability Act, and at odds with the specific provisions allowing member-management.

As for the second prong of the Ventron test, the court has found that Borne did not defraud in his use of the various entities. Nor did Borne use the limited liability form to perpetrate an injustice or a circumvention of the law. The court finds that Horton NJ has failed to establish by clear and convincing evidence-indeed, it has failed to establish by a preponderance of the evidence-that it has suffered an injustice by its failure to reach beyond the assets of Esplanade L.L.C. Esplanade L.L.C. disclosed its funding limitations. Horton NJ had no idea whether Dynastar was better capitalized than Esplanade L.L.C., or whether it was the other way around. To permit Horton NJ to reach beyond the parties who were liable under contract would not prevent an injustice, but create one. It would extend liability to parties with whom Horton NJ did not bargain and upon whose assets Horton NJ did not rely.

In sum, the court finds that Horton NJ has failed to establish a basis for piercing Esplanade L.L.C.'s veil.

Corporate Piercing Claims

As the *D.R. Horton Inc.* case illustrates, the relationship between creditor piercing claims in an LLC context and a corporate context is evolving. Creditor piercing claims often are directed at the protective veil provided by a corporation. See section F. of Chapter 3 for cases involving such claims, where the creditor uses various factors to support an argument that the corporation and shareholders are one and the same and that it would be unjust or inequitable to allow the shareholders to escape personal liability. As such cases illustrate, it is never an easy burden of proof for the plaintiff-creditor, and there are a host of factors (all potentially relevant in an LLC or limited partnership context) that often come into play.

3. CHARGING ORDER REALITIES

WEDDELL v. H2O, INC.
271 P.3d 743 (Nev. 2012)

By the Court, CHERRY, J.:

In this appeal, we consider distinct issues arising from a fall-out between business partners. We first consider whether a judgment creditor divests a dual member and manager of a limited-liability company of his managerial duties. We conclude that a judgment creditor has only the rights of an assignee of the member's interest, receiving only a share of the economic interests in a limited-liability company, including profits, losses, and distributions of assets. Therefore, the judgment creditor and holder of a charging order against appellant Rolland P. Weddell's membership interests is simply entitled to Weddell's economic interest in appellant Granite Investment Group, LLC. For this reason, we reverse the district court's judgment relating to the scope of the charging order against Weddell's membership interests and remand this matter to the district court for further proceedings concerning Weddell's managerial interests in Granite...

Stewart and Weddell were both involved in some respect with Granite Investment Group and appellant High Rock Holding, LLC. In December 2004, Weddell was elected manager of Granite. Several months later in May 2005, Stewart and Weddell signed an amended and restated operating agreement (Granite operating agreement).

According to the Granite operating agreement, Stewart received 1.5 votes and Weddell received 1 vote. Several years later, in October 2007, Stewart used his majority voting power to allegedly remove Weddell as manager. Thereafter, Stewart ostensibly elected himself manager of Granite. However, pursuant to section 5.10 of the Granite operating agreement, a manager can only be removed by the unanimous affirmative vote of all of the members. Additionally, section 5.2 does not prohibit more than one manager at a time.

When Weddell was elected manager of the Granite Investment Group, he was also elected manager of High Rock Holding. To reflect the management changes at High Rock, Stewart and Weddell entered into an amended and restated operating agreement whereby Stewart had 1.5 votes and Weddell had 1 vote (High Rock operating agreement). Likewise, in October 2007, Stewart used his superior voting power to remove Weddell as manager of High Rock. While the Granite operating agreement required a unanimous affirmative vote of the members, the similarly numbered section of the High Rock operating agreement only required an affirmative vote of the members.

In October 2008, in an unrelated matter, the district court granted an application by a creditor to charge Weddell's membership interest in Granite and High Rock, among other Weddell entities, for over $6 million. Pursuant to NRS 86.401, the charging order entitled the creditor to any and all disbursements and distributions, including interest, and all other rights of an assignee of the membership interest. Thereafter, Stewart purportedly purchased Weddell's remaining membership interest in Granite for $100 in accordance with section 10.2 of the Granite operating agreement.

The district court concluded that the charging order divested Weddell of *both* membership and managerial rights in Granite and High Rock upon the tender of purchase money made by Stewart. The district court also concluded that Stewart is the sole manager of Granite and High Rock.

To better understand the preeminent issue, we first review the general nature of limited liability companies, including the statutory framework pursuant to NRS Chapter 86. Next, we will present a historical overview of the charging order remedy. As part of this overview, we will analyze the rights of judgment creditors in the course of holding a charging order. Finally, we will explain the basis for our conclusion that, under Nevada law, judgment creditors have no right to participate in the management of the limited-liability company and only obtain the rights of an assignee of the member's interest—receiving only a share of the economic interests in a limited-liability company, including profits, losses, and distributions of assets. By limiting a creditor's right to exercise the debtor member's management rights, we ensure that creditors of a limited-liability company cannot disrupt and interfere with the management rights of other members. This conclusion rests on the uncontested right of a member to choose his or her associates and to encourage investing by enabling limited members to invest money and to share profits, but without risking more than the amount they contributed.

Limited-liability companies (LLCs) are business entities created "to provide a corporate-styled liability shield with pass-through tax benefits of a partnership." *White v. Longley,* 358 Mont. 268, 244 P.3d 753, 760 (2010); *Gottsacker v. Monnier,* 281 Wis.2d 361, 697 N.W.2d 436, 440 (2005) (stating that "[f]rom the partnership form, the LLC borrows characteristics of informality of organization and operation, internal governance by contract, direct participation by members in the company, and no taxation at the entity level. From the corporate form, the LLC borrows the characteristic of protection of members from investor-level liability."

In Nevada, an LLC is formed by signing and filing the articles of organization, together with the applicable filing fees, with the Secretary of State. An LLC may, but is not required to, adopt an operating agreement, NRS 86.286, which is defined as "any valid written agreement of the members as to the affairs of a limited-liability company and the conduct of its business." NRS 86.101. Unless the articles of organization or operating agreement provide otherwise, management of a limited-liability company is vested in its members in proportion to their contribution to capital. NRS 86.291. A member is "the owner of a member's interest in a limited-liability company or a noneconomic member." NRS 86.081. The term "[m]ember's interest" is defined as "a share of the economic interests in a limited-liability company, including profits, losses and distributions of assets." NRS 86.091.

The collection rights and remedies against a member's interest in a limited-liability company are governed by NRS 86.401. This provision recognizes the charging order as a remedy by which a judgment creditor of a member can seek satisfaction by petitioning a court to charge the member's interest with the amount of the judgment. NRS 86.401(1); *see Brant v. Krilich,* 835 N.E.2d 582, 592 (Ind.Ct.App.2005) (holding "that a charging order is the only remedy for a judgment creditor against a member's interest in an LLC," after interpreting a similar Indiana statute). A charging order directs the LLC to make distributions to the creditor that it would have made to the member. As a result, a charging order affects only the debtor's partnership interest and does not permit a creditor to reach partnership assets.

"Charging orders originated as a statutory solution to cumbersome common law collection procedures 'that were ill-suited for reaching partnership interests.'" *Green v. Bellerive,* 135 Md.App. 563, 763 A.2d 252, 256 (Md.Ct.Spec.App.2000). The charging order concept was first established in the United States in the 1914 Uniform Partnership Act and has since been replicated in some degree in nearly every United States jurisdiction, including Nevada.

Charging orders have been described as "nothing more than a legislative means of providing a creditor some means of getting at a debtor's ill-defined interest in a statutory bastard, surnamed 'partnership,' but corporately protecting participants by limiting their liability as [ ] corporate shareholders." *Bank of Bethesda v. Koch,* 408 A.2d 767, 770 (Md.Ct.Spec.App.1979). In short, "[a] charging order gives the charging creditor only limited access to the partnership interest of the indebted partner." *Green,* 763 A.2d at 257. Consequently, the judgment creditor does not unequivocally step into the shoes of a limited-liability member. *Id.* at 259. The limited access of a judgment creditor includes "*only* the rights of an assignee of the member's interest." NRS 86.401(1) (emphasis added). A judgment creditor, or assignee, is only entitled to the judgment debtor's share of the profit and distributions, takes no interest in the LLC's assets, and is not entitled to participate in the management or administration of the business. After the entry of a charging order, the debtor member no longer has the right to future LLC distributions to the extent of the charging order, but retains all other rights that it had before the execution of the charging order, including managerial interests.

Here, the charging order levied by Weddell's creditor directed Granite to divert Weddell's rights to LLC profits and distributions to the creditor. The charging order only divested Weddell of his economic opportunity to obtain profits and distributions from Granite—charging only his membership interest, not his managerial rights. *See* NRS 86.401. Prohibiting the creditor from exercising Weddell's management rights reflects the principle that LLC members should be able to choose those members with whom they associate.

We further conclude that the charging order triggered the involuntary transfer provision of the Granite operating agreement, section 10.4. Section 10.4 explicitly included charging orders in its purview. Therefore, we remand this case to the district court to resolve whether Stewart properly complied with section 10.4 and whether, as a result, Weddell was divested of his membership interest in Granite. In light of our conclusion, we direct the district court to determine whether Weddell has retained his managerial interests, and whether Stewart has elected himself co-manager pursuant to sections 5.2 and 5.10 of the Granite operating agreement. We also conclude that the district court did not err in finding that the April 2006 High Rock operating agreement signed by both parties controlled and that, under it, Weddell was voted out as manager of that LLC.

Pursuant to NRS 86.401, a judgment creditor may obtain the rights of an assignee of the member's interest, receiving only a share of the economic interests in a limited-liability company, including profits, losses, and distributions of assets. Thus, the charging order does not entitle the creditor to Weddell's managerial rights in Granite. Due to the district court's misinterpretation of NRS 86.401, we reverse the district court's judgment in part and remand this matter to the district court for further proceedings consistent with this opinion.

Example: Charging Order as Asset Protection Tool

George Judson is a surgeon. He has all the usual concerns. His malpractice rates have tripled over the last 10 years. He knows that there is a risk that 10 or 20 years down the road he might be held responsible for a surgical procedure that he performed today. He also knows that a damage suit could potentially produce a judgment that far exceeds the limits of his malpractice policy. George and his wife Betty have worked hard to build an estate valued at approximately $9 million.

George and Betty would like to lock- up a portion of their assets that could not readily be confiscated by a judgment creditor in the future. In short, they want an asset protection strategy. They know that an asset protection strategy probably will not work if a claim has already been made. This type of planning should be done in calm waters. They figure that now is the time. George also understands that the strategy may not be completely fool-proof, and there may be some uncertainties. They figure that something is better than nothing. They know that some strategies are designed to make things difficult, unbearable and, hopefully in some cases, downright impossible for the judgment creditor who is going after the assets. Obstacles can be created. The hope is that most creditors, when they discover the obstacles and the potential legal implications, will conclude that the carrot isn't worth the fight.

George and Betty have decided to form a limited partnership to help protect certain commercial properties and investments that they own. Initially, they will own the limited partnership units and have a corporate entity be the general partner. Over time, they will transfer limited partnership units to other family members, including their children and trusts for grandchildren. Any such transfers will increase their protection from creditors. But for now, let's focus on the value of the limited partnership structure itself as an asset protection device, apart from any transfers that may be made to other family members.

The limited partnership, if properly structured and funded with assets, can itself become a nuisance for a judgment creditor. If George has a large malpractice judgment entered against him, in many states a judgment creditor is limited to obtaining a charging order against the partnership. This charging order gives the creditor the right to receive distributions from the partnership when and if distributions are made to George. The creditor gets no rights to control or gain access to the assets that are owned by the limited partnership. The creditor has no right to become a general partner, nor can the creditor remove the general partner, vote in the partnership, or have any say in the management. All the creditor has is the right to receive the income and any other amounts that may be distributed to George. In some states, the creditor may petition to have the charging order "liquidated," which has the effect of transferring to the creditor all rights of the partnership interest.

The obvious question is: Can the creditor require that the partnership make distributions with respect to the partnership interest? Generally, the creditor has no such power. In this regard, if asset protection is a priority, it is usually advisable to include a clause in the partnership agreement that allows the general partners to retain cash in the partnership for the future business needs of the partnership.

There is one additional aspect of the limited partnership device that makes it an even greater nuisance for the judgment creditor. It's a tax twist, and it can hurt. Based on Revenue Ruling 77–137,[150] many professionals believe that if a creditor secures a charging order against the partnership units and is entitled to receive all of the income distributed by the partnership, there is a possibility that the creditor will be taxed on its share of the partnership income as the owner of the units. If that income is retained in the partnership, the creditor may end up having to book phantom income for tax purposes. In effect, the charging order may become a poison tax pill for the creditor. If the creditor becomes a limited partner by having the charging order liquidated, there is little question that the income will be taxed to the creditor.

Once the limited partnership structure is in place, George and Betty can take other steps to strengthen their defense against a future judgment creditor. They can transfer units to their children, either outright or in trust. If the transfers are timely made and properly structured, the transferred units will be completely beyond the reach of the creditors. If a creditor obtains a malpractice judgment against George, the creditor can only seek a charging order against partnership

---

150. 1977–1 C.B. 178.

units owned by George, and cannot pursue the limited partnership units owned by the children. If George wants to add another layer of potential protection, he could consider the possibility of using a foreign trust to hold his limited partnership units or a trust established in a state with favorable asset protection laws. Although such a trust will provide another obstacle for the judgment creditor, it is far from bullet-proof and likely will trigger some tough legal challenges if attacked by a tenacious creditor.[151]

E. FIDUCIARY DUTIES AND RISKS

CASE PROBLEM 2-7

Refer to Case Problem 2-4 in which Son and Dad form a manager-managed LLC where Son is the manager. The LLC operating agreement states that "all fiduciary duties of care and loyalty that would otherwise exist between the members are hereby eliminated." Son causes the LLC to license all rights in Strategy long-term to a new corporation owned equally by Son and an unrelated deep-pocket investor. The royalties payable under the license are clearly on the low side of reasonable and do not reflect the potential value of Strategy. Dad is livid.

1. Does Dad have a cause of action against Son for breach of Son's fiduciary duties?

2. If Son has breached his fiduciary duties, can Dad have the license declared void?

3. Would Dad's cause of action have to be asserted as a direct or derivative claim? What difference would it make in this case? Does any such difference make sense under these circumstances?

CONNORS v. HOWE ELEGANT, LLC
2009 WL 242324 (Conn.Super. 2009)

BRUCE L. LEVIN, Judge.

This action arises out of the breakdown of the relationship between the principals, the plaintiff, Rosa Connors, and the defendant, Jennifer Kiman, who are the sole members of the defendant Howe Elegant, LLC (hereafter Howe), a beauty and hair salon. Connors (hereafter the plaintiff) alleges that in February 2005, she informed Kiman (hereafter the defendant) that she wanted to sell her interest in Howe or dissolve the business, but that she and Kiman were unable to come to terms about the business' future or the terms of dissolution. The plaintiff further alleges that on May 19, 2005, Kiman locked her out of the business' premises, subsequently closed the business' bank account and transferred those funds to another account, to which the plaintiff did not have access, and withdrew about $4,500 in operating cash.

The plaintiff brought this action on June 30, 2005.

---

151. See, generally, D. Osborne and M. Osborne "*Asset Protection: Trust Planning*," The American Law Institute (2010).

The plaintiff is a skin care specialist; the defendant is a hairdresser. In February 2001, both parties left their prior employment, taking with them their respective clients, and created Howe. Howe's business was hair styling, and nail and skin care. The plaintiff and the defendant obtained a $70,000 bank loan that was guaranteed by the United States Small Business Association (SBA), for which they were individually liable. Howe entered into a five-year lease on February 12, 2001 for the premises at 500 Howe Avenue in Shelton, Connecticut, which the plaintiff and defendant individually guaranteed.

By mutual agreement, the incomes that the plaintiff and the defendant derived from the business varied in a manner not prescribed by the LLC's operating agreement. Initially, the plaintiff and the defendant each put $700 back into the business each week, over and above what each party had earned from her respective customers. There was no evidence as to what the parties' arrangement was after this initial period, except that the plaintiff and the defendant took draws only out of what they respectively earned from their own clients, not from the revenue produced by anyone else in the shop.

In addition to the plaintiff and the defendant, the business had six employees. Employees were paid on a commission basis. The commission was not uniform for all employees, but varied from 25 percent to 50 percent. The balance was put back into the business. The employees had their own clients who they brought to the business. All the employees were employees at will, as were the plaintiff and the defendant. There were no employment contracts nor covenants not to compete.

For over three years, the plaintiff was the dominant member of Howe. Although Howe's operating agreement provided that each party was a member-manager, the plaintiff, with the defendant's acquiescence, was the de facto sole manager of the business. In the latter half of 2004, however, the defendant began to take a more assertive role in the business. On February 8, 2005, the plaintiff and the defendant had a telephone conversation about an issue that had arisen at work. An argument erupted at the end of which the plaintiff and the defendant agreed that they no longer would be partners and that their association would be terminated.

In the ensuing two and one-half months, the business continued. The atmosphere in the business was tense, but professional. The parties spoke little to each other; they generally only communicated through counsel. In March, the plaintiff, by her attorney, offered to sell her interest in Howe to the defendant "at a price to be determined by mutual agreement." In the alternative, the plaintiff suggested that they dissolve Howe. These offers failed to result in an agreement.

In March, the plaintiff informed the employees that she would be leaving Howe to start her own business. The employees made it clear to the plaintiff that they would be following her to that business. The defendant approached one employee, Heather Fernandez, informed her that she and the plaintiff would not be working together and encouraged Fernandez to stay with her. Fernandez was, at best, equivocal.

In March 2005, the plaintiff found a new location one-half mile away from Howe, obtained a building permit and began fitting up the building for her business, Sona Bella Salon and Spa, LLC (Sona Bella). Employees talked openly with their customers about their going to the plaintiff's new establishment, so much so that the defendant could overhear the remarks. The plaintiff took customer information from Howe's computer and used it to send a mailing to some of her customers, and to customers of the employees, announcing that Sona Bella would be opening and would employ Howe's soon-to-be former employees. She also took Howe's appointment book home and copied it and sold a gift certificate for her competing salon while she was still working at Howe. The plaintiff told the employees to tell their customers that the employees would be moving to Sona Bella soon, and the customers should make their next appointments there.

On Monday, May 9, 2005, the defendant called the plaintiff to discuss terms for dissolving the LLC. The parties did not reach an agreement on terms. During the week of May 9, 2005, the plaintiff was in and out of Howe, taking care of some of her customers, then leaving to tend to the fitting up of Sona Bella, where her work station was not yet ready. Although the fit up for Sona Bella was not complete, its new employees started seeing customers there on May 10, 2005. The plaintiff continued seeing her customers at Howe until May 18 or 19, 2005; she had nowhere else to service them.

On Thursday, May 19, 2005, the defendant changed the locks to the premises at 500 Howe Avenue. That evening, after business hours, the plaintiff tried to gain entry to the business, unsuccessfully, to retrieve a make-up unit she needed to service teenage customers who were attending a high school prom that weekend. The plaintiff's husband then telephoned the defendant's husband and asked him to open the door to the business that evening. The defendant's husband refused and also refused a request to provide the plaintiff with a new key to the premises. The plaintiff retrieved the make-up unit the following day, when she arrived at the business with a police officer. She never entered the premises again. She also made no payments on the lease to 500 Howe Avenue or on the SBA loan.

Thereafter, the defendant ceased doing business at 500 Howe Avenue under the name Howe Elegant LLC and did business under Jennifer Lee, LLC. She never again consulted with the plaintiff, and she assumed the lease and used the equipment and improvements that were made to the premises in 2001, when Howe first began operating. She also used the existing inventory of supplies. The defendant took charge of Howe's bank account, closed it with a balance of about $23,000, and transferred the money to a new account entitled Howe Elegant Old Money. She used that money, however, only to pay obligations of Howe or the SBA loan.

Although the issue of the plaintiff's standing has not been raised by the defendants, the court raises it sua sponte because it implicates the court's jurisdiction. *Smith v. Snyder,* 267 Conn. 456, 460 n. 5, 839 A.2d 589 (2004).

"Standing is established by showing that the party claiming it is authorized by statute to bring suit or is classically aggrieved ... The fundamental test for determining aggrievement encompasses a well-settled twofold determination: first, the party claiming aggrievement must successfully demonstrate a specific, personal and legal interest in [the subject matter of the challenged action], as distinguished from a general interest, such as is the concern of all members of the community as a whole. Second, the party claiming aggrievement must successfully establish that this specific personal and legal interest has been specially and injuriously affected by the [challenged action] ... Aggrievement is established if there is a possibility, as distinguished from a certainty, that some legally protected interest ... has been adversely affected ..." *AvalonBay Communities, Inc. v. Orange,* 256 Conn. 557, 567-68, 775 A.2d 284 (2001).

"Since at least the middle of the [nineteenth] century, it has been accepted in this country that the law should permit shareholders to sue derivatively on their corporation's behalf under appropriate conditions ... [I]t is axiomatic that a claim of injury, the basis of which is a wrong to the corporation, must be brought in a derivative suit, with the plaintiff proceeding secondarily, deriving his rights from the corporation which is alleged to have been wronged ... *Fink v. Golenbock,* 238 Conn. 183, 200, 680 A.2d 1243 (1996).

"[I]n order for a shareholder to bring a direct or personal action against the corporation or other shareholders, that shareholder must show an injury that is separate and distinct from that suffered by any other shareholder or by the corporation. It is commonly understood that [a] shareholder-even the sole shareholder-does not have standing to assert claims alleging wrongs to the corporation." *Smith v. Snyder, supra,* 267 Conn. at 460-62.

Fink v. Golenbock, 238 Conn. 183, 680 A.2d 1243 (1996), has some similarities to and differences with the instant case. In *Fink,* the named parties were each 50 percent owners of a professional corporation (the corporation) that became a successful pediatric practice. The plaintiff's wife sued him for divorce and told an employee of the corporation, Joan Magner, that the plaintiff had engaged in sexual conduct with his young adopted children. After learning this information, the defendant informed the plaintiff that he was no longer part of the medical practice, that he would not be allowed to see patients, and that if he attempted to do so, the defendant would have him arrested. Soon thereafter, the defendant and Magner formed a new professional corporation and operated a pediatric medical practice in the same building, which building was owned by the parties' corporation, used the same telephone number as the corporation and used the equipment that belonged to the corporation. Furthermore, the defendant took $10,000 from the corporation's checking account to establish the new corporation, and he did not pay the corporation either for the use of its equipment or for the use of its building.

The plaintiff brought a derivative action on behalf of the corporation alleging conversion, tortuous interference with business expectancies, an unjust enrichment. On appeal, the defendant argued that the plaintiff did not have standing to sue on behalf of the corporation because the plaintiff's injuries were personal, and not derivative. The Supreme Court disagreed. It also declined to decide "whether the plaintiff could properly have brought a direct suit had he so chosen;" *id.,* at 200; although the court noted: "At least one authority has suggested that in the case of a closely held corporation, the court may choose to treat a derivative action as a direct action: 'In the case of a closely held corporation ... the court in its discretion may treat an action raising derivative claims as a direct action, exempt it from those restrictions and defenses applicable only to derivative actions, and order an individual recovery ...' 2 American Law Institute, Principles of Corporate Governance: Analysis and Recommendations (1994) § 7.01(d)." *Id.,* at 200 n. 14; see also *id.,* at 202 n. 17.

Subsequent cases have cast doubt on the current viability of this suggestion in *Fink.* In *Smith v. Snyder, supra,* 267 Conn. at 456, the plaintiffs, Patricia Smith, Carol Tartagnio and Lectron Labs, Inc., brought suit against the defendants, Bettina and Donald Snyder and CS Industries, alleging, *inter alia,* "that the named defendant, Charles Snyder, while serving as a director and officer of Lectron, breached a fiduciary duty that he owed to Lectron by engaging in a pattern of self dealing and other abuses of his position that were designed to destroy or devalue Lectron. On appeal, the Supreme Court addressed sua sponte the issue of the plaintiffs' standing; *id.,* at 460 n. 5; and concluded: that "Smith and Tartagni lacked standing to bring this action in their individual capacities because the allegations in the plaintiffs' complaint, if true, demonstrate that Lectron was harmed, but that no specific shareholder sustained an injury separate and distinct from that suffered by any other shareholder or by the corporation. Accordingly, the individual claims of Smith and Tartagni must be dismissed." *Id.,* at 462.

So too, here, the injuries that the defendant allegedly committed, transferring inventory, equipment and leasehold to Jennifer Lee, LLC, and even the "lock-out," were injuries to Howe, not to the plaintiff.

Based on *Smith v. Snyder,* the court holds that the plaintiff lacks standing to bring the tort claims in her individual capacity. Therefore, counts three through eighteen of the plaintiff's amended complaint are dismissed.

The defendants have filed a five-count counterclaim. In counts one and two of its counterclaim, Howe alleges that the plaintiff while she was a manager, member and employee of Howe, breached her fiduciary and statutory duties, pursuant to General Statutes § 34-141, in the following ways: "a. She obtained a location for a competing business within a short distance of the place of business of the defendant ... b. She recruited employees of the defendant ... for her competing salon; c. She and/or her recruited employees acting at her direction, compiled information relating to customers of Howe ... for the purpose of soliciting their business away from the defendant ... d. She and/or her recruited employees acting at her direction, communicated, directly or indirectly, to customers of Howe ... that the defendant ... was no longer going to be there; e. She and/or her recruited employees acting at her direction, sold gift certificates for her competing salon to customers of the defendant ... who came into the place of business of the defendant ... for the purpose of purchasing a gift certificate for the defendant ... and f. She, and/or her recruited employees acting at her direction, sent mailings and other advertisements to customers of the defendant ... in order to solicit their business for the competing salon opened by the plaintiff."

Howe claims: "As a result of the breach of fiduciary duty by the plaintiff, the defendant ... lost customers, sales gift certificates and products and the opportunity to develop new customers, all to its financial detriment. As a further result of [the] breach of duty by the plaintiff, the defendant ... suffered damage to its business reputation."

Each protagonist, the plaintiff and the defendant, established her own LLC with the knowledge of the other. Under all the circumstances, it was reasonable for them not to wait until the dissolution of Howe to do so. Indeed, this would have been unrealistic. These are not wealthy people; they are beauticians servicing the lower Connecticut valley area who could not afford to suspend their livelihood while awaiting the outcome of litigation, now three and one-half years old. Furthermore, as observed above, the plaintiff and the defendant each knew the other would be plying her trade under the guise of a new corporate entity. Cf. *Ostrowski v. Avery,* 243 Conn. 355, 376, 703 A.2d 117 (1997) ("[A]dequate disclosure of a corporate opportunity is an absolute defense to fiduciary liability for alleged usurpation of ... a corporate opportunity.")

Moreover, comment (e) to § 393 of the Restatement (Second) of Agency, as well as 19 C.J.S., Corporations § 603 (2007), support a conclusion that a corporate officer should be allowed to make preparations for a competing business, prior to his or her resignation or termination, in the absence of a restrictive agreement stating otherwise.

As observed *supra,* the parties did not execute a restrictive covenant. Pursuant to the Restatement cited above, the plaintiff was permitted to make arrangements to compete with the defendant prior to her resignation. It is noteworthy that the plaintiff did not solicit customers for her rival business until the end of her employment. The court finds that the plaintiff merely informed Howe's employees that she would be leaving to start her own business, several employees announced that they would be following her, and the employees spoke openly to their customers about going to the plaintiff's new establishment. This conduct does not amount to solicitation under the circumstances.

Case law from other jurisdictions reflects that courts have found that, in the absence of a restrictive covenant, it is not a breach of fiduciary duty for an employee to prepare to compete with an employer prior to the employee's resignation or termination. The Court of Special Appeals in Maryland in *Dworkin v. Blumenthal,* 77 Md.App. 774, 782, 551 A.2d 947 (1989), held that two dentists, who were members of a professional association, did not actively compete with the association during their employment, although they did make arrangements to compete while they were still employees. In that case, the defendants began compiling a patient list from the association's records prior to their resignation. *Id.,* at 779. The court noted that the defendants only notified those patients that they, themselves, had treated, that they would be leaving the association and opening a new practice. *Id.,* at 780. Similarly, here, the court found that the plaintiff compiled customer information from Howe's computer records and used it to notify her customers and her employee's customers that she would be opening a new salon. There is no evidence that the plaintiff solicited any of the defendant's customers prior to her departure from Howe.

By clear and convincing evidence, the court finds that the plaintiff did not breach any duty to Howe.

Derivative Action Obstacles

As the *Connors* case illustrates, often a member of an LLC will be denied the right to bring a direct action against other members for breach of fiduciary or contractual duties owed the LLC. The LLC statutes of many states require that such actions be brought as derivative actions on behalf of the LLC. Any recovery in a derivative suit against a wrongdoer goes to the LLC, not the member who prosecutes the lawsuit. Plus, before commencing the action, the plaintiff must make a demand on the LLC to prosecute or settle the charges or allege with particularity in the complaint that such a demand would be futile.[152] The demand requirement gives the LLC advance notice of the suit and, in theory, provides an opportunity for a pre-suit settlement and exhaustion of intra-LLC dispute resolution procedures. And it gives the LLC's management time to exercise its management prerogative in sizing up the situation and deciding whether the case should go forward. States that have adopted the latest version of the Revised Uniform Limited Liability Company Act statutorily permit the appointment of a special litigation committee composed of independent and disinterested members to represent the interests of the LLC in any derivative proceeding.[153]

See section C. of Chapter 9 for an extended discussion of derivative actions in the context of a corporation. The right of corporate shareholders to prosecute a derivative claim is an absolute necessity because it is the tool that reconciles the conflict between the fiduciary duties imposed on the officers and directors of a corporation and the board of directors' power to manage the enterprise. Without this right, the duties would mean little or nothing. A board is not going to authorize a suit against itself for its breach of the duties of care or loyalty. A shareholder, as an owner of the enterprise, must have the right to expose and prosecute the wrongdoing on behalf of the corporation. The lawsuit is labeled "derivative" because it is based on the rights of, and injuries to, the corporation. As discussed in Chapter 9, at times the line between direct and derivative actions is fuzzy. But, as illustrated by the *Connors* case, the line is important because often it is the difference between the case moving forward and being dismissed.

Many have claimed that the direct-derivative distinction often makes little sense in the context of a closely held corporation where some owners desire to bring an action against their co-owners, alleging breach of fiduciary duties.[154] These claims seek to distinguish the role of a derivative action in a publicly held company from the lack of a need for such a role in a closely held corporation. Thus, in limited situations involving closely held corporations, courts have

---

152. See RULLCA §§ 901 through 904.
153. See RULLCA §§ 901 through 905.
154. See, for example, *Crosby v. Beam*, 548 N.E.2d 217 (Ohio 1989), *Barth v. Barth*, 659 N.E.2d 559 (Ind. 1995), and ALI Principles § 7.01(d).

ignored derivative requirements and treated the conflict as the equivalent of a dispute among partners.[155] Any recovery flows to the prevailing party (not the corporation), there is no pre-suit demand requirement, and the parties can settle their dispute without court approval. As the *Connors* case illustrates, this movement to ignore derivative requirements has not caught on in the LLC context, and it's unlikely that it ever will in states that have specific LLC derivative statutes that are applicable to closely held enterprises.

AURIGA CAPITAL CORP. v. GATZ PROPERTIES
40 A.3d 839 (Del.Ch. 2012)

STRINE, Chancellor.

The manager of an LLC [Gatz] and his family acquired majority voting control over both classes of the LLC's equity during the course of its operations and thereby held a veto over any strategic option. The LLC was an unusual one that held a long-term lease on a valuable property owned by the manager and his family. The leasehold allowed the LLC to operate a golf course on the property.

The LLC intended to act as a passive operator by subleasing the golf course for operation by a large golf management corporation. A lucrative sublease to that effect was entered in 1998. The golf management corporation, however, was purchased early in the term of the sublease by owners that sought to consolidate its operations. Rather than invest in the leased property and put its full effort into making the course a success, the management corporation took short cuts, let maintenance slip, and evidenced a disinterest in the property. By as early as 2004, it was clear to the manager that the golf management corporation would not renew its lease.

This did not make the manager upset. The LLC and its investors had invested heavily in the property, building on it a first-rate Robert Trent Jones, Jr.—designed golf course and a clubhouse. If the manager and his family could get rid of the investors in the LLC, they would have an improved property, which they had reason to believe could be more valuable as a residential community. Knowing that the golf management corporation would likely not renew its sublease, the manager failed to take any steps at all to find a new strategic option for the LLC that would protect the LLC's investors. Thus, the manager did not search for a replacement management corporation, explore whether the LLC itself could manage the golf course profitably, or undertake to search for a buyer for the LLC. Indeed, when a credible buyer for the LLC came forward on its own and expressed a serious interest, the manager failed to provide that buyer with the due diligence that a motivated seller would typically provide to a possible buyer. Even worse, the manager did all it could to discourage a good bid, frustrating and misleading the interested buyer.

The manager then sought to exploit the opportunity provided by the buyer's emergence to make low-ball bids to the other investors in the LLC on the basis of materially misleading information. Among other failures, the manager made an offer at $5.6 million for the LLC without telling the investors that the buyer had

---

155. Id.

expressed a willingness to discuss a price north of $6 million. The minority investors refused the manager's offer. When the minority investors asked the manager to go back and negotiate a higher price with the potential buyer, the manager refused.

This refusal reflected the reality that the manager and his family were never willing to sell the LLC. Nor did they desire to find a strategic option for the LLC that would allow it to operate profitably for the benefit of the minority investors. The manager and his family wanted to be rid of the minority investors, whom they had come to regard as troublesome bothers.

Using the coming expiration of the golf management corporation's sublease as leverage, the manager eventually conducted a sham auction to sell the LLC. The auction had all the look and feel of a distress sale, but without any of the cheap nostalgic charm of the old unclaimed freight TV commercials. Ridiculous postage stamp-sized ads were published and unsolicited junk mail was sent out. Absent was any serious marketing to a targeted group of golf course operators by a responsible, mature, respected broker on the basis of solid due diligence materials. No effort was made to provide interested buyers with a basis to assume the existing debt position of the LLC if they met certain borrower responsibility criteria. Instead, interested buyers were told that they would have to secure the bank's consent but were given an unrealistic amount of time to do so. Worst of all, interested buyers could take no comfort in the fact that the manager—who controlled the majority of the voting power of the LLC—was committed to selling the LLC to the highest bidder, as the bidding materials made clear that the manager was also planning to bid and at the same time reserved the right to cancel the auction for any reason.

When the results of this incompetent marketing process were known and the auctioneer knew that no one other than the manager was going to bid, the auctioneer told the manager that fact. The manager then won with a bid of $50,000 in excess of the LLC's debt, on which the manager was already a guarantor. Only $22,777 of the bid went to the minority investors. For his services in running this ineffective process, the auctioneer received a fee of $80,000, which was greater than the cash component of the winning bid. Despite now claiming that the LLC could not run a golf course profitably and pay off the mortgage on the property, the manager has run the course himself since the auction and is paying the debt.

A group of minority investors have sued for damages, arguing the manager breached his contractual and fiduciary duties through this course of conduct. The manager, after originally disclaiming that he owed a fiduciary duty of loyalty to the minority, now rests his defense on two primary grounds. The first is that the manager and his family were able to veto any option for the LLC as their right as members. As a result, they could properly use a chokehold over the LLC to pursue their own interests and the minority would have to live with the consequences of their freedom of action. The second defense is that by the time of the auction, the LLC was valueless.

In this post-trial decision, I find for the plaintiffs. For reasons discussed in the opinion, I explain that the LLC agreement here does not displace the traditional duties of loyalty and care that are owed by managers of Delaware LLCs to their investors in the absence of a contractual provision waiving or modifying those duties. The Delaware Limited Liability Company Act (the "LLC Act") explicitly applies equity as a default and our Supreme Court, and this court, have consistently held that default fiduciary duties apply to those managers of alternative entities who would qualify as fiduciaries under traditional equitable principles, including managers of LLCs. Here, the LLC agreement makes clear that the manager could only enter into a self-dealing transaction, such as its purchase of the LLC, if it proves that the terms were fair. In other words, the LLC agreement essentially incorporates a core element of the traditional fiduciary duty of loyalty. Not only that, the LLC agreement's exculpatory provision makes clear that the manager is not exculpated for bad faith action, willful misconduct, or even grossly negligent action, i.e., a breach of the duty of care.

The manager's course of conduct here breaches both his contractual and fiduciary duties. Using his control over the LLC, the manager took steps to deliver the LLC to himself and his family on unfair terms. With a minimally competent and loyal fiduciary at the helm, the LLC could have charted a course that would have delivered real value to its investors.

The manager's defense that his voting power gave him a license to exploit the minority fundamentally misunderstands Delaware law. The manager was free not to vote his membership interest for a sale. But he was not free to create a situation of distress by failing to cause the LLC to explore its market alternatives and then to buy the LLC for a nominal price. The purpose of the duty of loyalty is in large measure to prevent the exploitation by a fiduciary of his self-interest to the disadvantage of the minority. The fair price requirement of that duty, which is incorporated in the LLC agreement here, makes sure that if the conflicted fiduciary engages in self-dealing, he pays a price that is as much as an arms-length purchaser would pay.

The manager is in no position to take refuge in uncertainties he himself created by his own breaches of duty. He himself is responsible for the distress sale conducted in 2009. Had he acted properly, the LLC could have secured a strategic alternative in 2007, when it was in a stronger position and the economy was too. A transaction at that time would have likely yielded proceeds for the minority of a return of their invested capital plus a 10% total return, an amount which reflects the reality that the manager's desire to retain control of the LLC would have pushed up the pricing of the transaction due to his incentive to top any third-party bidder. I therefore enter a remedy to that effect, taking into account the distribution received by the plaintiffs at the auction, and add interest, compounded monthly at the legal rate, from that time period. Because the manager has made this litigation far more cumbersome and inefficient than it should have been by advancing certain frivolous arguments, I award the plaintiffs one-half of their reasonable attorneys' fees and costs. This award is justified under the bad faith exception to the American Rule, and also ensures that the disloyal manager is not rewarded for making it unduly expensive for the minority investors to pursue their legitimate claims to redress his serious infidelity. I do not award full-fee shifting because I have not adopted all of the plaintiffs' arguments and because the manager's litigation conduct, while sanctionably disappointing, was not so egregious as to justify that result.

At points in this litigation, Gatz has argued that his actions were not subject to any fiduciary duty analysis because the LLC Agreement of Peconic Bay displaced any role for the use of equitable principles in constraining the LLC's Manager. As I next explain, that is not true.

The Delaware LLC Act starts with the explicit premise that "equity" governs any case not explicitly covered by the Act. But the Act lets contracting parties modify or even eliminate any equitable fiduciary duties, a more expansive constriction than is allowed in the case of corporations. For that reason, in the LLC context, it is typically the case that the evaluation of fiduciary duty claims cannot occur without a close examination of the LLC agreement itself, which often tailors the traditional fiduciary duties to address the specific relationship of the contracting parties.

It seems obvious that, under traditional principles of equity, a manager of an LLC would qualify as a fiduciary of that LLC and its members. Under Delaware law, "[a] fiduciary relationship is a situation where one person reposes special trust in and reliance on the judgment of another or where a special duty exists on the part of one person to protect the interests of another." other. *Metro Ambulance, Inc. v. E. Med. Billing, Inc.*, 1995 WL 409015, at 2 (Del.Ch. July 5, 1995). Corporate directors, general partners and trustees are analogous examples of those who Delaware law has determined owe a "special duty." *McMahon v. New Castle Assocs.*, 532 A.2d 601, 604–05 (Del.Ch.1987). Equity distinguishes fiduciary relationships from straightforward commercial arrangements where there is no expectation that one party will act in the interests of the other. *Wal–Mart Stores, Inc. v. AIG Life Ins. Co.*, 901 A.2d 106, 114 (Del.2006).

The manager of an LLC—which is in plain words a limited liability "company" having many of the features of a corporation—easily fits the definition of a fiduciary. The manager of an LLC has more than an arms-length, contractual relationship with the members of the LLC. Rather, the manager is vested with discretionary power to manage the business of the LLC.

Thus, because the LLC Act provides for principles of equity to apply, because LLC managers are clearly fiduciaries, and because fiduciaries owe the fiduciary duties of loyalty and care, the LLC Act starts with the default that managers of LLCs owe enforceable fiduciary duties.

The statute incorporates equitable principles. Those principles view the manager of an LLC as a fiduciary and subject the manager as a default principle to the core fiduciary duties of loyalty and care. But, the statute allows the parties to an LLC agreement to entirely supplant those default principles or to modify them in part. Where the parties have clearly supplanted default principles in full, we give effect to the parties' contract choice. Where the parties have clearly supplanted default principles in part, we give effect to their contract choice. But, where the core default fiduciary duties have not been supplanted by contract, they exist as the LLC statute itself contemplates.

I note at the outset that the Peconic Bay LLC Agreement contains no general provision stating that the only duties owed by the manager to the LLC and its investors are set forth in the Agreement itself. Thus, before taking into account the existence of an exculpatory provision, the LLC Agreement does not displace the traditional fiduciary duties of loyalty and care owed to the Company and its members by Gatz Properties and by Gatz, in his capacity as the manager of Gatz Properties. And although LLC agreements may displace fiduciary duties altogether or tailor their application, by substituting a different form of review, here § 15 of the LLC Agreement contains a clause reaffirming that a form akin to entire fairness review will apply to "Agreements with Affiliates," a group which includes Gatz Properties, that are not approved by a majority of the unaffiliated members' vote. In relevant part, § 15 provides:

> 15. Neither the Manager nor any other Member shall be entitled to cause the Company to enter ... into any additional agreements with affiliates on terms and conditions which are less favorable to the Company than the terms and conditions of similar agreements which could be entered into with arms-length third parties, without the consent of a majority of the non-affiliated Members (such majority to be deemed to be the holders of 66–2/3% of all Interests which are not held by affiliates of the person or entity that would be a party to the proposed agreement).

This court has interpreted similar contractual language supplying an "arm's length terms and conditions" standard for reviewing self-dealing transactions, and has read it as imposing the equivalent of the substantive aspect of entire fairness review, commonly referred to as the "fair price" prong.

Importantly, however, entire fairness review's procedural inquiry into "fair dealing" does not completely fall away, because the extent to which the process leading to the self-dealing either replicated or deviated from the behavior one would expect in an arms-length deal bears importantly on the price determination. Where a self-dealing transaction does not result from real bargaining, where there has been no real market test, and where the self-interested party's own conduct may have compromised the value of the asset in question or the information available to assess that value, these factors bear directly on whether the interested party can show that it paid a fair price. Thus, as written, § 15 permits Affiliate Agreements without the approval of the majority of the Minority Members, subject to a proviso that places the burden on the Manager (here, Gatz) to show that the price term of the Affiliate Agreement was the equivalent of one in an agreement negotiated at arms-length. But, "[i]mplicit in this proviso is the requirement that the [defendants] undertake some effort to determine the price at which a transaction with [Gatz] could be effected through a deal with a third party." In other words, in order to take cover under the contractual safe harbor of § 15, Gatz bears the burden to show that he paid a fair price to acquire Peconic Bay, a conclusion that must be supported by a showing that he performed, in good faith, a responsible examination of what a third-party buyer would pay for the Company. The record convinces me that Gatz has failed to meet the terms of this proviso.

The LLC Agreement does, however, contain an exculpatory provision, which is functionally akin to an exculpatory charter provision authorized by 8 Del. C. § 102(b)(7). In relevant part, § 16, governing "Exculpation and Indemnification," reads as follows:

> 16. No Covered Person [defined to include "the Members, Manager and the officers, equity holders, partners and employees of each of the foregoing"] shall be liable to the Company, [or] any other Covered Person or any other person or entity who has an interest in the Company for any loss, damage or claim incurred by reason of any act or omission performed or omitted by such Covered Person in good faith in connection with the formation of the Company or on behalf of the Company and in a manner reasonably believed to be within the scope of the authority conferred on such Covered Person by this Agreement, except that a Covered Person shall be liable for any such loss, damage or claim incurred by reason of such Covered Person's gross negligence, willful misconduct or willful misrepresentation.

Thus, by the terms of § 16, Gatz may escape monetary liability for a breach of his default fiduciary duties if he can prove that his fiduciary breach was not: (1) in bad faith, or the result of (2) gross negligence, (3) willful misconduct or (4) willful misrepresentation. Also, in order to fall within the terms of § 16, a Covered Person must first be acting "on behalf of the company" and "in a manner reasonably believed to be within the scope of authority conferred on [him] by [the LLC Agreement]." Thus, § 16 only insulates a Covered Person from liability for authorized actions; that is, actions taken in accordance with the other stand-alone provisions of the LLC Agreement. So, to the extent that the Auction and the follow-on Merger were effected in violation of the arms-length mandate set forth in § 15 (which they were), such a breach would not be exculpated by § 16. Moreover, even if I were to find that § 16 operated to limit Gatz's liability for actions taken in contravention of the terms of § 15, I find that his actions related to and in consummation of the Auction and follow-on Merger were taken in bad faith such that he would not be entitled to exculpation anyway.

Notably, the exculpation standard set forth in § 16 is both stronger and weaker than its corporate analogue in terms of limitation of liability. Whereas § 102(b)(7) authorizes a charter provision to exculpate a violation of the directors' duty of care (i.e., gross negligence), here § 16 does not exculpate for a breach of the duty of care. Gatz may still be liable for gross negligence. But, whereas § 102(b)(7) does not authorize exculpation for breaches of corporate directors' duty of loyalty, here § 16 does exculpate Gatz from liability for a breach of his fiduciary duty of loyalty (outside the context governed by § 15) to the extent he shows that the breach was not committed in bad faith or through willful misconduct.

The record convinces me that Gatz pursued a bad faith course of conduct to enrich himself and his family without any regard for the interests of Peconic Bay or its Minority Members. His breaches may be summarized as follows: (1) failing to take any steps for five years to address in good faith the expected loss of American Golf as an operator; (2) turning away a responsible bidder which could have paid a price beneficial to the LLC and its investors in that capacity; (3) using the leverage obtained by his own loyalty breaches to play "hardball" with the Minority Members by making unfair offers on the basis of misleading disclosures; and (4) buying the LLC at an auction conducted on terms that were well-designed to deter any third-party buyer, and to deliver the LLC to Gatz at a distress sale price.

Despite this, Gatz argues that he and his fellow defendant should not be held liable because even if they breached their fiduciary duties, they did not cause any economic harm because Peconic Bay was insolvent as of the time of the Auction.

By the time of his post-trial briefs, Gatz's defense was really one based on minimizing the damages he would owe. That defense melds with his defense based on § 15 of the LLC Agreement, which is that regardless of his misconduct, Gatz Properties in fact paid a fair price for Peconic Bay at the Auction and thus complied with its core mandate that Affiliate Agreements be entered into on "arms-length" terms and conditions. In support of that argument, Gatz points to testimony of Carr of Auriga. In that testimony, which was in response to questions from the court itself, Carr admitted that he considered bidding at the Auction, but did not because he could not come up with a model predicting positive returns high enough to meet his personal requirements.

Gatz himself is responsible for the evidentiary uncertainty caused by his own disloyalty. It was his own selfishly motivated acts of mismanagement that led to the distress sale. If he had acted properly, a liquidity event or some other sensible strategic alternative to the expiring American Golf Sublease would have been undertaken in 2007, when Galvin of RDC came on the scene. Gatz was the one who put Peconic Bay in a position of relative economic weakness by allowing the time on the Sublease to lapse and then choosing to put Peconic Bay on the auction block, and even then he chose an unduly rushed and compromised marketing process when there was time to do a professionally competent job. Given his own breaches of loyalty, the attendant uncertainties cut against Gatz, not against the victims of his infidelity.

In view of the persistent and serious nature of Gatz's breaches, and in view of his own 2008 claim that he was offering a deal that would have returned to the Minority Members their full initial capital contribution, I conclude that a remedy that awards the Minority Members their full capital contribution of $725,000 plus $72,500, is the equitable result. This is slightly less than the amount that would have been produced by a deal in 2007 of $6.5 million.

For all these reasons, I find for the Minority Members and will enter a final judgment for them.

The Value of Contractual Exculpation

Section 110(d) of the Revised Uniform Limited Liability Company Act authorizes liability exculpation provisions in an LLC operating agreement as follows:

(d) If not manifestly unreasonable, the operating agreement may:

(1) restrict or eliminate the duty:

(A) to account to the limited liability company and to hold as trustee for it any property, profit, or benefit derived by the member in the conduct or winding up of the company's business, from a use by the member of the company's property, or from the appropriation of a limited liability company opportunity;

(B) to refrain from dealing with the company in the conduct or winding up of the company's business as or on behalf of a party having an interest adverse to the company; and

(C) to refrain from competing with the company in the conduct of the company's business before the dissolution of the company;

(2) identify specific types or categories of activities that do not violate the duty of loyalty;

(3) alter the duty of care, except to authorize intentional misconduct or knowing violation of law;

(4) alter any other fiduciary duty, including eliminating particular aspects of that duty; and

(5) prescribe the standards by which to measure the performance of the contractual obligation of good faith and fair dealing.

(e) The operating agreement may specify the method by which a specific act or transaction that would otherwise violate the duty of loyalty may be authorized or ratified by one or more disinterested and independent persons after full disclosure of all material facts.

(f) To the extent the operating agreement of a member-managed limited liability company expressly relieves a member of a responsibility that the member would otherwise have under this [act] and imposes the responsibility on one or more other members, the operating agreement may, to the benefit of the member that the operating agreement relieves of the responsibility, also eliminate or limit any fiduciary duty that would have pertained to the responsibility.

(g) The operating agreement may alter or eliminate the indemnification for a member or manager.. and may eliminate or limit a member or manager's liability to the limited liability company and members for money damages, except for:

(1) breach of the duty of loyalty;

(2) a financial benefit received by the member or manager to which the member or manager is not entitled;

(3) a breach of a duty [for improper distritions];

(4) intentional infliction of harm on the company or a member; or

(5) an intentional violation of criminal law.

The breadth of these provisions creates powerful planning opportunities in drafting an LLC operating agreement. You will discover when you study fiduciary duties in the context of a corporation (Chapter 10) that the scope of these exculpation provisions exceeds anything in the corporate world. Careful drafting of an LLC operating agreement can reduce and, in some instances, completely eliminate fiduciary liability exposure. The limiting factor under the Revised Act is that the exculpation provisions cannot be "manifestly unreasonable." In explaining the role of this limitation under subparagraph (d), the official comments to the Revised Act state:

> **Subsection (d)** -Delaware recently amended its LLC statute to permit an operating agreement to fully "eliminate" fiduciary duty within an LLC. This Act rejects the ultra-contractarian notion that fiduciary duty within a business organization is merely a set of default rule and seeks instead to balance the virtues of "freedom of contract" against the dangers that inescapably exist when some have power over the interests of others. As one source has explained:
>
>> The open-ended nature of fiduciary duty reflects the law's long-standing recognition that devious people can smell a loophole a mile away. For centuries, the law has assumed that (1) power creates opportunities for abuse and (2) the devious creativity of those in power may outstrip the prescience of those trying, through ex ante contract drafting, to constrain that combination of power and creativity.[156]

F. AUTHORITY AND MANAGEMENT DISPUTES

SYNECTIC VENTURES I, LLC v. EVI CORP.
251 P.3d 216 (Or.App. 2011)

SERCOMBE, P.J.

These consolidated appeals involve an action by three investment funds to collect on a promissory note and foreclose on a security interest against defendant EVI Corporation (EVI) pursuant to the terms of a loan agreement. The dispute between the parties turns on whether an amendment to the loan agreement is binding on plaintiffs. The dispositive issue on appeal is whether the trial court correctly determined that plaintiffs' manager, Craig Berkman, had the authority to bind plaintiffs to the amendment. We affirm.

Plaintiffs are three investment funds that were organized as limited liability companies and originally managed by Berkman. The operating agreement for each plaintiff designates a separate management firm controlled by Berkman as

---

156. Carter G. Bishop and Daniel S. Kleinberger, *Limited Liability Companies: Tax and Business Law*, ¶ 14.05[4][a][ii]

the manager for each fund. Berkman was also the board chairman and treasurer of EVI, and served as the main fundraiser for EVI. His involvement with EVI was allowed under the terms of the operating agreements. On appeal, plaintiffs argue that Berkman lacked authority to bind them to the amendment. Initially, they assert that, because Berkman breached multiple duties to plaintiffs by executing the amendment, he did not have authority to bind them. Alternatively, plaintiffs argue that they limited Berkman's authority to act without prior approval before he signed the amendment, and that EVI had knowledge, through Berkman and EVI's CEO, Thomas Wiita, that Berkman lacked authority to enter into the amendment. Accordingly, plaintiffs claim that the amendment is not binding.

EVI contends that the amendment was valid, given that plaintiffs' operating agreements vest Berkman with exclusive management authority, and that he was acting within his authority when he entered into the amendment on behalf of plaintiffs. In addition, EVI argues that the operating agreements granted third parties the right to rely, without further inquiry, on a certificate signed by Berkman as the managing member. EVI also maintains that plaintiffs' operating agreements authorized the types of conflicts of interest that plaintiffs assert exist in this case. Finally, EVI asserts that plaintiffs ratified the amendment because they did not object to it until seven months after they discovered it.

The basic facts are undisputed. Plaintiffs are venture capital funds that were formed to invest in emerging companies. Each plaintiff is a fund that consists of individual investors. All three are governed by substantially similar operating agreements. Berkman's management entities are named in each operating agreement as the manager, and those documents generally grant the manager the exclusive authority to manage and control the interests of plaintiffs. EVI is an Oregon corporation in the medical device field.

Plaintiffs, along with two other investment funds—defendants Synectic Ventures IV, LLC (Fund IV), and Synectic Ventures V, LLC (Fund V)— advanced over $3 million to EVI before March 2003. In March 2003, the parties documented the terms of the advances in the loan agreement, which required EVI to pay the debt by December 31, 2004. If the debt was not timely paid, plaintiffs were entitled to foreclose on EVI's assets. However, if EVI received additional investments of at least $1 million before the deadline, EVI could force a conversion of the debt to equity (in the form of EVI stock).

Around the time that the parties executed the agreement, some, but not all, of the individual investors in plaintiffs hired a Portland law firm to investigate Berkman's management of the funds. After some initial investigation and communications with Berkman, the concerned investors and Berkman entered into a letter agreement in September 2003. The terms of the letter agreement provided that Berkman would inform the concerned investors of certain activities taken on behalf of plaintiffs, and that Berkman would not take on additional obligations or increase existing obligations for plaintiffs, without advance approval of the concerned investors.

The terms agreed to in the September 2003 letter agreement were reiterated in another letter agreement in June 2004. The June 2004 letter agreement also contemplated winding up the funds. Further communications on behalf of the concerned investors in late 2004 informed Berkman that the concerned investors intended to remove him as manager as soon as a replacement could be found.

Although the exact date is disputed, in September 2004, Berkman executed an amendment to the agreement on plaintiffs' behalf that extended EVI's repayment deadline until December 31, 2005. He also executed a Unanimous Consent on behalf of EVI's board of directors, which allowed Wiita to execute the amendment for EVI. Plaintiffs assert that they were unaware of the amendment at the time it was made. Pursuant to the process outlined in the operating agreements, plaintiffs removed Berkman as manager in December 2004 and hired another management company.

EVI did not pay the debt and did not receive additional investments of $1 million before December 31, 2004. In early 2005, plaintiffs discovered the existence of the amendment. In late August 2005, plaintiffs notified EVI that the amendment was not authorized and that EVI was in default. Subsequently, another investment fund managed by Berkman—Synectic Asset Ventures LLC (SAV)—invested $1 million in EVI by December 31, 2005. EVI then purportedly converted the loans subject to the agreement into equity in satisfaction of its debt.

Plaintiffs consolidate their argument on appeal, and maintain that the amendment is not binding on them for alternative reasons. They claim that Berkman breached several fiduciary duties owed to plaintiffs at the time of the amendment, and that, because EVI had actual knowledge of his conduct, the amendment is not binding on plaintiffs. Alternatively, plaintiffs assert that, even if Berkman did not breach any fiduciary duties, he lacked the authority to execute the amendment on plaintiffs' behalf, and, because EVI knew that he lacked authority, the amendment cannot be enforced against plaintiffs.

EVI responds that the amendment is enforceable for any of three reasons. First, EVI contends that Berkman, through plaintiffs' operating agreements, had actual authority to enter into and bind plaintiffs to the amendment. Second, EVI argues that, regardless of Berkman's actual authority, EVI was entitled to rely on Berkman's apparent authority given that the operating agreements specifically authorized third parties to rely on Berkman's actions without further inquiry. Third, EVI asserts that plaintiffs ratified the amendment because they knowingly acquiesced to its terms for seven months before challenging it.

We begin our analysis with a key provision from the statutes governing limited liability companies. ORS 63.140(2)(a) provides, in part:

"Each manager is an agent of the limited liability company for the purpose of its business, and an act of a manager, including the signing of an instrument in the limited liability company's name, for apparently carrying on in the ordinary course the business of the limited liability company, or business of the kind carried on by the limited liability company, binds the limited liability company unless the manager had no authority to act for the limited liability company in the particular matter and the person with whom the manager was dealing knew or had notice that the manager lacked authority."

As such, ORS 63.140(2)(a) sets forth the statutory standard for determining if a manager's act in carrying on in the ordinary course the business of the limited liability company is binding on that company. If the manager had no authority in that particular matter and the third party knew or had notice of the manager's lack of authority, then the company is not bound.

Determining whether a manager has authority requires us to look to the law of agency. Generally, a principal is bound by its agent's acts if the acts are within the scope of the agent's actual or apparent authority.

Plaintiffs' operating agreements each contain identical statements about the management and control of the companies. The operating agreements gave Berkman authority to exclusively manage and control the business and affairs of plaintiffs. His actual authority, expressly granted in the operating agreements, encompassed the ability to take action on behalf of plaintiffs without the consent of the members. The operating agreements also granted any third party the right to rely on Berkman's authority to bind plaintiffs without further inquiry. As such, at first blush it would appear that Berkman's act of executing the amendment was within the express authority granted to him in the operating agreements.

Plaintiffs, however, assert that Berkman's actual authority was limited in one of two ways: either the "letter agreements" that Berkman entered into with the concerned investors limited his authority to further obligate plaintiffs without approval of the concerned investors, or his authority was limited by his acts of self-dealing and his breach of the fiduciary duties he owed to plaintiffs.

We first examine the effect of the letter agreements. Plaintiffs contend that the trial court erroneously relied only on the text of the operating agreements and failed to consider other circumstances that existed at the time that Berkman entered into the amendment. They maintain that, through the series of communications and letter agreements, Berkman agreed that his authority was limited, and that any new obligations required the approval of plaintiffs. From that, they conclude that Berkman lacked the authority to execute the amendment on plaintiffs' behalf.

We agree with the trial court that the letter agreements did not limit Berkman's authority to bind plaintiffs because Berkman did not enter into these agreements *with plaintiffs*. The letter agreements confirmed an understanding between Berkman and the concerned investors. However, the concerned investors were acting in their capacity as a group of individual investors, not as the funds. Under general principles of the law of agency, any agreement between Berkman and a subset of individual investors who were not acting as plaintiffs did not limit Berkman's actual authority. *Restatement (Third) of Agency* § 3.06 (2006) (noting that termination of an agent's authority may occur by agreement between the agent and the *principal* or a manifestation of revocation by the *principal* to the agent).

In fact, the September 2003 letter agreement eschews the legal effect that plaintiffs currently seek. It advises that "[Berkman] will remain responsible for the Funds to the same extent as in the past." Moreover, while the record shows that Berkman did at times comply with the letter agreements, it also demonstrates that the concerned investors and their attorneys understood and communicated to Berkman that the letter agreements did not limit Berkman's authority to act on behalf of plaintiffs. For example, e-mail communications between the concerned investors' attorney and a company in a separate investment deal state that:

"the investors committee has no right to control the investment of Fund monies. That is the power, right, and responsibility of the Manager of the Funds. Even if the committee or individual investors whom we represent wanted to do so, they do not have the right to cause the Fund II Manager—[Berkman]—to invest or not invest further in [third party]. Moreover, there are other Fund II investors whose interests we do not represent. All of the Fund investors are free to express their preference to [Berkman], but he ultimately is the only one with responsibility for any Fund investment decisions."

Furthermore, the stated understanding of the concerned investors is consistent with the terms of the operating agreements, which set out a specific process for Berkman's removal as manager. Pursuant to the operating agreements, Berkman was removed in December 2004, but not before the amendment was executed.

Thus, the agreements purporting to limit Berkman's authority were ineffective to do so because they did not comply with the process set forth in the operating agreements. While the letter agreements may create an obligation that Berkman owed to the concerned investors, any breach of that obligation was between him and them, and it did not affect his authority to conduct business on plaintiffs' behalf.

Next, we address plaintiffs' contention that they were not bound by the amendment because Berkman breached his fiduciary duties to plaintiffs when he signed the amendment. Plaintiffs cite *Fine v. Harney Co. National Bank,* 181 Or. 411, 182 P.2d 379 (1947), and *Houck v. Feller Living Trust,* 191 Or.App. 39, 42–43, 79 P.3d 1140 (2003), for the proposition that an agent cannot bind the principal in a matter in which his own interest conflicts with the duty he owes to the principal—particularly when the third party with whom the agent is dealing knew that the agent was breaching his duties.

Plaintiffs maintain that ORS chapter 63 conferred duties of loyalty, care, and good faith and fair dealing on Berkman, and that the operating agreements contained a "standard of conduct" clause that explicitly required Berkman to act in accordance with those duties. Plaintiffs contend that Berkman breached the duties of loyalty, care, and good faith and fair dealing by executing the amendment without prior authorization from plaintiffs. Plaintiffs claim that, given Berkman's self-interest in the success of EVI, he was required by the operating agreements to seek plaintiffs' approval before executing the amendment. Further, plaintiffs claim that, given Berkman's position with EVI, knowledge of Berkman's conflicts was imputed to EVI.

Before considering whether Berkman owed certain duties to plaintiffs, and whether he breached those duties, we must determine if the remedy sought by plaintiffs for any such breach is available. That is, even if Berkman breached a duty to plaintiffs, can plaintiffs void the amendment? While the legal proposition is well established that an agent who breaches a duty to the principal is liable to the principal for any damages arising from that breach, *Restatement (Second) of Agency* § 401 (1958), it is not so clear that an agent's action that involves such a breach does not bind the principal.

Plaintiffs contend that *Fine* and *Houck* establish the principle that allows them to void the amendment based on Berkman's breach. EVI, of course, counters that *Fine* and *Houck* are inapposite. In neither *Fine* nor *Houck* did the fact that the agent breached a duty to the principal act to sever or limit the agent's authority. In *Fine*, the employee simply had no authority to receive deposits of his own checks, and it would have been illegal for the bank to authorize such an action. In *Houck*, the power of attorney did not authorize the actions of the grandson, and thus he acted outside the scope of the express authority granted in the power of attorney. These cases stand for the unremarkable proposition that, if a third party is aware that the agent is engaged in self-dealing in the transaction, the party must inquire into the agent's actual authority.

That basic proposition of the law of agency is reflected in the relevant statutory standard in ORS 63.140(2)(a)—the act of a manager binds the limited liability company "unless the manager had no authority to act for the limited liability company in the particular matter and the person with whom the manager was dealing knew or had notice that the manager lacked authority."

Therefore, under ORS 63.140(2)(a), even if we assume that Berkman owed plaintiffs the duties that they list, and even if we assume that he breached those duties, the question is still whether Berkman had the authority to act for plaintiffs. As we determined, Berkman retained the express authority to enter into the amendment. Plaintiffs took no action to limit his authority, and there was no operation of law that stripped him of his authority to bind plaintiffs in the ordinary course of business. An extension of the terms of the loan agreement is within the ordinary course of business and was expressly contemplated by the terms of the loan agreement. So, even if knowledge of Berkman's alleged self-dealing was imputed to EVI, any inquiry by EVI could only lead to the conclusion that Berkman had authority to enter into the amendment on plaintiffs' behalf. Moreover, we also note that the operating agreements contained a provision that explicitly authorized third parties to rely on Berkman's authority without further inquiry.

Finally, we address the related, but distinct, conflict of interest issues raised by plaintiffs. As recounted above, plaintiffs alleged that Berkman had multiple conflicts of interest that limited his authority to act to amend the loan agreement.

ORS 63.130(2) to (4) set forth the general provisions governing conflict of interest situations in manager-managed limited liability companies.

"(4) Unless otherwise provided in the * * * operating agreement, the following matters of a * * * manager-managed limited liability company require the consent of a majority of the members:

"(h) A transaction involving an actual or a potential conflict of interest between a member or a manager and the limited liability company[.]"

As the statute makes clear, a majority approval of the conflict of interest is required unless the operating agreement provides otherwise. In this instance, the operating agreements recognized the conflicts of interest that are alleged by plaintiffs. Specifically, the operating agreements state:

"Any Member or its Affiliates may engage independently or with others in other business and investment ventures of every nature and description and shall have no obligation to account to the Company for such business or investments or for business or investment opportunities. An 'Affiliate' shall mean any person or entity controlling, controlled by, or under common control with the person or entity in question, whether through beneficial ownership of securities, exercise of management control, or otherwise...

Accordingly, the type of conflict alleged here, where Berkman acted in his individual capacity as a board member and treasurer of a company in which plaintiffs invested, is authorized by the operating agreement, and ORS 63.130 does not apply. Affirmed.

G. DISSOLUTION CHALLENGES

HALEY v. TALCOTT
864 A.2d 86 (Del.Ch. 2004)

STRINE, Vice Chancellor.

Plaintiff Matthew James Haley has moved for summary judgment of his claim seeking dissolution of Matt and Greg Real Estate, LLC ("the LLC"). Haley and defendant Gregory L. Talcott are the only members of the LLC, each owning a 50% interest in the LLC. Haley brings this action in reliance upon § 18-802 of the Delaware Limited Liability Company Act which permits this court to "decree dissolution of a limited liability company whenever it is not reasonably practicable to carry on the business in conformity with a limited liability company agreement." The question before the court is whether dissolution of the LLC should be granted, as Haley requests, or whether, as Talcott contends, Haley is limited to the contractually-provided exit mechanism in the LLC Agreement.

Haley and Talcott have suffered, to put it mildly, a falling out. There is no rational doubt that they cannot continue to do business as 50% members of an LLC. But the path to separating their interests is complicated by a second company, Delaware Seafood, also known as the Redfin Seafood Grill ("Redfin Grill"), a restaurant that, at the risk of slightly oversimplifying, was owned by Talcott and, before the falling out, operated by Haley under an employment contract that gave him a 50% share in the profits. The LLC owns the land that the

Redfin Grill occupies under an expired lease. The resolution of the current case and the ultimate fate of the LLC therefore critically affect the continued existence of a second business that one party owns and that the other bitterly contends, in other litigation pending before this court, wrongly terminated him.

The question before the court is essentially how the interests of the members of the LLC are to be separated. Haley asserts that summary judgment is appropriate because it is factually undisputed that it is not reasonably practicable for the LLC to carry on business in conformity with a limited liability company agreement (the "LLC Agreement") that calls for the LLC to be governed by its two members, when those members are in deadlock. Therefore, urges Haley, the LLC should be judicially dissolved immediately. Such an end will force the sale of the LLC's real property, which is likely worth, at current market value, far more than the mortgage that the LLC must pay off if it sells.

In response, Talcott stresses that the LLC Agreement provides an alternative exit mechanism that allows the LLC to continue to exist, and argues that Haley should therefore be relegated to this provision if he is unhappy with the stalemate. In other words, Talcott argues that it is reasonably practicable for the LLC to continue to carry on business in conformity with its LLC Agreement because the exit mechanism creates a fair alternative that permits Haley to get out, receiving the fair market value of his share of the property as determined in accordance with procedures in the LLC Agreement, while allowing the LLC to continue. Critically, the exit provision would allow Talcott to buy Haley out with no need for the LLC's asset (i.e., the land) to be sold on the open market. The LLC could continue to exist and own the land (with its favorable mortgage arrangement) and Talcott, as owner of both entities, could continue to offer the Redfin Grill its favorable rent.

But the problem with Talcott's argument is that the exit mechanism is not a reasonable alternative. A principle attraction of the LLC form of entity is the statutory freedom granted to members to shape, by contract, their own approach to common business "relationship" problems. If an equitable alternative to continued deadlock had been specified in the LLC Agreement, arguably judicial dissolution under § 18-802 might not be warranted. In this case, however, Talcott admits that the exit mechanism provides no method to relieve Haley of his obligation as a personal guarantor for the LLC's mortgage. Haley signed an agreement with the lender personally guaranteeing the entire mortgage of the LLC (as did Talcott) in order to secure the loan. Without relief from the guaranty, Haley would remain personally liable for the mortgage debt of the LLC, even after his exit. Because Haley would be left liable for the debt of an entity over which he had no further control, I find that the exit provision specified in the LLC Agreement and urged by Talcott is not sufficient to provide an adequate remedy to Haley under these circumstances.

With no reasonable exit mechanism, I find that Haley is entitled to exercise the only practical deadlock-breaking remedy available to him, and one that is also alluded to in the LLC Agreement, the right to seek judicial dissolution. Haley argues, convincingly, that the analysis under § 18-802 for an evenly-split, two-owner LLC ordinarily should parallel the analysis under 8 *Del. C.* § 273, which enables this court to order the judicial dissolution of a joint venture corporation owned by deadlocked 50% owners. Because Haley has demonstrated an indisputable deadlock between the two 50% members of the LLC, and that deadlock precludes the LLC from functioning as provided for in the LLC Agreement, I also grant Haley's motion for summary judgment and order dissolution of Matt and Greg Real Estate, LLC.

Haley and Talcott each have a 50% interest in Matt & Greg Real Estate, LLC, a Delaware limited liability company they formed in 2003. In 2003, the parties formed Matt & Greg Real Estate, LLC to take advantage of the option to purchase the Property that was the subject of the Real Estate Agreement. The option price was $720,000 and the new LLC took out a mortgage from County Bank in Rehoboth Beach, Delaware, for that amount, exercised the option, and obtained the deed to the Property on or about May 23, 2003. Importantly, both Haley and Talcott, individually, signed personal guaranties for the entire amount of the mortgage in order to secure the loan. The Redfin Grill continued to operate at the site, paying the LLC $6,000 per month in rent, a payment sufficient to cover the LLC's monthly obligation under the mortgage. Thus by mid-2003, the parties appeared poised to reap the fruits of their labors; unfortunately, at that point their personal relationship began to deteriorate.

Haley, having managed the restaurant from the time it opened in May 2001, and having formalized his management position in the Employment Contract, apparently believed that the relationship would be reformulated to provide him a direct stock ownership interest in the Redfin Grill at some point. The reasons underlying that belief are not important here, but in late October they caused a rift to develop between the parties. On or about October 27, 2003, the conflict that had been brewing between the parties led to some kind of confrontation. As a result, Talcott sent a letter of understanding to Haley dated October 27, 2003, purporting to accept his resignation and forbidding him to enter the premises of the Redfin Grill.

Haley responded on November 3, 2003 with two separate letters from his counsel to Talcott. In the first, Haley asserts that he did not resign, and that he regarded Talcott's October 27, 2003 letter of understanding as terminating him without cause in breach of the Employment Contract. Haley goes on to express his intent to pursue legal remedies, an intent that he acted upon in the related case in this court.

The Redfin Grill's lease has expired and, as a consequence, the Redfin Grill continues to pay $6,000 per month to the LLC in a month-to-month arrangement. The $6,000 rent exceeds the LLC's required mortgage payment by $800 per month, so the situation remains stable. With only a 50% ownership interest, Haley cannot force the termination of the Redfin Grill's lease and evict the Redfin Grill as a tenant; neither can he force the sale of the Property, land that was appraised as of June 14, 2004 at $1.8 million. In short, absent intervention by this court, Haley is stuck, unless he chooses to avail himself of the exit mechanism provided in the LLC Agreement.

That exit mechanism, like judicial dissolution, would provide Haley with his share of the fair market value of the LLC, including the Property. Section 18 of the LLC Agreement provides that upon written notice of election to "quit" the company, the remaining member may elect, in writing, to purchase the departing member's interest for fair market value. If the remaining member elects to purchase the departing member's interest, the parties may agree on fair value, or have the fair value determined by three arbitrators, one chosen by each member and a third chosen by the first two arbitrators. The departing member pays the reasonable expenses of the three arbitrators. Once a fair price is determined, it may be paid in cash, or over a term if secured by: 1) a note signed by the company and personally by the remaining member; 2) a security agreement; and 3) a recorded UCC lien. Only if the remaining member fails to elect to purchase the departing member's interest is the company to be liquidated.

But despite this level of detail, the exit provision does not expressly provide a release from the personal guaranties that both Haley and Talcott signed to secure the mortgage on the Property. Nor does the exit provision state that any member dissatisfied with the status quo must break an impasse by exit rather than a suit for dissolution.

Haley argues that dissolution is required because the two 50% managers cannot agree how to best utilize the sole asset of the LLC, the Property, because no provision exists for breaking a tie in the voting interests, and because the LLC cannot take any actions, such as entering contracts, borrowing or lending money, or buying or selling property, absent a majority vote of its members. Because this circumstance resembles corporate deadlock, Haley urges that 8 *Del. C.* § 273 provides a relevant parallel for analysis.

In examining the record, I must draw every rational inference in Talcott's favor. Here, even if I find that there are no facts under which the LLC could carry on business in conformity with the LLC Agreement, the remedy of dissolution, by analogy to 8 *Del. C.* § 273, remains discretionary.

Here, the key facts about the parties' ability to work together are not rationally disputable. Therefore, my decision on the motion largely turns on two legal issues: 1) if the doctrine of corporate deadlock is an appropriate analogy for the analysis of a § 18-802 claim on these facts; and 2) if so, and if action to break the stalemate is necessary to permit the LLC to function, whether, because of the contract-law foundations of the Delaware LLC Act, Haley should be relegated to the contractual exit mechanism provided in the LLC Agreement.

Section 18-802 of the Delaware LLC Act is a relatively recent addition to our law, and, as a result, there have been few decisions interpreting it. Nevertheless, § 18-802 has the obvious purpose of providing an avenue of relief when an LLC cannot continue to function in accordance with its chartering agreement...

The relationship between Haley and Talcott indicates active involvement by both parties in creating a restaurant for their mutual benefit and profit, and the Employment Contract shows that Haley was to be the "Operations Director" of the Redfin Grill, a position that, according to the Side Letter Agreement, would only be terminated if the restaurant was sold. Haley was also entitled to a 50% share of the Redfin Grill's profits. In short, Haley and Talcott were in it together for as long as they owned the restaurant, equally sharing the profits as provided in the Employment Contract.

Most importantly, Haley never agreed to be a passive investor in the LLC who would be subject to Talcott's unilateral dominion. Instead, the LLC agreement provided that: "no member/managers may, *without the agreement of a majority vote of the managers' interest,* act on behalf of the company." Under these terms, as a 50% member/manager, no major action of the LLC could be taken without Haley's approval. Thus, Haley is entitled to a continuing say in the operation of the LLC.

Finally, the evidence clearly supports a finding of deadlock between the parties about the business strategy and future of the LLC. The very fact that dissolution has not occurred, combined with Talcott's opposition in this lawsuit, leads inevitably to the conclusion that Talcott opposes such a disposition of the assets. Neither is Talcott's opposition surprising given his economic interest in the continued success of the Redfin Grill, success that one must assume relies, in part, on a continuing favorable lease arrangement with the LLC.

For all these reasons, if the LLC were a corporation, there would be no question that Haley's request to dissolve the entity would be granted. But this case regards an LLC, not a corporation, and more importantly, an LLC with a detailed exit provision. That distinguishing factor must and is considered next.

The Delaware LLC Act is grounded on principles of freedom of contract. For that reason, the presence of a reasonable exit mechanism bears on the propriety of ordering dissolution under 6 *Del. C.* § 18-802. When the agreement itself provides a fair opportunity for the dissenting member who disfavors the inertial status quo to exit and receive the fair market value of her interest, it is at least arguable that the limited liability company may still proceed to operate practicably under its contractual charter because the charter itself provides an equitable way to break the impasse.

Here, that reasoning might be thought apt because Haley has already "voted" as an LLC member to sell the LLC's only asset, the Property, presumably because he knew he could not secure sole control of both the LLC and the Redfin Grill. Given that reality, so long as Haley can actually extract himself fairly, it arguably makes sense for this court to stay its hand in an LLC case and allow the contract itself to solve the problem.

Notably, this court's authority to order dissolution remains discretionary and may be influenced by the particular circumstances. Talcott rightly argues that the situation here is somewhat analogous to that in *In re Delaware Bay Surgical Services*, C.A. No. 2121-S (Del.Ch. Jan. 28, 2002), where this court declined to dissolve a corporation under § 273 in part because a mechanism existed for the repurchase of the complaining member's 50% interest.

But, this matter differs from *Surgical Services* in two important respects. First, in *Surgical Services,* the respondent doctor had owned the company before admitting the petitioner to his practice as a 50% stakeholder. The court found that both parties clearly intended, upon entering the contract, that if the parties ended their contractual relationship, the respondent would be the one permitted to keep the company. By contrast, no such obvious priority of interest exists here. Haley and Talcott created the LLC together and while the detailed exit provision provided in the formative LLC Agreement allows either party to leave voluntarily, it provides no insight on who should retain the LLC if both parties would prefer to buy the other out, and neither party desires to leave. In and of itself, however, this lack of priority might not be found sufficient to require dissolution, because of a case-specific fact; namely, that Haley has proposed-as a member of the LLC-that the LLC's sole asset be sold. But I need not-and do not-determine how truly distinguishing that fact is, because forcing Haley to exercise the contractual exit mechanism would not permit the LLC to proceed in a practicable way that accords with the LLC Agreement, but would instead permit Talcott to penalize Haley without express contractual authorization.

Why? Because the parties agree that exit mechanism in the LLC Agreement would not relieve Haley of his obligation under the personal guaranty that he signed to secure the mortgage from County Bank. If Haley is forced to use the exit mechanism, Talcott and he both believe that Haley would still be left holding the bag on the guaranty. It is therefore not equitable to force Haley to use the exit mechanism in this circumstance. While the exit mechanism may be workable in a friendly departure when both parties cooperate to reach an adequate alternative agreement with the bank, the bank cannot be compelled to accept the removal of Haley as a personal guarantor. Thus, the exit mechanism fails as an adequate remedy for Haley because it does not equitably effect the separation of the parties. Rather, it would leave Haley with no upside potential, and no protection over the considerable downside risk that he would have to make good on any future default by the LLC (over whose operations he would have no control) to its mortgage lender. Thus here, unlike in *Surgical Services,* the parties do not, in fact, "have at their disposal a far less drastic means to resolve their personal disagreement."

For the reasons discussed above, I find that it is not reasonably practicable for the LLC to continue to carry on business in conformity with the LLC Agreement. The parties shall confer and, within four weeks, submit a plan for the dissolution of the LLC. The plan shall include a procedure to sell the Property owned by the LLC within a commercially reasonable time frame. Either party may, of course, bid on the Property. IT IS SO ORDERED.

IN RE KECK, MAHIN & CATE
274 B.R. 740 (Bkrtcy.N.D.Ill. 2002)

CAROL A. DOYLE, Bankruptcy Judge.

This matter is before the court on plaintiff Jacob Brandzel's ("plaintiff") adversary complaint seeking a determination of defendants' liability under the Illinois Uniform Partnership Act ("IUPA"). The plaintiff is the plan administrator for the debtor Keck, Mahin & Cate ("Keck") pursuant to the chapter 11 plan ("Plan") confirmed by the bankruptcy court on December 16, 1999. The plaintiff seeks recovery for malpractice claims filed by Bank of Orange County and

Pacific Inland Bancorp (collectively, "Pacific Inland") and Wozniak Industries, Inc. ("Wozniak"), a claim filed by Citizens Commercial Leasing Corporation ("Citizens") and administrative claims allowed in the bankruptcy case as of December 16, 1999. Defendants Barbara P. Billauer and Thomas E. Ho'okano (collectively, "defendants") are former capital partners of Keck. Pursuant to the Plan, the plaintiff is the assignee of all allowed claims, and has the right to seek recovery from partners who did not participate in a settlement of partners' outstanding liabilities. Ms. Billauer and Mr. Ho'okano dispute any liability for allowed claims against Keck.

Keck was an Illinois partnership whose partners engaged in the practice of law. On December 16, 1997, some of Keck's creditors filed an involuntary chapter 7 bankruptcy petition against the partnership. On December 31, 1997, the bankruptcy court granted Keck's motion to convert the case to chapter 11 of the Bankruptcy Code. The Plan was confirmed on December 16, 1999. Under the confirmation order ("Order"), Jacob Brandzel was appointed plan administrator.

Ms. Billauer and Mr. Ho'okano are former capital partners of Keck. Ms. Billauer was a partner from July 2, 1990 until August 31, 1993. Mr. Ho'okano was a partner from June 24, 1991 until March 26, 1993. Pursuant to the Plan, all Keck partners had the option to pay a specified settlement amount for partnership liabilities and become "participating partners," or to decline to pay the settlement amount and become "non-participating partners." Non-participating partners potentially faced maximum liability for Keck's obligations. Ms. Billauer and Mr. Ho'okano chose not to participate in the settlement and are being sued for their liability with regard to the Pacific Inland, Wozniak, Citizens and administrative claims, totaling $5,483,189.96.

The plaintiff seeks to hold the defendants liable for administrative claims allowed in the bankruptcy case as of December 16, 1999, in the amount of approximately $2.1 million.

The plaintiff contends that the defendants are jointly and severally liable under section 13 of the IUPA, 805 ILCS 205/13, and the partnership agreement ("Agreement") for the Pacific Inland, Wozniak and Citizens claims. He asserts that each of these claims arose before or during the time the defendants were partners. Ms. Billauer and Mr. Ho'okano dispute any liability for the Pacific Inland, Wozniak and Citizens claims.

Ms. Billauer and Mr. Ho'okano first argue that no obligations to Wozniak or Pacific Inland existed at the time they left Keck. They assert that they are liable under paragraph 8(a) of the Agreement only for "Firm Obligations" that arose before they left the partnership. They further contend that the Wozniak and Pacific Inland malpractice claims did not become Firm Obligations until those claimants had a judgment entered against them or the malpractice claims were settled, which the defendants assert occurred after they left the partnership.

This argument is not persuasive. Sections 13 and 15 of the Illinois Uniform Partnership Act, 805 ILCS 205/13 & 15, determine the scope of Ms. Billauer's and Mr. Ho'okano's liability to third parties (which includes the plaintiff in this case). That liability is not limited to "Firm Obligations" as that phrase is used in paragraph 8(a) of the Agreement. Section 13 of the Act provides that "[w]here, by any wrongful act or omission of any partner acting in the ordinary course of the business of the partnership, ... loss or injury is caused to any person, ... the partnership is liable therefore to the same extent as the partners so acting or omitting to act." 805 ILCS 205/13. Under the language of section 13, it is the "wrongful act or omission" of a partner that gives rise to the liability of all other partners. The only reasonable interpretation of this provision is that the liability of all partners arises at the time of "any wrongful act or omission" by any partner. *Cf. In re Keck, Mahin & Cate,* 241 B.R. 583, 595 (Bankr.N.D.Ill.1999) (Barliant, J.) ("[I]f a professional's negligent conduct causes an injury, that professional's liability arises from his or her conduct."); *Garcia v. Pinto,* 258 Ill.App.3d 22, 25, 195 Ill.Dec. 795, 629 N.E.2d 103, 105 (1993) ("Generally, a cause of action for legal malpractice arises at the time of the negligent act when the attorney breaches his duty to act skillfully and diligently in representing his client.").

A partner cannot escape liability simply by leaving the partnership after the malpractice is committed but before the client wins or settles a malpractice claim. Courts have consistently held that, within the context of partnership dissolution, withdrawing partners remain liable for matters pending at the time of dissolution. *See, e.g.,* (holding that "the dissolution of a partnership does not relieve a partnership member from liability on existing contracts"); *Redman v. Walters,* 88 Cal.App.3d 448, 152 Cal.Rptr. 42, 45 (1979) ("In general a dissolution operates only with respect to future transactions; as to everything past the partnership continues until all pre-existing matters are terminated."). These cases support the conclusion that liability under section 13 of the IUPA arises at the time of the offending conduct.

[I]t is the act or omission by the attorney that gives rise to the partners' liability under the IUPA, not the subsequent liquidation of a client's damages. The court therefore finds that both the Wozniak and Pacific Inland claims arose before Ms. Billauer and Mr. Ho'okano left Keck in 1993, and they are both liable to the plaintiff for the full amount of each of those claims.

Ms. Billauer and Mr. Ho'okano argue that they are not liable for the Pacific Inland and Wozniak claims because the partnership dissolved when they withdrew from the firm and a new partnership was formed. They contend that the new partnership assumed any debts from the old partnership, and that therefore no liabilities against them now exist. However, whether the partnership dissolved and a new partnership was formed, or the old partnership continued by virtue of paragraph 15(b) of the Agreement without the defendants, the result is the same. The general rule under Illinois law is that "dissolution of the partnership does not of itself discharge the existing liability of any partners." 805 ILCS 205/36(1). As noted earlier, that liability can stem from prior contractual obligations, including those that give rise to malpractice claims.

In addition, partners cannot release one another from liability to third parties. *See Olin Corp. v. Fisons PLC,* No. Civil A. 93–11166–MLW, 1995 WL 811961, at 11 (D. Mass. Apr.24, 1995). Illinois law requires consent by the third party itself to release the liability of any partner. 805 ILCS 205/36(2). This consent may be express or inferred based on the third party's course of conduct after it learned of the dissolution. *Id.* Without this consent, partners cannot shield themselves from the rights of creditors. There is no evidence that either Wozniak or Pacific Inland consented to releasing Ms. Billauer and Mr. Ho'okano of their liability. Therefore, whether the partnership dissolved or the old partnership continued without the defendants, they are liable for debts incurred to the third-party claimants before their departure dates.

Under Illinois law and the Agreement, Ms. Billauer and Mr. Ho'okano are liable for claims arising before or during the time they were partners. *See* 805 ILCS 205/13 (establishing the liability of co-partners for the acts or omissions of a partner); Agreement ¶ 8(a)(1) (providing for the assumption of pre-existing Firm Obligations by incoming partners); *Magrini,* 17 Ill.App.2d at 356, 150 N.E.2d at 392 (holding that an incoming partner can be held personally liable for pre-existing partnership debts where there is an express assumption of liability). Keck is a general partnership subject to Illinois law. Under Illinois law, partners are jointly and severally liable to creditors of the partnership. Illinois law does not limit this liability with respect to innocent co-partners. 205 ILCS 210/13 & 15; *In re Georgou,* 145 B.R. 36, 37 (Bankr.N.D.Ill.1992) (Barliant, J.). As noted above, partners cannot release their liability to third parties without their consent. There is no evidence of any such consent.

Both defendants argue that they should not be held liable for any partnership debts because the firm was solvent when they left in 1993. However, neither party cites any support for this argument. The solvency of a partnership at the time a claim arises is not a defense to an action under section 13 of the IUPA.

Ms. Billauer asserts that the Agreement is void as against public policy. She contends that an amendment to the Agreement passed on May 3, 1996 reflects an intent by the partners in 1996 to fraudulently shield themselves from joint and several liability. The amendment in question, paragraph 15(r), attempts to limit a third party's recovery for liabilities arising after May 1, 1996 to general partnership assets. *See* Amendments to Agreement ¶ 15(r) (May 3, 1996) ("Notwithstanding anything to the contrary herein set forth, any ... payment or other obligation provided for under this [Partnership] Agreement in connection with events that occur or liabilities that arise on or after May 1, 1996 shall be limited to the general partnership assets of the Firm and none of the Partners shall have any personal liability therefore.").

This argument fails for two reasons. First, the amendment would only limit liabilities arising after May 1, 1996. Therefore, it would have no effect on the liability of partners with regard to the Wozniak and Pacific Inland claims, both of which arose prior to the defendants' departures in 1993. Second, even if the partners intended to limit their personal liability with regard to those claims, the amendment is unenforceable under the IUPA. *See* 805 ILCS 205/13 & 15.

For the foregoing reasons, the court finds that Mr. Ho'okano and Ms. Billauer are jointly and severally liable to the plaintiff in the amount of $775,000.00 for the Wozniak claim, $825,000.00 for the Pacific Inland claim and $2,177,787.73 for the administrative claims.

H. OPERATING AGREEMENT DESIGN

1. SCOPE AND LAWYER'S ROLE

The primary planning challenge during the organization of a partnership or LLC is to prepare a comprehensive operating agreement that incorporates all of the essential deal points between the co-owners of the business. Often the parties are tempted to short-circuit the front-end planning effort. They perpetuate the common (but false) perception that there is a "normal" or "accepted" way of documenting issues between co-owners. The result is that, in far too many cases, the operating agreement effort is limited to filling in blanks on a stock form, and the dialogue is limited to descriptive pronouncements from the lawyers. The operating agreement looks complete and official, but does little or nothing to reflect thoughtful, negotiated deal points that the owners have resolved with the assistance of skilled planning advisors.

In nearly all situations, the planning lawyer must take the lead in defining the scope of the front-end planning effort. This is done by identifying key planning issues, explaining the significance of the issues, and then helping the client carefully evaluate his or her objectives or priority concerns with respect to each issue. Usually customization of the operating agreement increases as the planning effort improves. More customization leads to more complexity and, most importantly, to a better mutual understanding of the key deal points between the owners of the business.

The identity of the client affects how the potential deal points are discussed and analyzed in any given partnership or LLC situation. If the client will own the controlling vote in the entity, the preferred choice may be to refrain from initiating any dialogue on many deal points with the other owners. The client knows that he or she has the power to dictate the outcome of any dispute by virtue of the voting control. Typically, the burden is on the minority owners to raise any operational issues that may require special treatment in the operating agreement. So the lawyer who represents the minority owners usually has the toughest job. Key issues must be identified, discussed, and prioritized. A plan must be developed for creating minority rights for those issues that are of greatest concern. Then the plan must be sold and eventually incorporated into the operating agreement.

The lawyer who is engaged to organize and represent the partnership or LLC, not a particular owner of group of owners, must be sensitive to the conflicts that many of the key planning issues might create between the owners. In this situation, usually the best approach is for the entity's lawyer to initiate a dialogue with all the owners in a meeting or series of meetings that addresses the most important issues, with input from lawyers representing specific owners. The process requires a modest commitment of time and expense, but it will go a long way in identifying and resolving on the front-end any fundamental differences between the parties.

Following is a brief description of certain key provisions of an operating agreement and related options for customizing these provisions. Specific references are to the LLC operating agreement in section B. of Chapter 17.

CASE PROBLEM 2-8

Refer to Case Problem 2-4 in which Son and Dad form a manager-managed LLC. Son lines up a deep-pocket investor ("Investor") who is willing to invest $1 million in the LLC if, and only if, the LLC operating agreement contains the following provisions:

1. Investor is the manager of the LLC and has the exclusive right to determine how Strategy is exploited, when it is sold, and the terms of any sale.

2. Investor is relieved of all liabilities to the LLC for any actions or omissions taken in good faith, even those that are determined to be grossly negligent or intentionally reckless.

3. All fiduciary duties of the Investor are eliminated.

4. The Investor is allocated 90 percent of the losses that are expected during the first three years of operation. This is regarded as a tax benefit for Investor.

5. Investor accrues an annual fee of $100,000 for management services, to be paid when the LLC has sufficient cash flow to pay this accrued compensation.

6. Investor is allocated 50 percent of all profits realized in any year or on the sale of Strategy.

7. Available cash flows from operations or the sale of Strategy are used: first, to pay any accrued management fees due Investor; second, to repay Investor's $1 million investment; and third, to pay Investor 50 percent of the excess and the other members the remaining 50 percent.

What problems, if any, will the parties encounter in designing the LLC operating agreement to meet these deal-braking demands of Investor?

2. AUTHORITY AND MANAGEMENT PROVISIONS

Purpose of the Company (Section 5). In a partnership or LLC, the preferred choice often is to use this provision to specifically define and limit the scope of the business activities of the entity. Partners and LLC members often want the comfort of knowing that their investment will not be diverted into activities that are outside the scope of what was originally discussed. Liability exposure may also be an issue, particularly where the managers of the venture have multiple business interests. Limiting the scope of the business activities may help eliminate the business entity's liability exposure for unrelated actions of its managers. A written activity limitation also may dash any expectations other owners may have relative to their other business activities by drawing an express, unequivocal line in the sand. Some partners and LLC member may object to a written limitation on the scope of the enterprise, arguing that it restricts flexibility, creates potential confusion for third parties, and fosters notions of "separateness" and "temporariness" between the owners.

Limits on Manager Authority. (Sections 11.1 and 11.6). Often the manager of the partnership or LLC is given broad authority to administer the business affairs of the enterprise. The planning challenge is to define those situations where the manager must seek approval of the partners or LLC members before taking action and what level of approval is required. In some circumstances, majority approval may be adequate. In other situations, a unanimous or super-majority vote may be justified. It all turns on the nature and scope of the business and the expectations and goals of the partners or LLC members. These are the sections of the agreement that can be used to define and protect minority rights and often justify significant dialogue during the planning process. Provisions that often require special attention in these sections include: required cash distributions; the admission of new partners or LLC members; outside or competitive activities of partners or LLC members; related party transactions; material changes to the business plan; debt limitations; confidentially covenants of managers, partners or LLC members; tax elections; selection of professionals; and dispute resolutions procedures.

Limited Liability of Manager (Section 11.3). The key issue is whether the manager should be relieved of personal liability to the partnership or LLC for actions taken or omitted by the manager with a good faith belief that such actions or omissions were in the best interests of the entity. Resolution of the issue in the partnership or LLC operating agreement often turns on the level of culpability that partners or LLC members are willing to forgive. Ordinary negligence usually isn't enough to override a good faith exculpation provision, while willful misconduct and criminal acts often render provision moot and trigger liability. But what about grossly negligence or intentionally reckless conduct? These are tougher issues in the planning process. Managers often do not want any liability exposure absent a showing of bad faith, willful misconduct or criminal activity. They don't want to get tangled up in line drawing between ordinary and gross negligence. In constrast, many owners want protection against a manager's gross negligence or intentionally reckless activities.

Resignation, Removal and Replacement of Manager (Section 15). This provision raises a number of potential issues in the design of the operating agreement. If a manager resigns in violation of specified conditions in the operating agreement, does the manager have any liability exposure to the entity? Will the manager be subject to any non-competition restrictions? What ongoing confidentiality covenants, if any, will apply to the manager? What level of partner or LLC member vote (majority, super-majority, unanimous) is required to remove and replace a manager? Is there any requirement to show "cause"? Is the manager entitled to any severance benefit if removed for no cause? Does the resignation or removal of manager entitle the partnership or LLC to purchase the partnership or LLC interest of the member or give the manager a right to compel such a purchase?

Indemnification (Section 11.4). Will partners and managers who act on behalf of the partnership or LLC be protected against any personal loss, damage or liability they incur as a result of their activities on behalf of the entity? Usually an indemnification and hold harmless provision is included in the operating agreement to protect against such liabilities and any associated legal fees, but limitations often need to be worked out between the partners or LLC members. The agreement may provide that the indemnification rights are limited to assets of the entity and are not obligations of the partners or LLC members. The owners may not want any personal exposure, and the primary assets of the business may have been pledged to secure financing. The net result is that the indemnification provision, as a practical matter, may mean little or nothing if the business fails. The indemnification provision may be limited to acts or omissions undertaken in good faith and with a belief that they were in the best interests of the entity, subject to exceptions for specified levels of culpability (see prior paragraph). The operating agreement also may condition any indemnification right on a tender of the defense or resolution of the claim to the partnership or LLC so that the entity can control expenses and dispose of the matter on its own terms. These indemnification limitations often create concerns for managers. A solution to ease these concerns may be an errors and omissions insurance policy for the managers that facilitates the agreed limitations while providing an additional level of protection for the managers of the enterprise.

Compensation of Managers (Section 11 Insertion). Often there is a need to specify how those partners or members who manage the enterprise are to be compensated for their services on behalf the partnership or LLC. Absent such an agreement, the statutory default rule usually will deny any compensation for services that are not related to dissolving and winding up the entity.

Time Devoted to Enterprise (Section 11.2). For partners or LLC members who manage the enterprise, key issues often include their service commitments and their right to be involved in other activities. Are they expected to devote all of their time and energies to the enterprise? Failure to adequately clarify this issue can lead to an early showdown when the investment partners or LLC members discover that the manager spends only a fraction of his or her time looking after the affairs of the enterprise and is heavily involved in other ventures. The stock language in many forms gives the manager significant flexibility to define the service level and pursue other ventures. This language won't do the job in many situations.

3. OWNER RIGHTS PROVISIONS

Owner Transfer Rights (Section 14). State statutes generally permit a partner or LLC member to transfer the economic (but not voting or management rights) rights of partnership or LLC interest to a third party transferee. Often, it is necessary and smart to prohibit any such voluntary or involuntary transfer unless specified conditions exist. These conditions usually include the death of a partner or LLC member or the approval by the managers or a designated percentage of the partners or LLC members. Absent such approval, partners are unable to transfer interests in the partnership or LLC. In many situations, the operating agreement also needs to specify the procedures and conditions that must be satisfied in order for a third party transferee to be admitted as an owner with all the rights and privileges of a partner or LLC member.

Buy-Sell Rights (Section 14 Insert). In many business enterprises, the operating agreement between the partners or LLC members needs to spell out buy-sell rights that are triggered when a partner or LLC member dies, becomes disabled, just desires to cash out and move on, experiences a messy divorce or bankruptcy, or needs to be expelled.   These buy-sell provisions and the associated planning may be used to accomplish various objectives, including to ensure that (1) ownership interests in the enterprise are never transferred or made available to third parties who are unacceptable to the owners, (2) there is a mechanism to fairly value and fund the equity interest of a departing owner, (3) control and ownership issues will be smoothly transitioned at appropriate times so as not to unduly interfere with and disrupt the operations of the business, (4) owners have a fair "market" for their shares at appropriate points of exit, (5) owners have the power to involuntarily terminate (expel) an owner who is no longer wanted, (6) the amount paid for the equity interest of a deceased owner determines the value of the deceased owner's equity interest for estate tax purposes, and (7) cash and funding challenges of owner departures are appropriately anticipated and covered.   An extended discussion of this planning challenge is included in section C. of Chapter 13.   The substance of that discussion, including certain of the common mistakes that are often made in the buy-sell planning process, is directly applicable to partnerships and LLCs.

Major Transaction Approval Rights (Section 11.6).   The operating agreement usually requires partner or LLC member approval of transactions that involve a merger of the partnership or LLC, a combination with another entity, or a sale of all or substantially all of the entity's assets. Majority approval works for many partnerships and LLCs. In some situations, the parties desire to require a super-majority vote, such as two-thirds. Often it helps to clarify if the manager's approval also is a condition to the transaction. And sometimes the often-used "substantially all" standard for determining whether an asset sale triggers owner approval rights is perceived as being too undefined or capable of manipulation. In such situations, the operating agreement lowers the threshold by specifying objective criteria (a designated percentage of assets or revenues, or both) for determining whether owner approval rights are required for a sale of assets.

Inspection Rights. (Section 13.4)   Some operating agreements provide partners and LLC members with broad document inspection rights, conditioned only on reasonable notice, inspection at the location where the documents are kept, and reimbursement of any reproduction costs. Often those who manage a limited partnership or a manager-managed LLC desire to limit the inspection rights of limited partners or LLC members who have no management rights. The rationale is that broad inspection rights for such investors will not benefit the entity in any way and may create opportunities for abuse that frustrate management efforts. When limited investor inspection rights are desired, the operating agreement often requires that the requesting partner or LLC member provide a written request that specifies the entity-related purpose for making the request, the particularized list of the documents requested, and how such documents relate to the stated purpose.   The manager has the final say on whether the conditions of the request have been satisfied.

Fiduciary Exculpatory Provisions. (Section 11.5 and Section 12 Insertion).   Statutory provisions impose fiduciary duties of care, loyalty, good faith, and fair dealing on those partners or LLC members who have the right to participate in the management of the enterprise. As explained in section E. of this Chapter, the operating agreement usually may include provisions that substantially reduce any liability for fiduciary breaches that do not involve bad faith. The only limitation in many states is that the exculpatory provision may not be "manifestly unreasonable." This presents a planning opportunity for those enterprises that want to deemphasize restrictions that come with the duties of care and loyalty.

Amendment Rights (Section 18). The power to amend the operating agreement is always an important consideration. In many situations, nothing short of unanimous consent will work. The agreement is viewed as a contract that protects minority rights. In those circumstances where ownership and management interests are separated (limited partnerships and manager-managed LLCs), the operating agreement specifies what may be amended by the approval of partners or members who own a majority or designated super-majority of the entity's interests. Also, in such situations, often the manager is authorized to amend the agreement without partner or member approval to cure ambiguities or inconsistencies in the agreement.

Owner Confidentiality Covenants. (Section 12 Insertion). Sometimes it is necessary to extend confidentially covenants to partners and LLC members, particularly in those enterprises where the owners may have access to trade secrets or proprietary information critical to the success of the business. Some investors may resist any such agreements or any mechanism that limits other investment options or exposes them to any future claims relating to the use of proprietary information.

Dissolutions Rights (Section 16). The operating agreement should specify the conditions for dissolving the partnership or LLC, which often track the applicable statutory provisions. A primary consideration is the approval requirement of the partners or LLC members to force a dissolution and winding up. Many require unanimous approval, while others impose a super-majority requirement. In limited partnerships and manager-managed LLCs, a dissolution decision generally always requires the consent of those who manage the enterprise.

Life After Rights (Section 12 Insertion). In professional organizations and other partnerships and LLCs where revenues are generated from the personal services of the owners, often it is advisable to spell out the "going forward" rights that each owner will have in the event there is a falling out and the group fractures. Absent such an agreement, the owners may find themselves tangled up with dissolution and wind-up issues that may make it difficult to immediately shift gears and preserve the continuity of their business activities. Most professionals and service providers cannot afford a major disruption that stops their careers. Key issues include the right to engage in the same business as the fractured entity, to pursue and service clients of the entity, to hire employees of the entity, to deal with vendors and financial institutions used by the entity, to make copies of client documents, files and other important documents, to use the same personal business email addresses and phone numbers, and to disclose the prior affiliation with the entity.

4. CAPITAL AND ALLOCATION PROVISIONS

Initial Capital Contributions (Sections 7.1 and 7.6). The operating agreement should describe the initial contribution obligations of the partners or LLC members. Most importantly, the value that is going to be assigned to non-cash contributions for capital account purposes should be specified in the agreement or an Exhibit. Such contributions may include tangible property (such as land or equipment), intellectual property rights, the business plan for the enterprise, past services rendered on behalf of the enterprise, future services to be rendered, and more. The planning challenge is to clarify the expectations of the parties with respect to any non-cash assets and properly value those assets that are going to be positive additions to the capital account of the contributing partner or LLC member. The agreement should authorize the partnership or LLC to take any action to enforce the contribution obligations of partners or LLC members, to recover any associated costs and attorney fees, and to settle any such disputes with a designated approval (usually majority) of the other partners or LLC members.

Future Contribution Obligations (Section 7.4). The issue of additional capital contribution obligations of the partners or LLC members should be documented in the operating agreement. Some owners, even those with deep pockets, may want to eliminate any expectations that they will provide additional capital to keep the venture afloat or fund growth. Others may be concerned with dilution; they do not want their equity interests reduced as those with greater means continually pony up more money and claim a bigger share of the enterprise. When this issue is a major concern (as it often is in start-up ventures), the owners need to talk through their concerns and, with the aid of counsel, reach an agreement that, to the fullest extent possible, addresses the objectives of the owners. One approach is to specify that each partner or LLC member must contribute his or her *pro rata* share of the capital needed to accomplish the purpose of the entity. Some owners may be unwilling to agree to an unlimited equity contribution requirement. In this situation, the agreement may have to place a cap on future required capital contributions. If there is no mandatory requirement for additional capital contributions, the operating agreement should spell out how future capital needs will be satisfied. Often this is done by specifying that owners may make additional contributions, as needed, and receive additional equity interests, while giving all partners or LLC members the right to participate in any such contributions on a *pro rata* basis.

Capital Account Maintenance (Section 7.5). The operating agreement must provide that a capital account will be maintained for each partner or member. This account ultimately determines what a partner or LLC member yields when the entity's business is sold or distributed and its affairs are wound up. The agreement should specify that each owner's account will be increased for capital contributions and allocations of income and will be decreased for distributions and loss allocations. It should also clarify the capital account impacts of contributions and distributions of non-cash assets and the rights of the partnership or LLC to restate and revalue capital account balances when a new owner is admitted and other designated conditions are satisfied. As section 7.5

illustrates, often this is accomplished by incorporating by reference the provisions of specific Treasury regulations to the Internal Revenue Code.

Allocations of Net Income and Net Loss (Section 8). The operating agreement should specify how the annual net income or net loss of the enterprise is going to be allocated to the partners or LLC members and reflected in their respective capital accounts. A benefit of partnerships and LLCs that are taxed as partnerships is that they have tremendous flexibility in structuring such allocations, far beyond that of a corporation. For example, one partner or LLC member may be allocated 60 percent of all income and 30 percent of all losses. A partnership allocation will be respected for tax purposes only if it has "substantial economic effect,"[157] three words that make section 704(b) of the Internal Revenue Code and its regulations one of the most complex subjects in the world of tax. Generally speaking (and I do mean generally), an allocation that does not produce a deficit capital account for a partner or LLC member will be deemed to have "economic effect" if capital accounts are maintained for all partners and, upon liquidation of the partnership, liquidating distributions are made in accordance with positive capital account balances.[158] In order for an allocation that produces a deficit capital account balance to have "economic effect," the partner or LLC member also must be unconditionally obligated to restore the deficit (i.e., pay cash to cover the shortfall) upon liquidation of the partnership,[159] or the partnership must have sufficient nonrecourse debt to assure that the partner's share of any minimum gain recognized on the discharge of the debt will eliminate the deficit.[160] An "economic effect," if present, will not be deemed "substantial" if it produces an after-tax benefit for one or more partners with no diminished after-tax consequences to other partners.[161] The most common examples of economic effects that are not deemed "substantial" are shifting allocations (allocations of different types of income and deductions among partners within a given year to reduce individual taxes without changing the partners' relative economic interests in the partnership) and transitory allocations (allocations in one year that are offset by allocations in later years).[162]

Required Cash Distributions (Section 10). The operating agreement should clarify how and when cash distributions are going to be made to the partners or LLC members. Some owners want to know that the plan includes regular distributions to the owners as the business ramps up and distributions that will cover the tax burden of partners or LLC members as the entity's income is allocated and taxed to them. Others may expect that all after-tax profits will be invested to finance growth or that cash distributions will be left to the discretion of the managers. This issue usually is tied to other key factors, including the growth rate of the business and the use of debt. Often the answer is to set guidelines regarding growth and debt that, once hit, will begin to trigger cash distributions to the owners. Typically, a provision is structured to ensure that

---

157. I.R.C. § 704(b).
158. Reg. §§ 1.704-1(b)(2)(ii) (b)(1), 1.704-(b)(2)(ii) (B)(2).
159. Reg. § 1.704-1(b)(2)(ii) (b)(3).
160. Reg. §§ 1.704-(2)(c), 1.704-(2)(f)(1), 1.704-(g)(1), 1.704-2(b)(1) & (e).
161. Reg. § 1.704-1(b)(2)(iii).
162. Reg. § 1.704-1(b)(2)(iii) (b) & (c).

cash is only distributed when all other cash needs of the business have been met, including ensuring appropriate reserves for working capital and targeted growth needs of the enterprise.

Cash Allocation Provisions. A related and equally important planning consideration is how cash distributions are allocated among the partners or LLC members. The most common and basic structure is to provide that any cash distributed will be allocated among the owners according to their respective percentage interests in the entity and then to insure, through forced allocations, that the respective capital account balances of the partners or LLC members at time of liquidation reflect these percentage interests. But there is flexibility in structuring the distribution provisions in the operating agreement. Consider the situation where there is a 50-50 ownership structure between two owners, one who puts up all the capital and one who provides services to the venture. The operating agreement might provide that cash distributions first will be allocated to the owner who provided the capital until that owner receives the equity contributed together with a specified preferred return equivalent to an interest rate. In addition, if the owner who put up the money also provided the personal guarantee that made outside institutional financing possible, the operating agreement may provide that owner an additional priority allocation of cash (e.g., two percent of the amount of the loan guaranteed) in consideration of providing the guarantee. Once these preferred distributions are made, all future cash distributions will be made to the owners according to their respective percentage interests. The important point is that, in partnerships and LLCs, there is flexibility in structuring cash rights among the owners, and preferences may be created in favor of certain owners.

Anti-Deficit Account Provisions (Section 8.3 through 8.8). Often the partners and LLC members want the operating agreement structured so that there is no risk that the capital account of a partner or member will have a negative balance when the affairs of the partnership or LLC are wound up. Such a negative balance would trigger an unwelcome contribution obligation to eliminate the negative balance. To protect against such a negative balance, the operating agreement often includes a number of relatively complicated provisions that limit net loss allocations, designate how net gains from non-recourse debt obligations ("Minimum Gain Chargebacks") are to be handled, force gross income allocations ("Qualified Income Offsets") in certain circumstances, authorize curative allocations and modifications, and clarify the overriding intention that no partner have a deficit capital account balance at liquidation. These provisions, illustrated by sections 8.3 through 8.8 of the form agreement, are a multifaceted attack on the risk of a negative capital account.

I. FAMILY PARTNERSHIPS AND LLCs

1. FLEXIBLE PLANNING TOOLS

Many business owners want financial plans that protect assets, preserve control, and save taxes. Perhaps no planning tools have been more effective in meeting these basic family objectives than the family partnership and the family limited liability company (LLC). These are flexible tools that can be crafted to accomplish specific, targeted objectives, including shifting income to other family members, maximizing wealth scattering gifting opportunities, protecting assets from creditors, and creating tax-saving valuation discounts in the parents' estate by repackaging investment assets into discounted limited partnership interests.

The powerful tax planning benefits of family partnerships and LLCs have made them a popular target of the IRS. The heat has been turned up over the last 15 years as the Service has pulled out all the stops to shut down techniques that are designed to produce extreme tax savings. The thrust of the fighting has made everything harder. This is not to suggest that the family partnership or LLC is doomed as a planning tool or is only suited for those who have a cast iron stomach and the will to invite an encounter with the government. What it does confirm is the importance of careful attention to detail, reasonable expectations, and a willingness to not push the evolving limits.

Most investment assets offer three potential benefits: income, value growth, and control. Many mistakenly assume that these three components are tied together and must reside in the same individual. A partnership or LLC makes it possible to separate these benefits. Valuable economic benefits can be transferred to another and separated from the control element.

Following are brief descriptions of four strategies for using a limited partnership or LLC in a family planning context. Although the examples focus on a family partnership, the planning opportunities and issues are the same for any family LLC that is taxed as a partnership.

2. FOUR MINI–CASE STUDIES

a. The Shift. Roger and Denise Moore have two children, ages 24 and 26. They also have strong incomes. Roger is a successful architect, and Denise owns and manages a profitable desktop publishing firm. Their combined taxable incomes exceed $450,000 a year. Their assets include a securities portfolio and real estate investments that produce a steady stream of interest, rental, and dividend income.

Roger and Denise's primary concern is income taxes. They pay big income taxes now and know that they will likely pay more as budgetary pressures promise higher rates for high-income taxpayers. Although they know that they are building an estate that will likely trigger an estate tax exposure on the death of the survivor, the estate tax threat is not their major concern at this time. The real issue now is income taxes.

In contrast to the parents' situation, each of their children is in a 15 percent tax bracket and will likely remain in that bracket for a long time. Simple arithmetic confirms that substantial income taxes could be saved if income could be shifted from the parents to the children. Plus, Roger and Denise would like to have a mechanism for transferring a steady income stream to each of their children. Since both children are over the age of 19, the Kiddie tax is not an issue.[163] The challenge is to figure out how to accomplish "The Shift."

After considering the alternatives, the Moores elect to use a family limited partnership to shift the income. A partnership is formed and funded with an income-producing securities portfolio and real estate investments. All of the general partner and limited partnership units initially are issued to Roger and Denise. Roger and Denise then embark on a program of gifting limited partnership units to each of their children. They initially make a gift of limited partnership units valued at $50,000 to each child. They use a portion of their combined unified credits to eliminate the gift tax impact of these initial transfers. They plan to gift to each child additional limited partnership units valued at $26,000 each year for the next five years. They will use their annual gift tax exclusions to shelter these gifts from gift taxes. They estimate that within five years, each child will have been given limited partnership units valued at approximately $180,000 for gift tax purposes. Appropriate minority interest and lack of marketability discounts will be used to maximize the value of the transfers to the children.

The income attributable to the gifted limited partnership units will be shifted and taxed to the children. This income will be used to help fund many of the children's financial needs down the road. The bottom line is that Roger and Denise have determined that a permanent shift of an income stream for the benefits of the children is a good idea. The family partnership accomplishes the shift.

b. The Scatter. Jim Bain is a 70-year-old, self-made real estate developer. He and his wife Lucy, age 66, have five children and 16 grandchildren. Jim's health is marginal; he has had some heart problems. Lucy's health is average. Jim and Lucy have a combined net worth of approximately $24 million. Most of their assets are illiquid real estate projects that Jim has developed over many years. Jim manages all of the assets. The couple's second son, Brandon, is the only child with any knowledge of the business. Brandon has worked with Jim for five years.

Jim and Lucy are concerned about their estate tax exposure. Although they have heard about estate taxes for many years, they've never really wanted to deal with the issue. Jim likes his real estate, and has never been able to get excited about the idea of transferring assets to his children and grandchildren. He has no intention of retiring and wants to keep developing. His desire to stay in the saddle is strengthened by the fact that Brandon is now involved in the business and wants to make real estate a career.

Jim and Lucy have determined that it's time to embark on a gifting program to save estate taxes. Income taxes have never been a serious issue; they have plenty of write-offs from their real estate projects. Their primary concern is estate taxes. They want to maximize the impact of the annual gift tax exclusion. They

---

163. In 2007, the Kiddie tax age limit was raised to include children under age 19 and students under age 24. The tax requires that the unearned income of any such child be taxed at his or her parents' highest marginal rate. I.R.C. § 11(g).

have figured that they have 24 potential donees each year. These include their five children, the spouses of their five children, and their 14 grandchildren. Jim and Lucy want to embark on a program of scattering their wealth to these 24 donees each year. Jim designs a wealth-scattering program that can be implemented over a 10-year period. He estimates, based on reasonable appreciation scenarios, that the plan could reduce their future estate value by at least $13 million.

As Jim considered such a program, he had some initial reservations. First, he knew that he didn't have cash to make the gifts each year, and he felt that it would be extremely cumbersome to transfer interests in specific real estate investments to 24 different individuals each year. Transfers of undivided interests through deeds would be cumbersome, complicated, costly, and confusing. Second, he was concerned that he would lose control as these transfers were made. Finally, he was concerned that it would be complicated to transfer an interest in real estate to a minor grandchild who had no legal capacity to deal with property.

A limited partnership or LLC would eliminate these concerns and made it possible for Jim and Lucy to embark on their family-scattering gifting program. Jim and Brandon would each contribute real estate interests to a newly formed S corporation, which in turn would contribute the interests to a new limited partnership in exchange for general partnership interests. Jim and Lucy would contribute a substantial block of low-leveraged real estate investments to the limited partnership in exchange for limited partnership interests. Jim and Lucy would then embark on a program of transferring limited partnership units to each of the 24 donees (or trusts established for their benefit) each year. They would structure the program so that, in even years, the gifts are made at the end of the year and, in odd years, the gifts are made at the beginning of the year. This technique would eliminate the need for annual valuations; valuations every other year would do the job.

The S corporation general partner provided a means of transitioning control to Brandon or others without impacting the family partnership. The family limited partnership would make it possible for Jim and Lucy to save substantial estate taxes by scattering their wealth to a broad range of descendants over an extended period of time.

c.　The Freeze. Sam and Joyce are both 65 years of age and looking forward to a long retirement. They have three children, and six grandchildren. Their estate is valued at approximately $25 million. A significant asset in their estate is an interest they hold in a bottling distribution LLC. They have owned this interest for about five years. This investment presently pays them an income of about $12,000 a month. They are looking forward to receiving this income for the rest of their lives.

They are concerned about estate taxes. They believe that their investment in the bottling distribution company will grow rapidly in value. It is postured to take off. Indeed, they anticipate that the value of the investment could increase eight to ten times over the next five to seven years. They are concerned that, as the value of the investment grows, their estate tax exposure will balloon. They want to take steps to reduce their estate tax exposure, without jeopardizing their current income stream.

The answer for Sam and Joyce may be a freeze family limited partnership. They would form a limited partnership with an S corporation general partner and then transfer their interest in the bottling distribution company LLC to that partnership. The LLC interest presently has a value of approximately $1.5 million.

The partnership would issue two kinds of limited partnership units. The first would be limited partnership units ("Income Units") that allow the holders of the units to receive a fixed, guaranteed income from the partnership every year. This would be an ongoing, cumulative obligation of the partnership. The Income Units would be owned by Sam and Joyce, and would be structured to pay them a guaranteed income of 12,000 a month.

The remaining units would be growth limited partnership units ("Growth Units"). Unlike the Income Units, these units would not offer any guaranteed income rights. However, all appreciation in the value of the investment held by the partnership would be allocated to these units. Sam and Joyce would gift the Growth Units to their children.

This structure is called a "Freeze Limited Partnership" because it is designed to freeze the value of the investment in Sam and Joyce's estate, while at the same time preserving the income stream for them. All of the future growth in value is allocated to the children, who own the Growth Units.

Great care should be exercised by anyone who is considering a family partnership freeze transaction. The limitations of section 2701 of the Internal Revenue Code are an insurmountable barrier in most situations, but not all. In order for the interest retained by the parents to have any value for gift tax purposes (and thus reduce the value of the interests transferred to the children), the parents must be entitled to receive a fixed, cumulative income interest that is the equivalent of a cumulative preferred stock interest.[164] In many cases, the required yield to be paid to the parents will exceed the anticipated increase of the value of the asset. In such a situation, the freeze transaction will be of no value. For this reason, the freeze strategy is best used in those situations, such as that faced by Sam and Joyce, where there is a real expectation of huge future appreciation that will balloon an existing significant estate tax exposure. It is important to realize that, if the income interest of the parents is not properly structured, any transfer of an interest to the children may trigger an enormous gift tax. Great care needs to be taken in structuring the parents' income interest and valuing the interest transferred to the children.

d. The Disappearing Act. Rubin, age 75, is a widower with a $20 million estate that consists primarily of a large stock and bond portfolio, various real estate investments, investments in a handful of passive limited partnership ventures, and an expensive home. He has one son, Bruce, and three

---

164. I.R.C. § 2701(c)(3).

grandchildren. His health is marginal, but he knows of no life threatening condition. He is distressed over his estate tax exposure.

Rubin decides to "get aggressive." He forms a limited partnership. A subchapter S corporation owned by his son, Bruce, is the sole general partner. Bruce separately funds the general partner, which owns one percent of the partnership. Rubin owns the remaining 99 percent of the partnership through limited partnership interests that are issued to him in exchange for all his assets except his home and $1.5 million of cash. Rubin estimates that the retained cash should cover his spending needs for the rest of his life. Bruce has complete control of the assets, and Rubin is relieved of all management burdens.

From a tax perspective, what Rubin hopes to accomplish with this technique is a substantial reduction in estate taxes at his death. As an owner of a limited partnership interest that provides no control and is subject to substantial marketability limitations, Rubin's estate would claim substantial lack of control and lack of marketability discounts in valuing the limited partnership interests. These discounts could total as much as 30 to 40 percent of the value of the underlying partnership assets attributable to the limited partnership units.

This strategy requires careful planning and a willingness to take some tax risks. Claiming these types of discounts to save big estate taxes when there has been a "circuitous recycling of value" can trigger a fight with the IRS. The Service has successfully attacked the use of this strategy in a number of "bad fact" cases where the taxpayer was too aggressive in pushing the limits of the strategy.[165] Use of this technique, and those described above, require the assistance of a competent planning attorney.

---

165. See, for example, *Estate of Rosen v. Commissioner*, T.C. Memo 2006-115, *Rector Estate v. Commissioner*, T.C. Memo 2007-367, *Estate of Erickson v. Commissioner*, T.C. Memo 2007-107, *Estate of Bigelow v. Commissioner*, 503 F.3d 955 (9th Cir. 2007); *Strangi v. Commissioner*, 417 F.3d 468 (5th Cir. 2005); *Estate of Hillgren v. Commissioner*, T.C. Memo 2004-46; *Kimbell v. United States*, 371 F.3d 257 (5th Cir. 2004); *Estate of Thompson v. Commissioner*, 382 F.3d 367 (3d Cir. 2004); *Estate of Bongard v. Commissioner*, 124 T.C. No. 8 (2005); *Estate of Jorgenson*, T.C. Memo 2009-66; *Estate of Malkin*, T.C. Memo 2009-212.

CHAPTER 3

CORPORATION BASICS

A. POPULARITY AND CORE BENEFITS

The purpose of this chapter is to provide basic information about corporations and foundational concepts that will facilitate the study of more difficult corporate concepts that are the subjects of later chapters.

The bulk of America's business is conducted through corporations. Some estimate as much as 84 percent. There are numerous public corporations whose stock is traded daily by thousands of shareholders. But most corporations are characterized as closely held because their stock is owned by only a few individuals, often members of the same family. Stock transfers in closely held corporations are a rare event, usually triggered only by a sale of the business or an event that requires a shareholder to cash out, such as death, disability, bankruptcy, or a falling out with other shareholders.

A corporation is a creature of state law. Every corporation is organized under and governed by the laws of a given state. State corporate matters are handled by a separate state division or department that is under the auspices of the attorney general's office of the state.

For legal purposes, a corporation is viewed as a separate being. It can own property; it can sue and be sued; it can enter into contracts; it can borrow money; it can commit a crime or a tort; it must pay taxes. In short, when it comes to property and business, a corporation generally has all the rights and liabilities of a human being.

A corporation can even have offspring. It can create and own subsidiary corporations, which can also spawn their own corporate offspring. Often this type of multi-tiered holding company structure is used to manage risk exposures by segregating liabilities, reduce expansion-related regulatory and tax hassles, enhance financing opportunities, develop and incent management teams, and facilitate a host of other key business objectives.

A corporation is immortal. Its existence can be perpetual. It can span multiple generations and become an institution that promotes permanence and stability.

A corporation can assemble capital by issuing stock to many individuals and institutions, while centralizing the control of the entire business in the hands of only a few. In a public corporation, stock can be bought or sold with a phone call to a broker. Ownership interests in a closely held enterprise can be transferred by handing over a simple document – a stock certificate – without impacting the assets, liabilities or operations of the business.

Limited liability is often trumpeted as a supreme benefit of a corporation. If the corporation defaults on a contact or loan, the aggrieved creditor generally has no claim against the shareholders, directors and officers unless they personally guaranteed the obligation. If an employee, while on the job, injures someone in an auto accident, the corporation can be held liable for the employee's actions, but the corporation's shareholders, directors and officers are not exposed personally. As sweet as the corporate shield may appear, it has its limits.

As we will see in Chapter 5, a corporation can offer attractive tax benefits. And the business and financial communities, worldwide, understand and accept the preeminent role of corporations.

These factors make the corporate structure a must for many businesses, both large and small.

B. GOOD OR BAD CITIZEN?

1. BEYOND THE PROFIT MOTIVE

Excerpts from Ross Bishop Article
"The Corporation and Society" (2006)

Regardless of how you feel about corporations, it is difficult to deny their contribution to our material well being. We are the best fed, dressed, equipped, housed and served people in human history. Legions of corporate employees look to our well being every day. There is virtually nothing in our lives that does not involve a corporate business. For all its failings, and there are many, the corporation has demonstrated itself to be the most efficient institution man has ever created for the application of resources to human endeavor.

Corporate efficiency however comes at a cost. We have freed corporations from societal constraints so that they might pursue material ends. Freed from the political, moral and ethical concerns that frustrate governmental and social organizations, corporations have benefited significantly from not having to be responsible for the long-term social consequences of their actions.

The hazy boundary between the corporation and society has always been a source of tension since the first corporation was formed in 12th century Germany. The hope was that a stable society would be in the organization's best interests and that the two could peacefully co-exist. And, up to the time of The American Revolution, there was some truth to that idea. The vast majority of goods were consumed close to the places of their production (usually within 20 miles). The producer was no more than a degree of separation from both his customers and his suppliers. He sold to or purchased from most of them directly and knew them by name. What we know about humans is that compassion comes naturally to most people in a proximate setting like that, and that it rapidly diminishes as the organization becomes institutionalized and the management is separated from its customers, suppliers, and employees.

In the period after the American Revolution, corporations grew dramatically both in reach and power. And as society began to feel the impacts of unregulated corporate self-interest, it swiftly put an end to the age of laissez-faire capitalism. Corporate charters could be revoked if the corporation violated its intended purpose. Charters had sunset dates and legislatures set rates that corporations could charge. Corporations were prohibited from owning other corporations and all corporate records and documents were open to the public (or public officials). Large and small investors were granted equal voting rights. Boards of directors and stockholders could be held personally liable for harms and debts. Then in the latter half of the century most of these restrictions were eliminated.

As with all human endeavors, the vast majority of corporate executives are honest, capable people who sincerely care about the world they live in. They may see things differently than say, Greenpeace or the Bioneers, but they are not motivated by malice. But unfortunately when greed and social concerns mix, greed and its resulting hubris all too often win out.

The Me First organizations leave a wake of social problems and environmental destruction that simply boggles the imagination. Whether it is sweatshops in Indonesia, outsourcing layoffs in the U.S., bankrupted suppliers, political payoffs, misappropriated pension funds, environmental destruction, the deforestation of the rain forests or impoverished employees who must live on welfare to survive, these companies want what they want, and they want it now! One cannot help but hearken to what seems like a return to the heartless days of greed and social irresponsibility that Charles Dickens despaired so in his England of the 1850's.

Fortunately, a contrary wind is blowing. A number of organizations, either from concern for the planet, recognition of what is better for their employees, or just because it makes them feel better, are taking a markedly different approach to doing business. Theirs is a Compassion First ethicality that puts them in polar conflict with the Me Firsters. Fundamental to many of these organizations is the belief that the company has many stakeholders and that employees, customers, the environment, vendors and the community, along with shareholders, can all gain meaning from the organization's existence.

Most notable are firms like: Procter & Gamble, Hewlett-Packard, John Deere, Intel, Avon, Herman Miller, Timberland, Cisco Systems, Southwest Airlines, AT&T, Starbucks, The St. Paul Companies, Pixar, AFLAC, Weight Watchers, Pepsi, Motorola, Agilent, Apple Computer, Fannie Mae, Green Mountain Coffee, Whole Foods and Eastman Kodak. Some of their hands aren't totally clean; after all, these are large organizations with histories. But, each of them is working today to create a sense of ethics with its various publics. Contrary to commonly held accounting values, they are also demonstrating that socially conscious policies can create a definite and measurable positive impact on profit. Compassionate management is not a new philosophy. Over the years many firms, usually smaller organizations with a dedicated individual owner, have done business this way. But, these organizations have generally been overshadowed by the raw market power of their corporate competitors.

The Compassionate Companies make the process of doing business more fulfilling, not just more profitable, for everyone. That, more than anything, may eventually spell the difference between them and the Me First organizations. This will be helped a great deal when consumers recognize the difference and respond accordingly.

In the West it is more likely that Compassionate Companies will succeed simply because they are simply just more enjoyable to work for and do business with. Robert Lane, Chairman and CEO of John Deere says, "It's the stuff that makes you want to get up in the morning." People are proud to be associated with these organizations. As John Mackey of Whole Foods puts it, "What the world wants business to do is to care about more than just making money. And that's what business must evolve to do."

True Story
Article "Just Blame It on the Board" (April 16, 2012)[1]

The starter at the golf course said the three guys were business colleagues and good golfers when he assigned me to play with them. I knew that he was only half right when we hit our tee shots on the first hole. The first two, subordinates to the trio's third member, Mr. CEO, were there solely to serve as fans of Mr. CEO and praise his golfing superiority. The next four hours would be painful for them. Mr. CEO would trounce his hapless mates, even with a swing that made him look like a badly wounded chicken.

As we strolled down the first fairway, I quickly learned that Mr. CEO loved to brag about himself and his company. He was the President, Chief Executive Officer and 80-percent owner of a distribution company that apparently was quite successful and employed about 150 people, the great bulk of whom were low-paid, blue-collar workers. As we approached the first green, he was telling me about his company's shrewd defined benefit retirement plan that socked away big tax-deferred dollars for the top dogs in the company every year.

He was explaining that the real key to the plan was an unwritten policy that only 15 percent of the company's employees would remain with the company for more than seven years. All other employees were to be cycled out of the company to protect against wage growth and limit any vesting under the retirement plan. As Mr. CEO spoke, his two fans smiled and gleefully shook their heads in agreement. Obviously, they were part of the protected 15 percent.

By the time I was standing over a four-foot putt on the first green, I had grown to hate Mr. CEO. When the putt lipped out, I hated him even more. So as we walked off the green, I couldn't help asking, "How do you feel about doing such an ugly number on all those employees who work hard for your company with the hope of permanence and stability?"

---

1. This article can be found at Dwight Drake's website www.plaintalkplanning.com.

Mr. CEO's defensive, knee-jerk response said it all: "Well, well, it's not about me. It is a policy of the board of directors, a matter that our corporate board feels is very important for the long-term stability of the company."

Many claim that "Corporations are people." Are they right? The point they try to make is that the economic benefits generated by corporate activity ultimately make their way to people – shareholders, employees, vendors, and all who deal with the corporation. But their economic benefit point, while accurate, should in no sense imply that a corporation can ever be viewed the same as a human being.

Sure, a corporation can own property, borrow money, sue, be sued, commit a tort or a crime, spawn offspring subsidiary corporations, and do just about anything that a human being can do when it comes to money and business. But, no matter how you cut it, a corporation has no values, no conscience, no ethics, no still small voice, nor any other similar descriptor applicable to human beings. It's a shell that is completely dependent on the values and ethics of the human beings who run the show.

And the sad reality, as my pitiful interface with Mr. CEO demonstrates, is that many human beings have no problem parking their values and ethics outside the door when they enter their corporate world. They will bust their tails to always insure political correctness, but the entity itself often provides a solid cover, a justification, even a compelling desire, for doing things that they would never feel comfortable doing as individual human beings. The entity is viewed as a separate being whose profit motives must always be served and never subordinated to matters of conscience. I've seen it more times than I can count. That's why I always have a visceral reaction when anyone, like Mr. CEO, tries to justify personal actions or decisions for the sake of the corporate good or pass the buck to artificial corporate machinery.

What this means is that the corporate world, while not inherently evil, is inherently dangerous. Personally, I would never say the same about human beings, but I suspect some might.

So we really do need corporate regulation. But it's foolish, and dangerous, to expect too much from such regulation. No amount of regulation will crack down on all the Mr. CEOs.

Smart regulation needs to be balanced and not pushed towards an extreme. If there is no leash, or the leash is useless, history has proven time and again that it's only a matter of time before unrestrained greed will take its toll. If the leash is being pulled too tight, the corporate world, like a scared dog, will sit tight for fear of the pain, and all will suffer as a result.

The regulators are the key, often far more important than the actual legislation that authorizes them to regulate. They have discretion that provides them with substantial powers. They can influence the fate of a particular company or an entire industry. What we badly need are tough, business savvy regulators who can get the job done with a smart, balanced approach that's consistent with robust business growth.

Corporate Charity

Many work hard to create the perception that corporations are big supporters of charitable causes. There is no question that corporations support many charities and often are regarded as easy targets by those who need to raise money for a particular project. But in no sense are corporations the largest or most significant players in the world of charitable giving.

According to the 2011 American Philanthropy Report of the of the American Association of Fundraising Counsel, corporations gave $14.55 billion to charities in 2011, a one percent decline over the 2010 giving level. This accounted for five percent of all charitable giving. An additional $46.1 billion (14 percent) came from foundations. For every dollar contributed by corporations, over $16 were contributed by individuals or through estates, who collectively gave over $242 billion.

This is not to suggest that corporations do not adequately support charitable causes. After all, their primary charge is to create returns for their shareholders. What it does suggest is that claims of corporate charitable giving, no matter how well publicized, should not be held out as a justification for actions that cross questionable boundaries in pursuit of those shareholder returns.

2. CORPORATE POLITICAL INFLUENCE?

CITIZENS UNITED v. FEDERAL ELECTION COMMISSION
558 U.S. 310 (2010)

Justice KENNEDY delivered the opinion of the Court.

Federal law prohibits corporations and unions from using their general treasury funds to make independent expenditures for speech defined as an "electioneering communication" or for speech expressly advocating the election or defeat of a candidate. 2 U.S.C. § 441b. Limits on electioneering communications were upheld in *McConnell v. Federal Election Comm'n*, 540 U.S. 93, 203–209, 124 S.Ct. 619, 157 L.Ed.2d 491 (2003). The holding of *McConnell* rested to a large extent on an earlier case, *Austin v. Michigan Chamber of Commerce*, 494 U.S. 652, 110 S.Ct. 1391, 108 L.Ed.2d 652 (1990). *Austin* had held that political speech may be banned based on the speaker's corporate identity.

In this case we are asked to reconsider *Austin* and, in effect, *McConnell*. It has been noted that "*Austin* was a significant departure from ancient First Amendment principles," We agree with that conclusion and hold that *stare decisis* does not compel the continued acceptance of *Austin*. The Government may regulate corporate political speech through disclaimer and disclosure requirements, but it may not suppress that speech altogether.

Citizens United is a nonprofit corporation. It brought this action in the United States District Court for the District of Columbia. A three-judge court later convened to hear the cause. The resulting judgment gives rise to this appeal.

Citizens United has an annual budget of about $12 million. Most of its funds are from donations by individuals; but, in addition, it accepts a small portion of its funds from for-profit corporations.

In January 2008, Citizens United released a film entitled *Hillary: The Movie*. We refer to the film as *Hillary*. It is a 90–minute documentary about then-Senator Hillary Clinton, who was a candidate in the Democratic Party's 2008 Presidential primary elections. *Hillary* mentions Senator Clinton by name and depicts interviews with political commentators and other persons, most of them quite critical of Senator Clinton. *Hillary* was released in theaters and on DVD, but Citizens United wanted to increase distribution by making it available through video-on-demand.

To implement the proposal, Citizens United was prepared to pay for the video-on-demand; and to promote the film, it produced two 10–second ads and one 30–second ad for *Hillary*. Each ad includes a short (and, in our view, pejorative) statement about Senator Clinton, followed by the name of the movie and the movie's Website address. Citizens United desired to promote the video-on-demand offering by running advertisements on broadcast and cable television.

Before the Bipartisan Campaign Reform Act of 2002 (BCRA), federal law prohibited—and still does prohibit—corporations and unions from using general treasury funds to make direct contributions to candidates or independent expenditures that expressly advocate the election or defeat of a candidate, through any form of media, in connection with certain qualified federal elections.

Citizens United wanted to make *Hillary* available through video-on-demand within 30 days of the 2008 primary elections. It feared, however, that both the film and the ads would be covered by § 441b's ban on corporate-funded independent expenditures, thus subjecting the corporation to civil and criminal penalties under § 437g. In December 2007, Citizens United sought declaratory and injunctive relief against the FEC. It argued that (1) § 441b is unconstitutional as applied to *Hillary;* and (2) BCRA's disclaimer and disclosure requirements, BCRA §§ 201 and 311, are unconstitutional as applied to *Hillary* and to the three ads for the movie.

The District Court denied Citizens United's motion for a preliminary injunction, and then granted the FEC's motion for summary judgment. The court held that § 441b was facially constitutional under *McConnell,* and that § 441b was constitutional as applied to *Hillary* because it was "susceptible of no other interpretation than to inform the electorate that Senator Clinton is unfit for office, that the United States would be a dangerous place in a President Hillary Clinton world, and that viewers should vote against her."

The First Amendment provides that "Congress shall make no law ... abridging the freedom of speech." Laws enacted to control or suppress speech may operate at different points in the speech process.

The law before us is an outright ban, backed by criminal sanctions. Section 441b makes it a felony for all corporations—including nonprofit advocacy corporations—either to expressly advocate the election or defeat of candidates or to broadcast electioneering communications within 30 days of a primary election and 60 days of a general election.

Section 441b's prohibition on corporate independent expenditures is thus a ban on speech. As a "restriction on the amount of money a person or group can spend on political communication during a campaign," that statute "necessarily reduces the quantity of expression by restricting the number of issues discussed, the depth of their exploration, and the size of the audience reached." *Buckley v. Valeo,* 424 U.S. 1, 19, 96 S.Ct. 612, 46 L.Ed.2d 659 (1976). Were the Court to uphold these restrictions, the Government could repress speech by silencing certain voices at any of the various points in the speech process. If § 441b applied to individuals, no one would believe that it is merely a time, place, or manner restriction on speech. Its purpose and effect are to silence entities whose voices the Government deems to be suspect.

Speech is an essential mechanism of democracy, for it is the means to hold officials accountable to the people. The right of citizens to inquire, to hear, to speak, and to use information to reach consensus is a precondition to enlightened self-government and a necessary means to protect it.

For these reasons, political speech must prevail against laws that would suppress it, whether by design or inadvertence. Laws that burden political speech are "subject to strict scrutiny," which requires the Government to prove that the restriction "furthers a compelling interest and is narrowly tailored to achieve that interest."

Premised on mistrust of governmental power, the First Amendment stands against attempts to disfavor certain subjects or viewpoints. Prohibited, too, are restrictions distinguishing among different speakers, allowing speech by some but not others. As instruments to censor, these categories are interrelated: Speech restrictions based on the identity of the speaker are all too often simply a means to control content...

Quite apart from the purpose or effect of regulating content, moreover, the Government may commit a constitutional wrong when by law it identifies certain preferred speakers. By taking the right to speak from some and giving it to others, the Government deprives the disadvantaged person or class of the right to use speech to strive to establish worth, standing, and respect for the speaker's voice. The Government may not by these means deprive the public of the right and privilege to determine for itself what speech and speakers are worthy of consideration. The First Amendment protects speech and speaker, and the ideas that flow from each.

We find no basis for the proposition that, in the context of political speech, the Government may impose restrictions on certain disfavored speakers. Both history and logic lead us to this conclusion.

The Court has recognized that First Amendment protection extends to corporations. *First Nat. Bank of Boston v. Bellotti,* 435 U.S. 765, 98 S.Ct. 1407, 55 L.Ed.2d 707. This protection has been extended by explicit holdings to the context of political speech. Under the rationale of these precedents, political speech does not lose First Amendment protection "simply because its source is a corporation."

Austin "uph[eld] a direct restriction on the independent expenditure of funds for political speech for the first time in [this Court's] history." There, the Michigan Chamber of Commerce sought to use general treasury funds to run a newspaper ad supporting a specific candidate. Michigan law, however, prohibited corporate independent expenditures that supported or opposed any candidate for state office. A violation of the law was punishable as a felony. The Court sustained the speech prohibition.

The Court is thus confronted with conflicting lines of precedent: a pre-*Austin* line that forbids restrictions on political speech based on the speaker's corporate identity and a post- *Austin* line that permits them. No case before *Austin* had held that Congress could prohibit independent expenditures for political speech based on the speaker's corporate identity. Before *Austin* Congress had enacted legislation for this purpose, and the Government urged the same proposition before this Court.

Political speech is "indispensable to decisionmaking in a democracy, and this is no less true because the speech comes from a corporation rather than an individual." This protection for speech is inconsistent with *Austin* 's antidistortion rationale. *Austin* sought to defend the antidistortion rationale as a means to prevent corporations from obtaining "'an unfair advantage in the political marketplace' " by using "'resources amassed in the economic marketplace.' " But *Buckley* rejected the premise that the Government has an interest "in equalizing the relative ability of individuals and groups to influence the outcome of elections." *Buckley* was specific in stating that "the skyrocketing cost of political campaigns" could not sustain the governmental prohibition. The First Amendment's protections do not depend on the speaker's "financial ability to engage in public discussion."

The appearance of influence or access, furthermore, will not cause the electorate to lose faith in our democracy. By definition, an independent expenditure is political speech presented to the electorate that is not coordinated with a candidate. The fact that a corporation, or any other speaker, is willing to spend money to try to persuade voters presupposes that the people have the ultimate influence over elected officials.

The Government contends further that corporate independent expenditures can be limited because of its interest in protecting dissenting shareholders from being compelled to fund corporate political speech. This asserted interest would allow the Government to ban the political speech even of media corporations. Under the Government's view, that potential disagreement could give the Government the authority to restrict the media corporation's political speech. The First Amendment does not allow that power. There is, furthermore, little evidence of abuse that cannot be corrected by shareholders "through the procedures of corporate democracy."

Those reasons are sufficient to reject this shareholder-protection interest; and, moreover, the statute is both underinclusive and overinclusive. As to the first, if Congress had been seeking to protect dissenting shareholders, it would not have banned corporate speech in only certain media within 30 or 60 days before an election. A dissenting shareholder's interests would be implicated by speech in any media at any time. As to the second, the statute is overinclusive because it covers all corporations, including nonprofit corporations and for-profit corporations with only single shareholders. As to other corporations, the remedy is not to restrict speech but to consider and explore other regulatory mechanisms. The regulatory mechanism here, based on speech, contravenes the First Amendment.

For the reasons above, it must be concluded that *Austin* was not well reasoned.

Austin is undermined by experience since its announcement. Political speech is so ingrained in our culture that speakers find ways to circumvent campaign finance laws. Our Nation's speech dynamic is changing, and informative voices should not have to circumvent onerous restrictions to exercise their First Amendment rights. Speakers have become adept at presenting citizens with sound bites, talking points, and scripted messages that dominate the 24–hour news cycle. Corporations, like individuals, do not have monolithic views. On certain topics corporations may possess valuable expertise, leaving them the best equipped to point out errors or fallacies in speech of all sorts, including the speech of candidates and elected officials.

Rapid changes in technology—and the creative dynamic inherent in the concept of free expression—counsel against upholding a law that restricts political speech in certain media or by certain speakers.. Soon, however, it may be that Internet sources, such as blogs and social networking Web sites, will provide citizens with significant information about political candidates and issues. Yet, § 441b would seem to ban a blog post expressly advocating the election or defeat of a candidate if that blog were created with corporate funds. The First Amendment does not permit Congress to make these categorical distinctions based on the corporate identity of the speaker and the content of the political speech. Due consideration leads to this conclusion: *Austin* should be and now is overruled. We return to the principle established in *Buckley* and *Bellotti* that the Government may not suppress political speech on the basis of the speaker's corporate identity. No sufficient governmental interest justifies limits on the political speech of nonprofit or for-profit corporations.

Impact of *Citizens United*?

Richard L. Hasen, an expert on campaign finance at the University of California at Irvine, wrote an article on March 9, 2012 for Slate titled, "The Numbers Don't Lie," in which he stated:

> Let's focus only on presidential election years, to keep the comparisons as simple as possible. In the 1992 election season, when it was entirely possible (under that 1976 Supreme Court decision) for Sheldon Adelson or George Soros to spend unlimited sums independently on elections, total outside spending up to March 8 was about $1.5 million. In 2000, total outside spending up to March 8 was $2.6 million. In 2004 and 2008, with the explosion of 527 organizations, total spending to

March 8 was $14 million and $37.5 million. What is the total for this election season through March 8? More than $88 million, *234 percent* of 2008's numbers and *628 percent* of 2004's. If this was not caused by *Citizens United*, we have a mighty big coincidence on our hands.

C. LAST TWO DECADES

History is full of experiences that illustrate the downside risks of entrusting a handful of individuals with ever-expanding amounts of private capital, ballooning capital markets to chase breakthroughs with expectations that defy logic, and pushing government mandates that encourage private enterprises to take actions that make no economic sense. We have experienced three huge traumas over the past two decades that have reminded us of these destructive risks and the capacity of corporate activities to impact, for better or worse, all sectors of our society. Before launching into a review of basic corporate legal concepts, it seems appropriate to provide a short recap of these recent traumas.

1. THE DOT.COM BOOM AND BUST

America enjoyed a powerful economic expansion that began in March 1991 and ended in March 2001. Players on both sides of the political aisle have always tried to claim credit for this boom period in an attempt to influence those who, because of age, ignorance or forgetfulness, don't know the truth. The Democrats argue that the driving force was President Bill Clinton and his policies, which included higher tax rates. Republicans point to their sweeping conquest of the House, the Gingrich-led crowd's "Contract with America," and the implementation of policies that ultimately forced Clinton to proclaim that "the era of big government is over." Both sides overstate their claims.

The driving force behind the '90s was the technology and dot.com boom and an associated abundance of confidence and optimism about the future. This force transcended all politics and parties. It produced plentiful capital that fueled all our markets, allowed innovators to innovate, and empowered businesses to increase productivity. Many, both inside and outside of government, believed and proclaimed that we had experienced a major structural change to a "new economy."

Americans benefited big time. Unemployment was down; wages were up; inflation was low; and individual portfolios were skyrocketing. The paper net wealth of Americans grew an astounding $18.3 trillion. The ratio of net wealth to disposable income grew from 4.9 percent to 6.4 percent, the highest level since 1952. Price/earnings ratios began to move out of sight – often out of existence because there were no earnings on which to calculate the ratios. Everyone's monthly investment statement showed growth each month. The only question was: how much growth? The Internet was becoming a reality and promised the future. Companies with an Internet strategy, but no earning and meager revenues, could attract investors, then more investors, and then watch their stock prices balloon as the demand fed on itself. It was up, up and away.

During the boom, Americans grew confident with their ever-escalating investment portfolios and were anxious to spend. Consumer spending outstripped all disposable income. As a result, Americans solidified their position as the worst savers in the industrial world. Experts estimate that the personal savings rate in America dropped from 8 percent to less than zero, and the share of Gross Domestic Product that households consumed rose 6 percent.

So a big question was: If Americans were spending all their income, where was the capital coming from – the capital that made everything possible? The answer: Offshore. Foreign money flooded into our stock markets, our financial institutions, and our government. The importing of foreign dollars allowed America to expand in the short run while its citizens progressively fueled demand by spending everything they earned. In 1993, net foreign investment was less than 5 percent of growth investments in the United States. By the end of the '90s, it had spiked to 23 percent.

The high employment and escalating income levels of the '90s heyday produced a bonanza for federal government coffers. By 1999, there was actually an on-budget surplus, something we hadn't seen since 1960. Higher earnings had pushed annual income tax revenues past the $1 trillion dollar mark for the first time, and the government's public debt had actually dropped. In early 2000, the Congressional Budget Office projected ever-escalating on-budget surpluses through the year 2010, which would reduce the total public debt to under $1 trillion dollars by 2010. Every year into the future was projected to just get better.

Of course, the surpluses never came. The new economy never materialized. Everything begin to shift in 2000 as the realization set in that this joyride was not a *bona fide* boom, but rather an over-hyped bubble that was about to burst. The difference between a boom and a bubble is the aftermath; the first retracts to something that resembles an acceptable norm, while the latter produces across-the-board misery. The burst began as some, then many, and then all concluded that the future profitability expectations of new investments were grossly overoptimistic, particularly those related to the technology and dot.com boom. Foreign capital began to disappear, which triggered a big drop in the value of the dollar.

All Americans witnessed that, just as capital giveth, the lack of capital taketh away. Unemployment skyrocketed. Our capital markets crashed. Monthly investment statements became something to hide from, not hang on the fridge. Companies quickly found themselves swimming in excess manufacturing capacity. Venture capital for new growth and innovation was nearly impossible to find.

As the equity markets crashed, the huge historic gains in the ratio of consumer wealth to disposable income completely disappeared, retracting to pre-1993 levels. The tech-heavy Nasdaq Composite lost 78 percent of its value, and even the stalwart S&P 500 got hammered, losing 49 percent of its value during the same time frame. Trillions of dollars in equity value had vanished in a few short years following the bubble's burst.

But for those who sucked up the hit, it wasn't about a trillion dollars. It was about having the nerve to open and look at monthly statements to see the losses that mounted every month. For many older players, it was about dashed retirement dreams or, at best, long-delayed retirement hopes. For younger players, who anxiously entered the market in the '90s, with expectations of riding the upward momentum to riches, it was about getting KO'd in their first round.

The pumping up and ultimate burst of the '90s bubble reminded us of the power of optimism and confidence about the future, our dependence on foreign capital, the importance of sound investing discipline, and the positive impact robust private sector growth can have on government coffers and employment and income levels.

2. ENRON AND SARBANES-OXLEY

The Enron scandal is one of the darkest stories in American corporate history. The root cause of the tragedy was not a function of bad market conditions. It was greed and the intellectual power of business manipulation, facilitated by a host of players who benefited by assuming the best and never demanding answers to tough, obvious questions. The collapse of giant Enron was triggered in 2001 when Lynn Brewer, an Enron executive, notified members of the U.S. government of her witness to corrupt dealing including bank fraud, espionage, unlawful price manipulation, and gross overstatements to the press and public. It eventually led to the bankruptcy of the Enron Corporation and the *de facto* dissolution of Arthur Andersen, one of the largest accounting firms in the world. Enron was the largest bankruptcy reorganization in American history at that time.

Enron was organized in 1985, when it started operations as an interstate pipeline company. It was the product of a merger of Houston Natural Gas and Omaha-based InterNorth. Kenneth Lay, the former chief executive officer of Houston Natural Gas, became the CEO and chairman of Enron. A sign in Enron's Houston headquarters announced that Enron was to become "the World's Greatest Company." Lay was widely hailed as a visionary, a man with strong political connections, and a friend of President George W. Bush, who referred to Lay as "Kenny boy."

In 1999, Enron launched EnronOnline, an Internet-based trading system for electricity, natural gas, crude oil and a wide range of other products. It soon became the largest business site in the world, with 90 percent of Enron's income coming from trades over EnronOnline. It was a perfect fit for the dot.com-driven stock market boom of the '90s. As Enron mushroomed on the Internet, Wall Street propelled its stock upward. At its peak, Enron was worth about $70 billion, with its shares trading in the $90 range.

Enron enjoyed spectacular growth with its revenues tripling from 1998 to 2000, reaching $100 billion in 2000. Enron had become the seventh-largest Fortune 500 company and the sixth-largest energy company in the world.

When things began to unravel, it was revealed that Enron had formed about a dozen "partnerships" with companies it had created to hide huge debts and heavy trading losses. Chief Financial Officer Andrew Fastow and others were successful in misleading Arthur Anderson and Enron's board of directors and audit committee on high-risk accounting practices. Everything crashed when Enron admitted that it had misstated its income and that its equity value had been overstated. Enron's natural gas trading desk, which dominated its business, was shut down. Soon credit rating agencies downgraded Enron to "junk bond" level, Enron stopped paying its bills, and others stopped doing business with Enron. Enron's stock plunged from a high of $90 a share to less than 61 cents in less than a year. Thousands of Enron employees were thrown out of work and, together with thousands of investors, lost billions as Enron's shares shrank to penny-stock levels.

Enron's collapse pulled down the stocks of Citigroup Inc. and J.P. Morgan Chase & Co., who had granted Enron several hundred million dollars of unsecured loans within weeks of the collapse. The hit to Citigroup and J.P. Morgan Chase, both Dow Jones companies, knocked more than 30 points off the Dow. The collapse also triggered widespread selling on Wall Street, with both the Standard & Poor's 500 and the Nasdaq composite index experiencing significant Enron-related declines.

Enron executives were indicted on a variety of charges and were later sentenced to prison. Arthur Andersen, Enron's auditor, was found guilty in a United States District Court, but the ruling was eventually overturned by the U.S. Supreme Court. Nevertheless, the firm lost the bulk of its clients during the scandal and was forced to close its doors. Enron employees and shareholders received limited returns in lawsuits, nothing close to the billions that had been lost in pensions and stock prices.

Enron wasn't the only corporate scandal during the dot.com bust period. Other corporate accounting scandals surfaced at Tyco International, WorldCom, and other companies, none quite as sensationally sinister as Enron, but all bad. These failures eventually led to new regulations and legislation designed to improve the quality of financial reporting for public companies, including the Sarbanes-Oxley Act of 2002 ("SOX"). SOX had huge bipartisan support, with 423 approving votes in the House and 99 in the Senate. When signing the bill, President George W. Bush heralded it as "the most far-reaching reforms of American business practices since the time of Franklin D. Roosevelt." Bush claimed, "The era of low standards and false profits is over; no boardroom in America is above or beyond the law."[2]

SOX ushered in a number of important changes, all designed to improve confidence in the capital markets of the U.S. and the veracity of corporate financial statements. Key provisions of SOX include the following:

• **A** Public Company Accounting Oversight Board was established to provide independent oversight of public accounting firms providing audit services. It also was tasked with registering auditors, defining the specific processes and procedures for compliance audits, inspecting and policing conduct and quality control, and enforcing compliance with the specific SOX mandates.

---

2. Bumiller, *"Bush Signs Bill Aimed at Fraud in Corporations,"* The New York Times (July 31, 2002).

• SOX enhanced reporting requirements for financial transactions, including off-balance-sheet transactions, pro-forma figures and stock transactions of corporate officers. It required internal controls for assuring the accuracy of financial reports and disclosures, and mandated both audits and reports on those controls. It also required timely reporting of material changes in financial condition and specific enhanced reviews by the SEC or its agents of corporate reports.

• **Standards** were established for external auditor independence, to limit conflicts of interest, to address requirements for new auditor approval, audit partner rotations, and auditor reporting, and to restrict auditing companies from providing non-audit services (e.g., consulting) for the same clients.

• SOX mandated that senior executives take individual responsibility for the accuracy and completeness of corporate financial reports. It defined the interaction of external auditors and corporate audit committees, and specified the responsibility of corporate officers for the accuracy and validity of corporate financial reports. It enumerated specific limits on the behaviors of corporate officers and described specific forfeitures of benefits and civil penalties for non-compliance.

• SOX included measures designed to help restore investor confidence in reporting by securities analysts by defining a code of conduct for securities analysts and requiring disclosure of knowable conflicts of interest.

• SOX defined the SEC's authority to censure or bar securities professionals from practice and defined conditions under which a person can be barred from practicing as a broker, advisor, or dealer.

• SOX required the Comptroller General and the SEC to perform various studies and report their findings.

• SOX included sections called the "Corporate and Criminal Fraud Accountability Act of 2002" which described specific criminal penalties for manipulation, destruction or alteration of financial records or other interference with investigations and provided certain protections for whistle-blowers.

• SOX's sections called "White Collar Crime Penalty Enhancement Act of 2002" increased criminal penalties associated with white-collar crimes and conspiracies, recommended stronger sentencing guidelines, and specified that the failure to certify corporate financial reports is a criminal offense.

• SOX required a company's Chief Executive Officer to sign the company's tax return.

• SOX's sections called "Corporate Fraud Accountability Act of 2002" identified corporate fraud and records tampering as criminal offenses and specified specific penalties, revised sentencing guidelines, strengthened penalties, and enabled the SEC to temporarily freeze transactions or payments deemed "large" or "unusual".

In looking back at the Enron tragedy, it's hard to comprehend how a company could grow so fast and promise so many people so much and then completely collapse even faster. A useful insight as to how it happened was provided by Lynn Brewer, the Enron executive who blew the whistle, in the following passage from her foreword to a book that I wrote in 2003:[3]

> I know crisis. I've felt it breed through an organization one office, one individual at a time. I've seen how the presence of opportunity with supporting pressures and available validation creates an environment ripe for self-serving acts with unfathomable consequences.

> I know crisis. I've watched leaders so preoccupied with short-term appearances and the security of their current power base that they lose all capacity to distinguish what is right, from what they believe may be justifiable. I've experienced the inertia of a large institution hurling itself into destruction as the fight to make right dies with determined avoidance of any conflict or murmur of transgression.

> I know lies. I've witnessed the posturing and manipulation of numbers, reports and financial records to defensibly mislead uninformed masses. I've observed first-hand how the need for money and capital can force subordination of intellectual honesty to practical pressures of delivering on expectations of empty promises. I've worked alongside good intentioned people who lose all capacity to acknowledge past blunders and wrongdoings for fear of what they know is inevitable.

> I know these things. In fact, I have lived them. It was my abhorrence of these realities that prompted me to do what I did at Enron. It is the continued presence of these realities that has driven me to devote my career to improving the position and practice of integrity in our corporate world and capital markets.

3. THE FINANCIAL CRISIS AND DODD-FRANK

Our economy is struggling to slowly crawl out of a protracted period of weakness that has delivered chronic unemployment numbers in the eight percent range, brought our largest financial institutions to their knees, and forced many businesses to close their doors. Millions have given up their job-seeking efforts and are not even included in the unemployment calculation. And millions more who do have jobs consider themselves grossly underemployed as they net only a fraction of what they used to earn.

For more than two decades, the world markets have been fueled by consumers in developed countries progressively spending at a faster pace. It was done with leverage – debt backed by assets that were supposed to continually grow in value and support perpetual borrowing and spending increases. The leverage occurred at all levels; government debt escalated; financial institutions leveraged derivative-based securities to the hilt; subprime mortgages were

---

3. Dwight Drake, *"Gutless Neglect: America's Biggest Money Crisis"* (Enterprise Actions 2003), p. i.

triggered by government mandates to push millions of families to buy homes they couldn't possibly afford; and households pumped up debt by refinancing based on escalating home prices and using easily available credit card leverage.

Then the momentum shifted. Asset values turned and headed in the wrong direction, spiraling down as demand shrank and fire sales escalated the descent. The largest financial institutions – those "too big to fail" – saw their balance sheet values crumble. They were soon on life support, begging the government for a lifeline. The value of just about every home in America plummeted, leaving millions of Americans underwater, with more debt than assets. The whole private sector was forced to deleverage by reducing debt and cutting spending. The resulting massive drop in demand forced employers to slash payrolls, which accelerated the drop in demand.

The government and the Federal Reserve kept money flowing by cutting short-term interest rates to nearly zero, driving annual federal deficits to trillion-dollar levels that no one could have imagined just a few years ago, and pumping trillions into the economy through the Federal Reserve's "quantitative easing" plans. The big question now is whether these measures can offset the effects of the private deleveraging that drove buyers to the sidelines without doing untold damage in the long term. The first signs were positive as financial spreads bounced back to normal, but then Ireland, Greece, Iceland and others hit the wall, and everyone started questioning and fearing the risks of massive, unsustainable government leverage. Meanwhile, nothing has seriously reduced the ugly unemployment rate and associated pain experienced by millions of America's businesses and families.

The experiences of the recent past have once again confirmed that unrestrained, irresponsible asset-based leveraging is a double-edged sword; it has the capacity to either fuel wonderful growth or quickly put large financial institutions and millions of businesses and families on their backs. Debates will forever rage over the effectiveness of various government actions designed to help offset the massive private sector de-leveraging and the debilitating drop in global demand.

Attacks were soon leveled at those responsible for the irresponsible lending, the exploitation of risk-spreading mortgage-backed derivatives, the massive leveraging of balance sheet financial assets, and the maintenance of an unregulated shadow banking industry that produced unprecedented bonuses and income levels for countless corporate executives. One huge result of these attacks was the Dodd-Frank Wall Street Reform and Consumer Protection Act of 2010, a massive 2,300-page act that mandates sweeping regulatory changes that affect all federal financial regulatory agencies and almost every part of the nation's financial services industry.

Dodd-Frank has been heralded as the most significant financial reform since the Great Depression. It will take years to fully implement and define the outer limits of Dodd-Frank. Generally speaking (and I really mean "generally"), Dodd-Frank in part:

- Establishes a Financial Stability Oversight Council to address systemic financial risks.

 • Provides authority to permit the orderly liquidation of companies deemed systemically risky.

 • Revises the bank and bank holding company regulatory regime and clarifies regulatory functions of the Federal Deposit Insurance Corporation (FDIC) and the Board of Governors of Federal Reserve (FRB).

 • Establishes regulations of all investment advisors, including hedge funds.

 • Establishes a new Federal Insurance Office to monitor the insurance industry and identify regulatory gaps that could contribute to systemic risk.

 • Restricts banks, bank affiliates and bank holding companies from proprietary trading or investing in a hedge fund or private equity fund.

 • Increases regulation and transparency of over-the-counter derivatives markets.

 • Establishes new regulations for credit rating agencies.

 • Establishes new requirements relating to executive compensation, including shareholders' "say on pay" rights (see Chapter 9).

 • Empowers a new independent office with broad authority and responsibilities under various current consumer financial protection laws.

 • Establishes extensive requirements applicable to the mortgage lending industry – everything from mortgage originator compensation to servicing, appraisals, counseling, and more.

 • Preserves enforcement powers of states with respect to financial institutions and restricts preemption of state laws by federal banking regulators.

D. THE CORPORATE PLAYERS

A corporation must act through human beings who wear various hats and are given varying degrees of authority to act for and on behalf of the corporation.

Incorporator. The incorporator is the person who actually forms the corporation, signs the articles of incorporation, and does what is necessary to bring the corporation into existence. Usually the incorporator is the driving force behind the new business or an attorney who represents that person.

Registered Agent. The registered agent of a corporation is the person, identified in the state's records, who is authorized to receive service of process in legal proceedings involving the corporation. Any person who wants to sue a corporation may check state records, secure the name and address of the registered agent, and serve that person.

Shareholders. The shareholders are the owners of the corporation's stock. In public companies, there are thousands of shareholders who regularly trade the corporation's stock. In closely held corporations, there may be only one shareholder or a few shareholders, and stock transfers are very rare events that are carefully controlled. The shareholders of a corporation elect the board of directors, approve major transactions (merges and the like), and vote on proposals. The shareholders do not manage the affairs of the company, although shareholders in closely held corporations may agree in writing to various deal points relating to the operation of the company that will preempt the management authority of the board.

Board of Directors. The board of directors is the ultimate management authority of a corporation. State law requires that the board manage the affairs of the corporation. Its members are elected by the shareholders. One board member is typically designated as the chairman, the leader of the board. The board members may also be shareholders and officers, although they need not be. All public corporations and many closely held corporations have outside directors who do not work for the company.

The board of directors elects the officers of the corporation and generally manages and approves all important matters relating to the affairs of the business. Often there are sub-committees of the board that are empowered to deal with specific matters. Popular sub-committees include a compensation committee, which deals with all officer-related compensation issues, and an audit committee, which deals with all accounting and audit matters.

Actions taken and approved by the board of directors are reflected in written resolutions. Official resolutions may be adopted by the vote of board members at a meeting or by all of the board members signing a written consent resolution that approves the resolutions.

Board members have a duty to manage the corporation for the benefit of the shareholders. This is a fiduciary duty that includes a duty of care and a duty of loyalty. A detailed discussion of these duties is provided in Chapter 10. The duty of care imposes on each director a responsibility to act in good faith and in a manner that the director reasonably believes to be in the best interests of the shareholders. This duty is softened by the well-established business judgment rule that provides that, absent self dealing or a breach of loyalty, a director is presumed to have acted in good faith and in the best interests of the shareholders. This presumption, of course, can be rebutted. The duty of loyalty requires a director to place the best interests of the corporation above any personal interests. The violation of this duty may surface when a director engages in self-dealing with the corporation or personally usurps business opportunities that should have first been offered to the corporation. A breach of any of these duties may expose a director to a derivative claim brought by a shareholder on behalf of the corporation.

Officers. The officers of the corporation are the ones who actually run the business and work daily to carry out the authority delegated to them by the organization documents of the corporation (the bylaws) and the board. Key officers typically include the President and Chief Operating Officer (CEO), the Chief Operating Officer (COO), the Chief Financial Officer (CFO), the Secretary, and the Treasurer. Often a single person wears multiple hats - the

CFO may, for example, be the Secretary and the Treasurer. Plus, the title of vice president is often used with many key players in the company, with various modifying adjectives. Examples: Senior VP in charge of hiring; Executive VP in charge of East Coast operations. In the corporate world, titles are a big deal and the combinations of available options are limitless.

Employees. Employees are those who work for the corporation but are not officers. They are managed by the officers. For most companies, a prerequisite to success is the ability to attract, retain and motivate quality employees. Effective employee motivation often is the key to achieving the company's goals and objectives. New technologies have increased productivity and enabled many companies to do more with fewer people; but, contrary to what some think, they have done nothing to reduce the importance of quality employees. Key challenges for most businesses today include improving employee skill levels, promoting employee stability, enhancing employee training, reducing employee turnover, and developing employees who care about the business.

DODGE v. FORD MOTOR CO.
204 Mich. 459, 170 N.W. 668 (1919)

Note: Ford Motor Company was founded in 1903 with an initial capitalization of $150,000. Henry Ford owned 58 percent of the stock, and the Dodge brothers owned 10 percent. The Dodge brothers brought this action to compel the company to pay dividends. The lower court ordered the company to pay $19 million in dividends to its shareholders.

Ostrander, C.J.

When plaintiffs made their complaint and demand for further dividends, the Ford Motor Company had concluded its most prosperous year of business. The demand for its cars at the price of the preceding year continued. It could make and could market in the year beginning August 1, 1916, more than 500,000 cars. Sales of parts and repairs would necessarily increase. The cost of materials was likely to advance, and perhaps the price of labor; but it reasonably might have expected a profit for the year of upwards of $60,000,000. It had assets of more than $132,000,000, a surplus of almost $112,000,000, and its cash on hand and municipal bonds were nearly $54,000,000. Its total liabilities, including capital stock, was a little over $20,000,000. It had declared no special dividend during the business year except the October, 1915, dividend. It had been the practice, under similar circumstances, to declare larger dividends. Considering only these facts, a refusal to declare and pay further dividends appears to be not an exercise of discretion on the part of the directors, but an arbitrary refusal to do what the circumstances required to be done.

These facts and others call upon the directors to justify their action, or failure or refusal to act. In justification, the defendants have offered testimony tending to prove, and which does prove, the following facts: It had been the policy of the corporation for a considerable time to annually reduce the selling price of cars, while keeping up, or improving, their quality. As early as in June, 1915, a general plan for the expansion of the productive capacity of the concern by a practical duplication of its plant had been talked over by the executive officers and directors and agreed upon; not all of the details having been settled, and no formal action of directors having been taken. The erection of a smelter was considered, and engineering and other data in connection therewith secured. In consequence, it was determined not to reduce the selling price of cars for the year beginning August 1, 1915, but to maintain the price and to accumulate a large surplus to pay for the proposed expansion of plant and equipment, and perhaps to build a plant for smelting ore. It is hoped, by Mr. Ford, that eventually 1,000,000 cars will be annually produced. The contemplated changes will permit the increased output.

The plan, as affecting the profits of the business for the year beginning August 1, 1916, and thereafter, calls for a reduction in the selling price of the cars. It is true that this price might be at any time increased, but the plan called for the reduction in price of $80 a car. The capacity of the plant, without the additions thereto voted to be made (without a part of them at least), would produce more than 600,000 cars annually. This number, and more, could have been sold for $440 instead of $360, a difference in the return for capital, labor, and materials employed of at least $48,000,000. In short, the plan does not call for and is not intended to produce immediately a more profitable business, but a less profitable one; not only less profitable than formerly, but less profitable than it is admitted it might be made. The apparent immediate effect will be to diminish the value of shares and the returns to shareholders.

It is the contention of plaintiffs that the apparent effect of the plan is intended to be the continued and continuing effect of it, and that it is deliberately proposed, not of record and not by official corporate declaration, but nevertheless proposed, to continue the corporation henceforth as a semi-eleemosynary institution and not as a business institution. In support of this contention, they point to the attitude and to the expressions of Mr. Henry Ford.

Mr. Henry Ford is the dominant force in the business of the Ford Motor Company. No plan of operations could be adopted unless he consented, and no board of directors can be elected whom he does not favor. One of the directors of the company has no stock. One share was assigned to him to qualify him for the position, but it is not claimed that he owns it. A business, one of the largest in the world, and one of the most profitable, has been built up. It employs many men, at good pay.

'My ambition,' said Mr. Ford, 'is to employ still more men, to spread the benefits of this industrial system to the greatest possible number, to help them build up their lives and their homes. To do this we are putting the greatest share of our profits back in the business.'

'With regard to dividends, the company paid sixty per cent. on its capitalization of two million dollars, or $1,200,000, leaving $58,000,000 to reinvest for the growth of the company. This is Mr. Ford's policy at present, and it is understood that the other stockholders cheerfully accede to this plan.'

He had made up his mind in the summer of 1916 that no dividends other than the regular dividends should be paid, 'for the present.'

'Q. For how long? Had you fixed in your mind any time in the future, when you were going to pay—— A. No.

'Q. That was indefinite in the future? A. That was indefinite; yes, sir.'

The record, and especially the testimony of Mr. Ford, convinces that he has to some extent the attitude towards shareholders of one who has dispensed and distributed to them large gains and that they should be content to take what he chooses to give. His testimony creates the impression, also, that he thinks the Ford Motor Company has made too much money, has had too large profits, and that, although large profits might be still earned, a sharing of them with the public, by reducing the price of the output of the company, ought to be undertaken. We have no doubt that certain sentiments, philanthropic and altruistic, creditable to Mr. Ford, had large influence in determining the policy to be pursued by the Ford Motor Company—the policy which has been herein referred to.

It is said by his counsel that——

'Although a manufacturing corporation cannot engage in humanitarian works as its principal business, the fact that it is organized for profit does not prevent the existence of implied powers to carry on with humanitarian motives such charitable works as are incidental to the main business of the corporation.'

And again:

'As the expenditures complained of are being made in an expansion of the business which the company is organized to carry on, and for purposes within the powers of the corporation as hereinbefore shown, the question is as to whether such expenditures are rendered illegal because influenced to some extent by humanitarian motives and purposes on the part of the members of the board of directors.'

There is committed to the discretion of directors, a discretion to be exercised in good faith, the infinite details of business, including the wages which shall be paid to employees, the number of hours they shall work, the conditions under which labor shall be carried on, and the price for which products shall be offered to the public.

It is said by appellants that the motives of the board members are not material and will not be inquired into by the court so long as their acts are within their lawful powers. As we have pointed out, and the proposition does not require argument to sustain it, it is not within the lawful powers of a board of directors to shape and conduct the affairs of a corporation for the merely incidental benefit of shareholders and for the primary purpose of benefiting others, and no one will contend that, if the avowed purpose of the defendant directors was to sacrifice the interests of shareholders, it would not be the duty of the courts to interfere.

We are not, however, persuaded that we should interfere with the proposed expansion of the business of the Ford Motor Company. In view of the fact that the selling price of products may be increased at any time, the ultimate results of the larger business cannot be certainly estimated. The judges are not business experts. It is recognized that plans must often be made for a long future, for expected competition, for a continuing as well as an immediately profitable venture. The experience of the Ford Motor Company is evidence of capable management of its affairs. It may be noticed, incidentally, that it took from the public the money required for the execution of its plan, and that the very considerable salaries paid to Mr. Ford and to certain executive officers and employés were not diminished. We are not satisfied that the alleged motives of the directors, in so far as they are reflected in the conduct of the business, menace the interests of shareholders. It is enough to say, perhaps, that the court of equity is at all times open to complaining shareholders having a just grievance.

Assuming the general plan and policy of expansion and the details of it to have been sufficiently, formally, approved at the October and November, 1917, meetings of directors, and assuming further that the plan and policy and the details agreed upon were for the best ultimate interest of the company and therefore of its shareholders, what does it amount to in justification of a refusal to declare and pay a special dividend or dividends? The Ford Motor Company was able to estimate with nicety its income and profit. It could sell more cars than it could make. Having ascertained what it would cost to produce a car and to sell it, the profit upon each car depended upon the selling price. That being fixed, the yearly income and profit was determinable, and, within slight variations, was certain.

There was appropriated—voted—for the smelter $11,325,000. As to the remainder voted, there is no available way for determining how much had been paid before the action of directors was taken and how much was paid thereafter; but assuming that the plans required an expenditure sooner or later of $9,895,000 for duplication of the plant, and for land and other expenditures $3,000,000, the total is $24,220,000. The company was continuing business, at a profit—a cash business. If the total cost of proposed expenditures had been immediately withdrawn in cash from the cash surplus (money and bonds) on hand August 1, 1916, there would have remained nearly $30,000,000.

Defendants say, and it is true, that a considerable cash balance must be at all times carried by such a concern. But, as has been stated, there was a large daily, weekly, monthly, receipt of cash. The output was practically continuous and was continuously, and within a few days, turned into cash. Moreover, the contemplated expenditures were not to be immediately made. The large sum appropriated for the smelter plant was payable over a considerable period of time. So that, without going further, it would appear that, accepting and approving the plan of the directors, it was their duty to distribute on or near the 1st of August, 1916, a very large sum of money to stockholders.

In reaching this conclusion, we do not ignore, but recognize, the validity of the proposition that plaintiffs have from the beginning profited by, if they have not lately, officially, participated in, the general policy of expansion pursued by this corporation. We do not lose sight of the fact that it had been, upon an occasion, agreeable to the plaintiffs to increase the capital stock to $100,000,000 by a stock dividend of $98,000,000. These things go only to answer other contentions now made by plaintiffs, and do not and cannot operate to estop them to demand proper dividends upon the stock they own. It is obvious that an annual dividend of 60 per cent. upon $2,000,000, or $1,200,000, is the equivalent of a very small dividend upon $100,000,000, or more.

The decree of the court below fixing and determining the specific amount to be distributed to stockholders is affirmed. In other respects, except as to the allowance of costs, the said decree is reversed.

E. THE INTERNAL AFFAIRS DOCTRINE

The traditional internal affairs doctrine is alive and well in nearly all states, including Delaware. Simply stated, the doctrine provides that the law of the state of incorporation will govern any matter related to the internal affairs of the corporation. Internal affairs generally include matters involving the relationship between the corporation and its officers, directors, and shareholders. Common examples of internal affairs subject to the doctrine include voting rights, the rights and liabilities of directors and officers, shareholder rights, distributions, indemnifications, mergers, and derivative litigation.

The internal affairs doctrine does not apply to matters unrelated to internal corporate relationships or procedures, such as taxes, antitrust, employment matters, environmental issues, securities laws, intellectual property matters, consumer protection, and most tort and contract claims.

Two states– California and New York – have statutes that apply their corporate law to resolve specific internal affairs of a corporation organized in another state (a "pseudo-foreign" corporation) that conducts most of its activities in California or New York, as the case may be, and has most of its outstanding stock owned by residents of the state. These pseudo-foreign corporation statutes will likely govern the outcome of any litigation in California or New York courts, but it is highly unlikely that they will have a controlling impact in a dispute that breaks out in another state.

For planning purposes, a legal advisor needs to understand the scope and impact of the internal affairs doctrine and potential wrinkles that may be triggered in New York or California under specific conditions. And, as discussed in Chapter 6, the legal advisor usually plays a key role in helping the client select the state of incorporation for the business.

MCDERMOTT INC. v. LEWIS
531 A.2d 206 (Del. 1987)

MOORE, Justice

We confront an important issue of first impression-whether a Delaware subsidiary of a Panamanian corporation may vote the shares it holds in its parent company under circumstances which are prohibited by Delaware law, but not the law of Panama. Necessarily, this involves questions of foreign law, and applicability of the internal affairs doctrine under Delaware law.

Plaintiffs, Harry Lewis and Nina Altman, filed these consolidated suits in the Court of Chancery in December, 1982 seeking to enjoin or rescind the 1982

Reorganization under which McDermott Incorporated, a Delaware corporation ("McDermott Delaware"), became a 92%-owned subsidiary of McDermott International, Inc., a Panamanian corporation ("International"). Lewis and Altman are stockholders of McDermott Delaware, which emerged from the Reorganization owning approximately 10% of International's common stock. Plaintiffs challenged this aspect of the Reorganization, and the Court of Chancery granted partial summary judgment in their favor, holding that McDermott Delaware could not vote its stock in International.

We conclude that the trial court erred in refusing to apply the law of Panama to the internal affairs of International. There was no nexus between International and the State of Delaware. Moreover, plaintiffs concede that the issues here do not involve the internal affairs of McDermott Delaware. We reaffirm the principle that the internal affairs doctrine is a major tenet of Delaware corporation law having important federal constitutional underpinnings.

International was incorporated in Panama on August 11, 1959, and is principally engaged in providing worldwide marine construction services to the oil and gas industry. Its executive offices are in New Orleans, Louisiana, and there are no operations in Delaware. International does not maintain offices in Delaware, hold meetings or conduct business here, have agents or employees in Delaware, or have any assets here.

McDermott Delaware and its subsidiaries operate throughout the United States in three principal industry segments: marine construction services, power generation systems and equipment, and engineered materials. McDermott Delaware's principal offices are in New Orleans.

Following the 1982 Reorganization, McDermott Delaware became a 92%-owned subsidiary of International. The public stockholders of International hold approximately 90% of the voting power of International, while McDermott Delaware holds about 10%.

The stated "principal purpose" of the reorganization, according to International's prospectus, was to enable the McDermott Group to retain, reinvest and redeploy earnings from operations outside the United States without subjecting such earnings to United States income tax. The prospectus also admitted that the 10% voting interest given to McDermott Delaware would be voted by International, "and such voting power could be used to oppose an attempt by a third party to acquire control of International if the management of International believes such use of the voting power would be in the best interests of the stockholders of International." An exchange offer, and thus the Reorganization, was supported by 89.59% of McDermott Delaware stockholders.

The applicable Panamanian law is set forth in the record by affidavits and opinion letters of Ricardo A. Durling, Esquire, and the deans of two Panamanian law schools, to support the claim that McDermott Delaware's retention of a 10% interest in International, and its right to vote those shares, is permitted by the laws of Panama. Significantly, the plaintiffs have not offered any contrary evidence...

We note at the outset that if International were incorporated either in

Delaware or Louisiana, its stock could not be voted by a majority-owned subsidiary. No United States jurisdiction of which we are aware permits that practice.

Relying on Norlin Corp. v. Rooney, Pace Inc., 744 F.2d 255 (2d Cir.1984), the Court of Chancery concluded that Panama in effect would refrain from applying its laws under the facts of this case. On that basis, the trial court then concluded that since both Delaware and Louisiana law prohibit a majority-owned subsidiary from voting its parent's stock, the device was improper. We consider this an erroneous application of both Delaware and Panamanian law..

It is apparent that under limited circumstances the laws of Panama permit a subsidiary to vote the shares of its parent. All three legal experts agreed that McDermott Delaware could vote the shares it held in International. Further, Dean Fernandez specifically stated that it "is a principle of law that in matters of public law one can only do what is expressly allowed by the law; while in private law all acts not prohibited by law can be performed." This fully accords with basic principles of Delaware corporate law.

Given the uncontroverted evidence of Panamanian law, establishing that a Panamanian corporation may place voting shares in a majority-owned subsidiary under the limited circumstances provided by Article 37, we turn to the fundamental issues presented by application of the internal affairs doctrine.

Internal corporate affairs involve those matters which are peculiar to the relationships among or between the corporation and its current officers, directors, and shareholders. The internal affairs doctrine requires that the law of the state of incorporation should determine issues relating to internal corporate affairs. Under Delaware conflict of laws principles and the United States Constitution, there are appropriate circumstances which mandate application of this doctrine.

Delaware's well established conflict of laws principles require that the laws of the jurisdiction of incorporation-here the Republic of Panama-govern this dispute involving McDermott International's voting rights...

The traditional conflicts rule developed by courts has been that internal corporate relationships are governed by the laws of the forum of incorporation. As early as 1933, the Supreme Court of the United States noted:

> It has long been settled doctrine that a court-state or federal-sitting in one state will, as a general rule, decline to interfere with, or control by injunction or otherwise, the management of the internal affairs of a corporation organized under the laws of another state but will leave controversies as to such matters to the courts of the state of the domicile.

Rogers v. Guaranty Trust Co. of New York, 288 U.S. 123, 130 (1933)

A review of cases over the last twenty-six years, however, finds that in all but a few, the law of the state of incorporation was applied without any discussion.

The policy underlying the internal affairs doctrine is an important one, and we decline to erode the principle:

> Under the prevailing conflicts practice, neither courts nor legislatures have maximized the imposition of local corporate policy on foreign corporations but have consistently applied the law of the state of incorporation to the entire gamut of internal corporate affairs. In many cases, this is a wise, practical, and equitable choice. It serves the vital need for a single, constant and equal law to avoid the fragmentation of continuing, interdependent internal relationships. The lex incorporationis, unlike the lex loci delicti, is not a rule based merely on the priori concept of territoriality and on the desirability of avoiding forum-shopping. It validates the autonomy of the parties in a subject where the underlying policy of the law is enabling. It facilitates planning and enhances predictability. In fields like torts, where the typical dispute involves two persons and a single or simple one-shot issue and where the common substantive policy is to spread the loss through compensation and insurance, the preference for forum law and the emphasis on the state interest in forum residents which are the common denominators of the new conflicts methodologies do not necessarily lead to unacceptable choices. By contrast, applying local internal affairs law to a foreign corporation just because it is amenable to process in the forum or because it has some local shareholders or some other local contact is apt to produce inequalities, intolerable confusion, and uncertainty, and intrude into the domain of other states that have a superior claim to regulate the same subject matter....

Kozyris, [*Corporate Wars and Choice of Law, 1985 Duke L.J. 1*] at 98.

Given the significance of these considerations, application of the internal affairs doctrine is not merely a principle of conflicts law. It is also one of serious constitutional proportions-under due process, the commerce clause and the full faith and credit clause-so that the law of one state governs the relationships of a corporation to its stockholders, directors and officers in matters of internal corporate governance. The alternatives present almost intolerable consequences to the corporate enterprise and its managers. With the existence of multistate and multinational organizations, directors and officers have a significant right, under the fourteenth amendment's due process clause, to know what law will be applied to their actions. Stockholders also have a right to know by what standards of accountability they may hold those managing the corporation's business and affairs. That is particularly so here, given the significant fact that in the McDermott Group reorganization, and after full disclosure, 89.59% of the total outstanding common shares of McDermott Delaware were tendered in the exchange offer.

Addressing the facts originally presented to the trial court and to us, we must conclude that due process and the commerce clause, in addition to principles of Delaware conflicts law, mandate reversal. Due process requires that directors, officers and shareholders be given adequate notice of the jurisdiction whose laws will ultimately govern the corporation's internal affairs. Under such circumstances, application of 8 Del.C. § 160(c) to International would unfairly and, in our opinion, unconstitutionally, subject those intimately involved with the management of the corporation to the laws of Delaware.

Moreover, application of Section 160(c) to International would violate the commerce clause. Delaware and Panama law clearly differ in their treatment of a subsidiary's voting rights under the facts originally presented here. For Delaware now to interfere in the internal affairs of a foreign corporation having no relationship whatever to this State clearly implies that International can be subjected to the differing laws of all fifty states on various matters respecting its internal affairs. Such a prohibitive burden has obvious commerce clause implications, and could not pass constitutional muster.

VANTAGEPOINT VENTURE PARTNERS 1996 V. EXAMEN, INC.
871 A.2d 1108 (Del. 2005)

HOLLAND, Justice

This is an expedited appeal from the Court of Chancery following the entry of a final judgment on the pleadings. We have concluded that the judgment must be affirmed.

Examen was a Delaware corporation engaged in the business of providing web-based legal expense management solutions to a growing list of Fortune 1000 customers throughout the United States. Following consummation of the merger on April 5, 2005, LexisNexis Examen, also a Delaware corporation, became the surviving entity. VantagePoint is a Delaware Limited Partnership organized and existing under the laws of Delaware. VantagePoint, a major venture capital firm that purchased Examen Series A Preferred Stock in a negotiated transaction, owned eighty-three percent of Examen's outstanding Series A Preferred Stock (909,091 shares) and no shares of Common Stock.

On February 17, 2005, Examen and Reed Elsevier executed the Merger Agreement, which was set to expire on April 15, 2005, if the merger had not closed by that date. Under the Delaware General Corporation Law and Examen's Certificate of Incorporation, including the Certificate of Designations for the Series A Preferred Stock, adoption of the Merger Agreement required the affirmative vote of the holders of a majority of the issued and outstanding shares of the Common Stock and Series A Preferred Stock, voting together as a single class. Holders of Series A Preferred Stock had the number of votes equal to the number of shares of Common Stock they would have held if their Preferred Stock was converted. Thus, VantagePoint, which owned 909,091 shares of Series A Preferred Stock and no shares of Common Stock, was entitled to vote based on a converted number of 1,392,727 shares of stock.

There were 9,717,415 total outstanding shares of the Company's capital stock (8,626,826 shares of Common Stock and 1,090,589 shares of Series A Preferred Stock), representing 10,297,608 votes on an as-converted basis. An affirmative vote of at least 5,148,805 shares, constituting a majority of the outstanding voting power on an as-converted basis, was required to approve the merger. If the stockholders were to vote by class, VantagePoint would have controlled 83.4 percent of the Series A Preferred Stock, which would have permitted VantagePoint to block the merger. VantagePoint acknowledges that, if Delaware law applied, it would not have a class vote.

According to VantagePoint, "the issue presented by this case is not a choice of law question, but rather the constitutional issue of whether California may promulgate a narrowly-tailored exception to the internal affairs doctrine that is designed to protect important state interests." VantagePoint submits that "Section 2115 was designed to provide an additional layer of investor protection by mandating that California's heightened voting requirements apply to those few foreign corporations that have chosen to conduct a majority of their business in California and meet the other factual prerequisite of Section 2115." Therefore, VantagePoint argues that "Delaware either must apply the statute if California can validly enact it, or hold the statute unconstitutional if California cannot."

In *CTS Corp. v. Dynamics Corp. of Am.*, 481 U.S. 69, 91, 107 S.Ct. 1637, 95 L.Ed.2d 67 (1987), the United States Supreme Court stated that it is "an accepted part of the business landscape in this country for States to create corporations, to prescribe their powers, and to define the rights that are acquired by purchasing their shares." In CTS, it was also recognized that "[a] State has an interest in promoting stable relationships among parties involved in the corporations it charters, as well as in ensuring that investors in such corporations have an effective voice in corporate affairs." The internal affairs doctrine is a long-standing choice of law principle which recognizes that only one state should have the authority to regulate a corporation's internal affairs-the state of incorporation.

The internal affairs doctrine is not, however, only a conflicts of law principle. Pursuant to the Fourteenth Amendment Due Process Clause, directors and officers of corporations "have a significant right ... to know what law will be applied to their actions" and "[s]tockholders ... have a right to know by what standards of accountability they may hold those managing the corporation's business and affairs." *McDermott Inc. v. Lewis,* 531 A.2d 206, 216 (Del.1987). Under the Commerce Clause, a state "has no interest in regulating the internal affairs of foreign corporations." Id. at 217. Therefore, this Court has held that an "application of the internal affairs doctrine is mandated by constitutional principles, except in the 'rarest situations,' " e.g., when "the law of the state of incorporation is inconsistent with a national policy on foreign or interstate commerce." Id.

VantagePoint argues that section 2115 "mandates application of certain enumerated provisions of California's corporation law to the internal affairs of 'foreign' corporations if certain narrow factual prerequisites [set forth in section 2115] are met." Under the California statute, if more than one half of a foreign corporation's outstanding voting securities are held of record by persons having addresses in California (as disclosed on the books of the corporation) on the record date, and the property, payroll and sales factor tests are satisfied, then on the first day of the income year, one hundred and thirty five days after the above tests are satisfied, the foreign corporation's articles of incorporation are deemed amended to the exclusion of the law of the state of incorporation. If the factual conditions precedent for triggering section 2115 are established, many aspects of a corporation's internal affairs are purportedly governed by California corporate law to the exclusion of the law of the state of incorporation.

Examen is a Delaware corporation. The legal issue in this case-whether a preferred shareholder of a Delaware corporation had the right, under the corporation's Certificate of Designations, to a Series A Preferred Stock class vote on a merger-clearly involves the relationship among a corporation and its shareholders. As the United States Supreme Court held in CTS, "[n]o principle of corporation law and practice is more firmly established than a State's authority to regulate domestic corporations, including the authority to define the voting rights of shareholders."

In CTS, the Supreme Court held that the Commerce Clause "prohibits States from regulating subjects that 'are in their nature national, or admit only of one uniform system, or plan of regulation,' " and acknowledged that the internal affairs of a corporation are subjects that require one uniform system of regulation. 481 U.S, at 89. In CTS, the Supreme Court concluded that "[s]o long as each State regulates voting rights only in the corporations it has created, each corporation will be subject to the law of only one State." Id. Accordingly, we hold Delaware's well-established choice of law rules and the federal constitution mandated that Examen's internal affairs, and in particular, VantagePoint's voting rights, be adjudicated exclusively in accordance with the law of its state of incorporation, in this case, the law of Delaware.

CASE PROBLEM 3-1

Five individuals are about to form a new corporation that will offer a unique fleet marketing service to car dealerships in states A and B. Each of the key players will own 20 percent of the company's outstanding stock. Four of the five will live in state A and manage the company's operations in state A. The fifth team member, Joe, resides in state B and will manage all operations in state B. The parties anticipate that approximately 25 percent of the company's business will come from state B.

As regards Joe, the other four shareholders are concerned that he might try to break off and take the business in State B for himself once the operation is fully established. Joe is an aggressive performer, but his track record reeks of greed, and loyalty has never been a priority. For this reason, the other shareholders want some protection against Joe trying to "confiscate" the state B business down the road.

State A has a well-established body of employment law that enforces non-competition agreements. State B has a public policy against enforcing such agreements under its employment laws. State B's business corporation act contains the following statute:

1.   An agreement among the shareholders of a corporation that complies with this section is effective among the shareholders and the corporation even though it is inconsistent with one or more other provisions of this title in that it establishes the terms and conditions of

any agreement for the transfer of property (including shares of stock of the corporation) or the provision of services between the corporation and any shareholder, director, or officer of the corporation or among any of them.

2. An agreement authorized by this section shall be (a) set forth in a written agreement that is signed by all persons who are shareholders at the time of the agreement and is made known to the corporation, (b) subject to amendment only by all persons who are shareholders at the time of the amendment, and (c) valid for ten years, unless the agreement provides otherwise.

State A has a similar statute that contains the following additional condition:

3.   If all of the common stock of a corporation owned by any shareholder who owns less than 25 percent of the corporation's outstanding common stock is acquired by the corporation or the other shareholders pursuant to the terms of such an agreement, such selling shareholder shall have the right to demand that the corporation, at its expense, employ a business appraiser acceptable to the corporation and the selling shareholder for the purposes of establishing a fair price for the stock. The determination of any such appraiser will be controlling between the parties. If the parties are unable to agree on a mutually acceptable appraiser, the selling shareholder may petition the Superior Court to appoint an appraiser.

You represent the other four shareholders. As regards the fears about Joe, should the new corporation be organized in state A or state B? Depending on which state is selected, how would you recommend dealing with such fears?

F. THE BUSINESS JUDGMENT RULE

BAYER v. BAYER
49 N.Y.S.2d 2 (Sup. Ct. 1944)

SHIENTAG, Justice

There derivative stockholders' suits present for review two transactions upon which plaintiffs seek to charge the individual defendants, who are directors, with liability in favor of the corporate defendant, the Celanese Corporation of America.

Directors of a business corporation are not trustees and are not held to strict accountability as such. Nevertheless, their obligations are analogous to those of trustees. Directors are agents; they are fiduciaries. The fiduciary has two paramount obligations: responsibility and loyalty. Those obligations apply with equal force to the humblest agent or broker and to the director of a great and powerful corporation. They lie at the very foundation of our whole system of free private enterprise and are as fresh and significant today as when they were formulated decades ago. The responsibility—that is, the care and the diligence—required of an agent or of a fiduciary, is proportioned to the occasion. It is a concept that has, and necessarily so, a wide penumbra of meaning—a concept, however, which becomes sharpened in its practical application to the given facts of a situation.

The concept of loyalty, of constant, unqualified fidelity, has a definite and precise meaning. The fiduciary must subordinate his individual and private interests to his duty to the corporation whenever the two conflict. In an address delivered in 1934, Mr. Justice, now Chief Justice, Stone declared that the fiduciary principle of undivided loyalty was, in effect, 'the precept as old as Holy Writ, that 'a man cannot serve two masters'. More than a century ago equity gave a hospitable reception to that principle and the common law was not slow to follow in giving it recognition. No thinking man can believe that an economy built upon a business foundation can long endure without loyalty to that principle'. He went on to say that 'The separation of ownership from management, the development of the corporate structure so as to vest in small groups control of resources of great numbers of small and uninformed investors, make imperative a fresh and active devotion to that principle if the modern world of business is to perform its proper function'.

A director is not an insurer. On the one hand, he is not called upon to use an extraordinary degree of care and prudence; and on the other hand it is established by the cases that it is not enough for a director to be honest, that fraud is not the orbit of his liability. The director may not act as a dummy or a figurehead. He is called upon to use care, to exercise judgment, the decree of care, the kind of judgment that one would give in similar situations to the conduct of his own affairs.

The director of a business corporation is given a wide latitude of action. The law does not seek to deprive him of initiative and daring and vision. Business has its adventures, its bold adventures; and those who in good faith, and in the interests of the corporation they serve, embark upon them, are not to be penalized if failure, rather than success, results from their efforts. The law will not permit a course of conduct by directors, which would be applauded if it succeeded, to be condemned with a riot of adjectives simply because it failed. Directors of a commercial corporation may take chances, the same kind of chances that a man would take in his own business. Because they are given this wide latitude, the law will not hold directors liable for honest errors, for mistakes of judgment. The law will not interfere with the internal affairs of a corporation so long as it is managed by its directors pursuant to a free, honest exercise of judgment uninfluenced by personal, or by any considerations other than the welfare of the corporation.

To encourage freedom of action on the part of directors, or to put it another way, to discourage interference with the exercise of their free and independent judgment, there has grown up what is known as the 'business judgment rule'. *Gamble v. Queens County Water Co.*, 123 N.Y. 91, 99, 25 N.E. 201, 202, 9 L.R.A. 527; *Weinberger v. Quinn*, 264 App. Div. 405, 408, 35 N.Y.S.2d 567, 570. 'Questions of policy of management, expediency of contracts or action, adequacy of consideration, lawful appropriation of corporate funds to advance corporate interests, are left solely to their honest and unselfish decision, for their powers therein are without limitation and free from restraint, and the exercise of them for the common and general interests of the corporation may not be questioned, although the results show that what they did was unwise or inexpedient.' *Pollitz v. Wabash R. Co.*, 207 N.Y. 113, 124, 100 N.E. 721, 724. Indeed, although the concept of 'responsibility' is firmly fixed in the law, it is only in a most unusual and extraordinary case that directors are held liable for negligence in the absence of fraud, or improper motive, or personal interest.

The 'business judgment rule', however, yields to the rule of undivided loyalty. This great rule of law is designed 'to avoid the possibility of fraud and to avoid the temptation of self-interest.' It is 'designed to obliterate all divided loyalties which may creep into a fiduciary relation. 'Included within its scope is every situation in which a trustee chooses to deal with another in such close relation with the trustee that possible advantage to such other person might influence, consciously or unconsciously, the judgment of the trustee. The dealings of a director with the corporation for which he is the fiduciary are therefore viewed 'with jealousy by the courts.' Such personal transactions of directors with their corporations, such transactions as may tend to produce a conflict between self-interest and fiduciary obligation, are, when challenged, examined with the most scrupulous care, and if there is any evidence of improvidence or oppression, any indication of unfairness or undue advantage, the transactions will be voided. 'Their dealings with the corporation are subjected to rigorous scrutiny and where any of their contracts or engagements with the corporation are challenged the burden is on the director not only to prove the good faith of the transaction but also to show its inherent fairness from the viewpoint of the corporation and those interested therein.'

While there is a high moral purpose implicit in this transcendent fiduciary principle of undivided loyalty, it has back of it a profound understanding of human nature and of its frailties. It actually accomplishes a practical, beneficent purpose. It tends to prevent a clouded conception of fidelity that blurs the vision. It preserves the free exercise of judgment uncontaminated by the dross of divided allegiance or self-interest. It prevents the operation of an influence that may be indirect but that is all the more potent for that reason. The law has set its face firmly against undermining 'the rule of undivided loyalty by the 'disintegrating erosion' of particular exceptions.'

The first, or 'advertising', cause of action charges the directors with negligence, waste and improvidence in embarking the corporation upon a radio advertising program beginning in 1942 and costing about $1,000,000 a year. It is further charged that they were negligent in selecting the type of program and in renewing the radio contract for 1943. More serious than these allegations is the charge that the directors were motivated by a noncorporate purpose in causing the radio program to be undertaken and in expending large sums of money therefore. It is claimed that this radio advertising was for the benefit of Miss Jean Tennyson, one of the singers on the program, who in private life is Mrs. Camille Dreyfus, the wife of the president of the company and one of its directors; that it was undertaken to 'further, foster and subsidize her career'; to 'furnish a vehicle' for her talents.

Eliminating for the moment the part played by Miss Tennyson in the radio advertising campaign, it is clear that the character of the advertising, the amount to be expended therefore, and the manner in which it should be used, are all matters of business judgment and rest peculiarly within the discretion of the board of directors. Under the authorities previously cited, it is not, generally speaking, the function of a court of equity to review these matters or even to consider them. Had the wife of the president of the company not been involved, the advertising cause of action could have been disposed of summarily. Her connection with the program, however, makes it necessary to go into the facts in some detail.

So far, there is nothing on which to base any claim of breach of fiduciary duty. Some care, diligence and prudence were exercised by these directors before they committed the company to the radio program. It was for the directors to determine whether they would resort to radio advertising; it was for them to conclude how much to spend; it was for them to decide the kind of program they would use. It would be an unwarranted act of interference for any court to attempt to substitute its judgment on these points for that of the directors, honestly arrived at. The expenditure was not reckless or unconscionable. Indeed, it bore a fair relationship to the total amount of net sales and to the earnings of the company. The fact that the company had offers of more business than it could handle did not, in law, preclude advertising.

Many corporations not now doing any business in their products because of emergency conditions advertise those products extensively in order to preserve the good will, the public interest, during the war period. The fact that the company's product may not now be identifiable did not bar advertising calculated to induce consumer demand for such identification. That a program of classical and semiclassical music was selected, rather than a variety program, or a news commentator program, furnishes no ground for legal complaint. True, variety programs have a wider popular appeal than do musicals, but it would be a very sad thing if the former were the only kind of radio programs to be used. Some of the largest industrial concerns in the country have recognized this and have maintained fine musical programs on the radio for many years.

Now we have to take up an unfortunate incident, one which cannot be viewed with the complacency displayed by some of the directors of the company. This is not a closely held family corporation. The Doctors Dreyfus and their families own about 135,000 shares of common stock, the other directors about 10,000 shares out of a total outstanding issue of 1,376,500 shares. Some of these other directors were originally employed by Dr. Camille Dreyfus, the president of the company. His wife, to whom he has been married for about twelve years, is known professionally as Miss Jean Tennyson and is a singer of wide experience.

Dr. Dreyfus, as was natural, consulted his wife about the proposed radio program; he also asked the advertising agency, that had been retained, to confer with her about it. She suggested the names of the artists, all stars of the Metropolitan Opera Company, and the name of the conductor, prominent in his field. She also offered her own services as a paid artist. All of her suggestions as to personnel were adopted by the advertising agency.

While the record shows Miss Tennyson to be a competent singer, there is nothing to indicate that she was indispensable or essential to the success of the program. She received $500 an evening. It would be far-fetched to suggest that the directors caused the company to incur large expenditures for radio advertising to enable the president's wife to make $24,000 in 1942 and $20,500 in 1943.

Of course it is not improper to appoint relatives of officers or directors to responsible positions in a company. But where a close relative of the chief executive officer of a corporation, and one of its dominant directors, takes a position closely associated with a new and expensive field of activity, the motives of the directors are likely to be questioned. The board would be placed in a position where selfish, personal interests might be in conflict with the duty it owed to the corporation. That being so, the entire transaction, if challenged in the courts, must be subjected to the most rigorous scrutiny to determine whether the action of the directors was intended or calculated 'to subserve some outside purpose, regardless of the consequences to the company, and in a manner inconsistent with its interests.'

After such careful scrutiny I have concluded that, up to the present, there has been no breach of fiduciary duty on the part of the directors. The president undoubtedly knew that his wife might be one of the paid artists on the program. The other directors did not know this until they had approved the campaign of radio advertising and the general type of radio program.

The evidence fails to show that the program was designed to foster or subsidize 'the career of Miss Tennyson as an artist' or to 'furnish a vehicle for her talents'. That her participation in the program may have enhanced her prestige as a singer is no ground for subjecting the directors to liability, as long as the advertising served a legitimate and a useful corporate purpose and the company received the full benefit thereof.

The musical quality of 'Celanese Hour' has not been challenged, nor does the record contain anything reflecting on Miss Tennyson's competence as an artist. There is nothing in the testimony to show that some other soprano would have enhanced the artistic quality of the program or its advertising appeal. There is no suggestion that the present program is inefficient or that its cost is disproportionate to what a program of that character reasonably entails.

Miss Tennyson's contract with the advertising agency retained by the directors was on a standard form, negotiated through her professional agent. Her compensation, as well as that of the other artists, was in conformity with that paid for comparable work. She received less than any of the other artists on the program. Although she appeared with a greater regularity than any other singer, she received no undue prominence, no special build-up. Indeed, all of the artists were subordinated to the advertisement of the company and of its products. The company was featured. It appears also that the popularity of the program has increased since it was inaugurated.

It is clear, therefore, that the directors have not been guilty of any breach of fiduciary duty, in embarking upon the program of radio advertising and in renewing it. It is unfortunate that they have allowed themselves to be placed in a position where their motives concerning future decisions on radio advertising may be impugned. The free mind should be ever jealous of its freedom. 'Power of control carries with it a trust or duty to exercise that power faithfully to promote the corporate interests, and the courts of this State will insist upon scrupulous performance of that duty.' Thus far, that duty has been performed and with noteworthy success. The corporation has not, up to the present time, been wronged by the radio advertising attacked in the complaints.

CASE PROBLEM 3-2

CompuSolve Inc. is a privately owned corporation that provides computer upgrade and maintenance services to a wide range of small and medium sized businesses. CompuSolve has 130 employees who are managed by Betty, the president and CEO, and Linda, the chief operating officer.

CompuSolve has 1,000 shares of voting common stock and 1,000 shares of non-voting common outstanding. Betty and Linda each own 200 shares of voting common and 200 shares of non-voting common. The remaining 600 shares of voting common is owned by Judd Wall, a wealthy investor who provided the initial funding for the company and serves as the chairman of the company's board of directors. Judd is not employed by the company. The remaining 600 non-voting shares are owned by Judd's two adult children, Sam and Lucy, neither of whom work for the company. As the majority owner of the voting shares, Judd has the power to elect the board of directors. There has always been a three-person board, composed of Judd, Sam and Lucy.

Judd and his wife Jane are very active in the community. They are wealthy by local standards. While they appreciate the dividend income that CompuSolve produces like clockwork each year, it is not a substantial component of their overall wealth.

Judd and Jane have decided that it's time to take their "giving back" commitment to a higher level. To this end, Judd has proposed two changes at CompuSolve, both of which were rubber stamped by his two children as directors in a 10-minute telephone conversation. First, old usable computer equipment that CompuSolve retrieves from a new upgrade or installation will be donated to local schools. Many clients do not want to mess with this equipment and agree to transfer it to CompuSolve as part of their contract with CompuSolve. CompuSolve has outlets for selling such equipment and generating extra revenues. Judd's proposal would eliminate this source of additional revenue. Second, Judd wants CompuSolve to commit to use up to seven percent of its capacity to provide free computer system maintenance services to local schools.

The proposals have made Betty and Linda fighting mad. According to their calculations, Judd's proposals would reduce revenues by 14 percent and slash the company's bottom line income and shareholder dividends by 35 percent. For Betty and Linda, their dividend income from CompuSolve is a major portion of their incomes. When Betty and Linda confronted Judd, he just exclaimed, "We've been blessed with a solid, profitable business, and the Board is convinced that it's time for us all to give back more." Betty sat silent as Linda blurted, "No, it's time for you to become a bigger deal with your wealthy buddies at our expense."

Judd has sought your advice. Primarily, he wants to know if Betty and Linda have any rights as minority shareholders that could disrupt his plans. Beyond this, he would appreciate any advice as to steps that he should take to strengthen his legal position. As for losing Betty or Linda, he is not concerned. Even with the projected cut in dividends, each of them will be earning far more than they could hope to earn outside the company. And if one of them chose to leave, the company's operations would not be adversely impacted because there is a stable of talented players.

SHLENSKY v. WRIGLEY
95 Ill.App.2d 173, 237 N.E.2d 776 (1968)

SULLIVAN, Justice

This is an appeal from a dismissal of plaintiff's amended complaint on motion of the defendants. The action was a stockholders' derivative suit against the directors for negligence and mismanagement. The corporation was also made a defendant. Plaintiff sought damages and an order that defendants cause the installation of lights in Wrigley Field and the scheduling of night baseball games.

Plaintiff is a minority stockholder of defendant corporation, Chicago National League Ball Club (Inc.), a Delaware corporation with its principal place of business in Chicago, Illinois. Defendant corporation owns and operates the major league professional baseball team known as the Chicago Cubs. The corporation also engages in the operation of Wrigley Field, the Cubs' home park, the concessionaire sales during Cubs' home games, television and radio broadcasts of Cubs' home games, the leasing of the field for football games and other events and receives its share, as visiting team, of admission moneys from games played in other National League stadia. The individual defendants are directors of the Cubs and have served for varying periods of years. Defendant Philip K. Wrigley is also president of the corporation and owner of approximately 80% of the stock therein.

Plaintiff alleges that since night baseball was first played in 1935 nineteen of the twenty major league teams have scheduled night games. In 1966, out of a total of 1620 games in the major leagues, 932 were played at night. Plaintiff alleges that every member of the major leagues, other than the Cubs, scheduled substantially all of its home games in 1966 at night, exclusive of opening days, Saturdays, Sundays, holidays and days prohibited by league rules. Allegedly this has been done for the specific purpose of maximizing attendance and thereby maximizing revenue and income.

The Cubs, in the years 1961-65, sustained operating losses from its direct baseball operations. Plaintiff attributes those losses to inadequate attendance at Cubs' home games. He concludes that if the directors continue to refuse to install lights at Wrigley Field and schedule night baseball games, the Cubs will continue to sustain comparable losses and its financial condition will continue to deteriorate.

Plaintiff alleges that, except for the year 1963, attendance at Cubs' home games has been substantially below that at their road games, many of which were played at night.

Plaintiff compares attendance at Cubs' games with that of the Chicago White Sox, an American League club, whose weekday games were generally played at night. The weekend attendance figures for the two teams was similar; however, the White Sox week-night games drew many more patrons than did the Cubs' weekday games.

Plaintiff alleges that the funds for the installation of lights can be readily obtained through financing and the cost of installation would be far more than offset and recaptured by increased revenues and incomes resulting from the increased attendance.

Plaintiff further alleges that defendant Wrigley has refused to install lights, not because of interest in the welfare of the corporation but because of his personal opinions 'that baseball is a 'daytime sport' and that the installation of lights and night baseball games will have a deteriorating effect upon the surrounding neighborhood.' It is alleged that he has admitted that he is not interested in whether the Cubs would benefit financially from such action because of his concern for the neighborhood, and that he would be willing for the team to play night games if a new stadium were built in Chicago.

Plaintiff alleges that the other defendant directors, with full knowledge of the foregoing matters, have acquiesced in the policy laid down by Wrigley and have permitted him to dominate the board of directors in matters involving the installation of lights and scheduling of night games, even though they knew he was not motivated by a good faith concern as to the best interests of defendant corporation, but solely by his personal views set forth above. It is charged that the directors are acting for a reason or reasons contrary and wholly unrelated to the business interests of the corporation; that such arbitrary and capricious acts constitute mismanagement and waste of corporate assets, and that the directors have been negligent in failing to exercise reasonable care and prudence in the management of the corporate affairs.

The question on appeal is whether plaintiff's amended complaint states a cause of action. It is plaintiff's position that fraud, illegality and conflict of interest are not the only bases for a stockholder's derivative action against the directors. Contrariwise, defendants argue that the courts will not step in and interfere with honest business judgment of the directors unless there is a showing of fraud, illegality or conflict of interest.

The cases in this area are numerous and each differs from the others on a factual basis. However, the courts have pronounced certain ground rules which appear in all cases and which are then applied to the given factual situation. The court in Wheeler v. Pullman Iron and Steel Company, 143 Ill. 197, 207, 32 N.E. 420, 423, said:

'It is, however, fundamental in the law of corporations, that the majority of its stockholders shall control the policy of the corporation, and regulate and govern the lawful exercise of its franchise and business. * * * Every one purchasing or subscribing for stock in a corporation impliedly agrees that he will be bound by the acts and proceedings done or sanctioned by a majority of the shareholders, or by the agents of the corporation duly chosen by such majority, within the scope of the powers conferred by the charter, and courts of equity will not undertake to control the policy or business methods of a corporation, although it may be seen that a wiser policy might be adopted and the business more successful if other methods were pursued. The majority of shares of its stock, or the agents by the holders thereof lawfully chosen, must be permitted to control the business of the corporation in their discretion, when not in violation of its charter or some public law, or corruptly and fraudulently subversive of the rights and interests of the corporation or of a shareholder.'

The standards set in Delaware are also clearly stated in the cases. In Davis v. Louisville Gas & Electric Co., 16 Del.Ch. 157, 142 A. 654, a minority shareholder sought to have the directors enjoined from amending the certificate of incorporation. The court said on page 659:

'We have then a conflict in view between the responsible managers of a corporation and an overwhelming majority of its stockholders on the one hand and a dissenting minority on the other-a conflict touching matters of business policy, such as has occasioned innumerable applications to courts to intervene and determine which of the two conflicting views should prevail. The response which courts make to such applications is that it is not their function to resolve for corporations questions of policy and business management. The directors are chosen to pass upon such questions and their judgment unless shown to be tainted with fraud is accepted as final. The judgment of the directors of corporations enjoys the benefit of a presumption that it was formed in good faith and was designed to promote the best interests of the corporation they serve.'

Plaintiff in the instant case argues that the directors are acting for reasons unrelated to the financial interest and welfare of the Cubs. However, we are not satisfied that the motives assigned to Philip K. Wrigley, and through him to the other directors, are contrary to the best interests of the corporation and the stockholders. For example, it appears to us that the effect on the surrounding neighborhood might well be considered by a director who was considering the patrons who would or would not attend the games if the park were in a poor neighborhood. Furthermore, the long run interest of the corporation in its property value at Wrigley Field might demand all efforts to keep the neighborhood from deteriorating. By these thoughts we do not mean to say that we have decided that the decision of the directors was a correct one. That is beyond our jurisdiction and ability. We are merely saying that the decision is one properly before directors and the motives alleged in the amended complaint showed no fraud, illegality or conflict of interest in their making of that decision.

While all the courts do not insist that one or more of the three elements must be present for a stockholder's derivative action to lie, nevertheless we feel that unless the conduct of the defendants at least borders on one of the elements, the courts should not interfere. The trial court in the instant case acted properly in dismissing plaintiff's amended complaint.

Finally, we do not agree with plaintiff's contention that failure to follow the example of the other major league clubs in scheduling night games constituted negligence. Plaintiff made no allegation that these teams' night schedules were profitable or that the purpose for which night baseball had been undertaken was fulfilled. Furthermore, it cannot be said that directors, even those of corporations that are losing money, must follow the lead of the other corporations in the field. Directors are elected for their business capabilities and judgment and the courts cannot require them to forego their judgment because of the decisions of directors of other companies. Courts may not decide these questions in the absence of a clear showing of dereliction of duty on the part of the specific directors and mere failure to 'follow the crowd' is not such a dereliction.

For the foregoing reasons the order of dismissal entered by the trial court is affirmed.

G. LIMITED LIABILITY LIMITATIONS

Limited liability is often trumpeted as a supreme benefit of a corporation. If the corporation defaults on a contract or loan, the aggrieved creditor cannot go after the shareholders, directors and officers unless they personally guaranteed the obligation. If an employee, while on the job, injures another in an auto accident, the corporation may be held liable for the employee's actions, but the corporation's shareholders, directors and officers are not exposed personally. As sweet as the corporate shield may appear, it has its limits.

There are various ways that shareholders of a closely held corporation may have personal liability exposure, including the following:

1. Key creditors, such as banks, other lenders, and important vendors often require the personal guarantees of the shareholders as a condition to extending credit.

2. If a shareholder or any person acting on behalf of a corporation negligently injures another, that person cannot escape personal responsibility for his or her tort even though the corporation is also legally responsible.

3. State corporate statutes personally obligate a shareholder, in certain situations, to return any dividend or distribution received by the shareholder if the shareholder, at the time of the distribution, knew that the corporation could not pay its creditors or that the corporation's liabilities exceeded its assets.

4. If a shareholder, acting as a promoter before the corporation is organized, enters into contracts on behalf of a soon-to-be formed corporation and the

corporation is never properly formed or fails to adopt or perform the contract, the shareholder/promoter may have personal liability for the contract. However, if the corporation was never officially formed and the creditor knew that the corporation was going to be the responsible party, courts have sometimes employed a *de facto* corporation doctrine to extend the protection of limited liability and prevent a windfall to the creditor.

5. Corporate directors and officers also face personal liability exposure. Directors may be exposed to shareholders if they violate their fiduciary duties of care and loyalty. Plus, there are various statutory liabilities: corporate state laws usually make directors personally liable if they approve payments to shareholders when the corporation cannot pay its debts or is insolvent; securities laws impose liability for insider trading or not properly disclosing facts; antitrust laws impose liability for price-fixing, market division schemes and other competitor-related activities that hurt the competitive process; tax laws impose personal liability for failing to properly handle employee withholdings; the list goes on.

6. Sometimes shareholders of a closely held corporation face a "piercing the corporate veil" or "alter ego" threat from creditors. The creditors seek to pierce the corporate veil to get to the personal assets of the shareholders, arguing that the corporation and shareholders are one and the same and that there would be an unjust or inequitable outcome if the shareholders escaped personal liability. As the following cases illustrate, it is never an easy burden of proof for the plaintiff-creditor, and there are a host of factors that often come into play.

MBCA § 6.22 Liability of Shareholders

(a) A purchaser from a corporation of its own shares is not liable to the corporation or its creditors with respect to the shares except to pay the consideration for which the shares were authorized to be issued (section 6.21) or specified in the subscription agreement (section 6.20).

(b) Unless otherwise provided in the articles of incorporation, a shareholder of a corporation is not personally liable for the acts or debts of the corporation except that he may become personally liable by reason of his own acts or conduct.

CASE PROBLEM 3-3

Last year Jerry found the yacht of his dreams, a posh 75-foot, 3-year-old pilothouse named "Magic." Jerry was able to purchase Magic for the bargain price of $2 million through a newly-formed corporation. A recently-retired couple, the Morgans, had purchased Magic three years earlier for $3.5 million, with the hope of endless luxury cruising.

The Morgans soon discovered that they could not safely handle their new, expensive toy. It quickly became something to fear, not enjoy. Plus, the moorage and maintenance costs (about $75,000 a year) were intolerable. Magic was soon on the used yacht market, with no interested buyers in a chronically sick economy.

But finally Jerry had surfaced, agreeing to pay $250,000 as a down payment and to provide the Morgans with a 10-year, 6-percent promissory note for $1,750,000 ("Note"). The obligor on the Note was Cruise Luxury, Inc, ("Cruise"), a new corporation that would use Magic 42 weeks a year to provide cruise trips to paying customers. Jerry planned to enjoy Magic for the balance of the time. The Note was guaranteed by Cruises' sole shareholder, Franklin Associates, Inc. ("Franklin"), a corporation that had been in existence for 10 years. Jerry was the sole shareholder of Franklin.

The Morgans weren't excited about the deal, but they figured that they didn't have an alternative for getting clear of their expensive boat. The bulk of the down payment would simply pay broker commissions. But the deal promised to end the high moorage and maintenance costs and to provide the Morgan's with interest and principle payments each month for the next 10 years.

The transaction was closed by the brokers and a yacht title company. Lawyer involvement was minimal. The Note was secured by a first lien on Magic and a guarantee from Franklin. When asked about Franklin, Jerry just said, "It's the company that I have conducted all my business through for years." Since Jerry projected substantial wealth, nothing more was said.

To fund the deal, Jerry contributed $250,000 to Franklin. Franklin loaned the $250,000 to Cruise and put a second lien on Magic (behind the Morgan interest) to secure its loan. Cruise insured Magic for only $1 million and secured $1.2 million of liability insurance.

On Cruise's sixth trip with paying customers, the captain made a fatal error and caused Magic to strike a long underwater cable that attached a tug to a huge barge. Four customers died, six others were seriously injured, and Magic was destroyed.

Cruise's only assets were the insurance proceeds. The $1 million Magic insurance was paid to the Morgans and the liability coverage was available to satisfy customer claims. The Morgans ended up with a loss on the Note in excess of $700,000, and the customers' claims far exceeded the insurance limits.

The focus has quickly turned to Franklin and Jerry. Franklin conducts substantial business (as Jerry represented), but it has never had any significant assets, and its note from Cruise is now worthless. Franklin's income is withdrawn by Jerry as dividends and salaries. Jerry's net worth is around $14 million.

The Morgans and the customers know that their only hope for any recovery is to reach Jerry's personal assets. What are their chances? What additional facts would help in making this assessment? What additional steps could Jerry have taken to help protect against the risks of such attempts to reach his assets?

WALKOVSZKY v. CARLTON
18 N.Y.2d 414, 223 N.E.2d 6 (1966)

FULD, Judge.

This case involves what appears to be a rather common practice in the taxicab industry of vesting the ownership of a taxi fleet in many corporations, each owning only one or two cabs.

The complaint alleges that the plaintiff was severely injured four years ago in New York City when he was run down by a taxicab owned by the defendant Seon Cab Corporation and negligently operated at the time by the defendant Marchese. The individual defendant, Carlton, is claimed to be a stockholder of 10 corporations, including Seon, each of which has but two cabs registered in its name, and it is implied that only the minimum automobile liability insurance required by law (in the amount of $10,000) is carried on any one cab. Although seemingly independent of one another, these corporations are alleged to be 'operated as a single entity, unit and enterprise' with regard to financing, supplies, repairs, employees and garaging, and all are named as defendants. The plaintiff asserts that he is also entitled to hold their stockholders personally liable for the damages sought because the multiple corporate structure constitutes an unlawful attempt 'to defraud members of the general public' who might be injured by the cabs.

The defendant Carlton has moved to dismiss the complaint on the ground that as to him it 'fails to state a cause of action'. The court at Special Term granted the motion but the Appellate Division, by a divided vote, reversed, holding that a valid cause of action was sufficiently stated. The defendant Carlton appeals to us, from the non-final order, by leave of the Appellate Division on a certified question.

The law permits the incorporation of a business for the very purpose of enabling its proprietors to escape personal liability but, manifestly, the privilege is not without its limits. Broadly speaking, the courts will disregard the corporate form, or, to use accepted terminology, 'pierce the corporate veil', whenever necessary 'to prevent fraud or to achieve equity'.   In determining whether liability should be extended to reach assets beyond those belonging to the corporation, we are guided, as Judge Cardozo noted, by 'general rules of agency'. In other words, whenever anyone uses control of the corporation to further his own rather than the corporation's business, he will be liable for the corporation's acts 'upon the principle of Respondeat superior applicable even where the agent is a natural person'. Such liability, moreover, extends not only to the corporation's commercial dealings.

In the 178, the plaintiff was injured as a result of the negligent operation of a cab owned and operated by one of four corporations affiliated with the defendant Terminal. Although the defendant was not a stockholder of any of the operating companies, both the defendant and the operating companies were owned, for the most part, by the same parties. The defendant's name (Terminal) was conspicuously displayed on the sides of all of the taxis used in the enterprise and, in point of fact, the defendant actually serviced, inspected, repaired and dispatched them. These facts were deemed to provide sufficient cause for piercing the corporate veil of the operating company—the nominal owner of the cab which injured the plaintiff—and holding the defendant liable. The operating companies were simply instrumentalities for carrying on the business of the defendant without imposing upon it financial and other liabilities incident to the actual ownership and operation of the cabs.

In the case before us, the plaintiff has explicitly alleged that none of the corporations 'had a separate existence of their own' and, as indicated above, all are named as defendants. However, it is one thing to assert that a corporation is a fragment of a larger corporate combine which actually conducts the business. It is quite another to claim that the corporation is a 'dummy' for its individual stockholders who are in reality carrying on the business in their personal capacities for purely personal rather than corporate ends. Either circumstance would justify treating the corporation as an agent and piercing the corporate veil to reach the principal but a different result would follow in each case. In the first, only a larger Corporate entity would be held financially responsible) while, in the other, the stockholder would be personally liable. Either the stockholder is conducting the business in his individual capacity or he is not. If he is, he will be liable; if he is not, then it does not matter—insofar as his personal liability is concerned—that the enterprise is actually being carried on by a larger 'enterprise entity'.

The individual defendant is charged with having 'organized, managed, dominated and controlled' a fragmented corporate entity but there are no allegations that he was conducting business in his individual capacity. Had the taxicab fleet been owned by a single corporation, it would be readily apparent that the plaintiff would face formidable barriers in attempting to establish personal liability on the part of the corporation's stockholders. The fact that the fleet ownership has been deliberately split up among many corporations does not ease the plaintiff's burden in that respect. The corporate form may not be disregarded merely because the assets of the corporation, together with the mandatory insurance coverage of the vehicle which struck the plaintiff, are insufficient to assure him the recovery sought. If Carlton were to be held individually liable on those facts alone, the decision would apply equally to the thousands of cabs which are owned by their individual drivers who conduct their businesses through corporations. These taxi owner-operators are entitled to form such corporations and we agree with the court at Special Term that, if the insurance coverage required by statute 'is inadequate for the protection of the public, the remedy lies not with the courts but with the Legislature.' It may very well be sound policy to require that certain corporations must take out liability insurance which will afford adequate compensation to their potential tort victims. However, the responsibility for imposing conditions on the privilege of incorporation has been committed by the Constitution to the Legislature and it may not be fairly implied, from any statute, that the Legislature intended, without the slightest discussion or debate, to require of taxi corporations that they carry automobile liability insurance over and above that mandated by the Vehicle and Traffic Law.

This is not to say that it is impossible for the plaintiff to state a valid cause of action against the defendant Carlton. However, the simple fact is that the plaintiff has just not done so here. While the complaint alleges that the separate corporations were undercapitalized and that their assets have been intermingled, it is barren of any 'sufficiently particular(ized) statements' that the defendant Carlton and his associates are actually doing business in their individual capacities, shuttling their personal funds in and out of the corporations 'without regard to formality and to suit their immediate convenience.' Such a 'perversion of the privilege to do business in a corporate form' would justify imposing personal liability on the individual stockholders. Nothing of the sort has in fact been charged, and it cannot reasonably or logically be inferred from the happenstance that the business of Seon Cab Corporation may actually be carried on by a larger corporate entity composed of many corporations which, under general principles of agency, would be liable to each other's creditors in contract and in tort.

In point of fact, the principle relied upon in the complaint to sustain the imposition of personal liability is not agency but fraud. Such a cause of action cannot withstand analysis. If it is not fraudulent for the owner-operator of a single cab corporation to take out only the minimum required liability insurance, the enterprise does not become either illicit or fraudulent merely because it consists of many such corporations. The plaintiff's injuries are the same regardless of whether the cab which strikes him is owned by a single corporation or part of a fleet with ownership fragmented among many corporations. Whatever rights he may be able to assert against parties other than the registered owner of the vehicle come into being not because he has been defrauded but because, under the principle of Respondeat superior, he is entitled to hold the whole enterprise responsible for the acts of its agents.

In sum, then, the complaint falls short of adequately stating a cause of action against the defendant Carlton in his individual capacity.

The order of the Appellate Division should be reversed

KEATING, Judge (dissenting).

The defendant Carlton, the shareholder here sought to be held for the negligence of the driver of a taxicab, was a principal shareholder and organizer of the defendant corporation which owned the taxicab. The corporation was one of 10 organized by the defendant, each containing two cabs and each cab having the 'minimum liability' insurance coverage. The sole assets of these operating corporations are the vehicles themselves and they are apparently subject to mortgages.

From their inception these corporations were intentionally undercapitalized for the purpose of avoiding responsibility for acts which were bound to arise as a result of the operation of a large taxi fleet having cars out on the street 24 hours a day and engaged in public transportation. And during the course of the corporations' existence all income was continually drained out of the corporations for the same purpose.

The issue presented by this action is whether the policy of this State, which affords those desiring to engage in a business enterprise the privilege of limited liability through the use of the corporate device, is so strong that it will permit that privilege to continue no matter how much it is abused, no matter how irresponsibly the corporation is operated, no matter what the cost to the public. I do not believe that it is.

Under the circumstances of this case the shareholders should all be held individually liable to this plaintiff for the injuries he suffered. At least, the matter should not be disposed of on the pleadings by a dismissal of the complaint. 'If a corporation is organized and carries on business without substantial capital in such a way that the corporation is likely to have no sufficient assets available to meet its debts, it is inequitable that shareholders should set up such a flimsy organization to escape personal liability. The attempt to do corporate business without providing any sufficient basis of financial responsibility to creditors is an abuse of the separate entity and will be ineffectual to exempt the shareholders from corporate debts. It is coming to be recognized as the policy of law that shareholders should in good faith put at the risk of the business unincumbered capital reasonably adequate for its prospective liabilities. If capital is illusory or trifling compared with the business to be done and the risks of loss, this is a ground for denying the separate entity privilege.'

In *Minton v. Cavaney*, 56 Cal.2d 576, 15 Cal.Rptr. 641, 364 P.2d 473, the Supreme Court of California had occasion to discuss this problem in a negligence case. The corporation of which the defendant was an organizer, director and officer operated a public swimming pool. One afternoon the plaintiffs' daughter drowned in the pool as a result of the alleged negligence of the corporation. Justice ROGER TRAYNOR, speaking for the court, outlined the applicable law in this area. 'The figurative terminology 'alter ego' and 'disregard of the corporate entity", he wrote, 'is generally used to refer to the various situations that are an abuse of the corporate privilege. * * * The equitable owners of a corporation, for example, are personally liable when they treat the assets of the corporation as their own and add or withdraw capital from the corporation at will * * *; when they hold themselves out as being personally liable for the debts of the corporation * * *; Or when they provide inadequate capitalization and actively participate in the conduct of corporate affairs'. affairs'. 56 Cal.2d, p. 579, 15 Cal.Rptr., p. 643, 364 P.2d p. 475

Examining the facts of the case in light of the legal principles just enumerated, he found that '(it was) undisputed that there was no attempt to provide adequate capitalization. The corporation never had any substantial assets. It leased the pool that it operated, and the lease was forfeited for failure to pay the rent. Its capital was 'trifling compared with the business to be done and the risks of loss". It seems obvious that one of 'the risks of loss' referred to was the possibility of drownings due to the negligence of the corporation. And the defendant's failure to provide such assets or any fund for recovery resulted in his being held personally liable.

The defendant Carlton claims that, because the minimum amount of insurance required by the statute was obtained, the corporate veil cannot and should not be pierced despite the fact that the assets of the corporation which owned the cab were 'trifling compared with the business to be done and the risks of loss' which were certain to be encountered. I do not agree.

The Legislature in requiring minimum liability insurance of $10,000, no doubt, intended to provide at least some small fund for recovery against those individuals and corporations who just did not have and were not able to raise or accumulate assets sufficient to satisfy the claims of those who were injured as a result of their negligence. It certainly could not have intended to shield those individuals who organized corporations, with the specific intent of avoiding responsibility to the public, where the operation of the corporate enterprise yielded profits sufficient to purchase additional insurance. Moreover, it is reasonable to assume that the Legislature believed that those individuals and corporations having substantial assets would take out insurance far in excess of the minimum in order to protect those assets from depletion. Given the costs of hospital care and treatment and the nature of injuries sustained in auto collisions, it would be unreasonable to assume that the Legislature believed that the minimum provided in the statute would in and of itself be sufficient to recompense 'innocent victims of motor vehicle accidents for the injury and financial loss inflicted upon them'.

The defendant contends that a decision holding him personally liable would discourage people from engaging in corporate enterprise. What I would merely hold is that a participating shareholder of a corporation vested with a public interest, organized with capital insufficient to meet liabilities which are certain to arise in the ordinary course of the corporation's business, may be held personally responsible for such liabilities. Where corporate income is not sufficient to cover the cost of insurance premiums above the statutory minimum or where initially adequate finances dwindle under the pressure of competition, bad times or extraordinary and unexpected liability, obviously the shareholder will not be held liable. The only types of corporate enterprises that will be discouraged as a result of a decision allowing the individual shareholder to be sued will be those such as the one in question, designed solely to abuse the corporate privilege at the expense of the public interest.

For these reasons I would vote to affirm the order of the Appellate Division.

SOERRIES v. DANCAUSE
546 S.E.2d 356 (Ga. App. 2001)

ELLINGTON, Judge.

In this dram shop liability case, William A. Soerries appeals from a jury verdict that pierced the corporate veil and held him personally liable for damages. Because we find that the evidence presented supported the jury's verdict, we affirm.

The facts, viewed in a light most favorable to the jury's verdict, show that Soerries was the sole shareholder of Chickasaw Club, Inc., which operated a popular nightclub in Columbus for 23 years until it closed in 1999. At approximately 11:45 p.m. on July 31, 1996, 18-year-old Aubrey Lynn Pursley was intoxicated when she entered the Chickasaw Club. Although a Columbus ordinance prohibits individuals under 21 years old from entering nightclubs, it is undisputed that club employees did not check Pursley's identification to establish her age. A friend testified that Pursley already was intoxicated when she arrived at the club. Even so, friends testified that Pursley drank additional alcohol at the club and was visibly intoxicated when she left at approximately 3:00 a.m. on August 1, 1996. Security videotapes showed that she left the club with a beer in her hand. Shortly thereafter, Pursley was killed when she lost control of her car and struck a tree.

Joseph Dancause, Pursley's stepfather, sued Chickasaw Club, Inc. and Soerries individually for the cost of the car and for punitive damages. Following a trifurcated jury trial, the trial court entered judgment on the jury's verdict, which pierced the corporate veil and found Soerries jointly liable with the corporation for $6,500 in compensatory damages and solely liable for $187,500 in punitive damages. Soerries appeals from this judgment.

Soerries argues that Dancause presented insufficient evidence to justify piercing the corporate veil. We disagree. As we have held:

> The concept of piercing the corporate veil is applied in Georgia to remedy injustices which arise where a party has overextended his privilege in the use of a corporate entity in order to defeat justice, perpetrate fraud or to evade contractual or tort responsibility. Because the cardinal rule of corporate law is that a corporation possesses a legal existence separate and apart from that of its officers and shareholders, the mere operation of corporate business does not render one personally liable for corporate acts. Sole ownership of a corporation by one person or another corporation is not a factor, and neither is the fact that the sole owner uses and controls it to promote his ends. There must be evidence of abuse of the corporate form. Plaintiff must show that the defendant disregarded the separateness of legal entities by commingling on an interchangeable or joint basis or confusing the otherwise separate properties, records or control. In deciding this enumeration of error, we are confronted with two maxims that sometimes conflict. On the one hand, we are mindful that great caution should be exercised by the court in disregarding the corporate entity. On the other, it is axiomatic that when litigated, the issue of piercing the corporate veil is for the jury, unless there is no evidence sufficient to justify disregarding the corporate form.

J-Mart Jewelry Outlets v. Standard Design, 462 S.E.2d 406 (1995).

In this case, the jury heard testimony from Larry Jones, who managed the Chickasaw Club for 20 years. Jones testified that the club was open four nights a week and regularly admitted an average of 250 people who paid cover charges of $3 to $4 each. Additional patrons were also admitted, so that the club sometimes exceeded its capacity of 477 people. According to Jones, he and the other employees were paid each night in cash by Soerries out of the proceeds of the club. Although Jones testified that 1996 was a "bad year" for the corporation and that he was paid between $10,000 and $12,000, corporate payroll records reported his earnings as only $5,690. Jones admitted that Soerries sometimes paid him extra cash that was not reported to the club's bookkeeper.

It is undisputed that Soerries paid his employees, suppliers, and entertainers in cash and not from existing corporate checking accounts. One employee admitted he was paid "under the table." The employee never appeared on corporate payroll records, although Soerries admitted giving him money to help out around the club.

Corporate tax returns showed that, even though the Chickasaw Club was a busy nightclub, it regularly declared business losses. On cross-examination, Soerries failed to explain the substantial difference between reported income on corporate and individual tax returns and evidence regarding cash proceeds from cover charges and alcohol sales. When asked how the club paid its employees and other operating expenses while operating at a loss, Soerries explained that he often paid the corporate expenses out of his personal funds.

Soerries owned the property on which the Chickasaw Club was located and testified that he paid his $4,830 monthly mortgage note from the club's cash proceeds. Although Soerries claimed that the club's payments were rent that he then used to pay the note, personal tax returns showed that he received only $34,173 in rent in 1996, even though the corporation reported paying $43,000 in rent in its 1996 corporate tax return. Further, both figures are significantly less than the $57,960 in rent that would have been due from the corporation, based upon 12 months of $4,830 rental payments. Additional evidence showed that Soerries also owned other rental property in 1996 that would have paid $3,150 per month, making the disparity between his alleged rental earnings and his reported income even greater.

A jury could construe this evidence to demonstrate that Soerries commingled individual and corporate assets by personally assuming the corporation's financial liabilities, waiving corporate rental payments, or using corporate funds to directly pay his personal mortgage notes and other expenses. As such, the totality of the evidence presented raised a jury issue on whether Soerries disregarded the separateness of legal entities by commingling and confusion of properties, records, control, etc. It is obvious that if the individual who is the principal shareholder or owner of the corporation conducts his private and corporate business on an interchangeable or joint basis as if they were one, then he is without standing to complain when an injured party does the same. Under such circumstances, the court may disregard the corporate entity. The question is whether the corporation serves as the alter ego or business conduit of its owner.").

On appeal, we construe all the evidence most strongly in support of the verdict, and if there is evidence to sustain the verdict, we cannot disturb it. We find that the evidence presented was sufficient to support the jury's decision to pierce the corporate veil.

KINNEY SHOE CORP. v. POLAN
939 F.2d 209 (4th Cir. 1991)

CHAPMAN, Senior Circuit Judge:

Plaintiff-appellant Kinney Shoe Corporation ("Kinney") brought this action in the United States District Court for the Southern District of West Virginia against Lincoln M. Polan ("Polan") seeking to recover money owed on a sublease between Kinney and Industrial Realty Company ("Industrial"). Polan is the sole shareholder of Industrial. The district court found that Polan was not personally liable on the lease between Kinney and Industrial. Kinney appeals asserting that the corporate veil should be pierced, and we agree.

The district court based its order on facts which were stipulated by the parties. In 1984 Polan formed two corporations, Industrial and Polan Industries, Inc., for the purpose of re-establishing an industrial manufacturing business. The certificate of incorporation for Polan Industries, Inc. was issued by the West Virginia Secretary of State in November 1984. The following month the certificate of incorporation for Industrial was issued. Polan was the owner of both corporations. Although certificates of incorporation were issued, no organizational meetings were held, and no officers were elected.

In November 1984 Polan and Kinney began negotiating the sublease of a building in which Kinney held a leasehold interest. The building was owned by the Cabell County Commission and financed by industrial revenue bonds issued in 1968 to induce Kinney to locate a manufacturing plant in Huntington, West Virginia. Under the terms of the lease, Kinney was legally obligated to make payments on the bonds on a semi-annual basis through January 1, 1993, at which time it had the right to purchase the property. Kinney had ceased using the building as a manufacturing plant in June 1983.

The term of the sublease from Kinney to Industrial commenced in December 1984, even though the written lease was not signed by the parties until April 5, 1985. On April 15, 1985, Industrial subleased part of the building to Polan Industries for fifty percent of the rental amount due Kinney. Polan signed both subleases on behalf of the respective companies.

Other than the sublease with Kinney, Industrial had no assets, no income and no bank account. Industrial issued no stock certificates because nothing was ever paid in to this corporation. Industrial's only income was from its sublease to Polan Industries, Inc. The first rental payment to Kinney was made out of Polan's personal funds, and no further payments were made by Polan or by Polan Industries, Inc. to either Industrial or to Kinney.

Kinney filed suit against Industrial for unpaid rent and obtained a judgment in the amount of $166,400.00 on June 19, 1987. A writ of possession was issued, but because Polan Industries, Inc. had filed for bankruptcy, Kinney did not gain possession for six months. Kinney leased the building until it was sold on September 1, 1988. Kinney then filed this action against Polan individually to collect the amount owed by Industrial to Kinney. Since the amount to which Kinney is entitled is undisputed, the only issue is whether Kinney can pierce the corporate veil and hold Polan personally liable.

The district court held that Kinney had assumed the risk of Industrial's undercapitalization and was not entitled to pierce the corporate veil. Kinney appeals, and we reverse.

We have long recognized that a corporation is an entity, separate and distinct from its officers and stockholders, and the individual stockholders are not responsible for the debts of the corporation. *See, e.g., DeWitt Truck Brokers, Inc. v. W. Ray Flemming Fruit Co.,* 540 F.2d 681, 683 (4th Cir.1976). This concept, however, is a fiction of the law and it is now well settled, as a general principle, that the fiction should be disregarded when it is urged with an intent not within its reason and purpose, and in such a way that its retention would produce injustices or inequitable consequences. *Laya v. Erin Homes, Inc.*, 352 S.E.2d 93, 97-98 (W.Va.1986).

Kinney seeks to pierce the corporate veil of Industrial so as to hold Polan personally liable on the sublease debt. The Supreme Court of Appeals of West Virginia has set forth a two prong test to be used in determining whether to pierce a corporate veil in a breach of contract case. This test raises two issues: first, is the unity of interest and ownership such that the separate personalities of the corporation and the individual shareholder no longer exist; and second, would an equitable result occur if the acts are treated as those of the corporation alone. *Laya,* 352 S.E.2d at 99. Numerous factors have been identified as relevant in making this determination.

(1) commingling of funds and other assets of the corporation with those of the individual shareholders;

(2) diversion of the corporation's funds or assets to noncorporate uses (to the personal uses of the corporation's shareholders);

(3) failure to maintain the corporate formalities necessary for the issuance of or subscription to the corporation's stock, such as formal approval of the stock issue by the board of directors;

(4) an individual shareholder representing to persons outside the corporation that he or she is personally liable for the debts or other obligations of the corporation;

(5) failure to maintain corporate minutes or adequate corporate records;

(6) identical equitable ownership in two entities;

(7) identity of the directors and officers of two entities who are responsible for supervision and management (a partnership or sole proprietorship and a corporation owned and managed by the same parties);

(8) failure to adequately capitalize a corporation for the reasonable risks of the corporate undertaking;

(9) absence of separately held corporate assets;

(10) use of a corporation as a mere shell or conduit to operate a single venture or some particular aspect of the business of an individual or another corporation;

(11) sole ownership of all the stock by one individual or members of a single family;

(12) use of the same office or business location by the corporation and its individual shareholder(s);

(13) employment of the same employees or attorney by the corporation and its shareholder(s);

(14) concealment or misrepresentation of the identity of the ownership, management or financial interests in the corporation, and concealment of personal business activities of the shareholders (sole shareholders do not reveal the association with a corporation, which makes loans to them without adequate security);

(15) disregard of legal formalities and failure to maintain proper arm's length relationships among related entities;

(16) use of a corporate entity as a conduit to procure labor, services or merchandise for another person or entity;

(17) diversion of corporate assets from the corporation by or to a stockholder or other person or entity to the detriment of creditors, or the manipulation of assets and liabilities between entities to concentrate the assets in one and the liabilities in another;

(18) contracting by the corporation with another person with the intent to avoid risk of nonperformance by use of the corporate entity; or the use of a corporation as a subterfuge for illegal transactions;

(19) the formation and use of the corporation to assume the existing liabilities of another person or entity.
entity.

Laya, 352 S.E.2d at 98-99

The district court found that the two prong test of *Laya* had been satisfied. The court concluded that Polan's failure to carry out the corporate formalities with respect to Industrial, coupled with Industrial's gross undercapitalization, resulted in damage to Kinney. We agree.

It is undisputed that Industrial was not adequately capitalized. Actually, it had no paid in capital. Polan had put nothing into this corporation, and it did not observe any corporate formalities. In this case, Polan bought no stock, made no capital contribution, kept no minutes, and elected no officers for Industrial.

In addition, Polan attempted to protect his assets by placing them in Polan Industries, Inc. and interposing Industrial between Polan Industries, Inc. and Kinney so as to prevent Kinney from going against the corporation with assets. Polan gave no explanation or justification for the existence of Industrial as the intermediary between Polan Industries, Inc. and Kinney. Polan was obviously trying to limit his liability and the liability of Polan Industries, Inc. by setting up a paper curtain constructed of nothing more than Industrial's certificate of incorporation. These facts present the classic scenario for an action to pierce the corporate veil so as to reach the responsible party and produce an equitable result. Accordingly, we hold that the district court correctly found that the two prong test in *Laya* had been satisfied.

For the foregoing reasons, we hold that Polan is personally liable for the debt of Industrial, and the decision of the district court is reversed and this case is remanded with instructions to enter judgment for the plaintiff.

GARDEMAL v. WESTIN HOTEL CO.
186 F.3d 588 (5th Cir. 1999)

DeMOSS, Circuit Judge:

Plaintiff-appellant, Lisa Cerza Gardemal ("Gardemal"), sued defendants-appellees, Westin Hotel Company ("Westin") and Westin Mexico, S.A. de C.V. ("Westin Mexico"), under Texas law, alleging that the defendants were liable for the drowning death of her husband in Cabo San Lucas, Mexico. The district court dismissed the suit in accordance with the magistrate judge's recommendation that the court grant Westin's motion for summary judgment, and Westin Mexico's motion to dismiss for lack of personal jurisdiction. We affirm the district court's rulings.

In June 1995, Gardemal and her husband John W. Gardemal, a physician, traveled to Cabo San Lucas, Baja California Sur, Mexico, to attend a medical seminar held at the Westin Regina Resort Los Cabos ("Westin Regina"). The Westin Regina is owned by Desarollos Turisticos Integrales Cabo San Lucas, S.A. de C.V. ("DTI"), and managed by Westin Mexico. Westin Mexico is a subsidiary of Westin, and is incorporated in Mexico. During their stay at the hotel, the Gardemals decided to go snorkeling with a group of guests. According to Gardemal, the concierge at the Westin Regina directed the group to "Lovers Beach" which, unbeknownst to the group, was notorious for its rough surf and strong undercurrents. While climbing the beach's rocky shore, five men in the group were swept into the Pacific Ocean by a rogue wave and thrown against the rocks. Two of the men, including John Gardemal, drowned.

Gardemal, as administrator of her husband's estate, brought wrongful death and survival actions under Texas law against Westin and Westin Mexico, alleging that her husband drowned because Westin Regina's concierge negligently directed the group to Lovers Beach and failed to warn her husband of its dangerous condition. Westin then moved for summary judgment, alleging that although it is the parent company of Westin Mexico, it is a separate corporate entity and thus could not be held liable for acts committed by its subsidiary. The magistrate judge agreed with Westin, and recommended that Westin be dismissed from the action. In reaching its decision the magistrate judge rejected Gardemal's assertion that the state-law doctrines of alter-ego and single business enterprise allowed the court to disregard Westin's separate corporate identity.

Gardemal timely objected to the magistrate judge's two recommendations. Applying a *de novo* standard of review, the district court accepted the magistrate judge's recommendations and dismissed Gardemal's suit. Gardemal now appeals, alleging that the district court erred in granting Westin's motion for summary judgment, and Westin Mexico's motion to dismiss. We affirm.

In this action Gardemal seeks to hold Westin liable for the acts of Westin Mexico by invoking two separate, but related, state-law doctrines. Gardemal first argues that liability may be imputed to Westin because Westin Mexico functioned as the alter ego of Westin. Gardemal next contends that Westin may be held liable on the theory that Westin Mexico operated a single business enterprise. We consider first the issue of whether Westin may be held liable on an alter-ego theory.

Under Texas law the alter ego doctrine allows the imposition of liability on a corporation for the acts of another corporation when the subject corporation is organized or operated as a mere tool or business conduit. It applies "when there is such unity between the parent corporation and its subsidiary that the separateness of the two corporations has ceased and holding only the subsidiary corporation liable would result in injustice." *Harwood Tire-Arlington, Inc. v. Young,* 963 S.W.2d 881, 885 (Tex.App.-Fort Worth 1998, writ dism'd by agr.). Alter ego is demonstrated "by evidence showing a blending of identities, or a blurring of lines of distinction, both formal and substantive, between two corporations." *Hideca Petroleum Corp. v. Tampimex Oil Int'l Ltd.,* 740 S.W.2d 838, 843 (Tex.App.-Houston [1st Dist.] 1987, no writ). An important consideration is whether a corporation is underfunded or undercapitalized, which is an indication that the company is a mere conduit or business tool.

On appeal Gardemal points to several factors which, in her opinion, show that Westin is operating as the alter ego of Westin Mexico. She claims, for example, that Westin owns most of Westin Mexico's stock; that the two companies share common corporate officers; that Westin maintains quality control at Westin Mexico by requiring Westin Mexico to use certain operations manuals; that Westin oversees advertising and marketing operations at Westin Mexico through two separate contracts; and that Westin Mexico is grossly undercapitalized. See *United States v. Jon-T Chemicals, Inc.,* 768 F.2d 686, 691-92 (5th Cir.1985). Gardemal places particular emphasis on the last purported factor, that Westin Mexico is undercapitalized. She insists that this factor alone is sufficient evidence that Westin Mexico is the alter ego of Westin. We are not convinced.

The record, even when viewed in a light most favorable to Gardemal, reveals nothing more than a typical corporate relationship between a parent and subsidiary. It is true, as Gardemal points out, that Westin and Westin Mexico are closely tied through stock ownership, shared officers, financing arrangements, and the like. But this alone does not establish an alter-ego relationship. As we explained in *Jon-T Chemicals, Inc.,* there must be evidence of complete domination by the parent. Thus, "one-hundred percent ownership and identity of directors and officers are, even together, an insufficient basis for applying the alter ego theory to pierce the corporate veil." *Id.* In this case, there is insufficient record evidence that Westin dominates Westin Mexico to the extent that Westin Mexico has, for practical purposes, surrendered its corporate identity. In fact, the evidence suggests just the opposite, that Westin Mexico functions as an autonomous business entity.

Gardemal is correct in pointing out that undercapitalization is a critical factor in our alter-ego analysis, especially in a tort case like the present one. But as noted by the district court, there is scant evidence that Westin Mexico is in fact undercapitalized and unable to pay a judgment, if necessary. This fact weighs heavily against Gardemal because the alter ego doctrine is an equitable remedy which prevents a company from avoiding liability by abusing the corporate form. In this case, there is insufficient evidence that Westin Mexico is undercapitalized or uninsured. Moreover, there is no indication that Gardemal could not recover by suing Westin Mexico directly. As a result, equity does not demand that we merge and disregard the corporate identities of Westin and Westin Mexico. We reject Gardemal's attempt to impute liability on Westin based on the alter-ego doctrine.

Likewise, we reject Gardemal's attempt to impute liability to Westin based on the single business enterprise doctrine. Under that doctrine, when corporations are not operated as separate entities, but integrate their resources to achieve a common business purpose, each constituent corporation may be held liable for the debts incurred in pursuit of that business purpose. *Old Republic Ins. Co. v. Ex-Im Serv. Corp.,* 920 S.W.2d 393, 395-96 (Tex.App.-Houston [1st Dist.] 1996). Like the alter-ego doctrine, the single business enterprise doctrine is an equitable remedy which applies when the corporate form is "used as part of an unfair device to achieve an inequitable result." *Id.* at 395.

On appeal, Gardemal attempts to prove a single business enterprise by calling our attention to the fact that Westin Mexico uses the trademark "Westin Hotels and Resorts." She also emphasizes that Westin Regina uses Westin's operations manuals. Gardemal also observes that Westin allows Westin Mexico to use its reservation system. Again, these facts merely demonstrate what we would describe as a typical, working relationship between a parent and subsidiary. Gardemal has pointed to no evidence in the record demonstrating that the operations of the two corporations were so integrated as to result in a blending of the two corporate identities. Moreover, Gardemal has come forward with no evidence that she has suffered some harm, or injustice, because Westin and Westin Mexico maintain separate corporate identities.

Reviewing the record in the light most favorable to Gardemal, we conclude that there is insufficient evidence that Westin Mexico was Westin's alter ego. Similarly, there is insufficient evidence that the resources of Westin and Westin Mexico are so integrated as to constitute a single business enterprise. Accordingly, we affirm the district court's grant of Westin's motion for summary judgment on that issue. We turn next to whether the district court erred in granting Westin Mexico's motion to dismiss for lack of personal jurisdiction.

AFFIRMED.

H. DIVIDEND LIMITATIONS

CASE PROBLEM 3-4

Two years ago, Doug, Linda and Laura, unrelated parties, formed a corporation ("Newco") under the laws of a state that has adopted the Model Business Corporation Act. Newco issued 200 shares of common stock to Doug for $200,000, 200 shares of common stock to Linda in return for a 10-year $200,000 promissory note ("Note'), and 200 shares of its common stock to Laura as a "signing bonus" under an employment agreement

Newco struggled through its first year in business. Doug was asked to put in more money, but refused when he saw how bad things were going. By the end of year two, prospects still looked bleak as the company continued to struggle with anemic sales. It was able to stay afloat by selling its accounts receivable at a discount for cash and stringing out the payment of all its suppliers and creditors.

Doug and Laura came up with a plan "to salvage what we can for ourselves." Newco would purchase from Linda her 200 common shares in return for a complete discharge of Linda's $200,000 promissory note held by Newco. Plus, Newco would either (1) pay a dividend of $50,000 to both Doug and Laura or (2) redeem 50 common shares from both Doug and Laura for $50,000.

You have been asked to advise the parties whether any element of their "salvage plan" is illegal." What additional facts (if any) would you like to have? How would your answer change if Newco was incorporated in Delaware?

*   *   *

There are three ways that a shareholder realizes a yield on an investment in the stock of a corporation. First, the shareholder can hold the stock until the corporations sells its business to a third party and liquidates. We discuss corporate sales in Chapter 15.

Second, the shareholder can sell the stock to a third party. An investment in a public corporation whose stock is actively traded can easily be sold at any time. The sale of stock in a closely held corporation presents a much tougher challenge. Usually there is no market for the stock, and the other shareholders do not want stock in the enterprise being shopped to third parties. This is why the buy-sell agreement between the owners of a closely held corporation (discussed in Chapter 13) is such a big deal. It spells out those situations where a shareholder's stock will be purchased by the corporation or the other shareholders and the terms and conditions of such a purchase. It also lays out the conditions that must be satisfied for a shareholder to sell stock to third parties.

Third, shareholders can receive dividends from the corporation which represent distributions of the company's earnings. As we will see in Chapter 7, preferred stocks often specify periodic dividends that are to be paid before any dividends are paid to those who own the common stock of the corporation. Payment of dividends on common stock is usually at the discretion of the board of directors. The dividend policies of the board can trigger problems if dividends are too low or nonexistent, or if dividends are too large.

When dividends are too low or nonexistent, minority shareholders of a closely held corporation may complain that they are being treated unfairly by those in control. We saw such a claim in the 1919 case of *Dodge V. Ford Motor Co.* presented in a prior section of this chapter. In many situations, the essence of the claim is that the minority shareholder is being oppressed and squeezed out, with no opportunity to realize any yield on the stock because it can't be sold and no dividends are being paid. Often the claim is accompanied by allegations that the controlling shareholder is able to generate income from the corporation through lucrative compensation payments. Such oppression claims and planning options to avoid them are discussed in Chapter s 12 and 13. Also, as explained in Chapter 5, failure to pay adequate dividends may expose a corporation to penalty taxes (the accumulated earnings and personal holding company tax traps) in select situations.

Legal problems also can surface when the board authorizes the payment of dividends that are too large. The overriding fear is that the corporation will be stripped of all its assets through generous payments to its shareholders and will not be able to meet its obligations to creditors. There have been statutory legal limitations on the payment of dividends from the beginning.

The old approach adopted a relatively complicated concept of legal capital – a designated minimum amount of capital (usually the par or stated value of the stock times the number of shares outstanding) that a corporation was required to maintain in the enterprise. Any capital or earnings in excess of the minimum capital was considered "surplus" that could be used to pay dividends or repurchase the corporation's stock. This minimum capital approach has proved inadequate over time because corporations routinely designated insignificant par or stated values that had no relationship to the stock's value or the corporation's capacity to honor its obligations. The result was that a corporation could pay large dividends, meet its minimum legal capital obligation, and be left with insufficient assets to pay its creditors. But this minimum capital approach is still part of the statutory schemes of certain states.

The modern statutory approach to excessive dividends, adopted by the Model Business Corporation Act and many states, imposes a two-prong test: a "Solvency" test and a "Balance Sheet" test. The Solvency test prohibits a corporation from paying dividends or repurchasing its own stock if the corporation is unable to pay its debts as they become due in the ordinary course of business. The Balance Sheet test prohibits a corporation from paying dividends or purchasing its own stock if the corporation's total assets are less than the sum of its total liabilities and any liquidation preferences that would be owed if the corporation dissolved at the time of distribution. State statutes often provide that, for purposes of the Balance Sheet test, asset values can be based on the corporation's financial statements prepared in accordance with generally accepted accounting principles or a reasonable fair valuation of the assets.

MBCA § 6.40(c), (d). Distributions to Shareholders

(c) No distribution may be made if, after giving it effect:

(1) the corporation would not be able to pay its debts as they become due in the usual course of business; or

(2) the corporation's total assets would be less than the sum of its total liabilities plus (unless the articles of incorporation permit otherwise) the amount that would be needed, if the corporation were to be dissolved at the time of the distribution, to satisfy the preferential rights upon dissolution of shareholders whose preferential rights are superior to those receiving the distribution.

(d) The board of directors may base a determination that a distribution is not prohibited under subsection (c) either on financial statements prepared on the basis of accounting practices and principles that are reasonable in the circumstances or on a fair valuation or other method that is reasonable in the circumstances.

* * *

Under the Model Act and many state statutes, these dividend limitations carry three significant consequences. First, board members can be held personally liable for consenting to the payment of any dividend that exceeds the statutory limitation.[4] Second, a corporation may not relieve a board member of such personal dividend liability exposure by a "good faith" exculpatory provision in the corporation's articles of incorporation or bylaws.[5] And third, any shareholder who receives such a dividend with knowledge that it exceeds the limitations may be required to repay the dividend to a director who has been held liable for the unlawful distribution.[6]

How does Delaware, the controlling law for many corporations, deal with the risks of excessive dividends? Delaware still has the old minimum capital/surplus scheme for controlling the payment of excessive dividends. Dividends and share repurchases may be made out of "surplus," defined to mean capital that exceeds the par or stated value of the shares and any addition amounts that the board elects to add to the minimum stated capital. As the following case illustrates, a board has tremendous flexibility in structuring dividends and share repurchases that fit within the limitations of this statutory scheme.

KANG v. SMITH'S FOOD & DRUG CENTERS, INC.
702 A.2d 150 (Del. 1997)

VEASEY, Chief Justice:

This appeal calls into question the actions of a corporate board in carrying out a merger and self-tender offer. Plaintiff in this purported class action alleges that a corporation's repurchase of shares violated the statutory prohibition against the impairment of capital.

No corporation may repurchase or redeem its own shares except out of "surplus," as statutorily defined, or except as expressly authorized by provisions of the statute not relevant here. Balance sheets are not, however, conclusive indicators of surplus or a lack thereof. Corporations may revalue assets to show surplus, but perfection in that process is not required. Directors have reasonable latitude to depart from the balance sheet to calculate surplus, so long as they evaluate assets and liabilities in good faith, on the basis of acceptable data, by methods that they reasonably believe reflect present values, and arrive at a determination of the surplus that is not so far off the mark as to constitute actual or constructive fraud.

We hold that, on this record, the Court of Chancery was correct in finding that there was no impairment of capital and there were no disclosure violations.

---

4. MBCA § 8.33.
5. MBCA § 2.02(b)(5).
6. MBCA § 8.33(b)(2).

Accordingly, we affirm.

Smith's Food & Drug Centers, Inc. ("SFD") is a Delaware corporation that owns and operates a chain of supermarkets in the Southwestern United States. Slightly more than three years ago, Jeffrey P. Smith, SFD's Chief Executive Officer, began to entertain suitors with an interest in acquiring SFD. At the time, and until the transactions at issue, Mr. Smith and his family held common and preferred stock constituting 62.1% voting control of SFD. Plaintiff and the class he purports to represent are holders of common stock in SFD.

On January 29, 1996, SFD entered into an agreement with The Yucaipa Companies ("Yucaipa"), a California partnership also active in the supermarket industry. Under the agreement, the following would take place:

(1) Smitty's Supermarkets, Inc. ("Smitty's"), a wholly-owned subsidiary of Yucaipa that operated a supermarket chain in Arizona, was to merge into Cactus Acquisition, Inc. ("Cactus"), a subsidiary of SFD, in exchange for which SFD would deliver to Yucaipa slightly over 3 million newly-issued shares of SFD common stock;

(2) SFD was to undertake a recapitalization, in the course of which SFD would assume a sizable amount of new debt, retire old debt, and offer to repurchase up to fifty percent of its outstanding shares (other than those issued to Yucaipa) for $36 per share; and

(3) SFD was to repurchase 3 million shares of preferred stock from Jeffrey Smith and his family.

SFD hired the investment firm of Houlihan Lokey Howard & Zukin ("Houlihan") to examine the transactions and render a solvency opinion. Houlihan eventually issued a report to the SFD Board replete with assurances that the transactions would not endanger SFD's solvency, and would not impair SFD's capital in violation of 8 *Del.C.* § 160. On May 17, 1996, in reliance on the Houlihan opinion, SFD's Board determined that there existed sufficient surplus to consummate the transactions, and enacted a resolution proclaiming as much. On May 23, 1996, SFD's stockholders voted to approve the transactions, which closed on that day. The self-tender offer was over-subscribed, so SFD repurchased fully fifty percent of its shares at the offering price of $36 per share.

A corporation may not repurchase its shares if, in so doing, it would cause an impairment of capital, unless expressly authorized by Section 160. A repurchase impairs capital if the funds used in the repurchase exceed the amount of the corporation's "surplus," defined by 8 *Del.C.* § 154 to mean the excess of net assets over the par value of the corporation's issued stock.

Plaintiff asked the Court of Chancery to rescind the transactions in question as violative of Section 160. As we understand it, plaintiff's position breaks down into two analytically distinct arguments. First, he contends that SFD's balance sheets constitute conclusive evidence of capital impairment. He argues that the negative net worth that appeared on SFD's books following the repurchase compels us to find a violation of Section 160. Second, he suggests that even allowing the Board to "go behind the balance sheet" to calculate surplus does not save the transactions from violating Section 160. In connection with this claim, he attacks the SFD Board's off-balance-sheet method of calculating surplus on the theory that it does not adequately take into account all of SFD's assets and liabilities. Moreover, he argues that the May 17, 1996 resolution of the SFD Board conclusively refutes the Board's claim that revaluing the corporation's assets gives rise to the required surplus. We hold that each of these claims is without merit.

In an April 25, 1996 proxy statement, the SFD Board released a pro forma balance sheet showing that the merger and self-tender offer would result in a deficit to surplus on SFD's books of more than $100 million. A balance sheet the SFD Board issued shortly after the transactions confirmed this result. Plaintiff asks us to adopt an interpretation of 8 *Del.C.* § 160 whereby balance-sheet net worth is controlling for purposes of determining compliance with the statute. Defendants do not dispute that SFD's books showed a negative net worth in the wake of its transactions with Yucaipa, but argue that corporations should have the presumptive right to revalue assets and liabilities to comply with Section 160.

Plaintiff advances an erroneous interpretation of Section 160. We understand that the books of a corporation do not necessarily reflect the current values of its assets and liabilities. Among other factors, unrealized appreciation or depreciation can render book numbers inaccurate. It is unrealistic to hold that a corporation is bound by its balance sheets for purposes of determining compliance with Section 160. Accordingly, we adhere to the principles of *Morris v. Standard Gas & Electric Co.,* Del.Ch., 63 A.2d 577 (1949), allowing corporations to revalue properly its assets and liabilities to show a surplus and thus conform to the statute.

It is helpful to recall the purpose behind Section 160. The General Assembly enacted the statute to prevent boards from draining corporations of assets to the detriment of creditors and the long-term health of the corporation. That a corporation has not yet realized or reflected on its balance sheet the appreciation of assets is irrelevant to this concern. Regardless of what a balance sheet that has not been updated may show, an actual, though unrealized, appreciation reflects real economic value that the corporation may borrow against or that creditors may claim or levy upon. Allowing corporations to revalue assets and liabilities to reflect current realities complies with the statute and serves well the policies behind this statute.

Plaintiff contends that SFD's repurchase of shares violated Section 160 even without regard to the corporation's balance sheets. Plaintiff claims that the SFD Board was not entitled to rely on the solvency opinion of Houlihan, which showed that the transactions would not impair SFD's capital given a revaluation of corporate assets. The argument is that the methods that underlay the solvency opinion were inappropriate as a matter of law because they failed to take into account all of SFD's assets and liabilities. In addition, plaintiff suggests that the SFD Board's resolution of May 17, 1996 itself shows that the transactions impaired SFD's capital, and that therefore we must find a violation of 8 *Del.C.* § 160. We disagree, and hold that the SFD Board revalued the corporate assets under appropriate methods. Therefore the self-tender offer complied with Section

160, notwithstanding errors that took place in the drafting of the resolution.

On May 17, 1996, Houlihan released its solvency opinion to the SFD Board, expressing its judgment that the merger and self-tender offer would not impair SFD's capital. Houlihan reached this conclusion by comparing SFD's "Total Invested Capital" of $1.8 billion-a figure Houlihan arrived at by valuing SFD's assets under the "market multiple" approach-with SFD's long-term debt of $1.46 billion. This comparison yielded an approximation of SFD's "concluded equity value" equal to $346 million, a figure clearly in excess of the outstanding par value of SFD's stock. Thus, Houlihan concluded, the transactions would not violate 8 *Del.C.* § 160.

Plaintiff contends that Houlihan's analysis relied on inappropriate methods to mask a violation of Section 160. Noting that 8 *Del.C.* § 154 defines "net assets" as "the amount by which total assets exceeds total liabilities," plaintiff argues that Houlihan's analysis is erroneous as a matter of law because of its failure to calculate "total assets" and "total liabilities" as separate variables. In a related argument, plaintiff claims that the analysis failed to take into account all of SFD's liabilities, i.e., that Houlihan neglected to consider current liabilities in its comparison of SFD's "Total Invested Capital" and long-term debt. Plaintiff contends that the SFD Board's resolution proves that adding current liabilities into the mix shows a violation of Section 160. The resolution declared the value of SFD's assets to be $1.8 billion, and stated that its "total liabilities" would not exceed $1.46 billion after the transactions with Yucaipa. As noted, the $1.46 billion figure described only the value of SFD's long-term debt. Adding in SFD's $372 million in current liabilities, plaintiff argues, shows that the transactions impaired SFD's capital.

We believe that plaintiff reads too much into Section 154. The statute simply defines "net assets" in the course of defining "surplus." It does not mandate a "facts and figures balancing of assets and liabilities" to determine by what amount, if any, total assets exceeds total liabilities. The statute is merely definitional. It does not require any particular method of calculating surplus, but simply prescribes factors that any such calculation must include. Although courts may not determine compliance with Section 160 except by methods that fully take into account the assets and liabilities of the corporation, Houlihan's methods were not erroneous as a matter of law simply because they used Total Invested Capital and long-term debt as analytical categories rather than "total assets" and "total liabilities."

We are satisfied that the Houlihan opinion adequately took into account all of SFD's assets and liabilities. Plaintiff points out that the $1.46 billion figure that approximated SFD's long-term debt failed to include $372 million in current liabilities, and argues that including the latter in the calculations dissipates the surplus. In fact, plaintiff has misunderstood Houlihan's methods. The record shows that Houlihan's calculation of SFD's Total Invested Capital is already net of current liabilities. Thus, subtracting long-term debt from Total Invested Capital does, in fact, yield an accurate measure of a corporation's net assets.

The record contains, in the form of the Houlihan opinion, substantial evidence that the transactions complied with Section 160. Plaintiff has provided no reason to distrust Houlihan's analysis. In cases alleging impairment of capital under Section 160, the trial court may defer to the board's measurement of surplus unless a plaintiff can show that the directors "failed to fulfill their duty to evaluate the assets on the basis of acceptable data and by standards which they are entitled to believe reasonably reflect present values." In the absence of bad faith or fraud on the part of the board, courts will not "substitute [our] concepts of wisdom for that of the directors." Here, plaintiff does not argue that the SFD Board acted in bad faith. Nor has he met his burden of showing that the methods and data that underlay the board's analysis are unreliable or that its determination of surplus is so far off the mark as to constitute actual or constructive fraud. Therefore, we defer to the board's determination of surplus, and hold that SFD's self-tender offer did not violate 8 *Del.C.* § 160.

The judgment of the Court of Chancery is affirmed.

I. CORPORATE AND PERSONAL WEALH PLANNING

1. CORPORATE TRANSITION PLANNING

Mom and Dad have labored a lifetime building a profitable corporation that services a market niche and regularly delivers a paycheck to two hundred hard-working employees. On paper, most would consider them rich, but they fully appreciate that the bulk of their wealth is tied up in a corporate operation that could be derailed by changing market conditions, a breakthrough technology, a new tenacious competitor, sloppy management, or a host of other factors. They have witnessed the demise of other businesses that were all considered "rock solid" at some point in their existence. The time has come for Mom and Dad to slow down, turn over the reins, and enjoy their retirement. One child is immersed in the business, fully prepared and anxious to run the show, and two other children are off pursing other careers. The family wants a plan that will ensure the parents' financial security, treat all children fairly, protect the business, promote family harmony, and minimize all tax bites. It's a tall order.

Family business transition planning is big business. Oft quoted statistics say it all. Family dominated businesses comprise more than 80 percent of U.S. enterprises, employ more than 50 percent of the nation's workforce, and account for the bulk (some estimate as much as 64 percent) of America's gross domestic product.[7] According to a 2007 survey of family businesses with annual gross sales of at least $5 million, 60 percent of the majority shareholders in family businesses are 55 or older, and 30 percent are at least age 65.[8] And although more than 80 percent of the senior family owners claim that they want the business to stay in the family, less than 30 percent acknowledge having a

---

7. See generally R. Duman, "Family Firms Are Different," Entrepreneurship Theory and Practice, 1992, pp. 13–21; and M. F. R. Kets de Vries, "The Dynamics of Family Controlled Firms: The Good News and the Bad News," Organizational Dynamics, 1993, pp. 59–71; W. G. Dyer, Cultural Change in Family Firms, Jossey–Bass, San Francisco, 1986; and P. L. Rosenblatt, M. R. Anderson and P. Johnson, The Family in Business, Jossey–Bass, San Francisco, 1985; Arthur Anderson/Mass Mutual, American Family Business Survey, 2002.

8. Family to Family: Laird Norton Tyee Family Business Survey 2007, page 5.

transition plan.[9] The result is that most family businesses do remain in the family, but at a dear cost. Best estimates are that less than 30 percent of family dominated businesses survive a second generation, and the survival rate is even uglier for those businesses that make it to generation three.[10]

Strategic transition planning takes time, energy, and a willingness to grapple with tough family, tax and financial issues. It cannot make a weak business strong or provide any guarantees of survival. But it can trigger an analytical process that prompts a frank assessment of available options, facilitates better long-term decision making, and saves taxes.

Although many successful family business owners enjoy a net worth that rivals or exceeds that of other well-heeled clients, the planning dynamics usually are much different when a family business takes center stage. For many clients, wealth transition planning focuses on a potpourri of investment and business assets, packaged in a medley of partnerships, trusts, limited liability companies (LLCs), and corporate entities. The challenge is to analyze, reposition where necessary, and ultimately transition the various marbles in the most tax efficient manner possible, consistent with the family objectives of the owners. With a family corporation, often it's not about rearranging marbles; it's about trying to move a mountain. In the recent survey referenced above, a startling 93 percent of the senior business owners acknowledged that the business is their primary source of income and security.[11] Little or no diversification makes everything tougher. Strategies that easily accommodate marble shifting often become more challenging, sometimes impossible, when applied to a sliver of the mountain. And, more often the not, the process is further complicated by strong emotional ties to the mountain and historical perceptions regarding essential bonds between the family and the mountain.

The plan design process for each family necessarily must be detail-oriented, strategic, and forward focused. Care must be exercised to avoid planning traps and the temptation to tack on complicated strategies that offer little or nothing for the particular family. Each situation is unique and should be treated as such. There is no slam-dunk solution; all strategies have limitations and disadvantages that mandate careful evaluation and some pose risks or legal uncertainties that many just can't stomach. Above all, the specific objectives of the family must drive the planning process. The objectives, once identified, must be prioritized to facilitate an effective analysis of the trade-offs and compromises that inevitably surface in the planning process. The ultimate goal is to design a plan that effectively accomplishes the highest priority objectives over a period of time and at a level of complexity that works for the family.

The owners of most successful family businesses sooner or later face a threshold question: Should the family business be sold or should it be

9. Id. The survey also indicated that (1) only 56 percent of the respondents have a written strategic business plan, (2) nearly 64 percent do not require that family members entering the business have any qualifications or business experience, and (3) 25 percent do not believe that the next generation is competent to move into leadership roles.

10. J. I. Ward, Keeping the Family Business Healthy, Jossey-Bass, San Francisco, 1987. This study suggests that the survival rate to generation three is less than 15 percent.

11. Family to Family: Laird Norton Tyee Family Business Survey 2007, page 5 (Executive Summary).

transitioned to the next generation? Of course, the decision to transition the business triggers a major obstacle: estate taxes. The government extracts a large price for the privilege of moving the ownership of a successful business to the next generation. There are ways that this estate tax obstacle can be planned for, massaged, reduced, frozen, and ultimately funded.

In many situations, the parents automatically will assume that the business is going to be kept in the family and transitioned to the next generation. The thought of selling the business to an outside party may have never seriously crossed the parents' mind. Some may even regard the issue as a taboo subject that is not to be discussed. The planning lawyer needs to be discerning in this situation and assess the risks of saying nothing. Often the lawyer does a client a disservice by ducking the issue at the first sign of any resistance. This is one area where a little artful devil's advocacy can shake loose the cobwebs, open minds, and get the thought process started by planting smart seeds.

It's important to remember that priorities, objectives, biases, family dynamics, and business risk factors continually evolve and change over time. So too, the answer to the sell-keep decision may change over time. The patriarch who would never consider selling out at age fifty-five may have a very different attitude at age seventy, particularly if he has been subjected to many enlightening discussions over the years that have focused on a number of key factors that rightfully influence the analysis and the decision.

Simply going through the process of evaluating the sell-keep decision factors often has considerable value even though the parents refuse to seriously consider the sellout alternative. By focusing on the key factors and business indicators that affect the decision, the parents will become more tuned-in to steps that should be taken to prepare the business for transitioning to the next generation. They will better understand and be more sensitive to the non-tax problems and obstacles that will be triggered when the transition kicks in. This increased sensitivity will often enable them to plan more effectively in structuring the business to face the challenges that will inevitably surface.

The form of entity usually has a significant impact in the plan design. Far and away, corporate entities are the preferred choice for family operating businesses. A 2002 survey of family businesses with average annual sales of $36 million confirmed that over 89 percent were corporations, split relatively equally between C and S status.[12] The differences between C and S corporations are discussed in Chapter 5. Both corporate forms present planning challenges. For C corporations, it is the double tax structure that drives up the cost of redemption and dividend strategies, the locked-in stock basis that discourages lifetime gifting and puts a premium on the basis step-up at death, and the alternative minimum tax threat that complicates corporate funding of life insurance. For S corporations, it is the eligibility requirements that preclude partnerships, corporations and most trusts from owning stock and prevents the use of any preferred stock.

---

12. Arthur Anderson/Mass Mutual, American Family Business Survey, 2002.

The plan design usually includes a program for transferring stock to other family members while one or both of the parents are living. The strategic options include gifts of stock to other family members or trusts established for their benefit, sales of stock to the corporation, and sales of stock to other family members or trusts. No option is clearly superior to the others; each has disadvantages and limitations that need to be carefully evaluated. Often a combination approach is the best alternative. Plus, in some cases the need to actually transfer stock while the parents are living may be mitigated or eliminated entirely by business restructuring techniques that have the effect of transitioning future value without actually transferring stock.

Timing is a critical element in the design of any corporate transition plan. The temperament and anxieties of the parents can affect all timing decisions. Some are anxious to move at full stream; many need to take it slow, to walk before they run. A variety of other factors can influence important timing decisions, including the stability of the business, the parents' capacity to accept and adapt to change, the demands and expectations of the children, the strength of parents' financial base outside of the business, the age and health of the parents, and personal relationships between specific family members. Often the pace of implementing specific plan elements accelerates as circumstances change and the parents become more comfortable with the transition process and their new roles.

The planning process usually is helped by focusing on three timeframes: the period both parents are living, the period following the death of the first parent, and the period following the death of the surviving parent. So long both parents are living, top priorities must include their financial needs and security, their willingness to let go and walk away from the business, and their appetite for living with any fallout resulting from the transition of serious wealth and control to their children.

The first parent's death often creates more flexibility. Any gifts to other family members after the first death may transfer high-basis assets. Any sales may be free of income taxes. If the deceased parent had the strongest ties to the business (as is so often the case), officially surrendering total control may no longer be an issue.

Of course, the death of the surviving parent triggers the moment of truth for the two big consequences that have been the focus of the planning from the outset: (1) the ultimate transition of the corporation and the parents' other assets, and (2) the estate tax bill. As regards the first, the goal is to ensure that the parents' objectives for the family are satisfied without compromising the strength and survival prospects of the business. The objective for the second is to keep the bill as small as possible, while ensuring a mechanism for payment that won't unduly strain the business.

Transitioning a family business is usually tougher when some children work in the business and others do not. This is a fairly common scenario. When only some of the children work in the business, there is always a potential income allocation conflict between the inside children, who have an interest in maximizing compensation and benefit payments, and the outside children, who know that their income rights will be negatively affected by any increase in compensation and benefit payments. It's the classic capital versus labor conflict.

When inside and outside children end up sharing corporate control, conflicts can easily surface. For example, the inside children may want to arrange for a new source of financing, develop a new line of products, expand into new territories, or take some other action that requires the consent of the outside children. The outside children must cast a vote on an issue that they do not really understand because they are not involved on a day-to-day basis. As a result, the outsiders, like many in their situation, tend to be suspicious and risk averse. Growth is slowed; opportunities are lost. The insiders, who are critical to the success of the enterprise, become frustrated. Their need to secure the approval of an uninformed, uninvolved, hard-nosed, suspicious brother or sister makes everything harder and can quickly become an obstacle to sound management and profitable decision-making. Too often, deep-seated personal emotions, the foundations of which may be events that occurred decades earlier, take priority over sound business judgment.

These types of problems can lead to imprudent business decisions, costly tax consequences, and conflicts that can drive a permanent wedge into sibling relationships. The planning challenge is to anticipate the potential conflicts, based on an honest assessment of the specific facts, and then implement one or more strategies that may mitigate any adverse effects. Often the best strategies are those that eliminate the source of the conflict - joint ownership of the business. Each child gets a fair share of the parents' estate, but the insiders end up with sole ownership of the family business. When this is not possible, other strategies, often perceived as less attractive, may be used to mitigate adverse tax and control issues triggered by the joint ownership by inside and outside children.

A successful business client once explained, "It's not the hunt that excites; it's the spoils from the effort, the rewards of success." For some clients, this simple statement says it all. The prospect of acquiring "enough" personal wealth is why they put it all on the line everyday to build successful businesses. These clients – the wealth managers – long for the time and freedom to enjoy their rewards with the comfort of knowing that all bases are covered. On the other end of the spectrum are those who can't focus beyond the chase. For them, the real thrill is in the challenge of first making it happen and then proving, time and again, that they still "have it." Why else would *so* many who have *so* much keep taking risks to conquer bigger prey? For these clients, the rush is in the victory and scoping out the next target, not in figuring out how to enjoy the last conquest. Personal wealth accumulation is just a wonderful byproduct of their efforts, the ultimate trophy. Their happiness is in chasing trophies. Many business owners, perhaps most, fall somewhere between these extremes. The rewards of wealth management are alluring, but they have a little trophy-chasing in their blood.

Where a client sits on this spectrum can have a powerful impact in the planning process. Nearly all can embrace planning challenges that directly impact their corporate business interests. But big differences begin to surface when the planning extends beyond the business to matters of family and intergenerational wealth preservation. Pure wealth managers are eager for the challenge—each component is viewed as another opportunity to get to the finish line faster. Some compulsive trophy-chasers are impossible. Their potential demise isn't a possibility worthy of serious discussion. Business challenges are viewed as comfortable, exciting opportunities; family challenges are uncomfortable, impossible burdens. When they do think beyond the next deal, they figure, "If I just keep raking it in, all will work out." Sometimes they are right, even when big saving opportunities are lost all along the way. And, of course, there are all those in the middle, some with wealth manager tendencies and others who naturally shy away from anything that isn't all business.

The quality business lawyer must be able to service all types. The advisor usually accomplishes little by even acknowledging a distinction between business and estate planning that gets very blurry and loses much of its significance when one or more closely held corporations are involved. Since the business activities are an integral part of everything, all the planning is about business. The planning typically incorporates corporate entities, one or more partnerships or LLCs, and the smart use of trusts. Planning, on its face, adds complexity. There are more entities, more pieces to deal with. The goal is to develop and implement over time an integrated multi-entity planning approach that accomplishes the wealth management objectives of the business owner.

2. MULTI–ENTITY PLANNING: AN EXAMPLE

Duncan and Sandy Smith, both age 62, have built an estate valued at approximately $22 million. They have three children, all married and in their 30's. They have six grandchildren. Duncan generates a substantial income in a consulting business ("Consulting") that he operates through a C corporation. He also owns the outstanding stock of Holding Inc. ("Holding"), an S corporation holding company that has a manufacturing subsidiary and a distribution subsidiary. Duncan plays an important role in the upper management and strategic decisions of Holding, but is not an employee of Holding. Sandy has always had an eye for quality real estate, principally raw land and small commercial properties. The couple owns two homes (in different states) and has significant stock and bond portfolios. The Smith's children and their spouses are all college-educated and gainfully employed. Their son works for Holding.

The Smiths have always been planners, but their serious planning started five years ago. They identified the following 10 objectives at that time, which still remain the focus of their planning:

1. Ensure that they always will have sufficient income and wealth for their personal needs, that they will never become a financial burden for their children, and that their privacy will be maintained with as little hassle as possible.

2. Ensure that their estate ultimately is shared equally by their children.

3. Establish a wealth accumulation program for each child that will provide a supplemental source of income and will be protected from the claims of creditors and the exposures of divorce.

4. Establish a wealth accumulation program for each grandchild that will help fund higher educational expenses and potentially provide some "getting started" support.

5. Provide their college alma maters with significant gifts that will fund in the future.

6. Defer any estate tax liabilities as long as possible.

7. Minimize their ultimate estate tax liability.

8. Ensure that their estate always has adequate liquidity, including sufficient cash to cover all estate taxes.

9. Minimize income and self-employment taxes.

10. Where possible, protect assets from exposure to unforeseen liabilities.

Duncan and Sandy have implemented a plan to accomplish these objectives. Following is a simple diagram of the plan components and a brief description of each component (moving clockwise from the bottom) and how it serves specific objectives.

Duncan and Sandy Smith Plan

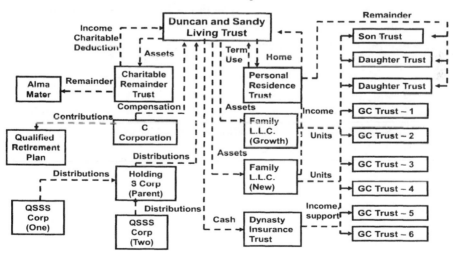

The operations of Holding are conducted in the S corporation that owns two qualified subchapter S subsidiaries. The separate subsidiaries protect each company's operations from any liability exposures of the other's operation and facilitate the development and compensation of separate managements. All of the operations are consolidated for tax purposes. The S structure allows Duncan to regularly receive substantial distributions free of any double income tax concerns and payroll tax burdens. Duncan and Sandy's plan is to transition the stock of Holding over time to their son who works in the business and to transfer other assets of equal value to their other two children.

Duncan's consulting business operates through the C corporation. The company funds a qualified defined benefit plan that primarily benefits Duncan, the sole shareholder and the highest paid employee. This enables Duncan to defer income taxes on a substantial portion of his consulting income. The C corporation structure also permits Duncan and the other employees to fund medical and insurance benefits with pre-tax dollars. Duncan "zeros out" the C corporation's taxable income each year with salary and bonus payments to himself.

The charitable remainder trust was set up principally to benefit Duncan and Sandy's alma maters, but it also provides some cash flow and tax benefits. Low basis, unencumbered raw land was contributed to the trust. The time had come to sale the land. The trust sold the land but, as a charitable remainder trust, paid no income taxes on the sale. The total sales proceeds were invested to fund a monthly annuity that is payable to Duncan and Sandy for so long as either of them is living. Upon the death of the survivor, the trust property will pass to their two alma maters in equal shares. In addition to the lifetime annuity payments, Duncan and Sandy received a charitable contribution deduction for the value of the trust's remainder interests designated for the charities.

The living trust is revocable. As such, it's a tax nullity. It holds title to Duncan and Sandy's personal assets. Its purpose is to eliminate the hassles and expense of probate (in their primary residence state and in any ancillary jurisdictions where they own real estate) and to protect the privacy of their affairs on death (with no probate, there is no public record of their holdings). The living trust provides for the establishment of an irrevocable qualified terminal interest property trust ("QTIP") on the death of the first spouse that will eliminate all estate taxes on the first death, provide the surviving spouse with a regular income stream and principal invasion rights as needed, protect the deceased spouse's remainder disposition preferences, and provide some creditor protection benefits. Duncan and Sandy also each have a will that pours over to the living trust any non-trust assets that they own at death.

Duncan and Sandy have established a separate trust for each of their children. These trusts have been funded for many years, primarily with interests in the two limited liability companies described below. The trusts provide protection from creditor claims and will help protect trust assets in a messy divorce proceeding.

A separate trust has been established for each grandchild. These trusts are designed to fund future college expenses, help with the purchase of a first home, and provide getting-started capital. The trusts will be funded over many years, primarily with interests in the two limited liability companies described below. The trusts also provide protection from creditor claims

The qualified personal residence trust was set up to hold title to Duncan and Sandy's personal residence, a quality property that has appreciated in value. The terms of the trust give Duncan and Sandy use of the residence for a specified term (there are 12 years remaining). The trust is designed to ensure that if

Duncan and Sandy outlive the trust term (a probability), the home will pass to the children's trusts free of any adverse gift tax consequences. If at the end of the trust term Duncan and Sandy want to continue residing in the home, they will lease the home from the trusts, which will create an additional opportunity to regularly transfer funds to the children free of any gift tax concerns.

The two family limited liability companies were established to facilitate the management of business and investment assets. Duncan and Sandy and two of their adult children are the managers. The "New" LLC invests in new undertakings and is funded with cash contributions from Duncan and Sandy and the children and grandchildren trusts, with the bulk of the cash coming from the trusts. The "Growth" LLC holds seasoned investments. Duncan and Sandy are the majority owners of the "Growth" LLC, but periodically gift membership interests to the children and grandchildren trusts.

The dynasty life insurance trust is an irrevocable life insurance trust structured to provide benefits for all Duncan and Sandy's descendants for as long as there are assets in the trust and the law will allow (in some states, in perpetuity). Hence, the name "Dynasty." The trust owns a $5 million second-to-die life insurance policy that will pay off on the death of the survivor of Duncan and Sandy. The premiums are funded by annual cash gifts to the trust from Duncan and Sandy. The trust is structured to avoid all gift, estate and generation skipping taxes.

The plan, as depicted in the picture and briefly summarized above, addresses all of Duncan and Sandy's objectives, at least in part. Duncan and Sandy receive income streams from the C corporation, the S corporation, the limited liability companies, the charitable remainder trust, and any assets owned by the living trust. The living trust provides probate and privacy protections. The children are treated equally, and the children and grandchildren's trusts, funded via the family limited liability companies and the personal residence trust, meet Duncan and Sandy's objectives for their descendants. Their alma maters are taken care of through the charitable remainder trust. Estate taxes are deferred through the QTIP trust in the living trust and are reduced through the children's and grandchildren's trusts, the dynasty trust, the personal residence trust, and the charitable remainder trust, all of which are excluded from Duncan and Sandy's taxable estate. Liquidity is ensured through the life insurance in the dynasty trust, which will escape all future estate and generation skipping taxes. There are no double income tax concerns, self-employment taxes are minimized, and taxable income can be shifted to children and grandchildren through the gifting of limited liability company units to the trusts. Duncan and Sandy have not surrendered any control of Consulting or Holding and have the opportunity to work with (and teach) two of their children in managing the limited liability companies. With the exception of the living trust, all the entities (the boxes) provide some level of protection against unforeseen liabilities.

CHAPTER 4

THE SCORECARDS AND NUMBERS OF BUSINESS

A. THE ABCs OF FINANCIAL STATEMENTS

The scorecards of every business are its financial statements. As a client once exclaimed, "A person who can't understand my scorecard will never be able to understand my business or appreciate how good I really am." Those who serve businesses need to know how to read the scorecards. There is no need to master the art of debits and credits or the details that go in to the preparation of financial statements, but there is a need to understand the components of each core financial statement, how the statements relate to one another, and how key transactions impact financial statements.

SEC Guide to Financial Statements [1]

If you can read a nutrition label or a baseball box score, you can learn to read basic financial statements. If you can follow a recipe or apply for a loan, you can learn basic accounting. The basics aren't difficult, and they aren't rocket science.

There are four main financial statements. They are: (1) balance sheets; (2) income statements; (3) cash flow statements; and (4) statements of shareholders' equity. Balance sheets show what a company owns and what it owes at a fixed point in time. Income statements show how much money a company made and spent over a period of time. Cash flow statements show the exchange of money between a company and the outside world also over a period of time. The fourth financial statement, called a "statement of shareholders' equity," shows changes in the interests of the company's shareholders over time.

Balance Sheets

A balance sheet provides detailed information about a company's assets, liabilities and shareholders' equity.

Assets are things that a company owns that have value. This typically means

---

1. U.S. Securities and Exchange Commission, Beginners' Guide to Financial Statements (February 5, 2007).

they can either be sold or used by the company to make products or provide services that can be sold. Assets include physical property, such as plants, trucks, equipment and inventory. It also includes things that can't be touched but nevertheless exist and have value, such as trademarks and patents. And cash itself is an asset. So are investments a company makes.

Liabilities are amounts of money that a company owes to others. This can include all kinds of obligations, like money borrowed from a bank to launch a new product, rent for use of a building, money owed to suppliers for materials, payroll a company owes to its employees, environmental cleanup costs, or taxes owed to the government. Liabilities also include obligations to provide goods or services to customers in the future.

Shareholders' equity is sometimes called capital or net worth. It's the money that would be left if a company sold all of its assets and paid off all of its liabilities. This leftover money belongs to the shareholders, or the owners, of the company.

> The following formula summarizes what a balance sheet shows:
>
> ### ASSETS = LIABILITIES + SHAREHOLDERS' EQUITY
>
> A company's assets have to equal, or "balance," the sum of its liabilities and shareholders' equity.

A company's balance sheet is set up like the basic accounting equation shown above. On the left side of the balance sheet, companies list their assets. On the right side, they list their liabilities and shareholders' equity. Sometimes balance sheets show assets at the top, followed by liabilities, with shareholders' equity at the bottom.

Assets are generally listed based on how quickly they will be converted into cash. Current assets are things a company expects to convert to cash within one year. A good example is inventory. Most companies expect to sell their inventory for cash within one year. Noncurrent assets are things a company does not expect to convert to cash within one year or that would take longer than one year to sell. Noncurrent assets include <u>fixed</u> assets. Fixed assets are those assets used to operate the business but that are not available for sale, such as trucks, office furniture and other property.

Liabilities are generally listed based on their due dates. Liabilities are said to be either current or long-term. Current liabilities are obligations a company expects to pay off within the year. Long-term liabilities are obligations due more than one year away.

Shareholders' equity is the amount owners invested in the company's stock plus or minus the company's earnings or losses since inception. Sometimes companies distribute earnings, instead of retaining them. These distributions are called dividends.

Sample Balance Sheet
Deere & Company
As of October 31, 2011 and 2010
(In millions of dollars except per share amounts)

	2011	2010
ASSETS		
Cash and cash equivalents	$ 3,647.2	$ 3,790.60
Marketable securities	787.3	227.9
Receivables from unconsolidated affiliates	48.0	38.8
Trade accounts and notes receivable - net	3,294.5	3,464.2
Financing receivables - net	19,923.5	17,682.2
Financing receivables securitized - net	2,905.0	2,238.3
Other receivables	1,330.6	925.6
Equipment on operating leases - net	2,150.0	1,936.2
Inventories	4,370.6	3,063.0
Property and equipment - net	4,352.3	3,790.7
Investments in unconsolidated affiliates	201.7	244.5
Goodwill	999.8	998.6
Other intangible assets - net	127.4	117.0
Retirement benefits	30.4	146.7
Deferred income taxes	2,858.6	2,477.1
Other assets	1,180.5	1,194.0
Assets held for sale		931.4
Total Assets	$ 48,207.40	$ 43,266.80
LIABILITIES AND STOCKHOLDERS' EQUITY		
LIABILITIES		
Short-term borrowings	$ 6,852.3	$ 5,325.7
Short-term securitization borrowings	2,777.4	2,208.8
Payables to unconsolidated affiliates	117.7	203.5
Accounts payable and accrued expenses	7,804.8	6,481.7
Deferred income taxes	168.3	144.3
Long-term borrowings	16,959.9	16,814.5
Retirement benefits and other liabilities	6,712.1	5,784.9
Total liabilities	41,392.5	36,963.4
Commitments and contingencies (Note 22)		
STOCKHOLDERS' EQUITY		
Common stock, $1 par value (authorized 1,200,000,000 shares;		
issued 536,431,204 shares in 2011 and 2010), at paid-in amount	3,251.7	3,106.3
Common stock in treasury, 130,361,345 shares in 2011, at cost	(7,292.8)	(5,789.5)
Retained earnings	14,519.4	12,353.1
Accumulated other comprehensive income (loss):		
Retirement benefits adjustment	(4,135.4)	(3,797.0)
Cumulative translation adjustment	453.8	436.0
Unrealized loss on derivatives	(8.3)	(29.2)
Unrealized gain on investments	11.9	10.6
Accumulated other comprehensive income (loss)	(3,678.0)	(3,379.6)
Total Deere & Company stockholders' equity	6,800.3	6,290.3
Noncontrolling interests	14.6	13.1
Total stockholders' equity	6,814.9	6,303.4
Total Liabilities and Stockholders' Equity	$ 48,207.4	$ 43,266.8

The notes to consolidated financial statements are an integral part of this statement.

A balance sheet shows a snapshot of a company's assets, liabilities and shareholders' equity at the end of the reporting period. It does not show the flows into and out of the accounts during the period.

Income Statements

An income statement is a report that shows how much revenue a company earned over a specific time period (usually for a year or some portion of a year). An income statement also shows the costs and expenses associated with earning that revenue. The literal "bottom line" of the statement usually shows the company's net earnings or losses. This tells you how much the company earned or lost over the period.

Income statements also report earnings per share (or "EPS"). This calculation tells you how much money shareholders would receive if the company decided to distribute all of the net earnings for the period. (Companies almost never distribute all of their earnings. Usually they reinvest them in the business.)

Sample Income Statement
Deere & Company
As of October 31, 2011, 2010 and 2009
(In millions of dollars except per share amounts)

	2011	2010	2009
Net Sales and Revenues			
Net sales	$29,466.1	$23,573.2	$20,756.1
Finance and interest income	1,922.6	1,825.3	1,842.1
Other income	623.8	606.1	514.2
Total	32,012.5	26,004.6	23,112.4
Costs and Expenses			
Cost of sales	21,919.4	17,398.8	16,255.2
Research and development expenses	1,226.2	1,052.4	977.0
Selling, administrative and general expenses	3,168.7	2,968.7	2,780.6
Interest expense	759.4	811.4	1,042.4
Other operating expenses	716.0	748.1	718.0
Total	27,789.7	22,979.4	21,773.2
Income of Consolidated Group before Income Taxes	4,222.8	3,025.2	1,339.2
Provision for income taxes	1,423.6	1,161.6	460.0
Income of Consolidated Group	2,799.2	1,863.6	879.2
Equity in income (loss) of unconsolidated affiliates	8.6	10.7	(6.3)
Net Income	2,807.8	1,874.3	872.9
Less: Net income (loss) attributable to noncontrolling interests	7.9	9.3	(0.6)
Net Income Attributable to Deere & Company	$ 2,799.9	$ 1,865.0	$ 873.5
Per Share Data			
Basic	$ 6.71	$ 4.4	$ 2.07
Diluted	$ 6.63	$ 4.35	$ 2.06
Dividends declared	$ 1.52	$ 1.16	$ 1.12
Average Shares Outstanding			
Basic	417.4	424	422.8
Diluted	422.4	428.6	424.4

The notes to consolidated financial statements are an integral part of this statement.

To understand how income statements are set up, think of them as a set of stairs. You start at the top with the total amount of sales made during the accounting period. Then you go down, one step at a time. At each step, you make a deduction for certain costs or other operating expenses associated with earning the revenue. At the bottom of the stairs, after deducting all of the expenses, you learn how much the company actually earned or lost during the accounting period. People often call this "the bottom line."

At the top of the income statement is the total amount of money brought in from sales of products or services. This top line is often referred to as gross revenues or sales. It's called "gross" because expenses have not been deducted from it yet. So the number is "gross" or unrefined.

The next line is money the company doesn't expect to collect on certain sales. This could be due, for example, to sales discounts or merchandise returns.

When you subtract the returns and allowances from the gross revenues, you arrive at the company's net revenues. It's called "net" because, if you can imagine a net, these revenues are left in the net after the deductions for returns and allowances have come out.

Moving down the stairs from the net revenue line, there are several lines that represent various kinds of operating expenses. Although these lines can be reported in various orders, the next line after net revenues typically shows the costs of the sales. This number tells you the amount of money the company spent to produce the goods or services it sold during the accounting period.

The next line subtracts the costs of sales from the net revenues to arrive at a subtotal called "gross profit" or sometimes "gross margin." It's considered "gross" because there are certain expenses that haven't been deducted from it yet.

The next section deals with operating expenses. These are expenses that go toward supporting a company's operations for a given period – for example, salaries of administrative personnel and costs of researching new products. Marketing expenses are another example. Operating expenses are different from "costs of sales," which were deducted above, because operating expenses cannot be linked directly to the production of the products or services being sold.

Depreciation is also deducted from gross profit. Depreciation takes into account the wear and tear on some assets, such as machinery, tools and furniture, which are used over the long term. Companies spread the cost of these assets over the periods they are used. This process of spreading these costs is called depreciation or amortization. The "charge" for using these assets during the period is a fraction of the original cost of the assets.

After all operating expenses are deducted from gross profit, you arrive at operating profit before interest and income tax expenses. This is often called "income from operations."

Next companies must account for interest income and interest expense. Interest income is the money companies make from keeping their cash in interest-bearing savings accounts, money market funds and the like. On the other hand, interest expense is the money companies paid in interest for money they borrow.

Some income statements show interest income and interest expense separately. Some income statements combine the two numbers. The interest income and expense are then added or subtracted from the operating profits to arrive at operating profit before income tax.

Finally, income tax is deducted and you arrive at the bottom line: net profit or net losses. (Net profit is also called net income or net earnings.) This tells you how much the company actually earned or lost during the accounting period. Did the company make a profit or did it lose money?

Earnings Per Share or EPS

Most income statements include a calculation of earnings per share or EPS. This calculation tells you how much money shareholders would receive for each share of stock they own if the company distributed all of its net income for the period.

To calculate EPS, you take the total net income and divide it by the number of outstanding shares of the company.

Cash Flow Statements

Cash flow statements report a company's inflows and outflows of cash. This is important because a company needs to have enough cash on hand to pay its expenses and purchase assets. While an income statement can tell you whether a company made a profit, a cash flow statement can tell you whether the company generated cash.

A cash flow statement shows changes over time rather than absolute dollar amounts at a point in time. It uses and reorders the information from a company's balance sheet and income statement.

The bottom line of the cash flow statement shows the net increase or decrease in cash for the period. Generally, cash flow statements are divided into three main parts. Each part reviews the cash flow from one of three types of activities: (1) operating activities; (2) investing activities; and (3) financing activities.

Operating Activities

The first part of a cash flow statement analyzes a company's cash flow from net income or losses. For most companies, this section of the cash flow statement reconciles the net income (as shown on the income statement) to the actual cash the company received from or used in its operating activities. To do this, it adjusts net income for any non-cash items (such as adding back depreciation expenses) and adjusts for any cash that was used or provided by other operating assets and liabilities.

Investing Activities

The second part of a cash flow statement shows the cash flow from all investing activities, which generally include purchases or sales of long-term assets, such as property, plant and equipment, as well as investment securities. If a company buys a piece of machinery, the cash flow statement would reflect this activity as a cash outflow from investing activities because it used cash. If the company decided to sell off some investments from an investment portfolio, the proceeds from the sales would show up as a cash inflow from investing activities because it provided cash.

Financing Activities

The third part of a cash flow statement shows the cash flow from all financing activities. Typical sources of cash flow include cash raised by selling stocks and bonds or borrowing from banks. Likewise, paying back a bank loan would show up as a use of cash flow.

Sample Cash Flow Statement
Deere & Company
As of October 31, 2011, 2010 and 2009
(In millions of dollars except per share amounts)

	2011	2010	2009
Cash Flows from Operating Activities			
Net income	$ 2807.8	$ 1874.3	$ 872.9
Adjustments to reconcile net income to net cash provided by operating activities			
Provision for doubtful receivables	13.5	106.4	231.8
Provision for depreciation and amortization	914.9	914.8	873.3
Goodwill impairment charges		27.2	289.2
Share-based compensation expense	69	71.2	70.5
Undistributed earnings of unconsolidated affiliates	11.1	(2.2)	7
Provision (credit) for deferred income taxes	(168.0)	175.0	171.6
Changes in assets and liabilities			
Trade, notes and financing receivables related to sales	(808.9)	(1,100.6)	481.8
Inventories	(1,730.5)	(1,052.7)	452.5
Accounts payable and accrued expenses	1,287.0	1,057.7	(1,168.3)
Accrued income taxes payable/receivable	1.2	22.1	(234.2)
Retirement benefits	495.3	(154.1)	(27.9)
Other	(566.1)	343.1	(35.4)
Net cash provided by operating activities	2,326.3	2,282.2	1,984.8
Cash Flows from Investing Activities			
Collections of receivables (excluding receivables related to sales)	12,151.4	11,047.1	11,252.0
Proceeds from maturities and sales of marketable securities	32.4	38.4	825.1
Proceeds from sales of equipment on operating leases	683.4	621.9	477.3
Government grants related to property and equipment		92.3	
Proceeds from sales of businesses, net of cash sold	911.1	34.9	
Cost of receivables acquired (excluding receivables related to sales)	(13,956.8)	(12,493.9)	(11234.2)
Purchases of marketable securities	(586.9)	(63.4)	(29.5)
Purchases of property and equipment	(1,056.6)	(761.7)	(906.7)
Cost of equipment on operating leases acquired	(624.2)	(551.1)	(401.4)
Acquisitions of businesses, net of cash acquired	(60.8)	(45.5)	(49.8)
Other	(113.7)	(28.1)	10.2
Net cash used for investing activities	(2,620.7)	(2,109.1)	(57.0)
Cash Flows from Financing Activities			
Increase (decrease) in total short-term borrowings	(226.1)	756.0	(1384.8)
Proceeds from long-term borrowings	5,655.0	2,621.1	6,282.8
Payments of long-term borrowings	(3,220.8)	(3,675.7)	(3,830.3)
Proceeds from issuance of common stock	170.0	129.1	16.5
Repurchases of common stock	(1,667.0)	(358.8)	(3.2)
Dividends paid	(593.1)	(483.5)	(473.4)
Excess tax benefits from share-based compensation	70.1	43.5	4.6
Other	(48.5)	(41.4)	(141.9)
Net cash provided by (used for) financing activities	139.6	(1,009.7)	470.3
Effect of Exchange Rate Changes on Cash and Cash Equivalents	11.4	(24.5)	42.2
Net Increase (Decrease) in Cash and Cash Equivalents	(143.4)	(861.1)	2,440.3
Cash and Cash Equivalents at Beginning of Year	3,790.6	4,651.7	2,211.4
Cash and Cash Equivalents at End of Year	$ 3,647.2	$ 3790.6	$ 4651.7

The notes to consolidated financial statements are an integral part of this statement.

Read the Footnotes

It's so important to *read the footnotes*. The footnotes to financial statements are packed with information. Here are some of the highlights:

<u>Significant accounting policies and practices</u> – Companies are required to disclose the accounting policies that are most important to the portrayal of the company's financial condition and results.

<u>Pension plans and other retirement programs</u> – The footnotes discuss the company's pension plans and other retirement or post-employment benefit programs.

<u>Stock options</u> – The notes also contain information about stock options granted to officers and employees, including the method of accounting for stock-based compensation and the effect of the method on reported results.

Read the MD&A

You can find a narrative explanation of a company's financial performance in a section of the quarterly or annual report entitled, "Management's Discussion and Analysis of Financial Condition and Results of Operations." MD&A is *management's* opportunity to provide investors with its view of the financial performance and condition of the company.

Sample Change in Stockholders' Equity Statement
Deere & Company
As of October 31, 2011, 2010 and 2009
(In millions of dollars except per share amounts)

	Total Stockholder's Equity	Comprehensive Income (Loss)	Deere & Company Stockholders Common Stock	Treasury Stock	Retained Earnings	Accumulated Other Comprehensive Income (Loss)	Non-Controlling Interests
Balance October 31, 2008	$ 6,537.2		$ 2,934	$ (5,594.6)	$ 10,580.6	$ (1,387.3)	$ 4.5
Net income (loss)	872.9	873.5			873.5		(0.6)
Other comprehensive income (loss)							
Retirement benefits adjustment	(2,536.6)	(2,536.6)				(2,536.6)	
Cumulative translation adjustment	327.4	326.8				326.8	.6
Unrealized loss on derivatives	(4.0)	(4.0)				(4.0)	
Unrealized gain on investments	7.8	7.8				7.8	
Total comprehensive income	(1,332.5)	$ (1,332.5)					
Repurchases of common stock	(3.2)			(3.2)			
Treasury shares reissued	33.1			33.1			
Dividends declared	(473.6)				(473.6)		
Stock options and other	61.8		62.2				(.4)
Balance October 31, 2009	4,822.8		2,996.2	(5,564.7)	10,980.5	(3,593.3)	4.1
Net income	1,874.3	1,865.0			1,865.0		9.3
Other comprehensive income (loss)							
Retirement benefits adjustment	158.0	158.0				158.0	
Cumulative translation adjustment	35.7	35.8				35.8	(.1)
Unrealized gain on derivatives	14.9	14.9				14.9	
Unrealized gain on investments	5.0	5.0				5.0	
Total comprehensive income	2,087.9	$ 2,078.7					9.2
Repurchases of common stock	(358.8)			(358.8)			
Treasury shares reissued	134.0			134.0			
Dividends declared	(492.7)				(492.3)		(.4)
Stock options and other	110.2		110.1		(.1)		.2
Balance October 31, 2010	6,303.4		3,106.3	(5,789.5)	12,353.1	(3,379.6)	13.1
Net income	2,807.8	$ 2,799.9			2,799.9		7.9
Other comprehensive income (loss)							
Retirement benefits adjustment	(338.4)	(338.4)				(338.4)	
Cumulative translation adjustment	17.8	17.8				17.8	
Unrealized gain on derivatives	20.9	20.9				20.9	
Unrealized gain on investments	1.3	1.3				1.3	
Total comprehensive income	2,509.4	$ 2,501.5					7.9
Repurchases of common stock	(1,667.0)			(1,667.0)			
Treasury shares reissued	163.7			163.7			
Dividends declared	(638.0)				(633.5)		(4.5)
Stock options and other	143.4		145.4		(.1)		(1.9)
Balance October 31, 2011	$ 6,814.9		$ 3,251.7	$ (7,292.8)	$ 14,519.4	$ (3,678.0)	$ 14.6

The notes to consolidated financial statements are an integral part of this statement.

The SEC's rules governing MD&A require disclosure about trends, events or uncertainties known to management that would have a material impact on reported financial information. The purpose of MD&A is to provide investors with information that the company's management believes to be necessary to an understanding of its financial condition, changes in financial condition and results of operations. It is intended to help investors to see the company through the eyes of management. It is also intended to provide context for the financial statements and information about the company's earnings and cash flows.

Financial Statement Ratios and Calculations

You've probably heard people banter around phrases like "P/E ratio," "current ratio" and "operating margin." But what do these terms mean and why don't they show up on financial statements? Listed below are just some of the many ratios that investors calculate from information on financial statements and then use to evaluate a company. As a general rule, desirable ratios vary by industry.

Debt-to-equity ratio compares a company's total debt to shareholders' equity. Both of these numbers can be found on a company's balance sheet. To calculate debt-to-equity ratio, you divide a company's total liabilities by its shareholder equity, or

Debt-to-Equity Ratio = Total Liabilities / Shareholders' Equity

If a company has a debt-to-equity ratio of 2 to 1, it means that the company has two dollars of debt to every one dollar shareholders invest in the company. In other words, the company is taking on debt at twice the rate that its owners are investing in the company.

Inventory turnover ratio compares a company's cost of sales on its income statement with its average inventory balance for the period. To calculate the average inventory balance for the period, look at the inventory numbers listed on the balance sheet. Take the balance listed for the period of the report and add it to the balance listed for the previous comparable period, and then divide by two. (Remember that balance sheets are snapshots in time. So the inventory balance for the previous period is the beginning balance for the current period, and the inventory balance for the current period is the ending balance.) To calculate the inventory turnover ratio, you divide a company's cost of sales (just below the net revenues on the income statement) by the average inventory for the period, or

Inventory Turnover Ratio = Cost of Sales / Average
Inventory for the Period

If a company has an inventory turnover ratio of 2 to 1, it means that the company's inventory turned over twice in the reporting period.

Operating margin compares a company's operating income to net revenues. Both of these numbers can be found on a company's income statement. To calculate operating margin, you divide a company's income from operations (before interest and income tax expenses) by its net revenues, or

Operating Margin = Income from Operations / Net Revenues

Operating margin is usually expressed as a percentage. It shows, for each dollar of sales, what percentage was profit.

P/E ratio compares a company's common stock price with its earnings per share. To calculate a company's P/E ratio, you divide a company's stock price by its earnings per share, or

P/E Ratio = Price per share / Earnings per share

If a company's stock is selling at $20 per share and the company is earning $2 per share, then the company's P/E Ratio is 10 to 1. The company's stock is selling at 10 times its earnings.

Working capital is the money leftover if a company paid its current liabilities (that is, its debts due within one-year of the date of the balance sheet) from its current assets.

Working Capital = Current Assets – Current Liabilities

Bringing It All Together

Although this discusses each financial statement separately, keep in mind that they are all related. The changes in assets and liabilities that you see on the balance sheet are also reflected in the revenues and expenses that you see on the income statement, which result in the company's gains or losses. Cash flows provide more information about cash assets listed on a balance sheet and are related, but not equivalent, to net income shown on the income statement. And so on. No one financial statement tells the complete story. But combined, they provide very powerful information for investors. And information is the investor's best tool when it comes to investing wisely.

CASE PROBLEM 4-1

Refer to the four financial statements of Deere & Company that are set forth above but ignore the reference that they are expressed in millions of dollars (that is, assume they are dollars only). Assume that Deere & Company determines that these statements need to be changed to account for an additional cash equipment sale that occurred in October 2011. The sales price was $1,000 and the cost of the item sold was $600. How would this transaction change specific line items in each of the four statements? Ignore tax considerations.

B. CORE BUSINESS CONCEPTS

A business legal advisor needs to understand core business concepts. Without such an understanding, the advisor will struggle to comprehend business objectives and to participate in intelligent business-focused conversations. The goal is to have a working knowledge of those basic concepts that drive all businesses: income, cash flow, leverage, opportunity costs, depreciation, return on equity, etc.

The following simple description of a tiny company's first three years of operation is designed to illustrate 10 core business concepts. It is designed for those students who need some basic business tutoring. The veteran business or accounting student is encouraged to skip this section and move on.

Party Time Inc.

Jane knows food and is a party animal. After much thought and analysis, she quit her job at the end of 2008 to start her own catering business in early 2009. She formed a corporation named Party Time, Inc., contributed $60,000 for the stock, and started the business on January 1. Initially, Party Time's targeted clients were high-income couples who wanted the very best when they threw a party. During the first year of operation, Jane was Party Time's sole employee and handled every detail of every event. When she needed assistance, Party Time hired temporary help for a flat hourly rate of $13. Party Time rented a small commercial kitchen and used $50,000 of its capital to buy a van and essential equipment items. In 2009, Party Time's gross client billings totaled $100,000, of which $80,000 was collected during the year. The uncollected $20,000 represented billings from the busy year-end holiday season that were collected during the first two months of 2010. Party Time's expenses in 2009 totaled $81,700, of which $11,000 remained unpaid at year-end. Key expenses included rent, food, advertising, temporary help, and gas. Jane took no compensation from the company during 2009.

1. Income. What was Party Time's income in 2009? Income is an essential concept of business, but it has different meanings based on what it is measuring. The starting point for most business owners is operating income, which is the earnings from the business before any reductions for interest, income taxes, depreciation, and amortization. It is commonly referred to as "EBITDA." EBITDA measures the profitability of the company's operations. Party Time's EBITDA in 2009 was $18,300, the excess of its total billings of $100,000 over its operating expenses of $81,700.

The next income definition is net income before taxes. This number factors in all expenses except the income taxes that the company must pay on its earnings. It is calculated by reducing the EBITDA by expenses for interest, depreciation, and amortization. Party Time had no interest expense in 2009 because it had no debt, nor did it have any amortizable assets. But it did own a van and equipment that will wear out over time and will need to be replaced. This wearing out cost is referred to as depreciation. It is not an expense that is based on a cash outlay; it reflects the diminution in value of assets owned by the business. Since the equipment purchased by Party Time for $50,000 at the beginning of 2009 was expected to wear out over a useful life of five years, Party Time's annual depreciation expense for that equipment was $10,000. Thus, Party Time's net income before taxes in 2009 was $8,300, its EBITDA of $18,300 less its depreciation expense of $10,000.

The third income component is net income after taxes. This component factors in the income taxes that need to be paid on the company's income. At a federal corporate tax rate of 15 percent on the first $50,000 of earnings, Party Time's income tax liability on its $8,300 of earnings in 2009 was $1,245. Thus, its net income after taxes equaled $7,055. All three of the income concepts described above are reflected in Party Time's income statement for 2009 (Exhibit 1, 2009 column).

Exhibit 1
Party Time Inc. Income Statements

	2009	2010	2011 No-Debt	2011 Debt
Revenues	$ 100,000	$ 180,000	$ 640,000	$ 640,000
Expenses				
Rent	$ 18,000	$ 18,000	$ 18,000	$ 18,000
Food	25,000	39,600	137,300	137,300
Advertising	22,000	22,000	22,000	22,000
Salaries	-	50,000	275,000	275,000
Payroll Taxes	-	4,500	24,750	24,750
Gas	1,100	1,900	7,500	7,500
Help	14,000	22,000	4,800	4,800
Misc. Expenses	1,600	2,900	3,400	3,400
Total	$ 81,700	$ 160,900	$ 492,750	$ 492,750
Operating Income	$ 18,300	$ 19,100	$ 147,250	$ 147,250
Depreciation	10,000	10,000	42,000	42,000
Interest Expense	-	-	-	13,500
Income Before Taxes	$ 8,300	$ 9,100	$ 105,250	$ 91,750
Income Taxes	1,245	1,365	24,297	19,445
Net Income	$ 7,055	$ 7,735	$ 80,953	$ 72,305

2. Cash Flow. Cash flow is a concept different than income, although it is heavily influenced by the income of the business. Cash flow is just what its name implies; it measures the cash that goes in and out of the business. The starting point for the cash flow analysis is the net income after taxes of the business, which was $7,055 in 2009.

To arrive at the cash flow, this income number must be increased for expenses that did not require any cash outlay during 2009, which for Party Time included the depreciation expense of $10,000, the $11,000 of operating expenses that remained unpaid at the end of the year (typically referred to as accounts payable increase), and the income tax liability of $1,245 that was not paid until the following year. For cash flow purposes, the net income must be decreased by the $20,000 of gross billings that were not actually collected during the year (the accounts receivable increase) and the $50,000 that was used to purchase the van and equipment. Exhibit 2 is Party Time's Cash Flow Summary for 2009.

As Exhibit 2 indicates, even though Party Time showed a net after-tax income of $7,055 in 2009, its cash resources plummeted from $60,000 at the beginning of the year to $19,300 at year-end. This is why many say "cash is king" in start-up operations and why undercapitalization is the reason so many promising businesses fail. The income statement and cash flow summary show the activity of the company over a given period of time, here calendar year 2009. This activity is reflected in the balance sheets of Party Time at the beginning and end of the year (Exhibit 3), each of which provides a snapshot of the assets and liabilities of the company at a specific point in time.

Exhibit 2
Party Time Inc. Cash Flow Summary

Beginning Cash	$ 60,000
Plus:	
Net Income	$ 7,055
Accounts Payable Increase	11,000
Income Tax Payable Increase	1,245
Depreciation	10,000
Total Additions	$ 29,300
Less:	
Equipment Purchases	$ 50,000
Accounts Receivable Increase	20,000
Total Reductions	$ 70,000
Net Change	(40,700)
Ending Cash	$ 19,300

3. Current Assets and Current Liabilities. A business needs to be able to meet its obligations as they become due. A popular technique for measuring a business' capacity to timely fund its obligations is to compare the company's current assets with its current liabilities.

Current assets are those assets that will be converted to cash within one year, and current liabilities are those debts that must be paid within a year. The number obtained by dividing the current assets by the current liabilities is known as the "current ratio." Party Time's current ratio at the end of 2009 was 3.2, strong by any standard. Another ratio that is often used is known as a "quick ratio" or "acid test" ratio. It is the same as the current ratio, except that inventories are excluded from current assets in making the calculation. Since Party Time had no inventories, its quick ratio would be the same as its current ratio.

4. Opportunity Costs. Beyond the costs actually incurred in operating the business, business owners must always consider the opportunity costs of any decision they make. Opportunity costs are the benefits that are lost because a particular course is pursued. In this case, Jane chose to form a new business that generated a bottom line profit of $7,055 in 2009 and sucked up a large portion of the $60,000 that she contributed to the business. She worked hard in 2009, but drew no salary or income from the business. This course of action triggered at least three opportunity costs. First, if she had left the $60,000 that she invested in the company in a bank certificate of deposit that earns five percent annually, she would have earned $3,000 of interest in 2009, and she would have had all of her cash at year end. Second, if she had stayed at her old job, she would have earned a salary and other benefits valued at $75,000 in 2009. Third, if she had remained at her old job, she would have racked up another year of experience and seniority. These are big opportunity costs that she incurred in starting the business.

Exhibit 3
Party Time Inc. Balance Sheet

	As of 1/1/2009	As of 12/31/2009
Assets		
Cash	$ 60,000	$ 19,300
Accounts Receivable		20,000
Total Current Assets		$ 39,300
Equipment		50,000
Less: Accum. Depreciation		(10,000)
Total Assets	$ 60,000	$ 79,300
Liabilities		
Accounts Payable		$ 11,000
Taxes Payable		1,245
Total Current Liabilities		$ 12,245
Owner Equity		
Contributed Capital	$ 60,000	$ 60,000
Retained Earnings		7,055
Total Owner Equity		$ 67,055
Total Liabilities and Equity	$ 60,000	$ 79,300

Smart business decisions are made by factoring in all costs, both real and opportunity. Standard financial statements do not reflect or account for opportunity costs. And often it isn't advisable to approach an opportunity cost analysis based solely on specific numbers. For example, when Jane decided to make her move in 2009, she knew that she would risk $60,000 of hard-earned capital, would work hard in 2009 for no pay, and would give up her secure job and all the benefits that it promised. Any short-term quantitative analysis of those opportunity costs likely would have encouraged Jane to sit tight and count her blessings. Many business plans never come to fruition because the short-term pain of making the move and taking the risks (the opportunity costs) is perceived as being too great. But in this case, Jane weighed these known opportunity costs against the opportunity benefits of doing something she loved and potentially building a valuable going concern that she would own. Although her numbers in 2009 were nothing to write home about, she knew momentum was building and the numbers would improve going forward. And they did.

5. Fixed vs. Variable Expenses. Through word of mouth, the demand for Party Time's custom catering services grew rapidly in 2010. By mid-year, Jane was regularly turning away more business than she accepted. As her revenue (her top line) number grew, she noticed that her bottom line income number grew at a faster rate. This was due to the fact that certain key expenses – rent and advertising – were fixed in amount and did not increase with the growth in revenues. Other expenses, such as food and temporary labor, were variable with the revenues. The ability to leverage fixed expenses is very important in the growth cycle of any business. In 2010, Jane grew Party Time's total revenues to $180,000, but profitability grew fast enough to allow Jane to draw personal compensation benefits of $50,000 from the business and still drop $7,735 to the bottom line as income. Party Time's income statement for 2010 is in Exhibit 1, 2010 column.

6. Economies of Scale. Although Jane was pleased with the activity in 2010, she was frustrated with the work she was being forced to turn away. Many of her clients owned or ran businesses or professional practices, and she was constantly being offered lucrative opportunities to cater business events. She was forced to turn down all but the smallest of these jobs because of her limited personnel and her one-truck operation. She soon discovered that the economy of scale of her business was not large enough to accommodate the kind of growth she wanted.

Every business must be geared to operate at a given level of activity. Its resources and planning are based on a defined level of activity, commonly referred to as its economy of scale. Some businesses are very "scalable," which means they can easily adjust their economy of scale to accommodate more volume. On the other end of the scalability spectrum are those businesses that must make huge additional investments and take on much greater risks to build an expanded economy of scale. Jane quickly determined that she needed to build a new economy of scale to meet the expanded demand for her services.

After careful analysis, she decided to purchase and outfit three large trucks and to hire three full-time "event lieutenants," each of whom would be paid compensation and benefits equal to $50,000 a year. Jane easily identified the best candidates from a talented pool of temporary assistants. She knew that each of the three candidates loved the business, would work hard, and would jump at the opportunity to have a full-time job that paid well. Jane's new economy of scale required an additional investment of $180,000 to cover the costs of the trucks and equipment and the necessary working capital to fund the expansion. Jane dipped deeper into her savings and made the additional investment.

Jane's expanded economy of scale was in full swing by the start of 2011. It all worked. Jane was able to effectively use her lieutenants to leverage her personal touch across all major events. As Party Time began catering larger corporate events, its reputation ballooned in all markets. Its gross revenues grew to $640,000 in 2011.

7. Leverage and Return on Equity. Jane's expansion plan required an additional investment of $180,000, bringing her total investment in Party Time to $240,000. And it all paid off. In 2011, she was able to pay herself $75,000 from the business and still generate a bottom line net profit of $80,953, as indicated by Party Time's 2011 income statement (See Exhibit 1, 2011 No-Debt column). This net profit represented a 33.73 percent annual return on her total equity investment of $240,000.

Suppose that Jane did not fund her expansion plan with more private investment capital. Assume instead that she went to her local bank, presented her operating history and future plans, and secured a bank line of credit for $180,000 at an annual interest cost of seven and one-half percent. Jane would be spared the burden of having to come up with more personal capital, but Party Time would have a new annual interest expense of $13,500. This interest expense, net of income tax impacts, would reduce Party Time's net income in 2011 to $72,305, as illustrated in Party Time's revised income statement for 2011 (see Exhibit 1, 2011 Debt column). Although the net income would be reduced by the net after-tax cost of the interest expense, the yield on Jane's equity investment would skyrocket. Her original equity investment of $60,000 would generate an annual yield in 2011 of $72,305, more than 120 percent. This is known as positive leverage. The business operations created the opportunity to leverage the existing equity by generating a yield off borrowed funds that far exceeded the cost of the funds. This leverage is the key to maximizing business equity. It is business 101.

8. Debt-to-Equity Ratio. The potential of debt leverage encourages some to overdo it. The ratio of the debt to the equity of the business must be reasonable for business and tax purposes. The reasonableness is measured by a debt-to-equity ratio, which is determined by dividing the company's debt by the equity of the business. Sometimes the ratio is based on all the debt of the business; other times it includes only the long-term debt. There is no mandated acceptable ratio. Debt-to-equity ratios vary widely among industries and particular businesses.

Generally (and I really mean generally), a ratio of less than 5-to-1 is considered reasonable, and any ratio in excess of 10-to-1 is usually suspect. If Jane had used the bank line to finance her expansion plan, the book value of the owner's equity on the company's balance sheet at the end of 2011 would equal $147,095. This is calculated by increasing the owner's equity balance at the end of 2009 (Exhibit 3) by the net retained income in 20010 and 2011 (Exhibit 1). Thus, even with a bank line of $180,000, her debt-to-equity ratio would have been less than 2-to-1, reasonable by any standard.

9. Gross Multipliers and Capitalization Rates. By the end of 2011, many were aware of Jane's success. Party Time had a superb reputation, and

Jane was known as the inspiration behind its success. A profitable high-end regional restaurant chain (Chain) had been planning a move into the corporate catering business. Chain was faced with a choice. It could endure the start-up expense and hassle of trying to compete with Party Time's reputation and Jane's golden touch, or it could try to buy Party Time and make Jane part of its team. Chain's management decided that a purchase would make sense if the purchased operation would generate a pre-tax operating yield of 13 percent on the price paid for the business. This is known as the capitalization rate, the rate used to determine the purchase price based on a known EBITDA. Party Time's EBITDA in 2011 was $147,250 (Exhibit 1, 2011 Debt column). Dividing this amount by the desired capitalization rate of 13 percent produced a purchase price of $1,132,692. If Jane accepted Chain's offer of this amount for the business, she would pay off the $180,000 bank line, pay her tax hit, put the rest in her pocket, and negotiate an employment agreement with Chain. Sometimes the capitalization rate is expressed as an equivalent income multiple. They are two sides of the same coin. In this case, an EBITDA income of $147,250 was the basis of a purchase price of $1,132,692 based on a 13 percent capitalization rate. This represents an income multiple of 7.69 (147,250/1,132,692). Thus, specifying an EBITDA income multiple of 7.69 is the equivalent of specifying a capitalization rate of 13 percent.

10. Goodwill and Going Concern Value. Under the forgoing analysis, the corporate equity owned by Jane at the time of sale had a value of approximately $953,000, after the purchase price of $1,132,692 was reduced by the $180,000 line of credit. But, as indicated above, the book value of Jane's equity on the company's balance sheet at the end of 2011 was only $147,095. Valuing the business' equity on the basis of the earnings power of the operation produced a value that was many times greater than the equity book value derived from the assets and liabilities of the company. This excess value, which is huge for many companies, is known as goodwill and going concern value. It recognizes that Jane has built an ongoing, profitable operation that has valued customers and employees and a coveted market reputation. A large, ever-growing goodwill and going concern value is the ultimate goal of all operating businesses.

CASE PROBLEM 4-2

Refer to the financial statements of Deere & Company in Section A of this chapter.

a. Based on such financial statements, what was Deere & Company's :

- Current ratio at the end of its 2011 year?

- Quick ratio at the end of its 2011 year?

- Total debt-to-equity ratio at the end of its 2011 year?

For these purposes, assume the inventories and all assets listed above the inventories are current assets.

b. What was Deere & Company's EBITDA for 2011? Refer to its Income Statement and Stockholders' Equity Statement.

c. Assume that the management of Deere & Company has decided to raise an additional $5 billion to finance its growth plans. There are two options for securing the needed capital: A 10-year loan (bond) or the sale of common stock. What factors would Deere & Company's management likely consider important in evaluating these two options? If the management would consider issuing more stock only on a basis that values the company's existing outstanding common stock at a capitalization rate of eight percent on its 2011 pre-tax consolidated income, what percentage of the total outstanding stock of Deere & Company would be issued for the $5 billion of new equity capital?

C. BUSINESS VALUATION BASICS

1. THE LAWYER'S NON-ROLE

Foolish is the lawyer who attempts to value a client's business or even express an opinion on its value. It's not the job of the lawyer. It is beyond the lawyer's expertise or training. Other professionals are trained to tackle the tough job of pinning a value on an ever-evolving bundle of assets and income-generating operations. Let them take the heat. Avoid any temptation to start sounding like a valuation expert with clients.

This does not mean that a lawyer should not understand the vocabulary and basic techniques of business valuations. Such an understanding is essential to being a good legal advisor to business owners. At the most basic level, it makes intelligent conversation possible with those business owners who regularly analyze and ponder the importance of events, both internal and external, that may impact the value of the business they have devoted their working lives to building. They regularly talk of intangible asset indicators, capitalization and discount rates, EBITDA multipliers, and the like.

But the need to know goes beyond client relationships. The issue of value goes right to the heart of the planning effort in countless situations. It, for example, is center stage in buy-sell planning among co-owners, new owner admission challenges, executive-based equity incentives, insurance planning, all estate planning and related family planning challenges, and all exit strategy planning. Valuation challenges are always present in major transaction, including acquisitions, mergers, leveraged buy-outs, and initial public offerings. Business valuation issues often arise in a litigation context in connection with marital dissolution, bankruptcy, breach of contract, dissenting shareholder and minority oppression cases, economic damages computations, and other cases.

While the lawyer is not the valuation expert in these situations, the lawyer's working knowledge of the relevant factors and techniques can strengthen the quality of the entire planning effort. It facilities dialogue with the experts that may help identify or eliminate sloppy valuations. It enables the lawyer to spot unreasonable client valuation expectations. Often it makes it possible for the lawyer to assist the client in understanding the factors that impact the valuation determination and to explain the valuation to other parties who are impacted by the determination. And in most situations, it helps the lawyer lead the planning process.

A knowledge of valuation factors and techniques also can make a lawyer a much better negotiator. Most business negotiations are about value. A primary challenge in the negotiation process is to convince the other side that it is being offered a fair deal based on the values. The lawyer who is equipped to use valuation lingo and measurement techniques to make the case is often very effective. This is one situation where the lawyer can become a valuation advocate by applying favorable factors, drawing comparisons, and expressing "heat-of-battle" opinions. The difference here (and it is huge) is that the lawyer is not seeking to advise a client, but rather is seeking to prevail in a negotiation with one who is not a client. Often the lawyer who gets on a valuation soapbox in a tough negotiation is well advised to privately remind any client who witnessed the show that negotiation dialogue is no substitute for quality advice from a valuation expert.

2. THE CHALLENGE

Revenue Ruling 59-60[2] is a useful starting point in assessing the nature of the business valuation challenge. Although ancient, this ruling continues to provide relevant guidance. In the context of business valuations, it states the classic definition of "fair market value" as "the price at which the property would change hands between a willing buyer and a willing seller when the former is not under any compulsion to buy and the latter is not under any compulsion to sell, both parties having reasonable knowledge of the relevant facts." In lieu of prescribing a specific mathematical valuation formula, the ruling discusses the following factors that should be considered in arriving at a fair market value determination:

1. The nature of the business and the history of the enterprise from its inception.

2. The economic outlook in general and the condition and outlook of the specific industry in particular.

3. The book value of the stock and financial condition of the business.

4. The earning capacity of the company.

5. The dividend-paying capacity.

6. Whether or not the enterprise has goodwill or other intangible value.

7. Sales of the stock and the size of the block of stock to be valued.

8. The market price of stocks of corporations engaged in the same or a similar line of business having their stocks actively traded in a free and open market, either on an exchange or over-the-counter.

---

2. 1959-1 C.B. 237. Years later in Revenue Ruling 68-609, 1968-2 C.B. 327, the Service stated that the valuation principles of 59-60 also would apply to partnership interests.

Although the fair market value standard has been around forever and nearly a half century ago the Internal Revenue Service provided guidance on how it should be applied in valuing business interests, serious valuation disputes routinely erupt. These disputes teach two important lessons. First, secure the services of a professional appraiser. Valuing a business interest requires judgment calls that must be made by a professional. Second, get the best appraiser available. If a dispute breaks out, the quality, reputation, and competence of the appraiser may be the ultimate deciding factor. The Tax Court, for example, has consistently refused to accept an appraisal on its face; it has followed a practice of carefully examining the underlying details and assumptions and the quality of the appraiser's analysis.[3]

Revenue Ruling 59-60 also recognized that the size of the block of stock is a relevant valuation factor in valuing an interest in a business enterprise, specifically noting that a minority interest would be more difficult to sell. In many situations, valuation discounts become the name of the game and play an essential role in the planning process. The two most significant discounts associated with an interest in a closely held business enterprise are the minority interest (lack of control) discount and the lack of marketability discount. The minority interest discount recognizes that a willing buyer will not pay as much for a minority interest; there is no control. The lack of marketability discount reflects the reality that a willing buyer will pay less for an interest in a closely held business if there is no ready market of future buyers for the interest. Usually both discounts are applied in valuing the transferred interest.[4] Often the two discounts total as much as 35 to 40 percent when a minority interest is being valued.[5]

Of course, publicly traded companies and closely held enterprises present different valuation challenges. A public company's value is impacted by the demand for its stock, which can be heavily influenced by general market conditions and factors that are unrelated to the company's performance. A closely held enterprise's value tends to be more closely tied to specify industry factors and the company's track record. Stockholders of public companies generally have no significant influence on how the company is managed; owners of closely held enterprises usually run the whole show. And whereas profit maximization is premier objective in publicly traded companies, income maximization often takes a back seat to tax planning for the owners of closely held businesses.

When it comes to business valuations, nothing is easy and uncertainty abounds. William Yegge, an experienced business valuation expert and author summed it as follows:

For nearly 30 years I have wrestled with the question: What is business

---

3. See, for example, Rabenhorst v. Commissioner, 71 TCM(CCH) 2271 (1996) and Estate of Kaufman v. Commissioner, 77 TCM (CCH) 1779 (1999).

4. See, for example, Dailey v. Commissioner, 82 TCM 710 (2001); Janda v. Commissioner, 81 TCM 1100 (2001); Barnes v. Commissioner, 76 TCM 881 (1998); Litchfield v. Commissioner, T.C. Memo 2009-21.

5. Id.

value? And to this day, assignment of intangible value in business remains the more perplexing task. There simply is no "pat" answer or formula. My way is neither right nor wrong, and the task is not really made easier with experience. If I have learned one common essential, it is to exercise caution in assigning intangible value and throughout the whole process. There will always be reams of theory and flames of discussion, because scientific formulas developed for intangible value can do no more than "attempt" to measure the art form of human enterprise.[6]

3. ALTERNATIVE VALUATION METHODS

It helps to have a basic understanding of the various methods that are used to value a business. The most appropriate method in any given situation depends on the nature and history of the business, market conditions, and a host of other factors. Often a combination of methods is used. In Section B above, the capitalized earnings method was illustrated. The business' value was determined by applying a capitalization rate to EBITDA or some other designated measure of income. Following is a brief description of select other methods.

Book Value Method. The book value method bases the value on the company's balance sheet. It is total assets less as total liabilities, using the balance sheet's historical dollar cost numbers. No attempt is made to account for the fair market value of the assets or the going concern value of the enterprise. For that reason, it is usually a poor measure of a company's real value. Its only virtue is its simplicity.

Adjusted Book Value Method. This is the same as the Book Value Method, with one important twist. Under this method, the assets are adjusted to reflect their current fair market values. The balance sheet is still the driving force, but asset values are restated. It works best in those situations where asset values are the key to the company's value. But it is a poor measure for an operating business whose value is predicated on its earning capacity and going concern value.

Hybrid Method. The hybrid method, in most situations, is a combination of the Adjusted Book Value Method and the capitalized earnings method illustrated in section B above (Item 9). A value is determined under each method and then the two values are weighted to arrive at a value for the business. For example, if a determination was made to base 20 percent of the value on the Adjusted Book Value Method and 80 percent on the capitalized earnings value, an amount equal to 20 percent of the Adjusted Book Value method would be added to an amount equal to 80 percent of the capitalized earnings value. The Hybrid Method works best in those situations where the business' value is attributable to a combination of asset values and its earning capacity.

Excess Earnings Method. This method incorporates the features of the Hybrid Method, but factors in the cost of carrying the assets of the business and financing impacts. The starting point is to multiply the "Net Tangible Assets"

---

6. Yegge, A Basic Guide to Valuing a Company (John Wiley & Sons Inc. 2002).

(aggregate fair market value of the tangible assets less liabilities) by a relevant applied lending interest rate to arrive at the annual cost of carrying the assets ("Cost of Money"). The designated income measure (EBITDA, for example) is reduced by the Cost of Money, and the result is divided by the designated capitalization rate to arrive at the business' "Intangible Value." The Intangible Value is then added to the Net Tangible Assets to arrive at the total value.

Discounted Cash Flow of Future Earnings. This method calculates the company's value by looking to the future. The applicable earnings measure (EBITDA, for example) is projected to increase at a given rate for a designated period of time, such as ten years. The present value of the projected EBITDA in each of such years is then calculated by applying a discount rate that reflects the level of risk and uncertainty associated with the business and the time value of money. The present value determinations for each of the years are then added together to arrive at the business' value. When this method it used, often it is done to confirm the conclusions of another method.

CASE PROBLEM 4-3

Refer to the four financial statements of Deere & Company that are set forth in Section A above, but ignore the reference that they are expressed in millions of dollars (that is, assume they are dollars only). Calculate the company's value under the following methods:

A. Book Value Method

B. Adjusted Book Value Method, assuming the following assets have the following values and each other asset has a value equal to its book value:

Equipment on Operating Leases: $ 3,250

Property and Equipment: $ 7,140

Investments in Unconsolidated Affiliates: $ 3,540

Goodwill: $ 4,210

Other Intangible Assets: $ 2,370

C. Capitalized earnings method based on the average consolidated pre-tax income for the last three years (2009 thru 2011) and a capitalization rate of 8.33 percent (equivalent to a multiplier of 12).

D. Hybrid of B and C, with 30 percent allocated to B and 70 percent allocated to C.

E. Excess earnings method based on consolidated pre-tax income for 2011, a seven percent applied lending rate, and a 12.5 percent yield rate (equivalent to a multiplier of 8). Assume the Net Intangible Assets total $12,957.

F. Discounted cash flow of future earnings method based on 10 year projections of consolidated pre-tax earnings, assuming consolidated pre-tax earnings increase at nine percent each year and the risk level return requirement is 18 percent.

CHAPTER 5

ENTITY TAXATION AND
CHOICE-OF-ENTITY PLANNING

A. ENTITY TAXATION CONCEPTS

Business owners need to be smart with taxes. The objective is to minimize the government's bite, consistent with other objectives, and to avoid look-back planning blunders – those situations where an owner, faced with an ugly tax bill that could have been avoided with some advance planning, exclaims in disgust, "I sure wish someone had told me that five years ago."

Smart tax planning requires more than just strategizing against a static set of rules. Changes in the rules must be anticipated and factored into the mix. Tax planning has always favored those who can wisely anticipate a moving target. And there is little question that today, perhaps more than ever, the target is moving faster and is harder to predict.

1. CORPORATION TAX BASICS – Q&As

5.1 What is a C corporation?

A C corporation is a regular corporation that pays its own taxes. It is a creature of state law, is recognized as a separate taxable entity, and is governed by the provisions of subchapter C of the Internal Revenue Code. Any corporation that does not properly elect to be taxed as an S corporation will be taxed as a C corporation.

5.2 What tax rates do C corporations pay?

The first $50,000 of a C corporation's taxable income each year is subject to a favorable 15 percent tax rate. The rate jumps to 25 percent on the next $25,000 of taxable income. Thus, the overall rate on the first $75,000 of taxable income is an attractive 18.33 percent, far less than the personal marginal rate applicable to most successful business owners. Beyond $75,000, the rate advantage disappears as the marginal rate jumps to 34 percent. Plus, if the corporation's income exceeds $100,000, the rate "bubbles" an additional five percent on taxable income over $100,000 until any rate savings on the first $75,000 is lost. The impact of this five percent "bubble" is that any C corporation with a taxable income of $335,000 or more will pay a rate of at least 34 percent from dollar one. Earnings of a C corporation in excess of $10 million are taxed at 35 percent, and a three percent "bubble" applies to C corporation earnings in excess of $15 million until the rate applicable to all income is 35 percent.[1]

There are no rate breaks for a professional service organization that is taxed as a C corporation; it is subject to a flat 35 percent rate from dollar one.[2]

5.3 What is the C corporations double tax structure?

The biggest negative of a C corporation is the double tax structure – a corporate level tax and a shareholder level tax. It surfaces whenever a dividend is paid or is deemed to have been paid. But the grief of the double tax structure is not limited to dividends; it kicks in whenever the assets of the business are sold and the proceeds distributed. It's all a result of the inherent double tax structure of a C corporation.

5.4 What are the federal tax rates that shareholders must pay on dividends received from a C corporation?

The economic stimulus package of 2003 resulted in a compromise that reduced the maximum tax rate on "qualifying corporate dividends" paid to non-corporate shareholders to 15 percent (5 percent for low-income shareholders otherwise subject to maximum marginal rates of 15 percent or less).[3] These reduced rates applied to all dividends received from January 1, 2003 to December 31, 2012. The American Taxpayer Relief Act of 2012 (the "fiscal cliff" legislation signed into law during the final days of 2012)[4] increased this low dividend rate to 20 percent starting in 2013 for couples with taxable incomes in excess of $450,000 and individuals with taxable incomes in excess of $400,000. Plus, in 2013, the 3.8 percent Medicare tax kicks in on interest, dividends, capital gains, and other "net investment income" to the extent that this income, when added to the taxpayer's other modified adjusted gross income, exceeds $200,000 in the case of unmarried individuals, $250,000 in the case of married individuals filing jointly, and $125,000 in the case of married individuals filing separately. The net result is that a couple with an adjusted income of less than $250,000 or a single person with an adjusted gross income of less than $200,000 will continue to pay the pre-2013 dividend rates (a maximum of 15 percent).[5] Couples or individuals with higher incomes will pay a combined income and Medicare dividend rate of either 18.8 percent or 23.8 percent, depending on whether the new $450,000 or $400,000 thresholds are exceeded.

5.5 How are C corporation dividends paid to C corporation shareholders taxed?

There is an attractive income tax deduction for dividends paid by one C corporation to another C corporation. The purpose of the deduction is to eliminate the potential of a triple tax on corporate earnings – one at the operating C corporation level, a second at the corporate shareholder level, and a third at the individual shareholder level. The deduction is at least 70 percent, and increases to 80 percent for corporate shareholders who own 20 percent of the operating

---

1. I.R.C. § 11(b)(1).
2. I.R.C. § 11(b)(2).
3. I.R.C. § 1(h)11(b).
4. Section 102 of the American Taxpayer Relief Act of 2012.
5. I.R.C. § 1411.

entity's stock and 100 percent for members of an affiliated group.[6]

5.6 How are tax losses of a C corporation treated?

Losses sustained by a C corporation are trapped inside the corporation. They may be carried backward or forward, but they will never be passed through to the shareholders.

5.7   How much flexibility does a C corporation have in selecting a tax year?

A great deal. A C corporation may adopt any fiscal year to ease its accounting and administrative burdens and to maximize tax deferral planning.[7]

5.8 Can a C corporation combine with other corporations on a tax-free basis?

Yes. A C corporation may participate in a tax-free reorganization with other corporate entities. It's possible for corporations to combine through mergers, stock-for-stock transactions, and assets-for-stock transactions on terms that eliminate all corporate and shareholder-level taxes.[8] This opportunity often is the key to the ultimate payday for those private business owners who cash in by "selling" their business to a public corporation. Cast as a reorganization, the transaction allows the acquiring entity to fund the acquisition with its own stock (little or no cash required) and enables the selling owners to walk with highly liquid, publicly traded securities and no tax bills until the securities are sold.

5.9 How is the gain recognized on the sale of C corporation stock taxed?

The stock of a C corporation is a capital asset that qualifies for long-term capital gain treatment if sold after being held for more than a year.[9] The problem for planning purposes is that it is usually difficult, if not impossible, to accurately predict when stock may be sold and even more difficult to speculate on what the state of the long-term capital gains break will be at that time. Too often, planning is based on the assumption that the status quo will remain the status quo. History, even very recent history, confirms the fallacy of this assumption with respect to the capital gains tax. Just over the past two decades, we have seen the gap between ordinary and capital gains rates completely eliminated, narrowed to levels that were not compelling for planning purposes, and, as now, widened to levels that get everyone excited.

5.10   What is the Section 1045 small business stock rollover deferral option?

Section 1045 of the Internal Revenue Code permits a non-corporate shareholder to defer the recognition of gain on the disposition of qualified small business stock held for more than six months by investing the proceeds into the stock of another qualified small business within 60 days of the sale.[10] This perk

---

6. I.R.C. § 243(a) & (c).
7. See generally I.R.C. § 441.
8. I.R.C. §§ 368, 354, 361.
9. I.R.C. §§ 1221(a), 1222(3).
10. Section 1045 incorporates the Section 1202(c) definition of "small business stock," which generally requires that the stock have been issued to the original issuee after the effective date of the Revenue

can excite the entrepreneur who is in the business of moving money from one deal to the next or the shareholder who has a falling out with his or her co-shareholders and wants to exit for another opportunity.

5.11 How is a loss recognized on the sale of C corporation stock treated for tax purposes?

Generally, any such loss is subject to all the limitations of capital losses. Thus, the loss usually is limited to offsetting capital gains or being recognized over time at a maximum pace of $3,000 a year.

There is a limited exception under Section 1244 of the Code. This exception grants individuals and partnerships ordinary loss treatment (as opposed to the less favorable capital loss treatment) on losses recognized on the sale or exchange of common or preferred stock of a "small business corporation" (generally defined as a corporation whose aggregate contributions to capital and paid-in surplus do not exceed $1 million). In order to qualify, the shareholder must be the original issuee of the stock and the stock must have been issued for money or property (services do not count).[11] This benefit often sounds better than it really is because the ordinary loss in any single year (usually the year of sale) is limited to $50,000 ($100,000 for married couples). This serious dollar limitation, together with the fact that bailout loss treatment is not an exciting topic during the start-up planning of any business, usually results in this perk having no impact in the planning process.

5.12 May C corporation shareholders who are also employees participate in a company's employee benefit programs?

Yes. A shareholder of a C corporation who is also an employee may participate in all employee benefit plans and receive the associated tax benefits. Such plans typically include group term life insurance, medical and dental reimbursement plans, section 125 cafeteria plans, dependent care assistance programs, and qualified transportation reimbursement plans. Partners and most S corporation shareholder/employees (those who own more than 2 percent of the outstanding stock) are not eligible for the tax benefits associated with such plans.[12]

5.13 May multiple C corporations that are commonly controlled file as a single entity for federal income tax purposes?

Yes. Often it is advantageous to use multiple corporations to conduct the operations of an expanding business. Multiple entities can reduce liability exposures, regulatory hassles, and employee challenges as the operations diversify and expand into multiple states and foreign countries. While there may be compelling business reasons for the use of multiple entities, business owners often prefer that all the entities be treated as a single entity for tax purposes in

---

Reconciliation Act of 1993 by a C corporation that actively conducts a trade or business and that has gross assets of $50 million or less at the time the stock is issued. I.R.C. § 1202(c), (d) & (e).

11. I.R.C. § 1244.

12. The benefits are available only to "employees," a status that partners can never obtain. Although S corporation shareholders may clearly qualify as "employees," Section 1372 provides that, for fringe benefit purposes, the S corporation will be treated as a partnership and any shareholder owning more than 2 percent of the stock will be treated as a partner.

order to simplify tax compliance, eliminate tax issues on transactions between the entities, and facilitate the netting of profits and losses for tax purposes. This is permitted under the consolidated return provisions of the Code.[13] The key is that the entities constitute an "affiliated group," which generally means that their common ownership must extend to 80 percent of the total voting power and 80 percent of the total stock value of each entity included in the group.[14]

5.14 Is the tax basis of the stock owned by a C corporation shareholder impacted by the corporation's retention and reinvestment of its earnings?

No. The basis of a shareholder's stock in a C corporation is not affected by the entity's income or losses. This can have a profound impact in a situation where a profitable C corporation has accumulated substantial earnings. Assume, for example, that XYZ Inc. has always had a single shareholder, Linda, who purchased her stock for $100,000, and that the company has accumulated $2 million of earnings over the last 10 years. Linda's stock basis at the end of year 10 is still $100,000. In contrast, if XYZ Inc. had been taxed as an S corporation or a partnership from day one, Linda's basis at the end of year 10 would have grown to $2.1 million.[15] On a sale, the difference would be a capital gains hit on $2 million. This basis step-up may be a compelling planning consideration in many situations.

5.15 Are C corporations subject to an alternative minimum tax?

Large C corporations are subject to an alternative minimum tax. There are blanket exceptions for a company's first year of operation, for any company with average annual gross receipts of not more than $5 million during its first three years, and for any company with average annual gross receipts of not more than $7.5 million during any three-year period thereafter.[16] The alternative minimum tax applies only to the extent it exceeds the corporation's regular income tax liability. The tax is calculated by applying a 20 percent rate to the excess of the corporation's alternative minimum taxable income (AMTI) over a $40,000 exemption.[17] AMTI is defined to include the corporation's taxable income, increased by a host of tax preference items and adjustments designed to reduce certain timing benefits (i.e., accelerated cost recovery deductions) of the regular corporate tax.[18] The greatest impact in recent years has been the expansion of AMTI to include an amount which, roughly speaking, is designed to equal 75 percent of the excess of the corporation's true book earnings over its taxable income.[19]

5.16 What are the disguised dividend traps of a C corporation?

Any payment from a C corporation to a shareholder may be scrutinized by the Service to see if the payment constitutes a disguised dividend. What's at

---

13. See generally I.R.C. §§ 1501-1504.

14. I.R.C. § 1504(a).

15. I.R.C. § 1367(a). Partners experience the same basis adjustment for accumulated earnings under I.R.C. § 705(a).

16. I.R.C. § 55(e).

17. I.R.C. §§ 55(b)(1)(B), 55(d)(2).

18. See generally I.R.C. § 56.

19. I.R.C. § 56(g).

stake are a deduction at the corporate level and an imputed taxable dividend at the shareholder level. Common examples of disguised dividends include excessive compensation payments to shareholder/employees or family members,[20] personal shareholder expenses that are paid and deducted as business expenses by the corporation,[21] interest payments on excessive shareholder debt that is reclassified as equity,[22] excess rental payments on shareholder property rented or leased to the corporation,[23] personal use of corporate assets, and bargain sales of corporate property to a shareholder.[24]

5.17 What is the C corporation accumulated earnings trap?

The C corporation double-tax structure produces more revenue for the government when larger dividends are paid and less income is accumulated in the corporation. For this reason, the tax code imposes a penalty tax on C corporations that accumulate excessive amounts of income accumulations by not paying sufficient dividends. The tax doesn't kick in until the aggregate accumulated earnings exceed $250,000 ($150,000 in the case of certain professional service organizations).[25] And the penalty tax can be avoided completely if the corporation can demonstrate that it accumulated the earnings in order to meet the reasonable business needs of the corporation.[26] There is a great deal of latitude in defining the reasonable business needs. For this reason, the accumulated earnings penalty usually is a trap for the uninformed who never saw it coming.

5.18 What is the C corporation personal holding company trap?

The personal holding company trap is a close cousin to the accumulated earnings trap. Its purpose is to prohibit C corporations from accumulating excess amounts of investment income, compensation payments (the incorporated movie star or other talent), and shareholder rental income (the corporate yacht scenario). Unlike the accumulated earnings tax, the personal holding company penalty cannot be avoided by documenting reasonable business needs. If the penalty becomes a threat, remedial actions include increasing compensation payments to shareholder/employees and paying dividends. Like the accumulated earnings penalty, it's a nuisance that has to be monitored in select situations.

5.19 What is the C corporation controlled group trap?

This trap is aimed primarily at the business owner who would like to use multiple C corporations to take multiple advantage of the low C corporation tax rates, the $250,000 accumulated earnings trap threshold, or the $40,000

---

20. See, e.g., Exacto Spring Corp. v. Commissioner, 196 F.3d 833 (7th Cir. 1999); Elliotts Inc. v. Commissioner, 716 F.2d 1241 (9th Cir. 1983); and Charles McCandless Tire Service v. United States, 422 F.2d 1336 (Ct. Cl. 1970).

21. See, e.g., Hood v. Commissioner, 115 T.C. 172 (2000).

22. See the related discussion Chapter 4. Also, see generally Hariton, "Essay: Distinguishing Between Equity and Debt in the New Financial Environment," 49 Tax L. Rev. 449 (1994).

23. See, e.g., International Artists, Ltd. v. Commissioner, 55 T.C. 94 (1970).

24. See, e.g., Honigman v. Commissioner, 466 F.2d 69 (6th Cir. 1972).

25. I.R.C. § 535(c).

26. I.R.C. § 532 provides that the tax is applicable to any corporation that is "formed or availed of for the purpose of avoiding the income tax with respect to its shareholders..." Section 533(a) then provides that, unless the corporation can prove by a preponderance of evidence to the contrary, any accumulation of earnings and profits "beyond the reasonable needs of the business shall be determinative of the purpose to avoid the income tax..."

alternative minimum tax exemption. If multiple corporations are deemed to be part of a controlled group, they are treated as a single entity for purposes of these tax perks, and the multiple-entity benefits are gone.[27] Section 1563 of the Internal Revenue Code defines three types of controlled groups: parent-subsidiary controlled group, brother-sister controlled groups, and combined controlled group.[28] The existence of this trap requires, as part of any business planning analysis, a disclosure of other C corporation interests owned by those who are going to own an interest in the new entity that is considering C corporation status.

5.20 What is the section 482 trap?

Section 482 is that ominous provision that gives the Internal Revenue Service authority to "distribute, apportion, or allocate gross income, deductions, credits or allowances between and among" commonly controlled business interests "whenever necessary to prevent evasion of taxes or clearly to reflect the income" of any such businesses. Although 482, by its terms, applies to any type of business organization, its application to related C corporations who do business with each other can trigger brutal double tax consequences. All business dealings between commonly controlled entities must be carefully monitored to avoid Section 482 exposure.

5.21 What is an S corporation?

An S corporation is a hybrid whose popularity has grown in recent years. It is organized as a corporation under state law and offers corporate limited liability protections. But it is taxed as a pass-through entity under the provisions of Subchapter S of the Internal Revenue Code. These provisions are similar, but not identical, to the partnership provisions of Subchapter K. The popularity of S status is attributable primarily to three factors: (1) accumulated earnings increase the outside stock basis of the shareholders' stock; (2) an S corporation is free of any threat of a double tax on shareholder distributions or sale and liquidation proceeds; and (3) S status can facilitate income shifting and passive income generation.

5.22 Can any corporation elect to be taxed as an S corporation?

No. There are certain limitations and restrictions with an S corporation that can pose serious problems in the planning process. Not every corporation is eligible to elect S status. If a corporation has a shareholder that is a corporation, a partnership, a non-resident alien or an ineligible trust, S status is not available.[29] Banks and insurance companies cannot elect S status.[30] Also, the election cannot be made if the corporation has more than 100 shareholders or has more than one class of stock.[31] For purposes of the 100-shareholder limitation, a husband and wife are counted as one shareholder and all the members of a family (six generations deep) may elect to be treated as one shareholder.[32] The one class of

---

27. I.R.C. § 1561
28. I.R.C. § 1563(a)(3).
29. I.R.C. § 1361(b).
30. I.R.C. § 1361(b)(2).
31. I.R.C. § 1361(b)(1)(A) & (D).
32. I.R.C. § 1361(c)(1).

stock requirement is not violated if the corporation has both voting and nonvoting common stock and the only difference is voting rights.[33] Also, there is a huge straight debt safe harbor provision that easily can be satisfied to protect against the threat of an S election being jeopardized by a debt obligation being characterized as a second class of stock.[34]

5.23 What trusts are eligible to own stock of an S corporation?

Trusts that are now eligible to qualify as S corporation shareholders include: (1) voting trusts; (2) grantor trusts; (3) testamentary trusts that receive S corporation stock via a will (but only for a two year period following the transfer); (4) testamentary trusts that receive S corporation stock via a former grantor trust (but only for a two year period following the transfer); (5) "qualified subchapter S" trusts (QSSTs), which generally are trusts with only one current income beneficiary who is a U.S. resident or citizen to whom all income is distributed annually and who elect to be treated as the owner of the S corporation stock for tax purposes; and (6) "electing small business" trusts (ESBTs), which are trusts whose beneficiaries are qualifying S corporation shareholders who acquired their interests in the trust by gift or inheritance, not purchase.[35] An ESBT must elect to be treated as an S corporation shareholder, in which case each current beneficiary of the trust is counted as one shareholder for purposes of the maximum 100 shareholder limitation and the S corporation income is taxed to the trust at the highest individual marginal rate under the provisions of Internal Revenue Code.[36]

5.24 How does a corporation elect in and out of S status?

An election to S status requires a timely filing of a Form 2553 and the consent of all shareholders.[37] A single dissenter can hold up the show. For this reason, often it is advisable to include in an organizational agreement among all the owners (typically a shareholder agreement) a provision that requires all owners to consent to an S election if a designated percentage of the owners at any time approve the making of the election. The election, once made, is effective for the current tax year if made during the preceding year or within the first two and one-half months of the current year.[38] If made during the first two and one-half months of the year, all shareholders who have owned stock at any time during the year, even those who no longer own stock at the time of the election, must consent in order for the election to be valid for the current year.[39] Exiting out of S status is easier than electing into it; a revocation is valid if approved by shareholders holding more than half of the outstanding voting and nonvoting

---

33. I.R.C. § 1361(c)(4).

34. I.R.C. § 1361(c)(5). To fit within the safe harbor, there must be a written unconditional promise to pay on demand or on a specified date a sum certain and (1) the interest rate and payment dates cannot be contingent on profits, the borrower's discretion, or similar factors; (2) there can be no stock convertibility feature; and (3) the creditor must be an individual, an estate, a trust eligible to be a shareholder, or a person regularly and actively engaged in the business of lending money. For planning purposes, it is an easy fit in most situations.

35. I.R.C. §§ 1361(c)(2), 1361(d), 1361(e).

36. I.R.C. §§ 1361 (e)(1)(A), 1361(c)(2)(b)(v).

37. I.R.C. § 1362(a). See generally Reg. § 1.1362-6.

38. I.R.C. § 1362(b)(1).

39. I.R.C. § 1362(b)(2). For potential relief on a late election where there is reasonable cause for the tardiness, see I.R.C. § 1362(b)(5) and Rev. Proc. 2004-48, 2004-2 C.B. 172.

shares.[40] For the organization that wants to require something more than a simple majority to trigger such a revocation, the answer is a separate agreement among the shareholders that provides that no shareholder will consent to a revocation absent the approval of a designated supermajority. The revocation may designate a future effective date. Absent such a designation, the election is effective on the first day of the following year, unless it is made on or before the 15th day of the third month of the current year, in which case it is retroactively effective for the current year.[41]

5.25 How is the income of an S corporation taxed?

The income of an S corporation is passed through and taxed to its shareholders. The entity itself pays no tax on the income,[42] and the shareholders' recognition of the income is not affected by the corporation's retention or distribution of the income. This eliminates the double tax threat and the need for the C corporation traps (e.g., accumulated earnings tax, and personal holding company tax) that are designed to maximize the double tax impact. Also, the income passing through an S corporation may qualify as passive income for those shareholders who are not deemed "material participants."

5.26 How are losses of an S corporation taxed?

An S corporation's losses also are passed through to its shareholders. , subject to the same three loss hurdles applicable to partnerships that are discussed in question 5.33 below.

5.27 Is the tax basis of the stock owned by an S corporation shareholder impacted by the corporation's allocation of income and losses and distributions?

Yes. An S corporation shareholder's stock basis is adjusted up and down for allocable income and losses and cash distributions, much as with a partnership.[43] There is no locked-in basis, as there is with a C corporation.

5.28 As compared to a C corporation, is it easier from a tax standpoint for an S corporation to make distributions to its shareholders?

Yes. The tax consequences of distributing money or property from an S corporation generally are much less severe than for a C corporation. Distributions of allocated S corporation income are tax-free to the shareholders.

5.29 How much flexibility does a S corporation have in selecting a tax year?

S corporations have very little flexibility, particularly as compared to the flexibility of C corporations. Partnerships, LLCs, S corporations and sole proprietorships generally are required to use a calendar year unless they can prove a business purpose for using a fiscal year (a tough burden in most cases) or make a tax deposit under Section 7519 that is designed to eliminate any deferral

---

40. I.R.C. § 1362(d)(1).
41. I.R.C. § 1362(d)(1)(C) & (D).
42. I.R.C. § 1363(a).
43. I.R.C. § 1367(a).

advantage.

5.30 Is it costly from a tax standpoint to convert from a C corporation to an S corporation?

A C corporation's conversion to an S corporation is far easier from a tax perspective than a conversion to a partnership. But there are traps even in an S conversion for built-in asset gains, accumulated earnings, LIFO inventory reserves, and excessive S corporation passive income. Usually these traps can be avoided or managed with smart planning.

2. LLC AND PARTNERSHIP TAX CONCEPTS – Q&As

5.31 Are limited liability companies and partnerships taxed the same?

Generally, yes. They are both treated as partnership-taxed entities under subchapter K of the Internal Revenue Code. However, as explained below, any limited liability company or partnership that has more than one owner may elect to be taxed as either a C corporation or an S corporation.

5.32 How is the income of a limited liability company or partnership taxed?

The income of the entity is passed through and taxed to its owners. The entity itself reports the income, but pays no taxes. The advantage, of course, is that there is no threat of a double tax. There is only one tax at the owner level. Unlike a C corporation, a distribution of cash or other assets generally does not trigger a tax at either the entity or owner level. Since there is no double-tax structure, all the C corporation traps tied to that menacing structure, including the redemption trap, the disguised dividend trap, the accumulated earnings tax trap, the personal holding company trap, and the consolidated group trap have no application to entities taxed as partnerships.

5.33 How are losses of a limited liability company or partnership taxed?

The losses of a partnership-taxed entity also pass through to its owners. Unlike a C corporation, the losses are not trapped inside the entity.

Does this mean the owners can use the losses to reduce the tax bite on their other income? Maybe. There are three hurdles that first must be overcome, and they can be very difficult in many situations. The first and easiest hurdle is the basis hurdle – the losses passed through to an owner cannot exceed that owner's basis in his or her interest in the entity.[44] This hurdle seldom presents a problem in a partnership-taxed entity, because each owner's share of the entity's liabilities, even its nonrecourse liabilities, is treated as a contribution of money by the owner for basis purposes.[45] The second hurdle, known as the at-risk hurdle, generally limits an owner's losses to only the amount that the owner actually has at risk.[46] An owner's at-risk amount typically includes property contributed to the entity by the owner and the owner's share of the entity's recourse liabilities

---

44. I.R.C. § 704(d).
45. I.R.C. § 752(a).
46. I.R.C. § 465(a).

(those liabilities that create personal exposure for the owners).[47]   Nonrecourse liabilities (those liabilities for which no owner has any personal exposure) generally do not count for purposes of the at-risk hurdle, but there is an important exception for qualified nonrecourse financing that makes it easy for many real estate transactions to satisfy the at-risk limitations.[48]   The third hurdle (and usually the toughest) is the passive loss rule,[49] a 1980s creation that is designed to prevent a taxpayer from using losses from a passive business venture to offset active business income or portfolio income (i.e., interest, dividends, gains from stocks and bonds, etc.).   It was created to stop doctors and others from using losses from real estate and other tax shelters to reduce or eliminate the tax on their professional and business incomes.   Losses passed through from a passive venture can only be offset against passive income from another source.   If there is not sufficient passive income to cover the passive losses, the excess passive losses are carried forward until sufficient passive income is generated or the owner disposes of his or her interest in the passive activity that produced the unused losses.[50]   Whether a particular business activity is deemed passive or active with respect to a particular partner is based on the owner's level of participation in the activity – that is, whether the owner is a "material participant" in the activity.   A limited partner is presumed not to be a material participant and, therefore, all losses allocated to a limited partner generally are deemed passive.[51] To meet the "material participation" standard and avoid the hurdle, an owner must show "regular, continuous, and substantial" involvement in the activity.[52] Given these three hurdles, in a choice-of-entity planning analysis, it is never safe to assume that use of a partnership-taxed entity will convert start-up losses into slam-dunk tax benefits for the owners.

5.34 Are there potential passive income benefits with a limited liability company or partnership?

Yes. Generally, taxable income is classified as portfolio income (dividends, interest, royalties, gains from stocks and bonds, and assets that produce such income), active income (income from activities in which the taxpayer materially participates), or passive income (income from passive business ventures). Passive income is the only type of income that can be sheltered by either an active loss or a passive loss.   So the passive loss rule, by limiting the use of passive losses, exalts the value of passive income.   An activity that generates

---

47. I.R.C. § 465(b).

48. I.R.C. § 465(b)(6).   To qualify as "qualified nonrecourse financing," the debt must be incurred in connection with the activity of holding real estate, must not impose any personal liability on any person, must not be convertible debt, and must have been obtained from a "qualified person" (generally defined to include a person who is in the business of lending money, who is not related to the borrower, and who is not the seller or related to the seller).

49. See generally I.R.C. § 469.

50. I.R.C. §§ 469(a), 469(b), 469(d)(1).

51. I.R.C. § 469(h)(2).

52. I.R.C. § 469(h)(1).   Under the temporary regulations, a taxpayer meets the material participation standard for a year by (1) participating in the activity for more than 500 hours in the year; (2) being the sole participant in the activity; (3) participating more than 100 hours in the activity and not less than any other person; (4) participating more than 100 hours in the activity and participating in the aggregate more than 500 hours in significant participation activities; (5) having been a material participant in the activity for any five of the last ten years; (6) having materially participated in the activity in any three previous years if the activity is a personal service activity; or (7) proving regular, continuous and substantial participation based on all facts and circumstances.   Temp. Reg. § 1.469-5T(a)(1)-(7).

passive income can breathe tax life into passive losses from other activities. A C corporation has no capacity to produce passive income; it pays dividends or interest (both classified as portfolio income) or compensation income (active income). In contrast, a profitable entity taxed as a partnership can pass through valued passive income to those owners who are not material participants.

5.35   Is the tax basis of the interest owned by the owner of a partnership-taxed entity impacted by the corporation's allocation of income and losses and distributions?

Yes. The owner's basis in his or her partnership interest is adjusted upward by capital contributions and income allocations and downward by distributions and loss allocations.[53]   Unlike stock in a C corporation, there is no locked-in basis. This can be a valuable perk to the owner of a thriving business that is retaining income to finance growth and expansion. In the case of Linda above (Question 5.14), the $2 million of retained earnings in an entity taxed as a partnership would have increased the outside basis in her partnership interest from $100,000 to $2.1 million.

5.36 How much flexibility does a partnership-taxed entity have in designing special allocations among its owners?

It has tremendous flexibility. An entity taxed as a partnership may structure special allocations of income and loss items among its various owners. For example, one owner may be allocated 60 percent of all income and 30 percent of all losses. Although a C corporation has some limited capacity to create allocation differences among owners through the use of different classes of stock and debt instruments, that capacity pales in comparison to the flexibility available to a partnership-taxed entity. A partnership-taxed entity allocation will be respected for tax purposes only if it has "substantial economic effect,"[54] three words that make section 704(b) and its regulations one of the most complex subjects in the world of tax. Generally speaking (and I do mean generally), an allocation that does not produce a deficit capital account for a partner will have "economic effect" if capital accounts are maintained for all partners and, upon liquidation of the partnership, liquidating distributions are made in accordance with positive capital account balances.[55] In order for an allocation that produces a deficit capital account balance to have "economic effect," the partner also must be unconditionally obligated to restore the deficit (i.e., pay cash to cover the shortfall) upon liquidation of the partnership,[56] or the partnership must have sufficient nonrecourse debt to assure that the partner's share of any minimum gain recognized on the discharge of the debt will eliminate the deficit.[57]   An "economic effect," if present, will not be deemed "substantial" if it produces an after-tax benefit for one or more partners with no diminished after-tax consequences to other partners.[58]   The most common examples of economic effects that are not deemed "substantial" are shifting allocations (allocations of

---

53. I.R.C. § 705(a).
54. I.R.C. § 704(b).
55. Reg. §§ 1.704-1(b)(2)(ii) (b)(1), 1.704-(b)(2)(ii) (B)(2).
56. Reg. § 1.704-1(b)(2)(ii) (b)(3).
57. Reg. §§ 1.704-(2)(c), 1.704-(2)(f)(1), 1.704-(g)(1), 1.704-2(b)(1) & (e).
58. Reg. § 1.704-1(b)(2)(iii).

different types of income and deductions among partners within a given year to reduce individual taxes without changing the partners' relative economic interests in the partnership) and transitory allocations (allocations in one year that are offset by allocations in later years).[59]

5.37 How easy is it from a tax standpoint to get money out of a limited liability company or a partnership?

It's easy to get money or property out of an entity that is taxed as a partnership. Both in the case of ordinary and liquidating distributions, the Code is structured to eliminate all taxes at the entity and owner level. There are a few exceptions. One is where a distribution of money to an owner exceeds the owner's basis in his or her entity interest; the excess is taxable.[60] Another is where the entity has unrealized accounts receivable or substantially appreciated inventory items; in these cases, ordinary income may need to be recognized to reflect any change in an owner's interest in such assets.[61] These easy bail-out provisions are a far cry from the harsh dividend, redemption, and liquidation provisions of C corporations, all of which are designed to maximize the tax bite at both the entity and owner levels on any money or property flowing from the corporation to its owners.

5.38 What is the tax-free profits interest benefit available to a limited liability company or a partnership?

Often a business entity desires to transfer an equity interest in future profits to one who works for the business. An entity taxed as a partnership can do this without triggering any current tax hit for the recipient.[62] A corporation generally cannot transfer an equity interest in return for services without creating a taxable event. Note that this benefit only applies to an equity interest in future profits, not an interest in existing capital.

5.39 What is the family partnership tax trap applicable to a limited liability company or a partnership?

Entities that are considered family partnerships for tax purposes are subject to a special trap that is designed to prevent the use of the entity to aggressively shift income among family members. If any person gifts an entity interest to another, the donor must be adequately compensated for any services rendered to the partnership; and the income allocated to the donee, calculated as a yield on capital, cannot be proportionately greater than the yield to the donor.[63] In effect, special allocations to favor donees are prohibited, as are attempts to shift service income. Any purchase among family members is considered a "gift" for purposes of this trap.[64]

5.40 Is it possible to convert a C corporation to a limited liability company or a partnership?

---

59. Reg. § 1.704-1(b)(2)(iii) (b) & (c).

60. I.R.C. § 731(a).

61. I.R.C. § 751; Reg. §§ 1.751-1(b)(2)(ii), 1.751-1(b)(3)(ii), 1.751-1(g).

62. See Rev. Proc. 93-27, 1993-2 C.B. 343 and Rev. Proc. 2001-43, 2001-2 C.B. 191.

63. I.R.C. § 704(e).

64. I.R.C. § 704(e)(3).

Technically it may be possible, but usually it is prohibitive from a tax standpoint to convert from a C corporation to an entity taxed as a partnership. Such a change will produce a double tax triggered by a liquidation of the C corporation. The far better option in most cases is to convert to S corporation status if pass-through tax benefits are desired.

3. SELF-EMPLOYMENT AND PAYROLL TAX BASICS

5.41 What impact does the self-employment and payroll tax have on the business planning process?

The self-employment/payroll tax is a regressive tax that's easy to ignore, but the consequences of neglect can be painful. The tax is levied at a flat rate of 15.3 percent on a base level of self-employment earnings ($113,700 for 2013) and 2.9 percent above the base. Starting in 2013, the rate jumps to 3.8 percent on a married couple's earnings in excess of $250,000 and an unmarried individual's earnings in excess of $200,000, and the new 3.8 percent rate applies to any interest, dividends, capital gains, and "net investment income" received by such taxpayers.[65] A self-employed person is entitled to an income tax deduction of one-half of self-employment taxes paid at the 15.3 percent and 2.9 percent rates.[66]

5.42 How does the payroll tax impact employees?

An employee has one-half of the tax (7.65 percent) come directly from his or her paycheck in the form of payroll taxes. The other half is paid by the employer who, in order to stay in business, must consider the tax burden in setting the employee's pay level.

5.43 How does the self-employment tax impact high-income taxpayers?

For high-income owners, including many business owners, the personal impact of the self-employment tax often is not significant because they are able to structure their affairs to reduce or eliminate its impact, or the base amount subject to the tax is considered small in relation to their overall earnings. The tax, by design, is structured to punish middle- and low-income workers. For 80 percent of American workers, the self-employment and payroll taxes paid on their earnings exceed the income tax bite, often by many times.[67]

5.44 Is the self-employment tax a factor to consider in choosing the best form of business entity to use in a given situation?

The answer is "yes" in many, but not all, situations. The form of business entity that is selected can affect the self-employment tax burden for the owners of the business.

5.45 What are the self-employment and payroll tax impacts with a C corporation?

---

65. I.R.C. § 1411.

66. I.R.C. § 164(f).

67. Report of the Congressional Budget Office, Economic Stimulus: Evaluating Proposed Changes in Tax Policy – Approaches to Cutting Personal Taxes (January 2002), footnote 7.

Compensation payments from a C corporation to owner/employees are subject to payroll taxes. Corporate dividends are now subject to the 3.8 percent tax to the extent a married couple's income exceeds $250,000 and an unmarried individual's income exceeds $200,000.[68] For other taxpayers, dividends are not subject to the tax. In a C corporation context, the negative trade-off is that the dividends are subject to the double income tax structure.

5.46 What are the self-employment tax impacts with an S corporation?

The C corporation double-tax trade-off disappears for an S corporation whose earnings are taxed directly through to its shareholders. Compensation payments to an S corporation shareholder are subject to payroll taxes. But a shareholder who works an S corporation avoids all self-employment taxes on dividends, including the 3.8 percent Medicare tax.[69] An S corporation investor who does not materially participate in the venture will also avoid any self-employment tax on dividends unless the applicable $250,000/$200,000 threshold is exceeded, in which case the 3.8 percent tax will kick in. Can a shareholder who works for an S corporation eliminate all self-employment and payroll taxes by paying only dividends? If a shareholder renders significant services to the S corporation and receives no compensation payments, the Service likely will claim that a portion of the dividends are compensation payments subject to payroll taxes.[70] The key is to be reasonable in taking advantage of the tax loophole for S corporation dividends paid to a shareholder/employee. Set a defensible compensation level and pay payroll taxes at that level. Then distribute the balance as dividends that are not subject to any self-employment or payroll tax burden.

5.47 What are the self-employment tax impacts with a partnership?

Section 1402(a) of the Code specifically provides that a partner's distributive share of income from a partnership constitutes earnings from self-employment tax purposes.[71] There is a limited statutory exception for retired partners[72] and a broader exception for limited partners, but the new 3.8 percent Medicare tax will still be applicable to the extent the triggering income thresholds ($250,000 or $200,000) are exceeded.[73] Thus, the key to minimizing the tax in a partnership structure is to fit within this limited partnership exception.

5.48 What are the self-employment tax impacts with a limited liability company?

It may be more difficult to avoid the tax for a member of a limited liability company that has no limited partners.

---

68. I.R.C. §§ 1402(a)(2), 1411.

69. If an S corporation shareholder materially participates in the venture, dividends paid to that shareholder do not fall within the definition of "net investment income" in IRC § 1411. See IRS Guidance in Reg.130507-11 (November 30, 2012).

70. See, for example, Joseph Radtke, S.C. v. United States, 712 F.Supp. 143 (E.D. Wis. 1989), affirmed 895 F.2d 1196 (7th Cir. 1990); Spicer Accounting, Inc. v. United States, 918 F.2d 90 (9th Cir. 1990); and Dunn & Clark, P.A. v. Commissioner, 57 F.3d 1076 (9th Cir. 1995).

71. I.R.C. § 1402(a).

72. I.R.C. § 1402(a)(10).

73. I.R.C. §§ 1402(a)(13), 1411.

The Service's first attempt to provide some guidance on the issue came in 1994 when it published its first Proposed Regulations. After public comment, new Proposed Regulations were issued in 1997, defining the scope of the limited partnership exception for all entities taxed as a partnership, without regard to state law characterizations.[74] Under the 1997 Proposed Regulations, an individual would be treated as a limited partner for purposes of the self-employment tax unless the individual was personally liable for the debts of the entity by being a partner, had authority to contract on behalf of the entity under applicable law, or participated for more than 500 hours in the business during the taxable year. The 1997 Proposed Regulations also drew criticism because LLC members who had authority to contract on behalf of the entity could never fit within the limited partner exception. The result was a statutory moratorium in 1997 on the issuance of any temporary or proposed regulations dealing with the limited partnership exception.[75]

For planning purposes, where does this history leave us now with respect to entities taxed as partnerships? Any general partner under state law is exposed to the tax. Any limited partner under applicable state law is probably safe. As for LLC members, any member who can fit within the 1997 Proposed Regulations' definition is justified in relying on the statutory limited partner exception. Beyond that definition, it becomes more difficult and uncertain to evaluate the facts and circumstances of each situation. The risk escalates in direct proportion to the individual's authority to act on behalf of the entity and the scope of any services rendered. Note, however, that any member will now be subject to the new 3.8 percent Medicare tax to the extent the applicable triggering income thresholds ($250,000 or $200,000) is exceeded.

5.49 Is it smart to design a plan that reduces or eliminates self-employment tax burdens for the owners of a business?

Most think it is. Of course, the payment of self-employment taxes may result in higher Social Security benefits down the road. The Social Security program, as presently structured, will become unsustainable in the future. Current benefit levels can be maintained long term only if tax rates or government borrowing levels are increased to unprecedented levels. There is a strong likelihood that, at some point in the not-too-distant future, forced structural reform of the program will reduce future government-funded benefits for all except those who are close to retirement or at the lowest income levels.[76]

CASE PROBLEM 5-1

Marsha is ready to start a new business that will generate about $150,000 of earnings each year. Marsha will work full time for the business. Her plan is to withdraw $100,000 of earnings from the business each year to fund her personal needs. She will leave the remaining earnings in the business to retire debt and fund future needs of the business. Marsha wants to minimize the overall tax bite

---

74. Proposed Reg. § 1.1402 (a)-2.

75. Tax Relief Act of 1997 § 935.

76. See generally The Interim and Final Reports of the President's Commission to Strengthen Social Security (August 2001 & December 2001).

on these earnings.

What will be the total entity and personal tax cost under each of the following scenarios, assuming Marsha's ordinary income tax rate is 25 percent, her dividend rate is 15 percent, and the applicable self-employment/payroll tax rate is 15.3 percent? Ignore all potential state income tax consequences.

1. Marsha's business is a C corporation that distributes Marsha a $100,000 dividend each year.

2. Marsha's business is a C corporation that pays Marsha a salary of $100,000 each year for services she renders to the corporation?

3. Marsha's business is an S corporation that pays Marsha a $40,000 salary each year and distributes a $60,000 dividend to Marsha each year.

4. Marsha's business is a limited liability company that is taxed as a partnership. Marsha owns 90 percent of the business, and Joe, an investor who does not work in the business, owns the remaining 10 percent. The LLC distributes $90,000 to Marsha each year and $10,000 to Joe. Assume Joe's marginal tax rate is also 25 percent.

B. SELECTING THE BEST ENTITY FORM

1. THE CHALLENGE

A primary planning challenge for all businesses is to select the best form of business organization. Too many business owners and executives mistakenly assume that this challenge is limited to new ventures. Many mature businesses have a need, albeit often unrecognized, to reevaluate their business structure from time to time to maximize the benefits of the enterprise for its owners.

Some perceive the "choice of entity" analysis solely as a tax-driven exercise. Although taxes are vitally important, there are many important non-tax factors that can impact the ultimate decision. The rules of the game have changed in recent years. Some factors, once deemed vitally important, no longer impact the final outcome, and there are new issues that now must be factored into the mix.

The analytical process usually requires the business owner or executive to predict and handicap what's likely to happen down the road. There usually is a need to consider and project earnings, losses, capital expansion needs, debt levels, the possibility of adding new owners, potential exit strategies, the likelihood of a sale, the estate planning needs of the owners, and a variety of other factors. The best answer is an easy call in some cases and a tough challenge in many others. The decision-making process is not an exact science that punches out a single, perfect answer for every client. There is a need to weigh and consider a number of factors, while being sensitive to the consequences of the alternative options.

The entity candidates include the C corporation, the S corporation, the limited liability company, the general partnership, and the limited partnership.

There are a few additional business entity forms that should be considered in select situations. The first is the professional limited liability company ("PLLC"), a state-chartered entity that many states now authorize in order to limit the liability exposure of professionals (i.e., doctors and lawyers) who render professional services. The entity does nothing to reduce a professional's personal liability for his or her own mistakes, but does eliminate a professional's liability for the errors, omissions, negligence, incompetence or malfeasance of other professionals who are not under his or her supervision and control. It also eliminates personal exposure for contract liabilities that the professional has not personally guaranteed. Some states require that a PLLC register with the applicable state licensing board before filing its organizational documents with the state. A close cousin to the PLLC is the registered limited liability partnership ("LLP"), a partnership that some state statutes allow to be registered for the sole purpose of providing liability protections to the partners of a partnership. Finally, there is the limited liability limited partnership ("LLLP"), a form of entity that some states authorize to permit a general partner of a limited partnership to eliminate his or her personal exposure for the entity's debts.

The complexity of the challenge often is enhanced by the need to use multiple entities to accomplish the objectives of the client. Multi-entity planning can be used to protect assets from liability exposure, limit or control value growth, scatter wealth among family members, segregate asset-based yields from operation-based risks and yields, shift or defer income, enhance tax benefits from recognized losses, facilitate exit strategy planning, satisfy liquidity needs, and promote a structured discipline that helps ensure that all financial bases are covered. It complicates the process, but the benefits usually far outweigh any burdens of added complexity. From the client's perspective, often the use of multiple entities actually promotes an understanding of the different planning challenges and objectives because each entity is being used for specific purposes. The entity options are not limited to the business entity forms reviewed in this chapter; they also include a broad menu of different trusts that can be used to promote targeted objectives.

2. "CHECK-THE-BOX" RULES

A mammoth choice-of-entity burden was eliminated in 1997 when the Internal Revenue Service decided to abandon the difficult corporate resemblance tests used for classifying unincorporated businesses and instead adopted an infinitely easier and more certain "check-the-box" regime. The analytical challenge of selecting the best entity form was not made any easier, but a business owner could now know for certain that the choice, once made, would stick. Prior to 1997, often there was a nerve-wracking uncertainty that some detail might trigger a retroactive tax reclassification of the entity by the Service – a disastrous result in nearly every situation. Great care was required to protect against this uncertainty. Often it required that less favorable substantive provisions be included in the governing documents in order to protect the entity's tax classification. It was a classic example of the tax tail wagging the dog.

This all changed in 1997. The Service threw in the towel on the difficult corporate characteristics test and opted for a simple "check-the-box" system. The system provides certainty and, unlike the prior system, contains default provisions that greatly reduce the likelihood of the uninformed being punished.

The "check-the-box" regulations apply to any business entity that is separate from its owner and that is not a trust.[77] Following is a brief description of the key provisions of the "check-the-box" system:

• **Corporations.** Any entity organized under a federal or state statute that uses the words "incorporated," "corporation," "body corporate," or "body politic" is taxed as a corporation.[78] Thus, any corporation formed under state law is taxed as a corporation, either as a C corporation under Subchapter C or as an S corporation under Subchapter S of the Internal Revenue Code.

• **Unincorporated Entity.** An unincorporated entity with two or more owners (i.e., a partnership, limited partnership, or limited liability company) is taxed as a partnership under the provisions of subchapter K unless the entity elects to be treated as a corporation for tax purposes.[79] Any such election may be effective up to 75 days before and 12 months after the election is filed.[80] The election must be signed by all members (including any former members impacted by a retroactive election) or by an officer or member specifically authorized to make the election.[81]

• **Single Owner Entity.** An unincorporated single-owner entity, such as a single-member limited liability company, is treated as a disregarded entity - a nullity - unless a corporate status election is made. Thus, the default is taxation as a sole proprietorship. A single-owner entity will never be subject to the partnership provisions of Subchapter K.[82]

• **Pre-1997 Entities.** With one exception, pre-1997 entities retain the same tax status they had under prior regulations unless a contrary election is made. The exception is for single-owner entities that were taxed as partnerships; they are now taxed as sole proprietorships unless a corporate election is made.[83]

• **Changes.** A classification election, once made, cannot be changed for 60 months unless the Service authorizes a new election or more than 50 percent of the ownership interests are acquired by persons who did not own any interest in the company at the time of the first election.[84] A change in the number of owners does not affect a classification unless the change results in a single-owner unincorporated entity (in which case it will be taxed as a sole proprietorship) or changes a single-owner unincorporated business into a multi-owner entity (in which case the entity will go from being taxed as a sole proprietorship to being taxed as a partnership).[85]

• **Election Tax Consequences.** If an entity that is taxed as a partnership

---

77. Reg. §§ 301.7701-1(a), 301.7701-2(a).

78. Reg. § 301.7701-2(b)(1).

79. Reg. §§ 301.7701-2(c)(1), 301.7701-3(a), 301.7701-3(b)(1).

80. Reg. § 301.7701-3(c)(1)(iii).

81. Reg. § 301.7701-3(c)(2).

82. Reg. §§ 301.7701-2(a), 301.7701-2(c)(2), 301.7701-3(a), 301.7701-3(b)(1).

83. Reg. § 301.7701-3(b)(3).

84. Reg. § 301.7701-3(c)(1).

85. Reg. § 301.7701-3(f).

elects to be taxed as a corporation, it will be deemed to have contributed all its assets and liabilities to the corporation in return for stock and then to have distributed the stock to the partners in liquidation of their partnership interests.[86] If an unincorporated entity that is taxed as a corporation elects to be taxed as a partnership, it will be deemed to have distributed its assets and liabilities to the shareholders, who, in turn, will be deemed to have contributed the assets and liabilities to a newly formed partnership.[87] Similar rules apply to a single-owner entity that elects corporate status or that, having elected and maintained corporate status for at least 60 months, elects sole proprietorship status.[88]

3. KEY FACTORS – FIVE EXAMPLE CASES

The choice of entity analysis requires a careful assessment of all relevant factors. This sections reviews 15 of the key factors, illustrated through five case studies. Each entity option offers certain benefits and traps that may pose problems down the road. The analysis should review the benefits and traps by carefully pondering their potential relevance under various scenarios that may be applicable to the specific situation.

In most cases, it is advisable to review all tax consequences, even those consequences that, at first blush, are not likely to impact the ultimate choice of entity decision. Such a review usually results in a deeper analysis and often triggers a detailed dialogue that significantly improves the quality of the analysis and enhances an appreciation of the issues. Plus, it can go a long way in protecting against the potential for a "no one told me" complaint when a tax trap, deemed unimportant upfront, kicks in because circumstances change. The individual who quickly jumps to an ultimate conclusion and then becomes a dogmatic advocate for that conclusion usually shortchanges the analytical process.

Everyone involved in the process should be ever mindful of the fact that taxes are a moving target; the rules often change. What works today may make no sense tomorrow. Advisors can make predictions and try hard to access the political winds, but uncertainty is a given that makes choice of entity planning more challenging and exciting.

Although each factor may be important, they never have equal weight in any given situation. It is not a game of adding up the factors to see which entity scores the most points. In many cases, one or two factors may be so compelling for the particular situation that they alone dictate the ultimate solution. But even in that situation, the other factors cannot be ignored because they help identify the collateral consequences of the decision that is about to be made.

The issue of limited liability protection for the owners of the business, once considered to be the most critical factor in the choice of entity analysis, is no longer included in the list of key factors. It's not that insulating the owners of a business from personal liability for the business' liabilities is no longer important;

---

86. Reg. § 301.7701-3(g)(1)(i).
87. Reg. § 301.7701-3(g)(1)(ii).
88. Reg. § 301.7701-3(g)(1)(iii) & (iv).

it's as important today as ever. Its absence from the critical factor list is due to the fact that, if desired, it can be accomplished in any given situation. Thus, it is a neutral consideration that no longer needs to affect the decision-making process. With the new check-the-box regime, there is no longer a fear that providing limited liability protection may result in an unincorporated business being inadvertently taxed as a corporation. Even a general partner can be protected by parking the ownership interest in a limited liability company or an S corporation.

Example Case One – Jason

Jason owns and manages three businesses. He now intends to start a fourth. His new business will offer specialized heavy equipment moving services in the western United States. Jason will own 60 percent of the new enterprise, and the remaining 40 percent will be owned equally by two investors, buddies of Jason. Jason will oversee the business, but will spend little time in the business.

The inspiration and driving force behind the business will be Joe, who has extensive experience in the industry. Joe will be given strong economic incentives as the CEO, but will not be an owner. In addition to Joe, the business will initially have about 30 employees. Jason anticipates that the business will be profitable from the get-go, and he plans on withdrawing profits on a regular basis. Plus, if things play out as planned, there might be a potential to sell to a larger strategic player down the road.

Jason wants an entity that will minimize all tax bites, always leave him in complete control, and avoid, to the fullest extent possible, any potential hassles with the minority owners.

The best option for Jason's new company would be an S corporation. This case illustrates six key factors.

Factor One: Earnings Bailout

In Jason's situation, an important factor in the choice of entity decision analysis is the tax cost of getting earnings out of the enterprise and into the hands of Jason and the other owners. Bailing out earnings in S corporations, LLCs, partnerships and sole proprietorships usually is no big deal. Profits generated by the business are passed through and taxed directly to the owners, so the distribution of those profits in the form of dividends or partnership distributions carries no tax consequences. In contrast, bailing out the fruits of a C corporation may trigger substantial income tax consequences, because a C corporation is not a pass-through entity.

When a C corporation bails out its earnings by distributing them to its shareholders in the form of dividends, the dividend distribution is not deductible to the corporation. The corporation pays a tax on the earnings, and the distribution of those earnings to the shareholders in the form of dividends is taxed a second time at the shareholder level. This double tax is one of the negatives of a C corporation.

For some businesses, this double tax risk is more academic than real. There are often ways to avoid it. The most common is for the shareholders to be employed by the corporation and to receive earnings in the form of taxable compensation. The payment of the compensation to the shareholders is deductible by the corporation, so that income is only taxed once, at the shareholder level. But the compensation must be reasonable for the services actually rendered. If it isn't, it may be re-characterized as a dividend. In service corporations where the services are rendered by the shareholders, stripping out all of the earnings of the business through the use of compensation payments usually can be easily justified. Since Jason does not plan on working for his new business, the compensation bailout structure isn't an option.

Factor Two: Self-Employment Taxes

Self-employment taxes can be an important choice of entity factor in some situations. In Jason's situation, use of an S corporation may create the opportunity to save self-employment taxes by just paying dividends that escape double income tax treatment by virtue of the S election.

If the plan is to bail out earnings as compensation payments to owners of a C corporation, the compensation payments will be subject to payroll taxes. Of course, except to the extent the new 3.8 percent Medicare tax is applicable to those with incomes above the triggering thresholds ($250,000 or $200,000), there is no self-employment tax imposed on dividends from a C corporation, but such dividends are subject to a double income tax structure.

In Jason's situation, the goal is for the owners to avoid the double income tax structure and self-employment taxes. S corporation dividends will do the job (subject to the 3.8 percent Medicare tax, where applicable), but distributions by a partnership-taxed entity, including a limited liability company, will not escape self-employment taxes unless the owners are limited partners. If the owners are limited partners of a limited partnership, there is a statutory exception that will protect them from self-employment taxes. The same exception should work in the context of a limited liability company where the owners have no management rights in the enterprise and are not personally responsible for the liabilities of the entity. The tough situation comes when a key owner, such a Jason, wants to exercise management rights. In Jason's case, reliance on the limited partnership exception in the LLC context may create an intolerable risk, given the uncertainty of current law. For self-employment tax purposes, a much smarter option would be an S corporation. Given the size of the self-employment tax, this factor may be the deciding issue in some cases.

Factor Three: Tax-Free Reorganization Potential

If Jason's business succeeds and a sellout opportunity surfaces, a corporate entity will be able to participate in a tax-free reorganization with a corporate buyer. Corporations may combine through mergers, stock-for-stock transactions, and assets-for-stock transactions on terms that eliminate all corporate and shareholder-level taxes. This benefit often is the key to the ultimate payday for those business owners who cash in by "selling" to a public corporation. Cast as a reorganization, the transaction allows the acquiring entity to fund the acquisition with its own stock (little or no cash required) and enables the selling owners to walk with highly liquid, publicly traded securities and no tax bills until the securities are sold.

A partnership-taxed entity, such as a limited liability company, can't enjoy the tax-free benefits of a corporate reorganization.

Factor Four: Control Rights

Jason wants complete control over all business decisions with as little discussion and fanfare as possible. A corporation, either C or S, or a limited partnership automatically offers this type of ultimate control in favor of the majority, absent a special agreement to the contrary. Minority corporate shareholders often have no control rights; the majority elects the board of directors, and the board has the authority to manage the affairs of the corporation. Limited partner status and the benefits associated with that status (i.e., liability protection and freedom from self-employment taxes) mandate little or no control. For the majority player who wants control of all the reins, the idea of easily getting it all "the normal way" can be appealing.

Limited liability companies and general partnerships are different only in that the control rights need to be spelled out in an operating agreement among the owners. In some cases, the fear is that the need for a single operating agreement may result in more dialogue, more negotiation, and more compromise. Minority owners may see that there is no "standard" or "normal" way of locking in voting requirements and that the agreement can be crafted to address the control concerns of all parties. Once minority expectations are elevated, the majority players' options become more difficult. One option, of course, is to throw down the gauntlet and demand ultimate majority control. Beyond the personal discomfort of having to overtly make such demands, the demands themselves may fuel suspicions, undermine loyalties, or, worst case, trigger the departure of a valuable minority player. The alternative option is to build into the operating agreement "mutually acceptable" minority rights.

For choice-of-entity planning purposes, suffice it to say that specific control interests of a dominant owner, such as Jason, and the dynamics between the various players (or lack thereof) may favor the use of a corporate entity or limited partnership in some cases.

Factor Five: Sellout Tax Hit

Most who start a new business or operate a seasoned business are not focused on selling out down the road. But the truth is that this factor can be extremely important in selecting the right form of business organization. If this factor is neglected, a business owner may find that, when it comes time to cash in, there is an added tax burden that could have been avoided.

If Jason's business flourishes and its assets are ultimately sold within a pass-through entity, such as an S corporation, partnership or LLC, the gains realized on the sale of the assets are taxed to the owners in proportion to their interests in the business. After those taxes are paid, the owners are free to pocket the net proceeds. Bailing out of a C corporation may carry a significant additional tax cost. A simple example illustrates the impact.

Assume Jason started a C corporation with a $250,000 investment, that the assets in the company have a present basis of $750,000, and that the company is worth $3 million. It's now time to cash in. The buyer does not want to buy the stock, but is willing to pay $3 million for the assets in the business.

The C corporation would sell the assets for $3 million to the buyer, and the corporation would recognize a $2.25 million gain – the difference between the $3 million purchase price and the corporation's $750,000 tax basis in the assets. After the corporation pays a corporate income tax on the gain, the balance of the proceeds would be distributed to the shareholders, who would pay a capital gains tax on the difference between the amount received and their low basis in the stock. The threat of this double tax at the time of sale is a major disadvantage for many C corporations.

Other important elements of this sellout factor should be kept in mind. First, if a C corporation accumulates earnings within the corporation over an extended period of time, those accumulations do nothing to increase the shareholders' tax basis in their stock. If the shareholder sells stock down the road, the shareholder recognizes capital gains based upon the shareholder's original cost basis in the stock. In contrast, if the business organization is operated in a pass-through entity, such as an LLC, an S corporation, or a partnership, the earnings accumulated in the business will boost, dollar for dollar, the owner's tax basis in his or her stock or partnership interest. So if the owner down the road sells the stock or partnership interest, the earnings accumulated within the enterprise reduce the tax bite to the owner. This is a significant consequence, and it should not be ignored if the business plans to accumulate earnings in anticipation of a sale at a future date.

A second consideration is that, if a C corporation already has substantial value, it is not easy to convert to a pass-through entity and eliminate the threat of double tax. The business cannot make the conversion a year before the sale and expect to get off tax free. Usually, it takes a significant period of time to wind out of the double-tax threat.

When all these factors are thrown into the mix, the S corporation looks pretty attractive to Jason with respect to this sellout factor. As a pass-through entity, it eliminates the double tax hit and provides the basis booster. Plus, as a corporate entity, it offers the potential of tax-free reorganization benefits and eliminates the potential ordinary income asset mix complications of an entity taxed as a partnership.

Factor Six: Passive Income Potential

If Jason uses a pass-through entity, such as an S corporation or an LLC, the income allocated to the owners who are not material participants in the business (a given in this situation) will be passive income that can be offset by tax losses, including passive losses. Even if the income is not distributed to the owners and is retained in the business to finance growth, the owners' losses from other activities can be used to reduce the tax bite on the business income. This capacity to use real estate and other passive losses of the owners to reduce current taxes on income from profitable activities often enhances the reinvestment of earnings in a profitable business to finance growth.

By comparison, if the business is operated as a C corporation, there is no way that the income of the business, whether retained in the business or distributed to the owners, can be sheltered by passive losses that the owners generate from other activities. The bottom line is that, for many income-producing enterprises, those owners who are not employed by the business (and perhaps the business itself) will be much better off with a pass-through entity.

Example Case 2: Sue and Joyce

Sue and Joyce are planning to form a new business that will offer specialized catering services. They will be the sole owners (in equal shares), and they will both work full time for the business. They will start out with eight other employees, but anticipate that the employee base could grow to 50 or more as they expand into neighboring markets.

They project that the business will need to reinvest $50,000 to $100,000 of earnings each year to finance growth and expansion. They will bailout the rest of the earnings as compensation income for the long hours they both will put into the business. They can't imagine ever selling the business and doubt anyone would be willing to pay much for it. The business is a means for them to each pursue a passion and earn a nice living along the way. It will be their careers. They want to maximize any fringe benefits for themselves.

The best option for the new company that is being organized by Sue and Joyce is a C corporation. This case illustrates three additional key choice-of-entity factors.

Factor Seven: Owner Fringe Benefits

Sue and Joyce's desire for employee fringe benefits may be a compelling factor in selecting a business form. There are a number of fringe benefits that are available to shareholder/employees of a C corporation that generally are not available to owner/employees of pass-through entities, such as a partnerships, LLCs, or S corporations. The significance of these fringe benefits depends on their importance to the particular owners. Investor owners could care less; employee owners, like Sue and Joyce, often view them as big deals. Each owner needs to assess whether the tax advantages of the fringe benefits are attractive enough to impact the choice-of-entity decision. The most significant fringe benefits available to shareholder-employees of C corporations include group-term life insurance plans under Section 79, medical-dental reimbursement plans under Section 106, Section 125 cafeteria plans,[89] and dependent care assistance programs under Section 129. Note that health insurance premiums are usually a neutral factor because they can be deducted in full by a self-employed person, a

---

89. A section 125 cafeteria plan may be adopted by a partnership, LLC, or S corporation, but S corporation shareholders holding two percent or more of the corporation's stock, partners of the partnership, and members of the LLC cannot participate in the plan. C corporation shareholders may participate so long as no more than 25 percent of the nontaxable benefits selected within the cafeteria plan go to key employees. Subject to the 25 percent limitation, C corporation shareholders can take full advantage of the tax benefits of the plan.

partner or an S corporation shareholder.

Factor Eight: The Bracket Racket

Only the C corporation offers the potential that the tax rate applied to the net income of the business may differ from the income tax rate applied to the owners of the business. All other entities (S corporations, LLCs, partnerships and sole proprietorships) are not separate taxpaying entities. Income earned by these entities is simply passed through and reported by the owners in proportion to their interests in the business. The C corporation may create an income splitting opportunity – to have the income retained in the business taxed at a rate lower than the rates paid by the owners. In Sue and Joyce's situation, the different rate structure can be used to their advantage. It's the bracket racquet.

C corporations have a tiered graduated rate structure. This structure imposes a low 15 percent tax on taxable income up to $50,000 and 25 percent on taxable income between $50,000 and $75,000. So if Sue and Linda can keep the corporation's taxable income to less than $100,000 each year, these low corporate rates will produce a significant bottom line tax savings. If this reinvested income were passed through to them, it is likely that the income tax rate would be at least 28 percent and perhaps more, and payroll taxes would be on top of the income tax hit. This bracket differential can be a big deal when the numbers are in these ranges.

Note that the potential negative consequences of a C corporation are no big deal in Sue and Linda's situation. They will avoid all double tax fears by bailing out all available earnings as deductible compensation. The C corporation accumulated earnings tax, personal holding company tax, and alternative minimum tax pose no threats. The locked-in stock basis and other sellout costs are not a factor because Sue and Joyce have no plans to sell.

Factor Nine: Tax Year Flexibility

Most C corporations may select any fiscal year for tax reporting purposes. Thus, use of a C corporation will give Sue and Joyce an opportunity to select a tax years that simplifies and accommodates their accounting and that may provide a tax deferral potential. Partnerships, LLCs, S corporations and sole proprietorships generally are required to use a calendar year unless they can prove a business purpose for using a fiscal year (a tough burden in most cases) or make a tax deposit under Section 7519 that is designed to eliminate any deferral advantage. C corporations that are personal service corporations may adopt a fiscal year with a deferral period of no more than three months, but the minimum distribution rules applicable to such personal service corporations under Section 280H substantially reduce any tax deferral potential.[90] When the plan is to bailout most of the corporate earning as deductible compensation to the shareholders, often a C corporation may offer an opportunity to defer the payment of income taxes by using a corporate fiscal year that is different than the shareholders' calendar tax year.

The ability to use this deferral technique is limited by the normal

---

90. I.R.C. §§ 444(b)(2), 280(H).

compensation reasonableness standards. Plus, the deferral impacts often are watered down by withholding and estimated tax payment requirements. But the technique is fairly common and is a legitimate means of deferring taxes if properly executed.

Example Case 3: Charles

Charles plans on opening a chain of indoor snow skiing facilities. Charles will put up 10 percent of the equity capital. The other 90 percent will come from four outside investors. The business will obtain debt financing equal to nearly four times the total equity capital, and is expected to generate substantial taxable losses during the first five years of operation, fueled in large part by big depreciation and amortization deductions.

Charles wants an entity that will allocate 99 percent of the losses to the investors, award him with 50 percent of the profits after the investors have recouped their investment, and, to the maximum extent possible, free him from minority owner hassles and contractual negotiations and dealings with minority owners. He wants total control. Plus, he would like to protect the investors from any self employment taxes.

Charles is going to need a partnership-taxed entity, either a limited liability company where he is the sole manager or a limited partnership where his investors are limited partners and his wholly-owned LLC or S corporation is the general partner. Of these two, the limited partnership option may make it easier for Charles to nail down his absolute control rights and reduce any self-employment tax risks for the investors. But either approach will work with some quality planning. This case illustrates two additional choice-of-entity factors.

Factor Ten: Different Ownership Interests

As Charles' deal illustrates, often owners want to structure different types of ownership interests in the entity. Income rights, loss rights, cash flow rights, or liquidation rights may need to be structured differently for select owners to reflect varying contributions to the enterprise. With a C corporation, different types of common and preferred stock may be issued to reflect the varying preferences. An S corporation is extremely limited in its ability to create different types of equity ownership interests. It is limited to voting and non-voting common stock, all of which must have the same income, loss, cash flow and liquidation rights.

Partnerships and limited liability companies offer the most flexibility in structuring different equity ownership interests. These partnership-taxed pass-through entities can customize and define the different interests in the entity's operating agreement. Although the design possibilities are almost unlimited, all allocations of profits, losses and credits will be respected for tax purposes only if the allocations are structured to have "substantial economic effect" within the meaning of section 704(b).

In Charles' situation, there's a clear need to use one of these flexible pass-through entities to create different types of ownership interests. This is particularly true in situations where one group of owners is providing capital and another group of owners is providing management, services and expertise. Often, an LLC is the answer; it offers the centralized management and limited liability benefits of a corporation, and the structuring and tax flexibility of a partnership.

Factor Eleven: Loss Utilization

Like many organizers of businesses that are projected to generate losses in the early years, Charles wants to insure that such losses are funneled to the tax returns that will trigger the highest tax savings. The threshold issue is whether the losses should be retained in the entity or passed through to the owners.

Losses generated by a C corporation are retained in the C corporation and are carried backward or forward to be deducted against income earned in previous or future years. Losses sustained by S corporations, LLCs, partnerships and sole proprietorships are passed through to the business owners. When losses are anticipated in the initial years of a business, using a pass-through entity may generate a tax advantage if the owners have other taxable income against which those losses can be offset, within certain limitations. The advantage is that the losses may produce immediate tax benefits.

In planning to pass through losses to the owners, never lose sight of the fact that the losses, even if passed through, may produce no benefit if one or more of the three loss hurdles mentioned get in the way. The at-risk and passive loss hurdles usually are not affected by the type of pass-through entity selected. The basis hurdle is different in this regard. The general rule is that losses generated by a pass-through entity are not available to an owner of the entity to the extent that the cumulative net losses exceed the owner's basis in the entity. For example, if an investor puts $50,000 into an S corporation, that owner's basis in the S corporation stock is $50,000. If the S corporation generates a loss of $150,000 in the first year and finances the loss through corporate indebtedness, the S corporation shareholder may only use $50,000 of the loss against his or her other income. The other $100,000 is suspended because it exceeds the owner's stock basis. It is carried forward to be used in future years if and when the basis is increased. In contrast, if the indebtedness is incurred in an entity taxed as a partnership, such as a limited liability company or a limited partnership, the indebtedness will increase the partners' basis in their partnership interests under the provisions of Section 752, and the basis limitation will no longer be a factor in assessing the current tax value of the losses.

This loss pass-through factor, perhaps more than any other factor, underscores the value of quality projections of the business operations for the first few years and an evaluation of the individual tax positions of the business owners.

Example Case 4: Jurden Inc.

Jurden Inc. is a successful C corporation that is poised to explode. It has five shareholders, all successful business investors. Then plan for the next five to10 years is to aggressively reinvest earnings to create a global presence and then sell out to a strategic buyer at the right time. The shareholders want to shed the C status now. They want the future tax benefits of a pass-though entity, including the stock basis booster for all reinvested earnings and the elimination or serious reduction of double tax bites at time of sale.

Jurden Inc's only option, as a practical matter, is to covert to an S corporation. This case illustrates a controlling choice-of-entity factor for many.

Factor Twelve: C Corporation Conversion Flexibility

As a C corporation, Jurden Inc. has only one option that makes any sense. If it converted to a partnership structure or an LLC, a gain on the liquidation of the corporation would be triggered at both the corporate and shareholder level at time of conversion – a disastrous scenario. The corporation would recognize a gain on all its assets, and the shareholders would recognize a gain on the liquidation of their stock. The tax costs of getting into a partnership or LLC pass-through entity usually are too great to even think about.

The only practical answer for Jurden Inc. is an S corporation. At the present time, a C corporation may convert to an S corporation without automatically triggering the type of gain that would be triggered on a deemed liquidation of a C corporation.

The S corporate conversion, while clearly the preferred choice in most situations, is not a perfect solution and may trigger some additional tax costs at the time of the conversion and later down the road. If, for example, the corporation values its inventories under the LIFO method, the corporation must recognize as income the LIFO reserve as a result of the S election conversion. Also, the conversion will not eliminate all threats of double taxation. If a C corporation converts to an S corporation and liquidates or sells out within 10 years after the election, the portion of the resulting gain that is attributable to the period prior to the election will be taxed at the corporate level as if the corporation had remained a C corporation. If the C corporation had accumulated earnings and profits before the conversion, the shareholders may end up with taxable dividends after the conversion. A completely clean break from C status often is not possible. But in most situations, these tax consequences of conversion can be managed and do not provide a basis for rejecting the conversion to S status.

Example Case 5: Peter

Peter has developed a business plan for creating and exploiting a series of new Internet games that promise the potential of a huge success. He has attracted the attention of various investors, none of whom want their personal tax returns exposed to any venture and all of whom would love to see Peter's unique talents showcased and exploited through a public company at the right time. The plan now is to reinvest all business earnings to build the business as fast as possible.

Peter is going to want a C corporation. This case illustrates three additional choice-of-entity factors, two of which usually are controlling when they are applicable to the situation.

Factor Thirteen: Going Public Prospects

When a company is funded with outside capital and the plan is to go public at the first solid opportunity, the C corporation often is the mandated choice. The interests of the outside investors and the potential of going public trump all other considerations. Usually the audited track record of the company leading up to the offering is best reflected in the same form of entity that will ultimately go public, which is a C corporation in nearly all cases.

Factor Fourteen: The "Not My Return" Factor

This factor is one of those considerations that sometimes preempts everything else when it is present. It is the owner who has no interest in anything that will implicate or complicate his or her personal tax return. Some just cannot buy into the concept of having to personally recognize and pay taxes on income from a pass-through entity that has never been (and may never be) received in the form of hard cash. Others are spooked by the accounting and audit risks. The thought that their personal tax return and their personal tax liability could be affected by the audit of a company managed by others is too much to bear. Still others are just adamant about keeping all personal matters as simple and as understandable as possible. A stack of K–1 forms flapping on the back of their return is not their concept of simple. When this factor is present and cannot be eliminated, the only option is a C corporation that offers the benefit of complete "separateness."

Factor Fifteen: Reinvestment Growth

Like many companies, Peter hopes to grow his company by reinvesting all earnings. In recent years, the tax rate differential between individual taxpayers and a C corporation has not been a big deal. Both have topped out at a maximum rate of 35 percent. So the choice-of-entity analysis has not turned on the potential to reinvest after tax earnings and grow the business.

But that has changed in 2013. The American Taxpayer Relief Act of 2012 (the "fiscal cliff" legislation signed into law during the final days of 2012)[91] increased individual ordinary income tax rates to 39.6 percent starting in 2013 for couples with taxable incomes in excess of $450,000 and individuals with taxable incomes in excess of $400,000. Plus, in 2013, the 3.8 percent Medicare tax kicks in for couples with a modified adjusted gross income in excess of $250,000 ($200,000 for individuals). The net result is that a successful business owner who is allocated profits through a pass-through S corporation or LLC could end up paying federal taxes at a combined income and Medicare rate of 43.4 percent. In contrast, political leaders on both sides of the aisle and the Obama administration have agreed that top corporate tax rates should be reduced to the 25 to 28 percent range to remain competitive with other countries. The result is that we could end up with a condition that we haven't had for decades – a mammoth gap between top individual rates and top corporate rates.

For a company looking to grow with reinvested earnings, such a huge rate differential between individual and corporate rates may compel use of a C

---

91. Section 101 of the American Taxpayer Relief Act of 2012.

corporation. The difference between reinvesting 56 cents on every earned dollar and reinvesting 75 cents, when compounded over five or 10 years and adjusted for leveraging differences, may impact a business' capacity to finance growth by as much as 50 percent or more. As the push for such rate differentials intensifies, this may emerge as the newest and most dominant choice-of-entity factor for businesses that need to grow. The old C Corporation could emerge as the ultimate comeback kid.

CASE STUDY 5-2

Jerry has plans to form a new company that will build large trawler yachts (measuring 55 to 65 feet) in China. At his own expense, he has completed the initial plans for the first four yachts, all of which will be built from the same mold. He has secured equity financing from five wealthy yacht enthusiasts, who collectively have agreed to put up $6 million for the first four yachts. The "deal" is that (1) Jerry will get a salary of $90,000 a year; (2) the investors will get their investment money back first; (3) Jerry will then be paid the $150,000 that he has invested in the initial plans; and (4) profits then will be distributed 30 percent to Jerry and 70 percent to the investors. Any losses will be allocated 99 percent to the investors and one percent to Jerry. Jerry wants to ensure that he always is in complete control of all business decisions.

You represent Jerry. What business form would you recommend?

CASE STUDY 5-3

Roger plans on opening a specialized machine shop. He will put up 55 percent of the capital, receive 55 percent of the equity interests in the business, work full-time as CEO of the business, and draw a salary and a bonus based on his performance. Three other individuals have committed to fund the balance of the needed capital in equal shares, and they will each receive 15 percent of the equity of the business. The business will have minimal debt and is expected to be profitable by year two. Roger wants a structure that ensures, to the maximum extent possible, freedom from minority owner hassles and contractual negotiations and dealings with minority owners. He wants total control. Plus, he wants to minimize income and self-employment taxes and have no personal liability for the entity's obligations.

You represent Roger. What form of business entity do you recommend?

CASE STUDY 5-4

ABC Inc. and Smith Enterprises Inc. are friendly competitors in the medical supply industry. They are both C corporations owned and operated as successful family businesses. They now desire to form a joint venture to market their respective products in Europe. The venture will be a separate U.S. entity owned by ABC Inc. and Smith Enterprises and will have its own employees and facilities. Both parties want flexibility in transferring funds into and out of the new entity and a clear written understanding of how decisions will be made and control exercised. What form of business entity would you recommend?

CHAPTER 6

CORPORATION FORMATION CHALLENGES

A. SELECTING THE STATE OF INCORPORATION

The legal advisor usually plays a key role in helping the client select the state of incorporation for a business. Hands down, Delaware is the darling of the corporate world. In the corporate charter game, Delaware is the reigning king, and it is highly unlikely that any other state will ever threaten its crown. For the organizers of most corporations, the question is: Should we incorporate in our home state or in Delaware? A number of factors may influence the answer to this basic question.

The starting point is to focus on the reasons that Delaware is the king, and whether those reasons have any relevance to the specific situation. Delaware's dominance in large part is attributable to its judiciary's demonstrated competence to resolve corporate matters in an efficient and fair manner. Many of its judges are accomplished corporate lawyers who have a massive body of corporate case law to work with and a deep appreciation of the importance of Delaware's corporate supremacy to the state. Corporate managers and lawyers generally love the predictability offered by Delaware's established case law and its favorable statutory provisions relating to compensation, self-dealing contracts, and indemnification. See 8 Del. C. §§ 143, 144, 145. Decades of doing deals in Delaware have caused money players and investment bankers to grow comfortable with Delaware's corporate mindset. Everyone understands and appreciates the importance of corporate franchise fees in Delaware and Delaware's strong incentive to remain corporate-friendly on cutting edge issues. Plus, unpopular statutory changes are unlikely given a state constitutional provision that requires a two-thirds vote of both legislative houses to change Delaware's corporation code. Del. Const. art. IX, § 1.

The importance of these factors in a given situation will depend in large part on the nature of the company's projected operations and ownership structure. If the company is going to do business in many states, it will be required to register as a foreign corporation in all such states and likely will deal with important third parties in multiple states. In such a case, the company may prefer to organize in Delaware to bolster its national or regional image and to remove any "local" taint. Similarly, a company that has any hope of going public – or that is, or may become, dependent on capital from established brokerage or venture firms – generally would be well advised to incorporate in Delaware from the get-go. The managers who run such firms, and their lawyers, will be saved the task of asking "Why not Delaware?" and taking necessary corrective actions. In contrast, a closely held corporation that is going to be owned and controlled by a select group of local shareholders often has no need to look beyond its local corporate law. The potential benefits of Delaware's deep body of case law and the trappings of being a Delaware player may not be worth the added hassle and expense of incorporating in Delaware and registering as a foreign corporation in the company's home state. In this very common situation, franchise fees and any specific oddities of the home state's corporate statutes may need to be factored into the mix. Often, the ultimate conclusion is to "stay local."

Excerpts from William L. Cary, *Federalism and Corporate Law: Reflections Upon Delaware*
83 Yale L.J. 663 (1974)

Delaware is both the sponsor and the victim of a system contributing to the deterioration of corporation standards. This unhappy state of affairs, stemming in great part from the movement toward the least common denominator, Delaware, seems to be developing on both the legislative and judicial fronts. In the management of corporate affairs, state statutory and case law has always been supreme, with federal intrusion limited to the field of securities regulation. Perhaps now is the time to reconsider the federal role.

In the early stages of the American economy there were grants of special franchises reminiscent of royal charters, but during the mid-nineteenth century there was a revulsion against them as anti-egalitarian, monopolistic, and scandalous. For this reason, in revising its constitution of 1846, New York provided that corporations might not be created by special act "except ... in cases where, in the judgment of the legislature, the objects of the corporation cannot be attained under general laws." By 1867 provisions of this character appeared in the constitutions of many states.

In 1896 New Jersey adopted what is regarded as the first of the modern liberal corporation statutes. As Mr. Justice Brandeis pointed out in *Liggett Co. v. Lee,* this act is commonly credited with attracting the incorporation of the New Jersey trusts, such as the old Standard Oil Company, which were not trusts at all but corporations operating as consolidated or holding companies. While corporation statutes had been restrictive, the leading industrial states began removing the limits upon both the size and powers of business units. The states, realizing that local restriction would be circumvented by foreign incorporation and eager for the revenue derived from the traffic in charters, joined in advertising their wares. In Brandeis' words, the race was not one of diligence but of laxity.

Shortly afterwards, Delaware, seeking new sources of revenue, copied very largely from the New Jersey act to establish its own statute. Then in 1913, at the insistence of Governor Woodrow Wilson, New Jersey drastically tightened its law relating to corporations and trusts with a series of provisions known as the seven sisters. Since Delaware did not amend its statute, it took the lead at that time and has never lost it, New Jersey by its own admission falling woefully behind. By 1915,the Delaware corporation law was commonly regarded as a modern and "liberal" act.

In all fairness it should be noted that if Delaware had not entered the race, other states would have joined in to attract the lucrative business of: incorporating. Indeed, Nevada has attempted to become the western Delaware but not with comparable success. At its birth in 1943 the Model Business Corporation Act presented an alternative draft corporation statute varying in major respects from the Delaware approach. It was prepared largely by lawyers of the Chicago Bar whose early experience had been in connection with the Illinois Business Corporation Act. Their spokesman commented that "[t]he Delaware statute bids for the corporate business of promotors [sic]. It makes little or no effort to protect the rights of investors. Hence in the opinion of the committee it was not the type of statute which the committee should present as a model for states intending to revise their laws." Over the years, however, the Model Act has been watered down to compete with the Delaware statute on its own terms rather than offering alternative approaches. Indeed, the recent indemnification provision of the Model Act is an exact duplicate of Delaware § 145. As stated by the chairman of the committee which prepared the 1962 amendments to the Model Act, "[C]orporate law has tended more and more in the direction of a simple set of workable ground rules for the corporate enterprise, leaving regulation either to the equitable jurisdiction of the courts or to regulation through statutes of a policing nature or through the informed judgment of administrative agencies." Because the Model Act has been endorsed by leaders of the corporate bar and is itself an American Bar Association committee product, it too accelerated the trend toward permissiveness. Indeed, the whole process is contagious. Other states understandably want to encourage companies to remain at home and therefore try to emulate Delaware by revising their acts along similar lines. Only two or three jurisdictions have resisted this temptation at all. This psychology has been responsible for much of the "modernization" of corporation laws everywhere. Today they are described as "enabling" acts— enabling management to operate with minimum interference...

Professor J. W. Hurst has provided an interesting rationale for these developments. Through the 1920's this style of corporation statute became a national norm, implying confidence in the productive rather than the speculative uses of the corporate device. Corporation law provided an open-ended opportunity for promoters and management to create the kind of vehicle they wanted. Since our country was growing at such breakneck speed, it would have been unthinkable then to hobble corporations in the performance of their functional role. At this stage, Professor Hurst says, the emphasis was upon utility...

Professor Hurst contrasts the principle of utility with the growing need for responsibility. The latter came to be recognized in the depression of the 1930's when speculative abuse in the corporate system became manifest. The marketplace had not provided adequate control for our free enterprise-expanding society. Because abuse was rampant, regulation was required for the protection of the market itself. But the regulation did not take the form of corporation law nor was it directed at the companies themselves, except where abuse had gone beyond all bounds in two major areas, the public utility holding company and the investment company. In Hurst's words, "[T]o define and enforce the responsibility of corporate power the law turned more and more to specialized regulation outside the structure of the corporation." In our mass capitalist society the market has been of such transcendent importance that regulation has been directed at the securities offered and sold rather than at the corporations themselves. In general, the controls that emerged can be labeled as securities regulation (at the federal level) as distinguished from corporate law (at the state level). These developments have been loosely referred to as the growth of federal corporation law.

Professor Hurst's analysis provides a philosophical base for the contrasting developments in state corporation law on the one hand and federal securities legislation on the other. At the state level there appears to have been a failure to recognize the difference between the goals of industrial capitalism and the abuses of finance capitalism—the stage in which we appear to be today. Yet there appears to be no way out of the syndrome that has developed and that permits incorporation in any jurisdiction that may provide management freedom from restrictions. North Carolina initially, and New York subsequently, attempted to adopt some provisions in an effort to regulate foreign corporations doing business in the state (so-called pseudo-foreign corporations), but their efforts have been futile and the restrictions have been largely amended out of the law. State action cannot be effective in providing a responsible corporate statute…

In light of these circumstances, Delaware understandably does not wish to surrender its lead. Amending its law in 1969, and again in 1970 and 1971, it is setting the pace. It likes to be number one. With some justification Delaware corporate counsel take pride in their role and enjoy the fees that flow from it. The system "engenders a volume of business for the bar which tends to be regarded as a vested interest, so that any attempt to retrace steps would encounter opposition in powerful quarters." Most important, the raison d'etre behind the whole system has been achieved—revenue for the state of Delaware.

Stimulating incorporation in Delaware has some of the flavor of a community chest drive. According to a state official, "The response 'has greatly exceeded our expectations.' So far this year 6,556 companies have incorporated themselves in Delaware. The total may hit 9,000 by Dec. 31. The influx boosted the state's incorporation tax take by $2.9 million in fiscal 1968" In 1971 corporation franchise taxes represented $52 million out of a total of $222 million in state tax collections, approximately one-quarter of the total. For revenue reasons, "creating a favorable climate" is declared to be the public policy of the state.

Some of the features of Delaware law demonstrating liberality have been recited in publications for practitioners. These include: greater freedom to pay dividends and make distributions; greater ease of charter amendment and less restrictions upon selling assets, mortgaging, leasing, and merging freedom from mandatory cumulative voting; permission to have staggered boards of directors; lesser pre-emptive rights for shareholders; [and] clearer rights of indemnification for directors and officers.

In addition, full faith and credit must be given to Delaware Corporation Law as to companies organized there but operating in other states. A few illustrations of the legislative approach reveal the Delaware position. For example, shareholders meetings may now be dispensed with if a consent is signed by the number of votes necessary to take the intended action, thus offering a technique to avoid disclosure. Protection from this abuse is provided through the proxy rules under federal law but they do not apply to firms that are unlisted or have less than 500 shareholders and minimal assets. Under § 109 of the Delaware law any corporation may in its certificate of incorporation confer the power to amend or repeal by-law provisions upon the directors and thus possibly foreclose any initiative outside the management.

The indemnification provisions relating to officers and directors have been criticized on several grounds. One is that the statutory remedy is nonexclusive as contrasted with the New York provisions. Furthermore, the new statute is broad and promises indemnity in areas where it is said that courts and commentators question the propriety of indemnification. Finally, Delaware authorizes insurance in situations where direct indemnity might not be permissible.

Judicial decisions in Delaware illustrate that the courts have undertaken to carry out the "public policy" of the state and create a "favorable climate" for management. Consciously or unconsciously, fiduciary standards and the standards of fairness generally have been relaxed. In general, the judicial decisions can best be reconciled on the basis of a desire to foster incorporation in Delaware. It is not clear, however, that the revenue thermometer should replace the chancellor's foot. This trend should be reversed.

Before proceeding to this inquiry certain underlying premises should be recognized. First, although there is not as much "free enterprise" as appears at first glance, ours is still a capitalist economy. At the same time, from the standpoint of legal rights and duties, we are tending toward a managerial, rather than a capitalist society—thanks in large part to the shift of authority to management.

Second, almost all of our business is transacted through corporations. For the year 1969 total business receipts amounted to $2.9 trillion, 84 percent of which was accounted for by active corporations. Moreover, a substantial and growing fraction of the major corporations is organized in Delaware. For this reason alone Delaware decisions have a profound impact upon the development of corporation law. Furthermore, similar to its influence on statutory modernization, Delaware's case law is cited constantly and relied upon in other jurisdictions. Every corporation law casebook for students is filled with Delaware decisions because it is the state where great companies are organized and where there is the most corporate experience to draw upon.

Next, it is of obvious importance that business should be conducted fairly, honestly, and competently. Indeed, these ingredients are essential to raise capital and make the system work. In another context I have adverted to a discussion in Washington some years ago with the Ambassador from a South American country. He came to seek advice because he wanted to encourage the investment of outside capital into private firms in his country and wondered how that could be achieved. I asked first, "Are your stock exchange facilities inadequate?" And he replied, "No, that really isn't the question. We have to get back to fundamentals .... My first concern is whether the public investor can trust anyone. The trouble with management in my country is that their only loyalty is to their relatives." This is not uncommon and it struck me forcefully; it emphasized the importance of confidence and a high standard of conduct by management as an essential ingredient before one can expect the private investor to entrust his funds to public companies. Such confidence can be sustained only by a combination of high standards coupled with disclosure and management accountability coupled with vulnerability to derivative or direct shareholder action.

Finally, it has been said that numerous members of the New York bar "felt Delaware was a more favorable forum than any other available." The necessary high standards of conduct cannot be maintained by courts shackled to public policy based upon the production of revenue, pride in being "number one," and the creation of a "favorable climate" for new incorporations. The view is widely held that Delaware corporate decisions lean toward the status quo and adhere to minimal standards of director responsibility both to the corporation and its shareholders.

The discussion thus far might seem to lead to the recommendation of federal incorporation. In my opinion, however, this is politically unrealistic. It has been raised many times in Congress and in the literature but has no public appeal. American business would unanimously reject such a convenient vehicle for government control of the major industries of this country.

It is true that business talks about free enterprise but asks for government intervention in the event of financial crisis or possible take-over bids. It is also true that many forms of federal regulation already exist. In the words of Professor Loss, "I think it's not too much to say that Section 12(g) of the Exchange Act ... is at least second cousin, if not first cousin, to federal incorporation in substance, not in form." Yet, I do not advocate, or even conceive of, federal incorporation as an imminent possibility except in the event of a catastrophic depression or a corporate debacle.

However, in order to remedy the Delaware syndrome it does appear that federal standards of corporate responsibility are called for. This can best be achieved by prescribing minimum corporation law provisions which shall be applicable to companies doing business in interstate commerce and construed by federal judicial standards. Uniformity is of the essence. Efforts must be made to insure that provisions are not interpreted differently owing to varying state interpretations of public policy. There should also be wide-ranging service of process upon directors and officers of corporations. The participation of a government agency such as the Securities and Exchange Commission is not contemplated in this proposal.

Ideally, consideration should be given to a much broader inquiry perceptively suggested by Professor Eisenberg. In his opinion "Traditional corporate statutes fail to deal with many important structural decisions which are common in today's business world." We might go even farther and ask what representation the modern constituency of the corporation—employees, consumers, and the public, as well as shareholders—should have in the governance of the corporation. Consideration of this issue is not contemplated here. The first step is to escape from the present predicament in which a pygmy among the 50 states prescribes, interprets, and indeed denigrates national corporate policy as an incentive to encourage incorporation within its borders, thereby increasing its revenue.

B. ORGANIZATIONAL PROCESS AND DOCUMENTS

Every corporation needs organizational documents to get it going. The number, scope and complexity of the documents depend on the composition of the owners, the number and type of entities used, and the quality of the planning effort on the front end. Usually customization of the organizational documents increases as the planning effort improves. More customization results in more complexity and, most importantly, a better mutual understanding of the key deal points between the organizers and owners of the business.

Too often the temptation is to short-circuit the planning process up front. The business organizers want to focus on start-up business challenges, not legal documents. Plus, the lawyers' job is much easier if the document customization effort is minimized or avoided altogether. Why trigger potentially contentious dialogue on tough hypothetical scenarios that may never develop? Why not just perpetuate the common (but false) perception that there is a "normal" or "accepted" way of documenting issues between co-owners? The result is that, in far too many cases, everyone opts for the "standard stuff." The documentation effort is limited to filling in blanks on stock forms, and the dialogue is limited to descriptive pronouncements from the lawyers. The documents look and read complete and official, but they do nothing to reflect thoughtful, negotiated "deal points" that the owners have resolved with the assistance of skilled planning advisors.

In nearly all situations, the lawyer must take the lead in defining the scope of the front-end planning effort. This is done by identifying key operational issues, explaining the significance of the issues, and then helping the client carefully evaluate his or her objectives or priority concerns with respect to each issue. Section D. of this chapter briefly reviews 20 of the most common operational issues that often need to be discussed and analyzed. In addition to the operational issues, there is the paramount challenge of structuring the buy-sell provisions between the co-owners of a closely held business. For most closely held businesses, the buy-sell provisions between the co-owners define how and when individual owners ultimately will realize a return on their investment in the venture. Although many business owners initially are confused by the need to give significant attention to provisions dealing with exit scenarios during the early planning stages of the business, the confusion usually disappears very quickly as the owners begin to realize that these provisions define what they will ultimately get in return for all of their invested capital and effort. This buy-sell agreement planning challenge is discussed in Chapter 13.

1. ORGANIZATIONAL DOCUMENTS

The advisor must have an understanding of the state corporate law that is going to be applicable to the entity in order to properly draft corporate organizational documents that will meet the client's objectives. This is essential because state corporate statutes specify important default rules that will apply unless the corporate organizational documents provide otherwise. These default rules vary from state to state. In many situations, a particular default rule will be perfectly consistent with a client's objectives, and there will be no need to call attention to the rule in the organizational documents and trigger the possibility of other owners raising an objection. In such a situation, saying nothing in the documents and letting the default rule automatically kick in may be the best course of action. In many other situations, a particular default rule will be inconsistent with the client's core objectives, and the organizational documents will need to be drawn to negate the default rule.

Articles of Incorporation. The Articles of Incorporation is the charter document mandated by state statute. When this document is filed with the appropriate state authority, the corporation comes into existence. This is a public document that can be easily accessed by anyone. For this reason, often it is drawn to include only the minimum provisions, which typically include the identity and address of the incorporators, the corporate name, the registered agent and office of the corporation, the number of shares of stock that the corporation is authorized to issue, and usually (but not always) the number and identity of the initial directors of the corporation. Here, it is critically important that the state's default rules regarding certain matters be carefully evaluated. If a default rule is ill advised or unacceptable, it must be negated in the articles of incorporation. If the state's default rules favor cumulative voting or preemptive rights, specific provisions denying these rights are often needed in the articles of incorporation. Similarly, the articles of incorporation often must contain specific provisions dealing with the limited liability of directors, the indemnification of directors and related expense advances, shareholder consent voting procedures, the authorization of "blank check" stock, and supermajority shareholder voting requirements. See Section C. of Chapter 17 for a sample from of Articles of Incorporation.

Bylaws. The bylaws serve as the owners' manual for the corporation. This document describes the roles of the shareholders, directors and officers and the mechanics for calling and holding meetings, approving consent resolutions, and handling other administrative and procedural matters. Key provisions often include the number of directors; the authorized use of electronic transmissions for shareholder notices; special meeting notice requirements; annual meeting time and place; authorized participation via communication equipment;

authorized board actions without a meeting; board of director compensation authorization; officer duties and titles; stock certificates and legends; stock transfer restrictions; indemnification provisions; fiscal year designation; bylaw amendment procedures; and special tax elections. See Section E. of Chapter 17 for a sample form of corporate bylaws.

Employment Agreements. These documents govern the employment relationship between the corporation and its key employees, including shareholders who are employed by the corporation. Often employment agreements are used to document important deal points between the owners.

Directors' Resolutions. These resolutions are approved by the board of directors and are essential for the organization and start-up of the business. The resolutions usually include provisions approving the articles of incorporation, adopting the bylaws, electing the officers, authorizing the issuance of stock and the receipt of consideration (money, property or services) for the stock, authorizing the establishment of corporate bank accounts, ratifying and approving any pre-incorporation business transactions, approving credit lines and other financing arrangements, authorizing the commencement of business operations, authorizing the execution of documents necessary for the acquisition of assets, leases, licenses and intellectual property rights, and approving any other significant matters related to the start-up of the business. The organizational directors' resolutions are documented either as written consent resolutions signed by all the directors or as minutes of an organizational meeting where the directors approved the resolutions. See Section D. of Chapter 17 for a sample form for Organization Directors' Resolutions.

Stock Register and Stock Certificates. Stock certificates are issued to the shareholders. Usually they include legends referencing the provisions of the Shareholder Agreement and transfer restrictions under applicable securities laws. The stock register is a record of when specific shares were issued and to whom they were issued.

Asset Transfer Documents. Often documents are needed to transfer specific assets to the corporation. Examples include bills of sale, lease assignments, license agreements and, in rare instances, real estate deeds. Often the documents include provisions requiring the corporation to assume liabilities related to the transferred assets.

Pre-Incorporation Agreement. In limited situations, the parties desire to document their mutual understandings regarding the formation of the corporation and their approval of the terms and conditions of all the organizational documents before steps are taken to officially form the corporation. This is accomplished with a pre-incorporation agreement, a comprehensive document that usually includes the other organizational documents as attachments. It is not a required document and is not used in many situations.

Required Government Filing. Each state requires that certain documents be filed and fees paid in order to form the corporation. Typically these documents include the Articles of Incorporation, the written consent of the registered agent for the corporation in the particular state, and an application to obtain a state tax identification number. Also, a Form SS-4 needs to be filed with the Internal Revenue Service to obtain a federal tax identification number, and a Form 2553 is required if an S election is desired.

Shareholder Agreement. An agreement between the shareholders of the corporation is critically important in nearly all situations involving closely held corporations. For planning purposes, this agreement is the most important document – by a long shot. It lays out the terms of the buy-sell agreements among shareholders and the details of those operational deal points that the shareholders have chosen to document. This is not a required document, and it is shamefully ignored in far too many situations. It takes more work, more dialogue and more customization than any other organizational document.

Although the authority to manage a corporation is vested in its board of directors, state corporate statutes generally authorize the use of shareholder agreements to establish rights among the shareholders of closely held corporations (those corporations whose stock is not publicly traded) that preempt the management authority of the board. Many such state statutes are modeled after The Model Business Act, which specifically authorizes any such agreements among the shareholders of a non-public company that "govern the exercise of corporate powers or the management of the business and affairs of the corporation or the relationship among the shareholders, the directors and the corporation, or any of them, and is not contrary to public policy." Model Business Corporation Act § 7.32(a)(8).

The shareholders agreement should be carefully drafted, specify how long it will remain in effect (absent such a term provision, applicable state statutes may terminate the agreement after a specified term, such as 10 years), and be conspicuously referenced in written legends on all stock certificates that are issued by the corporation.

2. ORGANIZATIONAL MECHANICS

CASE PROBLEM 6-1

You've been retained to help Darren form a new corporation that will be known as GhostGrip ("Ghost"). Ghost will develop and exploit a newly patented golf grip. Darren will be issued 40 percent of Ghost's common voting stock for his contribution of the patent to the venture. Ten other individuals, all avid golfers, will each be issued six percent of Ghost's common voting stock for a cash contribution. Except for the Dooby brother twins, the shareholders are unrelated.

The following questions have surfaced in your first meeting with Darren. Answer these questions based on your reading of the materials in this chapter and the assumption that the following provisions of the Model Business Corporation Act have been enacted in Idaho.

1. Darren is concerned about the state of incorporation. All of the shareholders have always lived in Idaho, and the corporation's offices will be in Idaho. What additional facts would you need to have in order to provide Darren

with some guidance on this issue?

2. The corporation will have five directors. If the corporation has cumulative voting, how many of the five directors will Darren be able to elect? How many will the Dooby brother twins, acting in concert, be able to elect? If the corporation does not have cumulative voting, how would the answers to these questions change? How would the answers change if the board had two-year staggered terms, with two directors being elected in the old years and three directors being elected in the even years? Are such staggered terms permissible?

3. Will preemptive rights always benefit Darren? Are there smart reasons for not having preemptive rights?

4. Does Darren, as the major shareholder, have to be Ghost's registered agent? Should he be the registered agent?

5. Do the names of the directors need to be in the articles of incorporation?

6. When does the corporation's existence start?

7. Darren anticipates that the corporation may need to raise additional capital in the future. He would like the board to be able to issue preferred stock on terms that the board sets without having to discuss the terms with the shareholders. Is this possible? If so, should such a provision be in the bylaws or the articles of incorporation?

8. If Darren determines that he would like to have the power to elect three of the five directors even though he owns only 40 percent of the voting stock, is this possible? If so, how should it be documented?

9. Can the corporation be named only "Ghost Grip."

10. Which of the following provisions must be in the articles of incorporation in order to be effective:

   a) A provision limiting the liability of directors.

   b) A provision allowing directors to approve resolutions by unanimous written consent without a meeting.

   c) A provision authorizing emergency bylaws.

   d) A provision indemnifying directors.

   e) A provision requiring a 67-percent shareholder approval vote for a transaction to sell substantially all the assets of the corporation.

   f) A provision limiting the purpose of the corporation.

Select Provisions of the Model Business Corporations Act

MBCA § 2.01. INCORPORATORS

One or more persons may act as the incorporator or incorporators of a corporation by delivering articles of incorporation to the secretary of state for filing.

MBCA § 2.02. ARTICLES OF INCORPORATION

(a) The articles of incorporation must set forth:

(1) a corporate name for the corporation that satisfies the requirements of section 4.01;

(2) the number of shares the corporation is authorized to issue;

(3) the street address of the corporation's initial registered office and the name of its initial registered agent at that office; and

(4) the name and address of each incorporator.

(b) The articles of incorporation may set forth:

(1) the names and addresses of the individuals who are to serve as the initial directors;

(2) provisions not inconsistent with law regarding:

(i) the purpose or purposes for which the corporation is organized;

(ii) managing the business and regulating the affairs of the corporation;

(iii) defining, limiting, and regulating the powers of the corporation, its board of directors, and shareholders;

(iv) a par value for authorized shares or classes of shares;

(v) the imposition of personal liability on shareholders for the debts of the corporation to a specified extent and upon specified conditions;

(3) any provision that under this Act is required or permitted to be set forth in the bylaws;

(4) a provision eliminating or limiting the liability of a director to the corporation or its shareholders for money damages for any action taken, or any failure to take any action, as a director, except liability for (A) the amount of a financial benefit received by a director to which he is not entitled; (B) an intentional infliction of harm on the corporation or the shareholders; (C) a violation of section 8.33; or (D) an intentional violation of criminal law; and

(5) a provision permitting or making obligatory indemnification of a director for liability (as defined in section 8.50(5)) to any person for any action taken, or any failure to take any action, as a director, except liability for (A) receipt of a financial benefit to which he is not entitled, (B) an intentional infliction of harm on the corporation or its shareholders, (C) a violation of section 8.33, or (D) an intentional violation of criminal law.

(c) The articles of incorporation need not set forth any of the corporate powers enumerated in this Act.

(d) Provisions of the articles of incorporation may be made dependent upon facts objectively ascertainable outside the articles of incorporation in accordance with section 1.20(k).

MBCA § 2.03. INCORPORATION

(a) Unless a delayed effective date is specified, the corporate existence begins when the articles of incorporation are filed.

(b) The secretary of state's filing of the articles of incorporation is conclusive proof that the incorporators satisfied all conditions precedent to incorporation except in a proceeding by the state to cancel or revoke the incorporation or involuntarily dissolve the corporation.

MBCA § 2.05. ORGANIZATION OF CORPORATION

(a) After incorporation:

(1) if initial directors are named in the articles of incorporation, the initial directors shall hold an organizational meeting, at the call of a majority of the directors, to complete the organization of the corporation by appointing officers, adopting bylaws, and carrying on any other business brought before the meeting;

(2) if initial directors are not named in the articles, the incorporator or incorporators shall hold an organizational meeting at the call of a majority of the incorporators:

(i) to elect directors and complete the organization of the corporation; or

(ii) to elect a board of directors who shall complete the organization of the corporation.

(b) Action required or permitted by this Act to be taken by incorporators at an organizational meeting may be taken without a meeting if the action taken is evidenced by one or more written consents describing the action taken and signed by each incorporator.

(c) An organizational meeting may be held in or out of this state.

MBCA § 2.06. BYLAWS

(a) The incorporators or board of directors of a corporation shall adopt initial bylaws for the corporation.

(b) The bylaws of a corporation may contain any provision for managing the business and regulating the affairs of the corporation that is not inconsistent with law or the articles of incorporation.

MBCA § 2.07. EMERGENCY BYLAWS

(a) Unless the articles of incorporation provide otherwise, the board of directors of a corporation may adopt bylaws to be effective only in an emergency defined in subsection (d). The emergency bylaws, which are subject to amendment or repeal by the shareholders, may make all provisions necessary for managing the corporation during the emergency, including:

(1) procedures for calling a meeting of the board of directors;

(2) quorum requirements for the meeting; and

(3) designation of additional or substitute directors.

(b) All provisions of the regular bylaws consistent with the emergency bylaws remain effective during the emergency. The emergency bylaws are not effective after the emergency ends.

MBCA § 3.01. PURPOSES

(a) Every corporation incorporated under this Act has the purpose of engaging in any lawful business unless a more limited purpose is set forth in the articles of incorporation.

(b) A corporation engaging in a business that is subject to regulation under another statute of this state may incorporate under this Act only if permitted by, and subject to all limitations of, the other statute.

MBCA § 3.02. GENERAL POWERS

Unless its articles of incorporation provide otherwise, every corporation has perpetual duration and succession in its corporate name and has the same powers as an individual to do all things necessary or convenient to carry out its business and affairs,

MBCA § 3.04. ULTRA VIRES

(a) Except as provided in subsection (b), the validity of corporate action may not be challenged on the ground that the corporation lacks or lacked power to act.

(b) A corporation's power to act may be challenged:

(1) in a proceeding by a shareholder against the corporation to enjoin the act;

(2) in a proceeding by the corporation, directly, derivatively, or through a receiver, trustee, or other legal representative, against an incumbent or former director, officer, employee, or agent of the corporation; or

(3) in a proceeding by the attorney general under section 14.30.

MBCA § 4.01. CORPORATE NAME

(a) A corporate name:

(1) must contain the word "corporation," "incorporated," "company," or "limited," or the abbreviation "corp.," "inc.," "co.," or "ltd.," or words or abbreviations of like import in another language; and

(2) may not contain language stating or implying that the corporation is organized for a purpose other than that permitted by section 3.01 and its articles of incorporation.

MBCA § 5.01. REGISTERED OFFICE AND REGISTERED AGENT

Each corporation must continuously maintain in this state:

(1) a registered office that may be the same as any of its places of business; and

(2) a registered agent, who may be:

(i) an individual who resides in this state and whose business office is identical with the registered office;

(ii) a domestic corporation or not-for-profit domestic corporation whose business office is identical with the registered office; or

(iii) a foreign corporation or not-for-profit foreign corporation authorized to transact business in this state whose business office is identical with the registered office.

§ 6.02. TERMS OF CLASS OR SERIES DETERMINED BY BOARD OF DIRECTORS

(a) If the articles of incorporation so provide, the board of directors is authorized, without shareholder approval, to:

(1) classify any unissued shares into one or more classes or into one or more series within a class,

(2) reclassify any unissued shares of any class into one or more classes or into one or more series within one or more classes, or

(3) reclassify any unissued shares of any series of any class into one or more classes or into one or more series within a class.

(b) If the board of directors acts pursuant to subsection (a), it must determine the terms, including the preferences, rights and limitations, to the same extent permitted under section 6.01, of:

(1) any class of shares before the issuance of any shares of that class, or

(2) any series within a class before the issuance of any shares of that series.

(c) Before issuing any shares of a class or series created under this section, the corporation must deliver to the secretary of state for filing articles of amendment setting forth the terms determined under subsection (a).

MBCA § 6.30. SHAREHOLDERS' PREEMPTIVE RIGHTS

(a) The shareholders of a corporation do not have a preemptive right to acquire the corporation's unissued shares except to the extent the articles of incorporation so provide.

(b) A statement included in the articles of incorporation that "the corporation elects to have preemptive rights" (or words of similar import) means that the following principles apply except to the extent the articles of incorporation expressly provide otherwise:

(1) The shareholders of the corporation have a preemptive right, granted on uniform terms and conditions prescribed by the board of directors to provide a fair and reasonable opportunity to exercise the right, to acquire proportional amounts of the corporation's unissued shares upon the decision of the board of directors to issue them.

(2) A shareholder may waive his preemptive right. A waiver evidenced by a writing is irrevocable even though it is not supported by consideration.

(3) There is no preemptive right with respect to:

(i) shares issued as compensation to directors, officers, agents, or employees of the corporation, its subsidiaries or affiliates:

(ii) shares issued to satisfy conversion or option rights created to provide compensation to directors, officers, agents, or employees of the corporation, its subsidiaries or affiliates;

(iii) shares authorized in articles of incorporation that are issued within six months from the effective date of incorporation;

(iv) shares sold otherwise than for money.

MBCA § 7.27. GREATER QUORUM OR VOTING REQUIREMENTS

(a) The articles of incorporation may provide for a greater quorum or voting requirement for shareholders (or voting groups of shareholders) than is provided for by this Act.

(b) An amendment to the articles of incorporation that adds, changes, or deletes a greater quorum or voting requirement must meet the same quorum requirement and be adopted by the same vote and voting groups required to take action under the quorum and voting requirements then in effect or proposed to be adopted, whichever is greater.

§ 7.28. VOTING FOR DIRECTORS; CUMULATIVE VOTING

(a) Unless otherwise provided in the articles of incorporation, directors are elected by a plurality of the votes cast by the shares entitled to vote in the election at a meeting at which a quorum is present.

(b) Shareholders do not have a right to cumulate their votes for directors unless the articles of incorporation so provide.

(c) A statement included in the articles of incorporation that "[all] [a designated voting group of] shareholders are entitled to cumulate their votes for directors" (or words of similar import) means that the shareholders designated are entitled to multiply the number of votes they are entitled to cast by the number of directors for whom they are entitled to vote and cast the product for a single candidate or distribute the product among two or more candidates.

§ 7.32. SHAREHOLDER AGREEMENTS

(a) An agreement among the shareholders of a corporation that complies with this section is effective among the shareholders and the corporation even though it is inconsistent with one or more other provisions of this Act in that it:

(1) eliminates the board of directors or restricts the discretion or powers of the board of directors;

(2) governs the authorization or making of distributions whether or not in proportion to ownership of shares, subject to the limitations in section 6.40;

(3) establishes who shall be directors or officers of the corporation, or their terms of office or manner of selection or removal;

(4) governs, in general or in regard to specific matters, the exercise or division of voting power by or between the shareholders and directors or by or among any of them, including use of weighted voting rights or director proxies;

(5) establishes the terms and conditions of any agreement for the transfer or use of property or the provision of services between the corporation and any shareholder, director, officer or employee of the corporation or among any of them;

(6) transfers to one or more shareholders or other persons all or part of the authority to exercise the corporate powers or to manage the business and affairs of the corporation, including the resolution of any issue about which there exists a deadlock among directors or shareholders;

(7) requires dissolution of the corporation at the request of one or more of the shareholders or upon the occurrence of a specified event or contingency; or

(8) otherwise governs the exercise of the corporate powers or the management of the business and affairs of the corporation or the relationship among the shareholders, the directors and the corporation, or among any of them, and is not contrary to public policy.

(b) An agreement authorized by this section shall be:

(1) set forth (A) in the articles of incorporation or bylaws and approved by all persons who are shareholders at the time of the agreement or (B) in a written agreement that is signed by all persons who are shareholders at the time of the agreement and is made known to the corporation;

(2) subject to amendment only by all persons who are shareholders at the time of the amendment, unless the agreement provides otherwise; and

(3) valid for 10 years, unless the agreement provides otherwise.

(c) The existence of an agreement authorized by this section shall be noted conspicuously on the front or back of each certificate for outstanding shares or on the information statement required by section 6.26(b). If at the time of the agreement the corporation has shares outstanding represented by certificates, the corporation shall recall the outstanding certificates and issue substitute certificates that comply with this subsection. The failure to note the existence of the agreement on the certificate or information statement shall not affect the validity of the agreement or any action taken pursuant to it. Any purchaser of shares who, at the time of purchase, did not have knowledge of the existence of the agreement shall be entitled to rescission of the purchase. A purchaser shall be deemed to have knowledge of the existence of the agreement if its existence is noted on the certificate or information statement for the shares in compliance with this subsection and, if the shares are not represented by a certificate, the information statement is delivered to the purchaser at or prior to the time of purchase of the shares. An action to enforce the right of rescission authorized by this subsection must be commenced within the earlier of 90 days after discovery of the existence of the agreement or two years after the time of purchase of the shares.

(d) An agreement authorized by this section shall cease to be effective when shares of the corporation are listed on a national securities exchange or regularly traded in a market maintained by one or more members of a national or affiliated securities association. If the agreement ceases to be effective for any reason, the board of directors may, if the agreement is contained or referred to in the corporation's articles of incorporation or bylaws, adopt an amendment to the articles of incorporation or bylaws, without shareholder action, to delete the agreement and any references to it.

(e) An agreement authorized by this section that limits the discretion or powers of the board of directors shall relieve the directors of, and impose upon the person or persons in whom such discretion or powers are vested, liability for acts or omissions imposed by law on directors to the extent that the discretion or powers of the directors are limited by the agreement.

MBCA § 8.06. STAGGERED TERMS FOR DIRECTORS

The articles of incorporation may provide for staggering the terms of directors by dividing the total number of directors into two or three groups, with each group containing one-half or one-third of the total, as near as may be.

MBCA § 8.21. ACTION WITHOUT MEETING

(a) Except to the extent that the articles of incorporation or bylaws require that action by the board of directors be taken at a meeting, action required or permitted by this Act to be taken by the board of directors may be taken without a meeting if each director signs a consent describing the action to be taken and delivers it to the corporation.

(b) Action taken under this section is the act of the board of directors.

C. DEFECTIVE INCORPORATION CHALLENGES

CRANSON v. IBM
200 A.2d 33 (Md. 1964)

HORNEY, Judge.

On the theory that the Real Estate Service Bureau was neither a de jure nor a de facto corporation and that Albion C. Cranson, Jr., was a partner in the business conducted by the Bureau and as such was personally liable for its debts, the International Business Machines Corporation brought this action against Cranson for the balance due on electric typewriters purchased by the Bureau. At the same time it moved for summary judgment and supported the motion by affidavit. In due course, Cranson filed a general issue plea and an affidavit in opposition to summary judgment in which he asserted in effect that the Bureau was a de facto corporation and that he was not personally liable for its debts.

The agreed statement of facts shows that in April 1961, Cranson was asked to invest in a new business corporation which was about to be created. Towards this purpose he met with other interested individuals and an attorney and agreed to purchase stock and become an officer and director. Thereafter, upon being advised by the attorney that the corporation had been formed under the laws of Maryland, he paid for and received a stock certificate evidencing ownership of shares in the corporation, and was shown the corporate seal and minute book. The business of the new venture was conducted as if it were a corporation, through corporate bank accounts, with auditors maintaining corporate books and records, and under a lease entered into by the corporation for the office from which it operated its business. Cranson was elected president and all transactions conducted by him for the corporation, including the dealings with I.B.M., were made as an officer of the corporation. At no time did he assume any personal obligation or pledge his individual credit to I.B.M. Due to an oversight on the part of the attorney, of which Cranson was not aware, the certificate of incorporation, which had been signed and acknowledged prior to May 1, 1961, was not filed until November 24, 1961. Between May 17 and November 8, the Bureau purchased eight typewriters from I.B.M., on account of which partial payments were made, leaving a balance due of $4,333.40, for which this suit was brought.

Although a question is raised as to the propriety of making use of a motion for summary judgment as the means of determining the issues presented by the pleadings, we think the motion was appropriate. Since there was no genuine dispute as to the material facts, the only question was whether I.B.M. was entitled to judgment as a matter of law. The trial court found that it was, but we disagree.

The fundamental question presented by the appeal is whether an officer of a defectively incorporated association may be subjected to personal liability under the circumstances of this case. We think not.

Traditionally, two doctrines have been used by the courts to clothe an officer of a defectively incorporated association with the corporate attribute of limited liability. The first, often referred to as the doctrine of de facto corporations, has been applied in those cases where there are elements showing: (1) the existence of law authorizing incorporation; (2) an effort in good faith to incorporate under the existing law; and (3) actual user or exercise of corporate powers. The second, the doctrine of estoppel to deny the corporate existence, is generally employed where the person seeking to hold the officer personally liable has contracted or otherwise dealt with the association in such a manner as to recognize and in effect admit its existence as a corporate body.

It is not at all clear what Maryland has done with respect to the two doctrines. There have been no recent cases in this State on the subject and some of the seemingly irreconcilable earlier cases offer little to clarify the problem.

In one line of cases, the Court, in determining the rights and liabilities of a defectively organized corporation, or a member or stockholder thereof, seems to have drawn a distinction between those acts or requirements which are a condition precedent to corporate existence and those acts prescribed by law to be done after incorporation. In so doing, it has been generally held that where there had been a failure to comply with a requirement which the law declared to be a condition precedent to the existence of the corporation, the corporation was not a legal entity and was therefore precluded from suing or being sued as such. . Boyce v. Trustees of etc. Methodist Episcopal Church, 46 Md. 359 (1877); Maryland Tube & Iron Works v. West End Imp. Co., 87 Md. 207, 39 A. 620, 39 L.R.A. 810 (1898); Cleaveland v. Mullin, 96 Md. 598, 54 A. 665 (1903); National Shutter Bar Co. v. Zimmerman, 110 Md. 313, 73 A. 19 (1909). These cases appear to stand for the proposition that substantial compliance with those formalities of the corporation law, which are made a condition precedent to corporate existence, was not only necessary for the creation of a corporation de jure, but was also a prerequisite to the existence of a de facto corporation or a corporation by estoppel.

In the Maryland Tube case, an action by a corporation for specific performance of a contract to convey land which it had entered into prior to its becoming a legal entity, the Court, having cited the statements in Jones v. Aspen Hardware Co., 21 Colo. 263, 40 P. 457, 29 L.R.A. 143 (1895), with approval for the propositions that "the doctrine of estoppel cannot be successfully invoked unless the corporation has [at least] a de facto existence," that "a de facto corporation can never be recognized in violation of a positive law" and that "there is a broad distinction between those acts made necessary by the statute as a prerequisite to the exercise of corporate powers, and those acts required of individuals seeking incorporation, but not made prerequisites to the exercise of such powers," went on to say that 'these principles were clearly recognized and applied' in the Boyce case.

In the National Shutter Bar case, an action by a corporation for an alleged libel which had occurred before the performance of a condition precedent necessary for legal incorporation, it was held-citing the Maryland Tube case for the proposition that statutory conditions precedent must have been complied with to give existence to corporations formed under general laws-that the corporation had no legal existence at the time of the alleged libel. In referring to the Boyce case, it was said that 'it has been held by our predecessors that a corporation cannot be actually or virtually created by estoppel in Maryland.' And, on the basis of the statements in Jones v. Aspen Hardware Co., supra (also relied on in the Maryland Tube case), it was concluded that the corporation could not maintain the action.

On the other hand, where the corporation has obtained legal existence but has failed to comply with a condition subsequent to corporate existence, this Court has held that such nonperformance afforded the State the right to institute proceedings for the forfeiture of the charter, but that such neglect or omission could never be set up by the corporation itself, or by its members and stockholders, as a defense to an action to enforce their liabilities. Hammond v. Straus, 53 Md. 1 (1880); Murphy v. Wheatley, 102 Md. 501, 63 A. 62 (1906).

In the Hammond case, an action by a creditor against a stockholder of a state bank on his statutory liability, the Court after stating that a corporation or a stock holder could not defeat an action by showing noncompliance with the requirements of the corporation law unless the acts required are conditions precedent to corporate existence, said:

'By holding otherwise, parties might avail themselves of the powers and privileges of a corporation, without in any manner subjecting themselves to its duties and obligations, and might set up their own neglect of duty, or wilful omission to comply with the requirements of the statute, as means of discharge from all their just obligations under the law. This is forbidden by every principle of law and justice, and hence such a defense could never be tolerated.'

It seems clear therefore that when a defect in the incorporation process resulted from a failure to comply with a condition subsequent, the doctrine of estoppel may be applied for the benefit of a creditor to estop the corporation, or the members or stockholders thereof, from denying its corporate existence.

In another line of Maryland cases which determined the rights and liabilities of a defectively organized corporation, or a member or stockholder thereof, the Court, apparently disregarding the distinction made between those requirements which are conditions precedent and those which are conditions subsequent to corporate existence, has generally precluded, on the grounds of estoppel or collateral attack, inquiry into the question of corporate existence. Maltby v. Northwestern Va. R. R. Co., 16 Md. 422 (1860); Franz v. Teutonia Building Ass'n, 24 Md. 259 (1866); Grape Sugar & Vinegar Mfg. Co. v. Small, 40 Md. 395 (1874).

When summarized, the law in Maryland pertaining to the de facto and estoppel doctrines reveals that the cases seem to fall into one or the other of two categories. In one line of cases, the Court, choosing to disregard the nature of the dealings between the parties, refused to recognize both doctrines where there had been a failure to comply with a condition precedent to corporate existence, but, whenever such noncompliance concerned a condition subsequent to incorporation, the Court often applied the estoppel doctrine. In the other line of cases, the Court, choosing to make no distinction between defects which were conditions precedent and those which were conditions subsequent, emphasized the course of conduct between the parties and applied the estoppel doctrine when there had been substantial dealings between them on a corporate basis.

There is, as we see it, a wide difference between creating a corporation by means of the de facto doctrine and estopping a party, due to his conduct in a particular case, from setting up the claim of no incorporation. Although some cases tend to assimilate the doctrines of incorporation de facto and by estoppel, each is a distinct theory and they are not dependant on one another in their application. Where there is a concurrence of the three elements necessary for the application of the de facto corporation doctrine, there exists an entity which is a corporation de jure against all persons but the state. On the other hand, the estoppel theory is applied only to the facts of each particular case and may be invoked even where there is no corporation de facto. Accordingly, even though one or more of the requisites of a de facto corporation are absent, we think that this factor does not preclude the application of the estoppel doctrine in a proper case, such as the one at bar.

I.B.M. contends that the failure of the Bureau to file its certificate of incorporation debarred all corporate existence. But, in spite of the fact that the omission might have prevented the Bureau from being either a corporation de jure or de facto, we think that I.B.M. having dealt with the Bureau as if it were a corporation and relied on its credit rather than that of Cranson, is estopped to assert that the Bureau was not incorporated at the time the typewriters were purchased. In 1 Clark and Marshall, Private Corporations, § 89, it is stated:

'The doctrine in relation to estoppel is based upon the ground that it would generally be inequitable to permit the corporate existence of an association to be denied by persons who have represented it to be a corporation, or held it out as a corporation, or by any persons who have recognized it as a corporation by dealing with it as such; and by the overwhelming weight of authority, therefore, a person may be estopped to deny the legal incorporation of an association which is not even a corporation de facto.'

In cases similar to the one at bar, involving a failure to file articles of incorporation, the courts of other jurisdictions have held that where one has recognized the corporate existence of an association, he is estopped to assert the contrary with respect to a claim arising out of such dealings.

Since I.B.M. is estopped to deny the corporate existence of the Bureau, we hold that Cranson was not liable for the balance due on account of the typewriters.

Judgment reversed; the appellee to pay the costs.

MBCA § 2.04
LIABILITY FOR PREINCORPORATION TRANSACTIONS

All persons purporting to act as or on behalf of a corporation, knowing there was no incorporation under this Act, are jointly and severally liable for all liabilities created while so acting.

STONE v. JETMAR PROPERTIES, LLC

733 N.W.2d 480 (Minn. App. 2007)

LANSING, Judge.

This appeal arises out of a series of real-estate transactions that resulted in the foreclosure sale of property that respondent Dale Stone had quitclaimed to a limited-liability company that was not yet organized when he attempted delivery. The foreclosure sale was initiated by Selwin Ortega, to whom the property had been mortgaged. Ortega appeals from an order establishing Stone's title to the property and providing damages. Ortega argues that the district court erred by concluding that the quitclaim deed was void, rejecting Ortega's claim that he was a good-faith purchaser for value, and failing to determine that Stone was equitably estopped from asserting an interest in the property and that Stone's claims constituted an impermissible collateral attack on a valid judgment. Because we conclude that the quitclaim deed was void and that Stone is not legally or equitably precluded from asserting his interest in the property, we affirm.

Keith Hammond drafted and signed articles of organization for Jetmar Properties, LLC, in November 2002, but he did not file the articles with the secretary of state. Later that same year, Hammond, acting as president of Jetmar, offered to buy commercial property from Selwin Ortega. Hammond and Ortega signed a purchase agreement, but the sale did not close because Hammond did not have the money. Nonetheless, based on Hammond's representation that he needed cash to develop the property into condominiums, Ortega gave Hammond a three-day, unsecured $200,000 loan, which Hammond failed to repay.

In April 2003 Hammond met Dale Stone, a retiree, and convinced him to invest in several of Jetmar's "real estate ventures." During the course of their relationship, Stone gave Hammond more than $50,000 in cashiers' checks for Jetmar's various projects. Sometime in May 2003, Hammond asked Stone to quitclaim a duplex to Jetmar to improve Jetmar's balance sheet, which would allow it to secure financing for a large condominium development. Stone was renting out the property to supplement his social-security income. In exchange for the deed, Hammond promised Stone an interest in the development. Hammond also told Stone that he would deed the property back to Stone "free and clear" in sixty days and that Stone could continue to collect rent. On May 14, 2003, Stone quitclaimed the property to Jetmar. Hammond purported to accept the deed as Jetmar's president and recorded it the same day.

On May 15, 2003, Hammond mortgaged the duplex to Ortega in exchange for an extension on the $200,000 loan. Ortega recorded the mortgage on May 20, 2003, after checking the title and determining that Jetmar had title to the property by virtue of a quitclaim deed from Stone.

Hammond did not repay the loan or deed the property back to Stone. Sometime around December 2003, Ortega began foreclosure proceedings. Ortega sent the duplex tenants a notice of foreclosure, which they passed along to Stone. Stone confronted Hammond about the mortgage, but he was told that there would be time to redeem and regain title to the property. Based on Hammond's assurances, Stone did not alert Ortega of his claimed interest. On March 2, 2004, Ortega conducted a sale under the foreclosure-by-advertisement procedures. Because there were no higher bidders, Ortega purchased the property in exchange for the surrender of his $200,000 claim against Jetmar. Hammond filed Jetmar's articles of organization on March 11, 2004, and received a certificate of organization.

Stone brought this action in October 2004, alleging that Hammond and Jetmar had defrauded him. Stone sought damages and a declaratory judgment that he was the owner of the duplex. Ortega filed an answer, but Hammond and Jetmar failed to respond. The district court concluded that, because Jetmar did not exist at the time of delivery, it was therefore incapable of taking title to land, and the quitclaim deed was void. Because the quitclaim deed was void, both the mortgage and the foreclosure were also void.. Based on these conclusions, the court awarded Stone damages and title to the duplex. This appeal followed.

Selwin Ortega argues that the district court erred by concluding that Dale Stone's quitclaim deed to Jetmar Properties, LLC, was void. Ortega claims that

Jetmar was a de facto corporation when the deed was delivered, and, alternatively, that Jetmar was not per se barred from accepting delivery of the deed despite its nonexistence at the time of transfer. Because Ortega's de facto-corporation claim raises an issue of statutory construction, it is subject to de novo review. Ortega's claim that a deed can be delivered to an entity that did not exist at the time of transfer is also subject to de novo review.

Ortega first argues that, although Jetmar had not filed its articles of organization when Stone delivered the quitclaim deed, Jetmar could accept the deed under the de facto-corporation doctrine. Historically, a de facto corporation could exist in Minnesota when there was "(1) some law under which a corporation with powers assumed might lawfully have been created; (2) a colorable and bona fide attempt to perfect an organization under such a law; and (3) user of the rights claimed to have been conferred by the law." *Evens v. Anderson,* 132 Minn. 59, 61, 155 N.W. 1040, 1041 (1916). Ortega's claim that the de facto-corporation doctrine applies in this case fails as a matter of fact because, as he acknowledges, there had been no colorable attempt to organize Jetmar under the LLC statute when Stone signed the deed. The LLC statute provides that an LLC is organized by filing articles of organization with the secretary of state. Hammond made no attempt to file Jetmar's articles of organization with the secretary of state. As a result, even if the de facto-corporation doctrine had not been abolished, it would not apply. We conclude, however, that the doctrine has been abolished in the context of business-corporation law and, by extension, in the context of LLC law.

The 1981 notes accompanying the business-corporations statute that sets the effective date of a corporation's articles of incorporation specifically provide that "the doctrine of de facto corporations is inapplicable in this state after the enactment of this act." Minn.Stat. Ann. § 302A.153. The rationale for the abolition of de facto corporations is that the process for incorporating is so simple that no one could ever make a "colorable attempt" to incorporate and fail.

We also reject Ortega's claim that even if the de facto-corporation doctrine was abolished for purposes of business corporations it has not been abolished for LLC purposes. The 1992 notes to the LLC statute explain that "[t]o the extent a chapter 322B provision resembles a chapter 302A provision in substance, the case law and Reporter's Notes of chapter 302A should be used to interpret and apply the chapter 322B provision." Because the law relevant to corporations guides our interpretation and application of the law relevant to LLCs, the prohibition against de facto corporations must extend to LLCs.

Ortega next argues that Jetmar's nonexistence at the time Stone executed the deed is not determinative of whether Jetmar could take title to the property. To transfer title, a deed must be delivered. *Slawik v. Loseth,* 207 Minn. 137, 139, 290 N.W. 228, 229 (1940). Ortega argues that when a deed is delivered to an "incipient" LLC, the transfer of title may take effect upon the LLC's formal organization. We disagree.

Under Minnesota law deeds cannot be delivered to nonexistent entities, whether the entities are natural or legal. A deed cannot be delivered to a deceased grantee, for example. *In re Estate of Savich*, 671 N.W.2d 746, 750 (Minn.App.2003). We can find no basis in Minnesota law for delaying transfer of title to some indeterminate future date when the grantee might come into existence.

We see no reason to deviate from the "ordinary rule" that a deed to an entity nonexistent at the time of conveyance is void. Limiting the question of delivery to the time of conveyance is not only consistent with Minnesota law, it is also a logical result given the ease of formal incorporation and organization. Allowing a form of future interest to vest in unorganized entities would be inconsistent with our public policy of encouraging legal organization.

Ortega next argues that the doctrine of corporation-by-estoppel prevents Stone from taking title to the property. The district court did not expressly address Ortega's equitable claims, but it implicitly denied them by granting Stone's request for a declaratory judgment establishing title in him.

Ortega argues that under the corporation-by-estoppel doctrine Stone cannot take title to the property because Stone obtained an advantage by entering into a contract with Jetmar acting as an LLC, and Stone cannot now question the organization of the LLC. Although section 302A.153 abolished the de facto-corporation doctrine, the reporter's notes to the same statute indicate that the corporation-by-estoppel doctrine "has nothing to do with the efficacy of an attempted incorporation, and may apply even where no documents have been filed with the secretary of state." Minn.Stat. Ann. § 302A.153. Thus, the corporation-by-estoppel doctrine survives in Minnesota despite the inapplicability of the de facto-corporation doctrine.

Even if we assume, without deciding, that the corporation-by-estoppel doctrine applies to LLCs, Ortega's claim fails. Stone treated Jetmar as a "corporation" when he executed the deed. But the estoppel doctrine does not apply when the acts forming the basis for an estoppel claim are induced by fraud. Similarly, a court may refuse to apply the doctrine of corporation-by-estoppel when the corporation is used to accomplish fraud. The district court found that Stone executed the quitclaim deed while "relying on the false representations, promises, and assurances of Hammond." Because Stone was fraudulently induced to sign the deed and treat Jetmar as a "corporation," the district court could reject Ortega's corporation-by-estoppel argument.

The district court did not err by concluding that the quitclaim deed was void and that neither law nor equity prevented Stone from asserting his interest in the property. Affirmed.

D. SHAREHOLDER OPERATIONAL DEAL POINTS

1. IDENTIFYING AND PRIORITIZING

The identity of the client affects how the potential deal points among the shareholders are discussed and analyzed in a given situation. If the client is a majority shareholder or a group that has voting control (over 50 percent of the voting interests), the preferred choice may be to refrain from initiating any dialogue with the other owners. The clients will resolve key issues among themselves, knowing that they are in the driver's seat by virtue of their control. The burden is on the minority shareholders to raise any issues that may require special treatment in a shareholders agreement. If the minority shareholders are not represented or are under-represented, nothing may surface as all shareholders get caught up in the exciting prospects of the new venture. The lawyer who represents a minority shareholder has a more difficult job. Key issues must be identified, discussed, and prioritized. A plan must be developed for creating minority rights for those issues that are of greatest concern. Then the plan must be sold and eventually incorporated into the shareholders agreement.

The lawyer who is engaged to organize and represent the corporation, not a particular shareholder or group of shareholders, must be sensitive to the conflicts that many of the key planning issues might create between the shareholders. In too many cases, the organization is formed "the normal way," with little or no dialogue on the potentially tough issues. The far better approach is for the entity's lawyer to initiate a dialogue with all the shareholders in a meeting or series of meetings that address the most important issues. Lawyers representing specific shareholders should be invited to attend. Following each session, a simply worded memo should be circulated to all the parties, summarizing what was agreed upon and any open issues, and soliciting corrections or additions. When the meetings have been concluded and the memos have been finished, a shareholders agreement should be drawn that reflects the understandings incorporated in the memos. A draft should be circulated to all shareholders and their individual lawyers. The process requires a modest commitment of time and expense, but it will go a long way in identifying and resolving on the front-end any fundamental differences between the parties. The corporation and the relationships between the shareholders will be stronger as a result.

2. TWENTY OPERATIONAL OWNER ISSUES

a. The Scope of the Enterprise. It is often desirable to limit in the shareholders agreement the scope of the business activities of the entity. Some shareholders may feel more comfortable about their investment in the venture if they do not have to worry about their money being diverted into activities that are outside the scope of what was originally discussed. Liability exposure may also be an issue, particularly where key players have multiple business interests. Limiting the scope of the business activities may help limit the business entity's liability exposure for unrelated actions of these players. And then there's the "Tag Along" problem. Often owners prefer a written activity limitation that removes any expectations that other owners may have relative to their other business activities. They like the idea of an express, unequivocal line in the sand that defines the limit of their relationship with their co-owners. Some shareholders may object to a written limitation on scope of the enterprise, arguing that it restricts flexibility, creates potential confusion for third parties, and fosters notions of "separateness" and "temporariness."

b. Business Plan Changes. The issue of business plan changes raises some of the same concerns as the scope of enterprise limitation. But here the issue is not whether the corporation can venture into different directions, but rather whether it can accelerate its plan for moving in its authorized direction. Turning up the volume usually triggers more risk and requires some combination of more capital or debt. Some shareholders may want the comfort of a written agreement that limits the capacity of their co-shareholders to overreact to early success by trashing the plan they all bought into up front in favor of a new model that promises greater pressure, more risk, and a potentially faster track to the gold.

c. Debt. Rare is the business that can grow and succeed without debt. The first lesson of Business 101 is the value of leveraging the borrowed dollar. In the business context, debt often raises two concerns among co-shareholders: (1) the amount of the debt relative to the size of the invested equity and the business operations; and (2) the need for personal guarantees from the shareholders. Most start-up operations require personal guarantees because the business operations are not mature enough to carry the debt. As the business grows, the guarantees may disappear unless a decision is made to accelerate the growth rate of the business. The big issues for the shareholders are: How much debt is going to be incurred during the start-up phase? What guarantees are the shareholders going to provide? What priority will be given to eliminating personal guarantees in the future? As the business grows and develops the ability to carry its own debt, what is an acceptable debt level? Some owners may want a written understanding on these key issues, particularly as they relate to personal guarantees. They may want to limit expectations of others relative to their willingness to provide guarantees beyond the levels agreed to, while being assured that their colleagues will step up to the plate and provide the level of guarantees that all have accepted.

d. Additional Capital Contributions. The issue of additional capital contributions from the shareholders often requires dialogue and a written understanding. Some shareholders, even those with deep pockets, may want to kill any expectations that they will help provide whatever is needed to keep the venture afloat or fund growth. Others may be concerned with dilution; they do not want their equity interests reduced as those with greater means continually pony up more money and claim a bigger share of the whole. Preemptive rights that give all owners the right to protect their percentage interests with additional contributions are usually inadequate. When this issue is a major concern, the owners need to talk through their concerns and, with the aid of counsel, reach an agreement that, to the fullest extent possible, addresses the objectives of the shareholders. One approach is to specify that each owner must contribute his or her *pro rata* share of the capital needed to accomplish the purpose of the entity. Some owners may be unwilling to agree to an unlimited equity contribution requirement. In this situation, the agreement may have to place a cap on future required capital contributions. If there is no mandatory requirement for additional capital contributions, the shareholders agreement may need to spell out how future capital needs will be satisfied. For example, it may permit but not require any one or more shareholders to make additional contributions and receive additional stock. Another approach is to authorize any shareholder to make a loan to the corporation if additional cash is required, and then to provide that the loan is to be paid back, together with interest, before any cash distributions are made to the shareholders. In some situations, the financial institution that finances the corporation's operations may limit or prohibit the corporation from borrowing additional funds from shareholders. If this is the case and additional capital is required, then the shareholders agreement may provide that any one or more of the owners may make additional capital contributions to the entity, which will have a priority right of repayment – no distributions will be made until these additional contributions have been fully repaid with a specified preferred return equivalent to an interest rate. Thus, the new money is treated like a loan for distribution purposes, but it is structured as an equity capital contribution that does not violate any restrictive covenant of the lender.

e. New Shareholders. The policy for admitting new shareholders is a critical issue in professional service and family organizations and many service businesses. It is a major event that, except in large firms, usually requires the consent of all the owners. Often it raises the same dilution concerns as additional capital contributions. Plus, there is the added factor of a new personality. Where the investors are truly passive and have no involvement in the operations, a new personality, even an unpleasant one, may be of little or no concern. But in most closely held businesses, the owners have input and have the capacity to be a positive or negative force. This reality, coupled with the fear that divisive factions may develop or be fed as more bodies are added, may warrant special provisions dealing with the admission of new shareholders.

f.   Shareholder Roles and Service Commitments. The roles of the shareholders need to be clarified in many situations. For those shareholders who are employed and compensated by the venture, the key issues are the level of their service commitment and their right to be involved in other activities. Are they expected to devote all of their time and energies to the enterprise? Many organizations quickly hit a wall when the shareholders discover that a key shareholder spends only a fraction of his or her time looking after the affairs of the business. For those shareholders who are not employed by the business, the challenge is to clarify expectations. Some shareholders may expect that they will be entitled to serve on the board or have some other advisory role that provides an opportunity for input. Having put up their money, they want a spot in the inner circle. Some may expect that the sage advice and wisdom of a particular shareholder will be available, when, in fact, that investor, although willing to put up a few dollars, has no interest in providing any input or otherwise being tied to the business.

g. Owner Employment Rights. Often there is a need to clarify the relationship between an owner's interest in the corporation and that owner's employment by the business. In many organizations, the two are tied together through the shareholders agreement – no employment, no equity. The issue usually surfaces in a few different ways. A key shareholder may have received stock for putting the deal together or as compensation for management services rendered or to be rendered or, as is usually the case, for some combination of all of these. Often that key shareholder wants assurance that his or her right to manage the business is protected and cannot be disturbed by the other shareholders, except under the most extreme circumstances. The other shareholders may want clearly defined termination rights if the key shareholder doesn't do the job to their satisfaction. And, to add injury to insult, the other shareholders may want the key shareholder to forfeit some or all of his or her stock in such an event or, at a minimum, to be obligated to sell any residual stock back to the corporation at a price determined pursuant to the shareholders agreement.

h. Business Location. In select situations, the location of the business' operations or headquarters may be a concern. There have been situations where shareholders have attempted to frustrate the rights of key shareholder/employees, by threatening to move the business to a location that, as a practical matter, makes it extremely inconvenient for the key employees. Usually, such a threatened move can withstand a bad faith claim because it is supported by valid business justifications, such as cheaper labor prices, lower taxes, or reduced shipping costs. The shareholder who has a vested interest in the business' headquarters staying in a particular city may want a contractual provision in the shareholders agreement that protects that interest. Usually it can be secured with no objection on the front end.

i. Outside Shareholder Activities. Beyond the issue of outside activities of shareholder/employees discussed previously, sometimes there is a need to consider limitations on the outside activities of other shareholders. Often there is a desire to restrict owners from investing in competitors, major suppliers, or important customers of the business. The fear is that such investments may create conflicts that could compromise future opportunities. Some shareholders may strongly resist such limitations. They may be unwilling to surrender their investment flexibility and options to a single investment, as they oppose any contractual corporate opportunity limitations. Often their willingness to participate will be conditioned on an express provision to the contrary.

j. Related Party Transactions. Transactions with related parties often are a source of contention in closely held businesses. Examples include leasing facilities from a major shareholder, purchasing supplies or raw materials from a business controlled by a shareholder or a relative, licensing proprietary rights from a shareholder, purchasing capital assets from a shareholder, and employing relatives of a shareholder. To avoid the conflicts and the uncomfortable embarrassments that often accompany these situations, the parties may include approval mechanisms in the shareholders agreement that assure that any such related party transactions are structured to include pricing terms, termination rights, and other provisions that serve the best interests of the corporation.

k. Tax Elections. To avoid future conflicts, often it is advisable to document how certain tax matters are going to be handled. Examples include the selection of a fiscal year, cost recovery deductions, and inventory valuation methods. There also is the issue of a potential future S election, which requires the consent of all owners, or the potential termination of an S election, which requires the consent of owners owning over half the outstanding stock. In both situations, a different approval percentage may be desired and fixed by agreement. For S election purposes, the preference may be a supermajority vote that gives no single shareholder a veto power. For S termination purposes, something more than a simple majority may be warranted before the S election is discarded. A shareholders agreement is an excellent tool for nailing down how key tax elections are going to be handled.

l. Confidentiality Covenants. Employees, including shareholders who are employees, are often required to sign confidentiality agreements that are structured to protect the trade secrets and proprietary rights of the business. Sometimes it is desirable to extend these agreements to all shareholders of the corporation, particularly in those situations where the shareholders may have access to trade secrets or proprietary information critical to the success of the business. Some investors may resist any such agreements or any mechanism that limits other investment options or exposes them to any future claims relating to the use of proprietary information. When the issue is important and the potential shareholders won't budge, it may be necessary to start shopping for some different investors.

m. Accounts Payable Management. There are different perceptions about paying bills. Some see it as an opportunity to generate easy, low-cost financing by implementing a practice of delayed payment that pushes the envelope but keeps all vendors on board. Others view it as an easy way to show strength, establish an admirable Dunn and Bradstreet rating, and build vendor loyalty and confidence (which may be badly needed in rough times) by not missing a due date. Plus, with the discounts many vendors offer for prompt payment, an on-time payment strategy may add to the bottom line. This issue can become a source of contention between shareholders as the business begins to mature. Some may not want to be involved with a slow-pay enterprise that always looks strapped for cash, while others may want to maximize all financing options within definable limits. Any up-front discussion between the shareholders may result in an understanding that avoids a future conflict when the business is in full swing and the issue is hot.

n. Cash Distributions and Allocations. Are cash distributions to the shareholders a priority concern? Some shareholders may want to know that the plan includes regular distributions to the shareholders as the business ramps up. Others may expect that all after-tax profits will be invested to finance growth and that no cash will flow for some time. It is a fundamental part of the plan that should be clear to all shareholders. The problem is that the issue is tied to other key factors, including the growth rate of the business and the use of debt. Often the answer is to set guidelines regarding growth and debt that, once hit, will begin to trigger cash distributions to the owners. Typically, a provision is structured to ensure that cash is only distributed when all other cash needs of the business have been met, including ensuring appropriate reserves for working capital and other potential future needs. Also, loan agreements with the business' bank likely will impose restrictions on the timing of cash distributions that the agreement should recognize. An agreement regarding cash distributions is particularly important with an S corporation, where the earnings of the corporation are not taxed to the entity but instead are passed through and taxed to the shareholders. The shareholders of an S corporation often want some contractual assurance that cash distributions will be made to fund their pass-through tax liabilities. It is not possible to structure such cash distributions based on the size of the respective tax liabilities of the individual S corporation shareholders. Any such attempt would likely result in a claim that the S corporation has more than one class of stock and end up killing the S election. In an S corporation, cash distributions must be allocated among the shareholders according to their respective common stockholdings. So when there is a need to contractually commit an S corporation to make cash distributions to cover the shareholders' pass-through tax liabilities, often the best approach is to specify in the shareholders agreement that a designated percentage of the income allocated to shareholders (e.g., 40 percent) will be distributed in cash to the shareholders in accordance with their respective stockholdings. Such a flat percentage approach will likely result in some shareholders getting more than is needed for their tax bill, and others may get slightly less than is needed, based on their unique tax situation.

o. Shareholder Compensation Benefits. In those situations where certain shareholders are employed by the corporation, there is a need to clarify the compensation rights of those shareholders and how such compensation rights will take priority over any dividends to the shareholders. The compensation rights may include a specified salary, period salary adjustments, cash bonuses based on the performance of the corporation, deferred compensation benefits, life insurance benefits, and compensation in the form of stock or stock rights. Typically, these compensation rights are spelled out in an executive employment agreement with a key shareholder/employee that is coordinated with the buy-out provisions of the shareholders agreement. A discussion of executive employment agreements is provided in Chapter 16.

p. Selection of Professionals. Business entities need the assistance of outside professionals, including lawyers, accountants, appraisers, actuaries, investment firms, employee benefit firms and so forth. The method of selecting such professionals is often a potential source of conflict. Too often the organizer selects professionals who have a history with, and a loyalty to, that person. Those selected may not be the best qualified, nor the best suited to represent the interests of the corporation. Depending on the circumstances leading up to the lawyer's involvement in the start-up planning process, this may be an uncomfortable issue to deal with during the organizational effort. Nevertheless, it is often smart to do so. It makes it easy for all shareholders to vent any concerns, and actually may help build credibility for the lawyer. Often it leads to a procedure for selecting and monitoring the performance of all outside professionals that eliminates future concerns or conflicts among the owners.

q. Indemnifications. Will those shareholders or employees who act on behalf of the entity be protected against any personal loss, damage or liability they incur as a result of such activity? The answer is usually "yes." An indemnification and hold harmless provision is included to protect against such liabilities and any associated legal fees. But significant limitations are often included. First, the agreement may provide that the indemnification may be recoverable only out of the assets of the entity and not from the owners of the entity. The shareholders may not want any personal exposure for the acts of others. If the primary assets of the business have been pledged to secure financing, the assets available for any such indemnity may be very limited. Second, the indemnification may extend only to acts or omissions undertaken in good faith and with a belief that they were in the best interests of the corporation. This places a proof burden on the employee or shareholder who is the target of the claim. Third, the agreement may require that the targeted employee or shareholder tender the defense or resolution of the claim to the company so that the company can control expenses and dispose of the matter on its own terms.

r. Dispute Resolution Procedures. An important issue that usually needs to be addressed by agreement is how disputes among shareholders are to be resolved. No matter how carefully the up-front planning is handled, there is always the possibility that a dispute may erupt among the shareholders. It's usually prudent to have all the shareholders agree to a method for quickly and inexpensively resolving any dispute that may surface. Absent such a mechanism, the likely result is expensive, time-consuming, destructive litigation. A common method of resolving any disputes is arbitration. The agreement lays out the necessary procedures, including where the arbitration will be held and how the costs will be shared and allocated. All agree that the decision of the arbiters will be binding on the parties. The agreement also may require mandatory mediation prior to any litigation or arbitration proceeding.

s. Life-After Rights. In many businesses, particularly in service and professional service organizations, it is advisable to spell out the "going forward" rights that each shareholder will have in the event there is a falling out and the group fractures. Absent such an agreement, the shareholders may find themselves tangled up with shutdown issues that may make it difficult for some to immediately shift gears and preserve the continuity of their business activities. Most professionals and service providers cannot afford a major disruption that stops their careers. Key issues include the right to engage in the same business as the fractured entity, the right to pursue and service clients of the entity, the right to hire employees of the entity, the right to deal with vendors and financial institutions used by the entity, the right to make copies of client documents, files and other important documents, the right to use the same personal business email addresses and phone numbers, and the right to disclose the prior affiliation with the entity. The shareholders often want the ability to immediately exercise these rights when things blow up, even while the affairs of the corporation are being resolved and settled.

t. Sell-Out Options. Often the shareholders desire to clarify how a decision will be made for the corporation to sell out and cash in down the road. Potential future transactions could include a sale of substantially all the assets and goodwill of the business, a sale of all the stock or equity interests of the business, or a merger of the corporation into a larger company whose stock is publicly traded. The owners may want to require something more than a majority vote for such a "that's the ball game" transaction, and may want the assurance of knowing that all are required to play ball and go along if the requisite percentage approves the transaction.

3. SOLUTION TECHNIQUES

Resolving a planning issue that is of concern to the shareholders requires a solution. The range of potential solutions in any given situation is limited only by the imagination of the parties involved. Following is a brief description of solution techniques that are often used.

a. Definitive Contractual Provision. The shareholders agreement resolves the issue by spelling out the "deal" and what is expected of each party. Examples: All owners must sign confidentiality agreements; accounts payable will be paid in a timely manner to take advantage of early pay discounts; an S elections will be made; arbitration is mandated in the event of a dispute; each owner will be required to make additional contributions equal to 25 percent of his or her original contribution if such funding is needed; all owners will have specified life-after rights in the event of a falling out; and so forth. The parties reach an agreement that is incorporated into the shareholder or operating agreement.

b. Supermajority Vote. The parties agree that resolution of the issue will require a supermajority approval vote of the shareholders. Seventy or 80 percent will be required in order to accelerate the business plan, to incur additional debt beyond the approved limits, to trigger or revoke an S election, to approve a merger or sale of substantially all the assets, and so forth. The provision comforts both those who want something more than a simple majority and those who want the assurances that individuals cannot block certain actions, such as the making of an S election.

c. Designated Board or Management Committee. Often the solution is to delegate all future decisions regarding an issue or group of issues to a board of directors that has been carefully structured by agreement to protect the interests of all parties. Assume, for example, a hybrid entity where 40 percent of the equity interests are owned by employees and 60 percent are owned by investors. The parties agree to have a four-person board, comprising two employee-shareholders and two investors. Since any decision will require a vote of at least three members, all shareholders have the comfort of knowing that any affirmative decision on a particular issue will require the approval of at least one of their representatives.

d. Specified Conditions. Sometimes an issue can be resolved by specifying the conditions that must exist in order for the board of directors of the corporation to move forward on a specific issue. Often such conditions are combined with a supermajority back-up provision. For example, the agreement might specify that, absent a 70 percent approval by the shareholders, the board will not incur any additional bank financing beyond the approved limits if such financing would cause the company's debt-to-equity ratio to exceed 4-to-1.

e. Individual Veto Right. In select situations, an issue can be resolved by giving a particular owner an individual veto right. For example, a key employee who is also an shareholder may be concerned that the board may choose to change the business plan by reducing employee health insurance benefits. The other shareholders appreciate their colleague's concern, but suspect that any changes in the short-term are unlikely. To resolve the issue, all agree that any reductions in employee health insurance benefits over the next five years are subject to the approval of the specific shareholder.

f. Opt-Out Rights. Sometimes an shareholder issue can be resolved by giving shareholders the right to opt out of the effects of a given decision. For example, any concerns regarding debt expansion may be eliminated by granting individual shareholders the right to opt out of any personal guarantee requirement for the additional debt. One or more individual dissenters may protect their own pocketbooks without stopping the entity from moving forward. Of course, if too many owners exercise the opt-out privilege, the additional financing becomes unobtainable.

g. Buy-Out Trigger. A buy-out trigger under the buy/sell provisions may be justified in some extreme situations. For example, a shareholder may be adamantly opposed to any business plan acceleration or debt expansion changes without his or her consent. To resolve the concern, that shareholder is given an option to trigger a purchase of his or her interest under the buy-sell agreement if the others choose to move forward with such a change in the future. The concerned owner is satisfied with the exit option protection, and the others are comfortable with a provision that may create an opportunity for them to increase their equity positions and rid themselves of a difficult colleague once things are going strong.

h. Cumulative Voting. In select situations, a cumulative voting provision may be used to give minority owners the capacity to elect an individual to the board of directors or managing committee of the organization. The provision grants each shareholder votes equal to the number of shares he or she owns multiplied by the number of directors to be elected and the right to cast those votes among one or more directors. A few states mandate cumulative voting; most states allow it if it is authorized in the Articles of Incorporation. The following basic formula helps in determining the number of minority shares (one vote per share) needed to elect a designated number of directors with cumulative voting, where "A" equals the total needed shares, "B" equals the total shares to be voted by all owners, "C" equals the number of directors the minority would like to elect, and "D" equals the total number of directors to be elected:

$$A = [(B \times C) / (D + 1)] + 1$$

For example, if the minority shareholders want the capacity to elect one of four directors and there are 1,000 votes outstanding, the minority shareholders would need 201 shares [((1,000 x 1) divided by 4 + 1) + 1]. For planning purposes, cumulative voting often sounds better than it really is. A single seat on the board may do little or nothing to enhance the minority's position on key issues. Plus, if the board seat is vitally important, it may be obtained by a specific agreement among the shareholders, without the complexity and arithmetic challenges of cumulative voting. But there are situations where the minority's counsel, hearkening back to his or her law school days, regards it as a big deal, and the majority concludes that it is a relatively harmless alternative to other solutions that may have more teeth.

i. Preemptive Rights. A preemptive rights provision in the Articles of Incorporation is sometimes used to pacify the concerns of those shareholders who fear that future fundraising efforts may dilute their interests in the enterprise. The provision gives each owner the right to acquire his or her proportionate share of any newly issued stock under specific conditions spelled out in the Articles of Incorporation or, in the absence of such conditions, according to the applicable state statute. There are three primary concerns from a planning perspective. First, although preemptive rights may seem harmless on their face, often they can stymie a company's flexibility to move quickly and decisively in resolving its capital needs. The rights can trigger delays and uncertainties that can hurt the company and cause potential new investors to quickly lose interest. Considerable thought should be given to the use (or better yet, the nonuse) of such rights. Second, if preemptive rights are to be granted, care should be taken to structure the necessary exceptions in the Articles of Incorporation and not to automatically rely on the default provisions of the applicable state statute. Important exceptions may include, among others, shares issued to compensate key employees, shares issued for property other than cash, shares issued in time of financial crisis to secure important financing guarantees, and shares issued to satisfy option and conversion rights. Finally, the timing requirements of the preemptive rights should be carefully structured. The company may be stuck on hold as shareholders ponder their decision to exercise or waive their preemptive rights and consult with their financial advisors. Short time requirements will turn up the heat, provide the company greater flexibility, and help preserve the interests of potential new investors.

j. Different Equity Interests. Sometimes conflicting objectives of the owners can be resolved by issuing different types of equity interests. Voting and nonvoting stock may be used to separate voting and control rights from growth and income interests in both C and S corporations. Preferred stock is not permitted in an S corporation. But in C corporations, preferred stock may be used to grant income, capital and liquidation preferences for specific shareholders. There is significant flexibility in structuring the terms and limitations of the preferences. The wise use of such different interests often can facilitate an agreement that addresses the competing objectives of different owners.

E. COMMON ETHICAL CHALLENGES[1]

1. IDENTIFYING THE REAL CLIENT

The threshold question a lawyer must always answer is: who is my client? For most lawyers, the answer is obvious—it's the person sitting across the desk, asking all the questions. The answer is not so easy, however, when the lawyer is being retained to represent a closely held business. In this situation, the general

---

1. The author of this section is Professor Scott Schumacher of the University of Washington School. This section is an excerpt from Dwight Drake's book, *Business Planning: Closely Held Enterprises* (West 3d Ed. 2011).

rule for identifying the client is set forth in ABA Model Rule 1.13, which provides simply that a "lawyer employed or retained by an organization represents the organization acting through its duly authorized constituents." With corporations, there usually is no confusion: It is well settled that a corporation is a separate legal entity, a separate legal "person." However, the law is much less settled with regard to partnerships, limited partnerships, limited liability partnerships, limited liability companies, and all of the other related hybrid entities.

Partnerships and LLCs are creatures of state law. Under § 101(b) of the Uniform Partnership Act of 1991, the term "partnership" means "an association of two or more persons to carry on as co-owners a business for profit." The predominate theory in cases that have examined this issue is that partnerships, LLCs, and similar structures are separate legal entities, rather than aggregates of their owners, and the lawyer represents the entity and not the partners or owners. However, other courts have found that the lawyer did in fact represent the owners as well as the entity. Nearly every court to have addressed this issue has based its determination on the facts of the individual case. The Supreme Court muddied the water in *Carden v. Arkoma Associates*, 494 U.S. 185 (1990), where the Court held that, for purposes of diversity jurisdiction to permit a suit in federal court, the citizenship of an unincorporated association is to be determined by the citizenships of all its members. Thus, the Court in essence held that a partnership or other unincorporated entity should be treated, at least in some instances, as an aggregate of its individual members.

The ABA has attempted to set forth a bright-line (or at least a brighter-line) rule on this issue of client identification in situations involving a partnership or a limited liability company. Model Rule 1.13(a) provides simply that a "lawyer employed or retained by an organization represents the organization acting through its duly authorized constituents." In ABA Formal Opinion 91–361 (1991), the ABA held that a partnership is an "organization" within the meaning of Rule 1.13, and that, generally, a lawyer who represents a partnership represents the entity rather than the individual partners. This rule would also be applicable to LLCs. Nevertheless, the ABA acknowledged that despite this general rule, an attorney-client relationship may nevertheless arise with the individual partners or owners, depending upon the facts of the case. Thus, while the ABA has clarified the issue as to whether an attorney represents the partnership as an entity (rather than an aggregate of individuals), the facts of any given case may well show that the attorney also represents one or more of the partners or owners.

2. DEFINITIVELY RESOLVING CLIENT IDENTITY

The way in which nearly every ethical duty must be discharged will depend upon who the client is, that is, to whom the duties under the various ethical rules are owed. And yet, this most fundamental question often is unanswerable in the absolute when dealing with certain entities. While the inconsistent treatment of entities and owners is bad enough, what is especially troubling is that the determination of who the client is may in some cases be based on the subjective beliefs *of the clients*. ABA Formal Op. 91–361 provides that whether a relationship between a lawyer and one or more of the partners has been created almost always will depend on an analysis of the specific facts involved, including "whether there was evidence of reliance by the individual partner on the lawyer as his or her separate counsel, or of the *partner's expectation* of personal representation."

It is therefore imperative that a lawyer (1) determine as many facts as possible about the case and the parties (partnership and partners); (2) decide which of the parties he or she will represent; (3) clearly communicate to all parties involved (whether being represented or not) who the practitioner will be representing; and (4) to the extent possible, obtain consents or acknowledgements from all of the parties as to the extent and limitations of that representation.

In ABA Formal Opinion 91–361, the ABA stated:

> Lest the difficulties of representing both a partnership and one or more of its partners appear impossible to overcome, however, Rule 1.7(b)(2) and, to a lesser extent, Rule 1.13(d) suggest a procedure that may be helpful in many situations. If an attorney retained by a partnership explains at the outset of the representation, preferably in writing, his or her role as counsel to the organization and not to the individual partners, and if, when asked to represent an individual partner, the lawyer puts the question before the partnership or its governing body, explains the implications of the dual representation, and obtains the informed consent of both the partnership and the individual partners, the likelihood of perceived ethical impropriety on the part of the lawyer should be significantly reduced.

In his *Ethics Chat* Newsletter (Issue 2, Vol. 7, Spring 2003), Professor Walter W. Steele, Jr. sets out two clauses to be used in retainer agreements in order to avoid the common misunderstandings about whom the lawyer represents:

Suggested Clause for Initial Retainer Letter to Entity Organizers

> It will be necessary to discuss numerous issues with each of you as the process of forming [name of entity] takes place. I have already advised you that I have agreed to serve as the lawyer for the entity—I am not the lawyer for any of you in this transaction. As I told you during our initial conference, you have the right to engage another lawyer of your choosing to represent your personal interests in this matter. The fact that I discuss issues with you during the process of forming [name of entity] must not be interpreted by you as any indication that I am your lawyer or that I am guarding your own individual interest in this matter. Because I am not your lawyer, I have the right, and perhaps the obligation at times, to share any information you provide to me with the other entity organizers.

Suggested Clause for Affirmation by Organizers—Post Entity Formation

We, the undersigned organizers of [name of entity] hereby ratify and confirm our agreement not to be represented personally as set forth in the retainer contract attached to this document, and we now confirm that at no point during the process of organizing [name of entity] did [lawyer] form an attorney-client relationship with any of us. Each of us were free at any point during this process to retain a lawyer to guard and protect our own personal interests, and the fact that we chose not to do so is not any evidence that we relied on [lawyer] for that purpose.

3. REPRESENTING BOTH ENTITIES AND OWNERS

Even though the general rule is that a lawyer represents the entity and not the individual owners, the situation routinely arises in which the lawyer may be asked to represent one or more of the owners in addition to the entity itself. In addition, lawyers representing an entity will inevitably develop a relationship with one or more of the owners and, if the lawyer has been effective on behalf of the entity, an owner may wish to retain the services of the lawyer in an unrelated legal matter. Is it acceptable under the rules to represent an owner while also representing the entity? Rule 1.7 sets out the rules governing a lawyer representing more than one client:

Rule 1.7 Conflict of Interest

(a) Except as provided in paragraph (b), a lawyer shall not represent a client if the representation involves a concurrent conflict of interest. A concurrent conflict of interest exists if:

(1) the representation of one client will be directly adverse to another client; or

(2) there is a significant risk that the representation of one or more clients will be materially limited by the lawyer's responsibilities to another client, a former client or a third person or by a personal interest of the lawyer.

(b) Notwithstanding the existence of a concurrent conflict of interest under paragraph (a), a lawyer may represent a client if:

(1) the lawyer reasonably believes that the lawyer will be able to provide competent and diligent representation to each affected client;

(2) the representation is not prohibited by law;

(3) the representation does not involve the assertion of a claim by one client against another client represented by the lawyer in the same litigation or other proceeding before a tribunal; and

(4) each affected client gives informed consent, confirmed in writing.

Under Rule 1.7, a lawyer may represent parties with potential conflicts of interest, but only if the lawyer believes his or her representation will not be affected, and each client consents in writing. It is therefore essential that the lawyer do a full conflicts check at the outset, obtain as many facts as possible, and secure written consents from each of the clients.

As in the case of any potential conflict involving multiple representations, a lawyer may represent an entity and one or more of the owners. However, Rule 1.13(g) imposes the additional requirement that the consent on behalf of the entity that is required by Rule 1.7 must be given by an owner other than the owner who will be represented by the lawyer. Accordingly, if a lawyer will be representing both a corporate client and one of the shareholders or a partnership client and one of the partners, it is essential that the lawyer obtain written consents from both the entity and the other individual to be represented, with the consent on behalf of the entity from an owner other than the one to be represented. It may be advisable, if the number of owners is sufficiently small to make it practicable, to have each of the owners who will not be represented by the lawyer consent to the dual representation.

4. DUTIES OWED TO FORMER CLIENTS AND PARTNERS

Another common conflict of interest involves former clients. For example, a lawyer represents an entity with several owners and, during the course of the representation, the lawyer learns information about one of the owners. Later, that owner is an opposing party in another case. Can the lawyer represent his client against the former owner? This issue is governed by Rule 1.9.

Rule 1.9: Duties to Former Clients

(a) A lawyer who has formerly represented a client in a matter shall not thereafter represent another person in the same or a substantially related matter in which that person's interests are materially adverse to the interests of the former client unless the former client gives informed consent, confirmed in writing.

(b) A lawyer shall not knowingly represent a person in the same or a substantially related matter in which a firm with which the lawyer formerly was associated had previously represented a client

(1) whose interests are materially adverse to that person; and

(2) about whom the lawyer had acquired information protected by Rules 1.6 and 1.9(c) that is material to the matter; unless the former client gives informed consent, confirmed in writing.

(c) A lawyer who has formerly represented a client in a matter or whose present or former firm has formerly represented a client in a matter shall not thereafter:

(1) use information relating to the representation to the disadvantage of the former client except as these Rules would permit or require with respect to a client, or when the information has become generally known; or

(2) reveal information relating to the representation except as these Rules would permit or require with respect to a client.

This is yet another reason to make sure about the identity of "the client." If the lawyer is not careful, numerous owners could be considered to be clients, thereby increasing the list of "former clients." Thus, Formal Opinion 91–361 opines that "a lawyer undertaking to represent a partnership with respect to a particular matter does not thereby enter into a lawyer-client relationship with each member of the partnership, so as to be barred, for example, by Rule 1.7(a) from representing another client on a matter adverse to one of the partners but unrelated to the partnership affairs."

Nevertheless, Rule 1.9(c) prohibits a lawyer from revealing "information relating to the representation" except as otherwise permitted by the Rules (e.g., Rule 1.6). This prohibition is absolute and is not waivable. Given the breadth of the attorney-client privilege and the inclusion of partners as agents of the partnership for purposes of the privilege, a lawyer should be extremely careful about using facts learned from or statements made by an owner during the course of the lawyer's representation of the entity against the owner in a later proceeding against the owner.

5. LAWYER AS A DIRECTOR

It has long been accepted practice for corporations to ask their outside counsel to serve as a director of the client. The practice is common among closely-held businesses, as well as public companies. However, merely because it is common practice does not mean it is a good idea nor free of ethical dilemmas. Among the problems associated with a lawyer serving his or her client as a director are the possibilities that the attorney-client privilege will be jeopardized, the lawyer's independent professional judgment may be hindered, and the lawyer may be disqualified due to a conflict of interest.

Most of the issues surrounding the lawyer as director must be analyzed under Rule 1.7, which governs conflicts of interest. In short, Model Rule 1.7(a) provides that a lawyer may not represent a client if the representation of one client will be directly adverse to another client, or if there is a significant risk that the representation of one or more clients will be materially limited by the lawyer's responsibilities to another client or other third party. There is nothing in Model Rule 1.7 prohibiting a lawyer from representing a client of which he or she is also a director. Nevertheless, given the numerous ethical pitfalls, members of the profession sought guidance from the ABA on this question.

In Formal Opinion 98–410, the ABA addressed whether it would be appropriate for an attorney to act as a director for a corporate client. Formal Opinion 98–410 enumerated the steps attorneys must take to mitigate the problems inherent in this dual role.

At the beginning of the relationship, the lawyer should take steps to ensure that the corporation's management and the other board members understand the different responsibilities of outside legal counsel and director. For example, management and the board must understand the importance of, as well as the limitations of, the attorney-client privilege, and that in some instances matters discussed at board meetings will not receive the protection of the attorney-client privilege that would attach to conversations between the client and the lawyer *qua* lawyer.

The client should also understand that conflicts of interest may arise that would require the lawyer to recuse himself or herself as a director or to withdraw from representing the corporation in a matter. The lawyer should also ensure that management and the other board members understand that, when acting as legal counsel, the lawyer represents only the corporate entity and not its individual officers and directors.

The Formal Opinion goes on to advise that during the course of the dual relationship, the lawyer should exercise care to protect the corporation's confidential information and to confront and resolve conflicts of interest that may arise. The opinion noted that it is essential that the lawyer be particularly careful when the client's management or board of directors consults him for legal advice. If the purpose of the meeting or consultation is to obtain legal advice from the lawyer in his or her capacity as lawyer, the lawyer-director should make clear that the meeting is solely for the purpose of providing legal advice, and the lawyer should avoid giving business or financial advice, except insofar as it affects legal considerations such as the application of the business judgment rule.

If during the course of the discussions the lawyer's presence and opinion is needed in his or her role as director, the lawyer should have another member of the firm present at the meeting to provide the legal advice. Vigilantly segregating the two roles of lawyer and director will provide the best support for a claim of privilege.

Formal Opinion 98–410 advises lawyers to "[m]aintain in practice the independent professional judgment required of a competent lawyer, recommending against a course of action that is illegal or likely to harm the corporation even when favored by management or other directors." It then advises the lawyer to "[p]erform diligently the duties of counsel once a decision is made by the board or management, even if, as a director, the lawyer disagrees with the decision, unless the representation would assist in fraudulent or criminal conduct, self-dealing or otherwise would violate the Model Rules."

Lawyers must also avoid conflicts of interest that may arise as a result of the insider status he or she enjoys on the board of directors. For example, a lawyer should recuse himself or herself as a director from board deliberations when the relationship of the corporation with the lawyer or the lawyer's firm is under consideration. Likewise, Formal Opinion 98–410 points out that a lawyer should decline any representation as counsel when the lawyer's interest as a director conflicts with his responsibilities of competent and diligent representation. For example, a lawyer should not represent a client matter if the lawyer is concerned about potential personal liability as a director resulting from a course approved by the board. *Id.; see also* Model Rule 1.7(a)(2).

Finally, Formal Opinion 98–410 points out what may be an unavoidable conflict: A director, who also is the corporation's lawyer, may be under a duty to disclose information to third parties that, in his role as attorney for the corporation, he could not disclose without obtaining consent from the client. In this situation, the lawyer-director's knowledge as a director may prove inseparable from the lawyer's acts and knowledge as outside legal counsel. The lawyer may have to resign his or her role as director in order to protect client confidences.

6. LAWYER AS AN OFFICER

An officer, depending on the duties assigned, could be everything from a figurehead who performs ministerial functions to an officer involved in every aspect of the corporation's day-to-day operations. Depending upon the nature and extent of the duties performed by the lawyer, acting as an officer may violate the rules of professional conduct if the lawyer undertakes legal representation of the entity. While it may be appropriate for a lawyer to act as corporate secretary and receive all legal documents served on the corporation, in most situations it would not be appropriate for a lawyer to represent a corporate client while serving as its chief financial officer. The ethical issues applicable to the lawyer-director are equally applicable, if not more so, depending on the duties of the lawyer-officer. A lawyer should keep each of the potential problems in mind when considering service as an officer of a corporate client.

7. ETHICAL ISSUES IN INVESTING WITH A CLIENT

May an attorney properly invest in a business with a client, either as payment for services or as an independent investment? The general rule on conflicts of interests with respect to current clients is found in Model Rule 1.8, which provides:

Rule 1.8: Conflict Of Interest: Current Clients: Specific Rules

(a) A lawyer shall not enter into a business transaction with a client or knowingly acquire an ownership, possessory, security or other pecuniary interest adverse to a client unless:

(1) the transaction and terms on which the lawyer acquires the interest are fair and reasonable to the client and are fully disclosed and transmitted in writing in a manner that can be reasonably understood by the client;

(2) the client is advised in writing of the desirability of seeking and is given a reasonable opportunity to seek the advice of independent legal counsel on the transaction; and

(3) the client gives informed consent, in a writing signed by the client, to the essential terms of the transaction and the lawyer's role in the transaction, including whether the lawyer is representing the client in the transaction.

Thus, a lawyer may invest in a venture with a client or may take stock in the client's business in lieu of fees only if the terms of the deal are fair and reasonable, the client is fully informed in writing about the terms of the deal, the client consents in writing to these terms, and the client is advised to seek independent legal counsel on the deal and is given the opportunity to seek that advice. Comment 1 to Model Rule 1.8 explains the reasons for this rule: "A lawyer's legal skill and training, together with the relationship of trust and confidence between lawyer and client, create the possibility of overreaching when the lawyer participates in a business, property or financial transaction with a client." If the transaction with the client involves one in which the lawyer will actually be advising the client, the risks highlighted by Comment 1 are even greater, since the knowledge, trust, and confidence that creates the risk of overreaching are even greater under these circumstances.

The ABA weighed-in on this issue in Formal Opinion 2000–418. First, the ABA answered what should be an obvious question by holding, "In our opinion, a lawyer who acquires stock in her client corporation in lieu of or in addition to a cash fee for her services enters into a business transaction with a client, such that the requirements of Model Rule 1.8(a) must be satisfied." After reviewing the requirements of Model Rule 1.8, the formal opinion then outlined situations where, despite satisfying the literal requirements of Rule 1.8, the transaction, and the lawyer's role in representing the client, may raise other ethical issues not contemplated by Rule 1.8. The opinion notes an example where the lawyer might have a duty when rendering an opinion on behalf of the corporation in a venture capital transaction to ask the client's management to reveal adverse financial information even though the revelation might cause the venture capital investor to withdraw. Under those circumstances, an attorney must evaluate his or her ability to exercise independent professional judgment in light of the adverse impact the advice may have on his or her own economic interests.

Formal Opinion 2000–418 notes that one way of reducing the risk that the stock-for-services fee arrangement will be deemed to be unreasonable is to establish a reasonable fee for the lawyer's services based on factors enumerated under Rule 1.5, and then accept an amount of stock that, at the time of the transaction, equals the reasonable fee. The difficulty of course, especially with start-up companies, is to determine the value of stock of the company. The opinion nevertheless encourages the stock to be valued at the amount per share that cash investors have agreed to pay for similar stock.

Joseph F. Troy has written a "Best Practices Checklist" for firms to follow when taking stock in clients, which is published in *Representing Start–Up Companies*, by Lee R. Petillon and Robert Joe Hull. Among the "Best Practices" Troy lists are:

• Impose firm control of all investments by lawyers in client's stock. Do not allow individual lawyers in the firm to make these investment decisions.

• Invest through a firm vehicle, and avoid direct investing by firm attorneys.

• Strictly limit the size of investments and the percentage of ownership. Troy lists a maximum of $25,000–50,000 or 1–2% of the company as typical or safe investment levels.

• Obtain a third-party valuation of the stock.

• Take all or the bulk of fees in cash.

• Do not take stock for future services without including vesting provisions and an express right of the client to terminate.

• Avoid flipping (immediate resale) of stock, and impose a voluntary lock-up.

• Impose strict insider trading rules.

• Require stock be held for investment and not with a view to resale. Do not permit trading of client stock.

• Disclose the stock ownership to third parties when appropriate.

• If you cannot fully and zealously represent your client on a matter because of your stock ownership, either do not invest or decline the representation.

• If your investment would compromise your independent professional judgment, either do not invest or decline the representation.

• Schedule a regular review of the conflicts and, when necessary, get a revised consent.

• Make a detailed and comprehensive disclosure of the conflicts; do not rely on boilerplate disclosures.

8. GENERAL DUTIES OWED TO BUSINESS OWNERS

The general rule is that a lawyer who is retained by a corporation, partnership, or LLC, represents the entity itself and not the individual owners. A lawyer may also represent an individual owner in the same matter or in an unrelated transaction, as long as he or she satisfies the requirements of Rule 1.7, dealing with conflicts of interest. The next question is what ethical duties are owed to the owners who are *not* clients? In one sense, the owners are merely third parties, and they are entitled, at a minimum, to the same treatment as other third parties. Model Rule 4.1 governs the treatment of third parties:

Rule 4.1: Truthfulness in Statements to Others.

In the course of representing a client a lawyer shall not knowingly:

> (a) make a false statement of material fact or law to a third person; or

> (b) fail to disclose a material fact to a third person when disclosure is necessary to avoid assisting a criminal or fraudulent act by a client, unless disclosure is prohibited by Rule 1.6.

Thus, Model Rule 4.1 requires at a minimum that a lawyer may not knowingly make a false statement of material fact or law to third persons, nor may the lawyer knowingly fail to disclose a material fact when disclosure is necessary to avoid assisting a criminal or fraudulent act by a client, unless disclosure is prohibited by Model Rule 1.6.

In addition, since many owners will not have their own representation, the lawyer may be required to treat the owners as "unrepresented persons" and comply with Model Rule 4.3:

Rule 4.3: Dealing With Unrepresented Persons

In dealing on behalf of a client with a person who is not represented by counsel, a lawyer shall not state or imply that the lawyer is disinterested. When the lawyer knows or reasonably should know that the unrepresented person misunderstands the lawyer's role in the matter, the lawyer shall make reasonable efforts to correct the misunderstanding. The lawyer shall not give legal advice to an unrepresented person, other than the advice to secure counsel, if the lawyer knows or reasonably should know that the interests of such a person are or have a reasonable possibility of being in conflict with the interests of the client.

Ideally, the lawyer will have set out in the engagement letter that he or she represents the entity and not the individual owners. As a result, there should not be a misunderstanding as to the lawyer's role in the matter. However, Rule 4.3 imposes a continuing duty to correct any misunderstanding that a third party (i.e., partner/member/shareholder) may have. Moreover, Model Rule 1.13(f) reinforces the requirement that the lawyer representing an entity must ensure that the owners are reminded of where the lawyer's duty of loyalty lies:

Model Rule 1.13(f)

In dealing with an organization's directors, officers, employees, members, shareholders or other constituents, a lawyer shall explain the identity of the client when the lawyer knows or reasonably should know that the organization's interests are adverse to those of the constituents with whom the lawyer is dealing.

The Rules and comments make it plain that when dealing with owners, lawyers should ensure that there is no confusion as to who the lawyer represents.

9. THE ATTORNEY–CLIENT PRIVILEGE

One of the most common issues in representing a partnership, corporation, or other entity involves the application of the attorney-client privilege. During the course of representing an entity, a lawyer must routinely determine whether statements by officers, directors, partners, employees or other "constituents" are subject to the attorney-client privilege. Privilege issues also may impact what a lawyer may disclose to individual owners and what the lawyer may refuse to disclose to owners. Whether a lawyer may refuse to divulge a given statement under the attorney-client privilege will depend upon (1) the identity of the declarant (i.e., his or her role within the entity); (2) the identity of the person seeking to obtain the statement (i.e., whether the person is also an owner of the entity or and outsider); (3) the purpose for which the statements were made to the lawyer; and (4) whether the privilege has been waived.

The general rule in dealing with confidences is found in Model Rule 1.6, which provides that "a lawyer shall not reveal information relating to the representation of a client unless the client gives informed consent, the disclosure is impliedly authorized in order to carry out the representation or the disclosure is permitted by paragraph (b)." The exceptions of 1.6(b) include: (1) To prevent reasonably certain death or substantial bodily harm; (2) to prevent the client from committing a crime or fraud that is reasonably certain to result in substantial injury to the financial interests or property of another and in furtherance of which the client has used or is using the lawyer's services; (3) to prevent, mitigate or rectify substantial injury to the financial interests or property of another that is reasonably certain to result or has resulted from the client's commission of a crime or fraud in furtherance of which the client has used the lawyer's services; (4) to secure legal advice about the lawyer's compliance with these Rules; and (5) to establish a claim or defense on behalf of the lawyer in a controversy between the lawyer and the client. How is this rule applied in the context of an entity client?

The seminal case in this area is *Upjohn Co. v. United States*, 449 U.S. 383, 101 S.Ct. 677 (1981), in which the Supreme Court adopted a fairly broad application of the attorney-client privilege in the corporate context, holding that where communications were made by corporate employees to counsel for the corporation acting at the direction of corporate superiors in order to secure legal advice from counsel, and the employees were aware that they were being questioned so that the corporation could obtain advice, these communications were protected. Thus, the Court in *Upjohn* examined the purposes for which the attorney obtained the statements from the employees. Since each of the disputed statements was elicited pursuant to the attorney's representation, the statements were protected by the privilege. While this is certainly the general rule, the *Upjohn* test has not been uniformly adopted. Accordingly, whether statements made by an employee or other constituent of an entity-client will be subject to the attorney-client privilege may depend upon the law of the jurisdiction involved.

In addition, whether a lawyer can refuse to disclose statements obtained from an owner or other constituent will depend upon who is seeking disclosure. In Formal Opinion 91–361, which is the Formal Opinion declaring that the partnership is the client, the ABA stated that "information received by a lawyer in the course of representing the partnership is 'information relating to the representation' of the partnership, and normally may not be withheld from individual partners." The ABA went on to explain its opinion as follows:

> The mandate of Rule 1.6(a), not to reveal confidences of the client, would not prevent the disclosure to other partners of information gained about the client (the partnership) from any individual partner(s). Thus, information thought to have been given in confidence by an individual partner to the attorney for a partnership may have to be disclosed to other partners, particularly if the interests of the individual partner and the partnership, or vis-a-vis the other partners, become antagonistic.

According to the ABA, since the partnership is the client, and not the individual partners, information received from the partners cannot be a "client confidence," at least with respect to the other partners. As a result, information received from a partner may not be withheld from other partners. Although the fiduciary duties owed by partners to their fellow partners are somewhat unique among business entities, the logic of Formal Opinion 91–361 would appear to apply equally to other entities types, and thus, in dealing with an entity and its owners, a lawyer may not normally refuse to disclose facts learned during the course or representing the entity. It is essential that the owners understand this and do not mistakenly make statements to an attorney, believing that the statement will be held in confidence. A lawyer should make this clear at the outset of the representation and remind owners of this during the course of the representation, if it appears that an owner may be mistaken as to the application of the attorney-client privilege...

On the other hand, Model Rule 1.13 suggests that statements by an owner or employee of an entity may be subject to attorney-client privilege if the person seeking disclosure is an outsider. Hence, the application of the privilege appears to depend upon who the declarant is, the declarant's role in the entity, the circumstances under which the lawyer sought and obtained the information and statements from the declarant, and who is seeking access to the statement or information. The lawyer must keep each of these factors in mind when dealing with owners and employees of the entity client in a situation that is or might soon become a sensitive or controversial matter. The problem, of course, is that statements are often obtained when neither the lawyer nor the client has any inkling that a controversy might soon erupt. The specific issue of an attorney's ethical duties when he or she learns of client misconduct is discussed in the following section.

Another common ethical issue concerns the situation where the lawyer learns that one or more of the owners, employees, or other constituents has done something that is either illegal or contrary to the best interests of the entity. As has been established, a lawyer represents the entity as a separate entity. Yet, entities can only act through individual owners and employees. Who speaks for the entity when there is a dispute and who should the lawyer listen to? Model Rule 1.13(a) provides that an organization acts through its "duly authorized constituents." However, particularly in the case of closely held businesses, it is not always clear who the duly authorized constituents are.

Comment 3 to Rule 1.13 emphasizes that the actions and decisions of the duly authorized constituent must generally be respected by lawyer: "When constituents of the organization make decisions for it, the decisions ordinarily must be accepted by the lawyer even if their utility or prudence is doubtful. Decisions concerning policy and operations, including ones entailing serious risk, are not as such in the lawyer's province."

One of the most difficult ethical issues a lawyer can face occurs when, for example, the general partner, who is the duly authorized constituent of the partnership, has taken some action that is either illegal or contrary to the interests of the partnership. Technically, the lawyer represents the partnership, not the general partner. However, in reality, the lawyer is retained by, paid by, and is answerable to a real person—the general partner. Lawyers must therefore resolve the inherent conflict in their duty to protect the "real" client (i.e., the partnership), not reveal confidences of a duly authorized constituent of the client, and still ensure that the best interests of the client and the other constituents are defended. Model Rule 1.13(b) sets out the basic rules on how the professional should act in these circumstances:

> Rule 1.13(b) If a lawyer for an organization knows that an officer, employee or other person associated with the organization is engaged in action, intends to act or refuses to act in a matter related to the representation that is a violation of a legal obligation to the organization, or a violation of law that reasonably might be imputed to the organization, and that is likely to result in substantial injury to the organization, then the lawyer shall proceed as is reasonably necessary in the best interest of the organization. Unless the lawyer reasonably believes that it is not necessary in the best interest of the organization to do so, the lawyer shall refer the matter to higher authority in the organization, including, if warranted by the circumstances to the highest authority that can act on behalf of the organization as determined by applicable law.

Thus, Rule 1.13(b) reemphasizes that the lawyer's primary duty is to act in the best interest of the organization. In addition, the lawyer must, if the circumstances warrant, report the misconduct to the "highest authority" within the organization. However, this does not answer the situation where the malevolent actor is the general partner who *is* the highest authority within the partnership.

Model Rule 1.13 was substantially revised in August of 2003... Under the revised version of Rule 1.13(c), a lawyer may reveal information about the organization's (or constituent's) misconduct, even though revealing that information would not normally be permitted by Rule 1.6. Thus, if the lawyer knows that an owner or employee is engaged in action in a matter related to the representation that is a violation of a legal obligation to the entity, or that the action is a violation of law that reasonably may be imputed to the entity and that will likely result in substantial harm to the entity, then the lawyer shall proceed as is reasonably necessary in the best interest of the entity. The lawyer's action will be determined by the circumstances, but ordinarily this means referral to a higher decision-making person or group within the organization. The lawyer may, but is not required to, reveal facts relating to the representation, even if not expressly permitted by Rule 1.6, but only if and to the extent the lawyer reasonably believes necessary to prevent substantial injury to the organization.

A common area of the law about which business lawyers routinely give advice involves the client's tax liability. Business lawyers can give prospective tax advice as to how clients should structure certain deals, provide advice on reporting positions for tax returns that are to be filed, and represent clients in tax disputes with the IRS. A significant issue in these contexts is whether statements between a client and its lawyer are subject to the attorney-client privilege.

The attorney-client privilege is affected in the tax area by how "legal advice" is defined. If the advice is considered "accounting advice," the privilege does not apply. This can include preparation of tax returns. The privilege does not apply to return advice because there is no expectation that communications from the client would remain confidential, given that the communications were made for the purpose of reporting transactions on a tax return. Hence, to the extent the privilege may have attached to any of the communications, it was waived when the return was filed. However, if there is an expectation of confidentiality and that confidentiality is not later waived, an attorney's tax advice is privileged if client confidences would be revealed by disclosure of the attorney's advice. The line between what is privileged and what is not has never been clear. As a result, a lawyer providing tax advice should assume that all communications may be discoverable by the IRS.

When a lawyer gives tax advice, the client's accountant often is involved in the conversations as well. In 1998, Congress enacted new § 7525 of the Internal Revenue Code that extends the attorney-client privilege to all authorized tax practitioners. Section 7525 extends the same common law protections of confidentiality that apply to communications between a taxpayer and an attorney to communications between a taxpayer and an accountant. However, the privilege may only be asserted in a non-criminal tax matter before the Service, and in non-criminal tax proceeding in Federal court brought by or against the United States.

Given the limited scope of the accountant client privilege, an attorney should be careful in retaining the services of an accountant in certain tax matters. If the case involves a dispute with the IRS and has a potential for a criminal prosecution of the client, a lawyer must only employ the services of an accountant under certain conditions. While the client will most likely wish to use its current accountant, the lawyer should insist on retaining a different accountant because of the difficulty in segregating the non-privileged tax return advice from the later privileged communications. Accountants retained under these circumstances are known as "Kovel" accountants, from the case *United States v. Kovel*, 296 F.2d 918 (2d Cir. 1961), where the court held that the attorney-client privilege extends to communications made by a client to an accountant *employed by the lawyer*, as part of the client receiving legal advice from the attorney. It is therefore essential that the *lawyer* retain the accountant directly and not have the client retain the accountant. In addition, all bills for services rendered by the accountant and all work-product produced by the accountant should go through the attorney before being distributed to the client.

CASE PROBLEM 6-2

Four years ago, you represented Jason, then age 28, in the implosion of a start-up venture. Four deep-pocket investors had funded a new company and selected Jason, boy wonder engineer, to be its president. Jason was given a "dream" employment contract that promised big riches if all played out as expected. Within six months, the investors were thoroughly dismayed with Jason's alleged incompetence, bizarre temper, and propensity to shade the truth. Jason was dismissed for cause and a brief legal battle ensued. You succeeded in quietly and quickly getting Jason out of the mess with a few bucks in his pocket.

Jason now has asked that you represent Lucy, Sam, and himself in organizing a new corporation ("Newco") that will develop and exploit a new product that is designed to make it easy to produce low-cost vinyl fencing. All three will serve on the board of Newco, and Jason and Lucy will be officers, employed full-time by Newco. Jason indicated that Newco may need your help in resolving a "frivolous" sexual harassment claim that likely will be triggered as a result of his efforts to recruit an office manager for the new venture. And Lucy has advised everyone that she has already signed a lease for office space in the name of the Newco because she thought Jason had already formed Newco.

Address the following:

1. May you collectively represent Jason, Lucy and Sam in the organization of Newco? Should you?

2. May you represent just Newco?

3. What precautions should you take in connection with your representation of Newco or any of its owners?

4. Must you or should you advise Lucy and Sam of your prior experiences with Jason?

5. Does Newco or any of its three owners have any liability for the new office lease or the potential sexual harassment claim? Sam would like to get Newco out of the lease. Can he?

6. May you invest $100,000 in Newco for six percent of its stock? Jason promises that, if you make such an investment, you will be guaranteed a position on the board, will be elected secretary of the corporation, will be assured all of the corporation's legal work, and will realize a great return on your investment. If you can do this, should you do it?

CASE PROBLEM 6-3

Refer to the facts of Case Problem 6-2.

Sam plans on investing $1.2 million in the new company ("Newco"), far more than Jason and Lucy. But, as things now stand, Sam will be only one of three directors. Sam wants some protection against Jason and Lucy (who control the board) taking the company in a direction that is not acceptable to him. Sam is concerned about any attempts to (1) change the basic business plan, (2) incur additional debt, (3) pay bonuses to officers, or (4) accelerate the growth targets. Sam feels strongly that he should have some additional control rights because of the size of his investment.

If you represent only Sam, how would you advise him? Be specific in addressing the four concerns that Sam has identified. If you represent only Jason, what suggestions would you have to accommodate Sam's concerns while preserving flexibility for Jason and Lucy?

CHAPTER 7

CAPITAL STRUCTURE AND SOURCING CHALLENGES

A. CAPITAL STRUCTURE Q&As

What does a corporation's capital structure reflect? It shows how a corporation has secured funds to finance its assets and operations. A corporation basically has three funding sources: sell stock, borrow funds, and reinvest earnings. The capital structure reflects how these sources have been used to create rights and values for different stakeholders. The sources appear on the right side of the balance sheet, not the left side that lists the assets of the corporation.

What is common stock? It is the foundational stock of a corporation. Every corporation has common stock. Common stockholders are the last in line in a bankruptcy proceeding and usually the big winners when a corporation performs well or is sold at a handsome profit. Dividends are often paid to common stockholders, but only after obligations to debt holders and preferred stockholders have been satisfied. Common stockholders usually have the exclusive right to elect the board of directors, are the primary beneficiaries of fiduciary duties imposed on the board of directors, and must approve major transactions, including substantial mergers and any sale of substantially all of the corporation's assets. Different classes of common stock and non-voting common stock may be issued.

Do the common stockholders manage the corporation? No. Management issues are the responsibility of the board of directors, which is elected by the shareholders. However, as explained in section D of Chapter 6, shareholders in a closely held corporation usually have the statutory right to contractually bind themselves to operational matters in a manner that preempts the authority of the board.

What is the difference between authorized stock and issued stock? Authorized stock refers to the number of shares of stock that the articles of incorporation authorize the board of directors to issue. Issued stock is the actual stock that the board has issued and that is currently outstanding. The authorized stock of a corporation typically exceeds by many times the number of issued and outstanding shares. If a corporation needs additional authorized stock, it must amend its articles of incorporation, and such an amendment requires shareholder approval.

What is par value? It's an ancient concept that many decades ago was designed to protect creditors of a corporation by designating a legal par value for stock and insuring that a corporation did not sell "watered stock" – stock that was supported only by water because it was sold below the designated par value. The entire concept fell apart as everyone discovered the safety of using very low par stock, and then the corporate laws were amended to permit no-par stock. The Model Business Corporation Act completely rejects the concepts of "par" or "stated" values, although a corporation may designate such a value in its articles of incorporation. MBCA § 6.21. The official comments to section 6.21 state, "there is no minimum price at which specific shares must be issued and therefore there can be no 'watered stock' liability for issuing shares below an arbitrarily fixed price."

What is the meaning of the following phrase that often appears on a corporation's balance sheet: "Paid-in capital in excess of par value"? If a corporation's articles of incorporation designate a par or stated value, then the par or stated value of the shares outstanding is disclosed in the owner's equity section of the corporation's financial statements. The amounts in excess of the par value that have actually been paid for the outstanding stock (usually many times the size of the par value) are reflected in this line item in the owner's equity section. If the corporation has no par or stated value, there is no need for this separate line item and the entire consideration paid for the stock is reflected as "Common Stock."

What constitutes valid consideration for common stock? The Model Business Corporation Act and most states define the scope of valid consideration broadly, permitting any "tangible or intangible property or benefit to the corporation, including cash, promissory notes, services performed, contracts for services to be performed, or other securities of the corporation." MBCA § 6.21. Historically, a promise of future services and promissory notes were not authorized consideration for common stock. Residues of these limitations still exist in certain states that have not implemented the expansion provision of the Model Act. Delaware, for example, did not amend its corporate laws to permit stock to be issued for future services until 2004.

Who decides the terms for issuing common stock? The board of directors. And state statures typically provide that the board's determination "is conclusive insofar as the adequacy of consideration for the issuance of shares relates to whether the shares are validly issued, fully paid, and nonassessable." MBCA § 6.21(c).

Why would a corporation ever want to use non-voting common stock? Often in closely held corporations, particularly those dominated by a single family, there is a desire to spread the economic benefits of stock ownership to heirs or other individuals without disrupting the existing voting power. And non-voting stock can help avoid an estate tax trap that is triggered when a parent transfers stock in a controlled corporation and, through some means, "directly or indirectly" retains the right to vote the stock. When this condition exists, Section

2036(b) kicks in and the stock is brought back into the parent's estate for estate tax purposes. The safest way to avoid this trap is to transfer nonvoting stock, an option available to both C and S family corporations. Plus, in addition to avoiding 2036(b) threats, use of nonvoting stock will usually enhance gift-tax free gifting options by buttressing application of a lack of control valuation discount.

What is treasury stock? It is that portion of a company's issued shares of stock that the company keeps in its own treasury. It may come from a repurchase or buyback of stock from shareholders or it may represent issued stock that was never sold to the public. Treasury shares have no dividend rights, no voting rights, and should not be included in any calculations that are based on the number of shares outstanding. Why have treasury shares? They may aid in meeting an urgent cash need (just sell the stock) and might help in warding off a hostile takeover (see Chapter 14).

What is preferred stock? It is any stock that has economic rights that are senior to the rights of common stock. The rights may be preferences in the event of liquidation, dividend preferences, call preferences, or any combination of these preferences.

Must preferred stock and its preferential terms be authorized in the articles of incorporation? The different classes of stock and the number of authorized shares in each class must be set forth in the articles of incorporation. Beyond this basic requirement, the articles of incorporation can give the board the right to establish the terms and preferences of any preferred stock at the time it is issued. See MBCA § 6.02. Such a "blank check" provision promotes flexibility, greatly simplifies the articles of incorporation, enhances the board's authority, and reduces the need for shareholder approval.

What is the difference between cumulative and non-cumulative preferred stock? Preferred stock dividends typically are due on an annual or quarterly basis. Cumulative preferred stock requires the payment of all dividends that have accrued, including any that have been missed, before any dividends can be paid on common stock. The preferred dividends "cumulate." With non-cumulative preferred, a dividend payment obligation lapses once if it is not paid and ceases to be an impediment to common stock dividends. Obviously, cumulative preferred stock is the preference of most investors.

What is the difference between participating and non-participating preferred stock? Participating preferred stock pays the owner the dividend and liquidation preferences of the stock plus permits the owner to share (participate) in dividend and liquidation distributions made on the common stock. Non-participating preferred stock does not offer this sharing right with the common stock.

What is callable preferred stock? It is preferred stock that, by its terms, can be purchased ("called") by the corporation at specified times or under specified conditions. Often, the corporation is required to pay a call premium to exercise this right.

What is convertible preferred stock? It is preferred stock that is convertible into common stock at a specified exchange ratio. This is an attractive option for many investment groups. The preferred stock provides liquidation and dividend preferences while the company's value is being built. The conversion feature insures a large common stock return when the corporation is sold or goes public.

May preferred stockholders have voting and control rights? Yes. It's a matter of negotiation, and often preferred investors drive a hard bargain, demanding seats on the boards and preferential voting rights. Corporate statutes typically provide preferred stockholders with the right to vote on any corporate structural change that would adversely impact their rights or preferences.

What is "subordinated" preferred stock? It is preferred stock that has rights that take a back seat (are subordinated) to the rights of another class of preferred shareholders. Subordination is common when multiple financing rounds are necessary to fund the growth of a business and the risks and stakes change with each round.

Why might a company prefer to issue preferred stock rather than common stock? The issuance of more common stock always dilutes the financial interests of the existing common stockholders in the growth in value of the business enterprise. For an investor who is looking for a fixed income yield, a non-convertible, cumulative, non-participating preferred stock may fit the bill without any serious dilution impacts to the existing common stockholders. Of course, if the preferred stock has a conversion feature, common stock dilution is likely if the business does well.

Why might a company prefer to issue preferred stock rather than debt? A preferred stock often resembles debt obligation because it offers a fixed periodic yield and may offer the potential of being called ("paid off") at some point down the road. The big difference, though, is that it is not a debt subject to debt legal payment obligations and default risks. The holder of a debt instrument usually has the right to accelerate payment of the entire obligation if interest payments are not made or other covenants in the instrument are not satisfied. Plus, all parties know that the debt must be paid off at a given point in time in accordance with its terms. In contrast, preferred stock usually is far more forgiving. If a dividend payment is missed, it may "cumulate" and move forward as an obstacle to common stock dividends, but it will not trigger the burdens of a default on a debt obligation. And with preferred stock, there may be the possibility, and perhaps even an expectation, that it will be retired through redemption at some future point, but usually there is no legal obligation comparable to that included in a debt instrument. The bottom line is that a preferred stock, as compared to a debt, is more flexible for the corporation and offers fewer guarantees to the investor. For that reason, the stated yield on a preferred stock often must be higher than a debt obligation in order to attract investors.

Are actively-traded preferred stocks rated? Yes. As with bonds, actively-traded preferred stocks are rated by the major credit rating companies, such as Standard & Poor's and Moody's. The rating of a company's preferred stock is generally one or two tiers below that of the same company's bonds because preferred dividends do not carry the same guarantees and they are junior to all creditors of the company.

What is a stock option? A stock option is a contract that gives a person, usually an executive, the right to buy stock from the company over a designated period of time on certain specified terms and conditions. With any stock option plan, there are three key points in time: the time the person is given the option (the "grant date"), the time the person acquires the stock through the exercise of the option and payment of the option price (the "exercise date"), and the time that the stock is sold and the sales price is realized in the form of cash (the "sale date").

Why do corporations issue stock options? Typically stock options are used to incentivize executives. They are a form of compensation that can handsomely reward those who cause a company's common stock price to escalate over time. There are two general types of stock options: incentive stock options ("ISOs" and sometimes called "qualified stock options") and non-qualified stock options. The requirements and tax consequences of these two types are very different. Details regarding these option types and the factors that impact the planning process in the use of such options are discussed in Section D of Chapter 16.

What is restricted stock? It is stock that is given to an executive as compensation with strings attached – restrictions. If one of the restrictions is violated, the company yanks the string and retrieves all or a portion of the stock. There is broad authority in structuring these restrictions. For example, the restriction may provide that if the executive leaves the company at any time during the next 10 years, he or she will forfeit all of the stock. Alternatively, it may allow the stock to "vest" at a designated rate, such as five percent, each year or may provide that all or a portion of the stock is forfeited if the executive fails to hit certain sales volumes or otherwise fails to satisfy some other objective measure of performance. Details regarding restricted stock and the factors that impact the planning process in the use of such stock are discussed in Section D of Chapter 16.

What are retained earnings? They are the portion of a company's net earnings that are not paid out as dividends, but rather are retained by the company to finance growth or retire debt. A company's total retained earnings are reflected in a line item in the shareholders' equity section of the balance sheet. Retained earnings are calculated by adding current net income to (or subtracting current net losses from) the beginning retained earnings balance and then subtracting any dividends paid to shareholders. Thus, it is possible to have a deficit balance in a retained earnings account. Retained earnings are sometimes referred to as "retained surplus," "earned surplus," or "retention ratio."

What are stock indexes? They are various indexes that track movements of stock values throughout every business day. Usually one can't avoid hearing of the most popular three indexes: the Dow Jones Industrial Average (an Index based on 30 stocks); the NASDAQ (which tracks thousands of stocks, many in the technology and communication sectors); and the S&P 500 (an index based on 500 stocks traded on the New York Stock exchange). Other much less visible, but highly regarded, indexes include the Russell 2000 Index (which tracks 2,000 stocks traded on the over-the-counter ("OTC") market) and the Wilson 5000 Equity Index (which is based on thousands of stocks of varying sizes).

What is a mutual fund? It's a pool of investment capital that thousands of investors, large and small, create by mutually contributing their savings. A professional manager then invests the funds in accordance with the stated objectives of the fund. The manager and all expenses of running the fund are paid out of the fund. A person can participate in some funds by investing a modest sum upfront and then adding as little as $50 or more to the account each month. A major advantage is instant diversification – each investor has a financial interest in every one of the fund's investments. Plus, the investor gets professional management and avoids the commissions and hassles of trading individual stocks and bonds. In 2010, the U.S. Statistical abstract reported that there were over 7,500 mutual funds that managed more than $11.8 trillion. Today, mutual funds are the vehicles that most investors use to purchase interest in corporate stocks and bonds. Each fund is characterized by its investment objective, and the range of investment objectives is huge. There are blue chip stock funds, international funds, sector funds, asset allocation funds, bond funds – a lengthy list. There are families of funds, which are large groups of funds with different investment objectives offered by a single fund company. Examples include Fidelity, Vanguard and Dreyfus. A person who invests with such a fund family can easily move money from fund to fund within the family at little or no cost.

What is the difference between a "load" and a "no-load" mutual fund? A "no load" fund means that no commissions are being paid to someone for selling the fund's shares. A person can buy the "no load" shares directly from the fund company or through a firm that offers "no load" funds. "Load" funds use a part of the investment to pay a commission to a salesperson.

What is the difference between an open-end and a closed-end mutual fund? An open-end fund, the most common, continually takes on new investment capital until the manager shuts off additional investments. There is no set maximum. New investors buy shares at the fund's net asset value, which is calculated daily by dividing the market value of the fund's investments by the shares outstanding. A closed-end fund has a fixed maximum amount of capital. Once the maximum is hit, no more capital flows into the fund, and the fund's shares are traded and valued like a stock.

What is the difference between a managed and an indexed mutual fund? A "Managed" fund is managed by a professional group who works to get the best possible return. Often one hears of funds boasting of beating the S&P 500 Index or the Dow Jones. An "Index" fund just mirrors an index. For example, an S&P Index Fund buys and holds the 500 stocks that make up the S&P 500. It'll never beat or loose to the index; it is the index. Why would one want an indexed fund? It offers some advantages. There's no need to fret over the fund manager's expertise, competence or track record. There are many fewer transactions in an index fund, so an investor pays fewer capital gains while in the fund. The total expenses of operating an index fund often are far less than a managed fund. And a person knows going in that he or she will never lose to the index.

CASE PROBLEM 7-1

Doug, Linda and Laura, unrelated parties, plan to form a new corporation ("Newco") under the laws of a state that has adopted the Model Business Corporation Act. Newco will issue 200 shares of common stock to Doug for $200,000. Linda has no money, but she has agreed to give Newco a $200,000 promissory note for 200 shares of Newco common stock. The note will bear interest at an annual rate of 4 percent, and all interest and principal will be due and payable in 10 years. Linda's hope is that dividends from Newco will be sufficient to cover required payments on the note. Laura will be issued 200 shares of common stock as a "signing bonus" under an employment agreement that will require that she manage the company for five years for a base salary and a cash bonus plan set forth in the agreement. The parties anticipate that Doug (a deep pocket player) will probably need to "pony up" more cash within a year or so. Their tentative thinking is that Doug will be issued preferred stock for any additional capital, and the specific terms of the preferred stock will be worked out at the time of his contribution. Regarding the formation of the corporation, the parties have asked that you advise them on the following questions:

1. Is it legal to issue common stock to the parties for the consideration each party has agreed to provide?

2. Will the terms for issuing the stock need to be included in the articles of incorporation of the company?

3. Should the common stock have a par value? Is this required? What are the benefits of having a par value?

4. Can any preferred stock issued to Doug in the future have voting rights?

5. Should any preferred stock issued to Doug in the future be participating or cumulative preferred stock? Why?

6. Can the preferred stock that Doug may receive down the road be authorized now in the articles of incorporation even though the specific terms of the preferred will not be ascertained until a later date?

B. CORPORATE DEBT

1. BONDS AND BOND LINGO

A bond is a debt security that allows institutions to borrow money directly from investors. The issuer of the bond promises to pay a fixed rate of interest over the life of the bond and to repay the principal amount on the designated maturity date. The description of a corporate bond generally includes the corporation's name, the coupon rate, and the maturity date. For example: "General Motors (GM) 5.25% due 12/31/2015" would mean the bond was issued by General Motors, pays an annual interest rate of 5.25 percent, and matures on December 31, 2015.

According to the Securities Industry and Financial Markets Association (SIFMA), the global bond market as of March 2012 totaled roughly $100 trillion. The United States has the largest bond market, approximately $32.3 trillion, 33 percent of the world market. The next closest country is Japan at 14 percent. Corporate bonds comprise about 24 percent ($7.7 trillion) of the total U.S. bond market.

Corporate bonds offer investors a consistent fixed income yield, long-term capital preservation, and liquidity - the capacity to sell the bond at any time. Bonds are often used by investors to hedge against the higher risks of stock investments. Some corporate bonds have a call option that allows the issuing corporation to redeem the bond before its maturity date. Other bonds offer a conversion feature that allows an investor to convert the bond into equity stock of the company.

The interest rate is usually the most important factor that influences a bond's market price and total return. Changes in the overall level of interest rates will cause the price of a bond owned by an investor to move in the opposite direction. If interest rates fall, an existing bond's value will move up, all other factors being equal. If interest rates rise, a bonds value will drop. And, of course, credit worthiness is always a factor. Rating agencies, such as Moody's and Standard & Poor's, rate bonds based on their credit strength. The value of the bond moves in the same direction of any rating change. Corporate bonds often are listed on major exchanges, although the bulk of the trading volume in corporate bonds is done through decentralized, dealer-based, over-the-counter markets.

Bonds have their own language. Following are the definitions of some of the key bond lingo terms:[1]

Ask Price (or Offer Price): The price at which a seller offers to sell a security.

Basis Point: Smallest measure used in quoting yields on bonds and notes. One basis point is 0.01 percent of yield. For example, a bond's yield that changed from 6.52 percent to 7.19 percent would be said to have moved 67 basis points.

Bid: Price at which a buyer is willing to purchase a security.

Bond year: An element in calculating average life of an issue and in calculating net interest cost and net interest rate on an issue. A bond year is the number of 12-month intervals between the date of the bond and its maturity date, measured in $1,000 increments. For example, the "bond years" allocable to a $5,000 bond dated April 1, 1980, and maturing June 1, 1981, is 5.830 [1.166 (14 months divided by 12 months) x 5 (number of $1,000 increments in $5,000 bond)]. Usual computations include "bond years" per maturity or per an interest rate, and total "bond years" for the issue.

Call: Actions taken to pay the principal amount prior to the stated maturity

---

1. See Sifma, Investing in Bonds.com/Glossary

date, in accordance with the provisions for "call" stated in the proceedings and the securities. Another term for call provisions is redemption provisions.

Call Premium: A dollar amount, usually stated as a percentage of the principal amount called, paid as a "penalty" or a "premium" for the exercise of a call provision.

Call Price: The specified price at which a bond will be redeemed or called prior to maturity, typically either at a premium (above par value) or at par.

Coupon: The rate of interest payable annually.

Covenant: The issuer's pledge, in the financing documents, to do or to avoid certain practices and actions.

Current Yield: The ratio of interest to the actual market price of the bond, stated as a percentage. For example, a bond with a current market price of $900 that pays $60 per year in interest would have a current yield of 6.67 percent.

Junk Bond: A debt obligation with a rating of Ba or BB or lower, generally paying interest above the return on more highly rated bonds, sometimes known as high-yield bonds.

Premium or Discount Price: When the dollar price of a bond is above its face value, it is said to be selling at a premium. When the dollar price is below face value, it is said to be selling at a discount.

Yield to Maturity: A yield on a security calculated by assuming that interest payments will be made until the final maturity date, at which point the principal will be repaid by the issuer. Yield to maturity is essentially the discount rate at which the present value of future payments (investment income and return of principal) equals the price of the security.

Zero-Coupon Bond: A bond for which no periodic interest payments are made. The investor receives one payment at maturity equal to the principal invested plus interest earned compounded semiannually at the original interest rate to maturity.

2. SHAREHOLDER DEBT: WHY AND HOW?

In the course of many corporation formations, the shareholders conclude that it is advantageous from a tax perspective to receive corporate debt in return for a significant portion of the money they contribute to the enterprise. Take Sam, Dick and Joy, each of whom has agreed to contribute $500,000 to a start-up corporation that they believe will "quickly take off." One option is to receive only common stock for their contributions. They would each end up owning one third of the equity, and all cash distributions to them would be taxed as double-taxed dividends. Suppose instead that they each receive stock for $150,000 of their contributed capital and corporate notes for the additional $350,000. They still each own one-third of the equity, with equal voting rights and value appreciation rights. But the tax impacts of cash distributions as the business "takes off" would have changed dramatically if (and it's a big "if") the debt works.

First, the double tax hit would be gone because the interest payments on the shareholder debt are deductible by the corporation. Even though interest is taxed to the shareholders at ordinary rates instead of the favorable dividends rates, the net aggregate tax cost for the corporation and the shareholders will still be reduced in nearly all situations. Second (and here's the really big deal), the principal balance of the debt ($350,000 for each shareholder) can be paid off tax free to the shareholders as a return of capital. This gives the corporation the capacity to repay 80 percent of the contributed capital free of any double tax hit. Any such payments to the shareholders with respect to their stock holdings would almost certainly be taxed as a dividend, particularly if the payments were *pro rata* among the shareholders.[2]

Will such a shareholder debt plan work? Maybe. Obviously, the IRS has an interest in trying to characterize the shareholder debt as equity for tax purposes. This re-characterization fight has been the subject of countless cases. What has emerged is a body of vague muss, characterized as a "jungle" by one court[3] and a "viper's tangle" by the leading commentator.[4] What we do know is that greed – pushing the concept too far – promises problems. We also know that key factors in assessing the greed include the debt-to-equity ratio (the higher the riskier), the real intent of the parties (as manifested by the terms of the documents and the capacity of the company to service and discharge the debt), proportionality among shareholders (the more proportionality, the more it is suspect), equity conversion rights (usually a killer), and subordination of the debt to other creditors (hurts, but not fatal).[5]

As the courts wrestled with the issue, Congress tried to offer some clarity by enacting Section 385 as part of the comprehensive Tax Reform Act of 1969, heralded as the 1969 Act's "most important" provision[6] because it empowered the Treasury to promulgate definitive regulations for determining whether and when a shareholder debt instrument would be treated as debt or equity. Temporary regulations came years later, followed by a second attempt, but then (over the cries of far too many) all was withdrawn and the effort was abandoned in 1983.[7] Nothing has happened since, suggesting that even the Treasury, specifically empowered by Congress, couldn't create acceptable standards that bring certainty to the muss.

So the muss remains. This does not mean that shareholder debt should not be used in planning the capital structure of a closely held enterprise. The advantages are powerful. It means that care and prudence are required, along with a willingness of the clients to live with a little uncertainty and risk. For planning purposes, there are a few semi-bright lights that have emerged from case law and the aborted 385 regulation effort that help in structuring shareholder

---

2. I.R.C. § 302(b).

3. See Commissioner v. Union Mutual Insurance Co. of Providence, 386 F.2d 974, 978 (1st Cir. 1967).

4. Bittker & Eustice, Federal Income Taxation of Corporations and Shareholders ¶ 4.04 (4th ed. 1979).

5. See, e.g., Hariton, "Essay: Distinguishing Between Equity and Debt in the New Financial Environment," 49 Tax L. Rev. 499 (1994).

6. Bittker & Eustice, Federal Income Taxation of Corporations and Shareholders ¶ 4.05 (3rd ed. 1971).

7. T.D. 7920, 48 Fed. Reg. 31054 (July 6, 1983). The temporary regulations were published in 45 Fed. Reg. 18957 (1980) and the final regulations in 45 Fed. Reg. 86438 (1980).

debt that doesn't cross over the line.

First, any hybrid equity characteristics, such as equity conversion rights, contingent interest obligations, or interest obligations tied to profitability, will kill any debt as debt for tax purposes.[8] They just can't exist.

Second, the debt-to-equity ratio is often the key factor in determining if the debt is "excessive." Under the old 385 regulations, the "excessive" tag was avoided if the outside debt-to-equity ratio (based on all liabilities of the corporation) did not exceed 10-to-1 and the inside debt-to-equity ratio (based only on the shareholder debt) did not exceed 3-to-1.[9]

Third, the intent of the parties to treat the debt as real debt requires that the debt instrument be a commercially "normal" debt instrument (unconditional promise to pay, sum certain, payment dates certain, reasonable interest rate, etc.) and that there is a reasonable basis (hopefully supported by reasonable projections) for concluding that the corporation will have no problem timely making all payments due under the debt instrument.

Fourth, shareholder debt that is proportional among the shareholders is highly suspect, but not necessarily deadly. It has a chance if it is issued for cash or property, bears a reasonable rate of interest, satisfies the old 385 regulation's debt-to-equity safe harbors (10-to-1 and 3-to-1), and has all the appropriate "intent" trappings.[10]

Fifth, subordination of shareholder debt to outside creditors should not be fatal if all other factors are solid, but it can become a big negative if the "intent" issue is equivocal, the debt-to-equity ratios are at or beyond the outer limits, and/or a proportionality condition exists.

Finally, no matter how safely the debt is structured, the client should be advised of the inherent uncertainties and the importance of treating the debt as real debt.

CASE PROBLEM 7-2

Lucy has operated a successful Italian import supply business as a sole proprietor for five years. She now plans to dramatically expand her business. To this end, she has lined up some new capital and developed the following plan:

1. She will form a C corporation that will have four shareholders: Lucy, Jim, Sue and Dave.

2. Lucy will contribute to the corporation accounts receivable that have a value of $100,000. She will be issued 100 shares of common stock in return.

3. Jim and Sue will each contribute $100,000 cash in return for 100 shares.

4. Dave will contribute a warehouse to the corporation in return for 100 shares of stock. The parties believe the warehouse has a value of $500,000.

---

8. Prop. Reg. §§ 1.385-3(d), 1.385-0(c)(2).

9. Prop. Reg. §§ 1.385-6(f)(2).

10. Prop. Reg. §§ 1.385-6.

There is an outstanding mortgage balance of $400,000 that the company will assume.

5. Each of the four shareholders also will loan the company $450,000. The loan, plus interest at prime, will be paid off in monthly installments over a 10-year period. No payments will be due the first 12 months, then interest-only payments will be due for three years, and then the principal plus interest will be amortized over a six-year period. The projections show that the company should have no problem with this payment schedule if things go as planned.

Advise Lucy as to the wisdom of her plan. What changes would you suggest? Why? What additional facts would you like to have?

C. SOURCES OF CAPTIAL

1. GOING PUBLIC REALITIES

Only a tiny fraction of businesses will ever consider "going public" – having their stock owned and regularly traded by a large number of public shareholders. All other businesses are just too small or not suited for public ownership and the associated regulatory hassles and horrendous expenses. But for those select few that are destined for the big time, going public is the ball game; it is their mission, their purpose, a prerequisite to their success. Their closely held status is merely preparatory to their real life as a public company. Typically, these companies are developing and preparing to exploit proprietary intellectual property rights and are financed and controlled by professional investment funds. All planning is focused on the unique objectives of the deep pockets that are writing the checks and calling the shots in preparation for the big day when the public is invited to the party.

The advantages of being a public company are compelling. The owners have liquid stock that facilitates the rapid growth and diversification of their wealth. The company has a larger, stronger capital base to fuel growth, pursue new ventures, or expand through the acquisition of other companies. The compensation paid to the corporation's executives often increases dramatically though higher salaries, bigger bonuses and stock equity incentives. There is often a perception that the prestige and presence of the entire enterprise and those who work for it has been pushed up to a whole new level.

Balanced against these advantages are risks, pressures, hassles, and costs that must be carefully considered and planned for. The pressure to show strength of earnings and growth is relentless and never-ending. It's all about the short-term, the here and now. The investing public, primarily though their guardians, the brokerage community, will scrutinize results and ask the tough questions. The challenges of public disclosure and confidentiality will demand serious time and attention to avoid litigation burdens that often accompany bad disclosures or breached confidences. Accounting, audit, internal control, and regulatory reporting and compliance pressures will balloon at all levels. Management will be directly accountable to an active board of directors, partially comprised of outside, independent members who will be the sole players on the all-important audit and compensation subcommittees. Sales and purchases of company stock by corporate executives will have to be publicly reported and carefully monitored to avoid securities law liability risks.

And then there are the costs – the costs to go public and the ongoing increased costs that come with being a public company. The baseline upfront costs to go public include substantial legal fees for a host of items, including preparation of the registration statement and securities law compliance, accounting and audit fees, printing costs, and various others direct fees and costs that are incurred during the launch period, which typically runs six to nine months. In a survey of 26 companies that went public during the 2009 to 2011 timeframe, Ernst & Young LLP[11] found that the companies, on average, engaged 11 third-party advisors in connection with the their IPO, including investment bankers, attorneys, auditors, printers, D&O insurance carriers, stock transfer agents, Sarbanes-Oxley consultants, compensation advisors, investor relations firms, tax advisors, road show consultants, compensation advisors to the board, and internal audit advisors. On average, the surveyed companies spent $13 million in one-time advisory costs associated with executing the IPO. Of course, the core offering costs will typically be much less in smaller offerings. But the bottom line is always the same – the up-front costs of an IPO, which are not predicated on a successful offering, are very expensive. And beyond these direct getting-started costs are the indirect and opportunity costs of personnel and management time and the substantial commissions and expenses that must be paid to those who sell the stock in the offering.

As for the additional costs that come with being a public company, in the same survey Ernst & Young reported that the new public companies, on average, incurred additional ongoing costs (not related to the IPO) of approximately $2.5 million a year as a public company. Of this amount, $1.5 million was attributable to executive compensation and directors' benefits, and the remaining $1 million represented increased compliance costs.

What does the process of going public involve? The starting point is a determination that the company is a good candidate for an initial public offering. This often requires discussions with consultants, underwriters, accountants and attorneys to assess the state of the market and the appeal of the company. The focus is on the proven ability of the company to maintain consistent growth, the experiences and track records of the management team, the type of product or service offered by the company (the "hotter" the better), how the company stacks up against its competition, and whether the audit requirements for a public offering have been or can be satisfied.

A key challenge is to get an underwriter committed to the offering. Often the creditability and experience of the management team is the primary factor in attracting a quality underwriter. And, of course, size matters. Most companies who are seriously exploring a public offering have annual sales of at least $100 million. It's often impossible to reasonably justify the increased costs and regulatory burdens of being a public company when the annual sales drop much

---

11. Ernst & Young IPO Cost Survey, November 2011. Ernst & Young is a global leader in assurance, tax, transaction and advisory services that employs 141,000 people worldwide.

below this threshold. In select situations, an underwriter may have an interest in smaller companies that have a cutting edge product and promise sustained, extreme annual growth (say, 25 percent) for the next five years.

The registration statement is always a major challenge in an initial public offering. It must be carefully drafted to include the history of the company, details related to the market for the product or services offered by the company, how the proceeds of the offering are going to be used, the risk factors that accompany an investment in the company, the backgrounds of the officers and directors, any transactions with related parties, the identifies of any major shareholders, and more. Of course, audited financial statements must be included in the registration statement. Once completed, the registration statement is submitted to the Securities and Exchange Commission for review.

The selling begins when the registration statement is approved and the offering is effective. Often the key to the sales effort is a high-quality "road show" that smartly and quickly lays out key facts and stimulates investor interest in the company. Institutional investors generally have no interest in visiting the companies they invest in. They want an informative presentation at the road show meetings that gives them what they need to make an investment decision. This is the ideal time (often the only time) for the company's senior management to communicate directly with potential investors. Usually the sales presentation is carefully scripted in various formats (everything from a full-blown presentation to a two-minute pitch) to accommodate different sales opportunities.

When the offering wraps up and the money has arrived, the governance, management, performance, disclosure, and compliance challenges of being a public company take center stage.

2. START-UP CAPITAL FORMATION CHALLENGES

Capital is usually the biggest obstacle for a new business. An idea has blossomed into a business plan, perhaps even a prototype or a few sales. But money is now needed to get the business started and fuel growth. Of course, the entrepreneur would love to secure the needed financing at the lowest possible cost. But, in most cases, cost isn't the driving factor. The challenge is availability or, perhaps better stated, the lack of available financing. This funding challenge often triggers the following key questions.

Is bank financing available?

Bank financing often is a godsend to growth for an established company that has a proven history of profitability. The business can leverage the bank debt by generating a return on its assets that far exceeds the interest cost of the debt. It is business 101 leverage at its best. The problem for a new business is that it lacks a proven income history and a solid asset base. Thus, absent a personal guarantee from a deep pocket player that moots the company's status as a start-up, bank debt just isn't available to a new venture.

Once the business is established, bank debt often is the best and lowest cost capital source to fund growth. A business can usually obtain asset-based bank financing for most hard assets that have a market value. It is common to secure financing for up to 85 to 90 percent of credit worthy accounts receivable, 50 percent of finished goods inventory, 80 percent of the cost of the equipment (repayable in fixed installments over a period of three to 10 years), and up to 75 to 85 percent of the value of marketable real estate. If asset-based financing doesn't work or there is a need to supplement such financing, banks often provide cash flow financing (through lines of credit or short-term debt) that allow a company to borrow against its demonstrated ability to generate sufficient cash to service and repay the financing. This ability is established through factors and ratios (debt coverage, debt-to-equity, working capital, senior debt restrictions, etc.), which factors and ratios often are built into the loan document as conditions that continually must be satisfied to keep the financing alive.

To assist with bank financing in select situations, the Small Business Administration, the Farmers Home Administration, and other government agencies will guarantee a bank loan to enable a business to obtain financing that it could not obtain on its own. For SBA programs, any owner of the business with an equity stake of 20 percent or more must personally guarantee the loan. Plus, there are SBA fees that must be paid, and often banks charge a higher interest rate on an SBA-guaranteed loan. Because an SBA lender's track record is important to the lender, most banks won't lend to start-up businesses that lack financial statements for two to three years and some significant owner's equity in the business.

What about angel or investment fund investors?

Angel investors range from family and friends to deep pocket individual investors who manage their own money. They can be fertile ground for the budding entrepreneur who needs capital. Angels often are advised and heavily influenced by their accountants, lawyers and other professionals, with whom the entrepreneur must deal. Some angel investors band together to develop specialized expertise, share due diligence burdens, and spread the cost of professional advisers.

Often friends, acquaintances and advisors are the only sources for finding angel investors. Many angels are well-suited for businesses that are too small for venture capital firms, but they are far less likely to help with future capital needs and sometimes become a frustrating source of complaints and naïve questions and demands.

As compared to angels, venture capital funds tend to be more sophisticated, more expensive and demanding, more interested in bigger deals. They often include pension funds and endowment investors, along with wealthy individual investors. Target annual returns of 50 to 60 percent are not uncommon hurdles when dealing with venture capital firms. These return objectives require that they negotiate tough terms that often gives the venture capital firm the power to control major corporate decisions and, in select cases, to dictate day-to-day operational decisions.

A venture capital firm will expend a great deal of effort investigating a potential investment. Its obligations to its investors permit nothing less. A business plan targeted at venture capital firms should be short, be concise and attempt to stimulate further interest, rather than present the business in exhaustive detail. The amount of needed financing should be discussed without proposing or mentioning the terms of a potential deal.   Generally, information that is proprietary or confidential should be left out of the document because such documents are often copied.

Seldom do venture capital firms just purchase common stock. The preferred form of investment usually is a mix of debt and equity, convertible debt, or convertible preferred security. The firm wants a preferred position in the event of a failure and liquidation and full upside equity benefits if things play out as all hope.

Are strategic investors an option?

In the right situation, a corporate partner or strategic investor is the best option by a long shot. Such investors are becoming a popular source of growth capital for many companies. Seldom will these deals work for a pure start-up because the unknowns and perceived risks are too high. But as the business matures and the needs and benefits of more capital are more clearly defined, strategic partners can be a great source of capital. Usually the partner is looking for something more than an investment. It may want the opportunity to get an inside track on a new or evolving technology or the first opportunity to buy the company at the right time.

What is crowdfunding?

Crowdfunding is where a group of individuals collectively contribute funds to a start-up effort in response to solicitations that usually come via the Internet. There are two kinds of crowdfunding: non-equity and equity.   Non-equity crowdfunding is where the individual does not receive any equity interest for his or her contribution to the cause. The contributor's motive may be completely charitable or with the hope of receiving a tangible item (not a security) promised by the company. Kickstarter.com is one of the leading non-equity crowdfunding sponsors. A company that has a creative idea but no money can use Kickstarter in hopes of raising modest amounts to "kick start" its business. The average yield from a success Kickstarter effort is about $5,000 – enough perhaps to make some noise about a creative idea, but not nearly enough to finance a real business.

Equity crowdfunding is a much different, and far more controversial, concept. It will soon be legal, but, as of this writing, nobody knows when or what it will mean. The JOBS ("Jumpstart Our Business Startups") Act of 2012 mandates that the SEC implement rules for a new crowdfunding securities registration exemption within 270 days of the April 5 passage date. The President heralded crowdfunding as a "game changer" for "small businesses and start-ups," stating "for the first time, ordinary Americans will be able to go online and invest in entrepreneurs that they believe in."[12]

---

12. President Obama's address on April 5, 2012 at signing of JOBs Act bill.

The concept of equity crowdfunding scares many. Within a short time, private business ventures of all types will be using the Internet to sell unregistered securities to "ordinary Americans" who will have no capacity to evaluate what's being offered. All the targeted investors will see are ground floor opportunities to play like the big dogs. The maximum amount that a business can raise through this crowdfunding tool in a 12-month period is $1 million – not serious money in the world of business development. Those who have an annual income and a net worth of less than $100,000 may invest the greater of $2,000 or five percent of their income or net worth in a single deal. Those who exceed the $100,000 threshold many invest 10 percent of their income or net worth up to a maximum of $100,000.

Proponents of equity crowdfunding compare it positively to buying lottery tickets. Opponents claim that the securities laws should at least seek to promote something greater than dumb luck gambling.

Here's the feared scenario. A budding entrepreneur with a hot-sounding business idea will use the internet to raise, say, $450,000 from 150 investors (average investment of $3,000) who have an average income and net worth of $60,000. The 150 investors will need attending to and will soon become a nuisance. They will have questions and concerns. They will want reports and information, to be assured that everything is on track. Of course, there will be no market for the stock, but some will want out anyway because of a lost job, a sickness, or a desire for a new car. A few will file bankruptcy, and their stock will end up in the hands of a bankruptcy trustee. An investor will die, and the heirs will demand the lowdown.

Meanwhile, the $450,000 will be spent on salaries, fees and start-up expenses. Soon more money will be needed to keep the plan alive. But what savvy investor will want to partner-up with 150 needy neophytes who can't bring any more to the table? If such an investor does surface, a plan will be developed to flush out the original 150 investors at the lowest possible cost. The more likely outcome is that the entrepreneur, having consumed the money, will just move on to the next deal after advising the investing crowd that there's no more money, the plan is dead, and they may be entitled to a tax deduction for a worthless investment.

Is this fraud? It might be. It might just be incompetence, stupidity or greed. Either way, the uninformed investors end up losing. Investing in unregistered securities of start-ups is a super high-risk game that always poses serious risks of fraud, abuse, and complete loss. That's why, to date, it's a game that has been off limits to general solicitation and advertising and has been limited to sophisticated investors and those with a certain level of wealth. Many believe that it's no place for unsophisticated investors of modest means.

This assessment is not unique. The President of the North American Securities Administration Association (NASAA) recently stated, "Congress has just released every huckster, scam artist, small business owner and salesman onto the internet." Ralph Nader claimed that it's a "return to the notorious boiler room practices" where any start-up "can sell stock to investors like the old Wild West days with little disclosure or regulation."

Will there be any serious oversight? In announcing the passage of the JOBS act, the President stated that the SEC would play an "important role" to ensure that "the websites where folks go to fund all these start-ups and small businesses will be subject to rigorous oversight." Opponents are quick to point out that this is the same SEC that failed to spot Enron, Worldcom, Madoff, the dot-com bust, the derivative showdown banking industry, the subprime mortgage lunacy, the financial meltdown, and a host of other huge messes. How about state securities regulators helping out with oversight and regulation? There is no hope there. The new law specifically provides that the federal exemption will cut off all state involvement.

As of this writing, the SEC has announced that it will not meet the 270-day deadline for the crowdfunding rules. It's unclear when we can expect the rules. When announced, the rules will clarify the opportunities and obstacles of equity crowdfunding. Although there are now many unknowns, it appears highly likely that, at some point in the not too distant future and for better or worse, many start-up companies will be using the Internet and social media to raise capital from large groups of small, uniformed investors.

Is "do-it-yourself" start-up funding the ultimate answer for most?

It's certainly the answer for many. The owners fund their dreams with their own resources: savings accounts, 401(k)s, credit cards, second mortgages, personally guaranteed loans, gifts from family members – you name it. It's tougher and lonelier, but it ensures 100 percent ownership and freedom from investor hassles during the early life of the enterprise. And for many, there is no other viable option to capitalize the operation until the business is up and running. A study conducted in the late 1980s concluded that 80 percent of the companies on Inc. Magazine's list of the 500 fastest growing companies were started and grown with no outside capital.[13]

D. SECURITIES LAW REGISTRATION EXEMPTIONS

1. REGISTRATION EXEMPTION BASICS

How much do I need? From whom can I get it? Many business owners mistakenly assume that these two basic questions sum up the capital challenges for a start-up or thriving business. But there's a third and, in many respects, a more fundamental question: How do I do it legally?

Since the immediate fallout of the great crash of 1929, our laws have recognized that there is a big difference between selling a security and selling a used car. The former is an intangible; it's not possible to get the lowdown by kicking the tires, looking under the hood, and taking a test spin. So over the past 80 years, a body of federal statutory securities laws has developed to provide

---

13. Amar Bhide, Bootstrap Finance: The Art of Start-ups, Harvard Business Review (Dec. 1992) p. 109.

special protections for those who entrust their investment dollars with others.[14] All states have followed suit with their own statutory schemes.[15] The purpose of these laws is to protect the public from some of the risks inherent in investing money in intangible assets. Various means are used to accomplish this overriding purpose, including mandated disclosure requirements, industry player regulation, government law enforcement, and expanded causes of action for private litigation. Most good business lawyers do not possess the know-how or the experience to navigate a client through the SEC and state regulatory mazes to take a client public; that rare effort is left to experts who play in those mazes every day. But a business lawyer should understand the basics of this all-important body of law, be sensitive to the flags that indicate that a client is near (or far over) an important line, and know how to discuss key issues with business clients. For most businesses, the three primary security law considerations are the registration requirements, the resale restrictions, and the anti-fraud prohibitions.

Sections 4 and 5 of the Securities Act of 1933 (the 1933 Act) establish the general requirement that any security offered for sale by an issuer, underwriter or dealer must be registered with the Securities and Exchange Commission (SEC).[16] As explained in the previous section, only a tiny fraction of businesses would ever consider going through the expense and hassle of such a registration process. For this reason, the important registration issues for most businesses in need of investors are the exceptions to the registration requirement. Is there an applicable exception that fits so that the money can be raised without enduring the burdens of registration?

There are two big statutory exceptions that become the ball game for most privately owned businesses that want outside investors. The first is found in Section 4(2) of the 1933 Act that exempts from registration any "transactions by an issuer not involving a public offering."[17] It is commonly referred to as the "private offering exemption." The second is in Section 3(a)(11) of the 1933 Act that exempts from registration securities offered and sold only to residents of a single state by an issuer who is a resident of and doing business within the same state.[18] It is commonly referred to as the "intrastate offering exemption." Of course, the challenge is to know what it takes to qualify for one of these exemptions. To this end, the SEC has published rules that set forth specific standards for meeting the exemptions. Rules 504 through 506 of Regulation D describe three private offering exemptions; SEC Rule 147 deals with the intrastate offering exemption.[19]

---

14. The federal securities statutes include the Securities Act of 1933 (15 U.S.C. §§ 77a et seq.), the Securities Exchange Act of 1934 (15 U.C.C. §§ 78a et seq.), the Public Utility Company Act of 1935 (15 U.S.C. §§ 79 et seq.), the Trust Indenture Act of 1939 (15 U.S.C. §§ 77aaa et seq.), the Investment Company Act of 1940 (15 U.S.C. §§ 80a-1 et seq.), the Investment Advisors Act of 1940 (15 U.S.C. §§ 80b-1 et seq.), the Securities Investor Protection Act of 1970 (15 U.S.C. §§ 78aaa et seq.) and the Sarbanes-Oxley Act of 2002 (miscellaneous provisions of 15 U.S.C.).

15. Most states have patterned their statutes after the Uniform Securities Act.

16. 15 U.S.C. §§ 77d and 77e.

17. 15 U.S.C. §§ 77d(2).

18. 15 U.S.C. § 77c(a)(11)

19. 17 C.F.R. §§ 230.504 thru 230.506. The definitions and other provisions of sections 230.501-230.503 should be read in conjunction with these three rules. See generally James Hagan, *Securities Laws for Start-Ups*, in Drake, *Business Planning: Closely Held Businesses* (West 3rd ed. 2011), pages 155 though 164.

Rule 504 Exemption

SEC Rule 504 allows a company to issue unregistered securities with a value of up to $1 million to an unlimited number of unsophisticated investors who purchase the securities for their own account and not for resale. The offering must be completed within a 12-month period, which starts when the first investment agreement is signed by an investor. The rule itself does not mandate any specific disclosures, but the issuer must satisfy the basic antifraud provisions of the securities laws (discussed below). The rule permits general solicitation, but often this is prohibited or limited by state securities laws. Securities issued under Rule 504 are freed of certain resale restrictions because they are not considered "restricted securities." The company must comply with the securities laws of each state in which a purchaser is a resident, and usually must file a notice with that state's commissioner of corporations or similar official. Any person who purchases a security under a Rule 504 offering should sign an investment agreement as proof of his or her investment intent and other required representations. A Form D must be filed with the SEC within 15 days after the first sale.

Rule 505 Exemption

SEC Rule 505 allows a company, within a 12-month period, to issue up to $5,000,000 worth of unregistered securities to 35 unsophisticated investors plus any number of "accredited investors." Generally, an "accredited investor" is an individual with a net worth of at least a $1,000,000 (primary home excluded) or an annual income of over $200,000 ($300,000 for a married couple) for the last two years. The definition also includes: banks and investment companies; private development companies; corporations, partnerships and trusts with assets over $5 million; and company insiders (officers, directors, and promoters). There are a number of required disclosures if any securities are sold to non-accredited investors. Advertising and general solicitations are prohibited. The securities are "restricted securities" and may not be readily resold. The company must comply with the securities laws of each state in which a person who buys the security is a resident, and usually must file a notice with that state's commissioner of corporations or similar official. Any person who acquires a security in a Rule 505 offering should sign an appropriate investment agreement. The company must file a Form D with the SEC within 15 days after the first sale.

Rule 506 Exemption

Rule 506 is the most popular registration exemption because there are no dollar limitations and (this is the big one) an exemption under 506 preempts all state securities law registration requirements. This can save a great deal of time, hassle or expense for the company that intends to raise money from investors in various states. Under Rule 506, there can be any number of accredited investors and up to 35 non-accredited investors if, and only if, each non-accredited investor (or an authorized representative) has knowledge and experience in financial and business matters and is capable of evaluating the risks of the investment. Historically, all advertising and general solicitations were prohibited under 506, but the JOBS Act of 2012 (discussed below) now permits general solicitation of accredited investors in a 506 offering if all the purchasers in the offering are accredited investors and reasonable steps are taken to ensure the accredited investor status of all investors. The company must file a form D with the SEC and with the corporation's commissioner in each state where stock is sold. Any person who buys stock in a Rule 506 offering should sign an appropriate investment agreement confirming that he or she is buying the stock for investment purposes, that there are serious restrictions on the resale of the stock, and that no attempt will be made to resell the stock without the approval of the company.

Rule 147 Exemption[20]

Rule 147 exempts from federal registration a company that sells securities in an "intrastate offering" to residents of only that state. To qualify as an "intrastate offering," the principal office of the company must be located in the state, at least 80 percent of the company's gross revenues must be derived from operations in the state, at least 80 percent of the company's assets must be located in the state, and at least 80 percent of the proceeds realized in the offering must be used in the state. The company must comply with the state's securities laws. Any person who acquires a security should sign an appropriate investment agreement containing proof of residence.

Regulation A Offerings

Regulation A provides an exemption allowing for public offers and sales of up to $5 million of securities in a 12-month period. It is sometimes referred to as a mini-registration. Investment companies and any company subject to the periodic reporting requirements of the Securities Exchange Act are not eligible. Regulation A requires the company to file an offering statement with the Securities and Exchange Commission containing disclosures similar to those made in a registration statement, certain exhibits, and financial statements prepared in accordance with generally accepted accounting principles (audited statements are not required). When the offering statement has been reviewed and qualified by the SEC, it must be delivered to prospective investors prior to any securities being sold. The company is required to file reports with the SEC detailing the securities sold and the use of proceeds from those sales. But once the offering is complete – and unlike all public companies – there are no ongoing reporting requirements. Securities sold in a Regulation A offering are unrestricted and may be transferred in a secondary market transaction. Regulation A offerings are seldom used because of the $5 million limitation and the amount of work they require.

JOBS Act of 2012

On April 5, 2012, President Obama signed the Jumpstart Our Business Startups (JOBS) Act with strong bi-partisan support. The Act is intended to increase American job creation and economic growth by improving access to the public capital markets for emerging growth companies. Key provisions of the Act include the following:

---

20. 17 C.F.R. § 240.147.

- The maximum number of shareholders of record that a private company can have before it must register with the SEC as a public company is increased from 500 to 2,000, so long as fewer than 500 are non-accredited investors.

- The prohibition on general solicitation and advertising in a private offering under Rule 506 of Regulation D must be removed by the SEC. In August 2012, the SEC released proposed changes to Rule 506 that would permit general solicitation and adverting if all the purchasers in the offering are accredited investors and reasonable steps are taken to ensure the accredited investor status of all investors.

- The SEC must adopt rules that permit "crowdfunding" activities so that entrepreneurs could raise up to $1 million from a large pool of small investors, subject to limitations based on investor income levels. (See related discussion of crowdfunding in the previous section of this chapter.)

- The SEC must raise the limit for offerings under Regulation A from $5 million to $50 million and exempting Regulation A offerings from state securities laws so long as the securities are offered or sold over a national securities exchange or are sold to a "qualified purchaser" (a term the SEC will need to define). The revised Regulation A will require a company to file audited financial statements annually with the SEC, and the SEC is directed to develop rules relating to periodic disclosure by Regulation A issuers.

- **A** category of issuer called an "emerging growth company" is created under the Act. This is a company that has under $1 billion in annual revenues. The regulatory burden on such companies is eased by permitting them to include only two years of audited financial statements and selected other information in their IPO registration statement, not requiring an auditor attestation of management's assessment of internal controls for financial reporting created under Sarbanes Oxley, and exempting them from certain other accounting requirements. Also, the Act eases offering-pending research disclosure rules, marketing communication conflict of interest rules, and pre-filing institutional investor communication limitations. Furthermore, an emerging growth company will be exempt from shareholder approval requirements of executive compensation

Antifraud Challenges

Beyond the registration exemptions are the anti-fraud prohibitions. Section 10(b) of the Securities Exchange Act of 1934 (the 1934 Act) prohibits "the use of a manipulative and deceptive device" in connection with the purchase or sale of any security.[21] SEC Rule 10b-5, promulgated under Section 10(b), makes it unlawful for any person, directly or indirectly in connection with the purchase and sale of a security, "to make any untrue statement of a material fact or to omit to state a material fact necessary in order to make the statements made, in the light of the circumstances under which they were made, not misleading."[22] This rule takes all dealings in securities to a higher level. The seller has an affirmative

---

21. 15 U.S.C. § 78j.
22. 17 C.F.R. § 240.10b-5.

duty to accurately state material facts and to not mislead; the buyer has a solid cause of action if the seller blows it. Rule 10b-5 and its state counterparts keep our courts packed with countless disgruntled investors who believe they were unfairly deceived when things didn't go as planned.

In offerings that are exempt from registration, the tool that is used to protect against antifraud risks is the private placement memorandum ("PPM"), a carefully prepared document that provides the necessary disclosures. Items typically included in a PPM include: The name, address, and telephone number of the issuer; a description and the price of the securities offered; the amount of the offering (minimum and maximum amounts, if any); the plan and cost of the distribution of the securities; an identification and description of the officers, directors, and advisers of the company; a description of company's business and products or services and the related technology; a discussion of the market for the issuer's products and services and related competition; a description of all risk factors, including those related to the company and those related to general market or economic conditions; a description of applicable resale restrictions and the related lack of liquidity impacts; and an explicit warning that the company could become insolvent or bankrupt and any investment in the company could be a total loss; recent financial statements of the company (audit not required); projections of future revenues, expenses, and profits or losses (optional); a description of how the proceeds realized from the offering will be used; a statement that neither the Securities and Exchange Commission nor any state securities commission has approved the securities or passed on the adequacy or accuracy of the disclosures in the PPM; a statement describing how the offering price was determined; a description of the company's present capital structure, prior offerings, and any outstanding stock plans or stock options; a description of the restrictions on the resale of the company's securities and the fact that no market now exists or may ever exist for the securities; a disclosure of any contracts or agreements with management; a disclosure of all significant contracts that the company has with third parties; copies of key documents related to the offering (legal opinions, Articles of Incorporation, etc.); and an offer for investors to meet with management, tour the company's facilities, and ask questions.

Resale Restrictions

The Securities Act of 1933 does not provide an exemption for private resale of restricted securities acquired through a private placement. In order to qualify for the private placement exemption, there can be no immediate distribution or resell by the initial purchasers of the securities. For that reason, companies should take precautions to protect against resells, which typically include confirming the investment intent of each purchaser, printing restrictive legends on the share certificates, issuing stop transfer instructions to any transfer agents, and obtaining purchaser representations in writing from each purchaser confirming that he or she is buying the security for his or her own account and not for resale or with a view to distribution.

There are options for a purchaser of restricted securities who desires to resell. SEC Rule 144[23] provides a non-exclusive safe harbor from registration for resells of restricted securities. Among other things, it imposes holding period and "dribble out" requirements. SEC Rule 144A[24] provides a separate safe harbor for resells to qualified institutional buyers. Also, the courts and the SEC have acknowledged an additional resale exception, known as the "Section 4(1 1/2)" exemption.[25] The SEC has characterized it as "a hybrid exemption not specifically provided for in the 1933 Act but clearly within its intended purpose" and has stated that it will apply "so long as some of the established criteria for sales under both section 4(1) and section 4(2) of the [1933] Act are satisfied."[26] Under this exemption, an investor holding restricted securities may resell the securities to another accredited investor who purchases them for his or her own account and not for distribution if the subsequent purchaser signs an appropriate investment letter and if the certificate issued bears appropriate legends for restricted securities.

2. COMMON SECURITY LAW MISCONCEPTIONS

The root cause of most trouble under the securities laws is ignorance. The client just didn't understand and didn't stop to think or ask for advice before charging ahead. There are many misconceptions that can get in the way. A challenge for the business advisor is to spot and eradicate these misconceptions before they become a problem. It's an ongoing educational effort with many business owners. Following is a brief summary of some of the most common misconceptions.

a. Big Guy Rules. Some business owners mistakenly assume that the securities laws apply only to public companies whose stock is regularly traded. It's the old "Why would the SEC want to mess with little old me?" notion. This misconception is supported by the little they read in the press (it's all focused on big companies), and the fact that none of their business owner friends have ever had to deal with the SEC. Although many securities law issues are uniquely directed at public companies and SEC efforts are focused on the public markets, the securities laws extend to any private security transaction between a company and individual investors. Size is not a prerequisite for Rule 10b-5. For most privately owned businesses, the fear is not a call from the SEC; it's a letter from a hungry plaintiff's lawyer who, armed with 10b-5 and a set of ugly facts, is making demands on behalf of unhappy investors at the worst possible time.

b. This Ain't a Security. The misconception is that the securities laws apply only to stocks. The term "security" is broadly defined in the 1933 Act to include, among other things, any note, bond, evidence of indebtedness, certificate of interest or participation in any profit-sharing agreement, and investment

---

23. 17 C.F.R. § 230.144.
24. 17 C.F.R. § 230.144A.
25. See SEC 1933 Act Release No. 33-6188 (Feb. 1, 1980) and Ackerberg v. Johnson, 892 F.2d 1328 (8th Cir. 1989).
26. SEC 1933 Act Release No. 33-6188 (Feb. 1, 1980). On this exemption, see Olander and Jacks, The Section 4 (1 1/2) Exemption – Reading Between the Lines of the Securities Act of 1933, 15 Sec. Reg. L.J. 339 (1988) and Schneider, Section 4 (1 1/2) – Private Resales of Restricted or Controlled Securities, 49 Ohio St. L.J. 501 (1988).

contract.[27] The Supreme Court has held that a "security" exists whenever money is invested in a common enterprise with profits to come solely from the efforts of others.[28] Applying this broad definition, courts have found a "security" in investment contracts involving worm farms, boats, silver foxes, oyster beds, vending machines, parking meters, cemetery plots, exotic trees, vineyards, fig orchards, chinchillas, beavers and more.[29] A flag should surface whenever a client claims or suggests that money can be raised by offering something that is *not* a "security."

c. The Safe, Dumb, Poor Crowd. Some mistakenly believe that it is "safer" to target unsophisticated investors who don't know the law and lack the means or the will to fight back if things go wrong. Plus, this group is "easier" because they don't know enough to ask the tough questions – that is, they can be fooled. This is dangerous thinking for a number of reasons. First, the most important registration exemption requires that the investors be accredited investors[30] or be non-accredited investors who are sophisticated in financial affairs or have representatives who possess such sophistication.[31] Second, the company loses the opportunity to bring in savvy investors who may contribute their wisdom and experience in addition to their money. Third (and this is the crux), besides just being a bad thing to do, the whole purpose of the securities laws is to protect the naive and uninformed from those who peddle intangible investments that promise riches. The dumb, poor investors may lack the capacity to evaluate what is being promised; but after things go bad, it doesn't take much to find an aggressive lawyer who is willing to spec the case against a contingent fee because, given the undisputed limitations of the plaintiffs, it's a slam dunk. Smart business owners generally limit their offers to accredited investors who have experience in financial and investment matters and who can afford the loss of their investment. In rare instances, they might consider a non-accredited individual, but only if that individual is sophisticated in financial matters and is investing a sum that he or she can afford to lose.

d. Only "Really Important" Stuff. The misconception is that only the "really important" information has to be disclosed because Rule 10b-5 speaks in terms of "material facts." Often this misconception is aggravated by the notion that the important information is the bottom-line conclusions that support the business plan. So, they reason, there's no need to sweat details that may complicate the money raising effort. The determination of a "material" fact within the meaning of Rule 10b–5 "depends on the significance the reasonable investor would place on the withheld or misrepresented information."[32] The "material" standard will be met if the misrepresentation or omission "would have been viewed by a reasonable investor as having significantly altered the 'total

---

27. 15 U.S.C. § 77b(1).

28. S.E.C. v. W.J. Howey Co., 328 U.S. 293 (1946).

29. See 2 L. Loss & J. Seligman, Securities Regulation (3rd ed. 1989-93) pp. 948-956.

30. Individuals are considered accredited investors if they have a net worth that exceeds $1 million (primary residence excluded) or an annual income of over $200,000 ($300,000 if married) for the most recent two years preceding the securities purchase. 15 U.S.C. § 77b(15) and 17 C.F.R. § 230.501(a).

31. The all-important Rule 506 exemption requires that nonaccredited investors be sophisticated investors. 17 C.F.R. § 230.506.

32. Basic Inc. v. Levinson, 485 U.S. 224, 240 (1988).

mix' of information made available."[33] It's a very broad definition that presents a mixed question of fact and law in most cases; it is decided as a matter of law only when reasonable minds would not differ on the issue.[34] It's a mistake to assume that the materiality requirement eliminates the need to provide details. Plus, there is another hard reality that always supports the conclusion that more, not less, should be disclosed. If things go bad and a significant contributing factor to the failure was not disclosed up front, it may be impossible, looking back, to claim that that factor was not material and worthy of disclosure. The wisest and safest approach is to lay out all known risk factors and the related details.

e. My Successes Say It All. Many business owners focus only on past successes when talking track record. Failures or disappointments are forgotten or "amended" to look like successes. The misconception is that it is appropriate to paint the best possible track record, even when it involves a little fudging or selective editing. A key executive's track record is important to any investor. What one has done in the past often is the best indicator of what might happen in the future. If things go bad, an investor who first learns after the fact that this was not the key person's first failure may be shocked into action. The challenge is to accurately and fairly summarize the background and experiences, both good and bad, of the key players in a way that suggests that they now possess the skills and abilities to successfully manage the proposed venture.

f. Good Advertising Is The Key. Some mistakenly assume that fundraising is all about advertising. They start a makeshift advertising campaign, only to learn that they have killed some of their best shots at a registration exemption. Although the JOBS Act of 2012 has opened up general solicitation and advertising in select Rule 506 offerings and presumably the crowdfunding world, usually the word of an exempt offering must be spread through friends, relatives and business associates.

g. Safety in Numbers. The misconception is that it is safer to have a large number of small investors, rather than one or two big players. It's based on the false assumption that a small investor will be more inclined to swallow a loss and less inclined to fight back. It ignores some basic realities. First, the size of one's investment does not govern the capacity to stomach a loss; many large players are better equipped to understand and suck up a loss than most small investors who have had unrealistic expectations from the get-go and can't afford any loss. Second, it ignores the capacity of many voices to stir each other up and to share the expense and burden of hiring a gladiator to fight their cause. Third, it ignores the burden, often horrendous, of having to respond to multiple ongoing inquiries all along the way from nervous, uninformed investors who just want to hear that all will pay off "as promised" and that there are "no problems." Finally, it ignores the significant value of binding a few key players to the effort. Inviting them into the inner circle gives the business the benefit of their advice and counsel and often eliminates any securities law exposure because they see it all, hear it all, and are part of it all.

h. Dodge the Downside. Some wrongfully assume that there is no need to

---

33. TSC Industries, Inc. v. Northway, Inc., 426 U.S. 438, 449 (1976).
34. Id. at 450.

talk about the potential of failure when trying to raise money. They figure that everyone knows there is risk. So why talk about it? The truth is that, from a securities law perspective, it is essential to spell out the risk factors in writing for any prospective investor. Nothing is more material than those factors that may potentially cause the business to fail. Thought should be given to risk factors that are specific to the business (competition, market condition changes, supply access, technology changes, skilled labor needs, capital and liquidity challenges, etc.) and the potential impact that general risks (e.g., interest rate increases) may have on the business. Often this is one of the most difficult tasks for business owners to embrace. As the risk factor list is committed to black and white, they begin to fear that everyone will be "spooked away." It helps to remind them that seasoned players are used to seeing such lists, and that they have all made money in ventures that started out with risk factor lists that were just as ugly as the one being created.

i. Projections Are Just Projections. The misconception is that since future projections, by their very nature, are speculative, they create an opportunity to strengthen the money raising effort by painting the rosiest possible picture of how things might play out. It's little wonder that such projections have been the driving force behind many securities law claims. The use of projections should be handled carefully. They should not be viewed as an opportunity to oversell, but rather as a means of illustrating the business' potential under a defined set of reasonable assumptions. If overdone, they may create unrealistic false expectations that cause an otherwise good performance to disappoint or, worse yet, fuel a legal dispute when things turn sour. There are a few important precautions that can be taken. First, make certain that the projections are based on reasonable assumptions that are spelled out. The operative word here is "reasonable;" the assumptions should not reflect an ideal, unrealistic set of conditions. Second, the predictions should be accompanied by a cautionary statement that identifies the predictions as forward-looking statements, warns that conditions and risks could cause actual results to differ substantially from the projections, and lists specific risks and conditions that may have such an effect. The effort may allow the company, if necessary, to rely on the "bespeaks caution doctrine" that provides a defense against allegations of false and misleading forward-looking statements when such precautionary language has been used.[35]

j. "Puffing" Works. Some business owners believe that the key to "legal money raising" is "puffing" – making vague overstated generalizations that get potential investors excited. Often they have heard about cases where defendants escaped securities law liability because the court concluded that the alleged misrepresentations were nothing more than "obviously immaterial puffery."[36] Statements like "our fundamentals are strong," "our product is revolutionary and could change the world," and "the stock is red hot" have been dismissed as immaterial puffing.[37] The problem is when it goes too far. What may appear as

---

35. See, e.g., In re Worlds of Wonder Sec. Litig., 35 F.3d 1407 (9th Cir. 1994); Gasner v. Board of Supervisors, 103 F.3d 351 (4th Cir. 1996); and Nadoff v. Duane Reade, Inc., 107 Fed. Appx. 250 (2d Cir. 2004).

36. See, e.g., Grossman v. Novell, Inc., 120 F.3d 1112 (10th Cir. 1997); Raab v. General Physics Corp., 4 F.3d 286 (4th Cir. 1993); and Helwig v. Vencor, Inc. 210 F.3d 612 (6th Cir. 2000).

37. Rosenzweig v. Azurix Corp., 332 F.3d 854 (5th Cir. 2003); Vosgerichian v. Commodore Int'l, 832

harmless puffing can trigger liability under the securities laws if the speaker had no reasonable basis for making the statement. The court will examine whether the speaker really believed that the statement was accurate and had a factual or historical basis for that belief.[38] There is some room for harmless puffing, but in no sense is it a free pass without limits.

k. Let 'Em Be. The misconception is that investors, once they've bought in, should be free to deal with their stock as they see fit. As described above, the private offering exemption requires that the investors not be used as a device to disseminate the stock to a broader audience and thereby convert what would otherwise be a private offering into a public offering. This important factor, coupled with the obvious antifraud challenges, gives the company a huge interest in what the investors do with their stock. For this reason, as described above, it is common practice to ascertain the investment intentions of purchasers up front, to place resale restrictive legends on share certificates, to issue stop transfer instructions to those who control the stock register, and to obtain written representations from all purchasers that they are acquiring the security for their own account and not for resale or with a view to distribute the stock.

l. Cashing In Is the Easy Part. This misconception surfaces when everybody just assumes that an acceptable exit strategy will present itself at the most opportune time. Often a business plan is developed with little or no thought given to the ultimate strategy that will be used to realize a return for the owners of the business. The organizers assume if things work out and the business becomes profitable, an opportunity will surface to cash in at the best time. No serious effort is made to research the practicality and possibility of specific exit scenarios. The details of operating the business and generating revenues have been thought through, but the broader picture is left to fuzzy notions of market options and base ignorance. This gets scary when an organizer with little knowledge starts speculating on return strategies with a potential investor who has even less knowledge. The organizer often has no specific knowledge regarding the appetite others may have for the business. The sad reality is that many business owner/managers are shocked and disappointed to discover that there is little or no market for their business. This disappointment can be magnified many times for the outside investor who draws no compensation and has assumed all along that a big payday was within reach. And then there are the baseless, overstated "going public" expectations. This sounds great to the naive investor, even though the organizer has no real clue as to what a public offering entails or requires. A primary challenge for many business owners is to develop a realistic expectation of the business' capacity to create returns for the owners. Seasoned entrepreneurs do this instinctively. Experience has taught them to always have their eye on the big picture and the entire life cycle of the business. Plus, they understand that conditions can change; what is solid and profitable today can be weak and vulnerable tomorrow. So timing is often the key when it comes to cashing in the marbles. Less experienced owners, particularly those who are wrapped up in their first effort, often fail to see, let alone focus on, the

---

F.Supp. 909 (E.D. Pa. 1993); Newman v. Rothschild, 651 F.Supp. 160 (S.D.N.Y. 1986).

38. See, e.g., Kline v. First Western Government Sec., 24 F.3d 480 (3d Cir. 1994), cert. denied 513 U.S. 1032 (1994) and In re Allaire Corp. Secs. Litig., 224 F.Supp.2d 319 (D. Mass. 2002).

broader picture and never develop such realistic expectations for themselves and those who have entrusted them with their money. As a result, they end up in a situation where they can only disappoint.

CASE PROBLEM 7-3

For the past three years, Wayne has been the sole owner and CEO of a corporation that manufactures and distributes a relatively expensive high-tech baby monitoring device known as "Hear All." The business has grown steadily, and Wayne is convinced that it's time to "shoot for the stars." To make this happen, Wayne needs $1.5 million of equity capital and an expanded bank line of credit that will be "doable without personal guarantees" based on the past record of the business and the new equity. Wayne is willing to give up 40 percent of the equity to secure the needed capital.

Wayne's brother-in-law Sam, a CPA and big fan of Wayne's product, claims to have "lined up the dough." Seven individuals will each contribute $200,000, and Sam will contribute $100,000. All Wayne knows is that the investors reside in three states, four of the seven are "doctor clients of Sam," two are mothers who "married right and love the product," and the last one is a "23-year-old kid who wants to be a musician and just inherited a bundle."

What additional facts do you need to advise Wayne relative to any registration exemptions under the federal securities laws? On the basis of the facts you have, which exemption likely will work best for Wayne?

CHAPTER 8

SHAREHOLDER VOTING AND PROPOSAL CHALLENGES

A. SHAREHOLDER VOTING

1. THE CONTROL - OWNERSHIP GAP

For decades economists and legal scholars have sought to explain and rationalize the role of shareholders in public corporations – or, perhaps better stated, the lack of a role. The roots of modern day analysis can be traced to a 1932 publication, *The Modern Corporation and Private Property*, where an economics professor (Gardiner Means) teamed up with a legal scholar (Adolf Berle) to study the 200 largest corporations listed on the New York Stock Exchange.

Means and Berle concluded that there is a distinct separation of control and ownership in a public corporation, shareholders have no control of the enterprise, management is a "self-perpetuating body" that runs the whole show, and enhanced legal protections are the only hope of protecting shareholders against the unfettered control and greed of management. As for the power of a shareholder at a meeting to impact the election of a slate of directors handpicked by management, Means and Berle aptly characterize the situation as follows, "As his personal vote will count for little or nothing at the meeting unless he has a very large block of stock, the stockholder is practically reduced to the alternative of not voting at all or else of *handing over his vote to individuals over whom he has no control and in whose selection he did not participate*." (Emphasis original).

No one has ever been able to credibly dispute the bottom line conclusions of Means and Berle. Many have tried to explain or rationalize them be developing various theories of how a public corporation should be viewed – everything from a team of producers that delegates control to a chosen few,[1] to an organization that is driven by political and economic forces,[2] to "nexus of contracts" arising from voluntary decisions of all stakeholders,[3] and more. But whatever the

---

1. See M. Blair and Lynn A. Stout, *A Team Production Theory of Corporate Law*, 85 Va. L. Rev. 247 (1999).
2. See Mark Roe, Strong Managers and Weak Owners: The Political Roots of the Separation of Ownership from Control (1994).
3. See Henry N. Butler, The Contractual Theory of the Corporation, 11 Geo. Mason U. L. Rev. 99 (1989).

theory, governance issues in a public corporation bear no resemblance to what happens in a closely held enterprise. A public corporation entrusts a small group of players with the power to manage a large pool of capital provided by many others. And as always, persuasive arguments will be advanced for the proposition that this concentration of power is necessary and proper to ensure the most efficient deployment of capital and labor for the common good.[4]

The inherent separation of control and ownership in a public corporation does not mean that the role of the shareholder is dead. Indeed, many factors that didn't exist in the days of Means and Berle continually push and facilitate greater shareholder awareness and oversight. These include the ever-growing concentration of economic power in institutional investors, new low-cost means of mass communication, and a heightened awareness of the dangers of unchecked greed in large organizations that operate on a world stage. Our laws have developed, and will continue to develop, in a direction that promotes management accountability and makes it easier for shareholders to be informed and have a voice. The general notion that enhanced shareholder involvement is good will drive many debates and regulatory changes. Many will applaud and seek to leverage these developments. But always undermining these efforts will be the hard reality that most public shareholders, out of laziness or a perceived lousy effort-benefit ratio, will not expend an ounce of energy looking beyond the movements in the price of the company's stock.

The Meeting Requirement. The shareholder meeting is the primary tool used for shareholder involvement. The Model Act and corporate statues mandate an annual meeting of the shareholders at a time and place specified in the bylaws.[5] Although an annual meeting of shareholders is required, corporate statutes typically provide that the failure to hold an annual meeting will "not affect the validity of any corporate action."[6] Common actions approved at an annual shareholders meeting include the election of directors, approval of the appointment of the company's auditors, approval of stock option plans and other executive compensation arrangements, ratification of select board actions, and consideration of shareholder proposals that have properly come before the meeting.

Special Meetings. At times a special meeting of the shareholders is necessary to approve a shareholder matter, such as a merger, that cannot await the next annual meeting. The Model Act and corporate statutes typically provide that a special meeting may be called by the board of directors, shareholders who own a designated percentage of the corporation's stock (i.e., 10 percent), and any other person authorized by the articles of incorporation or bylaws to call a special meeting.[7] The statutory percentage needed to call a special meeting usually may be changed by the articles of incorporation or bylaws so long as it does not exceed a stated maximum (25 percent under the Model Act).

---

4. See, for example, Stephan M. Bainbridge, *Director Primacy: The Means and Ends of Corporate Governance*, 97 NW. U. L. Rev. 547 (2003).

5. See, for example, MBCA § 7.01.

6. Id.

7. See MBCA § 7.02.

Notice. The corporation must set the date of the meeting and a date (the "record date") that will be used in determining the identity of the shareholders who are entitled to vote at the meeting. The officers of the corporation control these dates. Notice of the meeting must be sent to all shareholders who are entitled to vote at the meeting, typically 10 to 60 days in advance of the meeting date.[8] For special meetings, the purpose of the meeting must be described in the notice, and matters unrelated to the disclosed purpose may not be considered at the meeting.[9] In Delaware, the board has the option of setting two record dates: one to identify shareholders who are entitled to receive notice of the meeting, and another one closer to the meeting date to identify shareholders who are entitled to vote at the meeting.[10] Corporate statutes usually provide that notice of a meeting may be waived by a written waiver signed by the shareholder or by the shareholder attending the meeting and not objecting to lack of notice.[11]

Quorum. The successful passage of a matter at a meeting of shareholders requires the presence of a quorum and the casting of the requisite number of votes in support of the matter. Under the Model Act and most state statutes, the default shareholder quorum requirement usually is defined by statute as a majority of shares entitled to vote, although statutory authorization to establish a different quorum requirement in the articles of incorporation is common.[12] Delaware allows a corporation, by a majority vote of its shareholders, to amend its articles or bylaws to increase a quorum requirement or to decrease it to as low as one-third of the number of shares entitled to vote.[13]

Required Vote. As for the requisite voting requirement, once a quorum is present, corporate statutes usually specify that a matter will be deemed approved if a majority of the shares represented at the meeting vote in favor of the matter.[14] The result is that a shareholder matter often passes based on a favorable vote that is far less than a majority of the absolute number of shares outstanding. For director elections, the Model Business Corporation Act, as well as Delaware and most other states, provide that directors will be elected by a plurality of the votes cast.[15] On select matters, the articles of incorporation may require an approval vote of a majority of the total shares outstanding or may specify a super-majority voting requirement (i.e. two-thirds) based on either the shares represented at the meeting or the total number of shares outstanding. Some corporate statutes mandate such a super-majority requirement as a default rule that may be changed only in the corporation's articles of incorporation. Washington State, for example, has such a two-thirds default shareholder voting requirement for a merger, a share exchange, or the sale of substantially all of a corporation's assets.[16]

Consent Resolutions. In closely held corporations, shareholder matters that

---

8. See MBCA § 7.05.

9. See MBCA § 7.02(d).

10. 8 DGCL § 213(a).

11. See MBCA § 7.06.

12. See MBCA § 7.25.

13. 8 DGCL § 216.

14. See, for example, MBCA § 7.25(c) and 8 DGCL § 216.

15. See MBCA § 7.28 and 8 DGCL § 216(3)

16. RCW §§ 23B.11.030, 23B.12.020.

would typically require a meeting can often be handled without having an actual meeting. Most state corporate statutes authorize the use of written shareholder consent resolutions in lieu of a meeting. But unlike the requirements of director written consent statutes that uniformly require unanimous consent, the requirements of shareholder written consent statutes vary widely. The Model Business Corporation Act, for example, requires the written consent of all shareholders entitled to vote on the matter, determined as of the date the first shareholder consents in writing to the action.[17]

In contrast, Delaware permits approval of an action if shareholders owning a majority of the shares entitled to vote on the matter sign a written consent resolution. Written consents may be obtained over a 60 day period, and prompt notice that a matter has been approved by written consent must be sent to all non-consenting shareholders.[18] Other states permit action by unanimous written consent resolution, but authorize a corporation to include in its articles of incorporation a written consent procedure that requires only the number of votes that would be required at a meeting of the shareholders.[19]

However structured, a shareholder written consent procedure can be a valuable tool for any closely held corporation that wants to efficiently ensure that shareholder matters are appropriately approved and documented.

Proxies. The challenge is completely different for a public company. Shareholder meetings cannot possibly be avoided with written consent resolutions, and usually there is no hope of a quorum physically showing up at the meeting. That is why proxies are the name of the game for executives of a public company.

Every state has a statute that permits a shareholder to appoint another person as a proxy. It is done with a simple written document or electronic transmission that authorizes the other person to exercise the shareholder's voting rights at a meeting.[20] The appointed proxy may be granted discretion in voting the covered shares or may be specifically directed as to how the covered shares are to be voted on particular matters.

The appointment of a proxy usually may be revoked at any time unless it is an appointment coupled with an interest. For these purposes, a coupled interest typically includes an appointment to a pledgee, to a person who purchased or agreed to purchase the shares, to a creditor of the corporation who extended credit under terms requiring the appointment, to an employee of the corporation whose employment contract requires the appointment, or to a party of a voting agreement. Death or incapacity of the one appointing a proxy generally will not affect the right of the corporation to accept the proxy's authority unless notice of the death or incapacity is received by the secretary or other officer authorized to tabulate votes before the proxy exercises the authority under the appointment.[21]

---

17. MBCA § 7.04.
18. 8 DGCL § 228.
19. See, for example, Washington States statute, RCW 23B.07.040.
20. See, for example, MBCA § 7.22.
21. Id.

2. THE INDISPENSABLE ROLE OF PROXIES

The expectation and goal of the management of any public company is to make certain that, whenever they walk into a meeting room of stockholders (whether empty or packed), they have sufficient proxies in hand to ensure that a quorum is present and that every action supported by management passes by a wide margin. Huge sums of time and money are spent to get to this point. Proxy statements are carefully drafted, posted, printed, disbursed and filed with the SEC. Procedures and personnel are used to solicit and secure proxy appointments authorizing the company's management to vote the covered shares at the meeting.

Under the SEC's new, ever-evolving e-proxy rules,[22] a public corporation must post its proxy solicitation materials on a website (exclusive of the SEC's site) that is publicly available and "cookie free." The materials include proxy statements, proxy cards, information statements, annual reports to shareholders, notices of shareholder meetings, other soliciting materials, and any related amendments. The proxy materials also explain how a shareholder may vote in person, by mail, by phone (via a control number), or over the internet (via a control number). With this website posting, the corporation has two options, referred to as the "notice only" option and "full set delivery" option.

Many public corporations now use the "notice only" option. This option simply requires the corporation to mail shareholders, at least 40 days in advance of the meeting, a form that, in prominent, bold letters, states, "Important Notice Regarding the Availability of Proxy Materials for the Shareholder Meeting To Be Held on [*meeting date*]." The corporation is spared the expense and hassle of sending paper proxy materials to all shareholders. The notice to the shareholders should include:

1. A statement that the notice is not a form for voting;

2. A statement that the notice presents only an overview of the complete proxy materials, which contain important information and are available via the internet or by mail;

3. A statement that encourages shareholders to access and review the proxy materials before voting;

4. The internet website address where the proxy materials are available; and

5. Instructions on how shareholders may request a paper or email copy of the proxy materials at no charge, along with the date by which the request should be made and an explanation that, absent such a request, a paper or email copy of the materials will not be sent.

The second option available to public companies is the "full set delivery" option. This is the traditional paper model that companies have used for decades. The proxy materials are mailed to all shareholders. The company must still post all proxy materials on a "cookie free" internet website and send shareholders a "Notice of Internet Availability" with the proxy materials.

---

22. See generally SEC Rule 14a-16.

The proxy challenge is the primary corporate governance intersection of state and federal law. State corporate statutes dictate the circumstances that require proxies (where shareholder action is required) and authorize the use of proxies. But the regulation of proxies and the proxy solicitation process for all companies that must report under section 12 of the Securities Exchange Act of 1934, which include corporations whose securities are traded on a national exchange, are governed by federal law. Section 14(a) of the Securities Exchange Act makes it "unlawful" for any person "to solicit any proxy or consent or authorization in respect of any security" of a public company "in contravention of such rules and regulations as the Commission may prescribe as necessary or appropriate in the public interest or for the protection of investors." This statute puts the SEC in control of all matters related to public company proxy solicitations.

Of all the proxy rules promulgated by the SEC over the past eight decades, the most important (and frightening) is Rule 14a-9, which states:

> No solicitation subject to this regulation shall be made by means of any proxy statement, form of proxy, notice of meeting or other communication, written or oral, containing any statement which, at the time and in the light of the circumstances under which it is made, is false or misleading with respect to any material fact, or which omits to state any material fact necessary in order to make the statements therein not false or misleading or necessary to correct any statement in any earlier communication with respect to the solicitation of a proxy for the same meeting or subject matter which has become false or misleading.

Although neither section 14(a) of the Securities Exchange Act nor Rule 14a-9 refers to a private right of action for one who is injured by false or misleading proxy materials, the Supreme Court held that such a right existed in the celebrated case of in *J.J. Case Co. v. Borak*.[23] *Borak* and its aftermath have created a scope of personal liability that is a concern of every public company executive or director who participates in, or has responsibility for, the solicitation of proxies. Details of the *Borak* decision and liability exposure under Rule 14a-9 for false or misleading proxy materials are discussed in Section A. of Chapter 11.

The need to revise and update proxy regulations is an ongoing challenge for the SEC. New rules are needed to keep pace with technology advances, lessons learned from past experiences, and new matters that fall within the scope of shareholder governance. There is little question that many individual shareholders still end up with the same two options described by Means and Berle nearly 80 years ago – abstain or tender a proxy to those who are calling the shots. But, as discussed in the following section of this chapter, the scope of issues now presented to shareholders in public companies far exceeds anything Means and Berle saw in their survey.

One trend that has dramatically impacted the assessment of shareholder voting in public companies is the growth of institutional investors – mutual funds, state pension funds, hedge funds, labor union pension funds, corporate

---

23. 377 U.S. 426 (1964.

pension funds, and the like. In their working paper, "Institutional Investors and Stock Market Liquidity: Trends and Relationships," Wharton emeritus finance professor Marshall E. Blume and finance professor Donald B. Keim review trends in institutional stock ownership, noting that the growth of institutional investors in the stock market began after World War II. Before the war, from 1900 to 1945, the proportion of equities managed by institutional investors stayed close to five percent. After the war, institutional ownership ballooned. By 1980, institutions held $473 billion, 34 percent of the total market value of U.S. common stocks. By 2010, institutional ownership had grown to $11.5 trillion, or 67 percent of all stocks.

From a shareholder governance perspective, this concentration of equities in institutional investors is a mixed blessing. The sheer size of the amounts invested by an institution would suggest a close attention to detail and a willingness to be active in the affairs of its portfolio companies. And over the years, many institutional investors have been active, at times negotiating with management and, when necessary, using the shareholder proposal rules to fight director entrenchment efforts, the use of poison pills, excessive executive compensation plans, and more. But there are also many institutions that respond to the pressures of having to build their portfolios and perform for their investors by staying focused on short-term yield maximization, paths of least resistance, obedience to the norms of the investment community, liquidity options, avoiding conflicts and the appearance of conflicts, and cost reduction measures. It's not about the mantel of ownership; it's about an investment whose performance must be monitored against a market so that it can be sold at the right time.

For these reasons, pressure is building for more institutional investor transparency on shareholder governance initiatives. SEC Rule 30b1-4, which took effect on August 1, 2004, requires mutual fund managers to disclose how they voted on every shareholder proposal that surfaces in their portfolio companies. This change, which was staunchly opposed by the large mutual fund families, enables investors to see which fund managers, for their own sake, have a tendency to be rubber stamps for the managements of their portfolio companies.

Any attempt to evaluate the effectiveness of the proxy process is further complicated by the fact that 70 to 80 percent of the outstanding stock of public corporations is held in "street name" through custodians, such as banks and brokerage firms.[24] The custodians, in turn, hold the shares through accounts at Depository Trust Company (DTC), a depository institution and the record owner registered on the books of the company. The result is that it is difficult, often impossible, for a public company to ascertain the identity of the beneficial owners of all of its outstanding stock at a given point in time.

To satisfy the SEC proxy rules,[25] companies use a complicated, multi-tiered, circuitous process that, in theory, is designed to timely get proxy materials to the

---

24. See, generally, M. Kahan & E. Rock, *The Hanging Chads of Corporate Voting*, 96 The Georgetown L. J. 1227 (2008).

25. SEC Rules 14a-13, 14b-1, and 14b-2 mandate that a corporation implement procedures that attempt to communicate with beneficial owners through their nominees.

unidentified beneficial owners of its stock.[26] The process, by necessity, is fraught with unknowns in each application and produces results that cannot be verified. The company usually ends up with the proxies it needs, but many are signed by brokers who exercised their legal right to vote shares owned by clients who, for whatever reason, never responded to the proxy materials. And in some cases, the tallied results confirm multiple votes on the same shares that have been borrowed or lent to cover short sales.

What practical impact the new e-proxy procedures described above will have on this process and the inherent challenges of "street ownership" is yet to be determined. It will definitely reduce costs and hopefully will result in a higher percentage of beneficial owners actually receiving useful information that leads to a vote by proxy.

CASE PROBLEM 8-1

Franklin Engineering Inc. ("Franklin") provides custom concrete design and construction services for large commercial projects throughout the world. Franklin has a single class of voting common stock outstanding. Jason Rogers, age 64, is the president, chief executive officer, and chairman of the board of Franklin. Jason has a reputation of being a gifted engineer who cannot get along with anyone. He owns 15 percent of Franklin's outstanding common stock. The remaining 85 percent of Franklin's outstanding shares are owned as follows: 15 percent by nine other key executives of Franklin; 10 percent by Mary Lee; and 60 percent by 41 other individuals, none of whom owns more than three percent.

Franklin's articles of incorporation specify a seven-person board. The board consists of Jason, two Franklin executives, and four outsiders, all of whom were handpicked by Jason and own stock in Franklin (no one more than two percent). The board is fiercely loyal to Jason.

Eight months ago, Jason abruptly terminated Mary Lee, age 45, who at the time was second-in-command at Franklin. Mary was considered the "rising star" at Franklin and a tough competitor who had worked tirelessly to take the company to a new level. She enjoyed the admiration and respect of all Franklin's employees. Talk of when Mary would officially succeed Jason was frequent and always laced with an enthusiastic spin. Mary's termination shocked everyone. Jason, in a huff, just proclaimed that he was "finished with Mary's insubordination and know-it-all approach to virtually everything." Most chalked it up to Jason's ego and the "threat" Mary posed to Jason's "personal insecurities." Everyone considered it a major blow to the company.

As Mary left the annual shareholders meeting three weeks ago, she told many of her fellow shareholders, "Jason is losing it, and the company is badly losing traction and moving in the wrong direction." When most readily agreed, Mary started canvassing the shareholders. Within a week, she was convinced that shareholders owning 34 percent of the stock would "stand firm" behind a push to

---

26. For a thorough description of the process, see M. Kahan & E. Rock, *The Hanging Chads of Corporate Voting*, 96 The Georgetown L. J. 1227 (2008).

oust Jason and install her as Franklin's new CEO.

So with her 10 percent, Mary knows that she has a solid 44 percent that she can count on. Mary estimates that shareholders owning an additional 18 percent (the "Scared Minority") might support her bid if they do not have to face Jason in a meeting standoff. They shy away from meetings and are intimidated by Jason, but they sense something is wrong with the company, know Mary is popular with all the employees, and are concerned that Jason has lost the support of many around him. Shareholders owning the remaining 23 percent of the stock made it clear to Mary that they would not cross Jason, meaning that Jason (with his own shares) has a solid 38 percent support. Jason's supporters included the executive shareholders, all of whom claimed that they would "love to see Mary at the helm," but that they "couldn't possibly risk Jason's wrath" if Jason survived.

The net result is that Mary figures that if the Scared Minority stays away from any showdown or any votes from the Scared Minority split evenly, Mary would have a six point advantage over Jason.

Mary now needs help in deciding how she should proceed to unseat Jason. Assume that Franklin is incorporated in a state that has adopted the Model Business Corporation Act, which empowers shareholders to terminate directors with or without cause (MBCA § 8.08). How would you advise Mary to move forward? What additional facts would you like to have? Would your advice be any different if Franklin is incorporated in Delaware, which also empowers shareholders to remove directors with or without cause? 8 DGCL § 141(k).

3. INADVERTENT PROXY SOLICITATION RISKS

A communication to the shareholders of a corporation may constitute a proxy solicitation that is subject to the proxy rules even though the party responsible for the communication had no intention of moving into proxy territory. The source of this risk is the broad definition of a "solicitation" in Rule 14a-1(l):

(l) The terms "solicit" and "solicitation" include:

(i) Any request for a proxy whether or not accompanied by or included in a form of proxy[;]

(ii) Any request to execute or not to execute, or to revoke, a proxy; or

(iii) The furnishing of a form of proxy or other communication to security holders under circumstances reasonably calculated to result in the procurement, withholding, or revocation of a proxy.

If a communication is deemed a "solicitation" under this definition, all the proxy rules kick in, including the proxy statement and information rules,[27] the proxy card format rules,[28] the information disclosure format rules,[29] the filing requirements,[30] the antifraud rule for false or misleading statements,[31] and more.

---

27. Rule 14a-3.
28. Rule 14a-4.

Many courts have struggled with this inadvertent proxy solicitation risk. In *Union Pacific R.R. Co. v. Chicago & N.W. Ry Co.,*[32] for example, a report of a brokerage firm was sent by the firm to its clients at the same time the company sent copies of the report to its shareholders. The court held that the report constituted a proxy solicitation because, in the opinion of the court, the report was "reasonably calculated" to influence how the shareholders would vote on the matter that was the subject of the report. Similarly, in *Studebaker Corp. v. Gittlin,*[33] the Second Circuit held that a shareholder's written communication to other shareholders, requesting that they participate in a demand to inspect the corporation's shareholder list, constituted a proxy solicitation. Applicable law required that shareholders owning a least five percent of the company's outstanding stock participate in such a demand to inspect documents. The court reasoned that the written request to the other shareholders was part of a "continuous plan" to gain control of the board through shareholder action.

The following case took the issue to a whole new level.

LONG ISLAND LIGHTING COMPANY V. BARBASH
779 F.2d 793 (2nd Cir. 1985)

CARDAMONE, Circuit Judge:

A Long Island utility furnishing that area with power has scheduled a stockholders meeting for Thursday December 12, 1985. It has been embroiled in public controversy over its construction of the Shoreham Nuclear Power Plant and adverse publicity intensified recently because of extended loss of service to customers arising from damages to the transmission system caused by Hurricane Gloria.

In this setting, the company, believing that several groups had begun to solicit proxies during October in anticipation of the upcoming stockholders meeting, brought suit to enjoin them. The district court judge first slowed the matter by adjourning the case until the fall election was over, and then speeded it up by directing discovery to be completed in one day. Such handling only demonstrates again that in the law it is wise—even when expeditious action is required—to make haste slowly.

Long Island Lighting Company (LILCO) brings this expedited appeal from a November 8, 1985 order of the United States District Court for the Eastern District of New York (Weinstein, Ch.J.) that granted summary judgment dismissing LILCO's complaint against the Steering Committee of Citizens to Replace LILCO (the Citizens Committee), John W. Matthews and Island Insulation Corp. LILCO brought this action to enjoin defendants' alleged violations of § 14(a) of the Securities Exchange Act of 1934 and Rules 14a–9, 17 C.F.R. § 240.14a–9 and 14a–11, 17 C.F.R. 240.14a–11, promulgated under that statute, that govern proxy solicitations. The complaint alleges that defendants

---

29. Rule 14a-5.
30. Rule 14a-6.
31. Rule 14a-9.
32. 226 F.Supp. 400 (N.D. Ill. 1964).
33. 360 F.2d 692 (2nd Cir. 1966).

have committed such violations by publishing a false and misleading advertisement in connection with a special meeting of LILCO's shareholders scheduled for the purpose of electing a new LILCO Board of Directors. For the reasons explained below, this matter is remanded to the district court.

Plaintiff LILCO is a New York electric company serving Nassau and Suffolk Counties on Long Island, New York. Its common and preferred stocks are registered in accordance with Section 12(b) of the Securities Exchange Act and are traded on the New York Stock Exchange. Defendant John W. Matthews was an unsuccessful candidate for Nassau County Executive in the election held November 5, 1985. During the campaign he strongly opposed LILCO and its operation of the Shoreham Nuclear Power Plant. As an owner of 100 shares of LILCO's preferred stock and a manager of an additional 100 shares of common stock held by his company, Island Insulation Corp., Matthews initiated a proxy contest for the purpose of electing a majority of LILCO's Board of Directors. The stated purpose of the other defendants, the Citizens Committee, is to replace LILCO with a municipally owned utility company. The Citizens Committee was formed prior to this litigation, in order to challenge LILCO's construction of the Shoreham atomic energy plant, its service and its rates.

LILCO filed its complaint on October 21, 1985 alleging that defendants published a materially false and misleading advertisement in *Newsday,* a Long Island newspaper, and ran false and misleading radio advertisements throughout the New York area. The ads criticized LILCO's management and encouraged citizens to replace LILCO with a state-run company. The complaint sought an injunction against further alleged solicitation of LILCO shareholders until the claimed false and misleading statements had been corrected and a Schedule 14B had been filed. The district court granted LILCO an expedited hearing on its appeal from Magistrate Scheindlin's decision denying expedited discovery and also set for hearing defendants' motions to dismiss the complaint pursuant to Fed.R.Civ.P. 12(b)(6).

On October 30, 1985 Chief Judge Weinstein adjourned the hearing until November in order to prevent interference with Matthews' political campaign. The district court directed the defendants to bring the requested documents to the hearing on that date and told Matthews and others whom LILCO wished to depose to be available for such discovery. At the November 6 hearing the district judge directed LILCO's counsel to question Matthews under oath and overruled counsel's objections that he was unprepared to examine Matthews and that he had no prior opportunity to review the defendants' documents. The trial court also refused LILCO's request to question other defendants and told counsel that it must limit its questions to the alleged "conspiracy" between Matthews and the other defendants. Two days after this hearing the district court issued its Preliminary Memorandum Dismissing Complaint. Treating defendant's motion to dismiss as one for summary judgment, the district court granted summary judgment in favor of defendants on the ground that the proxy rules did not apply to the advertisements. This appeal followed.

In our view the district court further erred in holding that the proxy rules cannot cover communications appearing in publications of general circulation and that are indirectly addressed to shareholders. Regulation 14(a) of the Securities Exchange Act governs the solicitation of proxies with respect to the securities of publicly held companies, with enumerated exceptions set forth in the rules. 17 C.F.R. § 240.14a–1 *et seq.* Proxy rules promulgated by the Securities Exchange Commission (SEC) apply not only to direct requests to furnish, revoke or withhold proxies, but also to communications which may indirectly accomplish such a result or constitute a step in a chain of communications designed ultimately to accomplish such a result.

The question in every case is whether the challenged communication, seen in the totality of circumstances, is "reasonably calculated" to influence the shareholders' votes. Determination of the purpose of the communication depends upon the nature of the communication and the circumstances under which it was distributed.

Deciding whether a communication is a proxy solicitation does not depend upon whether it is "targeted directly" at shareholders. *See* Rule 14a–6(g), 17 C.F.R. § 240.14a–6(g) (requiring that solicitations in the form of "speeches, press releases, and television scripts" be filed with the SEC). As the SEC correctly notes in its amicus brief, it would "permit easy evasion of the proxy rules" to exempt all general and indirect communications to shareholders, and this is true whether or not the communication purports to address matters of "public interest."

Because discovery here was so abbreviated and the district court's determination was predicated on a mistaken notion of what constitutes a proxy solicitation and on the relationship between the proxy rules and the First Amendment, the case must be remanded to the district court.

WINTER, Circuit Judge, dissenting:

In order to avoid a serious first amendment issue, I would construe the federal regulations governing the solicitation of proxies as inapplicable to the newspaper advertisement in question. The content of the Committee's advertisement is of critical importance. First, it is on its face addressed solely to the public. Second, it makes no mention either of proxies or of the shareholders' meeting demanded by Matthews. Third, the issues the ad addresses are quintessentially matters of public political debate, namely, whether a public power authority would provide cheaper electricity than LILCO. Claims of LILCO mismanagement are discussed solely in the context of their effect on its customers. Finally, the ad was published in the middle of an election campaign in which LILCO's future was an issue.

On these facts, therefore, LILCO's claim raises a constitutional issue of the first magnitude. It asks nothing less than that a federal court act as a censor, empowered to determine the truth or falsity of the ad's claims about the merits of public power and to enjoin further advocacy containing false claims. We need not resolve this constitutional issue, however.

Where advertisements are critical of corporate conduct but are facially directed solely to the public, in no way mention the exercise of proxies, and debate only matters of conceded public concern, I would construe federal proxy regulation as inapplicable, whatever the motive of those who purchase them. This position, which is strongly suggested by relevant case law, maximizes public debate, avoids embroiling the federal judiciary in determining the rightness or wrongness of conflicting positions on public policy, and does not significantly impede achievement of Congress' goal that shareholders exercise proxy rights on the basis of accurate information.

It is of course true that LILCO shareholders may be concerned about public allegations of mismanagement on LILCO's part. However, shareholders are most unlikely to be misled into thinking that advertisements of this kind, particularly when purchased in the name of a committee so obviously disinterested in the return on investment to LILCO's shareholders, are either necessarily accurate or authoritative sources of information about LILCO's management. Such advertisements, which in no way suggest internal reforms shareholders might bring about through the exercise of their proxies, are sheer political advocacy and would be so recognized by any reasonable shareholder.

To be sure, the fact that a corporation has become a target of political advocacy might well justify unease among shareholders. No one seriously asserts, however, that the right to criticize corporate behavior as a matter of public concern diminishes as shareholders' meetings become imminent.

LILCO's Aftermath

The LILCO decision was one of many factors that sparked the SEC into taking a hard look at the need to amend the proxy rules. At the time of the LILCO decision, any communication deemed a proxy had to be preceded or accompanied by a written statement that complied with the federal proxy rules. Many argued that the board "solicitation" definition and the scary potential of violating the proxy rules discouraged shareholder communications, damaged the voting process, and further diminished the corporate governance role of shareholders. The upshot was four congressional hearing and years of debates and comments, all of which culminated in a major reform of the proxy rules in 1992. Following is a brief review of some of the key 1992 changes:

• The proxy rules no longer apply to solicitations conducted by persons ("disinterested parties") who do not seek proxy authority and who do not have a substantial interest in the subject matter of the vote. The antifraud provisions of Rule 14a-9 are still in play and there is a filing requirement for certain written communications, but the exemption eliminates all other proxy requirements. A person who owns more than $5 million of the company's securities must file with the SEC a notice within three days of any written solicitation, disclosing the person's name and address and a copy of the solicitation. The exemption does not apply to the company whose shares are the subject of the solicitation, any person acting on behalf of such company, a competitive bidder who is soliciting in opposition to a merger or other major transaction, persons seeking control of the company, or any person who would receive an extraordinary benefit (rather than share *pro rate* with other shareholders).

• A definition of "solicitation" no longer includes a public announcement of how a shareholder plans to vote on a particular matter and his or her rationale for doing so. Rule 14a-1. This definition refinement takes all such public communications outside the scope of all the proxy rules, including the antifraud provisions or Rule 14a-9. The provision will protect those, including fiduciaries and company officers and directors, who respond to requests from others about their voting intentions.

• Communications made in public speeches, press releases, newspapers, and other broadcast media do not need to be accompanied by a proxy statement so long as no proxy, consent or authorization accompanies the public statement and a proxy statement is on file with the SEC at the time of the communication. Rule 14a-3. This provision is designed to facilitate the use of public media in proxy contests.

• Most proxy solicitations are no longer be reviewed by the SEC's staff and, therefore, are no longer subject to a pre-filing requirement. Rules 14a-6, 14a-11, 14a-12, 14c-5. Such materials may be filed with the SEC and the national exchanges on the same day they are published or delivered directly to the shareholders. Solicitation may commence as soon as the materials are filed. Pre-filing reviews are still required for a company's initial proxy statement and certain transactions.

• A company's management may not group or bundle matters in order to force shareholders to cast a single vote on the bundled matters. Each item must be separately identified and voted on, although issues may be conditioned on one another so long as the voting consequences of the conditioning are clearly stated. Rules 14a-4(a),(b).

4. PLOYS TO FRUSTRATE SHAREHOLDER VOTING RIGHTS

SCHNELL v. CHRIS-CRAFT INDUS., INC.
285 A.2d 437 (Del. 1971)

HERRMANN, Justice.

This is an appeal from the denial by the Court of Chancery of the petition of dissident stockholders for injunctive relief to prevent management from advancing the date of the annual stockholders' meeting from January 11, 1972, as previously set by the by-laws, to December 8, 1971.

It will be seen that the Chancery Court considered all of the reasons stated by management as business reasons for changing the date of the meeting; but that those reasons were rejected by the Court below in making the following findings:

> I am satisfied, however, in a situation in which present management has disingenuously resisted the production of a list of its stockholders to plaintiffs or their confederates and has otherwise turned a deaf ear to plaintiffs' demands about a change in management designed to lift defendant from its present business doldrums, management has seized on a relatively new section of the Delaware Corporation Law for the

purpose of cutting down on the amount of time which would otherwise have been available to plaintiffs and others for the waging of a proxy battle. Management thus enlarged the scope of its scheduled October 18 directors' meeting to include the by-law amendment in controversy after the stockholders committee had filed with the S.E.C. its intention to wage a proxy fight on October 16.

Thus plaintiffs reasonably contend that because of the tactics employed by management (which involve the hiring of two established proxy solicitors as well as a refusal to produce a list of its stockholders, coupled with its use of an amendment to the Delaware Corporation Law to limit the time for contest), they are given little chance, because of the exigencies of time, including that required to clear material at the S.E.C., to wage a successful proxy fight between now and December 8. * * *."

In our view, those conclusions amount to a finding that management has attempted to utilize the corporate machinery and the Delaware Law for the purpose of perpetuating itself in office; and, to that end, for the purpose of obstructing the legitimate efforts of dissident stockholders in the exercise of their rights to undertake a proxy contest against management. These are inequitable purposes, contrary to established principles of corporate democracy. The advancement by directors of the by-law date of a stockholders' meeting, for such purposes, may not be permitted to stand.

When the by-laws of a corporation designate the date of the annual meeting of stockholders, it is to be expected that those who intend to contest the reelection of incumbent management will gear their campaign to the by-law date. It is not to be expected that management will attempt to advance the date in order to obtain an inequitable advantage in the contest.

Management contends that it has complied strictly with the provisions of the new Delaware Corporation Law in changing the by-law date. The answer to that contention, of course, is that inequitable action does not become permissible simply because it is legally possible.

Accordingly, the judgment below must be remanded, with instruction to nullify the December 8 date as a meeting date for stockholders; to reinstate January 11, 1972 as the sole date of the next annual meeting of the stockholders of the corporation; and to take such other proceedings and action as may be consistent herewith regarding the stock record closing date and any other related matters.

BLASIUS INDUSTRIES, INC. V. ATLAS CORP.
564 A.2d 651 (Del.Ch. 1988)

ALLEN, Chancellor.

The case was filed on December 30, 1987. As amended, it challenges the validity of board action taken at a telephone meeting of December 31, 1987 that added two new members to Atlas' seven member board. That action was taken as an immediate response to the delivery to Atlas by Blasius the previous day of a form of stockholder consent that, if joined in by holders of a majority of Atlas' stock, would have increased the board of Atlas from seven to fifteen members and would have elected eight new members nominated by Blasius.

As I find the facts of this first case, they present the question whether a board acts consistently with its fiduciary duty when it acts, in good faith and with appropriate care, for the primary purpose of preventing or impeding an unaffiliated majority of shareholders from expanding the board and electing a new majority. For the reasons that follow, I conclude that, even though defendants here acted on their view of the corporation's interest and not selfishly, their December 31 action constituted an offense to the relationship between corporate directors and shareholders that has traditionally been protected in courts of equity. As a consequence, I conclude that the board action taken on December 31 was invalid and must be voided.

Blasius is a new stockholder of Atlas. It began to accumulate Atlas shares for the first time in July, 1987. On October 29, it filed a Schedule 13D with the Securities Exchange Commission disclosing that, with affiliates, it then owed 9.1% of Atlas' common stock. It stated in that filing that it intended to encourage management of Atlas to consider a restructuring of the Company or other transaction to enhance shareholder values. It also disclosed that Blasius was exploring the feasibility of obtaining control of Atlas, including instituting a tender offer or seeking "appropriate" representation on the Atlas board of directors.

Blasius has recently come under the control of two individuals, Michael Lubin and Warren Delano. In May, 1987, with Drexel Burnham serving as underwriter, Lubin and Delano caused Blasius to raise $60 million through the sale of junk bonds. A portion of these funds were used to acquire a 9% position in Atlas. According to its public filings with the SEC, Blasius' debt service obligations arising out of the sale of the junk bonds are such that it is unable to service those obligations from its income from operations. The prospect of Messrs. Lubin and Delano involving themselves in Atlas' affairs, was not a development welcomed by Atlas' management.

Immediately after filing its 13D on October 29, Blasius' representatives sought a meeting with the Atlas management. At that meeting, Messrs. Lubin and Delano suggested that Atlas engage in a leveraged restructuring and distribute cash to shareholders. In such a transaction, which is by this date a commonplace form of transaction, a corporation typically raises cash by sale of assets and significant borrowings and makes a large onetime cash distribution to shareholders. The shareholders are typically left with cash and an equity interest in a smaller, more highly leveraged enterprise. Lubin and Delano gave the outline of a leveraged recapitalization for Atlas as they saw it.

Immediately following the meeting, the Atlas representatives expressed among themselves an initial reaction that the proposal was infeasible. On December 7, Mr. Lubin sent a letter detailing the proposal. This written proposal was distributed to the Atlas board on December 9 and Goldman Sachs was directed to review and analyze it. The proposal met with a cool reception from management. Blasius attempted on December 14 and December 22 to arrange a further meeting with the Atlas management without success. During this period, Atlas provided Goldman Sachs with projections for the Company. Lubin was told that a further meeting would await completion of Goldman's analysis. A meeting after the first of the year was proposed.

On December 30, 1987, Blasius caused Cede & Co. (the registered owner of its Atlas stock) to deliver to Atlas a signed written consent (1) adopting a precatory resolution recommending that the board develop and implement a restructuring proposal, (2) amending the Atlas bylaws to, among other things, expand the size of the board from seven to fifteen members-the maximum number under Atlas' charter, and (3) electing eight named persons to fill the new directorships. Blasius also filed suit that day in this court seeking a declaration that certain bylaws adopted by the board on September 1, 1987 acted as an unlawful restraint on the shareholders' right, created by Section 228 of our corporation statute, to act through consent without undergoing a meeting.

The reaction was immediate. Mr. Weaver conferred with Mr. Masinter, the Company's outside counsel and a director, who viewed the consent as an attempt to take control of the Company. They decided to call an emergency meeting of the board, even though a regularly scheduled meeting was to occur only one week hence, on January 6, 1988. The point of the emergency meeting was to act on their conclusion (or to seek to have the board act on their conclusion) "that we should add at least one and probably two directors to the board ..."

A quorum of directors, however, could not be arranged for a telephone meeting that day. A telephone meeting was held the next day. At that meeting, the board voted to amend the bylaws to increase the size of the board from seven to nine and appointed John M. Devaney and Harry J. Winters, Jr. to fill those newly created positions. Atlas' Certificate of Incorporation creates staggered terms for directors; the terms to which Messrs. Devaney and Winters were appointed would expire in 1988 and 1990, respectively.

In increasing the size of Atlas' board by two and filling the newly created positions, the members of the board realized that they were thereby precluding the holders of a majority of the Company's shares from placing a majority of new directors on the board through Blasius' consent solicitation, should they want to do so. Indeed the evidence establishes that that was the principal motivation in so acting.

The conclusion that, in creating two new board positions on December 31 and electing Messrs. Devancy and Winters to fill those positions the board was principally motivated to prevent or delay the shareholders from possibly placing a majority of new members on the board, is critical to my analysis of the central issue posed by the first filed of the two pending cases. If the board in fact was not so motivated, but rather had taken action completely independently of the consent solicitation, which merely had an incidental impact upon the possible effectuation of any action authorized by the shareholders, it is very unlikely that such action would be subject to judicial nullification..

Plaintiff attacks the December 31 board action as a selfishly motivated effort to protect the incumbent board from a perceived threat to its control of Atlas. Defendants, of course, contest every aspect of plaintiffs' claims. They claim the formidable protections of the business judgment rule..

While I am satisfied that the evidence is powerful, indeed compelling, that the board was chiefly motivated on December 31 to forestall or preclude the possibility that a majority of shareholders might place on the Atlas board eight new members sympathetic to the Blasius proposal, it is less clear with respect to the more subtle motivational question: whether the existing members of the board did so because they held a good faith belief that such shareholder action would be self-injurious and shareholders needed to be protected from their own judgment.

On balance, I cannot conclude that the board was acting out of a self-interested motive in any important respect on December 31. I conclude rather that the board saw the "threat" of the Blasius recapitalization proposal as posing vital policy differences between itself and Blasius. It acted, I conclude, in a good faith effort to protect its incumbency, not selfishly, but in order to thwart implementation of the recapitalization that it feared, reasonably, would cause great injury to the Company.

The real question the case presents, to my mind, is whether, in these circumstances, the board, even if it is acting with subjective good faith (which will typically, if not always, be a contestable or debatable judicial conclusion), may validly act for the principal purpose of preventing the shareholders from electing a majority of new directors. The question thus posed is not one of intentional wrong (or even negligence), but one of authority as between the fiduciary and the beneficiary.

The shareholder franchise is the ideological underpinning upon which the legitimacy of directorial power rests. Generally, shareholders have only two protections against perceived inadequate business performance. They may sell their stock (which, if done in sufficient numbers, may so affect security prices as to create an incentive for altered managerial performance), or they may vote to replace incumbent board members.

It has, for a long time, been conventional to dismiss the stockholder vote as a vestige or ritual of little practical importance. It may be that we are now witnessing the emergence of new institutional voices and arrangements that will make the stockholder vote a less predictable affair than it has been. Be that as it may, however, whether the vote is seen functionally as an unimportant formalism, or as an important tool of discipline, it is clear that it is critical to the theory that legitimates the exercise of power by some (directors and officers) over vast aggregations of property that they do not own. Thus, when viewed from a broad, institutional perspective, it can be seen that matters involving the integrity of the shareholder voting process involve consideration not present in any other context in which directors exercise delegated power.

The distinctive nature of the shareholder franchise context also appears when the matter is viewed from a less generalized, doctrinal point of view. From this point of view, as well, it appears that the ordinary considerations to which the business judgment rule originally responded are simply not present in the shareholder voting context. That is, a decision by the board to act for the primary purpose of preventing the effectiveness of a shareholder vote inevitably involves the question who, as between the principal and the agent, has authority with respect to a matter of internal corporate governance. That, of course, is true in a very specific way in this case which deals with the question who should constitute the board of directors of the corporation, but it will be true in every instance in which an incumbent board seeks to thwart a shareholder majority. A board's decision to act to prevent the shareholders from creating a majority of new board positions and filling them does not involve the exercise of the corporation's power over its property, or with respect to its rights or obligations; rather, it involves allocation, between shareholders as a class and the board, of effective power with respect to governance of the corporation. Action designed principally to interfere with the effectiveness of a vote inevitably involves a conflict between the board and a shareholder majority. Judicial review of such action involves a determination of the legal and equitable obligations of an agent towards his principal. This is not, in my opinion, a question that a court may leave to the agent finally to decide so long as he does so honestly and competently; that is, it may not be left to the agent's business judgment.

Plaintiff argues for a rule of per se invalidity once a plaintiff has established that a board has acted for the primary purpose of thwarting the exercise of a shareholder vote. A per se rule that would strike down, in equity, any board action taken for the primary purpose of interfering with the effectiveness of a corporate vote would have the advantage of relative clarity and predictability. It also has the advantage of most vigorously enforcing the concept of corporate democracy. The disadvantage it brings along is, of course, the disadvantage a per se rule always has: it may sweep too broadly.

In two recent cases dealing with shareholder votes, this court struck down board acts done for the primary purpose of impeding the exercise of stockholder voting power. In doing so, a per se rule was not applied. Rather, it was said that, in such a case, the board bears the heavy burden of demonstrating a compelling justification for such action.

In my view, our inability to foresee now all of the future settings in which a board might, in good faith, paternalistically seek to thwart a shareholder vote, counsels against the adoption of a per se rule invalidating, in equity, every board action taken for the sole or primary purpose of thwarting a shareholder vote, even though I recognize the transcending significance of the franchise to the claims to legitimacy of our scheme of corporate governance. It may be that some set of facts would justify such extreme action. This, however, is not such a case.

Defendants have demonstrated no sufficient justification for the action of December 31 which was intended to prevent an unaffiliated majority of shareholders from effectively exercising their right to elect eight new directors. The board was not faced with a coercive action taken by a powerful shareholder against the interests of a distinct shareholder constituency (such as a public minority). It was presented with a consent solicitation by a 9% shareholder. Moreover, here it had time (and understood that it had time) to inform the shareholders of its views on the merits of the proposal subject to stockholder vote. The only justification that can, in such a situation, be offered for the action taken is that the board knows better than do the shareholders what is in the corporation's best interest. While that premise is no doubt true for any number of matters, it is irrelevant (except insofar as the shareholders wish to be guided by the board's recommendation) when the question is who should comprise the board of directors. The theory of our corporation law confers power upon directors as the agents of the shareholders; it does not create Platonic masters. It may be that the Blasius restructuring proposal was or is unrealistic and would lead to injury to the corporation and its shareholders if pursued. Having heard the evidence, I am inclined to think it was not a sound proposal. The board certainly viewed it that way, and that view, held in good faith, entitled the board to take certain steps to evade the risk it perceived. It could, for example, expend corporate funds to inform shareholders and seek to bring them to a similar point of view. But there is a vast difference between expending corporate funds to inform the electorate and exercising power for the primary purpose of foreclosing effective shareholder action. A majority of the shareholders, who were not dominated in any respect, could view the matter differently than did the board. If they do, or did, they are entitled to employ the mechanisms provided by the corporation law and the Atlas certificate of incorporation to advance that view. They are also entitled, in my opinion, to restrain their agents, the board, from acting for the principal purpose of thwarting that action.

I therefore conclude that, even finding the action taken was taken in good faith, it constituted an unintended violation of the duty of loyalty that the board owed to the shareholders. I note parenthetically that the concept of an unintended breach of the duty of loyalty is unusual but not novel. See *AC Acquisitions Corp. v. Anderson, Clayton & Co.*, Del.Ch., 519 A.2d 103 (1986). That action will, therefore, be set aside by order of this court.

Advance Notice Bylaws (Round Two)

Many public companies have adopted advance notice bylaws that create an additional obstacle for shareholders who want to raise an issue at a meeting of shareholders. The purpose of an advance notice bylaw is to promote the smooth running of an annual meeting by requiring a shareholder to advise the company of an intention to introduce business at the meeting. If the mandated advance notice or other requirements of the bylaw are not satisfied, the officer running the meeting may prohibit the new business from being introduced at the meeting. The bylaw presumably helps management prepare for the meeting, facilitates advising other shareholders of what to expect at the meeting, and gives the company time to formulate its response and recommendations.

Two Delaware cases in 2008 leveled a blow at first generation advance notice bylaws. In *Jana Master Fund, Ltd. vs. CNET Networks, Inc. ("CNET")*, 2008 WL 660556 (Del. Ch. 2008), affirmed 947 A.2d 1120 (Del. 2008), Jana's goal was to gain control of CNET's classified board by replacing two existing directors, expanding the size of CNET's board by five directors, and electing its own slate to fill the seven open seats. When CNET received notice from Jana of its intent to conduct its own proxy solicitation, CNET claimed that Jana had not complied with CNET's advance notice bylaw requirement that proponents hold at least $1,000 worth of CNET stock for at least one year. In rejecting CNET's claim, the court held that the advance notice bylaw was applicable only to proposals that shareholders sought to have included in CNET's proxy statement under SEC Rule 14a-8 (discussed in next section) and, as a result, Jana's nominations and proposals were not subject to the advance notice bylaw.

In *Levitt Corp. vs. Office Depot, Inc.* 2008 WL 1724244 (Del. Ch. 2008), Levitt Corp. nominated its slate of directors and filed its own proxy materials after Office Depot had filed its definitive proxy materials with the SEC, but Levitt did not comply with Office Depot's advance notice bylaw that required advance notice to Office Depot's secretary for any "business to be properly brought before an annual meeting." The court broadly interpreted the word "business" in the bylaw, holding that Levitt was not required to comply with the bylaw because Office Depot had already brought to the meeting the "business" of nominating and electing directors through its own proxy materials.

The *CNET* and *Office Depot* cases helped spawn a new generation of the advance notice bylaws that have been fine tuned to better withstand the kind of interpretive attacks that were mounted in these cases. A round two advance notice bylaw typically:[34]

1. Requires detailed disclosure of the ownership interests of the proposal's proponents;

2. Specifies that compliance with the advance notice bylaws is the exclusive means by which a shareholder may bring a proposal or nomination before a meeting of shareholders;

3. Clarifies that the advance notice bylaw does not affect the right of a shareholder to include a proposal in the company's proxy statement under Rule 14a-8;

4. Mandates broad disclosure of relationships between any shareholder proponent and persons associated with such proponent in connection with any nomination or proposal;

5. States specifically that the presiding officer of a shareholder meeting has the authority to disregard any proposal or nomination that does not comply with the bylaw;

6. Often requires shareholder nominees to complete a questionnaire or provide specific information requested by the company; and

7. Specifies a window of time that proposals may be submitted in advance of a meeting, usually tied to the anniversary date of the prior year's annual meeting.

---

34. See generally, Kevin Douglas, Stephen Hinton and Eric Knox, *Advance Notice Bylaws: The Current State of Second Generation Provisions*, Deal Lawyers (July-August 2011).

As for the advance notice time window, a recent survey[35] showed that 84 percent of the public companies surveyed had a window notice period of 90-120 days prior to the meeting, nine percent had a notice period 60-90 days prior to the meeting, and seven percent had a notice period of 120-150 days prior to the meeting. The Delaware Court of Chancery in *Coggin v. Vermillion, Inc.*, C.A. No. 6465-VCN (Del. Ch. June 3, 2011), (which involved a proxy statement notice period, not a bylaw) suggested that an advance notice provision of 150 days would not be unreasonably long or unduly restrictive.

B. SHAREHOLDER PROPOSALS

1. HISTORY AND SCOPE

The first SEC rule relating to shareholder proposals (the predecessor to current Rule 14a-8) was adopted in 1942 on the heels of various laws and regulatory developments that prevented active investors from playing a role in the governance of public corporations. Shareholder proposals aimed at improving corporate performance and governance immediately started showing up, and the volume of proposals mushroomed over the next 30 years. In 1970, the landmark Dow Chemical decision[36] set forth below opened the door for shareholder proposals focused on social issues and the related impacts on the targeted corporation. The social issue agenda grew in both scope and volume. In 1978, for example, of the 790 shareholder proposals on public company agendas, 179 related to social issues.

Prior to the mid-1980s, individual activists drove the shareholder proposal movement. Often the roots of numerous proposals directed to many different companies could be traced to a handful of activists. In 1982, for example, a startling 29 percent of the 972 proposal requests received by 358 public companies came from three individuals.[37] Collective efforts began to take hold midway through the Reagan years. In 1986, T. Boone Pickens founded the United Shareholders Association for the express purpose of "upgrading shareholder awareness," and, for many years, this association actively targeted specific companies for corporate governance shareholder proposals. Since that time, the movement has been advanced by other coalitions, including the Investors' Rights Association of America that was founded in 1995 and The Investors for Director Accountability that was organized in 2006.[38]

And, of course, over the years the shareholder proposal agendas for public companies have been heavily influenced by the ever-growing presence of institutional investors. As described above, institutional ownership of public securities ballooned during the post-World War II period from a stable five

---

35. Id.

36. *Medical Committee for Human Rights v. Securities and Exchange Commission*, 432 F.2d 659 (C.A.D.C. 1970).

37. Remarks of SEC Commissioner James C. Treadway, Jr., *The Shareholder Proposal Rule*, Edison Electric Institute Seminar (June 23, 1983); Donald H Chew, Jr., Stuart L. Gillan, Donald H. Chew, *U.S. Corporate Governance* (Columbia University Press 2009), pp. 204-207.

38. Donald H Chew, Jr., Stuart L. Gillan, Donald H. Chew, *U.S. Corporate Governance* (Columbia University Press 2009), pp. 204-207.

percent of the market in the pre-war years to over 67 percent ($11.5 trillion) of all public stocks by 2010. A major event occurred in 1985 when Jesse Unruh, treasurer of the State of California, founded The Council of Institutional Investors. As California's treasurer, Unruh had direct responsibility for the performance of the California Public Employees Retirement System and the California State Teachers Retirement System. These funds were substantial investors in Texaco at the time Texaco paid a $137 million premium to redeem Texaco stock from a large investor who had acquired a substantial interest (9.8 percent) in the company. The redemption was a wakeup call for Unruh, who responded by forming the Council to serve as an activist and lobbying force for shareholder rights. The Council is now the vehicle that drives many institutional corporate governance advocates. It is comprised of more than 140 public, labor, and corporate pension funds whose financial assets collectively exceed more than $3 trillion.[39]

Another compelling institutional force has been advisory firms such as Institutional Shareholder Services (ISS), an organization that studies and provides information on corporate proxy votes, principally for the benefit of institutional investors (pension funds, college endowments, etc.). ISS also makes recommendations as to whether it is in a shareholder's best interest to vote for or against particular matters, and it advises a wide range of companies on corporate governance issues. Over its 25 year history, ISS has built a staff of over 600 professionals and a client base that includes more than 1,700 companies.[40]

A review of the shareholder proposal activity for the S&P 500 companies during the 2012 proxy season illustrates the vibrancy and scope of the shareholder proposal movement. In 2012, the shareholders of these 500 companies considered 369 proposals, 68 of which garnered enough shareholder support to pass. The proposals focused on governance issues, social issues and executive compensation issues.[41]

Governance Shareholder Proposals. The shareholders of the S&P 500 companies considered 164 corporate governance shareholder proposals in 2012. These included proposals (a) to separate the roles of the corporation's chief executive officer and chair of the board of directors (38 proposals), (b) to create a new right for shareholders to call a special meeting or to lower the percentage required to call a special meeting (13 proposals); (c) to grant shareholders the right to act through written consent resolutions (19 proposals); (d) to remove classified boards, (e) to adopt majority voting (instead of plurality voting) in director elections; and (f) to eliminate super-majority shareholder voting requirements for removing directors, amending the corporation's articles or bylaws, or approving major transactions. Many of these were precatory proposals that simply requested the board of directors to take action. Directors who do not implement a proposal that has passed should expect negative recommendations from proxy advisory firms when re-election time rolls around. ISS policies, for

---

39. Id.

40. See www.issgovernance.com.

41. For all of the following data on the 2012 proxy filing season and addition information regarding shareholder proposal activity during 2012, see the publication of Sullivan & Cromwell LLP entitled *2012 Proxy Season Review*, dated July 9, 2012.

example, mandate a negative recommendation for all incumbent directors if a precatory proposal is approved by holders of a majority of the company's outstanding shares and the board fails to promptly and responsibly act on the matter.

For the first time proposals relating to "exclusive forum" bylaw provisions surfaced in 2012. These bylaw provisions mandate that Delaware be the exclusive forum for specified corporate litigation, including shareholder class actions and derivative suits. The proposals (very small in number) came in two forms: proposals by shareholders seeking to remove an "exclusive form" bylaw adopted by the board, and proposals by management to have shareholders approve their adoption of such a bylaw. Although a board has the authority to adopt such a bylaw without shareholder approval, these management proposals were presumably made to discourage any shareholder attacks. Although ISS recommended against such bylaws, the shareholder proposals to remove the bylaws failed, and the management proposals to bless the bylaws received strong support. This result may say nothing about the advisability of such bylaws from a corporate governance perspective. It may just be further confirmation of managements' ability to get what it wants through the proxy voting process.

A total of 68 of the 164 governance shareholder proposals passed in 2012, up from 52 proposals in 2011. The significance of this improvement was enhanced by a New York Stock Exchange Information Memo released in January 2012 that prohibited brokers from voting on certain types of corporate governance proposals without instructions from the beneficial owners of the shares. In past years, brokers would generally vote uninstructed shares in favor of governance proposals that ISS and others supported. Because beneficial stock owners often do not provide voting instructions, this NYSE release had the effect reducing the number of positive votes for the proposals, measured as a percentage of total shares outstanding.

Social Issue Shareholder Proposals. The shareholders of the S&P 500 companies considered 139 social issue shareholder proposals in 2012. These included proposals dealing with political issues (66), environmental issues (30), sustainability reporting issues (11), labor issues (10), human rights issues (8), animal right issues (7), and various other social issues (7). The political issue proposals related primarily to additional disclosures on political expenditures and lobbying costs and, in select cases, requests for an advisory vote on political spending or the prohibition of such spending. As in 2011 and many prior years, none of the social issue proposals passed in 2012. They collectively received a total percentage vote of 19 percent, far less than the 51 percent total vote in favor of governance proposals. The range of support levels for various social issue proposals usually varies widely, with proposals calling for advisory votes or spending prohibitions often receiving no more than one percent support, and proposals calling for expanded disclosures often receiving well in excess of 40 percent support. Many activists argue that the value of a social issue shareholder proposal that is doomed to fail is the heightened awareness it creates for all corporate stakeholders, particularly the directors, and the momentum for support that it incrementally builds over many years.

Compensation-Related Shareholder Proposals. The shareholders of the S&P 500 companies considered 55 compensation-related shareholder proposals in 2012. These included proposals dealing with executive stock retention requirements (25), golden parachute limitations (10), pay and performance link requirements (6), and other compensation issues (14). The universal advisory say-on-pay voting requirement that took effect in 2011 (see section C. of Chapter 9) significantly reduced the volume of compensation-related shareholder proposals in 2011 and 2012. The primary focus of compensation-related proposals in 2012 – executive stock retention policies – is not a topic within the scope of the new say-on-pay rights. These proposals require executives to retain a specified amount (often as much as 75 percent) of shares acquired through compensation plans for a specified period that often extends beyond retirement. None of the compensation-related proposals passed in 2012, only two passed in 2011 (both golden parachute proposals), and the percentage of votes cast in favor of the proposals averaged only 26 percent.

2. ACCESSING THE PROXY MACHINE

The threshold challenge of every shareholder proposal effort is to force the company's management to include the proposal in the proxy materials for the next annual meeting of shareholders. This leveraging of the company's proxy machine saves big money and efficiently gets the proposal to the shareholders. Without this proxy help, the proposal's proponents may secure a list of shareholders under Rule 14a-7 and launch a solo effort to get the shareholders informed and excited. But it's an expensive, inefficient alternative that usually doesn't get past the first wave of brainstorming.

The company's management is the gatekeeper of the proxy machine and the agenda of the annual meeting of shareholders. Their natural tendency is to not "junk up" the proxy materials or the meeting agenda with multiple proposals that they often characterize as useless, distracting complaints from shareholder factions that do not understand the company's business and have a unique axe to grind. This is where Rule 14a-8 takes center stage. The function of the rule is to determine which shareholder proposals may be excluded by management and to establish a procedure that requires management to consider proposal requests and fairly assess the grounds for exclusion.

The rule imposes basic requirements on the proponent of a proposal.[42] The proponent must have owned the lesser of $2,000 worth of the company's stock or one percent of the company's outstanding stock for at least one year prior to submitting the proposal. A proponent may submit only one proposal for a meeting, and the proposal may not exceed 500 words. The proposal must be submitted at least 120 days prior to the anniversary date of the company's proxy statement for the prior year.

There is no prescribed form for a proposal request. Anything from a one page letter to a full blown memorandum with legal opinion attached will get the attention of the company's management. If a decision is made to include the

---

42. See, generally, SEC Rule 14a-8, which uses a question and answer format.

proposal, the proposal moves forward. It is included in the proxy materials, the proponent gears up to be heard at the shareholders meeting, and the company's management states whether they support or oppose the proposal and their related rationale.

If the company rejects the proposal, it must send a letter to the SEC that discloses its intention to reject the proposal. The letter is accompanied by a legal opinion that explains the grounds of the rejection. If the staff of the SEC agrees with the grounds for exclusion, it sends a simple letter that acknowledges (with no details) that there appears to be a basis for exclusion. If the SEC rejects the company's grounds for exclusion, the SEC's responsive letter states that it is unable to concur and explains the basis of its decision. On select occasions, the SEC suggests changes in the proposal (usually as to form) that will eliminate the grounds for exclusion.

In nearly all cases, the SEC's response is the final word. Although the proponent of the proposal may seek injunctive relieve to have the grounds of rejection reviewed by a court, the costs and uncertainties of such a proceeding are often prohibitive. And, of course, the company could choose to act contrary to the SEC's response and risk a more aggressive response from the SEC, but it is not something that happens. The SEC's no-action letter does the job in nearly all cases.

They key to the whole process, of course, is the permitted grounds for excluding a proposal, which are set forth in Rule 14a-8(i). Many are obvious and seldom trigger a dispute: the proposal that involves a violation of law, deals with a personal grievance or special interest, conflicts with a proposal of the company, is substantially implemented, is duplicative, or is a resubmission. The four grounds that generally define the battleground are:

1. The proposal is improper under state law because it infringes on the management authority of the board of directors;

2. The proposal is not relevant because it relates to less than five percent of the company's assets or less than 5 percent of the company's net income or gross sales and does not raise significant social policy issues related to the company's business;

3. The proposal relates to ordinary business and management functions that are part of the operating details for running the company's business; and

4. The proposal relates to elections.

CASE PROBLEM 8-2

Assume the same facts as in Case Problem 8-1, with the following changes:

1. Jason owns four percent of Franklin's outstanding shares; the other Franklin executives own five percent; Mary owns three percent; and the remaining shares are traded on the NASDAQ.

2. At the time of her departure from Franklin, Mary made the following observation in a short speech to many Franklin employees:

Jason's primary problem with me is that I have strongly opposed his efforts to source major projects in countries that support and sympathize with extreme radical organizations. I believe these projects pose intolerable safety risks to our employees, strain our credit capacity, and aid and abet those who seek to destroy our country. If Jason would just wake up and market Franklin's expertise in the ways I have suggested, Franklin could easily remain at full capacity without having to take such work.

3.   Mary's parting worlds sparked a firestorm among many Franklin shareholders. A contingent of shareholders (the "Contingent") who collectively own nine percent of Franklin's stock now want to "prohibit Franklin from undertaking any new engagements" in 22 countries that the Contingent describes as "risky terrorists states." They would like to present their proposal for a shareholders' vote at the next annual meeting of shareholders that will be held in seven months. Mary is not a member of the Contingent, but supports its cause.

4. When Jason heard of the Contingent's concerns, he simply stated, "Any proposal they have won't make it past my wastebasket."

5. Franklin is organized in a state that has adopted the Model Business Corporation Act.

The Contingent needs advice and has many questions. How should they word and frame the proposal? When should they submit the proposal? What can they do to help position the proposal for inclusion in Franklin's annual meeting proxy materials? Do Jason and the board have solid grounds for refusing the proposal's inclusion in the proxy materials? What happens if the board rejects the proposal? What recourse, if any, does the Contingent have in the event of such a rejection?

MEDICAL COMMITTEE FOR HUMAN RIGHTS v. SECURITIES AND EXCHANGE COMMISSION
432 F.2d 659 (C.A.D.C. 1970)

TAMM, Circuit Judge:

The instant petition presents novel and significant questions concerning implementation of the concepts of corporate democracy embodied in section 14 of the Securities Exchange Act of 1934, and of the power of this court to review determinations of the Securities and Exchange Commission made pursuant to its proxy rules. For reasons to be stated more fully below, we hold that the Commission's action in the present case is reviewable, and that the cause must be remanded for further administrative proceedings.

On March 11, 1968, Dr. Quentin D. Young, National Chairman of the Medical Committee for Human Rights, wrote to the Secretary of the Dow Chemical Company, stating that the Medical Committee had obtained by gift several shares of Dow stock and expressing concern regarding the company's manufacture of the chemical substance napalm . In part, Dr. Young's letter said:

After consultation with the executive body of the Medical

Committee, I have been instructed to request an amendment to the charter of our company, Dow Chemical. We have learned that we are technically late in asking for an amendment at this date, but we wish to observe that it is a matter of such great urgency that we think it is imperative not to delay until the shareholders' meeting next year. * * *

Copies of this letter were forwarded to the President and the General Counsel of Dow Chemical Company, and to the Securities and Exchange Commission. By letter dated March 21, 1968, the General Counsel of Dow Chemical replied to the Medical Committee's letter, stating that the proposal had arrived too late for inclusion in the 1968 proxy statement, but promising that the company would 'study the matter and * * * communicate with you later this year' regarding inclusion of the resolution in proxy materials circulated by management in 1969. Copies of this letter, and of all subsequent correspondence, were duly filed with the Commission.

The next significant item of record is a letter dated January 6, 1969, noting that the Medical Committee was 'distressed that 1968 has passed without our having received a single word from you on this important matter,' and again requesting that the resolution be included in management's 1969 proxy materials. The Secretary of Dow Chemical replied to this letter on January 17, informing the Medical Committee that Dow intended to omit the resolution from its proxy statement and enclosing an opinion memorandum from Dow's General Counsel.

On February 7, 1969, Dow transmitted to the Medical Committee and to the Commission a letter and memorandum opinion of counsel, which in essence reiterated the previous arguments against inclusion of the proposal and stated the company's intention to omit it from the proxy statement. Shortly thereafter, on February 18, 1969, the Commission's Chief Counsel of the Division of Corporation Finance sent a letter to Dow, with copies to the Medical Committee, concluding that 'for reasons stated in your letter and the accompanying opinion of counsel, both dated January 17, 1969, this Division will not recommend any action * * * if this proposal is omitted from the management's proxy material...

The Medical Committee's sole substantive contention in this petition is that its proposed resolution could not, consistently with the Congressional intent underlying section 14(a), be properly deemed a proposal which is either motivated by general political and moral concerns, or related to the conduct of Dow's ordinary business operations. These criteria are two of the established exceptions to the general rule that management must include all properly submitted shareholder proposals in its proxy materials. They are contained in Rule 14a-8(c), 17 C.F.R. § 240.14a-8(c) (1970), which provides in relevant part:

> * * * Management may omit a proposal * * * from its proxy statement and form of proxy under any of the following circumstances:

> (2) If it clearly appears that the proposal is submitted by the security holder * * * primarily for the purpose of promoting general economic, political, racial, religious, social or similar causes; or

> (5) If the proposal consists of a recommendation or request that the management take action with respect to a matter relating to the

conduct of the ordinary business operations of the issuer.

It is obvious to the point of banality to restate the proposition that Congress intended by its enactment of section 14 of the Securities Exchange Act of 1934 to give true vitality to the concept of corporate democracy. The depth of this commitment is reflected in the strong language employed in the legislative history:

> Even those who in former days managed great corporations were by reason of their personal contacts with their shareholders constantly aware of their responsibilities. But as management became divorced from ownership and came under the control of banking groups, men forgot that they were dealing with the savings of men and the making of profits became an impersonal thing. When men do not know the victims of their aggression they are not always conscious of their wrongs. * * * Fair corporate suffrage is an important right that should attach to every equity security bought on a public exchange. Managements of properties owned by the investing public should not be permitted to perpetuate themselves by the misuse of corporate proxies.

H.R.Rep. No. 1383, 73d Cong., 2d Sess. 5, 13 (1934).

In striving to implement this open ended mandate, the Commission has gradually evolved its present proxy rules... [I]n 1945 the Commission issued a release containing an opinion of the Director of the Division of Corporation Finance that was rendered in response to a management request to omit shareholder resolutions which bore little or no relationship to the company's affairs; for example, these shareholder resolutions included proposals 'that the anti-trust laws and the enforcement thereof be revised,' and 'that all Federal legislation hereafter enacted providing for workers and farmers to be represented should be made to apply equally to investors.' The Commission's release endorsed the Director's conclusion that 'proposals which deal with general political, social or economic matters are not, within the meaning of the rule, 'proper subjects for action by security holders.' The reason for this conclusion was summarized as follows in the Director's opinion:

> Speaking generally, it is the purpose of Rule X-14A-7 to place stockholders in a position to bring before their fellow stockholders matters of concern to them as stockholders in such corporation; that is, such matters relating to the affairs of the company concerned as are proper subjects for stockholders' action under the laws of the state under which it was organized. It was not the intent of Rule X-14A-7 to permit stockholders to obtain the consensus of other stockholders with respect to matters which are of a general political, social or economic nature. Other forums exist for the presentation of such views.

Several years after the Commission issued this release, it was confronted with the same kind of problem when the management of a national bus company sought to omit a shareholder proposal phrased as 'A Recommendation that Management Consider the Advisability of Abolishing the Segregated Seating

System in the South'- a proposal which, on its face, was ambiguous with respect to whether it was limited solely to company policy rather than attacking all segregated seating, and which quite likely would have brought the company into violation of state laws then assumed to be valid. The Commission staff approved management's decision to omit the proposal, and the shareholder then sought a temporary injunction against the company's solicitation in a federal district court. The injunction was denied because the plaintiff had failed to exhaust his administrative remedies or to show that he would be irreparably harmed by refusal to grant the requested relief. Peck v. Greyhound Corp., 97 F. Supp. 679 (S.D.N.Y.1951). The Commission amended its rules the following year to encompass the above-quoted exception for situations in which 'it clearly appears that the proposal is submitted by the security holder * * * primarily for the purpose of promoting general economic, political, racial, religious, social or similar causes.'

The origins and genesis of the exception for proposals 'relating to the conduct of the ordinary business operations of the issuer' are somewhat more obscure. This provision was introduced into the proxy rules in 1954, as part of amendments which were made to clarify the general proposition that the primary source of authority for determining whether a proposal is a proper subject for shareholder action is state law. See 19 Fed.Reg. 246 (1954). Shortly after the rule was adopted, the Commission explained its purpose to Congress in the following terms:

> The policy motivating the Commission in adopting the rule * * * is basically the same as the underlying policy of most State corporation laws to confine the solution of ordinary business problems to the board of directors and place such problems beyond the competence and direction of the shareholders. The basic reason for this policy is that it is manifestly impracticable in most cases for stockholders to decide management problems at corporate meetings.

These two exceptions are, on their face, consistent with the legislative purpose underlying section 14; for it seems fair to infer that Congress desired to make proxy solicitations a vehicle for corporate democracy rather than an all-purpose forum for malcontented shareholders to vent their spleen about irrelevant matters, and also realized that management cannot exercise its specialized talents effectively if corporate investors assert the power to dictate the minutiae of daily business decisions. However, it is also apparent that the two exceptions which these rules carve out of the general requirement of inclusion can be construed so as to permit the exclusion of practically any shareholder proposal on the grounds that it is either 'too general' or 'too specific.' Indeed, in the present case Dow Chemical Company attempted to impale the Medical Committee's proposal on both horns of this dilemma: in its memorandum of counsel, it argued that the Medical Committee's proposal was a matter of ordinary business operations properly within the sphere of management expertise and, at the same time, that the proposal clearly had been submitted primarily for the purpose of promoting general political or social causes...

The possibility that the Medical Committee's proposal could properly be omitted under Rule 14a-8(c)(2) appears somewhat more substantial in the circumstances of the instant case, although once again it may fairly be asked how Dow Chemical's arguments on this point could be deemed a rational basis for such a result: the paragraph in the company's memorandum of counsel purporting to deal with this issue, which is set forth in the margin, consists entirely of a fundamentally irrelevant recitation of some of the political protests which had been directed at the company because of its manufacture of napalm, followed by the abrupt conclusion that management is therefore entitled to exclude the Medical Committee's proposal from its proxy statement. Our own examination of the issue raises substantial questions as to whether an interpretation of Rule 14a-8(c)(2) which permitted omission of this proposal as one motivated primarily by general political or social concerns would conflict with the congressional intent underlying section 14(a) of the Act.

As our earlier discussion indicates, the clear import of the language, legislative history, and record of administration of section 14(a) is that its overriding purpose is to assure to corporate shareholders the ability to exercise their right- some would say their duty - to control the important decisions which affect them in their capacity as stockholders and owners of the corporation. Thus, the Third Circuit has cogently summarized the philosophy of section 14(a) in the statement that '(a) corporation is run for the benefit of its stockholders and not for that of its managers.' SEC v. Transamerica Corp., 163 F.2d 511, 517 (3d Cir. 1947), cert. denied, 332 U.S. 847 (1948). Here, in contrast to the situations detailed above which led to the promulgation of Rule 14a-8(c)(2), the proposal relates solely to a matter that is completely within the accepted sphere of corporate activity and control. No reason has been advanced in the present proceedings which leads to the conclusion that management may properly place obstacles in the path of shareholders who wish to present to their co-owners, in accord with applicable state law, the question of whether they wish to have their assets used in a manner which they believe to be more socially responsible but possibly less profitable than that which is dictated by present company policy. Thus, even accepting Dow's characterization of the purpose and intent of the Medical Committee's proposal, there is a strong argument that permitting the company to exclude it would contravene the purpose of section 14(a).

However, the record in this case contains indications that we are confronted with quite a different situation. The management of Dow Chemical Company is repeatedly quoted in sources which include the company's own publications as proclaiming that the decision to continue manufacturing and marketing napalm was made not because of business considerations, but in spite of them; that management in essence decided to pursue a course of activity which generated little profit for the shareholders and actively impaired the company's public relations and recruitment activities because management considered this action morally and politically desirable. The proper political and social role of modern corporations is, of course, a matter of philosophical argument extending far beyond the scope of our present concern; the substantive wisdom or propriety of particular corporate political decisions is also completely irrelevant to the resolution of the present controversy. What is of immediate concern, however, is the question of whether the corporate proxy rules can be employed as a shield to isolate such managerial decisions from shareholder control. After all, it must be remembered that 'the control of great corporations by a very few persons was the abuse at which Congress struck in enacting Section 14(a).' SEC v. Transamerica Corp., supra, 163 F.2d at 518. We think that there is a clear and compelling distinction between management's legitimate need for freedom to apply its expertise in matters of day-to-day business judgment, and management's patently illegitimate claim of power to treat modern corporations with their vast resources as personal satrapies implementing personal political or moral predilections. It could scarcely be argued that management is more qualified or more entitled to make these kinds of decisions than the shareholders who are the true beneficial owners of the corporation; and it seems equally implausible that an application of the proxy rules which permitted such a result could be harmonized with the philosophy of corporate democracy which Congress embodied in section 14(a) of the Securities Exchange Act of 1934.

In light of these considerations, therefore, the cause must be remanded to the Commission so that it may reconsider petitioner's claim within the proper limits of its discretionary authority as set forth above, and so that 'the basis for (its) decision (may) appear clearly on the record, not in conclusory terms but in sufficient detail to permit prompt and effective review.

Remanded for further proceedings consistent with this opinion.

Note: The social and political ground for exclusion referenced in the Medical Committee case is no longer a permitted ground for exclusion under Rule 14a-8. The "ordinary business operations" ground for exclusion remains.

LOVENHEIM v. IROQUOIS BRANDS, LTD.
618 F. Supp 554 (D.D.C. 1985)

GASCH, District Judge.

Plaintiff Peter C. Lovenheim, owner of two hundred shares of common stock in Iroquois Brands, Ltd. (hereinafter "Iroquois/Delaware"), seeks to bar Iroquois/Delaware from excluding from the proxy materials being sent to all shareholders in preparation for an upcoming shareholder meeting information concerning a proposed resolution he intends to offer at the meeting. Mr. Lovenheim's proposed resolution relates to the procedure used to force-feed geese for production of paté de foie gras in France, a type of paté imported by Iroquois/Delaware. Specifically, his resolution calls upon the Directors of Iroquois/Delaware to "form a committee to study the methods by which its French supplier produces paté de foie gras, and report to the shareholders its findings and opinions, based on expert consultation, on whether this production method causes undue distress, pain or suffering to the animals involved and, if so, whether further distribution of this product should be discontinued until a more humane production method is developed."

Iroquois/Delaware has refused to allow information concerning Mr. Lovenheim's proposal to be included in proxy materials being sent in connection with the next annual shareholders meeting. In doing so, Iroquois/Delaware relies on an exception to the general requirement of Rule 14a–8, Rule 14a–8(c)(5).

Iroquois/Delaware's reliance on the argument that this exception applies is based on the following information contained in the affidavit of its president: Iroquois/Delaware has annual revenues of $141 million with $6 million in annual profits and $78 million in assets. In contrast, its paté de foie gras sales were just $79,000 last year, representing a net loss on paté sales of $3,121. Iroquois/Delaware has only $34,000in assets related to paté. Thus none of the company's net earnings and less than .05 percent of its assets are implicated by plaintiff's proposal. These levels are obviously far below the five percent threshold set forth in the first portion of the exception claimed by Iroquois/Delaware.

Plaintiff does not contest that his proposed resolution relates to a matter of little economic significance to Iroquois/Delaware. Nevertheless he contends that the Rule 14a–8(c)(5) exception is not applicable as it cannot be said that his proposal "is not otherwise significantly related to the issuer's business" as is required by the final portion of that exception. In other words, plaintiff's argument that Rule 14a–8 does not permit omission of his proposal rests on the assertion that the rule and statute on which it is based do not permit omission merely because a proposal is not economically significant where a proposal has "ethical or social significance."

Iroquois/Delaware challenges plaintiff's view that ethical and social proposals cannot be excluded even if they do not meet the economic or five percent test. Instead, Iroquois/Delaware views the exception solely in economic terms as permitting omission of any proposals relating to a de minimis share of assets and profits. Iroquois/Delaware asserts that since corporations are economic entities, only an economic test is appropriate.

The Court would note that the applicability of the Rule 14a–8(c)(5) exception to Mr. Lovenheim's proposal represents a close question given the lack of clarity in the exception itself. In effect, plaintiff relies on the word "otherwise," suggesting that it indicates the drafters of the rule intended that other noneconomic tests of significance be used. Iroquois/Delaware relies on the fact that the rule examines other significance in relation to the issuer's business. Because of the apparent ambiguity of the rule, the Court considers the history of the shareholder proposal rule in determining the proper interpretation of the most recent version of that rule.

Prior to 1983, paragraph 14a–8(c)(5) excluded proposals "not significantly related to the issuer's business" but did not contain an objective economic significance test such as the five percent of sales, assets, and earnings specified in the first part of the current version. Although a series of SEC decisions through 1976 allowing issuers to exclude proposals challenging compliance with the Arab economic boycott of Israel allowed exclusion if the issuer did less than one percent of their business with Arab countries or Israel, the Commission stated later in 1976 that it did "not believe that subparagraph (c)(5) should be hinged solely on the economic relativity of a proposal." Securities Exchange Act Release No. 12,999, 41 Fed. Reg. 52,99 4, 52,997 (1976). Thus the Commission required inclusion "in many situations in which the related business comprised less than one percent" of the company's revenues, profits or assets "where the proposal has raised *policy questions* important enough to be considered 'significantly related' to the issuer's business."

As indicated above, the 1983 revision adopted the five percent test of economic significance in an effort to create a more objective standard. Nevertheless, in adopting this standard, the Commission stated that proposals will be includable notwithstanding their "failure to reach the specified economic thresholds if a significant relationship to the issuer's business is demonstrated on the face of the resolution or supporting statement." Securities Exchange Act Release No. 19,135, 47 Fed.Reg. 47,420, 47,428 (1982). Thus it seems clear based on the history of the rule that "the meaning of 'significantly related' is not *limited* to economic significance."

The Court cannot ignore the history of the rule which reveals no decision by the Commission to limit the determination to the economic criteria relied on by Iroquois/Delaware. The Court therefore holds that in light of the ethical and social significance of plaintiff's proposal and the fact that it implicates significant levels of sales, plaintiff has shown a likelihood of prevailing on the merits with regard to the issue of whether his proposal is "otherwise significantly related" to Iroquois/Delaware's business.

For the reasons discussed above, the Court concludes that plaintiff's motion for preliminary injunction should be granted.

APACHE CORP. v. NEW YORK CITY EMPLOYEES' RETIREMENT SYSTEM
621 F.Supp.2d 444 (S.D.Tex. 2008)

GRAY H. MILLER, District Judge.

Pending before the court are plaintiff Apache Corporation's Original Complaint seeking a declaratory judgment and application for a preliminary injunction... The court has carefully reviewed the application, all responsive and supplemental pleadings, declarations and other record evidence, arguments of counsel, and the applicable law. For the reasons discussed below, the court finds that Apache properly excluded defendants' proposal from proxy materials mailed to Apache's shareholders.

Apache is a Delaware corporation, is an independent energy company that explores for, develops, and produces natural gas, crude oil, and natural gas liquids. Defendants New York City Employees' Retirement System, New York City Teachers' Retirement System, New York City Police Pension Fund, New York City Fire Department Pension Fund, New York City Board of Education Retirement System (collectively, "Funds"), and Office of the Comptroller of the City of New York ("NYC Comptroller") are five New York pension funds and New York's chief fiscal and chief auditing officer, the custodian and trustee of the Funds.

On October 29, 2007, NYC Comptroller submitted to Apache, pursuant to Section 14(a) of the Securities Exchange Act of 1934, a shareholder proposal ("Proposal") for inclusion in the company's proxy statement to be mailed in advance of Apache's May 8, 2008, annual shareholders' meeting. The Proposal reads:

WHEREAS, corporations with non-discrimination policies relating to sexual orientation have a competitive advantage to recruit and retain employees from the widest talent pool;

Employment discrimination on the basis of sexual orientation diminishes employee morale and productivity;

The company has an interest in preventing discrimination and resolving complaints internally so as to avoid costly litigation and damage its reputation as an equal opportunity employer;

Atlanta, Seattle, Los Angeles, and San Francisco have adopted legislation restricting business with companies that do not guaranteed equal treatment for lesbian and gay employees and similar legislation is pending in other jurisdictions;

The company has operations in and makes sales to institutions in states and cities which prohibit discrimination on the basis of sexual orientation;

A recent National Gay and Lesbian Taskforce study has found that 16%–44% of gay men and lesbians in twenty cities nationwide experienced workplace harassment or discrimination based on their sexual orientation;

National public opinion polls consistently find more than three-quarters of the American people support equal rights in the workplace for gay men, lesbians, and bisexuals;

A number of Fortune 500 corporations have implemented non-discrimination policies encompassing the following principles:

1) Discrimination based on sexual orientation and gender identity will be prohibited in the company's employment policy statement.

2) The company's non-discrimination policy will be distributed to all employees.

3) There shall be no discrimination based on any employee's actual or perceived health condition, status, or disability.

4) There shall be no discrimination in the allocation of employee benefits on the basis of sexual orientation or gender identity.

5) Sexual orientation and gender identity issues will be included in corporate employee diversity and sensitivity programs.

6) There shall be no discrimination in the recognition of employee groups based on sexual orientation or gender identity.

7) Corporate advertising policy will avoid the use of negative stereotypes based on sexual orientation or gender identity.

8) There shall be no discrimination in corporate advertising and marketing policy based on sexual orientation or gender identity.

9) There shall be no discrimination in the sale of goods and services based on sexual orientation or gender identity, and

10) There shall be no policy barring on corporate charitable contributions to groups and organizations based on sexual orientation.

RESOLVED: The Shareholders request that management implement equal employment opportunity policies based on the aforementioned principles prohibiting discrimination based on sexual orientation and gender identity.

STATEMENT: By implementing policies prohibiting discrimination based on sexual orientation and gender identity, the Company will ensure a respectful and supportive atmosphere for all employees and enhance its competitive edge by joining the growing ranks of companies guaranteeing equal opportunity for all employees.

Apache refused to include the proposal in its proxy materials and on January 3, 2008, pursuant to Rule 14a–8(j), Apache requested a no-action letter from the Securities and Exchange Commission's ("SEC") Division of Corporation Finance. Apache asserted that the Proposal relates to the company's ordinary business operations and, therefore, is properly excludable from the proxy materials pursuant to Rule 14a–8(i)(7).. Both Apache and defendants extensively briefed the SEC on their respective positions. On March 5, 2008, the SEC's Division of Corporation Finance issued a no-action letter. The SEC found,

The proposal requests that management implement equal employment opportunity polices [sic] based on principles specified in the proposal prohibiting discrimination based on sexual orientation and gender identity.

There appears to be some basis for your view that Apache may exclude the proposal under rule 14a–8(i)(7). We note in particular that some of the principles relate to Apache's ordinary business operations. Accordingly, we will not recommend enforcement action to the Commission if Apache omits the proposal from its proxy materials in reliance on rule 14a–8(i)(7).

On March 31, 2008, Apache sent out notice of its annual meeting of stockholders and proxy statement. The proxy statement did not include the Proposal. On April 8, 2008, Apache filed a declaratory judgment action in this court. Apache seeks a declaration that it properly excluded the Proposal pursuant to Rule 14a–8(i)(7). The next day, defendants filed a parallel lawsuit in the Southern District of New York.

To resolve this dispute, the court must determine whether Apache properly excluded the Proposal from its proxy statement. Because the SEC found "some basis for [Apache's] view that [it] may exclude the proposal under rule 14a–8(i)(7)," the court must first determine whether it must defer to the SEC and adopt its position.

There are two types of rules, substantive and interpretive. Substantive, or legislative-type, rules are those that create new law, rights, or duties, in what amounts to a legislative act. *See Chrysler Corp. v. Brown*, 441 U.S. 281, 301–02 (1979). Substantive rules have the force of law. *See Batterton v. Francis*, 432 U.S. 416, 425 n. 9, 448 (1977). Conversely, "interpretative rules are statements as to what [an] administrative officer thinks [a] statute or regulation means." *Brown Express, Inc. v. United States*, 607 F.2d 695, 700 (5th Cir.1979). These rules do not have force of law, though they are entitled to some deference from the courts. *Batterton*, 432 U.S. at 425 n. 9, 97 S.Ct. 2399. "Varying degrees of deference are accorded to administrative interpretations, based on such factors as the timing and consistency of the agency's position, and the nature of its expertise." *Id.*

The proper weight to accord an SEC no-action letter is an issue of first impression in the Fifth Circuit. The Second Circuit, however, noted that no-action letters are interpretive because they do not impose or fix a legal relationship upon any of the parties. *See Amalgamated Clothing & Textile Workers Union v. Sec. & Exch. Comm'n*, 15 F.3d 254, 257 (2d Cir.1994). That court concluded that no-action letters are nonbinding, persuasive authority. *See id.* at 257 & n. 3. This court agrees. Therefore, a court must independently analyze the merits of a dispute even when affirming the SEC's conclusion.

Apache seeks to exclude the Proposal based on the Rule 14a–8(i)(7), exception. Rule 14a–8 requires, under certain circumstances, a public company to include "a shareholder's proposal in its proxy statement and identify the proposal in its form of proxy when the company holds an annual or special meeting of shareholders." If the shareholder submits a proposal in accordance with controlling regulations, the company must include the proposal in its proxy materials unless it is properly excludable for the substantive reasons listed in Rule 14a–8(i). Prior to excluding the proposal, Rule 14a–8(j) requires the company to "file its reasons with the Commission no later than 80 calendar days before it files its definitive proxy statement and form of proxy with the Commission." The company must show that the proposal fits within one or more of Rule 14a–8(i)'s exceptions...

Rule 14a–8(i)(7) permits exclusion of a proposal if it "deals with a matter relating to the company's ordinary business operations." The term "ordinary business operations" escapes formal definition. To gleam its scope, courts look to SEC guidance and state law. In adopting Rule 14a–8(i)(7),[FN5] the SEC stated:

> the term "ordinary business operations" has been deemed on occasion to include certain matters which have significant policy, economic or other implications inherent in them. For instance, a proposal that a utility company not construct a proposed nuclear power plant has in the past been considered excludable .... In retrospect, however, it seems apparent that the economic and safety considerations attendant to nuclear power plants are of such magnitude that a determination whether to construct one is not an "ordinary" business matter. Accordingly, proposals of that nature, as well as others that have major

implications, will in the future be considered beyond the realm of an issuer's ordinary business operations ....

Adoption of Amendments Relating to Proposals by Security Holders ("1976 Release"), 41 Fed. Reg. 52,994, 52,998 (December 3, 1976). Accordingly, only "business matters that are mundane in nature and do not involve any substantial policy" considerations may be omitted under the "ordinary business" exception. *Id.*

The policy underlying the ordinary business exclusion rests on two central considerations. The first relates to the subject matter of the proposal. Certain tasks are so fundamental to management's ability to run a company on a day-to-day basis that they could not, as a practical matter, be subject to direct shareholder oversight. Examples include the management of the workforce, such as the hiring, promotion, and termination of employees, decisions on production quality and quantity, and the retention of suppliers. However, proposals relating to such matters but focusing on sufficiently significant social policy issues (e.g., significant discrimination matters) generally would not be considered to be excludable, because the proposals would transcend the day-to-day business matters and raise policy issues so significant that it would be appropriate for a shareholder vote.

The second consideration relates to the degree to which the proposal seeks to "micro-manage" the company by probing too deeply into matters of a complex nature upon which shareholders, as a group, would not be in a position to make an informed judgment. This consideration may come into play in a number of circumstances, such as where the proposal involves intricate detail, or seeks to impose specific time-frames or methods for implementing complex policies. *Amendments to Rules on Shareholder Proposals ("1998 Release"),* 63 Fed. Reg. 29106, 29108 (May 28, 1998). As to the second factor, the SEC explained that the determination "will be made on a case-by-case basis, taking into account factors such as the nature of the proposal and the circumstances of the company to which it is directed." *Id.* at 29109.

A clear reading of the *1998 Release* informs this court's analysis. To read the guidance as directing proper exclusion of shareholder proposals only when those proposals do not implicate a significant social policy would make much of the statement superfluous and most of the no-action letters presented to the court by the parties incorrect. Because such a directive cannot be gleamed from the release language, the court finds that it must first determine whether the Proposal implicates a significant policy issue. A proposal that does not concern a significant policy issue but nevertheless implicates the ordinary business operations of a company is properly excludable under Rule 14a–8(i)(7). However, a proposal concerning the ordinary business operations of a company that implicates a significant policy issue is only excludable under Rule 14a–8(i)(7) if it "seeks to 'micro-manage' the company by probing too deeply into matters of a complex nature upon which shareholders, as a group, would not be in a position to make an informed judgment." *1998 Release,* 63 Fed. Reg. at 29108...

The court now turns to the Proposal. The "resolved" paragraph provides, "The Shareholders request that management implement equal employment opportunity policies based on the aforementioned principles prohibiting discrimination based on sexual orientation and gender identity." Defendants now argue that the enumerated principles merely illustrate how various Fortune 500 corporations implemented non-discrimination policies.

Nevertheless, a plain reading dictates the construction of the request. The shareholders seek that the company implement policies based on a list of principles. It is those principles that determine the employment opportunity policies, and not vice versa... With these in mind, the Proposal seeks to have Apache implement policies incorporating sexual orientation and gender identity into the company's employee benefits allocation, corporate advertising and marketing activities, sales activities, and charitable contributions.

Undoubtedly, advertising and marketing, sale of goods and services, and charitable contributions are ordinary business matters. Yet, the defendants, through the Proposal, seek to have Apache implement equal employment opportunity policies which incorporate anti-discrimination directives based on sexual orientation and gender identity into such activities. The court finds that only principles one through six are directed at discrimination in employment. To consider the remaining four principles as implicating employment discrimination would be a far stretch. Instead, principles seven through ten aim at discrimination in Apache's business conduct as it relates to advertising, marketing, sales, and charitable contributions. Therefore, because these principles do not implicate the social policy underlying the Proposal, and because the Proposal must be read with all of its parts, the Proposal is properly excludable under Rule 14a–8(i)(7).

Even were the court to find that principles seven through ten implicate the underlying social policy, the Proposal seeks to micromanage the company to an unacceptable degree. Shareholders, as a group, are not sufficiently involved in the day-to-day operations of Apache's business to fully appreciate its complex nature. For example, shareholders, as a group, are not positioned to make informed judgments as to the propriety of certain sales and purchases. Similarly, the complex implications stemming from the proposed principle forbidding discrimination in the sale of goods and services based on sexual orientation or gender identity preclude provident judgment on the part of the shareholders.

It would be imprudent to effectively cede control over such day-to-day decisions, traditionally within the purview of a company's executives and officers, to the shareholders. The aforementioned concerns are enhanced by the principle's implicit requirement that Apache determine whether its customers and suppliers discriminate on the basis of sexual orientation or gender identity. Such an inquiry is impractical and unreasonable, and the determination as to its propriety should properly remain with the company's management.

For the foregoing reasons, the court finds that pursuant to Rule 14a–8(i)(7), Apache properly excluded the Proposal from the proxy statement mailed to its shareholders.

3. BYLAW AMENDMENTS AND DIRECTOR NOMINATIONS

CASE PROBLEM 8-3

Assume the same facts as Case Problem 8-1, with the following changes:

1.   Jason owns four percent of Franklin's outstanding shares; the other Franklin executives own five percent; Mary owns three percent; and the remaining shares are traded on the NASDAQ.

2.   Mary is fighting mad over her termination and is determined to take on Jason at the next annual shareholders meeting that will occur in four months. She doesn't even try to assess the strength of her support as in Case Problem 8-1. Mary has recruited a slate of new directors (seven or eight, as needed) who would move to throw Jason out and install Mary as the new CEO of Franklin.

3.   Mary has identified three alternative strategies:

• Submit a proposed amendment to the articles of incorporation of Franklin that would increase the board's size to 15. Mary would then push hard to have her slate fill the newly-opened positions on the board. Mary perceives that this strategy would be "gentler" on the existing board members, many of whom may "swing her way" once they see that Jason is on his way out.

• Propose her slate as a complete replacement of the existing board. It would be a winner-take-all showdown at the next annual shareholders meeting. Mary would also submit a proposal that Franklin reimburse her for all costs and expenses that she incurs in connection with the effort. She considers this "only fair" because Jason and the exiting board will be using Franklin resources to preserve their positions.

• Propose an amendment to the bylaws of Franklin that would require Franklin to include in its proxy materials for an annual meeting any nominee for a director position who can demonstrate that he or she has the support of shareholders owning at least five percent of the company's outstanding stock. Mary would submit this proposal at a special meeting of shareholders that would be held a few months in advance of the annual meeting. If the proposal passes (she thinks it has a very good chance), she would propose her slate of directors in the company proxy materials for the next annual meeting.

Advise Mary on the challenges of each of the strategies, assuming Franklin is organized in a state that has adopted the Model Business Corporation Act. Would your counsel to Mary be any different if Franklin was organized in Delaware?

CA, INC. v. AFSCME EMPLOYEES PENSION PLAN
953 A.2d 227 (Del. 2008)

JACOBS, Justice.

This proceeding arises from a certification by the United States Securities and Exchange Commission (the "SEC"), to this Court, of two questions of law pursuant to Article IV, Section 11(8) of the Delaware Constitution and Supreme

Court Rule 41. On June 27, 2008, the SEC asked this Court to address two questions of Delaware law regarding a proposed stockholder bylaw submitted by the AFSCME Employees Pension Plan ("AFSCME") for inclusion in the proxy materials of CA, Inc. ("CA" or the "Company") for CA's 2008 annual stockholders' meeting. This Court accepted certification on July 1, 2008, and after expedited briefing, the matter was argued on July 9, 2008. This is the decision of the Court on the certified questions.

CA is a Delaware corporation whose board of directors consists of twelve persons, all of whom sit for reelection each year. CA's annual meeting of stockholders is scheduled to be held on September 9, 2008. CA intends to file its definitive proxy materials with the SEC on or about July 24, 2008 in connection with that meeting.

AFSCME, a CA stockholder, is associated with the American Federation of State, County and Municipal Employees. On March 13, 2008, AFSCME submitted a proposed stockholder bylaw (the "Bylaw" or "proposed Bylaw") for inclusion in the Company's proxy materials for its 2008 annual meeting of stockholders. The Bylaw, if adopted by CA stockholders, would amend the Company's bylaws to provide as follows:

> RESOLVED, that pursuant to section 109 of the Delaware General Corporation Law and Article IX of the bylaws of CA, Inc., stockholders of CA hereby amend the bylaws to add the following Section 14 to Article II:

> The board of directors shall cause the corporation to reimburse a stockholder or group of stockholders (together, the "Nominator") for reasonable expenses ("Expenses") incurred in connection with nominating one or more candidates in a contested election of directors to the corporation's board of directors, including, without limitation, printing, mailing, legal, solicitation, travel, advertising and public relations expenses, so long as (a) the election of fewer than 50% of the directors to be elected is contested in the election, (b) one or more candidates nominated by the Nominator are elected to the corporation's board of directors, (c) stockholders are not permitted to cumulate their votes for directors, and (d) the election occurred, and the Expenses were incurred, after this bylaw's adoption. The amount paid to a Nominator under this bylaw in respect of a contested election shall not exceed the amount expended by the corporation in connection with such election.

CA's current bylaws and Certificate of Incorporation have no provision that specifically addresses the reimbursement of proxy expenses. Of more general relevance, however, is Article SEVENTH, Section (1) of CA's Certificate of Incorporation, which tracks the language of 8 Del. C. § 141(a) and provides that:

> The management of the business and the conduct of the affairs of the corporation shall be vested in [CA's] Board of Directors.

It is undisputed that the decision whether to reimburse election expenses is presently vested in the discretion of CA's board of directors, subject to their fiduciary duties and applicable Delaware law.

On April 18, 2008, CA notified the SEC's Division of Corporation Finance (the "Division") of its intention to exclude the proposed Bylaw from its 2008 proxy materials. The Company requested from the Division a "no-action letter" stating that the Division would not recommend any enforcement action to the SEC if CA excluded the AFSCME proposal. CA's request for a no-action letter was accompanied by an opinion from its Delaware counsel, Richards Layton & Finger, P.A. ("RL & F"). The RL & F opinion concluded that the proposed Bylaw is not a proper subject for stockholder action, and that if implemented, the Bylaw would violate the Delaware General Corporation Law ("DGCL").

On May 21, 2008, AFSCME responded to CA's no-action request with a letter taking the opposite legal position. The AFSCME letter was accompanied by an opinion from AFSCME's Delaware counsel, Grant & Eisenhofer, P.A. ("G & E"). The G & E opinion concluded that the proposed Bylaw is a proper subject for shareholder action and that if adopted, would be permitted under Delaware law.

The Division was thus confronted with two conflicting legal opinions on Delaware law. Whether or not the Division would determine that CA may exclude the proposed Bylaw from its 2008 proxy materials would depend upon which of these conflicting views is legally correct. To obtain guidance, the SEC, at the Division's request, certified two questions of Delaware law to this Court.

The two questions certified to us by the SEC are as follows:

1. Is the AFSCME Proposal a proper subject for action by shareholders as a matter of Delaware law?

2. Would the AFSCME Proposal, if adopted, cause CA to violate any Delaware law to which it is subject?

The questions presented are issues of law which this Court decides de novo.

The first question presented is whether the Bylaw is a proper subject for shareholder action, more precisely, whether the Bylaw may be proposed and enacted by shareholders without the concurrence of the Company's board of directors. Before proceeding further, we make some preliminary comments in an effort to delineate a framework within which to begin our analysis.

First, the DGCL empowers both the board of directors and the shareholders of a Delaware corporation to adopt, amend or repeal the corporation's bylaws... Pursuant to Section 109(a), CA's Certificate of Incorporation confers the power to adopt, amend or repeal the bylaws upon the Company's board of directors. Because the statute commands that that conferral "shall not divest the stockholders ... of ... nor limit" their power, both the board and the shareholders of CA, independently and concurrently, possess the power to adopt, amend and repeal the bylaws.

Second, the vesting of that concurrent power in both the board and the shareholders raises the issue of whether the stockholders' power is coextensive with that of the board, and vice versa. As a purely theoretical matter that is possible, and were that the case, then the first certified question would be easily answered. That is, under such a regime any proposal to adopt, amend or repeal a bylaw would be a proper subject for either shareholder or board action, without distinction. But the DGCL has not allocated to the board and the shareholders the identical, coextensive power to adopt, amend and repeal the bylaws. Therefore, how that power is allocated between those two decision-making bodies requires an analysis that is more complex.

Moving from the theoretical to this case, by its terms Section 109(a) vests in the shareholders a power to adopt, amend or repeal bylaws that is legally sacrosanct, i.e., the power cannot be non-consensually eliminated or limited by anyone other than the legislature itself. If viewed in isolation, Section 109(a) could be read to make the board's and the shareholders' power to adopt, amend or repeal bylaws identical and coextensive, but Section 109(a) does not exist in a vacuum. It must be read together with 8 Del. C. § 141(a), which pertinently provides that:

> The business and affairs of every corporation organized under this chapter shall be managed by or under the direction of a board of directors, except as may be otherwise provided in this chapter or in its certificate of incorporation.

No such broad management power is statutorily allocated to the shareholders. Indeed, it is well-established that stockholders of a corporation subject to the DGCL may not directly manage the business and affairs of the corporation, at least without specific authorization in either the statute or the certificate of incorporation. Therefore, the shareholders' statutory power to adopt, amend or repeal bylaws is not coextensive with the board's concurrent power and is limited by the board's management prerogatives under Section 141(a).

Third, it follows that, to decide whether the Bylaw proposed by AFSCME is a proper subject for shareholder action under Delaware law, we must first determine: (1) the scope or reach of the shareholders' power to adopt, alter or repeal the bylaws of a Delaware corporation, and then (2) whether the Bylaw at issue here falls within that permissible scope. Where, as here, the proposed bylaw is one that limits director authority, that is an elusively difficult task. The tools that are available to this Court to answer those questions are other provisions of the DGCL and Delaware judicial decisions that can be brought to bear on this question.

Two other provisions of the DGCL, 8 Del. C. §§ 109(b) and 102(b)(1), bear importantly on the first question and form the basis of contentions advanced by each side. Section 109(b), which deals generally with bylaws and what they must or may contain, provides that:

> The bylaws may contain any provision, not inconsistent with law or with the certificate of incorporation, relating to the business of the corporation, the conduct of its affairs, and its rights or powers or the rights or powers of its stockholders, directors, officers or employees.

And Section 102(b)(1), which is part of a broader provision that addresses what the certificate of incorporation must or may contain, relevantly states that:

(b) In addition to the matters required to be set forth in the certificate of incorporation by subsection (a) of this section, the certificate of incorporation may also contain any or all of the following matters:

(1) Any provision for the management of the business and for the conduct of the affairs of the corporation, and any provision creating, defining, limiting and regulating the powers of the corporation, the directors and the stockholders, or any class of the stockholders ....; if such provisions are not contrary to the laws of this State. Any provision which is required or permitted by any section of this chapter to be stated in the bylaws may instead be stated in the certificate of incorporation.

AFSCME relies heavily upon the language of Section 109(b), which permits the bylaws of a corporation to contain "any provision ... relating to the ... rights or powers of its stockholders [and] directors...." The Bylaw, AFSCME argues, "relates to" the right of the stockholders meaningfully to participate in the process of electing directors, a right that necessarily "includes the right to nominate an opposing slate."

CA argues, in response, that Section 109(b) is not dispositive, because it cannot be read in isolation from, and without regard to, Section 102(b)(1). CA's argument runs as follows: the Bylaw would limit the substantive decision-making authority of CA's board to decide whether or not to expend corporate funds for a particular purpose, here, reimbursing director election expenses. Section 102(b)(1) contemplates that any provision that limits the broad statutory power of the directors must be contained in the certificate of incorporation. Therefore, the proposed Bylaw can only be in CA's Certificate of Incorporation, as distinguished from its bylaws. Accordingly, the proposed bylaw falls outside the universe of permissible bylaws authorized by Section 109(b).

Implicit in CA's argument is the premise that any bylaw that in any respect might be viewed as limiting or restricting the power of the board of directors automatically falls outside the scope of permissible bylaws. That simply cannot be. That reasoning, taken to its logical extreme, would result in eliminating altogether the shareholders' statutory right to adopt, amend or repeal bylaws. Bylaws, by their very nature, set down rules and procedures that bind a corporation's board and its shareholders. In that sense, most, if not all, bylaws could be said to limit the otherwise unlimited discretionary power of the board. Yet Section 109(a) carves out an area of shareholder power to adopt, amend or repeal bylaws that is expressly inviolate. Therefore, to argue that the Bylaw at issue here limits the board's power to manage the business and affairs of the Company only begins, but cannot end, the analysis needed to decide whether the Bylaw is a proper subject for shareholder action. The question left unanswered is what is the scope of shareholder action that Section 109(b) permits yet does not improperly intrude upon the directors' power to manage corporation's business and affairs under Section 141(a).

It is at this juncture that the statutory language becomes only marginally helpful in determining what the Delaware legislature intended to be the lawful scope of the shareholders' power to adopt, amend and repeal bylaws. To resolve that issue, the Court must resort to different tools, namely, decisions of this Court and of the Court of Chancery that bear on this question. Those tools do not enable us to articulate with doctrinal exactitude a bright line that divides those bylaws that shareholders may unilaterally adopt under Section 109(b) from those which they may not under Section 141(a). They do, however, enable us to decide the issue presented in this specific case.

It is well-established Delaware law that a proper function of bylaws is not to mandate how the board should decide specific substantive business decisions, but rather, to define the process and procedures by which those decisions are made. *Hollinger Intern., Inc. v. Black,* 844 A.2d 1022, 1078-79 (Del.Ch.2004), *aff'd,* 872 A.2d 559 (Del.2005). See also, *Gow v. Consol. Coppermines Corp.,* 165 A. 136, 140 (Del.Ch.1933). The process-creating function of bylaws provides a starting point to address the Bylaw at issue. It enables us to frame the issue in terms of whether the Bylaw is one that establishes or regulates a process for substantive director decision-making, or one that mandates the decision itself. Not surprisingly, the parties sharply divide on that question. We conclude that the Bylaw, even though infelicitously couched as a substantive-sounding mandate to expend corporate funds, has both the intent and the effect of regulating the process for electing directors of CA. Therefore, we determine that the Bylaw is a proper subject for shareholder action, and set forth our reasoning below.

Although CA concedes that "restrictive procedural bylaws (such as those requiring the presence of all directors and unanimous board consent to take action) are acceptable," it points out that even facially procedural bylaws can unduly intrude upon board authority. The Bylaw being proposed here is unduly intrusive, CA claims, because, by mandating reimbursement of a stockholder's proxy expenses, it limits the board's broad discretionary authority to decide whether to grant reimbursement at all. CA further claims that because (in defined circumstances) the Bylaw mandates the expenditure of corporate funds, its subject matter is necessarily substantive, not process-oriented, and, therefore falls outside the scope of what Section 109(b) permits.

Because the Bylaw is couched as a command to reimburse ("The board of directors shall cause the corporation to reimburse a stockholder"), it lends itself to CA's criticism. But the Bylaw's wording, although relevant, is not dispositive of whether or not it is process-related. The Bylaw could easily have been worded differently, to emphasize its process, as distinguished from its mandatory payment, component. By saying this we do not mean to suggest that this Bylaw's reimbursement component can be ignored. What we do suggest is that a bylaw that requires the expenditure of corporate funds does not, for that reason alone, become automatically deprived of its process-related character...

The context of the Bylaw at issue here is the process for electing directors-a subject in which shareholders of Delaware corporations have a legitimate and protected interest. The purpose of the Bylaw is to promote the integrity of that electoral process by facilitating the nomination of director candidates by stockholders or groups of stockholders. Generally, and under the current framework for electing directors in contested elections, only board-sponsored nominees for election are reimbursed for their election expenses. Dissident candidates are not, unless they succeed in replacing at least a majority of the entire board. The Bylaw would encourage the nomination of non-management board candidates by promising reimbursement of the nominating stockholders' proxy expenses if one or more of its candidates are elected. In that the shareholders also have a legitimate interest, because the Bylaw would facilitate the exercise of their right to participate in selecting the contestants.

The shareholders of a Delaware corporation have the right "to participate in selecting the contestants" for election to the board. The shareholders are entitled to facilitate the exercise of that right by proposing a bylaw that would encourage candidates other than board-sponsored nominees to stand for election. The Bylaw would accomplish that by committing the corporation to reimburse the election expenses of shareholders whose candidates are successfully elected. That the implementation of that proposal would require the expenditure of corporate funds will not, in and of itself, make such a bylaw an improper subject matter for shareholder action. Accordingly, we answer the first question certified to us in the affirmative.

That, however, concludes only part of the analysis. The DGCL also requires that the Bylaw be "not inconsistent with law." Accordingly, we turn to the second certified question, which is whether the proposed Bylaw, if adopted, would cause CA to violate any Delaware law to which it is subject.

In answering the first question, we have already determined that the Bylaw does not facially violate any provision of the DGCL or of CA's Certificate of Incorporation. The question thus becomes whether the Bylaw would violate any common law rule or precept. Were this issue being presented in the course of litigation involving the application of the Bylaw to a specific set of facts, we would start with the presumption that the Bylaw is valid and, if possible, construe it in a manner consistent with the law.

The factual context in which the Bylaw was challenged would inform our analysis, and we would "exercise caution [before] invalidating corporate acts based upon hypothetical injuries...." The certified questions, however, request a determination of the validity of the Bylaw in the abstract. Therefore, in response to the second question, we must necessarily consider any possible circumstance under which a board of directors might be required to act. Under at least one such hypothetical, the board of directors would breach their fiduciary duties if they complied with the Bylaw.

Accordingly, we conclude that the Bylaw, as drafted, would violate the prohibition, which our decisions have derived from Section 141(a), against contractual arrangements that commit the board of directors to a course of action that would preclude them from fully discharging their fiduciary duties to the corporation and its shareholders.

This Court has previously invalidated contracts that would require a board to act or not act in such a fashion that would limit the exercise of their fiduciary duties. In Paramount Communications, Inc. v. QVC Network, Inc., 637 A.2d 34 (Del.1994), we invalidated a "no shop" provision of a merger agreement with a favored bidder (Viacom) that prevented the directors of the target company (Paramount) from communicating with a competing bidder (QVC) the terms of its competing bid in an effort to obtain the highest available value for shareholders.

Similarly, in Quickturn Design Systems, Inc. v. Shapiro, 721 A.2d 1281 (Del.1998), the directors of the target company (Quickturn) adopted a "poison pill" rights plan that contained a so-called "delayed redemption provision" as a defense against a hostile takeover bid, as part of which the bidder (Mentor Graphics) intended to wage a proxy contest to replace the target company board. The delayed redemption provision was intended to deter that effort, by preventing any newly elected board from redeeming the poison pill for six months. This Court invalidated that provision, because it would "impermissibly deprive any newly elected board of both its statutory authority to manage the corporation under 8 Del. C. § 141(a) and its concomitant fiduciary duty pursuant to that statutory mandate."

Both QVC and Quickturn involved binding contractual arrangements that the board of directors had voluntarily imposed upon themselves. This case involves a binding bylaw that the shareholders seek to impose involuntarily on the directors in the specific area of election expense reimbursement. Although this case is distinguishable in that respect, the distinction is one without a difference. The reason is that the internal governance contract-which here takes the form of a bylaw-is one that would also prevent the directors from exercising their full managerial power in circumstances where their fiduciary duties would otherwise require them to deny reimbursement to a dissident slate. That this limitation would be imposed by a majority vote of the shareholders rather than by the directors themselves, does not, in our view, legally matter.

AFSCME contends that it is improper to use the doctrine articulated in QVC and Quickturn as the measure of the validity of the Bylaw. Because the Bylaw would remove the subject of election expense reimbursement (in circumstances as defined by the Bylaw) entirely from the CA's board's discretion (AFSCME argues), it cannot fairly be claimed that the directors would be precluded from discharging their fiduciary duty. Stated differently, AFSCME argues that it is unfair to claim that the Bylaw prevents the CA board from discharging its fiduciary duty where the effect of the Bylaw is to relieve the board entirely of those duties in this specific area.

That response, in our view, is more semantical than substantive. No matter how artfully it may be phrased, the argument concedes the very proposition that renders the Bylaw, as written, invalid: the Bylaw mandates reimbursement of election expenses in circumstances that a proper application of fiduciary principles could preclude.

That such circumstances could arise is not far fetched. Under Delaware law, a board may expend corporate funds to reimburse proxy expenses "[w]here the controversy is concerned with a question of policy as distinguished from personnel o[r] management." But in a situation where the proxy contest is motivated by personal or petty concerns, or to promote interests that do not further, or are adverse to, those of the corporation, the board's fiduciary duty could compel that reimbursement be denied altogether.

It is in this respect that the proposed Bylaw, as written, would violate Delaware law if enacted by CA's shareholders. As presently drafted, the Bylaw would afford CA's directors full discretion to determine what amount of reimbursement is appropriate, because the directors would be obligated to grant only the "reasonable" expenses of a successful short slate. Unfortunately, that does not go far enough, because the Bylaw contains no language or provision that would reserve to CA's directors their full power to exercise their fiduciary duty to decide whether or not it would be appropriate, in a specific case, to award reimbursement at all.

In arriving at this conclusion, we express no view on whether the Bylaw as currently drafted, would create a better governance scheme from a policy standpoint. We decide only what is, and is not, legally permitted under the DGCL. That statute, as currently drafted, is the expression of policy as decreed by the Delaware legislature. Those who believe that CA's shareholders should be permitted to make the proposed Bylaw as drafted part of CA's governance scheme, have two alternatives. They may seek to amend the Certificate of Incorporation to include the substance of the Bylaw; or they may seek recourse from the Delaware General Assembly.

Accordingly, we answer the second question certified to us in the affirmative.

Delaware's Response to Director Election Bylaws

The court in *AFSCME* concluded its analysis by setting forth two alternatives for the proponents of the defective bylaw change: amend the articles of incorporation or trigger a change in Delaware law. Unlike a bylaw amendment, an amendment of a corporation's articles of incorporation in Delaware, as in nearly all states, must be approved and proposed by the board of directors. 8 DGCL § 242. And usually there is little or no chance that a board of directors is going to approve an amendment to the articles of incorporation that restricts or limits its authority and flexibility going forward. So the specific issue at stake in *AFSCME* ended up triggering, and being resolved by, the following two 2009 additions to the Delaware General Corporation Law:

§ 112. Access to proxy solicitation materials.

The bylaws may provide that if the corporation solicits proxies with respect to an election of directors, it may be required, to the extent and subject to such procedures or conditions as may be provided in the bylaws, to include in its proxy solicitation materials (including any form of proxy it distributes), in addition to individuals nominated by the board of directors, 1 or more individuals nominated by a stockholder. Such procedures or conditions may include any of the following:

(1) A provision requiring a minimum record or beneficial ownership, or duration of ownership, of shares of the corporation's capital stock, by the nominating stockholder, and defining beneficial ownership to take into account options or other rights in respect of or related to such stock;

(2) A provision requiring the nominating stockholder to submit specified information concerning the stockholder and the stockholder's nominees, including information concerning ownership by such persons of shares of the corporation's capital stock, or options or other rights in respect of or related to such stock;

(3) A provision conditioning eligibility to require inclusion in the corporation's proxy solicitation materials upon the number or proportion of directors nominated by stockholders or whether the stockholder previously sought to require such inclusion;

(4) A provision precluding nominations by any person if such person, any nominee of such person, or any affiliate or associate of such person or nominee, has acquired or publicly proposed to acquire shares constituting a specified percentage of the voting power of the corporation's outstanding voting stock within a specified period before the election of directors;

(5) A provision requiring that the nominating stockholder undertake to indemnify the corporation in respect of any loss arising as a result of any false or misleading information or statement submitted by the nominating stockholder in connection with a nomination; and

(6) Any other lawful condition.

§ 113. Proxy expense reimbursement.

(a) The bylaws may provide for the reimbursement by the corporation of expenses incurred by a stockholder in soliciting proxies in connection with an election of directors, subject to such procedures or conditions as the bylaws may prescribe, including:

(1) Conditioning eligibility for reimbursement upon the number or proportion of persons nominated by the stockholder seeking reimbursement or whether such stockholder previously sought reimbursement for similar expenses;

(2) Limitations on the amount of reimbursement based upon the proportion of votes cast in favor of 1 or more of the persons nominated by the stockholder seeking reimbursement, or upon the amount spent by the corporation in soliciting proxies in connection with the election;

(3) Limitations concerning elections of directors by cumulative voting pursuant to § 214 of this title; or

(4) Any other lawful condition.

(b) No bylaw so adopted shall apply to elections for which any record date precedes its adoption.

SEC Tries to Get on Board

The SEC has tried to follow Delaware's lead in making it easier for shareholders to shake up board member elections. On August 25, 2010, the SEC adopted two changes in furtherance of this goal:

(1) A new Rule 14a-11 that would have permitted shareholders or shareholder groups who own not less than 3 percent in voting power of a public company for at least three years to include their nominees (up to 25 percent of the board) in the company's proxy materials, and

(2) A revision to Rule 14a-8 that requires companies to include in their proxy materials, under certain circumstances, shareholder proposals that seek to establish a procedure in the company's governing documents for the inclusion of one or more shareholder director nominees in a company's proxy materials.

The SEC entered a stay on October 4, 2010, of these changes when a lawsuit was filed in *Business Roundtable And Chamber Of Commerce Of The United States Of America v. Securities And Exchange Commission*, 647 F.3d 1144 (D.C. Cir. 2011), challenging new Rule 14a-11. On July 22, 2011, the District of Columbia Circuit vacated the new Rule 14a-11. The court held that the Commission acted arbitrarily and capriciously in failing to adequately assess the economic effects of the new rule and, thus, violated the Administrative Procedures Act and the SEC's obligation to consider the rule's effect upon efficiency, competition and capital formation. The court of stated:

> Here the Commission inconsistently and opportunistically framed the costs and benefits of the rule; failed adequately to quantify the certain costs or to explain why those costs could not be quantified; neglected to support its predictive judgments; contradicted itself; and failed to respond to substantial problems raised by commentators.

The SEC's final response to the court's decision was a press release on September 6, 2011, in which the SEC confirmed that it would not seek a rehearing of the court's decision. The release included the following statement of Chairman Mary L. Schapiro:

> I firmly believe that providing a meaningful opportunity for shareholders to exercise their right to nominate directors at their companies is in the best interest of investors and our markets. It is a process that helps make boards more accountable for the risks undertaken by the companies they manage. I remain committed to finding a way to make it easier for shareholders to nominate candidates to corporate boards.

> At the same time, I want to be sure that we carefully consider and learn from the Court's objections as we determine the best path forward. I have asked the staff to continue reviewing the decision as well as the comments that we previously received from interested parties."

The court's decision did not impact the change to Rule 14a-8, which became effective in September 2011. This change requires companies to include in their proxy materials, under certain circumstances, shareholder proposals that seek to establish a procedure in the company's governing documents for the inclusion of one or more shareholder director nominees in a company's proxy materials.

So the net result of this partially aborted SEC effort is an expanded capacity of shareholders to propose bylaw changes related to director election procedures and a confirmation that the SEC's mission to expand the director-election rights of shareholders will move forward. The lesson for all who have a stake in the matter is obvious: stay tuned.

The Intersection of State Law and the Proxy Rules

The *AFSCME* case aptly illustrates the point at which state corporate law becomes the focal point of a shareholder bylaw proposal effort. The right of shareholders under state law to propose bylaw amendments was considered long ago in *Auer v. Dressel*, 306 N.Y. 427, 118 N.E.2d 590 (1954), a case that involved the authority of shareholders to propose a bylaw amendment that would enable the shareholders to elect replacement directors. In finding that shareholders have an inherent right to make such a bylaw proposal, the court stated:

> Since these particular stockholders have the right to elect nine directors and to remove them on proven charges, it is not inappropriate that they should use their further power to amend the by-laws to elect the successors of such directors as shall be removed after hearing, or who shall resign pending hearing. Quite pertinent at this point is Rogers v. Hill, 289 U.S. 582, 589, 53 S.Ct. 731, 734, 77 L.Ed. 1385, which made light of an argument that stockholders, by giving power to the directors to make by-laws, had lost their own power to make them; quoting a New Jersey case, In re Griffing Iron Co., 63 N.J.L. 168, 41 A. 931, the United States Supreme Court said: "It would be preposterous to leave the real owners of the corporate property at the mercy of their agents, and the law has not done so".

But as the *AFSCME* case illustrates, the power of shareholders to propose bylaw amendments is not unlimited. The analysis used in the *AFSCME* case provides a helpful framework to test whether a particular proposal is a proper matter for shareholder action under applicable state law and whether the proposal, if approved, would violate applicable law by, for example, triggering a violation of the directors' duty of care or duty of loyalty. This should be a threshold consideration for any shareholder group that is pondering a creative or novel bylaw amendment proposal.

CHAPTER 9

CORE SHAREHOLDER RIGHTS

A. INSPECTION RIGHTS

1. STATUTORY SPINS ON A COMMON LAW RIGHT

At common law, the shareholder of a corporation had the right to inspect the corporation's books and records.[1] The source of the right was the shareholder's equitable interest in the entity's assets. Under the majority common law rule, a shareholder was presumed to have a proper purpose in making a demand to inspect corporate documents. The corporation had the burden of proving bad faith or an improper purpose.

This core common law right has been codified by the corporation statutes of every state. It is an important tool for the activist shareholder who wants to get the attention of management, force a dialogue with top executives, build a case for ousting a director or a slate of directors, submit a proposal for a shareholder vote, or commence a derivative lawsuit against officers or directors. Often it is the primary means by which a shareholder can secure the details and evidence to confirm suspicions and properly frame the allegations or the terms of a proposal.

The statutes of many states follow the Model Business Corporation Act in establishing a two-tier approach to shareholder inspection rights. The first tier provides that any shareholder who gives a corporation written notice of an inspection demand at least five business days in advance may inspect and copy, during regular business hours at the corporation's principal office, core organizational documents which include:

- The articles or restated articles of incorporation, all amendments to the articles currently in effect and any related notices to shareholders;

- The bylaws or restated bylaws and all amendments to them currently in effect;

- The minutes of all shareholders' meetings, and records of all action taken by shareholders without a meeting, for the past three years;

- Resolutions adopted by its board of directors creating one or more classes or series of shares, and fixing their relative rights, preferences, and limitations, if shares issued pursuant to those resolutions are outstanding;

---

1. See, generally, 5A Fletcher Cyc. Corp. § 2251 (perm. edition).

- All written communications to shareholders generally within the past three years, including financial statements furnished to the shareholders;

- A list of the names and business addresses of its current directors and officers; and

- The corporation's most recent annual report delivered to the secretary of state.

If a shareholder desires to inspect and copy other documents - financial records, excerpts from the minutes of any board meetings, records of any action of a committee of the board, minutes of any shareholder meeting or consent resolutions beyond the last three years, or the record of shareholders - the Model Act requires that the shareholder's demand (1) be made in "good faith and for a proper purpose," (2) describe with "reasonable particularity" the purpose and the requested records, and (3) be limited to records that are "directly connected" with the stated purpose.[2] The Model Act solidifies shareholder inspection rights by expressly stating, "The right of inspection granted by this section may not be abolished or limited by a corporation's articles of incorporation or bylaws."[3]

Some states create a third tier right – the right of any shareholder to inspect a list of shareholders entitled to vote at a meeting within 10 days of the meeting.[4] Other states limit certain inspection rights to shareholders who have owned a designated percentage of stock for a specified minimum period of time.[5] And, of course, many shareholder inspection disputes are governed by section 220 of Delaware's corporate law, which states in pertinent part:

> Any stockholder, in person or by attorney or other agent, shall, upon written demand under oath stating the purpose thereof, have the right during the usual hours for business to inspect for any proper purpose, and to make copies and extracts from: (1) The corporation's stock ledger, a list of its stockholders, and its other books and records...[6]

The common element in all state shareholder inspection statutes is the "proper purpose" requirement. This is the toughest hurdle for shareholders who want access to detailed documents that might exposure wrongdoing or faulty judgments.

2. THE "PROPER PURPOSE" CHALLENGE

CASE PROBLEM 9-1

Tolson Technologies, Inc. ("Tolson") is in the business of developing, producing and distributing sophisticated motion stabilization systems. One of its leading products is "StableSeas," a hi-tech stabilizer designed for large yachts and commercial boats. Tolson's stock is publically traded on the NASDAQ.

---

2. MBCA § 16.01 and 16.02.
3. MBCA § 16.02(d).
4. See, for example, Washington State's RCW 23B.07.200.
5. See, for example, N.Y.B.C.L. § 624(b), which limits certain shareholder inspection rights to shareholders who have owned at least five percent of a class of outstanding stock for at least six months.
6. 8 DGCL § 220(b)

Tolson's CEO is Dirk Lane, age 58, an avid yachtsman who is known as "commodore emeritus" at the local yacht club. Tolson's board has seven members – Dirk, Tolson's chief financial and chief operating officers, and four outsiders, all long-term acquaintances of Dirk.

Four years ago, Dirk got the idea that Tolson should own a corporate yacht that could be used to demonstrate StableSeas, entertain clients, host corporate meeting, and showcase StableSeas at boat shows and yacht festivals. Tolson's seven member board unanimously approved the purchase of a 130- foot pilot house yacht and named it "Stable."

Stable needed a captain and crew. For the first two years of Tolson's ownership of Stable, Dirk's son Luke (an expert, licensed captain) served as Stable's captain and managed a crew of three (including a chef). When Luke fell in love and secured an opportunity to captain a much larger yacht closer to his new wife's hometown, Dirk had to find a new captain.

After an exhaustive search, Dirk found and heavily recruited Marge Davis, a seasoned captain with a sterling reputation for always running "a very tight ship." As an added bonus, Marge's husband David was a superb chef and first mate who always worked with Marge. Marge and David advised Dirk that they would not leave their present jobs unless they were given "some assurances of long-term job security." Dirk handled this objection by providing a short letter that stated, "Tolson has no plans for selling Stable within the next five years, and you can count on continued employment during that period so long your performance meets our standards."

Until very recently, Marge and David believed that they were doing an excellent job. For each of the past two holiday seasons, Dirk personally transferred to Marge and David 5,000 shares of Tolson stock (average trading price $28) as a "Tip" for their "wonderful services to my family and friends." This stock came from Dirk, not Tolson.

Last week Marge and David received a short letter from Dirk advising them that their employment was being terminated, effective immediately, and directing them to immediately vacate Stable. The cited reason for the terminations was a Tolson board determination that "the crew was being poorly managed, the quality of food services was declining, complaints were coming from important guests, and a premier Tolson asset was not being properly maintained." A few calls to industry sources confirmed to Marge that Luke's "big gig busted," and that he and his bride were headed to Stable.

Marge and David are furious. Beyond losing annual salaries that totaled $310,000 and their house (Stable), their reputations have been tarnished in a tough market. David characterizes the board determination as "crap" and chalks the mess up to "shameful nepotism driven by Dirk's wife and her determination to 'get her son back.'" Marge goes farther and claims, "The whole Tolson thing is a ruse because everyone knows that Stable is Dirk's toy – his most cherished symbol of success, reserved only for friends, family and those he wants to impress. Tolson just pays the bills."

Marge and David want to take action. An important preliminary question is whether they can exercise their inspection rights as shareholders to obtain corporate reports and records that will prove that the cited reasons for their terminations are "bogus" and that the alleged board determination either didn't happen or was "just another uninformed rubber stamp for something Dirk wanted." Please advise Marge and David as to their inspection rights, assuming Tolson is incorporated in Delaware.

STATE EX REL. PILLSBURY v. HONEYWELL, INC.
191 N.W.2d 406 (Minn 1971)

KELLY, Justice.

Petitioner appeals from an order and judgment of the district court denying all relief prayed for in a petition for writs of mandamus to compel respondent, Honeywell, Inc., (Honeywell) to produce its original shareholder ledger, current shareholder ledger, and all corporate records dealing with weapons and munitions manufacture. We must affirm.

Petitioner attended a meeting on July 3, 1969, of a group involved in what was known as the 'Honeywell Project.' He was shocked at the knowledge that Honeywell had a large government contract to produce anti-personnel fragmentation bombs. Upset because of knowledge that such bombs were produced in his own community by a company which he had known and respected, petitioner determined to stop Honeywell's munitions production.

On July 14, 1969, petitioner ordered his fiscal agent to purchase 100 shares of Honeywell. He admits that the sole purpose of the purchase was to give himself a voice in Honeywell's affairs so he could persuade Honeywell to cease producing munitions.

Prior to the instigation of this suit, petitioner submitted two formal demands to Honeywell requesting that it produce its original shareholder ledger, current shareholder ledger, and all corporate records dealing with weapons and munitions manufacture. Honeywell refused.

On November 24, 1969, a petition was filed for writs of mandamus ordering Honeywell to produce the above mentioned records. In response, Honeywell answered the petition and served a notice of deposition on petitioner, who moved that the answer be stricken as procedurally premature and that an order be issued to limit the deposition. After a hearing, the trial court denied the motion, and the deposition was taken on December 15, 1969.

In the deposition petitioner outlined his beliefs concerning the Vietnam war and his purpose for his involvement with Honeywell. He expressed his desire to communicate with other shareholders in the hope of altering Honeywell's board of directors and thereby changing its policy. To this end, he testified, business records are necessary to insure accuracy.

A hearing was held on January 8, 1970, during which Honeywell introduced the deposition, conceded all material facts stated therein, and argued that petitioner was not entitled to any relief as a matter of law. Petitioner asked that alternative writs of mandamus issue for all the relief requested in his petition. On

April 8, 1970, the trial court dismissed the petition, holding that the relief requested was for an improper and indefinite purpose. Petitioner contends in this appeal that the dismissal was in error.

Honeywell is a Delaware corporation doing business in Minnesota. Both petitioner and Honeywell spent considerable effort in arguing whether Delaware or Minnesota law applies. The trial court, applying Delaware law, determined that the outcome of the case rested upon whether or not petitioner has a proper purpose germane to his interest as a shareholder. Del.Code Ann. tit. 8, s 220 (Supp. 1968). This test is derived from the common law and is applicable in Minnesota. See, Sanders v. Pacific Gamble Robinson Co., 250 Minn. 265, 84 N.W.2d 919 (1957). Minn.St. c. 300, upon which petitioner relies, applies only to firms incorporated under that chapter. We need not rule on whether the lower court applied the right state law since the test used was correct.

Under the Delaware statute the shareholder must prove a proper purpose to inspect corporate records other than shareholder lists. Del.Code Ann. tit. 8, s 220(c) (Supp.1968). This facet of the law did not affect the trial court's findings of fact. The trial court ordered judgment for Honeywell, ruling that petitioner had not demonstrated a proper purpose germane to his interest as a stockholder. Petitioner contends that a stockholder who disagrees with management has an absolute right to inspect corporate records for purposes of soliciting proxies. He would have this court rule that such solicitation is per se a 'proper purpose.' Honeywell argues that a 'proper purpose' contemplates concern with investment return. We agree with Honeywell.

This court has had several occasions to rule on the propriety of shareholders' demands for inspection of corporate books and records. Minn.St. 300.32, not applicable here, has been held to be declaratory of the common-law principle that a stockholder is entitled to inspection for a proper purpose germane to his business interests. While inspection will not be permitted for purposes of curiosity, speculation, or vexation, adverseness to management and a desire to gain control of the corporation for economic benefit does not indicate an improper purpose.

Several courts agree with petitioner's contention that a mere desire to communicate with other shareholders is, per se, a proper purpose. This would seem to confer an almost absolute right to inspection. We believe that a better rule would allow inspections only if the shareholder has a proper purpose for such communication. This rule was applied in McMahon v. Dispatch Printing Co., 101 N.J.L. 470, 129 A. 425 (1925), where inspection was denied because the shareholder's objective was to discredit politically the president of the company, who was also the New Jersey secretary of state.

The act of inspecting a corporation's shareholder ledger and business records must be viewed in its proper perspective. In terms of the corporate norm, inspection is merely the act of the concerned owner checking on what is in part his property. In the context of the large firm, inspection can be more akin to a weapon in corporate warfare. The effectiveness of the weapon is considerable:

'Considering the huge size of many modern corporations and the necessarily complicated nature of their bookkeeping, it is plain that to permit their thousands of stockholders to roam at will through their records would render impossible not only any attempt to keep their records efficiently, but the proper carrying on of their businesses.' Cooke v. Outland, 265 N.C. 601, 611, 144 S.E.2d 835, 842 (1965).

That one must have proper standing to demand inspection has been recognized by statutes in several jurisdictions. Courts have also balked at compelling inspection by a shareholder holding an insignificant amount of stock in the corporation.

Petitioner's standing as a shareholder is quite tenuous. He had previously ordered his agent to buy 100 shares, but there is no showing of investment intent. While his agent had a cash balance in the $400,000 portfolio, petitioner made no attempt to determine whether Honeywell was a good investment or whether more profitable shares would have to be sold to finance the Honeywell purchase.

Petitioner had utterly no interest in the affairs of Honeywell before he learned of Honeywell's production of fragmentation bombs. Immediately after obtaining this knowledge, he purchased stock in Honeywell for the sole purpose of asserting ownership privileges in an effort to force Honeywell to cease such production. We agree with the court in Chas. A. Day & Co. v. Booth, 123 Maine 443, 447, 123 A. 557, 558 (1924) that 'where it is shown that such stockholding is only colorable, or solely for the purpose of maintaining proceedings of this kind, (we) fail to see how the petitioner can be said to be a 'person interested,' entitled as of right to inspect * * *.' But for his opposition to Honeywell's policy, petitioner probably would not have bought Honeywell stock, would not be interested in Honeywell's profits and would not desire to communicate with Honeywell's shareholders. His avowed purpose in buying Honeywell stock was to place himself in a position to try to impress his opinions favoring a reordering of priorities upon Honeywell management and its other shareholders. Such a motivation can hardly be deemed a proper purpose germane to his economic interest as a shareholder.

We do not mean to imply that a shareholder with a bona fide investment interest could not bring this suit if motivated by concern with the long- or short-term economic effects on Honeywell resulting from the production of war munitions. Similarly, this suit might be appropriate when a shareholder has a bona fide concern about the adverse effects of abstention from profitable war contracts on his investment in Honeywell.

In the instant case, however, the trial court, in effect, has found from all the facts that petitioner was not interested in even the long-term well-being of Honeywell or the enhancement of the value of his shares. His sole purpose was to persuade the company to adopt his social and political concerns, irrespective of any economic benefit to himself or Honeywell. This purpose on the part of one buying into the corporation does not entitle the petitioner to inspect Honeywell's books and records.

Petitioner argues that he wishes to inspect the stockholder ledger in order that he may correspond with other shareholders with the hope of electing to the board one or more directors who represent his particular viewpoint. While a plan to elect one or more directors is specific and the election of directors normally would be a proper purpose, here the purpose was not germane to petitioner's or Honeywell's economic interest. Instead, the plan was designed to further petitioner's political and social beliefs. Since the requisite propriety of purpose germane to his or Honeywell's economic interest is not present, the allegation that petitioner seeks to elect a new board of directors is insufficient to compel inspection.

The order of the trial court denying the writ of mandamus is affirmed.

SAITO v. MCKESSON
806 A.2d 113 (Del. 2002)

BERGER, Justice.

In this appeal, we consider the limitations on a stockholder's statutory right to inspect corporate books and records. The statute, 8 *Del.C.* § 220, enables stockholders to investigate matters "reasonably related to [their] interest as [stockholders]" including, among other things, possible corporate wrongdoing. It does not open the door to the wide ranging discovery that would be available in support of litigation. For this statutory tool to be meaningful, however, it cannot be read narrowly to deprive a stockholder of necessary documents solely because the documents were prepared by third parties or because the documents predate the stockholder's first investment in the corporation. A stockholder who demands inspection for a proper purpose should be given access to all of the documents in the corporation's possession, custody or control, that are necessary to satisfy that proper purpose. Thus, where a § 220 claim is based on alleged corporate wrongdoing, and assuming the allegation is meritorious, the stockholder should be given enough information to effectively address the problem, either through derivative litigation or through direct contact with the corporation's directors and/or stockholders.

On October 17, 1998, McKesson Corporation entered into a stock-for-stock merger agreement with HBO & Company ("HBOC"). On October 20, 1998, appellant, Noel Saito, purchased McKesson stock. The merger was consummated in January 1999 and the combined company was renamed McKesson HBOC, Incorporated. HBOC continued its separate corporate existence as a wholly-owned subsidiary of McKesson HBOC.

Starting in April and continuing through July 1999, McKesson HBOC announced a series of financial restatements triggered by its year-end audit process. During that four month period, McKesson HBOC reduced its revenues by $327.4 million for the three prior fiscal years. The restatements all were attributed to HBOC accounting irregularities. The first announcement precipitated several lawsuits, including a derivative action pending in the Court of Chancery, captioned *Ash v. McCall,* Civil Action No. 17132. Saito was one of four plaintiffs in the *Ash* complaint, which alleged that: (i) McKesson's directors breached their duty of care by failing to discover the HBOC accounting irregularities before the merger; (ii) McKesson's directors committed corporate waste by entering into the merger with HBOC; (iii) HBOC's directors breached their fiduciary duties by failing to monitor the company's compliance with financial reporting requirements prior to the merger; and (iv) McKesson HBOC's directors failed in the same respect during the three months following the merger. Although the Court of Chancery granted defendants' motion to dismiss the complaint, the dismissal was without prejudice as to the pre-merger and post-merger oversight claims.

In its decision on the motion to dismiss, the Court of Chancery specifically suggested that Saito and the other plaintiffs "use the 'tools at hand,' most prominently § 220 books and records actions, to obtain information necessary to sue derivatively." Saito was the only *Ash* plaintiff to follow that advice. The stated purpose of Saito's demand was:

> (1) to further investigate breaches of fiduciary duties by the boards of directors of HBO & Co., Inc., McKesson, Inc., and/or McKesson HBOC, Inc. related to their oversight of their respective company's accounting procedures and financial reporting; (2) to investigate potential claims against advisors engaged by McKesson, Inc. and HBO & Co., Inc. to the acquisition of HBO & Co., Inc. by McKesson, Inc.; and (3) to gather information relating to the above in order to supplement the complaint in *Ash v. McCall, et al.*, ... in accordance with the September 15, 2000 Opinion of the Court of Chancery.

Saito demanded access to eleven categories of documents, including those relating to Arthur Andersen's pre-merger review and verification of HBOC's financial condition; communications between or among HBOC, McKesson, and their investment bankers and accountants concerning HBOC's accounting practices; and discussions among members of the Boards of Directors of HBOC, McKesson, and/or McKesson HBOC concerning reports published in April 1997 and thereafter about HBOC's accounting practices or financial condition.

Stockholders of Delaware corporations enjoy a qualified common law and statutory right to inspect the corporation's books and records. Inspection rights were recognized at common law because, "[a]s a matter of self-protection, the stockholder was entitled to know how his agents were conducting the affairs of the corporation of which he or she was a part owner." The common law right is codified in 8 *Del.C.* § 220, which provides in relevant part:

> (b) Any stockholder ... shall, upon written demand under oath stating the purpose thereof, have the right ... to inspect for any proper purpose the corporation's stock ledger, a list of its stockholders, and its other books and records, and to make copies or extracts therefrom. A proper purpose shall mean a purpose reasonably related to such person's interest as a stockholder.

Once a stockholder establishes a proper purpose under § 220, the right to relief will not be defeated by the fact that the stockholder may have secondary purposes that are improper. The scope of a stockholder's inspection, however, is limited to those books and records that are necessary and essential to accomplish the stated, proper purpose.

After trial, the Court of Chancery found "credible evidence of possible wrongdoing," which satisfied Saito's burden of establishing a proper purpose for the inspection of corporate books and records. But the Court of Chancery limited Saito's access to relevant documents in three respects. First, it held that, since Saito would not have standing to bring an action challenging actions that occurred before he purchased McKesson stock, Saito could not obtain documents created before October 20, 1998. Second, the court concluded that Saito was not entitled to documents relating to possible wrongdoing by the financial advisors to the merging companies. Third, the court denied Saito access to any HBOC documents, since Saito never was a stockholder of HBOC. We will consider each of these rulings in turn.

By statute, stockholders who bring derivative suits must allege that they were stockholders of the corporation "at the time of the transaction of which such stockholder complains...." The Court of Chancery decided that this limitation on Saito's ability to maintain a derivative suit controlled the scope of his inspection rights. As a result, the court held that Saito was "effectively limited to examining conduct of McKesson and McKesson HBOC's boards *following* the negotiation and public announcement of the merger agreement."

Although we recognize that there may be some interplay between the two statutes, we do not read § 327 as defining the temporal scope of a stockholder's inspection rights under § 220. The books and records statute requires that a stockholder's purpose be one that is "reasonably related" to his or her interest as a stockholder. The standing statute, § 327, bars a stockholder from bringing a derivative action unless the stockholder owned the corporation's stock at the time of the alleged wrong. If a stockholder wanted to investigate alleged wrongdoing that substantially predated his or her stock ownership, there could be a question as to whether the stockholder's purpose was reasonably related to his or her interest as a stockholder, especially if the stockholder's only purpose was to institute derivative litigation. But stockholders may use information about corporate mismanagement in other ways, as well. They may seek an audience with the board to discuss proposed reforms or, failing in that, they may prepare a stockholder resolution for the next annual meeting, or mount a proxy fight to elect new directors. None of those activities would be prohibited by § 327.

Even where a stockholder's only purpose is to gather information for a derivative suit, the date of his or her stock purchase should not be used as an automatic "cut-off" date in a § 220 action. In sum, the date on which a stockholder first acquired the corporation's stock does not control the scope of records available under § 220. If activities that occurred before the purchase date are "reasonably related" to the stockholder's interest as a stockholder, then the stockholder should be given access to records necessary to an understanding of those activities.

The Court of Chancery denied Saito access to documents in McKesson-HBOC's possession that the corporation obtained from financial and accounting advisors, on the ground that Saito could not use § 220 to develop potential claims against third parties. On appeal, Saito argues that he is seeking third party documents for the same reason he is seeking McKesson HBOC documents-to investigate possible wrongdoing by McKesson and McKesson HBOC. Since the trial court found that to be a proper purpose, Saito argues that he should not be precluded from seeing documents that are necessary to his purpose, and in McKesson HBOC's possession, simply because the documents were prepared by third party advisors.

We agree that, generally, the source of the documents in a corporation's possession should not control a stockholder's right to inspection under § 220. It is not entirely clear, however, that the trial court restricted Saito's access on that basis. The Court of Chancery decided that Saito's interest in pursuing claims against McKesson HBOC's advisors was not a proper purpose. It recognized that a secondary improper purpose usually is irrelevant if the stockholder establishes his need for the same documents to support a proper purpose. But the court apparently concluded that the categories of third party documents that Saito demanded did not support the proper purpose of investigating possible wrongdoing by McKesson and McKesson HBOC.

We cannot determine from the present record whether the Court of Chancery intended to exclude all third party documents, but such a blanket exclusion would be improper. The source of the documents and the manner in which they were obtained by the corporation have little or no bearing on a stockholder's inspection rights. The issue is whether the documents are necessary and essential to satisfy the stockholder's proper purpose. In this case, Saito wants to investigate possible wrongdoing relating to McKesson and McKesson HBOC's failure to discover HBOC's accounting irregularities. Since McKesson and McKesson HBOC relied on financial and accounting advisors to evaluate HBOC's financial condition and reporting, those advisors' reports and correspondence would be critical to Saito's investigation.

Finally, the Court of Chancery held that Saito was not entitled to any HBOC documents because he was not a stockholder of HBOC before or after the merger. Although Saito is a stockholder of HBOC's parent, McKesson HBOC, stockholders of a parent corporation are not entitled to inspect a subsidiary's books and records, "[a]bsent a showing of a fraud or that a subsidiary is in fact the mere alter ego of the parent...." *Skouras v. Admiralty Enterprises, Inc.,* 386 A.2d 674, 681 (Del.Ch.1978). The Court of Chancery found no basis to disregard HBOC's separate existence and, therefore, denied access to its records.

We reaffirm this settled principle, which applies to those HBOC books and records that were never provided to McKesson or McKesson HBOC. But it does not apply to relevant documents that HBOC gave to McKesson before the merger, or to McKesson HBOC after the merger. We assume that HBOC provided financial and accounting information to its proposed merger partner and, later, to its parent company. As with the third party advisors' documents, Saito would need access to relevant HBOC documents in order to understand what his company's directors knew and why they failed to recognize HBOC's accounting irregularities.

SEINFELD v. VERIZON COMMUNICATIONS, INC.
909 A.2d 117 (Del. 2006)

HOLLAND, Justice.

The plaintiff-appellant, Frank D. Seinfeld ("Seinfeld"), brought suit under section 220 of the Delaware General Corporation Law to compel the defendant-appellee, Verizon Communications, Inc. ("Verizon"), to produce, for his inspection, its books and records related to the compensation of Verizon's three highest corporate officers from 2000 to 2002. Seinfeld claimed that their executive compensation, individually and collectively, was excessive and wasteful. On cross-motions for summary judgment, the Court of Chancery applied well-established Delaware law and held that Seinfeld had not met his evidentiary burden to demonstrate a proper purpose to justify the inspection of Verizon's records.

The settled law of Delaware required Seinfeld to present some evidence that established a credible basis from which the Court of Chancery could infer there were legitimate issues of possible waste, mismanagement or wrongdoing that warranted further investigation. *Thomas & Betts Corp. v. Leviton Mfg. Co., Inc.,* 681 A.2d 1026, 1031 (Del.1996); *Security First Corp. v. U.S. Die Casting & Dev. Co.,* 687 A.2d 563, 567 (Del.1997); *Helmsman Mgmt. Servs., Inc. v. A & S Consultants, Inc.,* 525 A.2d 160, 166 (Del.Ch.1987). Seinfeld argues that burden of proof "erects an insurmountable barrier for the minority shareholder of a public company." We have concluded that Seinfeld's argument is without merit.

We reaffirm the well-established law of Delaware that stockholders seeking inspection under section 220 must present "some evidence" to suggest a "credible basis" from which a court can infer that mismanagement, waste or wrongdoing may have occurred. The "credible basis" standard achieves an appropriate balance between providing stockholders who can offer some evidence of possible wrongdoing with access to corporate records and safeguarding the right of the corporation to deny requests for inspections that are based only upon suspicion or curiosity. Accordingly, the judgment of the Court of Chancery must be affirmed.

Seinfeld asserts that he is the beneficial owner of approximately 3,884 shares of Verizon, held in street name through a brokerage firm. His stated purpose for seeking Verizon's books and records was to investigate mismanagement and corporate waste regarding the executive compensations of Ivan G. Seidenberg, Lawrence T. Babbio, Jr. and Charles R. Lee. Seinfeld alleges that the three executives were all performing in the same job and were paid amounts, including stock options, above the compensation provided for in their employment contracts. Seinfeld's section 220 claim for inspection is further premised on various computations he performed which indicate that the three executives' compensation totaled $205 million over three years and was, therefore, excessive, given their responsibilities to the corporation.

During his deposition, Seinfeld acknowledged he had no factual support for his claim that mismanagement had taken place. He admitted that the three executives did not perform any duplicative work. Seinfeld conceded he had no factual basis to allege the executives "did not earn" the amounts paid to them under their respective employment agreements. Seinfeld also admitted "there is a possibility" that the $205 million executive compensation amount he calculated was wrong.

The issue before us is quite narrow: should a stockholder seeking inspection under section 220 be entitled to relief without being required to show some evidence to suggest a credible basis for wrongdoing? We conclude that the answer must be no.

Section 220 provides stockholders of Delaware corporations with a "powerful right." *Disney v. Walt Disney Co.,* 857 A.2d 444, 447 (Del.Ch.2004). By properly asserting that right under section 220, stockholders are able to obtain information that can be used in a variety of contexts. Stockholders may use information about corporate mismanagement, waste or wrongdoing in several ways.

More than a decade ago, we noted that "[s]urprisingly, little use has been made of section 220 as an information-gathering tool in the derivative [suit] context." *Rales v. Blasband,* 634 A.2d 927, 934-35 n. 10 (Del.1993). Today, however, stockholders who have concerns about corporate governance are increasingly making a broad array of section 220 demands. The rise in books and records litigation is directly attributable to this Court's encouragement of stockholders, who can show a proper purpose, to use the "tools at hand" to obtain the necessary information before filing a derivative action. Section 220 is now recognized as "an important part of the corporate governance landscape."

The Court of Chancery determined that Seinfeld's deposition testimony established only that he was concerned about the large amount of compensation paid to the three executives. That court concluded that Seinfeld offered "no evidence from which [it] could evaluate whether there is a reasonable ground for suspicion that the executive's compensation rises to the level of waste." It also concluded that Seinfeld did not "submit any evidence showing that the executives were not entitled to [the stock] options." The Court of Chancery properly noted that a disagreement with the business judgment of Verizon's board of directors or its compensation committee is not evidence of wrongdoing and did not satisfy Seinfeld's burden under section 220. The Court of Chancery held:

> viewing the evidence in the light most favorable to Seinfeld, the court must conclude that he has not carried his burden of showing that there is a credible basis from which the court can infer that the Verizon board of directors committed waste or mismanagement in compensating these three executives during the relevant period of time. Instead, the record clearly establishes that Seinfeld's Section 220 demand was made merely on the basis of suspicion or curiosity.

In this appeal, Seinfeld asserts that the "Court of Chancery's ruling erects an insurmountable barrier for the minority shareholder of a public company." Seinfeld submits that "by requiring evidence, the shareholder is prevented from using the tools at hand."

In a section 220 action, a stockholder has the burden of proof to demonstrate a proper purpose by a preponderance of the evidence. It is well established that a stockholder's desire to investigate wrongdoing or mismanagement is a "proper purpose." Such investigations are proper, because where the allegations of mismanagement prove meritorious, investigation furthers the interest of all stockholders and should increase stockholder return.

The evolution of Delaware's jurisprudence in section 220 actions reflects judicial efforts to maintain a proper balance between the rights of shareholders to obtain information based upon credible allegations of corporation mismanagement and the rights of directors to manage the business of the corporation without undue interference from stockholders. In *Thomas & Betts*, this Court held that, to meet its "burden of proof, a stockholder must present some credible basis from which the court can infer that waste or mismanagement may have occurred." Six months later, in *Security First*, this Court held "[t]here must be some evidence of possible mismanagement as would warrant further investigation of the matter."

Investigations of meritorious allegations of possible mismanagement, waste or wrongdoing, benefit the corporation, but investigations that are "indiscriminate fishing expeditions" do not. "At some point, the costs of generating more information fall short of the benefits of having more information. At that point, compelling production of information would be wealth-reducing, and so shareholders would not want it produced." Accordingly, this Court has held that an inspection to investigate possible wrongdoing where there is no "credible basis," is a license for "fishing expeditions" and thus adverse to the interests of the corporation.

A stockholder is "not required to prove by a preponderance of the evidence that waste and [mis]management are actually occurring." Stockholders need only show, by a preponderance of the evidence, a credible basis from which the Court of Chancery can infer there is possible mismanagement that would warrant further investigation - a showing that "may ultimately fall well short of demonstrating that anything wrong occurred." That "threshold may be satisfied by a credible showing, through documents, logic, testimony or otherwise, that there are legitimate issues of wrongdoing."

Although the threshold for a stockholder in a section 220 proceeding is not insubstantial, the "credible basis" standard sets the lowest possible burden of proof. The only way to reduce the burden of proof further would be to eliminate any requirement that a stockholder show some evidence of possible wrongdoing. That would be tantamount to permitting inspection based on the "mere suspicion" standard that Seinfeld advances in this appeal. However, such a standard has been repeatedly rejected as a basis to justify the enterprise cost of an inspection...

Requiring stockholders to establish a "credible basis" for the Court of Chancery to infer possible wrongdoing by presenting "some evidence" has not impeded stockholder inspections. Although many section 220 proceedings have been filed since we decided Security First and Thomas & Betts, Verizon points out that Seinfeld's case is only the second proceeding in which a plaintiff's demand to investigate wrongdoing was found to be entirely without a "credible basis." In contrast, there are a myriad of cases where stockholders have successfully presented "some evidence" to establish a "credible basis" to infer possible mismanagement and thus received some narrowly tailored right of inspection.

We remain convinced that the rights of stockholders and the interests of the corporation in a section 220 proceeding are properly balanced by requiring a stockholder to show "some evidence of possible mismanagement as would warrant further investigation." The "credible basis" standard maximizes stockholder value by limiting the range of permitted stockholder inspections to those that might have merit. Accordingly, our holdings in Security First and Thomas & Betts are ratified and reaffirmed.

How Much is Enough?

There are limits on how much information a shareholder may request though the exercise of a statutory inspection right, particularly if the corporation has already made significant public disclosures related to the issue in dispute. In *Polygon Global Opportunities Master Fund v. West Corporation* 2006 WL 2947486 (Del.Ch. 2006), Polygon, an arbitrage fund, had purchased stock in West Corporation after West had announced a leveraged recapitalization that would squeeze out West's minority shareholders for a cash price that represented a 13 percent premium over the current trading price. In hopes of influencing enough minority shareholders to exercise their statutory appraisal rights to abort the recapitalization (the buyers had an "appraisal out" if too many shareholders exercised their appraisal rights), Polygon demanded from West valuation information under Delaware's section 220. In denying Polygon's request even though, in the court's view, Polygon had established a proper purpose, the court stated:

> There is a dichotomy in section 220 cases between publicly traded companies and closely held companies. With regard to the former, public SEC filings typically provide significant amounts of information about a company, and decisions granting section 220 demands are narrowly tailored to address specific needs, often in response to allegations of wrongdoing. In contrast, stockholders in non-publicly traded companies do not have the wealth of information provided in SEC filings and are often accorded broader relief in section 220 actions.

> In the case of a going private transaction governed by SEC Rule 13e-3, the amount of information made publicly available is even more comprehensive than that required in standard SEC periodic filings. Through its preliminary and final proxy materials, and its Schedule 13E-3, and amendments, West Corp. would appear to have disclosed all material information necessary for Polygon to determine whether or not to seek appraisal. This is not to say that there is a *per se* rule that the disclosure requirements under Rule 13e-3 are coextensive with the "necessary, essential and sufficient" information standard under section

220 demands for valuing stock in the case of a minority squeeze-out merger. Nevertheless, in the present case, the detail and scope of West Corp.'s disclosures makes this so. The disclosures include, among other things, all presentations made by Goldman Sachs and Morgan Stanley, detailed descriptions of their two fairness opinions, company projections, detailed descriptions of the board and special committee meetings, and terms of the Wests' investment in the surviving entity. This wealth of detailed information would appear to satisfy the obligation to disclose all facts material to the decision whether to demand appraisal.

Apparently anticipating the inherent problems with requesting additional information in the face of a transaction with comprehensive public disclosures, Polygon argues that it should be given access to the same information it would receive through discovery in an appraisal action. This argument misapprehends the significant difference in scope between a section 220 action and discovery under Rule 34. The two are, in fact, "entirely different procedures." Section 220 is not intended to supplant or circumvent discovery proceedings, nor should it be used to obtain that discovery in advance of the appraisal action itself. If Polygon wishes to receive the documents it seeks in this action, it must elect to seek appraisal and request them through the discovery process. To now permit Polygon additional information beyond the comprehensive disclosure already in the public domain simply because it could receive such information in a later appraisal action through discovery would be putting the cart before the horse.

B. MAJOR TRANSACTION APPROVAL RIGHTS

State corporate statutes give shareholders the right to approve certain major events that fundamentally change the corporation. At common law, such an event usually required unanimous shareholder consent on a contractual theory - the agreement among the owners of the enterprise was being altered. Corporate statutes have preserved the need for shareholder approval, but the unanimity requirement is long gone. Today, most state corporate statutes require only that the event or transaction be approved by those who hold a majority of the shares represented at a meeting in which a quorum is present. A few states, such as Washington,[7] boost the required approval vote to a higher percentage, such as two-thirds of the shares represented at such a meeting, unless the particular corporation's articles of incorporation specify only majority approval.

As we will see, often an event or transaction requires both board and shareholder approval. When approval by the board of directors is required, all issues relating to the board's fiduciary duties are in play - the duties of care and loyalty, the business judgment rule, and the related challenges discussed in Chapter 10. When shareholder approval is required, the proxy rules (discussed in Chapter 8) and the associated liability risks for false or misleading disclosures

---

7. See RCW §§ 23B.11.030, 23B.12.020.

(discussed in Chapter 11) are central challenges for all public corporations. In many closely held corporations, often a key planning challenge is to protect minority owners from the power of the majority, as discussed in Chapters 12 and 13. In some situations, the presence of a controlling shareholder who commands the shareholder vote poses unique challenges and liability risks, as discussed in Chapter12. When a fight for control of a corporation breaks out, as discussed in Chapter 14, it's all about the power of the shareholder vote. And often the strategic challenge of how best to structure the purchase or sale of a business or the combination of multiple businesses presents alternatives that require shareholder approval but that are driven primarily by tax and other considerations (as discussed in Chapter 15). The point is that much of what is discussed in the following chapters of this book is impacted by, or tied directly to, state law requirements that mandate shareholder approval in select situations.

1. AMENDMENTS TO THE ARTICLES OF INCORPORATION

State corporate statutes typically require both board and shareholder approvals in order to amend a corporation's articles of incorporation, with limited exceptions. Many states have used the Model Business Corporation Act to frame their statutory provisions regarding amendment's to a corporation's articles of incorporation. The Model Act specifically authorizes such amendments and states, "A shareholder of the corporation does not have a vested property right resulting from any provision in the articles of incorporation, including provisions relating to management, control, capital structure, dividend entitlement, or purpose or duration of the corporation."[8]

The Model Act empowers the board of directors, without shareholder approval, to make the following administrative changes to the articles of incorporation:[9]

1. To extend the duration of the corporation.

2. To delete the names and addresses of the initial directors or the initial registered agent.

3. To make certain authorized share changes if only one class of shares is outstanding.

4. To change the corporate name by substituting the word "corporation," "incorporated," "company," "limited," or the abbreviation "corp.," "inc.," "co.," or "ltd.," for a similar word or abbreviation in the name, or by adding, deleting, or changing a geographical attribution for the name.

5. To reflect a reduction in authorized shares when the corporation has acquired its own shares and the articles of incorporation prohibit the reissue of the acquired shares.

6. To delete a class of shares from the articles of incorporation when there are no remaining shares of the class because the corporation has acquired all

---

8. MBCA § 10.01(b).
9. MBCA § 10.05.

shares of the class and the articles of incorporation prohibit the reissue of the acquired shares.

As for other amendments to the articles of incorporation, the Model Act requires[10] that the amendment be adopted by the board of directors and then be submitted to the shareholders for their approval, along with a board recommendation that the shareholders approve the amendment or a statement as to why the board has determined that it cannot make such a recommendation ("conflicts of interest or other special circumstances"). The board of directors may condition its submission of the amendment to the shareholders on any basis. The corporation must then notify each shareholder, whether or not entitled to vote, of the meeting of shareholders at which the amendment is to be submitted for approval. The notice must state that the purpose of the meeting is to consider the amendment and must contain or be accompanied by a copy of the amendment. Unless the articles of incorporation or the board of directors requires a greater vote or a greater number of shares to be present, adoption of the amendment requires an approval vote of shareholders owning a majority of shares represented at a meeting at which a quorum consisting of at least a majority of the votes entitled to be cast on the amendment is present.

Delaware specifies a similar dual process of director and shareholder approvals for all amendments to the articles of incorporation.[11]

2. BYLAW AMENDMENTS

State corporate statutes typically provide that a corporation's bylaws may be amended by either the board of directors or the shareholders.[12] Dual approval is not required. This gives the board the authority to make bylaw changes as it sees fit, without having to endure the expense and hassle of a shareholder approval process. Although not required, in many situations the board chooses to seek shareholder ratification of its decision to amend the bylaws in order to promote shareholder goodwill and ward off any potential attacks. As discussed in Chapter 8, the power vested in shareholders to amend the bylaws often enhances shareholder governance authority by enabling shareholders to propose bylaw changes that likely would never be approved by the board.

3. CORPORATE DISSOLUTION

State corporate statutes (including Delaware's statute[13]) generally provide that the board of directors and shareholders may dissolve a corporation by following a dual board and shareholder approval process similar to that described above for amendments to the articles of incorporation. The Model Act requires[14] that a resolution to dissolve the corporation be approved by the board of directors and then be submitted to the shareholders for their approval, along with a board recommendation that the shareholders approve the dissolution or a statement as

---

10. See, generally, MBCA § 10.03.

11. 8 DGCL § 242(b).

12. See, for example, MBCA § 10.20 and 8 DGCL § 109. In Delaware, the power of the board to amend the bylaws must be set forth in the articles of incorporation. 8 DGCL § 109.

13. 8 DGCL § 275.

14. See, generally, MBCA § 10.02.

to why the board has determined that it cannot make such a recommendation ("conflicts of interest or other special circumstances"). The board of directors may condition its submission of the dissolution resolution to the shareholders on any basis. The corporation must then notify each shareholder, whether or not entitled to vote, of the meeting of shareholders at which the amendment is to be submitted for approval. The notice must state that the purpose of the meeting is to consider the dissolution of the corporation. Unless the articles of incorporation or the board of directors requires a greater vote or a greater number of shares to be present, adoption of the dissolution proposal requires an approval vote of shareholders owning a majority of shares represented at a meeting at which a quorum consisting of at least a majority of the votes entitled to be cast on the amendment is present.

4. MERGERS, CONSOLIDATIONS, SHARE EXCHANGES

A statutory merger is a transaction where two or more corporations combine to form a single entity.[15] Typically one corporation (the "Acquirer") is absorbing another corporation (the "Target"). All of assets, liabilities and rights of the Target pass by operation of law to the Acquirer, and the Acquirer is substituted in any pending litigation of the Target.[16] The Acquirer is the surviving entity, just bigger. The Target disappears. As consideration for their Target shares, the shareholders of Target either receive cash, property, or shares of the Acquirer's stock. The transaction is documented with a merger agreement that spells out the exchange terms and includes provisions that are typically included in an asset purchase agreement: covenants, representations and warranties, conditions, indemnifications, legal opinions, and the like (see Section B of Chapter 15). A document entitled "Articles of Merger" or "Certificate of Merger" is filed with the applicable state corporation divisions to evidence and complete the merger.[17]

A consolidation differs from a merger in one significant respect. With a consolidation, a new corporate entity is formed to be the surviving corporation. The existing corporate entities disappear. Consolidations are a rare event in today's world.

A share exchange is a transaction where one corporation, Acquirer, exchanges its stock for the outstanding stock another corporation, Target.[18] Target ends up being a wholly owned subsidiary of Acquirer.

CASE PROBLEM 9-2

ManHair, Inc. ("MH") is a company that provides a "macho look and experience" through a rapidly-growing string of retail hair salons that are located in the West and Midwest. MH's founder and CEO, Tim Lawson, owns 18 percent of MH's outstanding stock. Other MH executives own an additional 17 percent of the stock, and the balance of the stock is owned by 55 other individuals in roughly equal shares.

---

15. MBCA § 11.02, 8 DGCL § 251.
16. MBCA § 11.07, 8 DGCL § 259.
17. MBCA § 11.06, 8 DGCL § 251.
18. MBCA § 11.03

MH now desires to acquire StrongLook Incorporated ("SL"), a company that owns and operates similar retail outlets on the East Coast. SL is owned by 18 individuals. SL's founder and president is Duke Smith, age 75, who owns 30 percent of SL's outstanding stock and is ready to retire.

The key drivers for the combination are MH's strong management team, MH's momentum, Duke's need for cash and a desire to retire, the synergies that a nationwide presence may create for both companies, and the enhanced potential of higher values and better liquidity options for shareholders.

The boards of MH and SL have agreed to the basic terms of the deal. MH would be the surviving entity in the combination. As consideration for their shares in SL, the SL shareholders would receive $10 million in cash and shares of ML stock that would represent 35 percent of MH's outstanding stock after the combination. The cash and MH stock would be distributed pro rata to the shareholders of SL.

The question now: How best to structure the combination of MH and SL? Lawson and MH's board have identified the following basic objectives that should be considered in structuring the transaction:

1. They do not want the shareholders of MH to vote on the combination. They know that certain minority owners would voice loud opposition to an additional $10 million of debt that would be required to fund the deal.

2. They do not want the MH shareholders receiving any appraisal rights.

3. They want to minimize the risk of any "significant cash" having to be spent as a result of SL shareholders exercising appraisal rights. They are not concerned about the SL shareholder vote because they are confident that "Duke can deliver."

4. They want to minimize any disruptions to employees, customers, vendors and others who routinely deal with MH or SL.

5. They do not want MH, as the surviving entity, being liable for debts and obligations, known or unknown, of SL.

How should the combination be structured to accomplish these objectives, assuming MH and SL are both Delaware companies?

How would the analysis change, if at all, if both companies are incorporated in a state that has adopted the Model Business Corporation Act?

How would the answers to these questions change if both MH and SL are public corporations whose stocks are traded on the NASDAQ?

Appraisal Rights

The potential of shareholder appraisal rights is a planning consideration in any merger, consolidation, or share exchange. These rights are designed to provide an objecting shareholder with an opportunity to be paid a "fair value" cash price for his or her stock via a judicial proceeding where the price is determined. See Chapter 12 for a discussion of the procedures and limitations of dissenter appraisal rights. Every corporate statute authorizes such appraisal rights in select fundamental transaction, but state laws vary significantly in defining the scope and limitations of such rights.[19]

In 35 states (including Delaware) and under the Model Business Corporation Act, there is a significant market-out exception for public corporations that has the effect of taking appraisal rights off the table in most public company transaction.[20] Under the MBCA exception, dissenter appraisal rights are not available to shareholders who own stock if (1) there is a liquid market for the stock (traded on the New York Stock Exchange, American Stock Exchange, NASDAQ, or the stock is held by at least 2,000 shareholders with a $20 million public float) and (2) the transaction does not involve a controlling shareholder (defined as a shareholder who owns 20 percent or more of the corporation's stock or has the power to elect one-fourth of board) or a deal where officers of the target yield a financial benefit that is not available to the shareholders. The basis of this exception is that, under such circumstances, there is no need for court involvement to set a fair cash price for such shareholders because every shareholder has a market driven liquidity option that will adjust to reflect the value of the deal. Best estimates are that 91 percent of all public companies and 93 percent of Fortune 500 companies are incorporated in a state that provides this type of market-out exception to shareholder appraisal rights.[21]

Delaware also has a market-out exception to shareholder appraisal rights, but that exception contains a unique, important twist – an "exception to the exception." Unlike the Model Act, a transaction under Delaware law in which shareholders are required to accept cash for their shares will not trigger the market-out exception for such shareholders, and, thus, appraisal rights will be available. The result is that, in Delaware, the target company shareholders will always have appraisal rights in a cash merger. In *Louisiana Municipal Employees' Retirement System v. Crawford*, 918 A.2d 1172 (Del. Ch. 2007), the court held that this "exception to the exception" would apply to restore appraisal rights in a transaction where shareholders were "required" to receive both stock *and* cash, but in *Louisiana Municipal Employees' Retirement System v. Crawford*, 918 A.2d 1172 (Del. Ch. 2007), the court held it would not apply (and thus the market out exception would apply to eliminate appraisal rights) if all shareholders had an option to receive stock *or* cash.

Even when appraisal rights are available to dissenting minority shareholders, they trigger administrative details, costs, and uncertainties that must be seriously considered in any decision to assert such rights, as discussed in Chapter 12.

With any merger, consolidation or share exchange, there are three threshold questions: Which boards must approve the merger? Which shareholders must

---

19. In select situations, an amendment of the articles of incorporation may trigger shareholder appraisal rights if the articles, bylaws or directors' resolutions provide for such rights or others statutory conditions are satisfied. See, for example, MBCA § 13.02(4),(5).

20. See, generally, MBCA § 13.02(b), 8 DGCL § 262(b), and Jeff Goetz, *A Dissent Dampened by Timing: How the Stock Market Exception Systematically Deprives Public*, 15 Fordham Journal of Corporate and Financial Law 771-806 (2009).

21. See, generally, Lucian A. Bebchuck and Alma Cohen, *Firms' Decisions Where to Incorporate*, 46 J.L. & Econ. 383, 391 (2003).

approve the merger? Which shareholders are entitled to dissenter appraisal rights? The answers to these questions turn on applicable state law, any stock exchange rules that are applicable, and the relative positions of the parties in the transaction. The following scenarios illustrate the differences and the scope of the rights. Assume for these purposes that Acquirer is a Delaware corporation and Target is organized in a state that has adopted the Model Business Corporation Act.

Scenario 1: Non-Whale Merger

Acquirer and Target merge with Acquirer issuing two shares of its already authorized shares to the shareholders of Target for every three shares of Acquirer's stock outstanding before the merger. Thus, after the merger, the original shareholders of the Acquirer own 60 percent of the Acquirer's shares and the Target shareholders own the remaining 40 percent.

• Under Delaware law, the merger would have to be approved by the board of directors of Acquirer.[22]

• Under Delaware law, the merger would have to be approved by the shareholders of Acquirer because the number of shares issued in the transaction exceeds 20 percent of the number of Acquirer shares outstanding before the merger.[23]

• If the stock of Acquirer is traded on the New York Stock Exchange, the American Stock Exchange or the NASDAQ, exchange rules would require that the transaction be approved by the shareholders of Acquirer because the 20 percent threshold is exceeded. [24]

• Under the MBCA, the board of directors and shareholders of Target would have to approve the merger.[25]

• Dissenter appraisal rights would be available to all shareholders, subject to the market-out exception.[26]

• If the Acquirer was incorporated in a state that had adopted the MBCA, its shareholders would not have dissenter appraisal rights because all of their shares would remain outstanding after the merger.[27]

Scenario 2: Whale Merger

Acquirer and Target merge with Acquirer issuing one share of its already authorized shares to the shareholders of Target for every five shares of Acquirer's stock outstanding before the merger. Thus, after the merger, the original shareholders of the Acquirer would own 83.3 percent of Acquirer's shares and Target shareholders would own the remaining 16.7 percent.

---

22. 8 DGCL §§ 251, 252.
23. 8 DGCL §§ 251, 252.
24. See New York Stock Exchange *Listed Company Manual*, Section 312.03 Shareholder Approval; American Stock Exchange *Company Guide*, Section 712 Acquisitions; NASDAQ *Manual: Marketplace Rules*, Section 4350 Qualitative Listing Requirements for Nasdaq Issuers Except for Limited Partnerships.
25. MBCA § 11.04
26. MBCA § 13.02, 8 DGCL § 262(b).
27. MBCA § 13.02(a)(1).

- Under the MBCA, the board of directors and shareholders of Target would have to approve the merger.[28]

- Under Delaware law, the merger would have to be approved by the board of directors of Acquirer.[29]

- Under Delaware law, the shareholders of Acquirer would not have to approve the merger if the Acquirer is the surviving entity, there is no need to amend Acquirer's articles of incorporation, each share of Acquirer's existing stock remains unchanged and outstanding, and the number of shares of Acquirer to be issued in the merger does not exceed 20 percent of Acquirer's shares outstanding before the merger.[30] Similarly, because the 20 percent threshold is not exceeded, stock exchange rules would not require a vote of Acquirer's shareholders.[31]

- The same 20 percent no-shareholder-vote exception would apply if Acquirer was organized in a state that had adopted the Model Act.[32]

- As for dissenter appraisal rights, they would be available to the shareholders of Target, subject to the market exception, but would not be available to the shareholders of Acquirer. The same result would follow if the states of incorporation of Acquirer and Target were switched.[33]

Scenario 3: Short-Form Merger

Acquirer owns over 90 percent of the outstanding stock of Target and merges Target into Acquirer in a transaction that squeezes out the minority shareholders of Target by paying them cash for their shares. The details of such a short form squeeze out merger are discussed in Chapter 12.

- The merger would have to be approved only by the board of directors of Acquirer.[34]

- No vote of Target's board or shareholders would be required.

- As for dissenter appraisal rights, they would be available to the shareholders of Target, but would not be available to the shareholders of Acquirer.

- The same results would follow if the states of incorporation of Acquirer and Target were switched.[35]

Scenario 4: Triangular Merger

Acquirer forms a new wholly-owned subsidiary corporation ("Sub"), Sub and Target are then merged, and Acquirer issues its already authorized shares to the shareholders of Target. If Sub is the survivor in the merger, the transaction is

---

28. MBCA § 11.04
29. 8 DGCL §§ 251, 252.
30. 8 DGCL §§ 251(f).
31. See cited authority at note 24, *supra*.
32. MBCA § 11.04(g).
33. MBCA § 13.02, 8 DGCL § 262(b).
34. MBCA § 11.05, 8 DGCL § 253.
35. Id.

called a "forward triangular merger," and Target disappears, and Sub (now with all Target's assets) remains a wholly owned subsidiary of Acquirer. If Target is the surviving entity in the merger, the transaction is called a 'reverse triangular merger," Sub disappears, and Target ends up as a wholly-owned subsidiary of Acquirer. This triangular merger technique is popular because it provides the tax benefits of a merger while allowing the Acquirer to accomplish various non-tax objectives in structuring the transaction. (See Chapter 15).

- The board of directors and shareholders of Target would have to approve the triangular merger, whether Target is incorporated in Delaware or an MBCA state.[36]

- As a formality, Sub's board and its sole shareholder ('Acquirer") would need to approve the triangular merger.[37]

- Technically, Acquirer is not a party to the merger, but its board would have to approve the issuance of additional Acquirer stock and all matters related to the formation of Sub and the exercise of Sub rights.

- If Acquirer is incorporated in a state that has adopted the Model Act, Acquirer's shareholders would have to approve the share exchange in the triangular merger unless there is no need to amend Acquirer's articles of incorporation, each share of Acquirer's existing stock remains unchanged and outstanding, and the number of shares of Acquirer to be issued in the transaction does not exceed 20 percent of the Acquirer's shares outstanding before the transaction.[38]

- If Acquirer's stock is traded on the New York Stock Exchange, the American Stock Exchange or the NASDAQ, stock exchange rules would require a vote of Acquirer's shareholders if the 20 percent threshold is exceeded.[39]

- If Acquirer is a Delaware corporation and not subject to exchange rules, Acquirer's shareholders would not have to approve the transaction because Acquirer is not a party to the transaction and Delaware's corporate law does not have a share exchange provision. Thus, in many situations Delaware companies may cut off voting and appraisal rights of Acquirer's shareholders by structuring the transaction as a triangular merger.

- As for dissenter appraisal rights, they would be available to the shareholders of Target, subject to the market exception, but would not be available to the shareholders of Acquirer. This would be the result whether the Model Act or Delaware law applied.[40]

Scenario 5: Share Exchange

Acquirer issues its stock in exchange for all of the outstanding stock of Target. Many states (but not Delaware), including those that have adopted the

---

36. MBCA § 11.04, 8 DGCL § 251.
37. Id.
38. MBCA § 11.04.
39. See cited authority at note 24, *supra*.
40. MBCA § 13.02, 8 DGCL § 262(b).

Model Act, authorize this form of exchange and compel participation of the Target shareholders if the transaction is appropriately approved by the board and shareholders of Target.[41]

The parties end up in the same position as a reverse triangular merger (Target becoming a wholly-owned subsidiary of Acquirer), but, as described in Chapter 15, the tax requirements of a reverse triangular merger are much easier and more flexible than a straight share exchange. Also, this type of compulsory share exchange should not be confused with a tender offer transaction (discussed in Chapters 12 and 14), where the Acquirer offers to buy Target shares directly from the Target shareholders and each shareholder may elect to accept or reject the offer.

• The board of directors and shareholders of Target would have to approve the exchange if Target is incorporated in a Model Act state.[42] This type of compulsory share exchange is not authorized in Delaware.

• Acquirer's board of directors would have to approve the transaction.

• If Acquirer is incorporated in a state that has adopted the Model Act, Acquirer's shareholders would have to approve the share exchange unless there is no need to amend Acquirer's articles of incorporation, each share of Acquirer's existing stock remains unchanged and outstanding, and the number of shares of stock of Acquirer to be issued in the transaction does not exceed 20 percent of the Acquirer's shares outstanding before the transaction.[43]

• If Acquirer's stock is traded on the New York Stock Exchange, the American Stock Exchange or the NASDAQ, stock exchange rules would require a vote of Acquirer's shareholders if the 20 percent threshold is exceeded.[44]

• As for dissenter appraisal rights, they would be available to the shareholders of Target, subject to the market exception, but would not be available to the shareholders of Acquirer, whose shares would remain outstanding after the exchange.[45]

5. SALE OF ASSETS

The sale of a corporation's assets may also trigger shareholder voting and dissenter appraisal rights in certain situations. State corporate statutes[46] generally mandate such rights in a sale that involves substantially all of a corporation's assets, often referred to as a sale not "in the usual or regular course of business."[47]

In our case above, Acquirer could purchase all of Target's assets in return for cash or stock of Acquirer. In such a transaction, Target doesn't automatically disappear. The sale radically changes the composition of Target's assets, and

---

41. MBCA § 11.03.
42. MBCA § 11.04.
43. MBCA § 11.04(g).
44. See cited authority at note 24, *supra*.
45. MBCA § 13.02.
46. See, for example, MBCA § 12.02, 8 DGCL § 271.
47. See, for example, RCW 23B.12.020.

usually most or all of Target's known liabilities will have been transferred to, or assumed by, the buyer. Target then liquidates by discharging any residual liabilities and distributing the proceeds of the sale to its shareholders. Although the form of such an asset sale/liquidation transaction differs significantly from that of a merger, usually the parties, as a practical matter, end up in the same position: Acquirer has the assets and liabilities, Target is gone, and the shareholders of Target own stock of Acquirer.

In such a transaction, the board of directors and the shareholders of the selling corporation (Target) must approve the transaction.[48] As for dissenter appraisal rights, the Model Act gives the shareholders of the selling corporation such rights, subject to the market-out exception,[49] but no such rights are available to the shareholders of the selling corporation under Delaware law.[50]

As for the purchasing entity (Acquirer), Delaware law provides no shareholder voting or dissenter appraisal rights. It's a straight purchase of assets that requires only board approval in Delaware. The Model Act also provides no appraisal rights for the shareholders of the Acquirer, but shareholder approval is required unless there is no need to amend Acquirer's articles of incorporation, each share of Acquirer's stock remains unchanged and outstanding, and the number of shares of Acquirer to be issued in the transaction does not exceed 20 percent of the Acquirer's shares outstanding before the transaction.[51] If Acquirer's stock is traded on the New York Stock Exchange, the American Stock Exchange or the NASDAQ, stock exchange rules would require a vote of Acquirer's shareholders if the 20 percent threshold is exceeded.[52]

Shareholder voting and appraisal rights come into play only when there is a sale of assets to a third party. A transfer of assets to a wholly owned subsidiary or as a pledge or security for a loan (via a mortgage, deed of trust or other instrument) won't trigger the rights.[53]

The statutory requirement that the sale involve "substantially all" of the corporation's assets often can be a difficult challenge. The Model Act uses the phrase "significant continuing business activity" and provides that a selling corporation will be "conclusively" deemed to have retained such a continuing activity (and thus no shareholder voting rights kick in) if the retained business activity represents at least 25 percent of total assets and either 25 percent of after-tax operating income or 25 percent of revenues.[54] The quantitative and qualitative dimensions of the requirement are challenging, as illustrated by the following leading case on the issue.

GIMBEL v. SIGNAL COMPANIES, INC.
316 A2d 599 (Del.Ch. 1974), aff'd per curiam 316 A.2d 619 (Del. 1974)

QUILLEN, Chancellor:

---

48. MBCA § 12.02, 8 DGCL § 271.
49. MBCA § 13.02(3).
50. 8 DGCL § 262.
51. MBCA § 6.21(f).
52. See cited authority at note 24, *supra*.
53. See, for example, MBCA § 12.01, 8 DGCL §§ 271,272.
54. MBCA § 12.02.

This action was commenced on December 24, 1973 by plaintiff, a stockholder of the Signal Companies, Inc. ('Signal'). The complaint seeks, among other things, injunctive relief to prevent the consummation of the pending sale by Signal to Burmah Oil Incorporated ('Burmah') of all of the outstanding capital stock of Signal Oil and Gas Company ('Signal Oil'), a wholly-owned subsidiary of Signal. The effective sale price exceeds 480 million dollars. The sale was approved at a special meeting of the Board of Directors of Signal held on December 21, 1973.

The agreement provides that the transaction will be consummated on January 15, 1974 or upon the obtaining of the necessary governmental consents, whichever occurs later, but, in no event, after February 15, 1974 unless mutually agreed. The consents evidently have been obtained... It should be noted that the only parties who have appeared thus far are the plaintiff, Signal, Signal Oil and Burmah. It should also be noted that the plaintiff is part of an investment group which has some 2,400,000 shares representing 12% of the outstanding stock of Signal.

While the amount of money involved in this litigation is enormous and the values involved hotly disputed, the issues are basically simple to isolate and the Delaware law to be applied is, for the most part, well established and not open to question.

I turn first to the question of 8 Del.C. s 271(a) which requires majority stockholder approval for the sale of 'all or substantially all' of the assets of a Delaware corporation. A sale of less than all or substantially all assets is not covered by negative implication from the statute.

It is important to note in the first instance that the statute does not speak of a requirement of shareholder approval simply because an independent, important branch of a corporate business is being sold. The plaintiff cites several non-Delaware cases for the proposition that shareholder approval of such a sale is required. But that is not the language of our statute. Similarly, it is not our law that shareholder approval is required upon every 'major' restructuring of the corporation. Again, it is not necessary to go beyond the statute. The statute requires shareholder approval upon the sale of 'all or substantially all' of the corporation's assets. That is the sole test to be applied. While it is true that test does not lend itself to a strict mathematical standard to be applied in every case, the qualitative factor can be defined to some degree notwithstanding the limited Delaware authority. But the definition must begin with and ultimately necessarily relate to our statutory language.

In interpreting the statute the plaintiff relies on Philadelphia National Bank v. B.S.F. Co., 41 Del.Ch. 509, 199 A.2d 557 (Ch.1964). In that case, B.S.F. Company owned stock in two corporations. It sold its stock in one of the corporations, and retained the stock in the other corporation. The Court found that the stock sold was the principal asset B.S.F. Company had available for sale and that the value of the stock retained was declining. The Court rejected the defendant's contention that the stock sold represented only 47.4% of consolidated assets, and looked to the actual value of the stock sold. On this basis, the Court held that the stock constituted at least 75% of the total assets and the sale of the stock was a sale of substantially all assets.

The key language in the Court of Chancery opinion in Philadelphia National Bank is the suggestion that 'the critical factor in determining the character of a sale of assets is generally considered not the amount of property sold but whether the sale is in fact an unusual transaction or one made in the regular course of business of the seller.' (41 Del.Ch. at 515, 199 A.2d at 561). Professor Folk suggests from the opinion that 'the statute would be inapplicable if the assets sale is 'one made in furtherance of express corporate objects in the ordinary and regular course of the business " (referring to language in 41 Del.Ch. at 516, 199 A.2d at 561).

But any 'ordinary and regular course of the business' test in this context obviously is not intended to limit the directors to customary daily business activities. Indeed, a question concerning the statute would not arise unless the transaction was somewhat out of the ordinary. While it is true that a transaction in the ordinary course of business does not require shareholder approval, the converse is not true. Every transaction out of normal routine does not necessarily require shareholder approval. The unusual nature of the transaction must strike at the heart of the corporate existence and purpose. As it is written at 6A Fletcher, Cyclopedia Corporations (Perm.Ed. 1968 Rev.) s 2949.2, p. 648:

> 'The purpose of the consent statutes is to protect the shareholders from fundamental change, or more specifically to protect the shareholder from the destruction of the means to accomplish the purposes or objects for which the corporation was incorporated and actually performs.'

It is in this sense that the 'unusual transaction' judgment is to be made and the statute's applicability determined. If the sale is of assets quantitatively vital to the operation of the corporation and is out of the ordinary and substantially affects the existence and purpose of the corporation, then it is beyond the power of the Board of Directors. With these guidelines, I turn to Signal and the transaction in this case.

Signal or its predecessor was incorporated in the oil business in 1922. But, beginning in 1952, Signal diversified its interests. In 1952, Signal acquired a substantial stock interest in American President Lines. From 1957 to 1962 Signal was the sole owner of Laura Scudders, a nation-wide snack food business. In 1964, Signal acquired Garrett Corporation which is engaged in the aircraft, aerospace, and uranium enrichment business. In 1967, Signal acquired Mack Trucks, Inc., which is engaged in the manufacture and sale of trucks and related equipment. Also in 1968, the oil and gas business was transferred to a separate division and later in 1970 to the Signal Oil subsidiary. Since 1967, Signal has made acquisition of or formed substantial companies none of which are involved or related with the oil and gas industry. As indicated previously, the oil and gas production development of Signal's business is now carried on by Signal Oil, the sale of the stock of which is an issue in this lawsuit.

Based on the company's figures, Signal Oil represents only about 26% Of the total assets of Signal. While Signal Oil represents 41% of Signal's total net worth, it produces only about 15% of Signal's revenues and earnings.

While it is true, based on the experience of the Signal-Burmah transaction and the record in this lawsuit, that Signal Oil is more valuable than shown by the company's books, even if, as plaintiff suggests in his brief, the $761,000,000 value attached to Signal Oil's properties by the plaintiff's expert Paul V. Keyser, Jr., were substituted as the asset figure, the oil and gas properties would still constitute less than half the value of Signal's total assets. Thus, from a straight quantitative approach, I agree with Signal's position that the sale to Burmah does not constitute a sale of 'all or substantially all' of Signal's assets.

In addition, if the character of the transaction is examined, the plaintiff's position is also weak. While it is true that Signal's original purpose was oil and gas and while oil and gas is still listed first in the certificate of incorporation, the simple fact is that Signal is now a conglomerate engaged in the aircraft and aerospace business, the manufacture and sale of trucks and related equipment, and other businesses besides oil and gas. The very nature of its business, as it now in fact exists, contemplates the acquisition and disposal of independent branches of its corporate business. Indeed, given the operations since 1952, it can be said that such acquisitions and dispositions have become part of the ordinary course of business. The facts that the oil and gas business was historically first and that authorization for such operations are listed first in the certificate do not prohibit disposal of such interest. As Director Harold M. Williams testified, business history is not 'compelling' and 'many companies go down the drain because they try to be historic.'

It is perhaps true, as plaintiff has argued, that the advent of multi-business corporations has in one sense emasculated s 271 since one business may be sold without shareholder approval when other substantial businesses are retained. But it is one thing for a corporation to evolve over a period of years into a multi-business corporation, the operations of which include the purchase and sale of whole businesses, and another for a single business corporation by a one transaction revolution to sell the entire means of operating its business in exchange for money or a separate business. In the former situation, the processes of corporate democracy customarily have had the opportunity to restrain or otherwise control over a period of years. Thus, there is a chance for some shareholder participation. The Signal development illustrates the difference. For example, when Signal, itself formerly called Signal Oil and Gas Company, changed its name in 1968, it was for the announced 'need for a new name appropriate to the broadly diversified activities of Signal's multi-industry complex.'

I conclude that measured quantitatively and qualitatively, the sale of the stock of Signal Oil by Signal to Burmah does not constitute a sale of 'all or substantially all' of Signal's assets. This conclusion is supported by the closest case involving Delaware law which was been cited to the Court. Wingate v. Bercut, 146 F.2d 725 (9th Cir. 1944). Accordingly, insofar as the complaint rests on 8 Del.C. s 271(a), in my judgment, it has no reasonable probability of ultimate success.

CASE PROBLEM 9-3

Assume the same facts of Case Problem 11-2, except that SL's retail outlets in Florida are to be excluded from the combination because they do not reflect "the history, image, and quality of the other operations of MH and SL." These Florida outlets represent 28 percent of SL's assets, 19 percent of its revenues, and 22 percent of its profits. Plus, as a result of sexual harassment rumblings related to SL's Florida operations, the parties have agreed that such operations will remain in SL and that SL, as an entity, will continue to be owned by the existing shareholders of SL.

Under such circumstances, how should the combination be structured to accomplish the objectives of the parties, assuming MH and SL are both Delaware companies? How would the analysis change, if at all, if both companies are incorporated in a state that has adopted the Model Business Corporation Act?

De Facto Merger and Successor Liability Doctrines

Historically, a corporation's sale of substantially all of its assets sometimes triggered the consideration of two doctrines, one of which is effectively dead and the other of which is still alive in select situations.

The dead doctrine is the "de facto merger doctrine." This doctrine was created to protect shareholder rights that were cut off when a transaction was structured as an asset sale instead of a merger but the end result was the same as a merger.[55] The theory was that, in such a situation, the court should declare the transaction a "de facto merger" and should bestow the same shareholder voting and appraisal rights that would be required in a merger under applicable state law. The doctrine has been heavily criticized as being out of touch with the realities of modern capital challenges and the need to carefully structure the form of transactions to accommodate a host of different tax and non-tax objectives. In the world of major corporate transactions, the form of a transaction does matter and often has a co-equal role with substance in getting a deal done. The doctrine has been legislatively abolished in some states[56] and was effectively rejected by Delaware in *Hariton v. Arco Electronics, Inc.*, 182 A.2d 22 (Del. Ch. 1962), aff'd 188 A.2d 123 (Del. 1963), where the court stated:

> While plaintiff's contention that the doctrine of de facto merger should be applied in the present circumstances is not without appeal, the subject is one which, in my opinion, is within the legislative domain... The argument underlying the applicability of the doctrine of de facto merger, namely, that the stockholder is forced against his will to accept a new investment in an enterprise foreign to that of which he was a part has little pertinency. The right of the corporation to sell all of its assets for stock in another corporation was expressly accorded to Arco by § 271 of Title 8, Del.C. The stockholder was, in contemplation of law, aware of this right when he acquired his stock. He was also

---

55. See, for example, *Farris v. Glen Alden Corp.*, 143 A.2d 25 (Pa. 1958). The de facto merger doctrine was subsequently legislatively abolished in Pennsylvania. 15 Pa. Cons. Stat. § 1904.

56. Id.

aware of the fact that the situation might develop whereby he would be ultimately forced to accept a new investment, as would have been the case here had the resolution authorizing dissolution followed consummation of the sale.

> There is authority in decisions of courts of this state for the proposition that the various sections of the Delaware Corporation Law conferring authority for corporate action are independent of each other and that a given result may be accomplished by proceeding under one section which is not possible, or is even forbidden under another.

182 A.2d at 331-332.

The second doctrine is the "Successor Liability Doctrine." The focus of this doctrine is not on the lost rights of shareholders in an asset sale. It is on the plight of the creditor of the selling company whose claim was unknown at the time of sale but is discovered after the sale when the selling entity is long gone. Can such a creditor assert the claim against the purchaser in the transaction?

Of course, in a merger the surviving entity inherits by operation of law all of the liabilities of the merging parties, including any such unknown claims. But in an asset sale, typically the purchaser is responsible only for the known liabilities that are specifically assumed in the governing document. Hence, the need for an equitable doctrine that gives some relief to the creditor who is left out in the cold after the sale is wrapped up. This doctrine is similar to the de facto merger doctrine in that it seeks to import merger protections into an asset sale, and for that reason the doctrines are often confused or inappropriately linked. The purpose and thrust of the successor liability doctrine are entirely different than those of the de facto merger doctrine.

And, unlike the de facto merger doctrine, the successor liability doctrine still works in select situations,[57] particularly when there is a combination of factors that support relief: there were foreseeable unknown tort claims (such as product liability claims); the same business continued after the sale as before the sale; the creditor had no capacity to recover from the selling entity or its owners; and the purchaser had the opportunity to foresee and insure against the risk. Some courts are more hard-nosed in applying the doctrine, allowing its use only in situations where the end result is tantamount to a merger where the purchaser's stock is the primary consideration, the selling corporation disappears, and the business, assets and owners of the selling entity become part of the purchasing entity.[58]

State Law Variances

Of course, it goes without saying that the corporate laws of the state of incorporation always must be carefully considered in any transaction. But when it comes to the shareholder voting and appraisal rights in major transactions, this charge has an enhanced importance because the variances from state to state can be so significant.

---

57. See, for example, *Turner v. Bituminous Casualty Co.*, 244 N.W. 2d 873 (Mich. 1976) and *Ray v. Alad Corp.*, 560 P.2d 3 (Cal. 1977).
58. See, for example, *Niccum v Hydra Tool Corp.*, 438 N.W.2d 96 (Minn. 1989).

The foregoing discussion has illustrated key concepts by focusing on the provisions of the existing Model Act and Delaware law. In no sense do these provisions fairly represent the scope of corporate statutes dealing with shareholder voting and appraisal rights in major transactions. Some state statutes are modeled after the early version of the Model Act (before 1999), which, unlike the current version, did not mandate voting rights for the shareholders of the acquiring entity in triangular mergers and asset purchases.

Other states follow the lead of the American Law Institute Principles § 6.01(b) and have a statutory structure that seeks to grant identical shareholder voting and appraisal rights in all major transactions, no matter the form. There are states that seek to line up voting and appraisal rights so that they always go together, and states that do not have the market opt-out exception for appraisal rights. And, of course, there are those states that impose a super-majority shareholder voting requirement for major transactions. The components of the statutory schemes are varied and mixed.

The bottom line is that assumptions and generalizations in this area are ill advised. The specific statutes of the states in which the parties to the transaction are incorporated must be carefully assessed and satisfied.

C. THE RIGHT TO SUE

1. SHAREHOLDER LAWSUIT HARD REALITIES

Shareholders may use the courts to protect and enforce their rights as shareholders. Such lawsuits come in two forms. The first is a direct action where a shareholder seeks to enforce personal rights or to recover damages sustained as a result of a third party's breach of a duty (usually an officer, director, or controlling shareholder). Examples include an action to enforce inspection rights, a lawsuit to compel the inclusion of a shareholder's proposal in the company's proxy materials, or a claim based on false or misleading disclosures under the applicable securities laws. The second form, called a derivative action, is a lawsuit that a shareholder brings on behalf of the corporation. Actually, it's two equitable actions - a suit by the shareholder to compel the corporation to sue and a suit by the corporation, asserted by the shareholder, against those liable to the corporation.

As we will see, at times the line between direct and derivative actions is fuzzy. But the line is important for many reasons. A derivative action is a weird duck, created in equity to meet a compelling need. It is regulated by state statutes in varying degrees.[59] It serves an essential purpose and often exposes some hard realities.

Absolute Necessity. The right of shareholders to prosecute a derivative claim is an absolute necessity. It's the tool that reconciles the conflict between the fiduciary duties imposed on the officers and directors of a corporation and the board's power to manage the enterprise. Without this right, the duties would mean little or nothing. A board is not going to authorize a suit against itself for its

---

59. See, for example, MBCA §§ 7.40 through 7.47.

breach of the duties of care or loyalty. A shareholder, as an owner of the enterprise, must have the right to expose and prosecute the wrongdoing on behalf of the corporation. The lawsuit is labeled "Derivative" because it is based on the rights of, and injuries to, the corporation.

Corporation Recovers. Any recovery in a shareholder derivative suit against a wrongdoer goes to the corporation, not the shareholder who prosecutes the lawsuit. This is the fundamental difference between a direct claim and a derivative claim. The beneficiaries of a direct claim are the shareholders making the claim. In a derivative action, the shareholder prosecuting the claim reaps only the indirect proportionate benefit represented by his or her stock in the enterprise. So what's the financial incentive for a shareholder to be the named plaintiff in a derivative case? In a derivative action, it's not about the named plaintiff or the corporation. It's all about the lawyers.

Contingent Fee Bounty Hunters. Shareholder derivative lawsuits are driven by lawyers or, better stated, lawyer fees. The plaintiffs' lawyers know that a recovery on behalf of the corporation will yield a big payday funded out of corporate coffers. The lawyers, in effect, are contingent fee "bounty hunters" for the corporation and control all aspects of the litigation – everything from where and when the case is commenced, to the scope of discovery, to whether and on what terms the case settles. All legal fees, whether triggered by victory or settlement, must be approved by the court. The amount of the legal fees may be a function of the size of the recovery or settlement, a multiple of the attorneys' "lodestar" (actual hours multiplied by a prevailing hourly rate), and a host of other factors: the difficulty of the case, the risks of the litigation, the novelty of the issues, whether the case produced positive corporate governance changes, and other factors deemed important by the court. In some situations, the derivative action is accompanied by multiple private or class action direct claims based on allegations of false or misleading disclosures under proxy Rule 14a-9 or Rule 10b-5 (see Chapter 11). The consolidation of the cases often results in a separate contest to select the lead counsel for the plaintiffs – the firm that will direct the effort and reap the largest share of the fee award, which may be huge by any standard. As an example, the Southern District Court of New York approved lead counsel attorneys' fees totaling $336.1 million (based on a total lodestar of $83.2 million) in the $6.1 billion settlement of the securities litigation arising out of the collapse of telecommunications giant Worldcom, Inc. In approving the fee award, the court praised "the integral role that competent plaintiffs' counsel play in insuring the integrity of U.S. securities markets and supplementing the enforcement work of the SEC in that regard." 388 F.Supp.2d at 359.

The Named Plaintiff. State statutes typically require that the named plaintiff in a derivative action have owned common or preferred stock of the corporation at the time of the alleged wrongdoing,[60] and some states require that such ownership continue through the commencement and completion of the derivative lawsuit. Beneficial ownership through brokerage "street name" stock or a voting trust usually will qualify.[61] Although statutes typically mandate that

---

60. See, for example, MBCA § 7.41(1) and 8 DGCL § 3.27.
61. See MBCA § 7.40(2).

the named plaintiff "fairly and adequately" represent the interests of the corporation,[62] the presence of competent legal counsel will usually satisfy this requirement even if the named plaintiff has no clue as to what is happening. In *In re Fuqua Industries, Inc. Shareholder Litigation*, 752 A.2d 126 (Del. Ch. 1999), for example, the court refused to disqualify a derivative plaintiff who had lost her memory and faculties during the litigation and "lacked a meaningful grasp of the facts and allegations of the case prosecuted in her name." 752 A.2d at 129. The court stated:

> The allegation that attorneys bring actions through puppet plaintiffs while the real parties in interest are the attorneys themselves in search of fees is an oft-heard complaint from defendants in derivative suits. Sometimes, no doubt, the allegation rings true.

> By the same token, however, the mere fact that lawyers pursue their own economic interest in bringing derivative litigation cannot be held as grounds to disqualify a derivative plaintiff. To do so is to impeach a cornerstone of sound corporate governance. Our legal system has privatized in part the enforcement mechanism for policing fiduciaries by allowing private attorneys to bring suits on behalf of nominal shareholder plaintiffs. In so doing, corporations are safeguarded from fiduciary breaches and shareholders thereby benefit. Through the use of cost and fee shifting mechanisms, private attorneys are economically incentivized to perform this service on behalf of shareholders...

> Mr. and Mrs. Abrams retained counsel in an effort to redress their grievances. They placed their trust and confidence in their lawyers as clients have always done. Our legal system has long recognized that lawyers take a dominant role in prosecuting litigation on behalf of clients. A conscientious lawyer should indeed take a leadership role and thrust herself to the fore of a lawsuit. This maxim is particularly relevant in cases involving fairly abstruse issues of corporate governance and fiduciary duties.

752 A.2d at 133,135.

Abuse Risks. The lucrative dynamics of derivative litigation invite abuse. An aggressive plaintiff's attorney can cook up a marginal fiduciary claim against the directors of a corporation knowing that, when push comes to shove, the directors (personally named in the lawsuit) are going to favor a quick settlement that is covered by corporate indemnification provisions or insurance. When all is said and done, the interests of the corporation on whose behalf the case was brought are viewed as nothing more than an obstacle to getting the settlement approved. The attorney scores fast and starts looking for another derivative nuisance "strike suit." There are some safeguards that protect against the risks of such abuse. Beyond the normal litigation complaint verification requirements, some state statutes authorize the shifting of all litigation expenses, including the defendants' attorney fees, to the plaintiff in a strike suit. The Model Act permits such a shifting if the suit is commenced or maintained "without reasonable cause

---

62. See MBCA § 7.41(2).

or for an improper purpose."[63] And, of course, statutes usually require that any settlement of a derivative suit be approved by the court.[64] A number of factors may impact the approval, including the uncertainties of litigation, the costs of delay, disruption of business, negative publicity, additional indemnification burdens, the overall terms of the settlement, and any other consideration the court deems relevant. The challenge of the attorneys is to leverage these factors in convincing the court that the settlement is in the best interests of the corporation.

Lasting Impacts. The resolution of a derivative suit, whether by settlement or judgment, is binding on the corporation and any party who seeks to prosecute a derivative action based on the same claims raised in the original proceeding. This *res judicata* effect is significant. It underscores the importance of the court's role in approving any settlement. It sometimes opens up the opportunity for parties who were not involved in the lower court's approval of a settlement to prosecute an appeal of that decision.[65] And it may bar federal claims that arise out of the same facts as the derivative action even though the court that approved the derivative settlement had no jurisdiction over the federal claims.[66]

Weird Corporate Roles. The corporation has split and conflicting roles in a derivative proceeding. The named plaintiff is bringing the action on behalf of the corporation (and thus the corporation is the nominal plaintiff), and the corporation also is named as a defendant to compel it to assert its rights against the co-defendant wrongdoers. The weirdness continues because the corporation, controlled by the board, usually joins the other defendants in fighting against the claim that has been filed on its behalf. For this reason, the Supreme Court has held that, although technically a derivative claim is for the benefit of the corporation, the corporation should be treated as a defendant for federal diversity purposes if it joins the cause of the co-defendants.[67] Given this split role, a practical question that routinely surfaces is whether the same law firm (usually the company's regular outside counsel) can represent both the corporation and the other defendants (typically officers and directors) in fighting the derivative claim. The authority is split on this one: some cases strictly forbid such dual representation to insure protection of the corporation's interests[68] and other authorities permit dual representation unless the case involves charges of serious wrongdoing - fraud, intentional misconduct, or self-dealing.[69] And some argue that dual representation should be allowed if the corporation's disinterested directors conclude that there is no basis for the claims.[70] The safest, and often the most prudent, approach is to have separate counsel for the corporation.

---

63. MBCA § 7.46(2).

64. MBCA § 7.45.

65. See, for example, *Delvin v. Scardeletti*, 536 U.S. 1 (2002), and *In re PaineWebber Inc. Ltd. Partnerships Litigation*, 94 F.3d 49, 53 (C.A.2 1996).

66. *Matushita Elec. Indus. V. Epstein*, 516 U.S. 367 (1996) and *Marrese v. American Academy of Orthopaedic Surgeons*, 470 U.S. 373 (1985).

67. *Smith v. Sterling*, 354 U.S. 91 (1957).

68. See, for example, *Messing v. FDI, Inc.*, 439 F.Supp. 776 (D.C. N.J. 1977) and *In re Oracle Securities Litigation*, 829 F.Supp. 1176 (N.D. Cal. 1993).

69. See, for example, official comments to Rule 1.13 of the Model Rules of Professional Conduct, *Musheno v. Gensemer*, 897 F.Supp. 833 (M.D. Pa. 1995), and *Bell Atlantic v. Bolger*, 2 F.3d 1304 (3rd Cir. 1993).

70. See Comment to Section 131 of the Restatement (Third) of the Law Governing Lawyers (American Law Institute 2000).

Corporate Control? Whether and how a corporation exercises control in a derivative action filed on its behalf is the threshold legal challenge in most derivative actions. A sole shareholder, supported by a fee-hungry lawyer, can trigger a process that is destined to consume corporate time, effort and money and potentially damage reputation, momentum, morale, and business relationships. The board of directors, charged with the duty of managing the corporation and acting in the absolute best of faith, may conclude that it's in the best interests of the corporation to have the derivative action end quickly and the named plaintiff (with legal counsel) disappear. This is why statutes impose a demand requirement.

Demand Requirement. The demand requirement is designed to address the potential conflicting interests between the named plaintiff and the corporation. It requires the plaintiff, before commencing the action, to make a demand on the corporation to prosecute or settle the charges. The demand gives the corporation advance notice of the suit and, in theory, provides an opportunity for a pre-suit settlement and exhaustion of intra-corporate dispute resolution procedures. And it gives the corporation's board an opportunity to exercise its management prerogative in sizing up the situation and deciding whether the case should go forward.

Two Forms. This pre-suit demand requirement comes in two forms. The first form, used in Delaware and most states, allows the plaintiff to skip the demand by alleging in the complaint that such a demand would be futile because the corporation's board is not disinterested and independent. The second form, used in the Model Act, requires that a demand be made in all cases and that the plaintiff wait a designated time (i.e., 90 days) before filing a lawsuit. When the futility form is in play, a demand is never made because it would be an acknowledgment of the board's capacity to decide the fate of the case. In such a situation, absent a showing that the board was not properly informed (a long shot, at best), a decision of the board would put an end to the case before it is filed. So the strength of the plaintiff's futility claim becomes the deciding factor in determining whether the case can proceed over the objection of the corporation's board. When demand is mandated by statute and the board rejects the claim, the fate of the litigation still turns on the court's determination of whether the board's decision is entitled to protection under the business judgment rule.

Another Option. Even if the demand showdown doesn't put an end to the case, the corporation's board may have another option for terminating a derivative action. It may create what the Delaware Supreme Court has dubbed a "unique creature," a special litigation committee (SLC) comprised of disinterested, independent individuals. The SLC is delegated complete authority to evaluate the merits of the case continuing on behalf of the corporation and to bring a motion (unrelated to the demand requirement) at any time to end the litigation. Of course, an SLC may also be used to bolster a corporation's claim in the demand phase of the litigation. But, as we will see, when this option is used after the demand phase, it often imposes heightened burden of proof challenges and is never a slam dunk for the SLC.

CASE PROBLEM 9-4

Refer to the facts in Case Problem 11-1 and the plight of Marge and David. They hired a lawyer, Walter, who started digging into Tolson's ownership of Stable. Walter has gathered some interesting facts:

• Tolson paid $10.5 million for Stable;

• Tolson pays at least $800,000 a year to maintain Stable (captain and crew salaries and benefits, insurance, moorage fees, maintenance costs, food expenses, fuel costs, and more);

• Stable never attended a boat show or yacht festival during Marge's tenure, nor was it ever used to demonstrate StableSeas to potential buyers;

• Roughly 65 percent of Stable's on-water use was for Dirk and his family and friends;

• Use by three senior officers and board members accounted for the other 35 percent of Stable's on-water use;

• Marge and the crew were constantly admonished by Dirk to never mention Tolson's ownership of Stable to his friends and family; and

• Tolson held board meetings on Stable three times a year and used Stable for small corporate parties once or twice a year.

Walter is now excited that Marge and David, as shareholders, may have legitimate breach of fiduciary claims against Dirk and the members of Tolson's board. The claims would allege waste and associated breaches of the duties of care and loyalty.

Assume Tolson is a Delaware corporation. Advise Marge, David and Walter on the following questions and, where relevant, indicate what additional facts you would like to have in answering the questions:

1. Would the claims against Dirk and Tolson's directors need to be asserted as direct or derivative claims?

2. What are the impacts to Marge and David if the claims are asserted in a derivative action?

3. What risks do Marge and David take if the claims are dismissed as being frivolous?

4. Who pays the legal fees if Marge and David are victorious?

5. Would a formal demand of Tolson's board be required before commencing a lawsuit?

6. If Tolson's board determines that the claims are not meritorious, can Marge and David proceed with the lawsuit?

7. What steps should Marge and David anticipate that Dirk and Tolson's board will take to prevent the case from ever getting to a decision on the merits?

How would your answers to these questions change if Tolson is incorporated in a state that has adopted the Model Business Corporation Act?

2. DIRECT OR DERIVATIVE CLAIM?

TOOLEY V. DONALDSON, LUFKIN, & JENRETTE, INC.
845 A.2d 1031 (Del. 2004)

Veasey, Chief Justice:

Plaintiff-stockholders brought a purported class action in the Court of Chancery, alleging that the members of the board of directors of their corporation breached their fiduciary duties by agreeing to a 22-day delay in closing a proposed merger. Plaintiffs contend that the delay harmed them due to the lost time-value of the cash paid for their shares. The Court of Chancery granted the defendants' motion to dismiss on the sole ground that the claims were, "at most," claims of the corporation being asserted derivatively. They were, thus, held not to be direct claims of the stockholders, individually. Thereupon, the Court held that the plaintiffs lost their standing to bring this action when they tendered their shares in connection with the merger.

Although the trial court's legal analysis of whether the complaint alleges a direct or derivative claim reflects some concepts in our prior jurisprudence, we believe those concepts are not helpful and should be regarded as erroneous. We set forth in this Opinion the law to be applied henceforth in determining whether a stockholder's claim is derivative or direct. That issue must turn *solely* on the following questions: (1) who suffered the alleged harm (the corporation or the suing stockholders, individually); and (2) who would receive the benefit of any recovery or other remedy (the corporation or the stockholders, individually)?

Patrick Tooley and Kevin Lewis are former minority stockholders of Donaldson, Lufkin & Jenrette, Inc. (DLJ), a Delaware corporation engaged in investment banking. DLJ was acquired by Credit Suisse Group (Credit Suisse) in the Fall of 2000. Before that acquisition, AXA Financial, Inc.(AXA), which owned 71% of DLJ stock, controlled DLJ. Pursuant to a stockholder agreement between AXA and Credit Suisse, AXA agreed to exchange with Credit Suisse its DLJ stockholdings for a mix of stock and cash. The consideration received by AXA consisted primarily of stock. Cash made up one-third of the purchase price. Credit Suisse intended to acquire the remaining minority interests of publicly-held DLJ stock through a cash tender offer, followed by a merger of DLJ into a Credit Suisse subsidiary.

The tender offer price was set at $90 per share in cash. The tender offer was to expire 20 days after its commencement. The merger agreement, however, authorized two types of extensions. First, Credit Suisse could unilaterally extend the tender offer if certain conditions were not met, such as SEC regulatory approvals or certain payment obligations. Alternatively, DLJ and Credit Suisse could agree to postpone acceptance by Credit Suisse of DLJ stock tendered by the minority stockholders.

Credit Suisse availed itself of both types of extensions to postpone the closing of the tender offer. Plaintiffs challenge the second extension that resulted in a 22-day delay. They contend that this delay was not properly authorized and harmed minority stockholders while improperly benefitting AXA. They claim damages representing the time-value of money lost through the delay.

The order of the Court of Chancery dismissing the complaint, and the Memorandum Opinion upon which it is based, state that the dismissal is based on the plaintiffs' lack of standing to bring the claims asserted therein. Thus, when plaintiffs tendered their shares, they lost standing under Court of Chancery Rule 23.1, the contemporaneous holding rule. The ruling before us on appeal is that the plaintiffs' claim is derivative, purportedly brought on behalf of DLJ. The Court of Chancery, relying upon our confusing jurisprudence on the direct/derivative dichotomy, based its dismissal on the following ground: "Because this delay affected all DLJ shareholders equally, plaintiffs' injury was not a special injury, and this action is, thus, a derivative action, at most."

Plaintiffs argue that they have suffered a "special injury" because they had an alleged contractual right to receive the merger consideration of $90 per share without suffering the 22-day delay arising out of the extensions under the merger agreement. But the trial court's opinion convincingly demonstrates that plaintiffs had no such contractual right. Moreover, no other individual right of these stockholder-plaintiffs was alleged to have been violated by the extensions.

That conclusion could have ended the case because it portended a definitive ruling that plaintiffs have no claim whatsoever on the facts alleged. But the defendants chose to argue, and the trial court chose to decide, the standing issue, which is predicated on an assertion that this claim is a derivative one asserted on behalf of the corporation, DLJ.

The Court of Chancery correctly noted that "[t]he Court will independently examine the nature of the wrong alleged and any potential relief to make its own determination of the suit's classification.... Plaintiffs' classification of the suit is not binding." The trial court's analysis was hindered, however, because it focused on the confusing concept of "special injury" as the test for determining whether a claim is derivative or direct. The trial court's premise was as follows:

> In order to bring a *direct* claim, a plaintiff must have experienced some "special injury." A special injury is a wrong that "is separate and distinct from that suffered by other shareholders, ... or a wrong involving a contractual right of a shareholder, such as the right to vote, or to assert majority control, which exists independently of any right of the corporation."

In our view, the concept of "special injury" that appears in some Supreme Court and Court of Chancery cases is not helpful to a proper analytical distinction between direct and derivative actions. We now disapprove the use of the concept of "special injury" as a tool in that analysis.

The analysis must be based solely on the following questions: Who suffered the alleged harm - the corporation or the suing stockholder individually - and who would receive the benefit of the recovery or other remedy? This simple analysis is well imbedded in our jurisprudence, but some cases have complicated it by injection of the amorphous and confusing concept of "special injury."

The Chancellor, in the very recent *Agostino* case, correctly points this out and strongly suggests that we should disavow the concept of "special injury." In a scholarly analysis of this area of the law, he also suggests that the inquiry should be whether the stockholder has demonstrated that he or she has suffered an injury that is not dependent on an injury to the corporation. In the context of a claim for breach of fiduciary duty, the Chancellor articulated the inquiry as follows: "Looking at the body of the complaint and considering the nature of the wrong alleged and the relief requested, has the plaintiff demonstrated that he or she can prevail without showing an injury to the corporation?" We believe that this approach is helpful in analyzing the first prong of the analysis: what person or entity has suffered the alleged harm? The second prong of the analysis should logically follow.

Determining whether an action is derivative or direct is sometimes difficult and has many legal consequences, some of which may have an expensive impact on the parties to the action. For example, if an action is derivative, the plaintiffs are then required to comply with the requirements of Court of Chancery Rule 23.1, that the stockholder: (a) retain ownership of the shares throughout the litigation; (b) make presuit demand on the board; and (c) obtain court approval of any settlement. Further, the recovery, if any, flows only to the corporation. The decision whether a suit is direct or derivative may be outcome-determinative. Therefore, it is necessary that a standard to distinguish such actions be clear, simple and consistently articulated and applied by our courts.

[A] court should look to the nature of the wrong and to whom the relief should go. The stockholder's claimed direct injury must be independent of any alleged injury to the corporation. The stockholder must demonstrate that the duty breached was owed to the stockholder and that he or she can prevail without showing an injury to the corporation.

In this case it cannot be concluded that the complaint alleges a derivative claim. There is no derivative claim asserting injury to the corporate entity. There is no relief that would go the corporation. Accordingly, there is no basis to hold that the complaint states a derivative claim.

But, it does not necessarily follow that the complaint states a direct, individual claim. While the complaint purports to set forth a direct claim, in reality, it states no claim at all. The trial court analyzed the complaint and correctly concluded that it does not claim that the plaintiffs have any rights that have been injured. Their rights have not yet ripened. The contractual claim is nonexistent until it is ripe, and that claim will not be ripe until the terms of the merger are fulfilled, including the extensions of the closing at issue here. Therefore, there is no direct claim stated in the complaint before us.

Accordingly, the complaint was properly dismissed. But, due to the reliance on the concept of "special injury" by the Court of Chancery, the ground set forth for the dismissal is erroneous, there being no derivative claim. That error is harmless, however, because, in our view, there is no direct claim either.

For purposes of distinguishing between derivative and direct claims, we expressly disapprove both the concept of "special injury" and the concept that a claim is necessarily derivative if it affects all stockholders equally. In our view, the tests going forward should rest on those set forth in this opinion.

Closely Held Corporations

The direct-derivative distinction often makes little sense in the context of a closely held corporation where some shareholders desire to bring an action against their co-shareholders, alleging breach of fiduciary duties. In such situations, courts often ignore derivative requirements and treat the dispute as a conflict between owners, much the same as a dispute among partners.[71] Any recovery will flow to the prevailing party (not the corporation), there is no pre-suit demand requirement, and the parties can settle their dispute without court approval. However, precautions are sometimes necessary to insure that the resolution of the dispute does not encourage multiple claims, preclude a fair recovery for all interested parties, or unfairly prejudice creditors by compromising the financial viability of the corporation.[72]

In *Barth v. Barth*, 659 N.E.2d 559 (Ind. 1995), the court explained the rationale for treating closely held corporations differently by stating:

> While we affirm the general rule requiring a shareholder to bring a derivative rather than direct action when seeking redress for injury to the corporation, we nevertheless observe two reasons why this rule will not always apply in the case of closely-held corporations. First, shareholders in a close corporation stand in a fiduciary relationship to each other, and as such, must deal fairly, honestly, and openly with the corporation and with their fellow shareholders. Second, shareholder litigation in the closely-held corporation context will often not implicate the policies that mandate requiring derivative litigation when more widely-held corporations are involved...Because of the fundamental resemblance of the close corporation to the partnership, the trust and confidence which are essential to this scale and manner of enterprise, and the inherent danger to minority interests in the close corporation, we hold that stockholders in the close corporation owe one another substantially the same fiduciary duty in the operation of the enterprise that partners owe to one another. In our previous decisions, we have defined the standard of duty owed by partners to one another as the "utmost good faith and loyalty." Stockholders in close corporations must discharge their management and stockholder responsibilities in conformity with this strict good faith standard. They may not act out of avarice, expediency or self-interest in derogation of their duty of loyalty to the other stockholders and to the corporation.

> Because shareholders of closely-held corporations have very direct obligations to one another and because shareholder litigation in the closely-held corporation context will often not implicate the principles which gave rise to the rule requiring derivative litigation, courts in

---

71. See, for example, *Crosby v. Beam*, 548 N.E.2d 217 (Ohio 1989), *Barth v. Barth*, 659 N.E.2d 559 (Ind. 1995), and ALI Principles § 7.01(d).

72. See ALI Principles § 7.01(d).

many cases are permitting direct suits by shareholders of closely-held corporations where the complaint is one that in a public corporation would have to be brought as a derivative action.

659 N.E.2d at 561.

3. THE FUTILITY CHALLENGE

ARONSON v. LEWIS
473 A.2d 805 (Del. 1984)

Moore, Justice:

[W]hen is a stockholder's demand upon a board of directors, to redress an alleged wrong to the corporation, excused as futile prior to the filing of a derivative suit? We granted this interlocutory appeal to the defendants, Meyers Parking System, Inc. (Meyers), a Delaware corporation, and its directors, to review the Court of Chancery's denial of their motion to dismiss this action, pursuant to Chancery Rule 23.1, for the plaintiff's failure to make such a demand or otherwise demonstrate its futility. The Vice Chancellor ruled that plaintiff's allegations raised a "reasonable inference" that the directors' action was unprotected by the business judgment rule. Thus, the board could not have impartially considered and acted upon the demand.

We cannot agree with this formulation of the concept of demand futility. In our view demand can only be excused where facts are alleged with particularity which create a reasonable doubt that the directors' action was entitled to the protections of the business judgment rule. Because the plaintiff failed to make a demand, and to allege facts with particularity indicating that such demand would be futile, we reverse the Court of Chancery and remand with instructions that plaintiff be granted leave to amend the complaint.

The issues of demand futility rest upon the allegations of the complaint. The plaintiff, Harry Lewis, is a stockholder of Meyers. The defendants are Meyers and its ten directors, some of whom are also company officers.

In 1979, Prudential Building Maintenance Corp. (Prudential) spun off its shares of Meyers to Prudential's stockholders. Prior thereto Meyers was a wholly owned subsidiary of Prudential. Meyers provides parking lot facilities and related services throughout the country. Its stock is actively traded over-the-counter.

This suit challenges certain transactions between Meyers and one of its directors, Leo Fink, who owns 47% of its outstanding stock. Plaintiff claims that these transactions were approved only because Fink personally selected each director and officer of Meyers.

Prior to January 1, 1981, Fink had an employment agreement with Prudential which provided that upon retirement he was to become a consultant to that company for ten years. This provision became operable when Fink retired in April 1980. Thereafter, Meyers agreed with Prudential to share Fink's consulting services and reimburse Prudential for 25% of the fees paid Fink. Under this arrangement Meyers paid Prudential $48,332 in 1980 and $45,832 in 1981.

On January 1, 1981, the defendants approved an employment agreement between Meyers and Fink for a five year term with provision for automatic renewal each year thereafter, indefinitely. Meyers agreed to pay Fink $150,000 per year, plus a bonus of 5% of its pre-tax profits over $2,400,000. Fink could terminate the contract at any time, but Meyers could do so only upon six months' notice. At termination, Fink was to become a consultant to Meyers and be paid $150,000 per year for the first three years, $125,000 for the next three years, and $100,000 thereafter for life. Death benefits were also included. Fink agreed to devote his best efforts and substantially his entire business time to advancing Meyers' interests. The agreement also provided that Fink's compensation was not to be affected by any inability to perform services on Meyers' behalf. Fink was 75 years old when his employment agreement with Meyers was approved by the directors. There is no claim that he was, or is, in poor health.

Additionally, the Meyers board approved and made interest-free loans to Fink totaling $225,000. These loans were unpaid and outstanding as of August 1982 when the complaint was filed. At oral argument defendants' counsel represented that these loans had been repaid in full.

The complaint charges that these transactions had "no valid business purpose", and were a "waste of corporate assets" because the amounts to be paid are "grossly excessive", that Fink performs "no or little services", and because of his "advanced age" cannot be "expected to perform any such services". The plaintiff also charges that the existence of the Prudential consulting agreement with Fink prevents him from providing his "best efforts" on Meyers' behalf. Finally, it is alleged that the loans to Fink were in reality "additional compensation" without any "consideration" or "benefit" to Meyers.

The complaint alleged that no demand had been made on the Meyers board because such attempt would be futile for the following reasons:

(a) All of the directors in office are named as defendants herein and they have participated in, expressly approved and/or acquiesced in, and are personally liable for, the wrongs complained of herein.

(b) Defendant Fink, having selected each director, controls and dominates every member of the Board and every officer of Meyers.

(c) Institution of this action by present directors would require the defendant-directors to sue themselves, thereby placing the conduct of this action in hostile hands and preventing its effective prosecution.

The relief sought included the cancellation of the Meyers-Fink employment contract and an accounting by the directors, including Fink, for all damage sustained by Meyers and for all profits derived by the directors and Fink.

A cardinal precept of the General Corporation Law of the State of Delaware is that directors, rather than shareholders, manage the business and affairs of the corporation. 8 Del.C. § 141(a). The existence and exercise of this power carries with it certain fundamental fiduciary obligations to the corporation and its shareholders. Moreover, a stockholder is not powerless to challenge director action which results in harm to the corporation. The machinery of corporate democracy and the derivative suit are potent tools to redress the conduct of a torpid or unfaithful management. The derivative action developed in equity to enable shareholders to sue in the corporation's name where those in control of the company refused to assert a claim belonging to it. The nature of the action is two-fold. First, it is the equivalent of a suit by the shareholders to compel the corporation to sue. Second, it is a suit by the corporation, asserted by the shareholders on its behalf, against those liable to it.

By its very nature the derivative action impinges on the managerial freedom of directors. Hence, the demand requirement of Chancery Rule 23.1 exists at the threshold, first to insure that a stockholder exhausts his intracorporate remedies, and then to provide a safeguard against strike suits. Thus, by promoting this form of alternate dispute resolution, rather than immediate recourse to litigation, the demand requirement is a recognition of the fundamental precept that directors manage the business and affairs of corporations.

In our view the entire question of demand futility is inextricably bound to issues of business judgment and the standards of that doctrine's applicability. The business judgment rule is an acknowledgment of the managerial prerogatives of Delaware directors under Section 141(a). It is a presumption that in making a business decision the directors of a corporation acted on an informed basis, in good faith and in the honest belief that the action taken was in the best interests of the company. Absent an abuse of discretion, that judgment will be respected by the courts. The burden is on the party challenging the decision to establish facts rebutting the presumption.

The function of the business judgment rule is of paramount significance in the context of a derivative action. It comes into play in several ways—in addressing a demand, in the determination of demand futility, in efforts by independent disinterested directors to dismiss the action as inimical to the corporation's best interests, and generally, as a defense to the merits of the suit. However, in each of these circumstances there are certain common principles governing the application and operation of the rule.

First, its protections can only be claimed by disinterested directors whose conduct otherwise meets the tests of business judgment. From the standpoint of interest, this means that directors can neither appear on both sides of a transaction nor expect to derive any personal financial benefit from it in the sense of self-dealing, as opposed to a benefit which devolves upon the corporation or all stockholders generally. Thus, if such director interest is present, and the transaction is not approved by a majority consisting of the disinterested directors, then the business judgment rule has no application whatever in determining demand futility.

Second, to invoke the rule's protection directors have a duty to inform themselves, prior to making a business decision, of all material information reasonably available to them. Having become so informed, they must then act with requisite care in the discharge of their duties. While the Delaware cases use a variety of terms to describe the applicable standard of care, our analysis satisfies us that under the business judgment rule director liability is predicated upon concepts of gross negligence.

However, it should be noted that the business judgment rule operates only in the context of director action. Technically speaking, it has no role where directors have either abdicated their functions, or absent a conscious decision, failed to act. But it also follows that under applicable principles, a conscious decision to refrain from acting may nonetheless be a valid exercise of business judgment and enjoy the protections of the rule.

Delaware courts have addressed the issue of demand futility on several earlier occasions. See *Sohland v. Baker,* Del.Supr., 141 A. 277, 281–82 (1927); *McKee v. Rogers,* Del.Ch., 156 A. 191, 193 (1931); *Miller v. Loft,* Del.Ch., 153 A. 861, 862 (1931); *Fleer v. Frank H. Fleer Corp.,* Del.Ch., 125 A. 411, 414 (1924). The rule emerging from these decisions is that where officers and directors are under an influence which sterilizes their discretion, they cannot be considered proper persons to conduct litigation on behalf of the corporation. Thus, demand would be futile.

However, those cases cannot be taken to mean that any board approval of a challenged transaction automatically connotes "hostile interest" and "guilty participation" by directors, or some other form of sterilizing influence upon them. Were that so, the demand requirements of our law would be meaningless, leaving the clear mandate of Chancery Rule 23.1 devoid of its purpose and substance.

The trial court correctly recognized that demand futility is inextricably bound to issues of business judgment, but stated the test to be based on allegations of fact, which, if true, "show that there is a reasonable inference" the business judgment rule is not applicable for purposes of a pre-suit demand. The problem with this formulation is the concept of reasonable inferences to be drawn against a board of directors based on allegations in a complaint. As is clear from this case, and the conclusory allegations upon which the Vice Chancellor relied, demand futility becomes virtually automatic under such a test. Bearing in mind the presumptions with which director action is cloaked, we believe that the matter must be approached in a more balanced way.

Our view is that in determining demand futility the Court of Chancery in the proper exercise of its discretion must decide whether, under the particularized facts alleged, a reasonable doubt is created that: (1) the directors are disinterested and independent and (2) the challenged transaction was otherwise the product of a valid exercise of business judgment. Hence, the Court of Chancery must make two inquiries, one into the independence and disinterestedness of the directors and the other into the substantive nature of the challenged transaction and the board's approval thereof. As to the latter inquiry the court does not assume that the transaction is a wrong to the corporation requiring corrective steps by the board. Rather, the alleged wrong is substantively reviewed against the factual background alleged in the complaint. As to the former inquiry, directorial independence and disinterestedness, the court reviews the factual allegations to decide whether they raise a reasonable doubt, as a threshold matter, that the protections of the business judgment rule are available to the board. Certainly, if this is an "interested" director transaction, such that the business judgment rule is inapplicable to the board majority approving the transaction, then the inquiry ceases. In that event futility of demand has been established by any objective or subjective standard.

However, the mere threat of personal liability for approving a questioned transaction, standing alone, is insufficient to challenge either the independence or disinterestedness of directors, although in rare cases a transaction may be so egregious on its face that board approval cannot meet the test of business judgment, and a substantial likelihood of director liability therefore exists. In sum the entire review is factual in nature. The Court of Chancery in the exercise of its sound discretion must be satisfied that a plaintiff has alleged facts with particularity which, taken as true, support a reasonable doubt that the challenged transaction was the product of a valid exercise of business judgment. Only in that context is demand excused.

Having outlined the legal framework within which these issues are to be determined, we consider plaintiff's claims of futility here: Fink's domination and control of the directors, board approval of the Fink-Meyers employment agreement, and board hostility to the plaintiff's derivative action due to the directors' status as defendants.

Plaintiff's claim that Fink dominates and controls the Meyers' board is based on: (1) Fink's 47% ownership of Meyers' outstanding stock, and (2) that he "personally selected" each Meyers director. Plaintiff also alleges that mere approval of the employment agreement illustrates Fink's domination and control of the board. In addition, plaintiff argued on appeal that 47% stock ownership, though less than a majority, constituted control given the large number of shares outstanding, 1,245,745.

Such contentions do not support any claim under Delaware law that these directors lack independence. In Kaplan v. Centex Corp., Del.Ch., 284 A.2d 119 (1971), the Court of Chancery stated that "[s]tock ownership alone, at least when it amounts to less than a majority, is not sufficient proof of domination or control". Id. at 123. Moreover, in the demand context even proof of majority ownership of a company does not strip the directors of the presumptions of independence, and that their acts have been taken in good faith and in the best interests of the corporation. There must be coupled with the allegation of control such facts as would demonstrate that through personal or other relationships the directors are beholden to the controlling person. To date the principal decisions dealing with the issue of control or domination arose only after a full trial on the merits. Thus, they are distinguishable in the demand context unless similar particularized facts are alleged to meet the test of Chancery Rule 23.1.

The requirement of director independence inheres in the conception and rationale of the business judgment rule. The presumption of propriety that flows from an exercise of business judgment is based in part on this unyielding precept. Independence means that a director's decision is based on the corporate merits of the subject before the board rather than extraneous considerations or influences. While directors may confer, debate, and resolve their differences through compromise, or by reasonable reliance upon the expertise of their colleagues and other qualified persons, the end result, nonetheless, must be that each director has brought his or her own informed business judgment to bear with specificity upon the corporate merits of the issues without regard for or succumbing to influences which convert an otherwise valid business decision into a faithless act.

Thus, it is not enough to charge that a director was nominated by or elected at the behest of those controlling the outcome of a corporate election. That is the usual way a person becomes a corporate director. It is the care, attention and sense of individual responsibility to the performance of one's duties, not the method of election, that generally touches on independence.

We conclude that in the demand-futile context a plaintiff charging domination and control of one or more directors must allege particularized facts manifesting "a direction of corporate conduct in such a way as to comport with the wishes or interests of the corporation (or persons) doing the controlling". *Kaplan*, 284 A.2d at 123. The shorthand shibboleth of "dominated and controlled directors" is insufficient. In recognizing that *Kaplan* was decided after trial and full discovery, we stress that the plaintiff need only allege specific facts; he need not plead evidence. Otherwise, he would be forced to make allegations which may not comport with his duties under Chancery Rule 11.

Here, plaintiff has not alleged any facts sufficient to support a claim of control. The personal-selection-of-directors allegation stands alone, unsupported. At best it is a conclusion devoid of factual support. The causal link between Fink's control and approval of the employment agreement is alluded to, but nowhere specified. The director's approval, alone, does not establish control, even in the face of Fink's 47% stock ownership. The claim that Fink is unlikely to perform any services under the agreement, because of his age, and his conflicting consultant work with Prudential, adds nothing to the control claim. Therefore, we cannot conclude that the complaint factually particularizes any circumstances of control and domination to overcome the presumption of board independence, and thus render the demand futile.

Turning to the board's approval of the Meyers-Fink employment agreement, plaintiff's argument is simple: all of the Meyers directors are named defendants, because they approved the wasteful agreement; if plaintiff prevails on the merits all the directors will be jointly and severally liable; therefore, the directors' interest in avoiding personal liability automatically and absolutely disqualifies them from passing on a shareholder's demand.

Such allegations are conclusory at best. In Delaware mere directorial approval of a transaction, absent particularized facts supporting a breach of fiduciary duty claim, or otherwise establishing the lack of independence or disinterestedness of a majority of the directors, is insufficient to excuse demand. Here, plaintiff's suit is premised on the notion that the Meyers-Fink employment agreement was a waste of corporate assets. So, the argument goes, by approving such waste the directors now face potential personal liability, thereby rendering futile any demand on them to bring suit. Unfortunately, plaintiff's claim falls in its initial premise. The complaint does not allege particularized facts indicating that the agreement is a waste of corporate assets. Indeed, the complaint as now drafted may not even state a cause of action, given the directors' broad corporate power to fix the compensation of officers.

In essence, the plaintiff alleged a lack of consideration flowing from Fink to Meyers, since the employment agreement provided that compensation was not contingent on Fink's ability to perform any services. The bare assertion that Fink performed "little or no services" was plaintiff's conclusion based solely on Fink's age and the existence of the Fink-Prudential employment agreement. As for Meyers' loans to Fink, beyond the bare allegation that they were made, the complaint does not allege facts indicating the wastefulness of such arrangements. Again, the mere existence of such loans, given the broad corporate powers conferred by Delaware law, does not even state a claim.

Plaintiff's final argument is the incantation that demand is excused because the directors otherwise would have to sue themselves, thereby placing the conduct of the litigation in hostile hands and preventing its effective prosecution. This bootstrap argument has been made to and dismissed by other courts. Its acceptance would effectively abrogate Rule 23.1 and weaken the managerial power of directors. Unless facts are alleged with particularity to overcome the presumptions of independence and a proper exercise of business judgment, in which case the directors could not be expected to sue themselves, a bare claim of this sort raises no legally cognizable issue under Delaware corporate law.

In sum, we conclude that the plaintiff has failed to allege facts with particularity indicating that the Meyers directors were tainted by interest, lacked independence, or took action contrary to Meyers' best interests in order to create a reasonable doubt as to the applicability of the business judgment rule. Only in the presence of such a reasonable doubt may a demand be deemed futile. Hence, we reverse the Court of Chancery's denial of the motion to dismiss, and remand with instructions that plaintiff be granted leave to amend his complaint to bring it into compliance with the principles we have announced today.

Reversed and remanded.

RALES v. BLASBAND
634 A.2d 927 (Del. 1993)

VEASEY, Chief Justice:

This certified question of law comes before the Court pursuant to Article IV, Section 11(9) of the Delaware Constitution and Supreme Court Rule 41. The question of law was certified by the United States District Court for the District of Delaware (the "District Court"), and was accepted by this Court on June 16, 1993.

The underlying action pending in the District Court is a stockholder derivative action filed on March 25, 1991, by Alfred Blasband ("Blasband") on behalf of Danaher Corporation, a Delaware corporation ("Danaher").

In the context of this novel action, has plaintiff Alfred Blasband, in accordance with the substantive law of the State of Delaware, alleged facts to show that demand is excused on the board of directors of Danaher Corporation, a Delaware corporation? After consideration of the allegations of the amended complaint, the briefs, and the oral argument of the parties in this Court, it is our conclusion that the certified question must be answered in the affirmative. In the unusual context of this case, demand on the Board is excused because the amended complaint alleges particularized facts creating a reasonable doubt that a majority of the Board would be disinterested or independent in making a decision on a demand.

Blasband is currently a stockholder of Danaher. Prior to 1990 Blasband owned 1100 shares of Easco Hand Tools, Inc., a Delaware corporation ("Easco"). Easco entered into a merger agreement with Danaher in February 1990 whereby Easco became a wholly-owned subsidiary of Danaher (the "Merger").

Steven M. Rales and Mitchell P. Rales (the "Rales brothers") have been directors, officers, or stockholders of Easco and Danaher at relevant times. Prior to the Merger, the Rales brothers were directors of Easco, and together owned approximately 52 percent of Easco's common stock. They continued to serve as directors of Easco after the Merger.

The Rales brothers also own approximately 44 percent of Danaher's common stock. Prior to the Merger, Mitchell Rales was President and Steven Rales was Chief Executive Officer of Danaher. The Rales brothers resigned their positions as officers of Danaher in early 1990, but continued to serve as members of the Board. The Board consists of eight members. The other six members are Danaher's President and Chief Executive Officer, George Sherman ("Sherman"), Donald E. Ehrlich ("Ehrlich"), Mortimer Caplin ("Caplin"), George D. Kellner ("Kellner"), A. Emmett Stephenson, Jr. ("Stephenson"), and Walter Lohr ("Lohr"). A number of these directors have business relationships with the Rales brothers or with entities controlled by them.

The central focus of the amended complaint is the alleged misuse by the Easco board of the proceeds of a sale of that company's 12.875% Senior Subordinated Notes due 1998 (the "Notes"). On or about September 1, 1988, Easco sold $100 million of the Notes in a public offering (the "Offering"). The prospectus for the Offering stated that the proceeds from the sale of the Notes would be used for (1) repaying outstanding indebtedness, (2) funding corporate expansion, and (3) general corporate purposes. The prospectus further stated that "[p]ending such uses, the Company will invest the balance of the net proceeds from this offering in government and other marketable securities which are expected to yield a lower rate of return than the rate of interest borne by the Notes."

Blasband alleges that the defendants did not invest in "government and other marketable securities," but instead used over $61.9 million of the proceeds to buy highly speculative "junk bonds" offered through Drexel Burnham Lambert Inc. ("Drexel"). Blasband alleges that these junk bonds were bought by Easco because of the Rales brothers' desire to help Drexel at a time when it was under investigation and having trouble selling such bonds. The amended complaint describes the prior business relationship between the Rales brothers and Drexel in the mid–1980s, including Drexel's assistance in the Rales brothers' expansion of Danaher through corporate acquisitions and the role played by Drexel in the Rales brothers' attempt to acquire Interco, Inc. Moreover, Drexel was the underwriter of the Offering of Easco's Notes.

The amended complaint alleges that these investments have declined substantially in value, resulting in a loss to Easco of at least $14 million. Finally, Blasband complains that the Easco and Danaher boards of directors refused to comply with his request for information regarding the investments.

The stockholder derivative suit is an important and unique feature of corporate governance. In such a suit, a stockholder asserts a cause of action belonging to the corporation. Aronson, 473 A.2d at 811; Levine v. Smith, Del.Supr., 591 A.2d 194, 200 (1991). In a double derivative suit, such as the present case, a stockholder of a parent corporation seeks recovery for a cause of action belonging to a subsidiary corporation. See Sternberg v. O'Neil, Del.Supr., 550 A.2d 1105, 1123–24 (1988). Because directors are empowered to manage, or direct the management of, the business and affairs of the corporation, 8 Del.C. § 141(a), the right of a stockholder to prosecute a derivative suit is limited to situations where the stockholder has demanded that the directors pursue the corporate claim and they have wrongfully refused to do so or where demand is excused because the directors are incapable of making an impartial decision regarding such litigation. Levine, 591 A.2d at 200. Fed.R.Civ.P. 23.1, like Chancery Court Rule 23.1, constitutes the procedural embodiment of this substantive principle of corporation law.

Derivative suits have been used most frequently as a means of redressing harm to a corporation allegedly resulting from misconduct by its directors. Because such derivative suits challenge the propriety of decisions made by directors pursuant to their managerial authority, we have repeatedly held that the stockholder plaintiffs must overcome the powerful presumptions of the business judgment rule before they will be permitted to pursue the derivative claim. Our decision in Aronson enunciated the test for determining a derivative plaintiff's compliance with this fundamental threshold obligation: "whether, under the particularized facts alleged, a reasonable doubt is created that: (1) the directors are disinterested and independent [or] (2) the challenged transaction was otherwise the product of a valid exercise of business judgment." 473 A.2d at 814.

Although these standards are well-established, they cannot be applied in a vacuum. Not all derivative suits fall into the paradigm addressed by Aronson and its progeny. The essential predicate for the Aronson test is the fact that a decision of the board of directors is being challenged in the derivative suit.

Under the unique circumstances of this case, an analysis of the Board's ability to consider a demand requires a departure here from the standards set forth in Aronson. The Board did not approve the transaction which is being challenged by Blasband in this action. In fact, the Danaher directors have made no decision relating to the subject of this derivative suit. Where there is no conscious decision by directors to act or refrain from acting, the business judgment rule has no application. The absence of board action, therefore, makes it impossible to perform the essential inquiry contemplated by Aronson—whether the directors have acted in conformity with the business judgment rule in approving the challenged transaction.

Consistent with the context and rationale of the Aronson decision, a court should not apply the Aronson test for demand futility where the board that would be considering the demand did not make a business decision which is being challenged in the derivative suit. This situation would arise in three principal scenarios: (1) where a business decision was made by the board of a company, but a majority of the directors making the decision have been replaced; (2) where the subject of the derivative suit is not a business decision of the board; and (3) where, as here, the decision being challenged was made by the board of a different corporation.

Instead, it is appropriate in these situations to examine whether the board that would be addressing the demand can impartially consider its merits without being influenced by improper considerations. Thus, a court must determine whether or not the particularized factual allegations of a derivative stockholder complaint create a reasonable doubt that, as of the time the complaint is filed, the board of directors could have properly exercised its independent and disinterested business judgment in responding to a demand. If the derivative plaintiff satisfies this burden, then demand will be excused as futile.

In so holding, we reject the defendants' proposal that, for purposes of this derivative suit and future similar suits, we adopt either a universal demand requirement or a requirement that a plaintiff must demonstrate a reasonable probability of success on the merits. The defendants seek to justify these stringent tests on the need to discourage "strike suits" in situations like the present one. This concern is unfounded.

A plaintiff in a double derivative suit is still required to satisfy the Aronson test in order to establish that demand on the subsidiary's board is futile. The Aronson test was designed, in part, with the objective of preventing strike suits by requiring derivative plaintiffs to make a threshold showing, through the allegation of particularized facts, that their claims have some merit. Moreover, defendants' proposal of requiring demand on the parent board in all double derivative cases, even where a board of directors is interested, is not the appropriate protection against strike suits. While defendants' alternative suggestion of requiring a plaintiff to demonstrate a reasonable probability of success is more closely related to the prevention of strike suits, it is an extremely onerous burden to meet at the pleading stage without the benefit of discovery. Because a plaintiff must satisfy the Aronson test in order to show that demand is excused on the subsidiary board, there is no need to create an unduly onerous test for determining demand futility on the parent board simply to protect against strike suits.

In order to determine whether the Board could have impartially considered a demand at the time Blasband's original complaint was filed, it is appropriate to examine the nature of the decision confronting it. A stockholder demand letter would, at a minimum, notify the directors of the nature of the alleged wrongdoing and the identities of the alleged wrongdoers. The subject of the demand in this case would be the alleged breaches of fiduciary duty by the Easco board of directors in connection with Easco's investment in Drexel "junk bonds." The allegations of the amended complaint, which must be accepted as true in this procedural context, claim that the investment was made solely for the benefit of the Rales brothers, who were acting in furtherance of their business relationship with Drexel and not with regard to Easco's best interests. Such conduct, if proven, would constitute a breach of the Easco directors' duty of loyalty.

The task of a board of directors in responding to a stockholder demand letter is a two-step process. First, the directors must determine the best method to inform themselves of the facts relating to the alleged wrongdoing and the considerations, both legal and financial, bearing on a response to the demand. If a factual investigation is required, it must be conducted reasonably and in good faith. Spiegel v. Buntrock, Del.Supr., 571 A.2d 767, 777 (1990). Second, the board must weigh the alternatives available to it, including the advisability of implementing internal corrective action and commencing legal proceedings. See Weiss v. Temporary Inv. Fund, Inc., 692 F.2d 928, 941 (3d Cir.1982) (observing that directors, when faced with a stockholder demand, "can exercise their discretion to accept the demand and prosecute the action, to resolve the grievance internally without resort to litigation, or to refuse the demand"). See also Aronson, 473 A.2d at 811–12 (discussing the role of the demand requirement as a "form of alternate dispute resolution" that requires the stockholder to exhaust "his intracorporate remedies"). In carrying out these tasks, the board must be able to act free of personal financial interest and improper extraneous influences. We now consider whether the members of the Board could have met these standards.

The members of the Board at the time Blasband filed his original complaint were Steven Rales, Mitchell Rales, Sherman, Ehrlich, Caplin, Kellner, Stephenson, and Lohr. The Rales brothers and Caplin were also members of the Easco board of directors at the time of the alleged wrongdoing. Blasband's amended complaint specifically accuses the Rales brothers of being the motivating force behind the investment in Drexel "junk bonds." The Board would be obligated to determine whether these charges of wrongdoing should be investigated and, if substantiated, become the subject of legal action.

A director is considered interested where he or she will receive a personal financial benefit from a transaction that is not equally shared by the stockholders. Directorial interest also exists where a corporate decision will have a materially detrimental impact on a director, but not on the corporation and the stockholders. In such circumstances, a director cannot be expected to exercise his or her independent business judgment without being influenced by the adverse personal consequences resulting from the decision.

We conclude that the Rales brothers and Caplin must be considered interested in a decision of the Board in response to a demand addressing the alleged wrongdoing described in Blasband's amended complaint. Normally, "the mere threat of personal liability for approving a questioned transaction, standing alone, is insufficient to challenge either the independence or disinterestedness of directors...." Aronson, 473 A.2d at 815. Nevertheless, the Third Circuit has already concluded that "Blasband has pleaded facts raising at least a reasonable doubt that the [Easco board's] use of proceeds from the Note Offering was a valid exercise of business judgment." This determination is part of the law of the case, and is therefore binding on this Court. Such determination indicates that the potential for liability is not "a mere threat" but instead may rise to "a substantial likelihood."

Therefore, a decision by the Board to bring suit against the Easco directors, including the Rales brothers and Caplin, could have potentially significant financial consequences for those directors. Common sense dictates that, in light of these consequences, the Rales brothers and Caplin have a disqualifying financial interest that disables them from impartially considering a response to a demand by Blasband.

Having determined that the Rales brothers and Caplin would be interested in a decision on Blasband's demand, we must now examine whether the remaining Danaher directors are sufficiently independent to make an impartial decision despite the fact that they are presumptively disinterested. As explained in Aronson, "[i]ndependence means that a director's decision is based on the corporate merits of the subject before the board rather than extraneous considerations or influences." 473 A.2d at 816. To establish lack of independence, Blasband must show that the directors are "beholden" to the Rales brothers or so under their influence that their discretion would be sterilized. We conclude that the amended complaint alleges particularized facts sufficient to create a reasonable doubt that Sherman and Ehrlich, as members of the Board, are capable of acting independently of the Rales brothers.

Sherman is the President and Chief Executive Officer of Danaher. His salary is approximately $1 million per year. Although Sherman's continued employment and substantial remuneration may not hinge solely on his relationship with the Rales brothers, there is little doubt that Steven Rales' position as Chairman of the Board of Danaher and Mitchell Rales' position as Chairman of its Executive Committee place them in a position to exert considerable influence over Sherman. In light of these circumstances, there is a reasonable doubt that Sherman can be expected to act independently considering his substantial financial stake in maintaining his current offices.

Ehrlich is the President of Wabash National Corp. ("Wabash"). His annual compensation is approximately $300,000 per year. Ehrlich also has two brothers who are vice presidents of Wabash. The Rales brothers are directors of Wabash and own a majority of its stock through an investment partnership they control. As a result, there is a reasonable doubt regarding Ehrlich's ability to act independently since it can be inferred that he is beholden to the Rales brothers in light of his employment.

Therefore, the amended complaint pleads particularized facts raising a reasonable doubt as to the independence of Sherman and Ehrlich. Because of their alleged substantial financial interest in maintaining their employment positions, there is a reasonable doubt that these two directors are able to consider impartially an action that is contrary to the interests of the Rales brothers.

We conclude that, under the "substantive law" of the State of Delaware, the Aronson test does not apply in the context of this double derivative suit because the Board was not involved in the challenged transaction. Nevertheless, we do not agree with the defendants' argument that a more stringent test should be applied to deter strike suits. Instead, the appropriate inquiry is whether Blasband's amended complaint raises a reasonable doubt regarding the ability of a majority of the Board to exercise properly its business judgment in a decision on a demand had one been made at the time this action was filed. Based on the existence of a reasonable doubt that the Rales brothers and Caplin would be free of a financial interest in such a decision, and that Sherman and Ehrlich could act independently in light of their employment with entities affiliated with the Rales brothers, we conclude that the allegations of Blasband's amended complaint establish that DEMAND IS EXCUSED on the Board. The certified question is therefore answered in the AFFIRMATIVE.

Role of Inspection Rights

Aronson's "particularized facts" pleading requirement presents a formidable upfront challenge for the plaintiff in a derivative action. Facts need to be identified and alleged about the corporation's board before there has been any discovery. General conclusions and speculations won't cut it. The word "particularized" has the same import as the word "facts."

In recognition of this challenge, the Delaware courts have consistently encouraged derivative-action plaintiffs to develop their futility claims by exhausting their inspection rights before the derivative action is commenced. *In Beam ex rel. Martha Stewart Living Omnimedia, Inc. v. Stewart*, 845 A.2d 1040 (Del.Supr. 2004), for example, the court affirmed the Chancery court's dismissal of plaintiff Bean's derivative case for failure to prove demand futility. The court ruled that Bean had not alleged sufficient particularized facts to raise a reasonable doubt of the independence of outside directors by virtue of Martha Stewart's dominance. The court effectively chastised the plaintiff for not exhausting her inspection rights by stating:

> Beam's failure to plead sufficient facts to support her claim of demand futility may be due in part to her failure to exhaust all reasonably available means of gathering facts. As the Chancellor noted, had Beam first brought a Section 220 action seeking inspection of MSO's books and records, she might have uncovered facts that would have created a reasonable doubt... A books and records inspection might have revealed whether Stewart unduly controlled the nominating process or whether the process incorporated procedural safeguards to ensure directors' independence. Beam might also have reviewed the minutes of the board's meetings to determine how the directors handled Stewart's proposals or conduct in various contexts. Whether or not the result of this exploration might create a reasonable doubt would be sheer speculation at this stage. But the point is that it was within the

plaintiff's power to explore these matters and she elected not to make the effort.

In general, derivative plaintiffs are not entitled to discovery in order to demonstrate demand futility. The general unavailability of discovery to assist plaintiffs with pleading demand futility does not leave plaintiffs without means of gathering information to support their allegations of demand futility, however. Both this Court and the Court of Chancery have continually advised plaintiffs who seek to plead facts establishing demand futility that the plaintiffs might successfully have used a Section 220 books and records inspection to uncover such facts.

Because Beam did not even attempt to use the fact-gathering tools available to her by seeking to review MSO's books and records in support of her demand futility claim, we cannot know if such an effort would have been fruitless, as Beam claimed on appeal. Beam's failure to seek a books and records inspection that may have uncovered the facts necessary to support a reasonable doubt of independence has resulted in substantial cost to the parties and the judiciary.

845 A.2d at 1056-1057.

4. SPECIAL COMMITTEE LEGAL CHALLENGES

AUERBACH v. BENNETT
393 N.E.2d 994 (N.Y. Ct. App. 1979)

Jones, Judge.

While the substantive aspects of a decision to terminate a shareholders' derivative action against defendant corporate directors made by a committee of disinterested directors appointed by the corporation's board of directors are beyond judicial inquiry under the business judgment doctrine, the court may inquire as to the disinterested independence of the members of that committee and as to the appropriateness and sufficiency of the investigative procedures chosen and pursued by the committee. In this instance, however, no basis is shown to warrant either inquiry by the court. Accordingly we hold that it was error to reverse the lower court's dismissal of the shareholders' derivative action.

On April 21, 1976 the board of directors of the corporation adopted a resolution creating a special litigation committee "for the purpose of establishing a point of contract between the Board of Directors and the Corporation's General Counsel concerning the position to be taken by the Corporation in certain litigation involving shareholder derivative claims on behalf of the Corporation against certain of its directors and officers" and authorizing that committee "to take such steps from time to time as it deems necessary to pursue its objectives including the retention of special outside counsel." The special committee comprised three disinterested directors who had joined the board after the challenged transactions had occurred. The board subsequently additionally vested in the committee "all of the authority of the Board of Directors to determine, on behalf of the Board, the position that the Corporation shall take with respect to the derivative claims alleged on its behalf" in the present and similar shareholder derivative actions.

The special litigation committee reported under date of November 22, 1976. The committee determined that it would not be in the best interests of the corporation for the present derivative action to proceed, and, exercising the authority delegated to it, directed the corporation's general counsel to take that position in the present litigation as well as in pending comparable shareholders' derivative actions.

As all parties and both courts below recognize, the disposition of this case on the merits turns on the proper application of the business judgment doctrine, in particular to the decision of a specially appointed committee of disinterested directors acting on behalf of the board to terminate a shareholders' derivative action. That doctrine bars judicial inquiry into actions of corporate directors taken in good faith and in the exercise of honest judgment in the lawful and legitimate furtherance of corporate purposes.

In this instance our inquiry, to the limited extent to which it may be pursued, has a two-tiered aspect. The complaint initially asserted liability on the part of defendants based on the payments made to foreign governmental customers and privately owned customers, some unspecified portions of which were allegedly passed on to officials of the customers, i. e., the focus was on first-tier bribes and kickbacks. Then subsequent to the service of the complaint there came the report of a special litigation committee, particularly appointed by the corporation's board of directors to consider the merits of the present and similar shareholders' derivative actions, and its determination that it would not be in the best interests of the corporation to press claims against defendants based on their possible first-tier liability. The motions for summary judgment were predicated principally on the report and determination of the special litigation committee and on the contention that this second-tier corporate action insulated the first-tier transactions from judicial inquiry and was itself subject to the shelter of the business judgment doctrine. The disposition at Special Term was predicated on this analysis; its decision focused on the actions of the special litigation committee, and the motions for summary judgment were granted on the ground that the business judgment doctrine precluded the courts from going back of the decision of the special litigation committee on behalf of the corporation not to pursue the claims alleged in the complaint. Similarly the reversal at the Appellate Division was based on that court's perception of the proper application of the business judgment rule to the actions and determination of the special litigation committee. We proceed on the same analysis, concluding, however, on the record before us, at variance with the Appellate Division, that the determination of the special litigation committee forecloses further judicial inquiry in this case.

It appears to us that the business judgment doctrine, at least in part, is grounded in the prudent recognition that courts are ill equipped and infrequently called on to evaluate what are and must be essentially business judgments. The authority and responsibilities vested in corporate directors both by statute and decisional law proceed on the assumption that inescapably there can be no available objective standard by which the correctness of every corporate decision may be measured, by the courts or otherwise. Even if that were not the case, by definition the responsibility for business judgments must rest with the corporate directors; their individual capabilities and experience peculiarly qualify them for the discharge of that responsibility. Thus, absent evidence of bad faith or fraud (of which there is none here) the courts must and properly should respect their determinations.

Derivative claims against corporate directors belong to the corporation itself. As with other questions of corporate policy and management, the decision whether and to what extent to explore and prosecute such claims lies within the judgment and control of the corporation's board of directors. Necessarily such decision must be predicated on the weighing and balancing of a variety of disparate considerations to reach a considered conclusion as to what course of action or inaction is best calculated to protect and advance the interests of the corporation. This is the essence of the responsibility and role of the board of directors, and courts may not intrude to interfere.

In the present case we confront a special instance of the application of the business judgment rule and inquire whether it applies in its full vigor to shield from judicial scrutiny the decision of a three-person minority committee of the board acting on behalf of the full board not to prosecute a shareholder's derivative action. The record in this case reveals that the board is a 15-member board, and that the derivative suit was brought against four of the directors. Nothing suggests that any of the other directors participated in any of the challenged first-tier transactions. Indeed the report of the audit committee on which the complaint is based specifically found that no other directors had any prior knowledge of or were in any way involved in any of these transactions. Other directors had, however, been members of the board in the period during which the transactions occurred. Each of the three director members of the special litigation committee joined the board thereafter.

The business judgment rule does not foreclose inquiry by the courts into the disinterested independence of those members of the board chosen by it to make the corporate decision on its behalf here the members of the special litigation committee. Indeed the rule shields the deliberations and conclusions of the chosen representatives of the board only if they possess a disinterested independence and do not stand in a dual relation which prevents an unprejudicial exercise of judgment.

While the court may properly inquire as to the adequacy and appropriateness of the committee's investigative procedures and methodologies, it may not under the guise of consideration of such factors trespass in the domain of business judgment. At the same time those responsible for the procedures by which the business judgment is reached may reasonably be required to show that they have pursued their chosen investigative methods in good faith. What evidentiary proof may be required to this end will, of course, depend on the nature of the particular investigation, and the proper reach of disclosure at the instance of the shareholders will in turn relate inversely to the showing made by the corporate representatives themselves. The latter may be expected to show that the areas and subjects to be examined are reasonably complete and that there has been a good-faith pursuit of inquiry into such areas and subjects. What has been uncovered and the relative weight accorded in evaluating and balancing the several factors and considerations are beyond the scope of judicial concern. Proof, however, that the investigation has been so restricted in scope, so shallow in execution, or otherwise so pro forma or halfhearted as to constitute a pretext or sham, consistent with the principles underlying the application of the business judgment doctrine, would raise questions of good faith or conceivably fraud which would never be shielded by that doctrine.

ZAPATA CORP. v. MALDONADO
430 A.2d 779 (Del. 1981)

Quillen, Justice:

In June, 1975, William Maldonado, a stockholder of Zapata, instituted a derivative action in the Court of Chancery on behalf of Zapata against ten officers and/or directors of Zapata, alleging, essentially, breaches of fiduciary duty. Maldonado did not first demand that the board bring this action, stating instead such demand's futility because all directors were named as defendants and allegedly participated in the acts specified. In June, 1977, Maldonado commenced an action in the United States District Court for the Southern District of New York against the same defendants, save one, alleging federal security law violations as well as the same common law claims made previously in the Court of Chancery.

By June, 1979, four of the defendant-directors were no longer on the board, and the remaining directors appointed two new outside directors to the board. The board then created an "Independent Investigation Committee" (Committee), composed solely of the two new directors, to investigate Maldonado's actions, as well as a similar derivative action then pending in Texas, and to determine whether the corporation should continue any or all of the litigation. The Committee's determination was stated to be "final, ... not ... subject to review by the Board of Directors and ... in all respects ... binding upon the Corporation."

Following an investigation, the Committee concluded, in September, 1979, that each action should "be dismissed forthwith as their continued maintenance is inimical to the Company's best interests ...." Consequently, Zapata moved for dismissal or summary judgment in the three derivative actions.

On March 18, 1980, the Court of Chancery denied Zapata's motions, holding that Delaware law does not sanction this means of dismissal. More specifically, it held that the "business judgment" rule is not a grant of authority to dismiss derivative actions and that a stockholder has an individual right to maintain derivative actions in certain instances.

We begin with an examination of the carefully considered opinion of the Vice Chancellor which states, in part, that the "business judgment" rule does not confer power "to a corporate board of directors to terminate a derivative suit".

The "business judgment" rule is a judicial creation that presumes propriety, under certain circumstances, in a board's decision. Viewed defensively, it does not create authority. In this sense the "business judgment" rule is not relevant in corporate decision making until after a decision is made. It is generally used as a defense to an attack on the decision's soundness.

In the case before us, although the corporation's decision to move to dismiss or for summary judgment was, literally, a decision resulting from an exercise of the directors' (as delegated to the Committee) business judgment, the question of "business judgment", in a defensive sense, would not become relevant until and unless the decision to seek termination of the derivative lawsuit was attacked as improper. This question was not reached by the Vice Chancellor because he determined that the stockholder had an individual right to maintain this derivative action.

Thus, the focus in this case is on the power to speak for the corporation as to whether the lawsuit should be continued or terminated. As we see it, this issue in the current appellate posture of this case has three aspects: the conclusions of the Court below concerning the continuing right of a stockholder to maintain a derivative action; the corporate power under Delaware law of an authorized board committee to cause dismissal of litigation instituted for the benefit of the corporation; and the role of the Court of Chancery in resolving conflicts between the stockholder and the committee.

Accordingly, we turn first to the Court of Chancery's conclusions concerning the right of a plaintiff stockholder in a derivative action. We find that its determination that a stockholder, once demand is made and refused, possesses an independent, individual right to continue a derivative suit for breaches of fiduciary duty over objection by the corporation, as an absolute rule, is erroneous.

The language in Sohland relied on by the Vice Chancellor negates the contention that the case stands for the broad rule of stockholder right which evolved below. This Court therein stated that "a stockholder may sue in his own name for the purpose of enforcing corporate rights ... in a proper case if the corporation on the demand of the stockholder refuses to bring suit." The Court also stated that "whether ("(t)he right of a stockholder to file a bill to litigate corporate rights") exists necessarily depends on the facts of each particular case." Thus, the precise language only supports the stockholder's right to initiate the lawsuit. It does not support an absolute right to continue to control it.

Moreover, McKee v. Rogers, Del.Ch., 156 A. 191 (1931), stated "as a general rule" that "a stockholder cannot be permitted ... to invade the discretionary field committed to the judgment of the directors and sue in the corporation's behalf when the managing body refuses. This rule is a well settled one."

The McKee rule, of course, should not be read so broadly that the board's refusal will be determinative in every instance. Board members, owing a well-established fiduciary duty to the corporation, will not be allowed to cause a derivative suit to be dismissed when it would be a breach of their fiduciary duty.

Consistent with the purpose of requiring a demand, a board decision to cause a derivative suit to be dismissed as detrimental to the company, after demand has been made and refused, will be respected unless it was wrongful. A claim of a wrongful decision not to sue is thus the first exception and the first context of dispute. Absent a wrongful refusal, the stockholder in such a situation simply lacks legal managerial power.

In other words, when stockholders, after making demand and having their suit rejected, attack the board's decision as improper, the board's decision falls under the "business judgment" rule and will be respected if the requirements of the rule are met. That situation should be distinguished from the instant case, where demand was not made, and the power of the board to seek a dismissal, due to disqualification, presents a threshold issue. We recognize that the two contexts can overlap in practice. But it cannot be implied that, absent a wrongful board refusal, a stockholder can never have an individual right to initiate an action. For, as is stated in McKee, a "well settled" exception exists to the general rule.

> "(A) stockholder may sue in equity in his derivative right to assert a cause of action in behalf of the corporation, without prior demand upon the directors to sue, when it is apparent that a demand would be futile, that the officers are under an influence that sterilizes discretion and could not be proper persons to conduct the litigation."

This exception, the second context for dispute, is consistent with the Court of Chancery's statement below, that "(t)he stockholders' individual right to bring the action does not ripen, however, ... unless he can show a demand to be futile."

These comments in McKee and in the opinion below make obvious sense. A demand, when required and refused (if not wrongful), terminates a stockholder's legal ability to initiate a derivative action. But where demand is properly excused, the stockholder does possess the ability to initiate the action on his corporation's behalf.

These conclusions, however, do not determine the question before us. Rather, they merely bring us to the question to be decided. It is here that we part company with the Court below. Derivative suits enforce corporate rights and any recovery obtained goes to the corporation. "The right of a stockholder to file a bill to litigate corporate rights is, therefore, solely for the purpose of preventing injustice where it is apparent that material corporate rights would not otherwise be protected." We see no inherent reason why the "two phases" of a derivative suit, the stockholder's suit to compel the corporation to sue and the corporation's suit should automatically result in the placement in the hands of the litigating stockholder sole control of the corporate right throughout the litigation. To the contrary, it seems to us that such an inflexible rule would recognize the interest of one person or group to the exclusion of all others within the corporate entity. Thus, we reject the view of the Vice Chancellor as to the first aspect of the issue on appeal.

The question to be decided becomes: When, if at all, should an authorized board committee be permitted to cause litigation, properly initiated by a derivative stockholder in his own right, to be dismissed? As noted above, a board has the power to choose not to pursue litigation when demand is made upon it, so long as the decision is not wrongful. If the board determines that a suit would be detrimental to the company, the board's determination prevails. Even when demand is excusable, circumstances may arise when continuation of the litigation would not be in the corporation's best interests. Our inquiry is whether, under such circumstances, there is a permissible procedure under s 141(a) by which a corporation can rid itself of detrimental litigation. If there is not, a single stockholder in an extreme case might control the destiny of the entire corporation.

Before we pass to equitable considerations as to the mechanism at issue here, it must be clear that an independent committee possesses the corporate power to seek the termination of a derivative suit. Section 141(c) allows a board to delegate all of its authority to a committee. Accordingly, a committee with properly delegated authority would have the power to move for dismissal or summary judgment if the entire board did.

Even though demand was not made in this case and the initial decision of whether to litigate was not placed before the board, Zapata's board, it seems to us, retained all of its corporate power concerning litigation decisions. If Maldonado had made demand on the board in this case, it could have refused to bring suit. Maldonado could then have asserted that the decision not to sue was wrongful and, if correct, would have been allowed to maintain the suit. The board, however, never would have lost its statutory managerial authority. The demand requirement itself evidences that the managerial power is retained by the board. When a derivative plaintiff is allowed to bring suit after a wrongful refusal, the board's authority to choose whether to pursue the litigation is not challenged although its conclusion reached through the exercise of that authority is not respected since it is wrongful. Similarly, Rule 23.1, by excusing demand in certain instances, does not strip the board of its corporate power. It merely saves the plaintiff the expense and delay of making a futile demand resulting in a probable tainted exercise of that authority in a refusal by the board or in giving control of litigation to the opposing side. But the board entity remains empowered under s 141(a) to make decisions regarding corporate litigation. The problem is one of member disqualification, not the absence of power in the board.

The corporate power inquiry then focuses on whether the board, tainted by the self-interest of a majority of its members, can legally delegate its authority to a committee of two disinterested directors. We find our statute clearly requires an affirmative answer to this question.

We do not think that the interest taint of the board majority is per se a legal bar to the delegation of the board's power to an independent committee composed of disinterested board members. The committee can properly act for the corporation to move to dismiss derivative litigation that is believed to be detrimental to the corporation's best interest.

Our focus now switches to the Court of Chancery which is faced with a stockholder assertion that a derivative suit, properly instituted, should continue for the benefit of the corporation. At the risk of stating the obvious, the problem is relatively simple. If, on the one hand, corporations can consistently wrest bona fide derivative actions away from well-meaning derivative plaintiffs through the use of the committee mechanism, the derivative suit will lose much, if not all, of its generally-recognized effectiveness as an intra-corporate means of policing boards of directors. If, on the other hand, corporations are unable to rid themselves of meritless or harmful litigation and strike suits, the derivative action, created to benefit the corporation, will produce the opposite, unintended result. It thus appears desirable to us to find a balancing point where bona fide stockholder power to bring corporate causes of action cannot be unfairly trampled on by the board of directors, but the corporation can rid itself of detrimental litigation.

As we noted, the question has been treated by other courts as one of the "business judgment" of the board committee. We are not satisfied, however, that acceptance of the "business judgment" rationale at this stage of derivative litigation is a proper balancing point. While we admit an analogy with a normal case respecting board judgment, it seems to us that there is sufficient risk in the realities of a situation like the one presented in this case to justify caution beyond adherence to the theory of business judgment.

The context here is a suit against directors where demand on the board is excused. We think some tribute must be paid to the fact that the lawsuit was properly initiated. It is not a board refusal case. Moreover, this complaint was filed in June of 1975 and, while the parties undoubtedly would take differing views on the degree of litigation activity, we have to be concerned about the creation of an "Independent Investigation Committee" four years later, after the election of two new outside directors. Situations could develop where such motions could be filed after years of vigorous litigation for reasons unconnected with the merits of the lawsuit.

Moreover, notwithstanding our conviction that Delaware law entrusts the corporate power to a properly authorized committee, we must be mindful that directors are passing judgment on fellow directors in the same corporation and fellow directors, in this instance, who designated them to serve both as directors and committee members. The question naturally arises whether a "there but for the grace of God go I" empathy might not play a role. And the further question arises whether inquiry as to independence, good faith and reasonable investigation is sufficient safeguard against abuse, perhaps subconscious abuse.

Whether the Court of Chancery will be persuaded by the exercise of a committee power resulting in a summary motion for dismissal of a derivative action, where a demand has not been initially made, should rest, in our judgment, in the independent discretion of the Court of Chancery. We thus steer a middle course between those cases which yield to the independent business judgment of a board committee and this case as determined below which would yield to unbridled plaintiff stockholder control. In pursuit of the course, we recognize that "(t)he final substantive judgment whether a particular lawsuit should be maintained requires a balance of many factors ethical, commercial, promotional, public relations, employee relations, fiscal as well as legal." But we are content that such factors are not "beyond the judicial reach" of the Court of Chancery which regularly and competently deals with fiduciary relationships, disposition of trust property, approval of settlements and scores of similar problems. We recognize the danger of judicial overreaching but the alternatives seem to us to be outweighed by the fresh view of a judicial outsider. Moreover, if we failed to balance all the interests involved, we would in the name of practicality and judicial economy foreclose a judicial decision on the merits. At this point, we are not convinced that is necessary or desirable.

After an objective and thorough investigation of a derivative suit, an independent committee may cause its corporation to file a pretrial motion to dismiss in the Court of Chancery. The basis of the motion is the best interests of the corporation, as determined by the committee. The motion should include a thorough written record of the investigation and its findings and recommendations. Under appropriate Court supervision, akin to proceedings on summary judgment, each side should have an opportunity to make a record on the motion. As to the limited issues presented by the motion noted below, the moving party should be prepared to meet the normal burden under Rule 56 that there is no genuine issue as to any material fact and that the moving party is entitled to dismiss as a matter of law. The Court should apply a two-step test to the motion.

First, the Court should inquire into the independence and good faith of the committee and the bases supporting its conclusions. Limited discovery may be ordered to facilitate such inquiries. The corporation should have the burden of proving independence, good faith and a reasonable investigation, rather than presuming independence, good faith and reasonableness. If the Court determines either that the committee is not independent or has not shown reasonable bases for its conclusions, or, if the Court is not satisfied for other reasons relating to the process, including but not limited to the good faith of the committee, the Court shall deny the corporation's motion. If, however, the Court is satisfied under Rule 56 standards that the committee was independent and showed reasonable bases for good faith findings and recommendations, the Court may proceed, in its discretion, to the next step.

The second step provides, we believe, the essential key in striking the balance between legitimate corporate claims as expressed in a derivative stockholder suit and a corporation's best interests as expressed by an independent investigating committee. The Court should determine, applying its own independent business judgment, whether the motion should be granted. This means, of course, that instances could arise where a committee can establish its independence and sound bases for its good faith decisions and still have the corporation's motion denied. The second step is intended to thwart instances where corporate actions meet the criteria of step one, but the result does not appear to satisfy its spirit, or where corporate actions would simply prematurely terminate a stockholder grievance deserving of further consideration in the corporation's interest. The Court of Chancery of course must carefully consider and weigh how compelling the corporate interest in dismissal is when faced with a non-frivolous lawsuit. The Court of Chancery should, when appropriate, give special consideration to matters of law and public policy in addition to the corporation's best interests.

If the Court's independent business judgment is satisfied, the Court may proceed to grant the motion, subject, of course, to any equitable terms or conditions the Court finds necessary or desirable.

The interlocutory order of the Court of Chancery is reversed and the cause is remanded for further proceedings consistent with this opinion.

Standard of Review in Non-Demand SLC Actions

The *Auerbach* and *Zapata* cases illustrate different approaches (the extremes) that courts use in evaluating an SLC non-demand motion to end a derivative lawsuit. *Auerback* applies the same business judgment rule analysis that would be used in the demand-excusal context. *Zapata* imposes a far tougher dual procedural and substantive standard. Others have favored a middle ground approach, evaluating relevant facts to determine if an SLC member had a "relationship with the individual defendants or the corporation that would reasonably be expected to affect the member's judgment with respect to the litigation in issue." *Einhorn v. Culea*, 612 N.W.2d 78, 89 (Wisc. 2000).

Some have criticized the *Zapata* standard as adding an unnecessary complexity, fraught with uncertainty, that over complicates the litigation process (adds a suit within a suit) and stalls discovery on the merits while discovery proceeds on the independence of the special litigation committee that seeks to end it all. In the 2004 demand futility case of *In Beam ex rel. Martha Stewart Living Omnimedia, Inc. v. Stewart*, 845 A.2d 1040 (Del.Supr. 2004), the Delaware Supreme Court took the opportunity to explain the *Zapata* standard that had been established 23 years earlier. The court stated:

> An SLC is a unique creature that was introduced into Delaware law by *Zapata v. Maldonado* in 1981. The SLC procedure is a method sometimes employed where presuit demand has already been excused and the SLC is vested with the full power of the board to conduct an extensive investigation into the merits of the corporate claim with a view toward determining whether—in the SLC's business judgment— the corporate claim should be pursued. Unlike the demand-excusal context, where the board is presumed to be independent, the SLC has the burden of establishing its own independence by a yardstick that must be "like Caesar's wife"—"above reproach." Moreover, unlike the presuit demand context, the SLC analysis contemplates not only a shift in the burden of persuasion but also the availability of discovery into various issues, including independence.

> We need not decide whether the substantive standard of independence in an SLC case differs from that in a presuit demand case. As a practical matter, the procedural distinction relating to the diametrically-opposed burdens and the availability of discovery into independence may be outcome-determinative on the issue of independence. Moreover, because the members of an SLC are vested with enormous power to seek dismissal of a derivative suit brought against their director-colleagues in a setting where presuit demand is

already excused, the Court of Chancery must exercise careful oversight of the bona fides of the SLC and its process.

Under *Zapata*, the burden of having to prove independence can be difficult for any SLC. In the following case, the SLC seemed to have it all – stellar tenured professors from Stafford, its own active outside legal counsel, and a 1,100 page report supporting its conclusions. Note how the court cut through it all with some common sense notions of human nature.

IN RE ORACLE CORP. DERIVATIVE LITIGATION
824 A.2d 917 (Del.Ch. 2003)

STRINE, Vice Chancellor.

In this opinion, I address the motion of the special litigation committee ("SLC") of Oracle Corporation to terminate this action, "the Delaware Derivative Action," and other such actions pending in the name of Oracle against certain Oracle directors and officers. These actions allege that these Oracle directors engaged in insider trading while in possession of material, non-public information showing that Oracle would not meet the earnings guidance it gave to the market for the third quarter of Oracle's fiscal year 2001. The SLC bears the burden of persuasion on this motion and must convince me that there is no material issue of fact calling into doubt its independence. This requirement is set forth in Zapata Corp. v. Maldonado and its progeny.

The question of independence "turns on whether a director is, for any substantial reason, incapable of making a decision with only the best interests of the corporation in mind." *Parfi Holding AB v. Mirror Image Internet, Inc.,* 794 A.2d 1211, 1232 (Del.Ch.2001). That is, the independence test ultimately "focus[es] on impartiality and objectivity." Id. In this case, the SLC has failed to demonstrate that no material factual question exists regarding its independence.

During discovery, it emerged that the two SLC members - both of whom are professors at Stanford University - are being asked to investigate fellow Oracle directors who have important ties to Stanford, too. Among the directors who are accused by the derivative plaintiffs of insider trading are: (1) another Stanford professor, who taught one of the SLC members when the SLC member was a Ph.D. candidate and who serves as a senior fellow and a steering committee member alongside that SLC member at the Stanford Institute for Economic Policy Research or "SIEPR"; (2) a Stanford alumnus who has directed millions of dollars of contributions to Stanford during recent years, serves as Chair of SIEPR's Advisory Board and has a conference center named for him at SIEPR's facility, and has contributed nearly $600,000 to SIEPR and the Stanford Law School, both parts of Stanford with which one of the SLC members is closely affiliated; and (3) Oracle's CEO, who has made millions of dollars in donations to Stanford through a personal foundation and large donations indirectly through Oracle, and who was considering making donations of his $100 million house and $170 million for a scholarship program as late as August 2001, at around the same time period the SLC members were added to the Oracle board. Taken together, these and other facts cause me to harbor a reasonable doubt about the impartiality of the SLC.

It is no easy task to decide whether to accuse a fellow director of insider trading. For Oracle to compound that difficulty by requiring SLC members to consider accusing a fellow professor and two large benefactors of their university of conduct that is rightly considered a violation of criminal law was unnecessary and inconsistent with the concept of independence recognized by our law. The possibility that these extraneous considerations biased the inquiry of the SLC is too substantial for this court to ignore. I therefore deny the SLC's motion to terminate.

The Delaware Derivative Complaint centers on alleged insider trading by four members of Oracle's board of directors-Lawrence Ellison, Jeffrey Henley, Donald Lucas, and Michael Boskin (collectively, the "Trading Defendants"). Each of the Trading Defendants had a very different role at Oracle. According to the plaintiffs, each of these Trading Defendants possessed material, non-public information demonstrating that Oracle would fail to meet the earnings and revenue guidance it had provided to the market in December 2000.

The plaintiffs make two central claims in their amended complaint in the Delaware Derivative Action. First, the plaintiffs allege that the Trading Defendants breached their duty of loyalty by misappropriating inside information and using it as the basis for trading decisions...

Second, as to the other defendants - who are the members of the Oracle board who did not trade - the plaintiffs allege a Caremark violation, in the sense that the board's indifference to the deviation between the company's December guidance and reality was so extreme as to constitute subjective bad faith.

On February 1, 2002, Oracle formed the SLC in order to investigate the Delaware Derivative Action and to determine whether Oracle should press the claims raised by the plaintiffs, settle the case, or terminate it. Soon after its formation, the SLC's charge was broadened to give it the same mandate as to all the pending derivative actions, wherever they were filed. The SLC was granted full authority to decide these matters without the need for approval by the other members of the Oracle board.

Two Oracle board members were named to the SLC. The SLC members also share something else: both are tenured professors at Stanford University. Professor Hector Garcia-Molina is Chairman of the Computer Science Department at Stanford and holds the Leonard Bosack and Sandra Lerner Professorship in the Computer Science and Electrical Engineering Departments at Stanford. The other SLC member, Professor Joseph Grundfest, is the W.A. Franke Professor of Law and Business at Stanford University.

For their services, the SLC members were paid $250 an hour, a rate below that which they could command for other activities, such as consulting or expert witness testimony. Nonetheless, Garcia-Molina and Grundfest agreed to give up any SLC-related compensation if their compensation was deemed by this court to impair their impartiality.

The most important advisors retained by the SLC were its counsel from Simpson Thacher & Bartlett LLP. Simpson Thacher had not performed material amounts of legal work for Oracle or any of the individual defendants before its engagement, and the plaintiffs have not challenged its independence.

The SLC's investigation was, by any objective measure, extensive. The SLC reviewed an enormous amount of paper and electronic records. SLC counsel interviewed seventy witnesses, some of them twice. SLC members participated in several key interviews, including the interviews of the Trading Defendants...Importantly, the interviewees included all the senior members of Oracle's management most involved in its projection and monitoring of the company's financial performance, including its sales and revenue growth. These interviews combined with a special focus on the documents at the company bearing on these subjects, including e-mail communications....

During the course of the investigation, the SLC met with its counsel thirty-five times for a total of eighty hours. In addition to that, the SLC members, particularly Professor Grundfest, devoted many more hours to the investigation.

In the end, the SLC produced an extremely lengthy Report totaling 1,110 pages (excluding appendices and exhibits) that concluded that Oracle should not pursue the plaintiffs' claims against the Trading Defendants or any of the other Oracle directors serving during the 3Q FY 2001.

Consistent with its Report, the SLC moved to terminate this litigation.

In order to prevail on its motion to terminate the Delaware Derivative Action, the SLC must persuade me that: (1) its members were independent; (2) that they acted in good faith; and (3) that they had reasonable bases for their recommendations. If the SLC meets that burden, I am free to grant its motion or may, in my discretion, undertake my own examination of whether Oracle should terminate and permit the suit to proceed if I, in my oxymoronic judicial "business judgment," conclude that procession is in the best interests of the company. This two-step analysis comes, of course, from Zapata.

In that case, the Delaware Supreme Court also instructed this court to apply a procedural standard akin to a summary judgment inquiry when ruling on a special litigation committee's motion to terminate. In other words, the Oracle SLC here "should be prepared to meet the normal burden under Rule 56 that there is no genuine issue as to any material fact and that [it] is entitled to dismiss as a matter of law." Candidly, this articulation of a special litigation committee's burden is an odd one, insofar as it applies a procedural standard designed for a particular purpose - the substantive dismissal of a case - with a standard centered on the determination of when a corporate committee's business decision about claims belonging to the corporation should be accepted by the court.

As I understand it, this standard requires me to determine whether, on the basis of the undisputed factual record, I am convinced that the SLC was independent, acted in good faith, and had a reasonable basis for its recommendation. If there is a material factual question about these issues causing doubt about any of these grounds, I read Zapata and its progeny as requiring a denial of the SLC's motion to terminate.

Initially, I am satisfied that neither of the SLC members is compromised by a fear that support for the procession of this suit would endanger his ability to make a nice living. Both of the SLC members are distinguished in their fields and highly respected. Both have tenure, which could not have been stripped from them for making a determination that this lawsuit should proceed.

This is an important point of departure for discussing the multitude of ties that have emerged among the Trading Defendants, Oracle, and Stanford during discovery in this case. In evaluating these ties, the court is not faced with the relatively easier call of considering whether these ties would call into question the impartiality of an SLC member who was a key fundraiser at Stanford or who was an untenured faculty member subject to removal without cause. Instead, one must acknowledge that the question is whether the ties I am about to identify would be of a material concern to two distinguished, tenured faculty members whose current jobs would not be threatened by whatever good faith decision they made as SLC members.

The SLC contends that the ties among Oracle, the Trading Defendants, Stanford, and the SLC members do not impair the SLC's independence...From these more extreme arguments, however, one can distill a reasoned core that emphasizes what academics might call the "thickness" of the social and institutional connections among Oracle, the Trading Defendants, Stanford, and the SLC members.

These connections, the plaintiffs argue, were very hard to miss - being obvious to anyone who entered the SIEPR facility, to anyone who read the Wall Street Journal, Fortune, or the Washington Post, and especially to Stanford faculty members interested in their own university community and with a special interest in Oracle. Taken in their totality, the plaintiffs contend, these connections simply constitute too great a bias-producing factor for the SLC to meet its burden to prove its independence...

I begin with an important reminder: the SLC bears the burden of proving its independence. It must convince me. But of what? According to the SLC, its members are independent unless they are essentially subservient to the Trading Defendants - i.e., they are under the "domination and control" of the interested parties. If the SLC is correct and this is the central inquiry in the independence determination, they would win. Nothing in the record suggests to me that either Garcia-Molina or Grundfest are dominated and controlled by any of the Trading Defendants, by Oracle, or even by Stanford.

But, in my view, an emphasis on "domination and control" would serve only to fetishize much-parroted language, at the cost of denuding the independence inquiry of its intellectual integrity. Take an easy example. Imagine if two brothers were on a corporate board, each successful in different businesses and not dependent in any way on the other's beneficence in order to be wealthy. The brothers are brothers, they stay in touch and consider each other family, but each is opinionated and strong-willed. A derivative action is filed targeting a transaction involving one of the brothers. The other brother is put on a special litigation committee to investigate the case. If the test is domination and control, then one brother could investigate the other. Does any sensible person think that is our law? I do not think it is.

And it should not be our law. Delaware law should not be based on a reductionist view of human nature that simplifies human motivations on the lines of the least sophisticated notions of the law and economics movement. Homo sapiens is not merely homo economicus. We may be thankful that an array of other motivations exist that influence human behavior; not all are any better than greed or avarice, think of envy, to name just one. But also think of motives like love, friendship, and collegiality, think of those among us who direct their behavior as best they can on a guiding creed or set of moral values.

Nor should our law ignore the social nature of humans. To be direct, corporate directors are generally the sort of people deeply enmeshed in social institutions. Such institutions have norms, expectations that, explicitly and implicitly, influence and channel the behavior of those who participate in their operation. Some things are "just not done," or only at a cost, which might not be so severe as a loss of position, but may involve a loss of standing in the institution. In being appropriately sensitive to this factor, our law also cannot assume - absent some proof of the point - that corporate directors are, as a general matter, persons of unusual social bravery, who operate heedless to the inhibitions that social norms generate for ordinary folk.

At bottom, the question of independence turns on whether a director is, for any substantial reason, incapable of making a decision with only the best interests of the corporation in mind. That is, the Supreme Court cases ultimately focus on impartiality and objectivity.

Without backtracking from these general propositions, it would be less than candid if I did not admit that Delaware courts have applied these general standards in a manner that has been less than wholly consistent. Different decisions take a different view about the bias-producing potential of family relationships, not all of which can be explained by mere degrees of consanguinity. Likewise, there is admittedly case law that gives little weight to ties of friendship in the independence inquiry.

In this opinion, I will not venture to do what I believe to be impossible: attempt to rationalize all these cases in their specifics. Rather, I undertake what I understand to be my duty and what is possible: the application of the independence inquiry that our Supreme Court has articulated in a manner that is faithful to its essential spirit.

Special litigation committees are permitted as a last chance for a corporation to control a derivative claim in circumstances when a majority of its directors cannot impartially consider a demand. By vesting the power of the board to determine what to do with the suit in a committee of independent directors, a corporation may retain control over whether the suit will proceed, so long as the committee meets the standard set forth in Zapata.

I conclude that the SLC has not met its burden to show the absence of a material factual question about its independence. I find this to be the case because the ties among the SLC, the Trading Defendants, and Stanford are so substantial that they cause reasonable doubt about the SLC's ability to impartially consider whether the Trading Defendants should face suit.

In so concluding, I necessarily draw on a general sense of human nature. It may be that Grundfest is a very special person who is capable of putting these kinds of things totally aside. But the SLC has not provided evidence that that is the case. In this respect, it is critical to note that I do not infer that Grundfest would be less likely to recommend suit against Boskin than someone without these ties. Human nature being what it is, it is entirely possible that Grundfest would in fact be tougher on Boskin than he would on someone with whom he did not have such connections.

The inference I draw is subtly, but importantly, different. What I infer is that a person in Grundfest's position would find it difficult to assess Boskin's conduct without pondering his own association with Boskin and their mutual affiliations. Although these connections might produce bias in either a tougher or laxer direction, the key inference is that these connections would be on the mind of a person in Grundfest's position, putting him in the position of either causing serious legal action to be brought against a person with whom he shares several connections (an awkward thing) or not doing so (and risking being seen as having engaged in favoritism toward his old professor and SIEPR colleague).

The same concerns also exist as to Lucas. For Grundfest to vote to accuse Lucas of insider trading would require him to accuse SIEPR's Advisory Board Chair and major benefactor of serious wrongdoing - of conduct that violates federal securities laws. Such action would also require Grundfest to make charges against a man who recently donated $50,000 to Stanford Law School after Grundfest made a speech at his request.

The SLC's motion to terminate is DENIED. IT IS SO ORDERED.

D. SAY-ON-PAY RIGHTS

1. HISTORY AND PURPOSE

In the world of shareholder core rights, "say-on-pay" is the hot new kid on the block. Since January 21, 2011, section 951 of the Dodd-Frank Wall Street Reform and Consumer Protection Act ("Dodd-Frank") has required a public corporation to submit its executive compensation arrangements to a "yes" or "no" non-binding advisory vote of its shareholders. It's an up or down vote that gives the shareholders an opportunity to officially go on record as to whether they like or dislike the pay packages for the top dogs in the company. The significance of the right is heightened by the ever-growing presence of institutional investors who have the will and capacity to evaluate compensation packages, influence the results of the shareholder vote, and leverage the impact of a negative anti-management vote.

The say-on-pay concept was imported from the United Kingdom. Its roots can be traced to a 1999 announcement by U.K. officials, stating that they were considering a policy for shareholders to review executive "remuneration" reports. In 2002, the U.K. adopted its "Directors' Remuneration Report" regulations that mandated a shareholder vote on the company's remuneration report at each annual meeting. In 2005, the idea first gained attention in the U.S. when Escala

Group, Inc.'s proxy statement put the compensation packages of its top two officers to a shareholder vote. In 2007, the shareholders of roughly 50 companies considered proposals that would require a regular say-on-pay vote. The number jumped to 90 in 2008. Although these proposals received average shareholder support of only about 40 percent, they signaled a trend. In 2009, the SEC joined the movement, exercising rights under the American Recovery and Reinvestment Act to require a say-on-pay vote in companies (about 400) that received financial support from the federal government.

Early signs suggested say-on-pay might yield little or nothing, even for companies that made big headlines by promoting controversial executive pay packages amidst claims of abuse. The Merrill Lynch bonus headline mess did not prevent Bank of America from garnering a favorable say-on pay vote that exceeded 70 percent. Goldman Sachs' favorable number hit 98 percent, and Verizon's approval number was over 90 percent. Even Citigroup did well with a favorable vote of over 85 percent.

Meanwhile, pressure was building in Congress for a broader say-on-pay mandate, with specific bills being introduced by Representative Barney Frank and Senator Charles Schumer and heat coming from the Treasury Department, the SEC, and the White House. So when Congress developed Dodd-Frank to address the abuses that contributed to the financial crisis of 2008, the inclusion of say-on-pay was pretty much a legislative no-brainer.

Although the law calls for only a nonbinding vote, it's hard to overstate the significance of say-on-pay. It has quickly become the spotlight proxy issue, and all signs suggest that its impact will continue to grow. Although the tax code has always required shareholders to approve qualified stock option plans and the securities laws have mandated disclosures related to executive compensation, historically shareholders haven't had an official voice in the overall compensation packages for the corporation's top executives. That challenge has been delegated to a compensation committee of the board, comprised solely of outside directors, that receives professional expert advice from an outside consulting firm. The theory, of course, is that the committee and the consulting firm, both cloaked in objectivity, will act in the best interests of the corporation. But, in practice, everyone knows that the members of the compensation committee often are handpicked by the executives whose compensation is at issue and the consulting firm's ongoing involvement is predicated on delivering results that please those same executives. And then there is the sheer size of the numbers that often grab the headlines and put many CEO's in a league that movie stars and star athletes can only dream of. A recent study by Ernst & Young confirmed that escalating executive compensation levels is the highest cost burden of becoming a public company.[73]

Say-on-pay provides a new challenge for all those involved in the executive compensation process. A company's executives, directors, compensation committee, and outside advisors cannot ignore the consequences of the

---

73. Ernst & Young IPO Cost Survey, November 2011. Ernst & Young is a global leader in assurance, tax, transaction and advisory services that employs 141,000 people worldwide.

shareholder vote. A failing shareholder vote may insure conflict and trigger a need for changes. Often a passing grade won't be good enough. Norms are already developing that suggest that anything short of a 70 percent approval vote shows weakness and signals growing shareholder discontent in the future. The real goal is a solid approval vote north of 90 percent.

There are at least three dimensions to the say-on-pay challenge: (1) an analytical effort to insure that the corporation's compensation arrangements stack up against the key peer measures and make sense if light of the company's performance; (2) a political and sales effort to develop shareholder support for management's recommendations; and (3) smart response strategies to a bad shareholder vote that promise improved future vote outcomes and mitigate exposures for any enhanced legal risks. Obviously, everything is easier if the company is performing strong and hitting its benchmarks for the shareholders. But when the company's performance is stalled in a chronically sluggish economy, say-on-pay will often be the overriding consideration in any effort to inflate executive pay packages.

CASE PROBLEM 9-5

Falcon Industries, Inc. ("Falcon") is a Delaware corporation whose stock is traded on the American Stock Exchange. Falcon's primary business is providing customized inventory management and distribution systems to multi-national companies in various industries.

Last year, Falcon hired a new CEO, Jake Moss, to "bring a renewed energy and focus to Falcon." Falcon's board had determined that Jake's hiring was an "essential step to break a string of disappointing years for Falcon shareholders." To land Jake, who has a stellar reputation for being one of the absolute best CEO's in the industry, Falcon had to provide Jake a five-year contract that guaranteed an annual salary and cash bonuses of not less than $2.5 million and cash and stock performance incentives that potentially could pay up to an additional $5 million a year. Falcon's board understood at the time that this was the most generous arrangement provided to any CEO in the industry.

Jake has been the leader of Falcon for a year. He's discouraged. A successful turnaround of Falcon is going to take longer and be much tougher than he originally anticipated. Among other things, he's determined that Falcon has a "weak executive team that resists needed cultural changes." Jake sees little hope of earning his incentive compensation, and another opportunity has surfaced, offering Jake a more lucrative contract with a much more realistic upside potential.

Falcon's board is pleased with Jake and badly wants to keep him at the helm. They are convinced that Jake is the key to Falcon's future. In discussions with Jake, they've concluded that they can "hold onto Jake" if (1) Falcon convert's $1.5 million of Jake's annual incentive compensation payment to a guaranteed payment each year, and (2) Jake is authorized to hire new chief financial and operating officers with individual annual pay packages (inclusive of incentives) of up to $1.7 million. This represents a 35 percent increase over what is now being paid to the existing officers.

Falcon's board is concerned about its say-on-pay requirements if it honors these demands from Jake. It has five preliminary questions:

1. Must it condition Jake's demands on a favorable say-on-pay vote? Should it?

2. How can it minimize the number of say-on-pay votes until Jake has had an opportunity to get Falcon turned around?

3. What steps should it take to help insure a positive say-on-pay vote if it honors Jake's demands?

4. If Falcon honors Jake's demands and then experiences a negative say-on-pay vote, will it have to take steps to reduce Jake's compensation package and the packages offered Jake's two new executive colleagues?

5. If Falcon honors Jake's demands and then experiences a negative say-on-pay vote, will the personal legal exposure of Falcon's board members be increased if they take no actions in response to the negative vote and continue with the current plan in hopes that Jake can reverse Falcon's course?

2. THE LEGAL REQUIREMENTS

Section 951 of Dodd-Frank mandated say-on-pay for all public companies by adding new Section 14A(a) to the Securities Exchange Act of 1934. The SEC is authorized under Section 14A(e) to exempt certain classes of issuers. There are three basic requirements of the new section 14A(a).

1. Section 14A(a)(1) requires that all public companies, at least once every three years, provide shareholders with an opportunity to vote on a non-binding basis on the compensation of named executive officers. This same requirement is set forth in newly-adopted Rule 14a-21(a). Although the rule does not specify the form of the "say-on-pay" resolution to be voted on by shareholders, the SEC has provided the following "non-exclusive example" of a resolution that would satisfy the requirements of the rule:

> "RESOLVED, that the compensation paid to the company's named executive officers, as disclosed pursuant to Item 402 of Regulation S-K, including the Compensation Discussion and Analysis, compensation tables and narrative discussion, is hereby APPROVED."

The SEC has indicated that companies may use a resolution that substitutes plain English for the phrase "pursuant to Item 402 of Regulation S-K." The SEC provided the following as an acceptable example: "pursuant to the compensation disclosure rules of the Securities and Exchange Commission, including the compensation discussion and analysis, the compensation tables and any related material enclosed in this proxy statement."

2. Section 14A(a)(2) requires a "say-on-frequency" vote at least once every six years. This vote gives shareholders the opportunity to decide if the safe-on-pay vote is going to be required every year, every second year, or every third year. The first say-on-pay and say-on-frequency votes were required at the first

annual or other shareholder meeting occurring on or after January 21, 2011. Rule 14a-21(b) requires that the proxy card for the "say-on-frequency" vote include four choices: every 1 year, every 2 years, every 3 years, or abstain. The "say-on-frequency" doesn't have to be in the form of a resolution; a narrative explanation of the proposal is permitted.

3. Section 14A(b)(2) requires a separate vote to approve "golden parachute" compensation whenever a public company seeks shareholder approval for "an acquisition, merger, consolidation, or proposed sale or other disposition of all or substantially all the assets of an issuer." Disclosure is required for any agreements or understandings with any "named executive officer...concerning any type of compensation (whether present, deferred or contingent)" that is "based on or otherwise relates to" the transaction. This vote, also non-binding, is only required for golden parachute agreements that have not previously been subject to a shareholder pay-on-say vote under Section 14A(a). New SEC Rule 14a-21(c) requires such a vote for a golden parachute arrangement for "each named executive officer," which generally includes the company's principal executive officer (usually, the CEO), its principal financial officer (usually, the CFO) and the three other most highly-compensated executive officers for the year in question.

3. EARLY RESULTS

Say-on-pay was the buzz topic during the 2012 proxy season. When all was said and done, the median level of shareholder approval was just about 90 percent, and only three percent of all U.S. public companies had a failed vote. Many believe that these early rounds of say-on-pay taught two important lessons.

First, the Institutional Shareholder Services ("ISS") Proxy Advisory Services' recommendations and methodology must be taken very seriously.[74] Nearly 21 percent of the S&P 500 companies that received a negative ISS recommendation in 2012 had a failed shareholder vote – a stark contrast to the overall S&P failure rate of only 2.7 percent. Companies with a negative ISS recommendation received an average shareholder support vote of only 65 percent, compared to a 95 percent approval vote for those that had a positive ISS recommendation. An ISS negative recommendation is usually a strong indicator that there is a "pay for performance disconnect" – the CEO's pay is out of alignment with total shareholder return, as compared to the company's peer group performance. There is no question that the ISS's methodology for making its say-on-pay recommendations is quickly emerging as a threshold compensation consideration for many companies.

Second, a smart shareholder communication program can seriously boost the odds of securing a very favorable say-on-pay vote. Such a program will hone the message, communicate frequently, promote feedback (company listening), carefully use the best messengers, target the right people in each significant

---

74. See, generally, David A. Katz and Laura A. McIntosh, *"Say on Pay" in the 2012 Proxy Season*, (The Harvard Law School Forum on Corporate Governance and Financial Regulation 2012); Semler Brossy, *"2012 Say on Pay Results, Russell 3000,"* July 18, 2012; and John D. England, *"Say on Pay Soul Searching Required at Proxy Advisory Firms,"* Pay Governance, June 20, 2012.

institutional investor, and proactively anticipate and thwart negative spins.[75]

4. BAD VOTE LEGAL RISKS

Does a negative or poor shareholder say-on-pay vote increase the personal legal exposure of officers and directors who ignore the non-binding vote and take actions that, on their face, appear to be contrary to the expressed desires of the shareholders? New Section 14A(c) of the Exchange Act expressly provides that the say-on-pay and say-on-parachutes votes are not be construed as "overruling a decision by such issuer or board of directors," "to create or imply any change to the fiduciary duties," or to "create or imply any additional fiduciary duties for such issuer or board of directors." So is that the end of it? Probably not.

The neglect of a negative say-on-pay vote may be evidence to help support a claim that directors or officers have breached their duties of care or loyalty. But the statutory language is specific enough to negate the possibility of a separate private right of action based solely on a non-response to a failed say-on-pay vote. In *Assad v. Hart*, 2012 WL 33220 (S.D.Cal. 2012), the plaintiff tried just that. In dismissing the complaint, the court stated:

> Plaintiff asserts a claim for "breach of the fiduciary duty in connection with the failure to respond to the negative say on pay vote." Plaintiff alleges that Defendants breached their fiduciary duties "by failing to amend or alter 2010 executive compensation (or even issue a response) in connection with the negative say on pay vote"…

> "[A] court may not infer a private right of action from a federal statute unless Congress has displayed 'an intent to create not just a private right of action but also a private remedy.' " *Potter v. Hughes*, 546 F.3d 1051, 1064 (9th Cir.2008) (citing *Alexander v. Sandoval*, 532 U.S. 275, 286–89, (2001)). The language of the statute expressly states that it "may *not* be construed … to create or imply any *change* to fiduciary duties" nor does it " *create or imply* any additional fiduciary duties." *See* 15 U.S.C. § 78n–1(c) (emphasis added). The Dodd–Frank Wall Street Reform Act did not create a private right of action or create new fiduciary duties. The Court concludes that Plaintiff has failed to state a claim for breach of fiduciary duty based on the failure to respond to the negative say on pay vote pursuant to 15 U.S.C. § 78n–1. The motion to dismiss Plaintiff's third claim is GRANTED.

But might a failure to respond to a negative or poor say-on-pay vote help a plaintiff who brings a derivative action and needs to satisfy the *Aronson* demand futility test (see previous section) in order to keep the lawsuit alive? Is it evidence that raises a reasonable doubt concerning the directors' independence and business judgment? Following is one of the first cases (decided in 2102) to consider the issue. More will undoubtedly follow.

---

75. See, generally, David A. Katz and Laura A. McIntosh, *"Say on Pay" in the 2012 Proxy Season*, (The Harvard Law School Forum on Corporate Governance and Financial Regulation 2012).

LABORERS' LOCAL v. INTERSIL
2012 WL 762319 (N.D.Cal., March 7, 2012)

EDWARD J. DAVILA, District Judge.

This is a shareholders' derivative action suit brought for the benefit of Nominal Defendant Intersil against certain executives and directors of Intersil. According to the complaint, Plaintiff has been a shareholder of Intersil since July 2009. Intersil is a Delaware corporation, headquartered in Milpitas, California, which designs, develops, manufactures and markets high-performance analog and mixed-signal integrated circuits. Compensia, a citizen of California, is an executive compensation advisory firm that assisted the Intersil Board in connection with the 2010 executive pay. Compensia was retained by Intersil "to advise it on competitive market practices and other areas of Named Executive Officer compensation." The thirteen individually named defendants are directors and officers of Intersil.. Defendant Bell is the CEO, President, and a director of Intersil.. His pay was increased by 40.6 percent in 2010. Defendant Kennedy is the Chief Financial Officer of Intersil, and his pay was increased by 26.1 percent in 2010. Defendant Hardman is Senior Vice President of Intersil and her pay was increased by 38.6 percent. Defendant Oaklander is Senior Vice President of Intersil and his pay was increased by 36.7 percent. Defendant Loftus is also a Senior Vice President of Intersil and his pay increased by 66.6 percent. Defendants Conn, Diller, Gist, Johnson, Lang, Peeters, Pokelwaldt, and Urry were all Intersil directors at the time of the transaction and served either on the company's Compensation or Audit Committees, which approved the 2010 pay raises.

On March 26, 2011, the Intersil Board recommended shareholder approval of the 2010 executive compensation. The executive compensation plan raised the compensation of the company's named executives by an average of 41.7 percent, pursuant to Intersil's "pay for performance" policy. On May 4, 2011, pursuant to the Dodd–Frank Wall Street Reform and Consumer Protection Act ("Dodd–Frank Act"), a non-binding shareholder vote was held on executive compensation. In that vote, 56 percent of voting Intersil shareholders rejected the Board's 2010 CEO and top executive compensation.

On August 19, 2011, Plaintiff filed this action for breach of fiduciary duty and unjust enrichment on behalf of Intersil by one of its shareholders against several of Intersil's current executives and Board of Directors, alleging that the 2010 executive compensation approved by the Board of Directors was "excessive, irrational, and unreasonable" and that Intersil has been and continues to be severely injured by the executive pay. Plaintiff alleges that in 2010, Intersil suffered substantial financial declines in its net income, which declined by 31.6 percent, and earnings per share, which declined by 34.4 percent. At the same time, the Board approved substantial pay raises for its top executives, under the "pay for performance" program. Thus, Plaintiff claims that the relationship between executive pay and corporate performance was "tenuous at best."

Plaintiff also asserts a claim for aiding and abetting breach of fiduciary duty against Compensia, an independent compensation consultant. Plaintiff seeks recovery, on behalf of Intersil, and asks for damages, declaratory judgment, equitable and/or injunctive relief, implementation and administration of internal control and systems to prohibit and prevent payment of excessive executive compensation, and costs and fees associated with this action.

Before filing this action, Plaintiff did not make a pre-suit demand on Intersil's Board. However, Plaintiff alleges that demand would be futile because the entire board "faces a substantial likelihood of liability for breach of loyalty" and the Board's decision is not entitled to business judgment protection.

On October 17, 2011, Nominal Defendant Intersil, including the named individual defendants, and Defendant Compensia each filed a motion to dismiss Plaintiff's complaint. Additionally, Compensia filed a notice of joinder to Intersil's motion to dismiss.

Under Federal Rule of Civil Procedure 12(b)(6), a complaint may be dismissed if it fails to state a claim upon which relief can be granted. "To survive a motion to dismiss, a complaint must contain sufficient factual matter, accepted as true, 'to state a claim to relief that is plausible on its face.' " Ashcroft v. Iqbal, 556 U.S. 662, 129 S.Ct. 1937, 1949, 173 L.Ed.2d 868 (2009) (internal citations omitted). "A claim has facial plausibility when the plaintiff pleads factual content that allows the court to draw the reasonable inference that the defendant is liable for the misconduct alleged." Id. Recitals of the elements of a cause of action and conclusory allegations are insufficient. Id.

A shareholder derivative suit is a uniquely equitable remedy in which a shareholder asserts on behalf of a corporation a claim belonging not to the shareholder, but to the corporation. Aronson v. Lewis, 473 A.2d 805, 811 (Del.1984) (overruled on other grounds by Brehm v. Eisner, 746 A.2d 244 (Del.2000)). Pursuant to Federal Rule of Civil Procedure 23.1, which governs derivative actions, a shareholder's complaint must state with particularity "any effort by the plaintiff to obtain the desired action from the directors" and "the reasons for not obtaining the action or not making the effort." Fed.R.Civ.P. 23.1. Rule 23.1 imposes a higher standard of pleading than Rule 8(a).

Defendants move to dismiss the complaint on the ground that Plaintiff did not make a demand on Intersil's Board of Directors, as required by Delaware law, and that Plaintiff failed to plead particularized facts excusing the demand, as required under Rule 23.1. Plaintiff concedes that it did not make a pre-suit demand on Intersil's Board. However, Plaintiff contends that the demand upon the Board would have been futile.

Under Delaware law, "directors of a corporation and not its shareholders manage the business and affairs of the corporation, and accordingly, the directors are responsible for deciding whether to engage in derivative litigation." Levine v. Smith, 591 A.2d 194, 200 (Del. Ch.1991). Because directors are empowered to manage or direct the business affairs of the corporation, a shareholder seeking to bring a derivative action must first make a demand on that corporation's board of directors, giving the board an opportunity to examine the alleged grievance to determine whether pursuing the action is in the best interest of the corporation. Aronson, 473 A.2d at 812. The right of a shareholder to prosecute a derivative suit is limited to situations where the shareholder has demanded that the directors pursue the claim and they have wrongfully refused to do so or where demand is excused because the directors are incapable of making impartial decisions regarding such litigation.

To prove that demand is excused, a shareholder must plead with particularity the reasons why such demand would have been futile. Fed.R.Civ.P. 23.1. Under Delaware law, failure to make a demand may be excused if a plaintiff can raise a reasonable doubt that (1) a majority of the board is disinterested or independent, or (2) the challenged act was a product of the board's valid exercise of business judgment. Aronson, 473 A.2d at 814. If either part of the test is satisfied, demand is excused. Brehm, 746 A.2d at 256. However, where a plaintiff fails to adequately allege particularized facts demonstrating that either of the Aronson prongs has been met, the complaint must be dismissed.

Under the first part of the Aronson test, Plaintiff must raise a reasonable doubt that a majority of the board is disinterested or independent. Directorial interest exists whenever divided loyalties are present, where the director will receive a personal financial benefit from a transaction that is not equally shared by the stockholders, or when a corporate decision will have a "materially detrimental impact" on a director but not on the corporation or its stockholders. Aronson, 473 A.2d at 812. Independence exists when a director's decision is based on "the corporate merits of the subject before the board rather than extraneous considerations or influences." Aronson, 473 A.2d at 816.

Plaintiff insists that the complaint creates a reasonable doubt as to the independence of the whole Board because the Board of Directors faces a substantial likelihood of liability for breach of loyalty as a result of the approved 2010 executive compensation... Under Delaware law, "the mere threat of personal liability for approving a questioned transaction, standing alone, is insufficient to challenge either the independence or disinterestedness of directors ...." Aronson, 473 A.2d at 815. A plaintiff may not "bootstrap allegations of futility" by pleading merely that "the directors participated in the challenged transaction or that they would be reluctant to sue themselves." Blasband v. Rales, 971 F.2d 1034, 1049 (3rd Cir.1992) (citing Delaware law). Demand is not excused simply because the Board might be liable for a breach of duty of loyalty as a result of approving the 2010 executive compensation.

The court finds that Plaintiff does not meet its burden of proving that a majority of the directors are interested or not independent...Accordingly, Plaintiff has not met the first prong of the Aronson test for demand futility.

Under the second prong of the Aronson test, Plaintiff must raise a reasonable doubt that the transaction is entitled to the protection of the business judgment rule. The business judgment rule is "a presumption that in making a business decision the directors of a corporation acted on an informed basis, in good faith and in the honest belief that the action taken was in the best interest of the company." Aronson, 473 A.2d at 812... To rebut the business judgment rule presumption, "plaintiffs must plead particularized facts sufficient to raise (1) a reason to doubt that the action was taken honestly and in good faith or (2) a reason to doubt that the board was adequately informed in making the decision."

The complaint fails to allege facts showing that Intersil's Board was not adequately informed in making the decision regarding the 2010 executive compensation. With regards to the honesty and good faith of the Board, Plaintiff points to the shareholder vote to call the directors' decision into question.

Plaintiff claims that the Board's decision regarding increased 2010 executive pay was inconsistent with Intersil's "pay for performance" compensation policy, and therefore, not entitled to business judgment protection. Plaintiff alleges that the company's net income and earnings per share declined, whereas executive compensation rose. Plaintiff claims that the negative "say-on-pay" shareholder vote is evidence showing that directors failed to act in the shareholders' best interests and rebuts the presumption that the Board's decision regarding compensation is entitled to business judgment protection.

The Dodd–Frank Act was signed into law in July 2010 in light of the financial crisis in this country. It is described, in part, as "[a]n Act to promote the financial stability of the United States by improving accountability and transparency in the financial system...." In a report on The Restoring American Financial Stability Act of 2010, later renamed the Dodd–Frank Act, Senator Christopher Dodd noted that, "[i]n connection with the crisis ... investors need more protection; shareholders need a greater voice in corporate governance.... Congress is empowering shareholders in a public company to have a greater voice on executive compensation...." S.Rep. No. 111–176 at 35–37 (2010). The Senate Committee on Banking, Housing, and Urban Affairs held hearings for nearly three years in order to "identify[ ] and examin[e] gaps, overlaps, and shortfalls in a regulatory system that has not been updated since the 1930s" and, as a result, created "the reform our financial system needed and provided the American people with the economic stability that they deserve." Hearing on the Implementation of the Dodd–Frank Wall Street Reform and Consumer Protection Act Before the S. Comm. on Banking, Housing and Urban Affairs (Sept. 30, 2010) (statement of Sen. Christopher Dodd, Chairman, S. Comm. on Banking, Housing and Urban Affairs).

Section 951 of the Dodd–Frank Act requires public companies to conduct a non-binding shareholder vote on executive compensation at least once every three years. Senator Barney Frank noted that the "say on pay" provision was passed "to empower shareholders." The shareholder vote is meant to give shareholders "the ability to hold executives accountable, and to disapprove of misguided incentive schemes." 156 Cong. Rec. S5902–01, S5916 (2010) (statement of Sen. Jack Reed). Section 951 expressly states that the shareholder vote is not binding and it "may not be construed ... to create or imply any change to the fiduciary duties" nor "to create or imply any additional fiduciary duties." 15 U.S.C. § 78n–1(c). While the few courts analyzing section 951 of the Dodd–Frank Act agree that it does not create any new fiduciary duties, no court in California or Delaware has decided whether a negative shareholder vote under the Dodd–Frank Act can be used as evidence to rebut the business judgment rule presumption under Delaware law.

Congress was explicit that the shareholder vote on executive pay is non-binding, but the Act is silent on what consideration courts should give to the shareholder vote. Where resolution of a question of federal law turns on a statute and the intention of Congress, courts first look to the statutory language, and if it is unclear, then to the legislative history. Blum v. Stenson, 465 U.S. 886, 896 (1984). Congress must have intended for the shareholder vote to have some weight if, as discussed above, the goals of section 951 are to empower shareholders and to hold executives accountable. Furthermore, if the shareholder vote approving executive compensation is meant to have no effect whatsoever, it seems unlikely that Congress would have included a specific provision requiring such a vote.

Looking to precedent from other courts that have interpreted the shareholder vote provision of the Dodd–Frank Act, as well as the purpose of the Dodd–Frank Act, this court concludes that a shareholder vote on executive compensation under the Act has substantial evidentiary weight and may be used as evidence by a court in determining whether the second prong of the Aronson test has been met. Ruling only on the particular facts presented in the case before the court, where 56 percent of shareholders disapproved of Intersil's 2010 executive compensation package, the court finds that the shareholder vote alone is not enough to rebut the presumption of the business judgment rule. Additional facts are required for plaintiff to raise a reasonable doubt that the decision was not a valid exercise of business judgment.

Plaintiff relies heavily on NECA–IBEW Pension Fund on behalf of Cincinnati Bell, Inc. v. Cox, 2011 WL 4383368 (S.D.Ohio Sept. 20, 2011), a similar case recently decided in the United States District Court for the Southern District of Ohio applying Ohio state law to interpret the Dodd–Frank Act. The court found that where a majority of shareholders, in a shareholder vote, disapproved of the executive compensation, plaintiff has demonstrated sufficient facts to show that there is reason to doubt that the directors could exercise their independent business judgment over whether to bring suit against themselves for breach of fiduciary duty in awarding the challenged compensation. However, this case has been called into question by Plumbers Local No. 137 Pension Fund v. Davis, 2012 WL 104776 (D.Or. Jan. 11, 2012). The District Court for the District of Oregon noted that the Cincinnati Bell court apparently lacked subject matter jurisdiction and the plaintiff failed to disclose contrary authority in response to the court's specific inquiry. Id. at 5.

A recent case decided by the Georgia Superior Court, Teamsters Local 237 Additional Security Benefit Fund ("Beazer") v. McCarthy, No. 2011–cv197841, 2011 WL 4836230 (Superior Court of Fulton County, Ga., 9 Sept. 16, 2011), applied Delaware law in a situation similar to the case at hand. In Beazer, plaintiffs alleged that defendants had breached their duties of loyalty, candor, and good faith by approving "excessive" executive pay and that the results of the shareholder "say on pay" vote rebutted the presumption of the business judgment rule. Defendants in that case, as here, moved to dismiss the complaint, alleging that plaintiffs did not properly plead excuse from the demand requirement. The Georgia Superior Court decided that, under Delaware law, plaintiffs did not meet the first prong of the Aronson test, because only one of the directors was alleged to have received the challenged compensation. Furthermore, the court determined that plaintiffs did not meet the second prong of the Aronson test when plaintiffs pled that the negative "say on pay" vote constituted evidence to rebut the business judgment rule. First, the court noted that the vote was held after the challenged decision was made, so the Board could not have considered the result of the shareholder vote when making decisions regarding executive pay, and thus the directors did not fail to act on an informed basis when they did not take the vote's results into consideration. Second, the court reiterated that the Dodd–Frank Act preserves the preexisting fiduciary duty framework concerning directors' executive compensation decisions and that shareholders' independent business judgment does not rebut the presumption of business judgment. The court refused to conclude that "an adverse say on pay vote alone suffices to rebut the presumption of business judgment protection applicable to directors' compensation decisions." However, the court did not conclude that such a vote could not be used along with other facts to rebut the business judgment protection.

[T]he 56 percent negative vote by Intersil shareholders does not, on its own, rebut the business judgment presumption. Furthermore, Plaintiff has not pled sufficient facts to raise a reasonable doubt that the challenged act was a product of the board's valid exercise of business judgment. As such, Plaintiff has not met the second prong of the Aronson test for demand futility.

Accordingly, Plaintiff has not pled facts sufficient to prove that demand is excused. As such, Defendants' motions to dismiss the Complaint for failure to state a claim are GRANTED with leave to amend.

CHAPTER 10

DIRECTORS' DUTIES AND LIABILITIES

A. PUPPETS OR PROTECTORS?

Excerpts From
ROBERT JAEDICKE
CONGRESSIONAL TESTIMONY
Subcommittee on Oversight and Investigations
February 7, 2002

I am the Chairman of the Audit Committee of the Board of Directors of Enron Corporation. I have held that position since the mid-1980s.

Let me tell you about my background. I joined the faculty of the Stanford Graduate School of Business in 1961. I served as Dean of the Business School from 1983 until 1990. At that time, I returned to the faculty of the Business School, and retired in 1992.

What happened at Enron has been described as a systemic failure. As it pertains to the Board, I see it instead as a cautionary reminder of the limits of a director's role. We served as directors of what was then the seventh largest corporation in America. Our job as directors was necessarily limited by the nature of Enron's enterprise—which was worldwide in scope, employed more than 20,000 people, and engaged in a vast array of trading and development activities. By force of necessity, we could not know personally all of the employees. As we now know, key employees whom we thought we knew proved to be dishonest or disloyal.

The very magnitude of the enterprise requires directors to confine their control to the broad policy decisions. That we did this is clear from the record. At the meetings of the Board and its committees, in which all of us participated, these questions were considered and decided on the basis of summaries, reports and corporate records. These we were entitled to rely upon. Directors are also, as the Report recognizes, entitled to rely on the honesty and integrity of their subordinates and advisers until something occurs to put them on suspicion that something is wrong.

We did all of this, and more. Sadly, despite all that we tried to do, in the face of all the assurances we received, we had no cause for suspicion until it was too late.

Enron Director Numbers

Each Enron director was paid approximately $350,000 in annual compensation benefits for services as a director. Many questioned the plausibility of the directors' "see-no-evil, hear-no-evil" defense. The directors were charged with ignoring many red flags, including multiple warnings from Enron's outside auditors that Enron's accounting practices were "high-risk," "pushing the limits," and "at the edge" of acceptable practice. Ultimately, the directors settled the shareholders' legal claims by contributing $13 million to a $168 million settlement. It was widely reported that the Enron directors' $13 million personal contribution to the settlement represented about 10 percent of the profits realized by the directors from trading in Enron stock in the months leading up to the energy giant's collapse.

Excerpts from
*THE RISE OF INDEPENDENT DIRECTORS
IN THE UNITED STATES, 1950-2005: OF
SHAREHOLDERVALUE AND STOCK MARKET PRICES*
Stanford Law Review, April, 2007[1]

The now-conventional understanding of boards of directors in the diffusely held firm is that they reduce the agency costs associated with the separation of ownership and control. Elected by shareholders, directors are supposed to "monitor" the managers in view of shareholder interests. Who should serve on the board of a large public firm? Circa 1950, the answer was, as a normative and positive matter, that boards should consist of the firm's senior officers, some outsiders with deep connections with the firm (such as its banker or its senior outside lawyer), and a few directors who were nominally independent but handpicked by the CEO. Circa 2006, the answer is "independent directors," whose independence is buttressed by a range of rule-based and structural mechanisms. Inside directors are a dwindling fraction; the senior outside lawyer on the board is virtually an extinct species.

The move to independent directors, which began as a "good governance" exhortation, has become in some respects a mandatory element of corporate law. For controversial transactions, the Delaware courts condition their application of the lenient "business judgment rule" to board action undertaken by independent directors. The New York Stock Exchange requires most listed companies to have boards with a majority of independent directors and audit and compensation committees comprised solely of independent directors. The NASD requires that conflict transactions be approved by committees consisting solely of independent directors. Post-Enron federal legislation requires public companies to have an audit committee comprised solely of independent directors. But why has the move to independent directors been so pronounced?

One of the apparent puzzles in the empirical corporate governance literature is the lack of correlation between the presence of independent directors and the firm's economic performance. Various studies have searched in vain for an

1. Authored by Jeffrey N. Gordon, Alfred W. Bressler Professor of Law, Albert E. Cinelli Enterprise Professor of Law, Columbia Law School.

economically significant effect on the overall performance of the firm. Some would deny there is a puzzle: theory would predict that firms will select the board structure that enhances the chance for survival and success; if competitive market pressure eliminates out-of-equilibrium patterns of corporate governance, the remaining diversity is functional. Others would note that corporate governance in the United States is already quite good, and thus marginal improvements in a particular corporate governance mechanism would expectedly have a small, perhaps negligible, effect.

The rise of independent directors in the diffusely held public firm is not driven only by the need to address the managerial agency problem at any particular firm. "Independent directors" is the answer to a different question: how do we govern firms so as to increase social welfare (as proxied by maximization of shareholder value across the general market)? This maximization of shareholder value may produce institutions that are suboptimal for particular firms but optimal for an economy of such firms. Independent directors as developed in the U.S. context solve three different problems: First, they enhance the fidelity of managers to shareholder objectives, as opposed to managerial interests or stakeholder interests. Second, they enhance the reliability of the firm's public disclosure, which makes stock market prices a more reliable signal for capital allocation and for the monitoring of managers at other firms as well as their own. Third, and more controversially, they provide a mechanism that binds the responsiveness of firms to stock market signals but in a bounded way. The turn to independent directors serves a view that stock market signals are the most reliable measure of firm performance and the best guide to allocation of capital in the economy, but that a "visible hand," namely, the independent board, is needed to balance the tendency of markets to overshoot.

During [the post-World War II era to the present], the board's principal role shifted from the "advising board" to the "monitoring board," and director independence became correspondingly critical. Although other factors are at work, there were two main drivers of the monitoring model and genuine director independence. First, the corporate purpose evolved from stakeholder concerns that were an important element of 1950s managerialism to unalloyed shareholder wealth maximization in the 1990s and 2000s. Inside directors or affiliated outside directors were seen as conflicted in their capacity to insist on the primacy of shareholder interests; the expectations of director independence became increasingly stringent.

Second, fundamental changes in the information environment reworked the ratio of the firm's reliance on private information to its reliance on information impounded in prevailing stock market prices. Over the period, the central planning capabilities of the large public firm became suspect. Instead, a Hayekian spirit, embodied in the efficient capital market hypothesis, became predominant. The belief that markets "knew" more than the managers of any particular firm became increasingly credible as regulators and quasi-public standard setters required increasingly deep disclosure and this information was impounded in increasingly informative stock prices. The optimal boundaries of the firm changed as external capital markets advanced relative to internal capital markets in the allocation of capital. The richer public information environment changed the role of directors. Special access to private information became less important. Independent directors could use increasingly informative market prices to advise the CEO on strategy and evaluate its execution, as well as take advantage of the increasingly well-informed opinions of securities analysts. Independents had positional advantages over inside directors, who were more likely to overvalue the firm's planning and capital allocation capabilities. In the trade-off between advising and monitoring, the monitoring of managers in light of market signals became more valuable. The reliability of the firm's public disclosures became more important. Indeed, by the end of the period, boards came to have a particular role in assuring that the firm provided accurate information to the market.

Thus, fidelity to shareholder value and to the utility of stock market signals found unity in the reliance on stock price maximization as the measure of managerial success. From a social point of view, maximizing shareholder value may be desirable if fidelity to the shareholder residual (as opposed to balancing among multiple claimants) leads to maximization of the social surplus. This is the shareholder primacy argument. Independently, maximizing shareholder value may be socially desirable if stock prices are so informative that following their signals leads to the best resource allocation. This is the market efficiency argument.

Over the period, boards eventually undertook measures that assured management's responsiveness to stock market signals, in particular through the use of stock-related compensation and retention decisions based on stock market performance.

There were a number of innovations during the period aimed at creating incentives for good performance by outside directors. Circa 1950, director compensation was low and sometimes nonexistent. The tradition, going back to the nineteenth century, was not to pay directors, on the view that the opportunity to monitor management was reward enough for a substantial stockholder. As it became desirable for firms to put "outsiders" on the board and necessary to compensate them for their time, significant compensation became common; indeed, it became increasingly lavish throughout the period. Such compensation, of course, can undercut independence if the CEO has influence over director retention.

One 1990s-era governance innovation was to compensate directors in stock (or stock options) to strengthen the alignment of director and shareholder interests. Over time the stake accumulates, but this also undercuts director independence where the CEO has influence over director retention.

More seriously, perhaps, stock-based compensation may create a distinctive set of perverse incentives for the directors, as demonstrated by the wave of financial disclosure problems in the late 1990s and early 2000s. The director receiving stock-based compensation, like the similarly compensated CEO, may be tempted to accept aggressive accounting rather than stock-price-puncturing disclosure. It is important to remember that with respect to disclosure obligations,

Public Board Dual Duty

the public board has a dual duty--not only to the firm's shareholders, but to capital market participants more generally. This is because of the positive (negative) externalities associated with accurate (misleading) disclosure. With such divided duties, it's hard to know which way to set the optimal stock-based incentive effects.

Another important mechanism for director independence is the creative use of board structure to create a spirit of teamwork and mutual accountability among independent directors that helps foster independence-in-fact. Structural innovations multiplied over the period.

One particularly important innovation was the board committee assigned a specific key function. Beginning in the 1970s, "best practice" pronouncements called for three specific committees: the audit committee, the compensation committee, and the nominating committee, each with a majority of independent directors. Each committee is functionally tasked in areas where the interests of managers and the shareholders may conflict. Independence-in-fact may be enhanced in two respects. First, the ownership and accountability for a specific critical task may lead to greater autonomy from the CEO in performing that task. Second, the practice of acting jointly and autonomously in a targeted area may carry over to other important roles of the board, such as evaluating managerial performance and strategy. The potential for enhanced independence from this structural/functional mechanism source grew gradually over the period, beginning in the 1970s. One limiting factor was that only at the end of the period, via a NYSE rule, were these committees necessarily staffed solely by independent directors.

The most important board committee was the audit committee, a major objective of corporate governance reformers. Current standards, through both exchange listing rules and Sarbanes-Oxley, mandate audit committees for every publicly owned company, as well as stringent standards of independence and financial expertise.

At best, functionally tasked board committees should enhance independence, particularly in regard to the targeted task. Actual practices, until the post-Enron reform wave, made the committees less effective in that regard. For the audit committee, management hired (and fired) the auditor and also determined the level of more lucrative non-auditing consulting work assigned to the auditor, undercutting the auditor's allegiance to the audit committee. This managerial power over the auditor relationship was, of course, known to the audit committee members and would have dampened their independent engagement with significant auditing issues. Sarbanes-Oxley, passed in 2002, now gives the audit committee power (and responsibility) over the firm's auditor relationships and audit policies. This, in turn, should make the audit committee a stronger source of director independence.

The compensation committee also has a similar story of dampened independence. In setting executive pay, compensation committees typically have relied on the compensation consultant who also provided firm-wide compensation and human resources guidance. Such a management-retained consultant, earning the largest portion of its fees from the firm-wide assignment, is unlikely to make recommendations or offer viewpoints that senior management would find distressing.

The collapse of Enron, WorldCom, and similar but less catastrophic disclosure failures vividly demonstrated weaknesses in the board governance system produced by the 1990s and pointed the way towards new roles for independent directors and standards of independence. The 1990s system depended on an independent board's contracting with managers using stock market-based measures of managerial success to determine both compensation and tenure. Appropriate operation of the contracts critically depended upon the quality of the firm's disclosure, since otherwise stock prices would not reflect managerial performance. Yet the managers whose compensation and tenure depended on these stock prices were principally responsible for producing the disclosure on which the contracts relied. Boards had simply failed to appreciate and protect against some of the moral hazard problems that stock-based compensation created, in particular, the special temptations to misreport financial results. The principal objective of the Sarbanes-Oxley Act of 2002, then, was the protection of the integrity of financial disclosure, both through extensive new regulation of accountants and through new disclosure monitoring responsibilities imposed on directors.

Several recent studies find that the probability of accounting fraud, though small, nevertheless increases with the amount of stock-based compensation, and increases as well with the fraction of total compensation that is stock-based. The source of the temptation becomes apparent in comparing two forms of incentive compensation, cash bonuses and stock options. Bonus payments will typically increase linearly with earnings but the value of stock options can increase (decrease) exponentially because of the double effect that earnings changes have on stock prices.

Thus, as compensation came increasingly to consist of high-powered incentives like stock options and as the absolute level of potential stock option payout over a short period of time increased, management's temptations grew. This is the source of the most difficult moral hazard problem associated with the 1990s governance pattern.

The principle institutional failure that produced Enron and its ilk was the failure of the gatekeepers, especially the accountants, not the insufficiency of director independence. Yet boards had not performed well either, having failed to address management's undercutting of gatekeeper integrity. There certainly was a substantive case for enhancing the independence-in-fact of directors, particularly if the managerial agency problem was to be addressed through incentive-based compensation and termination contracts rather than through control markers. As post-Enron reform pressure mounted, managerial elites moved to ramp up board independence as an alternative to more intrusive regulation, in this way protecting managerial autonomy to the extent possible in the changed environment.

The post-Enron reforms lay the groundwork for a revised model of corporate governance. The model operates at many different levels. It ratchets up the liability for primary wrong-doers, particularly corporate officers. It imposes new duties, new liabilities, and a new regulatory structure on certain gatekeepers, accountants in particular but also lawyers and, in a fashion, securities analysts. The effect of the reforms on the board's role is to make the role of the independent director more important than ever. Both the federal securities law and the stock exchange listing requirements imposed more rigorous standards of director independence. Boards, particularly the audit committee, are given a specific mandate to supervise the firm's relationship with the accountants and thus to oversee the corporation's internal financial controls and financial disclosure. Boards are more likely to hear about their lawyers' concerns that the firm's managers are not in compliance with the federal securities laws or even state fiduciary duty. Directors, then, will have a particularized monitoring role, what might be called "controls monitoring," in addition to "performance monitoring."

B. THE DUTY OF CARE

1. BAD FAITH, WASTE, DERELICTION

FRANCIS v. UNITED JERSEY BANK
87 N.J. 432, 432 A.2d 814 (1981)

POLLOCK, J.

The primary issue on this appeal is whether a corporate director is personally liable in negligence for the failure to prevent the misappropriation of trust funds by other directors who were also officers and shareholders of the corporation.

Plaintiffs are trustees in bankruptcy of Pritchard & Baird Intermediaries Corp. (Pritchard & Baird), a reinsurance broker or intermediary. Defendant Lillian P. Overcash is the daughter of Lillian G. Pritchard and the executrix of her estate. At the time of her death, Mrs. Pritchard was a director and the largest single shareholder of Pritchard & Baird. Because Mrs. Pritchard died after the institution of suit but before trial, her executrix was substituted as a defendant. United Jersey Bank is joined as the administrator of the estate of Charles Pritchard, Sr., who had been president, director and majority shareholder of Pritchard & Baird.

This litigation focuses on payments made by Pritchard & Baird to Charles Pritchard, Jr. and William Pritchard, who were sons of Mr. and Mrs. Charles Pritchard, Sr., as well as officers, directors and shareholders of the corporation. Claims against Charles, Jr. and William are being pursued in bankruptcy proceedings against them.

The trial court, sitting without a jury, characterized the payments as fraudulent conveyances within N.J.S.A. 25:2-10 and entered judgment of $10,355,736.91 plus interest against the estate of Mrs. Pritchard. The judgment includes damages from her negligence in permitting payments from the corporation of $4,391,133.21 to Charles, Jr. and $5,483,799.02 to William.

The Appellate Division affirmed, but found that the payments were a conversion of trust funds, rather than fraudulent conveyances of the assets of the corporation. We granted certification limited to the issue of the liability of Lillian Pritchard as a director.

The initial question is whether Mrs. Pritchard was negligent in not noticing and trying to prevent the misappropriation of funds held by the corporation in an implied trust. A further question is whether her negligence was the proximate cause of the plaintiffs' losses. Both lower courts found that she was liable in negligence for the losses caused by the wrongdoing of Charles, Jr. and William. We affirm.

The matrix for our decision is the customs and practices of the reinsurance industry and the role of Pritchard & Baird as a reinsurance broker. Reinsurance involves a contract under which one insurer agrees to indemnify another for loss sustained under the latter's policy of insurance. Insurance companies that insure against losses arising out of fire or other casualty seek at times to minimize their exposure by sharing risks with other insurance companies. Thus, when the face amount of a policy is comparatively large, the company may enlist one or more insurers to participate in that risk. Similarly, an insurance company's loss potential and overall exposure may be reduced by reinsuring a part of an entire class of policies (e. g., 25% of all of its fire insurance policies). The selling insurance company is known as a ceding company. The entity that assumes the obligation is designated as the reinsurer.

The reinsurance broker arranges the contract between the ceding company and the reinsurer. In accordance with industry custom before the Pritchard & Baird bankruptcy, the reinsurance contract or treaty did not specify the rights and duties of the broker. Typically, the ceding company communicates to the broker the details concerning the risk. The broker negotiates the sale of portions of the risk to the reinsurers. In most instances, the ceding company and the reinsurer do not communicate with each other, but rely upon the reinsurance broker. The ceding company pays premiums due a reinsurer to the broker, who deducts his commission and transmits the balance to the appropriate reinsurer. When a loss occurs, a reinsurer pays money due a ceding company to the broker, who then transmits it to the ceding company.

Messrs. Pritchard and Baird initially operated as a partnership. Later they formed several corporate entities to carry on their brokerage activities. The proofs supporting the judgment relate only to one corporation, and we need consider only its activities. When incorporated under the laws of the State of New York in 1959, Pritchard & Baird had five directors: Charles Pritchard, Sr., his wife Lillian Pritchard, their son Charles Pritchard, Jr., George Baird and his wife Marjorie. William Pritchard, another son, became director in 1960. Upon its formation, Pritchard & Baird acquired all the assets and assumed all the liabilities of the Pritchard & Baird partnership. The corporation issued 200 shares of common stock. Charles Pritchard, Sr. acquired 120 shares, his sons Charles

Pritchard, Jr., 15 and William, 15; Mr. and Mrs. Baird owned the remaining 50. In June 1964, Baird and his wife resigned as directors and sold their stock to the corporation. From that time on the corporation operated as a close family corporation with Mr. and Mrs. Pritchard and their two sons as the only directors. After the death of Charles, Sr. in 1973, only the remaining three directors continued to operate as the board. Lillian Pritchard inherited 72 of her husband's 120 shares in Pritchard & Baird, thereby becoming the largest shareholder in the corporation with 48% of the stock.

The corporate minute books reflect only perfunctory activities by the directors, related almost exclusively to the election of officers and adoption of banking resolutions and a retirement plan. None of the minutes for any of the meetings contain a discussion of the loans to Charles, Jr. and William or of the financial condition of the corporation. Moreover, upon instructions of Charles, Jr. that financial statements were not to be circulated to anyone else, the company's statements for the fiscal years beginning February 1, 1970, were delivered only to him.

Charles Pritchard, Sr. was the chief executive and controlled the business in the years following Baird's withdrawal. Beginning in 1966, he gradually relinquished control over the operations of the corporation. In 1968, Charles, Jr. became president and William became executive vice president. Charles, Sr. apparently became ill in 1971 and during the last year and a half of his life was not involved in the affairs of the business. He continued, however, to serve as a director until his death on December 10, 1973. Notwithstanding the presence of Charles, Sr. on the board until his death in 1973, Charles, Jr. dominated the management of the corporation and the board from 1968 until the bankruptcy in 1975.

Contrary to the industry custom of segregating funds, Pritchard & Baird commingled the funds of reinsurers and ceding companies with its own funds. All monies (including commissions, premiums and loss monies) were deposited in a single account. Charles, Sr. began the practice of withdrawing funds from the commingled account in transactions identified on the corporate books as "loans." As long as Charles, Sr. controlled the corporation, the "loans" correlated with corporate profits and were repaid at the end of each year. Starting in 1970, however, Charles, Jr. and William began to siphon ever-increasing sums from the corporation under the guise of loans. As of January 31, 1970, the "loans" to Charles, Jr. were $230,932 and to William were $207,329. At least by January 31, 1973, the annual increase in the loans exceeded annual corporate revenues. By October 1975, the year of bankruptcy, the "shareholders' loans" had metastasized to a total of $12,333,514.47.

The designation of "shareholders' loans" on the balance sheet was an entry to account for the distribution of the premium and loss money to Charles, Sr., Charles, Jr. and William. As the trial court found, the entry was part of a "woefully inadequate and highly dangerous bookkeeping system."

Mrs. Pritchard was not active in the business of Pritchard & Baird and knew virtually nothing of its corporate affairs. She briefly visited the corporate offices in Morristown on only one occasion, and she never read or obtained the annual financial statements. She was unfamiliar with the rudiments of reinsurance and made no effort to assure that the policies and practices of the corporation, particularly pertaining to the withdrawal of funds, complied with industry custom or relevant law. Although her husband had warned her that Charles, Jr. would "take the shirt off my back," Mrs. Pritchard did not pay any attention to her duties as a director or to the affairs of the corporation.

After her husband died in December 1973, Mrs. Pritchard became incapacitated and was bedridden for a six-month period. She became listless at this time and started to drink rather heavily. Her physical condition deteriorated, and in 1978 she died. The trial court rejected testimony seeking to exonerate her because she "was old, was grief-stricken at the loss of her husband, sometimes consumed too much alcohol and was psychologically overborne by her sons." The court found that she was competent to act and that the reason Mrs. Pritchard never knew what her sons "were doing was because she never made the slightest effort to discharge any of her responsibilities as a director of Pritchard & Baird."

Individual liability of a corporate director for acts of the corporation is a prickly problem. Generally directors are accorded broad immunity and are not insurers of corporate activities. The problem is particularly nettlesome when a third party asserts that a director, because of nonfeasance, is liable for losses caused by acts of insiders, who in this case were officers, directors and shareholders. Determination of the liability of Mrs. Pritchard requires findings that she had a duty to the clients of Pritchard & Baird, that she breached that duty and that her breach was a proximate cause of their losses.

The New Jersey Business Corporation Act, which took effect on January 1, 1969, was a comprehensive revision of the statutes relating to business corporations. One section, N.J.S.A. 14A:6-14, concerning a director's general obligation makes it incumbent upon directors to discharge their duties in good faith and with that degree of diligence, care and skill which ordinarily prudent men would exercise under similar circumstances in like positions.

As a general rule, a director should acquire at least a rudimentary understanding of the business of the corporation. Accordingly, a director should become familiar with the fundamentals of the business in which the corporation is engaged. Because directors are bound to exercise ordinary care, they cannot set up as a defense lack of the knowledge needed to exercise the requisite degree of care.

Directors are under a continuing obligation to keep informed about the activities of the corporation. Otherwise, they may not be able to participate in the overall management of corporate affairs. Barnes v. Andrews, 298 F. 614 (S.D.N.Y.1924). Directors may not shut their eyes to corporate misconduct and then claim that because they did not see the misconduct, they did not have a duty to look. The sentinel asleep at his post contributes nothing to the enterprise he is charged to protect.

Directorial management does not require a detailed inspection of day-to-day activities, but rather a general monitoring of corporate affairs and policies.

Accordingly, a director is well advised to attend board meetings regularly. Indeed, a director who is absent from a board meeting is presumed to concur in action taken on a corporate matter, unless he files a "dissent with the secretary of the corporation within a reasonable time after learning of such action." Regular attendance does not mean that directors must attend every meeting, but that directors should attend meetings as a matter of practice. A director of a publicly held corporation might be expected to attend regular monthly meetings, but a director of a small, family corporation might be asked to attend only an annual meeting. The point is that one of the responsibilities of a director is to attend meetings of the board of which he or she is a member.

While directors are not required to audit corporate books, they should maintain familiarity with the financial status of the corporation by a regular review of financial statements. In some circumstances, directors may be charged with assuring that bookkeeping methods conform to industry custom and usage. The extent of review, as well as the nature and frequency of financial statements, depends not only on the customs of the industry, but also on the nature of the corporation and the business in which it is engaged. Financial statements of some small corporations may be prepared internally and only on an annual basis; in a large publicly held corporation, the statements may be produced monthly or at some other regular interval. Adequate financial review normally would be more informal in a private corporation than in a publicly held corporation.

Of some relevance in this case is the circumstance that the financial records disclose the "shareholders' loans". Generally directors are immune from liability if, in good faith, they rely upon the opinion of counsel for the corporation or upon written reports setting forth financial data concerning the corporation and prepared by an independent public accountant or certified public accountant or firm of such accountants or upon financial statements, books of account or reports of the corporation represented to them to be correct by the president, the officer of the corporation having charge of its books of account, or the person presiding at a meeting of the board.

In certain circumstances, the fulfillment of the duty of a director may call for more than mere objection and resignation. Sometimes a director may be required to seek the advice of counsel. The duty to seek the assistance of counsel can extend to areas other than the interpretation of corporation instruments. Modern corporate practice recognizes that on occasion a director should seek outside advice. A director may require legal advice concerning the propriety of his or her own conduct, the conduct of other officers and directors or the conduct of the corporation. In appropriate circumstances, a director would be "well advised to consult with regular corporate counsel (or his own legal adviser) at any time in which he is doubtful regarding proposed action ...." Sometimes the duty of a director may require more than consulting with outside counsel. A director may have a duty to take reasonable means to prevent illegal conduct by co-directors; in any appropriate case, this may include threat of suit. See Selheimer v. Manganese Corp., 423 Pa. 563, 572, 584, 224 A.2d 634, 640, 646 (Sup.Ct.1966) (director exonerated when he objected, resigned, organized shareholder action group, and threatened suit).

A director is not an ornament, but an essential component of corporate governance. Consequently, a director cannot protect himself behind a paper shield bearing the motto, "dummy director." The New Jersey Business Corporation Act, in imposing a standard of ordinary care on all directors, confirms that dummy, figurehead and accommodation directors are anachronisms with no place in New Jersey law.

The factors that impel expanded responsibility in the large, publicly held corporation may not be present in a small, close corporation. Nonetheless, a close corporation may, because of the nature of its business, be affected with a public interest. For example, the stock of a bank may be closely held, but because of the nature of banking the directors would be subject to greater liability than those of another close corporation. Even in a small corporation, a director is held to the standard of that degree of care that an ordinarily prudent director would use under the circumstances.

A director's duty of care does not exist in the abstract, but must be considered in relation to specific obligees. In general, the relationship of a corporate director to the corporation and its stockholders is that of a fiduciary. Shareholders have a right to expect that directors will exercise reasonable supervision and control over the policies and practices of a corporation. The institutional integrity of a corporation depends upon the proper discharge by directors of those duties.

While directors may owe a fiduciary duty to creditors also, that obligation generally has not been recognized in the absence of insolvency. With certain corporations, however, directors are seemed to owe a duty to creditors and other third parties even when the corporation is solvent. Although depositors of a bank are considered in some respects to be creditors, courts have recognized that directors may owe them a fiduciary duty. Directors of nonbanking corporations may owe a similar duty when the corporation holds funds of others in trust.

The most striking circumstances affecting Mrs. Pritchard's duty as a director are the character of the reinsurance industry, the nature of the misappropriated funds and the financial condition of Pritchard & Baird. The hallmark of the reinsurance industry has been the unqualified trust and confidence reposed by ceding companies and reinsurers in reinsurance brokers. Those companies entrust money to reinsurance intermediaries with the justifiable expectation that the funds will be transmitted to the appropriate parties. Consequently, the companies could have assumed rightfully that Mrs. Pritchard, as a director of a reinsurance brokerage corporation, would not sanction the comingling and the conversion of loss and premium funds for the personal use of the principals of Pritchard & Baird.

As a director of a substantial reinsurance brokerage corporation, she should have known that it received annually millions of dollars of loss and premium funds which it held in trust for ceding and reinsurance companies. Mrs. Pritchard should have obtained and read the annual statements of financial condition of Pritchard & Baird. Although she had a right to rely upon financial statements, such reliance would not excuse her conduct. The reason is that those statements disclosed on their face the misappropriation of trust funds. *Clearly misappropriation*

In summary, Mrs. Pritchard was charged with the obligation of basic knowledge and supervision of the business of Pritchard & Baird. Under the circumstances, this obligation included reading and understanding financial statements, and making reasonable attempts at detection and prevention of the illegal conduct of other officers and directors. She had a duty to protect the clients of Pritchard & Baird against policies and practices that would result in the misappropriation of money they had entrusted to the corporation. She breached that duty. *① Duty / ② was Breached*

Nonetheless, the negligence of Mrs. Pritchard does not result in liability unless it is a proximate cause of the loss. Kulas v. Public Serv. Elec. and Gas Co., 41 N.J. 311, 317, 196 A.2d 769 (1964). Analysis of proximate cause requires an initial determination of cause-in-fact. Causation-in-fact calls for a finding that the defendant's act or omission was a necessary antecedent of the loss, i.e., that if the defendant had observed his or her duty of care, the loss would not have occurred. Further, the plaintiff has the burden of establishing the amount of the loss or damages caused by the negligence of the defendant. *③ Proximate Cause? CIF?*

Cases involving nonfeasance present a much more difficult causation question than those in which the director has committed an affirmative act of negligence leading to the loss. Analysis in cases of negligent omissions calls for determination of the reasonable steps a director should have taken and whether that course of action would have averted the loss.

Usually a director can absolve himself from liability by informing the other directors of the impropriety and voting for a proper course of action. Even accepting the hypothesis that Mrs. Pritchard might not be liable if she had objected and resigned, there are two significant reasons for holding her liable. First, she did not resign until just before the bankruptcy. Consequently, there is no factual basis for the speculation that the losses would have occurred even if she had objected and resigned. Indeed, the trial court reached the opposite conclusion: "The actions of the sons were so blatantly wrongful that it is hard to see how they could have resisted any moderately firm objection to what they were doing." Second, the nature of the reinsurance business distinguishes it from most other commercial activities in that reinsurance brokers are encumbered by fiduciary duties owed to third parties. In other corporations, a director's duty normally does not extend beyond the shareholders to third parties. *How to Absolve* / *Two Reasons for Liability*

In this case, the scope of Mrs. Pritchard's duties was determined by the precarious financial condition of Pritchard & Baird, its fiduciary relationship to its clients and the implied trust in which it held their funds. Thus viewed, the scope of her duties encompassed all reasonable action to stop the continuing conversion. Her duties extended beyond mere objection and resignation to reasonable attempts to prevent the misappropriation of the trust funds. *Scope of Duties*

We conclude that even if Mrs. Pritchard's mere objection had not stopped the depredations of her sons, her consultation with an attorney and the threat of suit would have deterred them. That conclusion flows as a matter of common sense and logic from the record. Whether in other situations a director has a duty to do more than protest and resign is best left to case-by-case determinations. In this case, we are satisfied that there was a duty to do more than object and resign. Consequently, we find that Mrs. Pritchard's negligence was a proximate cause of the misappropriations.

Holding

To conclude, by virtue of her office, Mrs. Pritchard had the power to prevent the losses sustained by the clients of Pritchard & Baird. With power comes responsibility. She had a duty to deter the depredation of the other insiders, her sons. She breached that duty and caused plaintiffs to sustain damages.

The judgment of the Appellate Division is affirmed.

Model Business Corporation Act Provisions

MBCA § 8.30. STANDARDS OF CONDUCT FOR DIRECTORS

(a) Each member of the board of directors, when discharging the duties of a director, shall act: (1) in good faith, and (2) in a manner the director reasonably believes to be in the best interests of the corporation.

(b) The members of the board of directors or a committee of the board, when becoming informed in connection with their decision-making function or devoting attention to their oversight function, shall discharge their duties with the care that a person in a like position would reasonably believe appropriate under similar circumstances.

MBCA § 8.31 STANDARDS OF LIABILITY FOR DIRECTORS

(a) A director shall not be liable to the corporation or its shareholders for any decision to take or not to take action, or any failure to take any action, as a director, unless the party asserting liability in a proceeding establishes that:

(1) no defense interposed by the director based on [authorized provisions of the articles of incorporation or statutory provisions] does not preclude liability; and

(2) the challenged conduct consisted or was the result of:

(i) action not in good faith; or

(ii) a decision

(A) which the director did not reasonably believe to be in the best interests of the corporation, or

(B) as to which the director was not informed to an extent the director reasonably believed appropriate in the circumstances; or

(iii) a lack of objectivity due to the director's familial, financial or business relationship with, or a lack of independence due to the director's domination or control by, another person having a material interest in the challenged conduct

(A) which relationship or which domination or control could reasonably be expected to have affected the director's judgment respecting the challenged conduct in a manner adverse to the corporation, and

(B)   after a reasonable expectation to such effect has been established, the director shall not have established that the challenged conduct was reasonably believed by the director to be in the best interests of the corporation; or

(iv) a sustained failure of the director to devote attention to ongoing oversight of the business and affairs of the corporation, or a failure to devote timely attention, by making (or causing to be made) appropriate inquiry, when particular facts and circumstances of significant concern materialize that would alert a reasonably attentive director to the need therefore; or

(v) receipt of a financial benefit to which the director was not entitled or any other breach of the director's duties to deal fairly with the corporation and its shareholders that is actionable under applicable law.

(b) The party seeking to hold the director liable:

(1) for money damages, shall also have the burden of establishing that:

(i) harm to the corporation or its shareholders has been suffered, and   *Threshold*

(ii)   the harm suffered was proximately caused by the director's challenged conduct; or

(2) for other money payment under a legal remedy, such as compensation for the unauthorized use of corporate assets, shall also have whatever persuasion burden may be called for to establish that the payment sought is appropriate in the circumstances; or

(3) for other money payment under an equitable remedy, such as profit recovery by or disgorgement to the corporation, shall also have whatever persuasion burden may be called for to establish that the equitable remedy sought is appropriate in the circumstances.

(c) Nothing contained in this section shall (1) in any instance where fairness is at issue, such as consideration of the fairness of a transaction to the corporation under section 8.61(b)(3), alter the burden of proving the fact or lack of fairness otherwise applicable, (2) alter the fact or lack of liability of a director under another section of this Act, such as the provisions governing the consequences of an unlawful distribution under section 8 or a transactional interest under section 8.61, or (3) affect any rights to which the corporation or a shareholder may be entitled under another statute of this state or the United States.

MBCS § 2.02(b)(4) ARTICLES OF INCORPORATION

(b) The articles of incorporation may set forth:

(4) a provision eliminating or limiting the liability of a director to the corporation or its shareholders for money damages for any action taken, or any failure to take any action, as a director, except liability for (A) the amount of a financial benefit received by a director to which he is not entitled; (B) an

intentional infliction of harm on the corporation or the shareholders; (C) a violation of section 8.33; or (D) an intentional violation of criminal law.

IN RE THE WALT DISNEY COMPANY DERIVATIVE LITIGATION (II)
825 A.2d 275 (Del.Ch. 2003)

CHANDLER, Chancellor.

In this derivative action filed on behalf of nominal defendant Walt Disney Company, plaintiffs allege that the defendant directors breached their fiduciary duties when they blindly approved an employment agreement with defendant Michael Ovitz and then, again without any review or deliberation, ignored defendant Michael Eisner's dealings with Ovitz regarding his non-fault termination. Plaintiffs seek rescission and/or money damages from defendants and Ovitz, or compensation for damages allegedly sustained by Disney and disgorgement of Ovitz's unjust enrichment.

I conclude that plaintiffs' new complaint sufficiently pleads a breach of fiduciary duty by the Old and the New Disney Board of Directors so as to withstand a motion to dismiss under Chancery Rules 23.1 and 12(b)(6). Stated briefly, plaintiffs' new allegations give rise to a cognizable question whether the defendant directors of the Walt Disney Company should be held personally liable to the corporation for a knowing or intentional lack of due care in the directors' decision-making process regarding Ovitz's employment and termination. It is rare when a court imposes liability on directors of a corporation for breach of the duty of care, and this Court is hesitant to second-guess the business judgment of a disinterested and independent board of directors. But the facts alleged in the new complaint do not implicate merely negligent or grossly negligent decision making by corporate directors. Quite the contrary; plaintiffs' new complaint suggests that the Disney directors failed to exercise any business judgment and failed to make any good faith attempt to fulfill their fiduciary duties to Disney and its stockholders. Allegations that Disney's directors abdicated all responsibility to consider appropriately an action of material importance to the corporation puts directly in question whether the board's decision-making processes were employed in a good faith effort to advance corporate interests. In short, the new complaint alleges facts implying that the Disney directors failed to "act in good faith and meet minimal proceduralist standards of attention." *Gagliardi v. TriFoods Int'l, Inc.,* 683 A.2d 1049, 1052 (Del.Ch.1996).

Michael Eisner is the chief executive officer ("CEO") of the Walt Disney Company. In 1994, Eisner's second-in-command, Frank Wells, died in a helicopter crash. Eisner began looking for a new president for Disney and chose Michael Ovitz. Ovitz was founder and head of CAA, a talent agency; he had never been an executive for a publicly owned entertainment company. He had, however, been Eisner's close friend for over twenty-five years.

Eisner decided unilaterally to hire Ovitz. On August 13, 1995, he informed three Old Board members – Stephen Bollenbach, Sanford Litvack, and Irwin Russell (Eisner's personal attorney) – of that fact. Before informing Bollenbach, Litvack, and Russell on August 13, 1995, Eisner collected information on his own, through his position as the Disney CEO, on the potential hiring of Ovitz.

The compensation committee, consisting of defendants Ignacio Lozano, Jr., Sidney Poitier, Russell, and Raymond Watson, met on September 26, 1995, for just under an hour. Three subjects were discussed at the meeting, one of which was Ovitz's employment. According to the minutes, the committee spent the least amount of time during the meeting discussing Ovitz's hiring. In fact, it appears that more time was spent on discussions of paying $250,000 to Russell for his role in securing Ovitz's employment than was actually spent on discussions of Ovitz's employment. The minutes show that several issues were raised and discussed by the committee members concerning Russell's fee. All that occurred during the meeting regarding Ovitz's employment was that Russell reviewed the employment terms with the committee and answered a few questions. Immediately thereafter, the committee adopted a resolution of approval.

No copy of the September 23, 1995 draft employment agreement was actually given to the committee. Instead, the committee members received, at the meeting itself, a rough summary of the agreement. The summary, however, was incomplete. It stated that Ovitz was to receive options to purchase five million shares of stock, but did not state the exercise price. The committee also did not receive any of the materials already produced by Disney regarding Ovitz's possible employment. No spreadsheet or similar type of analytical document showing the potential payout to Ovitz throughout the contract, or the possible cost of his severance package upon a non-fault termination, was created or presented.

incomplete summary of employment

The committee also lacked the benefit of an expert to guide them through the process. The compensation committee was informed that further negotiations would occur and that the stock option grant would be delayed until the final contract was worked out. The committee approved the general terms and conditions of the employment agreement, but did not condition their approval on being able to review the final agreement. Instead, the committee granted Eisner the authority to approve the final terms and conditions of the contract as long as they were within the framework of the draft agreement.

The final version of Ovitz's employment agreement differed significantly from the drafts summarized to the compensation committee. The employment agreement had a term of five years. Ovitz was to receive a salary of $1 million per year, a potential bonus each year from $0 to $10 million, and a series of stock options (the "A" options) that enabled Ovitz to purchase three million shares of Disney stock at the October 16, 1995 exercise price. The options were to vest at one million per year for three years beginning September 30, 1998. At the end of the contract term, if Disney entered into a new contract with Ovitz, he was entitled to the "B" options, an additional two million shares. There was no requirement, however, that Disney enter into a new contract with Ovitz.

Should a non-fault termination occur, however, the terms of the final version of the employment agreement appeared to be even more generous. Under a non-fault termination, Ovitz was to receive his salary for the remainder of the contract, discounted at a risk-free rate keyed to Disney's borrowing costs. He was

Non-Fault termination conditions

also to receive a $7.5 million bonus for each year remaining on his contract, discounted at the same risk-free rate, even though no set bonus amount was guaranteed in the contract. Additionally, all of his "A" stock options were to vest immediately, instead of waiting for the final three years of his contract for them to vest. The final benefit of the non-fault termination was a lump sum "termination payment" of $10 million. The termination payment was equal to the payment Ovitz would receive should he complete his full five-year term with Disney, but not receive an offer for a new contract. Graef Crystal opined in the January 13, 1997, edition of California Law Business that "the contract was most valuable to Ovitz the sooner he left Disney."

Ovitz began serving as president of Disney on October 1, 1995, and became a Disney director in January 1996. Ovitz's tenure as Disney's president proved unsuccessful. Ovitz was not a good second-in-command, and he and Eisner were both aware of that fact. Instead of working to learn his duties as Disney's president, Ovitz began seeking alternative employment. He consulted Eisner to ensure that no action would be taken against him by Disney if he sought employment elsewhere. Eisner agreed that the best thing for Disney, Eisner, and Ovitz was for Ovitz to gain employment elsewhere.

Eisner agreed to help Ovitz depart Disney without sacrificing any of his benefits. Eisner and Ovitz worked together as close personal friends to have Ovitz receive a non-fault termination. Eisner, Litvack, and Ovitz met at Eisner's apartment on December 11, 1996, to finalize Ovitz's non-fault termination. Neither the Board of Directors nor the compensation committee had been consulted or given their approval for a non-fault termination. In addition, no record exists of any action by the Board once the non-fault termination became public on December 12, 1996.

No documents or board minutes currently exist showing an affirmative decision by the New Board or any of its committees to grant Ovitz a non-fault termination. New Board was already aware that Eisner was granting the non-fault termination as of December 12, 1996, the day it became public. No record of any action by the Board affirming or questioning that decision by Eisner either before or after that date has been produced. There are also no records showing that alternatives to a non-fault termination were ever evaluated by the New Board or by any of its committees.

When the plaintiff alleges a derivative claim, demand must be made on the board or excused based upon futility. To determine whether demand would be futile, the Court must determine whether the particular facts, as alleged, create a reason to doubt that: "(1) the directors are disinterested and independent" or "(2) the challenged transaction was otherwise the product of a valid exercise of business judgment." *Aronson v. Lewis,* 473 A.2d 805, 814 (Del.1984).

The primary issue before the Court is whether plaintiffs' new complaint survives the Rule 23.1 motion to dismiss under the second prong of Aronson v. Lewis. In order for demand to be excused under the second prong of Aronson, plaintiffs must allege particularized facts that raise doubt about whether the challenged transaction is entitled to the protection of the business judgment rule.

Plaintiffs may rebut the presumption that the board's decision is entitled to deference by raising a reason to doubt whether the board's action was taken on an informed basis or whether the directors honestly and in good faith believed that the action was in the best interests of the corporation. Thus, plaintiffs must plead particularized facts sufficient to raise (1) a reason to doubt that the action was taken honestly and in good faith or (2) a reason to doubt that the board was adequately informed in making the decision.

Defendants contend that the new complaint cannot be read reasonably to allege any fiduciary duty violation other than, at most, a breach of the directors' duty of due care. They further assert that even if the complaint states a breach of the directors' duty of care, Disney's charter provision, based on 8 Del. C. § 102(b)(7), would apply and the individual directors would be protected from personal damages liability for any breach of their duty of care. A § 102(b)(7) provision in a corporation's charter does not "eliminate or limit the liability of a director: (i)[f]or any breach of the director's duty of loyalty to the corporation or its stockholders; (ii) for acts or omissions not in good faith or which involve intentional misconduct or a knowing violation of the law; (iii) under § 174 of this title; or (iv) for any transaction from which the director derived an improper personal benefit." A fair reading of the new complaint, in my opinion, gives rise to a reason to doubt whether the board's actions were taken honestly and in good faith, as required under the second prong of Aronson. Since acts or omissions not undertaken honestly and in good faith, or which involve intentional misconduct, do not fall within the protective ambit of § 102(b)(7), I cannot dismiss the complaint based on the exculpatory Disney charter provision.

Defendants also argue that Ovitz's employment agreement was a reasonable exercise of business judgment. They argue that Ovitz's previous position as head of CAA required a large compensation package to entice him to become Disney's president. The Court is appropriately hesitant to second guess the business judgment of a disinterested and independent board of directors. As alleged in the new complaint, however, the facts belie any assertion that the Board exercised any business judgment or made any good faith attempt to fulfill the fiduciary duties they owed to Disney and its shareholders.

From the outset, Ovitz performed poorly as Disney's president. In short order, Ovitz wanted out, and, once again, his good friend Eisner came to the rescue, agreeing to Ovitz's request for a non-fault termination. Disney's board, however, was allegedly never consulted in this process. No board committee was ever consulted, nor were any experts consulted. Eisner and Litvack alone granted Ovitz's non-fault termination, which became public on December 12, 1996.

The new complaint, fairly read, also charges the Board with a similar ostrich-like approach regarding Ovitz's non-fault termination. On December 27, 1996, when Eisner and Litvack accelerated Ovitz's non-fault termination by over a month, with a payout of more than $38 million in cash, together with the three million "A" stock options, the board again failed to do anything. Instead, it appears from the new complaint that the Board played no role in Eisner's agreement to award Ovitz more than $38 million in cash and the three million "A" stock options, all for leaving a job that Ovitz had allegedly proven incapable of performing.

These facts, if true, do more than portray directors who, in a negligent or grossly negligent manner, merely failed to inform themselves or to deliberate adequately about an issue of material importance to their corporation. Instead, the facts alleged in the new complaint suggest that the defendant directors consciously and intentionally disregarded their responsibilities, adopting a "we don't care about the risks" attitude concerning a material corporate decision. Knowing or deliberate indifference by a director to his or her duty to act faithfully and with appropriate care is conduct, in my opinion, that may not have been taken honestly and in good faith to advance the best interests of the company. Put differently, all of the alleged facts, if true, imply that the defendant directors knew that they were making material decisions without adequate information and without adequate deliberation, and that they simply did not care if the decisions caused the corporation and its stockholders to suffer injury or loss. Viewed in this light, plaintiffs' new complaint sufficiently alleges a breach of the directors' obligation to act honestly and in good faith in the corporation's best interests for a Court to conclude, if the facts are true, that the defendant directors' conduct fell outside the protection of the business judgment rule.

Defendant Ovitz contends that the action against him should be dismissed because he owed no fiduciary duty not to seek the best possible employment agreement for himself. Ovitz did have the right to seek the best employment agreement possible for himself. Nevertheless, once Ovitz became a fiduciary of Disney on October 1, 1995, according to the new complaint, he also had a duty to negotiate honestly and in good faith so as not to advantage himself at the expense of the Disney shareholders. He arguably failed to fulfill that duty, according to the facts alleged in the new complaint.

The new complaint arguably charges that Ovitz engaged in a carefully orchestrated, self-serving process controlled directly by his close friend Eisner, all designed to provide Ovitz with enormous financial benefits. The facts, as alleged in the new complaint, belie an adversarial, arms-length negotiation process between Ovitz and the Walt Disney Company. Instead, the alleged facts, if true, would support an inference that Ovitz may have breached his fiduciary duties by engaging in a self-interested transaction in negotiating his employment agreement directly with his personal friend Eisner.

Although the strategy was economically injurious and a public relations disaster for Disney, the Ovitz/Eisner exit strategy allegedly was designed principally to protect their personal reputations, while assuring Ovitz a huge personal payoff after barely a year of mediocre to poor job performance. These allegations, if ultimately found to be true, would suggest a faithless fiduciary who obtained extraordinary personal financial benefits at the expense of the constituency for whom he was obliged to act honestly and in good faith.

It is of course true that after-the-fact litigation is a most imperfect device to evaluate corporate business decisions, as the limits of human competence necessarily impede judicial review. But our corporation law's theoretical justification for disregarding honest errors simply does not apply to intentional misconduct or to egregious process failures that implicate the foundational directoral obligation to act honestly and in good faith to advance corporate interests. Because the facts alleged here, if true, portray directors consciously indifferent to a material issue facing the corporation, the law must be strong enough to intervene against abuse of trust. Accordingly, all three of plaintiffs' claims for relief concerning fiduciary duty breaches and waste survive defendants' motions to dismiss.

The practical effect of this ruling is that defendants must answer the new complaint and plaintiffs may proceed to take appropriate discovery on the merits of their claims. To that end, a case scheduling order has been entered that will promptly bring this matter before the Court on a fully developed factual record.

Holding

IT IS SO ORDERED.

Daily Pay Rate of $350,000

Ovitz's severance package totaled $140 million, which amounted to a daily pay rate of over $350,000 for the time he spent at Disney. The case finally came to an end in 2006 when the Delaware Supreme Court upheld the trial court's decision in *In re the Walt Disney Company Derivative Litigation*, 906 A.2d 27 (Del. 2006). The Delaware Supreme Court carefully evaluated all the key facts, most of which were uncontroverted, in concluding that the Disney directors had not breached their duties of due care and good faith by approving the company's employment agreement with Ovitz and going along with the no-fault termination that yielded Ovitz the enormous payoff. The court took notice of the fact that the compensation committee must have known and expected that Ovitz would be provided with an exceptionally lucrative package and generous termination protections in order to entice him away from his dominant leadership position at Hollywood's premier talent agency.

MCPADDEN v. SIDHU
964 A.2d 1262 (Del.Ch. 2008)

CHANDLER, Chancellor.

Though what must be shown for bad faith conduct has not yet been completely defined, it is quite clearly established that gross negligence, alone, cannot constitute bad faith. Thus, a board of directors may act "badly" without acting in bad faith. This sometimes fine distinction between a breach of care (through gross negligence) and a breach of loyalty (through bad faith) is one illustrated by the actions of the board in this case.

Gross Negligence None

In June 2005, the board of directors of i2 Technologies, Inc. ("i2" or the "Company") approved the sale of i2's wholly owned subsidiary, Trade Services Corporation ("TSC"), to a management team led by then-TSC vice president, defendant Anthony Dubreville ("Dubreville") for $3 million. Two years later, after first rejecting an offer of $18.5 million as too low just six months after the sale, Dubreville sold TSC to another company for over $25 million. These transactions engendered this lawsuit and the motions to dismiss presently before me. Plaintiff alleges that the Company's directors caused the Company to sell

TSC to Dubreville's team for a price that the directors knew to be a mere fraction of TSC's fair market value.

Nominal defendant i2, a Delaware corporation headquartered in Dallas, Texas, sells supply-chain management software and related consulting services. i2's charter includes an exculpatory provision, which protects i2's directors from liability to the fullest extent under Delaware law. The Company operated a division known as the Content and Data Services Division ("CDSD"), which included both TSC and another subdivision known as CDS. TSC occupied a niche market unrelated to i2's main line of business.

Defendants Sanjiv S. Sidhu ("Sidhu"), Stephen Bradley ("Bradley"), Harvey B. Cash ("Cash"), Richard L. Clemmer ("Clemmer"), Michael E. McGrath ("McGrath"), Lloyd G. Waterhouse ("Waterhouse"), Jackson L. Wilson, Jr. ("Wilson"), and Robert L. Crandall ("Crandall" and, together, the "Director Defendants") were or still are members of the i2 board of directors. All Director Defendants approved the 2005 sale of TSC. Of these directors, defendants Cash, Crandall, Clemmer, Bradley, Waterhouse, and Wilson were members of the board's special committee that was charged with reviewing the Sonenshine fairness opinion. Defendant Dubreville was not a director of i2; he was vice president of CDCS, which, as described above, was a division of i2 that included TSC.

The gravamen of plaintiff's complaint is that i2's directors caused the Company to sell TSC, its wholly owned subsidiary, to members of TSC's management in bad faith for a price that defendants knew was a fraction of TSC's fair market value.

In early 2001, i2 acquired TSC and a related company for $100 million. By that time, Dubreville was CEO and president of TSC. After i2's acquisition of TSC, Dubreville remained in charge of TSC. By late 2004 or early 2005, i2 decided to sell TSC after determining that TSC was a non-core business that should be divested. In January 2003, VIS/ME sent a letter to Sidhu and i2's CFO stating that VIS/ME would be willing to pay up to $25 million for TSC. The i2 board discussed TSC at a meeting held a few days later. Director defendants Sidhu, Cash, and Crandall attended the meeting. In late 2004, Dubreville contacted VIS/ME's president and CEO to discuss Beutler's January 2003 letter.

In December 2004, the i2 board decided to sell TSC. An offering memorandum was prepared in January 2005 to convey information about TSC to prospective purchasers. At a board meeting on February 1, 2005, i2's investment banker, Sonenshine Partners ("Sonenshine"), gave a presentation that included various options for the sale of TSC. One of these options was to sell TSC for $4.2 million to TSC employees. At this meeting, the board was also apprised of the plan to let Dubreville conduct the sale process of TSC. By this time, Dubreville was aware that VIS/ME earlier had expressed interest in buying TSC for up to $25 million and Dubreville had already discussed with i2 the possibility of leading a management buyout of TSC. Sidhu, Clemmer, Cash, Crandall, and McGrath discussed the idea of a management buyout at the February 1, 2005 board meeting. Nevertheless, no business broker or investment banker was hired;

the board charged Dubreville with finding a buyer for TSC.

Plaintiff recounts Dubreville's limited efforts to market TSC. Dubreville did not solicit interest from any of TSC's direct competitors, which were its most likely buyers. In particular, Dubreville did not solicit interest from VIS/ME though he and at least three directors (Sidhu, Cash, and Crandall) knew VIS/ME had indicated a strong interest in buying TSC and had offered as much as $25 million for TSC in 2003.

While the search for a buyer for TSC was ongoing, on March 9, 2005, the board again discussed Dubreville's proposal to lead a management buyout of TSC. By this point, Dubreville had solicited only two bids for TSC. The process Dubreville employed ultimately produced three offers for TSC. First, an electronic parts distributor, HIS, offered $12 million for the entire CDSD division, of which $4.3 million was allocated to TSC. Because i2 did not want to bundle these two businesses for sale, it rejected IHS's offer. Ultimately, in 2006 IHS purchased CDS (the other CDSD subdivision) for approximately $29 million. A second offer was from an entity named Sunrise Ventures, the principal of which was Dubreville's former boss at TSC and his partner in a printing company. Sunrise Ventures offered $1.8 million for TSC, which plaintiff alleges was a "lowball" offer designed to make the Dubreville-led group's offer of $3 million appear generous. The third offer was from the Dubreville-led group, Trade Service Holdings, LLC ("TSH"), of which Dubreville was a principal owner. On March 18, 2005, TSH offered to buy TSC for $2 million in cash and $1 million in software licensing agreements, with TSH keeping all outstanding receivables and repayments. The offer also contemplated that TSC would sublease half its existing office space, that i2 would pay for TSC's relocation within its building, and that i2 would bear the costs of the office space that TSC would not use.

On April 18, 2005, the board met to discuss the proposed management buyout of TSC and the other two offers for TSC that had been received. As detailed in the Sonenshine Document, Sonenshine confirmed to the board that its preliminary valuation of TSC was around $3 to $7 million using the February management projections; and $6 to $10.8 million using the January projections. The board then authorized management to move forward with discussions to sell TSC to TSH (the company partially owned by Dubreville), even though the board knew that Dubreville had been responsible for conducting the sale of TSC and that TSC had not been offered to competitors. In addition, plaintiff contends that neither the board nor the special committee negotiated with Dubreville before the letter of intent was signed on April 22, 2005.

Sonenshine made a preliminary presentation to the special committee on June 21, 2005, and then an advisory presentation to the special committee and the board on June 23, 2005. On June 28, 2005, the special committee and the board met and approved the transaction. Plaintiff alleges that the fairness opinion that the board relied upon was "on its face grossly and blatantly unreliable" for a litany of reasons. The fairness opinion also failed to include TSC's competitors on the list of "potential suitors" and omitted the fees paid to TSC by VIS/ME as part of the litigation settlement.

In sum, the effect of these numerous alleged deficiencies is that the fairness opinion, because it was based on financial information, including projections and financial statements, provided or prepared by the buyers, favored the interests of Dubreville and TSH and produced a valuation that supported a sale at a price exceedingly favorable to the buyers. Because of the unreliability of the fairness opinion, plaintiff contends, the special committee and the board could not have relied in good faith on that opinion in its approval of the sale of TSC to Dubreville at an offer that represented 0.2X sales.

In the fall of 2005, TSH offered to sell TSC to VIS/ME. In December 2005, VIS/ME offered $18.5 million. TSH, through Dubreville, rejected this offer as too low and later, in 2007, sold TSC for more than $25 million. Plaintiff contends that no significant changes to TSC's business occurred during that period of time to justify the price difference and instead attributes it to the use of accurate financial statements, which supported a higher valuation of TSC.

In considering this motion to dismiss, the Court must assume the truthfulness of all well-pleaded facts in the complaint and is required to make all reasonable inferences that logically flow from the face of the complaint in favor of the plaintiff. Benefiting from such reasonable inferences, the complaint will then be dismissed for failure to state a claim only if it appears with reasonable certainty that, under any set of facts that could be proven to support the claims asserted, the plaintiff would not be entitled to the relief sought.

In evaluating the decisions of boards, the courts of this State have consistently noted the limited nature of such judicial determinations of due care: "Due care in the decision making context is *process* due care only." *Brehm v. Eisner,* 746 A.2d 244, 254 (Del.2000). Where, as here, the board has retained an expert to assist the board in its decision making process, the Delaware Supreme Court has specified that a complaint will survive a motion to dismiss in a due care case if it alleges particularized facts that, if proven, would show that "the subject matter ... that was material and reasonably available was so obvious that the board's failure to consider it was grossly negligent regardless of the expert's advice or lack of advice." Id. At 262. Contrary to defendants' cursory treatment of this argument, I conclude that the complaint does plead particularized facts demonstrating that material and reasonably available information was not considered by the board and that such lack of consideration constituted gross negligence, irrespective of any reliance on the Sonenshine fairness opinion.

The challenged transaction at issue – the sale of TSC to Dubreville's group – is analytically a series of discrete board actions. Plaintiff has sufficiently alleged facts to create a reasonable doubt that they, together, cannot be the product of a valid exercise of the board's business judgment. The board's first step in the series of actions culminating in the sale of TSC to Dubreville was also its most egregious: tasking Dubreville with the sale process of TSC when the board knew that Dubreville was interested in purchasing TSC. Certainly Dubreville's interest as a potential purchaser was material to the board's decision in determining to whom to assign the task of soliciting bids and offers for TSC.

Despite having tasked a potential purchaser of TSC with its sale, the board appears to have engaged in little to no oversight of that sale process, providing no check on Dubreville's half-hearted (or, worse, intentionally misdirected) efforts in soliciting bids for TSC. Dubreville's limited attempts to find a buyer for TSC did not include contacting the most obvious potential buyers: TSC's direct competitors, particularly a competitor that had previously offered as much as $25 million for TSC in 2003. Perhaps unsurprisingly, Dubreville's group emerged as the highest bidder for TSC from the sale process.

The board's actions are quite puzzling. In making its decisions, the board had no shortage of information that was both material – because it affected the process and ultimate result of the sale – and reasonably available (or, even, actually known as evidenced by the discussions at the board meetings): Dubreville's interest in leading a management buyout of TSC; Dubreville's limited efforts in soliciting offers for TSC, including his failure to contact TSC competitors, including one he knew had previously expressed concrete interest in purchasing TSC; the circumstances under which the January and February projections were produced; the use of those projections in Sonenshine's preliminary valuations of TSC; and that TSH was a group led by Dubreville. That the board would want to consider this information seems, to me, so obvious that it is equally obvious that the Directors Defendants' failure to do so was grossly negligent.

Though plaintiff has demonstrated gross negligence, plaintiff fails to state a claim against the Director Defendants, who have the benefit of a section 102(b)(7) exculpatory provision in the i2 certificate, because plaintiff has not adequately alleged that the Director Defendants acted in bad faith. In contrast, however, plaintiff has stated a claim for both breach of fiduciary duty and unjust enrichment as to Dubreville. Dubreville, though he, as an officer, owes the same duties to the Company as the Director Defendants, does not benefit from the same protections as the Director Defendants because the section 102(b)(7) provision operates to exculpate only directors, not officers.

As authorized by Section 102(b)(7),FN27 i2's certificate of incorporation contains an exculpatory provision, limiting the personal liability of directors for certain conduct. Certain conduct, however, cannot be exculpated, including bad faith actions. Gross negligence, in contrast, is exculpated because such conduct breaches the duty of care. Traditionally, "[i]n the duty of care context gross negligence has been defined as 'reckless indifference to or a deliberate disregard of the whole body of stockholders or actions which are without the bounds of reason.' " *Benihana of Tokyo, Inc. v. Benihana, Inc.*, 891 A.2d 150, 192 (Del.2005). Recently, however, the Supreme Court has modified Delaware's understanding of the definition of gross negligence in the context of fiduciary duty. In analyzing "three different categories of fiduciary behavior [that] are candidates for the 'bad faith' pejorative label," the Court made quite clear that gross negligence cannot be such an example of bad faith conduct: "[t]here is no basis in policy, precedent or common sense that would justify dismantling the distinction between gross negligence and bad faith." *In re Walt Disney Co. Derivative Litig.*, 906 A.2d at 64–65. Instead, the Court concluded that conduct motivated by subjective bad intent and that resulting from gross negligence are at opposite ends of the spectrum. The Court then considered a third category of conduct: the intentional dereliction of duty or the conscious disregard for one's responsibilities. The Court determined that such misconduct must be treated as a non-exculpable, non-indemnifiable violation of the fiduciary duty to act in good faith, a duty that the Court later confirmed was squarely within the duty of loyalty. Thus, from the sphere of actions that was once classified as grossly negligent conduct that gives rise to a violation of the duty of care, the Court has carved out one specific type of conduct – the intentional dereliction of duty or the conscious disregard for one's responsibilities – and redefined it as bad faith conduct, which results in a breach of the duty of loyalty. Therefore, Delaware's current understanding of gross negligence is conduct that constitutes reckless indifference or actions that are without the bounds of reason.

The conduct of the Director Defendants here fits precisely within this revised understanding of gross negligence. For the reasons explained above, the Director Defendants' actions, beginning with placing Dubreville in charge of the sale process of TSC and continuing through their failure to act in any way so as to ensure that the sale process employed was thorough and complete, are properly characterized as either recklessly indifferent or unreasonable. Plaintiff has not, however, sufficiently alleged that the Director Defendants acted in bad faith through a conscious disregard for their duties. Instead, plaintiff has ably pleaded that the Director Defendants quite clearly were not careful enough in the discharge of their duties – that is, they acted with gross negligence or else reckless indifference. Because such conduct breaches the Director Defendants' duty of care, this violation is exculpated by the Section 102(b)(7) provision in the Company's charter and therefore the Director Defendants' motion to dismiss for failure to state a claim must be granted.

As against Dubreville, however, the claim for breach of fiduciary duty may, without a doubt, proceed. Though an officer owes to the corporation identical fiduciary duties of care and loyalty as owed by directors, an officer does not benefit from the protections of a Section 102(b)(7) exculpatory provision, which are only available to directors. Thus, so long as plaintiff has alleged a violation of care or loyalty, the complaint proceeds against Dubreville. Here, plaintiff has more than sufficiently alleged a breach of fiduciary duty and defendants have done nothing to meet their burden of demonstrating with reasonable certainty that, under any set of facts that could be proven to support his claim for breach of fiduciary duty, plaintiff would not be entitled to the relief sought. I have no difficulty in concluding, based on plaintiff's allegations of wrongdoing by Dubreville and defendants' wholly inadequate arguments, which explicitly concede that the complaint states a claim, that the motion to dismiss Count 1 (breach of fiduciary duty) as to Dubreville must be denied.

Though this board acted "badly" – with gross negligence – this board did not act in bad faith. Therefore, with the benefit of the protections of the Company's exculpatory provision, the motion to dismiss Count 1 (breach of fiduciary duty) pursuant to Rule 12(b)(6) is granted as to the Director Defendants. Defendants' Rule 12(b)(6) motion is, however, flatly denied as to Dubreville as to Count 1. IT IS SO ORDERED.

CASE PROBLEM 10-1

Brand Promotion Inc. ("Brand") is in the business of offering specialized product rollout and event marketing services to large national and multinational companies who sell their products through dealer-based organizations. Brand's revenues come from fees and profits that it generates by selling branded merchandise to each client's dealer network pursuant to a licensing agreement.

The president, CEO and driving force behind Brand is Larry Walker, age 68. Larry and Jason Moro founded Brand 41 years ago as a tiny company that made plastic nametags. Moro died six years ago, and his Brand stock passed to his five children (the "Moro Clan") in equal shares.

Larry and the Moro Clan each own 30 percent of Brand's outstanding common stock. Linda Wayne ("Linda"), Brand's chief operating officer, Sam Duke ("Sam"), Brand's vice president of sales, and Clint Wright ("Clint"), Brand's vice president of product development, each own five percent of Brand's common stock. Eight investors own the remaining 25 percent of the outstanding Brand stock in roughly equal shares. Except for the Moro Clan, all the shareholders are unrelated. Brand has consistently paid an annual dividend to its shareholders. Larry often reminds the Moro Clan and other shareholders that the big payday will come when the economy picks up steam and Larry decides to cash in and sell Brand to a large advertising agency that wants Brand's product merchandising services and unique access to its client base.

Brand has seven members on its board of directors: Larry, Linda, Sam, Clint, Roger Duke, Walt Lake, and Jim Smith. Roger, a long-time friend of Larry, is an engineering professor at the local university. Walt is the owner of a local printing company that has provided printing services to Brand for over 20 years. Jim, a longtime golfing buddy of Larry, retired five years ago after selling a successful sporting goods chain in which Larry owned a minority stock interest. Roger, Walt and Jim are referred to as the "Outsiders," and each is paid an annual fee of $12,000 for his services as a director.

Eighteen months ago an officer of a Brand client introduced Larry to a Hollywood producer. The producer was raising money for an independent, low budget, feature length film entitled "Slingshot." The film was pitched to Larry as a "slam dunk financial success" with a "killer script," a star cast "already attached," and "a director to die for." A $4 million investment would buy Brand a 50 percent interest in the film, a chance to "easily triple" its investment, and the right (at no extra charge) to feature products of Brand's clients throughout the film. Larry saw it as a great opportunity to make "some serious" money, have fun, and offer a powerful, unique value-added service to Brand's best clients. He was sold.

Larry immediately sent a memorandum explaining the "Slingshot" opportunity to Brand's board members, along with a written consent resolution approving the investment. Each member signed and returned the consent resolution. Brand made the investment by tapping an unused bank credit line. Linda, Sam and Clint hated the idea, but didn't dare buck Larry. There was no dialogue among the "Outsiders," but Roger did call Larry to congratulate him on such a smart, strategic move.

Jim now needs some advice. After 18 months, Larry is back asking the board for authority to invest an additional $2 million in Slingshot. In a short memorandum, he explained that cost overruns are common when "a blockbuster is being made" and restated the benefits of the investment. Again, Larry sent a written consent resolution with the edict that "each board member needs to sign and return this document ASAP."

Jim is concerned about the risks of the Slingshot investments and any potential exposure he might have to the shareholders. The Moro Clan scares him because they openly claim that Larry never "played straight" with their dad. Jim wants to know if he, as a director, has any exposure on the first Slingshot investment and how he should deal with this latest demand from Larry. Assume for these purposes that Brand is incorporated in a state that has adopted the Model Business Corporation Act but that Brand's articles of incorporation have never been updated to include a provision authorized by MBCA § 2.02(b)(4).

How would your advice to Jim change as to Brand's original investment and Larry's new request if Brand's articles of incorporation had been amended 10 years ago to include a provision authorized by MBCA § 2.02(b)(4).

2. FAILURE TO GET INFORMED

SMITH v. VAN GORKOM
488 A.2d 858 (Del. 1985)

HORSEY, Justice.

This appeal from the Court of Chancery involves a class action brought by shareholders of the defendant Trans Union Corporation ("Trans Union" or "the Company"), originally seeking rescission of a cash-out merger of Trans Union into the defendant New T Company ("New T"), a wholly-owned subsidiary of the defendant, Marmon Group, Inc. ("Marmon"). Alternate relief in the form of damages is sought against the defendant members of the Board of Directors of Trans Union.

Following trial, the former Chancellor granted judgment for the defendant directors by unreported letter opinion dated July 6, 1982. Judgment was based on two findings: (1) that the Board of Directors had acted in an informed manner so as to be entitled to protection of the business judgment rule in approving the cash-out merger; and (2) that the shareholder vote approving the merger should not be set aside because the stockholders had been "fairly informed" by the Board of Directors before voting thereon. The plaintiffs appeal.

Speaking for the majority of the Court, we conclude that both rulings of the Court of Chancery are clearly erroneous. Therefore, we reverse and direct that judgment be entered in favor of the plaintiffs and against the defendant directors for the fair value of the plaintiffs' stockholdings in Trans Union. It has been stipulated that plaintiffs sue on behalf of a class consisting of 10,537 shareholders (out of a total of 12,844) and that the class owned 12,734,404 out of 13,357,758 shares of Trans Union outstanding.

We hold: (1) that the Board's decision, reached September 20, 1980, to approve the proposed cash-out merger was not the product of an informed business judgment; (2) that the Board's subsequent efforts to amend the Merger Agreement and take other curative action were ineffectual, both legally and factually; and (3) that the Board did not deal with complete candor with the stockholders by failing to disclose all material facts, which they knew or should have known, before securing the stockholders' approval of the merger.

Holding

Trans Union was a publicly-traded, diversified holding company, the principal earnings of which were generated by its railcar leasing business. During the period here involved, the Company had a cash flow of hundreds of millions of dollars annually. However, the Company had difficulty in generating sufficient taxable income to offset increasingly large investment tax credits (ITCs). Beginning in the late 1960's, and continuing through the 1970's, Trans Union pursued a program of acquiring small companies in order to increase available taxable income.

On August 27, 1980, Van Gorkom met with Senior Management of Trans Union. Van Gorkom reported on his desire to find a solution to the tax credit problem more permanent than a continued program of acquisitions. Various alternatives were suggested and discussed preliminarily, including the sale of Trans Union to a company with a large amount of taxable income.

On September 5, at another Senior Management meeting which Van Gorkom attended, Romans again brought up the idea of a leveraged buy-out as a "possible strategic alternative" to the Company's acquisition program. Romans and Bruce S. Chelberg, President and Chief Operating Officer of Trans Union, had been working on the matter in preparation for the meeting. According to Romans, they did not "come up" with a price for the Company. They merely "ran the numbers" at $50 a share and at $60 a share with the "rough form" of their cash figures at the time. At this meeting, Van Gorkom stated that he would be willing to take $55 per share for his own 75,000 shares.

Van Gorkom decided to meet with Jay A. Pritzker, a well-known corporate takeover specialist and a social acquaintance. Van Gorkom did so without consulting either his Board or any members of Senior Management except one: Carl Peterson, Trans Union's Controller. Telling Peterson that he wanted no other person on his staff to know what he was doing, but without telling him why, Van Gorkom directed Peterson to calculate the feasibility of a leveraged buy-out at an assumed price per share of $55.

secret meeting

Having thus chosen the $55 figure, based solely on the availability of a leveraged buy-out, Van Gorkom multiplied the price per share by the number of shares outstanding to reach a total value of the Company of $690 million. Van Gorkom directed Peterson to determine whether the debt portion of the purchase price could be paid off in five years or less if financed by Trans Union's cash flow as projected in the Five Year Forecast, and by the sale of certain weaker divisions identified in a study done for Trans Union by the Boston Consulting Group ("BCG study"). Peterson reported that, of the purchase price, approximately $50–80 million would remain outstanding after five years. Van

Gorkom was disappointed, but decided to meet with Pritzker nevertheless.

Van Gorkom arranged a meeting with Pritzker at the latter's home on Saturday, September 13, 1980. Van Gorkom reviewed with Pritzker his calculations based upon his proposed price of $55 per share. Although Pritzker mentioned $50 as a more attractive figure, no other price was mentioned.

On Monday, September 15, Pritzker advised Van Gorkom that he was interested in the $55 cash-out merger proposal and requested more information on Trans Union. Van Gorkom agreed to meet privately with Pritzker, accompanied by Peterson, Chelberg, and Michael Carpenter, Trans Union's consultant from the Boston Consulting Group.

On Thursday, September 18, Van Gorkom met again with Pritzker. At that time, Van Gorkom knew that Pritzker intended to make a cash-out merger offer at Van Gorkom's proposed $55 per share. Pritzker instructed his attorney, a merger and acquisition specialist, to begin drafting merger documents. There was no further discussion of the $55 price. However, the number of shares of Trans Union's treasury stock to be offered to Pritzker was negotiated down to one million shares; the price was set at $38—75 cents above the per share price at the close of the market on September 19. At this point, Pritzker insisted that the Trans Union Board act on his merger proposal within the next three days, stating to Van Gorkom: "We have to have a decision by no later than Sunday [evening, September 21] before the opening of the English stock exchange on Monday morning."

On Friday, September 19, Van Gorkom called a special meeting of the Trans Union Board for noon the following day. He also called a meeting of the Company's Senior Management to convene at 11:00 a.m., prior to the meeting of the Board. No one, except Chelberg and Peterson, was told the purpose of the meetings. Van Gorkom did not invite Trans Union's investment banker, Salomon Brothers or its Chicago-based partner, to attend.

Of those present at the Senior Management meeting on September 20, only Chelberg and Peterson had prior knowledge of Pritzker's offer. Van Gorkom disclosed the offer and described its terms, but he furnished no copies of the proposed Merger Agreement. Romans announced that his department had done a second study which showed that, for a leveraged buy-out, the price range for Trans Union stock was between $55 and $65 per share. Van Gorkom neither saw the study nor asked Romans to make it available for the Board meeting.

Ten directors served on the Trans Union Board, five inside (defendants Bonser, O'Boyle, Browder, Chelberg, and Van Gorkom) and five outside (defendants Wallis, Johnson, Lanterman, Morgan and Reneker). All directors were present at the meeting, except O'Boyle who was ill. Of the outside directors, four were corporate chief executive officers and one was the former Dean of the University of Chicago Business School. None was an investment banker or trained financial analyst. All members of the Board were well informed about the Company and its operations as a going concern.

Van Gorkom began the Special Meeting of the Board with a twenty-minute oral presentation. Copies of the proposed Merger Agreement were delivered too late for study before or during the meeting. He reviewed the Company's ITC and depreciation problems and the efforts theretofore made to solve them. He discussed his initial meeting with Pritzker and his motivation in arranging that meeting. Van Gorkom did not disclose to the Board, however, the methodology by which he alone had arrived at the $55 figure, or the fact that he first proposed the $55 price in his negotiations with Pritzker.

Van Gorkom outlined the terms of the Pritzker offer as follows: Pritzker would pay $55 in cash for all outstanding shares of Trans Union stock upon completion of which Trans Union would be merged into New T Company, a subsidiary wholly-owned by Pritzker and formed to implement the merger; for a period of 90 days, Trans Union could receive, but could not actively solicit, competing offers; the offer had to be acted on by the next evening, Sunday, September 21; Trans Union could only furnish to competing bidders published information, and not proprietary information; the offer was subject to Pritzker obtaining the necessary financing by October 10, 1980; if the financing contingency were met or waived by Pritzker, Trans Union was required to sell to Pritzker one million newly-issued shares of Trans Union at $38 per share.

Van Gorkom took the position that putting Trans Union "up for auction" through a 90-day market test would validate a decision by the Board that $55 was a fair price. He told the Board that the "free market will have an opportunity to judge whether $55 is a fair price." Van Gorkom framed the decision before the Board not as whether $55 per share was the highest price that could be obtained, but as whether the $55 price was a fair price that the stockholders should be given the opportunity to accept or reject.

Attorney Brennan advised the members of the Board that they might be sued if they failed to accept the offer and that a fairness opinion was not required as a matter of law. Romans attended the meeting as chief financial officer of the Company. He told the Board that he had not been involved in the negotiations with Pritzker and knew nothing about the merger proposal until the morning of the meeting. Romans told the Board that, in his opinion, $55 was "in the range of a fair price," but "at the beginning of the range."

The Board meeting of September 20 lasted about two hours. Based solely upon Van Gorkom's oral presentation, Chelberg's supporting representations, Romans' oral statement, Brennan's legal advice, and their knowledge of the market history of the Company's stock, the directors approved the proposed Merger Agreement.

The Merger Agreement was executed by Van Gorkom during the evening of September 20 at a formal social event that he hosted for the opening of the Chicago Lyric Opera. Neither he nor any other director read the agreement prior to its signing and delivery to Pritzker.

Salomon Brothers' efforts over a three-month period from October 21 to January 21 produced only one serious suitor for Trans Union—General Electric Credit Corporation ("GE Credit"), a subsidiary of the General Electric Company. However, GE Credit was unwilling to make an offer for Trans Union unless Trans Union first rescinded its Merger Agreement with Pritzker. When Pritzker refused, GE Credit terminated further discussions with Trans Union in early January.

On December 19, this litigation was commenced and, within four weeks, the plaintiffs had deposed eight of the ten directors of Trans Union, including Van Gorkom, Chelberg and Romans, its Chief Financial Officer. On January 21, Management's Proxy Statement for the February 10 shareholder meeting was mailed to Trans Union's stockholders. On January 26, Trans Union's Board met and, after a lengthy meeting, voted to proceed with the Pritzker merger. The Board also approved for mailing, "on or about January 27," a Supplement to its Proxy Statement. The Supplement purportedly set forth all information relevant to the Pritzker Merger Agreement, which had not been divulged in the first Proxy Statement.

On February 10, the stockholders of Trans Union approved the Pritzker merger proposal. Of the outstanding shares, 69.9% were voted in favor of the merger; 7.25% were voted against the merger; and 22.85% were not voted.

We turn to the issue of the application of the business judgment rule to the September 20 meeting of the Board.

The Court of Chancery concluded from the evidence that the Board of Directors' approval of the Pritzker merger proposal fell within the protection of the business judgment rule. The Court found that the Board had given sufficient time and attention to the transaction.

Under Delaware law, the business judgment rule is the offspring of the fundamental principle, codified in 8 Del.C. § 141(a), that the business and affairs of a Delaware corporation are managed by or under its board of directors. *Pogostin v. Rice,* Del.Supr., 480 A.2d 619, 624 (1984); *Aronson v. Lewis,* Del.Supr., 473 A.2d 805, 811 (1984. In carrying out their managerial roles, directors are charged with an unyielding fiduciary duty to the corporation and its shareholders. The determination of whether a business judgment is an informed one turns on whether the directors have informed themselves "prior to making a business decision, of all material information reasonably available to them." *Aronson, supra* at 812.

Here, there were no allegations of fraud, bad faith, or self-dealing, or proof thereof. Hence, it is presumed that the directors reached their business judgment in good faith, and considerations of motive are irrelevant to the issue before us. We think the concept of gross negligence is the proper standard for determining whether a business judgment reached by a board of directors was an informed one. It is against those standards that the conduct of the directors of Trans Union must be tested, as a matter of law and as a matter of fact, regarding their exercise of an informed business judgment in voting to approve the Pritzker merger proposal.

On the record before us, we must conclude that the Board of Directors did not reach an informed business judgment on September 20, 1980 in voting to "sell" the Company for $55 per share pursuant to the Pritzker cash-out merger proposal. The directors (1) did not adequately inform themselves as to Van Gorkom's role in forcing the "sale" of the Company and in establishing the per share purchase price; ②) were uninformed as to the intrinsic value of the Company; and ③) given these circumstances, at a minimum, were grossly negligent in approving the "sale" of the Company upon two hours' consideration, without prior notice, and without the exigency of a crisis or emergency.

As has been noted, the Board based its September 20 decision to approve the cash-out merger primarily on Van Gorkom's representations. None of the directors, other than Van Gorkom and Chelberg, had any prior knowledge that the purpose of the meeting was to propose a cash-out merger of Trans Union. No members of Senior Management were present, other than Chelberg, Romans and Peterson; and the latter two had only learned of the proposed sale an hour earlier. Both general counsel Moore and former general counsel Browder attended the meeting, but were equally uninformed as to the purpose of the meeting and the documents to be acted upon.

[margin note: Directors had no prior knowledge]

Without any documents before them concerning the proposed transaction, the members of the Board were required to rely entirely upon Van Gorkom's 20-minute oral presentation of the proposal. No written summary of the terms of the merger was presented; the directors were given no documentation to support the adequacy of $55 price per share for sale of the Company; and the Board had before it nothing more than Van Gorkom's statement of his understanding of the substance of an agreement which he admittedly had never read, nor which any member of the Board had ever seen.

[margin note: No written docs to make a decision w/]

Under 8 Del.C. § 141(e), "directors are fully protected in relying in good faith on reports made by officers." The term "report" has been liberally construed to include reports of informal personal investigations by corporate officers. However, there is no evidence that any "report," as defined under § 141(e), concerning the Pritzker proposal, was presented to the Board on September 20. Considering all of the surrounding circumstances—hastily calling the meeting without prior notice of its subject matter, the proposed sale of the Company without any prior consideration of the issue or necessity therefor, the urgent time constraints imposed by Pritzker, and the total absence of any documentation whatsoever—the directors were duty bound to make reasonable inquiry of Van Gorkom and Romans, and if they had done so, the inadequacy of that upon which they now claim to have relied would have been apparent.

[margin note: Reliance on a report]

A substantial premium may provide one reason to recommend a merger, but in the absence of other sound valuation information, the fact of a premium alone does not provide an adequate basis upon which to assess the fairness of an offering price.

The record also establishes that the Board accepted without scrutiny Van Gorkom's representation as to the fairness of the $55 price per share for sale of the Company—a subject that the Board had never previously considered. The Board thereby failed to discover that Van Gorkom had suggested the $55 price to Pritzker and, most crucially, that Van Gorkom had arrived at the $55 figure based on calculations designed solely to determine the feasibility of a leveraged buy-out. No questions were raised either as to the tax implications of a cash-out merger or how the price for the one million share option granted Pritzker was calculated.

We do not say that the Board of Directors was not entitled to give some credence to Van Gorkom's representation that $55 was an adequate or fair price. Under § 141(e), the directors were entitled to rely upon their chairman's opinion of value and adequacy, provided that such opinion was reached on a sound basis. Here, the issue is whether the directors informed themselves as to all information that was reasonably available to them. Had they done so, they would have learned of the source and derivation of the $55 price and could not reasonably have relied thereupon in good faith.

None of the directors, Management or outside, were investment bankers or financial analysts. Yet the Board did not consider recessing the meeting until a later hour that day (or requesting an extension of Pritzker's Sunday evening deadline) to give it time to elicit more information as to the sufficiency of the offer, either from inside Management (in particular Romans) or from Trans Union's own investment banker, Salomon Brothers, whose Chicago specialist in merger and acquisitions was known to the Board and familiar with Trans Union's affairs.

Thus, the record compels the conclusion that on September 20 the Board lacked valuation information adequate to reach an informed business judgment as to the fairness of $55 per share for sale of the Company. We conclude that Trans Union's Board was grossly negligent in that it failed to act with informed reasonable deliberation in agreeing to the Pritzker merger proposal on September 20.

A second claim is that counsel advised the Board it would be subject to lawsuits if it rejected the $55 per share offer. It is, of course, a fact of corporate life that today when faced with difficult or sensitive issues, directors often are subject to suit, irrespective of the decisions they make. However, counsel's mere acknowledgement of this circumstance cannot be rationally translated into a justification for a board permitting itself to be stampeded into a patently unadvised act. While suit might result from the rejection of a merger or tender offer, Delaware law makes clear that a board acting within the ambit of the business judgment rule faces no ultimate liability. Thus, we cannot conclude that the mere threat of litigation, acknowledged by counsel, constitutes either legal advice or any valid basis upon which to pursue an uninformed course.

We hold that the Trial Court committed reversible error in applying the business judgment rule in favor of the director defendants in this case.

McNEILLY, Justice, dissenting:

The majority opinion reads like an advocate's closing address to a hostile jury. And I say that not lightly. Throughout the opinion great emphasis is directed only to the negative, with nothing more than lip service granted the positive aspects of this case.

Trans Union's Board of Directors consisted of ten men, five of whom were "inside" directors and five of whom were "outside" directors. The "inside" directors were Van Gorkom, Chelberg, Bonser, William B. Browder, Senior

Vice-President-Law, and Thomas P. O'Boyle, Senior Vice-President-Administration. At the time the merger was proposed the inside five directors had collectively been employed by the Company for 116 years and had 68 years of combined experience as directors. The "outside" directors were A.W. Wallis, William B. Johnson, Joseph B. Lanterman, Graham J. Morgan and Robert W. Reneker. With the exception of Wallis, these were all chief executive officers of Chicago based corporations that were at least as large as Trans Union. The five "outside" directors had 78 years of combined experience as chief executive officers, and 53 years cumulative service as Trans Union directors.

The inside directors wear their badge of expertise in the corporate affairs of Trans Union on their sleeves. But what about the outsiders? Dr. Wallis is or was *math major* an economist and math statistician, a professor of economics at Yale University, dean of the graduate school of business at the University of Chicago, and Chancellor of the University of Rochester. Dr. Wallis had been on the Board of Trans Union since 1962. He also was on the Board of Bausch & Lomb, Kodak, Metropolitan Life Insurance Company, Standard Oil and others.

William B. Johnson is a University of Pennsylvania law graduate, President *vpenn* of Railway Express until 1966, Chairman and Chief Executive of I.C. Industries Holding Company, and member of Trans Union's Board since 1968.

Joseph Lanterman, a Certified Public Accountant, is or was President and *acctant* Chief Executive of American Steel, on the Board of International Harvester, Peoples Energy, Illinois Bell Telephone, Harris Bank and Trust Company, Kemper Insurance Company and a director of Trans Union for four years.

Graham Morgan is a chemist, was Chairman and Chief Executive Officer of *a chemist* U.S. Gypsum, and in the 17 and 18 years prior to the Trans Union transaction had been involved in 31 or 32 corporate takeovers.

Robert Reneker attended University of Chicago and Harvard Business Schools. He was President and Chief Executive of Swift and Company, director of Trans Union since 1971, and member of the Boards of seven other corporations including U.S. Gypsum and the Chicago Tribune.

Directors of this caliber are not ordinarily taken in by a "fast shuffle". I submit they were not taken into this multi-million dollar corporate transaction without being fully informed and aware of the state of the art as it pertained to the entire corporate panorama of Trans Union. True, even directors such as these, with their business acumen, interest and expertise, can go astray. I do not believe that to be the case here. These men knew Trans Union like the back of their hands and were more than well qualified to make on the spot informed business judgments concerning the affairs of Trans Union including a 100% sale of the corporation. Lest we forget, the corporate world of then and now operates on what is so aptly referred to as "the fast track". These men were at the time an integral part of that world, all professional business men, not intellectual figureheads.

The majority of this Court holds that the Board's decision, reached on September 20, 1980, to approve the merger was not the product of an informed business judgment. I disagree.

I have no quarrel with the majority's analysis of the business judgment rule. It is the application of that rule to these facts which is wrong. An overview of the entire record, rather than the limited view of bits and pieces which the majority has exploded like popcorn, convinces me that the directors made an informed business judgment which was buttressed by their test of the market.

Author's Note: The *Van Gorkom* decision was a bombshell. A $23.5 million judgment, rendered in favor of over 12,000 former Trans Union shareholders, was entered against a highly distinguished group of business players for approving a transaction that yielded the aggrieved shareholders a price that was 50 percent higher than the existing market price for their stock. Ultimately, no part of the judgment was actually paid by the defendant directors. Insurance proceeds covered $10 million of the judgment, and the remainder was paid by a party that was not a defendant in the case - the Pritzker Group. The *Van Gorkom* decision was a driving factor in Delaware's adoption, almost immediately following the decision, of Section 102(b)(7), which exculpates directors from personal liability for money damages for most duty of care breaches. The Model Business Corporation Act's counterpart provision is set forth above.

CEDE v. TECHNICOLOR, INC.
634 A.2d 345 (Del. 1994)

HORSEY, Justice:

Plaintiff Cinerama was at all times the owner of 201,200 shares of the common stock of Technicolor, representing 4.405 percent of the total shares outstanding. Cinerama did not tender its stock in the first leg of the MAF acquisition commencing November 4, 1982; and Cinerama dissented from the second stage merger, which was completed on January 24, 1983. In January 1986, Cinerama filed a suit in the Court of Chancery against Technicolor, seven of the nine members of the Technicolor board at the time of the merger, MAF, Macanfor and Ronald O. Perelman ("Perelman"), MAF's Chairman and controlling shareholder. Cinerama's personal liability action encompassed claims for fraud, breach of fiduciary duty and unfair dealing, and included a claim for rescissory damages, among other relief.

We conclude that the trial court has erred as a matter of law in reformulating the business judgment rule's elements for finding director breach of duty of care in the context of an arms-length, third-party transaction lacking evidence of director bad faith or director self-dealing. The Chancellor has erroneously imposed on Cinerama, for purposes of rebutting the rule, a burden of proof of board lack of due care which is unprecedented. We refer to the Chancellor's holding that a shareholder plaintiff such as Cinerama must prove injury resulting from a found board breach of duty of care, to rebut the business judgment presumption. The court has also erred in ruling that the damages recoverable by a wrongfully cashed-out shareholder such as Cinerama for board breach of fiduciary duty are limited to the difference between the fair value of its Technicolor stock, as determined for statutory appraisal purposes as of the date of the merger, and the cash tender offered. On the trial court's presumed findings of board breach of duty of care, we find the business judgment presumption accorded the Technicolor board action of October 29, 1982 to have been rebutted for board lack of due care. Therefore, we reverse and remand the personal liability action with instructions to the trial court to apply the entire fairness standard of review to the merger.

Our starting point is the fundamental principle of Delaware law that the business and affairs of a corporation are managed by or under the direction of its board of directors. 8 Del.C. § 141(a). In exercising these powers, directors are charged with an unyielding fiduciary duty to protect the interests of the corporation and to act in the best interests of its shareholders.

The business judgment rule is an extension of these basic principles. The rule operates to preclude a court from imposing itself unreasonably on the business and affairs of a corporation.

The rule posits a powerful presumption in favor of actions taken by the directors in that a decision made by a loyal and informed board will not be overturned by the courts unless it cannot be "attributed to any rational business purpose." *Sinclair Oil Corp. v. Levien,* Del.Supr., 280 A.2d 717, 720 (1971). To rebut the rule, a shareholder plaintiff assumes the burden of providing evidence that directors, in reaching their challenged decision, breached any one of the triads of their fiduciary duty – good faith, loyalty or due care. If a shareholder plaintiff fails to meet this evidentiary burden, the business judgment rule attaches to protect corporate officers and directors and the decisions they make, and our courts will not second-guess these business judgments. If the rule is rebutted, the burden shifts to the defendant directors, the proponents of the challenged transaction, to prove to the trier of fact the "entire fairness" of the transaction to the shareholder plaintiff..

Under the entire fairness standard of judicial review, the defendant directors must establish to the court's satisfaction that the transaction was the product of both fair dealing and fair price. Further, in the review of a transaction involving a sale of a company, the directors have the burden of establishing that the price offered was the highest value reasonably available under the circumstances.

As defendants concede, this Court has never interposed, for purposes of the rule's rebuttal, a requirement that a shareholder asserting a claim of director breach of duty of care (or duty of loyalty) must prove not only a breach of such duty, but that an injury has resulted from the breach and quantify that injury at that juncture of the case. No Delaware court has, until this case, imposed such a condition upon a shareholder plaintiff. That should not be surprising. The purpose of a trial court's application of an entire fairness standard of review to a challenged business transaction is simply to shift to the defendant directors the burden of demonstrating to the court the entire fairness of the transaction to the shareholder plaintiff. Requiring a plaintiff to show injury through unfair price would effectively relieve director defendants found to have breached their duty of care of establishing the entire fairness of a challenged transaction.

The Chancellor so ruled, notwithstanding finding from the record following trial that whether the Technicolor board exercised due care in approving the merger agreement was not simply a "close question" but one as to which he had "grave doubts." We adopt, as clearly supported by the record, the Chancellor's presumed findings of the directors' failure to reach an informed decision in approving the sale of the company. We disagree with the Chancellor's imposition on Cinerama of an additional burden, for overcoming the rule, of proving that the board's gross negligence caused any monetary loss to Cinerama.

The trial court's presumed findings of fact of board breach of duty of care clearly brought the case under the controlling principles of Van Gorkom and its holding that the defendant board's breach of its duty of care required the transaction to be reviewed for its entire fairness.

To inject a requirement of proof of injury into the rule's formulation for burden shifting purposes is to lose sight of the underlying purpose of the rule. Burden shifting does not create per se liability on the part of the directors; rather, it is a procedure by which Delaware courts of equity determine under what standard of review director liability is to be judged. To require proof of injury as a component of the proof necessary to rebut the business judgment presumption would be to convert the burden shifting process from a threshold determination of the appropriate standard of review to a dispositive adjudication on the merits.

This Court has consistently held that the breach of the duty of care, without any requirement of proof of injury, is sufficient to rebut the business judgment rule. In Van Gorkom, we held that although there was no breach of the duty of loyalty, the failure of the members of the board to adequately inform themselves represented a breach of the duty of care, which of itself was sufficient to rebut the presumption of the business judgment rule. A breach of either the duty of loyalty or the duty of care rebuts the presumption that the directors have acted in the best interests of the shareholders, and requires the directors to prove that the transaction was entirely fair. Cinerama clearly met its burden of proof for the purpose of rebutting the rule's presumption by showing that the defendant directors of Technicolor failed to inform themselves fully concerning all material information reasonably available prior to approving the merger agreement. Our basis for this conclusion is the Chancellor's own findings, enumerated above.

In sum, we find the Court of Chancery to have committed fundamental error in rewriting the Delaware business judgment rule's requirement of due care.

CASE PROBLEM 10-2

Assume the facts of Case Problem 10-1, except that, at the request of all three Outsides, Larry called a meeting of the board to discuss the second investment of $2 million. At the meeting, Slingshot's producer and line producer explained reasons for the cost overruns and delays and the need for additional funding. They claimed that "all could be lost without the added funds," but reiterated that the potential financial yields from the film were still very attractive. They explained that, even with no theater release or a weak release, substantial profits from such a low budget film could be realized through DVD, on-demand, and foreign rights sales. The board members were encouraged to ask questions at the meeting. In response to various questions, the producer opined that the "foreign market for this film's genre is very strong," that the cast wasn't really what they had hoped for (some of the "attached" stars had become "unattached"), and that at least two of Brand's clients had expressed no interest in having their products featured in the film because the script was "too extreme."

The board meeting adjourned with Larry stating "this is a must deal," encouraging members to call him with any questions, and indicating that another meeting would be held in three days to vote on the investment.

Jim seeks your advice on how he should deal with the situation. Based on what he heard at the meeting, Jim is inclined to vote for the additional investment in order to protect Brand's original investment and not disappoint Larry. But, above all, Jim doesn't want any legal exposure to the shareholders. Do these additional facts impact your advice to Jim, assuming Brand's articles of incorporation have not been amended to include a section 2.02(b)(4) provision? How would your advice change if Brand's articles of incorporation had been so amended?

3. POOR OVERSIGHT AND MONITORING

IN RE CAREMARK INTERNATIONAL INC. DERIVATIVE LITIGATION
698 A.2d 959 (Del.Ch. 1996)

ALLEN, Chancellor.

Pending is a motion to approve as fair and reasonable a proposed settlement of a consolidated derivative action on behalf of Caremark International, Inc. ("Caremark"). The suit involves claims that the members of Caremark's board of directors (the "Board") breached their fiduciary duty of care to Caremark in connection with alleged violations by Caremark employees of federal and state laws and regulations applicable to health care providers. As a result of the alleged violations, Caremark was subject to an extensive four year investigation by the United States Department of Health and Human Services and the Department of Justice. In 1994 Caremark was charged in an indictment with multiple felonies. It thereafter entered into a number of agreements with the Department of Justice and others. Those agreements included a plea agreement in which Caremark pleaded guilty to a single felony of mail fraud and agreed to pay civil and criminal fines. Subsequently, Caremark agreed to make reimbursements to various private and public parties. In all, the payments that Caremark has been required to make total approximately $250 million.

This suit was filed in 1994, purporting to seek on behalf of the company recovery of these losses from the individual defendants who constitute the board of directors of Caremark. The parties now propose that it be settled and, after notice to Caremark shareholders, a hearing on the fairness of the proposal was held on August 16, 1996.

Legally, evaluation of the central claim made entails consideration of the legal standard governing a board of directors' obligation to supervise or monitor corporate performance. For the reasons set forth below I conclude, in light of the discovery record, that there is a very low probability that it would be determined that the directors of Caremark breached any duty to appropriately monitor and supervise the enterprise. Indeed the record tends to show an active consideration by Caremark management and its Board of the Caremark structures and programs that ultimately led to the company's indictment and to the large financial losses incurred in the settlement of those claims. It does not tend to show knowing or intentional violation of law.

The complaint charges the director defendants with breach of their duty of attention or care in connection with the on-going operation of the corporation's business. The claim is that the directors allowed a situation to develop and continue which exposed the corporation to enormous legal liability and that in so doing they violated a duty to be active monitors of corporate performance. The complaint thus does not charge either director self-dealing or the more difficult loyalty-type problems arising from cases of suspect director motivation, such as entrenchment or sale of control contexts. The theory here advanced is possibly the most difficult theory in corporation law upon which a plaintiff might hope to win a judgment.

Director liability for a breach of the duty to exercise appropriate attention may, in theory, arise in two distinct contexts. First, such liability may be said to follow *from a board decision* that results in a loss because that decision was ill advised or "negligent". Second, liability to the corporation for a loss may be said to arise from an *unconsidered failure of the board to act* in circumstances in which due attention would, arguably, have prevented the loss. The first class of cases will typically be subject to review under the director-protective business judgment rule, assuming the decision made was the product of *a process* that was *either* deliberately considered in good faith or was otherwise rational. What should be understood, but may not widely be understood by courts or commentators who are not often required to face such questions, is that compliance with a director's duty of care can never appropriately be judicially determined by reference to *the content of the board decision* that leads to a corporate loss, apart from consideration of the good faith *or* rationality of the process employed. That is, whether a judge or jury considering the matter after the fact, believes a decision substantively wrong, or degrees of wrong extending through "stupid" to "egregious" or "irrational", provides no ground for director liability, so long as the court determines that the process employed was either rational or employed in *a good faith* effort to advance corporate interests. To employ a different rule-one that permitted an "objective" evaluation of the decision-would expose directors to substantive second guessing by ill-equipped judges or juries, which would, in the long-run, be injurious to investor interests. Thus, the business judgment rule is process oriented and informed by a deep respect for all *good faith* board decisions.

The second class of cases in which director liability for inattention is theoretically possible entail circumstances in which a loss eventuates not from a decision but, from unconsidered inaction. Most of the decisions that a corporation, acting through its human agents, makes are, of course, not the subject of director attention. As the facts of this case graphically demonstrate, ordinary business decisions that are made by officers and employees deeper in the interior of the organization can, however, vitally affect the welfare of the corporation and its ability to achieve its various strategic and financial goals. Financial and organizational disasters raise the question, what is the board's responsibility with respect to the organization and monitoring of the enterprise to assure that the corporation functions within the law to achieve its purposes?

Modernly this question has been given special importance by an increasing tendency, especially under federal law, to employ the criminal law to assure corporate compliance with external legal requirements, including environmental, financial, employee and product safety as well as assorted other health and safety regulations.

In 1963, the Delaware Supreme Court in *Graham v. Allis-Chalmers Mfg. Co.,* Del.Supr., 41 Del.Ch. 78, 188 A.2d 125 (1963), addressed the question of potential liability of board members for losses experienced by the corporation as a result of the corporation having violated the anti-trust laws of the United States. In notably colorful terms, the court stated that "absent cause for suspicion there is no duty upon the directors to install and operate a corporate system of espionage to ferret out wrongdoing which they have no reason to suspect exists." The Court found that there were no grounds for suspicion in that case and, thus, concluded that the directors were blamelessly unaware of the conduct leading to the corporate liability.

How does one generalize this holding today? Can it be said today that, absent some ground giving rise to suspicion of violation of law, that corporate directors have no duty to assure that a corporate information gathering and reporting systems exists which represents a good faith attempt to provide senior management and the Board with information respecting material acts, events or conditions within the corporation, including compliance with applicable statutes and regulations? I certainly do not believe so.

A broader interpretation of *Graham v. Allis-Chalmers*-that it means that a corporate board has no responsibility to assure that appropriate information and reporting systems are established by management-would not be accepted by the Delaware Supreme Court in 1996, in my opinion.

It would be a mistake to conclude that our Supreme Court's statement in *Graham* concerning "espionage" means that corporate boards may satisfy their obligation to be reasonably informed concerning the corporation, without assuring themselves that information and reporting systems exist in the organization that are reasonably designed to provide to senior management and to the board itself timely, accurate information sufficient to allow management and the board, each within its scope, to reach informed judgments concerning both the corporation's compliance with law and its business performance.

Obviously the level of detail that is appropriate for such an information system is a question of business judgment. And obviously too, no rationally designed information and reporting system will remove the possibility that the corporation will violate laws or regulations, or that senior officers or directors may nevertheless sometimes be misled or otherwise fail reasonably to detect acts material to the corporation's compliance with the law. But it is important that the board exercise a good faith judgment that the corporation's information and reporting system is in concept and design adequate to assure the board that appropriate information will come to its attention in a timely manner as a matter of ordinary operations, so that it may satisfy its responsibility.

Thus, I am of the view that a director's obligation includes a duty to attempt in good faith to assure that a corporate information and reporting system, which the board concludes is adequate, exists, and that failure to do so under some circumstances may, in theory at least, render a director liable for losses caused by non-compliance with applicable legal standards.

In order to show that the Caremark directors breached their duty of care by failing adequately to control Caremark's employees, plaintiffs would have to show either (1) that the directors knew or (2) should have known that violations of law were occurring and, in either event, (3) that the directors took no steps in a good faith effort to prevent or remedy that situation, and (4) that such failure proximately resulted in the losses complained of.

This case presents no occasion to apply a principle to the effect that knowingly causing the corporation to violate a criminal statute constitutes a breach of a director's fiduciary duty. It is not clear that the Board knew the detail found, for example, in the indictments arising from the Company's payments. But, of course, the duty to act in good faith to be informed cannot be thought to require directors to possess detailed information about all aspects of the operation of the enterprise. Such a requirement would simple be inconsistent with the scale and scope of efficient organization size in this technological age.

Since it does appears that the Board was to some extent unaware of the activities that led to liability, I turn to a consideration of the other potential avenue to director liability that the pleadings take: director inattention or "negligence". Generally where a claim of directorial liability for corporate loss is predicated upon ignorance of liability creating activities within the corporation, in my opinion only a sustained or systematic failure of the board to exercise oversight-such as an utter failure to attempt to assure a reasonable information and reporting system exists-will establish the lack of good faith that is a necessary condition to liability. Such a test of liability-lack of good faith as evidenced by sustained or systematic failure of a director to exercise reasonable oversight-is quite high. But, a demanding test of liability in the oversight context is probably beneficial to corporate shareholders as a class, as it is in the board decision context, since it makes board service by qualified persons more likely, while continuing to act as a stimulus to *good faith performance of duty* by such directors.

Here the record supplies essentially no evidence that the director defendants were guilty of a sustained failure to exercise their oversight function. The liability that eventuated in this instance was huge. But the fact that it resulted from a violation of criminal law alone does not create a breach of fiduciary duty by directors. The record at this stage does not support the conclusion that the defendants either lacked good faith in the exercise of their monitoring responsibilities or conscientiously permitted a known violation of law by the corporation to occur. The claims asserted against them must be viewed at this stage as extremely weak.

The proposed settlement provides very modest benefits. Given the weakness of the plaintiffs' claims, the proposed settlement appears to be an adequate, reasonable, and beneficial outcome for all of the parties. Thus, the proposed settlement will be approved.

STONE v. RITTER
911 A.2d 362 (Del. 2006)

HOLLAND, Justice:

This is an appeal from a final judgment of the Court of Chancery dismissing a derivative complaint against fifteen present and former directors of AmSouth Bancorporation ("AmSouth"), a Delaware corporation. The plaintiffs-appellants, William and Sandra Stone, are AmSouth shareholders and filed their derivative complaint without making a pre-suit demand on AmSouth's board of directors (the "Board"). The Court of Chancery held that the plaintiffs had failed to adequately plead that such a demand would have been futile.

The Court of Chancery characterized the allegations in the derivative complaint as a "classic Caremark claim," a claim that derives its name from In re Caremark Int'l Deriv. Litig. In Caremark, the Court of Chancery recognized that: "[g]enerally where a claim of directorial liability for corporate loss is predicated upon ignorance of liability creating activities within the corporation ... only a sustained or systematic failure of the board to exercise oversight—such as an utter failure to attempt to assure a reasonable information and reporting system exists-will establish the lack of good faith that is a necessary condition to liability."

In this appeal, the plaintiffs acknowledge that the directors neither "knew [n]or should have known that violations of law were occurring," i.e., that there were no "red flags" before the directors. Nevertheless, the plaintiffs argue that the Court of Chancery erred by dismissing the derivative complaint which alleged that "the defendants had utterly failed to implement any sort of statutorily required monitoring, reporting or information controls that would have enabled them to learn of problems requiring their attention."

During the relevant period, AmSouth's wholly-owned subsidiary, AmSouth Bank, operated about 600 commercial banking branches in six states throughout the southeastern United States and employed more than 11,600 people.

In 2004, AmSouth and AmSouth Bank paid $40 million in fines and $10 million in civil penalties to resolve government and regulatory investigations pertaining principally to the failure by bank employees to file "Suspicious Activity Reports" ("SARs"), as required by the federal Bank Secrecy Act ("BSA") and various anti-money-laundering ("AML") regulations.

The government investigations arose originally from an unlawful "Ponzi" scheme operated by Louis D. Hamric, II and Victor G. Nance. In August 2000, Hamric, then a licensed attorney, and Nance, then a registered investment advisor with Mutual of New York, contacted an AmSouth branch bank in Tennessee to arrange for custodial trust accounts to be created for "investors" in a "business venture." That venture (Hamric and Nance represented) involved the construction of medical clinics overseas. In reality, Nance had convinced more than forty of his clients to invest in promissory notes bearing high rates of return, by misrepresenting the nature and the risk of that investment. Relying on similar misrepresentations by Hamric and Nance, the AmSouth branch employees in Tennessee agreed to provide custodial accounts for the investors and to distribute monthly interest payments to each account upon receipt of a check from Hamric and instructions from Nance.

The Hamric–Nance scheme was discovered in March 2002, when the investors did not receive their monthly interest payments. Thereafter, Hamric and Nance became the subject of several civil actions brought by the defrauded investors in Tennessee and Mississippi (and in which AmSouth also was named as a defendant), and also the subject of a federal grand jury investigation in the Southern District of Mississippi. Hamric and Nance were indicted on federal money-laundering charges, and both pled guilty.

It is a fundamental principle of the Delaware General Corporation Law that "[t]he business and affairs of every corporation organized under this chapter shall be managed by or under the direction of a board of directors." Del. Code 8, § 141(a).

Critical is the fact that the directors' potential personal liability depends upon whether or not their conduct can be exculpated by the section 102(b)(7) provision contained in the AmSouth certificate of incorporation. Such a provision can exculpate directors from monetary liability for a breach of the duty of care, but not for conduct that is not in good faith or a breach of the duty of loyalty.

[T]he Caremark standard for so-called "oversight" liability draws heavily upon the concept of director failure to act in good faith. It is important, in this context, to clarify a doctrinal issue that is critical to understanding fiduciary liability under Caremark as we construe that case. The phraseology used in Caremark and that we employ here – describing the lack of good faith as a "necessary condition to liability" – is deliberate. The purpose of that formulation is to communicate that a failure to act in good faith is not conduct that results, ipso facto, in the direct imposition of fiduciary liability. The failure to act in good faith may result in liability because the requirement to act in good faith "is a subsidiary element[,]" i.e., a condition, "of the fundamental duty of loyalty." It follows that because a showing of bad faith conduct, in the sense described in Disney and Caremark, is essential to establish director oversight liability, the fiduciary duty violated by that conduct is the duty of loyalty.

This view of a failure to act in good faith results in two additional doctrinal consequences. First, although good faith may be described colloquially as part of a "triad" of fiduciary duties that includes the duties of care and loyalty, the obligation to act in good faith does not establish an independent fiduciary duty that stands on the same footing as the duties of care and loyalty. Only the latter two duties, where violated, may directly result in liability, whereas a failure to act in good faith may do so, but indirectly. The second doctrinal consequence is that the fiduciary duty of loyalty is not limited to cases involving a financial or other cognizable fiduciary conflict of interest. It also encompasses cases where the fiduciary fails to act in good faith.

We hold that Caremark articulates the necessary conditions predicate for director oversight liability: (a) the directors utterly failed to implement any reporting or information system or controls; or (b) having implemented such a system or controls, consciously failed to monitor or oversee its operations thus disabling themselves from being informed of risks or problems requiring their attention. In either case, imposition of liability requires a showing that the directors knew that they were not discharging their fiduciary obligations. Where directors fail to act in the face of a known duty to act, thereby demonstrating a conscious disregard for their responsibilities, they breach their duty of loyalty by failing to discharge that fiduciary obligation in good faith.

The Court of Chancery found that the plaintiffs did not plead the existence of "red flags"—"facts showing that the board ever was aware that AmSouth's internal controls were inadequate, that these inadequacies would result in illegal activity, and that the board chose to do nothing about problems it allegedly knew existed."

The KPMG Report evaluated the various components of AmSouth's longstanding BSA/AML compliance program. The KPMG Report reflects that AmSouth's Board dedicated considerable resources to the BSA/AML compliance program and put into place numerous procedures and systems to attempt to ensure compliance. According to KPMG, the program's various components exhibited between a low and high degree of compliance with applicable laws and regulations. The KPMG Report reflects that the directors not only discharged their oversight responsibility to establish an information and reporting system, but also proved that the system was designed to permit the directors to periodically monitor AmSouth's compliance with BSA and AML regulations.

Delaware courts have recognized that "[m]ost of the decisions that a corporation, acting through its human agents, makes are, of course, not the subject of director attention." *In re Caremark Int'l Inc. Deriv. Litig.*, 698 A.2d at 968. Consequently, a claim that directors are subject to personal liability for employee failures is "possibly the most difficult theory in corporation law upon which a plaintiff might hope to win a judgment." *Id.* at 967.

For the plaintiffs' derivative complaint to withstand a motion to dismiss, "only a sustained or systematic failure of the board to exercise oversight – such as an utter failure to attempt to assure a reasonable information and reporting system exists – will establish the lack of good faith that is a necessary condition to liability." *Id.* at 971.

The KPMG Report – which the plaintiffs explicitly incorporated by reference into their derivative complaint – refutes the assertion that the directors "never took the necessary steps ... to ensure that a reasonable BSA compliance and reporting system existed." Although there ultimately may have been failures by employees to report deficiencies to the Board, there is no basis for an oversight claim seeking to hold the directors personally liable for such failures by the employees.

With the benefit of hindsight, the plaintiffs' complaint seeks to equate a bad outcome with bad faith. The lacuna in the plaintiffs' argument is a failure to recognize that the directors' good faith exercise of oversight responsibility may not invariably prevent employees from violating criminal laws, or from causing the corporation to incur significant financial liability, or both. In the absence of red flags, good faith in the context of oversight must be measured by the directors' actions "to assure a reasonable information and reporting system exists" and not by second-guessing after the occurrence of employee conduct that results in an unintended adverse outcome. Accordingly, we hold that the Court of Chancery properly applied Caremark and dismissed the plaintiffs' derivative complaint for failure to excuse demand by alleging particularized facts that created reason to doubt whether the directors had acted in good faith in exercising their oversight responsibilities. The judgment of the Court of Chancery is affirmed.

CASE PROBLEM 10-3

Assume the facts of Case Problem 10-2. Immediately following the board meeting, Larry called Jim and asked that they privately meet at their golf club. Larry opened the meeting by acknowledging Jim's stress over the "unique investment" and Jim's "powerful influence" over the other directors. For these reasons, Larry wanted to privately share with Jim some information that was not known by the other directors or any officer of the company.

Larry reminded Jim that Brand's licensing agreements with its major clients require that Brand destroy unsold branded merchandise that is discontinued. The clients do not want branded, dealer-exclusive products showing up in general merchandise stores, gas stations, and other discount outlets that exist throughout the world. Each license agreement mandates that an allowance (usually two or three percent of sales) be set aside to cover the cost of the destroyed merchandise. All directors and officers of Brand are well aware of these allowances, the "duty to destroy," and the fact that the allowances have been used over the years to write off the costs of a huge volume of client-branded merchandise. What none of the directors have ever known is that much of the merchandise had not been destroyed, as required by the licenses.

Larry went on to explain that he had moved the merchandise to an off-site storage facility. It was easy to do with "some local Home Deport help" because Brand had no procedures for ensuring the destruction of the merchandise. Larry explained, "I just couldn't fathom the notion of destroying so much valuable product that we had worked so hard to create." No company officer or employee knew of the merchandise's existence. Larry indicated that he had never considered selling any of the "phantom inventory" until last year.

Larry further explained that, late last year, the producers of Slingshot quietly approached him and requested an additional $500,000 to "keep the movie going." The producers promised at that time that no additional funding requests would be necessary. For fear of "spooking" any of the directors or shareholders, Larry decided to fund this additional contribution by selling, in bulk, a large volume of the "phantom inventory" to a merchandise distributor for $500,000. No record of the bulk sale or the additional Slingshot investment ever showed up on Brand's books. In justifying this decision, Larry explained to Jim that the "investment" was for the benefit of Brand and there was no risk that any of the merchandise, if discovered (an "insane long shot" according to Larry), could ever be traced back to Brand. Any such discovery would be blamed on "Dealer Dumping," a common, unavoidable menace.

Jim's immediate concern was tax evasion on the $500,000 proceeds from the sale. Larry dismissed this concern by explaining that, because Brand's investments in Slingshot were currently deductible under a special tax provision for low budget films, the unrecorded transaction would result in an understatement of income and deductions in the same amount, producing "a wash for income tax purposes."

Larry stated that his real fear was "commotion" over the additional $2 million investment that could trigger questions about the "whole Slingshot deal" and potentially lead to the disclosure of his "phantom inventory" sale to fund Brand's "unrecorded" Slingshot investment. Such a disclosure could jeopardize the license agreements, the lifeblood of Brand's business. Larry emphasized to Jim that the only way "to get us out of this scary mess is to put up the last two million and hope for the best."

Again, Jim is requesting advice as to how he should proceed as a director. Beyond his questions regarding the additional Slingshot investment request, Jim wants to know whether he, as a director, could have any personal exposure if Larry's actions end up seriously damaging the value of the company. Assume first that Brand's articles of incorporation have not been amended to include a section 2.02(b)(4) provision, and then indicate whether and how your advice would change if Brand's articles of incorporation had been so amended.

4. DEFECTIVE DISCLOSURES

MALONE v. BRINCAT
722 A.2d 5 (Del. 1998)

HOLLAND, Justice:

Doran Malone, Joseph P. Danielle, and Adrienne M. Danielle, the plaintiffs-appellants, filed this individual and class action in the Court of Chancery. The complaint alleged that the directors of Mercury Finance Company ("Mercury"), a Delaware corporation, breached their fiduciary duty of disclosure. The individual defendant-appellee directors are John N. Brincat, Dennis H. Chookaszian, William C. Croft, Clifford R. Johnson, Andrew McNally, IV, Bruce I. McPhee, Fred G. Steingraber, and Phillip J. Wicklander. The complaint also alleged that the defendant-appellee, KPMG Peat Marwick LLP ("KPMG") aided and abetted the Mercury directors' breaches of fiduciary duty. The Court of Chancery dismissed the complaint with prejudice pursuant to Chancery Rule 12(b)(6) for failure to state a claim upon which relief may be granted.

The complaint alleged that the director defendants intentionally overstated the financial condition of Mercury on repeated occasions throughout a four-year period in disclosures to Mercury's shareholders. Plaintiffs contend that the complaint states a claim upon which relief can be granted for a breach of the fiduciary duty of disclosure.

This Court has concluded that the Court of Chancery properly granted the defendants' motions to dismiss the complaint. That dismissal, however, should have been without prejudice. Plaintiffs are entitled to file an amended complaint.

Mercury is a publicly-traded company engaged primarily in purchasing installment sales contracts from automobile dealers and providing short-term installment loans directly to consumers. The complaint alleged that the directors "knowingly and intentionally breached their fiduciary duty of disclosure because the SEC filings made by the directors and every communication from the company to the shareholders since 1994 was materially false" and that "as a direct result of the false disclosures ... the Company has lost all or virtually all of its value (about $2 billion)."

According to plaintiffs, since 1994, the director defendants caused Mercury to disseminate information containing overstatements of Mercury's earnings, financial performance and shareholders' equity. Mercury's earnings for 1996 were actually only $56.7 million, or $.33 a share, rather than the $120.7 million, or $.70 a share, as reported by the director defendants. Mercury's earnings in 1995 were actually $76.9 million, or $.44 a share, rather than $98.9 million, or $.57 a share, as reported by the director defendants. Mercury's earnings for 1994 were $83 million, or $.47 a share, rather than $86.5 million, or $.49 a share, as reported by the director defendants. Mercury's earnings for 1993 were $64.2 million, rather than $64.9 million, as reported by the director defendants. Shareholders' equity on December 31, 1996 was disclosed by the director defendants as $353 million, but was only $263 million or less. The complaint alleged that all of the foregoing inaccurate information was included or referenced in virtually every filing Mercury made with the SEC and every communication Mercury's directors made to the shareholders during this period of time.

Having alleged these violations of fiduciary duty, which (if true) are egregious, plaintiffs alleged that as "a direct result of [these] false disclosures ... the company has lost all or virtually all its value (about $2 billion)," and seeks class action status to pursue damages against the directors and KPMG for the individual plaintiffs and common stockholders. The individual director defendants filed a motion to dismiss, contending that they owed no fiduciary duty of disclosure under the circumstances alleged in the complaint. KPMG also filed a motion to dismiss the aiding and abetting claim asserted against it.

This Court has held that a board of directors is under a fiduciary duty to disclose material information when seeking shareholder action. The majority of opinions from the Court of Chancery have held that there may be a cause of action for disclosure violations only where directors seek shareholder action. The present appeal requires this Court to decide whether a director's fiduciary duty arising out of misdisclosure is implicated in the absence of a request for shareholder action. We hold that directors who knowingly disseminate false information that results in corporate injury or damage to an individual stockholder violate their fiduciary duty, and may be held accountable in a manner appropriate to the circumstances.

Although the fiduciary duty of a Delaware director is unremitting, the exact course of conduct that must be charted to properly discharge that responsibility will change in the specific context of the action the director is taking with regard to either the corporation or its shareholders. This Court has endeavored to provide the directors with clear signal beacons and brightly lined-channel markers as they navigate with due care, good faith, and loyalty on behalf of a Delaware corporation and its shareholders. This Court has also endeavored to mark the safe harbors clearly.

The shareholder constituents of a Delaware corporation are entitled to rely upon their elected directors to discharge their fiduciary duties at all times. Whenever directors communicate publicly or directly with shareholders about the corporation's affairs, with or without a request for shareholder action, directors have a fiduciary duty to shareholders to exercise due care, good faith and loyalty. It follows a fortiori that when directors communicate publicly or directly with shareholders about corporate matters the sine qua non of directors' fiduciary duty to shareholders is honesty.

The duty of disclosure is, and always has been, a specific application of the general fiduciary duty owed by directors. The duty of disclosure obligates directors to provide the stockholders with accurate and complete information material to a transaction or other corporate event that is being presented to them for action.

Shareholders are entitled to rely upon the truthfulness of all information disseminated to them by the directors they elect to manage the corporate enterprise. Delaware directors disseminate information in at least three contexts: public statements made to the market, including shareholders; statements informing shareholders about the affairs of the corporation without a request for shareholder action; and, statements to shareholders in conjunction with a request for shareholder action. Inaccurate information in these contexts may be the result of a violation of the fiduciary duties of care, loyalty or good faith. We will examine the remedies that are available to shareholders for misrepresentations in each of these three contexts by the directors of a Delaware corporation.

In the absence of a request for stockholder action, the Delaware General Corporation Law does not require directors to provide shareholders with information concerning the finances or affairs of the corporation. Even when shareholder action is sought, the provisions in the General Corporation Law requiring notice to the shareholders of the proposed action do not require the directors to convey substantive information beyond a statutory minimum.

The duty of directors to observe proper disclosure requirements derives from the combination of the fiduciary duties of care, loyalty and good faith. The directors of a Delaware corporation are required to disclose fully and fairly all material information within the board's control when it seeks shareholder action. When the directors disseminate information to stockholders when no stockholder action is sought, the fiduciary duties of care, loyalty and good faith apply. Dissemination of false information could violate one or more of those duties.

When corporate directors impart information they must comport with the obligations imposed by both the Delaware law and the federal statutes and regulations of the United States Securities and Exchange Commission ("SEC"). Historically, federal law has regulated disclosures by corporate directors into the general interstate market. This Court has noted that "in observing its congressional mandate the SEC has adopted a 'basic philosophy of disclosure.'" *Stroud v. Grace,* Del.Supr., 606 A.2d 75, 86 (1992). Accordingly, this Court has held that there is "no legitimate basis to create a new cause of action which would replicate, by state decisional law, the provisions of ... the 1934 Act." *Arnold v. Society for Savings Bancorp, Inc.,* Del.Supr., 678 A.2d 533, 539 (1996). In deference to the panoply of federal protections that are available to investors in connection with the purchase or sale of securities of Delaware corporations, this Court has decided not to recognize a state common law cause of action against the directors of Delaware corporations for "fraud on the market." Here, it is to be noted, the claim appears to be made by those who did not sell and, therefore, would not implicate federal securities laws which relate to the purchase or sale of securities.

The historic roles played by state and federal law in regulating corporate disclosures have been not only compatible but complementary. That symbiotic relationship has been perpetuated by the recently enacted federal Securities Litigation Uniform Standards Act of 1998. Although that statute by its terms does not apply to this case, the new statute will require securities class actions involving the purchase or sale of nationally traded securities, based upon false or misleading statements, to be brought exclusively in federal court under federal law. The 1998 Act, however, contains two important exceptions: the first provides that an "exclusively derivative action brought by one or more shareholders on behalf of a corporation" is not preempted; the second preserves the availability of state court class actions, where state law already provides that corporate directors have fiduciary disclosure obligations to shareholders. These exceptions have become known as the "Delaware carve-outs."

Delaware law also protects shareholders who receive false communications from directors even in the absence of a request for shareholder action. When the directors are not seeking shareholder action, but are deliberately misinforming shareholders about the business of the corporation, either directly or by a public statement, there is a violation of fiduciary duty. That violation may result in a derivative claim on behalf of the corporation or a cause of action for damages. There may also be a basis for equitable relief to remedy the violation.

Here the complaint alleges (if true) an egregious violation of fiduciary duty by the directors in knowingly disseminating materially false information. Then it alleges that the corporation lost about $2 billion in value as a result. Then it merely claims that the action is brought on behalf of the named plaintiffs and the putative class.

The allegation in paragraph 3 that the false disclosures resulted in the corporation losing virtually all its equity seems obliquely to claim an injury to the corporation. The plaintiffs, however, never expressly assert a derivative claim on behalf of the corporation or allege compliance with Court of Chancery Rule 23.1, which requires pre-suit demand or cognizable and particularized allegations that demand is excused.

The Court of Chancery properly dismissed the complaint before it against the individual director defendants, in the absence of well-pleaded allegations stating a derivative, class or individual cause of action and properly assertable remedy.

GANTLER v. STEPHENS
965 A.2d 695 (Del. 2009)

JACOBS, Justice.

First Niles, a Delaware corporation headquartered in Niles, Ohio, is a holding company whose sole business is to own and operate the Home Federal Savings and Loan Association of Niles ("Home Federal" or the "Bank").

In late 2003, First Niles was operating in a depressed local economy, with little to no growth in the Bank's assets and anticipated low growth for the future. At that time Stephens, who was Chairman, President, CEO and founder of First Niles and the Bank, was beyond retirement age and there was no heir apparent among the Company's officers. The acquisition market for banks like Home Federal was brisk, however, and First Niles was thought to be an excellent acquisition for another financial institution. Accordingly, the First Niles Board sought advice on strategic opportunities available to the Company, and in August 2004, decided that First Niles should put itself up for sale.

At the March 9 special Board meeting, Stephens distributed a memorandum describing [an offer to purchase] from First Place in positive terms. Without any discussion or deliberation, however, the Board voted 4 to 1 to reject that offer, with only Gantler voting to accept it. After the vote, Stephens discussed Management's privatization plan and instructed Legal Counsel to further investigate that plan.

Five weeks later, on April 18, 2005, Stephens circulated to the Board members a document describing a proposed privatization of First Niles ("Privatization Proposal"). That Proposal recommended reclassifying the shares of holders of 300 or fewer shares of First Niles common stock into a new issue of Series A Preferred Stock on a one-to-one basis (the "Reclassification"). The Series A Preferred Stock would pay higher dividends and have the same liquidation rights as the common stock, but the Preferred holders would lose all voting rights except in the event of a proposed sale of the Company. The Privatization Proposal claimed that the Reclassification was the best method to privatize the Company.

On June 5, 2006, the Board determined, based on the advice of Management and First Niles' general counsel, that the Reclassification was fair both to the First Niles shareholders who would receive newly issued Series A Preferred Stock, and to those shareholders who would continue to hold First Niles common stock. On June 19, the Board voted unanimously to amend the Company's certificate of incorporation to reclassify the shares held by owners of 300 or fewer shares of common stock into shares of Series A Preferred Stock that would have the features and terms described in the Privatization Proposal.

On November 16, 2006, the Board, disseminated a definitive proxy statement ("Reclassification Proxy" or "Proxy") to the First Niles shareholders. On November 20, the plaintiffs filed an amended complaint, alleging (inter alia) that the Reclassification Proxy contained material misstatements and omissions.

In the Reclassification Proxy, the Board represented that the proposed Reclassification would allow First Niles to "save significant legal, accounting and administrative expenses" relating to public disclosure and reporting requirements under the Exchange Act. The Reclassification Proxy also disclosed alternative transactions that the Board had considered, including a cash-out merger, a reverse stock-split, an issue tender offer, expense reduction and a business combination. The Proxy further disclosed that the Company had received one firm merger offer, and that "[a]fter careful deliberations, the board determined in its business judgment the proposal was not in the best interests of the Company or our shareholders and rejected the proposal."

We conclude that the Proxy disclosures concerning the Board's deliberations about the First Place bid were materially misleading.

It is well-settled law that "directors of Delaware corporations [have] a fiduciary duty to disclose fully and fairly all material information within the board's control when it seeks shareholder action." *Stroud v. Grace,* 606 A.2d 75, 84 (Del.1992); *In re Staples, Inc., S'holders Litig.,* 792 A.2d 934, 953–54 (Del.Ch.2001). That duty "attaches to proxy statements and any other disclosures in contemplation of stockholder action." *Arnold v. Soc'y for Savings Bancorp, Inc.,* 650 A.2d 1270, 1277 (Del.1994). The essential inquiry here is whether the alleged omission or misrepresentation is material. The burden of establishing materiality rests with the plaintiff, who must demonstrate "a substantial likelihood that the disclosure of the omitted fact would have been viewed by the reasonable investor as having significantly altered the 'total mix' of information made available." *Id.*

In the Reclassification Proxy, the Board disclosed that "[a]fter careful deliberations, the board determined in its business judgment that the [First Place merger] proposal was not in the best interest of the Company or our shareholders and rejected the [merger] proposal." Although boards are "not required to disclose all available information[,] ..." "once [they] travel[ ] down the road of partial disclosure of ... [prior bids] us[ing] ... vague language ..., they ha[ve] an obligation to   provide the stockholders with an accurate, full, and fair characterization of those historic events."

By stating that they "careful[ly] deliberat[ed]," the Board was representing to the shareholders that it had considered the Sales Process on its objective merits and had determined that the Reclassification would better serve the Company than a merger. The Court of Chancery found, however, that the Board's Reclassification Proxy disclosure of "careful deliberations" about terminating the Sales Process was immaterial, because it would not alter the total mix of information to "omit[ ] that phrase in its entirety." We disagree and conclude that that disclosure was materially misleading.

The Reclassification Proxy specifically represented that the First Niles officers and directors "ha[d] a conflict of interest with respect to the [Reclassification] because he or she is in a position to structure it in a way that benefits his or her interests differently from the interests of unaffiliated shareholders." Given the defendant fiduciaries' admitted conflict of interest, a reasonable shareholder would likely find significant—indeed, reassuring—a representation by a conflicted Board that the Reclassification was superior to a potential merger which, after "careful deliberations," the Board had "carefully considered" and rejected. In such circumstances, it cannot be concluded as a matter of law, that disclosing that there was little or no deliberation would not alter the total mix of information provided to the shareholders.

The Vice Chancellor's finding that the challenged phrase could have been omitted in its entirety has the same infirmity. Had the "careful deliberations" representation never been made, the shareholders might well have evaluated the Reclassification more skeptically, and perhaps even less favorably on its merits, for two reasons. First, the shareholders would have had no information about the Reclassification's desirability vis-à-vis other alternatives. Second, they were told that the Board and Management had a conflict of interest in the one transaction that their fiduciaries had determined to endorse.

We are mindful of the case law holding that a corporate board is not obligated to disclose in a proxy statement the details of merger negotiations that have "gone south," since such information "would be [n]either viably practical [n]or material to shareholders in the meaningful way intended by ... case law." Even so, a board cannot properly claim in a proxy statement that it had carefully deliberated and decided that its preferred transaction better served the corporation than the alternative, if in fact the Board rejected the alternative transaction without serious consideration. The complaint's allegation that at its March 9, 2005 meeting the Board voted to reject a merger with First Place without any discussion, supports a reasonable inference that the Board did not "carefully deliberate" on the merits of that transaction.

On this basis, the dismissal of Count II must be reversed.

CASE PROBLEM 10-4

Assume the facts of Case Problem 10-3. Jim decides to end his relationship with Brand. Citing his wife's troubling health challenges and "other pressures," Jim resigns as a director. This intensifies the uncomfortable pressure all directors are feeling over another Slingshot investment.

Larry decides to diffuse the pressure by calling for a shareholder vote on two resolutions: (1) approval of an amendment to Brand's articles of incorporation to include a section 2.01(b)(4) provision and (2) approval of an additional $2 million investment in Slingshot. Larry figures that the adoption of these resolutions will lead to an easy director vote approving the investment because the directors will have personal liability protection and a majority of the shareholders will have approved the investment.

Larry immediately sends an appropriate notice of a special meeting to all shareholders along with a memorandum explaining the need for the amendment to the articles and the history and benefits of the Slingshot investment. The memorandum makes no mention of the phantom inventory sale and related off-the-books investment in Slingshot. Larry anticipates objections from the Morro Clan, but is confident that he can secure a majority vote by pressuring Linda, Sam and Clint and convincing at least one other shareholder to approve the resolutions.

Does this move by Larry make sense? Has Larry correctly assessed the benefits of a majority shareholder vote approving the resolutions? Is the accuracy of Larry's assessment of such benefits even relevant if the remaining six directors end up unanimously approving the second Slingshot investment?

C. THE DUTY OF LOYALTY

1. SELF-DEALING TRANSACTIONS

STATE EX. REL HAYES OYSTER CO. v. KEYPOINT OYSTER CO.
391 P.2d 979 (Wash. 1964)

DENNEY, Judge.

This is an action to determine ownership of an interest in the capital stock of a corporation under circumstances requiring consideration of corporate morality and ethics in the conduct of the president, manager and director of a corporation in the sale of corporate assets.

The parties are Hayes Oyster Company, an Oregon corporation, hereinafter called Hayes Oyster; Coast Oyster Company, a Washington corporation, hereinafter called Coast; Keypoint Oyster Company, a Washington corporation, hereinafter called Keypoint; Joseph W. Engman, his wife, Edith M. Engman; Verne Hayes and Sam Hayes. Verne Hayes will be referred to as Hayes unless designated otherwise.

The action was commenced against Keypoint to require transfer of 50 per cent of its stock to Hayes Oyster. Keypoint disclaimed ownership of the stock and interpleaded other parties heretofore mentioned.

Hayes was one of the founders of Coast which, over the years, became a public corporation and acquired several large oyster property holdings, among which were oyster beds and facilities for harvesting oysters located at Allyn and Poulsbo, Washington. These properties will hereafter be referred to as Allyn and

Poulsbo. Hayes was an officer and director of Coast from its incorporation and was president and manager and owner of 23 per cent of its stock in the year 1960, and a portion of 1961, during which time the events leading to this litigation occurred.

On October 21, 1958, Coast and Hayes entered into a full employment contract by which Hayes was to act as president and manager of Coast for a 10-year period and to refrain directly or indirectly from taking part in any business which would be in competition with the business of Coast, except Hayes Oyster.

Hayes Oyster was a family-owned corporation in which Sam Hayes owned about 75 per cent and Verne Hayes about 25 per cent of its stock.

In the spring of 1960, Coast owed substantial amounts to several creditors and it became apparent that the corporation must have cash if it was to continue in business. Several alternatives were considered by the directors of Coast, among them Hayes' suggestion to sell Allyn and Poulsbo. In June, 1960, Hayes inquired of Engman, a long-time employee of Coast and a man thoroughly familiar with the operation of the oyster properties, if Engman would be interested in purchasing Allyn and Poulsbo. Engman was interested but needed capital with which to commence operations. Engman then asked Hayes if he would 'come in' with him. Hayes replied that his full-employment contract with Coast might forbid it, but he would consult Ward Kumm attorney for and long-time director of Coast.

Hayes testified that in July, 1960, he told Engman that he had consulted with Kumm and his brother Sam Hayes and that Hayes Oyster could aid Engman in securing the initial capital required by Engman. At this time, Engman told Hayes he would attempt to secure a loan from relatives.

On August 11, 1960, the board of directors of Coast approved the sale of Allyn and Poulsbo to Engman at a price of $250,000, nothing down, payment of $25,000 a year, interest at 5 per cent on unpaid balance. Hayes informed Engman of the action of the board of directors and put him in possession of Allyn and Poulsbo on August 16, 1960.

Engman instructed Kumm to draw the necessary documents to incorporate the new enterprise to be known as Keypoint Oyster Company, which was to enter into the contract with Coast for the purchase of Allyn and Poulsbo. Engman, his wife, and Sam Hayes were the incorporators, directors and officers of Keypoint. The initial paid in capital was $500. Certificate No. 1 for 250 shares of stock was issued to Engman, certificate No. 2 for 249 shares to Engman's wife, and certificate No. 3 for one qualifying share to Sam Hayes.

The incorporation of Keypoint was completed on October 1, 1960. Kumm believed that it was necessary, or at least prudent, to secure the approval of the shareholders of Coast to the contract for sale of such valuable properties. A shareholders' meeting was held on October 21, 1960, at which time Kumm explained the contract. Hayes held proxies, which, with his own stock, authorized him to vote a majority of Coast stock. He did so in favor of a resolution authorizing Hayes to sign the proposed contract on behalf of Coast. Hayes signed as president of Coast; Engman signed as president of Keypoint.

Shortly thereafter, Engman delivered to Verne Hayes Keypoint certificate of stock No. 2, issued to Edith Engman, together with the separate assignment signed by her in which the name of the assignee was left blank. It is undisputed that the words 'Hayes Oyster Company' as assignee were not typed in said assignment until July 5, 1962.

Hayes made no mention at the Coast directors' meeting on August 11, 1960, that Hayes or Hayes Oyster might acquire some interest in Keypoint. Hayes made no disclosure to any officer, director, stockholder or employee of Coast at the shareholders' meeting or at the time Hayes signed the contract for Coast on October 21, 1960, that Hayes or Hayes Oyster were to participate in or have a financial interest in Keypoint. Indeed, Coast acquired no knowledge of the Engman-Hayes deal until subsequent to the termination of Hayes' administrative duties as president and general manager of Coast in May, 1961.

On June 23, 1962, Verne and Sam Hayes made demand on Engman for transfer on Keypoint's books to Hayes Oyster of Mrs. Engman's 249 shares. Engman did not comply, but made full disclosure to Kumm of his agreement with Hayes to give Hayes or Hayes Oyster a one-half interest in Keypoint and that such had been done. Soon thereafter Engman made formal demand for return of the stock which had been delivered to Verne and Sam Hayes. Coast quickly followed with a formal demand on Verne and Sam Hayes for the Keypoint stock in their possession and return of any benefits received by Hayes from the Engman-Hayes agreement. This case was commenced shortly thereafter.

After a lengthy trial, the trial court acquitted Verne Hayes of any breach of duty to Coast, held the agreement between Engman and Hayes that Hayes Oyster should acquire one-half interest in Keypoint to be valid; held that Engman had no just claim to the stock; and ordered Keypoint to deliver the stock to Hayes Oyster, and transfer it on Keypoint's books.

Certain basic concepts have long been recognized by courts throughout the land on the status of corporate officers and directors. They occupy a fiduciary relation to a private corporation and the shareholders thereof akin to that of a trustee, and owe undivided loyalty, and a standard of behavior above that of the workaday world. Leppaluoto v. Eggleston, 57 Wash.2d 393, 357 P.2d 725; Arneman v. Arneman, 43 Wash.2d 787, 264 P.2d 256. Directors and other officers of a private corporation cannot directly or indirectly acquire a profit for themselves or acquire any other personal advantage in dealings with others on behalf of the corporation. Western States Life Ins. Co. v. Lockwood, 166 Cal. 185, 135 P. 496

Respondent is correct in his contention that this court has abolished the mechanical rule whereby any transaction involving corporate property in which a director has an interest is voidable at the option of the corporation. Such a contract cannot be voided if the director or officer can show that the transaction was fair to the corporation. However, nondisclosure by an interested director or officer is, in itself, unfair. This wholesome rule can be applied automatically without any of the unsatisfactory results which flowed from a rigid bar against any self-dealing. Corr v. Leisey, 138 So.2d 795 (Fla.App.1962).

The trial court found that any negotiations between Hayes and Engman up to the time of the loan by the Poulsbo Bank on September 1, 1960, resulted in no binding agreement that Hayes would have any personal interest for himself or as a stockholder in Hayes Oyster in the sale of Allyn and Poulsbo. The undisputed evidence, however, shows that Hayes knew he might have some interest in the sale. It would have been appropriate for Hayes to have disclosed his possible interest at the meeting of Coast's board of directors on August 11, 1960.

Hayes was required to divulge his interest in Keypoint. His obligation to do so arises from the possibility, even probability that some controversy might arise between Coast and Keypoint relative to the numerous provisions of the executory contract. Coast shareholders and directors had the right to know of Hayes' interest in Keypoint in order to intelligently determine the advisability of retaining Hayes as president and manager under the circumstances, and to determine whether or not it was wise to enter into the contract at all, in view of Hayes' conduct. In all fairness, they were entitled to know that their president and director might be placed in a position where he must choose between the interest of Coast and Keypoint in conducting Coast's business with Keypoint.

It is not necessary that an officer or director of a corporation have an intent to defraud or that any injury result to the corporation for an officer or director to violate his fiduciary obligation in secretly acquiring an interest in corporate property.

A corporation cannot ratify the breach of fiduciary duties unless full and complete disclosure of all facts and circumstances is made by the fiduciary and an intentional relinquishment by the corporation of its rights.

The decree ordering issuance of a new certificate of stock for 250 shares of Keypoint Oyster Company to Hayes Oyster Company is reversed with direction to order Keypoint Oyster Company to issue a new certificate for 250 shares of its stock to Coast Oyster Company and cancel the certificates heretofore standing in the name of or assigned to Hayes Oyster Company.

REMILLARD BRICK CO. v. REMILLIARD-DANDINI CO.
109 Cal.App.2d 405, 241 P.2d 66 (1952)

PETERS, Presiding Justice.

The present controversy involves four corporations and several members of their boards of directors. The corporations are:

1. Remillard Brick Company, which is wholly owned by Lillian Dandini.

2. Remillard-Dandini Company has 403 shares of stock, 150 shares of which are owned by the Remillard Brick Company, and 253 shares owned by the Sesennas and which were controlled by defendants Stanley and Sturgis, who at all times here involved had the Sesennas' proxy to vote the stock and a contract to buy it. The directors of the Remillard-Dandini Company at all times here involved were defendants Gatzert, Stanley and Sturgis, and Lillian Dandini and her lawyer Johnson.

3. San Jose Brick & Tile, Ltd., is owned by Remillard-Dandini Company. Its board of directors consists of Gatzert, Stanley, Sturgis, Den-Dulk, a law partner of Sturgis, and Davis, an employee of Remillard-Dandini Company. The San Jose Brick and Remillard Dandini compaines are engaged in the manufacture of bricks. Their legal positions are substantially similar, and they will be referred to hereafter as the manufacturing companies.

4. Remillard-Dandini Sales Corporation was organized and is wholly owned, controlled and operated by Stanley and Sturgis.

Stanley was president and general manager of both manufacturing companies. Sturgis was secretary and secretary-treasurer of the two companies, part-time jobs.

This action was brought by Remillard Brick Company to recover, on behalf of the two manufacturing companies, profits made by the sales corporation and Stanley and Sturgis, from the sale of bricks manufactured by the two manufacturing companies.

In 1948, while acting as directors and officers of the two manufacturing companies, Stanley and Sturgis conceived the idea of separating the sales functions of the two companies from their manufacturing functions, by having the two manufacturing companies, by contract, transfer their sales functions to the sales corporation, wholly owned by them. On January 29, 1948, at a directors' meeting, Stanley and Sturgis proposed that they, as officers of the two manufacturing companies, be authorized by the respective boards to enter into contracts on behalf of the two manufacturing companies with the sales corporation to the end that the sales corporation would handle, exclusively, the promotion and sales of all products manufactured by the manufacturing companies. This resolution was formally adopted by the vote of Stanley, Sturgis and Gatzert. The minority directors, Lillian Dandini and attorney Johnson, voted 'no.' In February of 1948, Stanley and Sturgis, acting as officers of the manufacturing companies, caused certain contracts to be entered into between the manufacturing companies and the sales corporation.

The contracts between the manufacturing companies and the sales corporation transferred to the latter full control over the sales of all products, including promotion of sales, manufactured by the manufacturing companies. The sales corporation agreed to sell all products manufactured by the two manufacturing companies 'that it is able to market and sell.' The sales corporation agreed to purchase all products manufactured by the manufacturing companies on such conditions and prices as sales corporation should judge to be fair and reasonable. A reasonable and fair price was defined as a price that would yield the manufacturing companies a gross profit, before taxes, of not less than $2.50 per thousand bricks manufactured and sold by the sales corporation.

In this fashion the sales corporation undertook to sell the products of the manufacturing companies using almost exclusively the facilities and equipment of the manufacturing companies. Undoubtedly, Stanley and Sturgis did a good job, not only in selling but in modernizing the two manufacturing plants. The trial court found that, under these contracts, the sales corporation, in 1948, received profits and paid salaries to Stanley, Sturgis and Gatzert of $55,727.73, while in 1949 such profits and salaries totalled $37,939.60. However, neither of the manufacturing companies declared a dividend in these years.

The trial court found that the 1949 contracts were unfair to the manufacturing companies, were void, and ordered them cancelled. It ordered the defendants (after making certain adjustments not here challenged) to repay $35,539.60, less $4,400 allowed to Stanley for extraordinary services, and $5,000 for the services of Sturgis. This left a balance ordered repaid of $26,139.60.

It is argued that, since the fact of common directorship was fully known to the boards of the contracting corporations, and because the Sesennas as majority stockholders consented to the transaction, the minority stockholder and directors of the manufacturing companies have no legal cause to complain. In other words, it is argued that if the majority directors and stockholders inform the minority that they are going to mulct the corporation, section 820 of the Corporations Code constitutes an impervious armor against any attack on the transaction short of actual fraud. If this interpretation of the section were sound, it would be a shocking reflection on the law of California. It would completely disregard the first sentence of section 820 setting forth the elementary rule that 'Directors and officers shall exercise their powers in good faith, and with a view to the interests of the corporation', and would mean that if conniving directors simply disclose their dereliction to the powerless minority, any transaction by which the majority desire to mulct the minority is immune from attack. That is not and cannot be the law.

Section 820 of the Corporations Code is based on former section 311 of the Civil Code. Before the adoption of that section it was the law that the mere existence of a common directorate, at least where the vote of the common director was essential to consummate the transaction, invalidated the contract. That rule was changed in 1931 when section 311 was added to the Civil Code. , If the conditions provided for in the section appear, the transaction cannot be set aside simply because there is a common directorate.

But neither section 820 of the Corporations Code nor any other provision of the law automatically validates such transactions simply because there has been a disclosure and approval by the majority of the stockholders. That section does not operate to limit the fiduciary duties owed by a director to all the stockholders, nor does it operate to condone acts which, without the existence of a common directorate, would not be countenanced. That section does not permit an officer or director, by an abuse of his power, to obtain an unfair advantage or profit for himself at the expense of the corporation. The director cannot, by reason of his position, drive a harsh and unfair bargain with the corporation he is supposed to represent. If he does so, he may be compelled to account for unfair profits made in disregard of his duty.

Even though the requirements of section 820 are technically met, transactions that are unfair and unreasonable to the corporation may be avoided. It would be a shocking concept of corporate morality to hold that because the majority directors or stockholders disclose their purpose and interest, they may strip a corporation of its assets to their own financial advantage, and that the minority is without legal redress. Here the unchallenged findings demonstrate that Stanley and Sturgis used their majority power for their own personal advantage and to the detriment of the minority stockholder.

It is hornbook law that directors, while not strictly trustees, are fiduciaries, and bear a fiduciary relationship to the corporation, and to all the stockholders. They owe a duty to all stockholders, including the minority stockholders, and must administer their duties for the common benefit. The concept that a corporation is an entity cannot operate so as to lessen the duties owed to all of the stockholders. Directors owe a duty of highest good faith to the corporation and its stockholders. It is a cardinal principle of corporate law that a director cannot, at the expense of the corporation, make an unfair profit from his position. He is precluded from receiving any personal advantage without fullest disclosure to and consent of *all* those affected. The law zealously regards contracts between corporations with interlocking directorates, will carefully scrutinize all such transactions, and in case of unfair dealing to the detriment of minority stockholders, will grant appropriate relief. Where the transaction greatly benefits one corporation at the expense of another, and especially if it personally benefits the majority directors, it will and should be set aside. In other words, while the transaction is not voidable simply because an interested director participated, it will not be upheld if it is unfair to the minority stockholders. These principles are the law in practically all jurisdictions. 3 Fletcher, Cyclopedia of Corps. (Perm.Ed.), p. 173, § 838, et seq.

The findings, and the evidence upon which they are based, compel the conclusion that the trial court correctly decided that the 1949 contracts were unfair and inequitable and constituted a fraud upon the manufacturing companies and their minority stockholder. The trial court correctly set aside those contracts.

Model Business Corporation Act Provisions

MBCA § 8.60. SUBCHAPTER DEFINITIONS

In this subchapter:

(1) "Conflicting interest" with respect to a corporation means the interest a director of the corporation has respecting a transaction effected or proposed to be effected by the corporation (or by a subsidiary of the corporation or any other entity in which the corporation has a controlling interest) if (i) whether or not the transaction is brought before the board of directors of the corporation for action, the director knows at the time of commitment that he or a related person is a party to the transaction or has a beneficial financial interest in or so closely linked to the transaction and of such financial significance to the director or a related person that the interest would reasonably be expected to exert an influence on the director's judgment if he were called upon to vote on the transaction; or (ii) the transaction is brought (or is of such character and significance to the corporation that it would in the normal course be brought) before the board of directors of the corporation for action, and the director knows at the time of commitment that any of the following persons is either a party to

the transaction or has a beneficial financial interest in or so closely linked to the transaction and of such financial significance to the person that the interest would reasonably be expected to exert an influence on the director's judgment if he were called upon to vote on the transaction: (A) an entity (other than the corporation) of which the director is a director, general partner, agent, or employee; (B) a person that controls one or more of the entities specified in subclause (A) or an entity that is controlled by, or is under common control with, one or more of the entities specified in subclause (A); or (C) an individual who is a general partner, principal, or employer of the director.

(2) "Director's conflicting interest transaction" with respect to a corporation means a transaction effected or proposed to be effected by the corporation (or by a subsidiary of the corporation or any other entity in which the corporation has a controlling interest) respecting which a director of the corporation has a conflicting interest.

(3) "Related person" of a director means (i) the spouse (or a parent or sibling thereof) of the director, or a child, grandchild, sibling, parent (or spouse of any thereof) of the director, or an individual having the same home as the director, or a trust or estate of which an individual specified in this clause (i) is a substantial beneficiary; or (ii) a trust, estate, incompetent, conservatee, or minor of which the director is a fiduciary.

(4) "Required disclosure" means disclosure by the director who has a conflicting interest of (i) the existence and nature of his conflicting interest, and (ii) all facts known to him respecting the subject matter of the transaction that an ordinarily prudent person would reasonably believe to be material to a judgment about whether or not to proceed with the transaction.

(5) "Time of commitment" respecting a transaction means the time when the transaction is consummated or, if made pursuant to contract, the time when the corporation (or its subsidiary or the entity in which it has a controlling interest) becomes contractually obligated so that its unilateral withdrawal from the transaction would entail significant loss, liability, or other damage.

MBCA § 8.61. JUDICIAL ACTION

(a) A transaction effected or proposed to be effected by a corporation (or by a subsidiary of the corporation or any other entity in which the corporation has a controlling interest) that is not a director's conflicting interest transaction may not be enjoined, set aside, or give rise to an award of damages or other sanctions, in a proceeding by a shareholder or by or in the right of the corporation, because a director of the corporation, or any person with whom or which he has a personal, economic, or other association, has an interest in the transaction.

(b) A director's conflicting interest transaction may not be enjoined, set aside, or give rise to an award of damages or other sanctions, in a proceeding by a shareholder or by or in the right of the corporation, because the director, or any person with whom or which he has a personal, economic, or other association, has an interest in the transaction, if:

(1) directors' action respecting the transaction was at any time taken in compliance with section 8.62;

(2) shareholders' action respecting the transaction was at any time taken in compliance with section 8.63; or

(3) the transaction, judged according to the circumstances at the time of commitment, is established to have been fair to the corporation.

MBCA § 8.62. DIRECTORS' ACTION

(a) Directors' action respecting a transaction is effective for purposes of section 8.61(b)(1) if the transaction received the affirmative vote of a majority (but no fewer than two) of those qualified directors on the board of directors or on a duly empowered committee of the board who voted on the transaction after either required disclosure to them (to the extent the information was not known by them) or compliance with subsection (b); provided that action by a committee is so effective only if:

(1) all its members are qualified directors, and

(2) its members are either all the qualified directors on the board or are appointed by the affirmative vote of a majority of the qualified directors on the board.

(b) If a director has a conflicting interest respecting a transaction, but neither he nor a related person of the director specified in section 8.60(3)(i) is a party to the transaction, and if the director has a duty under law or professional canon, or a duty of confidentiality to another person, respecting information relating to the transaction such that the director may not make the disclosure described in section 8.60(4)(ii), then disclosure is sufficient for purposes of subsection (a) if the director (1) discloses to the directors voting on the transaction the existence and nature of his conflicting interest and informs them of the character and limitations imposed by that duty before their vote on the transaction, and (2) plays no part, directly or indirectly, in their deliberations or vote.

(c) A majority (but no fewer than two) of all the qualified directors on the board of directors, or on the committee, constitutes a quorum for purposes of action that complies with this section. Directors' action that otherwise complies with this section is not affected by the presence or vote of a director who is not a qualified director.

(d) For purposes of this section, "qualified director" means, with respect to a director's conflicting interest transaction, any director who does not have either (1) a conflicting interest respecting the transaction, or (2) a familial, financial, professional, or employment relationship with a second director who does have a conflicting interest respecting the transaction, which relationship would, in the circumstances, reasonably be expected to exert an influence on the first director's judgment when voting on the transaction.

§ 8.63. SHAREHOLDERS' ACTION

(a) Shareholders' action respecting a transaction is effective for purposes of section 8.61(b)(2) if a majority of the votes entitled to be cast by the holders of all qualified shares were cast in favor of the transaction after (1) notice to shareholders describing the director's conflicting interest transaction, (2) provision of the information referred to in subsection (d), and (3) required disclosure to the shareholders who voted on the transaction (to the extent the information was not known by them).

(b) For purposes of this section, "qualified shares" means any shares entitled to vote with respect to the director's conflicting interest transaction except shares that, to the knowledge, before the vote, of the secretary (or other officer or agent of the corporation authorized to tabulate votes), are beneficially owned (or the voting of which is controlled) by a director who has a conflicting interest respecting the transaction or by a related person of the director, or both.

(c) A majority of the votes entitled to be cast by the holders of all qualified shares constitutes a quorum for purposes of action that complies with this section. Subject to the provisions of subsections (d) and (e), shareholders' action that otherwise complies with this section is not affected by the presence of holders, or the voting, of shares that are not qualified shares.

(d) For purposes of compliance with subsection (a), a director who has a conflicting interest respecting the transaction shall, before the shareholders' vote, inform the secretary (or other office or agent of the corporation authorized to tabulate votes) of the number, and the identity of persons holding or controlling the vote, of all shares that the director knows are beneficially owned (or the voting of which is controlled) by the director or by a related person of the director, or both

(e) If a shareholders' vote does not comply with subsection (a) solely because of a failure of a director to comply with subsection (d), and if the director establishes that his failure did not determine and was not intended by him to influence the outcome of the vote, the court may, with or without further proceedings respecting section 8.61(b)(3), take such action respecting the transaction and the director, and give such effect, if any, to the shareholders' vote, as it considers appropriate in the circumstances.

CASE PROBLEM 10-5

Assume the same facts as Case Problem 10-1, with the following changes:

1. Larry's daughter, Debby, introduced Larry to the producer of Slingshot. Debby, a graduate of the UCLA film school, is working hard to develop a career as a cinematographer.

2. The producer promised Larry that, if Brand invested $4 million in the film, Debby would be chosen as the film's assistant cinematographer, would be paid standard cinematographer compensation, would be given an "Assistant Producer" credit, and, as an AP, would be given a one percent interest in the film's back-end residuals. The producer made good on these promises.

3. Slingshot was made without a need for any investment by Brand beyond the original $4 million. The movie was a bust – poor reviews, no theatrical release, no on-demand interest, and small DVD and foreign sales. Brand ended

up losing over $3.5 million.

4. Brand is incorporated in a state that has adopted the Model Business Corporation Act and Brand's articles of incorporation include a provision authorized by MBCA § 2.02(b)(4).

5. Larry did not disclose Debbie's involvement in the film in the memorandum to the board members that accompanied the consent resolutions.

Does Larry, Debby or Brand's directors have any personal exposure to Brand for this loss? Does any party have a "conflicting interest" within the meaning of MBCA § 8.60? Does this qualify as a "conflicting interest transaction" within the meaning of MBCA § 8.60? How will MBCA § 8.61 impact any litigation by the shareholders to hold Larry or others responsible for the loss? How would your answers to these question change if Larry had fully disclosed Debby's role in the memorandum to the directors and all the directors had still signed and returned the resolution with no questions asked?

2. INDEPENDENT DIRECTORS' APPROVAL CHALLENGES

ORMAN v. CULLMAN
794 A.2d 5 (Del.Ch. 2002)

CHANDLER, Chancellor.

This purported class action involves alleged breaches of fiduciary duty in connection with the cash-out merger of the public shareholders of General Cigar Holdings, Inc. ("General Cigar" or the "Company"). According to the complaint, plaintiff Joseph Orman is and was the owner of General Cigar Class A common stock at all times relevant to this litigation. Orman brings this suit on behalf of himself and the Public Shareholders of General Cigar Class A common stock against General Cigar and its eleven-member board of directors (collectively the "Board").

On January 19, 2000 the Board unanimously approved a merger agreement pursuant to which a subsidiary of an unaffiliated third party, Swedish Match AB, would purchase the shares owned by the Unaffiliated Shareholders of General Cigar. On April 10, 2000 the Company filed with the Securities and Exchange Commission an amended proxy statement ("Proxy Statement") relating to this proposed merger.

The complaint first alleges breaches of fiduciary duty with respect to the Board's approval of (and the fairness of) the proposed merger. Orman contends that Board approval of the merger was ineffective and improper because a majority of the defendant directors was not independent and/or disinterested.

He further alleges that the defendant directors violated their fiduciary duty of loyalty by entering into a transaction that was unfair to the Public Shareholders of General Cigar and usurped for themselves corporate opportunities rightfully belonging to all General Cigar shareholders.

The motion to dismiss the duty of loyalty claims must be denied, as Orman has pled facts from which is it reasonable to question the independence and disinterest of a majority of the General Cigar Board.

In determining the sufficiency of factual allegations made by a plaintiff as to either a director's interest or lack of independence, the Delaware Supreme Court has rejected an objective "reasonable director" test and instead requires the application of a subjective "actual person" standard to determine whether a *particular* director's interest is material and debilitating or that he lacks independence because he is controlled by another.

General Cigar had an eleven-member board. In order to rebut the presumptions of the business judgment rule, Orman must allege facts that would support a finding of interest or lack of independence for a majority, or at least six, of the Board members. Orman asserts, and defendants appear to concede, that the four members of the Cullman Group were interested because they received benefits from the transaction that were not shared with the rest of the shareholders. Orman, therefore, would have to plead facts making it reasonable to question the interest or independence of two of the remaining seven Board members to avoid dismissal based on the business judgment rule presumption. With varying levels of confidence, Orman's complaint alleges that each of the seven remaining Board members—Israel, Vincent, Lufkin, Barnet, Sherren, Bernbach, and Solomon—were interested and/or lacked independence.[FN50]

FN50. Although interest and independence are two separate and distinct issues, these two attributes are sometimes confused by parties. Many plaintiffs allege facts which they assert establish that the defendant "lacked the disinterest and/or independence" necessary to consider the challenged transaction objectively. The plaintiff then asks the Court to select whichever type of disabling attribute is consistent with the facts alleged and that will support the plaintiff's claim. But it is not for the Court to divine the claims being made. A plaintiff must make clear to the Court the bases upon which his claims rest.

As described above, a disabling "interest," as defined by Delaware common law, exists in two instances. The first is when (1) a director personally receives a benefit (or suffers a detriment), (2) as a result of, or from, the challenged transaction, (3) which is not generally shared with (or suffered by) the other shareholders of his corporation, and (4) that benefit (or detriment) is of such subjective material significance to that particular director that it is reasonable to question whether that director objectively considered the advisability of the challenged transaction to the corporation and its shareholders. The second instance is when a director stands on both sides of the challenged transaction. *See* 8 *Del.C.* § 144. This latter situation frequently involves the first three elements listed above. As for the fourth element, whenever a director stands on both sides of the challenged transaction he is deemed interested and allegations of materiality have not been required.

"Independence" does not involve a question of whether the challenged director derives a benefit *from the transaction* that is not generally shared with the other shareholders. Rather, it involves an inquiry into whether the director's decision resulted from that director being *controlled* by another. A director can be controlled by another if in fact he is *dominated* by that other party, whether through close personal or familial relationship or through force of will. A director can also be controlled by another if the challenged director is *beholden* to the allegedly controlling entity. A director may be considered beholden to (and thus controlled by) another when the allegedly controlling entity has the unilateral power (whether direct or indirect through control over other decision makers), to decide whether the challenged director continues to receive a benefit, financial or otherwise, upon which the challenged director is so dependent or is of such subjective material importance to him that the threatened loss of that benefit might create a reason to question whether the controlled director is able to consider the corporate merits of the challenged transaction objectively.

Confusion over whether specific facts raise a question of interest or independence arises from the reality that similar factual circumstances may implicate *both* interest and independence, one but not the other, or neither. By way of example, consider the following: Director *A* is both a director and officer of company *X*. Company *X* is to be merged into company *Z*. Director *A* 's vote in favor of recommending shareholder approval of the merger is challenged by a plaintiff shareholder.

Scenario One. Assume that one of the terms of the merger agreement is that director *A* was to be an officer in surviving company *Z, and* that maintaining his position as a corporate officer in the surviving company was material to director *A*. That fact might, when considered in light of *all* of the facts alleged, lead the Court to conclude that director *A* had a disabling interest.

Scenario Two. Assume that director *C* is both a director and the majority shareholder of company *X*. Director *C* had the power plausibly to threaten director *A* 's position as officer of corporation *X* should director *A* vote against the merger. Assume further that director *A* 's position as a corporate officer is material to director *A*. Those circumstances, when considered in light of *all* of the facts alleged, might lead the Court to question director *A* 's independence from director *C*, because it could reasonably be assumed that director *A* was controlled by director *C*, since director *A* was beholden to director *C* for his position as officer of the corporation. Confusion over whether to label this disability as a disqualifying "interest" or as a "lack of independence" may stem from the fact that, colloquially, director *A* was "interested" in keeping his job as a corporate officer. Scenario Two, however, raises only a question as to director *A* 's independence since there is nothing that suggests that director *A* would receive something *from the transaction* that might implicate a disabling interest.

If a plaintiff's allegations combined all facts described in both Scenario One *and* Scenario Two, it might be reasonable to question *both* director *A* 's interest and independence. Conversely, if all the facts in both scenarios were alleged *except* for the materiality of Director *A* 's position as a corporate officer (perhaps because director *A* is a billionaire and his officer's position pays $20,000 per year and is not even of prestige value to him) then *neither* director *A* 's interest nor his independence would be reasonably questioned. The key issue is not simply whether a particular director receives a benefit from a challenged transaction not shared with the other shareholders, or solely whether another person or entity has the ability to take some benefit away from a particular director, but whether the possibility of gaining some benefit or the fear of losing a benefit is likely to be of such importance to that director that it is reasonable for the Court to question whether valid business judgment or selfish considerations animated that director's vote on the challenged transaction.

Perhaps the weakest allegations of interest and/or lack of independence are aimed at directors Israel and Vincent. The complaint states that these two defendants "had longstanding business relations with members of the Cullman Group which impeded and impaired their ability to function independently and outside the influence of the Cullman Group." To make clear my opinion as to the independence of directors Israel and Vincent, I conclude that the allegations in the complaint with regard to the lack of independence of these two directors fail as a matter of law. The naked assertion of a previous business relationship is not enough to overcome the presumption of a director's independence.

The *only* fact alleged in support of Orman's allegation of director Barnet's interest is that he "has an interest in the transaction since he will become a director of the surviving company." No case has been cited to me, and I have found none, in which a director was found to have a financialinterest *solely* because he will be a director in the surviving corporation. To the contrary, our case law has held that such an interest is not a disqualifying interest.

Orman alleges that director Bernbach was both interested in the merger and lacked the independence to make an impartial decision regarding that transaction because he has "a written agreement with the Company to provide consulting services [and that] [i]n 1998 ... Bernbach was paid $75,000 for such services and additional funds since that date."

Accepting Orman's allegations as true reveals that Bernbach does not meet this definition of "interest." Bernbach had a contract with General Cigar. If the merger were consummated, he would have a contract that the surviving company would be obligated to honor. If the merger were not consummated he would still have his contract with the existing General Cigar that it would be obligated to honor. Therefore, director Bernbach would have received no benefit *from the transaction* being challenged that was not shared by the other General Cigar shareholders. Orman's complaint, therefore, fails to plead adequately that director Bernbach was interested in the merger.

Orman also argues that Bernbach's consulting agreement suggests a lack of independence. At this stage of the litigation, the facts supporting this allegation are sufficient to raise a reasonable inference that director Bernbach was controlled by the Cullman Group because he was beholden to the controlling shareholders for future renewals of his consulting contract. Even though there is no bright-line dollar amount at which consulting fees received by a director become material, at the motion to dismiss stage and on the facts before me, I think it is reasonable to infer that $75,000 would be material to director Bernbach and that he is beholden to the Cullman Group for continued receipt of such fees. Although not determinative, the inference of materiality is strengthened when the allegedly disabling fee is paid for the precise services that comprise the principal occupation of the challenged director.

Orman alleges that "Defendant Solomon has an interest in the transaction since his company, PJSC, stands to reap fees of $3.3 million if the transaction is effectuated." The reasonable inference that can be drawn from this contention is that if the merger is consummated PJSC will receive $3.3 million. I think it would be naïve to say, as a matter of law, that $3.3 million is immaterial. In my opinion, therefore, it is reasonable to infer that director Solomon suffered a disabling interest when considering how to cast his vote in connection with the challenged merger when the Board's decision on that matter could determine whether or not his firm would receive $3.3 million.

Directors Bernbach and Solomon, at this stage, cannot be considered independent and disinterested. Orman has thus pled facts that make it reasonable to question the independence and/or disinterest of a majority of the General Cigar Board—the four Cullman Group directors, plus Bernbach and Solomon, or six out of the eleven directors. Accordingly, I cannot say, as a matter of law, that the General Cigar Board's actions are protected by the business judgment rule presumption. Defendants' motion to dismiss the fiduciary duty claims – based as it is on a conclusion that the challenged transaction was approved by a disinterested and independent board—must be denied

IN RE THE WALT DISNEY COMPANY
DERIVATIVE LITIGATION
731 A.2d 342 (Del.Ch. 1998)

CHANDLER, Chancellor.

This case arises from a corporate board's decision to approve a large severance package for its president. Certain shareholders of the corporation seek relief from the Court of Chancery because that board actually honored the corporation's employment contract when the president left the company. The sheer magnitude of the severance package undoubtedly sparked this litigation, as well as the intense media coverage of the ensuing controversy over the board's decision. Nevertheless, the issues presented by this litigation, while larger in scale, are not unfamiliar to this Court.

Just as the 85,000–ton cruise ships Disney Magic and Disney Wonder are forced by science to obey the same laws of buoyancy as Disneyland's significantly smaller Jungle Cruise ships, so is a corporate board's extraordinary decision to award a $140 million severance package governed by the same corporate law principles as its everyday decision to authorize a loan. Legal rules that govern corporate boards, as well as the managers of day-to-day operations, are resilient, irrespective of context. When the laws of buoyancy are followed, the Disney Magic can stay afloat as well as the Jungle Cruise vessels. When the Delaware General Corporation Law is followed, a large severance package is just as valid as an authorization to borrow. Nature does not sink a ship merely because of its size, and neither do courts overrule a board's decision to approve and later honor a severance package, merely because of its size.

At its heart, this case is about the decision of the Walt Disney Company ("Disney" or the "Company") Board of Directors to approve an employment contract with a large severance provision for Michael Ovitz, referred to by some as the "Most Powerful Man in Hollywood." Disney convinced Ovitz to leave his position as head of Creative Artists Agency ("CAA") and become president of Disney. This case arose after the Disney Board's decision, subsequent to Ovitz's failure to become an effective president, to honor their employment agreement with its attendant severance provisions. This is a noteworthy case because the severance payment is large—larger than even the expert hired by the Disney Board to explain the contract imagined it to be, larger than almost anyone anywhere will receive in the lifetime of any of the parties, and perhaps larger than any ever paid.

The facts, in summary, are as follows: Ovitz gave up his lucrative position at CAA to come to Disney and was rewarded handsomely for it, both in salary (on the upside) and in potential severance (on the downside). After fourteen months, all parties agreed that Ovitz was not working out as president, so he left the company. The parties disagree as to how he left, but the fact is that after he left the Board awarded him the significant amount of severance detailed in his employment agreement. Ovitz gave up options that he could have received had he stayed longer, and Disney avoided protracted litigation with Ovitz over his rights under that agreement.

The case appears to be exceptional because of the sheer dollar amount involved. But does that mean the amount is so large that this Court should use its equitable powers to stop its payment? Does that mean it is so large that the conventional corporate governance laws of Delaware do not apply? No. Unless Plaintiffs can plead with specificity facts that rebut the presumption of the business judgment rule, that the Board was corrupted and could not make a decision fairly and independently, in the best interests of the Corporation, then the Board's decision will stand.

I must decide whether the particularized facts alleged in the complaint create a reasonable doubt that: 1) the directors are disinterested and independent; or 2) the challenged transaction was otherwise the product of a valid exercise of business judgment.

In order to create a reasonable doubt that a director is disinterested, a derivative plaintiff must plead particular facts to demonstrate that a director "will receive a personal financial benefit from a transaction that is not equally shared by the stockholders" or, conversely, that "a corporate decision will have a materially detrimental impact on a director, but not on the corporation and the stockholders." In these situations, a director cannot be expected to act "without being influenced by the ... personal consequences" flowing from the decision. At the other end of the spectrum, a board member is considered to be disinterested when he or she neither stands to benefit financially nor suffer materially from the decision whether to pursue the claim sought in the derivative plaintiff's demand.

Plaintiffs offer several reasons for their assertion that the Board is not independent. Chief among them is Plaintiffs' assertion that Eisner dominates and controls the Board. Plaintiffs argue that at least twelve of the fifteen members of the Disney Board who would have considered such a demand (i.e., excluding Ovitz) had such strong ties to Eisner that they would not have been able to make an impartial decision with respect to any demand Plaintiffs may have made. In order to prove domination and control by Eisner, Plaintiffs must demonstrate first that Eisner was personally interested in obtaining the Board's approval of the Employment Agreement and, second, that a majority of the Board could not exercise business judgment independent of Eisner in deciding whether to approve the Employment Agreement.

Plaintiffs offer two grounds for finding that Eisner was interested in the Employment Agreement. First, Plaintiffs suggest that Eisner's long-time personal relationship with Ovitz caused him to be interested in obtaining the Board's approval of the Employment Agreement. This argument, however, finds no support under Delaware law. The fact that Eisner has long-standing personal and business ties to Ovitz cannot overcome the presumption of independence that all directors, including Eisner, are afforded.

Second, Plaintiffs allege that Eisner was interested because he wanted to maximize his own income from Disney. Plaintiffs explain that Eisner accomplished this objective by "(a) maximizing the payments made by Disney to Ovitz; and (b) minimizing, to the extent possible, the controversy surrounding Ovitz's severance pay." According to Plaintiffs' theory, by providing his second-in-command a lucrative compensation package, Eisner set a high baseline from which he could negotiate upward for increased compensation for himself.

Plaintiffs' allegation that Eisner was interested in maximizing his compensation at the expense of Disney and its shareholders cannot reasonably be inferred from the facts alleged in Plaintiffs' amended complaint. At all times material to this litigation, Eisner owned several million options to purchase Disney stock. Therefore, it would not be in Eisner's economic interest to cause the Company to issue millions of additional options unnecessarily and at considerable cost.

I turn now to the Disney directors whom Plaintiffs allege were under Eisner's control, to consider whether they could have exercised their business judgment independently of Eisner.

Plaintiffs allege that directors Roy E. Disney, Sanford M. Litvack, and Richard A. Nunis were unable to exercise independent business judgment with respect to a demand because they were Disney executive employees who reported to and were accountable to Eisner at the time Plaintiffs commenced this litigation. I note at the outset the general Delaware rule that "the fact that they hold positions with the company [controlled by Eisner] ... is no more disqualifying than is the fact that he designated them as directors."

I begin my analysis with Mr. Disney, who earns a substantial salary and receives numerous, valuable options on Disney stock. As a top executive, his compensation is set by the Board, not solely by Eisner. Furthermore, Mr. Disney, along with his family, owns approximately 8.4 million shares of Disney stock. At today's prices these shares are worth $2.1 billion. The only reasonable inference that I can draw about Mr. Disney is that he is an economically rational individual whose priority is to protect the value of his Disney shares, not someone who would intentionally risk his own and his family's interests in order to placate Eisner. Nothing in Plaintiffs' pleadings suggest that Mr. Disney would place Eisner's interests over Mr. Disney's own and over those of the Company in derogation of his fiduciary duties as a Disney director.

With respect to Nunis and Litvack, contrary to Plaintiffs' allegations, these directors do not necessarily lose their ability to exercise independent business judgment merely by virtue of their being officers of Disney and Disney's subsidiaries. Plaintiffs, however, have pleaded with some particularity that there is at least a reasonable doubt as to Litvack and Nunis's ability to vote independently of Eisner. Their salaries are presumably also set by the Board, but they do not hold the same level of shares as Roy E. Disney and his family, and so there is a reasonable possibility they are more beholden to Eisner. Since, as a matter of law, Plaintiffs are unable to show a reasonable doubt as to Eisner's absence of self-interest, his potential domination over these two directors is inconsequential.

Plaintiffs allege that director Stanley P. Gold similarly lacks independence from Eisner because, as Mr. Disney's personal attorney, and the president and chief executive officer of a company wholly-owned by Mr. Disney's family, he is beholden to Mr. Disney (who is allegedly controlled by Eisner). While Gold may hold such positions under Roy E. Disney, because Mr. Disney's ability to exercise his independent business judgment is not impaired by his connection with Eisner, the business judgment of Gold is similarly free from Eisner's alleged dominating influence.

Plaintiffs allege that director Robert A.M. Stern's financial dealings with Disney were sufficiently large to cast a reasonable doubt upon his ability to consider a demand disinterestedly. Plaintiffs point out that Stern, an architect, had been commissioned to design several buildings for the Company and one for Eisner, for which his firm had collected millions of dollars in fees from Disney and Eisner. Plaintiffs allege that because of these fees, Eisner controls Stern and there is a reasonable doubt as to whether Stern could consider a demand independent of Eisner's influence.

I agree with Plaintiffs: The fact that Stern's architectural firm has received, and perhaps continues to receive, payments from Disney over a period of years raises a reasonable doubt as to Stern's independent judgment with respect to the Employment Agreement. Fees have continued to flow from Disney to Stern's firm, and the fees received in the past, from both Disney and Eisner, have been quite substantial. Thus, as a matter of law, Plaintiffs have shown a reasonable doubt that Stern is independent of Eisner.

Plaintiffs assert that director E. Cardon Walker could not exercise business judgment independent of Eisner because, after Eisner became chairman of Disney, Walker consulted for Disney and has, in recent years, received substantial sums for his investments in certain Disney films. As for the substantial sums Plaintiffs allege Walker has received and continues to receive from Disney, these stem from contractual rights with the Company that are at least nineteen years old and that predate Eisner's reign with Disney. Plaintiffs have failed to demonstrate that Walker is somehow beholden to Eisner or otherwise incapable of exercising independent judgment.

Plaintiffs allege that director Gary L. Wilson lacked independence from Eisner as well. Wilson served under Eisner as Disney's executive vice president and chief financial officer from July 1985 through December 1989, receiving substantial compensation from Disney over which, Plaintiffs' allege, Eisner had considerable influence. Plaintiffs' claims do not raise a reasonable doubt that Wilson is interested in the Employment Agreement. Whatever rights Wilson had when he left Disney have already been paid to him.

Plaintiffs also allege that Father Leo J. O'Donovan, involved only in the decision to honor the Employment Agreement, is incapable of rendering independent business judgment. O'Donovan is the president of Georgetown University, the alma mater of one of Eisner's sons and the recipient of over $1 million of donations from Eisner since 1989. Accordingly, Plaintiffs allege that O'Donovan would not act contrary to Eisner's wishes.

The question is whether Eisner exerted such an influence on O'Donovan that O'Donovan could not exercise independent judgment as a director. Plaintiffs do not allege any personal benefit received by O'Donovan – in fact, they admit that O'Donovan is forbidden, as a Jesuit priest, from collecting any director's fee. I do not believe that Plaintiffs have presented a reasonable doubt as to the independence of O'Donovan.

Director Reveta F. Bowers is the principal of the elementary school that Eisner's children once attended. Plaintiffs suggest that because Bowers' salary as a teacher is low compared to her director's fees and stock options, "only the most rigidly formalistic or myopic analysis" would view Bowers as not beholden to Eisner.

Plaintiffs fail to recognize that the Delaware Supreme Court has held that "such allegations [of payment of director's fees], without more, do not establish any financial interest." *Grobow v. Perot,* Del.Supr., 539 A.2d 180, 188 (1988). To follow Plaintiffs' urging to discard "formalistic notions of interest and independence in favor of a realistic approach" expressly would be to overrule the

Delaware Supreme Court.

Furthermore, to do so would be to discourage the membership on corporate boards of people of less-than extraordinary means. Such "regular folks" would face allegations of being dominated by other board members, merely because of the relatively substantial compensation provided by the board membership compared to their outside salaries. I am especially unwilling to facilitate such a result. Without more, Plaintiffs have failed to allege facts that lead to a reasonable doubt as to the independence of Bowers.

Plaintiffs question the independence of Senator George J. Mitchell. Mitchell acts as special counsel to a law firm that has been engaged by Disney on various matters and that was paid $122,764 for its services in 1996. Disney has also retained Mitchell on an individual basis to provide consulting services to the Company. Plaintiffs allege that during 1996, Disney paid Mitchell $50,000 for performing these services. Accordingly, Plaintiffs allege that Mitchell is incapable of making business decisions independently of Eisner. Plaintiffs have not alleged any particularized facts that raise a reasonable doubt that Mitchell voted in favor of the Employment Agreement in order to obtain a specific financial benefit. Without such allegations, Plaintiffs' conclusory assertion that Mitchell was under Eisner's influence or otherwise interested in any aspect of the Employment Agreement is insufficient as a matter of law to raise a reasonable doubt as to Mitchell's independence.

Director Irwin E. Russell is an entertainment lawyer who serves as Eisner's personal counsel and has a long history of personal and business ties to Eisner. As a result, Plaintiffs allege Russell is unable to exercise independent business judgment. Russell practices in a small firm for which the fees derived from Eisner likely represent a large portion of the total amount of fees received by the firm. Accordingly, it appears Plaintiffs have raised a reasonable doubt as to Russell's independence of Eisner's influence for the purpose of considering a demand.

As for director Sidney Poitier, Plaintiffs do not allege that he is dominated by Eisner. Plaintiffs do allege, however, that Poitier is a longtime client of Creative Artists Agency—the talent agency that Ovitz founded—and through his relationship with CAA, he has earned millions of dollars. As a result, Plaintiffs suggest Poitier is "impermissibly conflicted" in his ability to render independent business judgment with respect to Ovitz's compensation. Although Poitier had enjoyed a successful relationship with Ovitz and CAA, (a) Ovitz is no longer the head of CAA, and (b) it does not follow that Poitier is incapable of considering Ovitz's compensation package without bias. Such an assertion is based on conjecture, and Plaintiffs have not raised a reasonable doubt as to Poitier's independence.

In sum, Plaintiffs have not raised a reasonable doubt as to the absence of self-interest of any of the directors in approving or honoring the Employment Agreement. If, however, Plaintiffs had shown a reasonable doubt on Eisner's part, then I would agree that they had demonstrated a reasonable doubt as to the independence only of directors Litvack, Nunis, Stern, and Russell, because of

Eisner's domination over them. Plaintiffs have not raised a reasonable doubt as to the independence from Eisner of directors Disney, Gold, Walker, Wilson, O'Donovan (involved only in the decision to honor the Employment Agreement), Bowers, Mitchell, and Poitier.

Thus, even assuming that Eisner was interested in the Employment Agreement – and, again, Plaintiffs have not shown a reasonable doubt as to Eisner's independence – Plaintiffs still come up short; ten of the fifteen directors who approved the Agreement and eleven of the sixteen who voted to honor the Agreement were independent in deciding the issues of Ovitz's compensation and free of domination from Eisner.

For the reasons assigned above, all counts of Plaintiffs' amended complaint must be dismissed for failure to make demand on the Disney Board in accordance with Chancery Rule 23.1 or for failure to state a claim under Chancery Rule 12(b)(6).

CASE PROBLEM 10-6

Assume the same facts as Case Problem 10-5, except a meeting of the directors was called to discuss the $4 million investment. At the meeting, the film's producer and line producer made a full presentation, Debby's role was thoroughly described and discussed, and the potential benefits to Brand and its clients were carefully evaluated. At the end of the meeting, the directors approved the investment by a vote of 6 to 1. Jim dissented.

How do these facts impact, if at all, the potential personal liability of Larry and others or the application of MBCA § 8.61 if a lawsuit is filed?

3. DISINTERESTED SHAREHOLDER RATIFICATION

LEWIS v. VOGELSTEIN
699 A.2d 327 (Del.Ch. 1997)

ALLEN, Chancellor.

This shareholders' suit challenges a stock option compensation plan for the directors of Mattel, Inc., which was approved or ratified by the shareholders of the company at its 1996 Annual Meeting of Shareholders. Two claims are asserted.

The facts as they appear in the pleading are as follows. The Plan was adopted in 1996 and ratified by the company's shareholders at the 1996 annual meeting. It contemplates two forms of stock option grants to the company's directors: a one-time grant of options on a block of stock and subsequent, smaller annual grants of further options. With respect to the one-time grant, the Plan provides that each outside director will qualify for a grant of options on 15,000 shares of Mattel common stock at the market price on the day such options are granted (the "one-time options"). The one-time options are alleged to be exercisable immediately upon being granted although they will achieve economic value, if ever, only with the passage of time. It is alleged that if not exercised, they remain valid for ten years.

With respect to the second type of option grant, the Plan qualifies each director for a grant of options upon his or her re-election to the board each year (the "Annual Options"). The maximum number of options grantable to a director pursuant to the annual options provision depends on the number of years the director has served on the Mattel board. Those outside directors with five or fewer years of service will qualify to receive options on no more than 5,000 shares, while those with more than five years service will qualify for options to purchase up to 10,000 shares. Once granted, these options vest over a four year period, at a rate of 25% per year. When exercisable, they entitle the holder to buy stock at the market price on the day of the grant. According to the complaint, options granted pursuant to the annual options provision also expire ten years from their grant date, whether or not the holder has remained on the board.

When the shareholders were asked to ratify the adoption of the Plan, as is typically true, no estimated present value of options that were authorized to be granted under the Plan was stated in the proxy solicitation materials.

I turn to the motion to dismiss the complaint's allegation to the effect that the Plan, or grants under it, constitute a breach of the directors' fiduciary duty of loyalty. As the Plan contemplates grants to the directors that approved the Plan and who recommended it to the shareholders, we start by observing that it constitutes self-dealing that would ordinarily require that the directors prove that the grants involved were, in the circumstances, entirely fair to the corporation. However, it is the case that the shareholders have ratified the directors' action. That ratification is attacked only on the ground just treated. Thus, for these purposes I assume that the ratification was effective. The question then becomes what is the effect of informed shareholder ratification on a transaction of this type (i.e., officer or director pay).

What is the effect under Delaware corporation law of shareholder ratification of an interested transaction? The answer to this apparently simple question appears less clear than one would hope or indeed expect. Four possible effects of shareholder ratification appear logically available: **First**, one might conclude that an effective shareholder ratification acts as a complete defense to any charge of breach of duty. **Second**, one might conclude that the effect of such ratification is to shift the substantive test on judicial review of the act from one of fairness that would otherwise be obtained (because the transaction is an interested one) to one of waste. **Third**, one might conclude that the ratification shifts the burden of proof of unfairness to plaintiff, but leaves that shareholder-protective test in place. **Fourth**, one might conclude (perhaps because of great respect for the collective action disabilities that attend shareholder action in public corporations) that shareholder ratification offers no assurance of assent of a character that deserves judicial recognition. Thus, under this approach, ratification on full information would be afforded no effect. Excepting the fourth of these effects, there are cases in this jurisdiction that reflect each of these approaches to the effect of shareholder voting to approve a transaction. *See, e.g., In re Wheelabrator Technologies, Inc., Shareholders Litig.*, Del.Ch., 663 A.2d 1194 (1995); *Michelson v. Duncan*, Del.Supr., 407 A.2d 211, 224 (1979); *Citron* *v. E.I. DuPont de Nemours & Co.,* Del.Ch., 584 A.2d 490, 500-502 (1990).

In order to state my own understanding I first note that by shareholder ratification I do not refer to every instance in which shareholders vote affirmatively with respect to a question placed before them. I exclude from the question those instances in which shareholder votes are a necessary step in authorizing a transaction. Thus the law of ratification as here discussed has no direct bearing on shareholder action to amend a certificate of incorporation or bylaws. Cf. Williams v. Geier, Del.Supr., 671 A.2d 1368 (1996); nor does that law bear on shareholder votes necessary to authorize a merger, a sale of substantially all the corporation's assets, or to dissolve the enterprise. For analytical purposes one can set such cases aside.

1. Ratification generally: I start with principles broader than those of corporation law. Ratification is a concept deriving from the law of agency which contemplates the ex post conferring upon or confirming of the legal authority of an agent in circumstances in which the agent had no authority or arguably had no authority. To be effective, of course, the agent must fully disclose all relevant circumstances with respect to the transaction to the principal prior to the ratification. Beyond that, since the relationship between a principal and agent is fiduciary in character, the agent in seeking ratification must act not only with candor, but with loyalty. Thus an attempt to coerce the principal's consent improperly will invalidate the effectiveness of the ratification.

Assuming that a ratification by an agent is validly obtained, what is its effect? One way of conceptualizing that effect is that it provides, after the fact, the grant of authority that may have been wanting at the time of the agent's act. Another might be to view the ratification as consent or as an estoppel by the principal to deny a lack of authority. In either event the effect of informed ratification is to validate or affirm the act of the agent as the act of the principal.

Application of these general ratification principles to shareholder ratification is complicated by three other factors. First, most generally, in the case of shareholder ratification there is of course no single individual acting as principal, but rather a class or group of divergent individuals-the class of shareholders. This aggregate quality of the principal means that decisions to affirm or ratify an act will be subject to collective action disabilities; that some portion of the body doing the ratifying may in fact have conflicting interests in the transaction; and some dissenting members of the class may be able to assert more or less convincingly that the "will" of the principal is wrong, or even corrupt and ought not to be binding on the class. In the case of individual ratification these issues won't arise, assuming that the principal does not suffer from multiple personality disorder. Thus the collective nature of shareholder ratification makes it more likely that following a claimed shareholder ratification, nevertheless, there is a litigated claim on behalf of the principal that the agent lacked authority or breached its duty. The second, mildly complicating factor present in shareholder ratification is the fact that in corporation law the "ratification" that shareholders provide will often not be directed to lack of legal authority of an agent but will relate to the consistency of some authorized director action with the equitable duty of loyalty. Thus shareholder ratification sometimes acts not to confer legal authority-but as in this case-to affirm that action taken is consistent with shareholder interests. Third, when what is "ratified" is a director conflict transaction, the statutory law-in Delaware Section 144 of the Delaware General Corporation Law-may bear on the effect.

2. Shareholder ratification: These differences between shareholder ratification of director action and classic ratification by a single principal, do lead to a difference in the effect of a valid ratification in the shareholder context. The principal novelty added to ratification law generally by the shareholder context, is the idea - no doubt analogously present in other contexts in which common interests are held - that, in addition to a claim that ratification was defective because of incomplete information or coercion, shareholder ratification is subject to a claim by a member of the class that the ratification is ineffectual (1) because a majority of those affirming the transaction had a conflicting interest with respect to it or (2) because the transaction that is ratified constituted a corporate waste. As to the second of these, it has long been held that shareholders may not ratify a waste except by a unanimous vote. *Saxe v. Brady*, Del.Ch., 184 A.2d 602, 605 (1962). The idea behind this rule is apparently that a transaction that satisfies the high standard of waste constitutes a gift of corporate property and no one should be forced against their will to make a gift of their property. In all events, informed, uncoerced, disinterested shareholder ratification of a transaction in which corporate directors have a material conflict of interest has the effect of protecting the transaction from judicial review except on the basis of waste.

The judicial standard for determination of corporate waste is well developed. Roughly, a waste entails an exchange of corporate assets for consideration so disproportionately small as to lie beyond the range at which any reasonable person might be willing to trade. *See Saxe v. Brady*, 184 A.2d 602, 610; *Grobow v. Perot*, Del.Supr., 539 A.2d 180, 189 (1988). Most often the claim is associated with a transfer of corporate assets that serves no corporate purpose; or for which no consideration at all is received. Such a transfer is in effect a gift. If, however, there is any substantial consideration received by the corporation, and if there is a good faith judgment that in the circumstances the transaction is worthwhile, there should be no finding of waste, even if the fact finder would conclude ex post that the transaction was unreasonably risky. Any other rule would deter corporate boards from the optimal rational acceptance of risk, for reasons explained elsewhere. Courts are ill-fitted to attempt to weigh the "adequacy" of consideration under the waste standard or, ex post, to judge appropriate degrees of business risk.

Before ruling on the pending motion to dismiss the substantive claim of breach of fiduciary duty, under a waste standard, I should make one other observation. The standard for determination of motions to dismiss is of course well established and understood. Where under any state of facts consistent with the factual allegations of the complaint the plaintiff would be entitled to a judgment, the complaint may not be dismissed as legally defective. It is also the case that in some instances "mere conclusions" may be held to be insufficient to withstand an otherwise well made motion. Since what is a "well pleaded" fact and what is a "mere conclusion" is not always clear, there is often and inevitably some small room for the exercise of informed judgment by courts in determining motions to dismiss under the appropriate test. Consider for example allegations that an arm's-length corporate transaction constitutes a waste of assets. In some instances the facts alleged, if true, will be so far from satisfying the waste standard that dismissal is appropriate.

This is not such a case in my opinion. Giving the pleader the presumptions to which he is entitled on this motion, I cannot conclude that no set of facts could be shown that would permit the court to conclude that the grant of these options, particularly focusing upon the one-time options, constituted an exchange to which no reasonable person not acting under compulsion and in good faith could agree. In so concluding, I do not mean to suggest a view that these grants are suspect, only that one time option grants to directors of this size seem at this point sufficiently unusual to require the court to refer to evidence before making an adjudication of their validity and consistency with fiduciary duty. Thus, for that reason the motion to dismiss will be denied.

HARBOR FINANCE PARTNERS v. HUIZENGA
751 A.2d 879 (Del.Ch. 1999)

STRINE, Vice Chancellor.

This matter involves a challenge to the acquisition of AutoNation, Incorporated by Republic Industries, Inc. A shareholder plaintiff contends that this acquisition (the "Merger") was a self-interested transaction effected for the benefit of Republic directors who owned a substantial block of AutoNation shares, that the terms of the transaction were unfair to Republic and its public stockholders, and that stockholder approval of the transaction was procured through a materially misleading proxy statement (the "Proxy Statement").

The affirmative stockholder vote on the Merger was informed and uncoerced, and disinterested shares constituted the overwhelming proportion of the Republic electorate. As a result, the business judgment rule standard of review is invoked and the Merger may only be attacked as wasteful. As a matter of logic and sound policy, one might think that a fair vote of disinterested stockholders in support of the transaction would dispose of the case altogether because a waste claim must be supported by facts demonstrating that "no person of ordinary sound business judgment" could consider the merger fair to Republic and because many disinterested and presumably rational Republic stockholders voted for the Merger. But under an unbroken line of authority dating from early in this century, a non-unanimous, although overwhelming, free and fair vote of disinterested stockholders does not extinguish a claim for waste. The waste vestige does not aid the plaintiff here, however, because the complaint at best alleges that the Merger was unfair, and does not plead facts demonstrating that no reasonable person of ordinary business judgment could believe the transaction advisable for Republic. Thus I grant the defendants' motion to dismiss under Chancery Court Rule 12(b)(6).

Although I recognize that our law has long afforded plaintiffs the vestigial right to prove that a transaction that a majority of fully informed, uncoerced independent stockholders approved by a non-unanimous vote was wasteful, I question the continued utility of this "equitable safety valve."

The origin of this rule is rooted in the distinction between voidable and void acts, a distinction that appears to have grown out of the now largely abolished ultra vires doctrine. Voidable acts are traditionally held to be ratifiable because the corporation can lawfully accomplish them if it does so in the appropriate manner. Thus if directors who could not lawfully effect a transaction without stockholder approval did so anyway, and the requisite approval of the stockholders was later attained, the transaction is deemed fully ratified because the subsequent approval of the stockholders cured the defect.

In contrast, void acts are said to be non-ratifiable because the corporation cannot, in any case, lawfully accomplish them. Such void acts are often described in conclusory terms such as "ultra vires" or "fraudulent" or as "gifts or waste of corporate assets." Because at first blush it seems it would be a shocking, if not theoretically impossible, thing for stockholders to be able to sanction the directors in committing illegal acts or acts beyond the authority of the corporation, it is unsurprising that it has been held that stockholders cannot validate such action by the directors, even on an informed basis.

One of the many practical problems with this seemingly sensible doctrine is that its actual application has no apparent modern day utility insofar as the doctrine covers claims of waste or gift, except as an opportunity for Delaware courts to second-guess stockholders. There are several reasons I believe this to be so.

First, the types of "void" acts susceptible to being styled as waste claims have little of the flavor of patent illegality about them, nor are they categorically ultra vires. Put another way, the oft-stated proposition that "waste cannot be ratified" is a tautology that, upon close examination, has little substantive meaning. I mean, what rational person would ratify "waste"? Stating the question that way, the answer is, of course, no one. But in the real world stockholders are not asked to ratify obviously wasteful transactions. Rather than lacking any plausible business rationale or being clearly prohibited by statutory or common law, the transactions attacked as waste in Delaware courts are ones that are quite ordinary in the modern business world. These are all garden variety transactions that may be validly accomplished by a Delaware corporation if supported by sufficient consideration, and what is sufficient consideration is a question that fully informed stockholders seem as well positioned as courts to answer. That is, these transactions are neither per se ultra vires or illegal; they only become "void" upon a determination that the corporation received no fair consideration for entering upon them.

Second, the waste vestige is not necessary to protect stockholders and it has no other apparent purpose. While I would hesitate to permit stockholders to ratify a blatantly illegal act – such as a board's decision to indemnify itself against personal liability for intentionally violating applicable environmental laws or bribing government officials to benefit the corporation – the vestigial exception for waste has little to do with corporate integrity in the sense of the corporation's responsibility to society as a whole. Rather, if there is any benefit in the waste vestige, it must consist in protecting stockholders. And where disinterested stockholders are given the information necessary to decide whether a transaction is beneficial to the corporation or wasteful to it, I see little reason to leave the door open for a judicial reconsideration of the matter.

The fact that a plaintiff can challenge the adequacy of the disclosure is in itself a substantial safeguard against stockholder approval of waste. If the corporate board failed to provide the voters with material information undermining the integrity or financial fairness of the transaction subject to the vote, no ratification effect will be accorded to the vote and the plaintiffs may press all of their claims. As a result, it is difficult to imagine how elimination of the waste vestige will permit the accomplishment of unconscionable corporate transactions, unless one presumes that stockholders are, as a class, irrational and that they will rubber stamp outrageous transactions contrary to their own economic interests.

Nor is the waste vestige necessary to protect minority stockholders from oppression by majority or controlling stockholders. As an initial matter, I note that property of the corporation is not typically thought of as personal property of the stockholders, and that it is common for corporations to undertake important value-affecting transactions over the objection of some of the voters or without a vote at all.

In any event, my larger point is that this solicitude for dissenters' property rights is already adequately accounted for elsewhere in our corporation law. Delaware fiduciary law ensures that a majority or controlling stockholder cannot use a stockholder vote to insulate a transaction benefiting that stockholder from judicial examination. Only votes controlled by stockholders who are not "interested" in the transaction at issue are eligible for ratification effect in the sense of invoking the business judgment rule rather than the entire fairness form of review. That is, only the votes of those stockholders with no economic incentive to approve a wasteful transaction count.

Third, I find it logically difficult to conceptualize how a plaintiff can ultimately prove a waste or gift claim in the face of a decision by fully informed, uncoerced, independent stockholders to ratify the transaction. The test for waste is whether any person of ordinary sound business judgment could view the transaction as fair.

If fully informed, uncoerced, independent stockholders have approved the transaction, they have, it seems to me, made the decision that the transaction is "a fair exchange." As such, it is difficult to see the utility of allowing litigation to proceed in which the plaintiffs are permitted discovery and a possible trial, at great expense to the corporate defendants, in order to prove to the court that the transaction was so devoid of merit that each and every one of the voters comprising the majority must be disregarded as too hopelessly misguided to be considered a "person of ordinary sound business judgment." In this day and age in which investors also have access to an abundance of information about corporate transactions from sources other than boards of directors, it seems presumptuous and paternalistic to assume that the court knows better in a particular instance than a fully informed corporate electorate with real money riding on the corporation's performance.

Finally, it is unclear why it is in the best interests of disinterested stockholders to subject their corporation to the substantial costs of litigation in a situation where they have approved the transaction under attack. Enabling a dissident who failed to get her way at the ballot box in a fair election to divert the corporation's resources to defending her claim on the battlefield of litigation seems, if anything, contrary to the economic well-being of the disinterested stockholders as a class. Why should the law give the dissenters the right to command the corporate treasury over the contrary will of a majority of the disinterested stockholders? The costs to corporations of litigating waste claims are not trifling.

For all these reasons, a reexamination of the waste vestige would seem to be in order. Although there may be valid reasons for its continuation, those reasons should be articulated and weighed against the costs the vestige imposes on stockholders and the judicial system. Otherwise, inertia alone may perpetuate an outdated rule fashioned in a very different time.

CASE PROBLEM 10-7

Assume the same facts as Case Problem 10-6, except a meeting of the shareholders was called to discuss the $4 million investment. At the meeting, the film's producer and line producer made a full presentation, Debby's role was thoroughly described and discussed, and the potential benefits to Brand and its clients were carefully evaluated. At the end of the meeting, shareholders owning 60 percent of the stock approved the investment. The approval votes came from Larry, Linda, Sam, Clint, and two minority shareholders who had been longtime friends of Larry. The Moro Clan and the other minority shareholders voted against the investment.

How do these facts impact, if at all, the potential personal liability of Larry and others or the application of MBCA § 8.61 if a lawsuit is filed?

4. THE CORPORATE OPPORTUNITY DOCTRINE

FARBER v. SERVAN LAND COMPANY, INC.
662 F.2d 371 (5th Cir. 1981)

TJOFLAT, Circuit Judge:

In 1959, Charles Serianni, a Broward County, Florida, businessman, initiated a plan to build and operate a golf course and country club near Ft. Lauderdale. With the assistance of several other investors he formed a corporation, the Servan Land Company, Inc. (the corporation), which was to own and operate the enterprise. The corporation acquired 160 acres of land on which to build the course. Shortly thereafter it acquired from James Farquhar twenty additional acres abutting the golf course, to be used as a dump site for top soil and as a nursery.

Serianni held 180 shares of the corporation's stock and served as President of the corporation throughout its existence. A. I. Savin, a resident of Connecticut, owned 216 1/2 shares of stock, and served as the corporation's Vice President. There were eight other stockholders, including Jack Farber, the plaintiff in this action. Farber owned sixty shares.

On several occasions the directors and stockholders discussed the possibility of acquiring more land abutting the golf course, but the corporation took no action. Then, at the 1968 annual stockholders' meeting, Servan Land Company director and stockholder Hamilton Forman informed his associates that James Farquhar was willing to sell 160 acres of abutting land to the corporation. This land was suitable for use as an additional golf course. At the time he made the statement, the stockholders were discussing refinancing the mortgage on the country club in order to obtain funds to redeem the corporation's preferred stock and pay debts owed to several stockholders. Forman suggested that the proceeds the stockholders received from the redemption could be used to buy additional stock in the corporation, thus generating the funds necessary for the corporation to acquire the Farquhar property.

A few months later, Serianni and Savin met with James Farquhar and negotiated to buy, in their individual capacities, the same 160 acres abutting the golf course that had been discussed at the corporation's annual stockholders' meeting. They closed the transaction in March 1969.

The minutes of the 1969 annual stockholders' meeting, held the following month, indicate no discussion of or reference to Serianni and Savin's purchase. During the following year Farber learned of the purchase from a third party, and at the 1970 annual stockholders' meeting, he inquired about it. Savin and Serianni acknowledged the purchase, but at this point the evidence varies. The official corporate minutes indicate that the stockholders discussed the purchase and found no impropriety, and that "(a) motion to approve this land purchase by Mr. Serianni and Mr. Savin individually was then moved, seconded and approved by everyone at the meeting, except (Mr. Farber's proxy)." Farber, however, having been at odds with the majority stockholders for some time, had sent a court reporter to the meeting, and the court reporter's transcript reports no motion to ratify Serianni and Savin's purchase.

Three years later, in 1973, Serianni, Savin and the corporation entered into an agreement with a purchaser to sell as a package the corporation's assets and the 160 acres of adjoining land Serianni and Savin had bought; each contract of sale was conditioned upon execution of the other. Of the aggregate sales price, the defendants allocated $5,000,000 to the corporation and $3,353,700 to Savin and Serianni, though this division was not based on any appraisal of the respective properties.

At a special directors' and stockholders' meeting, all the members of the corporation but Farber approved the sale and voted to liquidate Servan Land Company. After the sale was completed Farber brought a stockholders' derivative suit in the district court, based on diversity jurisdiction, alleging that Savin and Serianni had preempted a corporate opportunity by acquiring the 160 acres adjacent to the golf course. He also sought appointment of an appraiser to determine the proper allocation of the purchase price.

The appraiser subsequently valued the corporation's properties at $4,065,915, and the Serianni-Savin property at $3,950,925. Serianni and Savin had allotted to the corporation a greater percentage of the proceeds of the sale than would have been allocated using the appraiser's figures.

Following submission of the appraisal, the district court issued a memorandum opinion, which set forth its finding that "Serianni and Savin should have informed the directors of the opportunity to purchase Mr. Farquhar's 160 adjoining acres." But the court also noted that their purchase, "worked to the distinct advantage of the corporation and not to its detriment because it enhanced the value of the major corporate asset the golf course."

Farber appealed the district court's decision, and this court vacated and remanded it for clarification, stating: "if, as seems to be clearly expressed, there was no corporate opportunity, why should, as is three times stated, Serianni and Savin have offered the 160 adjacent acres to the corporation? The holdings are inconsistent." This court also questioned the district court's reliance on the theory that Savin and Serianni benefited the corporation by selling their 160 acres along with the corporation's assets. We stated, "If the corporate opportunity doctrine is otherwise applicable it is not made inapplicable by the realization of a substantial gain from a fortuitous sale of its assets at the same time as the sale of the property asserted to be a corporate opportunity to a lone buyer who would not have bought either property without the other. If a corporate opportunity existed the corporation and its stockholders would have been entitled to the profits from the sale of both parcels."

On remand, the district court failed to explain why it found that Serianni and Savin had a duty to offer the opportunity to purchase the 160 acres to the corporation, but it reaffirmed its finding that "Seriani (sic) and Savin had satisfactorily sustained the burden of establishing the propriety of the transaction." It stated that it based this conclusion on three grounds: "(1) the corporation, although it discussed Mr. Farquhar's abutting land ... took no action to acquire it at a previous annual meeting of the corporation; (2) the action of Seriani (sic) and Savin in purchasing the abutting land was ratified and approved by a special meeting of the stockholders on May 9th, 1973" and (3) Serianni and Savin were generous in valuing the corporation's assets above their worth when apportioning the proceeds of the package sale. The third fact, the court held, indicated that the defendants were not taking advantage of the corporation.

Farber appeals once again.

In reviewing the district court's decision we must evaluate its resolution of four key issues: whether a corporate opportunity existed; whether the stockholders declined the opportunity by failing to act; whether the stockholders ratified Serianni and Savin's purchase; and whether the subsequent benefit the corporation received in selling its assets in conjunction with Serianni and Savin's 160 acres rectifies any wrong it might have suffered through the defendants' initial purchase of the land.

If one occupying a fiduciary relationship to a corporation acquires, "in opposition to the corporation, property in which the corporation has an interest or tangible expectancy or which is essential to its existence," he violates what has come to be known as the "doctrine of 'corporate opportunity." 3 Fletcher Cyclopedia Corporations s 861.1 at 227 (rev'd ed. 1965). Florida has long recognized the doctrine of corporate opportunity, and has described a corporate opportunity as a business opportunity in which the corporation has an interest for a "valid and significant corporate purpose." Pan American Trading & Trapping v. Crown Paint, Inc., 99 So.2d 705, 706 (Fla.1957). The opportunity need not be "of the utmost importance to the welfare of the corporation," to be protected from preemption by the corporation's directors and officers. Pan American, 99 So.2d at 706. As we elaborated in the first appeal of this case, however, the opportunity must "fit into the present activities of the corporation or fit into an established corporate policy which the acquisition of the opportunity would forward." Farber, 541 F.2d at 1088.

It should be noted that the district court not only found that the stockholders frequently discussed acquisition of Mr. Farquhar's land at their meetings; it also found that the stockholders had discussed this matter at the last meeting, just shortly before Serianni and Savin made their purchase, and that they had "indicated a sense of approval to the idea of acquiring abutting land from Mr. Farquhar." Further, the court heard testimony that the corporation needed the land on the perimeter of the golf course, and evidence that the corporation had bought additional land from Mr. Farquhar in the past and that it had bought and operated a lodge located on part of that land. These facts make it clear that the opportunity to acquire the Farquhar land was an advantageous one that fit into a present, significant corporate purpose, as well as an ongoing corporate policy, and that the corporation had an active interest in it. Accordingly, the opportunity to buy the land constituted a corporate opportunity.

In addition to finding that no corporate opportunity existed, the district court found that if one did exist, "it was rejected by the corporation." The court apparently reached this conclusion because after deciding at their annual meeting that the opportunity to purchase the land should be investigated, the stockholders did not vote, at that meeting, to commit the funds available from the refinancing to purchase of the Farquhar property. We find that this failure does not indicate a decision to refrain from pursuing the opportunity to purchase. Because the other stockholders relied upon Serianni to initiate the investigation on the corporation's behalf, he may not now translate his own inaction into a corporate rejection of the opportunity, thus allowing him to buy the land personally. The district court's finding that the corporation rejected the opportunity is clearly erroneous.

As another ground for its decision, the district court held that the stockholders ratified Serianni and Savin's purchase at their May 9, 1970 meeting. Farber argues that even if the ratification vote did take place, it cannot be used to prohibit his derivative action. We agree. When ratification is possible and the proceedings are proper, stockholders may sanction the act of a corporate officer or director and thus abolish any cause of action that the corporation might have against that individual. Not all acts may be ratified, and the Florida courts have not indicated whether stockholders are capable of ratifying a director or officer's breach of fiduciary duty. We do not need to decide whether ratification was possible here, however, because even if it was, the manner of ratification in this case renders the ratification a nullity.

According to the corporate minutes, all of the directors present at the annual meeting, except the plaintiff, voted to ratify the land purchase. Both of the purchasing directors were present, and between the two of them, they held four-sevenths of the stock. While it is true that directors ordinarily may vote their stock on measures in which they have a personal interest, most authorities agree that "(t)he violation of their duty by corporate directors cannot be ratified by the action of those who were guilty of participation in the wrongful acts, even though they constitute a majority of the directors or of the stockholders." Chesapeake Construction Corp. v. Rodman, 256 Md. 531, 537, 261 A.2d 156, 159 (Md.App.1970). Thus, Serianni and Savin may not bind Farber by ratifying their own inappropriate acts. Farber is entitled to bring a derivative action.

Finally, in finding in favor of the defendants, the district court relied heavily on the notion that by valuing the two properties favorably for the corporation when they were sold jointly, and by selling the properties together, thus raising the value of each, Serianni and Savin benefitted the corporation. This benefit, according to the court, precluded any recovery for breach of fiduciary duty in obtaining the Farquhar acres in the first place. As we stated in the first appeal, however:

> If the corporate opportunity doctrine is otherwise applicable it is not made inapplicable by the realization of a substantial gain from a fortuitous sale of its assets at the same time as the sale of the property asserted to be a corporate opportunity to a lone buyer who would not have bought either property without the other.

We find that the opportunity to buy Mr. Farquhar's 160 acres constituted a corporate opportunity and that the defendants, Serianni and Savin, breached their fiduciary duties to the corporation by preempting that opportunity. We also find that the attempted ratification of the preemption does not preclude Farber from bringing a derivative suit on behalf of the corporation. The corporation is entitled to the profits of the directors' subsequent sale of the 160 acres. We remand the case to the district court to determine the proper amount of damages and the appropriate method for distributing those damages.

BROZ v. CELLULAR INFORMATION SYSTEMS, INC.
673 A.2d 148 (Del. 1996)

VEASEY, Chief Justice:

In this appeal, we consider the application of the doctrine of corporate opportunity. The Court of Chancery decided that the defendant, a corporate director, breached his fiduciary duty by not formally presenting to the corporation an opportunity which had come to the director individually and independent of the director's relationship with the corporation. Here the opportunity was not one in which the corporation in its current mode had an interest or which it had the financial ability to acquire, but, under the unique circumstances here, that mode was subject to change by virtue of the impending acquisition of the corporation by another entity.

We conclude that, although a corporate director may be shielded from liability by offering to the corporation an opportunity which has come to the director independently and individually, the failure of the director to present the opportunity does not necessarily result in the improper usurpation of a corporate opportunity. We further conclude that, if the corporation is a target or potential target of an acquisition by another company which has an interest and ability to entertain the opportunity, the director of the target company does not have a fiduciary duty to present the opportunity to the target company. Accordingly, the judgment of the Court of Chancery is REVERSED.

Robert F. Broz ("Broz") is the President and sole stockholder of RFB Cellular, Inc. ("RFBC"), a Delaware corporation engaged in the business of providing cellular telephone service in the Midwestern United States. At the time of the conduct at issue in this appeal, Broz was also a member of the board of directors of plaintiff below-appellee, Cellular Information Systems, Inc. ("CIS"). CIS is a publicly held Delaware corporation and a competitor of RFBC.

The conduct before the Court involves the purchase by Broz of a cellular telephone service license for the benefit of RFBC. The license in question, known as the Michigan-2 Rural Service Area Cellular License ("Michigan-2"), is issued by the Federal Communications Commission ("FCC") and entitles its holder to provide cellular telephone service to a portion of northern Michigan. CIS brought an action against Broz and RFBC for equitable relief, contending that the purchase of this license by Broz constituted a usurpation of a corporate opportunity properly belonging to CIS, irrespective of whether or not CIS was interested in the Michigan-2 opportunity at the time it was offered to Broz.

The principal basis for the contention of CIS is that PriCellular, Inc. ("PriCellular"), another cellular communications company which was contemporaneously engaged in an acquisition of CIS, was interested in the Michigan-2 opportunity. CIS contends that, in determining whether the Michigan-2 opportunity rightfully belonged to CIS, Broz was required to consider the interests of PriCellular insofar as those interests would come into alignment with those of CIS as a result of PriCellular's acquisition plans.

After trial, the Court of Chancery agreed with the contentions of CIS and entered judgment against Broz and RFBC. The court held that: (1) irrespective of the fact that the Michigan-2 opportunity came to Broz in a manner wholly independent of his status as a director of CIS, the Michigan-2 license was an opportunity that properly belonged to CIS; (2) due to an alignment of the interests of CIS and PriCellular arising out of PriCellular's efforts to acquire CIS, Broz breached his fiduciary duty by failing to consider whether the opportunity was one in which PriCellular would be interested; (3) despite the fact that CIS was aware of the opportunity and expressed no interest in pursuing it, Broz was required formally to present the transaction to the CIS board prior to seizing the opportunity for his own; and (4) absent formal presentation to the board, Broz' acquisition of Michigan-2 constituted an impermissible usurpation of a corporate opportunity. The trial court imposed a constructive trust on the agreement to purchase Michigan-2 and directed that the right to purchase the license be transferred to CIS. From this judgment, Broz and RFBC appeal.

Broz contends that the Court of Chancery erred in holding that he breached his fiduciary duties to CIS and its stockholders. Specifically, Broz asserts that he was under no obligation formally to present the corporate opportunity to the CIS Board of Directors. Broz further contends that PriCellular had not consummated its acquisition of CIS at the time of his decision to purchase Michigan-2, and that, accordingly, he was not obligated to consider the interests of PriCellular.

We agree with Broz and hold that: (1) the determination of whether a corporate fiduciary has usurped a corporate opportunity is fact-intensive and turns on, *inter alia,* the ability of the corporation to make use of the opportunity and the company's intent to do so; (2) while presentation of a purported corporate opportunity to the board of directors and the board's refusal thereof may serve as a shield to liability, there is no *per se* rule requiring presentation to the board prior to acceptance of the opportunity; and (3) on these facts, Broz was not required to consider the interests of PriCellular in reaching his determination whether or not to purchase Michigan-2.

The determination after trial of the Court of Chancery that Broz breached his fiduciary duty of loyalty involves both a question of law and a question of fact. As we have stated previously, a trial court's finding pertaining to a purported breach of the duty of loyalty, "being fact dominated," is, "on appeal, entitled to substantial deference unless clearly erroneous or not the product of a logical and deductive process." *Cede & Co. v. Technicolor, Inc.,* Del.Supr., 634 A.2d 345, 360 (1993).

The doctrine of corporate opportunity represents but one species of the broad fiduciary duties assumed by a corporate director or officer. A corporate fiduciary agrees to place the interests of the corporation before his or her own in appropriate circumstances. In light of the diverse and often competing obligations faced by directors and officers, however, the corporate opportunity doctrine arose as a means of defining the parameters of fiduciary duty in instances of potential conflict. The classic statement of the doctrine is derived from the venerable case of *Guth v. Loft, Inc,* Del.Supr., 5 A.2d 503 (1939). In *Guth,* this Court held that:

> if there is presented to a corporate officer or director a business opportunity which the corporation is financially able to undertake, is, from its nature, in the line of the corporation's business and is of practical advantage to it, is one in which the corporation has an interest or a reasonable expectancy, and, by embracing the opportunity, the self-interest of the officer or director will be brought into conflict with that of the corporation, the law will not permit him to seize the opportunity for himself.

Guth, 5 A.2d at 510-11.

The corporate opportunity doctrine, as delineated by *Guth* and its progeny, holds that a corporate officer or director may not take a business opportunity for his own if: (1) the corporation is financially able to exploit the opportunity; (2) the opportunity is within the corporation's line of business; (3) the corporation has an interest or expectancy in the opportunity; and (4) by taking the opportunity for his own, the corporate fiduciary will thereby be placed in a position inimicable to his duties to the corporation. The Court in *Guth* also derived a corollary which states that a director or officer *may* take a corporate opportunity if: (1) the opportunity is presented to the director or officer in his individual and not his corporate capacity; (2) the opportunity is not essential to the corporation; (3) the corporation holds no interest or expectancy in the opportunity; and (4) the director or officer has not wrongfully employed the resources of the corporation in pursuing or exploiting the opportunity.

Thus, the contours of this doctrine are well established. It is important to note, however, that the tests enunciated in *Guth* and subsequent cases provide guidelines to be considered by a reviewing court in balancing the equities of an individual case. No one factor is dispositive and all factors must be taken into account insofar as they are applicable. Cases involving a claim of usurpation of a corporate opportunity range over a multitude of factual settings. Hard and fast rules are not easily crafted to deal with such an array of complex situations. In the instant case, we find that the facts do not support the conclusion that Broz misappropriated a corporate opportunity.

We note at the outset that Broz became aware of the Michigan-2 opportunity in his individual and not his corporate capacity. This fact is not the subject of serious dispute. Nevertheless, this fact is not dispositive. The determination of whether a particular fiduciary has usurped a corporate opportunity necessitates a careful examination of the circumstances, giving due credence to the factors enunciated in *Guth* and subsequent cases.

We turn now to an analysis of the factors relied on by the trial court. First, we find that CIS was not financially capable of exploiting the Michigan-2 opportunity. Although the Court of Chancery concluded otherwise, we hold that this finding was not supported by the evidence. The record shows that CIS was in a precarious financial position at the time Mackinac presented the Michigan-2 opportunity to Broz. Having recently emerged from lengthy and contentious bankruptcy proceedings, CIS was not in a position to commit capital to the acquisition of new assets. Further, the loan agreement entered into by CIS and its creditors severely limited the discretion of CIS as to the acquisition of new assets and substantially restricted the ability of CIS to incur new debt.

The Court of Chancery based its contrary finding on the fact that PriCellular had purchased an option to acquire CIS' bank debt. Thus, the court reasoned, PriCellular was in a position to exercise that option and then waive any unfavorable restrictions that would stand in the way of a CIS acquisition of Michigan-2. The trial court, however, disregarded the fact that PriCellular's own financial situation was not particularly stable. At the time that Broz was required to decide whether to accept the Michigan-2 opportunity, PriCellular had not yet acquired CIS, and any plans to do so were wholly speculative. Thus, contrary to the Court of Chancery's finding, Broz was not obligated to consider the contingency of a PriCellular acquisition of CIS and the related contingency of PriCellular thereafter waiving restrictions on the CIS bank debt. Broz was required to consider the facts only as they existed at the time he determined to accept the Mackinac offer and embark on his efforts to bring the transaction to fruition.

Second, while it may be said with some certainty that the Michigan-2 opportunity was within CIS' line of business, it is not equally clear that CIS had a cognizable interest or expectancy in the license. Under the third factor laid down by this Court in *Guth,* for an opportunity to be deemed to belong to the fiduciary's corporation, the corporation must have an interest or expectancy in that opportunity. Despite the fact that the nature of the Michigan-2 opportunity was historically close to the core operations of CIS, changes were in process. At the time the opportunity was presented, CIS was actively engaged in the process of divesting its cellular license holdings. CIS' articulated business plan did not involve any new acquisitions. Further, as indicated by the testimony of the entire CIS board, the Michigan-2 license would not have been of interest to CIS even absent CIS' financial difficulties and CIS' then current desire to liquidate its cellular license holdings.

Where a corporation is engaged in a certain business, and an opportunity is presented to it embracing an activity as to which it has fundamental knowledge, practical experience and *ability to pursue,* which, logically and naturally, is adaptable to its business *having regard for its financial position,* and *is consonant with its reasonable needs and aspirations for expansion,* it may properly be said that the opportunity is within the corporation's line of business. This formulation of the definition of the term "line of business" suggests that the business strategy and financial well-being of the corporation are also relevant to a determination of whether the opportunity is within the corporation's line of business. Since we find that these considerations are decisive under the other factors enunciated by the Court in *Guth,* we do not reach the question of whether they are here relevant to a determination of the corporation's line of business.

Finally, the corporate opportunity doctrine is implicated only in cases where the fiduciary's seizure of an opportunity results in a conflict between the fiduciary's duties to the corporation and the self-interest of the director as actualized by the exploitation of the opportunity. In the instant case, Broz' interest in acquiring and profiting from Michigan-2 created no duties that were inimitable to his obligations to CIS. Broz, at all times relevant to the instant appeal, was the sole party in interest in RFBC, a competitor of CIS. CIS was fully aware of Broz' potentially conflicting duties. Broz, however, comported himself in a manner that was wholly in accord with his obligations to CIS. Broz took care not to usurp any opportunity which CIS was willing and able to pursue. Broz sought only to compete with an outside entity, PriCellular, for acquisition of an opportunity which both sought to possess. Broz was not obligated to refrain from competition with PriCellular. Therefore, the totality of the circumstances indicates that Broz did not usurp an opportunity that properly belonged to CIS.

In concluding that Broz had usurped a corporate opportunity, the Court of Chancery placed great emphasis on the fact that Broz had not formally presented the matter to the CIS board. In so holding, the trial court erroneously grafted a new requirement onto the law of corporate opportunity, *viz.*, the requirement of formal presentation under circumstances where the corporation does not have an interest, expectancy or financial ability.

The teaching of *Guth* and its progeny is that the director or officer must analyze the situation *ex ante* to determine whether the opportunity is one rightfully belonging to the corporation. If the director or officer believes, based on one of the factors articulated above, that the corporation is not entitled to the opportunity, then he may take it for himself. Of course, presenting the opportunity to the board creates a kind of "safe harbor" for the director, which removes the specter of a *post hoc* judicial determination that the director or officer has improperly usurped a corporate opportunity. Thus, presentation avoids the possibility that an error in the fiduciary's assessment of the situation will create future liability for breach of fiduciary duty. It is not the law of Delaware that presentation to the board is a necessary prerequisite to a finding that a corporate opportunity has not been usurped.

Thus, we hold that Broz was not required to make formal presentation of the Michigan-2 opportunity to the CIS board prior to taking the opportunity for his own. In so holding, we necessarily conclude that the Court of Chancery erred in grafting the additional requirement of formal presentation onto Delaware's corporate opportunity jurisprudence.

In concluding that Broz usurped an opportunity properly belonging to CIS, the Court of Chancery held that "[f]or practical business reasons CIS' interests with respect to the Mackinac transaction came to merge with those of PriCellular, even before the closing of its tender offer for CIS stock." Based on this fact, the trial court concluded that Broz was required to consider PriCellular's prospective, post-acquisition plans for CIS in determining whether to forego the opportunity or seize it for himself.

We disagree. Broz was under no duty to consider the interests of PriCellular when he chose to purchase Michigan-2. As stated in *Guth*, a director's right to "appropriate [an] ... opportunity depends on the circumstances existing at the time it presented itself to him without regard to subsequent events." *Guth*, 5 A.2d at 513. At the time Broz purchased Michigan-2, PriCellular had not yet acquired CIS. Any plans to do so would still have been wholly speculative. Accordingly, Broz was not required to consider the contingent and uncertain plans of PriCellular in reaching his determination of how to proceed.

In reaching our conclusion on this point, we note that certainty and predictability are values to be promoted in our corporation law. Broz, as an active participant in the cellular telephone industry, was entitled to proceed in his own economic interest in the absence of any countervailing duty. The right of a director or officer to engage in business affairs outside of his or her fiduciary capacity would be illusory if these individuals were required to consider every potential, future occurrence in determining whether a particular business strategy would implicate fiduciary duty concerns. In order for a director to engage meaningfully in business unrelated to his or her corporate role, the director must be allowed to make decisions based on the situation as it exists at the time a given opportunity is presented. Absent such a rule, the corporate fiduciary would be constrained to refrain from exploiting any opportunity for fear of liability based on the occurrence of subsequent events. This state of affairs would unduly restrict officers and directors and would be antithetical to certainty in corporation law.

The corporate opportunity doctrine represents a judicially crafted effort to harmonize the competing demands placed on corporate fiduciaries in a modern business environment. The doctrine seeks to reduce the possibility of conflict between a director's duties to the corporation and interests unrelated to that role. In the instant case, Broz adhered to his obligations to CIS.

Therefore, we hold that Broz did not breach his fiduciary duties to CIS. Accordingly, we **REVERSE** the judgment of the Court of Chancery holding that Broz diverted a corporate opportunity properly belonging to CIS and imposing a constructive trust.

Constructive Trust

As the *Farber* case illustrates, an officer or director who improperly usurps a corporate opportunity usually is deemed to hold any profits realized from the opportunity in a constructive trust for the benefit of the corporation. Expenditures made to exploit or develop the opportunity may be recovered by the offending party, along with reasonable compensation for services rendered.

Delaware's Safe Haven Provision

In 2000, Delaware added the following provision to its general corporation laws to provide protection against corporate opportunity claims. The protection is particularly helpful to entrepreneurs and investment groups who invest and hold board positions in companies that are in the same or related industries.

DGCL § 122 (17)

Every corporation created under this chapter shall have power to:

(17) Renounce, in its certificate of incorporation or by action of its board of directors, any interest or expectancy of the corporation in, or in being offered an opportunity to participate in, specified business opportunities or specified classes or categories of business opportunities that are presented to the corporation or 1 or more of its officers, directors or stockholders.

CASE PROBLEM 10-8

Baron Inc. ("Baron") is a publicly held corporation organized in a state that has adopted the Model Business Corporation Act. Baron has been in business 30 years. It became a public company 18 years ago. It provides custom concrete design and construction services for large commercial construction projects throughout the world.

Baron was founded by Luke Baron, a gifted engineer. Luke, now age 62, owns 22 percent of Baron's outstanding common stock and serves as the President, CEO and board chairman of Baron. Baron's board of directors consists of Luke, Jason Baron (Luke's oldest son and Baron's VP of marketing), David Spade (a partner in a local law firm that has represented Luke and Baron for many years), two close buddies of Luke (both of whom are smart businessman with no other ties to Baron), a local female radio talk show personality who has had strong social ties to the Baron family for two decades, and a professor at the local university.

Baron has recently relocated its office headquarters to a new high rise building. Immediately after signing an eight year lease (with a five year extension option) for six floors in a 34-story building, the building owner approached Luke and offered to give Baron a 10 percent equity interest in the building if Baron would extend its lease to 13 years, thereby making the extension option a "sure thing" for the building owner. The owner explained that such a longer lease would help with the building financing and would justify a transfer of a 10 percent equity interest to Baron.

Luke arranged an immediate conference call with the board. In the call, Luke explained the proposed deal and advised against the deal on the grounds that "it would compromise Baron's future flexibility." The board unanimously agreed to reject the offer on the phone. The next week Luke advised the building owner of the board's rejection of the deal. But as an alternative, Luke proposed to the building owner that Luke be issued the 10 percent building equity interest in return for his personal guarantee to take financial responsibility for the lease-up of the six floors for years nine through 13 if for any reason Baron did not exercise its five-year extension option. With such a personal guarantee from Luke, the building owner would have what he needed. The owner accepted Luke's proposal, and Luke was issued the 10 percent equity interest. Luke estimates that the 10 percent interest will be worth at least $2.5 million within the next eight years.

Does Luke have any personal liability exposure to Baron for his acquisition of this 10 percent interest? What actions could Luke have taken to mitigate the risk of any such exposure?

5. STATE LAW INSIDER TRADING EXPOSURE

Can an officer or director be held liable under state corporate law for insider trading of stock with nonpublic material information? When it comes to insider trading, nearly all of the action has centered on section 10b-5 of the Securities Exchange Act (See Section B of Chapter 11). But state corporate law has always lurked in the wings, and a recent decision of the Delaware Supreme Court suggests a possible move to center stage in select situations.

Courts have long recognized that state law liability may attach when a director or officer uses inside information in a direct face-to-face transaction with another shareholder. *Strong v. Repide*, 213 U.S. 419 (1909). As the court stated in *Taylor v. Wright*, 159 P.2d 980, 984-985, "[T]he detailed information a director has of corporate affairs is in a very real sense property of the corporation, and…no director should be permitted to use the information for his own benefit at the expense of his shareholders." Finding liability was often much tougher when the party on the other side of the transaction was not an existing shareholder, and nearly impossible when the director or officer bought or sold stock in the open market. *Goodwin v. Agassiz*, 186 N.E. 659 (Mass. 1933).

In *Brophy v. Cities Service Co.*, 70 A.2d 5 (Del. Ch. 1949), the court for the first time in Delaware held that a corporation could pursue insiders who traded in public markets with inside information. The case involved a confidential secretary to a corporate officer who generated substantial profits by buying and selling the company's stock with inside information. In stating that the employee was "analogous to a fiduciary," the court held that the corporation should recover for the "abuse" of trust and confidence even though the insider trading caused no loss to the corporation.

Many years later, in *In re Oracle Corp. Deriv. Litig.*, 808 A.2d 1206 (Del. Ch. 2002), Vice-Chancellor Strine strongly suggested that *Brophy* was questionable law, stating that *Brophy* pre-dated much of the "pertinent federal law," that "federal law developments" may have "undermined *Brophy,*" and that "allowing corporations to recover trading profits under state corporate law could potentially subject corporate insiders to double liability, given their exposure to liability under Rule 10b-5." Although Strine, for good reason, may have thought *Brophy* was nearly dead, the following recent case holds otherwise.

KAHN v. KOLBERG KRAVIS ROBERTS & CO., L.P.
23 A.3d 831 (Del.Supr.,2011)

STEELE, Chief Justice:

The Appellants in this derivative action, Linda Kahn and Alan Spiegal, who are shareholders of Primedia, Inc., appeal the Court of Chancery's decision granting the Primedia Special Litigation Committee's Motion to Dismiss claims arising out of a series of alleged violations of fiduciary duty by defendants, Kohlberg, Kravis, Roberts & Co., Primedia, Inc., and other Primedia officers and directors. Because we do not agree with the Court of Chancery's interpretation of a Brophy claim as explained in Pfeiffer, we must reverse the Court of Chancery's judgment of dismissal and remand the case for further proceedings consistent with this Opinion.

The nominal defendant in this action is Primedia, Inc., (the Company) a Delaware corporation whose main executive offices are located in New York City. Its common stock actively trades on the New York Stock Exchange.

Defendant below/appellee Kohlberg Kravis Roberts & Co. L.P. is an investment partnership that specializes in management buyouts of business entities. KKR indirectly controlled a majority of the common stock of Primedia. The remaining individual defendants below/appellees are eleven current and former directors of Primedia, several of whom are officers of the company. The plaintiffs below/appellants are two owners of Primedia common stock, Alan

Spiegal and Linda Parnes Kahn (collectively, Kahn).

On December 19, 2001, Primedia's board of directors approved a plan for Primedia to acquire up to $100 million dollars of its preferred shares, at 50% to 60% of redemption value, in exchange for common stock. As of December 19, 2001, KKR controlled approximately 60% of Primedia's outstanding stock and had three of its designees on Primedia's board. At the May 16, 2002 board meeting, Primedia's directors authorized an additional $100 million in buybacks of its preferred shares. On May 21, 2002, Primedia's KKR directors authored an advisory memo to KKR's Investment Committee and Portfolio Committee containing an update on Primedia's second quarter performance and advocating the purchase of Primedia's preferred shares. The May 21st memo contained nonpublic information about Primedia.

At some point in 2002, KKR sought from the Primedia board of directors permission for KKR to purchase Primedia's preferred shares, as long as Primedia was not purchasing those shares in the market. On July 2, 2002, Primedia director (and General Counsel) Beverley Chell circulated the unanimous written consent to the disinterested directors. After receiving advice from outside counsel, Chell circulated the written consent to Primedia's entire board on July 8, 2002. The written consent stated, in part, that KKR's purchase of up to $50 million in Primedia preferred stock was acceptable and not a usurpation of corporate opportunity. The board purportedly executed the written consent on July 8, 2002, without any serious deliberations. Between July 8 and November 5, 2002, KKR (through ABRA) purchased over $75 million of Primedia's preferred stock, an amount that exceeded the $50 million limit allowed by the written consent.

On September 26, 2002, Primedia's board of directors met and approved the sale of one of its biggest assets, the American Baby Group, for approximately $115 million in cash. Primedia did not publicly disclose the American Baby Group sale until November 4, 2002. Between September 26 and November 4, 2002, KKR spent $39 million to acquire Primedia's preferred stock. On November 5, 2002, Primedia's board of directors decided to explore repurchasing Primedia preferred shares. ABRA made its last purchase of Primedia's preferred shares on November 5, 2002.

Plaintiffs claimed that the KKR defendants breached their fiduciary duty to the Company by purchasing the preferred stock at a time when they possessed material, non-public information. On March 16, 2010, plaintiffs filed a Third Amended Complaint, which included the Brophy claim that KKR possessed material, non-public information. This latest complaint alleged that KKR knew that: (1) Primedia's earnings would be better than previously forecasted to the market, and (2) the Company anticipated at some point redeeming its outstanding preferred stock and KKR traded on this information during the period July 8 to November 5, 2002...

Here, the Vice Chancellor started from "the proposition that there is a Brophy claim that would blow by a motion to dismiss on failure to state a claim." Then the Vice Chancellor held that under the law, as explained in Pfeiffer v. Toll, 989 A.2d 683 (Del. Ch. 2010), disgorgement is not an available remedy for most of the Brophy claims. But, Pfeiffer's holding – which requires a plaintiff to show that the corporation suffered actual harm before bringing a Brophy claim – is not a correct statement of our law. To the extent Pfeiffer v. Toll conflicts with our current interpretation of Brophy v. Cities Service Co., Pfeiffer cannot be Delaware law.

In the venerable case of Brophy v. Cities Service Co., one of the defendants was an employee who had acquired inside information that the corporate plaintiff was about to enter the market and purchase its own shares. Using this confidential information, the employee, who was not an officer, bought a large block of shares and, after the corporation's purchases had caused the price to rise, resold them at a profit. Because the employee defendant occupied a position of trust and confidence within the plaintiff corporation, the court found his relationship analogous to that of a fiduciary. The employee defendant argued that the plaintiff had failed to state a claim because "it [did] not appear that the corporation suffered any loss through his purchase of its stock." The Court of Chancery expressly rejected that argument, stating that:

> In equity, when the breach of confidential relation by an employee is relied on and an accounting for any resulting profit is sought, loss to the corporation need not be charged in the complaint.... Public policy will not permit an employee occupying a position of trust and confidence toward his employer to abuse that relation to his own profit, regardless of whether his employer suffers a loss. *Brophy,* 70 A.2d at 8.

Thus, actual harm to the corporation is not required for a plaintiff to state a claim under Brophy. In Brophy, the court relied on the principles of restitution and equity, citing the Restatement of the Law of Restitution § 200, comment a, for the proposition that a fiduciary cannot use confidential corporate information for his own benefit. As the court recognized in Brophy, it is inequitable to permit the fiduciary to profit from using confidential corporate information. Even if the corporation did not suffer actual harm, equity requires disgorgement of that profit.

This Court has cited Brophy approvingly when discussing how the duty of loyalty governs the misuse of confidential corporate information by fiduciaries. The plaintiff must show that: "1) the corporate fiduciary possessed material, nonpublic company information; and 2) the corporate fiduciary used that information improperly by making trades because she was motivated, in whole or in part, by the substance of that information."

The defendants moved to dismiss the complaint, arguing, among other things, that Brophy is an outdated precedent in light of the federal securities laws, which govern insider trading claims. While on one hand upholding Brophy as good law, the Court of Chancery concluded that "[t]he purpose of a Brophy claim is to remedy harm to the corporation." By focusing on that harm, it "disposes of the defendants' contentions that Brophy is a misguided vehicle for recovering the same trading losses that are addressed by the federal securities laws ... [and] the contention that Brophy grants a remedy without underlying harm."

Next, the Vice Chancellor concluded that the harm to the corporation "is generally not measured by insider trading gains or reciprocal losses." Citing to this Court's precedent on two occasions, the Vice Chancellor found that Delaware law "does not provide a class-wide remedy for market based-harm" and "interpreting Brophy as a basis for recovering those measures of damages would conflict with [those holdings]." Moreover, the court found that "disgorgement of insider trading profits ... is also not the appropriate measure of damages because insiders who trade on an impersonal market typically are not engaging in the type of self-dealing transaction to which a disgorgement remedy historically applies." The court also held that market trading "typically does not involve the usurpation of a corporate opportunity, where disgorgement has been the preferred remedy."

To that end, the Vice Chancellor concluded that in the context of a Brophy claim, disgorgement is "theoretically available" in two circumstances: (1) "when a fiduciary engages directly in actual fraud and benefits from trading on the basis of the fraudulent information;" and (2) "if the insider used confidential corporate information to compete directly with the corporation." Brophy, in the Vice Chancellor's view, was an example of the second circumstance where disgorgement is an appropriate remedy. But, in most circumstances a corporation would only be able to recover for "actual harm causally related (in both the actual and proximate sense) to the breach of the duty of loyalty"—for example "costs and expenses for regulatory proceedings and internal investigations, fees paid to counsel and other professionals, fines paid to regulators, and judgments in litigation."

We decline to adopt [this] unduly narrow, interpretation of Brophy and its progeny. We also disagree with the conclusion that the purpose of Brophy is to "remedy harm to the corporation." In fact, Brophy explicitly held that the corporation did not need to suffer an actual loss for there to be a viable claim. Importantly, Brophy focused on preventing a fiduciary wrongdoer from being unjustly enriched. Moreover, we have found no cases requiring that the corporation suffer actual harm for a plaintiff to bring a Brophy claim. To read Brophy as applying only where the corporation has suffered actual harm improperly limits its holding.

We decline to adopt [the] interpretation that would limit the disgorgement remedy to a usurpation of corporate opportunity or cases where the insider used confidential corporate information to compete directly with the corporation. Brophy was not premised on either of those rationales. Rather, Brophy focused on the public policy of preventing unjust enrichment based on the misuse of confidential corporate information... The rule, inveterate and uncompromising in its rigidity, does not rest upon the narrow ground of injury or damage to the corporation resulting from a betrayal of confidence, but upon a broader foundation of a wise public policy that, for the purpose of removing all temptation, extinguishes all possibility of profit flowing from a breach of the confidence imposed by the fiduciary relation.

We find no reasonable public policy ground to restrict the scope of disgorgement remedy in Brophy cases – irrespective of arguably parallel remedies grounded in federal securities law.

D. DIRECTOR PROTECTIONS

Given the nature and scope of the charges that a corporate director might face, directors want protection against personal liability exposure and the risk of having to incur horrendous litigation costs. Without such protections, many qualified and responsible individuals could never be persuaded to serve on a corporation's board.

The protections come in three forms. The first form is corporate statutes that permit a corporation to include in its articles of incorporation a provision that eliminates or limits the liability of a director to the corporation or its shareholders for money damages for any action taken, or any failure to take any action, as a director unless the liability is for (1) the amount of a financial benefit received by a director to which he or she is not entitled, (2) an intentional infliction of harm on the corporation or the shareholders, (3) the approval of an unlawful dividend, or (4) an intentional violation of criminal law. Model Business Act § 202(b)(4) (set forth above) and Delaware General Corporate Law § 102(b)(7) (discussed in various cases above) are examples of such a provision.

The second form of protection is corporate statutes that obligate a corporation to indemnify a director in select situations and permit a corporation to include in its articles of incorporation a provision that imposes broader indemnification obligations on the corporation for director liabilities and related costs.

The third form of protection is an errors and omissions insurance policy, funded by the corporation, which provides each director added protection for acts taken in good faith.

Officers and directors typically want all three levels of protection.

1. INDEMNIFICATION AND ADVANCEMENT RIGHTS

An officer or director generally had no indemnification rights at common law, even if he or she prevailed on the merits. In the case of *New York Dock Co., Inc. v. McCollom*, 16 N.Y.S.2d 844 (N.Y.Sup. 1939), for example, the court held that a corporation lacked the power to reimburse defense costs of directors who prevailed in a derivative suit, reasoning that such costs provided no direct benefit to the corporation. The case ultimately sparked a push in New York to provide statutory rights of indemnification. Every other state followed.

Today, each state has statutory provisions that enable a corporation to indemnify its officers and directors under designated conditions. Beyond the basic indemnification rights, and in recognition of the onerous legal expenses that accompany claims against officers and directors, state statutes also authorize corporations to advance funds to cover legal and other expenses that an officer or director incurs to mount a defense in a civil, criminal or regulatory proceeding. Such advances usually are conditioned on a repayment obligation if it is ultimately determined that the officer or director is not entitled to indemnification by the corporation. See, for example, 8 DGCL § 145(e). But the rights of "indemnification" and "advancement" often are not tied together. In many situations, an advancement right turns on the specific provisions of the corporation's bylaws, which may obligate the corporation to advance funds in circumstance where indemnification is permissive or nonexistent.

There are two types of indemnification statutes – mandatory and permissive. A mandatory statute typically requires the corporation to indemnify a director or officer when that person prevails on the merits in defending against an asserted claim of liability. For example, Delaware entitles a present or former officer or director to indemnification for defense expenses "actually and reasonably incurred" when the officer or director "has been successful on the merits or otherwise in defense of" a claim based upon his or her actions on behalf of the corporation or a claim asserted by or on behalf of the corporation. 8 DGCL § 145(c).

A permissive statute allows, but does not obligate, a corporation to indemnify directors, officers and other persons if the person ends up settling or paying a claim and certain conditions are satisfied. For example, if a claim is made against an officer, director, employee or agent for actions taken on behalf of a corporation, Delaware's statute permits the corporation to indemnify such person for all defense expenses, fees, judgments, fines and settlements, actually and reasonably incurred, so long as the person acted in good faith, acted in the corporation's best interests; and had no reason to believe that his or her conduct was unlawful. 8 DGCL § 145(a). The statute specifically provides that an adverse termination or settlement does not create a presumption that the indemnification conditions have not been satisfied. If the threatened or actual claim is based on a charge made by or on behalf of the corporation, the permissive indemnification is conditioned on the same "good faith" and "best interest" requirements, plus a judicial determination that the indemnification is fair and reasonable when liability to the corporation is found to exist. 8 DGCL § 145(b).

In Delaware, as is common in most states, there are various ways for determining that the indemnification conditions have been satisfied. The determination can be made by (a) a majority vote of the directors who are not parties to such action, suit or proceeding, even though less than a quorum, (b) by a committee of such directors designated by majority vote of such directors, even though less than a quorum; (c) by a written opinion of legal counsel if there are no such directors, or if such directors so direct, or (d) by the stockholders. 8 DGCL § 145(b).

State indemnification statutes typically include a non-exclusivity provision that allows for additional indemnification and advancement protections through the corporation's articles of incorporation or bylaws or contracts with officers and directors. Delaware's statute, for example, states, "The indemnification and advancement of expenses provided by, or granted pursuant to, the other subsections of this section shall not be deemed exclusive of any other rights to which those seeking indemnification or advancement of expenses may be entitled under any bylaw, agreement, vote of stockholders or disinterested directors or otherwise, both as to action in such person's official capacity and as to action in another capacity while holding such office." 8 DGCL § 145(f).

The specific indemnification and advance provisions in a corporation's charter documents or specific contracts often are an important consideration in recruiting and retaining key people to serve in officer and director positions. Issues that often are dealt with in these documents include: criteria for determining if the officer or director has acted in "good faith" and "in the corporation's best interests;" the scope of individuals entitled to indemnification and advancement rights; conversion of permissive indemnification or advancement rights under a state statute to mandatory contractual or charter document rights; expanded contractual mandatory advancement rights; procedures for evaluating conflicts of interest that warrant separate defense counsel; mandatory liability insurance benefits for directors and officers; the duration of advancement rights; advancement rights in indemnification and advancement disputes; protections against indemnification and advancement rights being retroactively eliminated or reduced by subsequent bylaw amendments.

The potential of having indemnification or advancement rights stripped away is an important factor to consider in the planning process. In *Schoon v. Troy Corporation*, 948 A.2d 1157 (Del. Ch. 2008), a current director of Troy (Schoon) and a former director (Bohnen) sought advancement of legal fees incurred in defending against fiduciary duty breach claims. Troy denied the requests even though its bylaws had mandated advancement for current and former directors during the period that Bohnen had served. After Bohnen's resignation and before the litigation ensued, Troy had amended its bylaws to exclude former directors from receiving advancement rights. The court granted Schoon's advancement claims, but denied Bohnen's request. Rejecting the argument that Bohnen had a vested contractual advancement right that could not be divested through a bylaw amendment, the court held that rights to mandatory advancement through a bylaw provision do not vest until a triggering event actually occurs. Since the suit against Bohnen was neither threatened nor commenced before the bylaw amendment, Bohnen had no rights when the claim surfaced.

Schoon sparked an outcry that resulted in a 2010 amendment to Delaware's indemnification statute that reads, "A right to indemnification or to advancement of expenses arising under a provision of the certificate of incorporation or a bylaw shall not be eliminated or impaired by an amendment to the certificate of incorporation or the bylaws after the occurrence of the act or omission that is the subject of the civil, criminal, administrative or investigative action, suit or proceeding for which indemnification or advancement of expenses is sought, unless the provision in effect at the time of such act or omission explicitly authorizes such elimination or impairment after such action or omission has occurred." 8 DGCL § 145(f).

This provision would have protected Bohnen unless, at the time of Bohnen's service, Troy had a bylaw provision that explicitly permitted it to eliminate or impair rights after the questionable action or omission occurred. In Delaware, the presence of such an "eliminate or impair" bylaw is now a major planning consideration.

Various other issues often surface in contentious proceeding over indemnification and advancement rights. Use of the word "agent" in describing the covered parties can invite disputes. In *Jackson Walker, L.L.P. v. Spira Footwear, Inc.*, 2008 WL 2487256 (Del. Ch. June 23, 2008), for example, the court held that the term "agent" entitled the corporation's outside litigation counsel to advancement rights because the attorney had the right to represent and bind the company in litigation proceedings. The "fees-on-fees" issue arises in cases where a disgruntled officer or director seeks an advancement on fees to prosecute an action to enforce his or her indemnification or advancement rights. See, for example, *Stifel Financial Corp. v. Cochran*, 809 A.2d 555 (Del. Supr. 2002) (fees-on-fees claim allowed) and *Gentile v. SinglePoint Financial Inc.*, 788 A.2d 111 (Del.Supr. 2001), (fees-on-fees claim denied because of limited advancement right language in bylaws). There are cases where the corporation refuses to honor its advancement obligations on the grounds that the covered officer or director has unreasonably refused to settle a claim or unreasonably demands separate legal representation. See, for example, *Barrett v. American County Holdings, Inc.*, 951 A.2d 735 (Del. Ch. 2008), (holding that a refusal-to-settle defense to an advancement claim was lacking "in law, logic, or common sense"). And there are sometimes disputes over how long the advancement rights must continue. See, for example, *Sun Times Media Group, Inc., v. Black*, 954 A.2d 380 (Del. Ch. 2008) (advancement rights would continue until the "final non-appealable conclusion" even though the officers had already been convicted and sentenced).

Smart planning and careful bylaw drafting can go a long way in eliminating the risks of these types of disputes.

2. INSURANCE FOR OFFICERS AND DIRECTORS

Directors and Officers Liability Insurance
David M. Gische, Troutman Sanders LLP (2008)[2]

In recent years, directors and officers liability insurance has become a core component of corporate insurance. As many as 95% of Fortune 500 companies maintain directors and officers ("D&O") liability insurance today.

In the 1930s, in the wake of the depression, Lloyd's of London introduced coverage for corporate directors and officers. However, directors and officers did not perceive a great risk, and the insurance did not sell. Well into the 1960s, the market for D&O coverage was negligible. Then, during the 1960s changes in the interpretation of the securities laws created the realistic possibility that directors and officers themselves, and not only corporations, could face significant liability. Insurers responded to these changes by reviving specialty coverage for the "personal financial protection" of directors and officers. The D&O industry matured and evolved during the 1970s through the 1990s, and continues to do so today

At its most basic, D&O insurance protects directors and officers from

---

2. The views expressed in this article are not necessarily those of Troutman Sanders or its clients.

liability arising from actions connected to their corporate positions. Due to general expansion in the industry, market pressures and the industry's responses to the development of case law, D&O insurance has expanded beyond its original and basic coverage. Thus, a single policy now may provide multiple and varied options by standard form or endorsement.

Although each policy will employ its own language, Insuring Agreement A, often referred to as "A-Side Coverage," typically provides coverage directly to the directors and officers for loss – including defense costs – resulting from claims made against them for their wrongful acts. A-Side Coverage applies where the corporation does not indemnify its directors and officers. A corporation may not indemnify its directors or officers because it either (1) is prohibited by law from doing so, (2) is permitted to do so by law and the company's bylaws but chooses not to do so, or (3) is financially incapable of doing so, due to bankruptcy, liquidation, or lack of funds. The laws regarding indemnification differ from jurisdiction to jurisdiction. Insuring Agreement A additionally may specify that coverage is limited to those claims connected to an insured's capacity as an insured director or officer of the company. This issue of capacity recurs throughout D&O coverage analysis.

A typical Insuring Agreement B, or "B-side coverage," reimburses a corporation for its loss where the corporation indemnifies its directors and officers for claims against them. B-side coverage does not provide coverage for the corporation for its own liability. The language and conditions of Insuring Clause B typically mirror Insuring Clause A.

Many D&O policies offer an optional coverage to protect the corporation against securities claims. Such coverage provides protection for the corporation for its own liability. Entity coverage may be part of the policy form as "Insuring Agreement C" or may be added as an endorsement. **D.**

Employment Practices Liability ("EPL") coverage also has become a common addition to corporate coverage – often by endorsement to the D&O policy or as a stand-alone policy issued to the company. This coverage typically protects directors, officers, employees and/or the company against employment-related claims brought by employees and, in certain circumstances, specified third-parties.

Most D&O policies do not impose a duty to defend on the insurer. They do, however, provide coverage for defense costs and give the insurer the right to associate with the defense and approve defense strategies, expenditures, and settlements.

A D&O insurer cannot impose its choice of counsel on an insured – the insured generally has the right to select counsel, subject to the insurer's consent. D&O policies typically provide that an insurer may not unreasonably withhold approval of an insured's choice of counsel.

Although D&O insurers generally do not have a duty to defend, D&O policies do cover defense costs. Whether a D&O insurer must, or should, advance defense costs – that is, pay them as they are incurred – is a common question. Many of the issues affecting coverage cannot be resolved until the claim has been resolved. Specifically, certain exclusions only apply after a finding of fact has been made. A vigorous defense can be a costly endeavor that may be well beyond the means of an insured. Thus, many policies provide that insurers advance defense costs under the condition that, should the facts ultimately demonstrate a lack of coverage, the insured will reimburse the advanced monies.

Common to all coverages in a D&O policy is that each insuring clause generally provides coverage on a "claims-made" basis. In other words, it provides the coverage described for claims made during the period for which the coverage is purchased. Additionally, the insured typically must report the claim to the insurer during the policy period or within a reasonable time.

Loss generally includes damages, judgments, awards, settlements and defense costs. Loss usually excludes fines or penalties, taxes, treble (or other multiplied) damages, and matters uninsurable under law. Some states do not permit punitive or exemplary damages to be assessed at all. Those states prohibiting coverage of punitive damages generally base the prohibition on public policy concerns.

Dishonesty exclusions bar coverage for claims made in connection with an insured's dishonesty, fraud, or willful violation of laws or statutes. The dishonesty exclusion also may be coupled with a personal profit exclusion, barring coverage in connection with an insured's illicit gain. These exclusions typically are followed by a severability clause – that is, a caveat providing that the acts or knowledge of one insured will not be imputed to any other insured for the purposes of applying the exclusion. In other words, the exclusion only bars coverage for the insured(s) whose acts or knowledge are the basis of the claim at issue. Many dishonesty exclusions include an adjudication clause, which provides that the exclusion only applies if the fraud or dishonesty is established by a judgment or other final adjudication.

As the name implies, an insured versus insured ("IvI") exclusion bars coverage for claims made by an insured (e.g., a director, officer or corporate insured) against another insured. In addition, the exclusion may bar coverage for claims brought (1) by anyone directly or indirectly affiliated with an insured, (2) by a shareholder unless the shareholder is acting independently and without input from any insured, or (3) at the behest of an insured. The exclusion essentially prevents a company from suing or orchestrating a suit against its directors and officers in order to collect insurance proceeds. Questions regarding the application of the exclusion arise in the context of derivative lawsuits, bankruptcies and receiverships.

As a general matter, D&O policies do not provide coverage for liability associated with the provision of professional services. Thus, where a doctor is the president of a professional corporation, the D&O policy would only protect him or her against liability from acts as president of the corporation, and would not provide coverage for professional malpractice claims.

Prior acts exclusions bar coverage for claims arising out of an insured's wrongful acts prior to a specified date. Prior and pending litigation exclusions generally exclude coverage for (1) claims pending prior to the inception of the policy, or another agreed upon date, and (2) subsequent claims based on the same facts or circumstances.

In addition to the three insuring agreements discussed above, the D&O industry has expanded to include many sub-industries offering specialized coverages. Underwriters offer specialized policies addressing the specific issues of various industries. Directors and officers of non-profit organizations or condominium associations require different protections than directors and officers of banking and financial institutions or health care systems. The terms and conditions in these policies reflect the specific needs of these insureds.

A corporation's bankruptcy may have a great impact on its directors and officers insurance coverage. First, in dividing up the bankrupt estate, "some courts have held that insurance policies are part of the estate, although the proceeds may not be." Reliance Ins. Co. v. Weis, 148 B.R. 575 (E.D. Mo. 1992), (citing In re Daisy Systems Securities Litigation, 132 B.R. 752 (N.D. Cal. 1991); In re Louisiana World Exposition, 832 F.2d 1391 (5th Cir. 1987); In re Minoco Group of Companies, Ltd., 799 F.2d 517 (9th Cir. 1986)). If the policy and its proceeds are property of the estate, the insureds may need bankruptcy court approval to obtain proceeds from the insurer.

Second, where a claim is brought against a corporation's directors and officers and the entity is bankrupt, it will be unable to indemnify them. Thus, A-Side Coverage may be available.

Finally, claims by debtors in possession or trustees against directors or officers for the benefit of creditors may implicate the IvI exclusion. The analytical question is whether a trustee or debtor in possession stands in the shoes of the corporation. The case law addressing this question is growing but no consensus has emerged.

In the last few years, many insurers have offered multi-year, multi-line insurance policies that have combined several different types of coverages under one policy (and often subject to a single aggregate limit of liability). Insureds have used this approach to build "towers" of coverage that may often provide hundreds of millions of dollars for this combined risk. The combined policies often include D&O coverage (A-Side, B-Side and Entity Securities coverage), EPL coverage, fiduciary liability coverage, professional liability errors and omissions coverage (for financial institutions), and fidelity or crime bonds (for employee dishonesty and related losses).

CHAPTER 11

SECURITIES LAW RISKS

A. DISCLOSURE LIABILITY RISKS

1. A PRIVATE RIGHT OF ACTION

The federal securities laws pose ongoing risks for officers and directors who are charged with the responsibility of managing a public company. The focus is on the adequacy of disclosures. The primary statutory threat is Rule 10b-5, which Chief Justice Rehnquist described as "a judicial oak which has grown from little more than a legislative acorn."[1]

Rule 10b-5 makes it "unlawful for any person, directly or indirectly, by the use of any means or instrumentality of interstate commerce, or of the mails or of any facility of any national securities exchange, (a) To employ any device, scheme, or artifice to defraud, (b) To make any untrue statement of a material fact or to omit to state a material fact necessary in order to make the statements made, in the light of the circumstances under which they were made, not misleading, or (c) To engage in any act, practice, or course of business which operates or would operate as a fraud or deceit upon any person, in connection with the purchase or sale of any security."

Although a private right of action by injured shareholders predicated on a violation of federal securities laws is not expressly authorized by statute, the Supreme Court held that such a right existed in the landmark case of *J.I. Case Co. v. Borak,* 377 U.S. 426 (1964). The *Borak* holding brought federal securities laws directly into the boardroom and transformed the landscape of corporate governance litigation.

In *Borak*, the plaintiff was a shareholder in J.I. Case Co. ("Case") who brought an action to enjoin a merger between Case and American Tractor Company. The plaintiff alleged improper self-dealing by certain Case managers that resulted in the Case shareholders not being treated fairly. The statutory basis of the plaintiff's claim was section 14(a) of the Securities Exchange Act and related rule 14a-9, which makes it unlawful to use false or misleading statements in a proxy statement or solicitation. Key language from the Court's opinion follows.

---

1. Blue Chip Stamps v. Manor Drug Stores, 421 U.S. 723, 737 (1975).

572

J.I. CASE CO. V. BORAK
377 U.S. 426 (1964)

Mr. Justice CLARK delivered the opinion of the Court.

While the respondent contends that his Count 2 claim is not a derivative one, we need not embrace that view, for we believe that a right of action exists as to both derivative and direct causes.

The purpose of s 14(a) is to prevent management or others from obtaining authorization for corporate action by means of deceptive or inadequate disclosure in proxy solicitation. The section stemmed from the congressional belief that 'fair corporate suffrage is an important right that should attach to every equity security bought on a public exchange.' H.R.Rep. No. 1383, 73d Cong., 2d Sess., 13.

The injury which a stockholder suffers from corporate action pursuant to a deceptive proxy solicitation ordinarily flows from the damage done the corporation, rather than from the damage inflicted directly upon the stockholder. The damage suffered results not from the deceit practiced on him alone but rather from the deceit practiced on the stockholders as a group. To hold that derivative actions are not within the sweep of the section would therefore be tantamount to a denial of private relief. Private enforcement of the proxy rules provides a necessary supplement to Commission action. As in anti-trust treble damage litigation, the possibility of civil damages or injunctive relief serves as a most effective weapon in the enforcement of the proxy requirements. The Commission advises that it examines over 2,000 proxy statements annually and each of them must necessarily be expedited. Time does not permit an independent examination of the facts set out in the proxy material and this results in the Commission's acceptance of the representations contained therein at their face value, unless contrary to other material on file with it. Indeed, on the allegations of respondent's complaint, the proxy material failed to disclose alleged unlawful market manipulation of the stock of ATC, and this unlawful manipulation would not have been apparent to the Commission until after the merger.

We, therefore, believe that under the circumstances here it is the duty of the courts to be alert to provide such remedies as are necessary to make effective the congressional purpose.

Nor do we find merit in the contention that such remedies are limited to prospective relief. Our finding that federal courts have the power to grant all necessary remedial relief is not to be construed as any indication of what we believe to be the necessary and appropriate relief in this case. We are concerned here only with a determination that federal jurisdiction for this purpose does exist. Whatever remedy is necessary must await the trial on the merits.

Borak Questions

Borak established the private right of action, but raised a number of key questions relating to the scope of the liability exposure risks. What should be the requisite causation link between a defective disclosure and the plaintiffs' alleged injury? What standard should be used in determining whether a specific disclosure defect is sufficiently serious to trigger liability exposure? Should manifest unfairness alone be a basis for liability? The following Supreme Court decisions address these important questions and will help in answering the questions raised by the following Case Problems 11-1 through 11-3.

2. DEFINING THE SCOPE OF LIABILITY EXPOSURE

CASE PROBLEM 11-1

Wave Incorporated ("Wave") is a small Delaware public company that designs, installs and monitors customized data and communication systems. Wave has a five-person senior management team (the "Team"), headed by Burt Rogers, age 62, who has been the President and CEO of Wave for the past 15 years. Burt owns 10 percent of Wave's outstanding common stock, the other four members of the Team collectively own 15 percent, and the balance is owned by approximately 2,200 shareholders. Wave's stock is thinly traded over-the-counter at prices that have historically ranged from $15 to $23. The Team has never believed that these prices reflect the true value of the company.

Wave's board consists of seven members: Burt, two other members of the Team, and four outside directors (the "Outsiders"). Each Outsider owns Wave stock, has never worked for the company, has served on the board for at least five years, and considers Burt a friend.

Eleven months ago, Burt was rushed by ambulance to the hospital. A feared stroke turned out to be a false alarm, but the doctor's warning was ominous: "Slow up now or you will never enjoy your wealth or your grandkids." Burt took the warning to heart and decided to cash in, leave Wave, and move on. Burt knew that he would be able to realize a fair value on his Wave stock only if he seriously explored a sale of the company.

Burt advised the other Team members of his desire to explore a sale of the company and engaged an investment banking firm (the "Firm") to value the company and then to help find a buyer. After carefully evaluating the company, the Firm reported that the Wave shareholders could likely expect a price in the $28 to $35 range from a sale, assuming a qualified buyer could be found. Pleased with these numbers, Burt authorized the Firm to start looking for a buyer, with explicit instructions that Burt's ongoing personal services would not be part of the deal.

Within a few months, very preliminary discussions were underway with two potential buyers. The first candidate, Archer Inc., is a competitor of Wave that is many times Wave's size. Very interested in the strategic advantages of acquiring Wave, Archer expressed a willingness to pay up to $37 a share in a merger using Archer stock (traded on the NASDAQ). There were two problems with the Archer deal: the entire Team and many Wave employees would lose their jobs and an antitrust hurdle would need to be cleared. Although the antitrust issue was labeled "not a big deal" by the Firm, the job cuts were a major concern for the entire Team.

The other merger candidate was a large diversified company ("Folsum") that would pay $31 a share. A Folsum deal would not threaten the paychecks of the Team or other Wave employees, nor would it present any antitrust hurdles.

The entire Team, including Burt, opted for the Folsum deal. In discussions with the board in three separate meetings, Burt laid out all the facts, provided copies of the Firm's evaluation, encouraged questions from the Outsiders, and strongly recommended the Folsum deal. Ultimately, the board unanimously approved the Folsum merger. The merger was publically announced nine months after Burt's trip to the hospital.

The merger required a majority approval vote of the Wave shareholders. The proxy statement to Wave's shareholders appropriately advised the shareholders of their dissenter appraisal rights and included the following statement: "In assessing various options, the officers and directors of Wave have relied on their knowledge of the company and advice from experts in concluding that the Folsum proposal is the best overall option for all stakeholders in the company." The proxy statement made no mention of the Firm's estimated price range ($28-$35), the potential Archer deal at $37, or Burt's health scare and his related decisions. The Folsum merger was approved by 96 percent of Wave's shareholders. The prospect of netting $31 on a stock that was currently trading at $21 appealed to everyone. The merger was quickly closed.

Shortly after the closing, certain Wave shareholders heard rumors that "Burt Rogers had rejected a $37 price from big rival Archer to protect the jobs of his four buddies." As they pursued the rumors, they learned of all the facts leading to the merger. These shareholders now seek to recover an additional $6 a share from the officers and directors of Wave, Wave, and the Firm on the grounds that the merger price was "not fair" and that the proxy disclosures to the shareholders were false and misleading.

What additional facts would you like to have in assessing the merits of these claims? How should the shareholders frame their charges in a complaint? Who will have the burden of proof? What is the likelihood that the shareholders will prevail on their claims? What additional steps could the officers and directors of Wave have taken to reduce the risk of such claims?

MILLS v. ELECTRIC AUTO-LITE CO
396 U.S. 375 (1970)

Mr. Justice HARLAN delivered the opinion of the Court.

This case requires us to consider a basic aspect of the implied private right of action for violation of s 14(a) of the Securities Exchange Act of 1934, recognized by this Court in J. I. Case Co. v. Borak. As in Borak the asserted wrong is that a corporate merger was accomplished through the use of a proxy statement that was materially false or misleading. The question with which we deal is what causal relationship must be shown between such a statement and the merger to establish a cause of action based on the violation of the Act.

Petitioners were shareholders of the Electric Auto-Lite Company until 1963, when it was merged into Mergenthaler Linotype Company. They brought suit on the day before the shareholders' meeting at which the vote was to take place on the merger against Auto-Lite, Mergenthaler, and a third company, American Manufacturing Company, Inc. The complaint sought an injunction against the voting by Auto-Lite's management of all proxies obtained by means of an allegedly misleading proxy solicitation; however, it did not seek a temporary restraining order, and the voting went ahead as scheduled the following day. Several months later petitioners filed an amended complaint, seeking to have the merger set aside and to obtain such other relief as might be proper.

Petitioners alleged that the proxy statement sent out by the Auto-Lite management to solicit shareholders' votes in favor of the merger was misleading, in violation of s 14(a) of the Act and SEC Rule 14a-9 thereunder. Petitioners recited that before the merger Mergenthaler owned over 50% of the outstanding shares of Auto-Lite common stock, and had been in control of Auto-Lite for two years. American Manufacturing in turn owned about one-third of the outstanding shares of Mergenthaler, and for two years had been in voting control of Mergenthaler and, through it, of Auto-Lite. Petitioners charged that in light of these circumstances the proxy statement was misleading in that it told Auto-Lite shareholders that their board of directors recommended approval of the merger without also informing them that all 11 of Auto-Lite's directors were nominees of Mergenthaler and were under the 'control and domination of Mergenthaler.' Petitioners asserted the right to complain of this alleged violation both derivatively on behalf of Auto-Lite and as representatives of the class of all its minority shareholders.

On petitioners' motion for summary judgment with respect to Count II, the District Court for the Northern District of Illinois ruled as a matter of law that the claimed defect in the proxy statement was, in light of the circumstances in which the statement was made, a material omission. The District Court concluded, from its reading of the Borak opinion, that it had to hold a hearing on the issue whether there was 'a causal connection between the finding that there has been a violation of the disclosure requirements of s 14(a) and the alleged injury to the plaintiffs' before it could consider what remedies would be appropriate.

After holding such a hearing, the court found that under the terms of the merger agreement, an affirmative vote of two-thirds of the Auto-Lite shares was required for approval of the merger, and that the respondent companies owned and controlled about 54% of the outstanding shares. Therefore, to obtain authorization of the merger, respondents had to secure the approval of a substantial number of the minority shareholders. At the stockholders' meeting, approximately 950,000 shares, out of 1,160,000 shares outstanding, were voted in favor of the merger. This included 317,000 votes obtained by proxy from the minority shareholders, votes that were 'necessary and indispensable to the approval of the merger.' The District Court concluded that a causal relationship had thus been shown, and it granted an interlocutory judgment in favor of petitioners on the issue of liability, referring the case to a master for consideration of appropriate relief.

The respondents took an interlocutory appeal to the Court of Appeals for the Seventh Circuit. That court affirmed the District Court's conclusion that the proxy statement was materially deficient, but reversed on the question of causation. The court acknowledged that, if an injunction had been sought a sufficient time before the stockholders' meeting, 'corrective measures would have been appropriate.' However, since this suit was brought too late for preventive action, the courts had to determine 'whether the misleading statement and omission caused the submission of sufficient proxies,' as a prerequisite to a determination of liability under the Act. If the respondents could show, 'by a preponderance of probabilities, that the merger would have received a sufficient vote even if the proxy statement had not been misleading in the respect found,' petitioners would be entitled to no relief of any kind...

The Court of Appeals acknowledged that this test corresponds to the common-law fraud test of whether the injured party relied on the misrepresentation. However, rightly concluding that '(r)eliance by thousands of individuals, as here, can scarcely be inquired into,' the court ruled that the issue was to be determined by proof of the fairness of the terms of the merger. If respondents could show that the merger had merit and was fair to the minority shareholders, the trial court would be justified in concluding that a sufficient number of shareholders would have approved the merger had there been no deficiency in the proxy statement. In that case respondents would be entitled to a judgment in their favor.

As we stressed in Borak, s 14(a) stemmed from a congressional belief that '(f)air corporate suffrage is an important right that should attach to every equity security bought on a public exchange.' The provision was intended to promote 'the free exercise of the voting rights of stockholders' by ensuring that proxies would be solicited with 'explanation to the stockholder of the real nature of the questions for which authority to cast his vote is sought.' The decision below, by permitting all liability to be foreclosed on the basis of a finding that the merger was fair, would allow the stockholders to be by-passed, at least where the only legal challenge to the merger is a suit for retrospective relief after the meeting has been held. A judicial appraisal of the merger's merits could be substituted for the actual and informed vote of the stockholders.

The result would be to insulate from private redress an entire category of proxy violations those relating to matters other than the terms of the merger. Even outrageous misrepresentations in a proxy solicitation, if they did not relate to the terms of the transaction, would give rise to no cause of action under s 14(a). Particularly if carried over to enforcement actions by the Securities and Exchange Commission itself, such a result would subvert the congressional purpose of ensuring full and fair disclosure to shareholders.

Further, recognition of the fairness of the merger as a complete defense would confront small shareholders with an additional obstacle to making a successful challenge to a proposal recommended through a defective proxy statement. The risk that they would be unable to rebut the corporation's evidence of the fairness of the proposal, and thus to establish their cause of action, would be bound to discourage such shareholders from the private enforcement of the proxy rules.

Such a frustration of the congressional policy is not required by anything in the wording of the statute or in our opinion in the Borak case. Section 14(a) declares it 'unlawful' to solicit proxies in contravention of Commission rules, and SEC Rule 14a-9 prohibits solicitations 'containing any statement which * * * is false or misleading with respect to any material fact, or which omits to state any material fact necessary in order to make the statements therein not false or misleading * * *.' Use of a solicitation that is materially misleading is itself a violation of law, as the Court of Appeals recognized in stating that injunctive relief would be available to remedy such a defect if sought prior to the stockholders' meeting. In Borak, which came to this Court on a dismissal of the complaint, the Court limited its inquiry to whether a violation of s 14(a) gives rise to 'a federal cause of action for rescission or damages.' The Court stated: "But the causal relationship of the proxy material and the merger are questions of fact to be resolved at trial, not here. We therefore do not discuss this point further." In the present case there has been a hearing specifically directed to the causation problem. The question before the Court is whether the facts found on the basis of that hearing are sufficient in law to establish petitioners' cause of action, and we conclude that they are.

Where the misstatement or omission in a proxy statement has been shown to be 'material,' as it was found to be here, that determination itself indubitably embodies a conclusion that the defect was of such a character that it might have been considered important by a reasonable shareholder who was in the process of deciding how to vote. This requirement that the defect have a significant propensity to affect the voting process is found in the express terms of Rule 14a-9, and it adequately serves the purpose of ensuring that a cause of action cannot be established by proof of a defect so trivial, or so unrelated to the transaction for which approval is sought, that correction of the defect or imposition of liability would not further the interests protected by s 14(a).

There is no need to supplement this requirement, as did the Court of Appeals, with a requirement of proof of whether the defect actually had a decisive effect on the voting. Where there has been a finding of materiality, a shareholder has made a sufficient showing of causal relationship between the violation and the injury for which he seeks redress if, as here, he proves that the proxy solicitation itself, rather than the particular defect in the solicitation materials, was an essential link in the accomplishment of the transaction. This objective test will avoid the impracticalities of determining how many votes were affected, and, by resolving doubts in favor of those the statute is designed to protect, will effectuate the congressional policy of ensuring that the shareholders are able to make an informed choice when they are consulted on corporate transactions.

Our conclusion that petitioners have established their case by showing that proxies necessary to approval of the merger were obtained by means of a materially misleading solicitation implies nothing about the form of relief to which they may be entitled. We held in Borak that upon finding a violation the courts were 'to be alert to provide such remedies as are necessary to make effective the congressional purpose,' noting specifically that such remedies are not to be limited to prospective relief. In devising retrospective relief for violation of the proxy rules, the federal courts should consider the same factors that would govern the relief granted for any similar illegality or fraud. One important factor may be the fairness of the terms of the merger. Possible forms of relief will include setting aside the merger or granting other equitable relief, but, as the Court of Appeals below noted, nothing in the statutory policy 'requires the court to unscramble a corporate transaction merely because a violation occurred.' 403 F.2d, at 436. In selecting a remedy the lower courts should exercise "the sound discretion which guides the determinations of courts of equity," keeping in mind the role of equity as 'the instrument for nice adjustment and reconciliation between the public interest and private needs as well as between competing private claims.' Hecht Co. v. Bowles, 321 U.S. 321, 329-330, 64 S.Ct. 587, 591-592, 88 L.Ed. 754 (1944), quoting from Meredith v. Winter Haven, 320 U.S. 228, 235, 64 S.Ct. 7, 11, 88 L.Ed. 9 (1943).

Monetary relief will, of course, also be a possibility. Where the defect in the proxy solicitation relates to the specific terms of the merger, the district court might appropriately order an accounting to ensure that the shareholders receive the value that was represented as coming to them. On the other hand, where, as here, the misleading aspect of the solicitation did not relate to terms of the merger, monetary relief might be afforded to the shareholders only if the merger resulted in a reduction of the earnings or earnings potential of their holdings. These questions, of course, are for decision in the first instance by the District Court on remand.

In many suits under s 14(a), particularly where the violation does not relate to the terms of the transaction for which proxies are solicited, it may be impossible to assign monetary value to the benefit. Nevertheless, the stress placed by Congress on the importance of fair and informed corporate suffrage leads to the conclusion that, in vindicating the statutory policy, petitioners have rendered a substantial service to the corporation and its shareholders. Whether petitioners are successful in showing a need for significant relief may be a factor in determining whether a further award should later be made. But regardless of the relief granted, private stockholders' actions of this sort 'involve corporate therapeutics,' and furnish a benefit to all shareholders by providing an important means of enforcement of the proxy statute. To award attorneys' fees in such a suit to a plaintiff who has succeeded in establishing a cause of action is not to saddle the unsuccessful party with the expenses but to impose them on the class that has benefited from them and that would have had to pay them had it brought the suit.

For the foregoing reasons we conclude that the judgment of the Court of Appeals should be vacated and the case remanded to that court for further proceedings consistent with this opinion.

TSC INDUSTRIES, INC. v. NORTHWAY, INC.
426 U.S. 438 (1976)

Mr. Justice MARSHALL delivered the opinion of the Court.

The proxy rules promulgated by the Securities and Exchange Commission under the Securities Exchange Act of 1934 bar the use of proxy statements that are false or misleading with respect to the presentation or omission of material facts. We are called upon to consider the definition of a material fact under those rules, and the appropriateness of resolving the question of materiality by summary judgment in this case.

The dispute in this case centers on the acquisition of petitioner TSC Industries, Inc., by petitioner National Industries, Inc. In February 1969 National acquired 34% of TSC's voting securities by purchase from Charles E. Schmidt and his family. Schmidt, who had been TSC's founder and principal shareholder, promptly resigned along with his son from TSC's board of directors. Thereafter, five National nominees were placed on TSC's board; and Stanley R. Yarmuth, National's president and chief executive officer, became chairman of the TSC board, and Charles F. Simonelli, National's executive vice president, became chairman of the TSC executive committee. On October 16, 1969, the TSC board, with the attending National nominees abstaining, approved a proposal to liquidate and sell all of TSC's assets to National. The proposal in substance provided for the exchange of TSC common and Series 1 preferred stock for National Series B preferred stock and warrants. On November 12, 1969, TSC and National issued a joint proxy statement to their shareholders, recommending approval of the proposal. The proxy solicitation was successful, TSC was placed in liquidation and dissolution, and the exchange of shares was effected.

This is an action brought by respondent Northway, a TSC shareholder, against TSC and National, claiming that their joint proxy statement was incomplete and materially misleading in violation of s 14(a) of the Securities Exchange Act of 1934. The basis of Northway's claim under Rule 14a-3 is that TSC and National failed to state in the proxy statement that the transfer of the Schmidt interests in TSC to National had given National control of TSC... The Rule 14a-9 claim, insofar as it concerns us, is that TSC and National omitted from the proxy statement material facts relating to the degree of National's control over TSC and the favorability of the terms of the proposal to TSC shareholders.

As we have noted on more than one occasion, s 14(a) of the Securities Exchange Act "was intended to promote 'the free exercise of the voting rights of stockholders' by ensuring that proxies would be solicited with 'explanation to the stockholder of the real nature of the questions for which authority to cast his vote is sought.' " In Borak, the Court held that s 14(a)'s broad remedial purposes required recognition under s 27 of the Securities Exchange Act of an implied private right of action for violations of the provision. And in Mills, we attempted to clarify to some extent the elements of a private cause of action for violation of s 14(a). In a suit challenging the sufficiency under s 14(a) and Rule 14a-9 of a proxy statement soliciting votes in favor of a merger, we held that there was no need to demonstrate that the alleged defect in the proxy statement actually had a decisive effect on the voting. So long as the misstatement or omission was material, the causal relation between violation and injury is sufficiently established, we concluded, if "the proxy solicitation itself . . . was an essential link in the accomplishment of the transaction." 396 U.S., at 385, 90 S.Ct., at 622. After Mills, then, the content given to the notion of materiality assumes heightened significance.

The question of materiality, it is universally agreed, is an objective one, involving the significance of an omitted or misrepresented fact to a reasonable investor. Variations in the formulation of a general test of materiality occur in the articulation of just how significant a fact must be or, put another way, how certain it must be that the fact would affect a reasonable investor's judgment.

The Court of Appeals in this case concluded that material facts include "all facts which a reasonable shareholder might consider important." 512 F.2d, at 330 (emphasis added). This formulation of the test of materiality has been explicitly rejected by at least two courts as setting too low a threshold for the imposition of liability under Rule 14a-9. In these cases, panels of the Second and Fifth Circuits opted for the conventional tort test of materiality: whether a reasonable man would attach importance to the fact misrepresented or omitted in determining his course of action.

In formulating a standard of materiality under Rule 14a-9, we are guided, of course, by the recognition in Borak and Mills of the Rule's broad remedial purpose. That purpose is not merely to ensure by judicial means that the transaction, when judged by its real terms, is fair and otherwise adequate, but to ensure disclosures by corporate management in order to enable the shareholders to make an informed choice. See Mills, 396 U.S., at 381, 90 S.Ct., at 620. As an abstract proposition, the most desirable role for a court in a suit of this sort, coming after the consummation of the proposed transaction, would perhaps be to determine whether in fact the proposal would have been favored by the shareholders and consummated in the absence of any misstatement or omission. But as we recognized in Mills, such matters are not subject to determination with certainty. Doubts as to the critical nature of information misstated or omitted will be commonplace. And particularly in view of the prophylactic purpose of the Rule and the fact that the content of the proxy statement is within management's control, it is appropriate that these doubts be resolved in favor of those the statute is designed to protect..

The general standard of materiality that we think best comports with the policies of Rule 14a-9 is as follows: An omitted fact is material if there is a substantial likelihood that a reasonable shareholder would consider it important in deciding how to vote. This standard is fully consistent with Mills general description of materiality as a requirement that "the defect have a significant Propensity to affect the voting process." It does not require proof of a substantial likelihood that disclosure of the omitted fact would have caused the reasonable investor to change his vote. What the standard does contemplate is a showing of a substantial likelihood that, under all the circumstances, the omitted fact would have assumed actual significance in the deliberations of the reasonable shareholder. Put another way, there must be a substantial likelihood that the disclosure of the omitted fact would have been viewed by the reasonable investor as having significantly altered the "total mix" of information made available.

The issue of materiality may be characterized as a mixed question of law and fact, involving as it does the application of a legal standard to a particular set of facts. In considering whether summary judgment on the issue is appropriate, we must bear in mind that the underlying objective facts, which will often be free from dispute, are merely the starting point for the ultimate determination of materiality. The determination requires delicate assessments of the inferences a "reasonable shareholder" would draw from a given set of facts and the significance of those inferences to him, and these assessments are peculiarly ones for the trier of fact. Only if the established omissions are "so obviously important to an investor, that reasonable minds cannot differ on the question of materiality" is the ultimate issue of materiality appropriately resolved "as a matter of law" by summary judgment.

The Court of Appeals concluded that two omitted facts relating to National's potential influence, or control, over the management of TSC were material as a matter of law. First, the proxy statement failed to state that at the time the statement was issued, the chairman of the TSC board of directors was Stanley Yarmuth, National's president and chief executive officer, and the chairman of the TSC executive committee was Charles Simonelli, National's executive vice president. Second, the statement did not disclose that in filing reports required by the SEC, both TSC and National had indicated that National "may be deemed to be a 'parent' of TSC as that term is defined in the Rules and Regulations under the Securities Act of 1933." The Court of Appeals noted that TSC shareholders were relying on the TSC board of directors to negotiate on their behalf for the best possible rate of exchange with National. It then concluded that the omitted facts were material because they were "persuasive indicators that the TSC board was in fact under the control of National, and that National thus 'sat on both sides of the table' in setting the terms of the exchange."

We do not agree that the omission of these facts, when viewed against the disclosures contained in the proxy statement, warrants the entry of summary judgment against TSC and National on this record. Our conclusion is the same whether the omissions are considered separately or together.

The proxy statement prominently displayed the facts that National owned 34% of the outstanding shares in TSC, and that no other person owned more than 10%. It also prominently revealed that 5 out of 10 TSC directors were National nominees, and it recited the positions of those National nominees with National indicating, among other things, that Stanley Yarmuth was president and a director of National, and that Charles Simonelli was executive vice president and a director of National. These disclosures clearly revealed the nature of National's relationship with TSC and alerted the reasonable shareholder to the fact that National exercised a degree of influence over TSC. In view of these disclosures, we certainly cannot say that the additional facts that Yarmuth was chairman of the TSC board of directors and Simonelli chairman of its executive committee were, on this record, so obviously important that reasonable minds could not differ on their materiality.

Nor can we say that it was materially misleading as a matter of law for TSC and National to have omitted reference to SEC filings indicating that National "may be deemed to be a parent of TSC." The net contribution of including the contents of the SEC filings accompanied by such disclaimers is not of such obvious significance, in view of the other facts contained in the proxy statement, that their exclusion renders the statement materially misleading as a matter of law.

SANTA FE INDUSTRIES, INC. v. GREEN
430 U.S. 462 (1977)

Mr. Justice WHITE delivered the opinion of the Court.

The issue in this case involves the reach and coverage of s 10(b) of the Securities Exchange Act of 1934 and Rule 10b-5 thereunder in the context of a Delaware short-form merger transaction used by the majority stockholder of a corporation to eliminate the minority interest.

In 1936, petitioner Santa Fe Industries, Inc. (Santa Fe), acquired control of 60% of the stock of Kirby Lumber Corp. (Kirby), a Delaware corporation. Through a series of purchases over the succeeding years, Santa Fe increased its control of Kirby's stock to 95%; the purchase prices during the period 1968-1973 ranged from $65 to $92.50 per share. In 1974, wishing to acquire 100% ownership of Kirby, Santa Fe availed itself of s 253 of the Delaware Corporation Law, known as the 'short-form merger' statute. Section 253 permits a parent corporation owning at least 90% of the stock of a subsidiary to merge with that subsidiary, upon approval by the parent's board of directors, and to make payment in cash for the shares of the minority stockholders. The statute does not require the consent of, or advance notice to, the minority stockholders. However, notice of the merger must be given within 10 days after its effective date, and any stockholder who is dissatisfied with the terms of the merger may petition the Delaware Court of Chancery for a decree ordering the surviving corporation to pay him the fair value of his shares, as determined by a court-appointed appraiser subject to review by the court.

Santa Fe obtained independent appraisals of the physical assets of Kirby land, timber, buildings, and machinery and of Kirby's oil, gas, and mineral interests. These appraisals, together with other financial information, were submitted to Morgan Stanley & Co. (Morgan Stanley), an investment banking firm retained to appraise the fair market value of Kirby stock. Kirby's physical assets were appraised at $320 million (amounting to $640 for each of the 500,000 shares); Kirby's stock was valued by Morgan Stanley at $125 per share. Under the terms of the merger, minority stockholders were offered $150 per share.

The provisions of the short-form merger statute were fully complied with. The minority stockholders of Kirby were notified the day after the merger became effective and were advised of their right to obtain an appraisal in Delaware court if dissatisfied with the offer of $150 per share. They also received an information statement containing, in addition to the relevant financial data about Kirby, the appraisals of the value of Kirby's assets and the Morgan Stanley appraisal concluding that the fair market value of the stock was $125 per share.

Respondents, minority stockholders of Kirby, objected to the terms of the merger, but did not pursue their appraisal remedy in the Delaware Court of Chancery. Instead, they brought this action in federal court on behalf of the corporation and other minority stockholders, seeking to set aside the merger or to recover what they claimed to be the fair value of their shares. The amended complaint asserted that, based on the fair market value of Kirby's physical assets as revealed by the appraisal included in the information statement sent to minority shareholders, Kirby's stock was worth at least $772 per share…This course of conduct was alleged to be 'a violation of Rule 10b-5 because defendants employed a 'device, scheme, or artifice to defraud' and engaged in an 'act, practice or course of business which operates or would operate as a fraud or deceit upon any person, in connection with the purchase or sale of any security.''

The District Court dismissed the complaint for failure to state a claim upon which relief could be granted.

A divided Court of Appeals for the Second Circuit reversed. It first agreed that there was a double aspect to the case: first, the claim that gross undervaluation of the minority stock itself violated Rule 10b-5; and second, that 'without any misrepresentation or failure to disclose relevant facts, the merger itself constitutes a violation of Rule 10b-5' because it was accomplished without any corporate purpose and without prior notice to the minority stockholders.. As to the first aspect of the case, the Court of Appeals did not disturb the District Court's conclusion that the complaint did not allege a material misrepresentation or nondisclosure with respect to the value of the stock; and the court declined to rule that a claim of gross undervaluation itself would suffice to make out a Rule 10b-5 case. With respect to the second aspect of the case, however, the court fundamentally disagreed with the District Court as to the reach and coverage of Rule 10b-5. The Court of Appeals' view was that, although the Rule plainly reached material misrepresentations and nondisclosures in connection with the purchase or sale of securities, neither misrepresentation nor nondisclosure was a necessary element of a Rule 10b-5 action; the Rule reached 'breaches of fiduciary duty by a majority against minority shareholders without any charge of misrepresentation or lack of disclosure.'

We granted the petition for certiorari challenging this holding because of the importance of the issue involved to the administration of the federal securities laws. We reverse.

Section 10(b) of the 1934 Act makes it 'unlawful for any person . . . to use or employ . . . any manipulative or deceptive device or contrivance in contravention of (Securities and Exchange Commission rules)'; Rule 10b-5, promulgated by the SEC under s 10(b), prohibits, in addition to nondisclosure and misrepresentation, any 'artifice to defraud' or any act 'which operates or would operate as a fraud or deceit.' The court below construed the term 'fraud' in Rule 10b-5 by adverting to the use of the term in several of this Court's decisions in contexts other than the 1934 Act and the related Securities Act of 1933.

As we have indicated, the case comes to us on the premise that the complaint failed to allege a material misrepresentation or material failure to disclose. The finding of the District Court, undisturbed by the Court of Appeals, was that there was no 'omission' or 'misstatement' in the information statement accompanying the notice of merger. On the basis of the information provided, minority shareholders could either accept the price offered or reject it and seek an appraisal in the Delaware Court of Chancery. Their choice was fairly presented, and they were furnished with all relevant information on which to base their decision.

We therefore find inapposite the cases relied upon by respondents and the court below, in which the breaches of fiduciary duty held violative of Rule 10b-5 included some element of deception... [T]the cases do not support the proposition, adopted by the Court of Appeals below and urged by respondents here, that a breach of fiduciary duty by majority stockholders, without any deception, misrepresentation, or nondisclosure, violates the statute and the Rule.

It is also readily apparent that the conduct alleged in the complaint was not 'manipulative' within the meaning of the statute. 'Manipulation' is 'virtually a term of art when used in connection with securities markets.' No doubt Congress meant to prohibit the full range of ingenious devices that might be used to manipulate securities prices. But we do not think it would have chosen this 'term of art' if it had meant to bring within the scope of 10(b) instances of corporate mismanagement such as this, in which the essence of the complaint is that shareholders were treated unfairly by a fiduciary.

The language of the statute is, we think, 'sufficiently clear in its context' to be dispositive here, but even if it were not, there are additional considerations that weigh heavily against permitting a cause of action under Rule 10b-5 for the breach of corporate fiduciary duty alleged in this complaint. Congress did not expressly provide a private cause of action for violations of s 10(b). Although we have recognized an implied cause of action under that section in some circumstances, we have also recognized that a private cause of action under the antifraud provisions of the Securities Exchange Act should not be implied where it is 'unnecessary to ensure the fulfillment of Congress' purposes' in adopting that Act. As we noted earlier, the Court repeatedly has described the 'fundamental purpose' of the Act as implementing a 'philosophy of full disclosure'; once full and fair disclosure has occurred, the fairness of the terms of the transaction is at most a tangential concern of the statute... [W]e are reluctant to recognize a cause of action here to serve what is 'at best a subsidiary purpose' of the federal legislation.

A second factor in determining whether Congress intended to create a federal cause of action in these circumstances is "whether 'the cause of action (is) one traditionally relegated to state law . . .'" Piper v. Chris-Craft Industries, Inc., 430 U.S., at 40. The Delaware Legislature has supplied minority shareholders with a cause of action in the Delaware Court of Chancery to recover the fair value of shares allegedly undervalued in a short-form merger. Of course, the existence of a particular state-law remedy is not dispositive of the question whether Congress meant to provide a similar federal remedy, but... we conclude that 'it is entirely appropriate in this instance to relegate respondent and others in his situation to whatever remedy is created by state law.' 422 U.S., at 84

The reasoning behind a holding that the complaint in this case alleged fraud under Rule 10b-5 could not be easily contained. It is difficult to imagine how a court could distinguish, for purposes of Rule 10b-5 fraud, between a majority stockholder's use of a short-form merger to eliminate the minority at an unfair price and the use of some other device, such as a long-form merger, tender offer, or liquidation, to achieve the same result; or indeed how a court could distinguish the alleged abuses in these going private transactions from other types of fiduciary self-dealing involving transactions in securities. The result would be to bring within the Rule a wide variety of corporate conduct traditionally left to state regulation. In addition to posing a danger of vexatious litigation which could result from a widely expanded class of plaintiffs under Rule 10b-5,' this extension of the federal securities laws would overlap and quite possibly interfere with state corporate law. Federal courts applying a 'federal fiduciary principle' under Rule 10b-5 could be expected to depart from state fiduciary standards at least to the extent necessary to ensure uniformity within the federal system. Absent a clear indication of congressional intent, we are reluctant to federalize the substantial portion of the law of corporations that deals with transactions in securities, particularly where established state policies of corporate regulation would be overridden...

We thus adhere to the position that "Congress by s 10(b) did not seek to regulate transactions which constitute no more than internal corporate mismanagement." Superintendent of Insurance v. Bankers Life & Cas. Co., 404 U.S., at 12. There may well be a need for uniform federal fiduciary standards to govern mergers such as that challenged in this complaint. But those standards should not be supplied by judicial extension of s 10(b) and Rule 10b-5 to 'cover the corporate universe.'

The judgment of the Court of Appeals is reversed, and the case is remanded for further proceedings consistent with this opinion.

CASE PROBLEM 11-2

Same facts as in Case Problem 11-1. A class action is now being threatened against the officers and directors of Wave and the Firm on behalf of all those who sold Wave stock during the period (several months) that started when Burt decided that he wanted to explore selling the company (right after his health scare) and the date the Folsum merger was publically announced. The claim is that these selling shareholders were damaged as a direct result of inadequate disclosures regarding the plan to sell Wave and the potential yield from such a sale.

What additional facts would you like to have in assessing the merits of these claims? What is the likelihood that the shareholders will prevail on their claims? What additional steps could the officers and directors of Wave have taken to reduce the risk of such claims?

BASIC, INC. v. LEVINSON
485 U.S. 224 (1988)

Justice BLACKMUN delivered the opinion of the Court.

This case requires us to apply the materiality requirement of § 10(b) of the Securities Exchange Act of 1934, (1934 Act), 48 Stat. 881, as amended, 15

U.S.C. § 78a et seq. and the Securities and Exchange Commission's Rule 10b-5, 17 CFR § 240.10b-5 (1987), promulgated thereunder, in the context of preliminary corporate merger discussions. We must also determine whether a person who traded a corporation's shares on a securities exchange after the issuance of a materially misleading statement by the corporation may invoke a rebuttable presumption that, in trading, he relied on the integrity of the price set by the market.

Prior to December 20, 1978, Basic Incorporated was a publicly traded company primarily engaged in the business of manufacturing chemical refractories for the steel industry. As early as 1965 or 1966, Combustion Engineering, Inc., a company producing mostly alumina-based refractories, expressed some interest in acquiring Basic, but was deterred from pursuing this inclination seriously because of antitrust concerns it then entertained. In 1976, however, regulatory action opened the way to a renewal of Combustion's interest. The "Strategic Plan," dated October 25, 1976, for Combustion's Industrial Products Group included the objective: "Acquire Basic Inc. $30 million."

Beginning in September 1976, Combustion representatives had meetings and telephone conversations with Basic officers and directors, including petitioners here, concerning the possibility of a merger. During 1977 and 1978, Basic made three public statements denying that it was engaged in merger negotiations. On December 18, 1978, Basic asked the New York Stock Exchange to suspend trading in its shares and issued a release stating that it had been "approached" by another company concerning a merger. On December 19, Basic's board endorsed Combustion's offer of $46 per share for its common stock, and on the following day publicly announced its approval of Combustion's tender offer for all outstanding shares.

Respondents are former Basic shareholders who sold their stock after Basic's first public statement of October 21, 1977, and before the suspension of trading in December 1978. Respondents brought a class action against Basic and its directors, asserting that the defendants issued three false or misleading public statements and thereby were in violation of § 10(b) of the 1934 Act and of Rule 10b-5. Respondents alleged that they were injured by selling Basic shares at artificially depressed prices in a market affected by petitioners' misleading statements and in reliance thereon.

On the merits, the District Court granted summary judgment for the defendants. It held that, as a matter of law, any misstatements were immaterial: there were no negotiations ongoing at the time of the first statement, and although negotiations were taking place when the second and third statements were issued, those negotiations were not "destined, with reasonable certainty, to become a merger agreement in principle."

The United States Court of Appeals for the Sixth Circuit reversed the District Court's summary judgment, and remanded the case. The court reasoned that while petitioners were under no general duty to disclose their discussions with Combustion, any statement the company voluntarily released could not be "so incomplete as to mislead." In the Court of Appeals' view, Basic's statements that no negotiations where taking place, and that it knew of no corporate developments to account for the heavy trading activity, were misleading. With respect to materiality, the court rejected the argument that preliminary merger discussions are immaterial as a matter of law, and held that "once a statement is made denying the existence of any discussions, even discussions that might not have been material in absence of the denial are material because they make the statement made untrue."

The Court of Appeals joined a number of other Circuits in accepting the "fraud-on-the-market theory" to create a rebuttable presumption that respondents relied on petitioners' material misrepresentations, noting that without the presumption it would be impractical to certify a class under Federal Rule of Civil Procedure 23(b)(3).

We granted certiorari to resolve the split among the Courts of Appeals as to the standard of materiality applicable to preliminary merger discussions, and to determine whether the courts below properly applied a presumption of reliance in certifying the class, rather than requiring each class member to show direct reliance on Basic's statements.

The 1934 Act was designed to protect investors against manipulation of stock prices. Underlying the adoption of extensive disclosure requirements was a legislative philosophy: "There cannot be honest markets without honest publicity. Manipulation and dishonest practices of the market place thrive upon mystery and secrecy." H.R.Rep. No. 1383, 73d Cong., 2d Sess., 11 (1934). This Court "repeatedly has described the 'fundamental purpose' of the Act as implementing a 'philosophy of full disclosure.' " " *Santa Fe Industries, Inc. v. Green,* 430 U.S. 462, 477-478.

The Court previously has addressed various positive and common-law requirements for a violation of § 10(b) or of Rule 10b-5. The Court also explicitly has defined a standard of materiality under the securities laws, see TSC Industries, Inc. v. Northway, Inc., 426 U.S. 438 (1976), concluding in the proxy-solicitation context that "[a]n omitted fact is material if there is a substantial likelihood that a reasonable shareholder would consider it important in deciding how to vote." Acknowledging that certain information concerning corporate developments could well be of "dubious significance," the Court was careful not to set too low a standard of materiality; it was concerned that a minimal standard might bring an overabundance of information within its reach, and lead management "simply to bury the shareholders in an avalanche of trivial information-a result that is hardly conducive to informed decisionmaking." It further explained that to fulfill the materiality requirement "there must be a substantial likelihood that the disclosure of the omitted fact would have been viewed by the reasonable investor as having significantly altered the 'total mix' of information made available." We now expressly adopt the TSC Industries standard of materiality for the § 10(b) and Rule 10b-5 context.

The application of this materiality standard to preliminary merger discussions is not self-evident. Where the impact of the corporate development on the target's fortune is certain and clear, the TSC Industries materiality definition admits straightforward application. Where, on the other hand, the event is contingent or speculative in nature, it is difficult to ascertain whether the "reasonable investor" would have considered the omitted information significant at the time. Merger negotiations, because of the ever-present possibility that the contemplated transaction will not be effectuated, fall into the latter category.

Even before this Court's decision in TSC Industries, the Second Circuit had explained the role of the materiality requirement of Rule 10b-5, with respect to contingent or speculative information or events, in a manner that gave that term meaning that is independent of the other provisions of the Rule. Under such circumstances, materiality "will depend at any given time upon a balancing of both the indicated probability that the event will occur and the anticipated magnitude of the event in light of the totality of the company activity." SEC v. Texas Gulf Sulphur Co., 401 F.2d, at 849. Interestingly, neither the Third Circuit decision adopting the agreement-in-principle test nor petitioners here take issue with this general standard. Rather, they suggest that with respect to preliminary merger discussions, there are good reasons to draw a line at agreement on price and structure.

In a subsequent decision, the late Judge Friendly, writing for a Second Circuit panel, applied the Texas Gulf Sulphur probability/magnitude approach in the specific context of preliminary merger negotiations. After acknowledging that materiality is something to be determined on the basis of the particular facts of each case, he stated:

> "Since a merger in which it is bought out is the most important event that can occur in a small corporation's life, to wit, its death, we think that inside information, as regards a merger of this sort, can become material at an earlier stage than would be the case as regards lesser transactions-and this even though the mortality rate of mergers in such formative stages is doubtless high." SEC v. Geon Industries, Inc., 531 F.2d 39, 47-48 (1976).

We agree with that analysis.

Whether merger discussions in any particular case are material therefore depends on the facts. Generally, in order to assess the probability that the event will occur, a factfinder will need to look to indicia of interest in the transaction at the highest corporate levels. Without attempting to catalog all such possible factors, we note by way of example that board resolutions, instructions to investment bankers, and actual negotiations between principals or their intermediaries may serve as indicia of interest. To assess the magnitude of the transaction to the issuer of the securities allegedly manipulated, a factfinder will need to consider such facts as the size of the two corporate entities and of the potential premiums over market value. No particular event or factor short of closing the transaction need be either necessary or sufficient by itself to render merger discussions material.

As we clarify today, materiality depends on the significance the reasonable investor would place on the withheld or misrepresented information. The fact-specific inquiry we endorse here is consistent with the approach a number of courts have taken in assessing the materiality of merger negotiations. Because the standard of materiality we have adopted differs from that used by both courts below, we remand the case for reconsideration of the question whether a grant of summary judgment is appropriate on this record.

We turn to the question of reliance and the fraud-on-the-market theory. Succinctly put: "The fraud on the market theory is based on the hypothesis that, in an open and developed securities market, the price of a company's stock is determined by the available material information regarding the company and its business.... Misleading statements will therefore defraud purchasers of stock even if the purchasers do not directly rely on the misstatements.... The causal connection between the defendants' fraud and the plaintiffs' purchase of stock in such a case is no less significant than in a case of direct reliance on misrepresentations." *Peil v. Speiser*, 806 F.2d 1154, 1160-1161 (CA3 1986).

Our task, of course, is not to assess the general validity of the theory, but to consider whether it was proper for the courts below to apply a rebuttable presumption of reliance, supported in part by the fraud-on-the-market theory.

This case required resolution of several common questions of law and fact concerning the falsity or misleading nature of the three public statements made by Basic, the presence or absence of scienter, and the materiality of the misrepresentations, if any. In their amended complaint, the named plaintiffs alleged that in reliance on Basic's statements they sold their shares of Basic stock in the depressed market created by petitioners. Requiring proof of individualized reliance from each member of the proposed plaintiff class effectively would have prevented respondents from proceeding with a class action, since individual issues then would have overwhelmed the common ones. The District Court found that the presumption of reliance created by the fraud-on-the-market theory provided "a practical resolution to the problem of balancing the substantive requirement of proof of reliance in securities cases against the procedural requisites of [Federal Rule of Civil Procedure] 23." The District Court thus concluded that with reference to each public statement and its impact upon the open market for Basic shares, common questions predominated over individual questions.

Petitioners and their *amici* complain that the fraud-on-the-market theory effectively eliminates the requirement that a plaintiff asserting a claim under Rule 10b-5 prove reliance. They note that reliance is and long has been an element of common-law fraud and argue that because the analogous express right of action includes a reliance requirement, so too must an action implied under § 10(b).

We agree that reliance is an element of a Rule 10b-5 cause of action. Reliance provides the requisite causal connection between a defendant's misrepresentation and a plaintiff's injury. There is, however, more than one way to demonstrate the causal connection. Indeed, we previously have dispensed with a requirement of positive proof of reliance, where a duty to disclose material information had been breached, concluding that the necessary nexus between the plaintiffs' injury and the defendant's wrongful conduct had been established. See

Affiliated Ute Citizens v. United States, 406 U.S., at 153-154. Similarly, we did not require proof that material omissions or misstatements in a proxy statement decisively affected voting, because the proxy solicitation itself, rather than the defect in the solicitation materials, served as an essential link in the transaction. See *Mills v. Electric Auto-Lite Co.,* 396 U.S. 375 (1970).

The modern securities markets, literally involving millions of shares changing hands daily, differ from the face-to-face transactions contemplated by early fraud cases, and our understanding of Rule 10b-5's reliance requirement must encompass these differences.

"In face-to-face transactions, the inquiry into an investor's reliance upon information is into the subjective pricing of that information by that investor. With the presence of a market, the market is interposed between seller and buyer and, ideally, transmits information to the investor in the processed form of a market price. Thus the market is performing a substantial part of the valuation process performed by the investor in a face-to-face transaction.

Presumptions typically serve to assist courts in managing circumstances in which direct proof, for one reason or another, is rendered difficult. The courts below accepted a presumption, created by the fraud-on-the-market theory and subject to rebuttal by petitioners, that persons who had traded Basic shares had done so in reliance on the integrity of the price set by the market, but because of petitioners' material misrepresentations that price had been fraudulently depressed. Requiring a plaintiff to show a speculative state of facts, *i.e.,* how he would have acted if omitted material information had been disclosed, or if the misrepresentation had not been made, would place an unnecessarily unrealistic evidentiary burden on the Rule 10b-5 plaintiff who has traded on an impersonal market.

Arising out of considerations of fairness, public policy, and probability, as well as judicial economy, presumptions are also useful devices for allocating the burdens of proof between parties. The presumption of reliance employed in this case is consistent with, and, by facilitating Rule 10b-5 litigation, supports, the congressional policy embodied in the 1934 Act.

The presumption is also supported by common sense and probability. Recent empirical studies have tended to confirm Congress' premise that the market price of shares traded on well-developed markets reflects all publicly available information, and, hence, any material misrepresentations. Indeed, nearly every court that has considered the proposition has concluded that where materially misleading statements have been disseminated into an impersonal, well-developed market for securities, the reliance of individual plaintiffs on the integrity of the market price may be presumed. Commentators generally have applauded the adoption of one variation or another of the fraud-on-the-market theory. An investor who buys or sells stock at the price set by the market does so in reliance on the integrity of that price. Because most publicly available information is reflected in market price, an investor's reliance on any public material misrepresentations, therefore, may be presumed for purposes of a Rule 10b-5 action.

The Court of Appeals found that petitioners "made public, material misrepresentations and [respondents] sold Basic stock in an impersonal, efficient market. Thus the class, as defined by the district court, has established the threshold facts for proving their loss." The court acknowledged that petitioners may rebut proof of the elements giving rise to the presumption, or show that the misrepresentation in fact did not lead to a distortion of price or that an individual plaintiff traded or would have traded despite his knowing the statement was false.

Any showing that severs the link between the alleged misrepresentation and either the price received (or paid) by the plaintiff, or his decision to trade at a fair market price, will be sufficient to rebut the presumption of reliance. For example, if petitioners could show that the "market makers" were privy to the truth about the merger discussions here with Combustion, and thus that the market price would not have been affected by their misrepresentations, the causal connection could be broken: the basis for finding that the fraud had been transmitted through market price would be gone. Similarly, if, despite petitioners' allegedly fraudulent attempt to manipulate market price, news of the merger discussions credibly entered the market and dissipated the effects of the misstatements, those who traded Basic shares after the corrective statements would have no direct or indirect connection with the fraud.

Petitioners also could rebut the presumption of reliance as to plaintiffs who would have divested themselves of their Basic shares without relying on the integrity of the market. For example, a plaintiff who believed that Basic's statements were false and that Basic was indeed engaged in merger discussions, and who consequently believed that Basic stock was artificially underpriced, but sold his shares nevertheless because of other unrelated concerns, *e.g.*, potential antitrust problems, or political pressures to divest from shares of certain businesses, could not be said to have relied on the integrity of a price he knew had been manipulated.

In summary:

1. We specifically adopt, for the § 10(b) and Rule 10b-5 context, the standard of materiality set forth in *TSC Industries, Inc. v. Northway, Inc.*, 426 U.S., at 449, 96 S.Ct., at 2132.

2. We reject "agreement-in-principle as to price and structure" as the bright-line rule for materiality.

3. We also reject the proposition that "information becomes material by virtue of a public statement denying it."

4. Materiality in the merger context depends on the probability that the transaction will be consummated, and its significance to the issuer of the securities. Materiality depends on the facts and thus is to be determined on a case-by-case basis.

5. It is not inappropriate to apply a presumption of reliance supported by the fraud-on-the-market theory.

6. That presumption, however, is rebuttable.

CASE PROBLEM 11-3

Same facts as in Case Problem 11-1, except the Team, including Burt, collectively owned 55 percent of the stock of Wave. So at the time the proxy statement was sent, Burt and his team knew that they had the required number of votes to approve the merger. How would this fact impact (if at all) your assessment of the claims made by the minority shareholders? What additional steps could the officers and directors of Wave have taken to reduce the risk of such claims?

VIRGINIA BANKSHARES, INC. v. SANDBERG
501 U.S. 1083 (1991)

Justice SOUTER delivered the opinion of the Court.

Section 14(a) of the Securities Exchange Act of 1934, 48 Stat. 895, 15 U.S.C. § 78n(a), authorizes the Securities and Exchange Commission (SEC) to adopt rules for the solicitation of proxies, and prohibits their violation. In J.I. Case Co. v. Borak, we first recognized an implied private right of action for the breach of § 14(a) as implemented by SEC Rule 14a-9, which prohibits the solicitation of proxies by means of materially false or misleading statements.

The questions before us are whether a statement couched in conclusory or qualitative terms purporting to explain directors' reasons for recommending certain corporate action can be materially misleading within the meaning of Rule 14a-9, and whether causation of damages compensable under § 14(a) can be shown by a member of a class of minority shareholders whose votes are not required by law or corporate bylaw to authorize the corporate action subject to the proxy solicitation. We hold that knowingly false statements of reasons may be actionable even though conclusory in form, but that respondents have failed to demonstrate the equitable basis required to extend the § 14(a) private action to such shareholders when any indication of congressional intent to do so is lacking.

In December 1986, First American Bankshares, Inc. (FABI), a bank holding company, began a "freeze-out" merger, in which the First American Bank of Virginia (Bank) eventually merged into Virginia Bankshares, Inc. (VBI), a wholly owned subsidiary of FABI. VBI owned 85% of the Bank's shares, the remaining 15% being in the hands of some 2,000 minority shareholders. FABI hired the investment banking firm of Keefe, Bruyette & Woods (KBW) to give an opinion on the appropriate price for shares of the minority holders, who would lose their interests in the Bank as a result of the merger. Based on market quotations and unverified information from FABI, KBW gave the Bank's executive committee an opinion that $42 a share would be a fair price for the minority stock. The executive committee approved the merger proposal at that price, and the full board followed suit.

Although Virginia law required only that such a merger proposal be submitted to a vote at a shareholders' meeting, and that the meeting be preceded by circulation of a statement of information to the shareholders, the directors nevertheless solicited proxies for voting on the proposal at the annual meeting set for April 21, 1987. In their solicitation, the directors urged the proposal's adoption and stated they had approved the plan because of its opportunity for the minority shareholders to achieve a "high" value, which they elsewhere described as a "fair" price, for their stock.

Although most minority shareholders gave the proxies requested, respondent Sandberg did not, and after approval of the merger she sought damages in the United States District Court for the Eastern District of Virginia from VBI, FABI, and the directors of the Bank. She pleaded two counts, one for soliciting proxies in violation of § 14(a) and Rule 14a-9, and the other for breaching fiduciary duties owed to the minority shareholders under state law. Under the first count, Sandberg alleged, among other things, that the directors had not believed that the price offered was high or that the terms of the merger were fair, but had recommended the merger only because they believed they had no alternative if they wished to remain on the board. At trial, Sandberg invoked language from this Court's opinion in Mills v. Electric Auto-Lite Co., to obtain an instruction that the jury could find for her without a showing of her own reliance on the alleged misstatements, so long as they were material and the proxy solicitation was an "essential link" in the merger process.

The jury's verdicts were for Sandberg on both counts, after finding violations of Rule 14a-9 by all defendants and a breach of fiduciary duties by the Bank's directors. The jury awarded Sandberg $18 a share, having found that she would have received $60 if her stock had been valued adequately.

On appeal, the United States Court of Appeals for the Fourth Circuit affirmed the judgments, holding that certain statements in the proxy solicitation were materially misleading for purposes of the Rule, and that respondents could maintain their action even though their votes had not been needed to effectuate the merger. We granted certiorari because of the importance of the issues presented.

We consider first the actionability per se of statements of reasons, opinion, or belief. Because such a statement by definition purports to express what is consciously on the speaker's mind, we interpret the jury verdict as finding that the directors' statements of belief and opinion were made with knowledge that the directors did not hold the beliefs or opinions expressed, and we confine our discussion to statements so made. That such statements may be materially significant raises no serious question. The meaning of the materiality requirement for liability under § 14(a) was discussed at some length in TSC Industries, Inc. v. Northway, Inc., where we held a fact to be material "if there is a substantial likelihood that a reasonable shareholder would consider it important in deciding how to vote." We think there is no room to deny that a statement of belief by corporate directors about a recommended course of action, or an explanation of their reasons for recommending it, can take on just that importance. Shareholders know that directors usually have knowledge and expertness far exceeding the normal investor's resources, and the directors' perceived superiority is magnified even further by the common knowledge that state law customarily obliges them to exercise their judgment in the shareholders' interest. Naturally, then, the shareowner faced with a proxy request will think it important to know the directors' beliefs about the course they recommend and their specific reasons for urging the stockholders to embrace it.

But, assuming materiality, the question remains whether statements of reasons, opinions, or beliefs are statements "with respect to ... material fact [s]" so as to fall within the strictures of the Rule. Petitioners argue that we would invite wasteful litigation of amorphous issues outside the readily provable realm of fact if we were to recognize liability here on proof that the directors did not recommend the merger for the stated reason.

Attacks on the truth of directors' statements of reasons or belief, however, need carry no such threats. Such statements are factual in two senses: as statements that the directors do act for the reasons given or hold the belief stated and as statements about the subject matter of the reason or belief expressed... Reasons for directors' recommendations or statements of belief are characteristically matters of corporate record subject to documentation, to be supported or attacked by evidence of historical fact outside a plaintiff's control. Such evidence would include not only corporate minutes and other statements of the directors themselves, but circumstantial evidence bearing on the facts that would reasonably underlie the reasons claimed and the honesty of any statement that those reasons are the basis for a recommendation or other action, a point that becomes especially clear when the reasons or beliefs go to valuations in dollars and cents...

Under § 14(a), then, a plaintiff is permitted to prove a specific statement of reason knowingly false or misleadingly incomplete, even when stated in conclusory terms. In reaching this conclusion we have considered statements of reasons of the sort exemplified here, which misstate the speaker's reasons and also mislead about the stated subject matter (e.g., the value of the shares). A statement of belief may be open to objection only in the former respect, however, solely as a misstatement of the psychological fact of the speaker's belief in what he says..

The question arises, then, whether disbelief, or undisclosed belief or motivation, standing alone, should be a sufficient basis to sustain an action under § 14(a), absent proof by the sort of objective evidence described above that the statement also expressly or impliedly asserted something false or misleading about its subject matter. We think that proof of mere disbelief or belief undisclosed should not suffice for liability under § 14(a), and if nothing more had been required or proven in this case, we would reverse for that reason.

On the one hand, it would be rare to find a case with evidence solely of disbelief or undisclosed motivation without further proof that the statement was defective as to its subject matter. While we certainly would not hold a director's naked admission of disbelief incompetent evidence of a proxy statement's false or misleading character, such an unusual admission will not very often stand alone, and we do not substantially narrow the cause of action by requiring a plaintiff to demonstrate something false or misleading in what the statement expressly or impliedly declared about its subject.

On the other hand, to recognize liability on mere disbelief or undisclosed motive without any demonstration that the proxy statement was false or misleading about its subject would authorize § 14(a) litigation confined solely to what one skeptical court spoke of as the "impurities" of a director's "unclean heart"... We therefore hold disbelief or undisclosed motivation, standing alone, insufficient to satisfy the element of fact that must be established under § 14(a).

Since liability under § 14(a) must rest not only on deceptiveness but materiality as well (i.e., it has to be significant enough to be important to a reasonable investor deciding how to vote, see TSC Industries, 426 U.S., at 449, 96 S.Ct., at 2132), petitioners are on perfectly firm ground insofar as they argue that publishing accurate facts in a proxy statement can render a misleading proposition too unimportant to ground liability.

But not every mixture with the true will neutralize the deceptive. If it would take a financial analyst to spot the tension between the one and the other, whatever is misleading will remain materially so, and liability should follow. The point of a proxy statement, after all, should be to inform, not to challenge the reader's critical wits. Only when the inconsistency would exhaust the misleading conclusion's capacity to influence the reasonable shareholder would a § 14(a) action fail on the element of materiality.

The second issue before us, left open in Mills v. Electric Auto-Lite Co., is whether causation of damages compensable through the implied private right of action under § 14(a) can be demonstrated by a member of a class of minority shareholders whose votes are not required by law or corporate bylaw to authorize the transaction giving rise to the claim...

Although a majority stockholder in Mills controlled just over half the corporation's shares, a two-thirds vote was needed to approve the merger proposal. After proxies had been obtained, and the merger had carried, minority shareholders brought a Borak action. The question arose whether the plaintiffs' burden to demonstrate causation of their damages traceable to the § 14(a) violation required proof that the defect in the proxy solicitation had had "a decisive effect on the voting." The Mills Court avoided the evidentiary morass that would have followed from requiring individualized proof that enough minority shareholders had relied upon the misstatements to swing the vote. Instead, it held that causation of damages by a material proxy misstatement could be established by showing that minority proxies necessary and sufficient to authorize the corporate acts had been given in accordance with the tenor of the solicitation, and the Court described such a causal relationship by calling the proxy solicitation an "essential link in the accomplishment of the transaction." In the case before it, the Court found the solicitation essential, as contrasted with one addressed to a class of minority shareholders without votes required by law or by law to authorize the action proposed, and left it for another day to decide whether such a minority shareholder could demonstrate causation.

In this case, respondents address Mills' open question by proffering two theories that the proxy solicitation addressed to them was an "essential link" under the Mills causation test. They argue, first, that a link existed and was essential simply because VBI and FABI would have been unwilling to proceed with the merger without the approval manifested by the minority shareholders' proxies, which would not have been obtained without the solicitation's express misstatements and misleading omissions. On this reasoning, the causal connection would depend on a desire to avoid bad shareholder or public relations, and the essential character of the causal link would stem not from the enforceable terms of the parties' corporate relationship, but from one party's apprehension of the ill will of the other.

In the alternative, respondents argue that the proxy statement was an essential link between the directors' proposal and the merger because it was the means to satisfy a state statutory requirement of minority shareholder approval, as a condition for saving the merger from voidability resulting from a conflict of interest on the part of one of the Bank's directors, Jack Beddow, who voted in favor of the merger while also serving as a director of FABI. Under the terms of Va.Code Ann. § 13.1-691(A) (1989), minority approval after disclosure of the material facts about the transaction and the director's interest was one of three avenues to insulate the merger from later attack for conflict, the two others being ratification by the Bank's directors after like disclosure and proof that the merger was fair to the corporation. On this theory, causation would depend on the use of the proxy statement for the purpose of obtaining votes sufficient to bar a minority shareholder from commencing proceedings to declare the merger void.

Although respondents have proffered each of these theories as establishing a chain of causal connection in which the proxy statement is claimed to have been an "essential link," neither theory presents the proxy solicitation as essential in the sense of Mills' causal sequence, in which the solicitation links a directors' proposal with the votes legally required to authorize the action proposed. As a consequence, each theory would, if adopted, extend the scope of Borak actions beyond the ambit of Mills and expand the class of plaintiffs entitled to bring Borak actions to include shareholders whose initial authorization of the transaction prompting the proxy solicitation is unnecessary.

Assessing the legitimacy of any such extension or expansion calls for the application of some fundamental principles governing recognition of a right of action implied by a federal statute, the first of which was not, in fact, the considered focus of the Borak opinion. The rule that has emerged in the years since Borak and Mills came down is that recognition of any private right of action for violating a federal statute must ultimately rest on congressional intent to provide a private remedy. From this the corollary follows that the breadth of the right once recognized should not, as a general matter, grow beyond the scope congressionally intended.

This rule and corollary present respondents with a serious obstacle, for we can find no manifestation of intent to recognize a cause of action (or class of plaintiffs) as broad as respondents' theory of causation would entail...

The threats of speculative claims and procedural intractability are inherent in respondents' theory of causation linked through the directors' desire for a cosmetic vote. Causation would turn on inferences about what the corporate directors would have thought and done without the minority shareholder approval unneeded to authorize action. A subsequently dissatisfied minority shareholder would have virtual license to allege that managerial timidity would have doomed corporate action but for the ostensible approval induced by a misleading statement, and opposing claims of hypothetical diffidence and hypothetical boldness on the part of directors would probably provide enough depositions in the usual case to preclude any judicial resolution short of the credibility judgments that can only come after trial. Reliable evidence would seldom exist. Directors would understand the prudence of making a few statements about plans to proceed even without minority endorsement, and discovery would be a quest for recollections of oral conversations at odds with the official pronouncements, in hopes of finding support for ex post facto guesses about how much heat the directors would have stood in the absence of minority approval. The issues would be hazy, their litigation protracted, and their resolution unreliable. Given a choice, we would reject any theory of causation that raised such prospects, and we reject this one.

The theory of causal necessity derived from the requirements of Virginia law dealing with post-merger ratification seeks to identify the essential character of the proxy solicitation from its function in obtaining the minority approval that would preclude a minority suit attacking the merger. Since the link is said to be a step in the process of barring a class of shareholders from resort to a state remedy otherwise available, this theory of causation rests upon the proposition of policy that § 14(a) should provide a federal remedy whenever a false or misleading proxy statement results in the loss under state law of a shareholder plaintiff's state remedy for the enforcement of a state right. Respondents agree with the suggestions of counsel for the SEC and FDIC that causation be recognized, for example, when a minority shareholder has been induced by a misleading proxy statement to forfeit a state-law right to an appraisal remedy by voting to approve a transaction or when such a shareholder has been deterred from obtaining an order enjoining a damaging transaction by a proxy solicitation that misrepresents the facts on which an injunction could properly have been issued. Respondents claim that in this case a predicate for recognizing just such a causal link exists in Va.Code Ann. § 13.1-691(A)(2) (1989), which sets the conditions under which the merger may be insulated from suit by a minority shareholder seeking to void it on account of Beddow's conflict.

This case does not, however, require us to decide whether § 14(a) provides a cause of action for lost state remedies, since there is no indication in the law or facts before us that the proxy solicitation resulted in any such loss. The contrary appears to be the case. Assuming the soundness of respondents' characterization of the proxy statement as materially misleading, the very terms of the Virginia statute indicate that a favorable minority vote induced by the solicitation would not suffice to render the merger invulnerable to later attack on the ground of the conflict.

The statute bars a shareholder from seeking to avoid a transaction tainted by a director's conflict if, inter alia, the minority shareholders ratified the transaction following disclosure of the material facts of the transaction and the conflict. Assuming that the material facts about the merger and Beddow's interests were not accurately disclosed, the minority votes were inadequate to ratify the merger under state law, and there was no loss of state remedy to connect the proxy solicitation with harm to minority shareholders irredressable under state law. Nor is there a claim here that the statement misled respondents into entertaining a false belief that they had no chance to upset the merger, until the time for bringing suit had run out.

The judgment of the Court of Appeals is reversed.

Lost Appraisal Rights

In *Wilson v. Great American Industries, Inc.,* 979 F.2d 924 (2nd Cir. 1992), the Second Circuit considered whether minority shareholders who voted for a merger and lost their statutory appraisal rights could bring an action under section 14(a) based solely on the loss of such rights due to a false and misleading proxy statement. In holding that the loss of such rights provided a sufficient causal connection under Section 14(a), the court stated:

> As noted, *Virginia Bankshares* left open the possibility that § 14(a) might include this type of implied right to recover and did not address whether the causal relationship between a deceptive proxy and lost state remedies was sufficient to support a federal remedy.

> We continue to believe that a minority shareholder, who has lost his right to a state appraisal because of a materially deceptive proxy, may make "a sufficient showing of causal relationship between the violation and the injury for which he seeks redress." *Mills,* 396 U.S. at 385, 90 S.Ct. at 622. The transaction effected by a proxy involves not only the merger of the corporate entities, and the attendant exchange of stock, but also the forfeiture of shareholders' appraisal rights. The injury sustained by a minority shareholder powerless to affect the outcome of the merger vote is not the merger but the loss of his appraisal right. The deceptive proxy plainly constitutes an "essential link" in accomplishing the forfeiture of this state right.

> That the causal nexus between the merger and the proxy is absent when the minority stockholder's vote cannot affect the merger decision does not necessarily mean a causal link between the proxy and some other injury may not exist. We recognize that loss causation or economic harm to plaintiffs must be shown, as well as proof that the misrepresentations induced plaintiffs to engage in the subject transaction, that is, transaction causation.

> Here loss causation may be established when a proxy statement prompts a shareholder to accept an unfair exchange ratio for his shares rather than recoup a greater value through a state appraisal. And transaction causation may be shown when a proxy statement, because of material misrepresentations, causes a shareholder to forfeit his appraisal rights by voting in favor of the proposed corporate merger.

> Even though the proxy was not legally required in this case, when defendants choose to issue a proxy plaintiffs have a right to a truthful

one…The statute does not suggest that the prohibition of material misrepresentation in a proxy extends only to necessary proxies that are mailed to shareholders the solicitation of whose votes may affect the outcome of the proposed corporate action. That a controlling group of shareholders may accomplish any corporate change they want does not insulate them from liability for injury occasioned when they commit the sort of fraud that § 14(a) seeks to prevent.

3. SCIENTER OR NOT?

Is Ignorance a defense to a securities law claim based on defective shareholder disclosures? Suppose the defendant did not know of a fact that should have been disclosed, or had no knowledge that a disclosed fact was false or misleading, or assumed in good faith that a fact was not sufficiently material to warrant disclosure. Clearly, some level of culpability is required. The question is: How much culpability?

In *Ernst & Ernst v. Hockfelder*, 425 U.S. 185 (1976), the Supreme Court held that something more than ordinary negligence was required in a straight 10b-5 action that did not involve a proxy or registration statement. In that case, the victims of a fraudulent Ponzi scheme alleged that Ernst & Ernst had aided and abetted the perpetrator of the fraud by negligently conducting audits over many years. In rejecting the SEC's argument for a negligence standard, the Court stated:

> The argument simply ignores the use of the words "manipulate," "device," and "contrivance," terms that make unmistakable a congressional intent to proscribe a type of conduct quite different from negligence. Use of the word "manipulate" is especially significant. It is and was virtually a term of art when used in connection with securities markets. It connotes intentional or willful conduct designed to deceive or defraud investors by controlling or artificially affecting the price of securities. 425 U.S. at 193.

Although the Court in *Ernst & Ernst* left open the issue of whether recklessness would support a 10b-5 claim, the federal circuit courts answered the question by uniformly holding that reckless behavior was actionable under 10b-5. See *Hollinger v. Titan Capital Corp.*, 914 F.2d 1564 (9th Cir. 1990) and various circuit cases cited in footnote 6 of that opinion.

But does the 10b-5 scienter requirement disappear – that is, will ordinary negligence work – when a claim is made under section 14(a) based on a false or misleading proxy statement? In its *Virginia Bankshares* opinion, the Supreme Court held that, in order for an opinion to be deemed false or misleading and actionable under 14(a), it must be shown that the opinion was both objectively and subjectively false. Thus, scienter would need to be alleged and proved. Beyond false or misleading opinion allegations, the Supreme Court stated in footnote 5 of its decision in *Virginia Bankshares*, "In *TSC Industries, Inc. v. Northway, Inc...*, we reserved the question whether scienter was necessary for liability generally under § 14(a). We reserve it still."

Lower courts are split on the issue of whether ordinary negligence will do the job in a 14(a) claim. In *Gould v. American-Hawaiian S. S. Co.*, 535 F.2d 761 (3rd Cir. 1976), the Third Circuit held that ordinary negligence was the requisite standard by comparing a section 14(a) violation to a false or misleading registration statement claim under section 11. The court stated:

> We agree with the district court that section 14(a) and Rule 14a-9(a) may be more closely analogized to section 11 of the Securities Act of 1933, as amended by the Act of 1934, which deals with civil liability for false registration statements. Each section (section 14(a) as implemented by Rule 14a-9(a) and section 11) proscribes a type of disclosure or lack of it, i. e., false or misleading statements or omissions of material facts, and each enumerates specific classes of individuals who bear liability for failure to meet the required standard of disclosure. Moreover, each involves single specific documents which are of primary importance in two fundamental areas of securities regulation, sales of securities and the exercise of the shareholders' voting power. Since section 11 of the Securities Act clearly establishes negligence as the test for determining liability, the parallel between the two sections would strongly support adoption of negligence as the standard under section 14(a).

> All of the courts which have discussed the question, so far as the reported decisions indicate, have favored applying the rule of negligence as the criterion for determining liability under section 14(a). (Citations omitted) The language of section 14(a) and Rule 14a-9(a) contains no suggestion of a scienter requirement, merely establishing a quality standard for proxy material. The importance of the proxy provisions to informed voting by shareholders has been stressed by the Supreme Court, which has emphasized the broad remedial purpose of the section, implying the need to impose a high standard of care on the individuals involved. And, unlike sections 10(b) and 18 of the Act, which encompass activity in numerous and diverse areas of securities markets and corporate management, section 14(a) is specially limited to materials used in soliciting proxies. Given all of these factors the imposition of a standard of due diligence as opposed to actual knowledge or gross negligence is quite appropriate. We are confirmed in this view by the very recent case of *Ernst & Ernst v. Hochfelder*, 425 U.S. 185, fn. 28, 96 S.Ct. 1375, 47 L.Ed.2d 668 (1976), in which the Supreme Court pointed out that the "operative language and purpose" of each particular section of the Acts of 1933 and 1934 are important considerations in determining the standard of liability for violations of the section in question. We, therefore, conclude that the district court did not err in applying the standard of due diligence to determine Casey's liability in this case.

535 F.2d at 777.

In *Herskowitz v. Nutri/System, Inc.*, 857 F.2d 179 (3rd Cir. 1988), the Third Circuit applied the negligence standard to an investment banker in a proxy case, stating that any outside adviser should be held "to the same standard of liability as the management it is assisting." 857 F.2d at 190.

In contrast, the Sixth Circuit has held that 10b-5 scienter was the appropriate standard for an accountant who aided in the preparation of misleading financial statements in a proxy statement. *Adams v. Standard Knitting Mills*, 623 F.2d 422 (6th Cir. 1980). After observing that an "accountant's potential liability for relatively minor mistakes would be enormous under the negligence standard," the court in *Adams* said that it saw "no reason for a different standard of liability for accountants under the proxy provisions than under 10b-5." 623 F.2d at 429.

Whether scienter or negligence is the requisite standard, the Private Securities Litigation Reform Act of 1995 increased the state-of-mind allegation burden for plaintiffs who pursue a private right of action under the federal securities laws. The act requires that a plaintiff allege "with particularity facts giving rise to a strong inference that the defendant acted with the required state of mind." Section 21D(b)(2). Lower courts grappled with this "strong inference" pleading requirement until the Supreme Court clarified the process in *Tellabs, Inc. v. Makor Issues and Rights, LTD*, 551 U.S. 308 (2007). In *Tellabs*, the Court laid out a three step "workable construction" of the "strong inference" standard, summarizing the goal as follows: "[t]he inference of scienter must be more than merely 'reasonable' or 'permissible'– it must be cogent and compelling, thus strong in light of other explanations. A complaint will survive, we hold, only if a reasonable person would deem the inference of scienter cogent and at least as compelling as any opposing inference one could draw from the facts alleged."

B. INSIDER TRADING RISKS

1. DANGERS OF NONPUBLIC MATERIAL INFORMATION

IN THE MATTER OF CADY, ROBERTS & CO.
40 S.E.C. 907 (1961)

BY CARY, Chairman:

This is a case of first impression and one of signal importance in our administration of the Federal securities acts. It involves a selling broker who executes a solicited order and sells for discretionary accounts (including that of his wife) upon an exchange. The crucial question is what are the duties of such a broker after receiving nonpublic information as to a company's dividend action from a director who is employed by the same brokerage firm.

Early in November 1959, Roy T. Hurley, then President and Chairman of the Board of Curtiss-Wright Corporation, invited 2,000 representatives of the press, the military and the financial and business communities to a public unveiling on November 23, of a new type of internal combustion engine being developed by the company. From November 6, through November 23, Gintel had purchased approximately 11,000 shares of Curtiss-Wright stock for about 30 discretionary accounts of customers of registrant. With the rise in the price on November 24, he began selling Curtiss-Wright shares for these accounts and sold on that day a total of 2,200 shares on the Exchange.

On the morning of November 25, the Curtiss-Wright directors, including J. Cheever Cowdin ('Cowdin'), then a registered representative of registrant, met to consider, among other things, the declaration of a quarterly dividend. The company had paid a dividend, although not earned, of $.625 per share for each of the first three quarters of 1959. The Curtiss-Wright board, over the objections of Hurley, who favored declaration of a dividend at the same rate as in the prior quarters, approved a dividend for the fourth quarter at the reduced rate of $.375 per share. At approximately 11:00 a.m., the board authorized transmission of information of this action by telegram to the New York Stock Exchange. The Secretary of Curtiss-Wright immediately left the meeting room to arrange for this communication. There was a short delay in the transmission of the telegram because of a typing problem and the telegram, although transmitted to Western Union at 11:12 a.m., was not delivered to the Exchange until 12:29 p.m. It had been customary for the company also to advise the Dow Jones News Ticker Service of any dividend action. However, apparently through some mistake or inadvertence, the Wall Street Journal was not given the news until approximately 11:45 a.m. and the announcement did not appear on the Dow Jones ticker tape until 11:48 a.m.

Sometime after the dividend decision, there was a recess of the Curtiss-Wright directors' meeting, during which Cowdin telephoned registrant's office and left a message for Gintel that the dividend had been cut. Upon receiving this information, Gintel entered two sell orders for execution on the Exchange, one to sell 2,000 shares of Curtiss-Wright stock for 10 accounts, and the other to sell short 5,000 shares for 11 accounts. Four hundred of the 5,000 shares were sold for three of Cowdin's customers. According to Cowdin, pursuant to directions from his clients, he had given instructions to Gintel to take profits on these 400 shares if the stock took a 'run-up.' These orders were executed at 11:15 and 11:18 a.m. at 40 1/4 and 40 3/8, respectively.

When the dividend announcement appeared on the Dow Jones tape at 11:48 a.m., the Exchange was compelled to suspend trading in Curtiss-Wright because of the large number of sell orders. Trading in Curtiss-Wright stock was resumed at 1:59 p.m. at 36 1/2 ranged during the balance of the day between 34 1/8 and 37, and closed at 34 7/8.

So many times that citation is unnecessary, we have indicated that the purchase and sale of securities is a field in special need of regulation for the protection of investors. To this end one of the major purposes of the securities acts is the prevention of fraud, manipulation or deception in connection with securities transactions. Consistent with this objective, Section 17(a) of the Securities Act, Section 10(b) of the Exchange Act and Rule 10b–5, issued under that Section, are broad remedial provisions aimed at reaching misleading or deceptive activities, whether or not they are precisely and technically sufficient to sustain a common law action for fraud and deceit...

Section 17 and Rule 10b–5 apply to securities transactions by 'any person.' Misrepresentations will lie within their ambit, no matter who the speaker may be.

An affirmative duty to disclose material information has been traditionally imposed on corporate 'insiders,' particularly officers, directors, or controlling stockholders. We and the courts have consistently held that insiders must disclose material facts which are known to them by virtue of their position but which are not known to persons with whom they deal and which, if known, would affect their investment judgment. Failure to make disclosure in these circumstances constitutes a violation of the anti-fraud provisions. If, on the other hand, disclosure prior to effecting a purchase or sale would be improper or unrealistic under the circumstances, we believe the alternative is to forego the transaction.

The ingredients are here and we accordingly find that Gintel willfully violated Sections 17(a) and 10(b) and Rule 10b–5. We also find a similar violation by the registrant, since the actions of Gintel, a member of registrant, in the course of his employment are to be regarded as actions of registrant itself. It was obvious that a reduction in the quarterly dividend by the Board of Directors was a material fact which could be expected to have an adverse impact on the market price of the company's stock. The rapidity with which Gintel acted upon receipt of the information confirms his own recognition of that conclusion.

We have already noted that the anti-fraud provisions are phrased in terms of 'any person' and that a special obligation has been traditionally required of corporate insiders, e.g., officers, directors and controlling stockholders. These three groups, however, do not exhaust the classes of persons upon whom there is such an obligation. Analytically, the obligation rests on two principal elements; first, the existence of a relationship giving access, directly or indirectly, to information intended to be available only for a corporate purpose and not for the personal benefit of anyone, and second, the inherent unfairness involved where a party takes advantage of such information knowing it is unavailable to those with whom he is dealing. In considering these elements under the broad language of the anti-fraud provisions we are not to be circumscribed by fine distinctions and rigid classifications. Thus our task here is to identify those persons who are in a special relationship with a company and privy to its internal affairs, and thereby suffer correlative duties in trading in its securities. Intimacy demands restraint lest the uninformed be exploited.

The facts here impose on Gintel the responsibilities of those commonly referred to as 'insiders.' He received the information prior to its public release from a director of Curtiss-Wright, Cowdin, who was associated with the registrant. Cowdin's relationship to the company clearly prohibited him from selling the securities affected by the information without disclosure. By logical sequence, it should prohibit Gintel, a partner of registrant. This prohibition extends not only over his own account, but to selling for discretionary accounts and soliciting and executing other orders...

We cannot accept respondents' contention that an insider's responsibility is limited to existing stockholders and that he has no special duties when sales of securities are made to non-stockholders. This approach is too narrow. It ignores the plight of the buying public – wholly unprotected from the misuse of special information.

Neither the statutes nor Rule 10b–5 establish artificial walls of responsibility. Section 17 of the Securities Act, explicitly states that it shall be unlawful for any person in the offer or sale of securities to do certain prescribed acts. Although the primary function of Rule 10b–5 was to extend a remedy to a defrauded seller, the courts and this Commission have held that it is also applicable to a defrauded buyer. There is no valid reason why persons who *purchase* stock from an officer, director or other person having the responsibilities of an 'insider' should not have the same protection afforded by disclosure of special information as persons who *sell* stock to them.

Respondents further assert that they made no express representations and did not in any way manipulate the market, and urge that in a transaction on an exchange there is no further duty such as may be required in a 'face-to-face' transaction. We reject this suggestion. It would be anomalous indeed if the protection afforded by the antifraud provisions were withdrawn from transactions effected on exchanges, primary markets for securities transactions. If purchasers on an exchange had available material information known by a selling insider, we may assume that their investment judgment would be affected and their decision whether to buy might accordingly be modified. Consequently, any sales by the insider must await disclosure of the information.

Expanding on Cady Roberts

Cady Roberts opened the door to insider trading claims and criminal charges based on Rule 10b-5, which on its face makes no reference to insider trading and private rights of action. The case clarified that insider trading prohibitions under 10b-5 would extend to the firm and partner of a corporate director and would apply in open market transactions that involved a party who was not an existing stockholder of the corporation. But the case also triggered many compelling questions. Would liability extend to any person who trades a security while in the possession of nonpublic material information? Would liability exposure be limited only to insiders? Who qualifies as an insider? What constitutes material information? What if an insider did not know that the information hadn't been made available to the public? Is there a duty to investigate?

In *SEC v. Texas Gulf Sulphur Co.*, 401 F.2d 833 (2d Cir. 1968), the Second Circuit provided answers to certain key questions. In that case, officers, directors and employees of TGS had purchased shares of TGS stock with knowledge that recently discovered valuable mineral deposits owned by TGS had not been publicly disclosed. Kenneth Darke, a geologist in possession of the undisclosed information, was also named as a defendant, because of his trading activity. The court described the essence of the insider trading rule and the options available to one who possesses nonpublic material information as follows:

> The essence of the Rule is that anyone who, trading for his own account in the securities of a corporation has 'access, directly or indirectly, to information intended to be available only for a corporate purpose and not for the personal benefit of anyone' may not take 'advantage of such information knowing it is unavailable to those with whom he is dealing.' Insiders, as directors or management officers are,

of course, by this Rule, precluded from so unfairly dealing, but the Rule is also applicable to one possessing the information who may not be strictly termed an 'insider' within the meaning of Sec. 16(b) of the Act. Thus, anyone in possession of material inside information must either disclose it to the investing public, or, if he is disabled from disclosing it in order to protect a corporate confidence, or he chooses not to do so, must abstain from trading in or recommending the securities concerned while such inside information remains undisclosed. So, it is here no justification for insider activity that disclosure was forbidden by the legitimate corporate objective of acquiring options to purchase the land surrounding the exploration site; if the information was, as the SEC contends, material, its possessors should have kept out of the market until disclosure was accomplished. 401 F.2d at 848.

The court went on to explain that the "only regulatory objective" is that material information be "enjoyed equally," and that this overriding objective requires only that basic facts be disclosed to enable "outsiders" to use their own "evaluative expertise" with knowledge equal to that of the insiders. The court defined the materiality test as follows:

> This is not to suggest, however, as did the trial court, the 'the test of materiality must necessarily be a conservative one, particularly since many actions under Section 10(b) are brought on the basis of hindsight,' in the sense that the materiality of facts is to be assessed solely by measuring the effect the knowledge of the facts would have upon prudent or conservative investors. As we stated in List v. Fashion Park, Inc., 340 F.2d 457, 462, 'The basic test of materiality * * * is whether a reasonable man would attach importance * * * in determining his choice of action in the transaction in question. This, of course, encompasses any fact '* * * which in reasonable and objective contemplation might affect the value of the corporation's stock or securities * * *.' Such a fact is a material fact and must be effectively disclosed to the investing public prior to the commencement of insider trading in the corporation's securities. The speculators and chartists of Wall and Bay Streets are also 'reasonable' investors entitled to the same legal protection afforded conservative traders. Thus, material facts include not only information disclosing the earnings and distributions of a company but also those facts which affect the probable future of the company and those which may affect the desire of investors to buy, sell, or hold the company's securities. 401 F.2d at 849.

The Second Circuit went on to reverse the lower court's ruling that geologist Darke fell outside the scope of the 10b-5 prohibition. The court stated:

> [I]nequities based upon unequal access to knowledge should not be shrugged off as inevitable in our way of life, or, in view of the congressional concern in the area, remain uncorrected. We hold, therefore, that all transactions in TGS stock or calls by individuals apprised of the drilling results of K-55-1 were made in violation of

Rule 10b-5. Inasmuch as the visual evaluation of that drill core (a generally reliable estimate though less accurate than a chemical assay) constituted material information, those advised of the results of the visual evaluation as well as those informed of the chemical assay traded in violation of law. The geologist Darke possessed undisclosed material information and traded in TGS securities. Therefore we reverse the dismissal of the action as to him and his personal transactions. 401 F.2d at 852.

Two of the defendants in *Texas Gulf Sulphur* argued that they should not be liable under 10b-5 because their purchases of TGS stock occurred after the discovery was disclosed. Rejecting this argument, the court noted that the reading of a news release "is merely the first step in the process of dissemination required for compliance with the regulatory objective of providing all investors with an equal opportunity to make informed investment judgments" and then held that the defendants "should have waited until the news could reasonably have been expected to appear over the media of widest circulation, the Dow Jones broad tape, rather than hastening to insure an advantage to himself and his broker son-in-law." 401 F.2d at 854.

These same defendants then asserted a good faith defense, arguing that they honestly believed that the news of the strike had become public at the time they placed their orders. In rejecting this defense, the court held that due diligence, not ignorance, may be the basis of a defense by stating:

> More important, however, is the realization which we must again underscore at the risk of repetition, that the investing public is hurt by exposure to false or deceptive statements irrespective of the purpose underlying their issuance. It does not appear to be unfair to impose upon corporate management a duty to ascertain the truth of any statements the corporation releases to its shareholders or to the investing public at large. Accordingly, we hold that Rule 10b-5 is violated whenever assertions are made, as here, in a manner reasonably calculated to influence the investing public, e.g., by means of the financial media, if such assertions are false or misleading or are so incomplete as to mislead irrespective of whether the issuance of the release was motivated by corporate officials for ulterior purposes. It seems clear, however, that if corporate management demonstrates that it was diligent in ascertaining that the information it published was the whole truth and that such diligently obtained information was disseminated in good faith, Rule 10b-5 would not have been violated. 401 F.2d at 860-862.

CASE PROBLEM 11-4

Jerry, a doctor sitting in his country club's locker room, received a call from Pete, the chief financial officer of Bolton Inc, a large public company. In the call, Pete said, "I have to cancel our golf date today. Remember that potential merger that I told you about when we played last month? Well, it's happening. I am running in circles because it is huge. We're going to announce the merger tomorrow. There is no way that I can get away for golf today."

Jerry turned to Luke, a golfing buddy also sitting in the locker room, and said, "Pete can't make it today. He's tied up with some kind of big merger announcement that Bolton is going to make tomorrow. Being a CFO of a public company demands a lot. I'll meet you on the first tee in 10 minutes. I need to call my broker." Jerry then called his broker and bought 5,000 shares of Bolton stock. Luke did the same.

Has Jerry or Luke violated SEC Rule 10b-5 for illegal insider trading? What additional facts (if any) would you like to have in making this determination?

2. DEFINING THE OUTER LIMITS

CHIARELLA v. UNITED STATES
445 U.S. 222 (1980)

Mr. Justice POWELL delivered the opinion of the Court.

The question in this case is whether a person who learns from the confidential documents of one corporation that it is planning an attempt to secure control of a second corporation violates § 10(b) of the Securities Exchange Act of 1934 if he fails to disclose the impending takeover before trading in the target company's securities.

Petitioner is a printer by trade. In 1975 and 1976, he worked as a "markup man" in the New York composing room of Pandick Press, a financial printer. Among documents that petitioner handled were five announcements of corporate takeover bids. When these documents were delivered to the printer, the identities of the acquiring and target corporations were concealed by blank spaces or false names. The true names were sent to the printer on the night of the final printing.

The petitioner, however, was able to deduce the names of the target companies before the final printing from other information contained in the documents. Without disclosing his knowledge, petitioner purchased stock in the target companies and sold the shares immediately after the takeover attempts were made public. By this method, petitioner realized a gain of slightly more than $30,000 in the course of 14 months. Subsequently, the Securities and Exchange Commission (Commission or SEC) began an investigation of his trading activities. In May 1977, petitioner entered into a consent decree with the Commission in which he agreed to return his profits to the sellers of the shares. On the same day, he was discharged by Pandick Press.

In January 1978, petitioner was indicted on 17 counts of violating § 10(b) of the Securities Exchange Act of 1934 (1934 Act) and SEC Rule 10b–5. After petitioner unsuccessfully moved to dismiss the indictment, he was brought to trial and convicted on all counts.

The Court of Appeals for the Second Circuit affirmed petitioner's conviction. We granted certiorari, and we now reverse.

This case concerns the legal effect of the petitioner's silence. The District Court's charge permitted the jury to convict the petitioner if it found that he willfully failed to inform sellers of target company securities that he knew of a forthcoming takeover bid that would make their shares more valuable. In order to decide whether silence in such circumstances violates § 10(b), it is necessary to review the language and legislative history of that statute as well as its interpretation by the Commission and the federal courts.

Although the starting point of our inquiry is the language of the statute, § 10(b) does not state whether silence may constitute a manipulative or deceptive device. Section 10(b) was designed as a catch-all clause to prevent fraudulent practices. But neither the legislative history nor the statute itself affords specific guidance for the resolution of this case. When Rule 10b–5 was promulgated in 1942, the SEC did not discuss the possibility that failure to provide information might run afoul of § 10(b).

The SEC took an important step in the development of § 10(b) when it held that a broker-dealer and his firm violated that section by selling securities on the basis of undisclosed information obtained from a director of the issuer corporation who was also a registered representative of the brokerage firm. In Cady, Roberts & Co., 40 S.E.C. 907 1961), the Commission decided that a corporate insider must abstain from trading in the shares of his corporation unless he has first disclosed all material inside information known to him. The obligation to disclose or abstain derives from "[a]n affirmative duty to disclose material information[which] has been traditionally imposed on corporate 'insiders,' particular officers, directors, or controlling stockholders. We, and the courts have consistently held that insiders must disclose material facts which are known to them by virtue of their position but which are not known to persons with whom they deal and which, if known, would affect their investment judgment." Id., at 911.

The Commission emphasized that the duty arose from (i) the existence of a relationship affording access to inside information intended to be available only for a corporate purpose, and (ii) the unfairness of allowing a corporate insider to take advantage of that information by trading without disclosure.

That the relationship between a corporate insider and the stockholders of his corporation gives rise to a disclosure obligation is not a novel twist of the law. At common law, misrepresentation made for the purpose of inducing reliance upon the false statement is fraudulent. But one who fails to disclose material information prior to the consummation of a transaction commits fraud only when he is under a duty to do so. In its Cady, Roberts decision, the Commission recognized a relationship of trust and confidence between the shareholders of a corporation and those insiders who have obtained confidential information by reason of their position with that corporation. This relationship gives rise to a duty to disclose because of the "necessity of preventing a corporate insider from . . . tak[ing] unfair advantage of the uninformed minority stockholders."

[A]dministrative and judicial interpretations have established that silence in connection with the purchase or sale of securities may operate as a fraud actionable under § 10(b) despite the absence of statutory language or legislative history specifically addressing the legality of nondisclosure. But such liability is premised upon a duty to disclose arising from a relationship of trust and confidence between parties to a transaction. Application of a duty to disclose prior to trading guarantees that corporate insiders, who have an obligation to place the shareholder's welfare before their own, will not benefit personally through fraudulent use of material, nonpublic information.

In this case, the petitioner was convicted of violating § 10(b) although he was not a corporate insider and he received no confidential information from the target company. Moreover, the "market information" upon which he relied did not concern the earning power or operations of the target company, but only the plans of the acquiring company. Petitioner's use of that information was not a fraud under § 10(b) unless he was subject to an affirmative duty to disclose it before trading. In this case, the jury instructions failed to specify any such duty. In effect, the trial court instructed the jury that petitioner owed a duty to everyone; to all sellers, indeed, to the market as a whole. The jury simply was told to decide whether petitioner used material, nonpublic information at a time when "he knew other people trading in the securities market did not have access to the same information."

The Court of Appeals affirmed the conviction by holding that " [a]nyone — corporate insider or not—who regularly receives material nonpublic information may not use that information to trade in securities without incurring an affirmative duty to disclose." 588 F.2d, at 1365 (emphasis in original). Although the court said that its test would include only persons who regularly receive material, nonpublic information, id., at 1366, its rationale for that limitation is unrelated to the existence of a duty to disclose. The Court of Appeals, like the trial court, failed to identify a relationship between petitioner and the sellers that could give rise to a duty. Its decision thus rested solely upon its belief that the federal securities laws have "created a system providing equal access to information necessary for reasoned and intelligent investment decisions." Id., at 1362. The use by anyone of material information not generally available is fraudulent, this theory suggests, because such information gives certain buyers or sellers an unfair advantage over less informed buyers and sellers.

This reasoning suffers from two defects. First not every instance of financial unfairness constitutes fraudulent activity under § 10(b). See Santa Fe Industries, Inc. v. Green, 430 U.S. 462, 474–477 (1977). Second, the element required to make silence fraudulent—a duty to disclose—is absent in this case. No duty could arise from petitioner's relationship with the sellers of the target company's securities, for petitioner had no prior dealings with them. He was not their agent, he was not a fiduciary, he was not a person in whom the sellers had placed their trust and confidence. He was, in fact, a complete stranger who dealt with the sellers only through impersonal market transactions.

We cannot affirm petitioner's conviction without recognizing a general duty between all participants in market transactions to forgo actions based on material, nonpublic information. Formulation of such a broad duty, which departs radically from the established doctrine that duty arises from a specific relationship between two parties should not be undertaken absent some explicit evidence of congressional intent.

As we have seen, no such evidence emerges from the language or legislative history of § 10(b). Moreover, neither the Congress nor the Commission ever has adopted a parity-of-information rule. Instead the problems caused by misuse of market information have been addressed by detailed and sophisticated regulation that recognizes when use of market information may not harm operation of the securities markets. For example, the Williams Act limits but does not completely prohibit a tender offeror's purchases of target corporation stock before public announcement of the offer. Congress' careful action in this and other areas contrasts, and is in some tension, with the broad rule of liability we are asked to adopt in this case.

We see no basis for applying such a new and different theory of liability in this case. As we have emphasized before, the 1934 Act cannot be read " 'more broadly than its language and the statutory scheme reasonably permit.' " Touche Ross & Co. v. Redington, 442 U.S. 560 (1979). Section 10(b) is aptly described as a catchall provision, but what it catches must be fraud. When an allegation of fraud is based upon nondisclosure, there can be no fraud absent a duty to speak. We hold that a duty to disclose under § 10(b) does not arise from the mere possession of nonpublic market information. The contrary result is without support in the legislative history of § 10(b) and would be inconsistent with the careful plan that Congress has enacted for regulation of the securities markets.

In its brief to this Court, the United States offers an alternative theory to support petitioner's conviction. It argues that petitioner breached a duty to the acquiring corporation when he acted upon information that he obtained by virtue of his position as an employee of a printer employed by the corporation. The breach of this duty is said to support a conviction under § 10(b) for fraud perpetrated upon both the acquiring corporation and the sellers.

We need not decide whether this theory has merit for it was not submitted to the jury...

The jury instructions demonstrate that petitioner was convicted merely because of his failure to disclose material, nonpublic information to sellers from whom he bought the stock of target corporations. The jury was not instructed on the nature or elements of a duty owed by petitioner to anyone other than the sellers. Because we cannot affirm a criminal conviction on the basis of a theory not presented to the jury, we will not speculate upon whether such a duty exists, whether it has been breached, or whether such a breach constitutes a violation of § 10(b).

The judgment of the Court of Appeals is Reversed.

Mr. Chief Justice BURGER, dissenting.

I believe that the jury instructions in this case properly charged a violation of § 10(b) and Rule 10b–5, and I would affirm the conviction.

As a general rule, neither party to an arm's-length business transaction has an obligation to disclose information to the other unless the parties stand in some confidential or fiduciary relation. This rule permits a businessman to capitalize on his experience and skill in securing and evaluating relevant information; it provides incentive for hard work, careful analysis, and astute forecasting. But the policies that underlie the rule also should limit its scope. In particular, the rule should give way when an informational advantage is obtained, not by superior experience, foresight, or industry, but by some unlawful means.

The Court's opinion, as I read it, leaves open the question whether § 10(b) and Rule 10b–5 prohibit trading on misappropriated nonpublic information...The Court's reading of the District Court's charge is unduly restrictive. Fairly read as a whole and in the context of the trial, the instructions required the jury to find that Chiarella obtained his trading advantage by misappropriating the property of his employer's customers.

The evidence shows beyond all doubt that Chiarella, working literally in the shadows of the warning signs in the print shop, misappropriated—stole to put it bluntly – valuable nonpublic information entrusted to him in the utmost confidence. He then exploited his ill-gotten informational advantage by purchasing securities in the market. In my view, such conduct plainly violates § 10(b) and Rule 10b–5. Accordingly, I would affirm the judgment of the Court of Appeals.

CASE PROBLEM 11-5

Same facts as Case Problem 11-4, except that Roger, another club member who was unseen by Jerry and Luke, overheard the dialogue between Jerry and Luke. Roger called his broker and bought 3,000 shares of Bolton stock. Has Roger violated SEC Rule 10b-5 for illegal insider trading? What additional facts (if any) would you like to have in making this determination?

DIRKS v. SEC
463 U.S. 646 (1983)

Justice POWELL delivered the opinion of the Court.

Petitioner Raymond Dirks received material nonpublic information from "insiders" of a corporation with which he had no connection. He disclosed this information to investors who relied on it in trading in the shares of the corporation. The question is whether Dirks violated the antifraud provisions of the federal securities laws by this disclosure.

In 1973, Dirks was an officer of a New York broker-dealer firm who specialized in providing investment analysis of insurance company securities to institutional investors. On March 6, Dirks received information from Ronald Secrist, a former officer of Equity Funding of America. Secrist alleged that the assets of Equity Funding, a diversified corporation primarily engaged in selling life insurance and mutual funds, were vastly overstated as the result of fraudulent corporate practices. Secrist also stated that various regulatory agencies had failed to act on similar charges made by Equity Funding employees. He urged Dirks to verify the fraud and disclose it publicly.

Dirks decided to investigate the allegations. He visited Equity Funding's headquarters in Los Angeles and interviewed several officers and employees of the corporation. The senior management denied any wrongdoing, but certain corporation employees corroborated the charges of fraud. Neither Dirks nor his firm owned or traded any Equity Funding stock, but throughout his investigation he openly discussed the information he had obtained with a number of clients and investors. Some of these persons sold their holdings of Equity Funding securities, including five investment advisers who liquidated holdings of more than $16 million.

While Dirks was in Los Angeles, he was in touch regularly with William Blundell, the Wall Street Journal's Los Angeles bureau chief. Dirks urged Blundell to write a story on the fraud allegations. Blundell did not believe, however, that such a massive fraud could go undetected and declined to write the story. He feared that publishing such damaging hearsay might be libelous.

During the two-week period in which Dirks pursued his investigation and spread word of Secrist's charges, the price of Equity Funding stock fell from $26 per share to less than $15 per share. This led the New York Stock Exchange to halt trading on March 27. Shortly thereafter California insurance authorities impounded Equity Funding's records and uncovered evidence of the fraud. Only then did the Securities and Exchange Commission (SEC) file a complaint against Equity Funding and only then, on April 2, did the Wall Street Journal publish a front-page story based largely on information assembled by Dirks. Equity Funding immediately went into receivership.

The SEC began an investigation into Dirks' role in the exposure of the fraud. After a hearing by an administrative law judge, the SEC found that Dirks had aided and abetted violations of § 17(a) of the Securities Act of 1933, § 10(b) of the Securities Exchange Act of 1934, by repeating the allegations of fraud to members of the investment community who later sold their Equity Funding stock. The SEC concluded: "Where 'tippees'—regardless of their motivation or occupation—come into possession of material 'information that they know is confidential and know or should know came from a corporate insider,' they must either publicly disclose that information or refrain from trading." Recognizing, however, that Dirks "played an important role in bringing [Equity Funding's] massive fraud to light," the SEC only censured him.

Dirks sought review in the Court of Appeals for the District of Columbia Circuit. The court entered judgment against Dirks "for the reasons stated by the Commission in its opinion"… In view of the importance to the SEC and to the securities industry of the question presented by this case, we granted a writ of certiorari.. We now reverse.

In the seminal case of In re Cady, Roberts & Co., 40 S.E.C. 907 (1961), the SEC recognized that the common law in some jurisdictions imposes on "corporate 'insiders,' particularly officers, directors, or controlling stockholders" an "affirmative duty of disclosure ... when dealing in securities." Id., at 911, and n. 13. The SEC found that not only did breach of this common-law duty also establish the elements of a Rule 10b–5 violation, but that individuals other than corporate insiders could be obligated either to disclose material nonpublic information before trading or to abstain from trading altogether. Id., at 912. In Chiarella, we accepted the two elements set out in Cady Roberts for establishing a Rule 10b–5 violation: "(i) the existence of a relationship affording access to inside information intended to be available only for a corporate purpose, and (ii) the unfairness of allowing a corporate insider to take advantage of that information by trading without disclosure." 445 U.S., at 227. In examining whether Chiarella had an obligation to disclose or abstain, the Court found that there is no general duty to disclose before trading on material nonpublic information, and held that "a duty to disclose under § 10(b) does not arise from the mere possession of nonpublic market information." Id., at 235. Such a duty arises rather from the existence of a fiduciary relationship.

Not "all breaches of fiduciary duty in connection with a securities transaction," however, come within the ambit of Rule 10b–5. There must also be "manipulation or deception." In an inside-trading case this fraud derives from the "inherent unfairness involved where one takes advantage" of "information intended to be available only for a corporate purpose and not for the personal benefit of anyone." Thus, an insider will be liable under Rule 10b–5 for inside trading only where he fails to disclose material nonpublic information before trading on it and thus makes "secret profits."

We were explicit in Chiarella in saying that there can be no duty to disclose where the person who has traded on inside information "was not [the corporation's] agent, ... was not a fiduciary, [or] was not a person in whom the sellers [of the securities] had placed their trust and confidence." 445 U.S., at 232. Not to require such a fiduciary relationship, we recognized, would "depar[t] radically from the established doctrine that duty arises from a specific relationship between * two parties" and would amount to "recognizing a general duty between all participants in market transactions to forgo actions based on material, nonpublic information." Id., at 232, 233. This requirement of a specific relationship between the shareholders and the individual trading on inside information has created analytical difficulties for the SEC and courts in policing tippees who trade on inside information. Unlike insiders who have independent fiduciary duties to both the corporation and its shareholders, the typical tippee has no such relationships. In view of this absence, it has been unclear how a tippee acquires the Cady, Roberts duty to refrain from trading on inside information.

The SEC's position, as stated in its opinion in this case, is that a tippee "inherits" the Cady, Roberts obligation to shareholders whenever he receives inside information from an insider. This view differs little from the view that we rejected as inconsistent with congressional intent in Chiarella. Apparently recognizing the weakness of its argument in light of Chiarella, the SEC attempts to distinguish that case factually as involving not "inside" information, but rather "market" information, i.e., "information generated within the company relating to its assets or earnings." This Court drew no such distinction in Chiarella.

In effect, the SEC's theory of tippee liability in both cases appears rooted in the idea that the antifraud provisions require equal information among all traders. This conflicts with the principle set forth in Chiarella that only some persons, under some circumstances, will be barred from trading while in possession of material nonpublic information. We reaffirm today that "[a] duty [to disclose] arises from the relationship between parties ... and not merely from one's ability to acquire information because of his position in the market."

Imposing a duty to disclose or abstain solely because a person knowingly receives material nonpublic information from an insider and trades on it could have an inhibiting influence on the role of market analysts, which the SEC itself recognizes is necessary to the preservation of a healthy market. It is commonplace for analysts to "ferret out and analyze information," and this often is done by meeting with and questioning corporate officers and others who are insiders. And information that the analysts obtain normally may be the basis for judgments as to the market worth of a corporation's securities. The analyst's judgment in this respect is made available in market letters or otherwise to clients of the firm. It is the nature of this type of information, and indeed of the markets themselves, that such information cannot be made simultaneously available to all of the corporation's stockholders or the public generally.

The conclusion that recipients of inside information do not invariably acquire a duty to disclose or abstain does not mean that such tippees always are free to trade on the information. The need for a ban on some tippee trading is clear. Not only are insiders forbidden by their fiduciary relationship from personally using undisclosed corporate information to their advantage, but they may not give such information to an outsider for the same improper purpose of exploiting the information for their personal gain. Similarly, the transactions of those who knowingly participate with the fiduciary in such a breach are "as forbidden" as transactions "on behalf of the trustee himself." Mosser v. Darrow, 341 U.S. 267 (1951). Thus, the tippee's duty to disclose or abstain is derivative from that of the insider's duty. As we noted in Chiarella, "[t]he tippee's obligation has been viewed as arising from his role as a participant after the fact in the insider's breach of a fiduciary duty."

Thus, some tippees must assume an insider's duty to the shareholders not because they receive inside information, but rather because it has been made available to them improperly. And for Rule 10b–5 purposes, the insider's disclosure is improper only where it would violate his Cady, Roberts duty. Thus, a tippee assumes a fiduciary duty to the shareholders of a corporation not to trade on material nonpublic information only when the insider has breached his fiduciary duty to the shareholders by disclosing the information to the tippee and the tippee knows or should know that there has been a breach. Tipping thus properly is viewed only as a means of indirectly violating the Cady, Roberts disclose-or-abstain rule.

In determining whether a tippee is under an obligation to disclose or abstain, it thus is necessary to determine whether the insider's "tip" constituted a breach of the insider's fiduciary duty. All disclosures of confidential corporate information are not inconsistent with the duty insiders owe to shareholders. In contrast to the extraordinary facts of this case, the more typical situation in which there will be a question whether disclosure violates the insider's Cady, Roberts duty is when insiders disclose information to analysts. In some situations, the insider will act consistently with his fiduciary duty to shareholders, and yet release of the information may affect the market. For example, it may not be clear – either to the corporate insider or to the recipient analyst – whether the information will be viewed as material nonpublic information. Corporate officials may mistakenly think the information already has been disclosed or that it is not material enough to affect the market. Whether disclosure is a breach of duty therefore depends in large part on the purpose of the disclosure. This standard was identified by the SEC itself in Cady, Roberts: a purpose of the securities laws was to eliminate "use of inside information for personal advantage." 40 S.E.C., at 912, n. 15. Thus, the test is whether the insider personally will benefit, directly or indirectly, from his disclosure. Absent some personal gain, there has been no breach of duty to stockholders. And absent a breach by the insider, there is no derivative breach.

The SEC argues that, if inside-trading liability does not exist when the information is transmitted for a proper purpose but is used for trading, it would be a rare situation when the parties could not fabricate some ostensibly legitimate business justification for transmitting the information. We think the SEC is unduly concerned. In determining whether the insider's purpose in making a particular disclosure is fraudulent, the SEC and the courts are not required to read the parties' minds. Scienter in some cases is relevant in determining whether the tipper has violated his Cady, Roberts duty. But to determine whether the disclosure itself "deceive[s], manipulate[s], or defraud[s]" shareholders, Aaron v. SEC, 446 U.S. 680, (1980), the initial inquiry is whether there has been a breach of duty by the insider. This requires courts to focus on objective criteria, i.e., whether the insider receives a direct or indirect personal benefit from the disclosure, such as a pecuniary gain or a reputational benefit that will translate into future earnings. There are objective facts and circumstances that often justify such an inference. For example, there may be a relationship between the insider and the recipient that suggests a quid pro quo from the latter, or an intention to benefit the particular recipient. The elements of fiduciary duty and exploitation of nonpublic information also exist when an insider makes a gift of confidential information to a trading relative or friend. The tip and trade resemble trading by the insider himself followed by a gift of the profits to the recipient.

Determining whether an insider personally benefits from a particular disclosure, a question of fact, will not always be easy for courts. But it is essential, we think, to have a guiding principle for those whose daily activities must be limited and instructed by the SEC's inside-trading rules, and we believe that there must be a breach of the insider's fiduciary duty before the tippee inherits the duty to disclose or abstain. In contrast, the rule adopted by the SEC in this case would have no limiting principle.

Under the inside-trading and tipping rules set forth above, we find that there was no actionable violation by Dirks. It is undisputed that Dirks himself was a stranger to Equity Funding, with no pre-existing fiduciary duty to its shareholders. He took no action, directly or indirectly, that induced the shareholders or officers of Equity Funding to repose trust or confidence in him. There was no expectation by Dirk's sources that he would keep their information in confidence. Nor did Dirks misappropriate or illegally obtain the information about Equity Funding. Unless the insiders breached their Cady, Roberts duty to shareholders in disclosing the nonpublic information to Dirks, he breached no duty when he passed it on to investors as well as to the Wall Street Journal.

It is clear that neither Secrist nor the other Equity Funding employees violated their Cady, Roberts duty to the corporation's shareholders by providing information to Dirks. The tippers received no monetary or personal benefit for revealing Equity Funding's secrets, nor was their purpose to make a gift of valuable information to Dirks. As the facts of this case clearly indicate, the tippers were motivated by a desire to expose the fraud. In the absence of a breach of duty to shareholders by the insiders, there was no derivative breach by Dirks. Dirks therefore could not have been "a participant after the fact in [an] insider's breach of a fiduciary duty."

We conclude that Dirks, in the circumstances of this case, had no duty to abstain from use of the inside information that he obtained. The judgment of the Court of Appeals therefore is Reversed.

Justice BLACKMUN, with whom Justice BRENNAN and Justice MARSHALL join, dissenting.

The Court today takes still another step to limit the protections provided investors by § 10(b) of the Securities Exchange Act of 1934. The device employed in this case engrafts a special motivational requirement on the fiduciary duty doctrine. This innovation excuses a knowing and intentional violation of an insider's duty to shareholders if the insider does not act from a motive of personal gain. Even on the extraordinary facts of this case, such an innovation is not justified.

No one questions that Secrist himself could not trade on his inside information to the disadvantage of uninformed shareholders and purchasers of Equity Funding securities. Unlike the printer in Chiarella, Secrist stood in a fiduciary relationship with these shareholders. As the Court states, corporate insiders have an affirmative duty of disclosure when trading with shareholders of the corporation. This duty extends as well to purchasers of the corporation's securities...

The Court holds, however, that Dirks is not liable because Secrist did not violate his duty; according to the Court, this is so because Secrist did not have the improper purpose of personal gain. In so doing, the Court imposes a new, subjective limitation on the scope of the duty owed by insiders to shareholders. The novelty of this limitation is reflected in the Court's lack of support for it.

The insider's duty is owed directly to the corporation's shareholders. As Chiarella recognized, it is based on the relationship of trust and confidence between the insider and the shareholder. 445 U.S., at 228, 100 S.Ct., at 1114. That relationship assures the shareholder that the insider may not take actions that will harm him unfairly. The affirmative duty of disclosure protects against this injury

The fact that the insider himself does not benefit from the breach does not eradicate the shareholder's injury. It makes no difference to the shareholder whether the corporate insider gained or intended to gain personally from the transaction; the shareholder still has lost because of the insider's misuse of nonpublic information. The duty is addressed not to the insider's motives, but to his actions and their consequences on the shareholder. Personal gain is not an element of the breach of this duty.

The improper purpose requirement not only has no basis in law, but it rests implicitly on a policy that I cannot accept. The Court justifies Secrist's and Dirks' action because the general benefit derived from the violation of Secrist's duty to shareholders outweighed the harm caused to those shareholders – in other words, because the end justified the means. Under this view, the benefit conferred on society by Secrist's and Dirks' activities may be paid for with the losses caused to shareholders trading with Dirks' clients.

Although Secrist's general motive to expose the Equity Funding fraud was laudable, the means he chose were not. Moreover, even assuming that Dirks played a substantial role in exposing the fraud, he and his clients should not profit from the information they obtained from Secrist. Misprison of a felony long has been against public policy. A person cannot condition his transmission of information of a crime on a financial award. As a citizen, Dirks had at least an ethical obligation to report the information to the proper authorities. The Court's holding is deficient in policy terms not because it fails to create a legal norm out of that ethical norm, but because it actually rewards Dirks for his aiding and abetting.

Dirks and Secrist were under a duty to disclose the information or to refrain from trading on it. I agree that disclosure in this case would have been difficult. I also recognize that the SEC seemingly has been less than helpful in its view of the nature of disclosure necessary to satisfy the disclose-or-refrain duty. The Commission tells persons with inside information that they cannot trade on that information unless they disclose; it refuses, however, to tell them how to disclose. This seems to be a less than sensible policy, which it is incumbent on the Commission to correct. The Court, however, has no authority to remedy the problem by opening a hole in the congressionally mandated prohibition on insider trading, thus rewarding such trading.

In my view, Secrist violated his duty to Equity Funding shareholders by transmitting material nonpublic information to Dirks with the intention that Dirks would cause his clients to trade on that information. Dirks, therefore, was under a duty to make the information publicly available or to refrain from actions that he knew would lead to trading. Because Dirks caused his clients to trade, he violated § 10(b) and Rule 10b–5. Any other result is a disservice to this country's attempt to provide fair and efficient capital markets. I dissent.

Reg. FD Response to Dirks

One impact of the Dirks holding is that it provided comfort to insiders who discussed nonpublic material information with security analysts and market professionals. To help level the playing field between such analysts and market professionals and the general public, the SEC promulgated Regulation Fair Disclosure (Reg. FD) in 1999. Reg. FD provides that if a company discloses nonpublic material information to investment professionals (broker dealers, analysts, investment advisors, major shareholders), it must take steps to simultaneously disclose the information to the public.

The Lucky Eavesdropper

In *S.E.C. v. Switzer*, 590 F. Supp. 756 (D.C.Okl.,1984), the question before the court was whether Barry Switzer, the famous University of Oklahoma football coach, had violated 10b-5 when he traded stock based on nonpublic material information that he inadvertently overhead while sitting under the bleachers at a track meet. G. Platt, a corporate CEO, was discussing the information with another party and had no knowledge of Switzer's presence. In addition to trading for his own benefit, Switzer had passed the information on to select friends who he knew would trade on the information. In holding that neither Switzer nor his buddies were liable under 10b-5, the court stated:

> Since G. Platt did not breach a fiduciary duty to Phoenix shareholders, Switzer did not acquire nor assume a fiduciary duty to Phoenix's shareholders, and because Switzer did not acquire a fiduciary duty to Phoenix shareholders, any information he passed on to defendants Smith, Hodges, Amyx, Hoover, Kennedy and Deem was not in violation of Rule 10b–5... Since plaintiff did not meet its burden of proof as to the first prong of the two-prong *Dirks* test, *i.e.,* it was not proved that G. Platt breached a fiduciary duty to the shareholders of Phoenix, tippee liability cannot result from G. Platt's inadvertent disclosure to Switzer. 590 F.Supp. at 766.

CASE PROBLEM 11-6

Same facts as Case Problem 11-4, except that Linda, the manager of the club, overheard the dialogue between Jerry and Luke. Linda called her broker Mandy and said, "I love this club job. Just learned that Bolton will have a big merger announcement tomorrow. Buy 3,000 of Bolton stock ASAP."

The club's employee handbook states that every club employee "shall seek to carefully protect and not exploit the confidential information of each member."

Has Linda violated SEC Rule 10b-5 for illegal insider trading? What additional facts (if any) would you like to have in making this determination?

UNITED STATES v. O'HAGAN
521 U.S. 642 (1997)

Justice GINSBURG delivered the opinion of the Court.

This case concerns the interpretation and enforcement of § 10(b) and § 14(e) of the Securities Exchange Act of 1934, and rules made by the Securities and Exchange Commission pursuant to these provisions, Rule 10b–5 and Rule 14e–3(a). Two prime questions are presented. The first relates to the misappropriation of material, nonpublic information for securities trading; the second concerns fraudulent practices in the tender offer setting. In particular, we address and resolve these issues: (1) Is a person who trades in securities for personal profit, using confidential information misappropriated in breach of a fiduciary duty to the source of the information, guilty of violating § 10(b) and Rule 10b–5? (2) Did the Commission exceed its rulemaking authority by adopting Rule 14e–3(a), which proscribes trading on undisclosed information in the tender offer setting, even in the absence of a duty to disclose? Our answer to the first question is yes, and to the second question, viewed in the context of this case, no.

Respondent James Herman O'Hagan was a partner in the law firm of Dorsey & Whitney in Minneapolis, Minnesota. In July 1988, Grand Metropolitan PLC (Grand Met), a company based in London, England, retained Dorsey & Whitney as local counsel to represent Grand Met regarding a potential tender offer for the common stock of the Pillsbury Company, headquartered in Minneapolis. Both Grand Met and Dorsey & Whitney took precautions to protect the confidentiality of Grand Met's tender offer plans. O'Hagan did no work on the Grand Met representation. Dorsey & Whitney withdrew from representing Grand Met on September 9, 1988. Less than a month later, on October 4, 1988, Grand Met publicly announced its tender offer for Pillsbury stock.

On August 18, 1988, while Dorsey & Whitney was still representing Grand Met, O'Hagan began purchasing call options for Pillsbury stock. Each option gave him the right to purchase 100 shares of Pillsbury stock by a specified date in September 1988. Later in August and in September, O'Hagan made additional purchases of Pillsbury call options. By the end of September, he owned 2,500 unexpired Pillsbury options, apparently more than any other individual investor. O'Hagan also purchased, in September 1988, some 5,000 shares of Pillsbury common stock, at a price just under $39 per share. When Grand Met announced its tender offer in October, the price of Pillsbury stock rose to nearly $60 per share. O'Hagan then sold his Pillsbury call options and common stock, making a profit of more than $4.3 million.

The Securities and Exchange Commission (SEC or Commission) initiated an investigation into O'Hagan's transactions, culminating in a 57-count indictment. The indictment alleged that O'Hagan defrauded his law firm and its client, Grand Met, by using for his own trading purposes material, nonpublic information regarding Grand Met's planned tender offer. According to the indictment, O'Hagan used the profits he gained through this trading to conceal his previous embezzlement and conversion of unrelated client trust funds. A jury convicted O'Hagan on all 57 counts, and he was sentenced to a 41–month term of imprisonment.

A divided panel of the Court of Appeals for the Eighth Circuit reversed all of O'Hagan's convictions. Liability under § 10(b) and Rule 10b–5, the Eighth Circuit held, may not be grounded on the "misappropriation theory" of securities fraud on which the prosecution relied...

We address first the Court of Appeals' reversal of O'Hagan's convictions under § 10(b) and Rule 10b–5. Following the Fourth Circuit's lead, the Eighth

Circuit rejected the misappropriation theory as a basis for § 10(b) liability. We hold, in accord with several other Courts of Appeals, that criminal liability under § 10(b) may be predicated on the misappropriation theory.

Under the "traditional" or "classical theory" of insider trading liability, § 10(b) and Rule 10b–5 are violated when a corporate insider trades in the securities of his corporation on the basis of material, nonpublic information. Trading on such information qualifies as a "deceptive device" under § 10(b), we have affirmed, because "a relationship of trust and confidence [exists] between the shareholders of a corporation and those insiders who have obtained confidential information by reason of their position with that corporation." Chiarella v. United States, 445 U.S. 222, 228, 100 (1980). That relationship, we recognized, "gives rise to a duty to disclose [or to abstain from trading] because of the 'necessity of preventing a corporate insider from ... tak[ing] unfair advantage of ... uninformed ... stockholders.' " Id., at 228–229 (citation omitted). The classical theory applies not only to officers, directors, and other permanent insiders of a corporation, but also to attorneys, accountants, consultants, and others who temporarily become fiduciaries of a corporation. See Dirks v. SEC, 463 U.S. 646, 655, n. 14.

The "misappropriation theory" holds that a person commits fraud "in connection with" a securities transaction, and thereby violates § 10(b) and Rule 10b–5, when he misappropriates confidential information for securities trading purposes, in breach of a duty owed to the source of the information. Under this theory, a fiduciary's undisclosed, self-serving use of a principal's information to purchase or sell securities, in breach of a duty of loyalty and confidentiality, defrauds the principal of the exclusive use of that information. In lieu of premising liability on a fiduciary relationship between company insider and purchaser or seller of the company's stock, the misappropriation theory premises liability on a fiduciary-turned-trader's deception of those who entrusted him with access to confidential information.

The two theories are complementary, each addressing efforts to capitalize on nonpublic information through the purchase or sale of securities. The classical theory targets a corporate insider's breach of duty to shareholders with whom the insider transacts; the misappropriation theory outlaws trading on the basis of nonpublic information by a corporate "outsider" in breach of a duty owed not to a trading party, but to the source of the information. The misappropriation theory is thus designed to "protec [t] the integrity of the securities markets against abuses by 'outsiders' to a corporation who have access to confidential information that will affect th[e] corporation's security price when revealed, but who owe no fiduciary or other duty to that corporation's shareholders." Ibid.

In this case, the indictment alleged that O'Hagan, in breach of a duty of trust and confidence he owed to his law firm, Dorsey & Whitney, and to its client, Grand Met, traded on the basis of nonpublic information regarding Grand Met's planned tender offer for Pillsbury common stock. This conduct, the Government charged, constituted a fraudulent device in connection with the purchase and sale of securities.

We agree with the Government that misappropriation, as just defined, satisfies § 10(b)'s requirement that chargeable conduct involve a "deceptive device or contrivance" used "in connection with" the purchase or sale of securities. We observe, first, that misappropriators, as the Government describes them, deal in deception. A fiduciary who "[pretends] loyalty to the principal while secretly converting the principal's information for personal gain," "dupes" or defrauds the principal.

Deception through nondisclosure is central to the theory of liability for which the Government seeks recognition. As counsel for the Government stated in explanation of the theory at oral argument: "To satisfy the common law rule that a trustee may not use the property that [has] been entrusted [to] him, there would have to be consent.

The misappropriation theory advanced by the Government is consistent with Santa Fe Industries, Inc. v. Green, a decision underscoring that § 10(b) is not an all-purpose breach of fiduciary duty ban; rather, it trains on conduct involving manipulation or deception. In contrast to the Government's allegations in this case, in Santa Fe Industries, all pertinent facts were disclosed by the persons charged with violating § 10(b) and Rule 10b–5; therefore, there was no deception through nondisclosure to which liability under those provisions could attach. Similarly, full disclosure forecloses liability under the misappropriation theory: Because the deception essential to the misappropriation theory involves feigning fidelity to the source of information, if the fiduciary discloses to the source that he plans to trade on the nonpublic information, there is no "deceptive device" and thus no § 10(b) violation...

We turn next to the § 10(b) requirement that the misappropriator's deceptive use of information be "in connection with the purchase or sale of [a] security." This element is satisfied because the fiduciary's fraud is consummated, not when the fiduciary gains the confidential information, but when, without disclosure to his principal, he uses the information to purchase or sell securities. The securities transaction and the breach of duty thus coincide. A misappropriator who trades on the basis of material, nonpublic information, in short, gains his advantageous market position through deception; he deceives the source of the information and simultaneously harms members of the investing public.

The misappropriation theory targets information of a sort that misappropriators ordinarily capitalize upon to gain no-risk profits through the purchase or sale of securities. Should a misappropriator put such information to other use, the statute's prohibition would not be implicated. The theory does not catch all conceivable forms of fraud involving confidential information; rather, it catches fraudulent means of capitalizing on such information through securities transactions.

The Government notes another limitation on the forms of fraud § 10(b) reaches: "The misappropriation theory would not ... apply to a case in which a person defrauded a bank into giving him a loan or embezzled cash from another, and then used the proceeds of the misdeed to purchase securities." In such a case, the Government states, "the proceeds would have value to the malefactor apart from their use in a securities transaction, and the fraud would be complete as soon as the money was obtained." In other words, money can buy, if not anything, then at least many things; its misappropriation may thus be viewed as sufficiently detached from a subsequent securities transaction that § 10(b)'s "in connection with" requirement would not be met...

The misappropriation theory comports with § 10(b)'s language, which requires deception "in connection with the purchase or sale of any security," not deception of an identifiable purchaser or seller. The theory is also well tuned to an animating purpose of the Exchange Act: to insure honest securities markets and thereby promote investor confidence...Although informational disparity is inevitable in the securities markets, investors likely would hesitate to venture their capital in a market where trading based on misappropriated nonpublic information is unchecked by law. An investor's informational disadvantage vis-á-vis a misappropriator with material, nonpublic information stems from contrivance, not luck; it is a disadvantage that cannot be overcome with research or skill...

The Court of Appeals rejected the misappropriation theory primarily on two grounds. First, as the Eighth Circuit comprehended the theory, it requires neither misrepresentation nor nondisclosure. As we just explained, however, deceptive nondisclosure is essential to the § 10(b) liability at issue. Concretely, in this case, "it [was O'Hagan's] failure to disclose his personal trading to Grand Met and Dorsey, in breach of his duty to do so, that ma[de] his conduct 'deceptive' within the meaning of [§]10(b)."

Second and "more obvious," the Court of Appeals said, the misappropriation theory is not moored to § 10(b)'s requirement that "the fraud be 'in connection with the purchase or sale of any security.' " 92 F.3d, at 618 (quoting 15 U.S.C. § 78j(b)). The Court did not hold in Chiarella that the only relationship prompting liability for trading on undisclosed information is the relationship between a corporation's insiders and shareholders. That is evident from our response to the Government's argument before this Court that the printer's misappropriation of information from his employer for purposes of securities trading – in violation of a duty of confidentiality owed to the acquiring companies – constituted fraud in connection with the purchase or sale of a security, and thereby satisfied the terms of § 10(b). The Court declined to reach that potential basis for the printer's liability, because the theory had not been submitted to the jury. But four Justices found merit in it. And a fifth Justice stated that the Court "wisely le[ft] the resolution of this issue for another day."

Chiarella thus expressly left open the misappropriation theory before us today. Dirks, too, left room for application of the misappropriation theory in cases like the one we confront.

No showing had been made in Dirks that the "tippers" had violated any duty by disclosing to the analyst nonpublic information about their former employer. The insiders had acted not for personal profit, but to expose a massive fraud within the corporation. Absent any violation by the tippers, there could be no derivative liability for the tippee. Most important for purposes of the instant case, the Court observed in Dirks: "There was no expectation by [the analyst's] sources that he would keep their information in confidence. Nor did [the analyst] misappropriate or illegally obtain the information...." Dirks thus presents no suggestion that a person who gains nonpublic information through misappropriation in breach of a fiduciary duty escapes § 10(b) liability when, without alerting the source, he trades on the information.

In sum, the misappropriation theory, as we have examined and explained it in this opinion, is both consistent with the statute and with our precedent. Vital to our decision that criminal liability may be sustained under the misappropriation theory, we emphasize, are two sturdy safeguards Congress has provided regarding scienter. To establish a criminal violation of Rule 10b–5, the Government must prove that a person "willfully" violated the provision. Furthermore, a defendant may not be imprisoned for violating Rule 10b–5 if he proves that he had no knowledge of the Rule. O'Hagan's charge that the misappropriation theory is too indefinite to permit the imposition of criminal liability, thus fails not only because the theory is limited to those who breach a recognized duty. In addition, the statute's "requirement of the presence of culpable intent as a necessary element of the offense does much to destroy any force in the argument that application of the [statute]" in circumstances such as O'Hagan's is unjust.

The Eighth Circuit erred in holding that the misappropriation theory is inconsistent with § 10(b).

Justice THOMAS, with whom THE CHIEF JUSTICE joins, concurring in the judgment in part and dissenting in part.

Today the majority upholds respondent's convictions for violating § 10(b) of the Securities Exchange Act of 1934, and Rule 10b–5 promulgated thereunder, based upon the Securities and Exchange Commission's "misappropriation theory." Central to the majority's holding is the need to interpret § 10(b)'s requirement that a deceptive device be "use[d] or employ [ed], in connection with the purchase or sale of any security." 15 U.S.C. § 78j(b). Because the Commission's misappropriation theory fails to provide a coherent and consistent interpretation of this essential requirement for liability under § 10(b), I dissent.

I do not take issue with the majority's determination that the undisclosed misappropriation of confidential information by a fiduciary can constitute a "deceptive device" within the meaning of § 10(b). Nondisclosure where there is a pre-existing duty to disclose satisfies our definitions of fraud and deceit for purposes of the securities laws.

Unlike the majority, however, I cannot accept the Commission's interpretation of when a deceptive device is "use[d] ... in connection with" a securities transaction. Although the Commission and the majority at points seem to suggest that any relation to a securities transaction satisfies the "in connection with" requirement of § 10(b), both ultimately reject such an overly expansive construction and require a more integral connection between the fraud and the securities transaction. In upholding respondent's convictions under the new and improved misappropriation theory, the majority also points to various policy considerations underlying the securities laws, such as maintaining fair and honest markets, promoting investor confidence, and protecting the integrity of the securities markets. But the repeated reliance on such broad-sweeping legislative purposes reaches too far and is misleading in the context of the misappropriation theory. It reaches too far in that, regardless of the overarching purpose of the securities laws, it is not illegal to run afoul of the "purpose" of a statute, only its letter. The majority's approach is misleading in this case because it glosses over the fact that the supposed threat to fair and honest markets, investor confidence, and market integrity comes not from the supposed fraud in this case, but from the mere fact that the information used by O'Hagan was nonpublic.

As the majority concedes, because "the deception essential to the misappropriation theory involves feigning fidelity to the source of information, if the fiduciary discloses to the source that he plans to trade on the nonpublic information, there is no 'deceptive device' and thus no § 10(b) violation." Indeed, were the source expressly to authorize its agents to trade on the confidential information—as a perk or bonus, perhaps—there would likewise be no § 10(b) violation. Yet in either case—disclosed misuse or authorized use—the hypothesized "inhibiting impact on market participation," would be identical to that from behavior violating the misappropriation theory: "Outsiders" would still be trading based on nonpublic information that the average investor has no hope of obtaining through his own diligence.

The majority's statement that a "misappropriator who trades on the basis of material, nonpublic information, in short, gains his advantageous market position through deception; he deceives the source of the information and simultaneously harms members of the investing public," thus focuses on the wrong point. Even if it is true that trading on nonpublic information hurts the public, it is true whether or not there is any deception of the source of the information. Moreover, as we have repeatedly held, use of nonpublic information to trade is not itself a violation of § 10(b). E.g., Chiarella, 445 U.S., at 232–233, 100 S.Ct., at 1116–1117. Rather, it is the use of fraud "in connection with" a securities transaction that is forbidden. Where the relevant element of fraud has no impact on the integrity of the subsequent transactions as distinct from the nonfraudulent element of using nonpublic information, one can reasonably question whether the fraud was used in connection with a securities transaction. And one can likewise question whether removing that aspect of fraud, though perhaps laudable, has anything to do with the confidence or integrity of the market.

CASE PROBLEM 11-7

Same facts as Case Problem 11-6, except that Mandy sends an email to her top 100 clients that reads, "I now have a strong buy on Bolton stock. Suggest you consider buying immediately." Two-thirds of Mandy's clients buy Bolton stock within two hours.

Has Mandy or any of her clients violated SEC Rule 10b-5 for illegal insider trading? What additional facts (if any) would help in making this determination?

C. SHORT-SWING PROFIT CLAIMS

Section 16(b) of the Securities Exchange Act is designed to prevent corporation insiders and large shareholders from capitalizing on short-swing trades in a company's securities. This section requires any director, officer or greater than 10 percent stockholder of a company with equity securities registered under Section 12 of the Securities Exchange Act to give up ("disgorge") to the company all profits realized from the insider's purchases and sales of the company's equity securities within a six-month period.

Rule 16b-7 now exempts various transactions from the Section 16(b) disgorgement mandate under the theory that these types of transactions "do not significantly alter in an economic sense the investment the insider held before the transaction." August 2005 SEC Rule 16b-7 Release. Exempt transactions include reincorporations, a reorganization of a corporation's structure, and mergers and consolidations involving entities with at least 85 percent cross-ownership. Also, Rule 16b-7 now expressly includes the term "reclassification" so that insiders who acquire securities in a reclassification do not have to hold their investment for a six month period to avoid the reaches of section 16(b).

To encourage (force?) compliance with section 16(b), those subject to the statute are required to file periodic reports with the SEC that disclose their securities holdings and all recent transactions. Electronic reports must be filed within two days of any changes and posted on the company's website within one day after filing.

Who benefits from a 16(b) violation? The disgorged profits go to the corporation, but the lawyers prosecuting the claim can recover their fees. So, as is so often the case with suits initiated for the benefit of a corporation, the driving forces are attorneys in search of a pay day.

CHAPTER 12

CONTROLLING SHAREHOLDER
TRANSACTION RISKS

A. CASH MERGER MINORITY SQUEEZE-OUTS

CASE PROBLEM 12-1

InstruTech Inc. ("InstruTech") is a Delaware corporation whose stock is traded on the New York Stock Exchange. InstruTech develops and markets a wide range of specialized tools and precision instruments to many different industries through eight wholly-owned subsidiaries (the "Subs"). The Subs own many patents, obtained in the course of their product development efforts.

InstruTech owns 45 percent of the outstanding stock of HealthTools, Inc. ("HealthTools"), a Delaware corporation. The balance of HealthTools stock is traded on the NASDAQ. HealthTools has two divisions. Its medical division ("Medical"), which develops and markets specialized tools and precision instruments to medical healthcare providers, accounts for 75 percent of HealthTools' total sales. Its dental division ("Dental") develops and markets specialized tools and precision instruments to the dental industry and accounts for the remaining 25 percent of HealthTools' total sales.

HealthTools has a seven-member board, consisting of HealthTools' CEO and CFO, a senior officer of InstruTech, and four outside directors (the "Outsiders"). None of the Outsiders is employed by InstruTech, a Sub, or HeathTools. Each Outsider has a business background and is a personal acquaintance of InstruTech's CEO. Each year this director's slate is proposed, approved and never opposed.

Dental has recently completed the development of a new "soundless drill." HealthTools' management believes that this new drill "could take the market by storm," potentially doubling Dental's sales. The new drill is supported by two newly issued patents (the "Patents"). Although HealthTools' management and board hope and expect that the Patents have some value beyond the dental instrument market, they have done nothing to explore such possibilities in any depth at this time.

In contrast, InstruTech's CEO discreetly instructed a small, targeted group of engineers (the "Engineers") to carefully evaluate the broader potentials of the Patents. In a newly issued report (the "Report"), the Engineers described 14 "specific, extremely lucrative" patent pooling opportunities with the Subs and many other "amazingly profitable possibilities outside the InstruTech family."

In order to eliminate any "complications" relating to InstruTech's exploitation of the Patents, InstruTech's CEO determined that InstruTech "needed to become" the sole owner of HealthTools. To this end, InstruTech hired a reputable investment banking firm (the "Valuation Firm") to carefully evaluate HealthTools and propose the terms of a cash-out merger that would be fair to HealthTools' public shareholders. The Valuation Firm issued a written proposal (the "Proposal") that would merge HealthTools into InstruTech in a transaction that would pay the public shareholders of HealthTools $36 a share, a 50 percent premium over the existing trading price of $24.

A copy of the Proposal was delivered to each member of HealthTools' board three days in advance of a special meeting of the board. At the meeting, the Proposal was unanimously approved by the board after 30 minutes of discussion. Thereafter, proxies were sent to HealthTools' public shareholders, most of whom were institutional investors, seeking approval of the merger. Ninety percent of the public shareholders voted in favor of the merger. These votes, when added to InstruTech's shares, resulted in 94.5 percent of HealthTools' shareholders approving the merger.

A minority group (the "Group") of non-institutional HealthTools shareholders seeks to enjoin the consummation of the merger on the grounds that such a merger now is inherently unfair because time is necessary to exploit and determine the value of, the Patents. Alternatively, the Group claims that InstruTech should pay an additional $10 a share to HealthTools' public shareholders based on an expert valuation of HealthTools, commissioned by the Group, that "more appropriately considers the potential value" of the Patents.

What is the likelihood of the Group prevailing on its claims? What standard of review should the court use? Who bears the burden of proof? Is the business judgment rule a factor? Assume for these purposes that the Group has found out about the Report and that the Report's existence was never disclosed to the Valuation Firm, any board member of HealthTools, or the shareholders of HealthTools. How would your answers to these questions change (if at all) if the details of the Report were fully disclosed to the Valuation Firm, HealthTools' board, and HealthTools' shareholders via the proxy statement?

WEINBERGER v. UOP, INC.
457 A.2d 701 (Del. 1983)

Moore, Justice:

This post-trial appeal was reheard en banc from a decision of the Court of Chancery. It was brought by the class action plaintiff below, a former shareholder of UOP, Inc., who challenged the elimination of UOP's minority shareholders by a cash-out merger between UOP and its majority owner, The Signal Companies, Inc. Originally, the defendants in this action were Signal, UOP, certain officers and directors of those companies, and UOP's investment banker, Lehman Brothers Kuhn Loeb, Inc. The present Chancellor held that the terms of the merger were fair to the plaintiff and the other minority shareholders of UOP. Accordingly, he entered judgment in favor of the defendants.

Numerous points were raised by the parties, but we address only the following questions presented by the trial court's opinion:

1) The plaintiff's duty to plead sufficient facts demonstrating the unfairness of the challenged merger;

2) The burden of proof upon the parties where the merger has been approved by the purportedly informed vote of a majority of the minority shareholders;

3) The fairness of the merger in terms of adequacy of the defendants' disclosures to the minority shareholders;

4) The fairness of the merger in terms of adequacy of the price paid for the minority shares and the remedy appropriate to that issue; and

5) The continued force and effect of *Singer v. Magnavox Co.,* Del.Supr., 380 A.2d 969, 980 (1977), and its progeny.

In ruling for the defendants, the Chancellor re-stated his earlier conclusion that the plaintiff in a suit challenging a cash-out merger must allege specific acts of fraud, misrepresentation, or other items of misconduct to demonstrate the unfairness of the merger terms to the minority. We approve this rule and affirm it.

The Chancellor also held that even though the ultimate burden of proof is on the majority shareholder to show by a preponderance of the evidence that the transaction is fair, it is first the burden of the plaintiff attacking the merger to demonstrate some basis for invoking the fairness obligation. We agree with that principle. However, where corporate action has been approved by an informed vote of a majority of the minority shareholders, we conclude that the burden entirely shifts to the plaintiff to show that the transaction was unfair to the minority. But in all this, the burden clearly remains on those relying on the vote to show that they completely disclosed all material facts relevant to the transaction.

Here, the record does not support a conclusion that the minority stockholder vote was an informed one. Material information, necessary to acquaint those shareholders with the bargaining positions of Signal and UOP, was withheld under circumstances amounting to a breach of fiduciary duty. We therefore conclude that this merger does not meet the test of fairness, at least as we address that concept, and no burden thus shifted to the plaintiff by reason of the minority shareholder vote. Accordingly, we reverse and remand for further proceedings consistent herewith.

In considering the nature of the remedy available under our law to minority shareholders in a cash-out merger, we believe that it is, and hereafter should be, an appraisal under 8 *Del.C.* § 262 as hereinafter construed. We therefore overrule *Lynch v. Vickers Energy Corp.,* Del.Supr., 429 A.2d 497 (1981) (*Lynch II*) to the extent that it purports to limit a stockholder's monetary relief to a specific damage formula. But to give full effect to section 262 within the framework of the General Corporation Law we adopt a more liberal, less rigid and stylized, approach to the valuation process than has heretofore been permitted by our courts. While the present state of these proceedings does not admit the plaintiff to the appraisal remedy per se, the practical effect of the remedy we do grant him will be co-extensive with the liberalized valuation and appraisal methods we herein approve for cases coming after this decision.

Signal is a diversified, technically based company operating through various subsidiaries. Its stock is publicly traded on the New York, Philadelphia and Pacific Stock Exchanges. UOP, formerly known as Universal Oil Products Company, was a diversified industrial company engaged in various lines of business. Its stock was publicly held and listed on the New York Stock Exchange.

In 1974 Signal sold one of its wholly-owned subsidiaries for $420,000,000 in cash. While looking to invest this cash surplus, Signal became interested in UOP as a possible acquisition. Friendly negotiations ensued, and Signal proposed to acquire a controlling interest in UOP at a price of $19 per share. UOP's representatives sought $25 per share. In the arm's length bargaining that followed, an understanding was reached whereby Signal agreed to purchase from UOP 1,500,000 shares of UOP's authorized but unissued stock at $21 per share.

This purchase was contingent upon Signal making a successful cash tender offer for 4,300,000 publicly held shares of UOP, also at a price of $21 per share. This combined method of acquisition permitted Signal to acquire 5,800,000 shares of stock, representing 50.5% of UOP's outstanding shares.

Although UOP's board consisted of thirteen directors, Signal nominated and elected only six. Of these, five were either directors or employees of Signal. The sixth, a partner in the banking firm of Lazard Freres & Co., had been one of Signal's representatives in the negotiations and bargaining with UOP concerning the tender offer and purchase price of the UOP shares.

However, the president and chief executive officer of UOP retired during 1975, and Signal caused him to be replaced by James V. Crawford, a long-time employee and senior executive vice president of one of Signal's wholly-owned subsidiaries. Crawford succeeded his predecessor on UOP's board of directors and also was made a director of Signal.

The trial court found that at the instigation of certain Signal management personnel, including William W. Walkup, its board chairman, and Forrest N. Shumway, its president, a feasibility study was made concerning the possible acquisition of the balance of UOP's outstanding shares. This study was performed by two Signal officers, Charles S. Arledge, vice president (director of planning), and Andrew J. Chitiea, senior vice president (chief financial officer). Messrs. Walkup, Shumway, Arledge and Chitiea were all directors of UOP in addition to their membership on the Signal board.

Arledge and Chitiea concluded that it would be a good investment for Signal to acquire the remaining 49.5% of UOP shares at any price up to $24 each. Their report was discussed between Walkup and Shumway who, along with Arledge, Chitiea and Brewster L. Arms, internal counsel for Signal, constituted Signal's senior management. In particular, they talked about the proper price to be paid if the acquisition was pursued, purportedly keeping in mind that as UOP's majority shareholder, Signal owed a fiduciary responsibility to both its own stockholders as well as to UOP's minority. It was ultimately agreed that a meeting of Signal's executive committee would be called to propose that Signal acquire the remaining outstanding stock of UOP through a cash-out merger in the range of $20 to $21 per share.

The executive committee meeting was set for February 28, 1978. As a courtesy, UOP's president, Crawford, was invited to attend, although he was not a member of Signal's executive committee. Crawford voiced no objection to the $20 to $21 price range, nor did he suggest that Signal should consider paying more than $21 per share for the minority interests. Thus, it was the consensus that a price of $20 to $21 per share would be fair to both Signal and the minority shareholders of UOP. Signal's executive committee authorized its management "to negotiate" with UOP "for a cash acquisition of the minority ownership in UOP, Inc., with the intention of presenting a proposal to [Signal's] board of directors ... on March 6, 1978". Immediately after this February 28, 1978 meeting, Signal issued a press release. The announcement also referred to the fact that the closing price of UOP's common stock on that day was $14.50 per share.

Between Tuesday, February 28, 1978 and Monday, March 6, 1978, a total of four business days, Crawford spoke by telephone with all of UOP's non-Signal, i.e., outside, directors. Also during that period, Crawford retained Lehman Brothers to render a fairness opinion as to the price offered the minority for its stock. He gave two reasons for this choice. James W. Glanville, a long-time director of UOP and a partner in Lehman Brothers, had acted as a financial advisor to UOP for many years.

Crawford telephoned Glanville, who gave his assurance that Lehman Brothers had no conflicts that would prevent it from accepting the task. Glanville's immediate personal reaction was that a price of $20 to $21 would certainly be fair, since it represented almost a 50% premium over UOP's market price.

Glanville assembled a three-man Lehman Brothers team to do the work on the fairness opinion. The Lehman Brothers team concluded that "the price of either $20 or $21 would be a fair price for the remaining shares of UOP".

On March 6, 1978, both the Signal and UOP boards were convened to consider the proposed merger. Telephone communications were maintained between the two meetings. Walkup, Signal's board chairman, and also a UOP director, attended UOP's meeting with Crawford in order to present Signal's position and answer any questions that UOP's non-Signal directors might have. Arledge and Chitiea, along with Signal's other designees on UOP's board, participated by conference telephone. All of UOP's outside directors attended the meeting either in person or by conference telephone.

First, Signal's board unanimously adopted a resolution authorizing Signal to propose to UOP a cash merger of $21 per share as outlined in a certain merger agreement and other supporting documents. This proposal required that the merger be approved by a majority of UOP's outstanding minority shares voting at the stockholders meeting at which the merger would be considered, and that the minority shares voting in favor of the merger, when coupled with Signal's 50.5% interest would have to comprise at least two-thirds of all UOP shares. Otherwise the proposed merger would be deemed disapproved.

UOP's board then considered the proposal. Copies of the agreement were delivered to the directors in attendance, and other copies had been forwarded earlier to the directors participating by telephone. They also had before them UOP financial data for 1974–1977, UOP's most recent financial statements, market price information, and budget projections for 1978. In addition they had Lehman Brothers' hurriedly prepared fairness opinion letter finding the price of $21 to be fair.

Signal also suggests that the Arledge-Chitiea feasibility study, indicating that a price of up to $24 per share would be a "good investment" for Signal, was discussed at the UOP directors' meeting. The Chancellor made no such finding, and our independent review of the record, detailed *infra,* satisfies us by a preponderance of the evidence that there was no discussion of this document at UOP's board meeting. Furthermore, it is clear beyond peradventure that nothing in that report was ever disclosed to UOP's minority shareholders prior to their approval of the merger.

After consideration of Signal's proposal, Walkup and Crawford left the meeting to permit a free and uninhibited exchange between UOP's non-Signal directors. Upon their return a resolution to accept Signal's offer was then proposed and adopted.

Despite the swift board action of the two companies, the merger was not submitted to UOP's shareholders until their annual meeting on May 26, 1978. In the notice of that meeting and proxy statement sent to shareholders in May, UOP's management and board urged that the merger be approved. The proxy statement also advised:

> The price was determined after *discussions* between James V. Crawford, a director of Signal and Chief Executive Officer of UOP, and officers of Signal which took place during meetings on February 28, 1978, and in the course of several subsequent telephone conversations. (Emphasis added.)

In the original draft of the proxy statement the word "negotiations" had been used rather than "discussions". However, when the Securities and Exchange Commission sought details of the "negotiations" as part of its review of these materials, the term was deleted and the word "discussions" was substituted. The proxy statement indicated that the vote of UOP's board in approving the merger had been unanimous. It also advised the shareholders that Lehman Brothers had given its opinion that the merger price of $21 per share was fair to UOP's minority. However, it did not disclose the hurried method by which this conclusion was reached.

As of the record date of UOP's annual meeting, there were 11,488,302 shares of UOP common stock outstanding, 5,688,302 of which were owned by the minority. At the meeting only 56%, or 3,208,652, of the minority shares were voted. Of these, 2,953,812, or 51.9% of the total minority, voted for the merger, and 254,840 voted against it. When Signal's stock was added to the minority shares voting in favor, a total of 76.2% of UOP's outstanding shares approved the merger while only 2.2% opposed it.

By its terms the merger became effective on May 26, 1978, and each share of UOP's stock held by the minority was automatically converted into a right to receive $21 cash.

A primary issue mandating reversal is the preparation by two UOP directors, Arledge and Chitiea, of their feasibility study for the exclusive use and benefit of Signal. This document was of obvious significance to both Signal and UOP. It is clear from the record that neither Arledge nor Chitiea shared this report with their fellow directors of UOP. We are satisfied that no one else did either. This conduct hardly meets the fiduciary standards applicable to such a transaction.

None of UOP's outside directors who testified stated that they had seen this document. The Arledge-Chitiea report speaks for itself in supporting the Chancellor's finding that a price of up to $24 was a "good investment" for Signal. It shows that a return on the investment at $21 would be 15.7% versus 15.5% at $24 per share. This was a difference of only two-tenths of one percent, while it meant over $17,000,000 to the minority. Under such circumstances, paying UOP's minority shareholders $24 would have had relatively little long-term effect on Signal, and the Chancellor's findings concerning the benefit to Signal, even at a price of $24, were obviously correct.

Certainly, this was a matter of material significance to UOP and its shareholders. Since the study was prepared by two UOP directors, using UOP information for the exclusive benefit of Signal, and nothing whatever was done to disclose it to the outside UOP directors or the minority shareholders, a question of breach of fiduciary duty arises.

In assessing this situation, the Court of Chancery was required to examine what information defendants had and to measure it against what they gave to the minority stockholders, in a context in which 'complete candor' is required. In other words, the limited function of the Court was to determine whether defendants had disclosed all information in their possession germane to the transaction in issue. And by 'germane' we mean, for present purposes, information such as a reasonable shareholder would consider important in deciding whether to sell or retain stock. This is merely stating in another way the long-existing principle of Delaware law that these Signal designated directors on UOP's board still owed UOP and its shareholders an uncompromising duty of loyalty.

Given the absence of any attempt to structure this transaction on an arm's length basis, Signal cannot escape the effects of the conflicts it faced, particularly when its designees on UOP's board did not totally abstain from participation in the matter. There is no "safe harbor" for such divided loyalties in Delaware.

When directors of a Delaware corporation are on both sides of a transaction, they are required to demonstrate their utmost good faith and the most scrupulous inherent fairness of the bargain. *Gottlieb v. Heyden Chemical Corp.,* Del.Supr., 91 A.2d 57, 57–58 (1952). The requirement of fairness is unflinching in its demand that where one stands on both sides of a transaction, he has the burden of establishing its entire fairness, sufficient to pass the test of careful scrutiny by the courts. *Sterling v. Mayflower Hotel Corp.,* Del.Supr., 93 A.2d 107, 110 (1952); *Bastian v. Bourns, Inc.,* Del.Ch., 256 A.2d 680, 681 (1969).

There is no dilution of this obligation where one holds dual or multiple directorships, as in a parent-subsidiary context. Thus, individuals who act in a dual capacity as directors of two corporations, one of whom is parent and the other subsidiary, owe the same duty of good management to both corporations, and in the absence of an independent negotiating structure (see note 7, *supra*), or the directors' total abstention from any participation in the matter, this duty is to be exercised in light of what is best for both companies. *Warshaw v. Calhoun,* Del.Supr., 221 A.2d 487, 492 (1966). The record demonstrates that Signal has not met this obligation.

The concept of fairness has two basic aspects: fair dealing and fair price. The former embraces questions of when the transaction was timed, how it was initiated, structured, negotiated, disclosed to the directors, and how the approvals of the directors and the stockholders were obtained. The latter aspect of fairness relates to the economic and financial considerations of the proposed merger, including all relevant factors: assets, market value, earnings, future prospects, and any other elements that affect the intrinsic or inherent value of a company's stock. However, the test for fairness is not a bifurcated one as between fair dealing and price. All aspects of the issue must be examined as a whole since the question is one of entire fairness. However, in a non-fraudulent transaction we recognize that price may be the preponderant consideration outweighing other features of the merger. Here, we address the two basic aspects of fairness separately because we find reversible error as to both.

Part of fair dealing is the obvious duty of candor. Moreover, one possessing superior knowledge may not mislead any stockholder by use of corporate information to which the latter is not privy. *Lank v. Steiner,* Del.Supr., 224 A.2d 242, 244 (1966). Delaware has long imposed this duty even upon persons who are not corporate officers or directors, but who nonetheless are privy to matters of interest or significance to their company. company. *Brophy v. Cities Service Co.,* Del.Ch., 70 A.2d 5, 7 (1949). With the well-established Delaware law on the subject, and the Court of Chancery's findings of fact here, it is inevitable that the obvious conflicts posed by Arledge and Chitiea's preparation of their "feasibility study", derived from UOP information, for the sole use and benefit of Signal, cannot pass muster.

The Arledge-Chitiea report is but one aspect of the element of fair dealing. The structure of the transaction, again, was Signal's doing. So far as negotiations were concerned, it is clear that they were modest at best.

As we have noted, the matter of disclosure to the UOP directors was wholly flawed by the conflicts of interest raised by the Arledge-Chitiea report. All of those conflicts were resolved by Signal in its own favor without divulging any aspect of them to UOP.

This cannot but undermine a conclusion that this merger meets any reasonable test of fairness. The outside UOP directors lacked one material piece of information generated by two of their colleagues, but shared only with Signal.

Finally, the minority stockholders were denied the critical information that Signal considered a price of $24 to be a good investment. Since this would have meant over $17,000,000 more to the minority, we cannot conclude that the shareholder vote was an informed one. Under the circumstances, an approval by a majority of the minority was meaningless. Given these particulars and the Delaware law on the subject, the record does not establish that this transaction satisfies any reasonable concept of fair dealing, and the Chancellor's findings in that regard must be reversed.

Turning to the matter of price, plaintiff also challenges its fairness. His evidence was that on the date the merger was approved the stock was worth at least $26 per share. In support, he offered the testimony of a chartered investment analyst who used two basic approaches to valuation: a comparative analysis of the premium paid over market in ten other tender offer-merger combinations, and a discounted cash flow analysis.

In this breach of fiduciary duty case, the Chancellor perceived that the approach to valuation was the same as that in an appraisal proceeding. Consistent with precedent, he rejected plaintiff's method of proof and accepted defendants' evidence of value as being in accord with practice under prior case law. This means that the so-called "Delaware block" or weighted average method was employed wherein the elements of value, i.e., assets, market price, earnings, etc., were assigned a particular weight and the resulting amounts added to determine the value per share. This procedure has been in use for decades. However, to the extent it excludes other generally accepted techniques used in the financial community and the courts, it is now clearly outmoded. It is time we recognize this in appraisal and other stock valuation proceedings and bring our law current on the subject.

Accordingly, the standard "Delaware block" or weighted average method of valuation, formerly employed in appraisal and other stock valuation cases, shall no longer exclusively control such proceedings. We believe that a more liberal approach must include proof of value by any techniques or methods which are generally considered acceptable in the financial community and otherwise admissible in court. This will obviate the very structured and mechanistic procedure that has heretofore governed such matters.

Fair price obviously requires consideration of all relevant factors involving the value of a company. Although the Chancellor received the plaintiff's evidence, his opinion indicates that the use of it was precluded because of past Delaware practice. While we do not suggest a monetary result one way or the other, we do think the plaintiff's evidence should be part of the factual mix and weighed as such. Until the $21 price is measured on remand by the valuation standards mandated by Delaware law, there can be no finding at the present stage of these proceedings that the price is fair. Given the lack of any candid disclosure of the material facts surrounding establishment of the $21 price, the majority of the minority vote, approving the merger, is meaningless.

The plaintiff has not sought an appraisal, but rescissory damages. On remand the plaintiff will be permitted to test the fairness of the $21 price by the standards we herein establish, in conformity with the principle applicable to an appraisal—that fair value be determined by taking "into account all relevant factors" [see 8 Del.C. § 262(h), supra]. In our view this includes the elements of rescissory damages if the Chancellor considers them susceptible of proof and a remedy appropriate to all the issues of fairness before him.

Finally, we address the matter of business purpose. The defendants contend that the purpose of this merger was not a proper subject of inquiry by the trial court. The plaintiff says that no valid purpose existed—the entire transaction was a mere subterfuge designed to eliminate the minority. The Chancellor ruled otherwise, but in so doing he clearly circumscribed the thrust and effect of *Singer. Weinberger v. UOP,* 426 A.2d at 1342–43, 1348–50.

The requirement of a business purpose is new to our law of mergers and was a departure from prior case law. In view of the fairness test which has long been applicable to parent-subsidiary mergers, the expanded appraisal remedy now available to shareholders, and the broad discretion of the Chancellor to fashion such relief as the facts of a given case may dictate, we do not believe that any additional meaningful protection is afforded minority shareholders by the business purpose requirement. Accordingly, such requirement shall no longer be of any force or effect.

The judgment of the Court of Chancery, finding both the circumstances of the merger and the price paid the minority shareholders to be fair, is reversed. The matter is remanded for further proceedings consistent herewith. Upon remand the plaintiff's post-trial motion to enlarge the class should be granted.

REVERSED AND REMANDED.

KAHN v. LYNCH COMMUNICATION SYS., INC.
638 A.2d 1110 (Del. 1994)

Holland, Justice:

This is an appeal by the plaintiff-appellant, Alan R. Kahn ("Kahn"), from a final judgment of the Court of Chancery which was entered after a trial. The action, instituted by Kahn in 1986, originally sought to enjoin the acquisition of the defendant-appellee, Lynch Communication Systems, Inc. ("Lynch"), by the defendant-appellee, Alcatel U.S.A. Corporation ("Alcatel"), pursuant to a tender offer and cash-out merger.

Kahn alleged that Alcatel was a controlling shareholder of Lynch and breached its fiduciary duties to Lynch and its shareholders. According to Kahn,

Alcatel dictated the terms of the merger; made false, misleading, and inadequate disclosures; and paid an unfair price.

The Court of Chancery concluded that Alcatel was, in fact, a controlling shareholder that owed fiduciary duties to Lynch and its shareholders. It also concluded that Alcatel had not breached those fiduciary duties. Accordingly, the Court of Chancery entered judgment in favor of the defendants.

Kahn has raised three contentions in this appeal. Kahn's first contention is that the Court of Chancery erred by finding that "the tender offer and merger were negotiated by an independent committee," and then placing the burden of persuasion on the plaintiff, Kahn. Kahn asserts the uncontradicted testimony in the record demonstrated that the committee could not and did not bargain at arm's length with Alcatel. Kahn's second contention is that Alcatel's Offer to Purchase was false and misleading because it failed to disclose threats made by Alcatel to the effect that if Lynch did not accept its proposed price, Alcatel would institute a hostile tender offer at a lower price. Third, Kahn contends that the merger price was unfair. Alcatel contends that the Court of Chancery was correct in its findings, with the exception of concluding that Alcatel was a controlling shareholder.

This Court has concluded that the record supports the Court of Chancery's finding that Alcatel was a controlling shareholder. However, the record does not support the conclusion that the burden of persuasion shifted to Kahn. Therefore, the burden of proving the *entire* fairness of the merger transaction remained on Alcatel, the controlling shareholder. Accordingly, the judgment of the Court of Chancery is reversed. The matter is remanded for further proceedings in accordance with this opinion.

Lynch, a Delaware corporation, designed and manufactured electronic telecommunications equipment, primarily for sale to telephone operating companies. Alcatel, a holding company, is a subsidiary of Alcatel (S.A.), a French company involved in public telecommunications.

In 1981, Alcatel acquired 30.6 percent of Lynch's common stock pursuant to a stock purchase agreement. [O]n November 4, 1986, Alcatel made an offer to acquire the entire equity interest in Lynch, constituting the approximately 57 percent of Lynch shares not owned by Alcatel. The offering price was $14 cash per share.

On November 7, 1986, the Lynch board of directors authorized [its] Independent Committee [Kertz, Wineman, and Beringer] to negotiate the cash merger offer with Alcatel. At a meeting held that same day, the Independent Committee determined that the $14 per share offer was inadequate. The Independent's Committee's own legal counsel, Skadden, Arps, Slate, Meagher & Flom ("Skadden Arps"), suggested that the Independent Committee should review alternatives to a cash-out merger with Alcatel, including a "white knight" third party acquiror, a repurchase of Alcatel's shares, or the adoption of a shareholder rights plan.

On November 12, 1986, Beringer, as chairman of the Independent Committee, contacted Michiel C. McCarty ("McCarty") of Dillon Read, Alcatel's representative in the negotiations, with a counteroffer at a price of $17 per share. McCarty responded on behalf of Alcatel with an offer of $15 per share. When Beringer informed McCarty of the Independent Committee's view that $15 was also insufficient, Alcatel raised its offer to $15.25 per share. The Independent Committee also rejected this offer. Alcatel then made its final offer of $15.50 per share.

At the November 24, 1986 meeting of the Independent Committee, Beringer advised its other two members that Alcatel was "ready to proceed with an unfriendly tender at a lower price" if the $15.50 per share price was not recommended by the Independent Committee and approved by the Lynch board of directors. Beringer also told the other members of the Independent Committee that the alternatives to a cash-out merger had been investigated but were impracticable. After meeting with its financial and legal advisors, the Independent Committee voted unanimously to recommend that the Lynch board of directors approve Alcatel's $15.50 cash per share price for a merger with Alcatel. The Lynch board met later that day. With Alcatel's nominees abstaining, it approved the merger.

This Court has held that "a shareholder owes a fiduciary duty only if it owns a majority interest in or *exercises control* over the business affairs of the corporation." *Ivanhoe Partners v. Newmont Mining Corp.*, Del.Supr., 535 A.2d 1334, 1344 (1987). With regard to the exercise of control, this Court has stated:

> [A] shareholder who owns less than 50% of a corporation's outstanding stocks does not, without more, become a controlling shareholder of that corporation, with a concomitant fiduciary status. For a dominating relationship to exist in the absence of controlling stock ownership, a plaintiff must allege domination by a minority shareholder through actual control of corporation conduct.

Citron v. Fairchild Camera & Instrument Corp., Del.Supr., 569 A.2d 53, 70 (1989).

Alcatel held a 43.3 percent minority share of stock in Lynch. Therefore, the threshold question to be answered by the Court of Chancery was whether, despite its minority ownership, Alcatel exercised control over Lynch's business affairs. Based upon the testimony and the minutes of the August 1, 1986 Lynch board meeting, the Court of Chancery concluded that Alcatel did exercise control over Lynch's business decisions.

The standard of appellate review with regard to the Court of Chancery's factual findings is deferential. Those findings will not be set aside by this Court unless they are clearly erroneous or not the product of a logical and orderly deductive reasoning process. The record supports the Court of Chancery's factual finding that Alcatel dominated Lynch.

The record supports the Court of Chancery's underlying factual finding that "the non-Alcatel [independent] directors deferred to Alcatel because of its position as a significant stockholder and not because they decided in the exercise of their own business judgment that Alcatel's position was correct." The record also supports the subsequent factual finding that, notwithstanding its 43.3 percent minority shareholder interest, Alcatel did exercise actual control over Lynch by dominating its corporate affairs. The Court of Chancery's legal conclusion that Alcatel owed the fiduciary duties of a controlling shareholder to the other Lynch shareholders followed syllogistically as the logical result of its cogent analysis of the record.

A controlling or dominating shareholder standing on both sides of a transaction, as in a parent-subsidiary context, bears the burden of proving its entire fairness. The demonstration of fairness that is required was set forth by this Court in *Weinberger*. In this case, the Vice Chancellor noted that the Court of Chancery has expressed "differing views" regarding the effect that an approval of a cash-out merger by a special committee of disinterested directors has upon the controlling or dominating shareholder's burden of demonstrating entire fairness. One view is that such approval shifts to the plaintiff the burden of proving that the transaction was unfair. The other view is that such an approval renders the business judgment rule the applicable standard of judicial review.

It is often of critical importance whether a particular decision is one to which the business judgment rule applies or the entire fairness rule applies. In *Weinberger,* this Court held that because

> of the fairness test which has long been applicable to parent-subsidiary mergers, the expanded appraisal remedy now available to shareholders, and the broad discretion of the [Court of Chancery] to fashion such relief as the facts of a given case may dictate, we do not believe that any additional meaningful protection is afforded minority shareholders by the business purpose requirement. Accordingly, such requirement shall no longer be of any force or effect. *Weinberger v. UOP, Inc.*, 457 A.2d at 715

Thereafter, this Court recognized that it would be inconsistent with its holding in *Weinberger* to apply the business judgment rule in the context of an interested merger transaction which, by its very nature, did not require a business purpose. *See Rosenblatt v. Getty Oil Co.*, 493 A.2d at 937. Consequently, in *Rosenblatt,* in the context of a subsequent proceeding involving a parent-subsidiary merger, this Court held that the "approval of a merger, as here, by an informed vote of a majority of the minority stockholders, while not a legal prerequisite, shifts the burden of proving the unfairness of the merger entirely to the plaintiffs." *Id.*

Entire fairness remains the proper focus of judicial analysis in examining an interested merger, irrespective of whether the burden of proof remains upon or is shifted away from the controlling or dominating shareholder, because the unchanging nature of the underlying "interested" transaction requires careful scrutiny. The policy rationale for the exclusive application of the entire fairness standard to interested merger transactions has been stated as follows:

> Parent subsidiary mergers, unlike stock options, are proposed by a party that controls, and will continue to control, the corporation, whether or not the minority stockholders vote to approve or reject the transaction. The controlling stockholder relationship has the potential to

influence, however subtly, the vote of [ratifying] minority stockholders in a manner that is not likely to occur in a transaction with a noncontrolling party.

Even where no coercion is intended, shareholders voting on a parent subsidiary merger might perceive that their disapproval could risk retaliation of some kind by the controlling stockholder. At the very least, the potential for that perception, and its possible impact upon a shareholder vote, could never be fully eliminated. Consequently, in a merger between the corporation and its controlling stockholder – even one negotiated by disinterested, independent directors – no court could be certain whether the transaction terms fully approximate what truly independent parties would have achieved in an arm's length negotiation. Given that uncertainty, a court might well conclude that even minority shareholders who have ratified a merger need procedural protections beyond those afforded by full disclosure of all material facts. One way to provide such protections would be to adhere to the more stringent entire fairness standard of judicial review.

Citron v. E.I. Du Pont de Nemours & Co., 584 A.2d at 502.

Once again, this Court holds that the exclusive standard of judicial review in examining the propriety of an interested cash-out merger transaction by a controlling or dominating shareholder is entire fairness. *Weinberger v. UOP, Inc.*, 457 A.2d at 710–11. The initial burden of establishing entire fairness rests upon the party who stands on both sides of the transaction. *Id.* However, an approval of the transaction by an independent committee of directors or an informed majority of minority shareholders shifts the burden of proof on the issue of fairness from the controlling or dominating shareholder to the challenging shareholder-plaintiff. *See Rosenblatt v. Getty Oil Co.*, 493 A.2d at 937–38. Nevertheless, even when an interested cash-out merger transaction receives the informed approval of a majority of minority stockholders or an independent committee of disinterested directors, an entire fairness analysis is the only proper standard of judicial review. *See id.*

The same policy rationale which requires judicial review of interested cash-out mergers exclusively for entire fairness also mandates careful judicial scrutiny of a special committee's real bargaining power before shifting the burden of proof on the issue of entire fairness. A recent decision from the Court of Chancery articulated a two-part test for determining whether burden shifting is appropriate in an interested merger transaction. *Rabkin v. Olin Corp.*, In *Olin*, the Court of Chancery stated:

> The mere existence of an independent special committee ... does not itself shift the burden. At least two factors are required. First, the majority shareholder must not dictate the terms of the merger. Second, the special committee must have real bargaining power that it can exercise with the majority shareholder on an arms length basis.

This Court expressed its agreement with that statement by affirming the Court of Chancery decision in *Olin* on appeal.

The Independent Committee's assignment was to consider Alcatel's proposal to purchase Lynch. The Independent Committee proceeded on that task with full knowledge of Alcatel's demonstrated pattern of domination.

The Court of Chancery began its factual analysis by noting that Kahn had "attempted to shatter" the image of the Independent Committee's actions as having "appropriately simulated" an arm's length, third-party transaction. The Court of Chancery found that "to some extent, [Kahn's attempt] was successful." The Court of Chancery gave credence to the testimony of Kertz, one of the members of the Independent Committee, to the effect that he did not believe that $15.50 was a fair price but that he voted in favor of the merger because he felt there was no alternative.

The Court of Chancery also found that Kertz understood Alcatel's position to be that it was ready to proceed with an unfriendly tender offer at a lower price if Lynch did not accept the $15.50 offer, and that Kertz perceived this to be a threat by Alcatel. The Court of Chancery concluded that Kertz ultimately decided that, "although $15.50 was not fair, a tender offer and merger at that price would be better for Lynch's stockholders than an unfriendly tender offer at a significantly lower price." The Court of Chancery determined that "Kertz failed either to satisfy himself that the offered price was fair or oppose the merger."

In addition to Kertz, the other members of the Independent Committee were Beringer, its chairman, and Wineman. Wineman did not testify at trial. Beringer was called by Alcatel to testify at trial. Beringer testified that at the time of the Committee's vote to recommend the $15.50 offer to the Lynch board, he thought "that *under the circumstances,* a price of $15.50 was fair and should be accepted" (emphasis added).

The record reflects that Alcatel was "ready to proceed" with a hostile bid. This was a conclusion reached by Beringer, the Independent Committee's chairman and spokesman, based upon communications to him from Alcatel. Beringer testified that although there was no reference to a particular price for a hostile bid during his discussions with Alcatel, or even specific mention of a "lower" price, "the implication was clear to [him] that it probably would be at a lower price."

According to the Court of Chancery, the Independent Committee rejected three lower offers for Lynch from Alcatel and then accepted the $15.50 offer "after being advised that [it] was fair and after considering the absence of alternatives." The Vice Chancellor expressly acknowledged the impracticability of Lynch's Independent Committee's alternatives to a merger with Alcatel:

> Lynch was not in a position to shop for other acquirors, since Alcatel could block any alternative transaction. Alcatel also made it clear that it was not interested in having its shares repurchased by Lynch. The Independent Committee decided that a stockholder rights plan was not viable because of the increased debt it would entail.

Nevertheless, based upon the record before it, the Court of Chancery found that the Independent Committee had "appropriately simulated a third-party transaction, where negotiations are conducted at arms-length and there is no compulsion to reach an agreement." The Court of Chancery concluded that the Independent Committee's actions "as a whole" were "sufficiently well informed ... and aggressive to simulate an arms-length transaction," so that the burden of proof as to entire fairness shifted from Alcatel to the contending Lynch shareholder, Kahn. The Court of Chancery's reservations about that finding are apparent in its written decision.

A condition precedent to finding that the burden of proving entire fairness has shifted in an interested merger transaction is a careful judicial analysis of the factual circumstances of each case. Particular consideration must be given to evidence of whether the special committee was truly independent, fully informed, and had the freedom to negotiate at arm's length.

The Court of Chancery's determination that the Independent Committee "appropriately simulated a third-party transaction, where negotiations are conducted at arm's-length and there is no compulsion to reach an agreement," is not supported by the record. Under the circumstances present in the case *sub judice,* the Court of Chancery erred in shifting the burden of proof with regard to entire fairness to the contesting Lynch shareholder-plaintiff, Kahn. The record reflects that the ability of the Committee effectively to negotiate at arm's length was compromised by Alcatel's threats to proceed with a hostile tender offer if the $15.50 price was not approved by the Committee and the Lynch board. The fact that the Independent Committee rejected three initial offers, which were well below the Independent Committee's estimated valuation for Lynch and were not combined with an explicit threat that Alcatel was "ready to proceed" with a hostile bid, cannot alter the conclusion that any semblance of arm's length bargaining ended when the Independent Committee surrendered to the ultimatum that accompanied Alcatel's final offer.

Accordingly, the judgment of the Court of Chancery is reversed. This matter is remanded for further proceedings consistent herewith, including a redetermination of the entire fairness of the cash-out merger to Kahn and the other Lynch minority shareholders with the burden of proof remaining on Alcatel, the dominant and interested shareholder.

KAHN v. LYNCH COMMUNICATION SYS., INC.
669 A.2d 79 (Del. 1995)

WALSH, Justice:

This is the second appeal in this shareholder litigation after a Court of Chancery ruling in favor of the defendants. The underlying dispute arises from a cash-out merger of Lynch Communications System, Inc. ("Lynch") into a subsidiary of Alcatel USA, Inc. ("Alcatel"). In the previous appeal, this Court determined that Alcatel, as a controlling shareholder of Lynch, dominated the merger negotiations despite the fact that Lynch's board of directors has appointed an independent negotiating committee. We concluded, however, that such a determination did not necessarily preclude a finding that the transaction was entirely fair and remanded the matter to the Court of Chancery for a determination of entire fairness, with the burden of proof upon the defendants.

Upon remand, the Court of Chancery reevaluated the record under the appropriate burden of proof and concluded that the transaction was entirely fair to the Lynch minority shareholders. The court also rejected plaintiff's claim that the defendants violated their duty of disclosure in failing to describe specifically the threat of a lower priced tender offer. We affirm in both respects.

After examining the transaction for entire fairness, the Court of Chancery once again found for the defendants, holding that they had carried the burden of showing the entire fairness of the transaction. The Court of Chancery rejected the plaintiff's claim that the coercion of the Independent Committee should have been disclosed to the shareholders.

[T]he Court of Chancery examined the issue of fair price. Finding the evaluation of the plaintiffs' expert flawed, the court concluded that the defendants had also met their burden of establishing the fairness of the price received by the stockholders. Thus, the Court of Chancery held for the defendants after finding that they had established the entire fairness of the transaction.

With respect to the negotiations and structure of the transaction, the Court of Chancery, while acknowledging that the Court in *Lynch I* found the negotiations coercive, commented that the negotiations "certainly were no less fair than if there had been no negotiations at all". The court noted that a committee of non-Alcatel directors negotiated an increase in price from $14 per share to $15.50. The committee also retained two investment banking firms who were well acquainted with Lynch's prospects based. Moreover, the committee had the benefit of outside legal counsel.

It is true that the committee and the Board agreed to a price which at least one member of the committee later opined was not a fair price. But there is no requirement of unanimity in such matters either at the Independent Committee level or by the Board. A finding of unfair dealing based on lack of unanimity could discourage the use of special committees in majority dominated cash-out mergers.

Here Alcatel could have presented a merger offer directly to the Lynch Board, which it controlled, and received a quick approval. Had it done so, of course, it would have born the burden of demonstrating entire fairness in the event the transaction was later questioned. *See Weinberger v. UOP,* Del.Supr., 457 A.2d 701 (1983). Where, ultimately, it has been required to assume the same burden, it should fare no worse in a judicial review of the fairness of its negotiations with the Independent Committee.

In resolving issues of valuation the Court of Chancery undertakes a mixed determination of law and fact. When faced with differing methodologies or opinions the court is entitled to draw its own conclusions from the evidence. So long as the court's ultimate determination of value is based on the application of recognized valuation standards, its acceptance of one expert's opinion, to the exclusion of another, will not be disturbed. *Id.*

The Court of Chancery's finding that Alcatel had successfully born the initial burden of proving the fairness of the merger price is fully supportable by the evidence tendered by the experts retained by Alcatel and by the Independent

Committee. The Court of Chancery was not persuaded that Kahn had presented evidence of sufficient quality to prove the inadequacy of the merger price. We find that ruling to be logically determined and supported by the evidence and accordingly affirm.

Appraisal Proceeding Realities

Statutory appraisal rights are not the panacea for minority shareholders who believe they have been shortchanged by a majority shareholder in a squeeze out merger.

The procedural requirements are significant, as illustrated by sections 13.21 through 13.30 of the Model Business Corporations Act, and section 262 of the Delaware General Corporation Law. Under the Model Act, a shareholder who wants to trigger appraisal rights must first give written notice of his or her intent to dissent prior to the meeting at which the merger will be voted upon, must not vote in favor of the merger, and, if the merger is approved, must then timely demand payment for his or her shares and deposit the share certificates with the corporation. The corporation must then pay the shareholder the amount that it determines to be the fair value of the shares. If the shareholder disagrees with the corporation's determination of value, the shareholder is then required to notify the corporation of his or her estimate of fair value and demand payment from the corporation. The corporation then has a choice: it can honor the shareholder's demand or initiate a judicial appraisal proceeding. If a shareholder fails to comply with any of the procedural requirements and the related deadlines, the appraisal remedy is lost.

Beyond the procedural hassles is the risk that the whole effort may produce little or nothing. Prior to *Weinberger*, the valuation chore in a Delaware appraisal proceeding was handled with an antiquated block valuation method that used a weighted average of valuations based on asset value, earnings value, and market value. The net result in many cases was a lousy valuation for the shareholders that often bore little resemblances to the outcomes produced from current methods of valuation. Of course, *Weinberger* righted this wrong, rejected the block method as the exclusive means of valuation, and opened the door for all methods of valuation "generally considered acceptable in the financial community." Although this change improves the chances of a positive outcome for a dissenting shareholder, there is still the very real possibility that the shareholder's proposed valuation will be watered down or completely rejected, resulting in no yield or a pittance yield that didn't justify the effort.

Costs must also be factored into any decision to assert appraisal rights. An appraisal proceeding will trigger significant opportunity costs in terms of time, effort, and stress. Added to these opportunity costs are the actual costs for lawyers and valuation experts. Court costs, including compensation and expenses of court-appointed appraisers, will be assigned to the corporation unless the court determines that the shareholders acted arbitrarily, vexatiously, or in bad faith. But the expert legal and accounting fees of the shareholders are borne by the shareholders, subject only to a discretionary power of the court to have such fees recovered from the benefits reaped by a broader group of shareholders who benefited from the proceedings. See MBCA § 13.31.

The realities of the technical procedural requirements, the uncertainties of a profitable outcome, and the costs (both opportunity and actual) of pushing forward with a time-consuming appraisal proceeding often cause many minority shareholders to rethink an initial urge to fight for a higher price.

B. SHORT FORM MERGER SQUEEZE-OUTS

CASE PROBLEM 12-2

Assume the same facts as Case Problem 12-1, with the following changes:

1. InstruTech owns 91 percent of HealthTools' outstanding stock and the remaining nine percent is held by public shareholders.

2. InstruTech's board approved a short-form merger of HealthTools into InstruTech in accordance with 8 *Del. C.* § 253 (quoted below in *Glassman v. Unocal Exploration Corp*), with HealthTools' public shareholders being paid $36 a share.   Each public shareholder had the option of receiving $36 a share or pursing his or her statutory appraisal rights.

3. The Outsiders were appointed as a special committee to evaluate the terms of the merger on behalf of HealthTools' directors and shareholders. InstruTech's CEO advised the Outsiders that the committee was "just window dressing," and they were expected to "just rubber stamp the terms of the merger with no questions asked." The Outsiders approved the merger.

4. HealthTools shareholders never voted on the merger.

5. The Report's existence was never disclosed to the Valuation Firm, any board member of HealthTools, or the shareholders of HealthTools.

The Group now seeks to enjoin the consummation of the merger on the grounds that such a merger now is inherently unfair because time is necessary to exploit, and determine the value of, the Patents. Alternatively, the Group claims that InstruTech should pay an additional $10 a share to HealthTools' public shareholders based on an expert valuation of HealthTools, commissioned by the Group, that "more appropriately considers the potential value" of the Patents.

What is the likelihood of the Group prevailing on its claims? What standard of review should the court use? Who bears the burden of proof? Is the business judgment rule a factor?

8 DGCL § 253.
Merger of Parent Corporation and Subsidiary or Subsidiaries

(a) In any case in which at least 90% of the outstanding shares of each class of the stock of a corporation or corporations..., of which class there are outstanding shares that, absent this subsection, would be entitled to vote on such merger, is owned by another corporation and 1 of the corporations is a corporation of this State and the other or others are corporations of this State, or any other state or states, or the District of Columbia and the laws of the other state or states, or the District permit a corporation of such jurisdiction to merge with a corporation of another jurisdiction, the corporation having such stock ownership may either merge the other corporation or corporations into itself and assume all of its or their obligations, or merge itself, or itself and 1 or more of such other corporations, into 1 of the other corporations by executing, acknowledging and filing, in accordance with § 103 of this title, a certificate of such ownership and merger setting forth a copy of the resolution of its board of directors to so merge and the date of the adoption; provided, however, that in case the parent corporation shall not own all the outstanding stock of all the subsidiary corporations, parties to a merger as aforesaid, the resolution of the board of directors of the parent corporation shall state the terms and conditions of the merger, including the securities, cash, property, or rights to be issued, paid, delivered or granted by the surviving corporation upon surrender of each share of the subsidiary corporation or corporations not owned by the parent corporation, or the cancellation of some or all of such shares. Any of the terms of the resolution of the board of directors to so merge may be made dependent upon facts ascertainable outside of such resolution, provided that the manner in which such facts shall operate upon the terms of the resolution is clearly and expressly set forth in the resolution. The term "facts," as used in the preceding sentence, includes, but is not limited to, the occurrence of any event, including a determination or action by any person or body, including the corporation...

(d) In the event all of the stock of a subsidiary Delaware corporation party to a merger effected under this section is not owned by the parent corporation immediately prior to the merger, the stockholders of the subsidiary Delaware corporation party to the merger shall have appraisal rights as set forth in § 262 of this title.

GLASSMAN V. UNOCAL EXPLORATION CORP.
777 A.2d 242 (Del.Supr.,2001)

BERGER, Justice.

In this appeal, we consider the fiduciary duties owed by a parent corporation to the subsidiary's minority stockholders in the context of a "short-form" merger. Specifically, we take this opportunity to reconcile a fiduciary's seemingly absolute duty to establish the entire fairness of any self-dealing transaction with the less demanding requirements of the short-form merger statute. The statute authorizes the elimination of minority stockholders by a summary process that does not involve the "fair dealing" component of entire fairness. Indeed, the statute does not contemplate any "dealing" at all. Thus, a parent corporation cannot satisfy the entire fairness standard if it follows the terms of the short-form merger statute without more.

Unocal Corporation addressed this dilemma by establishing a special negotiating committee and engaging in a process that it believed would pass muster under traditional entire fairness review. We find that such steps were unnecessary. By enacting a statute that authorizes the elimination of the minority without notice, vote, or other traditional indicia of procedural fairness, the

General Assembly effectively circumscribed the parent corporation's obligations to the minority in a short-form merger. The parent corporation does not have to establish entire fairness, and, absent fraud or illegality, the only recourse for a minority stockholder who is dissatisfied with the merger consideration is appraisal.

Unocal Corporation is an earth resources company primarily engaged in the exploration for and production of crude oil and natural gas. At the time of the merger at issue, Unocal owned approximately 96% of the stock of Unocal Exploration Corporation ("UXC"), an oil and gas company operating in and around the Gulf of Mexico. In 1991, low natural gas prices caused a drop in both companies' revenues and earnings. Unocal investigated areas of possible cost savings and decided that, by eliminating the UXC minority, it would reduce taxes and overhead expenses.

In December 1991 the boards of Unocal and UXC appointed special committees to consider a possible merger. The UXC committee consisted of three directors who, although also directors of Unocal, were not officers or employees of the parent company. The UXC committee retained financial and legal advisors and met four times before agreeing to a merger exchange ratio of .54 shares of Unocal stock for each share of UXC. Unocal and UXC announced the merger on February 24, 1992, and it was effected, pursuant to 8 *Del. C.* § 253, on May 2, 1992. The Notice of Merger and Prospectus stated the terms of the merger and advised the former UXC stockholders of their appraisal rights.

Plaintiffs filed this class action, on behalf of UXC's minority stockholders, on the day the merger was announced. They asserted, among other claims, that Unocal and its directors breached their fiduciary duties of entire fairness and full disclosure. The Court of Chancery conducted a two day trial and held that: (i) the Prospectus did not contain any material misstatements or omissions; (ii) the entire fairness standard does not control in a short-form merger; and (iii) plaintiffs' exclusive remedy in this case was appraisal. The decision of the Court of Chancery is affirmed.

The short-form merger statute, as enacted in 1937, authorized a parent corporation to merge with its wholly-owned subsidiary by filing and recording a certificate evidencing the parent's ownership and its merger resolution. In 1957, the statute was expanded to include parent/subsidiary mergers where the parent company owns at least 90% of the stock of the subsidiary. The 1957 amendment also made it possible, for the first time and only in a short-form merger, to pay the minority cash for their shares, thereby eliminating their ownership interest in the company. In its current form, which has not changed significantly since 1957, 8 *Del. C.* § 253 provides in relevant part:

(a) In any case in which at least 90 percent of the outstanding shares of each class of the stock of a corporation... is owned by another corporation..., the corporation having such stock ownership may ... merge the other corporation ... into itself... by executing, acknowledging and filing, in accordance with § 103 of this title, a certificate of such ownership and merger setting forth a copy of the resolution of its board of directors to so merge and the date of the adoption; provided, however, that in case the parent corporation shall not own all the outstanding stock of ... the subsidiary corporation[ ],... the resolution ...shall state the terms and conditions of the merger, including the securities, cash, property or rights to be issued, paid delivered or granted by the surviving corporation upon surrender of each share of the subsidiary corporation....

(d) In the event that all of the stock of a subsidiary Delaware corporation ... is not owned by the parent corporation immediately prior to the merger, the stockholders of the subsidiary Delaware corporation party to the merger shall have appraisal rights as set forth in Section 262 of this Title.

The question presented to this Court was whether any equitable relief is available to minority stockholders who object to a short-form merger. In *Stauffer v. Standard Brands Incorporated,* Del.Supr., 187 A.2d 78 (1962), minority stockholders sued to set aside the contested merger or, in the alternative, for damages. They alleged that the merger consideration was so grossly inadequate as to constitute constructive fraud and that Standard Brands breached its fiduciary duty to the minority by failing to set a fair price for their stock. The Court of Chancery held that appraisal was the stockholders' exclusive remedy, and dismissed the complaint. This Court affirmed, but explained that appraisal would not be the exclusive remedy in a short-form merger tainted by fraud or illegality:

> [T]he exception [to appraisal's exclusivity] ... refers generally to all mergers, and is nothing but a reaffirmation of the ever-present power of equity to deal with illegality or fraud. But it has no bearing here. No illegality or overreaching is shown. The dispute reduces to nothing but a difference of opinion as to value. Indeed it is difficult to imagine a case under the short merger statute in which there could be such actual fraud as would entitle a minority to set aside the merger. This is so because the very purpose of the statute is to provide the parent corporation with a means of eliminating the minority shareholder's interest in the enterprise. Thereafter the former stockholder has only a monetary claim. 187 A.2d at 80.

One might have thought that the *Weinberger* court intended appraisal to be the exclusive remedy "ordinarily" in non-fraudulent mergers where "price ... [is] the preponderant consideration outweighing other features of the merger." In *Rabkin v. Philip A. Hunt Chemical Corp.,* however, the Court dispelled that view. The *Rabkin* plaintiffs claimed that the majority stockholder breached its fiduciary duty of fair dealing by waiting until a one year commitment to pay $25 per share had expired before effecting a cash-out merger at $20 per share. The Court of Chancery dismissed the complaint, reasoning that, under *Weinberger,* plaintiffs could obtain full relief for the alleged unfair dealing in an appraisal proceeding. This Court reversed, holding that the trial court read *Weinberger* too narrowly and that appraisal is the exclusive remedy only if stockholders' complaints are limited to "judgmental factors of valuation."

Rabkin, through its interpretation of *Weinberger,* effectively eliminated appraisal as the exclusive remedy for any claim alleging breach of the duty of entire fairness. But *Rabkin* involved a long-form merger, and the Court did not discuss, in that case or any others, how its refinement of *Weinberger* impacted short-form mergers. Two of this Court's more recent decisions that arguably touch on the subject are *Bershad v. Curtiss-Wright Corp.* and *Kahn v. Lynch Communication Systems, Inc.,* both long-form merger cases. In *Bershad,* the Court included § 253 when it identified statutory merger provisions from which fairness issues flow… and in *Lynch,* the Court described entire fairness as the "exclusive" standard of review in a cash-out, parent/subsidiary merger.

Mindful of this history, we must decide whether a minority stockholder may challenge a short-form merger by seeking equitable relief through an entire fairness claim. Under settled principles, a parent corporation and its directors undertaking a short-form merger are self-dealing fiduciaries who should be required to establish entire fairness, including fair dealing and fair price. The problem is that § 253 authorizes a summary procedure that is inconsistent with any reasonable notion of fair dealing. In a short-form merger, there is no agreement of merger negotiated by two companies; there is only a unilateral act—a decision by the parent company that its 90% owned subsidiary shall no longer exist as a separate entity. The minority stockholders receive no advance notice of the merger; their directors do not consider or approve it; and there is no vote. Those who object are given the right to obtain fair value for their shares through appraisal.

The equitable claim plainly conflicts with the statute. If a corporate fiduciary follows the truncated process authorized by § 253, it will not be able to establish the fair dealing prong of entire fairness. If, instead, the corporate fiduciary sets up negotiating committees, hires independent financial and legal experts, etc., then it will have lost the very benefit provided by the statute—a simple, fast and inexpensive process for accomplishing a merger. We resolve this conflict by giving effect the intent of the General Assembly. In order to serve its purpose, § 253 must be construed to obviate the requirement to establish entire fairness.

Thus, we hold that, absent fraud or illegality, appraisal is the exclusive remedy available to a minority stockholder who objects to a short-form merger. In doing so, we also reaffirm *Weinberger's* statements about the scope of appraisal. The determination of fair value must be based on *all* relevant factors, including damages and elements of future value, where appropriate. So, for example, if the merger was timed to take advantage of a depressed market, or a low point in the company's cyclical earnings, or to precede an anticipated positive development, the appraised value may be adjusted to account for those factors. We recognize that these are the types of issues frequently raised in entire fairness claims, and we have held that claims for unfair dealing cannot be litigated in an appraisal. But our prior holdings simply explained that equitable claims may not be engrafted onto a statutory appraisal proceeding; stockholders may not receive rescissionary relief in an appraisal. Those decisions should not be read to restrict the elements of value that properly may be considered in an appraisal.

Although fiduciaries are not required to establish entire fairness in a short-form merger, the duty of full disclosure remains, in the context of this request for stockholder action. Where the only choice for the minority stockholders is whether to accept the merger consideration or seek appraisal, they must be given all the factual information that is material to that decision. The Court of Chancery carefully considered plaintiffs' disclosure claims and applied settled law in rejecting them. We affirm this aspect of the appeal on the basis of the trial court's decision.

Based on the foregoing, we affirm the Court of Chancery and hold that plaintiffs' only remedy in connection with the short-form merger of UXC into Unocal was appraisal.

Defective Notice Impact

What happens in a short form merger if the merger is completed and material information is not disclosed in the notice advising the minority shareholders of the merger and their rights?

In *Berger v. Pubco Corporation*, 976 A.2d 132 (Del.Supr.2009), the Delaware Supreme Court held that, in such a situation, the appropriate remedy would be a "quasi-appraisal" proceeding that includes all minority stockholders (except those who opt out) and that does not require any minority stockholders to escrow a portion of their previously received merger consideration. The Pubco minority shareholders received a notice explaining that a short form merger had been completed and that they could receive $20 a share or pursue their appraisal rights. The notice did not disclose how the price was determined and included an outdated version of Delaware's appraisal statue. In holding that such notice defects were material, the court stated:

> Where, as here, a minority shareholder needs to decide only whether to accept the merger consideration or to seek appraisal, the question is partially one of trust: can the minority shareholder trust that the price offered is good enough, or does it likely undervalue the company so significantly that appraisal is a worthwhile endeavor?

> When faced with such a question, it would be material to know that the price offered was set by arbitrarily rolling dice. In a situation like Pubco's, where so little information is available about the company, such a disclosure would significantly change the landscape with respect to the decision of whether or not to trust the price offered by the parent. This does not mean that Kanner should have provided picayune details about the process he used to set the price; it simply means he should have disclosed in a broad sense what the process was, assuming he followed a process at all and did not simply choose a number randomly.

976 A.2d at 136.

C. TENDER OFFER - MERGER SQUEEZE-OUT

CASE PROBLEM 12-3

Assume the same facts as Case Problem 12-1, with the following changes:

1. The Outsiders were appointed as a special committee (the "Committee") to evaluate the terms of the merger on behalf of HealthTools' directors and shareholders, and the Report was made available to the Committee. The Committee carefully evaluated the entire record and unanimously objected to the terms of the merger. This led to HealthTools's board, by a 4-3 vote, rejecting the merger.

2. InstruTech's senior management responded by scrapping the merger plan and proposing a tender offer to HealthTools' public shareholders at a price of $36 a share. Management is confident that, given the heavy institutional representation among the shareholders, the tender offer will result in InstruTech owning more than 90 percent of HealthTools' stock. InstruTech would then have the ability to squeeze out the remaining HealthTools shareholders in a short form cash-out merger pursuant to 8 Del. C. § 253.

Will InstruTech's new plan work? How should InstruTech structure the tender offer to strengthen its position in moving forward with its plan? What is the likelihood of the Group prevailing in an action to enjoin the tender offer or to obtain an additional $10 a share? How should the Group frame its allegations? What standard of review should the court use? Who bears the burden of proof?

IN RE PURE RESOURCES, INC. SHAREHOLDERS LITIGATION
808 A.2d 421 (Del.Ch. 2002)

STRINE, Vice Chancellor.

This is the court's decision on a motion for preliminary injunction. The lead plaintiff in the case holds a large block of stock in Pure Resources, Inc., 65% of the shares of which are owned by Unocal Corporation. The lead plaintiff and its fellow plaintiffs seek to enjoin a now-pending exchange offer (the "Offer") by which Unocal hopes to acquire the rest of the shares of Pure in exchange for shares of its own stock.

The plaintiffs believe that the Offer is inadequate and is subject to entire fairness review, consistent with the rationale of Kahn v. Lynch Communication Systems, Inc. and its progeny. Moreover, they claim that the defendants, who include Unocal and Pure's board of directors, have not made adequate and non-misleading disclosure of the material facts necessary for Pure stockholders to make an informed decision whether to tender into the Offer.

By contrast, the defendants argue that the Offer is a non-coercive one that is accompanied by complete disclosure of all material facts. As such, they argue that the Offer is not subject to the entire fairness standard, but to the standards set forth in cases like Solomon v. Pathe Communications Corp., 672 A.2d 35 (Del.1996), standards which they argue have been fully met.

In this opinion, I conclude that the Offer is subject, as a general matter, to the Solomon standards, rather than the Lynch entire fairness standard. I conclude, however, that many of the concerns that justify the Lynch standard are implicated by tender offers initiated by controlling stockholders, which have as their goal the acquisition of the rest of the subsidiary's shares. These concerns should be accommodated within the Solomon form of review, by requiring that tender offers by controlling shareholders be structured in a manner that reduces the distorting effect of the tendering process on free stockholder choice and by ensuring minority stockholders a candid and unfettered tendering recommendation from the independent directors of the target board. In this case, the Offer for the most part meets this standard, with one exception that Unocal may cure.

But I also find that the Offer must be preliminarily enjoined because material information relevant to the Pure stockholders' decision-making process has not been fairly disclosed. Therefore, I issue an injunction against the Offer pending an alteration of its terms to eliminate its coercive structure and to correct the inadequate disclosures.

Unocal Corporation is a large independent natural gas and crude oil exploration and production company with far-flung operations. Before May 2000, Unocal also had operations in the Permian Basin of western Texas and southeastern New Mexico. During that month, Unocal spun off its Permian Basin unit and combined it with Titan Exploration, Inc. Titan was an oil and gas company operating in the Permian Basin, south central Texas, and the central Gulf Coast region of Texas. It also owned mineral interests in the southern Gulf Coast.

The entity that resulted from that combination was Pure Resources, Inc. Following the creation of Pure, Unocal owned 65.4% of Pure's issued and outstanding common stock. The remaining 34.6% of Pure was held by Titan's former stockholders, including its managers who stayed on to run Pure. The largest of these stockholders was Jack D. Hightower, Pure's Chairman and Chief Executive Officer, who now owns 6.1% of Pure's outstanding stock before the exercise of options. As a group, Pure's management controls between a quarter and a third of the Pure stock not owned by Unocal, when options are considered.

Several important agreements were entered into when Pure was formed. The first is a Stockholders Voting Agreement. That Agreement requires Unocal and Hightower to vote their shares to elect to the Pure board five persons designated by Unocal (so long as Unocal owns greater than 50% of Pure's common stock), two persons designated by Hightower, and one person to be jointly agreed upon by Unocal and Hightower.

During the summer of 2001, Unocal explored the feasibility of acquiring the rest of Pure. On August 20, 2002, Unocal sent the Pure board a letter that stated in pertinent part that:

> [Our Board of Directors has authorized us to make an exchange
> offer pursuant to which the stockholders of Pure (other than
> Union Oil) will be offered 0.6527 shares of common stock of

Unocal for each outstanding share of Pure common stock they own in a transaction designed to be tax-free. Based on the $34.09 closing price of Unocal's shares on August 20, 2002, our offer provides a value of approximately $22.25 per share of Pure common stock and a 27% premium to the closing price of Pure common stock on that date.

Unocal management [made] calls to the Pure board about the Offer. In their talking points, [they] were instructed to suggest that any Special Committee formed by Pure should have powers "limited to hiring independent advisors (bank and lawyers) and to coming up with a recommendation to the Pure shareholders as to whether or not to accept UCL's offer; any greater delegation is not warranted".

The next day the Pure board met to consider this event. The Pure board voted to establish a Special Committee comprised of Williamson and Covington to respond to the Unocal bid. The precise authority of the Special Committee to act on behalf of Pure was left hazy at first, but seemed to consist solely of the power to retain independent advisors, to take a position on the offer's advisability on behalf of Pure, and to negotiate with Unocal to see if it would increase its bid.

For financial advisors, the Special Committee hired Credit Suisse First Boston ("First Boston"), the investment bank assisting Pure with its consideration of the Royalty Trust, and Petrie Parkman & Co., Inc., a smaller firm very experienced in the energy field. For legal advisors, the Committee retained Baker Botts and Potter Anderson & Corroon. Baker Botts had handled certain toxic tort litigation for Unocal and was active as lead counsel in representing an energy consortium of which Unocal is a major participant in a major piece of litigation.

After the formation of the Special Committee, Unocal formally commenced its Offer, which had these key features:

• An exchange ratio of 0.6527 of a Unocal share for each Pure share.

• A non-waivable majority of the minority tender provision, which required a majority of shares not owned by Unocal to tender. Management of Pure, including Hightower and Staley, are considered part of the minority for purposes of this condition, not to mention Maxwell, Laughbaum, Chessum, and Ling.

• A waivable condition that a sufficient number of tenders be received to enable Unocal to own 90% of Pure and to effect a short-form merger under 8 Del.C. § 253.

• A statement by Unocal that it intends, if it obtains 90%, to consummate a short-form merger as soon as practicable at the same exchange ratio.

As of this time, this litigation had been filed and a preliminary injunction hearing was soon scheduled. Among the issues raised was the adequacy of the Special Committee's scope of authority.

Thereafter, the Special Committee sought to, in its words, "clarify" its authority. The clarity it sought was clear: the Special Committee wanted to be delegated the full authority of the board under Delaware law to respond to the Offer. With such authority, the Special Committee could have searched for alternative transactions, evaluated the feasibility of a self-tender, and put in place a shareholder rights plan (a.k.a., poison pill) to block the Offer.

The most reasonable inference that can be drawn from the record is that the Special Committee was unwilling to confront Unocal as aggressively as it would have confronted a third-party bidder. No doubt Unocal's talented counsel made much of its client's majority status and argued that Pure would be on uncertain legal ground in interposing itself – by way of a rights plan – between Unocal and Pure's stockholders. Realizing that Unocal would not stand for this broader authority and sensitive to the expected etiquette of subsidiary-parent relations, the Pure board therefore decided not to vote on the issue, and the Special Committee's fleeting act of boldness was obscured in the rhetoric of discussions about "clarifying its authority."

Contemporaneous with these events, the Special Committee met on a more or less continuous basis. On a few occasions, the Special Committee met with Unocal and tried to persuade it to increase its offer. On September 10, for example, the Special Committee asked Unocal to increase the exchange ratio from 0.6527 to 0.787. Substantive presentations were made by the Special Committee's financial advisors in support of this overture.

After these meetings, Unocal remained unmoved and made no counteroffer. Therefore, on September 17, 2002, the Special Committee voted not to recommend the Offer, based on its analysis and the advice of its financial advisors. The Special Committee prepared the 14D–9 on behalf of Pure, which contained the board's recommendation not to tender into the Offer. Hightower and Staley also announced their personal present intentions not to tender, intentions that if adhered to would make it nearly impossible for Unocal to obtain 90% of Pure's shares in the Offer.

During the discovery process, a representative of the lead plaintiff, which is an investment fund, testified that he did not feel coerced by the Offer. The discovery record also reveals that a great deal of the Pure stock held by the public is in the hands of institutional investors.

Distilled to the bare minimum, the plaintiffs argue that the Offer should be enjoined because: (i) the Offer is subject to the entire fairness standard and the record supports the inference that the transaction cannot survive a fairness review; (ii) in any event, the Offer is actionably coercive and should be enjoined on that ground; and (iii) the disclosures provided to the Pure stockholders in connection with the Offer are materially incomplete and misleading.

In order to prevail on this motion, the plaintiffs must convince me that one or more of its merits arguments have a reasonable probability of success, that the Pure stockholders face irreparable injury in the absence of an injunction, and that the balance of hardships weighs in favor of an injunction.

The primary argument of the plaintiffs is that the Offer should be governed by the entire fairness standard of review. In their view, the structural power of Unocal over Pure and its board, as well as Unocal's involvement in determining the scope of the Special Committee's authority, make the Offer other than a voluntary, non-coercive transaction. In the plaintiffs' mind, the Offer poses the same threat of (what I will call) "inherent coercion" that motivated the Supreme Court in Kahn v. Lynch Communication Systems, Inc. to impose the entire fairness standard of review on any interested merger involving a controlling stockholder, even when the merger was approved by an independent board majority, negotiated by an independent special committee, and subject to a majority of the minority vote condition.

In support of their argument, the plaintiffs contend that the tender offer method of acquisition poses, if anything, a greater threat of unfairness to minority stockholders and should be subject to the same equitable constraints. More case-specifically, they claim that Unocal has used inside information from Pure to foist an inadequate bid on Pure stockholders at a time advantageous to Unocal. Then, Unocal acted self-interestedly to keep the Pure Special Committee from obtaining all the authority necessary to respond to the Offer. As a result, the plaintiffs argue, Unocal has breached its fiduciary duties as majority stockholder, and the Pure board has breached its duties by either acting on behalf of Unocal or by acting supinely in response to Unocal's inadequate offer (the Special Committee and the rest of the board). Instead of wielding the power to stop Unocal in its tracks and make it really negotiate, the Pure board has taken only the insufficient course of telling the Pure minority to say no.

In response to these arguments, Unocal asserts that the plaintiffs misunderstand the relevant legal principles. Because Unocal has proceeded by way of an exchange offer and not a negotiated merger, the rule of Lynch is inapplicable. Instead, Unocal is free to make a tender offer at whatever price it chooses so long as it does not: i) "structurally coerce" the Pure minority by suggesting explicitly or implicitly that injurious events will occur to those stockholders who fail to tender; or ii) mislead the Pure minority into tendering by concealing or misstating the material facts. This is the rule of law articulated by, among other cases, Solomon v. Pathe Communications Corp. Because Unocal has conditioned its Offer on a majority of the minority provision and intends to consummate a short-form merger at the same price, it argues that the Offer poses no threat of structural coercion and that the Pure minority can make a voluntary decision. Because the Pure minority has a negative recommendation from the Pure Special Committee and because there has been full disclosure (including of any material information Unocal received from Pure in formulating its bid), Unocal submits that the Pure minority will be able to make an informed decision whether to tender. For these reasons, Unocal asserts that no meritorious claim of breach of fiduciary duty exists against it or the Pure directors.

This case therefore involves an aspect of Delaware law fraught with doctrinal tension: what equitable standard of fiduciary conduct applies when a controlling shareholder seeks to acquire the rest of the company's shares?

In building the common law, judges forced to balance these concerns cannot escape making normative choices, based on imperfect information about the world. This reality clearly pervades the area of corporate law implicated by this case. When a transaction to buy out the minority is proposed, is it more important to the development of strong capital markets to hold controlling stockholders and target boards to very strict (and litigation-intensive) standards of fiduciary conduct? Or is more stockholder wealth generated if less rigorous protections are adopted, which permit acquisitions to proceed so long as the majority has not misled or strong-armed the minority? Is such flexibility in fact beneficial to minority stockholders because it encourages liquidity-generating tender offers to them and provides incentives for acquirers to pay hefty premiums to buy control, knowing that control will be accompanied by legal rules that permit a later "going private" transaction to occur in a relatively non-litigious manner?

At present, the Delaware case law has two strands of authority that answer these questions differently. In one strand, which deals with situations in which controlling stockholders negotiate a merger agreement with the target board to buy out the minority, our decisional law emphasizes the protection of minority stockholders against unfairness. In the other strand, which deals with situations when a controlling stockholder seeks to acquire the rest of the company's shares through a tender offer followed by a short-form merger under 8 Del.C. § 253, Delaware case precedent facilitates the free flow of capital between willing buyers and willing sellers of shares, so long as the consent of the sellers is not procured by inadequate or misleading information or by wrongful compulsion.

These strands appear to treat economically similar transactions as categorically different simply because the method by which the controlling stockholder proceeds varies. This disparity in treatment persists even though the two basic methods (negotiated merger versus tender offer/short-form merger) pose similar threats to minority stockholders. Indeed, it can be argued that the distinction in approach subjects the transaction that is more protective of minority stockholders when implemented with appropriate protective devices—a merger negotiated by an independent committee with the power to say no and conditioned on a majority of the minority vote—to more stringent review than the more dangerous form of a going private deal—an unnegotiated tender offer made by a majority stockholder. The latter transaction is arguably less protective than a merger of the kind described, because the majority stockholder-offeror has access to inside information, and the offer requires disaggregated stockholders to decide whether to tender quickly, pressured by the risk of being squeezed out in a short-form merger at a different price later or being left as part of a much smaller public minority. This disparity creates a possible incoherence in our law.

The second strand of cases involves tender offers made by controlling stockholders— i.e., the kind of transaction Unocal has proposed. The prototypical transaction addressed by this strand involves a tender offer by the controlling stockholder addressed to the minority stockholders. In that offer, the controlling stockholder promises to buy as many shares as the minority will sell but may subject its offer to certain conditions. For example, the controlling stockholder might condition the offer on receiving enough tenders for it to obtain 90% of the subsidiary's shares, thereby enabling the controlling stockholder to consummate a short-form merger under 8 Del.C. § 253 at either the same or a different price.

As a matter of statutory law, this way of proceeding is different from the negotiated merger approach in an important way: neither the tender offer nor the short-form merger requires any action by the subsidiary's board of directors. The tender offer takes place between the controlling shareholder and the minority shareholders so long as the offering conditions are met. And, by the explicit terms of § 253, the short-form merger can be effected by the controlling stockholder itself, an option that was of uncertain utility for many years because it was unclear whether § 253 mergers were subject to an equitable requirement of fair process at the subsidiary board level. That uncertainty was recently resolved in Glassman v. Unocal Exploration Corp., an important recent decision, which held that a short-form merger was not reviewable in an action claiming unfair dealing, and that, absent fraud or misleading or inadequate disclosures, could be contested only in an appraisal proceeding that focused solely on the adequacy of the price paid.

Because no consent or involvement of the target board is statutorily mandated for tender offers, our courts have recognized that "[i]n the case of totally voluntary tender offers ... courts do not impose any right of the shareholders to receive a particular price. Delaware law recognizes that, as to allegedly voluntary tender offers (in contrast to cash-out mergers), the determinative factors as to voluntariness are whether coercion is present, or whether there are materially false or misleading disclosures made to stockholders in connection with the offer." *Solomon v. Pathe Communications Corp.,* 672 A.2d 35, 39 (Del.1996).

The differences between this approach, which I will identify with the Solomon line of cases, and that of Lynch are stark. To begin with, the controlling stockholder is said to have no duty to pay a fair price, irrespective of its power over the subsidiary. Even more striking is the different manner in which the coercion concept is deployed. In the tender offer context addressed by Solomon and its progeny, coercion is defined in the more traditional sense as a wrongful threat that has the effect of forcing stockholders to tender at the wrong price to avoid an even worse fate later on, a type of coercion I will call structural coercion. The inherent coercion that Lynch found to exist when controlling stockholders seek to acquire the minority's stake is not even a cognizable concern for the common law of corporations if the tender offer method is employed.

I turn more directly to that dispute now.

I begin by discussing whether the mere fact that one type of transaction is a tender offer and the other is a negotiated merger is a sustainable basis for the divergent policy choices made in Lynch and Solomon? Because tender offers are not treated exceptionally in the third-party context, it is important to ask why the tender offer method should be consequential in formulating the equitable standards of fiduciary conduct by which courts review acquisition proposals made by controlling stockholders. Is there reason to believe that the tender offer method of acquisition is more protective of the minority, with the result that less scrutiny is required than of negotiated mergers with controlling stockholders?

Unocal's answer to that question is yes and primarily rests on an inarguable proposition: in a negotiated merger involving a controlling stockholder, the controlling stockholder is on both sides of the transaction. That is, the negotiated merger is a self-dealing transaction, whereas in a tender offer, the controlling stockholder is only on the offering side and the minority remain free not to sell.

As a formal matter, this distinction is difficult to contest. When examined more deeply, however, it is not a wall that can bear the full weight of the Lynch/Solomon distinction. In this regard, it is important to remember that the overriding concern of Lynch is the controlling shareholders have the ability to take retributive action in the wake of rejection by an independent board, a special committee, or the minority shareholders. That ability is so influential that the usual cleansing devices that obviate fairness review of interested transactions cannot be trusted.

The problem is that nothing about the tender offer method of corporate acquisition makes the 800–pound gorilla's retributive capabilities less daunting to minority stockholders. Indeed, many commentators would argue that the tender offer form is more coercive than a merger vote. In a merger vote, stockholders can vote no and still receive the transactional consideration if the merger prevails. In a tender offer, however, a non-tendering shareholder individually faces an uncertain fate. That stockholder could be one of the few who holds out, leaving herself in an even more thinly traded stock with little hope of liquidity and subject to a § 253 merger at a lower price or at the same price but at a later (and, given the time value of money, a less valuable) time. The 14D–9 warned Pure's minority stockholders of just this possibility. For these reasons, some view tender offers as creating a prisoner's dilemma—distorting choice and creating incentives for stockholders to tender into offers that they believe are inadequate in order to avoid a worse fate. But whether or not one views tender offers as more coercive of shareholder choice than negotiated mergers with controlling stockholders, it is difficult to argue that tender offers are materially freer and more reliable measures of stockholder sentiment.

Furthermore, the common law of corporations has long had a structural answer to the formal self-dealing point Unocal makes: a non-waivable majority of the minority vote condition to a merger. By this technique, the ability of the controlling stockholder to both offer and accept is taken away, and the sell-side decision-making authority is given to the minority stockholders. That method of proceeding replicates the tender offer made by Unocal here, with the advantage of not distorting the stockholders' vote on price adequacy in the way that a tendering decision arguably does.

Lynch, of course, held that a majority of the minority vote provision will not displace entire fairness review with business judgment rule review. Critically, the Lynch Court's distrust of the majority of the minority provision is grounded in a concern that also exists in the tender offer context. The basis for the distrust is the concern that before the fact ("ex ante") minority stockholders will fear retribution after the fact ("ex post") if they vote no – i.e., they will face inherent coercion – thus rendering the majority of the minority condition an inadequate guarantee of fairness. But if this concern is valid, then that same inherent coercion would seem to apply with equal force to the tender offer decision-making process, and be enhanced by the unique features of that process. A controlling stockholder's power to force a squeeze-out or cut dividends is no different after the failure of a tender offer than after defeat on a merger vote.

Finally, some of the other factors that are said to support fairness review of negotiated mergers involving controlling stockholders also apply with full force to tender offers made by controlling stockholders. The informational advantage that the controlling stockholder possesses is not any different; in this case, for example, Unocal was able to proceed having had full access to non-public information about Pure. The tender offer form provides no additional protection against this concern.

Furthermore, the tender offer method allows the controlling stockholder to time its offer and to put a bull rush on the target stockholders. Here, Unocal studied an acquisition of Pure for nearly a year and then made a "surprise" offer that forced a rapid response from Pure's Special Committee and the minority stockholders.

Likewise, one struggles to imagine why subsidiary directors would feel less constrained in reacting to a tender offer by a controlling stockholder than a negotiated merger proposal. Indeed, an arguably more obvious concern is that subsidiary directors might use the absence of a statutory role for them in the tender offer process to be less than aggressive in protecting minority interests, to wit, the edifying examples of subsidiary directors courageously taking no position on the merits of offers by a controlling stockholder. Or, as here, the Special Committee's failure to demand the power to use the normal range of techniques available to a non-controlled board responding to a third-party tender offer.

For these and other reasons that time constraints preclude me from explicating, I remain less than satisfied that there is a justifiable basis for the distinction between the Lynch and Solomon lines of cases. Instead, their disparate teachings reflect a difference in policy emphasis that is far greater than can be explained by the technical differences between tender offers and negotiated mergers, especially given Delaware's director-centered approach to tender offers made by third-parties, which emphasizes the vulnerability of disaggregated stockholders absent important help and protection from their directors.

I admit being troubled by the imbalance in Delaware law exposed by the Solomon/Lynch lines of cases. Under Solomon, the policy emphasis is on the right of willing buyers and sellers of stock to deal with each other freely, with only such judicial intervention as is necessary to ensure fair disclosure and to prevent structural coercion. The advantage of this emphasis is that it provides a relatively non-litigious way to effect going private transactions and relies upon minority stockholders to protect themselves. The cost of this approach is that it arguably exposes minority stockholders to the more subtle form of coercion that Lynch addresses and leaves them without adequate redress for unfairly timed and priced offers. The approach also minimizes the potential for the minority to get the best price, by arguably giving them only enough protection to keep them from being structurally coerced into accepting grossly insufficient bids but not necessarily merely inadequate ones.

Admittedly, the Solomon policy choice would be less disquieting if Delaware also took the same approach to third-party offers and thereby allowed diversified investors the same degree of unrestrained access to premium bids by third-parties. In its brief, Unocal makes a brave effort to explain why it is understandable that Delaware law emphasizes the rights of minority stockholders to freely receive structurally, non-coercive tender offers from controlling stockholders but not their right to accept identically structured offers from third parties. Although there may be subtle ways to explain this variance, a forest-eye summary by a stockholder advocate might run as follows: As a general matter, Delaware law permits directors substantial leeway to block the access of stockholders to receive substantial premium tender offers made by third-parties by use of the poison pill but provides relatively free access to minority stockholders to accept buy-out offers from controlling stockholders.

In the case of third-party offers, these advocates would note, there is arguably less need to protect stockholders indefinitely from structurally non-coercive bids because alternative buyers can emerge and because the target board can use the poison pill to buy time and to tell its story. By contrast, when a controlling stockholder makes a tender offer, the subsidiary board is unlikely – as this case demonstrates – to be permitted by the controlling stockholder to employ a poison pill to fend off the bid and exert pressure for a price increase and usually lacks any real clout to develop an alternative transaction. In the end, however, I do not believe that these discrepancies should lead to an expansion of the Lynch standard to controlling stockholder tender offers.

Instead, the preferable policy choice is to continue to adhere to the more flexible and less constraining Solomon approach, while giving some greater recognition to the inherent coercion and structural bias concerns that motivate the Lynch line of cases. Adherence to the Solomon rubric as a general matter, moreover, is advisable in view of the increased activism of institutional investors and the greater information flows available to them. Investors have demonstrated themselves capable of resisting tender offers made by controlling stockholders on occasion, and even the lead plaintiff here expresses no fear of retribution. This does not mean that controlling stockholder tender offers do not pose risks to minority stockholders; it is only to acknowledge that the corporate law should not be designed on the assumption that diversified investors are infirm but instead should give great deference to transactions approved by them voluntarily and knowledgeably.

To the extent that my decision to adhere to Solomon causes some discordance between the treatment of similar transactions to persist, that lack of harmony is better addressed in the Lynch line, by affording greater liability-immunizing effect to protective devices such as majority of minority approval conditions and special committee negotiation and approval.

To be more specific about the application of Solomon in these circumstances, it is important to note that the Solomon line of cases does not eliminate the fiduciary duties of controlling stockholders or target boards in connection with tender offers made by controlling stockholders. Rather, the question is the contextual extent and nature of those duties, a question I will now tentatively, and incompletely, answer.

The potential for coercion and unfairness posed by controlling stockholders who seek to acquire the balance of the company's shares by acquisition requires some equitable reinforcement, in order to give proper effect to the concerns undergirding Lynch. In order to address the prisoner's dilemma problem, our law should consider an acquisition tender offer by a controlling stockholder non-coercive only when: 1) it is subject to a non-waivable majority of the minority tender condition; 2) the controlling stockholder promises to consummate a prompt § 253 merger at the same price if it obtains more than 90% of the shares; and 3) the controlling stockholder has made no retributive threats. Those protections – also stressed in this court's recent Aquila decision – minimize the distorting influence of the tendering process on voluntary choice. They also recognize the adverse conditions that confront stockholders who find themselves owning what have become very thinly traded shares. These conditions also provide a partial cure to the disaggregation problem, by providing a realistic non-tendering goal the minority can achieve to prevent the offer from proceeding altogether.

The informational and timing advantages possessed by controlling stockholders also require some countervailing protection if the minority is to truly be afforded the opportunity to make an informed, voluntary tender decision. In this regard, the majority stockholder owes a duty to permit the independent directors on the target board both free rein and adequate time to react to the tender offer, by (at the very least) hiring their own advisors, providing the minority with a recommendation as to the advisability of the offer, and disclosing adequate information for the minority to make an informed judgment. For their part, the independent directors have a duty to undertake these tasks in good faith and diligently, and to pursue the best interests of the minority.

When a tender offer is non-coercive in the sense I have identified and the independent directors of the target are permitted to make an informed recommendation and provide fair disclosure, the law should be chary about superimposing the full fiduciary requirement of entire fairness upon the statutory tender offer process. Here, the plaintiffs argue that the Pure board breached its fiduciary duties by not giving the Special Committee the power to block the Offer by, among other means, deploying a poison pill. Indeed, the plaintiffs argue that the full board's decision not to grant that authority is subject to the entire fairness standard of review because a majority of the full board was not independent of Unocal.

That argument has some analytical and normative appeal, embodying as it does the rough fairness of the goose and gander rule. I am reluctant, however, to burden the common law of corporations with a new rule that would tend to compel the use of a device that our statutory law only obliquely sanctions and that in other contexts is subject to misuse, especially when used to block a high value bid that is not structurally coercive. When a controlling stockholder makes a tender offer that is not coercive in the sense I have articulated, therefore, the better rule is that there is no duty on its part to permit the target board to block the bid through use of the pill. Nor is there any duty on the part of the independent directors to seek blocking power. But it is important to be mindful of one of the reasons that make a contrary rule problematic—the awkwardness of a legal rule requiring a board to take aggressive action against a structurally non-coercive offer by the controlling stockholder that elects it. This recognition of the sociology of controlled subsidiaries puts a point on the increased vulnerability that stockholders face from controlling stockholder tenders, because the minority stockholders are denied the full range of protection offered by boards in response to third party offers. This factor illustrates the utility of the protective conditions that I have identified as necessary to prevent abuse of the minority.

Turning specifically to Unocal's Offer, I conclude that the application of these principles yields the following result. The Offer, in its present form, is coercive because it includes within the definition of the "minority" those stockholders who are affiliated with Unocal as directors and officers. It also includes the management of Pure, whose incentives are skewed by their employment, their severance agreements, and their Put Agreements. This is, of course, a problem that can be cured if Unocal amends the Offer to condition it on approval of a majority of Pure's unaffiliated stockholders. Requiring the minority to be defined exclusive of stockholders whose independence from the controlling stockholder is compromised is the better legal rule (and result). Too often, it will be the case that officers and directors of controlled subsidiaries have voting incentives that are not perfectly aligned with their economic interest in their stock and who are more than acceptably susceptible to influence from controlling stockholders. Aside, however, from this glitch in the majority of the minority condition, I conclude that Unocal's Offer satisfies the other requirements of "non-coerciveness." Its promise to consummate a prompt § 253 merger is sufficiently specific, and Unocal has made no retributive threats.

D. CONTROLLED GROUP SALES

CASE PROBLEM 12-4

Assume the same facts as Case Problem 12-1, with the following changes:

1. The Outsiders were appointed as a special committee (the "Committee") to evaluate the terms of the merger on behalf of HealthTools' directors and shareholders, and the Report was made available to the Committee.   The Committee carefully evaluated the entire record and unanimously objected to the terms of the merger. This led to HealthTools' board, by a 4-3 vote, rejecting the merger.

2. InstruTech's senior management responded by scrapping the merger plan and proposing to purchase Dental from HealthTools for $65 million. The price was based on the findings of the Valuation Firm, which had complete access to the Report and all relevant information. The Committee carefully evaluated the proposed sale of Dental. In connection with its evaluation, the Committee had access to all relevant information and hired its own valuation expert and legal counsel. The Committee determined that the $65 million price was "fair and

reasonable." Base on the Committee's findings, HealthTools' board unanimously approved the sale.

The Group's valuation expert claims that the sales price should not be less than $80 million. What is the likelihood of the Group prevailing in an action to enjoin the sale or to cause the sales price to be increased $15 million? How should the Group frame its allegations? What standard of review should the court use? Who bears the burden of proof?

SINCLAIR OIL CORP v. LEVIEN
280 A.2d 717 (Del. 1971)

Wolcott, Chief Justice.

This is an appeal by the defendant, Sinclair Oil Corporation (hereafter Sinclair), from an order of the Court of Chancery,in a derivative action requiring Sinclair to account for damages sustained by its subsidiary, Sinclair Venezuelan Oil Company (hereafter Sinven), organized by Sinclair for the purpose of operating in Venezuela, as a result of dividends paid by Sinven, the denial to Sinven of industrial development, and a breach of contract between Sinclair's wholly-owned subsidiary, Sinclair International Oil Company, and Sinven.

Sinclair, operating primarily as a holding company, is in the business of exploring for oil and of producing and marketing crude oil and oil products. At all times relevant to this litigation, it owned about 97% of Sinven's stock. The plaintiff owns about 3000 of 120,000 publicly held shares of Sinven. Sinven, incorporated in 1922, has been engaged in petroleum operations primarily in Venezuela and since 1959 has operated exclusively in Venezuela.

Sinclair nominates all members of Sinven's board of directors. The Chancellor found as a fact that the directors were not independent of Sinclair. Almost without exception, they were officers, directors, or employees of corporations in the Sinclair complex. By reason of Sinclair's domination, it is clear that Sinclair owed Sinven a fiduciary duty. Getty Oil Company v. Skelly Oil Co., 267 A.2d 883 (Del.Supr.1970); Cottrell v. Pawcatuck Co., 35 Del.Ch. 309, 116 A.2d 787 (1955). Sinclair concedes this.

The Chancellor held that because of Sinclair's fiduciary duty and its control over Sinven, its relationship with Sinven must meet the test of intrinsic fairness. The standard of intrinsic fairness involves both a high degree of fairness and a shift in the burden of proof. Under this standard the burden is on Sinclair to prove, subject to careful judicial scrutiny, that its transactions with Sinven were objectively fair.

Sinclair argues that the transactions between it and Sinven should be tested, not by the test of intrinsic fairness with the accompanying shift of the burden of proof, but by the business judgment rule under which a court will not interfere with the judgment of a board of directors unless there is a showing of gross and palpable overreaching. A board of directors enjoys a presumption of sound business judgment, and its decisions will not be disturbed if they can be attributed to any rational business purpose. A court under such circumstances will not substitute its own notions of what is or is not sound business judgment.

We think, however, that Sinclair's argument in this respect is misconceived. When the situation involves a parent and a subsidiary, with the parent controlling the transaction and fixing the terms, the test of intrinsic fairness, with its resulting shifting of the burden of proof, is applied. David J. Greene & Co. v. Dunhill International, Inc., 249 A.2d 427 (Del.Ch.1968); Bastian v. Bourns, Inc., 256 A.2d 680 (Del.Ch.1969). The basic situation for the application of the rule is the one in which the parent has received a benefit to the exclusion and at the expense of the subsidiary.

A parent does indeed owe a fiduciary duty to its subsidiary when there are parent-subsidiary dealings. However, this alone will not evoke the intrinsic fairness standard. This standard will be applied only when the fiduciary duty is accompanied by self-dealing - the situation when a parent is on both sides of a transaction with its subsidiary. Self-dealing occurs when the parent, by virtue of its domination of the subsidiary, causes the subsidiary to act in such a way that the parent receives something from the subsidiary to the exclusion of, and detriment to, the minority stockholders of the subsidiary.

We turn now to the facts. The plaintiff argues that, from 1960 through 1966, Sinclair caused Sinven to pay out such excessive dividends that the industrial development of Sinven was effectively prevented, and it became in reality a corporation in dissolution.

From 1960 through 1966, Sinven paid out $108,000,000 in dividends ($38,000,000 in excess of Sinven's earnings during the same period). The Chancellor held that Sinclair caused these dividends to be paid during a period when it had a need for large amounts of cash. The Chancellor, applying the intrinsic fairness standard, held that Sinclair did not sustain its burden of proving that these dividends were intrinsically fair to the minority stockholders of Sinven.

Since it is admitted that the dividends were paid in strict compliance with 8 Del.C. s 170, the alleged excessiveness of the payments alone would not state a cause of action. Nevertheless, compliance with the applicable statute may not, under all circumstances, justify all dividend payments. If a plaintiff can meet his burden of proving that a dividend cannot be grounded on any reasonable business objective, then the courts can and will interfere with the board's decision to pay the dividend.

Sinclair contends that it is improper to apply the intrinsic fairness standard to dividend payments even when the board which voted for the dividends is completely dominated.

We do not accept the argument that the intrinsic fairness test can never be applied to a dividend declaration by a dominated board, although a dividend declaration by a dominated board will not inevitably demand the application of the intrinsic fairness standard. If such a dividend is in essence self-dealing by the parent, then the intrinsic fairness standard is the proper standard. For example, suppose a parent dominates a subsidiary and its board of directors. The subsidiary has outstanding two classes of stock, X and Y. Class X is owned by the parent and Class Y is owned by minority stockholders of the subsidiary. If the subsidiary, at the direction of the parent, declares a dividend on its Class X stock only, this might well be self-dealing by the parent. It would be receiving something from the subsidiary to the exclusion of and detrimental to its minority stockholders. This self-dealing, coupled with the parent's fiduciary duty, would make intrinsic fairness the proper standard by which to evaluate the dividend payments.

Consequently it must be determined whether the dividend payments by Sinven were, in essence, self-dealing by Sinclair. The dividends resulted in great sums of money being transferred from Sinven to Sinclair. However, a proportionate share of this money was received by the minority shareholders of Sinven. Sinclair received nothing from Sinven to the exclusion of its minority stockholders. As such, these dividends were not self-dealing. We hold therefore that the Chancellor erred in applying the intrinsic fairness test as to these dividend payments. The business judgment standard should have been applied.

We conclude that the facts demonstrate that the dividend payments complied with the business judgment standard and with 8 Del.C. s 170. The motives for causing the declaration of dividends are immaterial unless the plaintiff can show that the dividend payments resulted from improper motives and amounted to waste. The plaintiff contends only that the dividend payments drained Sinven of cash to such an extent that it was prevented from expanding.

The plaintiff proved no business opportunities which came to Sinven independently and which Sinclair either took to itself or denied to Sinven. As a matter of fact, with two minor exceptions which resulted in losses, all of Sinven's operations have been conducted in Venezuela, and Sinclair had a policy of exploiting its oil properties located in different countries by subsidiaries located in the particular countries.

Therefore, Sinclair usurped no business opportunity belonging to Sinven. Since Sinclair received nothing from Sinven to the exclusion of and detriment to Sinven's minority stockholders, there was no self-dealing. Therefore, business judgment is the proper standard by which to evaluate Sinclair's expansion policies.

Since there is no proof of self-dealing on the part of Sinclair, it follows that the expansion policy of Sinclair and the methods used to achieve the desired result must, as far as Sinclair's treatment of Sinven is concerned, be tested by the standards of the business judgment rule. Accordingly, Sinclair's decision, absent fraud or gross overreaching, to achieve expansion through the medium of its subsidiaries, other than Sinven, must be upheld.

Even if Sinclair was wrong in developing these opportunities as it did, the question arises, with which subsidiaries should these opportunities have been shared? No evidence indicates a unique need or ability of Sinven to develop these opportunities. The decision of which subsidiaries would be used to implement Sinclair's expansion policy was one of business judgment with which a court will not interfere absent a showing of gross and palpable overreaching. No such showing has been made here.

Next, Sinclair argues that the Chancellor committed error when he held it liable to Sinven for breach of contract.

In 1961 Sinclair created Sinclair International Oil Company (hereafter International), a wholly owned subsidiary used for the purpose of coordinating all of Sinclair's foreign operations. All crude purchases by Sinclair were made thereafter through International.

On September 28, 1961, Sinclair caused Sinven to contract with International whereby Sinven agreed to sell all of its crude oil and refined products to International at specified prices. The contract provided for minimum and maximum quantities and prices. The plaintiff contends that Sinclair caused this contract to be breached in two respects. Although the contract called for payment on receipt, International's payments lagged as much as 30 days after receipt. Also, the contract required International to purchase at least a fixed minimum amount of crude and refined products from Sinven. International did not comply with this requirement.

Clearly, Sinclair's act of contracting with its dominated subsidiary was self-dealing. Under the contract Sinclair received the products produced by Sinven, and of course the minority shareholders of Sinven were not able to share in the receipt of these products. If the contract was breached, then Sinclair received these products to the detriment of Sinven's minority shareholders. We agree with the Chancellor's finding that the contract was breached by Sinclair, both as to the time of payments and the amounts purchased.

Although a parent need not bind itself by a contract with its dominated subsidiary, Sinclair chose to operate in this manner. As Sinclair has received the benefits of this contract, so must it comply with the contractual duties.

Under the intrinsic fairness standard, Sinclair must prove that its causing Sinven not to enforce the contract was intrinsically fair to the minority shareholders of Sinven. Sinclair has failed to meet this burden. Late payments were clearly breaches for which Sinven should have sought and received adequate damages. As to the quantities purchased, Sinclair argues that it purchased all the products produced by Sinven. This, however, does not satisfy the standard of intrinsic fairness. Sinclair has failed to prove that Sinven could not possibly have produced or someway have obtained the contract minimums. As such, Sinclair must account on this claim.

Finally, Sinclair argues that the Chancellor committed error in refusing to allow it a credit or setoff of all benefits provided by it to Sinven with respect to all the alleged damages. The Chancellor held that setoff should be allowed on specific transactions, e.g., benefits to Sinven under the contract with International, but denied an over all setoff against all damages claimed. We agree with the Chancellor, although the point may well be moot in view of our holding that Sinclair is not required to account for the alleged excessiveness of the dividend payments.

We will therefore reverse that part of the Chancellor's order that requires Sinclair to account to Sinven for damages sustained as a result of dividends paid between 1960 and 1966, and by reason of the denial to Sinven of expansion during that period. We will affirm the remaining portion of that order and remand the cause for further proceedings.

Fairness Standard

Given Sinclair Oil's dominate ownership, is the court's reasoning regarding the large dividends and drilling opportunities persuasive? Should application of the fairness test in such situations turn on whether the parent corporation has received a benefit that was not available to the minority shareholders of the subsidiary corporation? Many believe that "entire fairness" is the standard that should be used in any transaction between a controlling parent corporation and a subsidiary. See ALI Principles of Corporate Governance §§ 5.10-5.12 and Siegel, *The Erosion of the Law of Controlling Shareholders*, 24 Del. J. Corp. L. 27 (1999).

E. SALE OF CONTROLLING INTEREST

CASE PROBLEM 12-5

Assume the same facts as Case Problem 12-1, with the following changes:

1. InstruTech owns 65 percent of HealthTools' outstanding stock.

2. The Outsiders were appointed as a special committee (the "Committee") to evaluate the terms of the merger on behalf of HealthTools' directors and shareholders, and the Report was made available to the Committee. The Committee carefully evaluated the entire record and unanimously objected to the terms of the merger. This led to HealthTools' board, by a 4-3 vote, rejecting the merger.

3. InstruTech's senior management responded by scrapping the merger plan and selling its 65 percent interest in HealthTools' common stock to Horton Industries, Inc. ("Horton") for $150 million. Horton's management team has a well-known reputation for taking aggressive actions to maximize its position at the expense of minority shareholders. The sale was unanimously approved by InstruTech's board.

4. HealthTools' board immediately resigned in mass pursuant to a provision in the stock sales agreement, and a new slate of directors, designated by Horton, was installed.

5. Pursuant to a provision in the stock sales agreement, Horton caused HealthTools' new board to approve the grant of a non-exclusive, 15-year license in the Patents to InstruTech on the same royalty terms that are used in stand-alone, arms-length licenses.

6. After the sale, Horton caused HealthTools to engage in a number of transactions with a Swedish corporation owned by Horton that allegedly reduced the value of HealthTools' business operations. Among other things, the Swedish entity was given substantial control rights over many of Healthtools' future product development efforts. The trading price of HealthTools' public stock has consistently declined.

What is the likelihood of the Group prevailing in an action to recover from InstruTech and its board members the losses they have sustained as a result of

InstruTech's block stock sale to Horton? How should the Group frame its allegations? What standard of review should the court use? Who bears the burden of proof?

HARRIS V. CARTER
582 A.2d 222 (Del.Ch. 1990)

ALLEN, Chancellor.

Two distinct groups of defendants have moved to dismiss the Amended and Supplemental Complaint in this action, ("amended complaint"). They assert that the amended complaint does not state a claim upon which relief may be granted. I conclude that the amended complaint does state a claim upon which relief may be granted against those defendants who are alleged to have negligently sold control of Atlas to a buyer who allegedly looted the corporation.

The litigation arises from the negotiation and sale by one group of defendants (the Carter group) of a control block of Atlas stock to Frederic Mascolo; the resignation of the Carter group as directors and the appointment of the Mascolo defendants as directors of Atlas, and, finally, the alleged looting of Atlas by Mascolo and persons associated with him. Insofar as the Carter defendants are concerned it is alleged that they were negligent and that their negligence breached a duty that, in the circumstances, they owed to the corporation. It is not claimed that they stand as an insurer of the corporation generally, but that the specific circumstances of their sale of control should have raised a warning that Mascolo was dishonest. The claims against Mascolo are more conventional: effectuation of self-dealing transactions on unfair terms. The Mascolo group is principally Messrs. Mascolo and Ager.

Plaintiff is a minority shareholder of Atlas. He brought this action after the change in control from the Carter group to the Mascolo group had occurred. The action was brought originally as a class action to enjoin a transaction that plaintiff alleged would constitute a breach of the directors' fiduciary duty; to rescind certain transactions effected by the Mascolo group; and, to collect damages from the Mascolo group. In addition the original complaint sought to collect damages from the Carter defendants for an alleged breach of a duty of care to minority shareholders in connection with the sale of control of Atlas to Mascolo.

In general the claims asserted against the Carter group in the amended complaint are of two types. More significantly it is alleged that the Carter group, qua shareholders, owed a duty of care to Atlas to take the steps that a reasonable person would take in the circumstances to investigate the bona fides of the person to whom they sold control. It is said that the duty was breached here, and that if it had been met the corporation would have been spared the losses that are alleged to have resulted from the transactions effected by the board under the domination of Mascolo. There is no allegation that the Carter group conspired with Mascolo. Indeed the Carter group did not sell for cash but for shares of common stock of a corporation that plaintiff claims was a worthless shell and which was later employed in the transactions that are said to constitute a looting of Atlas. Thus, accepting the allegations of the complaint, they suggest that the Carter group was misled to its own injury as well as the injury of Atlas and its other shareholders. This claim was set forth in the original pleading.

The second claim against the Carter defendants relates to a $100,000 payment made by Atlas after the change in control. It is alleged this amount was paid to a broker who acted for the Carter group in connection with the sale of its Atlas stock. It is thus said to constitute a corporate waste.

With respect to the second group of defendants – the Mascolo defendants – the amended complaint alleges a series of complex corporate transactions effectuated once Mascolo took control of Atlas, and claims that those transactions wrongfully injured Atlas.

Atlas Energy Corporation is a Delaware corporation which, before Mascolo acquired control of it, engaged in oil and gas exploration and production. It conducted its business primarily through the acquisition of oil and gas properties which were resold to drilling programs. It then acted as sponsor and general partner of the drilling programs.

The Carter group, which collectively owned 52% of the stock of Atlas, and Mascolo entered into a Stock Exchange Agreement dated as of March 28, 1986. That agreement provided that the Carter group would exchange its Atlas stock for shares of stock held by Mascolo in a company called Insuranshares of America ("ISA") and contemplated a later merger between ISA and Atlas. ISA was described in the preamble to the Stock Exchange Agreement as "a company engaged in the insurance field by and through wholly-owned subsidiaries."

In the course of negotiations, the Mascolo group furnished the Carter group with a draft financial statement of ISA that reflected an investment in Life Insurance Company of America, a Washington corporation ("LICA"). The existence of a purported investment by ISA in LICA was fictitious. It is alleged that the draft ISA financial statement was sufficiently suspicious to put any reasonably prudent business person on notice that further investigation should be made. Indeed Atlas' chief financial officer analyzed the financial statement and raised several questions concerning its accuracy, none of which were pursued by the Carter group.

The Stock Exchange Agreement further provided that Mascolo would place in escrow 50,000 shares of Louisiana Bankshares Inc. 8% cumulative preferred stock, $10 par value. It was agreed that if Atlas consummated an exchange merger for all of the outstanding common stock of ISA on agreed upon terms within 365 days of the date of the Stock Exchange Agreement, the bank stock would be returned to Mascolo. If no merger took place within the specified time, then that stock was to be distributed pro rata to the Carter group members.

It was agreed, finally, that as part of the stock exchange transaction, the members of the Carter group would resign their positions as Atlas directors in a procedure that assured that Mascolo and his designees would be appointed as replacements.

The gist of plaintiff's claim against the Carter defendants is the allegation that those defendants had reason to suspect the integrity of the Mascolo group, but failed to conduct even a cursory investigation into any of several suspicious aspects of the transaction: the unaudited financial statement, the mention of LICA in negotiations but not in the representations concerning ISA's subsidiaries, and the ownership of the subsidiaries themselves. Such an investigation, argues plaintiff, would have revealed the structure of ISA to be fragile indeed, with minimal capitalization and no productive assets.

The charges against the Mascolo defendants are that the Mascolo defendants caused the effectuation of self-dealing transactions designed to benefit members of the Mascolo group, at the expense of Atlas.

Mascolo purchased the Carter group's stock on March 28, 1986. Also on that day the newly elected Atlas board (i.e., the Mascolo defendants) adopted resolutions that, among other things: (a) changed Atlas' name to Insuranshares of America, Inc.; (b) effectuated a reverse stock split converting each existing Atlas share into .037245092 new shares, thus reducing the 26,849,175 Atlas shares to approximately 1,000,000 shares; (c) reduced Atlas authorized capitalization to 10,000,000 shares, $.10 par value; (d) approved the acquisition of all of the outstanding common stock of ISA in consideration for 3,000,000 post- reverse stock split Atlas shares; (e) elected defendant Mascolo as chairman of the board, Johnson as president, Devaney as treasurer and Ager as vice president; (f) approved the negotiation of the sale of Atlas' oil properties "with a series of potential buyers"; (g) approved the purchase of 200,000 shares of the common stock of Hughes Chemical Corporation at $3 per share with an option to acquire an additional 1,000,000 shares at $5 per share for a 12–month period and for $10 per share for a consecutive 12–month period; (h) ratified the actions of the company's prior officers and directors and released them from any liability arising as a consequence of their relationship to the company; and (i) authorized payment of a $100,000 commission to the company which found the buyers of the Carter group stock.

Plaintiff asserts that ISA is nothing more than a corporate shell. Pursuant to the Stock Exchange Agreement Mascolo acquired a controlling (52%) stock interest in Atlas in exchange for 518,335 ISA shares. Atlas then acquired all the outstanding ISA shares in exchange for 3,000,000 newly issued shares of Atlas common stock. As a result of that transaction, the Mascolo group as a whole came to own 75% of Atlas' shares. The minority shareholders of Atlas saw their proportionate ownership of Atlas reduced from 48% before the ISA transaction to 12% upon its consummation. For Atlas to exchange 3,000,000 of its shares for the stock of this "corporate shell" was, argues plaintiff, equivalent to issuing Atlas stock to the Mascolo group (the holders of the ISA stock) without consideration.

I turn to the Carter defendants motion to dismiss for failure to state a claim upon which relief may be granted. This motion raises novel questions of Delaware law. Stated generally the most basic of these questions is whether a controlling shareholder or group may under any circumstances owe a duty of care to the corporation in connection with the sale of a control block of stock. If such a duty may be said to exist under certain circumstances the questions in this case then become whether the facts alleged in the amended complaint would permit the finding that such a duty arose in connection with the sale to the Mascolo group and was breached. In this inquiry one applies the permissive standard appropriate for motions to dismiss: if on any state of facts that may reasonably be inferred from the pleaded facts plaintiff would be entitled to a judgment, a claim that will survive a Rule 12(b) motion has been stated..

A number of cases may be cited in support of the proposition that when transferring control of a corporation to another, a controlling shareholder may, in some circumstances, have a duty to investigate the bona fides of the buyer – that is, in those circumstances, to take such steps as a reasonable person would take to ascertain that the buyer does not intend or is unlikely to plan any depredations of the corporation. The circumstance to which these cases refer is the existence of facts that would give rise to suspicion by a reasonably prudent person. The leading case is Insuranshares Corporation, 35 F.Supp. 22 (E.D.Pa.1940).

In that case defendants, who comprised the entire board of directors of the corporation involved, sold their 27% stock interest in the corporation and resigned as directors. The resignations were done seriatim, in a way that permitted the designation of the buyers as successor directors. The buyers proceeded to loot the corporation. As here, the sellers contended that they could have no liability for the wrongs that followed their sale. They merely sold their stock and resigned. These were acts that they were privileged to do, they claimed. Judge Kirkpatrick rejected this position:

> Those who control a corporation, either through majority stock ownership, ownership of large blocks of stock less than a majority, office holding, management contracts, or otherwise, owe some duty to the corporation in respect of the transfer of the control to outsiders. The law has long ago reached the point where it is recognized that such persons may not be wholly oblivious of the interest of everyone but themselves, even in the act of parting with control, and that, under certain circumstances, they may be held liable for whatever injury to the corporation made possible by the transfer. Without attempting any general definition, and stating the duty in minimum terms as applicable to the facts of this case, it may be said that the owners of control are under a duty not to transfer it to outsiders if the circumstances surrounding the proposed transfer are such as to awaken suspicion and put a prudent man on his guard—unless a reasonably adequate investigation discloses such facts as would convince a reasonable person that no fraud is intended or likely to result.

> If, after such investigation, the sellers are deceived by false representations, there might not be liability, but if the circumstances put the seller on notice and if no adequate investigation is made and harm follows, then liability also follows.

35 F.Supp. at 25.

This statement represents the majority view on the subject. There is a minority view. Judging from a single fifty year old case, in New York a controlling shareholder may apparently not be held liable in any sale of control setting, other than one in which he had actual knowledge of a planned depredation by his buyer. In Gerdes v. Reynolds, 28 N.Y.S.2d 622, 652–654 (1941), [the] court concluded that a selling majority shareholder could be held to account for the looting of the corporation by his buyer only if he had knowledge of the improper purpose of his buyer.

Although there are few cases applying the principle of the Insuranshares case that do fix liability on a seller, it is the principle of Insuranshares and not the actual notice rule of Levy that has commanded the respect of later courts. In Swinney v. Keebler Company, 480 F.2d 573, 577 (1973), the Second Circuit Court of Appeals acknowledged Insuranshares as "the leading case." It aptly summarized the principle of that case:

> Liability was predicated upon breach of a duty not to transfer control since the circumstances surrounding the transfer were "such as to awaken suspicion and put a prudent man on his guard—unless a reasonably adequate investigation discloses such facts as would convince a reasonable person that no fraud is intended or likely to result." 35 F.Supp. at 25.

The appeals court went on:

> We agree with the district court that "[t]o require knowledge of the intended looting on the part of the seller in order to impose liability on him places a premium on the 'head in the sand' approach to corporate sales," [Swinney v. Keebler Co.] 329 F.Supp. [216] at 223, and with Judge Friendly that "[t]o hold the seller for delinquencies of the new directors only if he knew the purchaser was an intending looter is not a sufficient sanction." Essex Universal Corporation v. Yates, 305 F.2d 572, 581 (2nd Cir.1962) (concurring opinion).

While Delaware law has not addressed this specific question, one is not left without guidance from our decided cases. Several principles deducible from that law are pertinent. First, is the principle that a shareholder has a right to sell his or her stock and in the ordinary case owes no duty in that connection to other shareholders when acting in good faith. Frantz Manufacturing Co. v. EAC Industries, Del.Supr., 501 A.2d 401, 408 (1985).

Equally well established is the principle that when a shareholder presumes to exercise control over a corporation, to direct its actions, that shareholder assumes a fiduciary duty of the same kind as that owed by a director to the corporation. Sterling v. Mayflower Hotel Corp., Del.Supr., 93 A.2d 107, 109–10 (1952). A sale of controlling interest in a corporation, at least where, as is alleged here, that sale is coupled with an agreement for the sellers to resign from the board of directors in such a way as to assure that the buyer's designees assume that corporate office, does, in my opinion, involve or implicate the corporate mechanisms so as to call this principle into operation.

More generally, it does not follow from the proposition that ordinarily a shareholder has a right to sell her stock to whom and on such terms as she deems expedient, that no duty may arise from the particular circumstances to take care in the exercise of that right. It is established American legal doctrine that, unless privileged, each person owes a duty to those who may foreseeably be harmed by her action to take such steps as a reasonably prudent person would take in similar circumstances to avoid such harm to others. *Palsgraf v. Long Island Railroad Co.*, 248 N.Y. 339, 162 N.E. 99 (1928). While this principle arises from the law of torts and not the law of corporations or of fiduciary duties, that distinction is not, I think, significant unless the law of corporations or of fiduciary duties somehow privileges a selling shareholder by exempting her from the reach of this principle. The principle itself is one of great generality and, if not negated by privilege, would apply to a controlling shareholder who negligently places others foreseeably in the path of injury.

That a shareholder may sell her stock (or that a director may resign his office) is a right that, with respect to the principle involved, is no different, for example, than the right that a licensed driver has to operate a motor vehicle upon a highway. The right exists, but it is not without conditions and limitations, some established by positive regulation, some by common-law. Thus, to continue the parallel, the driver owes a duty of care to her passengers because it is foreseeable that they may be injured if, through inattention or otherwise, the driver involves the car she is operating in a collision. In the typical instance a seller of corporate stock can be expected to have no similar apprehension of risks to others from her own inattention. But, in some circumstances, the seller of a control block of stock may or should reasonably foresee danger to other shareholders; with her sale of stock will also go control over the corporation and with it the opportunity to misuse that power to the injury of such other shareholders. Thus, the reason that a duty of care is recognized in any situation is fully present in this situation. I can find no universal privilege arising from the corporate form that exempts a controlling shareholder who sells corporate control from the wholesome reach of this common-law duty. Certainly I cannot read the Supreme Court's opinion in Frantz, supra, as intending to lay down a rule applicable to the question here posed.

Thus, I conclude that while a person who transfers corporate control to another is surely not a surety for his buyer, when the circumstances would alert a reasonably prudent person to a risk that his buyer is dishonest or in some material respect not truthful, a duty devolves upon the seller to make such inquiry as a reasonably prudent person would make, and generally to exercise care so that others who will be affected by his actions should not be injured by wrongful conduct.

The cases that have announced this principle have laid some stress on the fact that they involved not merely a sale of stock, but a sale of control over the corporation. Thus, in Insuranshares, the agreement that the sellers would resign from the board in a way that would facilitate the buyers immediately assuming office was given importance. That circumstance is pleaded here as well.

One cannot determine (and may not on this type of motion determine) whether Mr. Carter and those who acted with him were in fact negligent in a way that proximately caused injury to the corporation. Indeed one cannot determine now whether the circumstances that surrounded the negotiations with Mascolo were such as to have awakened suspicion in a person of ordinary prudence. The test of a Rule 12(b)(6) motion is, as noted above, permissive. It is sufficient to require denial of this motion to dismiss that I cannot now say as a matter of law that under no state of facts that might be proven could it be held that a duty arose, to the corporation and its other shareholders, to make further inquiry and was breached. In so concluding I assume without deciding that a duty of care of a controlling shareholder that may in special circumstances arise in connection with a sale of corporate control is breached only by grossly negligent conduct. Cf. Lewis v. Aronson, 473 A.2d at 812.

That Mr. Carter may well have been misled to his own detriment may be a factor affecting the question whether a duty to inquire arose, as Carter might be assumed to be a prudent man when dealing with his own property. But that assumption is essentially evidentiary and can be given no weight on this motion.

For the foregoing reasons the pending motions will be denied.

ESSEX UNIVERSAL CORP. V. YATES
305 F.2d 572 (2d Cir. 1962)

Lumbard, Chief Judge.

This appeal from the district court's summary judgment in favor of the defendant raises the question whether a contract for the sale of 28.3 per cent of the stock of a corporation is, under New York law, invalid as against public policy solely because it includes a clause giving the purchaser an option to require a majority of the existing directors to replace themselves, by a process of seriatim resignation, with a majority designated by the purchaser. Despite the disagreement evidenced by the diversity of our opinions, my brethren and I agree that such a provision does not on its face render the contract illegal and unenforceable, and thus that it was improper to grant summary judgment. Judge Friendly would reject the defense of illegality without further inquiry concerning the provision itself (as distinguished from any contention that control could not be safely transferred to the particular purchaser). Accordingly, the grant of summary judgment is reversed and the case is remanded for trial of the question of the legality of the contested provision and such further proceedings as may be proper on the other issues raised by the pleadings.

The defendant Herbert J. Yates, a resident of California, was president and chairman of the board of directors of Republic Pictures Corporation, a New York corporation which at the time relevant to this suit had 2,004,190 shares of common stock outstanding. Republic's stock was listed and traded on the New York Stock Exchange. In August 1957, Essex Universal Corporation, a Delaware corporation owning stock in various diversified businesses, learned of the possibility of purchasing from Yates an interest in Republic. Negotiations proceeded rapidly, and on August 28 Yates and Joseph Harris, the president of Essex, signed a contract in which Essex agreed to buy, and Yates agreed 'to sell or cause to be sold' at least 500,000 and not more than 600,000 shares of Republic stock. The price was set at eight dollars a share, roughly two dollars above the then market price on the Exchange. In addition to other provisions not relevant to the present motion, the contract contained the following paragraph:

Upon and as a condition to the closing of this transaction if requested by Buyer at least ten (10) days prior to the date of the closing:

(a) Seller will deliver to Buyer the resignations of the majority of the directors of Republic.

(b) Seller will cause a special meeting of the board of directors of Republic to be held, legally convened pursuant to law and the by-laws of Republic, and simultaneously with the acceptance of the directors' resignations set forth in paragraph 6(a) immediately preceding will cause nominees of Buyer to be elected directors of Republic in place of the resigned directors.'

Before the date of the closing, as provided in the contract, Yates notified Essex that he would deliver 566,223 shares, or 28.3 per cent of the Republic stock then outstanding, and Essex formally requested Yates to arrange for the replacement of a majority of Republic's directors with Essex nominees pursuant to paragraph 6 of the contract. This was to be accomplished by having eight of the fourteen directors resign seriatim, each in turn being replaced by an Essex nominee elected by the others; such a procedure was in form permissible under the charter and by-laws of Republic, which empowered the board to choose the successor of any of its members who might resign.

Appellant's contention that the provision for transfer of director control is separable from the rest of the contract can quickly be rejected. We see no significance in the fact that the contract gave Essex only an option to have the directors replaced, rather than providing directly for such a transfer of control, and the most elementary application of the parol evidence rule forbids us to entertain Essex' argument that there is a factual issue as to whether the transfer clause was central to the negotiations or only an afterthought.

It is established beyond question under New York law that it is illegal to sell corporate office or management control by itself (that is, accompanied by no stock or insufficient stock to carry voting control). McClure v. Law, 161 N.Y. 78, 55 N.E. 388 (1899); Ballantine v. Ferretti, 28 N.Y.S.2d 668, 678-680 (N.Y. County Sup.Ct.1941). The same rule apparently applies in all jurisdictions where the question has arisen. The rationale of the rule is undisputable: persons enjoying management control hold it on behalf of the corporation's stockholders, and therefore may not regard it as their own personal property to dispose of as they wish. Any other rule would violate the most fundamental principle of corporate democracy, that management must represent and be chosen by, or at least with the consent of, those who own the corporation.

Essex was, however, contracting with Yates for the purchase of a very substantial percentage of Republic stock. If, by virtue of the voting power carried by this stock, it could have elected a majority of the board of directors, then the contract was not a simple agreement for the sale of office to one having no ownership interest in the corporation, and the question of its legality would require further analysis. Such stock voting control would incontestably belong to the owner of a majority of the voting stock, and it is commonly known that equivalent power usually accrues to the owner of 28.3% of the stock. For the purpose of this analysis, I shall assume that Essex was contracting to acquire a majority of the Republic stock, deferring consideration of the situation where, as here, only 28.3% is to be acquired.

Republic's board of directors at the time of the aborted closing had fourteen members divided into three classes, each class being 'as nearly as may be' of the same size. Directors were elected for terms of three years, one class being elected at each annual shareholder meeting on the first Tuesday in April. Thus, absent the immediate replacement of directors provided for in this contract, Essex as the hypothetical new majority shareholder of the corporation could not have obtained managing control in the form of a majority of the board in the normal course of events until April 1959, some eighteen months after the sale of the stock. The first question before us then is whether an agreement to accelerate the transfer of management control, in a manner legal in form under the corporation's charter and by-laws, violates the public policy of New York.

There is no question of the right of a controlling shareholder under New York law normally to derive a premium from the sale of a controlling block of stock. In other words, there was no impropriety per se in the fact that Yates was to receive more per share than the generally prevailing market price for Republic stock. Levy v. American Beverage Corp., 265 App.Div. 208, 218, 38 N.Y.S.2d 517, 526 (1st Dept. 1942).

The next question is whether it is legal to give and receive payment for the immediate transfer of management control to one who has achieved majority share control but would not otherwise be able to convert that share control into operating control for some time. I think that it is.

A fair generalization may be that a holder of corporate control will not, as a fiduciary, be permitted to profit from facilitating actions on the part of the purchasers of control which are detrimental to the interests of the corporation or the remaining shareholders. There is, however, no suggestion that the transfer of control over Republic to Essex carried any such threat to the interests of the corporation or its other shareholders.

Given this principle that it is permissible for a seller thus to choose to facilitate immediate transfer of management control, I can see no objection to a contractual provision requiring him to do so as a condition of the sale. Indeed, a New York court has upheld an analogous contractual term requiring the board of directors to elect the nominees of the purchasers of a majority stock interest to officerships. San Remo Copper Mining Co. v. Moneuse, 149 App.Div. 26, 133 N.Y.S. 509 (1st Dept. 1912). The court said that since the purchaser was about to acquire 'absolute control' of the corporation, 'it certainly did not destroy the validity of the contract that by one of its terms defendant was to be invested with this power of control at once, upon acquiring the stock, instead of waiting for the next annual meeting.' 149 App.Div. at 28, 133 N.Y.S. at 511.

The easy and immediate transfer of corporate control to new interests is ordinarily beneficial to the economy and it seems inevitable that such transactions would be discouraged if the purchaser of a majority stock interest were required to wait some period before his purchase of control could become effective. Conversely it would greatly hamper the efforts of any existing majority group to dispose of its interest if it could not assure the purchaser of immediate control over corporation operations. I can see no reason why a purchaser of majority control should not ordinarily be permitted to make his control effective from the moment of the transfer of stock.

Thus if Essex had been contracting to purchase a majority of the stock of Republic, it would have been entirely proper for the contract to contain the provision for immediate replacement of directors. Although in the case at bar only 28.3 per cent of the stock was involved, it is commonly known that a person or group owning so large a percentage of the voting stock of a corporation which, like Republic, has at least the 1,500 shareholders normally requisite to listing on the New York Stock Exchange, is almost certain to have share control as a practical matter. If Essex was contracting to acquire what in reality would be equivalent to ownership of a majority of stock, i.e., if it would as a practical certainty have been guaranteed of the stock voting power to choose a majority of the directors of Republic in due course, there is no reason why the contract should not similarly be legal. Whether Essex was thus to acquire the equivalent of majority stock control would, if the issue is properly raised by the defendants, be a factual issue to be determined by the district court on remand.

Because 28.3 per cent of the voting stock of a publicly owned corporation is usually tantamount to majority control, I would place the burden of proof on this issue on Yates as the party attacking the legality of the transaction. Thus, unless on remand Yates chooses to raise the question whether the block of stock in question carried the equivalent of majority control, it is my view that the trial court should regard the contract as legal and proceed to consider the other issues raised by the pleadings. If Yates chooses to raise the issue, it will, on my view, be necessary for him to prove the existence of circumstances which would have prevented Essex from electing a majority of the Republic board of directors in due course. It will not be enough for Yates to raise merely hypothetical possibilities of opposition by the other Republic shareholders to Essex' assumption of management control. Rather, it will be necessary for him to show that, assuming neutrality on the part of the retiring management, there was at the time some concretely foreseeable reason why Essex' wishes would not have prevailed in shareholder voting held in due course. In other words, I would require him to show that there was at the time of the contract some other organized block of stock of sufficient size to outvote the block Essex was buying, or else some circumstance making it likely that enough of the holders of the remaining Republic stock would band together to keep Essex from control.

Reversed and remanded for further proceedings not inconsistent with the judgment of this court.

FRIENDLY, Circuit Judge (concurring).

I have no doubt that many contracts, drawn by competent and responsible counsel, for the purchase of blocks of stock from interests thought to 'control' a corporation although owning less than a majority, have contained provisions like paragraph 6 of the contract sub judice. However, developments over the past decades seem to me to show that such a clause violates basic principles of corporate democracy. To be sure, stockholders who have allowed a set of directors to be placed in office, whether by their vote or their failure to vote, must recognize that death, incapacity or other hazard may prevent a director from serving a full term, and that they will have no voice as to his immediate successor. But the stockholders are entitled to expect that, in that event, the remaining directors will fill the vacancy in the exercise of their fiduciary responsibility. A mass seriatim resignation directed by a selling stockholder, and the filling of vacancies by his henchmen at the dictation of a purchaser and without any consideration of the character of the latter's nominees, are beyond what the stockholders contemplated or should have been expected to contemplate. This seems to me a wrong to the corporation and the other stockholders which the law ought not countenance, whether the selling stockholder has received a premium or not. Right in this Court we have seen many cases where sudden shifts of corporate control have caused serious injury. To hold the seller for delinquencies of the new directors only if he knew the purchaser was an intending looter is not a sufficient sanction. The difficulties of proof are formidable even if receipt of too high a premium creates a presumption of such knowledge, and, all too often, the doors are locked only after the horses have been stolen. Stronger medicines are needed – refusal to enforce a contract with such a clause, even though this confers an unwarranted benefit on a defaulter, and continuing responsibility of the former directors for negligence of the new ones until an election has been held.

Hence, I am inclined to think that if I were sitting on the New York Court of Appeals, I would hold a provision like Paragraph 6 violative of public policy save when it was entirely plain that a new election would be a mere formality-i.e., when the seller owned more than 50% of the stock. As a judge of this Court, my task is the more modest one of predicting how the judges of the New York Court of Appeals would rule, and I must make this prediction on the basis of legal materials rather than of personal acquaintance or hunch. Also, for obvious reasons, the prospective technique is unavailable when a Federal court is deciding an issue of state law.

At the very least the problems and uncertainties arising from the proposed line of demarcation are great enough, and its advantages small enough, that in my view a Federal court would do better simply to overrule the defense here, thereby accomplishing what is obviously the 'just' result in this particular case, and leave the development of doctrine in this area to the State, which has primary concern for it.

F. OPPRESSION IN CLOSELY HELD CORPORATIONS

CASE PROBLEM 12-6

Manu Inc. ("Manu") is a specialized manufacturing corporation that has been in business for 22 years. Walter and Jane Smith, husband and wife, founded the business and own 60 percent of Manu's outstanding common stock.

They are Manu's only directors. Manu has always been profitable. Walter annually draws a salary and bonuses totaling $400,000 to $500,000.

Manu has had four key employees, including Linda, for many years. Approximately five years ago, they were each granted, as additional compensation, 10 percent of Manu's outstanding common stock. Historically, they have each annually been paid a salary and bonus equal to $180,000 to $210,000. There has never been a shareholder buy-sell agreement between Manu and its stockholders.

Seven months ago, Walter and Linda had a major falling out over the termination of a junior employee. Linda wailed in protest until Walter finally exclaimed, "That's it, Linda. I've had it with you and your complaining. You are finished." Linda was instantly terminated and paid six months of severance pursuant to a simple employment agreement.

After cooling off for a month, Linda sent Walter an email requesting that either Manu or Walter buy her Manu stock. Walter's respond was curt: "Manu doesn't need your stock. I don't want your stock. There is no market for the stock, and there never will be. Manu has never paid a dividend and never will. As you well know, Manu pays its earnings to the team that makes it happen. You are no longer part of that team."

Linda wants to know if she has any rights as a minority shareholder in this situation. What additional facts would you like to have? In a legal proceeding, how should the issues and allegations be framed on behalf of Linda? What standard of review should the court use?

BONAVITA v. CORDO
692 A.2d 119 (Ch. Div. 1996)

LESEMANN, J.S.C.

Gerald Bonavita, the holder of one-half the stock of Corbo Jewelers, Inc., instituted this suit claiming that the corporation was deadlocked and that he was the victim of oppression by Alan Corbo, holder of the other 50% of the corporation's stock, who is also its president and chief executive officer. He sought relief under *N.J.S.A.* 14A:12-7 and also under this court's common-law power to remedy such oppression. Gerald Bonavita died before trial, and the suit has been continued by his executrix and widow, Julia Bonavita.

The oppression claim is based on Alan Corbo's rejection of plaintiff's attempt to have the corporation either pay dividends or buy out the Bonavita stock interests. With both demands rejected, plaintiff claims she is locked into a corporation which provides her with no benefit of any kind. At the same time, she says, Alan Corbo and his three sons are employed full time by the corporation, and his wife and daughter are employed part time. Thus, the Corbo half of the stock ownership receives substantial benefits-with fringe benefits, the total annual family compensation is between $300,000 and $400,000-while the Bonavita half receives nothing.

Defendants deny any obligation to buy the Bonavita stock. They also maintain that the refusal to pay dividends is merely an application of the "business judgment rule" and is amply justified by sound business reasons. There is no evidence that defendant's "no-dividend" policy is motivated by animus toward plaintiff, or by anything other than their view of what is best for the corporation. Thus, the case presents the question of the extent to which the business judgment rule will insulate a corporation's power structure from a claim of oppression when application of that rule has the effect of providing substantial benefits to some of the holders of the corporation's stock and no benefits to the others.

In the mid 1980's, as Gerald Bonavita aged and his health deteriorated, he told Alan Corbo that he wanted to retire and wanted to have the corporation (or Alan) purchase his stock. Some discussions ensued, but the parties did not reach agreement on a buy out. Gradually, Bonavita reduced the time he was spending on corporate business, until he completely retired in March 1991. Julia continued working for a short time thereafter, until she too ceased all work in January 1992.

Plaintiff's complaint was filed in December 1991. It alleges a deadlock within the meaning of *N.J.S.A.* 14A:12-7 and also alleges stockholder "oppression" within the meaning of that statute. Plaintiff sought interim relief, and the court, pursuant to Subsection (1) of *N.J.S.A.* 14A:12-7 appointed Thomas Herten, Esq., as a "provisional director" to function while the litigation proceeded.

In early 1994, Bonavita formally requested the corporation to pay a dividend of approximately $650,000 to each of the two shareholders-a total of $1,300,000. That sum represented a portion of the corporation's retained earnings on which income tax had already been paid-a point discussed further below. The request was denied, with Alan Corbo opposed to the request and the provisional director declining to join Bonavita in what he regarded as a matter of "business judgment." An attempt to have the court overrule that decision while the suit was pending was unsuccessful and thus no dividend was paid. Bonavita thereafter modified his request to propose a smaller dividend, but that, too, was denied, and Alan Corbo has remained, ever since, adamantly opposed to the payment of any substantial dividend.

Although plaintiff claims there is a corporate "deadlock," that charge is not sharply drawn, and it is not clear just what constitutes the alleged deadlock of which plaintiff complains. *N.J.S.A.* 14A:12-7 contains two deadlock provisions. Subsection (1)(a) provides that the court may take remedial action upon proof that:

> [t]he shareholders of the corporation are so divided in voting power that, for a period which includes the time when two consecutive annual meetings were or should have been held, they have failed to elect successors to directors whose terms have expired or would have expired upon the election and qualification of their successors.

As noted above, the Corbo certificate of incorporation requires three directors. A by-law provision of questionable validity provides for two directors and, in fact, the corporation has functioned for many years with just two directors.

Plaintiff seems to claim that three directors are required; that the by-law amendment providing for a two-member board is invalid; and that the failure to select a three-member board evidences deadlock. The claim is not persuasive. Gerald Bonavita had long acquiesced in a board composed of two directors and had voted to amend the by-laws to authorize such a board. An attempt to change that position now would raise substantial issues of waiver and estoppel.

Plaintiff claims that the rejection of her demand for payment of a dividend or a buy-out of the Bonavita stock constitutes such an inability to effect corporate action. However, rather than characterizing the refusal to accede to her demands as an inability "to effect action," it is more accurate to describe those decisions as what they really are: determinations by defendants to reject plaintiff's demands.

In short, this is not a case where a corporation is unable to act. It can act. And it did act. It acted by denying plaintiff's demands. And it is the result of that action-not an inability to act-which is the basis for plaintiff's claim that she has been left in a hopeless, "no-win" situation. Whether those actions, leading to those results, constitute shareholder oppression is the significant issue presented.

The essence of plaintiff's claim is that the corporation, as operated by defendant Alan Corbo, provides substantial benefits for Alan Corbo and his family but no benefits for Bonavita. That is certainly an accurate statement.

As noted, the six Corbo family members on the corporate payroll realize approximately $400,000 per year in salary and other benefits. And while there is no claim that the salaries are excessive, neither was there a showing that if the "inside" employment were terminated those family members could earn as much elsewhere. In addition, of course, a job in the family business probably provides considerably more security than one might find in other employment.

Such employment is, of course, a frequent and perfectly proper benefit of stockholders in a closed corporation. The difficulty here is that the benefit flows in one direction only: to the Corbos, and not to Bonavita, and there is no compensating, alternative benefit for the Bonavita interests.

Mrs. Bonavita testified that she and her husband had no children who could move into the jewelry stores' operation. She also said, as did her husband in his *de bene esse* deposition before trial, that Mr. Bonavita had hoped to receive some benefits from the corporation before he died, and she has a similar hope now for herself. Otherwise, as she put it, her husband's interest, which she now owns, will be locked forever within Corbo Jewelers, Inc., and will be of absolutely no benefit to her, as it was of no benefit to her husband.

Absent employment, and absent any thought of long-term growth (inapplicable to Julia Bonavita as it was to Gerald Bonavita because of age), the normal corporate benefit which one in the position of Mr. or Mrs. Bonavita might expect would be the payment of dividends. This corporation, however, pays no dividends.

Plaintiff argues that Alan Corbo's "no dividend" policy is particularly harsh in view of the extraordinary financial condition of the corporation. That argument has considerable merit. As of June 30, 1993, the corporate balance sheet showed retained earnings of more than $5,000,000 and, after adjustment for treasury stock held as a liability, showed total stockholders' equity of approximately $4,600,000. In addition, on June 30, 1993, the corporation had cash, or liquid assets easily convertible into cash, of approximately $1,100,000 and current liabilities of only $12,000.

Defendants' stated reason for the refusal to pay dividends is the corporation's need for cash. Alan Corbo testified that the business is seasonal and that the corporation's continued profitability requires it to have substantial cash available to buy quickly when "bargains" become available. The ability to do that, without the need to borrow money and pay interest, he maintained, is one reason for the corporation's success over the years. Alan Corbo also pointed to the anticipated need for substantial renovation expenses for two of the corporation's stores which were approaching the end of leaseholds. In each case, he said, the landlord would require such expenditures as a condition to lease renewal.

While the facts just described strongly indicate that the corporation can well afford to pay dividends, a contrary decision could hardly be called irrational. Indeed, from Alan Corbo's point of view, the "no dividend" policy undoubtedly makes good sense. Since the primary benefit that he receives from the corporation is continued employment for himself and his family, the maintenance of a $5,000,000 earned surplus, large cash balances, and the non-payment of dividends is certainly in his best interest.

If the Corbo's and Bonavita were in essentially the same position, and each was similarly affected by the decision against paying dividends, that policy could hardly be characterized as anything other than a permissible exercise of business judgment. It would, presumably, be unassailable under the principle that a court will not normally overturn the exercise of such judgment..

But that, of course, is not this case. The problem here is that the operation of the corporation benefits only one of its shareholders-Alan Corbo. It provides no benefit of any kind to Julia Bonavita. She receives, and she will receive, no salary. The long range future of the corporation will not benefit her. And the "no dividend" policy is not a short term measure adopted to meet some pressing financial necessity. It is what Alan Corbo sees as the norm, and a policy from which he does not intend to deviate.

What Julia Bonavita has, and what she will continue to have so long as Alan Corbo is able to make the kinds of decisions he has been making, is a block of stock which has absolutely no value. Alan Corbo has made and will continue to make decisions which are in his best interests (and those of his family) and which ignore the wishes, needs, and best interests of his co-shareholder.

Given the effect of those actions on plaintiff, and regardless of whether defendants' actions might otherwise be termed "wrongful" or "illegal," there is no question that defendants' conduct has destroyed any reasonable expectation that plaintiff may have enjoyed respecting her stock interests. As such, it is clear from the decision of our Supreme Court in *Brenner v. Berkowitz*, 134 *N.J.* 488, 634 *A.*2d 1019 (1993), from other New Jersey case law, from comments and analyses by leading text writers, and from decisions in other states, that defendants' actions do indeed constitute "oppression" within the meaning of *N.J.S.A.* 14A:12-7.

N.J.S.A. 14A:12-7 sets out four remedies which a court "may" order to remedy "oppression." A court may appoint a custodian, appoint a provisional director, order a sale of the corporation's stock as provided below, or enter a judgment dissolving the corporation...The statutory power to order a stock sale, is a power to order an unwilling party to *sell* stock. It does not authorize a mandatory *purchase* by someone otherwise unwilling to buy.

In *Brenner v. Berkowitz, supra,* however, the Court held that the statutory list of remedies was non-exclusive and that the statute "was not intended to supersede the inherent, common law power of the Chancery Division to achieve equity." One of those equitable remedies, it held, is the power to order an involuntary *purchase* of stock held by one of the corporation's shareholders. That power, however, should be exercised sparingly.

Dissolution, of course, is a "last resort" remedy and something which neither defendant nor plaintiff wants here. What plaintiff does want is an order directing the corporation, or Alan Corbo, to purchase the Bonavita stock. That remedy, as noted, is available, but should be imposed only if the court is satisfied that it represents "the only practical alternative" to dissolution and that some lesser remedy will not suffice.

Neither side in this case has focused on any such alternative remedy. The reason for that seems clear: there is no reasonable, practical lesser remedy which will solve the problem inherent in this relationship and provide plaintiff with the long-range relief to which she is entitled. In short, no other remedy will work.

Thus, the corporation could certainly be ordered to pay the dividend which plaintiff requests-or at least some smaller dividend. But if that were done, what about next year? Or the year after? Alan Corbo will continue to see such payments as antithetical to the best interests of the corporation. And as he defines the best interests of the corporation-consistent with his best interests and those of his family-his viewpoint would hardly be irrational. But it will continue to be inconsistent with the reasonable expectations of the Bonavita interests.

Similarly, the court could continue the appointment of the present provisional director or appoint someone else with a direction for that person to participate more actively in the business of the corporation. But given the ongoing divergence between the interests of the two shareholders, no such appointment could "solve" the existing problem.

In sum, there is no rational basis on which this corporation can continue to exist and operate with half its shares owned by the Corbo interests and half by the Bonavita interests. There must be a "divorce." One method of accomplishing that, raised and explored at trial but shown to be unworkable, would be a division of the corporation's stores between the two shareholders. The difficulty with such a division is that there is nothing that Mrs. Bonavita could do with three or four of the seven Corbo stores. She is not in a position to operate them. And Alan Corbo made emphatically clear that there is today no market for retail jewelry stores. She would not be able to sell them.

That brings us back, then, to plaintiff's request for a compulsory buy out of her stock. And since such a mandatory purchase by the corporation or Alan Corbo represents a less drastic measure than dissolution of the corporation, it is clear that the only feasible, rational remedy here is an order that the corporation (or perhaps Alan Corbo) be required to purchase the Bonavita stock interests.

Based on an analysis and evaluation of the extensive evidence submitted at trial as to the value of the Bonavita stock interests, the court has concluded that the price at which that sale should take place is $1,900,000.

What remains to be resolved, however, are the terms and conditions under which a sale at that price should take place....To investigate and consider all of these issues, and any others that must be resolved in order to effect the purchase of the Bonavita stock, this court will appoint a special fiscal agent. The agent will consult with the attorneys for the parties; make such independent investigation as may be deemed necessary or appropriate; and may consult with banks, other possible lending sources, accountants, and anyone else deemed helpful. The agent will then submit a proposal as to the terms and conditions on which the sale will take place. The parties will have an opportunity to be heard concerning the agent's report, and thereafter, the court will enter a final order fixing the terms and conditions of sale.

Grounds for Dissolution

State corporate statutes typically authorize a court to dissolve a corporation in a proceeding initiated by a shareholder if (a) the directors are deadlocked, the shareholders can't break the deadlock, and there is a threat of irreparable injury or the business and affairs of the corporation can no longer be conducted; (2) the directors or those in control of the corporation have acted in a manner that is illegal, oppressive, or fraudulent; (3) the shareholders are deadlocked in voting power and have failed, for a designated period of time, to appoint successors to directors whose terms have expired; or (4) corporate assets are being misapplied or wasted. MBCA § 14.30.

KIRIAKIDES v. ATLAS FOOD SYSTEMS & SERVICES, INC.
541 S.E.2d 257 (S.C. 2001)

TOAL, Chief Justice:

This is a case in which respondents, minority shareholders in a closely held family corporation, claim the majority shareholders have acted in a manner which is fraudulent, oppressive and unfairly prejudicial. They seek a buyout of their shares under South Carolina's judicial dissolution statutes.

Respondents are 72–year–old John Kiriakides and his 74–year–old sister Louise Kiriakides. John and Louise are the minority shareholders in the family business, Atlas Food Systems & Services, Inc. (Atlas). Petitioners are their older brother, 88–year–old Alex Kiriakides, Jr., and the family business and its subsidiaries, Marica Enterprises, Ltd. (MEL), and Marica, Inc. (Marica).

Atlas is a food vending service which provides refreshments to factories and other businesses. Atlas was incorporated in 1956. Currently, Alex is the majority stockholder, owning 57.68%; John owns 37.7%, and Louise owns 3%.

Throughout Atlas' history, Alex has been in charge of the financial and corporate affairs of the family business; he has had overall control and is Chairman of the Board of Directors. John is also on the three member Board. In 1986, John became President of Atlas, after years of running client relations and field operations. Two of Alex' children are also employed by Atlas, his son Alex III, and his daughter Mary Ann. Alex III is (since John's departure as discussed below) President and is on the Board; Mary Ann is a CPA who performs accounting and financial functions; their brother Michael worked for Atlas in the past, but is no longer employed there.

For years, Atlas operated as a prototypical closely held family corporation. Troubles developed, however, in 1995, when a rift began between Alex and John. The relationship between the two became very strained. Several incidents served to heighten the tension.

In December 1995, the Board and shareholders of Atlas decided to convert Atlas from a subchapter C corporation to a subchapter S corporation. However, in March 1996, Alex, without bringing a vote, unilaterally determined the company would remain a C corporation. Later, in mid–1996, a dispute arose over Atlas' contract to purchase a piece of commercial property. Notwithstanding the contract, John, Alex III and William Freitag (Senior Vice President of Finance and Administration) decided not to go through with the sale. Alex however, without consulting or advising John, elected to go through with the sale. When John learned of Alex' decision, he became extremely upset and allegedly advised Alex III he was quitting his job as President. The next day, Alex III made plans with managers to continue operations in John's absence; John, however, went to the Atlas office in Greenville and visited Atlas offices in Columbia, Orangeburg and Charleston.

The following Monday, John went to work at Atlas doing "business as usual." He was told later that day (by Alex' son Michael) that management was planning John would no longer be President of Atlas. John circulated a memo indicating he intended to remain President; Alex III replied in a memo prepared with the aid of his father, refusing to allow John to continue as president of the company. The following day, Alex refused to allow John to stay on as president of Atlas, and designated Alex III as President. John was offered, but refused a position as a consultant.

In September 1996, Atlas offered to purchase John's interest in Atlas, MEL and K Enterprises, for one million dollars, plus the cancellation of $800,000 obligations owed by John. John refused this offer, believing it too low. John filed this suit in November 1996, seeking to obtain corporate records. The complaint was subsequently amended, naming Louise as a plaintiff, and adding claims for fraud under the judicial dissolution statute. The complaint sought an accounting, a buyout of John and Louise's shares, and damages for fraud. The trial was bifurcated on the issues of liability and damages.

After a five day hearing, the referee found Alex had engaged in fraud in numerous respects, and found Atlas had engaged in conduct which was fraudulent, oppressive and unfairly prejudicial toward John and Louise. The referee held a buyout was the appropriate remedy under S.C.Code Ann. § 33–14–300(2)(ii) and § 33–14–310(d)(4). The referee found that, at the bifurcated damages hearing, it would be determined whether John and Louise had suffered any damages from the fraud in this regard. The Court of Appeals affirmed in result.

Atlas contends the Court of Appeals applied an improper standard of review to the referee's findings of fraud. We disagree.

An appellate court's scope of review in cases of fraud, where the proof must be by clear, cogent and convincing evidence, is limited to determining whether there is any evidence reasonably supporting the circuit court's findings. It is not for the appellate court to weigh the evidence to determine whether it is sufficient to meet the burden of proof. We find evidentiary support in the record for each of the referee's findings of fraud. Townes Associates, Ltd. v. City of Greenville, supra; Burns v. Wannamaker, supra. Accordingly, the referee's findings of fraud are affirmed.

The referee found that, taken together, the majority's actions were "illegal, fraudulent, oppressive or unfairly prejudicial," justifying a buyout of John and Louise's interests under S.C.Code Ann. § 33–14–300(2)(ii) and § 33–14–310(d)(4).

The Court of Appeals affirmed the referee's holdings. In making this ruling, the Court of Appeals defined the statutory terms "oppressive" and "unfairly prejudicial" as follows:

1) A visible departure from the standards of fair dealing and a violation of fair play on which every shareholder who entrusts his money to a company is entitled to rely; or

2) A breach of the fiduciary duty of good faith and fair dealing; or

3) Whether the reasonable expectations of the minority shareholders have been frustrated by the actions of the majority; or

4) A lack of probity and fair dealing in the affairs of a company to the prejudice of some of its members; or

5) A deprivation by majority shareholders of participation in management by minority shareholders.

Atlas contends the Court of Appeals' definitions of oppressive, unfairly prejudicial conduct are beyond the scope of our judicial dissolution statute. We agree. In our view, the Court of Appeals' broad view of oppression is contrary to the legislative intent and is an unwarranted expansion of section 33–14–300.

South Carolina's judicial dissolution statute was amended in 1963 in recognition of the growing trend toward protecting minority shareholders from abuses by those in the majority. Section § 33–14–300(2)(ii) now permits a court to order dissolution if it is established by a shareholder that "the directors or those in control of the corporation have acted, are acting, or will act in a manner that is illegal, fraudulent, oppressive, or unfairly prejudicial either to the corporation or to any shareholder (whether in his capacity as a shareholder, director, or officer of the corporation)." The official comment to section 33–14–300 provides:

> No attempt has been made to define oppression, fraud, or unfairly prejudicial conduct. These are elastic terms whose meaning varies with the circumstances presented in a particular case, and it is felt that existing case law provides sufficient guidelines for courts and litigants.

Given the Legislature's deliberate exclusion of a set definition of oppressive and unfairly prejudicial conduct, we find the Court of Appeals' enunciation of rigid tests is contrary to the legislative intent.

Under the Court of Appeals' holding, a finding of fraudulent/oppressive conduct may be based upon any one of its alternative definitions. We do not believe the Legislature intended such a result. In particular, we do not believe the Legislature intended a court to judicially order a corporate dissolution solely upon the basis that a party's "reasonable expectations" have been frustrated by majority shareholders. To examine the "reasonable expectations" of minority shareholders would require the courts of this state to microscopically examine the dealings of closely held family corporations, the intentions of majority and minority stockholders in forming the corporation and thereafter, the history of family dealings, and the like. We do not believe the Legislature, in enacting section 33–14–300, intended such judicial interference in the business philosophies and day to day operating practices of family businesses.

In adopting the "reasonable expectations" approach, the Court of Appeals cited the North Carolina case of Meiselman v. Meiselman, 309 N.C. 279, 307 S.E.2d 551 (1983). In Meiselman, a minority shareholder in a family owned close corporation was "frozen out" of the family corporation in much the same fashion as John and Louise claim they have been frozen out of Atlas. The minority shareholder brought an action requesting a buyout of his interests under N.C.G.S. § 55–125.1(a)(4), which permits a North Carolina court to liquidate assets when it is "reasonably necessary for the protection of the rights or interests of the complaining shareholders." (Emphasis supplied).

In holding the minority shareholder was entitled to relief, the Meiselman court noted that the trial court had focused on the conduct of the majority shareholder, using standards of "oppression," "overreaching," "unfair advantage," and the like. The Court found this was error because the North Carolina statute in question required the trial court to focus on the plaintiff's "rights and interests," his "reasonable expectations" in the corporate defendants, and determine whether those rights or interests were in need of protection. The focus in Meiselman, based upon the language of the North Carolina statute, was upon the interests of the minority shareholder, as opposed to the conduct of the majority.

Unlike the North Carolina statute in Meiselman, section 33–14–300 does not place the focus upon the "rights or interests" of the complaining shareholder but, rather, specifically places the focus upon the actions of the majority, i.e., whether they "have acted, are acting, or will act in a manner that is illegal, fraudulent, oppressive, or unfairly prejudicial either to the corporation or to any shareholder." Given the language of our statute, a "reasonable expectations" approach is simply inconsistent with our statute.

We recognize that a number of leading authorities advocate a "reasonable expectations" approach to oppressive conduct. Although several jurisdictions have adopted "reasonable expectations" as a guide to the meaning of "oppression," it has been noted by one commentator that "no court has adopted the reasonable expectations test without the assistance of a statute." Ralph A. Peeples, *The Use and Misuse of the Business Judgment Rule in the Close Corporation,* 60 Notre Dame L.Rev. 456, 505 (1985). One criticism of the "reasonable expectations" approach is that it "ignores the expectations of the parties other than the dissatisfied shareholder." See Lerner v. Lerner Corp., 132 Md.App. 32, 750 A.2d 709, 722 (Md.2000). Similarly, it has been suggested that the reasonable expectations approach is "based on false premises, invites fraud, and is an unnecessary invasion of the rights of the majority." J.C. Bruno, Reasonable Expectations:A Primer on An Oppressive Standard, 71 Mich. B.J. 434 (May 1992).

We find adoption of the "reasonable expectations" standard is inconsistent with section 33–14–300, which places an emphasis not upon the minority's expectations but, rather, on the actions of the majority. We decline to adopt such an expansive approach to oppressive conduct in the absence of a legislative mandate. We find, consistent with the Legislature's comment to section 33–18–400, that the terms "oppressive" and "unfairly prejudicial" are elastic terms whose meaning varies with the circumstances presented in a particular case. As noted by one commentator:

> While business corporation statutes may attempt to provide certainty and clarity in the law to enhance the attractiveness of doing business, the definition of oppression has been left to judicial construction on a case-by-case basis. Such an approach has been suggested by the Model Close Corporation Supplement which expressly indicates that no attempt has been made to statutorily define oppression, fraud or prejudicial conduct, leaving these "elastic terms" to judicial interpretation.... The judicial construction of the definition of oppressive conduct is well-suited to the diversified, fact-specific disputes among shareholders of closely-held corporations. However, the judicial development of a meaningful standard for defining oppressive conduct, apart from fraud or mismanagement, is a difficult task.

Sandra K. Miller, *Should the Definition of Oppressive Conduct by the Majority Shareholders Exclude a Consideration of Ethical Conduct And Business Purpose?* 97 Dick. L.Rev. 227, 229–230 (Winter 1993).

We find a case-by-case analysis, supplemented by various factors which may be indicative of oppressive behavior, to be the proper inquiry under S.C.Code § 33–14–300. Accordingly, the Court of Appeals' opinion is modified to the extent it adopted a "reasonable expectations" approach.

The question remains whether the conduct of Atlas toward John and Louise was "oppressive" and "unfairly prejudicial" under the factual circumstances presented. We find this case presents a classic example of a majority "freeze-out," and that the referee properly found Atlas had engaged in conduct which was fraudulent, oppressive and unfairly prejudicial. Accordingly, the referee properly ordered a buyout of their shares pursuant to S.C.Code Ann. § 33–14–310(d)(4).

The right of the majority to control the enterprise achieves a meaning and has an impact in close corporations that it has in no other major form of business organization under our law. Only in the close corporation does the power to manage carry with it the de facto power to allocate the benefits of ownership arbitrarily among the shareholders and to discriminate against a minority whose investment is imprisoned in the enterprise. The essential basis of this power in the close corporation is the inability of those so excluded from the benefits of proprietorship to withdraw their investment at will.

This unequal balance of power often leads to a "squeeze out" or "freeze out" of the minority by the majority shareholders. At its extreme, this harm manifests itself as the classic freeze out where the minority shareholder faces a trapped investment and an indefinite exclusion from participation in business returns. The position of the close corporation shareholder, therefore, is uniquely precarious.

Common freeze out techniques include the termination of a minority shareholder's employment, the refusal to declare dividends, the removal of a minority shareholder from a position of management, and the siphoning off of corporate earnings through high compensation to the majority shareholder. Often, these tactics are used in combination. In a public corporation, the minority shareholder can escape such abuses by selling his shares; there is no such market, however, for the stock of a close corporation. "The primary vulnerability of a minority shareholder is the specter of being 'locked in,' that is, having a perpetual investment in an entity without any expectation of ever receiving a return on that investment." Charles Murdock, *The Evolution of Effective Remedies for Minority Shareholders and Its Impact Upon Valuation of Minority Shares,* 65 Notre Dame L.Rev. 425, 477 (1990).

The present case presents a classic situation of minority "freeze out." The referee considered the following factors: 1) Alex' unilateral action to deprive Louise of the benefits of ownership in her shares in Atlas, and subsequent reduction in her distributions based upon the reduced number of shares, 2) Alex' conduct in depriving John and Louise of the 21% interest of Marica stock, 3) the fact that there is no prospect of John and Louise receiving any financial benefit from their ownership of Atlas shares, 4) the fact that Alex and his family continue to receive substantial benefit from their ownership in Atlas, 5) the fact that Atlas has substantial cash and liquid assets, very little debt and that, notwithstanding its ability to declare dividends, it has indicated it would not do so in the foreseeable future, 6) the fact that Alex, majority shareholder in total control of Atlas, is totally estranged from John and Louise, 7) Atlas' extremely low buyout offers to John and Louise, and 8) the fact that Atlas is not appropriate for a public stock offering at the present time.

These factors, when coupled with the referee's findings of fraud, present a textbook example of a "freeze out" situation. Short of a buyout of their shares, it is unlikely John and Louise will ever receive any benefit from their ownership interests in Atlas. We find the referee properly concluded the totality of the circumstances demonstrated that the majority had acted "oppressively" and "unfairly prejudicially" to John and Louise. Accordingly, we affirm the referee's finding that a buyout of John and Louise's shares is the appropriate remedy under the circumstances of this case.

Under South Carolina's judicial dissolution statute, the Court of Appeals erred in attempting to define oppressive and unfairly prejudicial conduct. Further, we reject the "reasonable expectations" approach adopted by the Court of Appeals. Under section 33–14–300, the proper focus is not on the reasonable expectations of the minority but, rather, on the conduct of the majority. Such an inquiry is to be performed on a case-by-case basis, with an inquiry of all the circumstances and an examination of the many factors hereinabove recited. We believe such an inquiry is in keeping with the Legislature's intention in enacting sections 33–14–300 and 33–14–310.

Under the factual circumstances presented here, we find the majority's conduct clearly constitutes oppressive and unfairly prejudicial conduct entitling John and Louise to a buyout of their shares.

The Delaware Approach

Delaware has taken a hard-nosed approach in dealing with minority shareholders who fail to protect their investment with a shareholder buy-sell agreement or another appropriate arrangement. In *Nixon v. Blackwell*, 626 A.2d 1366 (Del. 1993), the corporation, through the adoption of an employee stock ownership plan and the purchase of key person life insurance, had provided employees of the corporation with the means to sell their stock. The plaintiffs, holders of class B nonvoting stock, had not been provided a comparable liquidity option and had no means of selling their stock. The Delaware Supreme Court agreed with the lower court that the plaintiffs had not received equal benefits, but held that it "would do violence to normal corporate practice and our corporation law to fashion an ad hoc ruling which would result in a court-imposed stockholder buy-out for which the parties had not contracted." 626 A.2d at 1380. Key language from the court's opinion is quoted in section A of Chapter 13.

CHAPTER 13

OWNER PROTECTIONS IN CLOSE CORPORATIONS

A. CHALLENGES AND OBJECTIVES

1. THE CO-OWNER PLANNING PROCESS

For closely held businesses, the planning process among the owners often is the most critical component of the overall planning for the business. It likely will define the value of an owner's equity interest in the business – what the owner will yield when it comes time to cash out. And, as we saw in Chapter 6, this process, if done right, will identify and prioritize the operational deal points between the owners and employ the best solution techniques to protect all owners, including the otherwise powerless minority.

In far too many cases, this co-owner planning process is given inadequate attention. When the entrepreneurial bug bites a group of charged-up business owners, they usually are focused on making the business succeed, maximizing revenues, and minimizing expenses. They have little interest in discussing potential breakups, the risks of the three big "Ds"– death, disability and divorce – and all the other issues that should be addressed in a well-structured buy-sell agreement. A good advisor will help the owners look at the big picture and consider the entire life cycle of the business.

Business owners need to prepare early for the day when they will part company for whatever reason. At some point down the road, they are each going to want to or have to cash out their equity interest in the business. Somebody is going to leave the business, die, become disabled, or experience a messy divorce. Plus, the owners should acknowledge the simple reality that no matter how good they feel about one another going into the enterprise, tough business decisions may create friction along the way. Friction often leads to a buyout or, worse yet, a legal blowup.

Often the question is asked: What happens if a dispute breaks out and there is no shareholder buy-sell agreement? It can trigger a serious problem that tests the will of the combatants and may threaten the health or survival of the business. The minority shareholders may have no effective remedy other than a potential claim, often nearly impossible to prove, that the controlling owners have been oppressive. As for statutory remedies, most states have corporate statutes patterned after the Model Business Corporation Act that empower a court to dissolve the corporation if a shareholder can prove that (a) the directors are deadlocked, the deadlock cannot be broken by the shareholders, and the deadlock is injuring the corporation or impairing the conduct of its business; (b) the shareholders are deadlocked and have not been able to elect directors for two years; (c) corporate assets are being wasted; or (d) those in control are acting "in a manner that is illegal, oppressive, or fraudulent."[1] As regards any oppression claim, the Official Comments to this section of the Model Act indicate that courts should be "cautious" so as "to limit such cases to genuine abuse rather than instances of acceptable tactics in a power struggle for control of a corporation."[2]

A disgruntled minority shareholder, armed with such a statute, may have nothing more than a feeble threat to bring an action to dissolve the entity. And often there is no basis for believing that a court will go beyond the confines of the applicable corporation code.

The sentiment of many courts, when faced with a claim of an unhappy minority shareholder, was aptly described by the Delaware Supreme Court in *Nixon v. Blackwell*[3] as follows:

> We wish to address one further matter which was raised at oral argument before this Court: Whether there should be any special, judicially-created rules to "protect" minority stockholders of closely-held Delaware corporations.
>
> The case at bar points up the basic dilemma of minority stockholders in receiving fair value for their stock as to which there is no market and no market valuation. It is not difficult to be sympathetic, in the abstract, to a stockholder who finds himself or herself in that position. A stockholder who bargains for stock in a closely-held corporation and who pays for those shares (unlike the plaintiffs in this case who acquired their stock through gift) can make a business judgment whether to buy into such a minority position, and if so on what terms. One could bargain for definitive provisions of self-ordering permitted to a Delaware corporation through the certificate of incorporation or by-laws by reason of the provisions in 8 Del.C. §§ 102, 109, and 141(a). Moreover, in addition to such mechanisms, a stockholder intending to buy into a minority position in a Delaware corporation may enter into definitive stockholder agreements, and such agreements may provide for elaborate earnings tests, buyout provisions, voting trusts, or other voting agreements. See, e.g., 8 Del.C. § 218.
>
> The tools of good corporate practice are designed to give a purchasing minority stockholder the opportunity to bargain for protection before parting with consideration. It would do violence to normal corporate practice and our corporation law to fashion an ad hoc

---

1. Model Business Corporation Act § 14.30(a)(2). If a shareholder petitions to dissolve the corporation under the statute, the corporation or other shareholders may elect to purchase the shares of the petitioning shareholder at the fair value of such shares and, thereby, turn the proceeding into a valuation case. Model Business Corporation Act § 14.34.

2. Model Business Corporation Act Official Comment 2. B. to § 14.30.

3. 626 A.2d 1366 (Del. 1993).

ruling which would result in a court-imposed stockholder buy-out for which the parties had not contracted.[4]

So the planning challenge, in the words of the Delaware Supreme Court, is to use the "tools of good corporate practice" and "bargain for protection before parting with consideration."

Potential separation issues are best addressed in a calm, planning-oriented atmosphere, not at the point of crisis. Preferably, the job should be done at the outset of the business when all parties are making important decisions to devote capital and energy to the business enterprise. Encouraging clients to collectively think about the key issues up front often will bring to the surface diverse expectations that may surprise everyone. It usually helps to have these expectations out in the open before irrevocable commitments are made to the venture. Too often, the parties plunge ahead with little regard for the consequences of their inevitable separation down the road.

The buy-sell agreement planning process usually involves a series of meetings of all of the owners where questions are asked and opinions are expressed. Two factors permeate these discussions: "control" of the business enterprise and "the need for liquidity" at the right time. An understanding of the importance of these factors is critical to the process of designing a buy-sell agreement.

The control of a closely held organization is always a major consideration. The impact of a future change in ownership on the control of the business must be considered in structuring the agreement among the owners. Often parties misunderstand the significance of shareholder voting control. The shareholders of a corporation elect the board of directors and approve major corporate transactions, such as mergers, consolidations and sales of the business. The shareholders do not manage the business; the business is managed by the board. Therefore, the composition of the board becomes a vital issue. Absent specific provisions in the shareholders agreement or cumulative voting rights provisions, a minority shareholder usually will have no power to impact the election of board members.

The liquidity factor also is important in structuring the provisions of the agreement. Most owners want to be assured that, at the right time in the future, there will be a buyer for their interest and funds will be available to cover the purchase price. They want the comfort of knowing that their business interest will be fairly valued. They do not want an untimely death to leave a family member with the burden of having to negotiate price and payment terms with little knowledge and no leverage.

In a closely held corporation, these control, buyout, and liquidity issues are dealt with in a separate contract between the shareholders. In partnerships and limited liability companies, the issues are dealt with in the partnership agreement or the LLC operating agreement.

4.　626 A.2d at pages 1379-80.

2. BASIC OBJECTIVES OF THE PLANNING PROCESS

A carefully designed buy-sell agreement will accomplish many important objectives of the parties. Often, it is helpful to start the process by identifying and prioritizing the primary objectives. Following is a brief summary of seven of the key objectives that often are considered in the planning process:

a. Control Who Gets In. The objective is to ensure that ownership interests in the company are never transferred or made available to third parties who are unacceptable to the owners. This objective may not be a big deal in some organizations that only have passive investors, but it usually is a top priority in all other situations. Absent careful planning, an untimely death, disability, bankruptcy, or employment termination may trigger a condition that exposes an equity interest to an unwanted third party.

b. Fairness. The objective is to ensure that there is a mechanism to fairly value and fund the equity interest of a departing owner. The goal is to avoid the necessity of divisive negotiations at a point of crisis, where one party may be in a weak position with no leverage. The agreement should contain fair provisions that will apply evenly to all parties.

c. Smooth Transition. The objective is to ensure that control and ownership issues will be smoothly transitioned at appropriate times so as not to unduly interfere with and disrupt the operations of the business. Unless properly planned, business ownership changes may create anxieties for lenders, key suppliers, employees, and customers of any business. The goal is to plan for a seamless transition that generates as little concern as possible for those who regularly deal with the business.

d. Market. The objective is to ensure that all owners have a fair "market" for their shares at appropriate points of exit. Absent a well-structured buy-sell agreement, there may be no market either inside or outside of the company. As a practical matter, the only viable exit opportunity for a departing owner may be an inside sale to the other owners pursuant to the terms of a carefully structured and funded buy-sell agreement.

e. Expulsion Right. The objective is to ensure that the owners have the power to involuntarily terminate (expel) an owner who is no longer wanted. This may not be a concern in some organizations, but it is important in all service organizations, professional service organizations, and most companies that are partially owned by those who work in the business.

f. Estate Tax Exposure. The objective is to ensure that the amount paid for the equity interest of a deceased owner determines the value of the deceased owner's equity interest for estate tax purposes. This can be an important consideration in many situations. Few can accept the concept of having to pay estate taxes on a value that exceeds the amount actually received for the equity interest.

g. Cash. The objective is to ensure that the cash and funding challenges of owner departures are appropriately anticipated and covered. Often this will require the smart use of life and disability insurance. But insurance won't cover all the exit triggers. To protect the business, usually there is a need to spell out payment terms in the agreement, including mechanisms for determining the duration of the payments, the interest rate, and any special relief provisions for the company.

B. POOLED VOTING ARRANGEMENTS

Minority shareholders sometimes seek to protect themselves and strengthen their power through arrangements that combine their voting rights. Several shareholders create a united block of votes that might help satisfy voting requirements for calling a meeting, deterring a hostile takeover, facilitating a sale of the corporation's business, or accomplishing any other action that is conditioned on a stock ownership requirement. Proxies, voting agreements, and voting trusts may be used for these purposes.

Proxies

A proxy is a power of attorney document that a shareholder uses to empower another to vote that shareholder's stock. As explained in Chapter 8, proxy solicitations by public companies are regulated by rules of the Securities and Exchange Commission. A proxy is revocable unless coupled with an interest. The following provision of the Model Business Corporation Act or something very similar thereto has been adopted in each state.

MBCA § 7.22 PROXIES

(a) A shareholder may vote his shares in person or by proxy.

(b) A shareholder or his agent or attorney-in-fact may appoint a proxy to vote or otherwise act for the shareholder by signing an appointment form, or by an electronic transmission. An electronic transmission must contain or be accompanied by information from which one can determine that the shareholder, the shareholder's agent, or the shareholder's attorney-in-fact authorized the electronic transmission.

(c) An appointment of a proxy is effective when a signed appointment form or an electronic transmission of the appointment is received by the inspector of election or the officer or agent of the corporation authorized to tabulate votes. An appointment is valid for 11 months unless a longer period is expressly provided in the appointment form.

(d) An appointment of a proxy is revocable unless the appointment form or electronic transmission states that it is irrevocable and the appointment is coupled with an interest. Appointments coupled with an interest include the appointment of:

(1) a pledgee;

(2) a person who purchased or agreed to purchase the shares;

(3) a creditor of the corporation who extended it credit under terms requiring the appointment;

(4) an employee of the corporation whose employment contract requires the appointment; or

(5) a party to a voting agreement created under section 7.31.

(e) The death or incapacity of the shareholder appointing a proxy does not affect the right of the corporation to accept the proxy's authority unless notice of the death or incapacity is received by the secretary or other officer or agent authorized to tabulate votes before the proxy exercises his authority under the appointment.

(f) An appointment made irrevocable under subsection (d) is revoked when the interest with which it is coupled is extinguished.

(g) A transferee for value of shares subject to an irrevocable appointment may revoke the appointment if he did not know of its existence when he acquired the shares and the existence of the irrevocable appointment was not noted conspicuously on the certificate representing the shares or on the information statement for shares without certificates.

(h) Subject to section 7.24 and to any express limitation on the proxy's authority stated in the appointment form or electronic transmission, a corporation is entitled to accept the proxy's vote or other action as that of the shareholder making the appointment.

Voting Trusts

With a voting trust arrangement, shares owned by various shareholders are transferred to a trustee for a specified period of time. The trustee is authorized to vote the shares as a block and, in some voting trusts, is granted additional powers, such as the power to sell the shares. At the end of the trust period, the shares are transferred back to the shareholders. State statutes usually limit the trust term to 10 years, with provisions to extend the term by agreement.

MBCA § 7.30 VOTING TRUSTS

(a) One or more shareholders may create a voting trust, conferring on a trustee the right to vote or otherwise act for them, by signing an agreement setting out the provisions of the trust (which may include anything consistent with its purpose) and transferring their shares to the trustee. When a voting trust agreement is signed, the trustee shall prepare a list of the names and addresses of all owners of beneficial interests in the trust, together with the number and class of shares each transferred to the trust, and deliver copies of the list and agreement to the corporation's principal office.

(b) A voting trust becomes effective on the date the first shares subject to the trust are registered in the trustee's name. A voting trust is valid for not more than 10 years after its effective date unless extended under subsection (c).

(c) All or some of the parties to a voting trust may extend it for additional terms of not more than 10 years each by signing written consent to the extension. An extension is valid for 10 years from the date the first shareholder signs the extension agreement. The voting trustee must deliver copies of the extension agreement and list of beneficial owners to the corporation's principal office. An extension agreement binds only those parties signing it.

Voting Agreements

A voting agreement is a contractual arrangement used by corporate shareholders to agree on how their shares will be voted on designated matters. The agreement usually is specifically enforceable by stature.

MBCA § 7.31 VOTING AGREEMENTS

(a) Two or more shareholders may provide for the manner in which they will vote their shares by signing an agreement for that purpose. A voting agreement created under this section is not subject to the provisions of section 7.30.

(b) A voting agreement created under this section is specifically enforceable.

C. BUY-SELL AGREEMENT PLANNING

1. CASE STUDY AND KEY PLANNING ISSUES

ABC Inc. is a manufacturing corporation that has been in business for 17 years. The business was started by Jim and Sue Olson, husband and wife. Jim is the president of the corporation and the driving person behind its success. Sue has always been involved in the business and, during the early years, played an important role in keeping the books and providing general business advice. Sue considers herself to be part of the business and still works part-time in the business. They have one son, Sam, age 26, who now works full-time in the business. Jim and Sue together own 60 percent of the stock of the business.

The business has two key employees, Roger and Joyce. They both have worked in the business for over 12 years. Approximately five years ago, they each acquired a 20 percent stock interest in the business. So at the present time, Jim and Sue jointly own 60 percent of the stock of the business, and Roger and Joyce each own 20 percent.

Following is a review of some of the key planning issues that the owners of ABC Inc. should consider in structuring a buy-sell agreement and eight common planning blunders that they should seek to avoid.

a. What buyout triggers should be structured into the shareholders buy-sell agreement?

The buyout triggers are those events that give one party the right to buy out another party, obligate a party to buy out another party, or give a party the right to have his or her shares purchased by the corporation or the other shareholders. The triggering event often results in a transfer of voting shares and may result in a shift in voting control. The most common triggers in any buy-sell agreement include:

- Death of an owner

- Disability of an owner

- Voluntary termination of an owner/employee

- Divorce of an owner

- Bankruptcy of an owner

- Desire of an owner to cash out and move on

- Expulsion of an owner

Each of these triggering events creates a unique set of problems and may require a different solution.

Take death as an example. In the case of ABC Inc., it's likely that the agreement should be structured to provide that if one of the 20 percent stockholders dies, his or her stock would be purchased by the other shareholders or the corporation. Certainly, Jim and Sue, the majority owners, would want the comfort of knowing that they could purchase the stock of Roger or Joyce if one of them died. Roger and Joyce also would want the comfort of knowing that the stock they own would be cashed out at a fair price in the event of an untimely death. But if Jim were to die, it's doubtful that his stock should be bought by the other shareholders or redeemed by the company. Sue may want the stock, or perhaps Jim would want the stock to be left to his son, who is moving up in the business. There's no requirement that all shareholders be treated the same under each of the various triggering events.

Disability presents unique problems. Usually a disability trigger applies only to owners whose ownership interests in the business are tied to their employment in the business. Often the trigger operates in favor of both the company and the disabled employee; that is, either party can trigger the buyout. The parties initially must agree on a definition of disability and a process for determining whether a shareholder/employee is disabled. As in the case of death, there is no requirement that the disability provision apply to all of the shareholders.

One of the questions often asked is: Why is it advisable to have divorce and bankruptcy included as triggering events in the agreement? The purpose of these provisions is to protect the company and the other shareholders if a shareholder's stock becomes tangled up in a messy divorce or bankruptcy proceeding. The other owners or the company are given the option to purchase that stock at a fair value to keep the company out of the mess. If the particular proceeding does not disrupt the company or pose any threat, there may be no reason for the company or other shareholders to exercise their rights under the agreement. But if an estranged spouse's attorney or a bankruptcy trustee attempts to cause problems or create uncertainty for the company by exercising control over a block of stock, the buyout rights can be effectively used to neutralize the actions of the attorney or trustee.

Expulsion usually is a difficult trigger for owners to discuss and resolve.

Nobody likes to think about kicking out one of their own. But in many privately owned businesses, the owners are the primary employees in the business. If there are a number of business owners, usually there is a need to develop a mechanism that permits the group to discharge a colleague who is causing problems and purchase any stock owned by that colleague. The trigger usually is structured to require a unanimous or super-high majority (75 percent) vote of the other owners.

b. What are the trade-offs between using a redemption approach versus a cross-purchase approach in structuring the agreement?

When the corporation purchases the shares of a departing shareholder, it's called a redemption. When the other owners purchase the stock, it's called a cross-purchase. Typically, whether a redemption or cross-purchase approach is used, the fundamental control results are the same. The remaining shareholders end up with the same resulting percentage ownership interests under either approach. Plus, under either approach the departing shareholder, or his or her estate, is given cash or other property in exchange for the interest in the business. But beyond these common end results, there are important factors that may favor one approach over the other in any given situation.

An important tax factor is the impact on the outside tax basis of the stock owned by the other shareholders of a C corporation. A stock redemption by a C corporation will not increase the basis of the stock held by the remaining owners. By contrast, stock acquired in a cross-purchase transaction will have a basis equal to the purchase price. This will result in a higher basis in the stock owned by the other shareholders. They will realize a lower capital gain on any subsequent sale.

Let's assume, for example, that in the case of ABC Inc., Roger, one of the 20 percent shareholders, leaves the company, his 20 percent interest has a fair market value of $400,000 at the time of departure, and his tax basis in the stock is $100,000. If ABC Inc. redeems his stock on his departure for $400,000, Jim and Sue, the original 60 percent owners, would own 75 percent of the outstanding stock of the company, and Joyce, the other owner, would end up owning 25 percent of the outstanding stock of the company. If Joyce's basis in her 20 percent interest was $100,000, her total basis in her increased 25 percent interest would still be $100,000. As for Jim and Sue, if their original 60 percent interest had a very low basis, say $30,000, the basis in their 75 percent interest would remain at $30,000. The stock redemption approach generates no step-up in basis for the other owners.

If the remaining shareholders acquired Roger's shares through a cross-purchase on a proportionate basis, Jim and Sue would acquire three-fourths of Roger's 20 percent interest, and Joyce would acquire the other one-fourth. Roger and Sue would still end up owning 75 percent, and Joyce would end up owning 25 percent. But the basis in their stock would have changed. Under a cross-purchase, Jim and Sue would have paid $300,000 for three-fourths of Roger's stock, resulting in a total basis in their shares of $300,000 plus $30,000, or $330,000. Joyce will now have a basis in her shares equal to her original investment of $100,000, plus the $100,000 that she would pay to Roger for one-fourth of his stock. So her total basis would have increased to $200,000. On a subsequent sale of the stock or liquidation of the company, Jim and Sue have an additional $300,000 that could be recovered tax-free, and Joyce has an additional $100,000 that could be recovered tax-free.

This basis issue is not a factor for S corporations, partnerships, and limited liability companies. In these pass-through entities, the owners will receive a basis step-up whether a redemption or cross-purchase approach is used. If the transaction is structured as a redemption, the receipt of life insurance proceeds or entity income to fund the redemption will increase the outside basis of the equity interests held by the other owners.[5]

Does this basis difference make the cross-purchase approach the best choice for C corporations? Not always. In cases where there are many shareholders, the cross-purchase approach may be too cumbersome, particularly when there are multiple life insurance policies that need to be reshuffled every time an owner dies or is bought out. Beyond the complexity of the reshuffling are serious transfer-for-value problems that can destroy the tax-free character of life insurance death benefits and ultimately force a conversion to a redemption strategy.[6] Also, often the shareholders do not have sufficient capital to fund a cross-purchase buyout. The capital is in the corporation, and there is no effective tax way to get the cash out of the company and into the hands of the shareholders to fund the buyout of their departing partner. Another factor that may favor a redemption strategy in a C corporation is the deductibility of interest payments on any installment obligation paid to the departing owner or his or her heirs. Interest paid by a C corporation pursuant to a redemption is deductible as trade or business interest, whereas interest paid by the shareholders in a cross-purchase would be subject to the investment interest limitations.[7] So in many cases, as a practical matter, the redemption approach is preferred simply from a funding standpoint.

In some situations, there are other factors that make the redemption approach unattractive. If the C corporation is large enough to be subject to the alternative minimum tax (AMT) (annual gross receipts over $5 million during the first three years and over $7.5 million thereafter), receipt of life insurance proceeds may trigger an AMT for the corporation.[8] Plus, accumulation of funds to buy out a major shareholder may not qualify as a reasonable business need for purposes of the accumulated earnings tax.[9] State law restrictions may limit the corporation's ability to redeem its own stock if it lacks sufficient capital surplus

---

5. I.R.C. § 1367 sets forth the basis adjustments for stock held by S corporation shareholders. The counterpart provision for entities taxed as partnerships is I.R.C. § 705.

6. I.R.C. § 101(a)(2) eliminates the tax free death benefit on life insurance policies that are transferred for valuable consideration. There are exceptions for transfers among partners, transfers to a partnership in which the insured is a partner, and transfers to a corporation in which the insured was an officer or officer. But there is no exception for transfers among co-shareholders of a corporation.

7. I.R.C. § 163(d).

8. I.R.C. §§ 55(b)(2), 55(e), 56(g).

9. I.R.C. §§ 535(c)(1), 537; see, e.g., John B. Lambert & Associates v. United States, 212 Ct. Cl. 71 (1976); Lamark Shipping Agency, Inc. v. Commissioner, 42 T.C.M. 38 (1981).

or retained earnings to fund the redemption.[10] At a minimum, such state law restrictions may trigger additional costs (e.g. appraisal fees) to get the deal done. Finally, restrictive covenants in loan agreements often limit a corporation's capacity to redeem stock by making substantial payments to the owners of the business. All of these factors should be evaluated in considering the redemption approach.

Note that many of these factors do not come into play with a pass-through entity, such as an S corporation, a partnership, or an LLC. As stated above, the outside basis differential is not an issue. Plus, getting money out of the entity and into the hands of the owners to fund a cross purchase usually presents no difficult tax issues.[11] There are no AMT or accumulated earnings tax issues to worry about. The deductibility of the interest on any installment purchase will turn on other factors. It may qualify as trade or business deductible interest for those who are material participants in the venture; for all other owners, it will be passive or investment interest or both, depending on the investment assets held by the entity. State law and loan agreement restrictions may be just as applicable.

In some situations, the solution is to draft the agreement to provide flexibility. The agreement allows for a redemption or a cross-purchase and gives the company and the other shareholders the right to select the preferred approach when a trigger is pulled. This flexible approach sounds better than it really is because advance planning for the funding – whether through the use of life insurance, disability insurance, or internal funding – usually requires a decision on which approach will be used at the time the funding vehicle is put in place.

c. What mandatory buyout obligations should be in the buy-sell agreement?

The business owners need to decide whether a triggering event requires a mandatory purchase or simply grants an option to purchase. And if it's optional, which party will have the option? For example, upon the death of a shareholder, the remaining shareholders typically want an option to purchase the shares of the deceased shareholder to preserve control. The deceased shareholder's heirs will want a put, which is an option to require the corporation or remaining shareholders to buy their stock, or a mandatory purchase obligation. It also is possible to give options to both the heirs and the remaining shareholders, permitting either side to trigger the purchase. Making the purchase mandatory or at the option of the heirs of the deceased shareholder puts the remaining shareholders in the position of having to come up with the purchase price at death. Life insurance often is essential.

---

10. In any such redemption, the applicable state corporate law must be carefully analyzed to ascertain any restrictions. Appraisals are often necessary. The Model Business Corporation Act prohibits a "distribution" (broadly defined to include proceeds from a redemption) if "after giving it effect: (1) the corporation would not be able to pay its debts as they become due in the ordinary course of business, or (2) the corporation's total assets would be less than the sum of its total liabilities plus (unless the articles of incorporation permit otherwise) that amount that would be needed, if the corporation were to be dissolved at the time of the distribution, to satisfy the preferential rights upon the dissolution of shareholders whose preferential rights are superior to those receiving the distribution." MBCA §§ 1.04, 6.40(c). These two tests, referred to as the "equity insolvency test" and the "balance sheet test," have been widely incorporated into state corporate statutes.

11. If an S corporation has accumulated earnings and profits from a prior C period, distributions that exceed its accumulated adjustment account may trigger taxable dividends. I.R.C. § 1368(c).

Similar issues arise if an owner simply wants to cash out. Most owners view this event as a voluntary event and have less concern for the cash and liquidity desires of the owner who wants to exit. The shareholders agreement may give the remaining owners the option to buy the interest of the departing owner, but impose no obligation. In other situations, the owners will recognize the need for owners to come and go, particularly in service organizations and professional groups. In these cases, there is often a provision for a payout upon voluntary withdrawal, but the payment terms are usually over an extended period of time to avoid creating an undue burden on the cash flow of those who remain.

d. Is it advisable to tie business ownership to continued employment?

Many businesses restrict stock ownership to those who are employed by the business. For these businesses, termination of employment is an important triggering event. This is typically true for professional service corporations, as well as numerous service organizations and many companies where a portion of the stock is owned by employees. For these businesses, it's advisable to provide for a mandatory buyout upon the termination of employment of an owner. Funding is a challenge for the remaining owners. It is common for the departing owner to be paid in installments over a time frame that accommodates the cash needs of the business.

The question is often asked: What happens if one of the owners wants out and none of the other owners wants to buy that person's stock? Usually the agreement should be structured to give the parties significant time to negotiate a solution to the stalemate. If the stalemate continues for a designated time, often the owner who wants out is given the right to trigger a sale or liquidation of the business or to find an outside buyer for his or her stock.

e. What types of special exceptions should be structured into the agreement for unique shareholders?

There is no requirement that all shareholders be treated equally in a shareholders agreement. Often the expectations and the needs of the shareholders will result in different rights, particularly in organizations that have a dominant owner. ABC Inc. is an example. Upon the death of one of the primary owners, Jim or Sue, the surviving spouse will not want the two minority shareholders to have the right or the obligation to purchase the stock of the deceased. Upon the death of the survivor of Jim and Sue, their stock will likely pass to their son, Sam. A similar exception may give Jim and Sue the right to transfer stock to Sam at any time. They also may want the flexibility to transfer stock to a trust for the benefit of their grandchildren for estate planning purposes. In most situations, dominant owners like Jim and Sue would not tolerate the minority shareholders having similar rights.

f. Is there a need to structure special voting restrictions into the agreement?

Sometimes. For example, one shareholder may be willing to purchase 25 percent of the stock on the condition that he or she is assured a seat on the board of directors. The shareholders agreement could provide that all of the shareholders must vote their stock to maintain that shareholder's board position.

That same 25 percent shareholder may want to have veto power over certain major corporate events, such as the liquidation of the business or a sale of the business. The agreement could provide that no such act will occur without at least a 76 percent approval by the shareholders. By carefully designing a shareholder agreement, a minority shareholder can be given important voting rights at the time of his or her investment in the enterprise.

In the case of ABC Inc., the two minority shareholders, Roger and Joyce, insisted on such a provision to protect themselves against a substantial change in the direction of the business by Sam, the owners' son, at the time he inherits his parents' 60 percent interest. They wanted to prevent Sam from unilaterally starting a new business, shutting down existing plants, or incurring debt beyond certain limits without a supermajority approval by the shareholders.

In Chapter 6, there is a short discussion of 20 potential operating deal points that may require special treatment and the different solution techniques that may be considered.

g. How do the parties select the most appropriate method for valuing equity ownership interest and the business?

Carefully. Often the most difficult element in a buy-sell agreement is the determination of how an ownership interest will be priced upon the occurrence of a triggering event. There are a number of options. One common (and usually bad) approach is to use book value. Its only virtue in most cases is simplicity. The problem with book value is that it does not reflect changes in the asset values or the goodwill and going concern value of the business. For these reasons, a modified book value approach is sometimes used. It adjusts the value of the balance sheet assets to reflect their current fair market values, but it too usually fails to account for the going concern and goodwill value of an operating business.

The third common approach is to have a formula based on the recent average earnings of the business. This approach focuses on the earning capacity of the business and is used to reflect the going concern and goodwill value of the enterprise. Perhaps its biggest drawback is that it is based on historical earnings and may not fairly reflect recent changes, good or bad, in the future prospects of the business.

A fourth approach is to agree on a mechanism for having the business appraised when a triggering event occurs. The comparative advantage of this approach is that it is designed to derive the current fair market value of the business. The problem is that appraisals can be expensive, and often businesses are so unique that even appraisers are incapable of accurately assessing their true value.

The fifth approach is to specify in the agreement that the price will be a fixed price, subject to adjustment by the shareholders at their annual meeting each year. Then each year the shareholders establish a new price that will govern any transaction for the following year. The appeal of the approach is that it requires the owners to focus on the valuation issue each year and to reach an agreement for a limited future time frame under calm circumstances that are not stressed by the demands of an immediate deal. A key to the approach is a specified backup valuation method if the shareholders neglect or are unable to resolve the valuation issue for a period of time. For example, the agreement might require that the price be re-examined each year at the annual meeting, but that if it has not been re-examined within two years of the date of an event that triggers the buy-sell agreement, the value will be determined by mutual agreement between the interested parties. If the interested parties cannot reach an agreement on price within 30 days, then each party selects an appraiser and the two appraisers jointly determine the price. This gives the interested parties an opportunity to agree on a price before incurring the expense and the time delay of a formal appraisal, but also provides a binding mechanism for ultimately determining the price.

A three-tiered approach of this type often is used in situations where the owners cannot agree on a formula for valuing the business. Some may view this as avoiding the issue rather than facing it. But often the job of agreeing on a value at a given point in time is easier than the task of developing a formula that will work in the future, especially for a business that has not matured or that is growing rapidly.

h. Should the same valuation method apply for all triggers?

Often the owners will want to establish a different price or price formula, depending upon the event that triggers the buyout. Providing a discount from the regular price for a departing owner/employee who does not give the remaining owners adequate advance notice of departure can be an effective means of ensuring a smooth transition in the case of key employees. Another possible use of a discounted fair market value is the situation where the departing owner/employee may become a competitor of the business. The departing owner moves across the street and wants his or her former colleagues to help fund a new competitive business venture. A heavy discount in this situation may be justified in many cases.

i. Will the amount paid under the agreement to the heirs of a deceased owner govern for estate tax purposes?

Not necessarily. The buyout price paid under a buy-sell agreement on the death of an owner may not be the same value used to determine the federal estate tax liability of the deceased. It is possible that the IRS could determine that the actual fair market value of the interest for tax purposes is greater than the buyout price under the agreement. The owner's family would end up receiving a payment for the deceased's interest in the business that is substantially less than the value that is used to compute estate taxes. This could be disastrous for the family, particularly in situations where the business is the largest asset in the estate.

A buy-sell agreement often can be structured to fix the value of the transferred business interest for estate tax purposes. The difficulty of accomplishing this desired result depends, in part, on whether the business is considered a family business for purposes of Section 2703 of the Internal

Revenue Code.[12] If non-family parties own more than 50 percent of the equity interests in the business, the requirements of Section 2703 will not be an issue. In such a situation, the value determined pursuant to the agreement will govern for estate tax purposes if: (1) the price for the interest is specified or readily ascertainable pursuant to the terms of the agreement and the price was reasonable when the agreement was entered into; (2) the decedent's estate was obligated to sell at death for the price established by the agreement; and (3) the deceased was restricted from selling or transferring the interest during life.[13] This third condition is not satisfied if the decedent had the right to transfer the interest by gift during life to a person who was not subject to the restrictions imposed by the agreement. At a minimum, this provision generally requires that the interest have been subject to a right of first refusal at a fixed or determinable price under the agreement during the decedent's life.

If family members control the company, then the price determined pursuant to the buy-sell agreement will govern for estate tax purposes only if the forgoing three conditions are satisfied, along with the requirements of Section 2703. Section 2703 requires that the agreement be a *bona fide* business arrangement, not be used as a device to transfer property for less than full value, and contain terms that are comparable to similar arrangements entered into by persons in arms-length arrangements.[14] The "arms-length" requirement is the most difficult in almost every family situation. It requires a determination of what unrelated parties are doing in the same industry or similar types of businesses owned by unrelated parties.[15] Industry research and the assistance of a quality appraiser are often necessary at this stage of the planning process.

2. COMMON BLUNDERS TO AVOID

a. Blunder One: Improper Use of the Showdown Clause

The first common blunder is the improper use of the showdown clause. A showdown clause is a mechanism that is often used in a buy-sell agreement to deal with an owner who wants to cash out. Here's how it works. If an owner wants to withdraw from the company, that owner presents an offer to the other owners in the form of a purchase price and payment terms. The other owners then have the choice to be either buyers or sellers, at the specified price and payment terms. The showdown clause, in theory, forces the price and payment terms to be fair, since the one proposing them doesn't know if he or she is going to be a buyer or a seller.

The attraction of a showdown clause is its simplicity and apparent fairness.

---

12. Reg. § 25.2703-1(b)(3). Family members include the transferor's spouse, any ancestor of the transferor or the transferor's spouse, any spouse of any such ancestor, and any lineal descendant of the parents of the transferor or the transferor's spouse (but not spouses of such descendants). Reg. § 25.2703-1(b)(3); Reg. § 25.2701-2(b)(5). Broad entity attribution rules are used to determine ownership, with an interest being deemed a family interest if it is attributed to both a family and non-family member. Reg. § 25.2703-1(b)(3); Reg. § 25.2701-6(a)(2)-(4).

13. Reg. § 20.2031-2(h).

14. I.R.C. § 2703(b).

15. Reg. § 25.2703-1(b)(4)(i).

Many advisers wrongly believe that it is the ultimate solution to all difficult buyout situations, and, therefore, they use it as a standard in structuring buy-sell agreements. But in many types of businesses, the appearance of simplicity and fairness is deceiving. Take, for example, a business that has a majority shareholder and one or more minority owners. The showdown clause usually gives the majority owner a huge advantage. Not only is the larger owner likely to have a bigger net worth and more capacity to pay, but he or she only faces the possibility of having to buy a minority interest in the business. By contrast, the smaller owner is not only likely to have a smaller net worth, but also has to pay a much larger price to buy out the interest of the majority owner. In this type of business, the showdown clause may be nothing more than an easy way for the majority owner to dictate price and payment terms for squeezing out the minority. Similarly, the showdown clause can be unfair in a business where all of the owners work in the business and have relatively equal interests, but one or more of them have a greater net worth. Again the showdown clause may become a means for the richer owners to squeeze out those who do not have sufficient means to be buyers in a showdown situation.

The third type of business where a showdown clause may be inappropriate is the business where some of the owners work in the business and others do not. If some of the owners depend upon the business for their jobs, a showdown clause may force these inside owners to become unwilling buyers simply to preserve their jobs. The importance of their employment relationship with the company and the lack of other comparable job opportunities may leave the insiders no choice any time the showdown clause is triggered by one of the outside owners. For all practical purposes, the outside owners have a put at a price and terms that they can dictate.

The showdown clause works best in organizations where all the players are passive owners, no owner depends on the business for his or her employment, each owner owns roughly the same percentage interest in the business, and each owner has the financial capacity to be a buyer when the clause is triggered.

b. Blunder Two: Failure to Recognize the Unique Rights of the Majority Owner

The second big mistake is found in businesses dominated by a single controlling owner. The buy-sell agreement too often is structured on the assumption that all owners should be treated the same. In fact, many provisions under a buy-sell agreement should apply differently to the majority owner than to the other owners. If the owners stop to think about it and ask all the appropriate "what if" questions, they will usually see the importance of this unequal treatment.

One area where this unintended equal treatment shows up is in the control of the board of directors of a corporation. Some majority shareholders assume that they control the operations of the corporation solely by virtue of the fact that they own a majority of the voting shares. As stated above, the shareholders of any corporation, whether public or private, do little more than elect the board of directors. The real control of the operation of the business rests with the board.

Unless the majority shareholder also controls the board, that majority shareholder does not control the operation of the business. The problem surfaces when the shareholders agreement grants certain shareholders the right to serve on the board of directors.

Take, for example, ABC Inc. where Jim and Sue own 60 percent of the stock and Roger and Joyce each own 20 percent. If the shareholders agreement specifies a board of three members and ensures Jim, Roger and Joyce each a seat on the board, Roger and Joyce, the 20 percent owners, would control the board and the company. If Roger and Joyce are adamant about their board positions, Jim will want to restructure the board to protect control in his family. He could easily do this by expanding the board to five members. With a five-member board, Jim, the majority owner, could elect Sue and Sam to the board and, thereby, preserve board control in the family. A buy-sell agreement that deals with the composition of the board needs to be structured to ensure that the control of the corporation by a majority shareholder is not inadvertently forfeited.

Other buy-sell provisions that often have unintended results for a dominant shareholder involve equal application of the buyout rights that arise in certain events, such as death, disability, or retirement. In the typical buy-sell agreement, when one of these triggering events occurs, the other owners have the right, and often the obligation, to purchase the stock of the departing owner. This is appropriate and works well in an organization where all of the owners have substantially equal interests. But in an enterprise with a dominant owner, the majority owner may have never intended that he or she would be subject to the provisions. While it may be entirely appropriate to permit the majority owner to purchase the stock of a departing minority owner, it may not be consistent with the majority owner's intention that the same rights exist when he or she dies, retires or is disabled.

c. Blunder Three: The Constructive Dividend Trap

A mistake occurs in the context of a C corporation when the agreement imposes a primary and unconditional cross-purchase obligation on the shareholders, and the parties want to preserve the flexibility of a potential redemption by the corporation. Often the mistake is aggravated by sloppily putting ownership of life insurance policies in the corporation to facilitate the payment of premiums with corporate dollars. If there is a primary and unconditional obligation of the shareholders to purchase the stock of the deceased or departing shareholder and that obligation is paid and discharged by the corporation, all payments by the corporation to redeem the stock of the deceased or departing owners will be taxed as constructive dividends to the remaining shareholders.[16]

The key to avoiding this trap and preserving flexibility is to structure any cross-purchase obligation of the shareholders as a secondary, backup obligation. This is done by first giving the corporation the right to redeem the stock, and then providing that the shareholders will purchase the stock if the corporation fails to exercise its right to purchase. It may look like form over substance, but it can be

---

16. Rev. Rule 69-608, 1969-2 C.B. 42.

the difference between a clean deal and a costly constructive dividend.[17]

d. Blunder Four: Use of Inappropriate Payment Terms

A common mistake regarding the payment terms of an installment obligation provided a departing owner is the failure to provide for adequate security. At a minimum, the obligations under the installment note should be secured by a pledge of the stock or the equity interest that is being purchased. When a stock pledge is used, the buy-sell agreement should specify its terms. For example, usually it should provide that, as long as the payments remain current, the voting rights and the right to receive dividends and other distributions with respect to the stock are retained by the purchasers and that those rights automatically shift back to the departed owner if there is any default in the payment of the installment obligation.

Consideration also should be given to the need for other forms of security. For example, if the departing owner's stock is being redeemed by the company, should the other shareholders be required to personally guarantee the payment of the redemption price by the corporation? The issue can be very important, particularly in situations where the redemption price is being paid over an extended period of time. Owners sometimes, but not always, agree that it is appropriate for those who stay behind and reap the benefits of the ongoing business to personally guarantee the payment of the deferred price. Also, consideration should be given to restrictions on the payment of compensation or dividends to the remaining owners so long as the deferred purchase price is outstanding. Often this is done by requiring that the business maintain designated income levels and certain debt-to-equity, quick-asset, or other ratios as conditions to making distributions to the other owners.

e. Blunder Five: Poor Structuring of Life Insurance Ownership

A fifth common blunder in structuring buy-sell agreements (and an expensive one) relates to the purchase of life insurance to fund a buyout obligation on the death of an owner. Most properly structured buy-sell agreements will permit the buyout of the deceased owner to be made by either the corporation or the remaining owners. The surviving owners can examine the circumstances existing at the death of one of the owners and determine then whether it's most appropriate to have the corporation buy the stock of the deceased owner or to have that stock purchased by the remaining owners. As stated above, various factors may impact the decision to structure the purchase as a redemption or a cross-purchase.

The mistake is made when life insurance is purchased to fund that obligation. Because of habit, simplicity, lack of thought, or a combination of all these, the life insurance often is purchased by the corporation. The corporation pays the premiums, and the corporation is named as the beneficiary. Upon the death of an owner, the corporation collects the life insurance proceeds. The mistake is that the decision relating to the ownership of the life insurance also, by

---

17. Compare Situations 1 and 2 with Situation 5 in Rev. Rule 69-608, 1969-2 C.B. 42.

necessity, decides the redemption-versus-cross-purchase issue. So even though the buy-sell agreement has been carefully structured to retain the flexibility to have either a redemption or a cross-purchase buyout, the purchase of the life insurance by the corporation forces the election of the redemption approach. The life insurance proceeds cannot be made available to the other owners to fund a cross purchase without significant adverse tax consequences.

There are two advantages of a cross-purchase that need to be carefully examined at the time the life insurance is acquired. The first advantage is that, with a cross-purchase, each of the shareholders receives a stepped-up basis in the acquired stock. No such step-up occurs with a redemption by a C corporation. The second advantage of having the owners directly own the policies is that the risk of triggering a corporate alternative minimum tax on the receipt of the insurance is avoided.

Another life insurance structuring blunder sometimes is made in a corporation that has a dominant owner. A life insurance policy is acquired on each owner, including the dominant owner, to provide liquidity at the death an owner. The premiums are funded by the corporation, and the buy-sell agreement is structured to require that the insurance be used to purchase an owner's stock at death. Upon the dominant owner's death, the family ends up with the policy's death benefit, subject to estate taxes, and loses all equity in the business. The minority shareholders end up with the entire business. For many majority shareholders, an infinitely better structure would eliminate all buyout rights of the minority shareholders. The life insurance on the majority owner would be held for the benefit of his or her family in a life insurance trust that would not be subject to estate taxes. The majority owner's family would end up with the life insurance death benefit, tax-protected in trust, and still own the majority interest in the business. Most majority owners, when presented with the huge contrasts in these two scenarios, will enthusiastically opt for the latter.

f. Blunder Six: Misused Right of First Refusal

A common provision in many buy-sell agreements is the right of first refusal. It provides that, if an owner wants out of the business, that owner must find a third party who is willing to buy his or her interest, and then the other owners have the first right to buy the interest on the same price and terms offered by the third party. It is a method of dealing with the owner who wants out while giving the other owners the capacity to preserve ownership within the group. Each owner has the comfort of knowing that he or she will have the ability to prevent an unwanted owner from becoming part of the ownership group. In most cases, the provision just doesn't work.

The first problem with the right of first refusal provision is that it assumes there is a market for the stock when, in fact, there is no market for a minority equity interest. A minority owner usually finds it impossible to locate a third party who will make a reasonable, *bona fide* offer to trigger the right of first refusal provision. The result is that the right of first refusal provision becomes an absolute prohibition on sale. The problem with the provision is that it is based on the assumption that each owner has the capacity to liquidate his or her interest when, in fact, there is no such capacity. It also may encourage individual owners to try to market their interests to uninformed third parties who know nothing about the business. It is usually not in the best interests of the company or the owners to have details relating to the business being shopped to strangers who are being invited to kick the tires. Apart from requiring executive time and expense to ensure full disclosure of all material facts, the effort may be counterproductive to the strategic development of the company's business plan. Most private business owners, if they stop to think, will quickly conclude that they do not want to do anything that encourages minority owners to shop the stock to third parties.

The second problem with a right of first refusal provision surfaces in the rare situation where the departing owner actually finds someone who wants to buy into the business. The prospective buyer is willing to pay a premium to get a foothold in the enterprise. It may be a competitor, a potential competitor, a strategic supplier, a huge customer, an obnoxious relative of the departing owner, or some other party that the other owners do not want. This puts the remaining owners in a tough position. They either have to come up with a large sum to match the price and terms or end up with a co-owner they don't like or want or who may pose a threat to the business.

A right of first refusal provision usually gives the task of finding the new owner to the wrong person. The departing owner doesn't care who the new owner is going to be; he or she just wants the best price and terms for the stock. Yet, the right of first refusal provision puts the onus on the departing owner to find a potential candidate in order to trigger the provision. Those who really care about any new owner are the remaining owners, who are going to have to embrace the new owner as a colleague.

What's the alternative? It is to structure a mechanism that permits an owner to withdraw and get cashed out, without creating the problems described above that are often triggered with a right of first refusal. For example, the buy-sell agreement could provide that if an owner wants out, that owner must trigger Stage One by giving the others significant advance notice, say three months. Stage One is a reaction period for the other owners. They have a period of time to find a new owner or prepare for the purchase of the departing owner's stock. The pricing mechanism and payment terms are set forth in the agreement, but they are optional for the remaining owners. If, at the end of the three-month period, the existing owners have not found an acceptable replacement owner or developed a plan to pay the price specified in the agreement, Stage Two kicks in. This is a time (say, an additional 60 days) designated for negotiation between the owner who wants out and the other owners. Everyone will have had time to ponder the realities of the situation and assess their options. Of course, the remaining owners can always buy the departing owners interest for the price and terms specified in the agreement. But if Stage Two is triggered, the remaining owners will be looking for some concessions from the owner who wants out. If there is still no deal at the end of Stage Two, there is an additional period of time, say six months, for the existing owners to find a replacement owner. This is Stage Three. During all these stages, the departing owner remains an owner and is entitled to all the benefits of ownership. If at the end of the extended period a replacement owner has not been found and the remaining owners are still unwilling to purchase the interest of the departing owner on the stated terms or on mutually acceptable renegotiated terms, the departing owner has the option to force a sale of the business. This is Stage Four. If the option is exercised, any owner or group of owners may be the purchaser. Essentially, the company is put up for sale and anyone can be a bidder. If sold, the owner who wants to depart is cashed out at a price that reflects the value of the business.

As a practical matter, it is highly unlikely that the process will ever get to Stage Four. The remaining owners will have had plenty of time to find a replacement owner, secure financing to fund the buyout pursuant to the terms of the agreement, or renegotiate a more palatable deal with the departing owner. A staged exit procedure of this type, or any version thereof, can provide the remaining owners with the time and the opportunity to solve the problem of the departing owner, while at the same time providing the departing owner with a means of ultimately getting cashed out.

There are a number of variations of this approach. The important point is that the right of first refusal should not be the automatic solution to the problem of an owner who wants to depart. A better mechanism usually can be structured to provide a more realistic solution to the problem.

g. Blunder Seven: Failure to Cover the Downside

Another common mistake in structuring buy-sell agreements is to neglect the downside – the disaster scenario. Most buy-sell agreements are entered into when all parties are anticipating a successful company. Most don't even want to think about the business failing. But it frequently happens. It helps to deal with the potential fallout up front.

The most common problem in a disaster scenario is that one or more of the owners end up getting stuck with a disproportionately large share of the liabilities because of personal guarantees or other commitments made in connection with the business. Most guarantees by multiple owners are joint and several. The lender can go after any one or more of the owners to collect the entire debt. The owners should agree up front as to how they will share the debt burdens of the business. Typically, the agreement should provide that if an owner is forced to fund a company debt, the portion of the payment that exceeds that owner's percentage interest in the business constitutes a loan to the other owners, in proportion to their respective percentage interests in the business. The agreement should set forth a mechanism for the repayment of the loan and perhaps collateral to secure the obligation.

h. Blunder Eight: Ignore S Corporation Issues

A common mistake in buy-sell agreements relates to S corporations. The mistake is the failure to address in the buy-sell agreement specific S corporation issues. The first and most obvious issue is the failure to prohibit a shareholder from making any stock transfer that would result in the termination of the S election. There are a number of shareholder requirements that must be met in order for a corporation to be taxed as an S corporation. There are limits on the number of shareholders and the permissible types of shareholders. The buy-sell agreement should prohibit any transfer of stock that would terminate the S election and should provide that any such attempted transfer is void.

An S corporation also has the option of making certain tax elections. These elections often require the consent of all shareholders. In order to prevent a single shareholder or a minority group of shareholders from vetoing an election that the majority wants to make, the buy-sell agreement may provide that all shareholders will consent to any tax election that is approved by a specified percentage of shareholders (e.g., 70 percent). An example would be an S corporation that has C corporation earnings and profits. An S corporation may elect to treat distributions as first coming from its C corporation earnings and profits rather than from its accumulated adjustment account.[18] Many owners of an S corporation might desire such an election to accommodate their personal tax planning. This election requires the unanimous consent of all shareholders. A buy-sell agreement can soften the impact of the unanimous consent requirement.

Another important issue that usually should be addressed in an S corporation buy-sell agreement relates to the payment of dividends. It's an issue that is common to all pass-through entities, including partnerships and limited liability companies. The income of the entity is passed through and taxed to the owners, even if it is not distributed. The owners may end up with a tax bill and no cash. To ensure that the owners will be distributed enough cash to cover their tax liabilities, the shareholders or operating agreement may contain a provision that obligates the entity to distribute cash to fund the tax liabilities of the owners. In order to avoid any risk that such a provision creates a second class of stock (a condition that would kill the S election), the tax distribution to the shareholders should not be based on the specific tax liabilities of the different shareholders. Rather, the total distribution should be based on a stated percentage of the entity's total allocated taxable income for the year and should be distributed to the shareholders based on their respective stockholdings in the company.

The Bottom Line. An effective and workable buy-sell agreement requires considerable thought by the business owners and guidance from their legal advisors. The owners should be encouraged to spend sufficient time to think through and hash out the issues. A careful record should be kept of the decision points in the discussions so that the agreement can be periodically reviewed to determine if the reasons for the various provisions remain or have changed. As time passes, circumstances will change that will necessitate revisions.

3. JUDICIAL ENFORCEMENT

CONCORD AUTO AUCTION, INC. v. RUSTIN
627 F.Supp. 1526 (D.Mass.,1986)

YOUNG, District Judge.

Close corporations, Concord Auto Auction, Inc. ("Concord") and E.L. Cox Associates, Inc. ("Associates") brought this action for the specific performance

---

18. I.R.C. § 1368(e)(3).

of a stock purchase and restriction agreement (the "Agreement"). Concord and Associates allege that Lawrence H. Rustin ("Rustin") as the administrator of E.L. Cox's estate ("Cox") failed to effect the repurchase of Cox's stock holdings as provided by the Agreement.

Rustin alleges in his defense that Concord and Associates are not entitled to specific performance because 1) they have breached the Agreement which they seek to enforce; 2) they have unclean hands because they failed to effect a review and revaluation of the shares; 3) the value of the stock increased so substantially that specific enforcement would be unfair and unjust to Cox's estate; and 4) specific performance is conditional upon an annual review of share value to be held no later than the third Tuesday of February, here February 21, 1984.

Rustin alleges that all parties intended an annual revaluation, that Betsy Cox Powell ("Powell") and Nancy Cox Thomas ("Thomas"), sisters of the decedent Cox, as the only other shareholders in both Concord and Associates, knew that a revaluation would result in a higher price and failed to effect the annual review required by the Agreement, that this failure breached the Agreement and was "undertaken with the intent and effect of depriving the estate of E. Leroy Cox from receiving fair value for its shares of Concord and Associates." Rustin further alleges that by failing to establish new prices, Powell in particular as well as Thomas breached their fiduciary duties to the estate of Cox in light of their direct pecuniary interest in the value of the shares. Finally, Rustin alleges that the actions of Powell, Thomas, Concord and Associates constitute a willful violation of Mass.Gen.Laws, ch. 93A, § 11.

Concord and Associates move for summary judgment, specific performance of the Agreement and dismissal of the counterclaims. Pursuant to Fed.R.Civ.P. 56, the Court will treat the motion for dismissal as a motion for summary judgment because the Court has gone beyond the pleadings to consider various affidavits and exhibits. For the reasons set forth below, the Court allows the motions for summary judgment.

Both Concord and Associates are Massachusetts Corporations. Concord operates a used car auction for car dealers, fleet operators, and manufacturers. Associates operates as an adjunct to Concord's auction business by guaranteeing checks and automobile titles. Both are close corporations with the same shareholders, all siblings: Cox (now his estate), Powell, and Thomas. At all times relevant to this action, each sibling owned one-third of the issued and outstanding stock in both Concord and Associates.

To protect "their best interests" and the best interests of the two corporations, the three shareholders entered into a stock purchase and restriction agreement on February 1, 1983. The Agreement provides that all shares owned by a shareholder at the time of his or her death be acquired by the two corporations, respectively, through life insurance policies specifically established to fund this transaction. This procedure contemplates the "orderly transfer of the stock owned by each deceased Shareholder." At issue in the instant action are the prerequisites for and effect of the repurchase requirements as set forth in the Agreement.

This dispute arises because Rustin failed to tender Cox's shares as required by Paragraph 2, *Death of Shareholder*. Rustin admits this but alleges a condition precedent: that Powell, specifically, and Thomas failed to effect both the annual meeting and the annual review of the stock price set in the Agreement as required by Paragraph 6, *Purchase Price:* "Each price shall be reviewed at least annually no later than the annual meeting of the stockholders ... (commencing with the annual meetings for the year 1984) ...," here February 21, 1984. Rustin implies that, had the required meeting been held, revaluation would or should have occurred and that, after Cox's accidental death in a fire on March 14, 1984, Powell in particular as well as Thomas were obligated to revalue the stock prior to tendering the repurchase price.

There is no dispute that the By-Laws call for an annual meeting on the third Tuesday of February, here February 21, 1984. There is no dispute that none took place or that, when Cox died, the stocks of each corporation had not been formally revalued. No one disputes that Paragraph 6 of the Agreement provides for a price of $672.00 per share of Concord and a price of $744.00 per share for Associates. This totals $374,976 which is covered by insurance on Cox's life of $375,000. There is no substantial dispute that the stock is worth a great deal more, perhaps even twice as much. No one seriously disputes that Paragraph 6 further provides that:

> ... all parties may, as a result of such review, agree to a new price by a written instrument executed by all the parties and appended to an original of this instrument, and that any such new price shall thereupon become the basis for determining the purchase price for all purposes hereof unless subsequently superceded pursuant to the same procedure. The purchase price shall remain in full force and effect and until so changed.

Rustin asserts that the explicit requirement of a yearly price review "clashes" with the provision that the price shall remain in effect until changed. He argues a trial is required to determine the intent of the parties:

> The question then arises, presenting this Court with a material issue of fact not susceptible to determination on a motion for summary judgment: Did the parties intend, either to reset, or at least to monitor, yearly, the correspondence between the Paragraph 6 price and the current value of the companies? If so, who, if anyone, was principally responsible for effecting the yearly review required by the Agreement, and for insuring an informed review?

In answering these questions the Court first outlines its proper role in the interpretation of this contract.

A Court sitting in diversity will apply the substantive law of the forum state. *Erie R.R. Co. v. Tompkins,* 304 U.S. 64, (1938), here Massachusetts. In Massachusetts as elsewhere, absent ambiguity, contracts must be interpreted and enforced exactly as written. *Freelander v. G. & K. Realty Corp.,* 357 Mass. 512, 515, 516, 258 N.E.2d 786 (1970). Where the language is unambiguous, the interpretation of a contract is a question of law for the court. *Edwin R. Sage v.*

Foley, 12 Mass.App. 20, 28, 421 N.E.2d 460 (1981). Further, contracts must be construed in accordance with their ordinary and usual sense.

Contrary to Rustin's assertion, the Court in applying these standards holds that there is no ambiguity and certainly no "clash" between the dual requirements of Paragraph 6 that there be an annual review of share price and that, absent such review, the existing price prevails. When, as here, the Court searches for the meaning of a document containing two unconditional provisions, one immediately following the other, the Court favors a reading that reconciles them. *Kates v. St. Paul Fire & Marine Ins. Co.,* 509 F.Supp. 477, 485 (D.Mass.1981). The Court rules that the Agreement covers precisely the situation before it: no revaluation occurred, therefore the price remains as set forth in the Agreement. This conclusion is reasonable, for the Agreement is not a casual memorialization but a formal contract carefully drafted by attorneys and signed by all parties.

Moreover, the Court interprets Paragraph 2 to provide, in unambiguous terms:

> "In the event of the death of any Shareholder subject to this agreement, his respective ... administrator ... *shall,* within sixty (60) days after the date of death ... give written notice thereof to each Company which notice *shall* specify a purchase date not later than sixty (60) days thereafter, *offering to each Company for purchase* as hereinafter provided, and *at the purchase price set forth in Paragraph 6,* all of the Shares owned on said date by said deceased Shareholder...." [Emphasis by the Court].

Rustin, therefore, was unambiguously obligated as administrator of Cox's estate to tender Cox's shares for repurchase by Concord and Associates. His failure to do so is inexcusable unless he raises cognizable defenses.

All of Rustin's defenses turn on two allegations: that his performance is excused because the surviving parties failed to review and to adjust upward the $374,976 purchase price. Rustin contends that the parties meant to review the price per share on an annual basis. No affidavit supports this assertion, nor does any exhibit. In fact, absent any evidence for this proposition, Rustin's assertion is no more than speculation and conjecture. While Rustin contends that the failure to review and revalue constitutes "unclean hands" and a breach of fiduciary duty which excuses his nonperformance, he places before the Court only argument not facts.

It simply does not follow that because a meeting was not held and the prices were not reviewed that a trial of the parties' intentions is required. The Agreement is the best evidence of the parties' intent. Although the text of the Agreement provides that share price "shall" be reviewed "at least annually," the Agreement also states that "The purchase price shall remain in full force and effect unless and until so changed."

Even giving all intendments to Rustin, the "favorable inferences" generally afforded parties opposing summary judgment must be reasonable and based on facts, not conjecture. *Hahn v. Sargent,* 523 F.2d 461, 464 (1st Cir.1975). There must be sufficient evidence supporting the claimed factual dispute to require a trial to resolve the parties' different versions; the evidence manifesting the dispute must be substantial. Although, as the party opposing the motion, Rustin is entitled to inferences from the evidence in the records, he "is not entitled to build a case on the gossamer threads of whimsey, speculation and conjecture." *Manganaro v. Delaval Separator Co.,* 309 F.2d 389, 393 (1st Cir.1962). Thus, conclusory allegations unsupported by facts, do not create an issue which should be reserved for trial. Rustin presents no evidence that would tend to suggest that Cox intended to depart from or rescind the Agreement. He presents only bare allegations that a revaluation would have occurred had the annual meeting been held.

Even if competent evidence adduced at trial would support Rustin's allegations, his proposition would of necessity require judicial intervention, a course this Court does not favor. Rustin produces not a shred of evidence that the parties intended that a court should intercede to set the share price in the event the parties failed to do so themselves. Every first year law student learns that although the courts can lead an opera singer to the concert hall, they cannot make her sing. *Lumley v. Guy,* 118 Eng.Rep. 749 (1853). While this Court will specifically enforce a consensual bargain, memorialized in an unambiguous written document, it will not order the revision of the share price. Such intrusion into the private ordering of commercial affairs offends both good judgment and good jurisprudence. Moreover, the record before the Court indicates that the parties fully intended what their competent counsel drafted and they signed.

Moreover, the nucleus of Rustin's premise is that somehow Powell should have guaranteed the review and revision of the share prices. On the contrary, nothing in the record indicates that a reasonable trier of fact could find that Powell's duties and responsibilities included such omnipotence. More to the point, the By-Laws suggest that several individuals shared the responsibility for calling the required annual meeting: "In case the annual meeting for any year shall not be duly called or held, the Board of Directors or the President shall cuase (sic) a special meeting to be held...." Pursuant to the By-Laws, Cox himself had the power, right, and authority to call a meeting of the stockholders of both companies, in order to review the price per share—or for any other purpose for that matter.

Furthermore, nothing in the record indicates that somehow Powell, Thomas, Concord, or Associates was charged with the duty of raising the share price. In fact, this is discretionary and consensual: "all parties *may,* as a result of such review, *agree to* a new price by a written instrument *executed by all parties....*" Nowhere can the Court find any affirmative duty to guarantee either an annual meeting or a share price revision. To fault Powell for not doing by fiat what must be done by consensus credits Powell with powers she simply does not have. The mere fact that, as a shareholder of Concord and Associates, Powell benefits from the enforcement of the Agreement at the $374,976 purchase price does not, as matter of law, create an obligation on her part to effect a review or revision of the purchase price. One cannot breach a duty where no duty exists, and Rustin cannot manufacture by allegation a duty where neither the Agreement nor the By-Laws lends any support.

Of Rustin's defense that the value of the stock increased so substantially that specific enforcement would be unfair and unjust to Cox's estate, little need be said. This defense as well as Rustin's counterclaims rest on the allegation that Powell, in particular, and Thomas "knew" that a revaluation would result in a higher price and "failed to effect an annual review." Of Powell, Rustin argues that she had a "special responsibility" to effect a review of the purchase price because her siblings looked to her for financial expertise and to call a meeting. Nowhere is this "special responsibility" supported by the Agreement or the By-Laws. Rustin also implies that the sisters "knew" that failure to revalue would inure to their benefit. This presumes they knew that Cox would die in an accidental fire three weeks after the deadline for the annual meeting. To call this preposterous understates it, for nothing immunized the sisters from an equally unforeseeable accident. Rustin's argument withers in the light of objectivity to a heap of conclusory straws.

Rustin goes on to argue that the sisters had a fiduciary duty to revalue the shares *after Cox's death* and *before tender*. Nowhere in the Agreement is there the slightest indication they were so obligated. Nowhere is there evidence of willfulness, intent to deceive, or knowing manipulation. As a result, Rustin's counterclaim that the Companies, Powell, or Thomas violated Mass.Gen.Laws, ch. 93A, § 11 must fail.

Agreements, such as those before the Court, "among shareholders of closely held corporations are common and the purpose of such contracts are clear." *Brigham v. M & J Corporation*, 352 Mass. 674, 678, 227 N.E.2d 915 (1967). Moreover, such agreements are valid, bind the stockholder and his administrator or executor, and may be specifically enforced. *Donahue v. Rodd Electrotype Company of New England, Inc.*, 367 Mass. 578, 598, 328 N.E.2d 505 (1975), as limited by *Wilkes v. Springside Nursing Home, Inc.*, 370 Mass. 842, 848–852, 353 N.E.2d 657 (1976); *Smith v. Atlantic Properties, Inc.*, 12 Mass.App. 201, 205–206, 422 N.E.2d 798 (1981).

The validity of such agreements will be upheld absent any fraud, overreaching, undue influence, duress, or mistake at the time the deceased entered into the agreement, these conditions rendering the agreement void. *New England Trust Co. v. Abbott*, 162 Mass. at 155, 38 N.E. 432; *see Renberg v. Zarrow*, 667 P.2d at 470. Thus "fairness" and "good faith" in a closely held corporation generally means that each stockholder must have an equal opportunity to sell his or her shares to the corporation for an identical price. *Donahue v. Rodd Electrotype Company of New England, Inc.*, 367 Mass. at 598, 328 N.E.2d 505. The effect of the Agreement is "blind": regardless of who dies first, his or her administrator is required to sell the shares held to the corporations by set procedure for a set price. These circumstances are "fair": "[T]he stipulated price provision wherein no one knows for certain at the time the price is set whether he is to be a buyer or a seller is inherently fair and provides mutuality of risk." *Renberg v. Zarrow*, 667 P.2d at 471.

Moreover, specific performance of an agreement to convey will not be refused merely because the price is inadequate or excessive. *New England Trust Co. v. Abbott*, 162 Mass. at 155, 38 N.E. 432; *see Lee v. Kirby*, 104 Mass. 420,

430 (1870); *Allen v. Biltmore Tissue Corp.*, 2 N.Y.2d 534, 543, 161 N.Y.S.2d 418, 141 N.E.2d 812 (1957) ("The validity of the restriction on transfer does not rest on any abstract notion of intrinsic fairness of price. To be invalid, more than mere disparity between option price and current value of the stock must be shown"); *Renberg v. Zarrow*, 667 P.2d at 470 ("In the absence of fraud, overreaching, or bad faith, an agreement between the stockholders that upon the death of any of them, the stock may be acquired by the corporation is binding. Even great disparity between the price specified in a buy-sell agreement and the actual value of the stock is not sufficient to invalidate the agreement.") The fact that surviving shareholders were allowed to purchase Cox' shares on stated terms and conditions which resulted in the purchase for less than actual value of the stock does not subject the agreement to attack as a breach of the relation of trust and confidence, there being no breach of fiduciary duty.

Rather than evidence of any impropriety, the Court rules that the purchase prices were carefully set, fair when established, evidenced by an Agreement binding all parties equally to the same terms without any indication that any one sibling would reap a windfall. The courts may not rewrite a shareholder's agreement under the guise of relieving one of the parties from the hardship of an improvident bargain. The Court cannot protect the parties from a bad bargain and it will not protect them from bad luck. Cox, the party whose estate is aggrieved, had while alive every opportunity to call the annual meeting and persuade his sisters to revalue their stock. Sad though the situation be, sadness is not the touchstone of contract interpretation.

In the absence any genuine issues of material fact, Concord and Associates are entitled to judgment as matter of law. The Agreement shall be specifically enforced.

SO ORDERED.

CASE PROBLEM 13-1

Alton Inc. provides take-out laundry services to hospitals and health-care providers in the Northwest. It is a C corporation with three shareholders, all of whom work full time for the business. The three owners have been "buddies and partners" since high school, but now they are all over age 40. The business has 80 employees and continual growth. The owners have decided that they need some kind of "buyout" agreement in case something happens to one of them. What "triggers" would you recommend be included in the shareholders buy-sell agreement? How would you suggest structuring each trigger?

CASE PROBLEM 13-2

Clint Wade owns 70 percent of the stock of Knock-Down Inc., a demolition and gravel supply company. The remaining 30 percent of the stock is owned in equal shares by three of the key managers of the business. The minority owners recently had their attorney draw up a "standard" buy-sell agreement to protect them in case one of them dies, retires, or wants out of the business. The agreement gives all the shareholders equal rights in the event of a triggering event. You represent Wade. How would you advise him?

CASE PROBLEM 13-3

Sports Limited owns a small chain of profitable sporting goods stores. The company has three shareholders: Sam, who owns 40 percent of the stock and does not work in the business; and Lewis and Jake, each of whom owns 30 percent of the stock and works in the business full-time. Sam is independently wealthy; his investment in the company represents a tiny portion of his wealth. Lewis and Jake have their company stock and their salaries and nothing else.

Sports Unlimited has a shareholder agreement that contains a standard right of first refusal provision and a showdown clause. The right of first refusal requires any shareholder who wants out to obtain a bid for his stock from a third party and then gives the company or the remaining shareholders a first right to match the third-party's offer. The showdown clause gives any shareholder the right to set a price for the stock and then force the other shareholders to elect to buy or sell at that price.

You represent Jake. Advise him on the wisdom of having these provisions in the agreement. What alternatives would you suggest?

CHAPTER 14

FIGHTS FOR CORPORATE CONTROL AND OWNERSHIP

A. HIGH STAKES, INHERENT CONFLICTS

Public companies are "public." Unlike a closely held corporation, the management and ownership of a public corporation, at least theoretically, are always up for grabs. If someone wants to replace the board so that a new executive management team can be installed, a showdown proxy battle can be triggered to let the shareholders decide. And to hedge all bets that the shareholders will collectively approve the shakeup, the proponents of change (often a deep-pocket private equity firm or hedge fund) may use their capital to influence or dictate the vote by increasing their ownership in the enterprise. An effective tool to quickly and dramatically boost ownership in a public corporation is the tender offer – an offer made to all shareholders to buy a designated amount of stock at a price that nearly always reflects a premium over the current trading price of the stock.

Tender offers are classified and defined in different ways. A friendly offer is an offer that is blessed by the target company's management; a hostile offer is one that threatens management and, in the opinion of management, is not in the best interests of the corporation or its shareholders. A coercive offer is an offer for a limited number shares that threatens misery for the remaining shareholders of the target who are left at the mercy of the new controlling owners. Its opposite is the unlimited all-cash offer that places no limits on shareholder participation. A single tier (or one-step) offer is an offer that does not contemplate a follow-up transaction between the bidder and the target company. A two-tier offer contemplates such a follow up (back-end) transaction at some point following the successful completion of the tender offer.

Are tender offers that rattle and threaten the status quo a good thing? Some passionately argue "yes" because they promote (force?) management accountability and provide a powerful punitive incentive to keep corporate performance and stock values at high levels. The best defense to a hostile proxy battle is superior performance, and few things discourage a tender more than a strong stock price. Others argue that tender offers, on balance, are just necessary evils that provide deep-pocketed profiteers with a mechanism to leverage the capital markets with schemes that, in the end, damage multiple corporate stakeholders – employees, creditors, communities, vendors, states and, yes, even shareholders. But, whether good or bad, two realities about tender offers are undeniable.

First, a tender offer usually drives stock prices up, at least temporarily, for the shareholders of the target corporation and often for the shareholders of the bidder. Various theories have been advanced to explain this price-escalating reality, including that a tender offer exposes the potential of stronger management in the future, the profitable synergistic possibilities between the bidder and target, the value of "bigness," the inherent market under-valuing of long-term stock values, and the impact of boosting shareholder value at the expense of other corporate stakeholders. Whatever the theory, just the mention of a tender offer often sparks shareholder enthusiasm because it suggests the opportunity for a sellout at a premium price.

Second, a tender offer can dramatically showcase the conflicts and tensions that exist between those who own the corporation and those who manage the corporation. Who should have the final say in any decision to fight or oppose a tender offer? Should management sit tight and let the shareholders play it out? Should management confine its efforts to maximizing the net yield to the shareholders? At what point does management's push to preserve the status quo violate duties owned to the shareholders? When and how can management "lock up" a friendly deal with a third party that cannot be dismantled by a hostile tender offer? Of course, these questions are often complicated by others who have a powerful, vested stake in the outcome – those who count on the corporation for a job, tax revenues, local business, community support, and long-term stability.

Given the high stakes and inherent conflicts that surface when management and ownership control of a public corporation are put into play, multiple legal challenges are common and expected. Some of the key ones have been covered in previous chapters of this book. Any use of the proxy machine (very common in control disputes) will be subject to the proxy rules discussed in Chapter 8 and the antifraud proxy risks of Rule 14a-9 discussed in Chapter 11. Management must carefully regulate and monitor disclosures during a control showdown to not trigger 10b-5 liabilities, as discussed in Chapter 11. Management efforts to frustrate shareholder voting rights (of the bidder or others) to protect their positions may run afoul of the *Blasius* "compelling justification" standard discussed in Chapter 8. As we will see, this standard has triggered some serious challenges for the Delaware courts in a tender offer context. And, of course, the directors' fiduciary duties of care and loyalty and the role of the business judgment rule (discussed in Chapter 10) often are central issues when an attempt is made to thwart a tender offer.

This Chapter adds to these previous discussions by focusing on three dimensions of the legal challenges triggered by tender offers. The following section reviews federal regulation of public company tender offers under the Williams Act amendments to the Securities Exchange Act of 1934. Section C discusses the history and impacts of state antitakeover statutes (all states have them) that now play a central role in the design of tender offers. And section D discusses defensive actions that target companies often take (poison pills and the like) and the legal challenges triggered by such actions.

B. FEDERAL REGULATION

The 1968 Williams Act amendments to the Securities Exchange Act of 1934 were designed to improve federal regulation of transactions that impact corporate control. They apply to all public corporations registered under section 12 of the '34 Act. Following is a brief description of the key Williams Act provisions that are applicable in a tender offer situation.

Five Percent Notice. Any person or group that acquires beneficial ownership of more than five percent of a public corporation's outstanding equity securities must file a "Schedule 13D" disclosure with the SEC. Beneficial ownership is predicated on "voting power and/or investment power." The Schedule 13d must be filed within 10 days of acquiring the triggering five-percent interest and must include:

- The identity and background of the acquiring person or group.

- The source and amount of funds used in making the stock purchases.

- The number of the corporation's shares held by the person or group.

- Details regarding any arrangements with others relating to shares of the corporation's stock.

- The purpose of the acquisition and the intentions of the acquiring person or group regarding the corporation.

Tender Offer Notice. A disclosure document ("Schedule TO") must be filed with the SEC on the same day that a person ("bidder") commences a tender offer. The document must set forth the information required on a Schedule 13d filing, along with the terms and conditions of the tender offer, past negotiations between the bidder and the corporation, any applicable regulatory requirements, and other information that the bidder deems material. Financial statements of the bidder should also be included if they are material to the tender offer.

Mandatory Offer Terms. A tender offer is subject to the following terms:

- The offer must stay open 20 business days and at least 10 business days after any change in the offer price or the percentage of shares covered by the offer.

- Any shareholder can revoke a tender of shares while the tender offer is open.

- The tender offer must be available to all shareholders holding the same class of shares.

- All shareholders must be offered the same price and the same choices as to the form of consideration if any such choices are offered.

- If the number of tendered shares exceeds the number of shares covered by the tender offer, the bidder must purchase shares on a *pro rata* basis from the tendering shareholders.

- The bidder is prohibited from purchasing shares of the corporation's stock outside of the tender offer while the offer is open.

Target Cooperation. The target corporation must assist in distributing the bidder's tender materials to the shareholders either by mailing them or providing a current shareholders mailing list to the bidder. All expenses must be borne by the bidder. Plus, the management of the target corporation must submit a responding statement to the tender offer within 10 business days following the commencement of the offer. The statement should explain the management's reasons for opposing the offer, supporting the offer, or taking no position with respect to the offer.

Self-Tender Rules. Any self-tender offer made by a corporation to buy its own shares (usually made as a defensive move against a third party offer) must comply with the same rules that are applicable to third party offers, except (1) the corporation may purchase its stock while its self-tender offer is open, and (2) no purchases may be made by the corporation during a 10 business day cooling off period after the termination of the self-tender.

False or Misleading Statements. Tender offers are subject to the following broad antifraud provision of section 14(e) of the '34 Act:

> (e) It shall be unlawful for any person to make any untrue statement of a material fact or omit to state any material fact necessary in order to make the statements made, in the light of the circumstances under which they are made, not misleading, or to engage in any fraudulent, deceptive, or manipulative acts or practices, in connection with any tender offer or request or invitation for tenders, or any solicitation of security holders in opposition to or in favor of any such offer, request, or invitation.

Although the language of section 14(e) is similar to Rule 10b-5, there is one major difference – 14(e) does not require a "sale or purchase" of a security. Its protection could extend to a person who elected not to participate in a tender offer. Of course, in many battles for control, 10b-5 will be applicable to disclosures that may impact stock trading, and the antifraud proxy provisions of section Rule 14a-9 will be in play to the extent proxy solicitations are made in connection with the tender offer. (See Chapter 11). The focus of section 14(e) is on false or misleading disclosures, not whether the tender offer is fair. In *Schreider v. Burlington Northern, Inc.*, 472 U.S. 1 (1985) the plaintiff alleged that management's orchestration of the substitution of a friendly tender for a more favorable hostile offer constituted an illegal "manipulation" under section 14(e). In rejecting the claim, the Court stated:

> Nowhere in the legislative history is there the slightest suggestion that § 14(e) serves any purpose other than disclosure, or that the term "manipulative" should be read as an invitation to the courts to oversee the substantive fairness of tender offers; the quality of any offer is a matter for the marketplace. To adopt the reading of the term "manipulative" urged by petitioner would not only be unwarranted in light of the legislative purpose but would be at odds with it. Inviting judges to read the term "manipulative" with their own sense of what

constitutes "unfair" or "artificial" conduct would inject uncertainty into the tender offer process. An essential piece of information-whether the court would deem the fully disclosed actions of one side or the other to be "manipulative"-would not be available until after the tender offer had closed. This uncertainty would directly contradict the expressed congressional desire to give investors full information.

472 U.S. at 11-12.

Insider Trading. The SEC has promulgated a broad tender offer insider trading prohibition under Rule 14(e)(3). This rule prohibits any person from trading during a tender offer if that person possesses nonpublic, material information about the offer that the person has reason to know was obtained from the bidder or management of the target company. It extends to anyone; the tipper "personal benefit" requirement of 10b-5 (see Chapter 11) does not apply.

C. STATE ANTITAKEOVER STATUTES

1. HISTORY AND CONSTITUTIONAL CHALLENGES

States have always had a vested interest in the activities of outsiders who seek to take control of a local public company and disrupt the *status quo* by moving, consolidating or dismantling the target corporation for profit. These efforts can destroy jobs, deplete a tax base, and damage all elements of a state's economy. The following list of legislative findings to support Washington State's antitakeover statute (an example only) perhaps says it best:

RCW 23B.19.010
Legislative findings — Intent

The legislature finds that:

(1) Corporations that offer employment and health, retirement, and other benefits to citizens of the state of Washington are vital to the economy of this state and the well-being of all of its citizens;

(2) The welfare of the employees of these corporations is of paramount interest and concern to this state;

(3) Many businesses in this state rely on these corporations to purchase goods and services;

(4) Hostile or unfriendly attempts to gain control of or influence otherwise publicly held corporations can cause corporate management to dissipate a corporation's assets in an effort to resist the takeover by selling or distributing cash or assets, redeeming stock, or taking other steps to increase the short-term gain to shareholders and to dissipate energies required for strategic planning, market development, capital investment decisions, assessment of technologies, and evaluation of

competitive challenges that can damage the long-term interests of shareholders and the economic health of the state by reducing or eliminating the ability to finance investments in research and development, new products, facilities and equipment, and by undermining the planning process for those purposes;

(5) Hostile or unfriendly attempts to gain control or influence otherwise publicly held corporations are often highly leveraged pursuant to financing arrangements which assume that an acquirer will promptly obtain access to an acquired corporation's cash or assets and use them, or the proceeds of their sale, to repay acquisition indebtedness;

(6) Hostile or unfriendly attempts to gain control of or influence otherwise publicly held corporations can harm the economy of the state by weakening corporate performance, and causing unemployment, plant closings, reduced charitable donations, declining population base, reduced income to fee-supported local government services, reduced tax base, and reduced income to other businesses; and

(7) The state has a substantial and legitimate interest in regulating domestic corporations and those foreign corporations that have their most significant business contacts with this state and in regulating hostile or unfriendly attempts to gain control of or influence otherwise publicly held domestic corporations and those foreign corporations that employ a large number of citizens of the state, pay significant taxes, and have a substantial economic base in the state.

State efforts to regulate takeovers initially faced constitutional challenges. The winning argument in *Edgar v. Mite Corp.*, 457 U.S. 625 (1982), was that the Illinois statute in question was preempted by the Williams Act and violated the dormant commerce clause by placing an undue burden on out-of-state tender offers that outweighed the state's interest in shareholder protections. The statute in *Mite*, like most first generation state antitakeover statutes, focused on shareholder protection by requiring a 20-day preannouncement waiting period and a fairness review by state officials, and by extending its provisions to non-Illinois companies that had significant contacts with the state. In striking down the statute, the Supreme Court stated:

> It is therefore apparent that the Illinois statute is a direct restraint on interstate commerce and that it has a sweeping extraterritorial effect. Furthermore, if Illinois may impose such regulations, so may other States; and interstate commerce in securities transactions generated by tender offers would be thoroughly stifled... Because the Illinois Act purports to regulate directly and to interdict interstate commerce, including commerce wholly outside the State, it must be held invalid...

> The Illinois Act is also unconstitutional under the test of *Pike v. Bruce Church, Inc.*, 397 U.S., at 142, 90 S.Ct., at 847, for even when a state statute regulates interstate commerce indirectly, the burden

imposed on that commerce must not be excessive in relation to the local interests served by the statute...The effects of allowing the Illinois Secretary of State to block a nationwide tender offer are substantial. Shareholders are deprived of the opportunity to sell their shares at a premium. The reallocation of economic resources to their highest valued use, a process which can improve efficiency and competition, is hindered. The incentive the tender offer mechanism provides incumbent management to perform well so that stock prices remain high is reduced...

Appellant claims the Illinois Act furthers two legitimate local interests. He argues that Illinois seeks to protect resident security holders and that the Act merely regulates the internal affairs of companies incorporated under Illinois law. We agree with the Court of Appeals that these asserted interests are insufficient to outweigh the burdens Illinois imposes on interstate commerce... Insofar as the Illinois law burdens out-of-state transactions, there is nothing to be weighed in the balance to sustain the law.

457 U.S. at 642.

Mite sent states back to the drawing board to start crafting, with the aid of pro-management advocates, a second generation of antitakeover statutes that would apply only to corporations incorporated within the state, focus on regulating corporate internal governance, and heavily target the destructive impacts of coercive tender offers. Soon Indiana's second generation version was before the Supreme Court. The statute applied only to Indiana corporations that had significant ties to the state and provided that shares acquired by a tender offer bidder could not be voted by the bidder until disinterested shareholders (management excluded) voted to authorize such voting rights. To the surprise of many, the court upheld this version of an antitakeover statute in *CTS Corp. v. Dynamics Corp. of America,* 481 U.S. 69 (1987), by stating:

The Indiana Act operates on the assumption, implicit in the Williams Act, that independent shareholders faced with tender offers often are at a disadvantage. By allowing such shareholders to vote as a group, the Act protects them from the coercive aspects of some tender offers. If, for example, shareholders believe that a successful tender offer will be followed by a purchase of nontendering shares at a depressed price, individual shareholders may tender their shares—even if they doubt the tender offer is in the corporation's best interest—to protect themselves from being forced to sell their shares at a depressed price. As the SEC explains: "The alternative of not accepting the tender offer is virtual assurance that, if the offer is successful, the shares will have to be sold in the lower priced, second step." Two-Tier Tender Offer Pricing and Non-Tender Offer Purchase Programs, SEC Exchange Act Rel. No. 21079 (June 21, 1984).

In such a situation under the Indiana Act, the shareholders as a group, acting in the corporation's best interest, could reject the offer, although individual shareholders might be inclined to accept it. The desire of the Indiana Legislature to protect shareholders of Indiana corporations from this type of coercive offer does not conflict with the Williams Act. Rather, it furthers the federal policy of investor protection...

The principal objects of dormant Commerce Clause scrutiny are statutes that discriminate against interstate commerce. The Indiana Act is not such a statute. It has the same effects on tender offers whether or not the offeror is a domiciliary or resident of Indiana. Thus, it "visits its effects equally upon both interstate and local business," *Lewis v. BT Investment Managers, Inc., supra,* 447 U.S., at 36.

Dynamics nevertheless contends that the statute is discriminatory because it will apply most often to out-of-state entities. This argument rests on the contention that, as a practical matter, most hostile tender offers are launched by offerors outside Indiana. But this argument avails Dynamics little. "The fact that the burden of a state regulation falls on some interstate companies does not, by itself, establish a claim of discrimination against interstate commerce." *Exxon Corp. v. Governor of Maryland,* 437 U.S. 117, 126, 98 S.Ct. 2207, 2214, 57 L.Ed.2d 91 (1978)...

Dynamics' argument that the Act is unconstitutional ultimately rests on its contention that the Act will limit the number of successful tender offers. There is little evidence that this will occur. But even if true, this result would not substantially affect our Commerce Clause analysis. We reiterate that this Act does not prohibit any entity— resident or nonresident—from offering to purchase, or from purchasing, shares in Indiana corporations, or from attempting thereby to gain control. It only provides regulatory procedures designed for the better protection of the corporations' shareholders.

We have rejected the "notion that the Commerce Clause protects the particular structure or methods of operation in a ... market." *Exxon Corp. v. Governor of Maryland,* 437 U.S., at 127. The very commodity that is traded in the securities market is one whose characteristics are defined by state law. Similarly, the very commodity that is traded in the "market for corporate control"—the corporation—is one that owes its existence and attributes to state law. Indiana need not define these commodities as other States do; it need only provide that residents and nonresidents have equal access to them. This Indiana has done. Accordingly, even if the Act should decrease the number of successful tender offers for Indiana corporations, this would not offend the Commerce Clause. 481 U.S. at 83 – 94.

Armed with a victory in *CTS* and guidance from the Supreme Court, states soon tackled the challenge of developing a third generation of antitakeover statutes. Today, there are various statutory schemes included in this third generation, some of which test the limits of the *CTS* holding. Following is a brief recap of the types of statutes in play today.

2. STATUTORY SCHEMES

The Delaware Moratorium Scheme. Delaware's scheme is one of the least onerous. Section 203 of Delaware's General Corporation Law prohibits an interested shareholder (defined as one who acquires 15 percent or more of the stock of a Delaware corporation in a tender offer) from engaging in any merger or business combination ("Business Combination") with the corporation for a three-year period following the tender offer. This prohibition does not apply if (1) the corporation's board approved the Business Combination before the tender offer that triggered the 15 percent triggering threshold, (2) the interested person acquires at least 85 percent of the corporation's stock (excluding management shares) through the tender offer, or (3) the Business Combination is approved by the corporation's board and shareholder who own at least two-thirds of the other outstanding shares. So the options available to a bidder who wants to trigger a second-tier combination to terminate the interests of other target company shareholders are to wait three years, acquire at least 85 percent through the tender, secure approval of the corporation's board before the tender, or secure approval of the corporation's board and holders of two-thirds of the other shares after the tender.

Control Purchase Schemes. Under these schemes, a bidder whose holdings hit a designated threshold (such as 33 percent) of a corporation's stock is prohibited from acquiring "control shares" unless the shareholders of the corporation, at a meeting usually called no more than 50 days after the bidder's notice, approve the acquisition of control shares by the bidder. As the Court noted in *CTS*, this type of scheme protects against coercive tender offers by forcing collective action of the shareholders.

Control Voting Schemes. This is the scheme that was at issue in *CTS*. It's similar to the prior scheme, except the focus is on the voting rights of the bidder. The bidder can buy stock beyond a designated threshold, but the voting rights of those shares are contingent on a vote of the other shareholders.

Fair-Price Schemes. This scheme prohibits a bidder who acquires control of a corporation though a tender offer to engage in a second-tier (sometimes called a "back-end") transaction with the corporation unless the price paid in the second-tier transaction equals or exceeds a statutorily designated fair price, which often is based on the tender price in the first-tier transaction or the market value of the stock during a designated time-frame. The objective is to ensure that the bidder does not use the newly-acquired control to force a second transaction that yields an unfair price to the other shareholders.

Combo Moratorium/Fair Price Scheme. Some state statutes incorporate both moratorium and a fair price schemes. An example is Washington State,[1] which imposes a five-year moratorium on transactions between the bidder and the corporation following a tender offer (with exceptions similar to those in Delaware) and imposes a fair price scheme on certain mergers and liquidations

---

1. RCW 23B.19.040.

that fall outside of the five-year window.

Foreign Corporation Schemes. Some state statutes apply to a corporation organized in another state if the corporation has key ties to the state; maintains its principal executive in the state; has a designated percentage (often 10 percent) of its shareholders, or a designated percentage of its outstanding shares, owned by residents of the state; has a majority of its employees in the state; and has the majority of its assets or assets with a designated value ($50 million) located in the state.[2] Other states, including Delaware,[3] limit the scope of their statute to corporations organized in the state.

Optional or Mandatory?

Are the provisions of a state's antitakeover statute optional or mandatory? That is, may a corporation opt out of the provisions? Delaware permits such an opt out by a provision in the corporation's articles of incorporation, provided that any opt-out amendment to the articles of incorporation is not effective for 12 months.[4] Other states do not provide for such an opt-out, but instead confirm that the statutory requirements are "in addition to, not in lieu of" other protective provisions that may be included in the articles of incorporation or bylaws of the corporation[5] – such as poison pill and staggered board provisions and specific authorization for the board to consider a broad range of corporate stakeholders (shareholders, employees, vendors, customers, creditors, employees, communities) in developing a response to an unsolicited tender offer.

D. CORPORATE DEFENSES TO HOSTILE BIDS

1. WHEN CREATIVITY AND FEAR LINK UP

Corporate managers often have strong incentives to protect against the job security risks of a hostile tender offer. They know that the strength of their continued lucrative employment is tied to the stability of the board. This reality has prompted pro-management groups, with the support of many clever lawyers, to develop an arsenal of tools that can be used to fight a tender offer. Some of these defensive tools are designed to fight the offer when it arrives; others create obstacles that discourage tender offers by complicating or devaluing any hostile effort. It's what happens when there's a need for creativity.

In many situations, the interests of the target company shareholders (which often include a potential bidder) are squarely aligned with the plans of a potential takeover bid. The shareholders do not want defensive tools that entrench management, drive away bidders, and destroy opportunities for a premium yield that come when a company's true long-term value is exposed in a control showdown. Such shareholders have a few options. They can prevent a defensive tool from ever being adopted or implemented by the smart use of shareholder proposals (see Chapter 9) or by putting pressure on the board. They can

---

2. See, for example, RCW 23B.10.020(19(b).
3. 8 DGCL § 203.
4. 8 DGCL § 203(a)(3).
5. See, for example, RCW 25B.19.050.

collectively organize (often with a bidder who owns stock) to force (via a proxy battle) changes in the board's membership that will lead to the termination or deactivation of a defensive tool. And, as discussed in the following section, they can seek injunctive and other equitable judicial relief to prevent management from protecting its interests at the expense of shareholders.

It's beyond the scope of this effort to describe in any detail the breadth of the potential tools that a corporation may consider for inclusion in its antitakeover arsenal. Following is a brief description of some of the most popular.

Poison Pills. This defensive tool is designed to create an intolerable valuation obstacle for a hostile bidder. It can be structured in many ways, but the core feature is that shareholders of the target corporation (excluding the bidder) are given rights to buy stock at a deep discount if a triggering event occurs (the bidder acquires a designated percentage of the target's stock, such as 15 or 20 percent) and the target's board does not redeem the rights and prevent release of the poison within a short time (usually 10 days) following the triggering event. The dilution risks to the bidder are prohibitive if the discount purchase rights become effective (the poison is released). So the bidder's only options, as a practical matter, are to negotiate a deal with the target's existing management to redeem the rights (at a nominal value specified in the plan) or put an end to the rights by gaining control of the target's board. A "flip-in" plan gives the shareholders the right to buy target shares at a deep discount. A "flip-over" plan gives the shareholders the right, usually through convertible preferred stock, to buy shares of the bidder at a deep discount in the event of a merger or other combination after the triggering event. Poison pills are very effective in preventing hostile tender offers and, for that very reason, many institutional investors and investor advisory firms oppose their use. Some companies have "shelf poison pills," plans that have not been officially approved but that can be instantly adopted by a bylaw amendment approved by the target's board if the need arises.

Shark Repellents. These are corporate governance defensive measures that are implemented (usually by bylaw amendment) before any tender offer threat is made. The most popular repellents are:

• A *staggered board* provision that gives directors varying terms of more than one year and substantially lengthens the time for a successful bidder to replace the target's board,

• A *supermajority shareholder voting* requirement for any merger or business combination following a successful tender offer, and

• A *"fair price" provision* requiring that any price in a "back-end" transaction following a tender offer be at least equal to the price offered in the "front-end" tender offer.

Pacman Attack. This occurs when the target company's management reacts to a hostile takeover attempt by initiating a tender offer to gain control of the hostile bidder. For management, it's the ultimate "winner-take-all" showdown. For shareholders, it often guarantees super-escalating premiums for their stock.

White Squire Sale. This occurs when the target's management dilutes the efforts of the hostile bidder by selling additional target shares (often at a discount) to an investor ("squire") who is friendly to management. The squire is not a competitive bidder for control, but the squire's acquisition of stock makes it tougher for the hostile bidder to succeed.

White Knight Recruit. This occurs when the target's management seeks to drive up the price offered by the hostile bidder or force the hostile bidder to retreat by finding another party (a "knight" friendly to management) to engage in a competitive bidding contest with the hostile bidder.

Crown Jewel Sale. This tactic is where the target's management gives a white knight or another party a contractual right or option to purchase a valuable part of the target's business (the "Crown Jewel") at a bargain price. This is considered a "scorched earth" defensive move that is designed to make the target unattractive to any hostile bidder.

Golden Parachute Hikes. This tool drives up the costs of a takeover bid by increasing golden parachute benefits to senior executives and automatically vesting restricted stock and supplemental retirement benefits in the event of a takeover.

Greenmail Payment. This is where the target's management causes the target to purchase a large block of stock held by a potential hostile bidder to remove the risk of a tender offer. It's akin to blackmail in that it nets the potential hostile bidder a "greenmail" price that reflects a substantial premium over the current market price of the stock. It's sometimes called a "bon voyage bonus" or a "goodbye kiss."

Macaroni Defense. This tactic involves the target company issuing bonds that come with a guarantee that the bonds will be redeemed at a substantial premium price by the target company if there is a successful hostile takeover bid. The high costs of the bonds are designed to discourage a hostile bidder. The term "macaroni" refers to the fact that the redemption price expands with the heat of a hostile bid.

People Pill. This defense is possible when retention of the target's management team is deemed essential to the success of the company. In such a situation, the management team threatens to leave *in masse* if the hostile bid is successful. The goal of the strategy is to discourage offers in those situations where the bidder needs existing management.

Share Buyback. This strategy involves the company borrowing funds to buy back its own shares in a self-tender offer that competes with the hostile bidder. It has a dual deterrent impact on the hostile bidder – it forces the bidder to pay more as the stock price is driven up by the competition, and the company gets weaker as it takes on more debt. This tactic is often referred to as a "leveraged recapitalization." When taken to extremes, the strategy can become a "suicide pill" because it can threaten the survival of the company.

BankMail. This tactic involves an agreement between the target company and its bank to terminate any existing financing arrangements if control of the company changes as a result of a hostile takeover. It discourages hostile bids because it forces the bidder to find new financing sources for the target's business, drives up transaction costs, and gives the target's management time to implement other defensive strategies.

2. DEFENSES UNDER JUDICIAL ATTACK – NOTHING EASY

Antitakeover defense jurisprudence has been a core challenge for Delaware's Chancery and Supreme courts for decades. The overriding question has always focused on the standard of review that a court should apply in resolving the inherent conflict between a board's statutory authority to manage a corporation and shareholder interests when actions are taken to preserve that authority in a dispute with a hostile bidder. Related questions are the role of the business judgment rule and who should bear the burden of proof when shareholders attack a management-installed defensive measure designed to deter or thwart hostile actions.

In the early days, before the creation of the present smorgasbord of defensive options, the central question was whether management could use corporate funds to end the threat of a hostile bid by purchasing the bidder's stock at a premium. There was never any question of the board's statutory authority to use corporate funds to purchase stock of the corporation. The issue was whether the board members were exercising that authority "solely or primarily" for an improper purpose – to perpetuate their position of control.[6] In *Bennett v. Propp*, the court stated:

> We must bear in mind the inherent damager in the purchase of shares with corporate funds to remove a threat to corporate policy when a threat to control is involved. The directors are of necessity confronted with a conflict of interest, and an objective decision is difficult. Hence, in our opinion, the burden should be on the directors to justify such a purchase as one primarily in the corporate interest.

187 A.2d at 49.

Given this burden of proof for directors, the Delaware Supreme Courts reversal of the Chancery Court's decision in *Cheff v. Mathews*, 199 A.2d 548 (Del. Supr.1964), came as a surprise to many. In that case, the directors of Holland Furnace Company ("Holland") caused Holland to purchase the shares of a shareholder ("Maremont") who had acquired a 15 percent stake in Holland and was threatening a tender offer for the balance of the corporation's stock. One director ("Cheff") was an officer of Holland and another ("Trenkamp") was Holland's attorney. The other directors were outsiders who owned Holland stock. A derivative action was brought by shareholders, claiming that the purchase was made to protect the control of the incumbent board and demanding that the purchase be rescinded and the directors be required to personally account

---

6. See *Kors v. Carey*, 158 A.2d 136 (Del.Ch. 1960), *Bennett v. Propp*, 187 A.2d 405 (Del. Ch. 1962), and *Yasik v. Wachtel*, 17 A.2d 309 (Del.Ch. 1941).

for any damages to Holland. In reversing the lower court decision that the directors had not sustained their burden of proof and ruling for the defendants, the court stated:

> To say that the burden of proof is upon the defendants is not to indicate, however, that the directors have the same 'self-dealing interest' as is present, for example, when a director sells property to the corporation. The only clear pecuniary interest shown on the record was held by Mr. Cheff, as an executive of the corporation, and Trenkamp, as its attorney. The mere fact that some of the other directors were substantial shareholders does not create a personal pecuniary interest in the decisions made by the board of directors, since all shareholders would presumably share the benefit flowing to the substantial shareholder. Accordingly, these directors other than Trenkamp and Cheff, while called upon to justify their actions, will not be held to the same standard of proof required of those directors having personal and pecuniary interest in the transaction...

> Plaintiffs urge that the sale price was unfair in view of the fact that the price was in excess of that prevailing on the open market. However, as conceded by all parties, a substantial block of stock will normally sell at a higher price than that prevailing on the open market, the increment being attributable to a 'control premium'. Plaintiffs argue that it is inappropriate to require the defendant corporation to pay a control premium, since control is meaningless to an acquisition by a corporation of its own shares. However, it is elementary that a holder of a substantial number of shares would expect to receive the control premium as part of his selling price, and if the corporation desired to obtain the stock, it is unreasonable to expect that the corporation could avoid paying what any other purchaser would be required to pay for the stock... The Vice Chancellor made no finding as to the fairness of the price other than to indicate the obvious fact that the market price was increasing as a result of open market purchases by Maremont, Mrs. Cheff and Holland.

> The question then presented is whether or not defendants satisfied the burden of proof of showing reasonable grounds to believe a danger to corporate policy and effectiveness existed by the presence of the Maremont stock ownership. It is important to remember that the directors satisfy their burden by showing good faith and reasonable investigation; the directors will not be penalized for an honest mistake of judgment, if the judgment appeared reasonable at the time the decision was made...

> [W]e are of the opinion that the evidence presented in the court below leads inevitably to the conclusion that the board of directors, based upon direct investigation, receipt of professional advice, and personal observations of the contradictory action of Maremont and his explanation of corporate purpose, believed, with justification, that there was a reasonable threat to the continued existence of Holland, or at

least existence in its present form, by the plan of Maremont to continue building up his stock holdings. We find no evidence in the record sufficient to justify a contrary conclusion.

199 A.2d at 555-556.

Cheff provided a wobbly analytical framework for examining actions taken by boards to end hostile tender offer threats. The business judgment rule was in play, predicated on the board satisfying an unspecified proof burden of good faith and reasonable investigation.

This framework continued to shape the law as hostile takeover bids ballooned and grabbed headlines from the late '70s to the early '90s and pro-management forces pulled out all stops to create the menu of defensive measures described above. The Delaware courts were constantly being challenged to use an undefined standard of review in high-stakes cases that posed unique facts that went right to the heart of the core conflict between those who manage and those who own a corporation. Half-way through the tender offer activity surge, the Delaware Supreme Court decided the landmark case of *Unocal Corporation v. Mesa Petroleum Co*, which established a standard that would be the foundational starting point for all future decisions.

Strategy Going Forward

It's a formidable challenge to figure out how best to use a reasonable number of pages in a text on business organizations to introduce students to an ever-evolving body of complicated corporate law where smart judges regularly craft opinions approaching 100 pages to resolve specific corporate control disputes that usually involve hundreds of millions of dollars. I've given this challenge a fair amount of thought and do not profess to have the best solution. But I do have a strategy.

Start by carefully reading the *Unocal* opinion. Then carefully consider the specific questions raised by Case Problem Case 15-1 that follows *Unocal*. Study the opinions in the *Unitrin* and *Chesapeake* cases that follow and analyze the questions raised in Case Problem Case 15-1 based on the reasoning used by the courts in those cases.

Following the *Chesapeake* case, a lengthy discussion will introduce you to Revlon-Land, an outgrowth of Unocal that deals with the obligations of a board when a change in the control of a corporation is inevitable. After reading the discussion's short descriptions of a few key Revlon-Land cases, study Case Problem 15-2 and attempt to analyze the questions based on the reasoning used by the Delaware Chancery Court in the 2011 case of *In re Smurfit-Stone Container Corp. Shareholder Litigation*.

These exercises will likely leave you uncertain about your answers and a bit confused as to how the standards established by the Delaware courts should be applied in a specific case. This just confirms that you are normal; uncertainty and confusion are the norm. It also confirms that you probably are right. Anyone who professes certainty has likely oversimplified the analysis.

Please note that, out of necessity, the following court opinions in this Chapter have been heavily edited.

3. APPLYING UNOCAL'S TWO-PRONG TEST

UNOCAL CORPORATION v. MESA PETROLEUM CO.
493 A.2d 946 (Del. Supr. 1985)

Moore, Justice.

We confront an issue of first impression in Delaware—the validity of a corporation's self-tender for its own shares which excludes from participation a stockholder making a hostile tender offer for the company's stock.

The Court of Chancery granted a preliminary injunction to the plaintiffs, Mesa Petroleum Co., Mesa Asset Co., Mesa Partners II, and Mesa Eastern, Inc. (collectively "Mesa"), enjoining an exchange offer of the defendant, Unocal Corporation (Unocal) for its own stock. The trial court concluded that a selective exchange offer, excluding Mesa, was legally impermissible. We cannot agree with such a blanket rule. The factual findings of the Vice Chancellor, fully supported by the record, establish that Unocal's board, consisting of a majority of independent directors, acted in good faith, and after reasonable investigation found that Mesa's tender offer was both inadequate and coercive. Under the circumstances the board had both the power and duty to oppose a bid it perceived to be harmful to the corporate enterprise. On this record we are satisfied that the device Unocal adopted is reasonable in relation to the threat posed, and that the board acted in the proper exercise of sound business judgment. We will not substitute our views for those of the board if the latter's decision can be "attributed to any rational business purpose." Accordingly, we reverse the decision of the Court of Chancery and order the preliminary injunction vacated.

The factual background of this matter bears a significant relationship to its ultimate outcome.

On April 8, 1985, Mesa, the owner of approximately 13% of Unocal's stock, commenced a two-tier "front loaded" cash tender offer for 64 million shares, or approximately 37%, of Unocal's outstanding stock at a price of $54 per share. The "back-end" was designed to eliminate the remaining publicly held shares by an exchange of securities purportedly worth $54 per share. However, pursuant to an order entered by the United States District Court for the Central District of California on April 26, 1985, Mesa issued a supplemental proxy statement to Unocal's stockholders disclosing that the securities offered in the second-step merger would be highly subordinated, and that Unocal's capitalization would differ significantly from its present structure. Unocal has rather aptly termed such securities "junk bonds".

Unocal's board consists of eight independent outside directors and six insiders. It met on April 13, 1985, to consider the Mesa tender offer. Thirteen directors were present, and the meeting lasted nine and one-half hours. The directors were given no agenda or written materials prior to the session. However, detailed presentations were made by legal counsel regarding the board's obligations under both Delaware corporate law and the federal securities laws. The board then received a presentation from Peter Sachs on behalf of Goldman Sachs & Co. (Goldman Sachs) and Dillon, Read & Co. (Dillon Read) discussing the bases for their opinions that the Mesa proposal was wholly inadequate. Mr. Sachs opined that the minimum cash value that could be expected from a sale or orderly liquidation for 100% of Unocal's stock was in excess of $60 per share. In making his presentation, Mr. Sachs showed slides outlining the valuation techniques used by the financial advisors, and others, depicting recent business combinations in the oil and gas industry. The Court of Chancery found that the Sachs presentation was designed to apprise the directors of the scope of the analyses performed rather than the facts and numbers used in reaching the conclusion that Mesa's tender offer price was inadequate.

Mr. Sachs also presented various defensive strategies available to the board if it concluded that Mesa's two-step tender offer was inadequate and should be opposed. One of the devices outlined was a self-tender by Unocal for its own stock with a reasonable price range of $70 to $75 per share. The cost of such a proposal would cause the company to incur $6.1—6.5 billion of additional debt, and a presentation was made informing the board of Unocal's ability to handle it. The directors were told that the primary effect of this obligation would be to reduce exploratory drilling, but that the company would nonetheless remain a viable entity.

The eight outside directors, comprising a clear majority of the thirteen members present, then met separately with Unocal's financial advisors and attorneys. Thereafter, they unanimously agreed to advise the board that it should reject Mesa's tender offer as inadequate, and that Unocal should pursue a self-tender to provide the stockholders with a fairly priced alternative to the Mesa proposal. The board then reconvened and unanimously adopted a resolution rejecting as grossly inadequate Mesa's tender offer. Despite the nine and one-half hour length of the meeting, no formal decision was made on the proposed defensive self-tender.

On April 15, the board met again with four of the directors present by telephone and one member still absent. This session lasted two hours. Unocal's Vice President of Finance and its Assistant General Counsel made a detailed presentation of the proposed terms of the exchange offer. A price range between $70 and $80 per share was considered, and ultimately the directors agreed upon $72. The board's decisions were made in reliance on the advice of its investment bankers, including the terms and conditions upon which the securities were to be issued. Based upon this advice, and the board's own deliberations, the directors unanimously approved the exchange offer. Their resolution provided that if Mesa acquired 64 million shares of Unocal stock through its own offer (the Mesa Purchase Condition), Unocal would buy the remaining 49% outstanding for an exchange of debt securities having an aggregate par value of $72 per share. The board resolution also stated that the offer would be subject to other conditions that had been described to the board at the meeting, or which were deemed necessary by Unocal's officers, including the exclusion of Mesa from the proposal (the Mesa exclusion). Any such conditions were required to be in accordance with the "purport and intent" of the offer.

Unocal's exchange offer was commenced on April 17, 1985, and Mesa promptly challenged it by filing this suit in the Court of Chancery. On April 22, the Unocal board met again and was advised by Goldman Sachs and Dillon Read to waive the Mesa Purchase Condition as to 50 million shares. This recommendation was in response to a perceived concern of the shareholders that, if shares were tendered to Unocal, no shares would be purchased by either offeror. The directors were also advised that they should tender their own Unocal stock into the exchange offer as a mark of their confidence in it.

Another focus of the board was the Mesa exclusion. Legal counsel advised that under Delaware law Mesa could only be excluded for what the directors reasonably believed to be a valid corporate purpose. The directors' discussion centered on the objective of adequately compensating shareholders at the "back-end" of Mesa's proposal, which the latter would finance with "junk bonds". To include Mesa would defeat that goal, because under the proration aspect of the exchange offer (49%) every Mesa share accepted by Unocal would displace one held by another stockholder. Further, if Mesa were permitted to tender to Unocal, the latter would in effect be financing Mesa's own inadequate proposal.

On April 29, 1985, the Vice Chancellor temporarily restrained Unocal from proceeding with the exchange offer unless it included Mesa. The trial court recognized that directors could oppose, and attempt to defeat, a hostile takeover which they considered adverse to the best interests of the corporation. However, the Vice Chancellor decided that in a selective purchase of the company's stock, the corporation bears the burden of showing: (1) a valid corporate purpose, and (2) that the transaction was fair to all of the stockholders, including those excluded.

The issues we address involve these fundamental questions: Did the Unocal board have the power and duty to oppose a takeover threat it reasonably perceived to be harmful to the corporate enterprise, and if so, is its action here entitled to the protection of the business judgment rule?

Mesa contends that the discriminatory exchange offer violates the fiduciary duties Unocal owes it. Mesa argues that because of the Mesa exclusion the business judgment rule is inapplicable, because the directors by tendering their own shares will derive a financial benefit that is not available to all Unocal stockholders. Thus, it is Mesa's ultimate contention that Unocal cannot establish that the exchange offer is fair to all shareholders, and argues that the Court of Chancery was correct in concluding that Unocal was unable to meet this burden.

Unocal answers that it does not owe a duty of "fairness" to Mesa, given the facts here. Specifically, Unocal contends that its board of directors reasonably and in good faith concluded that Mesa's $54 two-tier tender offer was coercive and inadequate, and that Mesa sought selective treatment for itself. Furthermore, Unocal argues that the board's approval of the exchange offer was made in good faith, on an informed basis, and in the exercise of due care. Under these circumstances, Unocal contends that its directors properly employed this device to protect the company and its stockholders from Mesa's harmful tactics.

We begin with the basic issue of the power of a board of directors of a Delaware corporation to adopt a defensive measure of this type. Absent such authority, all other questions are moot. Neither issues of fairness nor business judgment are pertinent without the basic underpinning of a board's legal power to act.

The board has a large reservoir of authority upon which to draw. Its duties and responsibilities proceed from the inherent powers conferred by 8 Del.C. § 141(a), respecting management of the corporation's "business and affairs". Additionally, the powers here being exercised derive from 8 Del.C. § 160(a), conferring broad authority upon a corporation to deal in its own stock. From this it is now well established that in the acquisition of its shares a Delaware corporation may deal selectively with its stockholders, provided the directors have not acted out of a sole or primary purpose to entrench themselves in office.

Finally, the board's power to act derives from its fundamental duty and obligation to protect the corporate enterprise, which includes stockholders, from harm reasonably perceived, irrespective of its source. *See e.g. Panter v. Marshall Field & Co.,* 646 F.2d 271, 297 (7th Cir.1981); *Crouse-Hinds Co. v. Internorth, Inc.,* 634 F.2d 690, 704 (2d Cir.1980); *Heit v. Baird,* 567 F.2d 1157, 1161 (1st Cir.1977). Thus, we are satisfied that in the broad context of corporate governance, including issues of fundamental corporate change, a board of directors is not a passive instrumentality.

Given the foregoing principles, we turn to the standards by which director action is to be measured. In Pogostin v. Rice, Del.Supr., 480 A.2d 619 (1984), we held that the business judgment rule, including the standards by which director conduct is judged, is applicable in the context of a takeover. The business judgment rule is a "presumption that in making a business decision the directors of a corporation acted on an informed basis, in good faith and in the honest belief that the action taken was in the best interests of the company." *Aronson v. Lewis,* Del.Supr., 473 A.2d 805, 812 (1984). A hallmark of the business judgment rule is that a court will not substitute its judgment for that of the board if the latter's decision can be "attributed to any rational business purpose." *Sinclair Oil Corp. v. Levien,* Del.Supr., 280 A.2d 717, 720 (1971).

When a board addresses a pending takeover bid it has an obligation to determine whether the offer is in the best interests of the corporation and its shareholders. In that respect a board's duty is no different from any other responsibility it shoulders, and its decisions should be no less entitled to the respect they otherwise would be accorded in the realm of business judgment. There are, however, certain caveats to a proper exercise of this function. Because of the omnipresent specter that a board may be acting primarily in its own interests, rather than those of the corporation and its shareholders, there is an enhanced duty which calls for judicial examination at the threshold before the protections of the business judgment rule may be conferred.

This Court has long recognized that we must bear in mind the inherent danger in the purchase of shares with corporate funds to remove a threat to corporate policy when a threat to control is involved. The directors are of necessity confronted with a conflict of interest, and an objective decision is difficult. *Bennett v. Propp,* Del.Supr., 187 A.2d 405, 409 (1962). In the face of this inherent conflict directors must show that they had reasonable grounds for believing that a danger to corporate policy and effectiveness existed because of another person's stock ownership. *Cheff v. Mathes,* 199 A.2d at 554–55. However, they satisfy that burden "by showing good faith and reasonable investigation...." *Id.* at 555. Furthermore, such proof is materially enhanced, as here, by the approval of a board comprised of a majority of outside independent directors who have acted in accordance with the foregoing standards.

In the board's exercise of corporate power to forestall a takeover bid our analysis begins with the basic principle that corporate directors have a fiduciary duty to act in the best interests of the corporation's stockholders. As we have noted, their duty of care extends to protecting the corporation and its owners from perceived harm whether a threat originates from third parties or other shareholders. But such powers are not absolute. A corporation does not have unbridled discretion to defeat any perceived threat by any Draconian means available.

The restriction placed upon a selective stock repurchase is that the directors may not have acted solely or primarily out of a desire to perpetuate themselves in office. Of course, to this is added the further caveat that inequitable action may not be taken under the guise of law. The standard of proof established in Cheff v. Mathes is designed to ensure that a defensive measure to thwart or impede a takeover is indeed motivated by a good faith concern for the welfare of the corporation and its stockholders, which in all circumstances must be free of any fraud or other misconduct. However, this does not end the inquiry.

A further aspect is the element of balance. If a defensive measure is to come within the ambit of the business judgment rule, it must be reasonable in relation to the threat posed. This entails an analysis by the directors of the nature of the takeover bid and its effect on the corporate enterprise. Examples of such concerns may include: inadequacy of the price offered, nature and timing of the offer, questions of illegality, the impact on "constituencies" other than shareholders (i.e., creditors, customers, employees, and perhaps even the community generally), the risk of nonconsummation, and the quality of securities being offered in the exchange. While not a controlling factor, it also seems to us that a board may reasonably consider the basic stockholder interests at stake, including those of short term speculators, whose actions may have fueled the coercive aspect of the offer at the expense of the long term investor. Here, the threat posed was viewed by the Unocal board as a grossly inadequate two-tier coercive tender offer coupled with the threat of greenmail.

Specifically, the Unocal directors had concluded that the value of Unocal was substantially above the $54 per share offered in cash at the front end. Furthermore, they determined that the subordinated securities to be exchanged in Mesa's announced squeeze out of the remaining shareholders in the "back-end" merger were "junk bonds" worth far less than $54. It is now well recognized that such offers are a classic coercive measure designed to stampede shareholders into tendering at the first tier, even if the price is inadequate, out of fear of what they will receive at the back end of the transaction. Wholly beyond the coercive aspect of an inadequate two-tier tender offer, the threat was posed by a corporate raider with a national reputation as a "greenmailer".

In adopting the selective exchange offer, the board stated that its objective was either to defeat the inadequate Mesa offer or, should the offer still succeed, provide the 49% of its stockholders, who would otherwise be forced to accept "junk bonds", with $72 worth of senior debt. We find that both purposes are valid. However, such efforts would have been thwarted by Mesa's participation in the exchange offer. First, if Mesa could tender its shares, Unocal would effectively be subsidizing the former's continuing effort to buy Unocal stock at $54 per share. Second, Mesa could not, by definition, fit within the class of shareholders being protected from its own coercive and inadequate tender offer.

Thus, we are satisfied that the selective exchange offer is reasonably related to the threats posed. It is consistent with the principle that "the minority stockholder shall receive the substantial equivalent in value of what he had before." *Sterling v. Mayflower Hotel Corp.,* Del.Supr., 93 A.2d 107, 114 (1952). This concept of fairness, while stated in the merger context, is also relevant in the area of tender offer law. Thus, the board's decision to offer what it determined to be the fair value of the corporation to the 49% of its shareholders, who would otherwise be forced to accept highly subordinated "junk bonds", is reasonable and consistent with the directors' duty to ensure that the minority stockholders receive equal value for their shares.

Mesa contends that it is unlawful, and the trial court agreed, for a corporation to discriminate in this fashion against one shareholder. However, as we have noted earlier, the principle of selective stock repurchases by a Delaware corporation is neither unknown nor unauthorized. The only difference is that heretofore the approved transaction was the payment of "greenmail" to a raider or dissident posing a threat to the corporate enterprise. All other stockholders were denied such favored treatment, and given Mesa's past history of greenmail, its claims here are rather ironic.

However, our corporate law is not static. It must grow and develop in response to, indeed in anticipation of, evolving concepts and needs. Merely because the General Corporation Law is silent as to a specific matter does not mean that it is prohibited. In the days when Cheff, Bennett, Martin and Kors were decided, the tender offer, while not an unknown device, was virtually unused, and little was known of such methods as two-tier "front-end" loaded offers with their coercive effects. Then, the favored attack of a raider was stock acquisition followed by a proxy contest. Various defensive tactics, which provided no benefit whatever to the raider, evolved. Thus, the use of corporate funds by management to counter a proxy battle was approved. Litigation, supported by corporate funds, aimed at the raider has long been a popular device.

More recently, as the sophistication of both raiders and targets has developed, a host of other defensive measures to counter such ever mounting threats has evolved and received judicial sanction. These include defensive charter amendments and other devices bearing some rather exotic, but apt, names: Crown Jewel, White Knight, Pac Man, and Golden Parachute. Each has highly selective features, the object of which is to deter or defeat the raider.

Thus, while the exchange offer is a form of selective treatment, given the nature of the threat posed here the response is neither unlawful nor unreasonable. If the board of directors is disinterested, has acted in good faith and with due care, its decision in the absence of an abuse of discretion will be upheld as a proper exercise of business judgment.

To this Mesa responds that the board is not disinterested, because the directors are receiving a benefit from the tender of their own shares, which because of the Mesa exclusion, does not devolve upon all stockholders equally. However, Mesa concedes that if the exclusion is valid, then the directors and all other stockholders share the same benefit. The answer of course is that the exclusion is valid, and the directors' participation in the exchange offer does not rise to the level of a disqualifying interest. Nor does this become an "interested" director transaction merely because certain board members are large stockholders. As this Court has previously noted, that fact alone does not create a disqualifying "personal pecuniary interest" to defeat the operation of the business judgment rule.

Mesa also argues that the exclusion permits the directors to abdicate the fiduciary duties they owe it. However, that is not so. The board continues to owe Mesa the duties of due care and loyalty. But in the face of the destructive threat Mesa's tender offer was perceived to pose, the board had a supervening duty to protect the corporate enterprise, which includes the other shareholders, from threatened harm.

Mesa contends that the basis of this action is punitive, and solely in response to the exercise of its rights of corporate democracy. Nothing precludes Mesa, as a stockholder, from acting in its own self-interest. However, Mesa, while pursuing its own interests, has acted in a manner which a board consisting of a majority of independent directors has reasonably determined to be contrary to the best interests of Unocal and its other shareholders. In this situation, there is no support in Delaware law for the proposition that, when responding to a perceived harm, a corporation must guarantee a benefit to a stockholder who is deliberately provoking the danger being addressed.

In conclusion, there was directorial power to oppose the Mesa tender offer, and to undertake a selective stock exchange made in good faith and upon a reasonable investigation pursuant to a clear duty to protect the corporate enterprise. Further, the selective stock repurchase plan chosen by Unocal is reasonable in relation to the threat that the board rationally and reasonably believed was posed by Mesa's inadequate and coercive two-tier tender offer. Under those circumstances the board's action is entitled to be measured by the standards of the business judgment rule. Thus, unless it is shown by a preponderance of the evidence that the directors' decisions were primarily based on perpetuating themselves in office, or some other breach of fiduciary duty such as fraud, overreaching, lack of good faith, or being uninformed, a Court will not substitute its judgment for that of the board.

With the Court of Chancery's findings that the exchange offer was based on the board's good faith belief that the Mesa offer was inadequate, that the board's action was informed and taken with due care, that Mesa's prior activities justify a reasonable inference that its principle objective was greenmail, and implicitly, that the substance of the offer itself was reasonable and fair to the corporation and its stockholders if Mesa were included, we cannot say that the Unocal directors have acted in such a manner as to have passed an "unintelligent and unadvised judgment". The decision of the Court of Chancery is therefore REVERSED, and the preliminary injunction is VACATED.

The Challenges of *Unocal* and *Blasius*

Unocal clarified the gateway to the presumption of the business judgment rule when corporate directors are challenged for their adoption of an antitakeover defense provision. When defensive actions are questioned, directors are not entitled to the protection of the business judgment rule and the rule's related shift of the burden to rebut its presumption to the plaintiff until the board has sustained its own burden of satisfying a two-prong test. The first prong is a *reasonableness test,* which is satisfied by the directors demonstrating that they had reasonable grounds to believe that a danger to corporate policy and effectiveness existed. The second prong is a *proportionality test,* which is satisfied by the directors demonstrating that their response was reasonable in relation to the threat posed.

Unocal involved a self-tender offer in response to a grossly inadequate two-tier coercive offer. Looking back, it was a relatively easy fact pattern for drawing lines. Its two-prong test has triggered, and continues to trigger, challenging questions in cases where the facts are tougher. What grounds will satisfy the reasonableness test? Could the interests of non-shareholders form a basis for such grounds? How will the proportionality test play out in a situation where the hostile bid is not coercive? Or how about where the board is acting to protect against an unknown potential future risk? Or how about the situation where the directors' objective is to "lock up" a friendly deal that could be derailed by a hostile bid? The challenge of these questions in difficult high-stakes cases has been and remains the legacy of *Unocal's* two-prong test.

In the same year the Delaware Supreme Court decided *Unocal*, it applied *Unocal's* two-pong test to a board's adoption of a poison pill rights plan in response to coercive tender offer in *Moran v. Household International, Inc.*, 500 A.2d 1346 (Del. 1985). In holding that Household's adoption of the bill satisfied *Unocal's* proportionate test, the court stated:

> There are no allegations here of any bad faith on the part of the Directors' action in the adoption of the Rights Plan. There is no allegation that the Directors' action was taken for entrenchment purposes. Household has adequately demonstrated, as explained above, that the adoption of the Rights Plan was in reaction to what it perceived to be the threat in the market place of coercive two-tier tender offers...[T]o meet their burden, the Directors must show that the defensive mechanism was "reasonable in relation to the threat posed". The record reflects a concern on the part of the Directors over the

increasing frequency in the financial services industry of "boot-strap" and "bust-up" takeovers. The Directors were also concerned that such takeovers may take the form of two-tier offers. In addition, on August 14, the Household Board was aware of Moran's overture on behalf of D–K–M. In sum, the Directors reasonably believed Household was vulnerable to coercive acquisition techniques and adopted a reasonable defensive mechanism to protect itself.

500 A.2d at 1356-57

Three year later, the Delaware Chancery Court decided *Blasius Industries v. Atlas Corp*, 564 A.2d 651 (Del. Ch. 1988) (see opinion in Chapter 8) where the court held that "when [a board] acts ... for the primary purpose of preventing or impeding an unaffiliated majority of shareholders from expanding the board and electing a new majority," its action "constitute[s] an offense to the relationship between corporate directors and shareholders that has traditionally been protected...." 564 A.2d at 652. Such disenfranchising actions, although not "invalid *per se,*" require that "the board bears the heavy burden of demonstrating a compelling justification for such action." *Blasius,* 564 A.2d at 661.

As you will see, the point at which *Blasius'* "compelling justification" standard intersects with *Unocal's* two-prong test in an antitakeover defense battle has presented a difficult challenge for defendants and the courts. There is no denying that various popular "shark repellents" are specifically designed to create voting obstacles for those who, for example, seek to replace board members to ensure that a poison pill is never released. And there is little question that the "onerous" *Blasius* "compelling interest" standard poses a tougher burden for a board than Unocal's two-prong "reasonable" and "proportionate" tests.

The remedy sought in *Unocal* was an injunction. That is common in disputes over corporate control. The goal is to shutdown the defensive strategy. The injunction request requires the court to focus on the likelihood of the plaintiff prevailing on the merits and the potential of irreparable harm. A money damage award for breach of fiduciary duties is possible, but often is rendered moot, as a practical matter, by a Delaware Code § 102(b)(7) provision in the corporation's articles of incorporation that eliminates any director liability for money absent a showing of bad faith (see Chapter 10). And although minority appraisal rights are an option in cases where the market opt-out is not applicable, they focus only the fairness of the here-and-now value and trigger administrative challenges, costs, and inherent outcome uncertainties (see Chapter 12).

CASE PROBLEM 14-1

Troy Walton is the founder, chief executive officer, and chairman of the board of Kfiber Inc. ("Kfiber"), a Delaware corporation that designs and manufactures a broad range of kevlar products. Troy, age 75, frequently talks of retiring but has done nothing to slow down. Troy's son, Julian, age 47, has made Kfiber his career and presently serves as Kfiber's executive vice president in charge of sales.

Troy is Kfiber's largest shareholder, owning 18 percent of the outstanding common stock. An additional 10 percent of Kfiber's stock is owned by key Kfiber executives (including Julian). The remaining 72 percent of the stock is owned and publicly traded by outside investors, heavily represented by institutional investors. The attraction of Kfiber has been its ever-growing profitability, its products' strategic *niche* positions in many markets, and Troy's historic *blasé* attitude about Kfiber's stock price. Troy's focus has always been on product development and operational efficiencies, not the current trading price of Kfiber stock, which currently hovers in the $20 range. As a result, many believe that Kfiber's stock is seriously undervalued in the market and that substantial values will be realized when Troy finally steps aside and the company is sold to a strategic buyer.

Kfiber has a nine member board: Troy, Julian, two other Kfiber executives, and five outsiders, all of whom are loyal friends of Troy.

Warfield Industries Incorporated ("Warfield"), a Delaware corporation, is a large diversified investment company that is forever on the lookout for undervalued companies that are ripe for a management change. It has a reputation for "busting up companies and destroying jobs." Two months ago, Warfield's CEO approached Troy about the possibility of Warfield buying Kfiber. Troy rejected the overture out of hand, stating that "Kfiber will always be run in accordance with a firmly established Walton culture that employees customers, and shareholders all have a stake in the enterprise." Troy advised members of Kfiber's board of his short interchange with Warfield's CEO.

Troy and other members of Kfibers board recently learned that Warfield has purchased nine percent of Kfiber's stock. They also have heard rumors that Warfield is considering a tender offer for Kfiber's stock at a price in the $32 range. It's likely that such a price would excite many of Kfiber's shareholders. It was unclear whether such an offer would be for all or only a portion of Kfiber's outstanding stock. Troy arranged a meeting with Kfiber's legal counsel and a reputable outside investment firm. After a lengthy discussion over many hours, the meeting ended with the following ideas on the table:

Recommendation A. Kfiber's board should appoint the outside members of the board as a special committee (the "Committee") to obtain an independent valuation of Kfiber's business and to consider the advisability of Kfiber taking actions to protect against the risks of a hostile tender offer that would seek to capitalize on Kfiber's undervalued stock.

Recommendation B. The Committee should consider the advisability of recommending that Kfiber's board adopt (by way of bylaw amendment) a "standard" flip-in shareholder rights poison pill plan that would empower the board to issue rights to existing Kfiber shareholders to purchase additional Kfiber stock at a substantial discount if and when a hostile bidder acquired more than 20 percent of Kfiber's stock. The board would have the right to redeem and cancel such rights at any time for a nominal consideration. The Committee was advised that, as is usually the case with a poison pill, the threatened valuation impacts of such a plan will prevent a hostile tender offer from going forward so long as there is any possibility of the rights becoming effective.

Recommendation C. The Committee should consider the advisability of recommending that Kfiber's board adopt an amendment to Kfiber's bylaws to provide that a special meeting of shareholders can be called by shareholders only if shareholders owning at least two-thirds of Kfiber's outstanding shares participate in the request.

Recommendation D. The Committee should consider the advisability of recommending that Kfiber's board adopt an amendment to Kfiber's bylaws to provide that Kfiber's bylaws may be amended by shareholders only if shareholders owning at least two-thirds of Kfiber's outstanding shares vote in favor of the amendment.

Recommendation E. The Committee should consider the advisability of recommending that Kfiber's board adopt an amendment to Kfiber's bylaws to provide that any shareholder-initiated changes to Kfiber's board of directors between annual meetings must be approved by shareholders owning at least two-thirds of Kfiber's outstanding shares.

Recommendation F. The Committee should consider the advisability of recommending that Kfiber's board approve a sale of authorized common stock to Bolton Industries, Inc, ("Bolton"), a strategic supplier of Kfiber that has always expressed an interest in owning Kfiber stock. Bolton would be loyal to Troy's interests and would have no interest in any plans of Warfield. Bolton would pay $19 a share. After the sale, Troy, existing Kfiber executives, and Bolton would collectively own 34 percent of Kfieber's outstanding stock. The capital generated from the stock sale would be used to fund a new Kfiber plant in San Diego.

In explaining the logic of the recommendations, the advisers explained that the poison pill would stop any hostile bid until the bidder could secure enough shareholder support to trigger a shareholder-approved bylaw amendment or a change in the composition of the board. Recommendations C, D, and E would create serious obstacles to any attempts by a bidder or shareholders to eliminate the risk of the pill, particularly since the next annual meeting of shareholders wouldn't be held for 10 months. The "White Squire" stock sale to Bolton would "breathe defensive life" into the two-thirds voting requirements of the other recommendations.

Please help Troy and his colleagues with the following questions that have surfaced regarding how the recommendations will stack up under *Unocal's* two-prong test:

1. Will each defensive action be evaluated separately under Unocal's "reasonableness" test?

2. What factors should be considered in assessing whether Kfiber's board can sustain its burden of proof under the "reasonableness" test? What additional facts should the Committee seek to obtain in this regard?

3. What procedural steps should the Committee take to ensure that it can sustain its burden under *Unocal's* "reasonableness" test?

4. Will any of these defensive measures be considered "preclusive"? If so,

what's the impact?

5. Will any of the defensive measures be considered "substantively coercive"? If so, what's the impact?

6. Will any of the defensive measures be subject to *Blasius'* "compelling interest" standard? If so, what would have to be shown to meet that standard?

7. What factors should be considered in assessing whether Kfiber's board can sustain its burden of proof under *Unocal's* proportionality test? Will each defensive measure be separately evaluated under this test or will the adopted measures be collectively evaluated under the test?

UNITRIN, INC. v. AMERICAN GENERAL CORP.
651 A.2d 1361 (Del. 1995)

HOLLAND, Justice.

American General, which had publicly announced a proposal to merge with Unitrin for $2.6 billion at $50– 3/8 per share, and certain Unitrin shareholder plaintiffs, filed suit in the Court of Chancery, *inter alia,* to enjoin Unitrin from repurchasing up to 10 million shares of its own stock (the "Repurchase Program"). On August 26, 1994, the Court of Chancery temporarily restrained Unitrin from making any further repurchases. After expedited discovery, briefing and argument, the Court of Chancery preliminarily enjoined Unitrin from making further repurchases on the ground that the Repurchase Program was a disproportionate response to the threat posed by American General's inadequate all cash for all shares offer, under the standard of this Court's holding in *Unocal Corp. v. Mesa Petroleum Co.,* Del.Supr., 493 A.2d 946 (1985) (" *Unocal* ").

Unitrin has raised several issues in this appeal. First, it contends that the Court of Chancery erred in assuming that the outside directors would subconsciously act contrary to their substantial financial interests as stockholders and, instead, vote in favor of a subjective desire to protect the "prestige and perquisites" of membership on Unitrin's Board of Directors. Second, it contends that the Court of Chancery erred in holding that the adoption of the Repurchase Program would materially affect the ability of an insurgent stockholder to win a proxy contest. According to Unitrin, that holding is unsupported by the evidence, is based upon a faulty mathematical analysis, and disregards the holding of *Moran v. Household Int'l, Inc.,* Del.Supr., 500 A.2d 1346, 1355 (1985). Furthermore, Unitrin argues that the Court of Chancery erroneously substituted its own judgment for that of Unitrin's Board. Third, Unitrin submits that the Court of Chancery erred in finding that the plaintiffs would be irreparably harmed absent an injunction (a) because the Court of Chancery disregarded Unitrin's proffered alternative remedy of sterilizing the increased voting power of the stockholder directors and (b) because there was no basis for finding that stockholders who sold into the market during the pendency of the Repurchase Program would be irreparably harmed.

This Court has concluded that the Court of Chancery erred in applying the proportionality review *Unocal* requires by focusing upon whether the Repurchase Program was an "unnecessary" defensive response. The Court of Chancery should have directed its enhanced scrutiny: first, upon whether the Repurchase Program the Unitrin Board implemented was draconian, by being either preclusive or coercive and; second, if it was not draconian, upon whether it was within a range of reasonable responses to the threat American General's Offer posed. Consequently, the interlocutory preliminary injunctive judgment of the Court of Chancery is reversed. This matter is remanded for further proceedings in accordance with this opinion.

American General is the largest provider of home service insurance. On July 12, 1994, it made a merger proposal to acquire Unitrin for $2.6 billion at $50– /8 per share. Following a public announcement of this proposal, Unitrin shareholders filed suit seeking to compel a sale of the company. American General filed suit to enjoin Unitrin's Repurchase Program.

Unitrin is also in the insurance business. It is the third largest provider of home service insurance. The other defendants-appellants are the members of Unitrin's seven person Board of Directors (the "Unitrin Board" or "Board"). Two directors are employees, Richard C. Vie ("Vie"), the Chief Executive Officer, and Jerrold V. Jerome ("Jerome"), Chairman of the Board. The five remaining directors are not and have never been employed by Unitrin.

The record reflects that the non-employee directors each receive a fixed annual fee of $30,000. They receive no other significant financial benefit from serving as directors. At the offering price proposed by American General, the value of Unitrin's non-employee directors' stock exceeded $450 million...

On July 12, 1994, American General sent a letter to Vie proposing a consensual merger transaction in which it would "purchase all of Unitrin's 51.8 million outstanding shares of common stock for $50– 3/8 per share, in cash" (the "Offer"). The Offer was conditioned on the development of a merger agreement and regulatory approval. The Offer price represented a 30% premium over the market price of Unitrin's shares. In the Offer, American General stated that it "would consider offering a higher price" if "Unitrin could demonstrate additional value." American General also offered to consider tax-free "[a]lternatives to an all cash transaction."

Upon receiving the American General Offer, the Unitrin Board's Executive Committee (Singleton, Vie, and Jerome) engaged legal counsel and scheduled a telephonic Board meeting for July 18. At the July 18 special meeting, the Board reviewed the terms of the Offer. The Board was advised that the existing charter and bylaw provisions might not effectively deter all types of takeover strategies. It was suggested that the Board consider adopting a shareholder rights plan and an advance notice provision for shareholder proposals.

The Unitrin Board met next on July 25, 1994 in Los Angeles for seven hours. All directors attended the meeting. The principal purpose of the meeting was to discuss American General's Offer. Vie reviewed Unitrin's financial condition and its ongoing business strategies. The Board also received a presentation from its investment advisor, Morgan Stanley & Co. ("Morgan Stanley"), regarding the financial adequacy of American General's proposal. Morgan Stanley expressed its opinion that the Offer was financially inadequate.

Legal counsel expressed concern that the combination of Unitrin and American General would raise antitrust complications due to the resultant decrease in competition in the home service insurance markets.

The Unitrin Board unanimously concluded that the American General merger proposal was not in the best interests of Unitrin's shareholders and voted to reject the Offer. The Board then received advice from its legal and financial advisors about a number of possible defensive measures it might adopt, including a shareholder rights plan ("poison pill") and an advance notice bylaw provision for shareholder proposals. Because the Board apparently thought that American General intended to keep its Offer private, the Board did not implement any defensive measures at that time.

On July 26, 1994, Vie faxed a letter to Tuerff, rejecting American General's offer. On August 2, 1994, American General issued a press release announcing its Offer to Unitrin's Board to purchase all of Unitrin's stock for $50– 3/8 per share. The press release also noted that the Board had rejected American General's Offer. After that public announcement, the trading volume and market price of Unitrin's stock increased.

At its regularly scheduled meeting on August 3, the Unitrin Board discussed the effects of American General's press release. The Board noted that the market reaction to the announcement suggested that speculative traders or arbitrageurs were acquiring Unitrin stock. The Board determined that American General's public announcement constituted a hostile act designed to coerce the sale of Unitrin at an inadequate price. The Board unanimously approved the poison pill and the proposed advance notice bylaw that it had considered previously.

Beginning on August 2 and continuing through August 12, 1994, Unitrin issued a series of press releases to inform its shareholders and the public market: first, that the Unitrin Board believed Unitrin's stock was worth more than the $50– 3/8 American General offered; second, that the Board felt that the price of American General's Offer did not reflect Unitrin's long term business prospects as an independent company; third, that "the true value of Unitrin [was] not reflected in the [then] current market price of its common stock," and that because of its strong financial position, Unitrin was well positioned "to pursue strategic and financial opportunities;" fourth, that the Board believed a merger with American General would have anticompetitive effects and might violate antitrust laws and various state regulatory statutes; and fifth, that the Board had adopted a shareholder rights plan (poison pill) to guard against undesirable takeover efforts.

The Unitrin Board met again on August 11, 1994. The minutes of that meeting indicate that its principal purpose was to consider the Repurchase Program. At the Board's request, Morgan Stanley had prepared written materials to distribute to each of the directors. Morgan Stanley gave a presentation in which alternative means of implementing the Repurchase Program were explained. Morgan Stanley recommended that the Board implement an open market stock repurchase. The Board voted to authorize the Repurchase Program for up to ten million shares of its outstanding stock.

On August 12, Unitrin publicly announced the Repurchase Program. The Unitrin Board expressed its belief that "Unitrin's stock is undervalued in the market and that the expanded program will tend to increase the value of the shares that remain outstanding." The announcement also stated that the director stockholders were not participating in the Repurchase Program, and that the repurchases "will increase the percentage ownership of those stockholders who choose not to sell."

Unitrin's August 12 press release also stated that the directors owned 23% of Unitrin's stock, that the Repurchase Program would cause that percentage to increase, and that Unitrin's certificate of incorporation included a supermajority voting provision. The following language from a July 22 draft press release revealing the antitakeover effects of the Repurchase Program was omitted from the final press release.

Under the [supermajority provision], the consummation of the expanded repurchase program would enhance the ability of nonselling stockholders, including the directors, to prevent a merger with a greater-than-15% stockholder if they did not favor the transaction.

Unitrin sent a letter to its stockholders on August 17 regarding the Repurchase Program which stated:

Your Board of Directors has authorized the Company to repurchase, in the open market or in private transactions, up to 10 million of Unitrin's 51.8 million outstanding common shares. This authorization is intended to provide an additional measure of liquidity to the Company's shareholders in light of the unsettled market conditions resulting from American General's unsolicited acquisition proposal. The Board believes that the Company's stock is undervalued and that this program will tend to increase the value of the shares that remain outstanding.

Between August 12 and noon on August 24, Morgan Stanley purchased nearly 5 million of Unitrin's shares on Unitrin's behalf. The average price paid was slightly above American General's Offer price.

In this case, before the Court of Chancery could evaluate the reasonable probability of the plaintiffs' success on the merits, it had to determine the nature of the proceeding. When shareholders challenge directors' actions, usually one of three levels of judicial review is applied: the traditional business judgment rule, the *Unocal* standard of enhanced judicial scrutiny, or the entire fairness analysis. "Because the effect of the proper invocation of the business judgment rule is so powerful and the standard of entire fairness so exacting, the determination of the appropriate standard of judicial review frequently is determinative of the outcome of [the] litigation." *Mills Acquisition Co. v. Macmillan, Inc.*, 559 A.2d at 1279.

The plaintiffs argued that the conduct of the Unitrin Board should be examined under the entire fairness standard. The Court of Chancery concluded that the Board's implementation of the poison pill and the Repurchase Program, in response to American General's Offer, did not constitute self-dealing that would require the Unitrin Board to demonstrate entire fairness. *See Nixon v.*

Blackwell, Del.Supr., 626 A.2d 1366, 1376 (1993); *Weinberger v. UOP, Inc.,* Del.Supr., 457 A.2d 701, 710 (1983). Consequently, the Court of Chancery addressed the plaintiffs' third alternative argument, that the Unitrin Board's actions should be examined under the standard of enhanced judicial scrutiny this Court set forth in *Unocal.*

Before a board of directors' action is subject to the *Unocal* standard of enhanced judicial scrutiny, the court must determine whether the particular conduct was defensive. The stockholder-plaintiffs asked the Court of Chancery to review both the poison pill and the Repurchase Program pursuant to the *Unocal* standard. American General requested the Court of Chancery to apply *Unocal* and enjoin the Repurchase Program only. Unitrin acknowledged that the poison pill was subject to the enhanced scrutiny *Unocal* requires but argued that the Court of Chancery should evaluate the Repurchase Program under the business judgment rule.

According to the Unitrin Board, the Repurchase Program was enacted for a valid business purpose and, therefore, should not be evaluated as a defensive measure under *Unocal.* The Court of Chancery agreed that, had the Board enacted the Repurchase Program independent of a takeover proposal, its decision would be reviewed under the traditional business judgment rule. The Court of Chancery concluded, however, that the Unitrin Board perceived American General's Offer as a threat and, from the timing of the consideration and implementation of the Repurchase Program, adopted the Repurchase Program as one of several defensive measures in response to that threat. Unitrin does not dispute that conclusion for the purpose of this interlocutory appeal.

The Court of Chancery held that all of the Unitrin Board's defensive actions merited judicial scrutiny according to *Unocal.* Therefore, the Court of Chancery properly concluded the facts before it required an application of *Unocal* and its progeny. The evolution of that jurisprudence is didactic.

The business judgment rule applies to the conduct of directors in the context of a takeover. The business judgment rule is a "presumption that in making a business decision the directors of a corporation acted on an informed basis, in good faith and in the honest belief that the action taken was in the best interests of the company." *Aronson v. Lewis,* 473 A.2d at 812. An application of the traditional business judgment rule places the burden on the "party challenging the [board's] decision to establish facts rebutting the presumption." *Id.* If the business judgment rule is not rebutted, a "court will not substitute its judgment for that of the board if the [board's] decision can be 'attributed to any rational business purpose.'" *Unocal,* 493 A.2d at 954 (citation omitted).

When a board addresses a pending takeover bid it has an obligation to determine whether the offer is in the best interests of the corporation and its shareholders. In that respect a board's duty is no different from any other responsibility it shoulders, and its decisions should be no less entitled to the respect they otherwise would be accorded in the realm of business judgment.

In *Unocal,* this Court reaffirmed "the application of the business judgment rule in the context of a hostile battle for control of a Delaware corporation where board action is taken to the exclusion of, or in limitation upon, a valid stockholder vote." *Stroud v. Grace,* 606 A.2d at 82. This Court has recognized that directors are often confronted with an "'inherent conflict of interest' during contests for corporate control '[b]ecause of the omnipresent specter that a board may be acting primarily in its own interests, rather than those of the corporation and its shareholders.' " *Id.* (quoting *Unocal,* 493 A.2d at 954). Consequently, in such situations, before the board is accorded the protection of the business judgment rule, and that rule's concomitant placement of the burden to rebut its presumption on the plaintiff, the board must carry its own initial two-part burden:

First, a *reasonableness test,* which is satisfied by a demonstration that the board of directors had reasonable grounds for believing that a danger to corporate policy and effectiveness existed, and

Second, a *proportionality test,* which is satisfied by a demonstration that the board of directors' defensive response was reasonable in relation to the threat posed. *Unocal,* 493 A.2d at 955. The common law pronouncement in *Unocal* of enhanced judicial scrutiny, as a threshold or condition precedent to an application of the traditional business judgment rule, is now well known.

The enhanced judicial scrutiny mandated by *Unocal* is not intended to lead to a structured, mechanistic, mathematical exercise. Conversely, it is not intended to be an abstract theory. The *Unocal* standard is a flexible paradigm that jurists can apply to the myriad of "fact scenarios" that confront corporate boards.

The correct analytical framework is essential to a proper review of challenges to the decision-making process of a corporate Board. The ultimate question in applying the *Unocal* standard is: what deference should the reviewing court give "to the decisions of directors in defending against a takeover?" The question is usually presented to the Court of Chancery, as in the present case, in an injunction proceeding, a posture which is known as "transactional justification." To answer the question, the enhanced judicial scrutiny *Unocal* requires implicates both the substantive and procedural nature of the business judgment rule.

The business judgment rule has traditionally operated to shield directors from personal liability arising out of completed actions involving operational issues. Conversely, in transactional justification cases involving the adoption of defenses to takeovers, the director's actions invariably implicate issues affecting stockholder rights. In transactional justification cases, the directors' decision is reviewed judicially and the burden of going forward is placed on the directors... If the directors' actions withstand *Unocal's* reasonableness and proportionality review, the traditional business judgment rule is applied to shield the directors' defensive decision rather than the directors themselves.

The litigation between Unitrin, American General, and the Unitrin shareholders in the Court of Chancery is a classic example of a transactional justification case. The Court of Chancery's determination that the conduct of Unitrin's Board was subject to *Unocal's* enhanced judicial scrutiny required it to evaluate each party's ability to sustain its unique burden in the procedural context of a preliminary injunction proceeding. The plaintiff's burden in such a proceeding is to demonstrate a reasonable probability of success after trial.

In general, to effectively defeat the plaintiff's ability to discharge that burden, a board must sustain its burden of demonstrating that, even under *Unocal's* standard of enhanced judicial scrutiny, its actions deserved the protection of the traditional business judgment rule. Thus, the plaintiff's likelihood of success in obtaining a preliminary injunction was initially dependent upon the inability of the Unitrin Board to discharge the burden placed upon it first by *Unocal.* Accordingly, having concluded that the Board's actions were defensive, the Court of Chancery logically began with an evaluation of the Unitrin Board's evidence.

The first aspect of the *Unocal* burden, the reasonableness test, required the Unitrin Board to demonstrate that, after a reasonable investigation, it determined in good faith, that American General's Offer presented a threat to Unitrin that warranted a defensive response. This Court has held that the presence of a majority of outside independent directors will materially enhance such evidence. An "outside" director has been defined as a non-employee and non-management director, (*e.g.,* Unitrin argues, five members of its seven-person Board). Independence "means that a director's decision is based on the corporate merits of the subject before the board rather than extraneous considerations or influences." *Aronson v. Lewis,* Del.Supr., 473 A.2d 805, 816 (1984).

The Unitrin Board identified two dangers it perceived the American General Offer posed: inadequate price and antitrust complications. The Court of Chancery characterized the Board's concern that American General's proposed transaction could never be consummated because it may violate antitrust laws and state insurance regulations as a "makeweight excuse" for the defensive measure. It determined, however, that the Board reasonably believed that the American General Offer was inadequate and also reasonably concluded that the Offer was a threat to Unitrin's uninformed stockholders.

The Court of Chancery held that the Board's evidence satisfied the first aspect or reasonableness test under *Unocal.* The Court of Chancery then noted, however, that the threat to the Unitrin stockholders from American General's inadequate opening bid was "mild," because the Offer was negotiable both in price and structure. The court then properly turned its attention to *Unocal's* second aspect, the proportionality test because "[i]t is not until both parts of the *Unocal* inquiry have been satisfied that the business judgment rule attaches to defensive actions of a board of directors." *See Unocal,* 493 A.2d at 955.

The second aspect or proportionality test of the initial *Unocal* burden required the Unitrin Board to demonstrate the proportionality of its response to the threat American General's Offer posed. The record reflects that the Unitrin Board considered three options as defensive measures: the poison pill, the advance notice bylaw, and the Repurchase Program. The Unitrin Board did not act on any of these options on July 25.

On August 2, American General made a public announcement of its offer to buy all the shares of Unitrin for $2.6 billion at $50–3/8 per share. The Unitrin

Board had already concluded that the American General offer was inadequate. It also apparently feared that its stockholders did not realize that the long term value of Unitrin was not reflected in the market price of its stock.

On August 3, the Board met to decide whether any defensive action was necessary. The Unitrin Board decided to adopt defensive measures to protect Unitrin's stockholders from the inadequate American General Offer in two stages: first, it passed the poison pill and the advance notice bylaw; and, a week later, it implemented the Repurchase Program.

With regard to the second aspect or proportionality test of the initial *Unocal* burden, the Court of Chancery analyzed each stage of the Unitrin Board's defensive responses separately. Although the Court of Chancery characterized Unitrin's antitrust concerns as "makeweight," it acknowledged that the directors of a Delaware corporation have the prerogative to determine that the market undervalues its stock and to protect its stockholders from offers that do not reflect the long term value of the corporation under its present management plan. The Court of Chancery concluded that Unitrin's Board believed in good faith that the American General Offer was inadequate and properly employed a poison pill as a proportionate defensive response to protect its stockholders from a "low ball" bid.

The Court of Chancery did not view either its conclusion that American General's Offer constituted a threat, or its conclusion that the poison pill was a reasonable response to that threat, as requiring it, *a fortiori,* to conclude that the Repurchase Program was also an appropriate response. The Court of Chancery then made two factual findings: first, the Repurchase Program went beyond what was "necessary" to protect the Unitrin stockholders from a "low ball" negotiating strategy; and second, it was designed to keep the decision to combine with American General within the control of the members of the Unitrin Board, as stockholders, under virtually all circumstances. Consequently, the Court of Chancery held that the Unitrin Board failed to demonstrate that the Repurchase Program met the second aspect or proportionality requirement of the initial burden *Unocal* ascribes to a board of directors.

The Court of Chancery framed the ultimate question before it as follows:

This case comes down to one final question: Is placing the decision to sell the company in the hands of stockholders who are also directors a disproportionate response to a low price offer to buy all the shares of the company for cash?

The Court of Chancery then answered that question:

I conclude that because the only threat to the corporation is the inadequacy of an opening bid made directly to the board, and the board has already taken actions that will protect the stockholders from mistakenly falling for a low ball negotiating strategy, a repurchase program that intentionally provides members of the board with a veto of any merger proposal is not reasonably related to the threat posed by American General's negotiable all shares, all cash offer.

In explaining its conclusion, the Court of Chancery reasoned that:

> I have no doubt that a hostile acquiror can make an offer high enough to entice at least some of the directors that own stock to break ranks and sell their shares. Yet, these directors undoubtedly place a value, probably a substantial one, on their management of Unitrin, and will, at least subconsciously, reject an offer that does not compensate them for that value.... The prestige and perquisites that accompany managing Unitrin as a member of its Board of directors, even for the non-officer directors that do not draw a salary, may cause these stockholder directors to reject an excellent offer unless it includes this value in its "price parameter."

The Court of Chancery concluded that, although the Unitrin Board had properly perceived American General's inadequate Offer as a threat and had properly responded to that threat by adopting a "poison pill," the additional defensive response of adopting the Repurchase Program was unnecessary and disproportionate to the threat the Offer posed. Accordingly, it concluded that the plaintiffs had "established with reasonable probability that the [Unitrin Board] violated its duties under *Unocal* [by authorizing the Repurchase Program]" because the Board had not sustained its burden of demonstrating that the Repurchase Program was a proportionate response to American General's Offer. Therefore, the Court of Chancery held that the plaintiffs proved a likelihood of success on that issue and granted the motion to preliminarily enjoin the Repurchase Program.

Before the Repurchase Program began, Unitrin's directors collectively held approximately 23% of Unitrin's outstanding shares. Unitrin's certificate of incorporation already included a "shark-repellent" provision barring any business combination with a more–than–15% stockholder unless approved by a majority of continuing directors or by a 75% stockholder vote ("Supermajority Vote"). Unitrin's shareholder directors announced publicly that they would not participate in the Repurchase Program and that this would result in a percentage increase of ownership for them, as well as for any other shareholder who did not participate.

The Court of Chancery found that by not participating in the Repurchase Program, the Board "expected to create a 28% voting block to support the Board's decision to reject [a future] offer by American General." From this underlying factual finding, the Court of Chancery concluded that American General might be "chilled" in its pursuit of Unitrin:

> Increasing the board members' percentage of stock ownership, combined with the supermajority merger provision, does more than protect uninformed stockholders from an inadequate offer, it chills any unsolicited acquiror from making an offer.

The parties are in substantial disagreement with respect to the Court of Chancery's ultimate factual finding that the Repurchase Program was a disproportionate response under *Unocal*. Unitrin argues that American General or another potential acquiror can theoretically prevail in an effort to obtain control of Unitrin through a proxy contest. American General argues that the record supports the Court of Chancery's factual determination that the adoption of the Repurchase Program violated the principles of *Unocal,* even though American General acknowledges that the option of a proxy contest for obtaining control of Unitrin remained theoretically available. The stockholder-plaintiffs argue that even if it can be said, as a matter of law, that it is acceptable under certain circumstances to leave potential bidders with a proxy battle as the sole avenue for acquiring an entity, the Court of Chancery correctly determined, as a factual matter, that the Repurchase Program was disproportionate to the threat American General's Offer posed.

This Court has been and remains assiduous in its concern about defensive actions designed to thwart the essence of corporate democracy by disenfranchising shareholders. Nevertheless, this Court has upheld the propriety of adopting poison pills in given defensive circumstances. Keeping a poison pill in place may be inappropriate, however, when those circumstances change dramatically. Similarly, this Court has recognized the propriety of implementing certain repurchase programs (as in *Unocal* itself), as well as the unreasonableness and non-proportionality of responding defensively to a takeover bid with a coercive and preclusive partial self-tender offer.

More recently, this Court stated: "we accept the basic legal tenets," set forth in *Blasius Indus., Inc. v. Atlas Corp.,* Del.Ch., 564 A.2d 651 (1988), that "[w]here boards of directors deliberately employ [ ] ... legal strategies either to frustrate or completely disenfranchise a shareholder vote, ... [t]here can be no dispute that such conduct violates Delaware law." *Stroud v. Grace,* 606 A.2d at 91. In *Stroud,* we concluded, however, that a *Blasius* analysis was inappropriate. We reached that conclusion because it could not be said "that the 'primary purpose' of the board's action was to interfere with or impede exercise of the shareholder franchise," and because the shareholders had a "full and fair opportunity to vote." *Stroud v. Grace,* 606 A.2d at 92.

This Court also specifically noted that boards of directors often interfere with the exercise of shareholder voting when an acquiror *launches both a proxy fight and a tender offer. Id.* at 92 n. 3. We then stated that such action "necessarily invoked both *Unocal* and *Blasius* " because "both [tests] recognize the inherent conflicts of interest that arise when shareholders are not permitted free exercise of their franchise." *Id.* Consequently, we concluded that, "[i]n certain circumstances, [the judiciary] must recognize the special import of protecting the shareholders' franchise within *Unocal's* requirement that any defensive measure be proportionate and 'reasonable in relation to the threat posed.' " *Id.*

We begin our examination of Unitrin's Repurchase Program mindful of the special import of protecting the shareholder's franchise within *Unocal's* requirement that a defensive response be reasonable and proportionate. For many years the "favored attack of a [corporate] raider was stock acquisition followed by a proxy contest." *Unocal,* 493 A.2d at 957. Some commentators have noted that the recent trend toward tender offers as the preferable alternative to proxy contests appears to be reversing because of the proliferation of sophisticated takeover defenses. Lucian A. Bebchuk & Marcel Kahan, *A Framework for*

Analyzing Legal Policy Towards Proxy Contests, 78 Cal.L.Rev. 1071, 1134 (1990). In fact, the same commentators have characterized a return to proxy contests as "the only alternative to hostile takeovers to gain control against the will of the incumbent directors." *Id.*

The Court of Chancery concluded that Unitrin's adoption of a poison pill was a proportionate response to the threat its Board reasonably perceived from American General's Offer. Nonetheless, the Court of Chancery enjoined the additional defense of the Repurchase Program as disproportionate and "unnecessary."

The record reflects that the Court of Chancery's decision to enjoin the Repurchase Program is attributable to a continuing misunderstanding, i.e., that in conjunction with the longstanding Supermajority Vote provision in the Unitrin charter, the Repurchase Program would operate to provide the director shareholders with a "veto" to preclude a successful proxy contest by American General…The premise was the Court of Chancery's *sua sponte* determination that Unitrin's outside directors, who are also substantial stockholders, would not vote like other stockholders in a proxy contest, *i.e.,* in their own best economic interests. At American General's Offer price, the outside directors held Unitrin shares worth more than $450 million. Consequently, Unitrin argues the stockholder directors had the same interest as other Unitrin stockholders generally, when voting in a proxy contest, to wit: the maximization of the value of their investments.

In rejecting Unitrin's argument, the Court of Chancery stated that the stockholder directors would be "subconsciously" motivated in a proxy contest to vote against otherwise excellent offers which did not include a "price parameter" to compensate them for the loss of the "prestige and perquisites" of membership on Unitrin's Board. The Court of Chancery's subjective determination that the *stockholder directors* of Unitrin would reject an "excellent offer," unless it compensated them for giving up the "prestige and perquisites" of directorship, appears to be subjective and without record support. It cannot be presumed.

It must be the subject of proof that the Unitrin directors' objective in the Repurchase Program was to forego the opportunity to sell their stock at a premium. In particular, it cannot be presumed that the prestige and perquisites of holding a director's office or a motive to strengthen collective power prevails over a stockholder-director's economic interest. Even the shareholder-plaintiffs in this case agree with the legal proposition Unitrin advocates on appeal: stockholders are presumed to act in their own best economic interests when they vote in a proxy contest.

The first objective premise relied upon by the Court of Chancery, unsupported by the record, is that the shareholder directors needed to implement the Repurchase Program to attain voting power in a proxy contest equal to 25%. The Court of Chancery properly calculated that if the Repurchase Program was completed, Unitrin's shareholder directors would increase their absolute voting power to 25%. It then calculated the odds of American General marshalling enough votes to defeat the Board and its supporters.

The Court of Chancery and all parties agree that proxy contests do not generate 100% shareholder participation. The shareholder plaintiffs argue that 80–85% may be a usual turnout. Therefore, *without* the Repurchase Program, the director shareholders' absolute voting power of 23% would already constitute *actual voting power greater than* 25% in a proxy contest with normal shareholder participation below 100%.

The second objective premise relied upon by the Court of Chancery, unsupported by the record, is that American General's ability to succeed in a proxy contest depended on the Repurchase Program being enjoined because of the Supermajority Vote provision in Unitrin's charter. Without the approval of a target's board, the danger of activating a poison pill renders it irrational for bidders to pursue stock acquisitions above the triggering level. Instead, "bidders intent on working around a poison pill must launch and win proxy contests to elect new directors who are willing to redeem the target's poison pill." Joseph A. Grundfest, *Just Vote No: A Minimalist Strategy for Dealing with Barbarians Inside the Gates,* 45 Stan.L.Rev. 857, 859 (1993).

As American General acknowledges, a less than 15% stockholder bidder need not proceed with acquiring shares to the extent that it would ever implicate the Supermajority Vote provision. In fact, it would be illogical for American General or any other bidder to acquire more than 15% of Unitrin's stock because that would not only trigger the poison pill, but also the constraints of 8 *Del.C.* § 203. If American General were to initiate a proxy contest *before* acquiring 15% of Unitrin's stock, it would need to amass only 45.1% of the votes assuming a 90% voter turnout. If it commenced a tender offer at an attractive price contemporaneously with its proxy contest, it could seek to acquire 50.1% of the outstanding voting stock.

American General also calculated the votes available to the Board or the bidder with and without the Repurchase Program:

> Assuming no Repurchase [Program], the [shareholder directors] would hold 23%, the percentage collectively held by the [directors] and the bidder would be 37.9%, and the percentage of additional votes available to either side would be 52.1%.

> Assuming the Repurchase [Program] is fully consummated, the [shareholder directors] would hold 28%, the percentage collectively held by the bidder and the [directors] would be 42.9%, and the percentage of additional votes available to either side would be 47.1%.

American General then applied these assumptions to reach conclusions regarding the votes needed for the 14.9% stockholder bidder to prevail: first, in an election of directors; and second, in the subsequent vote on a merger. With regard to the election of directors, American General made the following calculations:

> Assume 90% stockholder turnout. To elect directors, a plurality must be obtained; assuming no abstentions and only two competing slates, one must obtain the votes of 45.1% of the shares.

The percentage of additional votes the bidder needs to win is: 45.1% − 14.9% (maximum the bidder could own and avoid the poison pill, § 203 and supermajority) = **30.2%**.

A merger requires approval of a majority of outstanding shares, 8 *Del.C.* § 251, not just a plurality. In that regard, American General made the following calculations:

Assume 90% stockholder turnout. To approve a merger, one must obtain the favorable vote of 50.1% of the shares.

The percentage of additional votes the bidder needs to win is 50.1% − 14.9% = **35.2%**.

Consequently, to prevail in a proxy contest with a 90% turnout, the percentage of additional shareholder votes a 14.9% shareholder bidder needs to prevail is 30.2% for directors and 35.2% in a subsequent merger. The record reflects that institutional investors held 42% of Unitrin's stock and 20 institutions held 33% of the stock. Thus, American General's own assumptions and calculations in the record support the Unitrin Board's argument that "it is hard to imagine a company more readily susceptible to a proxy contest concerning a pure issue of dollars."

The conclusion of the Court of Chancery that the Repurchase Program would make a proxy contest for Unitrin a "theoretical" possibility that American General could not realistically pursue may be erroneous and appears to be inconsistent with its own earlier determination that the "repurchase program strengthens the position of the Board of Directors to defend against a hostile bidder, but will not deprive the public stockholders of the 'power to influence corporate direction through the ballot.' " Even a complete implementation of the Repurchase Program, in combination with the pre-existing Supermajority Vote provision, would not appear to have a preclusive effect upon American General's ability successfully to marshall enough shareholder votes to win a proxy contest. A proper understanding of the record reflects that American General or any other 14.9% shareholder bidder could apparently win a proxy contest with a 90% turnout.

The key variable in a proxy contest would be the merit of American General's issues, not the size of its stockholdings. *Moran v. Household Int'l, Inc.,* Del.Supr., 500 A.2d 1346, 1355 (1985). If American General presented an attractive price as the cornerstone of a proxy contest, it could prevail, irrespective of whether the shareholder directors' absolute voting power was 23% or 28%.

Consequently, a proxy contest apparently remained a viable alternative for American General to pursue notwithstanding Unitrin's poison pill, Supermajority Vote provision, and a fully implemented Repurchase Program.

This Court has recognized "the prerogative of a board of directors to resist a third party's unsolicited acquisition proposal or offer." *Paramount Communications, Inc. v. QVC Network, Inc.,* Del.Supr., 637 A.2d 34, 43 n. 13 (1994). The Unitrin Board did not have unlimited discretion to defeat the threat it perceived from the American General Offer by any draconian means available.

Pursuant to the *Unocal* proportionality test, the nature of the threat associated with a particular hostile offer sets the parameters for the range of permissible defensive tactics. Accordingly, the purpose of enhanced judicial scrutiny is to determine whether the Board acted reasonably in "relation ... to the threat which a particular bid allegedly poses to stockholder interests." *Mills Acquisition Co. v. Macmillan, Inc.,* Del.Supr., 559 A.2d 1261, 1288 (1989)...

The record reflects that the Unitrin Board perceived the threat from American General's Offer to be a form of substantive coercion. The Board noted that Unitrin's stock price had moved up, on higher than normal trading volume, to a level slightly below the price in American General's Offer. The Board also noted that some Unitrin shareholders had publicly expressed interest in selling at or near the price in the Offer. The Board determined that Unitrin's stock was undervalued by the market at current levels and that the Board considered Unitrin's stock to be a good long-term investment. The Board also discussed the speculative and unsettled market conditions for Unitrin stock caused by American General's public disclosure. The Board concluded that a Repurchase Program would provide additional liquidity to those stockholders who wished to realize short-term gain, and would provide enhanced value to those stockholders who wished to maintain a long-term investment. Accordingly, the Board voted to authorize the Repurchase Program for up to ten million shares of its outstanding stock on the open market.

The record appears to support Unitrin's argument that the Board's justification for adopting the Repurchase Program was its reasonably perceived risk of substantive coercion, *i.e.,* that Unitrin's shareholders might accept American General's inadequate Offer because of "ignorance or mistaken belief" regarding the Board's assessment of the long-term value of Unitrin's stock. The adoption of the Repurchase Program also appears to be consistent with this Court's holding that economic inadequacy is not the only threat presented by an all cash for all shares hostile bid, because the threat of such a hostile bid could be exacerbated by shareholder "ignorance or ... mistaken belief." *Paramount Communications, Inc. v. Time, Inc.,* 571 A.2d at 1153.

The Court of Chancery applied an incorrect legal standard when it ruled that the Unitrin decision to authorize the Repurchase Program was disproportionate because it was "unnecessary." The Court of Chancery stated:

> Given that the Board had already implemented the poison pill and the advance notice provision, the repurchase program was unnecessary to protect Unitrin from an inadequate bid.

A court applying enhanced judicial scrutiny should be deciding whether the directors made *a reasonable* decision, not *a perfect* decision. If a board selected one of several reasonable alternatives, a court should not second guess that choice even though it might have decided otherwise or subsequent events may have cast doubt on the board's determination. Thus, courts will not substitute their business judgment for that of the directors, but will determine if the directors' decision was, on balance, within a range of reasonableness. The Court of Chancery did not determine whether the Unitrin Board's decision to implement the Repurchase Program fell within a "range of reasonableness."

The record reflects that the Unitrin Board's adoption of the Repurchase Program was an apparent recognition on its part that all shareholders are not alike. This Court has stated that distinctions among types of shareholders are neither inappropriate nor irrelevant for a board of directors to make, *e.g.,* distinctions between long-term shareholders and short-term profit-takers, such as arbitrageurs, and their stockholding objectives.. In *Unocal* itself, we expressly acknowledged that "a board may reasonably consider the basic stockholder interests at stake, including those of short term speculators, whose actions may have fueled the coercive aspect of the offer at the expense of the long term investor." *Unocal,* 493 A.2d at 955–56.

The Court of Chancery's determination that the Unitrin Board's adoption of the Repurchase Program was unnecessary constituted a substitution of its business judgment for that of the Board, contrary to this Court's "range of reasonableness" holding in *Paramount Communications, Inc. v. QVC Network, Inc.,* 637 A.2d at 45–46.

In assessing a challenge to defensive actions by a target corporation's board of directors in a takeover context, this Court has held that the Court of Chancery should evaluate the board's overall response, including the justification for each contested defensive measure, and the results achieved thereby. Where all of the target board's defensive actions are inextricably related, the principles of *Unocal* require that such actions be scrutinized collectively as a unitary response to the perceived threat. Thus, the Unitrin Board's adoption of the Repurchase Program, in addition to the poison pill, must withstand *Unocal* 's proportionality review. *Id.*

An examination of the cases applying *Unocal* reveals a direct correlation between findings of proportionality or disproportionality and the judicial determination of whether a defensive response was draconian because it was either coercive or preclusive in character. In *Time,* for example, this Court concluded that the Time board's defensive response was reasonable and proportionate since it was not aimed at "cramming down" on its shareholders a management-sponsored alternative, *i.e.,* was not coercive, and because it did not preclude Paramount from making an offer for the combined Time–Warner company, *i.e.,* was not preclusive. *See Paramount Communications, Inc. v. Time, Inc.,* Del.Supr., 571 A.2d 1140, 1154–55 (1990).

This Court also applied *Unocal's* proportionality test to the board's adoption of a "poison pill" shareholders' rights plan in *Moran v. Household Int'l, Inc.,* Del.Supr., 500 A.2d 1346 (1985). After acknowledging that the adoption of the rights plan was within the directors' statutory authority, this Court determined that the implementation of the rights plan was a proportionate response to the theoretical threat of a hostile takeover, in part, because it did not "strip" the stockholders of their right to receive tender offers *and* did not fundamentally restrict proxy contests, *i.e.,* was not preclusive.

If a defensive measure is not draconian, however, because it is not either coercive or preclusive, the *Unocal* proportionality test requires the focus of enhanced judicial scrutiny to shift to "the range of reasonableness." *Paramount Communications, Inc. v. QVC Network, Inc.,* Del.Supr., 637 A.2d 34, 45–46 (1994). Proper and proportionate defensive responses are intended and permitted to thwart perceived threats. When a corporation is not for sale, the board of directors is the defender of the metaphorical medieval corporate bastion and the protector of the corporation's shareholders. The fact that a defensive action must not be coercive or preclusive does not prevent a board from responding defensively before a bidder is at the corporate bastion's gate.

The *ratio decidendi* for the "range of reasonableness" standard is a need of the board of directors for latitude in discharging its fiduciary duties to the corporation and its shareholders when defending against perceived threats. The concomitant requirement is for judicial restraint. Consequently, if the board of directors' defensive response is not draconian (preclusive or coercive) and is within a "range of reasonableness," a court must not substitute its judgment for the board's.

In this case, the initial focus of enhanced judicial scrutiny for proportionality requires a determination regarding the defensive responses by the Unitrin Board to American General's offer. We begin, therefore, by ascertaining whether the Repurchase Program, as an addition to the poison pill, was draconian by being either coercive or preclusive.

A limited nondiscriminatory self-tender, like some other defensive measures, may thwart a current hostile bid, but is not inherently coercive. Moreover, it does not necessarily preclude future bids or proxy contests by stockholders who decline to participate in the repurchase. A selective repurchase of shares in a public corporation on the market, such as Unitrin's Repurchase Program, generally does not discriminate because all shareholders can voluntarily realize the same benefit by selling. Here, there is no showing on this record that the Repurchase Program was coercive.

We have already determined that the record in this case appears to reflect that a proxy contest remained a viable (if more problematic) alternative for American General even if the Repurchase Program were to be completed in its entirety. Nevertheless, the Court of Chancery must determine whether Unitrin's Repurchase Program would only inhibit American General's ability to wage a proxy fight and institute a merger or whether it was, in fact, preclusive because American General's success would either be mathematically impossible or realistically unattainable. If the Court of Chancery concludes that the Unitrin Repurchase Program was not draconian because it was not preclusive, one question will remain to be answered in its proportionality review: whether the Repurchase Program was within a range of reasonableness?

The Court of Chancery found that the Unitrin Board reasonably believed that American General's Offer was inadequate and that the adoption of a poison pill was a proportionate defensive response. Upon remand, in applying the correct legal standard to the factual circumstances of this case, the Court of Chancery may conclude that the implementation of the limited Repurchase Program was also within a range of reasonable additional defensive responses available to the Unitrin Board. In considering whether the Repurchase Program was within a range of reasonableness the Court of Chancery should take into consideration whether: (1) it is a statutorily authorized form of business decision which a board of directors may routinely make in a non-takeover context; (2) as a defensive response to American General's Offer it was limited and corresponded in degree or magnitude to the degree or magnitude of the threat, (*i.e.,* assuming the threat was relatively "mild," was the response relatively "mild?"); (3) with the Repurchase Program, the Unitrin Board properly recognized that all shareholders are not alike, and provided immediate liquidity to those shareholders who wanted it...

In this case, the Court of Chancery erred by substituting its judgment, that the Repurchase Program was unnecessary, for that of the Board. The Unitrin Board had the power and the duty, upon reasonable investigation, to protect Unitrin's shareholders from what it perceived to be the threat from American General's inadequate all-cash for all-shares Offer. The adoption of the poison pill *and* the limited Repurchase Program was not coercive and the Repurchase Program may not be preclusive. Although each made a takeover more difficult, individually and collectively, if they were not coercive or preclusive the Court of Chancery must determine whether they were within the range of reasonable defensive measures available to the Board.

If the Court of Chancery concludes that individually and collectively the poison pill and the Repurchase Program were proportionate to the threat the Board believed American General posed, the Unitrin Board's adoption of the Repurchase Program and the poison pill is entitled to review under the traditional business judgment rule. The burden will then shift "back to the plaintiffs who have the ultimate burden of persuasion [in a preliminary injunction proceeding] to show a breach of the directors' fiduciary duties." *Moran v. Household Int'l, Inc.,* Del.Supr., 500 A.2d 1346, 1356 (1985)...

We hold that the Court of Chancery correctly determined that the *Unocal* standard of enhanced judicial scrutiny applied to the defensive actions of the Unitrin defendants in establishing the poison pill and implementing the Repurchase Program. The Court of Chancery's finding, that the Repurchase Program was a disproportionate defensive response, was based on faulty factual predicates, unsupported by the record. This error was exacerbated by its application of an erroneous legal standard of "necessity" to the Repurchase Program as a defensive response.

The interlocutory judgment of the Court of Chancery, in favor of American General, is REVERSED. This matter is REMANDED for further proceedings in accordance with this opinion.

CHESAPEAKE CORP. v. SHORE
771 A.2d 293 (Del.Ch. 2000)

STRINE, Vice Chancellor.

This case involves a contest for control between two corporations in the specialty packaging industry, the plaintiff Chesapeake Corporation and the defendant Shorewood Packaging Corporation, whose boards of directors both believe that the companies should be merged. The boards just disagree on which company should acquire the other and who should manage the resulting entity.

Shorewood started the dance by making a 41%, all-cash, all-shares premium offer for Chesapeake. The Chesapeake board rejected the offer as inadequate, citing the fact that the stock market was undervaluing its shares. Chesapeake countered with a 40%, all-cash, all-shares premium offer for Shorewood. The Shorewood board, all of whose members are defendants in this case, turned down this offer, claiming that the market was also undervaluing Shorewood.

Recognizing that Chesapeake, a takeover-proof Virginia corporation, might pursue Shorewood, a Delaware corporation, through a contested tender offer or proxy fight, the Shorewood board adopted a host of defensive bylaws to supplement Shorewood's poison pill. The bylaws were designed to make it more difficult for Chesapeake to amend the Shorewood bylaws to eliminate its classified board structure, unseat the director-defendants, and install a new board amenable to its offer. These bylaws, among other things, eliminated the ability of stockholders to call special meetings and gave the Shorewood board control over the record date for any consent solicitation.

Most important, the bylaws raised the votes required to amend the bylaws from a simple majority to 66 2/3% of the outstanding shares. Because Shorewood's management controls nearly 24% of the company's stock, the 66 2/3% Supermajority Bylaw made it mathematically impossible for Chesapeake to prevail in a consent solicitation without management's support, assuming a 90% turnout.

Chesapeake then increased its offer, went public with it in the form of a tender offer and a consent solicitation, and initiated this lawsuit challenging the 66 2/3% Supermajority Bylaw. Shortly before trial, the Shorewood board amended the Bylaw to reduce the required vote to 60%.

Chesapeake challenges the 60% Supermajority Bylaw's validity on several grounds. Principally, Chesapeake contends that the Shorewood board, which is dominated by inside directors, adopted the Bylaw so as to entrench itself and without informed deliberations. It argues that the Bylaw raises the required vote to unattainable levels and is grossly disproportionate to the modest threat posed by Chesapeake's fully negotiable premium offer. Moreover, it claims that the defendants' argument that the Bylaw is necessary to protect Shorewood's sophisticated stockholder base, which is comprised predominately of institutional investors and management holders, from the risk of confusion is wholly pretextual and factually unsubstantiated.

In this post-trial opinion, I conclude that the defendants have not met their burden to sustain the Supermajority Bylaw under either the Unocal v. Mesa Petroleum Co. In sum, the Supermajority Bylaw is a preclusive, unjustified impairment of the Shorewood stockholders' right to influence their company's policies through the ballot box.

In this opinion, I also address the defendants' claim that the Shorewood stockholders are prohibited from voting to eliminate the company's classified board structure and subsequently seating a new board. I reject that claim as inconsistent with the plain language of 8 Del. C. § 141 and the policy of our corporation law that stockholders have the authority to determine the governance structure of their corporations in the bylaws, absent a certificate provision to the contrary…

Chesapeake and the defendant-directors part company on the standard of review that should apply to examine the validity of the Supermajority Bylaw. For its part, Chesapeake contends that the defendant-directors' primary purpose in adopting the Supermajority Bylaw was to interfere with or impede the exercise of the shareholder franchise. As such, Chesapeake argues that the compelling justification standard set forth in Blasius Industries, Inc. v. Atlas Corp. applies.

The defendant directors counter that the Supermajority Bylaw is not preclusive of stockholder action to amend the Shorewood bylaws. Moreover, the Bylaw was adopted as a defensive measure against a hostile tender offer. Therefore, the defendant directors argue that that the Unocal standard of review is singularly applicable. This clash of arguments forces me to address an issue that our courts have struggled with for over a decade: to what extent is the Blasius standard of review viable as a standard of review independent of Unocal in a case where Unocal would otherwise be the standard of review?

In the wake of Blasius, Delaware courts have struggled with how broadly that case should be applied. In retrospect, this difficulty might have been anticipated. Because the test is so exacting—akin to that used to determine whether racial classifications are constitutional—whether it applies comes close to being outcome-determinative in and of itself. Therefore, in a moment of rather remarkable candor, the Delaware Supreme Court stated: the Blasius "burden of demonstrating a 'compelling justification' is quite onerous, and is therefore applied rarely." *Williams v. Geier,* Del.Supr., 671 A.2d 1368, 1376 (1996).

Of course, the fact that a test is "onerous" is not a reason not to apply it if the circumstances warrant. But it is not easy in most cases to determine whether the Blasius standard should be invoked. It is important to remember that it was undisputed in Blasius that the board's actions precluded the election of a new board majority and that the board intended that effect. As such, Chancellor Allen had no difficulty in concluding that the "board acted for the primary purpose of thwarting the exercise of a shareholder vote."

In the more typical case involving board actions touching upon the electoral process, the question of whether the board's actions are preclusive is usually hotly contested. And the preclusion question and the issue of the board's "primary purpose" are not easily separable. The line between board actions that influence the electoral process in legitimate ways (e.g., delaying the election to provide more time for deliberations or to give the target board some reasonable breathing room to identify alternatives) and those that preclude effective stockholder action is not always luminous. Absent confessions of improper purpose, the most important evidence of what a board intended to do is often what effects its actions have.

In such a case, the court must be rather deep in its analysis before it can even determine if the Blasius standard properly applies. Put another way, rather than the standard of review determining how the court looks at the board's actions, how the court looks at the board's actions influences in an important way what standard of review is to apply.

In addition, the Delaware Supreme Court and this court have both recognized the high degree of overlap between the concerns animating the Blasius standard of review and those that animate Unocal. For example, in Stroud v. Grace, Del.Supr., 606 A.2d 75, 82 (1992), the Delaware Supreme Court held that Unocal must be applied to any defensive measure touching upon issues of control, regardless of whether that measure also implicates voting rights. In so ruling, the Court noted that "[b]oard action interfering with the exercise of the franchise often ar [ises] during a hostile contest for control where an acquiror launch[es] both a proxy fight and a tender offer." *Id.* at 92 n. 3. When a case involves defensive measures of such a nature, the trial court is not to ignore the teaching of Blasius but must "recognize the special import of protecting the shareholders' franchise within Unocal's requirement that any defensive measure be proportionate and 'reasonable in relation to the threat posed.' " Therefore, a "board's unilateral decision to adopt a defensive measure touching upon issues of control that purposely disenfranchises its shareholders is strongly suspect under Unocal, and cannot be sustained without a compelling justification." *Id.*

The Supreme Court's Unitrin opinion seems to go even further than Stroud in integrating Blasius's concern over manipulation of the electoral process into the Unocal standard of review. At issue in Unitrin (and discussed in greater detail in the next section of this opinion) was the arguably preclusive effect of a stock repurchase program that would have placed up to 28% of Unitrin's stock in the hands of its directors on a proxy contest to elect a new Unitrin board by another company, American General, that had made an all-cash, all-shares tender offer. In determining to reverse the trial court's decision to strike down the repurchase program, the Supreme Court focused a section of its opinion on the "Shareholder Franchise." In that section, the Court emphasized the "assiduous[ness of] its concern about defensive actions designed to thwart the essence of corporate democracy by disenfranchising shareholders" and its acceptance of the " 'basic tenets' " of Blasius. Because the board's actions came in the face of a tender offer coupled with a proxy fight, the Court cited extensively to Stroud's discussion of the interrelationship of Blasius and Unocal in such circumstances.

But when it came time to assess whether the Chancery Court's determination that the repurchase program was invalid was correct, the Supreme Court appeared to eschew any application of the compelling justification test. The Court never cited to Blasius after that point in its opinion, never referenced or applied the compelling justification standard, and, to the contrary, emphasized the latitude a board of directors must be given to adopt reasonable defensive measures in its business judgment.

Stroud and Unitrin thus left unanswered the question most important to litigants: when will the compelling justification test be used, whether within the Unocal analysis or as a free-standing standard of review? Assuming the compelling justification language is to be taken seriously, whether that language applies could, of course, tilt the outcome of a Unocal analysis in an important way. After Unitrin, this question became even more consequential, because that opinion appeared to accord target boards of directors quite a bit of leeway to take defensive actions that made it more difficult for an insurgent slate to win a proxy fight...

In reality, invocation of the Blasius standard of review usually signals that the court will invalidate the board action under examination. Failure to invoke Blasius, conversely, typically indicates that the board action survived (or will survive) review under Unocal.

Given this interrelationship and the continued vitality of Schnell v. Chris-Craft, one might reasonably question to what extent the Blasius "compelling justification" standard of review is necessary as a lens independent of or to be used within the Unocal frame. If Unocal is applied by the court with a gimlet eye out for inequitably motivated electoral manipulations or for subjectively well-intentioned board action that has preclusive or coercive effects, the need for an additional standard of review is substantially lessened. Stated differently, it may be optimal simply for Delaware courts to infuse our Unocal analyses with the spirit animating Blasius and not hesitate to use our remedial powers where an inequitable distortion of corporate democracy has occurred. This is especially the case when a typical predicate to the invocation of Blasius is the court's consideration of Unocal factors, such as the board's purpose and whether the board's actions have preclusive or coercive effects on the electorate.

For purposes of this case, however, I must apply the law as it exists. That means that Unocal must be applied to the Supermajority Bylaw because of its defensive origin. To the extent that I further conclude that the Supermajority Bylaw was adopted for the primary purpose of interfering with or impeding the stockholder franchise, the Bylaw cannot survive a Unocal review unless it is supported by a compelling justification.

To apply this approach in a reasoned manner, I will first examine the Supermajority Bylaw employing purely the Unocal standard. After examining the defendant's justifications for the Bylaw and whether the Bylaw is a proportionate response under Unocal, I will then determine whether the compelling justification standard of Blasius is implicated.

In some respects, this case unavoidably brings to the fore certain tensions in our corporation law. For example, several cases have stated that a corporate board may consider a fully-financed all-cash, all-shares, premium to market tender offer a threat to stockholders on the following premise: the board believes that the company's present strategic plan will deliver more value than the premium offer, the stock market has not yet bought that rationale, the board may be correct, and therefore there is a risk that "stockholders might tender ... in ignorance or based upon a mistaken belief ...." A rather interesting term has emerged to describe this threat: "substantive coercion."

One might imagine that the response to this particular type of threat might be time-limited and confined to what is necessary to ensure that the board can tell its side of the story effectively. That is, because the threat is defined as one involving the possibility that stockholders might make an erroneous investment or voting decision, the appropriate response would seem to be one that would remedy that problem by providing the stockholders with adequate information. The corporate board has, of course, many tools to accomplish that, but may legitimately need more time to ensure that it can get its message out to the marketplace.

In addition, it may be that the corporate board acknowledges that an immediate value-maximizing transaction would be advisable but thinks that a better alternative than the tender offer might be achievable. A time period that permits the board to negotiate for a better offer or explore alternatives would also be logically proportionate to the threat of substantive coercion.

But our law has, at times, authorized defensive responses that arguably go far beyond these categories. Paradoxically, some of these defensive responses have caused our law to adopt a view of stockholder voting capabilities that is a bit hard to reconcile. In Unitrin, for example, the Supreme Court held that the target Unitrin board could protect its stockholder base from an all-cash, all-shares premium tender offer from American General on the grounds that the Unitrin stockholders were susceptible to accepting an inadequate price ignorantly or mistakenly. At the same time, the Supreme Court held that it was not necessarily a disproportionate response to the American General offer for the Unitrin board to buy its stock in a selective repurchase program at a price comparable to the tender offer price (thus arguably "substantively coercing" participants itself) even though the selective repurchase program thereby increased the percentage of the company's stock in directors' hands to as much as 28%.

In order of importance, three reasons seemed to underlie the Supreme Court's conclusion that the repurchase program might not be preclusive. First, Unitrin's stockholder base was heavily concentrated within a small number of institutional investors. This concentration "facilitat[ed the] bidder's ability to communicate the merits of its position." Second, the fact that the insurgent would have to receive majorities from the disinterested voters uncommon in hotly contested elections in republican democracies was of " de minimis " importance "because 42% of Unitrin's stock was owned by institutional investors." As such, the Supreme Court found that "it is hard to imagine a company more readily susceptible [than Unitrin] to a proxy contest concerning a pure issue of dollars." Finally, the Supreme Court was unwilling to presume that the directors' block—which was controlled almost entirely by non-management directors—would not sell for the right price or vote themselves out of office to facilitate such a sale.

The first two premises of the Court's rejection of the Chancery Court's finding of preclusion seem somewhat contradictory to its acceptance of substantive coercion as a rationale for sweeping defensive measures against the American General bid. On the one hand, a corporate electorate highly dominated by institutional investors has the motivation and wherewithal to understand and act upon a proxy solicitation from an insurgent, such that the necessity for the insurgent to convince over 64% of the non-aligned votes to support its position in order to prevail is not necessarily preclusive. On the other, the same electorate must be protected from substantive coercion because it (the target board thinks) is unable to digest management's position on the long-term value of the company, compare that position to the view advocated by the tender offeror, and make an intelligent (if not risk-free) judgment about whether to support the election of a board that will permit them to sell their shares of stock.

If the consistency in this approach is not in the view that stockholders will always respond in a lemming-like fashion whenever a premium offer is on the table, then a possible reading of Unitrin is that corporate boards are allowed to have it both ways in situations where important stockholder ownership and voting rights are at stake. In approaching the case at hand, I apply a different reading of Unitrin, however.

Without denying the analytical tension within that opinion, one must also remember that the opinion did not ultimately validate the Unitrin defensive repurchase program. Rather, the Supreme Court remanded the case to the Chancery Court to conduct a further examination of the repurchase program, using the refined Unocal analysis the Court set forth. That analysis emphasized the need for trial courts to defer to well-informed corporate boards that identify legitimate threats and implement proportionate defensive measures addressing those threats. It was open for the court on remand to conclude, after considering the relevant factors articulated by the Supreme Court, that the repurchase program was invalid.

I therefore believe it is open to and required of me to examine both the legitimacy of the Shorewood board's identification of "substantive coercion" or "stockholder confusion" as a threat and to determine whether the Supermajority Bylaw is a non-preclusive and proportionate response to that threat. Indeed, the importance to stockholders of a proper Unocal analysis can hardly be overstated in a case where a corporate board relies upon a threat of substantive coercion as its primary justification for defensive measures. Several reasons support this assertion.

As a starting point, it is important to recognize that substantive coercion can be invoked by a corporate board in almost every situation. There is virtually no CEO in America who does not believe that the market is not valuing her company properly. Moreover, one hopes that directors and officers can always say that they know more about the company than the company's stockholders— after all, they are paid to know more. Thus, the threat that stockholders will be confused or wrongly eschew management's advice is omnipresent.

Therefore, the use of this threat as a justification for aggressive defensive measures could easily be subject to abuse. The only way to protect stockholders is for courts to ensure that the threat is real and that the board asserting the threat is not imagining or exaggerating it. In this respect, it bears emphasis that one of corporate management's functions is to ensure that the market recognizes the value of the company and that the stockholders are apprised of relevant information about the company. This informational responsibility would include, one would think, the duty to communicate the company's strategic plans and prospects to stockholders as clearly and understandably as possible. If management claims that its communication efforts have been unsuccessful, shouldn't it have to show that its efforts were adequate before using the risk of confusion as a reason to deny its stockholders access to a bid offering a substantial premium to the company's market price? Where a company has a high proportion of institutional investors among its stockholder ranks, this showing is even more important because a "relatively concentrated percentage of [such] stockholdings would facilitate [management's] ability to communicate the merits of its position."

This confusion rationale should also be tested against the information currently available to investors. The proliferation of computer technology and changes in the broadcast media industry have given investors access to abundant information about the companies in which they invest. The capability of corporations to communicate with their stockholders has never been greater. And the future promises even easier and more substantial information flows.

Our law should also hesitate to ascribe rube-like qualities to stockholders. If stockholders are presumed competent to buy stock in the first place, why are they not presumed competent to decide when to sell in a tender offer after an adequate time for deliberation has been afforded them?

Another related concern is the fact that corporate boards that rely upon substantive coercion as a defense are unwilling to bear the risk of their own errors. Corporate America would rightfully find it shocking if directors were found liable because they erroneously blocked a premium tender offer, the company's shares went into the tank for two years thereafter, and a court held the directors liable for the investment losses suffered by stockholders the directors barred from selling. But, because directors are not anxious to bear any of the investment risk in these situations, courts should hesitate before enabling them to make such fundamental investment decisions for the company's owners. It is quite different for a corporate board to determine that the owners of the company should be barred from selling their shares than to determine what products the company should manufacture. Even less legitimate is a corporate board's decision to protect stockholders from erroneously turning the board out of office.

It is also interesting that the threat of substantive coercion seems to cause a ruckus in boardrooms most often in the context of tender offers at prices constituting substantial premiums to prior trading levels. In the case of Shorewood, for example, shareholders had been selling in the market at the pre-Chesapeake tender offer price, which was much lower. Did Shorewood management make any special efforts to encourage these shareholders to hold? While I recognize that the sale of an entire company is different from day-to-day sales of small blocks, one must remember that the substantive coercion rationale is not one advanced on behalf of employees or communities that might be adversely affected by a change of control. Rather, substantive coercion is a threat to stockholders who might sell at a depressed price. The stockholder who sells in a depressed market for the company's stock without a premium is obviously worse off than one who sells at premium to that depressed price in a tender offer. But it is only in the latter situation that corporate boards commonly swing into action with extraordinary measures. The fact that the premium situation usually involves a possible change in management may play more than a modest role in that difference.

This leads to a final point. As Unocal recognized, the possibility that management might be displaced if a premium-producing tender offer is successful creates an inherent conflict between the interests of stockholders and management. There is always the possibility that subjectively well-intentioned, but nevertheless interested directors, will subconsciously be motivated by the profoundly negative effect a takeover could have on their personal bottom lines and careers.

Allowing such directors to use a broad substantive coercion defense without a serious examination of the legitimacy of that defense would undercut the purpose the Unocal standard of review was established to serve...To support an allegation of substantive coercion, a meaningful proportionality test requires a coherent statement of management's expectations about the future value of the company. From the perspective of shareholders, substantive coercion is possible only if management plausibly expects to better the terms of a hostile offer— whether by bargaining with the offeror, by securing a competitive bid, or by managing the company better than the market expects. To make such a claim requires more than the standard statement that a target's board and its advisers believe the hostile offer to be "grossly inadequate." In particular, demonstrating the existence of a threat of substantive coercion requires a showing of how—and when—management expects a target's shareholders to do better.

The discipline imposed by requiring management to state clearly just how it intends to cause the price of the company's shares to increase is a critical check on knee-jerk resort to assertions that a hostile offer's price is inadequate. For example, if management believes that the price of a hostile offer is inadequate because the market undervalues the company[ ] ... an acceptable statement of the threat to shareholders would require management to describe the steps that it planned to correct the market's valuation.

[S]ubstantive coercion is a slippery concept. To note abstractly that management might know shareholder interests better than shareholders themselves do cannot be a basis for rubber-stamping management's pro forma claims in the face of market skepticism and the enormous opportunity losses that threaten target shareholders when hostile offers are defeated. Preclusive defensive tactics are gambles made on behalf of target shareholders by presumptively self-interested players. Although shareholders may win or lose in each transaction, they would almost certainly be better off on average if the gamble were never made in the absence of meaningful judicial review. By minimizing management's ability to further its self-interest in selecting its response to a hostile offer, an effective proportionality test can raise the odds that management resistance, when it does occur, will increase shareholder value.

When the board of a Delaware corporation acts to oppose or defend against a hostile bid for corporate control, a heightened standard of judicial review applies. In order for the board's defensive actions to survive this enhanced judicial scrutiny, the board must establish: (1) that it had reasonable grounds to believe that the hostile bid for control threatened corporate policy and effectiveness; and (2) that the defensive measures adopted were reasonable in relation to the threat posed. *Unocal*, 493 A.2d at 955.

The "presence of a majority of outside, independent directors will materially enhance" a board's ability to meet this burden. *Unitrin*, 651 A.2d at 1375. In this case, I have concluded that six of the nine members of the Shorewood board cannot be considered outside, independent directors. Therefore, the board's actions are entitled to less deference.

The first prong of Unocal requires the defendants to establish that the Shorewood board, "after a reasonable investigation, ... determined in good faith, that the [Chesapeake Tender Offer and Consent Solicitation] presented a threat ... that warranted a defensive response." *Unitrin*, 651 A.2d at 1375. Although the defendants would have me focus almost entirely on their actions in December 1999 and January 2000, a reasoned analysis requires a consideration of all their relevant actions, starting principally with the November board meetings.

In examining this prong of Unocal, I will focus on the two major threats that the defendants have relied upon to justify the Supermajority Bylaw: (1) price inadequacy; and (2) the risk of stockholder confusion. Although no one will ever point to the Shorewood board's actions as a model of how to analyze an acquisition bid, I am persuaded that the board had sufficient, good faith reasons to conclude that both the $16.50 and $17.25 a share offers were inadequate from a price perspective. Both of these offers trailed Shorewood's one-year high and, according to information provided to the board by O'Donnell and unrebutted by Chesapeake, lagged the price at which comparable transactions had been effected in the specialty packaging industry. The price offered also trailed the values placed on the company's stock by independent analysts.

On the other hand, the defendants have not convinced me that the threat posed by Chesapeake's all-shares, all-cash Tender Offer was a particularly dangerous one. The defendants must concede that there was nothing structurally coercive about Chesapeake's bid—for example, it was not in any sense a front-end loaded, two-tiered tender offer. At the time of the $17.25 Tender Offer, Shorewood also had in place a poison pill and had eliminated Chesapeake's ability to call a special stockholders' meeting. Thus Chesapeake was forced to present its Tender Offer indirectly, through the more deliberative consent solicitation process. Even after a successful consent solicitation, the Tender Offer could not go forward until a new Shorewood board was seated and redeemed the pill after proper deliberations.

Another factor requiring a characterization of the price inadequacy threat as mild is the board's failure to show that its current plans will generate a higher realizable value than $17.25 in the relatively near future. Having cloaked itself in the business strategy privilege, the Shorewood board has cut off any ability of the court to assess how inadequate the Chesapeake offer really is. Given that the Shorewood board is barring its stockholders access to a substantial premium, it is critical, therefore, that Shorewood's defenses be proportionate to this modestly justified threat.

I reach a different conclusion about whether the Shorewood board legitimately identified the second threat it relies upon: the risk of stockholder confusion. Though the defendants claim that this issue first came to the fore in November, there is no persuasive evidence that this is so. Rather, this threat appears to have emerged out of Shorewood's "A Team" of advisors in December. The evidence that the board actually—in its very brief November meetings—concentrated on whether stockholders would be unable to sort out the relevant issues after effective disclosures from management is not convincing. The board has not come close to demonstrating that it identified this threat at any time "after a reasonable investigation" and "in good faith."

On the basis of this record, the threat of confusion emerges more as a post hoc, litigation-inspired rationale for the previously adopted 66 2/3% Supermajority Bylaw than as a serious threat identified as a genuine concern by the board. The defendants have not persuaded me that they made an informed, good faith judgment that the Shorewood electorate would be confused about Shorewood's value and vote with Chesapeake as a result of confusion, rather than informed self-interest. Nor have they proven that such a threat of confusion actually exists.

Therefore, I conclude that the defendants have only met their burden on the first prong of Unocal as to the issue of price inadequacy.

The second prong of Unocal requires the defendants to establish that the Supermajority Bylaw was a proportionate response to the legitimate threats facing Shorewood. In this case, that means that the defendants must show that the Supermajority Bylaw was: (1) not preclusive; and (2) within the range of reasonable defensive responses to Chesapeake's Tender Offer and Consent Solicitation. I have already found that the Shorewood board did not satisfy its burden of showing that it identified the threat of "stockholder confusion" or of "substantive coercion" in a good faith and informed manner.

Nonetheless, I will test the Supermajority Bylaw against both the threat of price inadequacy (which was legitimately identified) and the "stockholder confusion threat" (which was not).

To meet their burden to show that the Supermajority Bylaw is not preclusive, the defendants must show, per Unitrin, that it is "realistically" attainable for Chesapeake to prevail in a consent solicitation to amend the Shorewood bylaws. I read Unitrin as mandating that this court give some reasonable deference to the considered business judgment of a board in addressing this issue and that this court should not quibble around the margins if a board determined that a measure was reasonable after informed and good faith deliberations. But I do not read Unitrin as a reformulation of Unocal 's focus on the actual substantive reasonableness of defensive measures and whether a board in fact made a good faith and informed business judgment in adopting those measures.

In this case, the Shorewood board simply made no judgment at all whether it was "realistically" attainable for Chesapeake to amend the Shorewood bylaws in the face of either the 66 2/3% Supermajority Bylaw or the final 60% Supermajority Bylaw. The Shorewood board did not even discuss this issue. An indication of how blind the Shorewood board was to the relevance of whether the Supermajority Bylaw was preclusive was its adoption of the 66 2/3% Supermajority Bylaw. Under that measure, it was "mathematically impossible" for Chesapeake to prevail in a consent solicitation involving a 90% turnout, assuming that the Shorewood board followed its announced intention to oppose such a solicitation. At the time the board lowered the requirement to 60%, it again ignored whether Chesapeake could "realistically" attain the necessary votes to amend the Shorewood bylaws if the Shorewood board continued to oppose that endeavor.

Not only that, the Shorewood board failed to consider a host of other relevant issues, including the historical turnout in Shorewood elections, the composition of the Shorewood electorate, and the self-interest of the management holders. The board's impoverished deliberations were only once supplemented by expertise, and that consisted of less than five minutes of input from Crozier of Innisfree, who opined without much preparation that 95% of the electorate would vote. Crozier appears to have been asked no questions and never was asked to advise whether an insurgent could realistically attain victory in the face of the Supermajority Bylaw.

Therefore, nothing in the Shorewood board's deliberations is sufficient to help them carry the day.

Even if the Supermajority Bylaw was not preclusive, the board has not met its burden to show that it was a proportionate response to the threat posed by Chesapeake. The Supreme Court has instructed this court to consider this issue in light of whether the defensive measure at issue "is a statutorily authorized form of business decision which a board of directors may routinely make in a non-takeover context" and is "limited and corresponded in degree or magnitude to the degree or magnitude of the threat ...."

Both questions must be answered in the negative. As to the first, I do not reach Chesapeake's argument that a board of directors may not, by bylaw, require a supermajority vote to amend the bylaws. But I agree with Chesapeake's contention that a board decision to adopt a supermajority bylaw is not one "routinely" made in the "non-takeover" context. Rather, such bylaws are almost always a method of minimizing the ability of stockholders to interfere with the board's control or management of the company.

The more important proportionality problem is the fact that the Supermajority Bylaw is an extremely aggressive and overreaching response to a very mild threat. The board already had a poison pill in place that gave it breathing room and precluded the Tender Offer. The Defensive Bylaws had eliminated Chesapeake's ability to call a special meeting, at which a majority of a quorum could act. This forced Chesapeake to proceed through the slower route of a consent solicitation with the minimum support of a majority of the outstanding shares. The Shorewood board controlled, per the Defensive Bylaws, the record date. This guaranteed adequate time for communications and counter-solicitation efforts, as well as for the board to develop and consider strategic alternatives.

Given these factors, the board could have addressed the threat at hand through an aggressive communications plan. The board could have also taken Chesapeake up on its offer to negotiate price and structure, if the board truly believed that price inadequacy was the problem. It never considered these less extreme and more proportionate options.

Instead, the board adopted a Supermajority Bylaw that can only be surmounted by obtaining over 88% of the disinterested votes, assuming a 90% turnout. Yet the board has been unable to demonstrate that such an outcome can be achieved. Ironically, its primary argument in that regard is that Shorewood's stockholder base is overwhelmingly comprised of sophisticated and highly mobilized stockholders who will turn out in droves. These, of course, are the very same stockholders who are, the defendants say, unable to sort out the issues and make a rational judgment for themselves.

The Shorewood board adopted the Supermajority Bylaw as a way of reducing the voting power of Chesapeake and Ariel. It reached a determination about the 60% threshold by subtracting out the shares held by Chesapeake and Ariel from the denominator. By doing so, it treated those votes as less equal than others and acted to impede Chesapeake's voting power.

The primary purpose for this action was to impair Chesapeake's ability to win the Consent Solicitation by increasing the required majority Chesapeake needed to obtain to preclusive levels.

Compounding this intentional impairment of the franchise was the defendants' decision to apply a very different standard to their own self-interest than they did to that of Chesapeake and Ariel.

Hence, I conclude that the defendants clearly acted to "interfere with or impede ... [the exercise of] the shareholder franchise." Therefore, the compelling justification standard applies. The mild threat posed to Shorewood by Chesapeake's all-shares, all-cash Tender Offer and supporting Consent Solicitation does not provide a compelling justification for the Bylaw. The defendants' belief that they "know[ ] better than ... the stockholders" about "who should comprise the board of directors" provides no legitimate justification at all. As a result, the Supermajority Bylaw is invalid under the Blasius standard.

For the foregoing reasons, a partial final judgment shall be entered in Chesapeake's favor on its claim that the Supermajority Bylaw should be enjoined.

4. REVLON-LAND

In *Revlon, Inc. v. MacAndrews & Forbes Holdings*, 506 A.2d 173 (Del. 1986), the Delaware Supreme Court was confronted with the challenge of having to apply the *Unocal* tests in the context of a case where a change of control was inevitable. In that case, Pantry Pride aggressively pursued the acquisition of Revlon, continually upping its offer while threatening a tender offer. Revlon's board considered Pantry Pride "a small, highly leveraged company bent on a 'bust up' takeover by using 'junk bond' financing to buy Revlon cheaply, sell the assets to pay the debts incurred, and retain the profit for itself." Revlon's board initially responded to Pantry Pride's unsolicited bids by adopting a shareholders' rights poison bill and agreed to purchase 10 million shares of its own stock for notes ("Notes") that contained a covenant against any additional debt. As to these defensive measures, the court found that "the board acted in good faith, and on an informed basis, with reasonable grounds to believe that there existed a harmful threat to the corporate enterprise." Citing *Unocal* and upholding these defensive measures, the court stated, "The adoption of a defensive measure, reasonable in relation to the threat posed, was proper and fully accorded with the powers, duties, and responsibilities conferred upon directors under our law." 506 A.2d 181.

The court then focused on the steps Revlon's board had taken when Pantry Pride's offer hit $53 a share and a sale of the company was inevitable. The board authorized Revlon's management to negotiate a sale of the company to a third party. This led to a friendly agreement to sell Revlon to Forstmann for $57.25 a share and Forstmann's agreement to support the market price of the Notes. To secure the deal in the face of Pantry Pride's threat "to top" any offer, Forstmann was given "lock up" protections: a Revlon "no-shop" covenant supported by a $25 million cancellation fee and the right to buy two Revlon divisions at a deeply discounted price. Pantry Pride responded by raising its offer to $58 a share and suing to nullify the rights plan, to terminate the Note's covenants, and to obtain an injunction against the lock-up provision. In holding that Revlon's board had breached its duty of care by approving lock-up protections that shut down the bidding process, the court stated:

> The Revlon board's authorization permitting management to negotiate a merger or buyout with a third party was a recognition that the company was for sale. The duty of the board had thus changed from the preservation of Revlon as a corporate entity to the maximization of the company's value at a sale for the stockholders' benefit. This significantly altered the board's responsibilities under the *Unocal* standards. It no longer faced threats to corporate policy and effectiveness, or to the stockholders' interests, from a grossly inadequate bid. The whole question of defensive measures became moot. The directors' role changed from defenders of the corporate bastion to auctioneers charged with getting the best price for the stockholders at a sale of the company.

> This brings us to the lock-up with Forstmann and its emphasis on shoring up the sagging market value of the Notes in the face of threatened litigation by their holders. Such a focus was inconsistent with the changed concept of the directors' responsibilities at this stage of the developments. The impending waiver of the Notes covenants had caused the value of the Notes to fall, and the board was aware of the noteholders' ire as well as their subsequent threats of suit. The directors thus made support of the Notes an integral part of the company's dealings with Forstmann, even though their primary responsibility at this stage was to the equity owners.

> The original threat posed by Pantry Pride—the break-up of the

company—had become a reality which even the directors embraced. Selective dealing to fend off a hostile but determined bidder was no longer a proper objective. Instead, obtaining the highest price for the benefit of the stockholders should have been the central theme guiding director action. Thus, the Revlon board could not make the requisite showing of good faith by preferring the noteholders and ignoring its duty of loyalty to the shareholders. The rights of the former already were fixed by contract. The noteholders required no further protection, and when the Revlon board entered into an auction-ending lock-up agreement with Forstmann on the basis of impermissible considerations at the expense of the shareholders, the directors breached their primary duty of loyalty.

A board may have regard for various constituencies in discharging its responsibilities, provided there are rationally related benefits accruing to the stockholders. *Unocal,* 493 A.2d at 955. However, such concern for non-stockholder interests is inappropriate when an auction among active bidders is in progress, and the object no longer is to protect or maintain the corporate enterprise but to sell it to the highest bidder.

A lock-up is not *per se* illegal under Delaware law. Such options can entice other bidders to enter a contest for control of the corporation, creating an auction for the company and maximizing shareholder profit. Current economic conditions in the takeover market are such that a "white knight" like Forstmann might only enter the bidding for the target company if it receives some form of compensation to cover the risks and costs involved. However, while those lock-ups which draw bidders into the battle benefit shareholders, similar measures which end an active auction and foreclose further bidding operate to the shareholders' detriment.

The Forstmann option had a destructive effect on the auction process. Forstmann had already been drawn into the contest on a preferred basis, so the result of the lock-up was not to foster bidding, but to destroy it. The board's stated reasons for approving the transactions were: (1) better financing, (2) noteholder protection, and (3) higher price. As the Court of Chancery found, and we agree, any distinctions between the rival bidders' methods of financing the proposal were nominal at best, and such a consideration has little or no significance in a cash offer for any and all shares. The principal object, contrary to the board's duty of care, appears to have been protection of the noteholders over the shareholders' interests.

While Forstmann's $57.25 offer was objectively higher than Pantry Pride's $56.25 bid, the margin of superiority is less when the Forstmann price is adjusted for the time value of money. In reality, the Revlon board ended the auction in return for very little actual improvement in the final bid. The principal benefit went to the directors, who avoided personal liability to a class of creditors to whom the board owed no further duty under the circumstances. Thus, when a board ends an intense bidding contest on an insubstantial basis, and where a significant by-product of that action is to protect the directors against a perceived threat of personal liability for consequences stemming from the adoption of previous defensive measures, the action cannot withstand the enhanced scrutiny which *Unocal* requires of director conduct. *See Unocal,* 493 A.2d at 954–55.

After the directors authorized management to negotiate with other parties, Forstmann was given every negotiating advantage that Pantry Pride had been denied: cooperation from management, access to financial data, and the exclusive opportunity to present merger proposals directly to the board of directors. Favoritism for a white knight to the total exclusion of a hostile bidder might be justifiable when the latter's offer adversely affects shareholder interests, but when bidders make relatively similar offers, or dissolution of the company becomes inevitable, the directors cannot fulfill their enhanced *Unocal* duties by playing favorites with the contending factions. Market forces must be allowed to operate freely to bring the target's shareholders the best price available for their equity. Thus, as the trial court ruled, the shareholders' interests necessitated that the board remain free to negotiate in the fulfillment of that duty.

Having concluded that Pantry Pride has shown a reasonable probability of success on the merits, we address the issue of irreparable harm. The Court of Chancery ruled that unless the lock-up and other aspects of the agreement were enjoined, Pantry Pride's opportunity to bid for Revlon was lost. The court also held that the need for both bidders to compete in the marketplace outweighed any injury to Forstmann. Given the complexity of the proposed transaction between Revlon and Forstmann, the obstacles to Pantry Pride obtaining a meaningful legal remedy are immense. We are satisfied that the plaintiff has shown the need for an injunction to protect it from irreparable harm, which need outweighs any harm to the defendants.

In conclusion, the Revlon board was confronted with a situation not uncommon in the current wave of corporate takeovers. A hostile and determined bidder sought the company at a price the board was convinced was inadequate. The initial defensive tactics worked to the benefit of the shareholders, and thus the board was able to sustain its *Unocal* burdens in justifying those measures. However, in granting an asset option lock-up to Forstmann, we must conclude that under all the circumstances the directors allowed considerations other than the maximization of shareholder profit to affect their judgment, and followed a course that ended the auction for Revlon, absent court intervention, to the ultimate detriment of its shareholders. No such defensive measure can be sustained when it represents a breach of the directors' fundamental duty of care. *See Smith v. Van Gorkom,* Del.Supr., 488 A.2d 858, 874 (1985). In that context the board's action is not entitled to the deference accorded it by the business judgment rule. The measures were properly enjoined. The decision of the Court of Chancery, therefore, is AFFIRMED.

506 A.2d at 182-185

The standards announced *in Revlon* (dubbed the "Revlon duties") have raised some tough questions. At what point in the process do the duties kick in? Does there have to be an auction for the duties to apply? What do the Revlon duties require a board to do when there are multiple potential buyers? Can a board use lockup protections in a deal the board believes is good for the shareholders? Without such lockup protections, can a potential buyer reasonably be expected to commit to a deal that can be dismantled by a competitive bid? In discharging its *Revlon* duties, can a board consider the interests of others, such as employees or creditors, or must the sole focus be short-term maximization for the shareholders? Do the Revlon duties ever apply in a stock-for-stock merger where no shareholders are being cashed out? What about a part-cash, part-stock transaction? Are the Revlon duties a special standard apart from the *Unocal* tests or are they just an example of the *Unocal* rules applied to a special fact situation? In numerous subsequent cases, the Delaware courts have struggled with these questions.

In *Paramount Communications, Inc. v. Time*, Inc. 571 A.2d 1140 (1989), the Delaware Supreme Court helped clarify when *Revlon* duties may be triggered. Time and Warner had entered into a stock-for-stock merger. Paramount sought to stop the merger by making cash tender offers to Time's shareholders on the condition that the Time-Warner merger be terminated. Fearful that its shareholders might opt for Paramount's offer, Time restructured its deal with Warner as a cash purchase for 51 percent of Warner's stock in a transaction that would not require the approval of Time's shareholders. As a result, Time's shareholders never had a vote on the condition that would have made Paramount's offer operative. The court held that Time's outside directors had not violated their *Unocal* duties, finding that the directors had acted in good faith in determining that the Paramount offer was inadequate and that Time's shareholders may lack the capacity to appreciate the strategic benefit of a merger with Warner. The court also held that no *Revlon* duties were triggered by stating:

> Under Delaware law there are, generally speaking and without excluding other possibilities, two circumstances which may implicate *Revlon* duties. The first, and clearer one, is when a corporation initiates an active bidding process seeking to sell itself or to effect a business reorganization involving a clear break-up of the company. However, *Revlon* duties may also be triggered where, in response to a bidder's offer, a target abandons its long-term strategy and seeks an alternative transaction involving the breakup of the company. Thus, in *Revlon,* when the board responded to Pantry Pride's offer by contemplating a "bust-up" sale of assets in a leveraged acquisition, we imposed upon the board a duty to maximize immediate shareholder value and an obligation to auction the company fairly. If, however, the board's reaction to a hostile tender offer is found to constitute only a defensive

response and not an abandonment of the corporation's continued existence, *Revlon* duties are not triggered, though *Unocal* duties attach.

The plaintiffs insist that even though the original Time–Warner agreement may not have worked "an objective change of control," the transaction made a "sale" of Time inevitable. Plaintiffs rely on the subjective intent of Time's board of directors and principally upon certain board members' expressions of concern that the Warner transaction *might* be viewed as effectively putting Time up for sale. Plaintiffs argue that the use of a lock-up agreement, a no-shop clause, and so-called "dry-up" agreements prevented shareholders from obtaining a control premium in the immediate future and thus violated *Revlon.*

We agree with the Chancellor that such evidence is entirely insufficient to invoke *Revlon* duties; and we decline to extend *Revlon*'s application to corporate transactions simply because they might be construed as putting a corporation either "in play" or "up for sale." *See Citron v. Fairchild Camera,* Del.Supr., 569 A.2d 53, (1989).; *Macmillan,* 559 A.2d at 1285 n. 35. The adoption of structural safety devices alone does not trigger *Revlon.* Rather, as the Chancellor stated, such devices are properly subject to a *Unocal* analysis.

Finally, we do not find in Time's recasting of its merger agreement with Warner from a share exchange to a share purchase a basis to conclude that Time had either abandoned its strategic plan or made a sale of Time inevitable. The Chancellor found that although the merged Time–Warner company would be large (with a value approaching approximately $30 billion), recent takeover cases have proven that acquisition of the combined company might nonetheless be possible. The legal consequence is that *Unocal* alone applies to determine whether the business judgment rule attaches to the revised agreement.

571 A.2d at 1150 – 1151.

Paramount found itself again with a losing *Revlon* argument in a subsequent case that further clarified when *Revlon* duties may be triggered – *Paramount Communications, Inc. v. QVC Networks, Inc.* 637 A.2d 34 (Del. 1994). Rebounding from its failed Time bid, Paramount entered into a merger agreement with Viacom, under which Paramount shareholders would receive a combination of cash and Viacom stock valued at $69 a share and Viacom was protected by a no-shop covenant, a termination fee, and unique stock option – the right to buy 19.9 percent of Paramount's stock at $69.14 per share with a senior subordinated note if the termination fee was triggered. When QVC announced a competitive tender offer for Paramount's stock at a higher price on the condition that the stock option be invalidated, Paramount's board characterized the QVC offer as "illusory" and continued to show its preference for the Viacom deal. The court held that Paramount's board had violated its *Revlon* duties with the "draconian" stock option, its refusal to negotiate with QVC, its uninformed "illusory" characterization of QVC's offer, and its unwavering allegiance to Viacom. The big issue was whether the *Revlon* duties were even triggered. In holding that the *Revlon* duties applied, the court emphasized that a change of control was inevitable in which a "fluid aggregation of unaffiliated shareholders" would sell their voting control to a single buyer. In distinguishing its holding in *Time*, the court noted that in *Time* there was no "substantial evidence to conclude that Time's board, in negotiating with Warner, made the dissolution or break-up of the corporate entity inevitable" and then stated:

> Under Delaware law there are, generally speaking and without excluding other possibilities, two circumstances which may implicate *Revlon* duties. The first, and clearer one, is when a corporation initiates an active bidding process seeking to sell itself or to effect a business reorganization involving a clear break-up of the company. However, *Revlon* duties may also be triggered where, in response to a bidder's offer, a target abandons its long-term strategy and seeks an alternative transaction involving the breakup of the company.

> The Paramount defendants have misread the holding of *Time–Warner.* Contrary to their argument, our decision in *Time–Warner* expressly states that the two general scenarios discussed in the above-quoted paragraph are not the **only** instances where "*Revlon* duties" may be implicated. The Paramount defendants' argument totally ignores the phrase "without excluding other possibilities." Moreover, the instant case is clearly within the first general scenario set forth in *Time–Warner.* The Paramount Board, albeit unintentionally, had "initiate[d] an active bidding process seeking to sell itself" by agreeing to sell control of the corporation to Viacom in circumstances where another potential acquiror (QVC) was equally interested in being a bidder.

> The Paramount defendants' position that **both** a change of control **and** a break-up are **required** must be rejected. Such a holding would unduly restrict the application of *Revlon,* is inconsistent with this Court's decisions in *Barkan* and *Macmillan,* and has no basis in policy. There are few events that have a more significant impact on the stockholders than a sale of control or a corporate break-up. Each event represents a fundamental (and perhaps irrevocable) change in the nature of the corporate enterprise from a practical standpoint. It is the significance of **each** of these events that justifies: (a) focusing on the directors' obligation to seek the best value reasonably available to the stockholders; and (b) requiring a close scrutiny of board action which could be contrary to the stockholders' interests.

> Accordingly, when a corporation undertakes a transaction which will cause: (a) a change in corporate control; **or** (b) a break-up of the corporate entity, the directors' obligation is to seek the best value reasonably available to the stockholders. This obligation arises because the effect of the Viacom–Paramount transaction, if consummated, is to shift control of Paramount from the public stockholders to a controlling stockholder, Viacom. Neither *Time–Warner* nor any other decision of this Court holds that a "break-up" of the company is essential to give

rise to this obligation where there is a sale of control. (*Emphasis Original*)

637 A.2d at 47-48.

CASE PROBLEM 14-2

Refer to the basic facts of Case Problem 14-1. As Kfiber's Committee pursed discussions with their "white squire" Bolton, the concept of Bolton becoming a "white knight" started to take hold. Bolton would acquire Kfiber through a triangular merger in which Kfiber would be merged into a newly-formed subsidiary of Bolton and thus become a wholly owned subsidiary of Bolton. Kfiber shareholders would receive a combination of cash and Bolton stock valued at $32 a share. The mix of cash and stock has not yet been resolved, but all agree that, for tax reasons, the cash portion will not exceed 50 percent of the consideration. After the merger, former Kfiber shareholders would own from 18 to 35 percent of Bolton's outstanding stock, depending on the cash-stock mix. Troy and Julian would join Bolton's board, the "Walton culture" would continue at Kfiber, and no Kfiber jobs would be threatened.

Troy is "pumped" by the prospects of this merger. He believes that it would provide a "great answer" to troubling questions about Kfiber's future while generating "a superb price and liquidity options" for Kfiber's shareholders.

Bolton is willing to proceed with the transaction only if it can have comfort that "those Warfield vultures can't upset the deal or drive up the price." To protect Bolton and the strength of the deal, the Committee and Bolton have agreed to the following:

- Kfiber's board will adopt the poison plan rights plan described in Recommendation A in Case Problem 14-1.

- Kfiber will agree to a no-shop provision in its agreement with Bolton.

- Kfiber will agree to pay Bolton a termination fee equal to four percent of the deal's consideration (estimated at $48 million) if the deal is cancelled due to an offer from another party.

- If the conditions of the termination fee are triggered, Kfiber will sell to Bolton its Chicago and Houston plants for $325 million, a bargain price by any standard.

The overriding question now is whether Wardfield or other Kfiber shareholders will be able to enjoin the enforcement of these protective actions by successfully alleging that Kfiber's board has violated its fiduciary duties to Kfiber's shareholders. In evaluating this overall question, consider the following specific issues:

1. Will *Revlon* duties be trigger in this situation?

2. How can the transaction be structured to reduce the potential of triggering *Revlon* duties?

3. How do the proof and substantive challenges change for Kfiber's board

if *Revlon* duties are triggered?

4. Are the *Unocal* standards still applicable to this transaction?

5. Are the interests of preserving Kfiber's culture and jobs for Kfiber's workforce legitimate considerations for Kfiber's board in deciding to ignore Warfield's offers?

6. What procedural and substantive record should Kfiber's board attempt to establish in order to protect its board members from any potential fiduciary breach claims?

IN RE SMURFIT–STONE CONTAINER CORP. SHAREHOLDER LITIGATION
2011 WL 2028076 (Del.Ch. 2011)

PARSONS, Vice Chancellor.

This matter involves a stockholder challenge to a merger in which a third-party strategic acquiror has agreed to merge with the target corporation for consideration valued at $35 per share. The agreed-upon deal provides that each of the target's stockholders will receive approximately half of the merger consideration in cash and the other half in stock of the acquiror. Plaintiffs allege that the $35 merger price is unreasonable and that the target's board failed adequately to inform itself as to the true value of the company and maximize stockholder value under Delaware's Revlon line of cases. Furthermore, Plaintiffs allege that the target's board breached its fiduciary duties by agreeing unreasonably to a number of deal protection measures that had a preclusive, deterrent effect on any bidders who otherwise might have made a higher offer.

Importantly, this case provides cause for the Court to address a question that has not yet been squarely addressed in Delaware law; namely, whether and in what circumstances Revlon applies when merger consideration is split roughly evenly between cash and stock. Plaintiffs have moved for a preliminary injunction and request that the Court delay the target's stockholder vote and enjoin the deal protections for a period of 45 to 60 days so as to allow the target to seek higher bids. For the reasons stated in this Opinion, however, I deny Plaintiffs' motion for a preliminary injunction.

The target in this consolidated action is Defendant Smurfit–Stone Container Corp. ("Smurfit–Stone" or the "Company"), a Delaware corporation with its headquarters in Chicago, Illinois. It is a manufacturer of paperboard and paper-based packaging, including containerboard and corrugated containers...

On January 23, 2011, the board of directors of Smurfit–Stone unanimously approved an agreement and plan of merger (the "Merger Agreement" or "Agreement") to be acquired by Defendants Rock–Tenn Company ("Rock–Tenn") and Sam Acquisition, LLC ("SA") in a cash and stock transaction worth approximately $3.5 billion (the "Proposed Transaction" or "Transaction"). Rock–Tenn is incorporated in Georgia where it has its principal executive office.

As a result of the economic downturn beginning in 2008 and the concomitant reduction in demand for packaging materials, Smurfit–Stone filed a voluntary petition on January 26, 2009 to restructure itself under Chapter 11 of the United States Bankruptcy Code. Approximately a year and a half later, on June 30, 2010, the Company emerged from bankruptcy after shedding significant debt, closing several underperforming mills, and reducing its workforce by approximately ten percent.

Upon its exit from bankruptcy, Smurfit–Stone's creditors' committee chose a new board of directors based on an interview process conducted by an executive recruiting firm. The reconstituted Board, consisted of eleven individuals, including: two inside directors, Moore and Klinger; one hold-over outside director, O'Connor; and eight new outside directors.

A byproduct of the creditors' committee's work to create a new board was the extension of new employment contracts to Moore, Klinger, and Smurfit–Stone's chief administrative officer and general counsel, Craig A. Hunt. The contracts provided for certain payments to these individuals in the event that the Company entered into a change of control transaction before certain specified dates.

Facing significant challenges in its efforts to return to profitability after bankruptcy, the Company sought to find a permanent management team, in particular a new CEO to replace Moore once his interim contract expired.

On September 16, 2010, representatives of Evercore Partners ("Evercore") indicated to Davis that a prominent private equity firm, Company A, was interested in exploring a transaction with Smurfit–Stone.

On November 11, Evercore informed Moore that Company A likely was interested in purchasing the entire company. Eleven days later, Company A sent Hake a nonbinding, all-cash offer to buy the Company for $29 per share, which constituted a premium of 24.2% to the prior day's closing price... After reviewing the terms of the offer, the Board created a special committee composed of the entire Board except Moore and Klinger, the only inside directors (the "Special Committee" or "Committee"). The Special Committee also formed an informal subcommittee consisting of Hake, Foster, and Haberli (the "Subcommittee"), to oversee the deal process on a day-to-day basis.

The Committee's first order of business was retaining Lazard Freres & Co. LLC ("Lazard") and Wachtell, Lipton, Rosen & Katz ("Wachtell") to be its independent financial and legal advisors, respectively.

Over the next three weeks, Lazard worked on preparing its valuations and Company A continued to perform due diligence. Among other things, the Board asked Lazard to evaluate the Levin Report and determine whether its estimate that Smurfit–Stone's stock could garner $40 per share was realistic.

After Lazard presented its findings, the Special Committee discussed the possibility of reaching out to other potential bidders, but concluded that the benefits of doing so were outweighed by the "risk of leaks, the disruption to management of multiple parties conducting due diligence, and the potential impact on customers, employees, and the Company's business." In addition, both the Special Committee and Lazard allegedly believed that, as a practical matter,

Smurfit–Stone had conducted the functional equivalent to a two-year market check in the form of its bankruptcy because it had engaged in discussions with potential financial and strategic acquirors during that time.

Ultimately, the Special Committee directed Lazard to tell Company A that its $29 per share offer was inadequate, but the Company would entertain a possible transaction at a "significantly higher valuation range." On December 17, Company A withdrew its offer and notified Smurfit–Stone that it would not proceed with the process further.

Rock–Tenn became interested in contacting Smurfit–Stone about a potential acquisition in late 2010. According to its CEO, James Rubright, Rock–Tenn regularly monitors publicly available information about its competitors, including Smurfit–Stone, and was aware of the Company's bankruptcy, the fact that by the middle of 2010 it still had not appointed a permanent CEO, and that industry analysts speculated that it might be an acquisition target...

On January 9, Rock–Tenn made a nonbinding offer to acquire all of the Company's shares at a price of $32 per share, including consideration of 50% cash and 50% stock at a fixed exchange ratio, subject to the negotiation of a definitive merger agreement, limited confirmatory due diligence, and stockholder approval.

The next day, the Special Committee, along with Moore and Hunt, convened to consider Rock–Tenn's offer and request for additional due diligence. The Committee determined that $32 per share was inadequate, but authorized Lazard to permit Rock–Tenn to conduct reasonable additional due diligence to improve its offer.

The Committee also discussed whether it should attempt to reopen negotiations with Company A or solicit offers from other potential acquirors. In particular, it discussed the "risks involved in contacting other parties," including burdens of multiple parties conducting due diligence at the same time, the risk of information leaks, the potential negative impact on customers, employees, and other constituencies, as well as the possibility of jeopardizing a proposed transaction with Rock–Tenn. The Committee also discussed certain analysts' speculation that Smurfit–Stone was a takeover candidate and the possibility that another acquiror would be interested in offering a higher price than Rock–Tenn. On the subject of trying to reopen negotiations with Company A, Lazard advised the Committee that, based on "the history of the prior discussions with [Company A], [it] did not believe that such party would be likely to offer a higher price than Rock–Tenn would be willing to offer." In addition, the Committee recognized that, even if the Company entered into a transaction with Rock–Tenn, it still could consider competing offers, if they should arise, subject to "customary no-shop and breakup fee provisions." As such, the Committee resolved not to contact Company A or other parties about a potential transaction.

Contemporaneously, Wachtell, on behalf of the Committee, and King & Spalding, LLP ("King & Spalding"), Rock–Tenn's counsel, negotiated a draft merger agreement. The Committee "set objectives" for Wachtell so that Smurfit–Stone could obtain a merger agreement that would not "deter[ ] another bidder in the unlikely event that another bidder came along." After rejecting King & Spalding's first draft agreement circulated on January 18, which certain representatives of Smurfit–Stone characterized as "problematic" and "a complete non-starter," Wachtell negotiated for reciprocal deal protection devices and a significantly reduced termination fee.

Following the reciprocal due diligence presentations and the initial draft merger negotiations, Rock–Tenn informed the Company that any deal between the parties had to be finalized by January 23. Smurfit–Stone then asked for Rock–Tenn's best and final offer. On Thursday, January 20, Rubright indicated to Hake that Rock–Tenn would offer $35 per share, split equally between stock and cash as in its previous offer. This price represented a 27% premium to the Company's then-current trading price. The effect of the deal would be that Smurfit–Stone stockholders would own approximately 45% of outstanding Rock–Tenn common shares following consummation.

On Sunday, January 23, the Smurfit–Stone directors convened a joint meeting of the Board and the Special Committee to consider Rock–Tenn's latest offer. Hake, Moore, Wachtell, and Lazard reviewed with the Board the negotiations and discussions between the two companies since the previous meeting on January 20. Moore also expressed his view that it was not to Smurfit–Stone's advantage to remain a stand-alone company.

Lazard presented its analysis regarding the fairness of Rock–Tenn's offer, including valuations of Smurfit–Stone, Rock–Tenn, and the combination of the two companies. Lazard's analyses of the Company generated a valuation range of $27–$39 per share. After Lazard reported that it found the offer to be fair from a financial point of view and Wachtell reviewed the terms of the proposed Merger Agreement, Moore excused himself so the Special Committee could put the offer to a vote. The Committee unanimously agreed to recommend to the Board that it accept Rock–Tenn's offer. Upon Moore's return, the Board unanimously voted to accept Rock–Tenn's offer.

[T]he Merger Agreement contains several so-called deal protection devices, which Plaintiffs claim are unreasonable. In particular, the Agreement contains a "no shop" clause which prevents Smurfit–Stone from "initiat[ing], solicit[ing], induc[ing], or knowingly encourag[ing] or facilitat[ing]" a potentially superior acquisition bid from another prospective acquiror. This restriction is tempered by a "fiduciary out" clause, whereby the Company retains the ability to consider an unsolicited "Company Superior Proposal," as defined in the Agreement, in line with the Board's fiduciary duties.

In addition, the Agreement contains a "matching rights" provision. In pertinent part, that provision gives Rock–Tenn the right to receive details of an unsolicited Superior Proposal received by the Company, as well as the bidder's identity, and, within three calendar days, revise its proposal to try to match or exceed the competing bid.

Finally, the Agreement contains a termination fee of $120 million. This amount would be payable to Rock–Tenn if the Smurfit–Stone Board fails to recommend the Proposed Transaction to its stockholders in the companies' joint proxy statement or if it terminates such transaction in favor of a Superior Proposal.

Count I of the Complaint accuses the Board of breaching its fiduciary duties of care and loyalty by failing to take steps to maximize the value of Smurfit–Stone to its public stockholders. Specifically, Plaintiffs argue that the Proposed Transaction constitutes a "change of control" transaction as to which the Board failed to comply with its obligations under Revlon, Inc. v. MacAndrews & Forbes Holdings, Inc. by conducting an inadequate sales process and obtaining an inadequate price from Rock–Tenn. Count II accuses Rock–Tenn of aiding and abetting the Board in violating its fiduciary duties by way of the challenged conduct. Plaintiffs seek, among other types of relief, a preliminary injunction to delay the stockholder vote on the Proposed Transaction and lift temporarily the deal protection devices.

Defendants begin by challenging Plaintiffs' contention that the Proposed Transaction warrants heightened scrutiny under Revlon and argue that the Court, instead, should review the Board's actions under the more deferential business judgment rule. But, even if Revlon does apply, Defendants assert that the Board fully complied with its fiduciary duties to secure the best value reasonably available for Smurfit–Stone stockholders.

Plaintiffs contend that the Proposed Transaction constitutes a "change of control" transaction and, as such, the Court should apply the heightened Revlon standard. They bolster this argument by characterizing the Transaction as the Smurfit–Stone stockholders' relinquishing majority ownership of the Company in favor of minority ownership of Rock–Tenn and arguing that, because approximately half of the Merger Consideration is in cash, the stockholders are losing the last opportunity to maximize the value of a significant amount of their investment in Smurfit–Stone.

Defendants, for their part, argue that heightened Revlon scrutiny is inapplicable here and urge the Court to review Plaintiffs' claims through the lens of the business judgment rule. They contend that the Board never put Smurfit–Stone up "for sale" and the Proposed Transaction is not a "change of control" transaction under relevant Supreme Court precedent. Specifically, Defendants assert that control of the post-merger entity here will remain, as it was in Smurfit–Stone's case before the merger, in a large, fluid, changeable and changing public market. This, they argue, gives Smurfit–Stone stockholder's a "tomorrow" whereby they, by virtue of the stock portion of the Merger Consideration, can participate in Rock–Tenn's future successes and possibly obtain a future control premium should Rock–Tenn be acquired in a change of control transaction. In Defendants' view, the fact that the Transaction contemplates an approximately 50/50 mix of cash and stock consideration does not change this conclusion.

Based on my review of the law and facts of this case, I conclude that Plaintiffs have not shown a reasonable probability of success on their claim that the Board breached its fiduciary duties by approving the Rock–Tenn merger. As to the governing standard, I believe Plaintiffs are likely to prevail on their argument that Revlon applies here, even though the Delaware Supreme Court has not yet addressed this issue directly. As such, this position is not free from doubt. Nevertheless, in the circumstances of this case, even if I assume without deciding that the Revlon standard applies, the result would be the same. That is, Plaintiffs have not demonstrated that they are likely to succeed on the merits of their claim that the actions of the admittedly independent and disinterested Special Committee (as well as the vast majority of the Company's Board) in negotiating and approving the Merger Agreement failed to satisfy their obligations under Revlon.

Under § 141(a) of the Delaware General Corporation Law, a corporation's board of directors is empowered to manage the business and affairs of the corporation. The business judgment rule ("BJR"), a deferential standard of review, reflects the common law's recognition of § 141(a). In short, it is a "presumption that in making a business decision the directors of a corporation acted on an informed basis, in good faith and in the honest belief that the action taken was in the best interests of the company." *Emerald P'rs v. Berlin*, 787 A.2d 85, 90–91 (Del.2001); *Revlon, Inc.*, 506 A.2d at 180; *Moran v. Household Int'l, Inc.*, 500 A.2d 1346, 1356 (Del.1985). This standard of review is respectful to director prerogatives to manage the business of a corporation; in cases where it applies, courts must give "great deference" to directors' decisions and, as long as the Court can discern a rational business purpose for the decision, it must "not invalidate the decision ... examine its reasonableness, [or] substitute [its] views for those of the board...." *Paramount Commc'ns Inc. v. QVC Network Inc.*, 637 A.2d 34, 45 n. 17 (Del.1994).

In limited circumstances, however, the Delaware Supreme Court has imposed special obligations of reasonableness on boards of corporations who oversee the sale of control of their corporation. *See, e.g., QVC Network Inc.*, 637 A.2d at 42; *Revlon, Inc. v. MacAndrews & Forbes Hldgs., Inc.*, 506 A.2d 173, 182 (Del.1986). When a board leads its corporation into so-called Revlon territory, its subsequent actions will be reviewed by this Court not under the deferential BJR standard, but rather under the heightened standard of reasonableness. In addition, and as discussed in greater detail below, the Board's fiduciary obligations shift to obtaining the best value reasonably available to the target's stockholders.

While the differences between directors' obligations under business judgment and Revlon review are not insignificant, the standard of review is not necessarily outcome determinative. Nonetheless, "absent a limited set of circumstances as defined under Revlon, a board of directors, while always required to act in an informed manner, is not under any per se duty to maximize shareholder value in the short term ...." *Paramount Commc'ns, Inc. v. Time Inc.*, 571 A.2d 1140, 1150 (Del.1989); *Air Prods. & Chems., Inc. v. Airgas, Inc.*, 16 A.3d 48, 101–02 (Del.Ch.2011). Therefore, a question of much ongoing debate, and one to which the parties devoted much ink in this case, is when does a corporation enter Revlon mode such that its directors must act reasonably to maximize short-term value of the corporation for its stockholders.

The Delaware Supreme Court has determined that a board might find itself faced with such a duty in at least three scenarios: "(1) when a corporation initiates an active bidding process seeking to sell itself or to effect a business reorganization involving a clear break-up of the company[ ]; (2) where, in response to a bidder's offer, a target abandons its long-term strategy and seeks an alternative transaction involving the break-up of the company; or (3) when approval of a transaction results in a sale or change of control [.]" *See, e.g., In re Santa Fe Pac. Corp. S'holder Litig.,* 669 A.2d 59, 71 (Del.1995).

Here, Plaintiffs do not allege that the Board initiated an active bidding process to sell itself or effected a reorganization involving the break-up of Smurfit–Stone. Nor do they argue that the Board abandoned its long-term strategy in response to a bidder's offer and sought an alternative transaction involving the break-up of the Company. Rather, they allege that Revlon should apply to this case because the Merger Consideration was comprised of 50% cash and 50% stock at the time the parties entered into the Agreement, which qualifies the Proposed Transaction as a "change of control" transaction. A question remains, however, as to when a mixed stock and cash merger constitutes a change of control transaction for Revlon purposes.

On the one hand, pure stock-for-stock transactions do not necessarily trigger Revlon. If, for example, the resulting entity has a controlling stockholder or stockholder group such that the target's stockholders are relegated to minority status in the combined entity, Delaware Courts have found a change of control would occur for Revlon purposes. But, if ownership shifts from one large unaffiliated group of public stockholders to another, that alone does not amount to a change of control. In this event, the target's stockholders' voting power will not be diminished to minority status and they are not foreclosed from an opportunity to obtain a control premium in a future change of control transaction involving the resulting entity.

On the other hand, Revlon will govern a board's decision to sell a corporation where stockholders will receive cash for their shares. Revlon applies in the latter instance because, among other things, there is no tomorrow for the corporation's present stockholders, meaning that they will forever be shut out from future profits generated by the resulting entity as well as the possibility of obtaining a control premium in a subsequent transaction. Heightened scrutiny is appropriate because of an "omnipresent specter" that a board, which may have secured a continuing interest of some kind in the surviving entity, may favor its interests over those of the corporation's stockholders.

The Supreme Court has not yet clarified the precise bounds of when Revlon applies in the situation where merger consideration consists of an equal or almost equal split of cash and stock. Thus, to make such a determination, I evaluate the circumstances of the Proposed Transaction based on its economic implications and relevant judicial precedent.

[I]n In re Lukens Inc., Vice Chancellor Lamb considered a transaction in which Bethlehem Steel would acquire 100% of Lukens' common stock for a value of $25 per common share. Under the terms of the merger, which were subject to dispute on the defendants' motion to dismiss, "each Lukens shareholder would have the right to elect to receive the consideration in cash, subject to a maximum total cash payout equal to 62% of the total consideration." *In re Lukens Inc.*, 757 A.2d at 725. While the Court did not have occasion to determine definitively whether Revlon should apply—it assumed that it did—it offered sage guidance on transactions involving both cash and stock merger consideration, which informs this Court's opinion here. Vice Chancellor Lamb opined that, though the Supreme Court had not yet established a bright line rule for what percentage of merger consideration could be cash without triggering Revlon, he would find that under the circumstances of the Lukens case Revlon would apply. In pertinent part, he explained as follows:

> I cannot understand how the Director Defendants were not obliged, in the circumstances, to seek out the best price reasonably available. The defendants argue that because over 30% of the merger consideration was shares of Bethlehem common stock, a widely held company without any controlling shareholder, Revlon and QVC do not apply. I disagree. Whether 62% or 100% of the consideration was to be in cash, the directors were obliged to take reasonable steps to ensure that the shareholders received the best price available because, in any event, for a substantial majority of the then-current shareholders, "there is no long run." ... I do not agree with the defendants that Santa Fe, in which shareholders tendered 33% of their shares for cash and exchanged the remainder for common stock, controls a situation in which over 60% of the consideration is cash.... I take for granted ... that a cash offer for 95% of a company's shares, for example, even if the other 5% will be exchanged for the shares of a widely held corporation, will constitute a change of corporate control. Until instructed otherwise, I believe that purchasing more than 60% achieves the same result.

757 A.2d at 732 n. 25.

Thus far, this Court has not been instructed otherwise, and, while the stock portion of the Merger Consideration is larger than the portion in Lukens, I am persuaded that Vice Chancellor Lamb's reasoning applies here, as well. Defendants attempt to distinguish Lukens on its facts, arguing that "they offer no support to plaintiffs' position." I disagree. While the factual scenarios are not identical, there are some material similarities. Most important of these is that the Court in Lukens was wary of the fact that a majority of holders of Lukens common stock potentially could have elected to cash out their positions entirely, subject to the 62% total cash consideration limit. In this case, Defendants emphasize that no Smurfit–Stone stockholder involuntarily or voluntarily can be cashed out completely and, after consummation of the Proposed Transaction, the stockholders will own slightly less than half of Rock–Tenn. While the facts of this case and Lukens differ slightly in that regard, Defendants lose sight of the fact that while no Smurfit–Stone stockholder will be cashed out 100%, 100% of its stockholders who elect to participate in the merger will see approximately 50% of their Smurfit–Stone investment cashed out. As such, like Vice Chancellor Lamb's concern that potentially there was no "tomorrow" for a substantial majority of Lukens stockholders, the concern here is that there is no "tomorrow" for approximately 50% of each stockholder's investment in Smurfit–Stone. That each stockholder may retain a portion of her investment after the merger is insufficient to distinguish the reasoning of Lukens, which concerns the need for the Court to scrutinize under Revlon a transaction that constitutes an end-game for all or a substantial part of a stockholder's investment in a Delaware corporation.

Finally, I note that factors identified by Plaintiffs and Defendants as having been considered by Delaware courts in determining whether to apply Revlon review are important to a robust analysis of the issue. In QVC, for example, the Supreme Court noted the importance of considering whether a target's stockholder's voting rights would be relegated to minority status in the surviving entity of a merger and whether such stockholders still could obtain a control premium in future transactions as part of the postmerger entity in determining whether a "change of control" had occurred. But, the fact that control of Rock–Tenn after consummation will remain in a large pool of unaffiliated stockholders, while important, neither addresses nor affords protection to the portion of the stockholders' investment that will be converted to cash and thereby be deprived of its long-run potential.

Based on the foregoing, therefore, I conclude that Plaintiffs are likely to succeed on their argument that the approximately 50% cash and 50% stock consideration here triggers Revlon.

When the Board explored whether to enter into the Proposed Transaction, which, as discussed above, warrants review under Revlon, its fiduciary duties required it to obtain the best value reasonably available to Smurfit–Stone stockholders. There is no single path that a board must follow in order to maximize stockholder value, but directors must follow a path of reasonableness which leads toward that end. Importantly, a board's actions are not reviewed upon the basis of price alone. In reviewing a board's actions under Revlon, the Court must (1) make a determination as to whether the information relied upon in the decision-making process was adequate and (2) examine the reasonableness of the directors' decision viewed from the point in time during which the directors acted. Director defendants have the burden of proving they were adequately informed and acted reasonably.

Plaintiffs first attack the process the Special Committee undertook in the run up to its recommendation to the Smurfit–Stone Board that it approve the Proposed Transaction. Specifically, they assert that the Committee impermissibly: (a) engaged in exclusive negotiations with Rock–Tenn and approved a deal with it based on inadequate information and without previously canvassing the market; (b) agreed to restrictive deal protections that preclude a meaningful post-signing market check and discourage the submission of competing bids; (c) permitted certain members of senior Smurfit–Stone management with conflicting interests to play significant roles in negotiating the deal terms; (d) relied on a financial advisor with no experience in the containerboard industry and with a financial incentive to close a transaction; and (e) accepted an inadequate price. I address each of these contentions in turn.

Plaintiffs contend that the Board breached its fiduciary duties by engaging in a flawed negotiating process, approving the Proposed Transaction without having adequate information, and agreeing to deal exclusively with Rock–Tenn even though the latter never requested such a restriction.

At the outset, I note that the process followed by the Board and Special Committee was not perfect. But, reasonableness, and not perfection, is what Revlon requires. After carefully reviewing the record, I find that the process undertaken by the Board included sufficient indicia of reasonableness under the circumstances to satisfy Revlon.

Preliminarily, I reject Plaintiffs' contention that the Board and Special Committee were not adequately informed when they authorized the signing of the Merger Agreement. First, the record reflects that nine out of the current ten Smurfit–Stone directors are outside, independent directors. These individuals are sophisticated business executives with experience in a diverse range of industries. Although a substantial majority of these directors took their seats after Smurfit–Stone exited bankruptcy, they educated themselves about the Company and took their positions as directors seriously. Moreover, upon receiving notice of the first offer from Company A, the Board created a Special Committee, which retained competent advisors. Specifically, it obtained financial counsel from Lazard, an advisory company with significant experience working with Smurfit–Stone in its bankruptcy, and legal counsel from Wachtell Lipton, an established leader in the M & A space. Finally, Plaintiffs have not demonstrated any reason to doubt the independence or disinterestedness of any of the outside Board members.

In addition, despite Plaintiffs' claims otherwise, the Board made appropriate use of the Special Committee, which was comprised of all nine of the Company's outside directors. The Committee asserted its control over the negotiations with Company A and Rock–Tenn, as well as their own personnel, from a very early stage. Indeed, Hake appointed a special Subcommittee of three outside directors to "drive the nitty-gritty work that gets done in analyzing a proposal" on a day-to-day basis because of his belief that the process should be driven by the Company's outside directors. While management did play an active role in negotiating with Company A and Rock–Tenn, as discussed further below, members of the Special Committee made clear that potential acquirors needed to direct their communications and inquiries to the outside directors, through their financial advisor, Lazard. Furthermore, the Committee did not accept projections from management or other sources at face value and held regular and robust discussions regarding them, including pushing back against management to make sure they were not "in any way ... intentionally or unintentionally ... sharing with us projections that were excessively conservative."

Further, Plaintiffs took issue with the relatively short duration between the date the Board received Rock–Tenn's first concrete indication of interest, approximately January 4, 2011, and the date the Board approved the Proposed Transaction, January 23, 2011. They contend this was an insufficient amount of time to understand adequately the Company's value, especially to other potential strategic bidders. While the length of time a company has to determine its options is important in assessing the reasonableness of a board's actions under Revlon, it is not dispositive, and a relatively quick sales process is not a per se ground for a Revlon violation.

In Lyondell Chemical Co. v. Ryan, 970 A.2d 235 (Del.2009), for example, the Supreme Court indicated that the Lyondell directors did not breach their duties of loyalty to the company even though they took only approximately one week to consider Basell's offer to purchase the company for $48 per share—one-third the time the Smurfit–Stone Board spent negotiating with Rock–Tenn. Importantly, the Supreme Court explained that the Lyondell board's process, while short in duration, was thorough enough to satisfy the directors' fiduciary duty of loyalty under Revlon because, among other things, they: (1) met several times during the week they considered Basell's offer; (2) permitted their CEO to try to negotiate better terms with Basell; (3) evaluated the price offered and the likelihood of obtaining a better price; (4) were generally aware of their company's value and understood its market; (5) solicited the assistance of competent financial and legal advisors; and (6) attempted to persuade Basell to improve its offer even though evidence indicated that $48 was a " 'blowout' price."

Similarly, in this case, the Board met multiple times in January to consider Rock–Tenn's offers, permitted Lazard and Hake to try to persuade Rubright to improve Rock–Tenn's $35 offer, evaluated that offer using Lazard's valuations, Wachtell's legal expertise, and its own knowledge of the Company's market, and discussed the likelihood that a better offer would materialize. FN125 Moreover, the Board benefited not just from its and Lazard's work in January, but also from their work in previous months when the Special Committee was evaluating Company A's offer.

I also note that, notwithstanding Plaintiffs' pejorative characterizations, the Special Committee's conduct in January 2011 was assertive and apparently devoid of undue influence by management.

Similarly, and for many of the same reasons, I do not find that Plaintiffs are likely to succeed on their claim that the Board breached its fiduciary duties by agreeing to deal exclusively with Rock–Tenn and failing to conduct a presigning market check. In the context of a merger transaction, directors have a duty to maximize stockholder value, but they are under "no duty to employ a specific device such as the auction or market check mechanism." Even without such a market check, I find that the members of the Special Committee had enough information by the time they received Rock–Tenn's best and final offer reasonably to determine that a topping bid was unlikely. First, Smurfit–Stone was in Chapter 11 bankruptcy for approximately a year and a half, ending on June 30, 2010, and had received some interest from potential acquirors during this time, but nothing concrete had materialized. The Board was notified about these indications of interest and considered the bankruptcy time period to be a functional equivalent of a market check...

In the face of this information, the Board also considered the dangers of delaying a signing with Rock–Tenn. Conducting a prolonged presigning market check would have increased the risk of information leaks pertaining to a possible imminent sale of Smurfit–Stone, which may have disrupted the Company's personnel and business. In addition, the Board understood that there were only a few potential strategic buyers who might be interested in acquiring Smurfit–Stone and, by virtue of being in the same industry, those potential buyers likely would have been aware of Smurfit–Stone's receptiveness to a transaction. Plaintiffs also make much of the fact that Smurfit–Stone, and not Rock–Tenn, requested exclusive dealings, but this duty was reciprocal. With the knowledge that other bidders were not likely to step forward and a reasonable belief that Rock–Tenn's offer was superior to remaining as a stand-alone company, the Board reasonably could have sought to sign an exclusive deal with Rock–Tenn to prevent the latter from considering other acquisitions, subject to its fiduciary duties.

Therefore, I find that the Board possessed a sufficient amount of reliable evidence from which it reasonably could conclude that a market check was not worth the risks of jeopardizing the Rock–Tenn Transaction and that dealing exclusively with Rock–Tenn would maximize stockholder value. As such, Plaintiffs are not likely to prevail on their claim that the Board unreasonably failed to perform a formal market check before or after signing the Merger Agreement.

Plaintiffs next argue that, having decided to forego conducting a presigning market check, the Board impermissibly agreed to several preclusive deal protection devices in the Merger Agreement...Specifically, the three items challenged by Plaintiffs are the no shop provision, the matching rights provision, and the termination fee, which are included in §§ 6.4, 6.5, and 8.2 of the Merger Agreement, respectively. According to Plaintiffs, the no shop provision, which, as mentioned supra, contains a fiduciary out that allows the Board to consider Superior Proposals, substantially reduces the likelihood of a topping bid because it prohibits the Board from actively soliciting potential interested parties. Similarly, they object to the matching rights provision, under which Rock–Tenn has three days to match a Superior Proposal, on the ground that it significantly reduces the likelihood of such a proposal. Moreover, Plaintiffs allege that the $120 million termination fee, which constitutes approximately 3.4% of equity value, is excessively large and significantly diminishes the probability of a competing buyer making a bid. Lastly, Plaintiffs contend that these three protective devices have an unreasonably preclusive effect in combination, even if none is preclusive in isolation.

Under the relevant case law, Plaintiffs are not likely to succeed in showing that the no shop and matching rights provisions are unreasonable either separately or in combination. Potential suitors often have a legitimate concern that they are being used as a stalking horse merely to draw others into a bidding war. This presumably was a concern for Rock–Tenn based on the facts that while the Company had been the subject of persistent takeover rumors for several months, potential buyers had shown little interest, with the exception of Company A, and that Rock–Tenn's initial draft of the Merger Agreement contained both a no shop and matching rights provisions. Therefore, in an effort to entice an acquirer to make a strong offer, it is reasonable for a seller to provide a buyer some level of assurance that he will be given an adequate opportunity to buy the seller, even if a higher bid later emerges. Plaintiffs have not shown that any alternative bidder was precluded by the challenged provisions from successfully making a higher offer. Accordingly, they have not demonstrated a likelihood of success on the merits of their objections to either the no shop or matching rights provisions.

Plaintiffs also take issue with the $120 million termination fee, which represents approximately 3.4% of equity value. While the termination fee is toward the upper boundary of permissibility under Delaware law, this Court has approved several termination fees of similar size. The relative size of the Termination Fee is further mitigated by the fact that it is reciprocal, applying to Rock–Tenn as well as Smurfit–Stone. Accordingly, because the Termination Fee is generally within the range previously found to be reasonable and appears to have resulted from good faith, arm's-length negotiations, I conclude that Plaintiffs are not likely to succeed on their claim that the Board acted unreasonably in assenting to that fee.

In addition, I am not persuaded that, collectively, the Merger Agreement's three primary deal protections unreasonably inhibit another bidder from making a Superior Proposal. The challenged provisions are relatively standard in form and have not been shown to be preclusive or coercive, whether they are considered separately or collectively. Accordingly, on the record presented, I am not convinced that Plaintiffs are likely to be able to prove that the Board acted unreasonably in agreeing to give Rock–Tenn these deal protections.

Plaintiffs next take issue with the Special Committee's decision to permit Moore and Hunt, whom they characterize as having significant conflicts, to take active roles in negotiating the Proposed Transaction with Rock–Tenn. Plaintiffs cite as the source of these conflicts the employment agreements of Moore and Hunt, which provide for change of control bonuses that, according to Plaintiffs, incentivized them to negotiate a change of control without regard to whether it was in the Company's stockholders' best interests…

Plaintiffs merely have established that certain of Smurfit–Stone's management had potential pecuniary conflicts of interest based on the existence of change of control bonuses in their employment contracts. The evidence shows that the Defendant outside directors had nothing to do with negotiating or approving those contracts. Moreover, Plaintiffs have not shown that the executives involved acted on their conflicts at Smurfit–Stone's expense or that the Committee impermissibly permitted them to do so. Therefore, Plaintiffs are not likely to succeed in proving that Moore and Hunt, and Klinger to the extent Plaintiffs include him in their conflict argument, materially tainted the sales process here through their involvement in it.

Plaintiffs further contend that the Special Committee's hiring and reliance on Lazard, whom they characterize as conflicted and inexperienced, contributes to the unreasonableness of their conduct under Revlon. They argue first that the Lazard team had no experience in the paper and fiberboard industry or with mergers involving corporations that recently had exited bankruptcy. In addition, Plaintiffs fault the Committee for hiring Lazard without conducting a formal interview process or receiving a presentation by Lazard.

These criticisms are largely unfounded. While the Board did not conduct a formal interview process or "beauty pageant," it did meaningfully consider the issue of hiring an experienced and independent financial advisor. Several members of the Special Committee recommended hiring Lazard based on their belief that it had significant M & A experience and that it would be independent because it had no previous relationship with the Special Committee or the other Transaction participants. Equally important, the Committee determined Lazard would be a good fit because of its prior experience advising Smurfit–Stone when it was in bankruptcy and its resultant ability to get up to speed quickly.FN150 I also note that the Board did not take lightly the terms under which it retained Lazard. In that regard, the Board negotiated to reduce Lazard's fees and obtained a lower contingent success fee.

This segues into Plaintiffs' next criticism; namely, that the Special Committee agreed to retain Lazard under terms that include a "significant success fee, whereby Lazard will receive substantially greater compensation if a deal closes—even a bad deal—than if there is no transaction." Plaintiffs argue this type of fee structure is appropriate in an auction setting where a corporation is choosing among competing bids, but not where the corporation is choosing between selling itself or remaining as a going concern. In the latter situation, Plaintiffs assert that a success fee creates a "strong incentive" for Lazard to push through any deal, even a bad deal, to collect its fee. This, they contend, is what happened here because Lazard made no good faith attempt to push Rock–Tenn to increase its offer above $35 per share.

Contingent fees for financial advisors in a merger context are somewhat "routine" and previously have been upheld by Delaware courts. Moreover, a sales process is not unreasonable under Revlon merely because a special committee is advised by a financial advisor who might receive a large contingent success fee, even if the special committee is considering only one bidder. Rather, the Court can take that fact into consideration in determining whether the financial advisor failed to assist the committee in maximizing stockholder value or whether the committee failed to oversee adequately the advisor's work. Here, Plaintiffs failed to allege any colorable wrongdoing or conflict on the part of Lazard. Even if they did, I find that the Special Committee maintained continuous and diligent oversight of Lazard's work and negotiations with Rock–Tenn and Wells Fargo. Indeed, even if Lazard merely "went through the motions" in half-heartedly asking Rock–Tenn to improve its $35 bid as Plaintiffs claim, the Special Committee independently verified that Rock–Tenn would not budge past $35.

Therefore, I find that the Special Committee's decision to retain and rely upon the work of Lazard was not unreasonable and, as such, is not likely to provide a predicate for a violation of its members' fiduciary duties.

Plaintiffs further contend that the price of the Proposed Transaction is inadequate. They have provided little basis, however, on which to question the reasonableness of the Board's decision that $35 per share was a fair price. To support their claim, Plaintiffs rely primarily on the projections made by Rock–Tenn's investment banker, Wells Fargo, and those made by the Levin Group in July 2010. The Smurfit–Stone Board, however, was not privy to the calculations made by Wells Fargo. Moreover, reasonable minds may differ as to the value of the Company because, ultimately, valuation is an art and not a science. As to the presentation by the Levin Group, Lazard and the Special Committee specifically focused on that information. Moreover, it was acknowledged that the Levin Group's analysis was based on several speculative assumptions, some of which, including the Company's ability to divest certain of its Mills, later proved to be unrealistic.

On the whole, I am not convinced Plaintiffs are likely to be able to prove that the Board's decision was unreasonable. Lazard provided extensive analysis that indicated that $35 per share was a reasonable price based on measures such as a discounted cash flow, EBITDA multiples for comparable companies, and comparable transactions. While Plaintiffs question whether Lazard offered unbiased advice, I have rejected that argument for the reasons discussed supra. Furthermore, a quasi-appraisal process is inappropriate at this point because even a dispute over valuation between two financial advisors will not support a preliminary injunction.

In some situations where a target's board breaches its duties under Revlon, a Court may find that stockholders face a threat of irreparable harm because the board failed to adequately shop the company in advance of recommending that stockholders approve a proposed merger. This is because after-the-fact inquiries into what might have been had directors adequately tested the market necessarily involve speculation and guesswork. Yet, in the absence of concomitant disclosure violations and where a plaintiff's complaint boils down to an allegation of inadequate price, Delaware courts have found that money damages can provide a sufficient remedy for a board's Revlon violations. *See Norberg v. Young's Mkt. Co.,* 1989 WL 155462, at 3 (Del.Ch. Dec.19, 1989).

In the circumstances of this case, Plaintiffs have not established that permitting the Proposed Transaction to close would cause irreparable harm to Smurfit–Stone stockholders. First, as discussed above, the Board reasonably concluded that a topping bid was not likely to materialize imminently... Moreover, the Company arguably has been "for sale" for approximately four months since the Board approved the Transaction and no other bidder has indicated an interest in making an offer, or even indicated that the Merger Agreement's lock up provisions chilled it from doing so. In addition, Plaintiffs concede that all relevant facts relating to the Transaction are before the stockholders including, for example, the rise in the price of Rock–Tenn's stock since the announcement of the Transaction, which Plaintiffs assert reflects the market's view that Rock–Tenn is purchasing Smurfit–Stone "on the cheap." On these facts, I find Plaintiffs' argument that an injunction might provide a possibility of permitting a topping bid to materialize is speculative and insufficient to constitute irreparable harm.

In addition, Smurfit–Stone stockholders who agree with Plaintiffs that $35 per share undervalues their investment in the Company are not without recourse in the absence of injunctive relief. Plaintiffs still may seek money damages as compensation for the Board's alleged breaches of their fiduciary duties. (Admittedly, however, this remedy may be of limited value based on the presence of an 8 Del. C. § 102(b)(7) exculpation clause in Smurfit–Stone's certificate of incorporation.) They also may vote against the merger and seek appraisal for their shares under 8 Del. C. § 262. Thus, I hold that Plaintiffs have failed to carry their burden to show they face a threat of irreparable harm in the absence of preliminary injunctive relief.

Here, Plaintiffs have not made a strong showing of a likelihood of success on the merits or the existence of irreparable harm if injunctive relief is denied. Moreover, the Proposed Transaction offers a significant premium to Smurfit–Stone's stockholders and, as of the date of this Opinion, no topping bid has been made or even suggested. Enjoining the Transaction now would create a risk that Smurfit–Stone's stockholders could lose out on this Transaction altogether.

For the reasons stated, I find that Plaintiffs have failed to carry their burden to prove they are likely to succeed on the merits of their claims, will suffer imminent irreparable harm if injunctive relief is not granted, and are favored by the equities. Therefore, I deny Plaintiffs' motion for a preliminary injunction.

IT IS SO ORDERED.

CHAPTER 15

BUYING AND SELLING A BUSINESS

A. STRUCTURING THE DEAL

1. THE NON-TAX AGENDA

Businesses are bought and sold every day. For most owners, it's a momentous event. They are using their power and means to grow through acquisition; or they are selling out, cashing in on a profitable adventure that may have lasted a lifetime. But whether they are buying or selling, and whether they are dealing with a business that's lasted three generations or three months, the structure of the transaction is a big deal. It sets the parameters for getting the deal done and allocates risks, liabilities, and administrative burdens. Most importantly, it directly impacts the net cost to the buyer and the net yield to the seller.

Many mistakenly assume that it's only about taxes. Tax consequences are always important and often drive the structure of the deal. But in some transactions, non-tax factors, deemed critically important by one or both of the parties, will trump all other considerations and dictate whether the transaction should be structured as a sale of assets or a sale of the entity itself. In many more situations, important non-tax objectives, while not controlling, must be evaluated and prioritized against the tax consequences of alternative structures. A useful starting point in any transaction is to identify key non-tax considerations that are impacted by structure and then assess their relative importance. Some of the most compelling non-tax factors that often surface include the following:

a. **Undisclosed Liability Exposure.** Often buyers fear exposure to undisclosed liabilities attributable to the operation of the business prior to the acquisition. Such liabilities may come in many different forms – product liability exposures; employee claims, including sexual harassment, discrimination or wrongful termination claims; environmental liabilities; unpaid taxes; contractual disputes and related expenses and exposures; regulatory violations; and many more. The buyer knows that if the entity is acquired, either through merger or stock purchase, it comes with all its skeletons. The acquisition agreement usually includes seller representations and warranties, indemnification provisions, and escrow holdback procedures, all designed to shift the ultimate risk of any material undisclosed liabilities back to the seller. But even with these, there is still the possibility – often the probability – that the buyer, as the new owner of the old entity, will get tangled up in a dispute over issues that pre-date the buyer's involvement. Many buyers want a structure that provides protections greater than those offered through a contract. For them, an asset acquisition, though not completely bullet-proof from all pre-acquisition liabilities, is a preferred structure because the old entity remains with the seller.

b. **Third-Party Disruptions**. The impact of the transaction on employees, customers, vendors, and other third parties often is an important consideration. Banks and key executives usually are knee-deep in the details, no matter the structure of the deal. But an acquisition that keeps the old entity intact and functioning, just with new owners, often can be accomplished with no knowledge of, let alone any involvement with, rank-and-file employees, customers and vendors. If the business and assets are transferred to a new entity, these other players soon discover that they too are being transferred. The result may be heightened insecurities, the need for additional assurances or, worse yet, new demands.

c. **Third-Party Consents**. An asset acquisition structure usually requires more third-party consents. Typically, such consents are required for leases, licenses, permits, and contracts that the new buyer needs to maintain in order to run the business. The consent process itself may result in added costs and delays. Also, and much worse, the need for the consent may provide a key third party with an exit opportunity that wouldn't exist otherwise. This opportunity may result in the loss of a valuable contract right or a forced unfavorable renegotiation. Although an entity acquisition, either through merger or stock purchase, often requires some third-party consents based on the breadth of transfer-of-control provisions in specific contracts, the burden is usually much tougher with an asset structure.

d. **Unwanted Assets.** Sometimes the buyer wants to cherry-pick specific assets that are necessary for the operation of the core business. The remaining assets are left for the seller to deal with. An entity acquisition structure can work in this situation if the seller can get the unwanted assets out of the entity before the deal is done. But, depending on the nature and value of the unwanted assets, often an asset structure is preferred because the old entity remains with the owner of the unwanted assets and, as a result, the seller has greater flexibility in dealing with any future transfers of the unwanted assets and the associated tax impacts.

e. **Sales and Use Taxes.** A sale of tangible assets often triggers a state sales tax or use tax, typically paid by the buyer. This is often an added expense of using an asset acquisition structure. In some transactions, it is a material cost that affects the structural decision.

f. **Insurance Rating.** Sometimes the selling entity has a favorable historical workmen's compensation insurance rating that will be lost if only assets, not the entity, are transferred. This can be a major factor in some situations. When it is, an entity acquisition structure becomes more appealing.

g. **Closing Complexities**. The closing of an entity deal is usually much easier than an asset deal. A stock certificate or ownership interest is transferred.

In an asset transaction, there is a need for transfer documents (e.g. assignments, bills of sale, deeds, assumption agreements, etc.) covering the tangible assets, licenses, leases, contract rights, intangibles, and other assets being transferred and all the liabilities being assumed by the buyer. It requires more effort, more paperwork and more attention to detail. Usually this factor is less important than other considerations. Often it is cited as an added reason or excuse by a party who, for more compelling reasons, is advocating an entity structure.

h. **Securities Law Exposures**. Some sellers are spooked by the anti-fraud provisions of the securities laws. They hate the idea of being legally obligated to eliminate all misleading material facts related to a complex business operation and its potential acquisition by a buyer who may see only the surface. Often their fear is grounded in a prior bad experience involving securities. They feel safer with an asset structure that does not involve the sale of stock. Usually in any transaction, either entity or asset, the buyer will expect and demand extensive representations and warranties from the seller; and often it is standard practice to include a catchall representation that is the verbatim equivalent of Rule 10b-5, the securities law antifraud provision.[1] A seller who is spooked enough by the burdens of 10b-5 to let it influence the structure of the deal will often refuse to make such a catchall representation. This can complicate the negotiation. If the seller is adamant, the solution, in many situations, is to have the seller represent that he or she has not "knowingly misrepresented any material facts" (usually the specific "knowingly" limitation removes any objection) and to carefully design other representations and warranties to give the buyer the comfort needed to move forward.

2. CASE STUDY FACTS

Michael Manufacturing (Seller) has been in business 30 years. Its two equal owners, Larry and Sue, both age 58, have decided that it's time to sell. They both have worked for the company their entire careers. Each currently pulls about $300,000 a year from the business. They have concluded that a transition to family members is out of the question. And although the business has a seasoned second level management team that would love to own what it has built, the economics of an inside sale make no sense. Larry and Sue would end up bearing all the risk, against the hope that they would receive a fair yield over a very long time. These factors and a serious offer from a strategic deep-pocketed C corporation buyer (Buyer) have convinced them that it is time to cash in and start enjoying the good life.

The value of Seller's equity is $12 million, the excess of the $17 million fair market value of its assets over its liabilities of $5 million. The book value of Seller's equity is $5 million, the excess of the book value of its assets ($10 million) over its liabilities of $5 million. Of the $7 million of asset value in excess of book value, $1 million is attributable to tangible assets (equipment) and $6 million to goodwill and going concern value. The company's tangible assets –

---

1. 17 C.F.R. § 240.10b-5.

primarily cash, accounts receivable, inventories and equipment – have a book value and basis of $10 million and a fair market value of $11 million. For the last three years, the company's earnings, before interest, taxes, depreciation, amortization and any payments to Larry and Sue, have averaged $2.4 million on average sales of $30 million.

The following sections review the tax consequences to Seller, Buyer, Larry, and Sue under different transaction structure scenarios. The first section assumes that Seller is a C corporation, that Larry and Sue each have a $250,000 basis in their stock, that Larry and Sue are subject to a combined federal and state marginal income tax rate of 40 percent on ordinary income and 20 percent on long-term capital gains, and that Seller and Buyer, both C corporations, are subject to a combined federal and state marginal income tax rate of 40 percent (remember, C corporations get no capital gains tax rate break).

3. C CORPORATIONS – 11 SCENARIOS

a. Asset Sale-Liquidation

Under this common scenario, Buyer pays Seller $12 million for all the assets of the business and assumes all the liabilities of the business. Seller pays its taxes and then distributes the net after-tax proceeds to Larry and Sue in a complete liquidation of Seller. Larry and Sue pay a long-term capital gains tax on the excess of the proceeds received over their stock basis. Seller disappears. The net result is a double tax – a corporate level tax and a shareholder level tax. [2]

Here's how the numbers shake out. Seller would recognize a taxable gain of $7 million, the excess of $17 million (the sum of the $12 million received and the $5 million of liabilities assumed by Buyer) over its assets' basis of $10 million. At a 40 percent combined federal and state tax rate, seller's tax hit would total $2.8 million. The net distributed to Larry and Sue would be $9.2 million, the excess of the $12 million paid by Buyer over the $2.8 million in taxes paid by Seller. Larry's and Sue's recognized long-term capital gains would total $8.7 million ($9.2 million less their $500,000 combined stock basis), and their tax hit at a combined federal and state rate of 20 percent would total $1.74 million. All said and done, they walk with $7.46 million after tax ($3.73 million each). The taxes on the deal total $4.54 million – $2.8 million at the corporate level and $1.74 million at the shareholder level. See Illustration A.

When faced with such consequences, Larry and Sue may ask: Can the $12 million paid by Buyer be allocated to reduce the overall tax bite? If it all goes to Seller, the answer is usually "No" because, as a C corporation, all of Seller's income is taxed at the same rate. The only exception is where Seller has an unused capital loss, a rare situation. In that case, care should be taken to create enough capital gain for Seller to use up any available capital loss. Also, there may be an opportunity to reduce overall taxes by having a portion of the consideration paid directly to Larry and Sue for their personal covenants not to compete with Buyer. Assume, for example, that $1 million of the price was paid

---

2. I.R.C. § 331.

for such personal covenants. This would be ordinary income to Larry and Sue, triggering a tax of $400,000. Seller's tax bite would drop by $400,000, and Larry and Sue's capital gains tax would drop by $120,000 (20 percent of $600,000). The net result would be a tax savings of $120,000.

Illustration A: Asset Sale-Liquidation

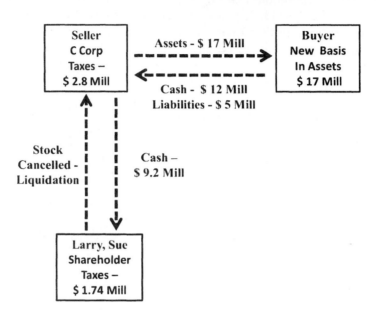

For tax purposes, the big winner under this scenario is Buyer, who gets to allocate the full purchase price to the acquired assets. This results in a basis step-up that will produce larger depreciation or amortization deductions in the future. Section 197 permits a buyer to amortize intangible assets ratably over a 15-year period.[3] Such assets include goodwill, going concern value, covenants not to compete, information bases, customer lists, know-how, licenses, franchises, trade names and more.[4] No longer does the Buyer need to sweat out a fight with the IRS over how much of the price constitutes goodwill or some other type of intangible that, prior to Section 197, produced no future tax benefit. Now there's a solid 15-year write-off period for intangibles.

So, asks Buyer, how much latitude is there in allocating the price to tangible assets that have a depreciation life of less than 15 years? After all, Seller has no interest in the allocations because it pays the same tax on all its income. Section 1060[5] spells out the rules for allocating the total consideration paid in an asset acquisition to the various assets. It mandates a priority residual approach that breaks assets into seven classes and then requires that the total consideration

---

3. I.R.C. § 197.
4. I.R.C. § 197(d)(1).
5. I.R.C. § 1060.

(which includes all liabilities assumed) be allocated to the assets (up to their fair market value) in each priority class.[6] In this case, Buyer would allocate the $17 million total consideration ($12 million paid plus $5 million of assumed liabilities) in the following priority: cash and cash equivalents (Class I priority); marketable securities, foreign currencies, certificates of deposits (Class II priority); accounts receivable, mortgages and credit card receivables (Class III priority); inventories and other dealer property (Class IV priority); all other tangible assets, including equipment (Class V priority); intangible assets other than goodwill and going concern value (Class VI priority); and, lastly, goodwill and going concern value (Class VII priority).[7] Seller and Buyer may, without changing the allocation priority, agree on the value of various assets in their agreement, and any such agreement will be binding on both parties for tax purposes unless the IRS determines that the value is not appropriate.[8] The IRS may use any appraisal method to challenge any allocation of value, especially in those situations (like this) where there are no conflicting interests between the parties to provide a basis for an arm's-length value negotiation.[9]

b. Liquidation-Asset Sale

Under this scenario, the liquidation of Seller precedes the asset sale to Buyer. Seller distributes all of its assets to Larry and Sue in a complete liquidation, and Larry and Sue then sell the assets to Buyer. The bottom line tax results are identical to the first scenario, although the road traveled is different.

The liquidation of Seller triggers a gain for Seller equal to the excess of the fair market value of its assets ($17 million) over the assets' basis of $10 million.[10] The result is a $7 million gain that triggers a corporate tax of $2.8 million that Larry and Sue must pay because Seller no longer has any assets. Larry and Sue receive assets that have a value of $17 million, and their capital gain is determined by reducing this total asset value by the $5 million of corporate liabilities they assume, the $2.8 million in taxes they pay on behalf of Seller, and their combined stock basis of $500,000. The net result is a long-term capital gain of $8.7 million that, as in the first scenario, triggers a tax of $1.74 million.

Following the liquidation of Seller, Larry and Sue have a tax basis of $17 million in the assets they have just acquired by virtue of the taxes they've paid and the liabilities they've assumed. So the sale to Buyer for $12 million plus the assumption of the $5 million of liabilities produces no gain. The end result is taxes totaling $4.54 million, the same as in scenario one. Again, Larry and Sue each walk with $3.73 million after tax.

As an asset purchaser, the consequences for Buyer under this scenario also are the same as in scenario one. Intangibles qualify for 15-year amortization treatment under Section 197, and the whole Section 1060 priority regime will apply. See Illustration B.

---

6. I.R.C. § 1060(c); Reg. §§ 1.1060-1(a)(1), 1.1060-1(b)(1).

7. Reg. §§ 1.1060-1(c), 1.338-6.

8. I.R.C. § 1060(a); Staff of the Joint Committee on Taxation, General Explanation of the Tax Reform Act of 1986, 100th Cong., 1st Sess. 355-360 (1987).

9. Reg. § 1.1060-1(c).

10. I.R.C. § 336(a).

Illustration B: Liquidation-Asset Sale

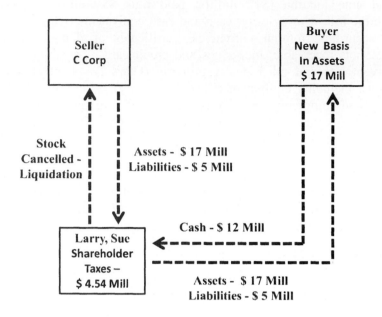

c. Cash Merger

Under this scenario, Seller is merged into Buyer or a subsidiary of Buyer in a statutory merger, and Buyer distributes cash directly to Larry and Sue. The value of the structure is that the statutory merger will automatically transfer all of Seller's assets and liabilities to Buyer or its subsidiary, thereby eliminating the need to document the transfer of specific assets and the assumption of specific liabilities. For tax purposes, the IRS treats this scenario the same as an asset sale by Seller followed by a complete liquidation of Seller – scenario one.[11]

Since the surviving entity in the merger (Buyer or its subsidiary) is going to have a $2.8 million tax bill as a result of the merger, the cash paid to Larry and Sue in the merger will be $9.2 million ($12 million less $2.8 million). Again, they incur a capital gains tax of $1.74 million, and they each end up netting $3.73 million. Since Buyer is deemed an asset purchaser, its tax consequences are the same as under the first two scenarios.

d. Installment Asset Sale – Liquidation

This scenario is the same as scenario one, with an important twist. A portion of the $12 million paid by Buyer is represented by an installment note that, with interest, will be paid off over many years. Let's assume in this case that the note obligation is equal to $7 million.

The tax issue is whether the note obligation will permit Seller or Larry and Sue to defer the taxes they would otherwise have to pay. There is no hope for Seller; the distribution of the installment obligation on the liquidation of Seller

---

11. Rev. Rule 69-6, 19690-1 C.B. 104.

triggers an immediate recognition of all gain that might otherwise have been deferred for Seller's benefit under the note.[12] So Seller still owes $2.8 million in taxes that it will pay out of the $5 million cash received from Buyer.

Although Seller gets no deferred tax benefits from the note obligation, Larry and Sue will get a deferral benefit if Seller adopts a plan of complete liquidation and then sells its assets and distributes the note and any other proceeds to its shareholders within 12 months following the adoption of the plan.[13] So Larry and Sue would end up receiving $2.2 million in cash ($5 million less the $2.8 million of taxes paid by Seller) and a $7 million note issued by Buyer, for a total of $9.2 million. Their total capital gain, after subtracting their combined basis, is $8.7 million. So their gross profit fraction is 94.5 percent (8.7/9.2). Of the $2.2 million cash they receive on the liquidation, $2.079 million (94.5 percent) will be taxable as a long-term capital gain. Then 94.5 percent of all future principal payments they receive under the note will be taxable as long-term capital gain.

e. Asset Sale – No Liquidation

Under this scenario, Seller sells its assets to Buyer, but Seller is not liquidated. The proceeds from the sale ($12 million) are used to pay Seller's $2.8 million tax bill and the remainder ($9.2 million) are kept inside of Seller. There is no liquidation. This scenario raises two questions: Why would any shareholder want to do it? What are the tax consequences of leaving the money in Seller?

The answer to the "Why" question is found in Section 1014 of the Code. If Larry, for example, dies before Seller is liquidated, the basis in his Seller stock is stepped up to its fair market value at death.[14] So if the liquidation follows Larry's death, Larry's estate or heirs will not recognize any capital gain to the extent the proceeds do not exceed the stock's fair market value on Larry's death. The strategy makes little sense for a 58 year-old in good health. But for someone twenty years older or a shareholder dealing with serious health issues, the prospect of completely avoiding the tax at the shareholder level might be appealing, which raises the second question.

If the proceeds of the sale are maintained in Seller and invested to generate portfolio income (interests, dividends, rents, etc.), Seller will become a personal holding company subject to the personal holding company tax penalty. What this means, as a practical matter, is that Seller will need to distribute its earned portfolio income as dividend income to Larry and Sue to avoid the personal holding company penalty tax. Although this results in a double tax on the portfolio income, it may not be a serious problem if the double tax burden continues only for a short period. It might end up being a relatively small cost for eliminating a huge capital gain in the deceased shareholder's estate.

What about converting to S status after the sale in order to eliminate the double tax hit on the portfolio income as Seller holds the proceeds and waits for a shareholder to die? Won't work. Section 1375 imposes an entity level tax at the

---

12. I.R.C. § 453B(a).
13. I.R.C. § 453(h).
14. I.R.C. § 1014(a).

maximum corporate rate on any S corporation with C corporation earnings and profits (which Seller would have in spades by virtue of the sale) that has net investment income in excess of 25 percent of its total gross receipts. Plus, if the condition persists for three consecutive years, the S election is terminated.[15] The Code drafters saw this one coming.

f. Straight Stock Sale

This scenario is the easiest and one of the most popular. Larry and Sue just sell their stock in Seller to Buyer. Buyer becomes the new sole shareholder of Seller. Since Seller is not a party to the transaction, it recognizes no income. The only income recognized is the capital gain at the shareholder level – the excess of the amount Larry and Sue receive from Buyer over the basis in their stock.

The trade-off for the single tax hit is that Buyer takes Seller with its historic basis in its assets. There is no basis step-up at the corporate level for the additional value paid by Buyer. In this case, the basis loss is $7 million (the excess of the $17 million fair market value over the $10 million basis). Had the transaction been structured under any of the prior scenarios, Buyer would have received additional future tax write-offs of $7 million. Since Buyer loses this tax benefit under this scenario, it is reasonable to expect that Buyer will not be willing to pay as much.

The big question then becomes: How large of a haircut in price will the Buyer require for this structure? If we assume that Buyer's combined federal and state marginal income tax rate will remain at 40 percent, the additional $7 million in basis would produce future tax savings of $2.8 million. But this number must be reduced by two factors to arrive at a fair estimate of the value of the lost tax benefits to Buyer. First, if the transaction were structured as an asset sale under any of the prior scenarios, Buyer would have to start new depreciation and amortization periods for all assets acquired. Many of these new write-off periods may be longer than the historic write-off periods that would be inherited under this scenario. Thus, while future write-offs will clearly be less under this scenario, this scenario may result in faster write-offs (and thus faster tax benefits) for some assets. Second, the difference in the future annual tax benefits of the write-offs under an asset scenario and this scenario, as adjusted, must be discounted by an interest factor to arrive at the present value of such benefits. Since much of the difference will be realized over a 15-year period, this present value discount often is huge. In theory, the present value of the lost tax benefits represents the additional tax cost of this scenario to the Buyer and would be the basis of any price reduction. If in this case these two reduction factors result in a present value of $1.5 million (from a starting point of $2.8 million), the price Buyer would pay for the stock of Seller would be reduced from $12 million to $10.5 million.

Note that even with such a $1.5 million price reduction, Larry and Sue net more on an after-tax basis under this scenario than under any of the previous asset sale scenarios. Their recognized long-term capital gain would be $10

---

15. I.R.C. § 1362(d)(3).

million (the excess paid by Buyer over their $500,000 stock basis). Using the assumed combined capital gains rate of 20 percent, Larry and Sue's tax hit would equal $2 million, reducing their net yield to $8.5 million. They would each net $4.25 million, nearly a 14 percent increase over the $3.73 million realized under the prior asset scenarios.

Now, suppose the parties agree to a total stock price of $10.5 million, but Buyer only wants to purchase 80 percent of Larry and Sue's stock for $8.4 million (80 percent of $10.5 million). The remaining $2.1 million will come from Seller, who will pay this amount to Larry and Sue to redeem the balance of their Seller stock. Larry and Sue end up getting their $10.5 million, and Buyer ends up owning all of Seller's outstanding stock by using only $8.4 million of its cash. Of course, Seller is out $2.1 million.

Illustration C: Bootstrap Stock Acquisition

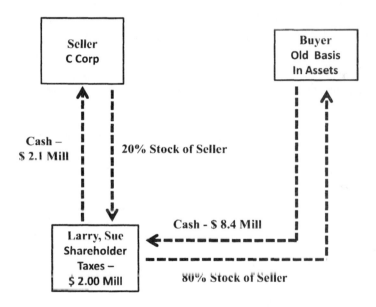

The question: Will this "bootstrap" acquisition create any different tax consequences for the parties? If Larry and Sue's entire stock interest is terminated by the coordinated transactions, the redemption will qualify for sale or exchange treatment (as opposed to dividend treatment), and they will end up in the same after-tax position.[16] The only significant difference is that Buyer's basis in its newly-acquired Seller stock will be $2.1 million less. See Illustration C.

There is one other potential twist under this bootstrap scenario. Suppose Seller's stock is owned by a C corporation ("LS"), not Larry and Sue. Could the transaction be structured so that the amount paid by Seller to LS would qualify as a dividend that would trigger a dividend deduction under 243 (available only to corporate shareholders) and eliminate the tax on $2.1 million of the proceeds

---

16. Zenz v. Quinlivan, 213 F.2d 914 (6th Cir. 1954); Rev. Rule 75-447, 1975-2 C.B. 113.

realized in the transaction? This technique will not work if the transactions are linked for tax avoidance purposes and not supported by independent business purposes.[17] The proceeds will not be treated as dividends subject to the 243 deduction.

g. Statutory Merger

In this scenario, Seller and Buyer merge under state law and Buyer issues to Seller's shareholders, Larry and Sue, its stock as part of the purchase price. The goal is to qualify the transaction as a tax-free A reorganization under Section 368(a)(1)(A).[18] Assume in this case that the consideration paid to Larry and Sue totals $10.5 million – $2.5 million in cash and $8 million in Buyer's common stock. If the transaction qualifies as an A reorganization, Seller recognizes no taxable income,[19] Buyer recognizes no taxable income,[20] and Larry and Sue recognize only $2.5 million of taxable income – the amount of cash that they receive.[21] Their total tax hit, at a combined federal and state rate of 20 percent, is $500,000, a far cry from the total tax bill under any of the previous scenarios.

There are a few trade-offs for this wonderful tax treatment. First, Larry and Sue's basis in the Buyer stock they receive would equal their basis in their old Seller stock ($500,000), increased by their recognized gain ($2.5 million) and decreased by the cash received ($2.5 million).[22] Thus, in this case, their basis remains at $500,000 ($250,000 each). If either of them sells their Buyer stock before death, a large capital gain will be triggered on the sale because of the low carryover basis. If they hold the Buyer stock until death, its basis will be stepped up to its fair market value at death.[23] Second, Seller's basis in the assets acquired by Buyer in the merger carries over to Buyer.[24] There is no step up in basis. And third, in select situations, the income recognized by the shareholders, Larry and Sue in this case, may be taxed as dividend income, but will never exceed their gain realized in the exchange.[25] So long as the dividend rate and the long-term capital gains rate remain the same, this possibility will be of no significance to individual shareholders.

So now the big question: What does it take to qualify as an A reorganization? Four requirements must be satisfied. First, there must be a statutory merger or consolidation under applicable state law.[26] With the merger in this case, all assets and liabilities of Seller are transferred to Buyer without the need for specific asset or liability transfer documents, and Seller is dissolved by operation of law.

---

17. See Waterman Steamship Corp. v. Commissioner, 430 F.2d 1185 (5th Cir. 1970). Also see TSN Liquidating Corp. v. United States, 624 F.2d 1328 (5th Cir. 1980) and Litton Industries v. Commissioner, 89 T.C. 1086 (1987) where technique worked under the specific facts of the case.
18. I.R.C. § 368(a)(1)(A).
19. I.R.C. § 361(a).
20. I.R.C. § 1032(a).
21. I.R.C. §§ 354(a)(1), 356(a)(1).
22. I.R.C. § 358(a)(1).
23. I.R.C. § 1014.
24. I.R.C. § 362(b).
25. I.R.C. § 356(a)(2).
26. I.R.C. § 368(a)(1)(A).

Second, the continuity of interest doctrine must be satisfied. In this case, the doctrine requires that the stock issued by Buyer in the transaction equal a certain percentage of the total consideration paid by Buyer.[27] How large must that percentage be? Case law suggests that 40 percent will do the job,[28] and the IRS has said that 50 percent will qualify for a favorably ruling.[29] In this case, the percentage is in excess of 76 percent ($8 million as a percent of $10.5 million). Note that the percentage requirement focuses on the nature of the consideration paid by Buyer, not the shareholder's ownership percentage in the merged entity, which often is very small. Also, this requirement places no limitation on Larry or Sue's capacity to sell some of their Seller stock to a party unrelated to Seller or Buyer immediately before the merger, nor their capacity to sell any of their Buyer stock to a party unrelated to Buyer immediate after the merger (even if prearranged).[30]

Third, the continuity of business enterprise doctrine must be satisfied. This requires that the purchaser continues the business of the selling entity or uses a significant portion of the selling entity's assets for business purposes.[31] The requirement would not prevent Buyer from transferring Seller's business or assets to a subsidiary corporation or a partnership that is controlled by Buyer.[32]

Finally, there must be a business purpose for the merger. In a merger designed to strengthen two corporate entities, the business purpose requirement usually is not a problem.

h. Stock Swap

This scenario is designed to qualify as a tax-free B reorganization under Section 368(a)(1)(B).[33] Here, Buyer would transfer its voting stock to Larry and Sue in exchange for all of their stock in Seller. The tax consequences for all the parties would be the same as in the previous merger scenario, except that Larry and Sue would not recognize any taxable income on the exchange because they would not receive any cash.

What does it take to qualify as a tax-free B reorganization? The big factor (and major difference from other reorganizations) is the "solely" requirement – the consideration paid by the purchaser must consist solely of the purchaser's voting stock.[34] Thus, Buyer could not use any other consideration, including nonvoting stock, without killing the tax-free treatment of the exchange. In addition to the "solely" requirement, the continuity of interest (a slam dunk with only voting stock), continuity of business enterprise, and business purpose requirements must also be satisfied. The "solely requirement makes the B reorganization one of the least favored strategies.

---

27. Reg. § 1.368-1(e)(1).
28. See, for example, John A. Nelson Co. v. Helvering, 296 U.S. 374 (1935), Miller v. Commissioner, 84 F.2d 415 (6th Cir. 1936), and Ginsburg and Levin, Mergers, Acquisitions and Buyouts ¶ 610 (2004 edition).
29. Rev. Proc. 77-37, 1977-2 C.B. 568.
30. Reg. § 1.368-1(e)(1).
31. Reg. § 1.368-1(d).
32. Reg. § 1.368-1(d)(4) & (5).
33. I.R.C. § 368(a)(1)(B).
34. I.R.C. § 368(a)(1)(B); Reg. § 1.368-2(c).

i. Stock for Assets

Under this scenario, Buyer would transfer its voting stock to Seller as consideration for Seller's assets and business. Seller would then liquidate by distributing the Buyer stock to Larry and Sue. The goal would be to qualify the transaction as a tax-free C reorganization. If successful, the tax consequences to all the parties would be the same as in the previous two reorganization scenarios. One is hard pressed to imagine why this scenario would ever be preferred over a statutory merger ("A") reorganization. The execution is far more difficult because specific assets and liabilities must be transferred; with a merger, this happens automatically by operation of law. Plus, as we will see, the qualification requirements are more demanding.

As for what it takes to qualify, the continuity of interest, continuity of business enterprise, and business purpose requirements must be satisfied. That's the easy part. There also is a "solely" voting stock requirement similar to the stock swap B reorganization, but it is not as strict.[35] It is not violated by the purchaser's assumption of liabilities.[36] Plus, consideration other than voting stock is permitted if (and this is a big "if") the value of the other consideration and the assumed liabilities do not exceed 20 percent of the total consideration paid. In this case, for example, Buyer's assumption of Seller's liabilities of $5 million would not violate the C reorganization "solely" requirement. But because those liabilities exceed 20 percent of the total consideration paid by Buyer ($15.5 million if Buyer issues $10.5 million of voting stock and assumes $5 million of liabilities), no other consideration can be paid. If the liabilities were less than 20 percent of the total, different consideration would be permitted up to the 20 percent mark. So, unlike the statutory merger, there is no capacity for Larry and Sue to get any cash out of the deal without killing the tax-free treatment for all parties.

There are a few additional C reorganization requirements that aren't a problem in this and many cases, but can be issues in select situations. C reorganization treatment requires that Buyer purchase "substantially all" of Seller's property, which, to be safe, means it must acquire at least 90 percent of the fair market value of Seller's net assets and 70 percent of the fair market value of its gross assets.[37] Finally, Seller must distribute all its assets (principally the Buyer's stock) to its shareholders pursuant to the reorganization plan.[38]

j. Forward Triangular Merger

Under this very popular scenario, Buyer forms a wholly owned subsidiary ("Subsidiary"), Seller is merged into Subsidiary, and Buyer's stock is issued to Seller's shareholders, Larry and Sue. Buyer ends up owning Seller's assets and business through its new subsidiary, Seller disappears, and Larry and Sue get Buyer stock. The tax consequences for all the parties are the same as under a

---

35. I.R.C. § 368(a)(1)(C).
36. I.R.C. § 368(a)(1)(C).
37. I.R.C. § 368(a)(1)(C); Rev. Proc. 77-37, 1977-2 C.B. 568, 569.
38. I.R.C. § 368(a)(2)(G). The statute authorizes the Treasury Secretary to waive this requirement in accordance with conditions prescribed by the Secretary. See Rev. Proc. 89-50, 1989-2 C.B. 631.

statutory merger ("A") reorganization. The key is to qualify under Section 368(a)(2)(D), which specifically permits tax-free reorganization treatment for such a triangular merger.

In addition to the regular continuity of interest, continuity of business enterprise, and business purpose requirements, three other conditions must be satisfied. First, Subsidiary must acquire substantially all of Seller's property.[39] It's the same "substantially all" requirement applicable to C reorganizations. No problem here. Second, none of Subsidiary's stock can be used in the transaction. Again, no problem. Third, the transaction must be structured so that it would have qualified as a statutory merger ("A") reorganization if Seller had been merged into Buyer.[40] This third condition (and here's the good news) just requires that the continuity of interest requirement for an A reorganization must have been satisfied.[41] Thus, a substantial portion of the consideration paid by Buyer (50 to 60 percent) may be property other than its stock and the transaction will still qualify as a tax-free reorganization. Of course, Seller's shareholders, Larry and Sue, must still recognize income for the non-stock consideration (as in the case of an A reorganization), but otherwise the tax-free treatment applies.

Illustration D: Forward Triangular Merger

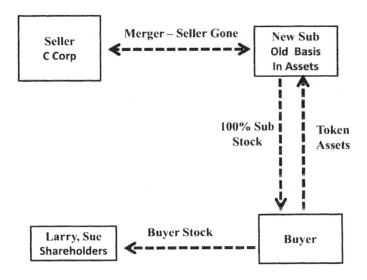

The value of this strategy is that it offers the flexibility and simplicity of a statutory merger, enables the purchaser to acquire the assets in a new subsidiary, and permits the use of substantial non-stock consideration without threatening the tax-free character of the reorganization. See Illustration D.

---

39. I.R.C. § 368(a)(2)(D).
40. I.R.C. § 368(a)(2)(D).
41. Reg. § 1.368-2(b)(2).

k. Reverse Triangular Merger

This scenario is a close cousin to the last. The difference is that Seller, not Subsidiary, is the surviving entity of the merger. As in the last scenario, Buyer forms Subsidiary, Subsidiary merges with Seller, and Buyer's stock is issued to Seller's shareholders, Larry and Sue. Here, Seller ends up as a wholly owned subsidiary of Buyer, and Subsidiary disappears. This reverse triangular merger[42] is attractive in those situations where Seller's continued existence is important for non-tax reasons (e.g., contractual rights, leases, licenses, franchises, etc.). The tax consequences to all parties are the same as under the prior scenario, but qualification is slightly tougher.

With one major exception, the qualification requirements for a reverse triangular merger generally are the same as a forward triangular merger. The exception relates to the amount of non-stock consideration that may be paid to the shareholders, Larry and Sue. For a reverse triangular merger to qualify as a tax-free reorganization, 80 percent of the Seller's stock must be acquired with voting stock of Buyer.[43] So the non-stock consideration cannot exceed 20 percent of the total consideration. As compared to a forward triangular merger, the reverse merger allows the selling entity to survive (which is important in many situations), but offers less flexibility with regard to the amount of non-stock consideration that can be used in the transaction.

4. S CORPORATION SCENARIOS

How do the structural scenarios change if Seller is an S corporation, not a C corporation? The impact of four primary factors must be assessed. First, if Seller has been an S corporation for a significant length of time, Larry and Sue's basis in their stock will be higher. Their basis in their S corporation stock is increased as the earnings of the S corporation are passed through and taxed to them but retained inside the company.[44] Seller's equity now has a book value of $5 million. Thus, depending on when Seller elected S status, Larry and Sue's basis in their stock may be as high as $5 million, a ten-fold increase over their $500,000 stock basis in a C corporation. This stock basis increase, a big benefit for S corporation shareholders, pays off at time of sale. Under all structural scenarios, the shareholder's stock basis affects the amount of gain recognized at the time of sale or, in the case of a reorganization, the amount that carries over to become the basis of the stock acquired in the reorganization.

Second, any corporate level gain triggered on the sale of assets or a liquidation of the S corporation will be passed through and taxed to the S corporation shareholders, Larry and Sue. The character of the gain is based on the assets transferred by the S corporation.[45] The real plus is that the shareholder's basis in their stock is increased by the amount of the gain.[46] As a result, there is little or no shareholder-level tax triggered on the distribution to the

---

42. I.R.C. § 368(a)(2)(E).
43. I.R.C. §§ 368(a)(2)(E), 368(c).
44. I.R.C. § 1367.
45. I.R.C. § 1366(b).
46. I.R.C. § 1367.

shareholders. Thus, the double tax hit is eliminated even in those situations where the transaction is structured to give the purchaser a basis step-up in the acquired assets.

For example, assume in this case that Buyer purchases all of Seller's assets (which have a value of $17 million), assumes the liabilities of $5 million, and pays $12 million cash (first scenario above). As an S corporation, Seller recognizes a $7 million gain, $1 million of which is ordinary income (1245 recapture) and $6 million of which is capital gain. This income is passed through and taxed to Larry and Sue, resulting in a tax of $1.6 million (40 percent of $1 million and 20 percent of $6 million). Larry and Sue's basis in their stock also is increased $7 million. If we assume that Seller has always been an S corporation and that Larry and Sue's basis in their stock before the sale equaled the book value of Seller's equity before the sale ($5 million), Larry and Sue would have a basis of $12 million in their stock when the $12 million of sales proceeds are distributed to them. Thus, the $12 million distribution triggers no additional tax on its receipt. Plus, as a purchaser of assets, Buyer gets a basis step-up. The net after-tax yield to Larry and Sue is $10.4 million ($5.2 million each), a 36 percent increase over the $3.73 million they each would have netted after the double tax hit with a C corporation.

The practical effect of this difference is huge. No longer is there a need to balance the purchaser's desire for a step up in basis against the burdens of a double tax hit, or to hassle with a negotiated price reduction to induce the purchaser to forego the basis step-up. Even when the transaction (for whatever reason) is structured as a stock purchase with the purchaser buying the stock of the S corporation shareholders, the parties may jointly make an election under 338(h)(10) to have the transaction treated as an asset sale followed by a liquidation. The purchaser ends up with a basis step-up, and no double tax is generated.

Third, if the S corporation has a C past, the potential impacts of the built-in gains (BIG) tax must be assessed.[47] The BIG tax applies when an S corporation disposes of assets that it owned at the time of its conversion to S status within 10 years of the conversion. It's an entity level tax imposed at the maximum corporate rate on the built-in gain at the time of conversion. This tax is in addition to the tax that is realized and passed through to the S corporation's shareholders on the sale. Its purpose is to preserve, at least in part and for a period of ten years, the double tax burdens of the corporation's C past.

Finally, an S corporation may be a party to any of the tax-free reorganization scenarios described above. The challenge is to assess the impact of the reorganization on the corporation's continued S status if the corporation survives the reorganization. If the stock of the S corporation ends up being owned by a C corporation after the reorganization (as might happen in a B reorganization or a reverse triangular merger), S status will be lost. If the S corporation is the purchaser in the reorganization, care should be taken to ensure that no S corporation eligibility requirements are violated (e.g., the 100

---

47. See generally I.R.C. § 1374.

shareholder limitation, no corporate or partnership shareholders, etc.).

5. Partnership-Taxed Entity Scenarios

How do the structural scenarios change if Seller is a partnership-taxed entity? If Buyer's stock is used in the deal, the tax-free reorganization options are out. They require corporate status of all parties. So any Buyer stock used in the transaction will be treated the same as any other consideration. As for the other structural options, the partnership's presence eliminates the burden of a double tax. The basis increase on the income passed through is the same as with an S corporation – both as income is accumulated during the life of the entity and when it is recognized at the time of sale.[48] Thus, the tax consequences are similar, but not identical, to those for an S corporation.

If Seller, as a partnership-taxed entity, sells all its assets to Buyer for $12 million and Buyer's assumption of all liabilities, a $7 million gain will be triggered and passed through to the partners, Larry and Sue. The character of the gain will be determined at the partnership level; thus, $1 million will be ordinary income (1245 recapture) and $6 million will be capital gain (goodwill and going concern value). Larry and Sue's basis in their partnership interests will be increased by the $7 million pass-through gain. Thus, assuming Larry and Sue had a combined basis in their partnership interests of $5 million before the transaction, there will be no second tax on the gain when the proceeds from the sale are distributed to Larry and Sue. Buyer will get a stepped-up basis in the assets under the 1060 regime and the ability to write off intangibles over 15 years under Section 197.

Although the consequences of this asset sale scenario look just like its S corporation counterpart, there are a few potential differences. First, if Larry or Sue had contributed to Seller any of the property sold by Seller and that contributed property had a built-in gain or built-in loss at the time of contribution (that is, a fair market value different from its transferred basis), any gain recognized on the sale of the contributed property would first be allocated to the contributing partner to account for such built-in gain or loss, and the balance would then be allocated to the two partners.[49] Thus, although the total gain recognized by Larry and Sue on such a sale would be the same as with an S corporation, the gain would be allocated differently among the owners. Second, unlike an S corporation with a prior C past, a partnership-taxed entity that sells its assets need not worry about any entity level tax comparable to the ten-year BIG tax under Section 1374. If the business had a prior C history, it would have taken its tax lumps at the time of its conversion from C to partnership status.

Suppose Larry and Sue liquidate Seller and receive all Seller's assets and liabilities and then sell all the assets to Buyer for $12 million and Buyer's assumption of the liabilities. The partnership would terminate on the liquidation,

---

48. I.R.C. § 705(a).
49. I.R.C. § 704(c)(1); Reg. § 1.704-3(a)(3).

and its tax year would close.[50] Generally, Larry and Sue, as the partners of Seller, would not recognize any gain or loss on the liquidation of Seller.[51] Their basis in their partnership interests would carry over to the basis in the assets received in the liquidation.[52] Their subsequent sale of the assets would trigger a taxable gain equal to the excess of the amount they received over their basis in the assets ($7 million under these facts). The character of the gain would be based on the assets sold; thus, $1 million would be ordinary income and $6 million would be capital gain. But, again, the gain might be allocated differently between Larry and Sue if, within the seven years preceding the liquidation, one of them had contributed some of the property distributed in the liquidation.[53] Also, any attempt to allocate the ordinary income element of the gain disproportionately between the Larry and Sue (if, for example, one of them was in a lower personal tax bracket) by distributing more equipment (1245 recapture property) to one partner and more of the other assets to the other partner will fail.[54] As a purchaser of the assets, Buyer would get a new basis in the assets.

Suppose, as an alternative, Buyer purchased Larry and Sue's interests in the partnership for $12 million. Seller, the partnership, would terminate for tax purposes. Larry and Sue would recognize income equal to the excess (here $7 million) of the amount received over their basis in the partnership interests.[55] But, unlike a sale of corporate stock, the sale of a partnership interest may trigger ordinary income if the partnership holds ordinary income assets (e.g., unrealized receivables and inventory items).[56] Thus, the gain represented by such assets will affect the character of the gain recognized by a partner on the sale of a partnership interest. Here, $1 million of the gain recognized by Larry and Sue would be taxed as ordinary income. As for Buyer, the transaction would be treated as a purchase, as if Seller had made a liquidating distribution to Larry and Sue followed by Buyer's purchase of the former partnership assets – exactly as in the prior scenario.[57]

CASE PROBLEM 15-1

Circle Inc. (CI) is a calendar year C corporation that has two equal shareholders Doug and Jane. Doug, age 81, owns 1,000 shares of CI's common stock, with a basis of $300,000. Jane, age 34, also owns 1,000 shares, but her basis is $7 million. Jane inherited the stock from her father. CI's balance sheet assets and liabilities are set forth below.

Olson Inc. (Olson) wants to buy CI, and Doug and Jane are ready to sell. Assume that CI is subject to a combined federal and state income tax rate of 40 percent, and Doug and Jane's combined federal and state ordinary marginal income tax rate is 40 percent and capital gain rate is 20 percent.

---

50. I.R.C. § 708(b).
51. I.R.C. § 731(a).
52. I.R.C. § 732(b).
53. I.R.C. § 704(c)(1)(B).
54. I.R.C. § 751(b); Reg. § 1.751-1.
55. I.R.C. § 741.
56. I.R.C. § 751(a); Reg. § 1.751-1(d).
57. Rev. Rule 99-6, 1999-1 C.B. 432.

CI's Assets and Liabilities

	Book Value Basis	Fair Market Value
Cash	$ 1,500,000	$ 1,500,000
Inventory	2,500,000	3,000,000
Accounts Receivable	2,000,000	2,000,000
Equipment	2,000,000	3,000,000
Customer Lists	-	500,000
Copyrights	200,000	500,000
Goodwill	-	11,000,000
Total Assets	$ 8,200,000	$ 21,500,000
Accounts Payable	$ 1,500,000	$ 1,500,000

a. CI sells its assets to Olson for $20 million plus an assumption of all liabilities. CI pays its taxes and distributes all remaining proceeds to Doug and Jane. Calculate the tax impacts to CI, Doug, and Jane. What is Olson's basis in the assets? Any suggestions for Doug or Jane?

b. Olson buys CI's stock from Doug and Jane for $18 million. Is this a sensible price under the circumstances? Calculate the tax impacts to CI, Doug, and Jane. What is Olson's basis in its CI stock?

c. Olson buys 70 percent of CI's stock from Doug and Jane for $12.6 million. CI redeems the remaining 30 percent by paying $2.7 million cash to Doug (it will borrow an additional $1.2 million) and distributing the equipment to Jane. Calculate the tax impacts to CI, Doug, and Jane. What is Olson's basis in its CI stock?

d. Olson forms a new subsidiary (S). CI is merged into S, and Doug and Jane are each issued 100,000 shares (value $90 per share) of Olson's common stock. What are the tax impacts to CI, Doug, Jane, Olson and S in such a reorganization? If Doug and Jane wanted some cash out of the deal, how much cash could they be paid without destroying the tax free character of the reorganization for everyone?

e. Same as **d.**, except S is merged into CI. What are the tax impacts to CI, Doug, Jane, Olson and S in such a reorganization? If Doug and Jane wanted some cash out of the deal, how much cash could they be paid without destroying the tax free character of the reorganization for everyone?

f. Same as **a.** except CI is and always has been an S corporation and Doug's basis in his stock is $3 million and Jane's basis is $8 million.

g. Same as **b.** except CI is and always has been an LLC taxed as a partnership, and Doug's basis in his partnership interest is $3 million and Jane's basis is $8 million.

B. DOCUMENTING THE DEAL

NEGOTIATING THE PURCHASE AGREEMENT
Richard A. Goldberg[44]

1. Introduction

a. Function of the acquisition agreement. In addition to setting forth the principal financial terms of a transaction, the acquisition agreement also sets forth the legal rights and obligations of the parties with respect to the transaction. It provides the buyer with a detailed description of the business being acquired and affords the buyer remedies where the description proves to be materially inaccurate. The agreement indicates the actions which must be taken by the parties to properly consummate the transaction and requires the parties to take these actions. Finally, the acquisition agreement allocates the risks associated with the purchased business among the parties to the agreement. Special consideration may be applicable to the structuring of an acquisition and/or sale of divisions and subsidiaries. Certain legal issues are unique to these divestiture transactions, and may require particular attention, such as: fiduciary issues, financials; shared assets and liabilities; antitrust issues, taxes and employee matters.

b. Main components. The objectives of the purchase agreement are accomplished through the operation of the representations and warranties, covenants, conditions and indemnification provisions.

(1) Representations and warranties. The primary function of the representations and warranties is to provide the buyer with a "snapshot" of the acquired business at a particular point in time, typically on the date the agreement is signed and again on the date of the closing.

(2) Covenants. The covenants govern the relationship of the parties over a certain time period. Certain covenants apply from the signing of the agreement until the closing date and provide assurance that the proper actions are taken to facilitate the closing of the transaction and preserve the business pending the closing. Other covenants survive the closing for a certain length of time, such as covenants requiring cooperation of the parties with respect to the post-closing transition of the business or sharing of facilities.

(3) Conditions. Acquisition agreements contain conditions precedent that must be met in order for the party receiving the benefit of the condition to be legally obligated to consummate the transaction. If one party fails to satisfy a condition by the date of the closing, the other party has the right to terminate the agreement and walk away from the transaction.

(4) Indemnification. The indemnification portion of the agreement

---

58. Copyright © Practicing Law Institute and the author. Reprinted with permission. Mr. Goldberg is a partner in the law firm of Dechert LLP. His practice focuses on mergers and acquisitions, and he has counseled public and private companies, as well as investment banking firms. He has lectured and written extensively on legal topics, including mergers and acquisitions.

requires the parties to pay damages in the event of a breach of their respective representations, warranties and covenants. Indemnification provisions also serve to allocate specific post-closing risks associated with the transferred business.

c. Simultaneous versus delayed closing.

(1) Purposes of a delayed closing. In most instances, the parties would prefer to sign the agreement and close without any delay. However, it is often necessary to delay the closing to provide time to obtain third party and/or governmental consents which are required to consummate the transaction or to facilitate the financing of the transaction. For example, transactions exceeding a certain size require the approval of the Federal Trade Commission, and others necessitate filings with the Securities and Exchange Commission (SEC), e.g., where securities of the purchaser are issued as consideration for the transaction in a manner which constitutes a public offering. In addition, the seller and possibly the buyer may need to obtain shareholder consent to the transaction. In such an event, if the seller or the buyer, as the case may be, is a public reporting company, subject to the SEC's proxy rules, an SEC filing would also be required. The two-part signing and closing allows the parties to reach an agreement as early as possible and attend to these matters after the agreement is signed.

The Delaware Supreme Court held, in a 1996 decision, that in a two-step merger, the value added to the business being acquired following a change in majority control and during the transition period "accrues to the benefit of all shareholders and must be included in the appraisal process on the date of the merger." Accordingly, when a buyer is considering a two-step acquisition, the buyer should consider the possibility that dissenting shareholders who do not sell their shares in the first step of an acquisition may be entitled to their pro rata share of the value added to the business being acquired by the buyer during the transition period, thereby forcing the buyer to pay a higher price to such shareholders at the second step of the acquisition than the original price paid.

(2) Effects on the agreement. Acquisition agreements involving a simultaneous signing and closing are much simpler than those involving delayed closings. The reason for this is that the covenants which govern between the signing and the closing and the conditions to closing may be eliminated. For example, no shop provisions, options and break-up fees are only necessary in the event of a delayed closing (see section IIIC "Specific covenants; effects of termination: no shops, options and break-up fees" below). Other than the principal financial terms, only the representations and warranties, the related indemnification provisions and the post-closing covenants need to be included in the Agreement.

(3) Disclosure. During the period between the signing and the closing, the buyer is typically given full access to the seller's books, records and other pertinent data. Prior to the signing, the buyer's access will be less extensive because of the seller's reluctance to provide certain information in the absence of a signed agreement.

2. Representations and Warranties

a. Seller's representations. The seller's representations and warranties serve various purposes from the buyer's perspective. First, the buyer seeks assurance that the seller has the authority and power to enter into the transaction, and that once the buyer pays the consideration, it will own the business being acquired. Second, the representations serve as a means to acquire information from the seller regarding the nature and value of the business. Representations force the seller to carefully consider and disclose material that may not otherwise be discoverable by the buyer through due diligence. In addition, through the operation of the conditions to closing, the representations provide the buyer with the right to terminate the agreement in the event that any of the representations prove to be false at the time of the closing. The representations also provide the groundwork for indemnification after the closing.

b. Buyer's representations. The seller will also want to obtain representations to the effect that the transaction is properly authorized and is binding on the buyer. Aside from these, the form of payment will govern the extent of any other representations and warranties that the seller will require from the buyer. If the consideration is in the form of cash, the seller will usually not seek many other representations and warranties, provided that it is satisfied with the buyer's ability to pay. However, if the consideration includes securities of the buyer, the viability of the buyer's business and associated risks become material to the seller. Accordingly, in these situations, the seller will seek the same type of business disclosure that it is providing to the buyer.

c. Specific seller representations. The following is a brief discussion regarding specific types of representations typically made by the seller.

(1) Financial statements. The seller's financial statements are a significant source of information regarding the seller's business. A set of year end and stub period (if applicable) financial statements is usually attached as an exhibit to the acquisition agreement or otherwise delivered to the buyer. The seller represents that the financial statements are complete and correct, fairly represent the financial condition of the business (including the liabilities of the seller) for the periods indicated, and were prepared in accordance with generally accepted accounting principles (GAAP). Additional representations might also be sought that mirror Sarbanes Oxley certification requirements. See section 13 below.

(2) Assets and liabilities. The seller will frequently also be asked to make representations about specific assets and liabilities included in the financial statements. This gives the buyer greater protection than the financial statement representation alone because a representation that the financial statements have been prepared in accordance with GAAP may not be breached for a minor variation from the balance sheet with respect to the value of certain assets which are of particular importance to the buyer. The following are examples of these types of representations:

(i) Accounts receivable. Negotiations frequently revolve around the seller's reluctance to state that the accounts receivable are collectible, which is in effect a guarantee of collection. Although the seller typically refuses to give such a guarantee, it will usually agree to represent that the accounts receivable arose in the ordinary course of business and represent the actual obligations of its customers. The seller also typically agrees to represent that, except for amounts reserved in allowance for doubtful accounts, there are no known claims or offsets against the receivables. If the collectability of the accounts receivable is an integral part of the value of the business being acquired, the parties sometimes agree that the buyer has the right to "put" or sell back to the seller the receivables that remain uncollected after a certain period of time. A buyer may be reluctant, however, to turn over the collection process to the seller who may not have the same customer sensitivities as the buyer.

(ii) **Inventory.** The objective of a representation regarding inventory is to flush out obsolete or unsalable inventory that has not been written off and to make sure that the inventory has been accounted for on a consistent basis.

(iii) **Plant and equipment**. The seller typically represents that the plant and equipment is in good operating condition and that no fundamental structural problems exist. The seller may also be asked to represent that the plant and equipment is sufficient to run the business. The seller will not want to make this representation so stringent as to turn it into a warranty that the equipment will not break down.

(iv) **Liabilities**. A representation stating that the financial statements have been prepared in accordance with GAAP will not cover liabilities which are not required to be included on a balance sheet (e.g. certain contingent liabilities and lease liabilities which are not capitalized) or which occur after the date of the financial statements. As a result, it is important to obtain a representation that there are no undisclosed liabilities except as set forth in the financial statements or on an attached schedule and except those that have been incurred in the ordinary course of business subsequent to the date of the balance sheet. The schedule typically excludes liabilities below an agreed upon dollar threshold.

(v) **Taxes.** A buyer will typically want a representation that all of the require tax returns have been properly prepared and filed and that all taxes shown to be due thereon have been paid, e.g., income taxes, excise taxes, customs taxes, sales taxes, etc. It is helpful for the representation to specify the years through which the seller's income tax returns have been audited and to indicate whether the seller has waived the statute of limitations with respect to any tax years. Of course, a tax representation is less significant in a sale of assets than a sale of stock.

(3) **Leases, contracts and other commitments**. The buyer needs to be familiar with all of the seller's material agreements in order to be forewarned about the obligations that the buyer will be undertaking. In addition, the buyer will review these documents to be sure that they are assignable. The buyer typically seeks a schedule of material agreements and a representation that the seller is not in default under any material agreement. The definition of a "material" contract will depend upon the size of the business being acquired and the cost to the seller of compiling the agreements.

(4) Customers and suppliers. Where material, the seller is asked to represent that customer and supplier relations are satisfactory. Frequently, a schedule of the principal customers and suppliers is provided.

(5) Employee matters. This representation covers the seller's potential liability under employee benefit plans such as health plans, pension plans, retirement plans, etc. and their respective compliance with ERISA. Typically, the representation also covers unions, if any, and labor relations, as well as a statement that there are no unfair labor practices or proceedings pending.

(6) Patents, trademarks, copyrights, trade names, etc. Where material, all patents, trademarks and licenses are listed on a schedule to the purchase agreement. In addition, the seller may be asked to represent that to its knowledge, its intellectual property is not being infringed upon by any third party and that it is not infringing the intellectual property rights of a third party.

(7) Litigation and compliance with law. This representation typically covers threatened as well as pending claims. Knowledge qualifications are usually permitted for threatened litigations but not for those that are pending.

(8) Absence of certain changes. This representation assures the buyer that there have been no material adverse changes in the business subsequent to the date of the most recent financial statements. Frequently, the representation will also cover changes in the industry in which the seller operates

(9) Insurance. This representation typically provides that the seller maintains adequate insurance with reputable insurance companies. In addition, the buyer will often want to know whether the seller has been refused any insurance or has experienced any insurance cancellations, as these are often indications of operational problems or uninsurable risks. A schedule of all the types and amounts of insurance maintained by the seller is sometimes included as part of the representation. Care should be taken to identify insurance coverage that is maintained on a "claims made" basis, e.g., product liability or directors and officers liability insurance. "Tail" coverage is often available for purchase by the buyer to avoid gaps in coverage which would otherwise arise under a "claims made" policy. It is also useful to ascertain whether there is "entity" coverage as part of any directors and officers liability insurance policy.

(10) Environmental protection. Representations with respect to environmental protection are often one of the more significant representations in the acquisition agreement. If lenders are involved, they are particularly concerned with these representations in view of the potential lender liability associated with environmental noncompliance. Environmental representations typically encompass compliance with applicable environmental laws. However, this is often an area of negotiation because environmental laws are so comprehensive that sellers are typically unwilling to represent that they are in compliance will all such laws.

(11) Data Backup and Redundancy. In an environment of heightened concern about data redundancy capabilities, a representation should be sought which provides assurances about protections against loss of critical data.

(12) Regulation FD. Regulation FD adopted by the Securities and Exchange Commission (SEC) and effective as of October 23, 2000, generally applies whenever a senior official of a U.S. public company or another employee or agent who regularly communicates with the investment community discloses material nonpublic information to a security market professional or to a security holder where it was reasonably foreseeable that the security holder would trade based on the information. When the disclosure obligations of Regulation FD are triggered, the issuer is required to either simultaneously, for intentional disclosures or promptly, for non-intentional disclosures, make public disclosure of the same information. Thus, the buyer might ask the seller to represent that no disclosure violating Regulation FD has been made since the effective date of the Regulation.

(13) Sarbanes-Oxley. The Sarbanes-Oxley Act of 2002 (SOX) was enacted on July 30, 2002, with the aim of increasing corporate responsibility. Among other things, SOX imposes two separate certification requirements on the chief executive officer (CEO) and chief financial officer (CFO) of a public company. Section 302 of SOX requires that the CEO/CFO make specific representations in their respective certifications to each annual report on Form 10K and each quarterly report on 10Q. Section 906 creates a new CEO/CFO certification requirement in connection with all periodic reports that contain financial statements.

In 2003, the SEC adopted requirements relating to executive management internal control over financial reporting as required under the SOX mandate. The rules adopted pursuant to Section 404 of SOX require that the CEO/CFO include in their annual reports a report of management on the company's internal control over financial reporting. A company that is an "accelerated filer" as defined in Exchange Act Rule 12b-2, commencing with reports for its fiscal year ending on or after November 15, 2004, must comply with Rule 404 management report on internal control over financial reporting disclosure requirements in its annual report for that fiscal year. A company that is not an "accelerated filer" must comply with Rule 404 disclosure requirements commencing with reports for its first fiscal year ending on or after July 15, 2005. The CEO's/CFO's internal report must certify their responsibility for establishing and maintaining adequate control over financial reporting for the company; assess the effectiveness of the company's internal control over financial reporting as of the end of the company's most recent fiscal year; identify the framework used by management to evaluate the effectiveness of the company's internal control over financial reporting; and certify that the public accounting firm that audited the Company's financial statements included in the annual report has issued an attestation report on management's assessment of the company's internal control over financial reporting. Furthermore, the CEO/CFO must evaluate any change in the company's internal control over financial reporting that occurred during a fiscal quarter that has materially affected or is reasonably likely to materially affect, the company's internal control over financial reporting. In view of the requirements of SOX, the buyer might ask a public company seller to represent that it has complied with the requirements of SOX and to make further representations that mirror the contents of these certifications.

The effect of complying with Section 404 of SOX may add significant challenges to due diligence. With a looming deadline for certification of internal controls, there may be pressure to integrate an acquired division or subsidiary rapidly so that the certification can be made. Due diligence will be necessary to determine whether there are weaknesses in internal controls that will prevent certification in a timely manner. Poor internal controls of a target company were once less significant during the due diligence process because it was viewed that the poor internal controls would be fixed post-acquisition. Poor internal controls can now impact the acquirer to the extent that management and the auditor may conclude that the acquirer and the target, taken as a whole do not have effective internal control over financial reporting. In addition, some seemingly small acquisitions can affect the acquirer's Section 404 compliance process if the operations of the new entity represent specific risks to the acquirer or cause a previously insignificant business location to become significant when combined with the acquired entity. Acquisitions of private companies may cause additional difficulties in this area because private companies are less likely to have devoted much time to documenting their controls. If an acquisition is closed before the end of a buyer's fiscal year end, the SEC recognizes that it is not always possible to conduct an assessment of an acquired business' internal control over financial reporting in the period between the consummation date and the date of management's assessment. Management may exclude the acquired business from their assessment and explain why they have done so. This is, in effect, a one year grace period for compliance for acquisitions made late in the year. However, management may not make this exclusion for more than one year after the acquisition date or in more than one annual management report. Although the acquirer may have an extended period of time to prepare its report under Section 404 covering the acquired entity, the first Section 302 certification under SOX after acquisition must include the operations of the acquired entity, and that certification must be made as of the end of the quarter in which the acquisition closes. As also required by the SOX mandate, the SEC has implemented two additional disclosure requirements pursuant to Sections 406 and 407 of SOX. Section 406 of SOX requires a company to disclose whether it has adopted a code of ethics that applies to the company's executive management including the CEO, CFO, Controller, or other persons performing similar functions. Section 407 requires a company to disclose whether its audit committee includes at least one member who is a financial expert. Rules 406 and 407 are effective for annual reports for fiscal years ending on or after July 15, 2003. If a company does not adopt a code of ethics nor appoint an audit committee financial expert, the company must disclose these facts. This disclosure should be reviewed as part of due diligence and might result in additional representations in the purchase agreement.

It is also worth noting that the requirements of SOX may affect public companies acquiring private companies that were not subject to the same SEC oversight prior to the acquisition. Under the securities laws, if the acquisition is large enough, as defined by SEC regulations, a buyer that is a public company must disclose the historical audited financial statements of the seller on a Form 8-K and in some cases, in a proxy statement or registration statement related to the proposed acquisition. Depending upon the size and nature of the transaction, the buyer may have to include the target company's audited financial statements from the previous year or up to three years prior to the transaction. These requirements make it incumbent upon the buyer to ensure that the audited financial statements are available or can be made available prior to the due date of the SEC filing. In addition, though SOX does not impose new obligations on the officers of the buyer to certify the target company's historical financial reports, it does create new criminal penalties and increase already existing civil and criminal penalties under pre-existing securities laws. For example, Sections 13(a) and 18 of the Securities Exchange Act of 1934 (Exchange Act) impose personal liability (and criminal liability) on the CEO and CFO of a buyer for the contents of any Exchange Act filings and corporate officers signing such filings can be held liable for material misstatements or omissions under Section 10(b) of the Exchange Act. As SOX increases, considerably, the civil and criminal penalties for violations of these laws it is critical that the parties to a merger or purchase agreement conduct extensive due diligence throughout the process in order to carefully review the financial statements and information concerning the target.

(14) Catch-all representations. The buyer will sometimes ask the seller to make the general representation that there are no material misstatements or omissions in the representations. This type of representation can be a shortcut in cases where the principals desire to consummate the transaction quickly, without extensive due diligence or time spent on preparing schedules to the agreement.

d. Schedules. Schedules are typically the most illuminating portions of an acquisition agreement because they disclose all of the exceptions to the representations and warranties. For example, a representation will often provide that there are no defaults in material agreements except as set forth in the attached schedule. In evaluating a potential acquisition candidate, a review of schedules to previous acquisition agreements by such candidate (which may be publicly available if the candidate is publicly held) can provide a useful source for due diligence.

The information contained in the schedules can often be competitively sensitive. For example, the schedule may contain a list of the seller's largest customers and the volume of business done with these customers during a certain time period. If the buyer is a public company and the acquisition agreement is material to the buyer, the schedules must be filed with the SEC as exhibits to the purchase agreement. In these circumstances, the buyer may be willing to accept, in lieu of a schedule, a representation in the agreement that would have an exclusion for items "previously disclosed to the buyer." This may refer to items delivered during the due diligence process. If this approach is used, thought should be given as to whether these items are intended to be included within the integration clause of the agreement.

It should also be noted that under 8-K disclosure requirements, which became effective August 23, 2004, a merger or similar asset or stock purchase agreement must be disclosed on Form 8-K and filed as an exhibit within four business days of execution. Under prior 8-K rules, while some issuers filed merger agreements earlier, they were not required to be filed until the date of filing of the next quarterly report on Form 10Q or annual report on Form 10K after the execution of the merger agreement.

c. Limitations on representations and warranties.

(1) Materiality qualification. The manner in which a representation is drafted plays an important role in the allocation of risk between the parties. It will determine whether the existence of certain previously undisclosed facts will permit the buyer to terminate the transaction or, after the closing, seek indemnification. One way to shift risk to the buyer is to qualify some or all of the representations with materiality exceptions, e.g., "except for those which do not have a material adverse effect upon the Company, its financial condition or the transaction contemplated hereby." Accordingly, the buyer bears the risk and costs with respect to any non-material items.

Different materiality standards may be used in the various sections of the acquisition agreement. For example, the seller may agree to disclose all litigation (without any materiality qualification) but limit the right to indemnification to situations in which exposure from the undisclosed litigation exceeds a certain dollar threshold. This option allows the buyer to flush out any potential problems with the seller's business through detailed disclosure schedules, but without triggering indemnification obligations for immaterial matters. Another alternative would be to require disclosure and indemnification for all litigation, but permit the buyer to terminate the agreement only in the event that the undisclosed litigation has a material adverse effect on the acquired business. The parties typically arrive at compromises on these issues depending on the particular facts related to the transaction.

(2) Double materiality. The buyer should bear in mind the pitfall of double materiality. This occurs when a representation is qualified by materiality and the corresponding indemnification provision is conditioned upon the breaches resulting in a certain threshold level of damages. The result is that the representation would not be breached, and any resulting loss would not be counted toward the minimum threshold level, unless there exists a material obligation or liability which is not disclosed. Due to the interplay of these provisions, the buyer may suffer substantial damages without triggering indemnification, leaving the buyer without adequate protection.

(3) Knowledge qualification. The seller can also limit the scope of its representations by having them qualified by a phrase such as "to the best of Seller's knowledge." This qualification limits the duty to disclose to only such information as is within the seller's knowledge. Often, the seller will argue that it can only make representations as to what it knows. However, the issue is not the veracity or trustworthiness of the seller. Instead, it is purely a question of who among the parties will bear the risk of unknown liabilities. By adding a knowledge qualifier, the risk is shifted from the seller to the buyer.

Frequently, the parties negotiate over what the appropriate meaning of "knowledge" should be. The seller will sometimes argue that it cannot be held responsible for the knowledge of all of its employees while the buyer will claim that, as between the seller and buyer, the seller should bear the risk of information known by its low level employees. A frequent compromise is to define the individual(s) whose knowledge is subsumed within the meaning of the term. Often, these individuals will be limited to the seller's officers (or just its executive officers) and its directors. The definition of knowledge may also clarify whether it includes constructive knowledge.

f. Incorporation of SEC filings into representations and warranties. In situations where the party providing the representations and warranties is a public company, it may be sufficient to simply have a representation regarding the accuracy of the company's SEC filings coupled with limited additional representations concerning transaction specific matters, such as the authorization and execution of the agreement. However, the buyer is likely to want more specific representations about specialized areas of concern such as environmental and ERISA compliance and customer relations.

3. Covenants

a. General. Many of the covenants contained in the acquisition agreement require the parties to obtain the necessary approvals and consents from various governmental agencies and third parties, which are required for the consummation of the transaction. The delayed closing provides the parties with sufficient time to perform these covenants. Other covenants ensure that the seller's status quo is preserved during the hiatus between the signing and the closing. Where the parties have a simultaneous signing and closing, the covenants will be limited to post-closing items such as payment of relevant taxes, filing of tax forms and the general covenant to take any further actions which may become necessary to consummate the transaction.

b. Covenants pending the closing.

(1) Best efforts qualification. When a third-party consent is necessary to consummate the transaction, the buyer may seek an affirmative covenant that the seller will use its "best efforts" to obtain such consent. "Best efforts" is an ambiguous phrase which parties are sometimes reluctant to use. For example, a party may be concerned that such a covenant may require it to commence litigation, if necessary, in order to obtain such consent. A compromise sometimes entails the phrase "reasonable efforts" instead of "best efforts."

(2) Stringency of certain covenants. The buyer will typically desire strict covenants aimed at preserving the seller's status quo by requiring the seller to seek the buyer's consent prior to taking certain actions. However, the covenants should not be drafted so strictly as to materially interfere with the business of the seller pending the closing.

(3) Examples of specific covenants.

(i) Affirmative:

- To obtain all necessary consents;

- To carry on the business only in the ordinary course;

- To maintain plant, property and equipment;

- To comply with all applicable laws;

- To pay all taxes when due and avoid liens; and

- To maintain qualifications to do business in appropriate jurisdictions.

(ii) Negative:

- Not to introduce any method of accounting inconsistent with that used in prior periods;

- Not to enter into any transaction other than in the ordinary course of business, e.g., sales or purchases of a material amount of assets, bank borrowings;

- Not to amend the seller's charter and by-laws or principal agreements, except in the ordinary course;

- Not to grant any increase in the salary or other compensation of any employee, except in the ordinary course of business (absent previously anticipated increases or scheduled bonuses);

- Not to enter into any long-term contracts or commitments (specific dollar thresholds can be employed);

- Not to release any claims or waive any rights against third parties.

    c. Covenants effective after the closing. Earn outs provide flexibility in determining a purchase price of the acquired business. Earn outs allow the buyer to pay most of the agreed upon purchase price at the closing, and then make subsequent additional payments which are contingent upon how the business performs after the acquisition. When using earn out provisions, it is important to clearly define the performance criteria that trigger the additional payments. Performance criteria may include attaining specified revenue or earnings levels, or other defined targets such as completing the development of a new product line or receipt of awards relating to the acquired business' performance or products. It is critical to clearly define the accounting terms to be used in earn out provisions (reference to generally accepted accounting rules is helpful). In that regard, it would be advisable to have an accountant review the earn out provisions to lessen the potential for ambiguity in interpretation, e.g. review by one or more certified public accounting firms. Further, the period of time over which the contingent payments may be earned, and the timing of computation and payment of the subsequent payments (whether annually or incrementally) must be clearly stated in the earn out provision. Since disputes with respect to earn out provisions are common, a clause providing for an alternate dispute resolution method may be useful.

    d. Specific covenants; effects of termination: no shops, options and break-up fees. In the event that the agreement has a delayed closing and the seller is publicly held, the seller's board of directors could be faced with an unsolicited offer between signing and closing which it could not ignore without violating its fiduciary duties. To protect against this possibility, the buyer often requests certain covenants which minimize the actions the seller can take in respect of a third party, discourage third-party offers and compensate the buyer if a transaction is consummated with a third party. These protections generally prohibit the seller's board from soliciting or negotiating with alternate purchasers (subject to the seller board's fiduciary duties, as discussed below). The provisions may also grant the buyer certain rights in the event that the contemplated transaction is never consummated, such as reimbursement of the potential purchaser's expenses, a specified termination fee or an option to purchase certain assets or stock of the seller. These provisions are discussed below.

(1) **No shop provisions**. The agreement will generally contain a no shop provision prohibiting the seller from soliciting other offers. However, the seller will generally insist upon an exception that enables the seller to entertain unsolicited third party offers if the failure to do so would violate the fiduciary duties of the seller's board to its shareholders. This exemption is typically referred to as a "fiduciary out." The "fiduciary out" generally plays a more important role when the seller is a publicly held, as opposed to a closely held, company for two reasons. First, in a closely held company, it is likely that the shareholders have agreed to the transaction with the initial purchaser and may indeed all be parties to the acquisition agreement. Second, since there is no public market for the shares, it is less likely that a competing bid would emerge without cooperation of the shareholders.

(2) **Stock or asset options**. As a result of the "fiduciary out" typically included in the no shop provision, the potential buyer is at risk of the transaction not being consummated due to a competing bid. Accordingly, a purchaser will often ask for an option to purchase stock or assets of the seller upon the occurrence of a triggering event in order to deter, and give itself an advantage over, other potential purchasers. The triggering event is typically the termination of the acquisition agreement or the acquisition by another potential purchaser of a certain percentage of the seller's stock.

(i) **Stock options**. A stock option grants the initial purchaser the right to purchase authorized but unissued stock of the seller upon the occurrence of a triggering event. Such an option is advantageous to the initial purchaser in three respects. First, in the event the seller is considering a competing offer from another potential buyer, the initial purchaser can exercise its options and vote the shares in favor of its transaction with the seller and against the competing offer. Second, by increasing the number of shares outstanding, the issuance of the option would make the purchase by a competing bidder more costly. Finally, in the event a competing offer is commenced and the initial purchaser is outbid, the initial purchaser can realize a profit by exercising its options and tendering its shares for the higher bid.

(ii) **Asset options**. An asset option provides a buyer with the option to purchase a particular asset of the seller at an advantageous price upon the occurrence of a triggering event. Since the particular asset underlying the option is often a significant division or subsidiary of the seller (sometimes referred to as a "crown jewel"), the asset option can be successful in deterring potential purchasers who are mainly interested in, or unwilling to consummate the transaction if the seller were to lose, that asset.

(3) Expense reimbursement or break-up fees. Often, the acquisition agreement will contain a provision whereby the seller will be required to reimburse the initial purchaser for expenses incurred in connection with the transaction and/or pay a termination fee in the event that the acquisition agreement is terminated because of a specified reason, including the consummation, or recommendation to the seller's shareholders, of an alternative offer. These payments deter competing offers by making them more expensive and reimburse an unsuccessful potential purchaser for expenses incurred in connection with the failed acquisition.

(4) Legality. In the event of a change of control, the primary objective of the seller's board of directors must be "to secure the transaction offering the best value reasonably available for [its] stockholders." No shop provisions, options and termination fees are generally material features of a transaction to be considered by the board of directors in the exercise of their fiduciary duties to further that end.

(i) No shop provisions. While no shop provisions are not per se illegal, they must not limit the fiduciary duties of the seller's board of directors or they will be unenforceable.

(ii) Options. Asset and stock options have generally been upheld in Delaware courts if the granting of the option is necessary, and is used, to encourage either the initial offer or other competing offers on terms more favorable to the seller's shareholders. However, these options generally have been enjoined where they have been used to favor one buyer over another in the bidding process, and to exclude or limit competing offers, to the detriment of the seller's shareholders.

(iii) Break-up fees Break-up fees are generally upheld if they are reasonable in relation to the size of the whole transaction. In each case, the test would be whether the defensive measure used enhanced the bidding process in order to maximize the value to the seller's shareholders. In addition, Courts will take into account the overall effect that all of the protective measures have collectively on competing bids. Break-up fees average generally between 1 percent and 3.5 percent of the overall deal value, with smaller deals at the higher end of the range. In 2003, break-up fees, as a percent of transaction value, ranged from a high of 6.0 percent to a low of 0.3 percent, with a mean of 3.2 percent and a median of 3.2 percent. One significant break-up fee paid to a spurned buyer was $200 million, paid to First Bank System of Minneapolis; although seemingly large, this amount represented less than 2 percent of the overall deal. The Delaware Court of Chancery indicated that although the break-up fee was significantly large in the aggregate, it was not inappropriate with respect to the total value of the transaction.

4. Conditions

a. General. The parties' obligation to close the transaction is subject to certain conditions precedent which, absent a waiver, must be fulfilled before the party to whom the condition runs is obligated to close. Certain conditions are reciprocal, such as the requirement to obtain the necessary governmental or third party consents to the transaction. Other conditions encompass circumstances beyond the parties' control, such as the absence of an injunction against the transaction. In addition, there may be conditions that are specific to the seller, such as the absence of a material adverse change in the seller's business.

b. Material Adverse Effect/Change. The Delaware Court of Chancery, in a 2001 decision in the Tyson case, highlighted the importance of the careful drafting of a "material adverse effect" (MAE) or "material adverse change" (MAC) clause. Basing its decision on New York law (because the merger agreement was governed by New York law), the Court determined that the seller had not suffered a MAE and ordered the buyer's specific performance of the merger agreement. In its analysis of the MAE clause, the Court looked at the information available to the parties during and after closing. The Court paid particular attention to the buyer's access to information during its due diligence review and to any additional material disclosed in the schedules to the merger agreement. Despite a significant drop-off in earnings during the seller's first quarter, the Court found that, when examined in connection with the cyclical nature of the seller's business and its consistently fluctuating economic performance over time, the drop-off did not indicate a material change in the financial situation of the seller over a long period. In addition, rather than judging the buyer's dealings under the standard of a reasonable purchaser, the Court subdivided the reasonableness standard into that of an acquirer looking at the long-term prospects of the business and a short-term speculator. The Court reasoned that a short-term speculator may well consider a first-quarter drop-off in earnings as "material" while a long-term acquirer would need to look at the seller's earnings over a long period of time: "a MAC embraces a development that is consequential to a company's earning power over a commercially reasonable period, measured in years rather than months." The Court's analysis leaves the interpretation of a MAC clause dependent on the nature of the buyer. For example, the MAC clause in a highly leveraged transaction (which is dependent on financing) is more likely to be judged on a short-term basis.

A well-drafted MAE clause should provide exceptions to a MAE to account for unavoidable circumstances such as changes to general industry conditions or natural disasters. The parties in the case discussed above had not included such exceptions and though the Court determined that in that specific case it was not necessary, subsequent Delaware decisions have since held that if the parties desire that such exceptions apply they must be written into the agreement and will not be assumed by the court. The tense of the MAE is also important. The clause should be both immediate and prospective in nature. For example, a clause that outlines events that "have" a MAE would be more narrowly construed and include only those consequences that occur simultaneously with the happening of the MAE and have an immediate effect on the seller's business, such as the destruction of the seller's primary manufacturing plant. In contrast, a clause outlining events that are "reasonably likely to have" or "could" have a

MAE involves a more sweeping definition and might include an event that is more difficult to measure, such as the loss of a major supplier or employee.

There is no definitive test for determining whether a MAE has occurred. The "materiality" of an event is normally a question of fact. Case law provides no definitive standard for evaluating the concept of materiality. The Tyson case, though very specific in its application, emphasizes the importance of the parties paying greater attention to the drafting of the MAE clause. Proper language and the tailoring of the MAE clause to the nature of the business involved are critical.

c. Standards of compliance with conditions. Covenants may also include materiality qualifiers, requiring only that the condition be satisfied in all material respects. However, this will usually be inappropriate with respect to regulatory approvals.

d. Effect of failure of certain conditions. The failure to satisfy a condition will generally provide the non-breaching party with the option to terminate. However, the agreement may also permit the non-breaching party to seek damages for breach of the covenant not performed. Under certain circumstances (e.g. where a buyer ends a deal on MAC grounds) the non-terminating party may seek legal remedies against the terminating party for terminating the deal. Another potential consequence that a buyer terminating a deal must consider is that the target company's shareholders may commence an action against the buyer. Shareholders may seek to enforce the acquisition agreement, to recover damages based upon a theory of diminution in value of the target company's stock, or may make securities fraud claims alleging that the buyer failed to disclose that it was aware of material adverse information about the target at some point prior to its termination of the agreement or that buyer misrepresented its intention to close the transaction to the detriment of the target's shareholders. A review of case law in this area indicates that, absent exceptional circumstances, the Courts will generally deny shareholders' claims based on a lack of standing to sue or in the case of securities fraud claims, on the grounds that the buyer does not owe a duty to disclose information about the target to the target's shareholders. The Courts generally stress the importance of drafting a merger or acquisition agreement with precise language to make clear the intent of the parties. Most merger agreements contain explicit language providing that neither the agreement nor the transaction itself is intended to confer any rights or remedies on anyone who is not a "party" to the agreement. Current case law suggests that a court will deny shareholders the ability to sue the buyer directly where the agreement includes such language and, if other documents accompany the agreement, the agreement includes an integration clause, and nothing in the agreement suggests an intent to grant such rights to a third party. Despite the failure of the majority of such claims, their increasing frequency suggests that the buyer should be aware from the inception of a deal through post-closing of the risk of shareholder lawsuits not only in the drafting of the purchase agreement but in its internal statements and public disclosures, including e-mails, concerning the transaction.

e. Legal opinions. The scope of legal opinions is typically the subject of much negotiation.

(1) Purpose. The main purpose of a legal opinion is to force opposing counsel to perform the due diligence required to ensure that the transaction is handled properly. It is not a vehicle for making the opinion giver a guarantor of his client's representations.

(2) Who can rely on the opinion. The opinion giver will explicitly specify who is entitled to rely on the opinion. Typically, the opinion giver limits such reliance to only the opposing party. However, in certain instances the buyer's financing sources will also be entitled to rely on the opinion.

(3) Opinion giver. The opinion can be given by either inside or outside counsel. In most instances, the recipient of the opinion will prefer to receive an opinion from outside counsel as an independent party and a deeper pocket.

(4) Contents of opinion. The contents of a legal opinion are usually negotiated as part of the operative document. In most cases, the opinion will be limited to providing the opposing party with comfort that the objectives of the transaction have been accomplished. Typical portions of the opinion include the following:

(i) Incorporation and good standing. A basic component of most legal opinions is an opinion as to the due incorporation and valid existence of the opinion giver's corporate client. As a safeguard, the opinion giver should obtain and explicitly rely upon one or more certificates from state authorities attesting that the corporation is an existing corporation, in good standing and that all franchise tax returns have been filed to date.

(ii) Qualification. Opinion givers may be reluctant to opine that their corporate client and all of its subsidiaries are qualified to do business in every state in which such qualification is necessary, because businesses are often not in full compliance with these provisions. A frequent compromise is the use of a materiality qualification whereby the opinion giver states that his client is qualified in specific states and all other states wherein the failure to be qualified would have a material adverse effect on the seller.

(iii) Enforceable in accordance with its terms. Unless the only obligation under the agreement is a cash payment, many opinion givers are unwilling to give an unqualified opinion that such agreement is "enforceable in accordance with its terms" because of the uncertainty surrounding the meaning of the phrase. However, as a compromise, the opinion giver will make this opinion subject to creditors' rights and equitable principles. Care should be taken that the governing law clause of each of the operative agreements provides for the law of a state in which the opinion giver is qualified to opine.

(iv) Consents. The opinion giver will also be asked to give the opinion that no consents are required in order to consummate the transaction or that the required consents have been obtained.

(5) Transaction specific matters. It is typical for the opinion giver to opine that the transaction contemplated by the acquisition agreement will not result in any violation of law known to be applicable to their client or breach the certificate of incorporation or bylaws or any material agreement to which their client is a party.

(6) Factual matters. The party receiving the opinion will often ask the opinion giver to opine as to factual matters such as the existence of any breach of current agreements or the existence of any pending litigations. Most firms resist giving opinions involving such factual matters. For example, in order to opine as to the absence of breaches of existing agreements, the opinion giver would have to rely almost entirely on his client's representation that no breaches exist. Some firms will agree to provide such an opinion to the best of their knowledge. In such cases, they will typically limit the scope of the opinion to specified agreements and will exclude compliance with financial covenants. An opinion as to the absence of pending legal claims should specify, if true, that no search of court dockets was made. Otherwise, even if such opinion is qualified as being given to the best of the opinion giver's knowledge, an assumption can be drawn that a docket search was made.

(7) Multiple jurisdictions. In certain instances, opinions will be required as to matters that involve the laws of a number of different jurisdictions. Often, the principal counsel for the parties will not be an expert in the laws of each of these jurisdictions. This issue can be dealt with in various ways. The opinion giver can assume that the laws of each jurisdiction, other than the jurisdiction in which he is an expert, is identical to the laws of such counsel's jurisdiction or limit the scope of the opinion to the text of a particular statute, such as the corporate law of such state. In the alternative, the parties may retain local counsel in each jurisdiction for the purpose of giving an opinion. When making this decision, the parties weigh the sensitivity or importance of the issue requiring local counsel and the cost of retaining such counsel. Local counsel's opinion may be rendered directly to the opposing party or to the principal opinion giver, who in turn relies on such opinion in rendering its own opinion to the opposing party. Choosing the latter alternative ensures that the principal opinion giver is confident with the choice of local counsel.

5. Indemnification

a. General. The indemnification provisions are the principal mechanism in the purchase agreement for monetary risk shifting among the parties. The most common effect of the indemnification provisions is to provide the buyer with a remedy for any losses or expenses suffered in the event that the seller breaches the agreement or any of the representations or warranties. The indemnification may come in the form of a direct claim by the buyer against the seller for damages, or as a demand by the buyer to be indemnified from a third party claim regarding a matter for which the seller has assumed the risk.

(1) Who should be the indemnitors? One of the most hotly debated issues in an acquisition agreement, regardless of the form of the transaction, is whether the shareholders of the acquired company will be required to stand behind the seller's indemnification provisions. In the case of a sale of stock, if the shareholders do not agree to provide indemnification, there is no party available to provide the indemnity. If the seller is publicly held, its shareholders can provide indemnity in the form of a hold-back from the consideration paid by the buyer or some form of deferred or contingent consideration. Alternatively, if there are one or more principal shareholders of a publicly held company who are intimately familiar with the seller's business, they may be willing to provide indemnity, at least to a limited extent. The seller's shareholders often argue that the buyer has ample opportunity to perform a complete investigation of the seller's business through due diligence prior to the signing of the agreement. They also argue that they no longer wish to be subject to any potential liability relating to the business after the closing. That, in essence, is why they are selling the business. (The second argument is especially relevant to shareholders who are individuals.) The buyer typically argues that the due diligence process never uncovers all liabilities and that they are unwilling to assume all of the risks in the transaction. If the seller is an individual and the buyer is relatively comfortable with the potential risks, the buyer may compromise by not seeking the shareholders' indemnity in return for a reduction in the purchase price. However, if the seller has a parent company, the buyer will typically insist on indemnification by the parent entity.

(2) Scope of the indemnity.

(i) Substantive elements. The general indemnification provision will ensure that the buyer is made whole for breaches of the seller's representations and warranties or covenants. Typical examples include misrepresentations as to the value of inventory and the absence of undisclosed liabilities of the seller. The parties may also agree that the seller will continue to be liable with respect to certain specific liabilities, which will be stated separately from the general indemnification provision. For example, the seller may agree to remain liable for liability under specified ongoing litigation.

(ii) Fees and expenses. The indemnified party will be entitled to indemnification for fees and expenses incurred in the process of enforcing its indemnification claims. Such fees and expenses include attorneys' fees, accountants' fees and fees of experts. Expenses that are not recoverable by the buyer include consequential damages (unless the indemnification provision explicitly allows such recovery).

(iii) Third party claims. The indemnification provisions will also cover post-closing claims by third parties against the buyer. Examples of these include products liability litigation based on products sold by the seller prior to the closing, claims for unpaid taxes and environmental liabilities. The agreement will typically enable the indemnifying party to control the defense of the claim and require the indemnified party to cooperate in the defense of the claim (with appropriate reimbursement). In addition, the indemnifying party will be prohibited from settling a claim without the indemnified party's consent, unless the latter is released in full.

(3) Who may be indemnified? The indemnification provision typically covers the buyer, the seller and their respective directors, officers, employees, shareholders, affiliates and funding sources or other assignees.

(4) The amount of indemnification. The amount of indemnification is usually left for negotiation at the time the breach is discovered or ultimately to the courts. However, the parties are also free to agree in advance on liquidated damages in order to define the amount of indemnification. This is useful where the determination of damages is ambiguous. However, if the amount agreed upon is too high and is in effect a penalty, courts may not enforce such a provision.

b. Limitations on indemnification.

(1) The "basket." The seller will want to include a provision setting a minimum loss requirement beneath which the buyer will not be entitled to indemnification. Minimum loss provisions may take the form of a threshold or a deductible.

(i) Threshold. If a threshold is built into the indemnity, the buyer will be entitled to indemnification only if the damages exceed a specified amount, e.g., if the damages exceed 5 percent of the purchase price. Once the damages exceed this amount, the buyer recovers from the first dollar of the loss.

(ii) Deductible. If a deductible is built into the indemnity, the buyer will only be indemnified for losses that exceed the agreed specified minimum amount. The buyer therefore bears the loss up to that minimum amount.

(iii) Specific concerns. If the representations and warranties include materiality exceptions, the inclusion of a basket in the indemnity section can result in having an overprotected seller. Buyers may seek to side-step the basket by suing directly under the representations and warranties. To avoid this, seller should include a provision that provides that the sole remedy for breach of representations is through a claim for indemnification.

(2) Survival. Sellers generally impose time limitations on the survival period of representations and warranties, and indemnification rights. This refers to the period during which a claim for indemnification must be asserted. The survival period should be long enough to allow discovery of inherent problems in the acquired business. A typical survival period is about two years, however, certain representations are typically held open for longer. At a minimum, the buyer should seek survival until the first audited financial statements following the closing are available. Representations concerning taxes, ERISA and environmental compliance often extend until the expiration of the applicable statute of limitations. Representations on issues that go to the essence of the transaction such as capitalization, corporate organization and authority to enter into the transaction are often perpetual. If the agreement simply provides for the survival of representations and warranties, and indemnification rights, without any time limitation, the survival will be equal to the appropriate statute of limitations within which to bring any actions under the acquisition agreement.

(3) Caps on amount of indemnification. Sellers may try to limit their liability by including a specified amount beyond which the buyer will not be entitled to indemnification. This may apply only with respect to the seller's shareholders and may be agreed to in the context of negotiating whether the selling shareholder will stand behind the indemnity.

(4) Defense of actual knowledge of buyer before the closing. Seller may seek to include a provision prohibiting the buyer from recovering for the breach of a representation if the buyer had actual knowledge of such breach on or before the closing of the misrepresentation. This provision can make it more difficult for the buyer to obtain indemnification by imposing a burden on it to prove that it was not aware of such breach prior to the closing. Often the buyer will insist that the agreement affirmatively state that the indemnification provision will apply regardless of any investigations conducted on behalf of the buyer.

c. Arbitration clauses. A clause requiring arbitration can facilitate a speedy and inexpensive resolution of indemnification claims. Such clause should specify the method of selecting the arbitrator or arbitrators and the rules and jurisdiction for arbitrating. However, arbitration does have certain disadvantages. Often, the arbitrators are not lawyers and may have difficulty resolving complex legal issues. In addition, the discovery process in arbitration is limited. For the party who is likely to have to provide indemnification rather than receive it, litigation provides greater opportunities for delay which in turn benefit the payor. Another typical complaint about arbitration is that arbitrators tend to push the parties to compromise and settle on a middle ground.

CASE PROBLEM 15-2

Roger is preparing to purchase all of the stock of FlyNet Inc., a successful C corporation that is owned by five individuals. He knows that there are others in the wings, ready to make an offer for the stock. He needs to move fast, and he needs to be reasonable.

The term sheet for the deal sets the price of the stock at $18 million and lays out the other key terms. It also references one of Roger's real concerns with the deal – a potential dispute over a patented product ("the Patent") owned by FlyNet and developed by Walter Larson. The term sheet states that this concern "will be appropriately addressed to the mutual satisfaction of all parties in the definitive agreement between the parties."

FlyNet claims that Larson owns no financial interest in FlyNet, that it purchased the Patent from Larson for $250,000, and that it has documents to support these claims. Roger's preliminary due diligence has confirmed that Larson has a reputation as a trouble maker and has stated to others on various occasions that FlyNet "did a number on me when FlyNet stole my patent." Three weeks ago, in a drunken stupor, Larson called the CEO of FlyNet and ranted that he still owned the Patent because he was never given the 20,000 shares of FlyNet stock that he was promised.

Roger is concerned that a dispute with Larson could surface after the acquisition is closed and Larson discovers that each of the five stockholders of FlyNet walked with millions from the sale. If FlyNet's ownership of the Patent was lost, Roger would still have an interest in purchasing the stock of FlyNet, but the price would be no more than $15 million.

Describe how Roger's concerns with respect to the Patent may be addressed in drafting each of the following elements of the definitive stock purchase agreement between the parties: (1) the recitals; (2) the covenants; (3) the representations and warranties; (4) the conditions; (5) the indemnification provisions; and (6) the legal opinions provided by FlyNet's counsel. Which of these would be most effective from Roger's perspective? Should certain of these options be used in combination? What options will reduce an overkill risk that may incent the owners of FlyNet to reopen discussions with other interested buyers?

CHAPTER 16

EXECUTIVE COMPENSATION PLANNING

A. THE EVOLUTION OF EXECUTIVE COMPENSATION

U.S. Executive Compensation in Historical Perspective (Excerpts)
Professor Harwell Wells[1]

Before the twentieth century, there was no debate over executive compensation, for there were no executives, at least as we understand the term. The great majority of business enterprises were comparatively small, run by managers who had significant ownership stakes and whose economic rewards came chiefly through that ownership rather than a fixed salary or similar compensation. If a firm needed to recruit new managers from outside its circle of ownership, they were typically promised or given ownership interests upon recruitment or when ascending the ranks. While railroads, the largest corporate enterprises, developed a professional, salaried middle management in the nineteenth century, decisions at the top were most often made not by autonomous senior officers but by active boards of directors…

Executives – top managers whose compensation was not chiefly derived from an ownership stake – appeared with rapid economic changes that occurred at the beginning of the twentieth century. A "great merger movement" swept the industrial sector as almost 2000 small manufacturing firms combined into approximately 150 large corporations. Owners who had run the small manufacturers often wanted to cash out, and their successors were frequently experienced managers who neither owned a large part of the new firm, nor whose wealth was concentrated in it.

These new managers were compensated by salaries. Proprietary management began to give way to executive management. Few gave much thought to whether these new executives should be paid differently than any other employee. Before World War I, according to the only useful survey, senior executives at large industrial firms were compensated almost completely through fixed salaries. (Taussig & Barker 1925). The authors of the survey contrasted this

---

[1]. Harwell Wells is an Associate Professor of Law at the Temple University James E. Beasley School of Law. Citations have been omitted from these excerpts.

with European management systems where top executives' pay was incentive-based, often linked to company profits. They also noted that the average executive's annual salary at a large firm (defined as having capital above $1,500,000) was $9,958 (approximately $220,000 in 2010 dollars), a sum the study's authors deemed "modest." While a fair number of surveyed executives did have significant ownership in their firms, attesting to the slow transition from proprietary to executive management, some senior managers, even at the largest firms surveyed, owned no stock at all, meaning they were compensated solely through salary.

Even before World War I, however, a few prescient business leaders concluded that a fixed salary could never replicate the incentives provided by ownership.... As American Tobacco's James B. Duke put it, these new managers, no longer having a major ownership stake, still needed to believe that "they are part owners of the business and that their personal success and prosperity are measured by the success and prosperity they achieve for the company." To link the executive's "personal success and prosperity" to that of his firm, a number of large corporations, beginning in the 1910s with American Tobacco and U.S. Steel, adopted bonus systems for senior executives. These bonus plans typically paid the senior most managers a percentage of annual firm profits as well as a base salary.

The new plans, the first modern executive compensation systems, looked both backwards to older traditions of a "moral economy" that saw salaried work as servile and valorized the man who owned his own business, and forward to the twentieth century's concern with the separation of ownership and control in the modern corporation and search for ways to align managers' incentives with shareholders' interests.

The available evidence gives us only a rough sense of executive compensation during the 1920s because, before the mid-1930s, data on executive compensation was not gathered or publicly available. Compensation reporting was not mandated, and firms treated executives' compensation as proprietary information, unavailable even to shareholders. Legal checks on executive compensation at public corporations were also minimal, while directors were prohibited from setting their own compensation, they were free to fix officers' compensation, and so long as proper procedures were followed compensation agreements were generally upheld...

In the 1930s a series of government investigations and shareholder lawsuits thrust executives' pay into the spotlight and generated a wave of protest and reforms that would transform executive compensation. For the first time, executive compensation became a public issue.

The conflicts can be dated to 1930, when a fairly mundane lawsuit against Bethlehem Steel, challenging not pay levels but a proposed acquisition, revealed that Bethlehem president W. R. Grace had received over $1,600,000 as compensation in 1929, and that the steel firm had paid senior managers millions in bonuses during the late 1920s, even in years when it did not pay shareholders a dividend. (Wells 2010). Reports of Grace's "million dollar a year" income were front page news, astonishing observers and infuriating Bethlehem shareholders. It soon turned out that his pay was not unique.

Later that year a lawsuit against American Tobacco revealed that the firm's president, G. W. Hill, was scheduled to receive nearly $2 million compensation that year, mostly from stock and bonus plans, compensation again not disclosed to shareholders. The next few years saw similar disclosures at other firms, culminating at Congress's 1932-33 Pecora hearings into the securities industry, where it was revealed that National City Bank's Charles Mitchell, a man blamed for much of Wall Street's frenzy leading up to the crash of 1929, had taken home more than a million dollars a year in the late 1920s. These sums were not typical – most executives made far less – but they were taken by the public as representative. A million dollars a year soon became a byword for greed.

Executive compensation came before the courts when shareholders at several firms sued their boards of directors, alleging that the huge compensation packages awarded lacked a rational business purpose and so constituted "waste" under well established corporate law doctrine forbidding, in essence, giving away corporate assets.

Initially, the suits enjoyed some success. In 1933, the U.S. Supreme Court held, in Rogers v. Hill (a challenge to the American Tobacco payments), that compensation having "no relation to the value of services for which it is given" constituted waste. The Court did not, however, reach the question of whether Hill's pay package met this standard, instead remanding the case to the district court for that determination. While some at the time believed Rogers augured more vigorous judicial oversight of compensation, that promise proved false. Rogers settled before the district court could rehear it, and over the rest of the decade courts retreated from the case's activist implications back to their traditional deference to business judgments made by boards of directors. Indeed, despite Rogers and several other cases challenging executive compensation, no court ever found an executive pay package waste on account of its size.

With greater long-term effect, executive compensation also became an issue for Congress…The legislative fix for this was simply to limit salaries at recipients of government aid (at airlines receiving mail contracts, for instance, Congress capped executives' salaries at $17,500). Others in Congress were apparently outraged by the mere size of executives' pay packages, regardless of how earned, leading to unsuccessful proposals to cap pay through confiscatory marginal tax rates.

The most popular and effective response, however, turned on disclosure…The collapse of securities markets following the 1929 Crash, and the perception that the Crash occurred in part because of widespread deception in securities offerings and trading, created further support for disclosure-based reforms. Compensation reform was swept up into the national push for greater disclosure, and found its way into the new Securities Acts of 1933 and the Securities Exchange Act of 1934. Both Acts mandated disclosure of senior officers' pay, the 1934 Act's requirements being most consequential.

World War II marked the beginning of a new era of executive

compensation, one that would stretch into the 1970s. This pay regime was characterized by slower growth in compensation packages and even intermittent declines in executive compensation. During much of this period, executives' compensation would grow at a slower pace than that of the average worker...

The composition of executive compensation changed from the 1940s to the 1970s, often in response to changes in tax policy. Marginal tax rates had risen as the war drew near, and remained high afterwards. From war's end to the late 1950s, the marginal tax rate for incomes over $100,000 hovered around 90%, and into the 1970s the marginal rate for incomes over $200,000 was 70%, developments that encouraged forms of compensation that would not be characterized as ordinary income. The postwar period, for example, saw the continued popularity of health and life insurance and retirement plans, benefits not generally counted as taxable income.

High marginal tax rates made popular a new kind of compensation, stock options. While stock options were occasionally offered at firms in the 1930s, they were uncommon.

By 1960, a majority of firms listed on the New York Stock Exchange offered stock options plans. While stock options were popular, however, they were not exorbitant, and appeared more as a supplement to traditional salaries than a substitute for them.

Executive compensation remained a minor issue through the 1960s and early 1970s, perhaps because social changes of the time overshadowed it, or because of its slow growth. This lag in growth was not a secret; while the general public seemed to believe that executives' pay was rapidly growing, and a few scholars agreed, more careful observers recognized that it had stagnated for decades, with a few even concluding, wrongly, that average executives' compensation had shrunk since the end of the war...Pay patterns would change quickly, however, in the 1970s, making executive compensation again a national issue.

Executive compensation began growing at a faster rate in the mid-1970s, starting in roughly 1973. The general trend is well known. The average CEO was paid approximately 24 times more than an average worker in 1965, 35 times the more in 1979, 71 times more in 1989, and 299 times more than an average worker's pay at the end of the century. While executive compensation dipped some after the bursting of the Internet bubble in 2000 and the financial crisis of 2008-09, the trend of accelerating growth of executive compensation does not appear to have stopped. And even as executive pay rose, the income of the average American worker began to stagnate, another development which often lay behind popular discontent with executive compensation.

Rising executive compensation drew new scrutiny by the early 1980s. This scrutiny had a different tone than in the past, for the new growth in executive compensation coincided with broader economic problems. After nearly thirty relatively flush years, a series of shocks that commenced with the appearance of "stagflation" (high inflation and low growth) in the early 1970s, and was followed by the Arab oil embargo of 1973-74, an ongoing decline in industrial productivity, and foreign challenges to American industry, led many to conclude that the American economy, and American industry, were in serious trouble. Well-publicized corporate scandals, especially the collapse of the Penn Central Railroad and the discovery of widespread illegal corporate donations in the wake of Watergate, further emphasized shortcomings in corporate governance and created doubts about the competence and integrity of CEOs and Boards of Directors. Issues of executive compensation were often folded into these larger developments.

As executive pay rose, so did public criticism. Some hostility surely stemmed from executive pay's new visibility, which may have begun when CEO pay packages crossed the million-dollar-a-year threshold in the late 1970s, an important psychological barrier for several decades. The main source of discontent, though, was a growing impression that executives were taking home large compensation packages while their workers suffered .

Academic attention also returned to executive compensation in the 1980s, for obvious reasons: the desire to explain the rise in compensation, and the apparent disconnect between high compensation and poor corporate performance... Unlike popular criticism, which often targeted the high level of compensation, the new academic work focused on the structure of compensation, and argued that compensation's problem (to the extent there was one) was it was poorly designed. Compensation should be structured, economists and legal scholars claimed, to incentivize senior executives to pursue strategies that would most benefit shareholders.

Executive compensation both grew and changed during the 1980s. It was, clearly, higher than it had been a decade before. During the 1970s, median CEO compensation, in a sample of large publicly traded firms, was approximately $1.17 million; during the 1980s, $1.81 million; during the 1990s, $4.09 million (all in 2000 dollars).. By 1990, CEO pay had returned to (inflation-adjusted) levels not seen since the 1930s. The composition of pay packages was also evolving, as a larger share of compensation was linked to short- and long-term shareholder value.

In the early 1990s popular discontent with executive pay boiled over. In the 1992 presidential campaign, Bill Clinton targeted executive compensation in his stump speeches, and Time magazine called executive pay "the populist issue no politician can resist."

In response to populist pressures, in 1992 both Congress and the SEC adopted new measures to rein in and refocus executive compensation. Congress altered the tax rules concerning compensation, adding §162(m) to the Tax Code to prevent public corporations from deducting compensation in excess of $1,000,000 paid to the firm's top executives unless the compensation was both "performance-based," defined as linked to performance goals determined by a compensation committee composed solely of independent directors, and part of a plan approved in a separate shareholder vote. The SEC adopted new disclosure requirements mandating more detailed disclosure of policies used in setting compensation as well as tabular reporting of senior executive compensation…The SEC also modified rules concerning shareholder proposals, allowing shareholders to include nonbinding proposals criticizing pay practices in corporate proxies. These measures did not aim directly to reduce executive pay; rather, they embraced a "pay-for-performance" approach that accepted high compensation so long as it was both incentive-based and disclosed to shareholders. In effect, the shareholder value vision of executive compensation had won out; high compensation was fine, the new measures implied, so long as it was disclosed to shareholders and designed to increase shareholder wealth. While popular discontent surely reflected a lingering belief that no one deserved to earn as much as some executives did, proposals aimed simply at pushing high pay down by, for instance, imposing punitive taxation on firms that paid CEOs above some multiple of the average worker's wage were rejected in Congress.

Whether these reforms can be said to have succeeded depends on what their goal was. They did little to stall overall growth of executive compensation. While exact measures varied, executive compensation, as discussed above, continued its growth during the 1990s, in both absolute terms and relative to ordinary workers' wages.

Despite their popularity, it is not clear whether the new pay-for-performance arrangements actually tied executive pay more closely to firm performance. Options grants in particular were promoted as a way to link executive compensation to shareholder value. Several features of the new options grants, however, led critics to claim they were not as sensitive to firm performance as promised, and were open to manipulation.

While changes in the tax code, and the new SEC disclosure requirements, may have had marginal effect on executive compensation, other legal attempts to curb executive pay largely failed. Shareholder litigation proved of little use in changing broader pay trends. For the most part, courts asked to second-guess a Board's compensation decision continued to adhere to the business judgment rule, declining to become entangled in compensation disputes so long as proper procedures were followed and blatant self-dealing avoided. At the end of the 1990s, it briefly appeared that this might change through the Disney litigation. Disney had paid Michael Ovitz $140 million when he left the firm after serving as president for less than a year, and shareholders sued the board, arguing that in both his hiring and firing Disney board members had violated their fiduciary duties and committed waste. Early on in the protracted litigation, plaintiffs received some encouragement from Delaware courts hearing the case; the Delaware Supreme Court, for instance, warned that the "sheer size" of the payment to Ovitz "pushes the envelope of judicial respect for the business judgment of directors in making compensation decisions." In 2005, however, the Delaware courts declined to find Disney's board liable for Ovitz's payments, holding that, while procedures may have been sloppy, the board did not violate its fiduciary duties or commit waste. Disney seemed the death-knell to hopes that courts would impose substantive limits on executive compensation, no matter how high it rose.

The Internet bubble burst in 2000, leading to a sharp drop in CEO pay in 2001-03, as stock prices plunged far below many options' strike price. The bubble's bursting, followed a year later by the collapse of Enron and other major American corporations, led to speculation that this marked a change in America's regulation of corporations and thus executive compensation. But it was not to be. Executive pay resumed its rise in 2003, and continued on an upward slope until the financial crisis of 2008-09. The Sarbanes-Oxley Act of 2002, passed in Enron's wake, made significant changes in aspects of corporate governance but only tweaked executive compensation practices... Public anger and disgust with executive pay remained, but was ineffectual.

New proposals to curb executive pay arose, particularly campaigns by academics and activist institutional investors to implement "Say-on-Pay" advisory shareholder votes, but they did not enjoy significant success before the 2008-09 crisis. The options backdating scandals of 2006, during which journalists revealed that a large number of companies had backdated options grants to executives and other senior employees, created a momentary firestorm but did not result in broad-gauged compensation reform. Only two developments held out any promise for real change: the adoption by the Securities and Exchange Commission, in 2006, of new and expanded compensation reporting requirements, including a mandatory "Compensation Disclosure and Analysis," (CD&A) and the change to accounting rules in 2004 that required firms to expense stock options grants to employees. This last development led some firms to move from options to restricted stock. Whether more fundamental reforms will follow the financial crisis of 2008-09 and the Dodd-Frank "Wall Street Reform and Consumer Protection Act," remains to be seen.

B. THE EXECUTIVE EMPLOYMENT AGREEMENT

1. COMMON MYTHS

The use of carefully crafted employment agreements in large organizations is forever expanding down to deeper levels to hedge against the risk of expensive litigation and the loss or dilution of valued proprietary rights. Many closely held businesses still resist the need to get things in writing with those who can do the most damage. The owners cling to the old notion that a piece of paper can't make a bad employee good or a good one better. So why bother?

Usually the reluctance to come of age on this one is a result of inertia and ignorance. A program of using smart agreements with key employees takes real effort. Since many closely held businesses do not have a separate human resources person (much less a department), the burden of the effort falls on the chief executive officer or some other high-ranking officer who already has a more-than-full plate. Add to this a few common myths that question the whole value of the effort and it's easy to let this "priority" drop to the bottom of the stack. Following are a few of the myths that often get in the way.

Myth 1: Advantage Employee. The myth is that the document produces more for the employee, less for the company. Why else would only a privileged few in the company have their own agreement? The truth is that nearly all of the key provisions in an executive employment agreement primarily benefit the company in a big way. Such provisions include termination rights, confidentiality covenants, post-employment competition restrictions, intellectual property protections, work effort requirements, dispute resolution procedures, choice of law designations and more. Even the compensation provisions benefit the company by spelling out the limits and defining expectations.

Myth 2: A Front-End Downer. The myth is that it's counterproductive to get tangled up in legal minutiae during the courting phase with a new key executive. The focus should be on positive business challenges and synergies, not potential problems that may never surface between the company and its newest arrival. The myth ignores a basic truth – nearly all prospective employees long for the details of the whole deal. Showing that the key issues have been fairly thought through and incorporated into a document tailored for the new executive will not be viewed as a negative or an unjustified preoccupation with the dark side of business relationships. If done right, it will confirm that the company has its act together, values relationships based on detailed mutual understandings, and regards the prospective employee as a valuable part of the management team. It can actually be an "upper" that removes uncertainties and facilitates a more complete understanding of the objectives and priorities of both parties. And if an insurmountable conflict surfaces during the process, all will benefit from its early detection.

Myth 3: It's Easier After the Honeymoon. The myth is that the details of the employment relationship with a key employee are easier to hash out after the employee has been on board for a while. Everyone knows more; expectations are clearer. It's wrong. The problem is that the job won't get done. Once the employee is in the saddle, what interest will the employee have in dealing with post-employment noncompetition restrictions, broad employer termination rights, dispute resolution procedures and the like? In most situations, the company will be left with two lousy options to push the agenda along. It can get tough and demand its agreement, which may undermine morale, mutual respect, and all the other intangibles that strengthen individual business relationships; or it can offer something more, which can get expensive. Far and away the best time to work out the details and document the deal is just before the starting gun when both parties are anxious to find common ground and move forward.

Myth 4: Money Vagueness Works. The myth is that it's always smarter to not spell out the details of incentive compensation in an employment agreement. Far too often the matter is settled with a salary and some vague bonus discussions that create expectations of more money but do nothing to perpetuate individual performance objectives. The difference between real success and baseline mediocrity in many businesses is the ability and drive of the key employees who are charged with making it happen. The ability factor is tied directly to the executive's focus on specific targets of success. The drive factor is a function of how badly the executive wants to be better than good. Smart incentive compensation can keep the fire hot under both factors. Here are the key factors to consider.

- **Understandable.** The executive must be able to understand all specifics of the incentive. It can't be too complicated or tied to factors that are foreign to the executive.

- **Measurable.** The incentive should be objectively measurable. It should not be based totally on someone's discretion or will, although some subjectivity may be factored into the process. For example, the incentive for an accounts receivable manager may be a percentage of salary based on the percentage of accounts collected within 90 days (e.g., a 7 percent bonus for an 85 percent collection rate, a 10 percent bonus for a 90 percent collection rate, etc.). The plan also may give the company's CEO the discretion to increase any earned bonus by up to an additional 50 percent if the employee turnover rate in the accounts receivable department in a given year is less than 75 percent of the company's average. Such a bonus plan would be measurable and keep the manager focused on two critical success elements – collection percentages and employee turnover.

- **True Incentive.** The incentive must be large enough to matter. If the amount at stake is insignificant, the employee may pay lip service to the objectives without ever believing that there are serious concerns that warrant additional effort and commitment.

- **Calculation Factors.** The factors that affect the calculation of the bonus should be within the control of the executive. For the CEO and CFO, it may be the overall performance of the company. But there is usually a need for more specificity down the executive ladder. For the vice president of sales, it may be the volume from new customers. For a production VP, it may be the average employee cost for each unit produced. The key is to identify specific success factors that will result in the company becoming stronger as the executive makes more. It is the classic win-win.

- **Visible Time Monitors.** Techniques that enable the company and its executives to track and monitor progress on a regular basis, at least once a month, are vital. This need for regular monitoring may require some special periodic accounting reports or some custom adjustments to the company's computer information system, but the benefits usually easily justify any added up-front effort or expense.

2. Key Elements of the Agreement

Ten Essential Considerations for
Any Employment Agreement[2]
Theodora Lee, Lisa Chagala
Littler Mendelson, P.C.

As employment agreements become increasingly common, company counsel and human resources professionals must be alert to the specific terms of every employment contract. Failure to consider each and every term and how it will affect the employment relationship of each and every applicant and employee may have disastrous consequences. Thus, whether or not the agreement is a highly-tailored, long-negotiated agreement for an executive, or a

---

2. Copyright © 2004 Practicing Law Institute and the authors. Reprinted here with the permission of the Practicing Law Institute and the authors. Ms. Lee is a partner in Littler, Mendelson, P.C.; Ms. Chagala is an associate in the firm.

standardized contract used for a rank-and-file employee, several key considerations apply. The following provides an overview of certain considerations; however, given the complexity of the subject matter, consultation with an experienced employment attorney is highly recommended.

1. Defining the Term of Employment

The determination of the employment term is essentially a question of management objective. Does management wish to have maximum flexibility to terminate the employment relationship at any time without notice? Or, does management wish to create a contractual incentive to encourage an employee to remain in employment for a certain period of time? There are essentially three types of employment provisions that may be applied to achieve these management objectives. These provisions are commonly referred to as "at-will," "drop dead," and "evergreen" clauses.

In an at-will employment relationship, either party may terminate the employment relationship at any time. The primary advantage of an at-will employment relationship is flexibility. The main disadvantage of the at-will employment relationship is that there is no incentive, in the form of a "stick," for the employee to remain employed for any period of time. Some employers choose to combine an at-will provision with a notice period. This provides the employer – and the employee – a minimum time period to make alternative arrangements in light of the upcoming termination.

A "drop dead" clause is a provision that provides that the employment relationship will end upon a particular date. The advantage of this approach is that it provides a specific end to the employment relationship. The main disadvantage of this approach is that the employer will be bound to employing the individual through the specified date. This may be costly for the employer if, for example, technologies change or it is later discovered that the individual does not possess the necessary skills for the job. To address the chance that the employment relationship will continue beyond the specified date, employers may combine a "drop dead" provision with an at-will provision, providing that the employment relationship will continue for a specific period of time (until the "drop dead" date) and thereafter will be at-will.

An "evergreen" provision is a clause that states that the employment relationship will continue for a certain period of time and then automatically renew for successive periods unless either party gives notice of intent to terminate within a certain timeframe. This has the advantage of permitting the contract to continue indefinitely, such that the incentive to remain in the employment relationship continues indefinitely. However, the automatic renewal may become more of a hindrance than help. As years pass, the employer may forget to provide notice of termination within the required timeframe.

Regardless of what employment term the employer chooses, the duration of the contractual employment relationship should be defined within the contract. Even if employment is for a stated period, it should be clear that employment may be terminated for cause at any time and cause should be defined. If a "drop dead" or "evergreen" provision is used, the employer should include a provision that allows the employer to terminate the employment relationship "for cause" without penalty.   Cause is normally defined within the contract and varies, including extreme levels of dishonesty and nonperformance on the part of the employee.   The employer will, in most cases, want the contract to survive termination of the employment relationship, to ensure that contractual protections relating to intellectual property and arbitration, for example, are effective beyond the end of the term of the employment relationship.

2. Compensation

Traditionally, employment contracts set forth the terms of compensation for the individual, including the amount of base salary the individual is entitled to receive, when pay raises would occur, and what formula would apply to calculation of incentive compensation.   Employers traditionally set forth each aspect of the total rewards structure, including base salary, future salary increases, incentive compensation arrangements such as bonus programs, commissions, and stock options, and benefits programs such as medical, retirement, and stock purchase programs.

3. Arbitration

An arbitration clause is a provision that secures an employee's consent to binding arbitration as a means of resolving disputes between the employee and the employer.   Such clauses can be especially valuable in disputes over termination of employment, which often trigger large claims for damages.   The value of arbitration clauses in the employment context have been debated among legal professionals and human resources professionals (and within the popular press) for years.   Most employers have determined resolution of disputes through arbitration offer several advantages.   Arbitration can be significantly less costly than resolving a dispute through the court.   Disputes are often resolved much faster through arbitration than through the courts.   Disputes resolved through arbitration are significantly more private than those resolved through the courts.   Additionally, the outcome of the case may be more predictable with the use of an arbitrator than a jury.   On the other hand, employers have also experienced several disadvantages in arbitration.   Some employers experience an increased number of disputes, due to the reduced cost to an employee of bringing a claim.   Judicial review (through appeal or otherwise) is extremely limited, leaving little wiggle room in the event of a disappointing arbitration result.   Furthermore, arbitration may have negative employee relations consequences, as employees may believe (perhaps incorrectly) that arbitration erodes their substantive rights.   These advantages and disadvantages must be weighed before deciding whether or not to implement a mandatory arbitration policy.

4. Protections of Intellectual Property

In today's increasingly competitive marketplace, employers must protect and preserve the key assets that are essential to competitive advantage.   Often, these assets are in the form of intellectual property.   Employers are willing to take great efforts to preserve confidential information and intellectual property from walking out the door (and to a competitor) with a terminated employee. Employment agreements are simply one factor within a program for protecting intellectual property. Normally, such program includes informing employees and others on an ongoing basis of confidentiality requirements and adopting company-wide policies for trade secret protection. Without a comprehensive, company-wide policy, it is not likely that any clause within any employment agreement will be effective.

One means of protecting valuable intellectual property is with a covenant not to compete. Such covenants restrict the activities of an employee after the employee stops working for the employer. Because non-compete covenants are post-employment restrictions on an employee's ability to earn a living, they are viewed in most states with disfavor and are narrowly construed. Generally, courts view covenants not to compete as enforceable only to the extent they are necessary to protect the employer's interest in its goodwill, confidential information, and customer relationships. Covenants not to compete must be narrowly tailored as to the time, geographic scope, and prohibited activity necessary to protect a legitimate employer interest. Defining what activity is prohibited is critical. Typically, the covenant will prevent persons from working for a competitor for a specific period of time in specific locations, may even name the competitors to which the clause applies, and specifies the particular work that is prohibited.

State law considerations cannot be ignored. States impose varying standards to determine whether or not covenants not to compete are enforceable, and some states altogether do not permit covenants not to compete. California is famous (or infamous) in this regard. An employer who uses a non-compete clause in California not only risks having the clause declared unenforceable, but also risks being found to have committed an unlawful business practice by including the clause in its agreements. For this reason, state law must be carefully analyzed before placing such a covenant into an employment agreement.

Non-disclosure covenants are clauses that preclude the employee from disclosing or making use of the employer's confidential information. Whether or not such provision is enforceable is a matter of state law. Generally, in order to be enforceable, such provision must be properly restricted as to time and territory and the employer must have a strong proprietary interest in protecting trade secrets. Again, analysis of state law is essential for ensuring that such a clause is enforceable and that the employer does not act unlawfully in requesting that the applicant or employee enter into such a covenant.

5. Work Effort

A provision regarding "work effort" generally states that the employee shall apply his or her best efforts at all times. The provision may also state that the employee must devote his or her entire work time and effort to the employer and will not engage in other gainful employment during the term of employment with the employer. This type of provision has certain advantages that are appealing to any employer. Restrictions on the employee's time avoids scheduling conflicts and prevents situations where transfer of intellectual property may occur. However, important legal considerations exist for such provisions. Many jurisdictions prohibit certain restrictions on an individual's personal time. For these reasons, "work effort" provisions must be carefully drafted. A blanket prohibition on moonlighting may be replaced with a requirement that employees must avoid actual or potential conflicts of interest, or the appearance of conflicts of interest, as well as outside activities that would interfere with the employee's loyalty to the employer and ability to fulfill all job responsibilities.

6. Prior Commitments

A "prior commitments" clause is a clause that requires the employee (or applicant) to certify that he or she is not subject to any contractual commitments (such as employment agreement with former employers) that conflict with the obligations to the new employer. Such clause is important for two reasons. As a practical matter, an employer will want to know if it will only receive the benefit of part of the employee's knowledge.

7. Choice of Law Provision

A "choice of law" provision is a clause within an agreement that indicates what state law will apply in the event of a dispute. The choice of law provision is particularly important in the arena of the employment relationship. Many aspects of the employment relationship are governed by state law. Choice of law provisions are presumptively valid in most jurisdictions. However, a choice of law provision may be overcome if, for example, the jurisdiction does not have a reasonable relationship to the circumstances of the employment relationship. Choice of law provisions may also be overcome if they pose a hardship that effectively eliminates an individual's substantive rights. A provision that effectively precludes an individual from having his or her day in court (for example, requiring a disabled or financially-strapped individual to travel cross-country for litigation) will not likely be enforced. Furthermore, statutory protections (such as state wage and hour or anti-discrimination laws) may set forth specific provisions for extra-territorial reach and, thus, cannot be overcome with a contractual choice of law provision.

8. Integration and Amendment

An integration clause states that the terms of the contract constitute the complete and exclusive statement of the terms of the agreement, and that no other agreements, oral, written, or otherwise, which are not stated in the agreement will be valid. The integration clause is particularly important in the employment setting.

The provision for amendment of the agreement is similarly important. The provision for amendment specifies how the agreement may be amended. Such provision is important in the event that the employee claims that the agreement was modified after execution.

9. Liquidated Damages

A "liquidated damages" provision states an amount of money the employee will have to pay if he or she breaches the contract. Liquidated damages provisions will be enforceable only if the actual damages would be extremely difficult to ascertain. Additionally, the amount of the liquidated damages must be "reasonable." Determining whether to include a liquidated damages provision is not an exact science and is, thus, a matter of balance and judgment. With little or no potential for damages, the employee will have little incentive to comply with the terms of the agreement. For example, an employee considering termination before the end of the employment relationship will balance the cost of the breach of the employment agreement with the value he or she will receive by going to work for the new employer. Similarly, an employee considering improper use of an employer's confidential information will weigh the costs of violating the contract with the value he or she will receive from exploiting that confidential information.

10. Execution and Document Retention Strategies

After all the effort in drafting the agreement, the final steps are most crucial: making sure the agreement is executed and retained. Retention and accessibility of the executed employment agreement is key. Steps must be taken to ensure that executed employment agreements make their way from supervisors' desks and file drawers to the company's formal document retention system.

CASE PROBLEM 16-1

Larry Smyth is the primary owner and CEO of a growing computer hardware distribution company. The company has 120 employees, which includes 10 managers. Larry feels that there is a compelling need to boost employee morale. He believes the problem is at the top. Seven of his 10 managers are "just logging time." Most employees are paid by the hour. The managers are all salaried. The company has sporadically paid bonuses in the past, but bonuses are not something any employee expects.

Larry has decided to adopt a cash bonus program for his 10 managers, in hopes that the plan will fire up the managers to get the place hopping. He has decided to divide 25 percent of the pre-tax income of the business among the 10 managers in equal shares each year. The bonuses will be paid within two weeks of the completion of the year-end financials.

Larry has asked you to draft a bonus plan document that can be reviewed and approved by the other two shareholders (both of whom serve on the Board) and the managers. He has also asked you to share your thoughts on his plan. What do you think of Larry's plan? Why might it be a waste of money? How might it backfire and create bigger morale problems? Is it oversimplified? What are the components of an effective cash bonus plan that Larry should consider? Is this something that a lawyer should even be concerned about? Why do you think Larry would ask your opinion?

CASE PROBLEM 16-2

Duke Longer, the CEO of Waldon Technologies, has just completed a negotiation to hire Jane Smith, a talented software designer. Jane will relocate from Boston to San Diego. Jane's salary will be high by Waldon's standards. Duke wants to ensure that Jane is "tied to the company for at least three years" but that the company "can get out of the deal after three years." Duke also wants to ensure that everything that Jane creates while working for the company will remain the exclusive property of the company.

Jane wants assurance that her high salary will be protected for the long-term. Her move from her hometown of Boston and her family is viewed as a sacrifice that is justified only by the promise of "big bucks" for the long-term. Plus, Jane routinely creates software on her off hours that has nothing to do with her job. She wants to make it clear that she will own all rights to such off-hour creations.

What middle-ground solutions should the attorneys for Waldon and Jane explore in putting together the employment agreement?

C. DEFERRED COMPENSATION: SERPs

1. THE RETIREMENT CHALLENGE

Many executives rank retirement planning as their number one financial concern. They want to know that they are going to "have enough" and are not going to outlive their financial resources. For many executives, the solution is a special supplemental executive retirement plan (SERP) provided by their employer. The company's regular qualified retirement plan is too watered down to do the job. An old-fashioned savings program is too tough, and social security, even if available, is hopelessly inadequate.

For decades companies have recognized the value of individually-tailored retirement arrangements for their key executives. These arrangements are routinely used to recruit and retain valuable executives. The substantial benefits that accrue under the plan over time create a powerful incentive for the executive to toe the line and not even consider flirting with the competition.

A key factor in many SERPs is life insurance. Often, it is the life insurance that breathes life into the SERP, hedges the financial risks for the company, and makes the whole effort "doable." The question is often asked: Why life insurance as opposed to some other investment? The answer lies in the three "tax-frees" of life insurance: the tax-free death benefit, the tax-free inside buildup within the policy, and the tax-free loan withdrawal privileges.

2. A SERP EXAMPLE

Peter is 55 years of age. He is the chief executive officer of a growing manufacturing company and has served in that capacity for five years. The company is privately owned, and Peter has no hope of ever receiving any equity. The stockholders consider Peter indispensable to the ongoing success of the company and want to ensure that he remains in his position for at least another 10 years. They want to bind him to the business. Peter is concerned about his retirement needs and has voiced that concern to the owners.

A deal has been worked out to provide Peter a special supplemental retirement benefit that will commence on his retirement at age 65. The benefit, equal to 70 percent of Peter's highest average salary during any remaining three-year period of his employment with the company, will be paid monthly so long as Peter or his wife is living. Peter estimates that the annual benefit should be at least $250,000 if he continues to receive salary increases as he has in the past. Absent death or disability, Peter must remain with the company to age 65 in order to receive the benefit. If he dies or becomes disabled before age 65, the benefit will commence on the second month following his death or permanent disability.

The plan accomplishes the objectives of both parties. The company and its owners are assured of Peter's continued service and loyalty, and Peter's retirement concerns are put to rest. Following are brief reviews of the tax traps, structural options, collateral consequences, and funding alternatives that often need to be considered in the planning process for such a plan.

3. SERP TAX TRAPS

The plan for Peter is based on the premise that no income taxes will need to be paid on any SERP benefits accrued under the plan until the benefits are actually paid to Peter or his wife. As a deferred compensation plan, a SERP is subject to the tax traps that need to be carefully watched whenever income is deferred.

a. The Constructive Receipt Trap

The first tax trap is the constructive receipt doctrine. Income is taxable in the year in which it is "received by the taxpayer."[3] If the constructive receipt doctrine applies to a SERP, the executive will be in the unfavorable position of having to pay taxes on money that he or she has not received. The mere deferral of the actual receipt of income will not guarantee deferral for tax purposes because the phrase "received by the taxpayer" encompasses "constructive receipt" as well as actual receipt of income.[4] Income is constructively received by a taxpayer when it is "credited to his account, set apart for him, or otherwise made available so that he may draw upon it at any time, or so that he could have drawn upon it during the taxable year if notice of intention to withdraw had been given."[5]

The constructive receipt trap can be an issue in those situations (unlike Peter's) where an executive elects to defer the receipt of compensation in order to fund a SERP benefit. The key is such situations is to ensure that the executive makes the election to defer the income before the services are rendered and the compensation is earned.[6] The constructive receipt doctrine may also become a problem if the executive at any point in time is given the unrestricted right to draw money out of the plan.[7]

b. The Economic Benefit Trap

The second trap is the economic benefit doctrine. Even if the employee is not deemed to have constructively received the income, the employee's

---

3. I.R.C. § 451(a).
4. Reg. § 1.451-1(a).
5. Reg. § 1.451-2(a).
6. Rev. Proc. 71-19, 1971-1 C.B. 698, amplified Rev. Proc. 92-65, 1992 C.B. 428; I.R.C. 409A(a)(4)(B)(i).
7. Reg. § 1.451-2(a). See Martin v. Commissioner, 96 T.C. 814 (1991) for a discussion of the facts that impact such an application of the constructive receipt doctrine.

opportunity to defer taxation may be derailed if he or she receives an economic benefit from the deferred amount that is the equivalent of cash.[8]

The doctrine usually surfaces when the employer's obligation to pay the deferred compensation is somehow "funded" and the employee acquires an interest in the funding vehicle. Examples include an escrow account for the executive, a trust vehicle to fund benefits for an executive,[9] an annuity contract naming the executive as an owner,[10] and a life insurance policy that guarantees the executive the cash value of the policy in the event of employment termination.[11]

In structuring any deferred compensation arrangement, the planner needs to keep both the constructive receipt doctrine and the economic benefit doctrine in mind. The economic benefit doctrine is clearly the more nebulous of the two and the one that often causes the greatest concern. A red flag should go up whenever an employee (1) receives a substantial economic or financial benefit from a non-qualified funding vehicle, particularly if the benefit is not forfeitable; (2) has the ability to assign his or her rights under that funding vehicle to an outside third party; or (3) has any other right or capacity to convert his or her rights under the funding vehicle to cash.

c. The Section 83 Trap

The third trap is found in Section 83 of the Internal Revenue Code. It's similar to the economic benefit trap. Section 83 provides that, when property is transferred to an employee as compensation for services, the employee is taxed on the fair market value of the property at the time it is received if the property is transferable or is not subject to a substantial risk of forfeiture.[12] If the property is subject to a substantial risk of forfeiture, as is the case when the employee's rights to the property are contingent upon the employee remaining in the service of the employer, no tax will be incurred until that risk of forfeiture lapses or the property becomes transferable.

As regards a deferred compensation plan such as a SERP, the positive news is that the regulations under Section 83 provide that an unsecured and unfunded promise of an employer to pay deferred compensation does not constitute "property" for purposes of Section 83.[13] If the participant receives nothing more than the unsecured contractual promise of the company, there is no Section 83 problem. In all other cases where the participant is offered something extra, it is necessary to take a hard look to see whether Section 83 has been triggered. Plus, as described below, section 409A has now breathed new life into Section 83 when an offshore funding vehicle or an employer financial health trigger is used

---

8. Rev. Rule 60-31, 1960-1 C.B. 174 (Example 4); Sproull v. Commissioner, 16 T.C. 244 (1951), affirmed per curiam 194 F.2d 541 (6th Cir. 1952); Rev. Rule 62-74, 1962-1 C.B. 68; Commissioner v. Smith, 324 U.S. 177 (1945).

9. Sproull v. Commissioner, 16 T.C. 244 (1951), affirmed per curiam 194 F.2d 541 (6th Cir. 1952); Jacuzzi v. Commissioner, 61 T.C. 262 (1973).

10. Brodie v. Commissioner, 1 T.C. 275 (1942).

11. See, for example, Frost v. Commissioner, 52 T.C. 89 (1969).

12. I.R.C. § 83(a).

13. Reg. § 1.83-3(e).

in connection with a nonqualified deferred compensation arrangement.[14] If Section 83 applies and the deferred amounts are not subject to a substantial risk of forfeiture, the employee will be hit with a current tax.

d. The Reasonable Compensation Trap

The fourth trap is the old "reasonable compensation" requirement of Section 162. This trap focuses on the tax treatment to the company, not the participant. The company wants to secure a deduction when the deferred compensation is paid to the employee. If the compensation is being paid to a shareholder/employee and is determined to be excessive within the meaning of Section 162, the company will lose its deduction.[15] The result is a double tax. Reasonableness is based on the facts and circumstances that exist at the time the contract is made, not those that exist when the contract is called into question.[16] For planning purposes, the challenge in any potentially troublesome situation is to carefully document the facts and circumstances that support a "reasonableness" determination at the time the plan is adopted by the company so that, if required, a sound case can be made at a later date.

e. The 409A Traps

As deferred compensation tax traps go, the newest and toughest kid on the block is section 409A,[17] which was added by the America Jobs Creation Act of 2004. This section imposes specific statutory requirements that every nonqualified deferred compensation plan must meet. It does not replace the traps described above; it adds to them.[18] The 409A statutory requirements are not unduly burdensome in most normal situations; they are primarily designed to cause problems for those who play on the outer limits of the other traps. But they have real teeth. If a Section 409A requirement is violated, the participant is immediately taxed on all deferred amounts that are not subject to a substantial risk of forfeiture, plus he or she gets hit with an interest charge calculated at a rate one percent above the normal underpayment rate *and an extra 20 percent tax* on the deferred amount included in income.[19] Section 409A is not a "no harm, no foul" statute. It can hurt. Here are brief descriptions of some of the key Section 409A requirements:[20]

- Amounts deferred under the plan may not be distributed[21] before the participant's separation from service,[22] the participant's disability,[23] the

---

14. I.R.C. § 409A(b).

15. Reg. § 1.162-7(b)(1).

16. Reg. § 1.162-7(b)(3).

17. I.R.C. § 409A.

18. I.R.C. § 409A(c).

19. I.R.C. § 409A(a)(1).

20. Extensive regulations to Section 409A were finalized in 2007. Reg. § 1.409A.

21. I.R.C. § 409A(2).

22. For a "specified employee," the separation from service requirement is not met if a payment is made before the date which is six months after the separation of service. A "specified employee" is a key employee (as defined in section 416(i) without regard to paragraph (5)) of a corporation any stock of which is publicly traded. I.R.C. § 409A(a)(2)(B); Reg. § 1.409A-1(i)(1).

23. Disability generally requires a condition that can be expected to result in death or can be expected to last for at least 12 continuous months and that prevents any "substantial gainful activity" or that entitles the participant to receive income replacement benefits for not less than three months under an accident and health plan covering employees of the company. I.R.C. § 409A(a)(2)(C); Reg. § 1.409A-3(i)(4)(i).

participant's death, the specified time or payment schedule in the plan, a change in the ownership or control of the corporate employer or a substantial portion of the assets of the corporate employer,[24] or the occurrence of an unforeseeable emergency.[25] What is not permitted is fuzzy payout language or schedules designed to give executives discretion over when they can get the deferred amounts.

- The plan may not permit the acceleration of the time or schedule for the payment of benefits, except as provided by regulations.[26]

- The plan may not give an employee an election to defer compensation earned during a taxable year after that year begins. The election must be made by the close of the preceding taxable year.[27] There are two exceptions. If it's the employee's first year in the plan, the election may be made within 30 days after the employee becomes eligible, but the election may relate only to services performed after the election.[28] Also, for performance-based bonuses that are based on services rendered over a period of at least 12 months, the deferral election may be made no later than 6 months before the end of the period.[29]

- The plan may not give an employee an election to further delay the payment of benefits under the plan unless the plan requires that (i) any such election not take effect until at least 12 months after it is made, (ii) the extended deferral period is not less than five years (except in the case of death, disability and unforeseeable emergency), and (iii) any additional delay in an election relating to a specified time or fixed payment schedule provision must be made at least 12 months before the first scheduled payment under such provision.[30]

- Assets held outside the United States and set aside (directly or indirectly) to pay benefits under a deferred compensation plan will be considered property under Section 83, thus triggering a recognition of taxable income for the employees, plus the 409A interest charge and the 409A extra 20 percent tax.[31] Lesson: Do not earmark any assets that are held in offshore accounts as having anything to do with a deferred compensation plan.

- Employer assets that become restricted to the provisions of a deferred compensation plan as a result of a change in the employer's financial health will be considered property under Section 83, thus triggering a recognition of taxable income for the employees, plus the 409A interest charge and the 409A extra 20

---

24. See Reg. § 1.409A-3(i)(5).

25. An "unforeseeable emergency" means a severe financial hardship resulting from (i) an illness or accident of the employee, a spouse or a dependant, (ii) a loss of property due to casualty, or (iii) similar extraordinary and unforeseen circumstances beyond the control of the employee. I.R.C. § 409A(a)(2)(B)(ii); Reg. § 1.409A-3(i)(3)(i).

26. I.R.C. § 409A(a)(3). The Regulations provide that accelerated payments may be permitted to fulfill a domestic relations order, to pay income taxes due upon a vesting event under a plan subject to section 457(f), and to pay FICA taxes on compensation deferred under the plan. Reg. § 1.409A-3(i)(4).

27. I.R.C. § 409A(a)(4)(B)(i); Reg. § 1.409A-2(a)(3).

28. I.R.C. § 409A(a)(4)(B)(ii); Reg. § 1.409A-2(a)(7).

29. I.R.C. § 409A(a)(4)(B)(iii). Reg. § 1.409A-2(a)(8). At a minimum, the bonus must be contingent on performance criteria and may not be substantially certain at time of deferral. Reg. § 1.409A-1(e)(1).

30. I.R.C. § 409A(a)(4)(C); Reg. § 1.409A-2(b).

31. I.R.C. § 409A(b)(1),(3),(4).

percent tax.[32] Lesson: Don't include in the plan any provision dealing with a change in the employer's financial health.

• If the company maintains a single-employer defined benefit plan that has not been adequately funded (i.e., is considered "at risk" within the meaning of Section 430(i)), any assets set aside for the payment of deferred compensation benefits to the company's chief executive officer, the company's four highest paid officers, or any individual subject to Section 16(a) of the Securities Exchange Act of 1934 will be treated as property taxable under Section 83.[33]

4. STRUCTURAL BASICS AND COLLATERAL CONSEQUENCES

A SERP is a private contract between the company and the executive. The primary components of the contract are: (1) the formula or basis for determining the amount of the SERP retirement payments; (2) the circumstances under which the SERP payments will be paid or not paid; and (3) the method of payment, such as a lump-sum cash-out, monthly installments, a life annuity, or some combination of these. The contract may contain other provisions based on the circumstances and the purpose of the SERP. The company gets no tax deduction until the amounts are actually paid to the executive, and the executive realizes no taxable income until the benefits are received.

a. Plan Early. The key to preserving the tax deductibility of the benefit payments under a SERP, particularly when the employee is also an owner of the business, is to establish the SERP many years prior to the date of retirement. If a SERP is established just prior to retirement, the IRS may challenge the company's deduction for the payments on the ground that they represent unreasonable compensation for a short period. If the employee is a stockholder, there is always the risk that the payments will be considered dividends or buy-out payments rather than true retirement benefits. In such a situation, the key is to make sure that the retirement benefit accrues over a sufficient number of years such that it is fair and reasonable compensation for services rendered during the years of accrual.

b. Benefit Formula. The company has flexibility in structuring the benefit accrual formula under the contract. The only limitation in structuring the arrangement is that it be reasonable. The formula may accrue a fixed sum each year, may be based on a defined monthly benefit at retirement, may be adjusted for inflation, may be based on accumulated years of service, or may consider any other factors that are reasonable. The retirement benefit accrual should be prospective, not retroactive. Typically a SERP does not involve deferral elections by the executive; it just specifies the benefits that will be paid by the company and the conditions of payment. From a tax standpoint, the safest approach is to structure the SERP so that the supplemental retirement benefit accrues after the date the agreement is executed. And, as previously noted, the amount of the accrued benefit under the plan each year plus the amount of the current

---

32. I.R.C. § 409A(b)(2),(3),(4).

33. I.R.C. § 409A(b)(3).

compensation must, in combination, constitute reasonable compensation for services rendered during the period.

c. Elective Deferrals. The SERP benefit can be structured as an elective benefit, similar to a 401(k) plan. With this approach, the employee is given the right each year to elect to defer an amount of compensation that will be paid out at retirement or termination of employment. Alternatively, the SERP can be structured as an add-on, employer-provided benefit that doesn't involve any employee election. If the elective approach is used, the key is to make sure that the deferral election is in writing and that the election to defer compensation for any given taxable year is made prior to the beginning of that year. If the election to defer compensation earned during a given year is made after the year begins, the employee will be taxed currently on the deferred amount and will be subject to the interest and extra 20 percent tax provision of Section 409A – a disaster.

d. Method of Payout. Another issue that must be addressed in the SERP agreement is the method of paying out the benefit. Typically the payout form is described in terms of a monthly payment for life or a term of years. Often the SERP provides for a lump-sum payment upon the death of the employee prior to retirement. The key is to ensure that the payout options are definitive enough to conform to the permissible payout options of Section 409A. Another important feature of many SERPs is a provision that gives the company the option to cash out any accrued benefits if the company is sold. This provision will help the company bail out proceeds received from the sale with tax-deductible dollars. Also, such a cash-out feature will benefit the purchaser who has no interest in picking up the SERP liability or perpetuating the SERP plan. A SERP can be structured to impose golden handcuffs on key employees. There are no restrictions on conditions or forfeiture limitations. The plan may provide that the benefits are reduced or eliminated if a key employee signs on with a competitor or voluntarily departs before retirement.

e. Regulatory Requirements. As with other nonqualified deferred compensation plans, SERPs are not subject to the same type of IRS and Department of Labor regulatory requirements that plague qualified retirement plans. A SERP needs to steer clear of any Section 409A foul-ups and the other tax traps. ERISA regulations are no big deal so long as the benefits are unfunded at all times and are made available only to a select group of highly compensated employees.

f. Funding. The SERP should be an unfunded obligation of the company in order to qualify for the ERISA exemption and avoid an early tax hit to the employee. This means that the company cannot set aside funds in a separate trust that is legally earmarked for the benefit of the SERP participants and is beyond the reach of the company's creditors. Although legal funding is taboo, the company can still prepare for the day when the SERP payments will commence. This is done by establishing an informal funding program. The company sets aside cash or other property to cover its future payment obligations to the executive. The key is that the assets set aside must continue to be owned by the company and be subject to the claims of the company's creditors.

g. FICA and Social Security. The SERP offers a potential FICA benefit. SERP benefits are considered earned for FICA purposes when the benefit is accrued and no longer subject to a substantial risk of forfeiture.[34] So, for example, if an executive accrues a $70,000 annual SERP benefit and is already receiving cash compensation in excess of the social security taxable wage base, the additional $70,000 of SERP accrual does not increase the amount of non-medical FICA taxes either for the executive or the corporation. And since the SERP benefit was potentially subject to non-medical FICA taxes when accrued, no non-medical FICA taxes are due when the SERP benefit is paid. The other social security issue is whether the SERP benefits, when paid, will reduce social security benefits. Fortunately, SERP benefits are counted as earned income when accrued, not when paid, for purposes of determining the benefit offset. So the receipt of the SERP benefit will not reduce social security benefits if the SERP recipient is otherwise eligible.

h. Impact on Qualified Retirement Benefits. Another aspect of a SERP that has to be kept in mind is its potential impact on qualified retirement plan benefits. If an executive's current income is less than it would be if a SERP benefit were not being accrued, this lower income level may reduce the amount that is being accrued for the executive under the company's qualified retirement plan. It depends on the benefit accrual formula of the qualified plan.

i. Financial Statement Impact. A factor to consider in designing a SERP is the effect it will have on the company's financial statements. Since the accrued SERP benefit is a liability of the company, it must show up on the books as a liability. Care will need to be taken to make sure that the SERP liability does not cause the company to violate any loan-to-net-worth ratios or other covenants in loan agreements that are tied to the company's book net worth. Loan agreements should be reviewed and possibly revised to avoid this result.

j. The foregoing are some of the basic factors to consider in structuring a SERP. Since the SERP offers a nonqualified benefit through a private contract between the employee and the company, there is considerable flexibility in structuring the terms to meet important objectives.

5. THE NO-FUND FUNDING OPTIONS

Let's return to the indispensable executive, Peter, in the above example. Peter understands that the supplemental retirement benefit he has worked out with the company is a special nonqualified benefit designed specifically for him. He further understands that the company's payment obligation is a general unsecured liability of the company. His payment rights are no better than those of a general, unsecured creditor of the company. Finally, Peter understands that if the company takes any steps to formally fund the benefit by legally earmarking a pot of money for him, the odds are that he will be taxed currently on the amount of the accrued benefit. Peter likes the idea of knowing that he will not have to pay any taxes under the program until he begins receiving benefits at age 65.

---

34. I.R.C. § 3121(v)(2)(A).

With all this understood, Peter would like to have the company take action to start informally funding the benefit. He realizes that the benefit could represent a significant liability of the company by the time he reaches age 65. He is concerned that, as he grows older, the owners may become nervous about the size of that liability and may try to renegotiate the liability or take some other action that could jeopardize his right to receive the promised benefit. Peter figures that the best way to head off any future problem is for the company to start preparing for the day when it will have to write his retirement checks.

a. Company-Owned Insurance Funding

One option for funding the benefit is a high-cash-value life insurance contract owned by the company. The company would be both the owner and the beneficiary of the policy. Substantial premium payments would be made on the policy for the next 10 years. The earnings within the policy would accumulate on a tax-deferred basis. When Peter reaches age 65, there would be a substantial cash value in the policy that would offset, at least in part, the company's liability to Peter. The company could commence a program of borrowing from the policy the after-tax cost of the retirement payment that would be due Peter. The company's interest deduction on such borrowings would be limited.[35] When Peter dies, the company would receive a tax-free death benefit that would reimburse the company for all or a substantial portion of its payments to Peter under the program. Peter would have the comfort of knowing that the company has affirmatively taken steps to fund the program for his benefit. Although the policy would internally be tied to Peter's agreement, he would have no legal rights to the policy.

Illustration A: Corporate Owned Insurance Funding

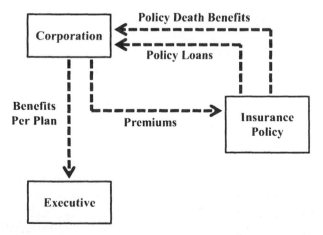

b. Rabbi Trust Option

A second option would be a "Rabbi" trust. The Rabbi trust is an irrevocable

---

35. I.R.C. § 264(e)(1) limits interest deductions on indebtedness against policies insuring the lives of key employees to interest charges on $50,000 of such indebtedness.

trust established by the company. The company would make periodic contributions to the trust that would be invested by the trustee. The trustee of the trust would be authorized to make investments and to use the assets of the trust for only two purposes. First, the assets could be used to pay Peter's benefit under his SERP. Second, the assets could be used to pay claims of the creditors of the company. Although the Rabbi trust would lock up funds for Peter's retirement benefit, it would not protect those funds from claims of the company's creditors. If the company were to experience serious financial problems, Peter's benefit might be lost.

The value of the Rabbi trust is that it provides some protection to Peter while preserving the tax deferral. The trust precludes the company from using trust assets to finance other corporate priorities. For ruling purposes, the IRS has imposed a number of requirements in order for a Rabbi trust to qualify: trust assets must be held for the sole purpose of paying benefits under the plan, except the assets may revert to the company if the company becomes bankrupt or insolvent; the company's management must have an express duty to notify the trustee of the company's bankruptcy or insolvency; if the trustee receives such a notice, the trustee must stop all payments from the trust and hold the assets until directed to make payments by appropriate court order; state law must not grant Peter any priority rights to the amounts held in the trust; the trust cannot be funded with securities of the company; and the trust may not contain an insolvency trigger or any other provision that might frustrate the rights of other creditors of the company.[36] In addition, Section 409A prohibits use of a Rabbi trust that holds assets outside the United States or that springs into existence or becomes subject to new restrictions upon a change in the company's financial health.[37]

Illustration B: Rabbi Trust Option

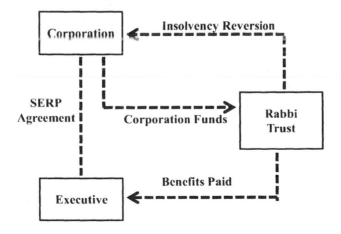

---

36. Rev. Proc. 92-64, 1992-2 C.B. 422.
37. I.R.C. § 409A(b)(1) & (2).

The bottom line is that the Rabbi trust strategy may provide Peter with some protection in the event of a change in control, a change in management, or a change in the company's desire to pay the benefit.

c. Rabbi-Owned Insurance Option

A third option is to combine the life insurance with the Rabbi trust. Here the trust is both the owner and the beneficiary of the policy that insures Peter's life. The trust makes all the premium payments with the amounts contributed to the trust by the company. The earnings in the policy accumulate on a tax-deferred basis. When Peter reaches age 65, there will be a substantial cash value in the policy that will be owned by the trust and used to fund Peter's benefits. The company could commence a program of borrowing from the policy to use such borrowings and other trust assets to make the retirement payments to Peter. When Peter dies, the trust would receive a tax-free death benefit that would cover all amounts due Peter's estate or spouse following his passing under the terms of the plan and potentially allow the company to recover a substantial portion of its payments to the trust. In this situation, Peter would have the added comfort of knowing that the company would not own and control the policy, so there would be no risk of the company choosing to use the policy to help fund some other corporate priority. The Rabbi trust would provide these added protections with respect to the policy.

Illustration C: Rabbi Owned Insurance Option

d. The Split-Dollar SERP

As Peter studies the insurance options for his SERP, he may decide that he would like to structure the insurance program to provide his family with an insured death benefit and to save substantial estate taxes. He proposes that the company fund the SERP with a split-dollar insurance program.

A split-dollar insurance contract is entered into between Peter and the company as part of the SERP agreement. The contract provides that the company is entitled to receive the cash value benefit under the policy, and Peter is entitled to receive the excess death benefit under the policy. The company is the owner of the policy, and Peter's rights under the split-dollar agreement are evidenced by an endorsement on the policy. If Peter's only right under the policy is a portion of the death benefit, the endorsement split dollar arrangement itself will not be considered a deferred compensation arrangement subject to Section 409A.[38] As the policy owner, the company has the right to borrow against the cash value to fund the after-tax cost of payments under the SERP. The contract is structured to have the company pay the entire premium. Peter must recognize as taxable income each year the value of the death benefit that he is provided, determined pursuant to a schedule published by the IRS. Peter transfers his rights in the policy to an irrevocable life insurance trust established for the benefit of his family. The value of the death benefit taxable to Peter each year is also deemed a gift from Peter to the trust.

Illustration D: Split Dollar Insurance SERP

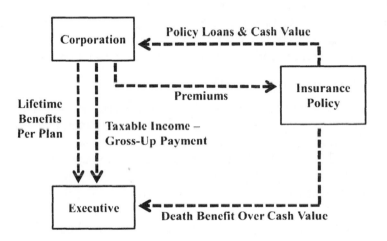

What has Peter accomplished with this structure? From Peter's perspective, the one negative is that he is going to have a current tax hit each year. Usually this tax hit is minimal, although it will grow each year. Also, the company gets a corresponding tax deduction, and it may choose to use the tax benefit from the deduction each year to fund Peter's tax hit with a grossed-up bonus. The trade-offs for the annual tax burden are a few significant benefits for Peter. First, the split-dollar agreement obligates the company to fund the insurance premium each year. Peter has more than a SERP agreement that he hopes the company will informally fund with insurance each year; he has a contractual promise that the insurance will be funded. Second, he has the assurance that, if he dies, the death benefit under the policy (to the extent it exceeds the cash value) will immediately be paid to his family. This is because the family trust owns that death benefit. Peter does not have to worry about the company collecting the death benefit and

---

38. See IRS notice 2007-34, which specifically discusses the impact of Section 409A on split-dollar arrangements.

then deciding to pay his family out over time. Finally, the structure permits the family to receive the death benefit free of income and estate taxes, assuming the trust's rights in the proceeds are established at least three years before Peter's death. In contrast, if the company collects the death benefit and makes payments under the SERP contract, the payments are subject to estate taxes and to income taxes as income in respect of a decedent.[39]

How does the structure stack up for the company? The structure contractually obligates the company to fund the insurance. In return, the company is relieved of any liability under the SERP at the death of Peter, whether that death is pre-or post-retirement. Perhaps the most negative impact is that, while the company does receive the cash surrender value under the policy at Peter's death, it does not receive all the life insurance proceeds. If the portion of the proceeds payable to the trust established for Peter's family exceeds the amount the company would otherwise be required to pay at Peter's death under the plan, such excess would represent an added cost to the company and an added benefit to Peter's family.

The bottom line is that the split-dollar structure represents a stronger commitment by the company and will probably cost the company more in the long run. The employee has a great death benefit, some tax benefits at death, and more assurance that the company will stick with the program.

e. Bonus Insurance SERP

Assume the same facts, with one important twist. Peter has determined that security for the payment of the benefit is far more important than the tax deferral. He is willing to take a tax hit now for the security of knowing that his benefit is going to be paid, no matter what happens to the company. Also, he has figured out that if he has to take a current tax hit, the company gets a current tax deduction. He has convinced the owners of the company that the company should pass on to him the benefit of its early tax deduction by paying him a cash bonus to cover his current tax bill. He figures that he will have the perfect plan if he can just figure out a way to legally earmark funds to cover his benefit. Peter wants something simple and easy – something that everyone can understand.

The answer for Peter may be a bonus insurance plan, which involves no trust at all and no tax deferral. Here's how it works.

The company would adopt a bonus insurance plan for Peter. Peter would be the owner of the policy. Each year the company would bonus to Peter the amount necessary to fund the policy for Peter's retirement benefit, along with a gross-up bonus to cover any associated tax hit. The after-tax amount paid as a bonus to Peter each year would be structured to ensure that the value of the policy at Peter's retirement would be large enough to provide Peter his desired monthly benefits.

Peter would enter into an agreement with the company that would provide that, if Peter terminates his employment early, he would be obligated to repay to

---

39. I.R.C. § 691.

the company all or a portion of the amounts that the company had paid to Peter to fund the policy. This repayment obligation would arise by virtue of the employment contract, and the company would have no special right to enforce its rights against the insurance contract. If Peter terminates his employment and does not repay the amounts, the company would have a legal right to pursue Peter for all amounts due. When Peter retires, he could borrow against the cash value of the police to fund his monthly retirement benefits. At death, his family would be paid any residual death benefit under the policy.

Illustration E: Bonus Insurance SERP

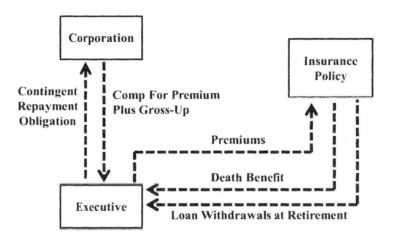

This strategy may be an attractive candidate in those rare situations where the executive wants a secure asset, tax deferral is not an objective, the company wants some golden handcuff protections, and the company is willing to take the risk of recovering any forfeited amounts from Pete.

f. The Guarantor Option

Another option that may be used to provide Peter with added protection that his promised benefits will be paid is to have the payment of the benefits guaranteed by a third party that has deep pockets. If the company goes under and is unable to pay the benefits, Peter can look to the third party for payment. An alternative is a surety bond that would guarantee the company's payment obligation to Peter. The IRS has ruled that if the company neither pays the premium on the bond nor reimburses Peter for the bond, the mere existence of the surety bond will not trigger tax on the deferred income, even though the employee has essentially acquired a guarantee of the payment.[40] If the company secures the bond and pays for the coverage, the likely result is that the employee will get hit with a current tax under the reaches of the economic benefit doctrine. Although some have felt that the surety bond may be the ultimate answer for the

---

40. PLR 84060022.

employee who has been promised a large supplemental retirement benefit, such surety bonds are not widely available and can be very expensive when they are available.

CASE PROBLEM 16-3

Jurden Windows Inc. hired Justin, a new sales vice president, two years ago. Justin is 51 years old. In the words of the company CEO, Justin has "taken the company to the moon." He has used his contacts in the industry to cherry-pick the best salespersons and to put together a sales effort that has everyone talking. That's the good news. The scary news is that everyone wants Justin and his sales team, whose loyalty is more to Justin than to the company. Bottom line: the company needs to lock Justin up.

The CEO of the company knows that Justin, a big spender, is concerned about his retirement down the road. The CEO doesn't know much about Justin's financial situation, but suspects that Justin doesn't save and invest much. Justin has inquired on a number of occasions if something can be done to enhance the company's retirement plan, which is a vanilla 401(k) plan that puts the funding onus on the employee.

The CEO would like to adopt a special retirement plan just for Justin. Ideally, it would be a plan that would bind Justin to the company for the duration. The CEO has many questions: Is such a plan for one person legal? What are the tax impacts? How would the benefits under the plan be funded? The CEO feels strongly that the plan must offer Justin more than just a "naked promise" down the road. There needs to be "some teeth" to show that the benefits will be paid. Plus, the CEO says it "can't create a bunch of tax problems for Justin before he starts collecting following his retirement from the company."

Advise the company.

D. COMPENSATING WITH STOCK AND STOCK RIGHTS

Highly motivated executives often get to a point in their careers where something more than a salary and a bonus is required as an incentive. They want to own a portion of the business. They want to work *with* the business owner – not just *for* the business owner. Often the executive really doesn't understand or appreciate what an interest in the business represents. All the executive knows is that he or she wants to feel like an owner and be treated like an owner.

The lawyer may advise the employer who is faced with the challenge or the key executive who wants to be its beneficiary. Many employers view the challenge as a necessary evil and approach the task with suspicion, fear, and a natural propensity to drag out and procrastinate on the process. The employer usually recognizes the value of the key executive and wants to preserve loyalty and dedication. What the employer does not want to do is create a structure fraught with legal and tax complexities that unduly inflates the executive's expectations, diverts the executive's commitment or, worse yet, funds the executive's departure.

The advisor for the executive has a specific challenge – to clearly identify the real value of what is being offered or promised, and the associated pitfalls. This can be a formidable task, particularly sorting through the tax and legal tradeoffs. Complexity is the order of the day in dealing with stock options, restricted stock plans, phantom stock plans, stock right plans, and other types of ownership incentive programs.

1. BENEFITS AND BURDENS OF STOCK OWNERSHIP

For purposes of this discussion, let's assume that XYZ, Inc. is a closely held manufacturing corporation that is equally owned by two individuals, Larry and Sue. The company has 150 employees and is very profitable. Jim, age 42, has become a key ingredient in the company's success. Jim manages the day-to-day field operations of the company and is the primary contact with certain of the company's most important customers. Jim has reached a point where he feels that he should own part of the company.

What are the real benefits to Jim if he acquires stock of the company? Whenever stock is acquired by an executive, there are seven potential benefits. Depending on the circumstances, some of these benefits may be of great value, and others may be of no significance. Let's review the seven benefits in light of Jim's situation

The first benefit is the privilege to vote the shares. If Jim is issued voting stock, he will have a vote that he didn't have before. Sharcholders of a corporation have the power to elect the board of directors of the corporation and to vote on major transactions involving the corporation, such as mergers, liquidations, and sales of the corporation's assets. This new vote may be of no real value to Jim. As a minority stockholder, he can always be outvoted, and there's no assurance that he'll be given an opportunity to serve on the board of directors. Since it is the board of directors of the company that really controls its affairs, the opportunity to serve on the board may be far more important than the opportunity to vote a few shares.

The second benefit that Jim receives is the right to receive dividends. In a publicly held company that regularly pays a dividend, that right may have real economic value. Most closely held C corporations, however, such as XYZ, Inc., do not pay any significant dividends. Since dividends are subject to a double tax, the closely held corporation would rather bail out its earnings in the form of tax-deductible payments to its shareholders through salaries, bonuses, rental payments and other arrangements. For this reason, the dividend advantage in the closely held corporation often is not significant as a practical matter.

The third potential benefit of stock ownership is the right to participate in any sale or liquidation of the business. If Larry and Sue decide to dispose of XYZ, Inc. down the road and Jim owns a share of its stock, he will be in a position to participate in the rewards generated from the sale. This can produce a significant economic benefit if the company is sold at a handsome profit. But the prospects of any such sale may be nonexistent or, at best, remote. Maybe Larry and Sue have no interest in selling the business and want to preserve the business for their next generation. Maybe there is no market for the particular business. This is an important factor that needs to be analyzed in reviewing the potential benefits of any ownership program.

The fourth potential benefit is growth potential. By acquiring an interest in the stock of the company, Jim acquires an asset that has growth potential. As the earnings of the business increase, the value of his stock also should increase. The real question to ask is: How is Jim going to realize a profit on the value of that stock? There is no established market for XYZ, Inc. stock. Since XYZ, Inc. is a closely held corporation, there should be a buy-sell agreement between the shareholders of the company. That agreement will specify the terms and conditions for buying stock owned by a shareholder. In many closely held corporations, the terms of the shareholder buy-sell agreement are the most important factors in assessing the value of the stock incentive program that is offered to the executive. It is through that agreement that the minority shareholder executive will realize the value of the equity interest.

The fifth potential benefit is the capital gains tax break realized on the sale of a capital asset. One of the principal incentives for issuing an executive stock as compensation is the opportunity to generate capital gains that are taxed at favorable rates.

The last two benefits that executives usually long for in these types of programs are the "feel better" benefit and the "treat me more equal" benefit. These are purely subjective factors. Many executives are convinced that they will feel better and be more secure in their jobs if they own a part of the company. They also believe that the owners of the company will treat them more as equals, more like partners, if they own an interest in the business. Often these subjective factors are of greater importance to the executive than those factors related directly to the economic benefits of the program.

Frequently the question is asked: Are there any disadvantages to an executive receiving an equity ownership interest in the company that he or she works for? There are a few potential disadvantages that should be carefully reviewed in every situation.

First, there is the potential disadvantage of triggering the recognition of phantom taxable income – taxable income that is not accompanied by any cash. In many stock ownership programs, the executive ends up with a stock certificate and a tax bill, but no cash. More on this potential disadvantage later.

Second, in rare situations there is the possibility that the executive may take on some additional liability exposure by becoming an owner of the business. If there are uninsured risks in operating the business and the affairs of the corporation are neglected, there is a risk that the shareholders of the corporation may become personally exposed for certain debts and liabilities of the company. The executive may end up on the wrong side of a lawsuit in which a creditor of the corporation is trying to pierce the corporate veil to get directly to the corporate shareholders. Usually this risk can be mitigated or eliminated entirely by properly taking care of the corporate, legal and insurance affairs of the business. Suffice it to say, the executive who acquires stock in the corporation will want to be satisfied that the corporate legal affairs are in order.

There also are the potential disadvantages associated with the business losing money or possibly needing additional capital from its shareholders. If Jim is issued 10 percent of the stock of XYZ, Inc. and XYZ, Inc. then gets into financial trouble, Jim may have pressure put on him by Larry or Sue to help fund the operations of XYZ, Inc. by coughing up his share of the additional needed capital. Although Jim may have no legal obligation to make such a contribution, the pressure of being a co-owner with Larry and Sue may push him into having to fund his share of the shortfall.

Usually the biggest disadvantage is the opportunity cost in any situation where an executive takes an equity interest as part of his or her pay package. By taking stock in the company, Jim may lose the right to receive some alternative form of compensation that, in the end, may prove more valuable to him.

In each situation, the potential benefits and burdens of owning an interest in the company need to be carefully analyzed. In some situations, the executive may conclude that the benefits do not justify the burdens, the hassle, and the opportunity costs of alternative forms of compensation.

2. FACTORS IN ASSESSING AN OWNERSHIP PROGRAM

There are factors that should be analyzed in structuring or reviewing any equity ownership incentive program. Following are brief descriptions of eight key planning factors.

1. The Real Cost Factor

Does the program require that the executive bear a real cost by making an investment to acquire his or her stock in the company? Most stock option programs are structured to require that the executive write a check and make an investment before the executive can acquire stock in the company. Employers often feel that such an investment on the part of the executive is essential to accomplish the real objectives of the plan. They argue that, absent such an investment, the executive can't really lose any money and may not fully appreciate the value of what's been given. In contrast, many executives do not want to make an investment or lack the resources to make a significant investment to acquire an interest in the company. Their argument is that their investment has been and will continue to be in the form of quality executive services to the company and their willingness to forgo other opportunities. This issue of whether the executive is going to be required to come "out of pocket" to acquire his or her interest is a threshold issue in structuring and analyzing any program.

2. The "Value Now" Factor

Will the program be structured so that the executive is given a stock interest that has a built-in economic value to the executive at the time it is given? As we will see, many programs are structured to simply give the executive an economic interest in future appreciation that accrues in the company's stock. The emphasis is on the future, not the present. Many stock option programs, stock appreciation right programs, and phantom stock programs are designed to give the executive an economic interest in future appreciation. There is no immediate economic value in the option or the right at the time it is given to the executive. In contrast, other programs are structured to give the executive an interest in the company that has a demonstrable economic value at the time it is given. Under such a program, the executive's net worth is increased at the time the executive is granted the option or the right. Many employers are willing to part with a portion of the future value in their company, but are unwilling to simply grant the executive, free of charge, an interest in the value that has already been created.

3. The Golden Handcuffs Factor

Is the program going to be structured to ensure that the executive can enjoy the full economic benefits only if the executive satisfies certain specified employment criteria? Many programs are structured to provide executives with significant economic benefits that depend entirely on the executive's willingness to remain loyal and dedicated to the company. If the executive prematurely terminates his or her employment with the company, fails to measure up to designated performance criteria, or elects to go to work for a competitor, the executive forfeits some or all of the economic benefits that accrued under the particular plan.

This factor can be extremely important from the executive's perspective. The executive has been given something of value, but it is conditional and contingent. It can be lost. Often specified, custom-tailored conditions need to be negotiated with each executive in order to satisfy the interests of all parties.

4. The Cash-Out Factor

This factor focuses on the mechanism that will be used to allow the executive to convert his or her stock interest to cash at an appropriate point in the future. This factor is not a consideration for the publicly held company whose stock is registered and regularly traded. In contrast, this Cash-Out Factor is particularly important to the executive of the closely held business. How is that executive going to realize a profit on the investment? A carefully drafted shareholder buy-sell agreement that specifies a reasonable basis for valuing the stock at appropriate points in time is critically important. It also is essential to develop a funding mechanism in many situations. This often requires that the business purchase a life insurance policy on the life of the executive to ensure that the company will have the required funds to cash out the executive if there is an untimely death. Cash-out provisions also have to be negotiated to deal with issues of employment severance, disability, retirement and expulsion.

5. The Phantom Income Factor

Is the program going to create taxable income for the executive before the executive has any cash to pay the tax liability? Many programs are structured to confer an economic value for the executive at the time the particular option or right is granted. The result is that the executive may be taxed on the fair market value of that economic benefit at the time it is received, even though no cash has been paid to the executive. This can create an intolerable situation for the executive from a tax standpoint. To remedy the situation, employers often are forced to bonus additional cash sums to the executive to cover the tax liability. As we'll see, many programs attempt to deal with this Phantom Income Factor by eliminating the Value Now Factor – that is, by granting no present economic benefit – or by maximizing the Golden Handcuffs Factor, which presents a substantial risk of forfeiture to the executive. The trade-offs can be significant for any executive.

6. Employer's Tax Factor

The sixth factor focuses on the tax consequence for the employer. Does the program produce any tax advantages for the employer? The employer often find that the program has been structured to provide a tax deduction for options or rights granted to the executive, even though the employer has not expended any cash or liquid resources. Such a plan may reduce the tax liability of the employer and the overall costs of the plan. The executive, on the other hand, may be demanding that at least a portion of those tax savings should be reallocated to him or her to reduce the burden of any phantom taxable income.

7. The Fall-Out Leverage Factor

This factor focuses on the relevant positions of the executive and the company if there is a major blow-up between them. Who has the most leverage? If there is a falling-out and the executive believes that he or she has been abused in the process, the executive may have substantially more leverage by exercising rights as a stockholder. For this reason alone, many employers prefer plans that grant stock equivalency rights or phantom stock rights, but never provide real stock. Carefully drafted transfer restrictions and buy-sell agreements can help mitigate the fear generated by this Fall-Out Leverage Factor when real stock is issued. Often it is difficult to get a handle on the significance of this factor in a given situation because the parties don't want to even acknowledge the prospect of a major blow-up.

8. The Real Thing Factor

As we will see, incentive ownership programs can be structured without offering the executive any real equity interest in the company. Instead, the executive receives contractual payment rights structured to produce economic benefits that are the equivalent of stock ownership. Often these programs are unacceptable to the executive simply because they do not offer the "real thing." The executive isn't satisfied with anything less than stock, even though, from a tax and structuring standpoint, the executive may be better off receiving a carefully drafted stock substitute.

These eight factors are important considerations in analyzing any ownership incentive program. The following planning strategies focus on these factors. It is common to find that the company and the executive disagree on the importance of a particular factor or how it should be structured into the particular program.

3. SIX PLANNING STRATEGIES

1. Incentive Stock Options

The incentive stock option (ISO) is the strategy that presents the most technical requirements. It is available only to corporate entities, not entities taxed as partnerships.[41] The ISO gives the executive the right to buy stock from the company over a designated period of time on certain specified terms and conditions. It is designed to provide a tax benefit to the executive who receives the option.

With any stock option plan, there are three key points in time: the time the executive is given the option, the time the executive acquires stock through the exercise of the option and payment of the option price, and the time that the stock is sold by the executive and the sales price is realized in the form of cash. The appeal of an ISO is that the executive does not have to recognize any taxable income at the time of grant or the time of exercise, but rather only recognizes taxable income at the time of sale – when cash is available.[42] And any income recognized at the time of sale can qualify as capital gain income. There is one slight tax hitch. Although the executive does not have to recognize any phantom taxable income at the time of grant or at the time of exercise, if the fair market value of the stock at the time of exercise exceeds the option price (a circumstance that will exist in almost every case, for why else would the executive have exercised the option?), such excess fair market value at time of exercise will be treated as a tax preference item for purposes of the alternative minimum tax.[43]

What does it take for an option to qualify as an ISO so that the executive can enjoy the tax benefits of ISO treatment? There are a number of technical requirements, including the following:[44]

First, the plan under which the option is granted must be approved by the shareholders of the company within 12 months before or after the date the plan is adopted by the board of directors.

Second, each option must be granted within 10 years of the plan adoption. In other words, the plan is good for 10 years.

Third, the option period cannot be longer than 10 years, so the executive must make his or her election to exercise the option and acquire the stock within a 10-year time frame after it is granted.

Fourth, the option price cannot be less than the fair market value of the company's stock at the time the option is granted. Determining the fair market value of the stock of a closely held corporation can be a challenge. For this reason, there is a special provision that the ISO will qualify as long as a good faith effort is made to determine the fair market value of the stock.

Fifth, the option cannot be transferred, except in the case of the death of the executive.

---

41. I.R.C. § 422(b) requires that the recipient be an employee of a corporation.
42. I.R.C. § 421(a).
43. I.R.C. § 56(b)(3).
44. See, generally, I.R.C. § 422(a)-(d).

Sixth, the executive who gets the ISO cannot own over 10 percent of the stock of the company.

Seventh, the total fair market value of all stock subject to ISOs which are first exercisable by the executive in any calendar year cannot exceed $100,000. The fair market value of the stock is determined at the time of grant.

Eighth, to claim the ISO benefits, the executive cannot sell the stock within two years of the date the option is granted, nor within one year from the date the stock is acquired through the exercise of the option. After exercising the option, the executive, Jim in our case, must hold the stock long enough to satisfy these periods in order to enjoy capital gains tax treatment.

Finally, the executive must have been an employee of the company or an affiliate of the company at all times from the date the option is granted until at least three months prior to the date upon which the option is exercised. In other words, if the executive leaves the employ of the company, the ISO must be exercised within three months of leaving in order to preserve the favorable ISO tax treatment.

The obvious question is this: Why wouldn't any executive and company (such as Jim and XYZ, Inc.) only want options that qualify as ISOs? After all, there is no taxable income until time of sale. The phantom income tax risks are eliminated. Also, the ISO can be structured with Golden Handcuffs features to protect the company. Usually this is done by providing that portions of the ISO can be exercised only after the executive has satisfied certain designated employment periods with the company. And once the option is exercised, the executive acquires the real thing – stock in the company.

Although certain advantages and structural opportunities exist, there are some major disadvantages to ISOs that are compelling in many situations. The result is that the ISO, although once very popular, has lost much of its appeal. First, from the executive's perspective, the ISO, by definition, flunks the Real Cost Factor and the Value Now factor tests. The executive must make a real investment before getting any stock, and the purchase price of the stock, by definition, must be equal to the fair market value of the stock at the time the option is granted. The option offers only a hope of future appreciation and no existing value. Jim may want some value now.

Second, the employer gets no deduction for the ISO. If the stock goes up in value and the employee, Jim in our case, recognizes a gain at time of sale, Jim will pay tax and the company will get no tax deduction. On a net tax basis, this is a costly, inefficient approach for moving value from the company to the executive. The executive is paying a tax bill with no offsetting tax benefit to the employer.

Finally, if the executive has an alternative minimum tax problem, the ISO may significantly aggravate that problem by creating an additional tax preference item at the time the option is exercised.

For these reasons, the ISO, although still a viable candidate and strategy, has lost much of its glitter. Many companies and their executives would be well advised to consider one of the less technical strategies.

2. The Nonqualified Stock Option

The second strategy is the nonqualified stock option. A nonqualified stock option is an option that does not qualify as an incentive stock option; it flunks one of the technical requirements. The executive still is given the right to buy a designated number of shares of the company's stock on specific terms and conditions. However, there are no rules governing the option price, the option period, or any other items. The parties are completely free to sculpt their own deal.

Are nonqualified options taxed the same as ISOs? Not a chance. Generally, the executive will not have to recognize any taxable income at the time the option is granted unless the option can be transferred by the executive or the option itself is tradable and has a readily ascertainable fair market value. [45] Because such options are almost never transferable by the executive and usually never have readily ascertainable fair market values, the time of grant is not a problem – certainly not in a situation involving a closely held business such as XYZ, Inc.

The tax problem comes at the point of exercise. When Jim exercises the option by paying the price and receiving the stock, Jim is required to recognize taxable income equal to the excess of the fair market value of the stock over the option price. If, in our example, Jim is given an option to buy 100,000 shares of stock at a price of $1.00 per share (for a total of $100,000) and Jim exercises the option at a time when the shares have a fair market value of $3.00 per share (or $300,000), Jim would be required to recognize $200,000 of taxable ordinary income at the time of exercise. Yet Jim has no cash from the transaction at this point. Jim's tax basis in the stock would be $300,000. At the time that Jim sells the stock, he would only have to recognize income to the extent the sale price exceeds $300,000.

It's important to note that there is a tax benefit to the corporation at the time of exercise. When the exercise occurs, the corporation gets a tax deduction equal to the income that Jim is required to recognize.[46] In our example, the corporation would get a $200,000 deduction at time of exercise.

If the parties have determined that they want to use stock options, nonqualified options offer great flexibility in structuring their arrangement. The option requires some investment, so there is a Real Cost Factor. But the option price can be below the existing fair market value of the stock. If, in our example, the stock has a value of $2.00 per share at the time of grant and the option price is $1.00 per share, Jim effectively would have been transferred $1.00 of real value for each share at the time the option is granted. From Jim's perspective, this circumstance would satisfy the Value Now Factor because he has been given some of the existing equity in the company through the structure of the option price. Many employers have used these types of options to set exercise prices that are substantially below the existing fair market value of the stock at time of

---

45. I.R.C. § 83(e)(3); Reg. §§ 1.83-7(b)(1) & (2).
46. I.R.C. § 83(h).

grant.

If some Value Now is built into a nonqualified option, care must be taken to comply with the requirements of Section 409A. Under Regulation § 1.409A-1(b)(5), a nonqualified stock option will be treated as a deferred compensation plan if the option price does not at least equal to the fair market value of the stock at time of option grant. Thus, a nonqualified option that has a preferred Value Now option price will lose a great deal of flexibility as to the timing of its exercise. To comply with Section 409A, the time of exercise would have to be specified at time of grant or be tied to a permissible payout event under Section 409A (separation for service, disability, death, change of control, or unforeseen emergency). The executive would lose the capacity to pick the time to exercise the option. In view of the penalties triggered by a violation of 409A, any company that issues nonqualified options that are not intended to comply with the exercise limitations of Section 409A should take extreme care to ensure that the option price is not less than the stock's fair market value at time of grant. In recognition of the difficulty of valuing closely held business interests (and the high stakes for Section 409A non-compliance), the regulations to Section 409A permit the use of any reasonable valuation method, describe factors that will be used to determine the reasonableness of the valuation, impose consistency requirements, create a presumption of reasonableness for a one-year period, and create a special presumption for the good faith valuation of a start-up company's stock during the first 10 years of its active conduct of a trade or business. [47]

There is really no limit on the Golden Handcuffs feature that can be attached to the nonqualified option. For example, XYZ, Inc. could grant to Jim an option to purchase 200,000 shares of the company's common stock at a specified price. The option could be structured to provide that Jim would have the right to exercise the option with respect to one-tenth (1/10) of such shares (20,000) each year that Jim remains in the employ of XYZ, Inc. The effect is that Jim would vest in his right to acquire the full 200,000 shares over a 10-year time frame. If the company does well, Jim would have a strong incentive to remain loyal for a long period of time.

From Jim's perspective, the phantom taxable income created at the time of exercise is a real problem, but even this problem can often be resolved. Remember, the corporation is getting an offsetting tax deduction. The transaction is often structured so that the corporation lends the amount of its tax benefit at the time of exercise to the executive. This provides the executive with a source of funding to cover his tax liability at the time of exercise. Interest would be paid or accrued on the loan. The loan would be paid off at the time the stock is sold.

As an alternative, the company could elect to simply bonus to the executive the amount of its tax saving from the exercise of the option. A calculation would have to be made to gross-up the bonus to take into account taxes also saved as a result of the bonus paid to Jim. This would provide Jim with a source of cash to cover his tax liability at the time of exercise. The net effect from Jim's standpoint

---

47. Reg. § 1.409A-1(b)(5).

is that the nonqualified option gives him some real value now, provides a source of funding his phantom tax liability, and presents no alternative minimum tax problems.

Stock options are viable strategies. The nonqualified option provides more structural flexibility, but does raise a phantom income issue that needs to be addressed in the planning process. One major disadvantage of any stock option program is that the executive doesn't own the stock – the real thing – until he or she steps up and pays the option price. So the benefits of actual stock ownership usually are delayed. This may be a real negative from the standpoint of many executives.

3. Bonus Stock

Bonus stock perhaps is the least technical and most straightforward strategy of all. Under this approach, XYZ, Inc. would adopt a stock bonus plan and transfer to Jim a specified number of its shares as compensation for services rendered. From Jim's standpoint, bonus stock offers some real pluses. There is no need to make a cash investment; there is no real cost. There is immediate value now; the existing value of the stock belongs to the executive, and the transfer of the stock is not deemed to be a deferred compensation plan subject to Section 409A.[48] A shareholder buy-sell agreement can be drafted to ensure that the Cash-Out Factor is satisfied. The executive owns the real thing now; there is no delayed enjoyment, as in the case of an option. Finally, the executive is entitled to vote the shares now and can immediately participate in all dividends and other rights.

But there are also disadvantages to bonus stock from the executive's perspective. Usually the executive is given fewer shares under a bonus stock plan than under some other type of plan, such as an option plan. It's only natural to expect that the company will be willing to transfer, free of charge, fewer shares under a bonus plan than it would be willing to sell for full value under an option program. The resulting disadvantage is that the executive has less opportunity to participate in the future appreciation of the company.

Bonus stock also presents a major phantom taxable income problem. The fair market value of the stock is taxed to Jim at the time the stock is transferred to him. As in the case of a nonqualified option, the company may find itself in the position of having to lend money to Jim to enable him to pay his phantom tax liability, or it may simply couple the stock bonus grant with a grossed-up cash bonus to cover the tax liability.

4. Restricted Stock

Restricted stock is bonus stock with a twist. The twist is that the stock has strings attached – restrictions. If one of these restrictions is violated, the company yanks the string and retrieves all or a portion of the stock. Suppose, for example, that XYZ, Inc. is willing to transfer to Jim $100,000 worth of stock now. No investment is required on Jim's part. There is immediate value now.

---

48. Reg. § 1.409A-1(b)(6).

Jim gets the real thing now. And, presumably, there is a buy-sell agreement to ensure the Cash-Out Factor. Further, suppose that XYZ, Inc. wants to make certain that the stock will cement Jim's loyalty and dedication to the company. So it places a restriction on the stock. For example, the restriction may provide that, if Jim leaves the company at any time during the next 10 years, he will forfeit all of the stock. Alternatively, it may provide that Jim vests in his right to keep the stock at a rate of 10 percent each year. So if he leaves at the end of five years, for example, he will be paid for 50 percent of the stock under the buy-sell agreement, and he will forfeit the remaining 50 percent. Alternatively, the restriction may provide that all or a portion of the stock is forfeited if Jim fails to hit certain sales volumes, or otherwise fails to satisfy some other objective measure of performance.

There is a significant tax consequence to this forfeiture feature. As long as a substantial risk of forfeiture exists, the executive does not have to pay tax on the stock that's been transferred.[49] In our example, Jim could be transferred $100,000 worth of stock and pay no tax at the time of transfer. If, after 10 years, the forfeiture feature goes away, Jim would be taxed on the full value of the stock at that time. Often the forfeiture provisions are structured to lapse over a period of years so that only a portion of the tax liability is recognized in any year. On the other side, the company gets a tax deduction equal to the amount of taxable income that Jim is required to report in the same year that Jim reports the income.[50]

There is another tax planning option that should be considered whenever restricted stock is used. The executive may elect to be taxed on the stock at the time the stock is received, rather than at the time the forfeiture provision lapses.[51] Why would an executive ever want to elect to recognize taxable income at an earlier point in time? If the stock value at the time the stock is received is very low and there is a substantial prospect that it is going to appreciate rapidly in the future, the executive may prefer to recognize the taxable income at the time the stock is granted at the much lower value. If the election is made to recognize income at the time of grant, there is no need to recognize any future taxable income until the stock is actually sold. There is a disadvantage with this election. If the executive elects to recognize the income at the time the stock is granted and the stock is then forfeited, the executive gets no offsetting deduction at the time of the forfeiture. Thus, the executive may be in a position of having paid tax on something that never produced any value. It's a calculated risk. If the executive's choice is to make the election, the company gets a deduction at the same time the executive recognizes the income.

Restricted stock is a flexible tool that can be used in many situations. As many stock option programs have lost their appeal, the restricted stock alternative has become more popular.

---

49. I.R.C. § 83(a)(1); Reg. § 1.83-3(c). The existence of the forfeiture feature and the related tax deferral does not make the arrangement a deferred compensation plan subject to the new section 409A requirements. Proposed Reg. § 1.409A-1(a)(6).

50. I.R.C. § 83(h).

51. See, generally, I.R.C. § 83(b).

5. Stock Appreciation Right Strategy

The next strategy is different from the four previous strategies in one significant respect: the executive never gets the real thing. There is no stock. In lieu of receiving stock, the executive is given a contractual right to compensation that is structured to provide the same economic benefits as stock. Here is how it works.

Suppose XYZ, Inc. wants to give Jim the right to fully receive the value of all appreciation that accrues on 100,000 shares of its stock in the future. Jim doesn't want any stock options for a number of reasons. He doesn't want to have to pay a real cost, as is required by an option. The tax traps of options also are a problem for the parties. An ISO will produce no tax deduction for the company and may present an alternative tax problem for Jim. A nonqualified option, on the other hand, will produce phantom taxable income for Jim at time of exercise.

A stock appreciation right contract may be the answer. A contract is drawn that essentially states that the parties will pretend that Jim owns 100,000 shares of stock. He never really owns the stock. Usually the contract would establish a base price of the stock – say $1.00 per share – that would equal the current value of the stock. The contract would offer a number of economic benefits based on the pretend stock. It would provide that if a dividend is paid to the real shareholders of the company, then a corresponding amount of compensation would be paid to Jim on his 100,000 pretend shares. It would also provide that if the company is sold, merged, or goes public, Jim would receive the excess in the value of his pretend shares, at that time, over the base value of such phantom shares at the time the contract was awarded to him. For example, if the company is sold at a price of $3.00 per share down the road, Jim would be entitled to receive compensation income at a rate of $2.00 per share for the 100,000 pretend shares awarded to him under the contract. The contract would also provide that the stock appreciation rights would be valued at the time Jim dies, is disabled, or otherwise terminates his employment. The excess of the value of the rights at that time over the base value of $1.00 per share would be paid as additional compensation income to Jim. Golden Handcuffs features may be structured into the contract to provide Jim with incentives to remain loyal and dedicated to the company. Essentially, the contract is designed to provide Jim with the same economic benefits, in the form of compensation under the contract, that he would otherwise receive in the form of stockholder economic benefits if he actually owned the real stock.

What are the advantages to such a stock appreciation right arrangement? There are a number of benefits. First, there is no threat of phantom income. Since all amounts paid to Jim are compensation under the contract, Jim will not have any taxable income until he actually receives payment. Second, there is no alternative minimum tax threat. Third, since all amounts paid to Jim represent compensation, the company receives a full deduction at the time of payment. This is a significant benefit to the company and may allow the company to pay Jim a larger benefit. In many ways, a stock appreciation right contractual arrangement is one of the most efficient strategies, from a tax perspective, for transferring upside stock value from the company to the executive.

Is there any tax disadvantage to such an arrangement? Historically, the biggest disadvantage to any such arrangement has been the absence of any capital gains or favorable dividend tax break for the executive. Because the executive never owns any stock, there is no possibility of creating a capital gain at time of sale or receiving dividends. To sweeten the deal for the executive, an added bonus may be provided to produce a net after-tax yield to the executive that is equal to the yield that would result if the pretend stock payment were taxed as a capital gain or dividend. Again, the company gets a full deduction for all amounts paid. Often, this capital gains or dividend bonus can be paid with the company still incurring a net after-tax cost that is less than what would be incurred if it purchased stock or paid a dividend under another strategy.

A stock appreciation right arrangement provides a number of flexible alternatives. There is no requirement that the executive make an investment in order to acquire rights to future appreciation in the stock. There is no risk of phantom income. The company gets a deduction. There is no alternative minimum tax risk. The Golden Handcuffs Factor and the Cash-Out Factor can both be accommodated in a variety of different ways through the contract. The company often prefers this type of arrangement because of the Fall-out Leverage Factor. If there is a major problem between the executive and the company down the road, the executive has a contractual right to payment, but does not own any stock in the company. Accordingly, the executive is not in a position to cause problems as a shareholder.

With a stock appreciation right plan, care must be taken to ensure that it avoids the reach of Section 409A or that it is structured to comply with the Section 409A requirements (i.e., no executive election rights as to timing or method of payout after the grant of the rights). There is no room for ambiguity. A stock appreciation right plan can avoid 409A treatment if there is no Value Now Factor (only appreciation following the grant is considered) and the plan includes no other deferred compensation element. [52]

The biggest disadvantage from the executive's perspective is that he or she never owns the real thing. The arrangement is a fancy employment contract. The subjective desires of being viewed and treated like an owner may never be realized. Often it's possible to overcome this fear by reemphasizing that the contract is being drawn to provide a real piece of the rock by offering economic benefits that, dollar for dollar, are structured to be the same as those that would be realized if stock were actually owned.

6. Phantom Stock Plan

The next strategy is the phantom stock plan. This strategy is the same as the stock appreciation right strategy described previously, with one significant twist. The strategy is structured to give full effect to the Value Now Factor and falls squarely within the reach of Section 409A. A contract is drawn that gives the executive the right to be compensated on the basis of certain pretend shares, but there is no existing base value price. At the time the contract is entered into, the

---

52. Reg. § 1.409A-(b)(5)(i)(C)(3).

executive is promised payments down the road based on the current value of the phantom shares, together with all future appreciation on those shares. It's as if the executive actually owned the stock now. Hence, the name "phantom stock."

Jim, for example, could be provided a phantom stock benefit that gives him the right to 100,000 phantom shares that have an existing value of $2.00 per share. This would be an attractive contractual right from Jim's perspective. Moreover, as the value of the stock in the company increases, the value of Jim's phantom shares would similarly increase.

Since such a phantom stock plan is subject to Section 409A, Jim can have no timing or payout elections after the grant of the rights. To comply with Section 409A, the time and method of payout must be specified at time of grant or tied to a permissible payout event under Section 409A (separation from service, disability, death, change of control, or unforeseen emergency).

Assuming the requirements of Section 409A are satisfied, is Jim required to recognize this Value Now Factor ($200,000 in our example) at the time the contract is entered into? The answer is "no" so as long as Jim simply has the contractual right to receive a payment for this amount as compensation in the future.[53] Thus, unlike the bonus stock and the restricted stock strategies described previously, Jim can receive a Real Value Now factor and avoid any phantom taxable income. The key variable is that he has received a contractual right to future payments, rather than a property right represented in the form of stock.

Again, the biggest disadvantage from Jim's perspective is that he has not received real stock in the company. Also, because Jim never receives stock, there is no opportunity for capital gains treatment. These potential disadvantages may pale in significance compared to the economic benefits being offered under the program and the fact that there is no threat of phantom taxable income. Plus, as described above, the plan can be structured to pay Jim compensation for any lost capital gains benefits and put him in the exact economic position as if he had received real stock. When the plan is dolled up to include such benefits, it is sometimes referred to as a "stock equivalency plan" – a term that may sound more appealing than "phantom stock."

CASE PROBLEM 16-4

Refer to Case Problem 16-3 and Jurden Industries' challenge to lock in its star VP of sales, Justin. The CEO opened up discussions with Justin and, to everyone's surprise, Justin demanded a piece of the rock. He wants to participate in the equity growth of the company. He wants the rights of an owner. Specifically, Justin has requested (demanded?) the following:

1. He wants equity value now in recognition of the value he has already brought to the company. He doesn't want a deal that is based solely on the future

---

53. An unfunded and unsecured right to receive money or property does not constitute "property" under the provisions of Section 83. Reg. § 1.83-3(e).

appreciation of the company's stock.

2. He doesn't want to pay anything for his equity interest in the company. He figures that he has already paid through his efforts on behalf of the company.

3. He wants an official vote in the management affairs of the company. He isn't asking for control – just the right to be part of the inner circle.

4. He doesn't want to pay any income taxes on the equity interest that he receives until the stock is sold and cash is realized.

5. He wants the tax benefits of stock ownership – specifically preferred tax treatment on dividends and capital gains benefits at the time of sale.

Jurden's CEO is overwhelmed. He doesn't want to give Justin anything that is not tied to his future long-term performance on behalf of the company. The CEO asks: What happens if we give Justin stock and he stops performing or quits? How do we get the stock back? Do we have to buy it back? What happens to Justin's stock if there is a falling out down the road?

The CEO wants your advice. What do you recommend?

CHAPTER 17

SELECT FORMS

A. SMART USE OR MISUSE?

A good form library is a blessing for any lawyer. It's a necessity; no one has the time or the competence to start from scratch with every important document. A quality form jumpstarts the drafting process and becomes a valuable aid in the planning process. The competent lawyer knows his or her forms—what they say and, far more important, what they do *not* say. The limitations, shortcomings, and imperfections of each form (they all have them) are well understood. A form never becomes a tool for short-circuiting or cheating the planning process.

Forms become curses when they are misused. They make it possible for the lazy or ill-informed to create complete, official-looking documents without ever embracing the planning process. Often the form's misuse is rationalized by perpetuating a dangerously false notion that there is a "standard" or "normal" way of doing things. The perpetrator sometimes lacks a thorough knowledge of what the form really says and usually has no clue as to the form's flaws or shortcomings. The foolishness of such a practice should be obvious to anyone who has read the foregoing pages.

Sample forms are included in the following sections of this chapter. They were taken directly from the form file of one of the top Seattle-based firms.[1] As forms go, they are fine but nothing special. They are offered here not as examples of extraordinary quality, but rather as tools to assist the learning effort. The educational value of analyzing a form is in identifying and understanding its limitations and shortcomings. This can be an individual or group effort. You will discover that these forms, like all their counterparts, contain limitations that a quality planning lawyer will easily spot and a phony often will often miss. The

---

1. The forms in this Chapter, included for educational purposes only, are from the form files of Foster Pepper PLLC, a Northwest-based firm with regional and national practices.

hope is that your analysis of each form will enhance your understanding of the relevant planning challenges and promote a healthy respect for the value and limitations of all forms.

B. FORM: LIMITED LIABILITY COMPANY OPERATIING AGREEMENT

OPERATING AGREEMENT OF

_____   _____

A Washington Limited Liability Company

This Operating Agreement (the "Agreement") is made and entered into as of the ___ day of _____, 2011, by and between _____ ("_____") and _____ ("_____") (the "Members"). The parties agree to operate as a limited liability company under the laws of the state of Washington as follows.

The parties hereto agree as follows:

1. DEFINITIONS. The following terms used in the Agreement shall have the meanings specified below:

1.1 "Act" means the Washington Limited Liability Company Act, as amended from time to time.

1.2 "Adjusted Contribution Amount" with respect to each Member means the Capital Contributions pursuant to Sections 7.1 and 7.4, as reduced from time to time by distributions pursuant to Section 10.

1.3 "Agreement" means this Operating Agreement of the ABC, LLC as it may be amended from time to time.

1.4 "Assignee" means a person who has acquired a Member's Interest in whole or part and has not become a Substitute Member.

1.5 "Capital Account" means the account maintained for each Member in accordance with Section 7.5. In the case of a transfer of an interest, the transferee shall succeed to the Capital Account of the transferor or, in the case of a partial transfer, a proportionate share thereof.

1.6 "Capital Contribution" means the total amount of money and the fair market value of all property contributed to the Company by each Member pursuant to the terms of the Agreement. Capital Contribution shall also include any amounts paid directly by a Member to any creditor of the Company in respect of any guarantee or similar obligation undertaken by such Member in connection with the Company's operations. Any reference to the Capital Contribution of a Member shall include the Capital Contribution made by a predecessor holder of the interest of such Member.

1.7 "Cash Available for Distribution" means all cash receipts of the Company, excluding cash available upon liquidation of the Company, in excess of amounts reasonably required for payment of operating expenses, repayment of current liabilities, repayment of such amounts of Company indebtedness as the

Manager shall determine necessary or advisable, and the establishment of and additions to such cash reserves as the Manager shall deem necessary or advisable, including, but not limited to reserves for capital expenditures, replacements, contingent or unforeseen liabilities or other obligations of the Company.

1.8 "Code" means the United States Internal Revenue Code of 1986, as amended. References to specific Code Sections or Treasury Regulations shall be deemed to refer to such Code Sections or Treasury Regulations as they may be amended from time to time or to any successor Code Sections or Treasury Regulations if the Code Section or Treasury Regulation referred to is repealed.

1.9 "Company" means the Washington limited liability company named ABC, LLC governed by the Agreement.

1.10 "Company Property" means all the real and personal property owned by the Company.

1.11 "Deemed Capital Account" means a Member's Capital Account, as calculated from time to time, adjusted by (i) adding thereto the sum of (A) the amount of such Member's Mandatory Obligation, if any, and (B) each Member's share of Minimum Gain (determined after any decreases therein for such year) and (ii) subtracting therefrom (A) allocations of losses and deductions which are reasonably expected to be made as of the end of the taxable year to the Members pursuant to Code Section 704(e)(2), Code Section 706(d) and Treasury Regulation Section 1.751–1(b)(2)(ii), and (B) distributions which at the end of the taxable year are reasonably expected to be made to the Member to the extent that said distributions exceed offsetting increases to the Member's Capital Account (including allocations of the Qualified Income Offset pursuant to Section 8.7 but excluding allocations of Minimum Gain Chargeback pursuant to Section 8.6) that are reasonably expected to occur during (or prior to) the taxable years in which such distributions are reasonably expected to be made.

1.12 "Interest" or "Company Interest" means the ownership interest of a Member in the Company at any particular time, including the right of such Member to any and all benefits to which such Member may be entitled as provided in the Agreement and in the Act, together with the obligations of such Member to comply with all the terms and provisions of the Agreement and the Act.

1.13 "Manager(s)" means those Member(s) and other persons who are appointed in accordance with this Agreement to exercise the authority of Manager under this Agreement and the Act. If at any time a Member who is a Manager ceases to be a Member for any reason, that Member shall simultaneously cease to be a Manager. The initial Manager of the Company shall be [_____].

1.14 "Mandatory Obligation" means the sum of (i) the amount of a Member's remaining contribution obligation (including the amount of any Capital Account deficit such Member is obligated to restore upon liquidation) provided that such contribution must be made in all events within ninety (90) days of liquidation of the Member's interest as determined under Treasury Regulation

Section 1.704–1(b)(2)(ii)(g) and (ii) the additional amount, if any, such Member would be obligated to contribute as of year end to retire recourse indebtedness of the Company if the Company were to liquidate as of such date and dispose of all of its assets at book value.

1.15 "Member(s)" means those persons who execute a counterpart of this Agreement and those persons who are hereafter admitted as members under Section 14.4 below.

1.16 "Minimum Gain" means the amount determined by computing, with respect to each nonrecourse liability of the Company, the amount of gain, if any, that would be realized by the Company if it disposed of the Company Property subject to such nonrecourse liability in full satisfaction thereof in a taxable transaction, and then by aggregating the amounts so determined. Such gain shall be determined in accordance with Treasury Regulation Section 1.704–2(d). Each Member's share of Minimum Gain at the end of any taxable year of the Company shall be determined in accordance with Treasury Regulation Section 1.704–2(g)(1).

1.17 "Net Income" or "Net Loss" means taxable income or loss (including items requiring separate computation under Section 702 of the Code) of the Company as determined using the method of accounting chosen by the Manager and used by the Company for federal income tax purposes, adjusted in accordance with Treasury Regulation Section 1.704–1(b)(2)(iv)(g), for any property with differing tax and book values, to take into account depreciation, depletion, amortization and gain or loss as computed for book purposes.

1.18 "Percentage Interest" means the percentage interest of each Member as set forth on Appendix A.

1.19 "Substitute Member" means an Assignee who has been admitted to all of the rights of membership pursuant to Section 14.4 below.

2. FORMATION. The Members hereby agree to form and to operate the Company under the terms and conditions set forth herein. Except as otherwise provided herein, the rights and liabilities of the Members shall be governed by the Act.

2.1 Defects as to Formalities. A failure to observe any formalities or requirements of this Agreement, the articles of organization for the Company or the Act shall not be grounds for imposing personal liability on the Members or Manager for liabilities of the Company.

2.2 No Partnership Intended for Nontax Purposes. The Members have formed the Company under the Act, and expressly do not intend hereby to form a partnership under either the Washington Uniform Partnership Act or the Washington Uniform Limited Partnership Act or a corporation under the Washington Business Corporation Act. The Members do not intend to be partners one to another, or partners as to any third party. The Members hereto agree and acknowledge that the Company is to be treated as a partnership for federal income tax purposes.

2.3 Rights of Creditors and Third Parties. This Agreement is entered into among the Company and the Members for the exclusive benefit of the Company, its Members and their successors and assigns. The Agreement is expressly not intended for the benefit of any creditor of the Company or any other person. Except and only to the extent provided by applicable statute, no such creditor or third party shall have any rights under the Agreement or any agreement between the Company and any Member with respect to any Contribution or otherwise.

2.4 Title to Property. All Company Property shall be owned by the Company as an entity and no Member shall have any ownership interest in such Property in the Member's individual name or right, and each Member's interest in the Company shall be personal property for all purposes. Except as otherwise provided in this Agreement, the Company shall hold all Company Property in the name of the Company and not in the name or names of any Member or Members.

2.5 Payments of Individual Obligations. The Company's credit and assets shall be used solely for the benefit of the Company, and no asset of the Company shall be transferred or encumbered for or in payment of any individual obligation of any Member unless otherwise provided for herein.

3. NAME. The name of the Company shall be ABC, LLC. The Manager may from time to time change the name of the Company or adopt such trade or fictitious names as they may determine to be appropriate.

4. OFFICE; AGENT FOR SERVICE OF PROCESS. The principal office of the Company shall be _____. The Company may maintain such other offices at such other places as the Manager may determine to be appropriate. The agent for service of process for the Company shall be _____ at the above address.

5. PURPOSES OF THE COMPANY. The Company shall be in the business of providing _____ marketing products and services. In addition, the Company may engage in any other business and shall have such other purposes as may be necessary, incidental or convenient to carry on the Company's primary purpose or as determined by the Manager and Members from time to time in accordance with the terms of this Agreement.

6. TERM. The term of the Company shall commence on the date of the filing of the Articles of Organization for the Company in the office of the Washington Secretary of State, and shall continue until dissolved, wound up and terminated in accordance with the provisions of this Agreement and the Act.

7. PERCENTAGE INTERESTS AND CAPITAL CONTRIBUTIONS.

7.1 Initial Capital Contributions; Percentage Interests. The Members shall make the initial Capital Contributions to the Company in the amounts set forth on Appendix A for the Percentage Interests in the Company as shown on Appendix A.

7.2 No Interest on Capital. No Member shall be entitled to receive interest on such Member's Capital Contributions or such Member's Capital Account.

7.3 No Withdrawal of Capital. Except as otherwise provided in this Agreement, no Member shall have the right to withdraw or demand a return of any or all of such Member's Capital Contribution. It is the intent of the Members that no distribution (or any part of any distribution) made to any Member pursuant to Section 10 hereof shall be deemed a return or withdrawal of Capital Contributions, even if such distribution represents (in full or in part) a distribution of revenue offset by depreciation or any other non-cash item accounted for as an expense, loss or deduction from, or offset to, the Company's income, and that no Member shall be obligated to pay any such amount to or for the account of the Company or any creditor of the Company. However, if any court of competent jurisdiction holds that, notwithstanding the provisions of this Agreement, any Member is obligated to make any such payment, such obligation shall be the obligation of such Member and not of any other Member, including the Manager.

7.4 Additional Capital. Except as otherwise provided for herein or mutually agreed upon by the Members, no Member shall be obligated to make an additional Capital Contribution to the Company.

7.5 Capital Accounts. The Company shall establish and maintain a Capital Account for each Member in accordance with Treasury Regulations issued under Code Section 704. The initial Capital Account balance for each Member shall be the amount of initial Capital Contributions made by each Member under Section 7.1. The Capital Account of each Member shall be increased to reflect (i) such Member's cash contributions, (ii) the fair market value of property contributed by such Member (net of liabilities securing such contributed property that the Company is considered to assume or take subject to under Code Section 752), (iii) such Member's share of Net Income (including all gain as calculated pursuant to Section 1001 of the Code) of the Company and (iv) such Member's share of income and gain exempt from tax. The Capital Account of each Member shall be reduced to reflect (a) the amount of money and the fair market value of property distributed to such Member (net of liabilities securing such distributed property that the Member is considered to assume or take subject to under Section 752), (b) such Member's share of non-capitalized expenditures not deductible by the Company in computing its taxable income as determined under Code Section 705(a)(2)(B), (c) such Member's share of Net Loss of the Company and (d) such Member's share of amounts paid or incurred to organize the Company or to promote the sale of Company Interests to the extent that an election under Code Section 709(b) has not properly been made for such amounts. The Manager shall determine the fair market value of all property which is distributed in kind, and the Capital Accounts of the Members shall be adjusted as though the property had been sold for its fair market value and the gain or loss attributable to such sale allocated among the Members in accordance with Section 8.1 or 8.2, as applicable. In the event of a contribution of property with a fair market value which is not equal to its adjusted basis (as determined for federal income tax purposes), a revaluation of the Members' Capital Accounts upon the admission of new members to the Company, or in other appropriate situations as permitted by Treasury Regulations issued under Code Section 704, the Company shall separately maintain "tax" Capital Accounts solely for purposes of taking into account the variation between the adjusted tax basis and book value of Company property in tax allocations to the Members consistent with the principles of Code Section 704(c) in accordance with the rules prescribed in Treasury Regulations promulgated under Code Section 704.

7.6 Default. In the event any Member shall fail to contribute any cash or property when due hereunder, such Member shall remain liable therefor to the Company, which may institute proceedings in any court of competent jurisdiction in connection with which such Member shall pay the costs of such collection, including reasonable attorneys' fees. Any compromise or settlement with a Member failing to contribute cash or property due hereunder may be approved by a majority by Percentage Interest of the other Members.

8. ALLOCATIONS.

8.1 Allocation of Net Loss from Operations. Except as otherwise provided in this Section 8 and in Section 16.3, the Company shall allocate Net Loss to the Members in proportion to each Member's Percentage Interest.

8.2 Allocation of Net Income from Operations. Except as otherwise provided in this Section 8 and Section 16.3, the Company shall allocate all Net Income as follows:

1. First, to the Members in proportion to the aggregate distributions of Cash Available for Distribution made to the Members in the current year and all prior years pursuant to Section 10 until such time as each Member has been allocated Net Income pursuant to this Section 8.3 in an amount equal to the excess of (i) the amount of Cash Available for Distribution distributed to such Member for the current year and all prior years pursuant to Section 10, over (ii) the amount of Net Income previously allocated to such Member pursuant to this Section 8.3; and thereafter, all remaining Net Income shall be allocated in proportion to each Member's Percentage Interest.

8.3 Limitation on Net Loss Allocations. Notwithstanding anything contained in this Section 8, no Member shall be allocated Net Loss to the extent such allocation would cause a negative balance in such Member's Deemed Capital Account as of the end of the taxable year to which such allocation relates.

8.4 Minimum Gain Chargeback. If there is a net decrease in Minimum Gain during a taxable year of the Company, then notwithstanding any other provision of this Section 8 or Section 16.3, each Member must be allocated items of income and gain for such year, and succeeding taxable years to the extent necessary (the "Minimum Gain Chargeback"), in proportion to, and to the extent of, an amount required under Treasury Regulation Section 1.704–2(f).

8.5 Qualified Income Offset. If at the end of any taxable year and after operation of Section 10, any Member shall have a negative balance in such Member's Deemed Capital Account, then notwithstanding anything contained in this Section 8, there shall be reallocated to each Member with a negative balance in such Member's Deemed Capital Account (determined after the allocation of income, gain or loss under this Section 8 for such year) each item of Company gross income (unreduced by any deductions) and gain in proportion to such negative balances until the Deemed Capital Account for each such Member is increased to zero.

8.6 Curative Allocations. The allocations set forth in Sections 8.3, 8.4 and 8.5 (the "Regulatory Allocations") are intended to comply with certain requirements of the Treasury Regulations issued pursuant to Code Section 704(b). It is the intent of the Members that, to the extent possible, all Regulatory Allocations shall be offset either with other Regulatory Allocations or with special allocations of other items of Company income, gain, loss, or deduction pursuant to this Section 8. Therefore, notwithstanding any other provision of this Section 8 (other than the Regulatory Allocations), the Manager shall make such offsetting special allocations of Company income, gain, loss, or deduction in whatever manner they determine appropriate so that, after such offsetting allocations are made, each Member's Capital Account balance is, to the extent possible, equal to the Capital Account balance such Member would have had if the Regulatory Allocations were not part of the Agreement and all Company items were allocated pursuant to other provisions of this Section 8.

8.7 Modification of Company Allocations. It is the intent of the Members that each Member's distributive share of income, gain, loss, deduction, or credit (or items thereof) shall be determined and allocated in accordance with this Section 8 to the fullest extent permitted by Section 704(b) of the Code. In order to preserve and protect the determinations and allocations provided for in this Section 8, the Manager shall be, and hereby is, authorized and directed to allocate income, gain, loss, deduction or credit (or items thereof) arising in any year differently from the manner otherwise provided for in this Section 8 if, and to the extent that, allocation of income, gain, loss, deduction or credit (or items thereof) in the manner provided for in this Section would cause the determination and allocation of each Member's distributive share of income, gain, loss, deduction or credit (or items thereof), not to be permitted by Section 704(b) of the Code and Treasury Regulations promulgated thereunder. Any allocation made pursuant to this Section 8.9 shall be made only after the Manager has secured an opinion of counsel that such modification is the minimum modification required to comply with Code Section 704(b) and shall be deemed to be a complete substitute for any allocation otherwise provided for in this Section and no amendment of this Agreement or approval of any Member shall be required. The Members shall be given notice of the modification within thirty (30) days of the effective date thereof, such notice to include the text of the modification and a statement of the circumstances requiring the modification to be made.

8.8 Deficit Capital Accounts at Liquidation. It is understood and agreed that one purpose of the provisions of this Section 8 is to insure that none of the Members has a deficit Capital Account balance after liquidation and to insure that all allocations under this Section 8 will be respected by the Internal Revenue Service. The Members and the Company neither intend nor expect that any Member will have a deficit Capital Account balance after liquidation and, notwithstanding anything to the contrary in this Agreement, the provisions of this Agreement shall be construed and interpreted to give effect to such intention. However, if following a liquidation of a Member's interest as determined under Treasury Regulation Section 1.704–1(b)(2)(ii)(g), a Member has a deficit balance in such Member's Capital Account after the allocation of Net Income pursuant to this Section 8 and Section 16.3 and all other adjustments have been made to such

Member's Capital Account for Company operations and liquidation, no Member shall have any obligation to restore such deficit balance, as provided in Section 8.9.

8.9 Deficit Restoration Obligation. No Member shall have an obligation to restore a deficit Capital Account balance upon liquidation of the Company or liquidation of its interest in the Company.

9. COMPANY EXPENSES. The Company shall pay, and the Manager shall be reimbursed for, all costs and expenses of the Company, which may include, but are not limited to:

9.1 All organizational expenses incurred in the formation of the Company and the selling of interests in the Company;

9.2 All costs of personnel employed by the Company;

9.3 All costs reasonably related to the conduct of the Company's day-to-day business affairs, including, but without limitation, the cost of supplies, utilities, taxes, licenses, fees and services contracted from third parties;

9.4 All costs of borrowed money, taxes and assessments on Company property, and other taxes applicable to the Company;

9.5 Legal, audit, accounting, brokerage and other fees;

9.6 Printing and other expenses and taxes incurred in connection with the issuance, distribution, transfer, registration and recording of documents evidencing ownership of an interest in the Company or in connection with the business of the Company;

9.7 Fees and expenses paid to service providers, including affiliates of the Manager;

9.8 The cost of insurance obtained in connection with the business of the Company;

9.9 Expenses of revising, amending, converting, modifying or terminating the Company;

9.10 Expenses in connection with distributions made by the Company to, and communications and bookkeeping and clerical work necessary in maintaining relations with, Members;

9.11 Expenses in connection with preparing and mailing reports required to be furnished to Members for investment, tax reporting or other purposes that the Manager deems appropriate; and

9.12 Costs incurred in connection with any litigation, including any examinations or audits by regulatory agencies.

10. DISTRIBUTIONS OF CASH AVAILABLE FOR DISTRIBUTION. At such times and in such amounts as the Manager in its discretion determines appropriate, Cash Available for Distribution shall be distributed in the following order of priority:

10.1 First, among the Members in proportion to their Adjusted Contribution Amounts until such balances are reduced to zero; and

10.2 Thereafter, among the Members in proportion to their Percentage Interests.

11. POWERS, RIGHTS AND OBLIGATIONS OF MANAGER.

11.1 General Authority and Powers of Manager. Except as provided in Section , the Manager shall have the exclusive right and power to manage, operate and control the Company and to do all things and make all decisions necessary or appropriate to carry on the business and affairs of the Company. All decisions required to be made by the Manager or action to be taken by the Manager shall require the approval and action of only one Manager, acting alone, except as otherwise specifically provided in this Agreement. The authority of one Manager, acting alone, shall include, but shall not be limited to the following:

(a) To spend the capital and revenues of the Company;

(b) To manage, develop, and operate the business of the Company and the Company properties;

(c) To employ service providers to assist in the operation and management of the Company's business and for the operation and development of the property of the Company, as the Manager shall deem necessary in its sole discretion;

(d) To acquire, lease and sell personal and/or real property, hire and fire employees, and to do all other acts necessary, appropriate or helpful for the operation of the Company business;

(e) To execute, acknowledge and deliver any and all instruments to effectuate any of the foregoing powers and any other powers granted the Manager under the laws of the state of Washington or other provisions of this Agreement;

(f) To enter into and to execute agreements for employment or services, as well as any other agreements and all other instruments a Manager deems necessary or appropriate to operate the Company's business and to operate and dispose of Company properties or to effectively and properly perform its duties or exercise its powers hereunder;

(g) To borrow money on a secured or unsecured basis from individuals, banks and other lending institutions to meet Company obligations, provide Company working capital and for any other Company purpose, and to execute promissory notes, mortgages, deeds of trust and assignments of Company property, and such other security instruments as a lender of funds may require, to secure repayment of such borrowings;

(h) To enter into such agreements and contracts and to give such receipts, releases and discharges, with respect to the business of the Company, as a Manager deems advisable or appropriate;

(i) To purchase, at the expense of the Company, such liability and other insurance as the Manager, in its sole discretion, deems advisable to protect the Company's assets and business; however, the Manager shall not be liable to the Company or the other Members for failure to purchase any insurance; and

(j) To sue and be sued, complain, defend, settle and/or compromise, with respect to any claim in favor of or against the Company, in the name and on behalf of the Company.

11.2 Time Devoted to Company; Other Ventures. The Manager shall devote so much of its time to the business of the Company as in its judgment the conduct of the Company's business reasonably requires. The Manager and the other Members may engage in business ventures and activities of any nature and description independently or with others, whether or not in competition with the business of the Company, and shall have no obligation to disclose business opportunities available to them, and neither the Company nor any of the other Members shall have any rights in and to such independent ventures and activities or the income or profits derived therefrom by reason of their acquisition of interests in the Company. This Section 11.2 is intended to modify any provisions or obligations of the Act to the contrary and each of the Members and the Company hereby waives and releases any claims they may have under the Act with respect to any such activities or ventures of the Manager or other Members.

11.3 Liability of Manager to Members and Company. In carrying out its duties and exercising the powers hereunder, the Manager shall exercise reasonable skill, care and business judgment. A Manager shall not be liable to the Company or the Members for any act or omission performed or omitted by it in good faith pursuant to the authority granted to it by this Agreement as a Manager or Tax Matters Partner (as defined in the Code) unless such act or omission constitutes gross negligence or willful misconduct by such Manager.

11.4 Indemnification. The Company shall indemnify and hold harmless the Manager from any loss or damage, including attorneys' fees actually and reasonably incurred by it, by reason of any act or omission performed or omitted by it on behalf of the Company or in furtherance of the Company's interests or as Tax Matters Partner; however, such indemnification or agreement to hold harmless shall be recoverable only out of the assets of the Company and not from the Members. The foregoing indemnity shall extend only to acts or omissions performed or omitted by a Manager in good faith and in the belief that the acts or omissions were in the Company's interest or not opposed to the best interests of the Company.

11.5 Fiduciary Responsibility. The Manager shall have a fiduciary responsibility for the safekeeping and use of all funds and assets of the Company, and all such funds and assets shall be used in accordance with the terms of this Agreement.

11.6 Restrictions on Authority of Manager.

(a) Except as provided in Section 11.6(b), the following Company decisions shall require the written consent of the Manager and Members holding a majority of the Percentage Interests in the Company:

(i) The dissolution and winding up of the Company;

(ii) The sale, exchange or other transfer of all or substantially all the assets of the Company other than in the ordinary course of business; or

(iii) A change in the nature of the business of the Company.

(b) Notwithstanding the provisions of Section 11.6(a), no consent or approval of the Members shall be required prior to a transfer of the Project or other Company property for no consideration other than full or partial satisfaction of Company indebtedness such as by deed in lieu of foreclosure or similar procedure.

(c) Notwithstanding the provisions of Section 11.6(a)(i), the dissolution and winding up or insolvency filing of the Company shall require the unanimous consent of all Members.

12. STATUS OF MEMBERS.

12.1 No Participation in Management. Except as specifically provided in Section 11.6 above, no Member shall take part in the conduct or control of the Company's business or the management of the Company, or have any right or authority to act for or on the behalf of, or otherwise bind, the Company (except a Member who may also be a Manager and then only in such Member's capacity as a Manager within the scope of such Member's authority hereunder).

12.2 Limitation of Liability. No Member shall have, solely by virtue of such Member's status as a Member in the Company, any personal liability whatever, whether to the Company, to any Members or to the creditors of the Company, for the debts or obligations of the Company or any of its losses beyond the amount committed by such Member to the capital of the Company, except as otherwise required by the Act.

12.3 Death or Incapacity of Non–Manager Member. The death, incompetence, withdrawal, expulsion, bankruptcy or dissolution of a Member, or the occurrence of any other event which terminates the continued membership of a Member in the Company, shall not cause a dissolution of the Company unless such Member is a Manager of the Company. Upon the occurrence of such event, the rights of such non-Manager Member to share in the Net Income and Net Loss of the Company, to receive distributions from the Company and to assign an interest in the Company pursuant to Section 14 shall, on the happening of such an event, devolve upon such Member's executor, administrator, guardian, conservator, or other legal representative or successor, as the case may be, subject to the terms and conditions of this Agreement, and the Company shall continue as a limited liability company. However, in any such event, such legal representative or successor, or any assignee of such legal representative or successor shall be admitted to the Company as a Member only in accordance with and pursuant to all of the terms and conditions of Section 14 hereof.

12.4 Death or Incapacity of a Manager Member. The death, incompetence, withdrawal, expulsion, bankruptcy or dissolution of a Member that is a Manager, or the occurrence of any other event which terminates the continued membership of such Member in the Company, shall cause a dissolution of the Company, unless the Company is continued in accordance with Section 16. If the Company is continued in accordance with Section 16, the rights of such Member to share in the Net Income and Net Loss of the Company, to receive distributions from the Company and to assign an interest in the Company pursuant to Section 14 hereof shall, on the happening of such an event, devolve upon such Member's executor, administrator, guardian, conservator, or other legal representative or successor, as the case may be, subject to the terms and conditions of this Agreement, and the Company shall continue as a limited liability company. However, in any such event such legal representative or successor, or any assignee of such legal representative or successor shall be admitted to the Company as a Member only in accordance with and pursuant to all of the terms and conditions of Section 14 hereof.

12.5 Recourse of Members. Each Member shall look solely to the assets of the Company for all distributions with respect to the Company and such Member's Capital Contribution thereto and share of Net Income and Net Loss thereof and shall have no recourse therefore, upon dissolution or otherwise, against any Manager or any other Member.

12.6 No Right to Property. No Member, regardless of the nature of such Member's contributions to the capital of the Company, shall have any right to demand or receive any distribution from the Company in any form other than cash, upon dissolution or otherwise.

13. BOOKS AND RECORDS, ACCOUNTING, REPORTS AND STATEMENTS AND TAX MATTERS.

13.1 Books and Records. The Manager shall, at the expense of the Company, keep and maintain, or cause to be kept and maintained, the books and records of the Company on the same method of accounting as utilized for federal income tax purposes, which shall be kept separate and apart from the books and records of the Manager.

13.2 Annual Accounting Period. All books and records of the Company shall be kept on the basis of an annual accounting period ending December 31 of each year, except for the final accounting period which shall end on the date of termination of the Company. All references herein to the "fiscal year of the Company" are to the annual accounting period described in the preceding sentence, whether the same shall consist of twelve months or less.

13.3 Manager's Reports to Members. The Manager shall send at Company expense to each Member the following:

(a) Within seventy-five (75) days after the end of each fiscal year of the Company, such information as shall be necessary for the preparation by such Member of such Member's federal income tax return which shall include a computation of the distributions to such Member and the allocation to such Member of profits or losses, as the case may be; and

(b) Within one hundred twenty (120) days after the end of each fiscal quarter of the Company, a quarterly report, which shall include:

(i) A balance sheet;

(ii) A statement of income and expenses;

(iii) A statement of changes in Members' capital; and

(iv) A statement of the balances in the Capital Accounts of the Members.

13.4 Right to Examine Records. Members shall be entitled, upon written request directed to the Company, to review the records of the Company at all reasonable times and at the location where such records are kept by the Company.

13.5 Tax Matters Partner. Should there be any controversy with the Internal Revenue Service or any other taxing authority involving the Company, the Manager may expend such funds as they deem necessary and advisable in the interest of the Company to resolve such controversy satisfactorily, including, without being limited thereto, attorneys' and accounting fees. _____ is hereby designated as the "Tax Matters Partner" as referred to in Section 6231(a)(7)(A) of the Code, and is specially authorized to exercise all of the rights and powers now or hereafter granted to the Tax Matters Partner under the Code. Any cost incurred in the audit by any governmental authority of the income tax returns of a Member (as opposed to the Company) shall not be a Company expense. The Manager agrees to consult with and keep the Members advised with respect to (i) any income tax audit of a Company income tax return, and (ii) any elections made by the Company for federal, state or local income tax purposes.

13.6 Tax Returns. The Manager shall, at Company expense, cause the Company to prepare and file a United States Partnership Return of Income and all other tax returns required to be filed by the Company for each fiscal year of the Company.

13.7 Tax Elections. The Manager shall be permitted in its discretion to determine whether the Company should make an election pursuant to Section 754 of the Code to adjust the basis of the assets of the Company. Each of the Members shall, upon request, supply any information necessary to properly give effect to any such election. In addition, the Manager, in its sole discretion, shall be authorized to cause the Company to make and revoke any other elections for federal income tax purposes as they deem appropriate, necessary, or advisable.

14. TRANSFERS OF COMPANY INTERESTS; WITHDRAWAL AND ADMISSION OF MEMBERS.

14.1 General Prohibition. No Member may voluntarily or involuntarily, directly or indirectly, sell, transfer, assign, pledge or otherwise dispose of, or mortgage, pledge, hypothecate or otherwise encumber, or permit or suffer any encumbrance of, all or any part of such Member's interest in the Company, except as provided in this Section 14. Any other purported sale, transfer, assignment, pledge or encumbrance shall be null and void and of no force or effect whatsoever.

14.2 Withdrawal of Member. A Member shall have no power to withdraw voluntarily from the Company, except that a Member may withdraw upon written approval of a majority of the non-withdrawing Members voting by Percentage Interests, which approval shall include the terms for redemption by the Company of the Interest of the such Member.

14.3 Transfers by Members.

(a) Subject to any restrictions on transferability required by law or contained elsewhere in this Agreement, a Member may transfer such Member's entire interest in the Company upon satisfaction of the following conditions:

(i) The transfer shall (A) be by bequest or by operation of the laws of intestate succession, or (B) be approved in writing by the Manager, which approval shall be withheld only if the proposed transfer does not comply with the requirements of this Section 14.

(ii) The transferor and transferee shall have executed and acknowledged such reasonable and customary instruments as the Manager may deem necessary or desirable to effect such transfer; and

(iii) The transfer does not violate any applicable law or governmental rule or regulation, including without limitation any federal or state securities laws.

(b) At the time of a transfer of any Member's interest, whether or not such transfer is made in accordance with this Section 14, all the rights possessed as a Member in connection with the transferred interest, which rights otherwise would be held either by the transferor or the transferee, shall terminate against the Company unless the transferee is admitted to the Company as a Substitute Member pursuant to the provisions of Section 14.4 hereof; provided, however, that if the transfer is made in accordance with this Section 14, such transferee shall be entitled to receive distributions to which his transferor would otherwise be entitled from and after the Effective Date. The Effective Date shall be the date that is the later of the following dates: (a) the effective date of such transfer as agreed to by the transferee and transferor and set forth in writing in the transfer documentation, or (b) the last day of the calendar month following the date that the Manager has received notice of the transfer and all conditions precedent to such transfer provided for in this Agreement have been satisfied including receipt by the Manager of all documents necessary to comply with the requirements of Section , provided that the Manager, in its sole discretion, may agree to an earlier effective date if an earlier date is requested by the transferor and transferee. The Company and the Manager shall be entitled to treat the transferor as the recognized owner of such interests until the Effective Date and shall incur no liability for distributions made in good faith to the transferor prior to the Effective Date.

(c) Notwithstanding any other provision of this Agreement, a Member may not transfer such Member's interest in any case if such a transfer, when aggregated with all other transfers within a twelve (12) month period, would cause the termination of the Company as a partnership for federal income tax purposes pursuant to Section 708 of the Code, unless such transfer has been previously approved by the Manager.

(d) A change in the custodian or trustee of a Member that is a IRA, Trust, or pension or profit sharing plan, will be reflected on Appendix A in connection with an amendment completed in the first quarter of each year following notification to the Company of such change by the Member and the new custodian or trustee. The IRA, trust or pension or profit sharing plan shall pay the costs incurred by the Company to amend the Company documents to reflect the change in custodian or trustee.

14.4 Admission of Transferees as Members.

(a) No transferee of a Member shall be admitted as a Member unless all of the following conditions have been satisfied:

    (i) The transfer complies with Section 14.3;

    (ii) The further written consent of the Manager, to such transferee being admitted as a Member is first obtained, which consent may be arbitrarily withheld;

    (iii) The prospective transferee has executed an instrument, in form and substance satisfactory to the Manager, accepting and agreeing to be bound by all the terms and conditions of this Agreement, including the power of attorney set forth in Section 17 hereof, and has paid all expenses of the Company in effecting the transfer;

    (iv) All requirements of the Act regarding the admission of a transferee Member have been complied with by the transferee, the transferring Member and the Company; and

    (v) Such transfer is effected in compliance with all applicable state and federal securities laws.

(b) In the event of a transfer complying with all the requirements of Section 14.3 hereof and the transferee being admitted as a Member pursuant to this Section 14.4, the Manager, for itself and for each Member pursuant to the Power of Attorney granted by each Member, shall execute an amendment to this Agreement and file any necessary amendments to the articles of organization for the Company. Unless named in this Agreement, as amended from time to time, no person shall be considered a Member.

(c) In the event of a change in the custodian or trustee of a Member that is a IRA, trust, or pension or profit sharing plan that complies with Section hereof, the Manager, for itself and for each Member pursuant to the Power of Attorney granted by each Member, shall execute an amendment to this Agreement to reflect such change.

14.5 Assignment as Security Permitted. Notwithstanding any other provision of this Article 14, a Member may assign, as security for a loan or other indebtedness incurred by such Member, such Member's right to receive distributions from the Company, and the Manager, upon receipt of notification of any such assignment, shall acknowledge such assignment and shall agree to pay or distribute proceeds in accordance with instructions from such Member subject to such conditions, including indemnification, as the Manager may reasonably require; provided, however, that such lender shall acknowledge in writing to the Manager that such assignment of proceeds shall not entitle such lender to foreclose or otherwise acquire or sell the Company Interest and that the only right acquired by such lender shall be the right to receive distributions of cash and property, if any, made by the Company to the Members in accordance with this Agreement.

15. RESIGNATION AND ADMISSION OF MANAGER.

15.1 Resignation of Manager. A Manager shall be entitled to resign as a Manager 120 days after delivery of written notice to the Company and the Members of the Manager's intention to resign, or upon such earlier date as the Manager's resignation is accepted by Members holding a majority of the Percentage Interests in the Company. Resignation of a Manager, who is a Member, pursuant to this Section shall not affect its interest as a Member of the Company. Notwithstanding the foregoing, the transfer by a Manager, who is also a Member, of its Interest in the Company, shall constitute a resignation by such Member as a Manager, which resignation shall be effective as of the date of such transfer.

15.2 Death or Incompetency of Manager. A Manager who is a Member in the Company, shall cease to be a Manager upon the death, incompetence, bankruptcy or dissolution of such Manager, or any other event which terminates the continued membership of the Manager as a Member of the Company.

15.3 Removal of a Manager. A Manager may be removed as a Manager upon the written approval of Members holding a majority of the Percentage Interests of the Company. Removal of Manager who is a Member of the Company, pursuant to this Section shall not affect such Manager's interest as a Member of the Company.

15.4 Appointment of a New or Replacement Manager. A new or replacement Manager may be appointed with the written approval of Members holding a majority of the Percentage Interests of the Company.

16. DISSOLUTION, WINDING UP AND TERMINATION.

16.1 Events Causing Dissolution. The Company shall be dissolved and its affairs shall be wound up upon the happening of the first to occur of any of the following events:

(a) Expiration of the term of the Company stated in Section 6 hereof;

(b) Entry of a decree of administrative or judicial dissolution pursuant to the Act;

(c) The sale or other disposition of all or substantially all of the assets of the Company;

(d) The death, incompetence, withdrawal, expulsion, resignation, removal, bankruptcy or dissolution of a Manager, who is a Member, which is the last remaining Manager of the Company, unless (i) within 120 days of such occurrence, Members owning at least a majority of Percentage Interests in the Company, consent to the appointment of a new Manager(s) in accordance with

Section 15.4, in which case the business of the Company shall be carried on by the newly appointed Manager(s), and (ii) the conditions of Section 14 are also satisfied;

(e) The death, incompetence, withdrawal, expulsion, bankruptcy, resignation, or dissolution of a Manager, who is a Member, or any other event that terminates the continued membership of such Manager unless at the time of the occurrence of any of such event there are at least two other Members, and within 120 days of such occurrence, remaining Members owning at least a majority of the Percentage Interests in the Company (or, if greater, remaining Members owning at least a "majority in interest" in the capital and profits of the Company as such term is used in Treas. Reg. Section 301.7701–2(b)(1)), consent to the continuation of the Company, in which case the business of the Company shall be carried on by the remaining Manager(s); or

(f) The unanimous vote of Members.

16.2 Winding Up. Upon dissolution of the Company for any reason, the Manager shall commence to wind up the affairs of the Company and to liquidate its assets. In the event the Company has terminated because the Company lacks a Manager, then the remaining members shall appoint a new Manager solely for the purpose of winding up the affairs of the Company. The Manager shall have the full right and unlimited discretion to determine the time, manner and terms of any sale or sales of Company property pursuant to such liquidation. Pending such sales, the Manager shall have the right to continue to operate or otherwise deal with the assets of the Company. A reasonable time shall be allowed for the orderly winding up of the business of the Company and the liquidation of its assets and the discharge of its liabilities to creditors so as to enable the Manager to minimize the normal losses attendant upon a liquidation, having due regard to the activity and condition of the relevant markets for the Company properties and general financial and economic conditions. Any Member may be a purchaser of any properties of the Company upon liquidation of the Company's assets, including, without limitation, any liquidation conducted pursuant to a judicial dissolution or otherwise under judicial supervision; provided, however, that the purchase price and terms of sale are fair and reasonable to the Company.

16.3 Allocation of Net Income and Net Loss Upon Termination or Sale. All Net Income and Net Loss upon dissolution of the Company or from sale, conversion, disposition or taking of all or substantially all of the Company's property, including, but not limited to the proceeds of any eminent domain proceeding or insurance award (respectively, "Gain on Sale" or "Loss on Sale") shall be allocated as follows:

(a) Loss on Sale shall be allocated among the Members as follows:

(i) First, proportionately to those Members having positive Capital Account balances until all positive Capital Accounts have been reduced to zero; and

(ii) Thereafter, among the Members in proportion to their Percentage Interests.

(b) Gain on Sale to the extent available shall be allocated among the Members as follows:

(i) First to those Members having negative Capital Account balances in proportion to such negative balances until they are increased to zero; and

(ii) Thereafter, any remaining Gain on Sale shall be allocated to the Members in proportion to their Percentage Interests.

16.4 Distributions. Prior to making distributions in dissolution to the Members, the Manager shall first pay or make provision for all debts and liabilities of the Company, including payment of any Manager Loans, and other loans to Members and their affiliates, and all expenses of liquidation. Subject to the right of the Manager to set up such cash reserves as it deems reasonably necessary for any contingent or unforeseen liabilities or obligations of the Company, the proceeds of liquidation and any other funds of the Company shall be distributed in the following order of priority:

(a) First, to Members in proportion to their Capital Account balances as adjusted by the allocations provided for in Section above; and

(b) Thereafter, the balance, if any, to the Members in proportion to their Percentage Interests.

It is intended and anticipated that the amount of cash distributable upon a termination or dissolution of the Company should equal the sum of the Members' Capital Accounts, after adjustment of such balances in accordance with Sections 16.3(a) and 16.3(b), and that therefore all cash will be distributable under this Section 16.4.

16.5 Certificate of Cancellation; Report; Termination. Upon the dissolution and commencement of winding up of the Company, the Manager shall execute and file articles of dissolution for the Company. Within a reasonable time following the completion of the liquidation of the Company's assets, the Manager shall prepare and furnish to each Member, at the expense of the Company, a statement which shall set forth the assets and liabilities of the Company as of the date of complete liquidation and the amount of each Member's distribution pursuant to Section 16.4 hereof. Upon completion of the liquidation and distribution of all Company funds, the Company shall terminate and the Manager shall have the authority to execute and file all documents required to effectuate the termination of the Company.

17. SPECIAL AND LIMITED POWER OF ATTORNEY.

17.1 The Manager, with full power of substitution, shall at all times during the existence of the Company have a special and limited power of attorney as the authority to act in the name and on the behalf of each Member to make, execute, swear to, verify, acknowledge and file the following documents and any other documents deemed by the Manager to be necessary for the business of the Company:

(a) This Agreement, any separate articles of organization, fictitious business name statements, as well as any amendments to the foregoing which, under the laws of any state, are required to be filed or which the Manager deems it advisable to file;

(b) Any other instrument or document which may be required to be filed by the Company under the laws of any state or by an governmental agency, or which the Manager deems it advisable to file; and

(c) Any instrument or document which may be required to effect the continuation of the Company, the admission of a Manager or Member, the transfer of an interest in the Company, the change in custodian or trustee of any IRA, trust or pension or profit sharing plan Member, or the dissolution and termination of the Company (provided such continuation, admission or dissolution and termination are in accordance with the terms of this Agreement), or to reflect any increases or reductions in amount of contributions of Members.

17.2 The special and limited power of attorney granted to the Manager hereby:

(a) Is a special and limited power of attorney coupled with an interest, is irrevocable, shall survive the dissolution or incompetency of the granting Member, and is limited to those matters herein set forth;

(b) May be exercised by the Manager (or by any authorized officer of the Manager, if not a natural person) for each Member by referencing the list of Members on Appendix A and executing any instrument with a single signature acting as attorney-in-fact for all of them;

(c) Shall survive a transfer by a Member of such Member's interest in the Company pursuant to Section 14 hereof for the sole purpose of enabling the Manager to execute, acknowledge and file any instrument or document necessary or appropriate to admit a transferee as a Member; and

(d) Notwithstanding the foregoing, in the event that a Manager ceases to be a Manager in the Company, the power of attorney granted by this Section 17 to such Manager shall terminate immediately, but any such termination shall not affect the validity of any documents executed prior to such termination, or any other actions previously taken pursuant to this power of attorney or in reliance upon its validity, all of which shall continue to be valid and binding upon the Members in accordance with their terms.

18. AMENDMENTS. Except as otherwise provided by law, this Agreement may be amended in any respect by a majority vote of the Members voting by Percentage Interests; provided, however, that:

18.1 This Agreement may not be amended so as to change any Member's rights to or interest in Net Income, Net Loss or distributions unless (i) such amendment is made in connection with an additional capital contribution to the Company or an additional guarantee of Company indebtedness, (ii) each Member is given the first opportunity maintain its Percentage Interest by participating in such contribution or guarantee in proportion to their existing Percentage Interest, and (iii) the amendment is approved by a sixty-six and two-thirds (66 2/3) of the Members voting by Percentage Interests;

18.2 Without the consent of each Member to be adversely affected by the amendment, this Agreement may not be amended so as to increase the liability of or change the capital contributions required by a Member;

18.3 In the case of any provision hereof which requires the action, approval or consent of a specified Percentage Interest of Members, such provision may not be amended without the consent of the Members owning such specified Percentage Interest; and

18.4 In addition to any amendments otherwise authorized herein, amendments may be made to this Agreement from time to time by the Manager without the consent or approval of the Members, (i) to cure any ambiguity or to correct any typographical errors in this Agreement or (ii) to correct or supplement any provision herein which may be inconsistent with any other provision herein.

19. MISCELLANEOUS.

19.1 Notices. Any notice, offer, consent or other communication required or permitted to be given or made hereunder shall be in writing and shall be deemed to have been sufficiently given or made when delivered personally to the party (or an officer of the party) to whom the same is directed, or (except in the event of a mail strike) five days after being mailed by first class mail, postage prepaid, if to the Company or to a Manager, to the office described in Section 4 hereof, or if to a Member, to such Member's last known address or when received by facsimile if to the Company or Manager to the facsimile number for the office described in Section hereof, or if to a Member, to such Member's facsimile number. Any Member may change such Member's address for the purpose of this Section 19.1 by giving notice of such change to the Company, such change to become effective on the tenth day after such notice is given.

19.2 Entire Agreement. This Agreement constitutes the entire agreement among the parties and supersedes any prior agreement or understandings among them, oral or written, all of which are hereby cancelled. This Agreement may not be modified or amended other than pursuant to Section 18 hereof.

19.3 Captions; Pronouns. The paragraph and section titles or captions contained in this Agreement are inserted only as a matter of convenience of reference. Such titles and captions in no way define, limit, extend or describe the scope of this Agreement nor the intent of any provision hereof. All pronouns and any variation thereof shall be deemed to refer to the masculine, feminine or neuter, singular or plural, as the identity of the person or persons may require.

19.4 Counterparts. This Agreement may be executed in any number of counterparts and by different parties hereto in separate counterparts, each of which when so executed shall be deemed to be an original and all of which when taken together shall constitute one and the same agreement. Delivery of any executed counterpart of a signature page to this Agreement by facsimile shall be effective as delivery of an executed original counterpart of this Agreement.

19.5 Governing Law. This Agreement shall be governed by and construed in accordance with the internal laws of the state of Washington.

IN WITNESS WHEREOF the parties have executed this Agreement as of the date first hereinabove written.

MANAGER/MEMBER:_____

MANAGER/MEMBER:_____

MANAGER/MEMBER:_____

SPOUSAL CONSENT

The undersigned acknowledges that she has read the foregoing Agreement, knows and understands its contents, and has had ample opportunity to consult with legal counsel of her own choosing. The undersigned is aware that by its provisions, her spouse agrees to hold their Percentage Interest in the Company subject to certain restrictions. The undersigned hereby approves of the provisions of this Agreement and consents to the imposition of certain restrictions on any interest he may have in the Percentage Interests, and agrees that she will not make any transfer of, or otherwise deal with, the Percentage Interests or with any interest she may have in the Percentage Interests except as expressly permitted by such Agreement.

DATED:_____

_____

APPENDIX A

Member	Cash Contribution	Percentage Interest	
	$	_____	%
	$	_____	%
	$	_____	%
TOTAL	$	100	%

C. FORM: ARTICLES OF INCORPORATION

ARTICLES OF INCORPORATION

OF

_____

_____ hereby executes these Articles of Incorporation for the purpose of forming a corporation under Title 23B of the Revised Code of Washington, the Washington Business Corporation Act.

ARTICLE 1

Name

The name of this corporation is:

_____

ARTICLE 2

Capital Stock

☐ This corporation has the authority to issue _____ shares, the par value of each of which is $_____.

☐ This corporation has the authority to issue _____ shares, and each share shall be without par value.

☐ The shares shall be classified as follows:

** Insert Text **

ARTICLE 3

Preemptive Rights

☐ The shareholders of this corporation have no preemptive rights to acquire additional shares of this corporation.

☐ The shareholders of this corporation shall have preemptive rights to acquire additional shares of this corporation.

ARTICLE 4

Cumulative Voting

☐ The shareholders of this corporation shall not be entitled to cumulative voting at any election of directors.

☐ Shareholders entitled to vote at any election of directors are entitled to cumulate votes by multiplying the number of votes they are entitled to cast by the number of directors for whom they are entitled to vote and to cast the product for a single candidate or distribute the product among two or more candidates.

ARTICLE 5

Action by Consent

Any action required or permitted to be taken at a shareholders' meeting may be taken without a meeting or a vote if either:

(i)   the action is taken by written consent of all shareholders entitled to vote on the action; or

(ii)   so long as the Corporation does not have any capital stock registered under the Securities Exchange Act of 1934, as amended, the action is taken by written consent of shareholders holding of record, or otherwise entitled to vote, in the aggregate not less than the minimum number of votes that would be necessary to authorize or take such action at a meeting at which all shares entitled to vote on the action were present and voted.

To the extent prior notice of any such action is required by law to be given to nonconsenting or nonvoting shareholders, such notice shall be made before the date on which the action becomes effective. The form of the notice shall be sufficient to apprise the nonconsenting or nonvoting shareholder of the nature of the action to be effected, in a manner approved by the board of directors of this Corporation or by the board committee or officers to whom the board of directors has delegated that responsibility.

ARTICLE 6

Approval by Majority Vote

Unless these Articles of Incorporation provide for a greater voting requirement for any voting group of shareholders, any action which would otherwise require the approval of two-thirds (2/3) of all the votes entitled to be cast, including without limitation the amendment of these Articles of Incorporation, the approval of a plan of merger or share exchange, the sale, lease, exchange or other disposition of all, or substantially all of the Corporation's property otherwise than in the usual and regular course of business, and the dissolution of the Corporation, shall be authorized if approved by each voting group entitled to vote thereon by a simple majority of all the votes entitled to be cast by that voting group.

ARTICLE 7

Limitation of Liability

A director of this Corporation shall not be personally liable to the Corporation or its shareholders for monetary damages for conduct as a director, except for liability of the director *(i)* for acts or omissions that involve intentional misconduct by the director or a knowing violation of law by the director, *(ii)* for conduct violating RCW 23B.08.310 of the Act, or *(iii)* for any transaction from which the director will personally receive a benefit in money, property or services to which the director is not legally entitled. If the Washington Business Corporation Act is amended in the future to authorize corporate action further eliminating or limiting the personal liability of directors, then the liability of a director of this Corporation shall be eliminated or limited to the full extent permitted by the Washington Business Corporation Act, as so amended, without any requirement of further action by the shareholders.

ARTICLE 8

Indemnification

The Corporation shall indemnify any individual made a party to a proceeding because that individual is or was a director of the Corporation and shall advance or reimburse the reasonable expenses incurred by such individual in advance of final disposition of the proceeding, without regard to the limitations in RCW 23B.08.510 through 23B.08.550 of the Act, or any other limitation which may hereafter be enacted to the extent such limitation may be disregarded if authorized by the Articles of Incorporation, to the full extent and under all circumstances permitted by applicable law.

Any repeal or modification of this Article by the shareholders of this Corporation shall not adversely affect any right of any individual who is or was a director of the Corporation which existed at the time of such repeal or modification.

ARTICLE 9

Directors

☐ The initial board of directors shall consist of _____ (_____) directors. The names and addresses of the persons who are to serve as initial directors are:

_____

_____

_____

_____

_____

_____

_____

_____

_____

☐ The initial board of directors shall consist of one director. The name and address of the person who is to serve as the sole initial director is:

_____

_____

_____

Except with respect to the initial board of directors, the number of directors constituting the board of directors shall be determined in the manner specified in the bylaws. In the absence of such a provision in the bylaws, the board shall consist of the number of directors constituting the initial board of directors.

ARTICLE 10

Registered Office and Registered Agent

The street address of the initial registered office of this corporation is:

☐   1780 Barnes Blvd. S.W.

Tumwater, WA 98512-0410

☐   1111 Third Avenue, Suite 3400

Seattle, WA 98101-3299

☐   _____

_____

_____

_____

and the name of its initial registered agent at that address is:

☐National Registered Agents, Inc.

☐FPS Corporate Services, Inc.

☐[Client]

ARTICLE 11

Incorporator

The name and address of the incorporator is:

☐   _____

1111 Third Avenue, Suite 3400

Seattle, WA 98101

☐   _____

_____

_____

Executed   this   _____   day   of   _____,

_____.

_____,

Incorporator

CONSENT TO SERVE AS REGISTERED AGENT

National Registered Agents, Inc. ("NRAI"), hereby consents to serve as Registered Agent in the State of Washington for _____ (the "Corporation"). NRAI understands that as agent for the Corporation, it will be its responsibility to receive service of process in the name of the Corporation; to forward all mail to the Corporation; and to immediately notify the office of the Secretary of State in the event of its resignation, or of any changes in the registered office address of the Corporation for which it is agent.

NATIONAL REGISTERED AGENTS, INC.

By:_____

Name: _____

Title: _____

NAME OF REGISTERED AGENT: National Registered Agents, Inc.

ADDRESS OF REGISTERED AGENT: 1780 Barnes Blvd. S.W.

Tumwater, WA 98512-0410

ARTICLE II

TEXT INSERTS

[**INSERT:** Voting and Non-Voting Classes of Common Stock.]

The shares consist of _____ shares designated as "Class A Common Stock" and _____ shares designated as "Class B Common Stock". Each share of Class A Common Stock shall have unlimited voting rights. Class B Common Stock shall have no voting rights, and no separate vote of the holders of Class B Common Stock as a class shall be required for any purpose except as may be required by law. Other than with respect to voting rights, Class A Common Stock and Class B Common Stock shall have identical rights.

[**INSERT:** Special Class of Stock to Elect Designated Directors.]

The shares consist of _____ shares designated as "Class A Common Stock" and _____ shares designated as "Class B Common Stock". With respect to the election of directors, the holders of Class A Common Stock shall have the sole and exclusive right to elect _____ director(s), and the balance of the directors will be elected by the holders of Class B Common Stock. The holders of each class of stock shall have the sole and exclusive right to remove at any time the director(s) elected by such holders. The election and removal of the director(s) to be elected by the holders of any class of stock may be effected by unanimous written consent of all such holders, at a special meeting of such holders called for that purpose, or at an annual meeting of shareholders. Any vacancy with respect to a director elected by the holders of any class of stock shall be filled by a special election by the holders of that class, and not by a vote of the remaining directors. Other than with respect to rights relating to the election and removal of directors, Class A Common Stock and Class B Common Stock shall have identical rights.

The Board of Directors shall consist of not less than _____ directors.

[**INSERT:** Special Class of Stock to Elect Designated Directors. [All stock to elect balance of directors.]]

The shares consist of _____ shares designated as "Class A Common Stock" and _____ shares designated as "Class B Common Stock". With respect to the election of directors, the holders of Class B Common Stock shall have the sole and exclusive right to elect _____ director(s), and the balance of the directors will be elected by holders of all shares. The holders of Class B Common Stock shall have the sole and exclusive right to remove at any time the director(s) elected by such holders. The election and removal of the director(s) to be elected by the holders of Class B Common Stock may be effected by unanimous written consent of all such holders, at a special meeting of such holders called for that purpose, or at an annual meeting of shareholders. Any vacancy with respect to a director elected by the holders of Class B Common Stock shall be filled by a special election by the holders of Class B Common Stock, and not by a vote of the remaining directors. Other than with respect to rights relating to the election and removal of directors, Class A Common Stock and Class B Common Stock shall have identical rights.

The Board of Directors shall consist of not less than _____ directors.

[**INSERT:** "Blank Check" Stock Authorized.]

The shares consist of _____ shares designated as "Common Stock" and _____ shares designated as "Preferred Stock."

Except to the extent such rights are granted to Preferred Stock or one or more series thereof, Common Stock has unlimited voting rights and is entitled to receive the net assets of the corporation upon dissolution.

The preferences, limitations, and relative rights of Preferred Stock are undesignated. The Board of Directors may designate one or more series within Preferred Stock, and the designation and number of shares within each series, and shall determine the preferences, limitations, and relative rights of any shares of Preferred Stock, or of any series of Preferred Stock, before issuance of any shares of that class or series. [Preferred Stock, or any series thereof, may be designated as common or preferred, and may have rights that are identical to those of Common Stock.]

Shares of one class or series may be issued as a share dividend in respect to shares of another class or series.

OPTIONAL PROVISIONS

[**INSERT:** Simple Majority Vote to Amend Articles, etc.]

ARTICLE ____

Amendment of the articles of incorporation, approval of a plan of merger or share exchange, authorizing the sale, lease, exchange, or other disposition of all, or substantially all of the corporation's property, otherwise than in the usual and regular course of business, and authorizing dissolution of the corporation, shall be approved by each voting group entitled to vote thereon by a simple majority of all the votes entitled to be cast by that voting group.

ARTICLE V

TEXT INSERTS

To the maximum extent allowable bylaw, any action which may be authorized or approved by a vote of the shareholders at a meeting thereof at any time prior to the registration of any Corporation securities under the Securities Exchange Act of 1934, as amended, may be taken with the written consent of shareholders holding that number of shares as could authorize or approve the action at a meeting of all shareholders entitled to vote on such action. Except as otherwise provided by law, a notice describing the action taken and the effective date of such action shall be provided to each nonconsenting shareholder no later than ten (10) days prior to the effective date of any action approved pursuant to the preceding sentence

D. FORM: BOARD OF DIRECTORS' ORGANIZATIONAL CONSENT RESOLUTIONS

CONSENT IN LIEU OF ORGANIZATIONAL MEETING OF [SOLE] DIRECTOR(S)

OF

_____

The undersigned, being [all the] [the sole] director(s) of _____, a Washington corporation (the "Company"), pursuant to Section 23B.08.210 of the Washington Business Corporations Act (the "Act") hereby consent(s) to, and by this action approve(s) and adopt(s) the following resolutions:

FORMATION

WHEREAS, the original Articles of Incorporation of the Company were filed in the office of the Secretary of State of Washington on _____; therefore it is

RESOLVED, that a certified copy of said Articles of Incorporation be inserted in the minute book of the Company; and

RESOLVED, that all the acts of the incorporator of the Company in forming and organizing the Company are hereby approved, ratified, and adopted as valid and binding acts of the Company.

BYLAWS

RESOLVED, that the Bylaws, consisting of fifteen (15) pages inserted in the minute book following the Articles of Incorporation, are hereby adopted as the Bylaws of the Company.

AGENT FOR SERVICE OF PROCESS

RESOLVED, that the appointment of _____ as the Company's registered agent for service of process in Washington is hereby ratified, approved and confirmed.

FISCAL YEAR

RESOLVED, that the Company's fiscal year shall end on _____ each year.

PAYMENT OF ORGANIZATIONAL EXPENSES

RESOLVED, that the officers of the Company or any of them be, and each hereby is, authorized and directed to pay the expenses of incorporation and organization of the Company.

DIRECTORS

WHEREAS, the Bylaws of the Company allow for the number of directors to be set by the Articles of Incorporation or by resolution of the board of directors; therefore it is

RESOLVED, that the number of directors of the Company be fixed at _____ (_____) until such time as such number is amended by action of the Board of Directors or the shareholders of the Company.

OFFICERS

RESOLVED, that the following persons be, and they hereby are, elected, effective immediately, as officers of the Company to serve until the next annual meeting of directors and until the election and qualification of their successors:

Name	Title
_____	President
_____	Vice President
_____	Secretary
_____	Treasurer

FORM OF STOCK CERTIFICATE

RESOLVED, that the form of stock certificate attached hereto be, and the same hereby is, approved and adopted for use by the Company.

ISSUANCE OF SHARES

WHEREAS, the Company is authorized to issue up to

_____

(_____) shares of Common Stock, [no] [$_____] par value, and none yet have been sold or issued;

RESOLVED, that the board of directors hereby determines that $_____ per share is adequate consideration to be received by the Company for its Common Stock;

RESOLVED, that subject to compliance with the applicable state securities laws and the Securities Act of 1933, as amended ("1933 Act"), the Company shall issue shares of its Common Stock to the persons listed below at a price of $_____ per share, in cash, and for the number of shares set forth opposite their name:

Name	Number of Shares
_____	_____
_____	_____
_____	_____

RESOLVED, that upon receipt of the stated consideration and payment in full of any amounts payable pursuant to the terms thereof, such shares shall be duly and validly issued, fully paid and nonassessable.

RESOLVED, that the appropriate officers of the Company are hereby authorized and directed for and on behalf of the Company (i) to take all action necessary to comply with applicable state securities laws and the 1933 Act with respect to the above offer and issuance of shares, (ii) to thereafter issue shares on behalf of the Company pursuant to the above authorization, and (iii) to take such other action as they may deem appropriate to carry out the offer and issuance of shares and the intent of these resolutions.

BANK ACCOUNT

RESOLVED, that the officers, or any of them, be, and each of them are hereby authorized to execute on behalf of the Company any and all forms of bank resolutions dealing with corporate banking matters, including the establishing and maintaining of corporate bank accounts, which in their judgment from time to time may be required for the proper fiscal management of the Company, including the designation thereon of such authorized signatures of corporate officers or other agents as may to them seem appropriate. Such officers may execute such banking resolution or resolutions as if authorized to do so by a specific resolution of the board of directors adopted on the date this resolution was adopted by the board. A copy of any such banking resolutions shall be placed in the corporate minute book.

REGISTRATIONS AND LICENSES

RESOLVED, that the officers of the Company are hereby authorized and directed to cause the Company to be registered with federal and state taxing authorities, to obtain all necessary business licenses, and otherwise take all actions that are necessary or appropriate to enable the Company to commence business.

* * * [S CORPORATION OPTION] * * *

S CORPORATION ELECTION

RESOLVED, that for the first taxable year that is hereby designated to end on December 31, _____, the corporation shall make an election pursuant to Section 1362 of the Internal Revenue Code of 1986, as amended, to be treated as an "S corporation." The shareholders shall execute such consents as are required thereby and the corporation shall timely file Internal Revenue Service Form 2553 and the required consents.

OMNIBUS

RESOLVED, that any and all actions heretofore taken by the incorporator and/or officers of the Company resolutions are hereby ratified and confirmed as the acts and deeds of the Company; and

FURTHER RESOLVED, that the officers of the Company be, and each of them hereby is, authorized, directed and empowered to do all such other acts and things and to execute and deliver all such certificates or other documents and to take such other action as they deem necessary or desirable to carry out the purposes and intent, but within the limitations, of the above resolutions.

DATED this _____ day of _____, _____.

DIRECTOR(S):

_____

_____

_____

_____

E. FORM: CORPORATE BYLAWS

BYLAWS

OF

_____

ARTICLE I. OFFICES

The principal office and place of business of the corporation in the state of Washington shall be located at _____.

The corporation may have such other offices within or without the state of Washington as the board of directors may designate or the business of the corporation may require from time to time.

ARTICLE II. DEFINITIONS

As used in these bylaws, the following terms shall have the following meanings:

"*Electronic transmission*" means an electronic communication not directly involving the physical transfer of a Record in a tangible medium and that may be retained, retrieved and reviewed by the sender and the recipient and that may be directly reproduced in a tangible medium by the sender and recipient.

"*Execute*," "*executes*" or "*executed*" means signed with respect to a written Record or electronically transmitted along with sufficient information to determine the sender's identity with respect to an electronic transmission.

"*Record*" means information inscribed on a tangible medium or contained in an electronic transmission.

"*Tangible medium*" means a writing, copy of a writing or facsimile, or a physical reproduction, each on paper or on other tangible material.

"*Writing*" or "*written*" means embodied in a tangible medium, and excludes an electronic transmission.

ARTICLE III. NUMBER OF DIRECTORS

The board of directors of this corporation shall consist of _____ (_____) director(s).

ARTICLE IV. NOTICE

Section 4.1 Types of Notice Allowed.

4.1.1. Notice Provided in a Tangible Medium. Notice may be provided in a tangible medium and may be transmitted by mail, private carrier or personal delivery; telegraph or teletype; or telephone, wire or wireless equipment that transmits a facsimile of the notice.

4.1.2. Notice Provided in an Electronic Transmission. Notice may be given in an electronic transmission and be electronically transmitted. Notice to shareholders or directors in an electronic transmission is effective only with respect to shareholders and directors that have consented, in the form of a Record, to receive electronically transmitted notices and designated in the consent the address, location or system to which these notices may be electronically transmitted. Notice provided in an electronic transmission includes material required or permitted to accompany the notice by the Washington Business Corporation Act or other applicable statute or regulation. A shareholder or director that has consented to receipt of electronically transmitted notices may revoke the consent by delivering a revocation to the corporation in the form of a Record. The consent of a shareholder or director to receive notice by electronic transmission is revoked if the corporation is unable to electronically transmit two consecutive notices given by the corporation in accordance with the consent, and this inability becomes known to the secretary of the corporation, the transfer agent or any other person responsible for giving the notice. The inadvertent failure by the corporation to treat this inability as a revocation does not invalidate any meeting or other action. Notice to shareholders or directors that have consented to receipt of electronically transmitted notices may be provided by posting the notice on an electronic network and delivering to the shareholder or director a separate Record of the posting, together with comprehensible instructions regarding how to obtain access to the posting on the electronic network.

4.1.3. Other Types of Notice. In addition, any other type of notice may be given that is allowed by applicable law.

Section 4.2 Effectiveness of Notice.

(i) Notice by Mail. Notice given by mail is effective when deposited in the United States mail, first-class postage prepaid, addressed to the shareholder or director at the shareholder's or director's address as it appears in the corporation's current records.

(ii) Notice by Registered or Certified Mail. Notice is effective on the date shown on the return receipt, if sent by registered or certified mail, return receipt requested, and the receipt is signed by or on behalf of the addressee.

(iii) Notice by Telegraph, Teletype or Facsimile Equipment. Notice given by telegraph, teletype or facsimile equipment that transmits a facsimile of the notice is effective when dispatched to the shareholder's or director's address, telephone number or other number appearing on the records of the corporation.

(iv) Notice by Air Courier. Notice given by air courier is effective when dispatched, if prepaid and properly addressed to the shareholder or director at the shareholder's or director's address as it appears in the corporation's current records.

(v) Notice by Personal Delivery. Notice given by personal delivery is effective when received by a shareholder or director.

(vi) Notice by Electronic Transmission. Notice provided in an electronic transmission, if in comprehensible form, is effective when it is (1) electronically transmitted to an address, location or system designated by the recipient for that purpose, or (2) has been posted on an electronic network and a separate Record of the posting has been delivered to the recipient together with comprehensible instructions regarding how to obtain access to the posting on the electronic network.

(vii) Notice by Publication. Notice given by publication is effective five days after first publication.

ARTICLE V. SHAREHOLDERS

Section 5.1 Annual Meeting. The annual meeting of the shareholders shall be held on the _____ in the month of _____ in each year, beginning with the year_____, at _____ m., or at such other date or time as may be determined by the board of directors, for the purpose of electing directors and for the transaction of such other business as may come before the meeting. If the day fixed for the annual meeting shall be a legal holiday in the state of Washington, the meeting shall be held on the next succeeding business day. If the election of directors is not held on the day designated herein for any annual meeting of the shareholders or at any adjournment thereof, the board of directors shall cause the election to be held at a meeting of the shareholders as soon thereafter as may be convenient.

Section 5.2 Special Meetings. Special meetings of the shareholders for any purpose or purposes unless otherwise prescribed by statute may be called by the president, by the board of directors, or by request of any director set forth in an executed written Record or an executed electronically transmitted Record (if the corporation has designated an address, location or system to which the request may be electronically transmitted and the request is electronically transmitted to the designated address, location, or system). A special meeting of the shareholders shall be held by request set forth in an executed written Record or an executed electronically transmitted Record (if the corporation has designated an address, location, or system to which the request may be electronically transmitted and the request is electronically transmitted to the designated address, location, or system) of any holders of at least ten percent (10%) of the votes entitled to be cast on each issue.

Section 5.3 Place of Meetings. Meetings of the shareholders shall be held at either the principal office of the corporation or at such other place within or without the state of Washington as the board of directors or the president may designate.

Section 5.4 Fixing of Record Date. For the purpose of determining shareholders entitled to notice of or to vote at any meeting of shareholders or any adjournment thereof, or shareholders entitled to receive payment of any dividend or distribution, or in order to make a determination of shareholders for any other proper purpose, the board of directors may fix in advance a date as the record date for any such determination of shareholders, which date in any case shall not be more than seventy (70) days prior to the date on which the particular action requiring such determination of shareholders is to be taken. If no record date is fixed for the determination of shareholders entitled to notice of or to vote at a meeting of shareholders, or shareholders entitled to receive payment of a dividend or distribution, the day before the first notice of a meeting is dispatched to shareholders or the date on which the resolution of the board of directors authorizing such dividend or distribution is adopted, as the case may be, shall be the record date for such determination of shareholders. When a determination of shareholders entitled to notice of or to vote at any meeting of shareholders has been made as provided in this section, such determination shall apply to any adjournment thereof unless the board of directors fixes a new record date, which it must do if the meeting is adjourned to a date more than one hundred twenty (120) days after the date fixed for the original meeting.

Section 5.5 Voting Lists. At least ten (10) days before each meeting of the shareholders, the officer or agent having charge of the stock transfer books for shares of the corporation shall prepare an alphabetical list of all its shareholders on the record date who are entitled to vote at the meeting or any adjournment thereof, arranged by voting group, and within each voting group by class or series of shares, with the address of and the number of shares held by each, which record for a period of ten (10) days prior to the meeting shall be kept on file at the principal office of the corporation or at a place identified in the meeting notice in the city where the meeting will be held. Such record shall be produced and kept open at the time and place of the meeting and shall be subject to the inspection of any shareholder, shareholder's agent or shareholder's attorney at any time during the meeting or any adjournment thereof. Failure to comply with the requirements of this bylaw shall not affect the validity of any action taken at the meeting.

Section 5.6 Notice of Meetings. Notice stating the date, time, and place of a meeting of shareholders and, in the case of a special meeting of shareholders, the purpose or purposes for which the meeting is called, shall be given in the form of a Record, in accordance with Article IV, by or at the direction of the president, the secretary, or the officer or persons calling the meeting to each shareholder of record entitled to vote at such meeting (unless required by law to send notice to all shareholders regardless of whether or not such shareholders are entitled to vote), not less than ten (10) days and not more than sixty (60) days before the meeting, except that notice of a meeting to act on an amendment to the articles of incorporation, a plan of merger or share exchange, a proposed sale, lease, exchange, or other disposition of all or substantially all of the assets of the corporation other than in the usual course of business, or the dissolution of the corporation shall be given not less than twenty (20) days and not more than sixty (60) days before the meeting.

Section 5.7 Adjourned Meeting. If an annual or special shareholders' meeting is adjourned to a different date, time or place, notice need not be given of the new date, time or place if the new date, time or place is announced at the meeting before adjournment unless a new record date is or must be fixed. If a new record date for the adjourned meeting is or must be fixed, however, notice of the adjourned meeting must be given to persons who are shareholders as of the new record date.

Section 5.8 Waiver of Notice. A shareholder may waive any notice required to be given under the provisions of these bylaws, the articles of incorporation, or by applicable law, whether before or after the date and time stated therein. A valid waiver is created by any of the following three methods: (a) in either an executed and dated written Record or in an executed and dated electronically transmitted Record (if the corporation has designated an address location or system to which the waiver may be electronically transmitted and the waiver is electronically transmitted to the designated address, location, or system) and delivered to the corporation for inclusion in its corporate records; (b) by attendance at the meeting, in person or by proxy, unless the shareholder at the beginning of the meeting objects to holding the meeting or transacting business at the meeting; or (c) by failure to object at the time of presentation of a matter not within the purpose or purposes described in the meeting notice.

Section 5.9 Manner of Acting; Proxies. A shareholder may vote either in person or by proxy. A shareholder may vote by proxy by means of a proxy appointment form which is executed in writing by the shareholder, his agent, or by his duly authorized attorney-in-fact; or authorizing another person or persons to act for the shareholder as proxy by transmitting or authorizing the transmission of a recorded telephone call, voice mail, or other electronic transmission to the corporation or the person who will be the holder of the proxy or to a proxy solicitation firm, proxy support service organization, or like agent duly authorized by the person who will be the holder of the proxy to receive the transmission, provided that the transmission must either set forth or be submitted with information, including any security or validation controls used, from which it can reasonably be determined that the transmission was authorized by the shareholder. If it is determined that the transmission is valid, the inspectors of election or, if there are no inspectors, any officer or agent of the corporation making that determination on behalf of the corporation shall specify the information upon which they relied. The corporation shall require the holders of proxies received by transmission to provide to the corporation copies of the transmission and the corporation shall retain copies of the transmission for at least sixty days. An appointment of a proxy is effective when a signed appointment form or telegram, cablegram, recorded telephone call, voicemail or other transmission of the appointment is received by the inspectors of election or the officer or agent of the corporation authorized to tabulate votes. All proxy appointment forms shall be filed with the secretary of the corporation before or at the commencement of meetings. No unrevoked proxy appointment form shall be valid after eleven (11) months from the date of its execution unless otherwise expressly provided in the appointment form. No proxy appointment may be effectively revoked until notice of such revocation has been given to the secretary of the corporation by the shareholder appointing the proxy. Notice of such revocation shall be set forth in an executed written Record or, if the corporation has designated an address, location or system to which the notice may be electronically transmitted and the notice is electronically transmitted to the designated address, location or system, in an executed electronically transmitted Record.

Section 5.10 Participation by Communications Equipment. At the discretion of the board of directors, shareholders or proxies may participate in a meeting of the shareholders by any means of communication by which all persons participating in the meeting can hear each other during the meeting, and participation by such means shall constitute presence in person at the meeting.

Section 5.11 Quorum. At any meeting of the shareholders, a majority in interest of all the shares entitled to vote on a matter, represented by shareholders of record, shall constitute a quorum of that voting group for action on that matter. Once a share is represented at a meeting, other than to object to holding the meeting or transacting business, it is deemed to be present for purposes of a quorum for the remainder of the meeting and for any adjournment of that meeting unless a new record date is or must be fixed for the adjourned meeting. At such reconvened meeting, any business may be transacted that might have been transacted at the adjourned meeting. If a quorum exists, action on a matter is approved by a voting group if the votes cast within the voting group favoring the action exceed the votes cast within the voting group opposing the action, unless the question is one upon which a different vote is required by express provision of law or of the articles of incorporation or of these bylaws.

Section 5.12 Voting of Shares. Each outstanding share, regardless of class, shall be entitled to one vote on each matter submitted to a vote at a meeting of shareholders, except as may be otherwise provided in the articles of incorporation.

Section 5.13 Voting for Directors. The shareholders of the corporation shall not be entitled to cumulative voting at any election of directors. Unless otherwise provided in the articles of incorporation, in any election of directors the candidates elected are those receiving the largest numbers of votes cast by the shares entitled to vote in the election, up to the number of directors to be elected by such shares.

Section 5.14 Acceptance of Votes.

5.14.1. Vote by Named Shareholder. If the name signed on a vote, consent, waiver, or proxy appointment corresponds to the name of a shareholder, the corporation may accept the vote, consent, waiver, or proxy appointment as the shareholder's act.

5.14.2. Vote Not Corresponding to Named Shareholder. If the name signed on a vote, consent, waiver, or proxy appointment does not correspond to the name of its shareholder, the corporation may accept the vote, consent, waiver or proxy appointment as the shareholder's act if:

 (i) the shareholder is an entity and the name signed purports to be that of an officer, partner, or agent of the entity;

 (ii) the name signed purports to be that of an administrator, executor, guardian, or conservator representing the shareholder and evidence of fiduciary status acceptable to the corporation has been presented with respect to the vote, consent, waiver or proxy appointment;

 (iii) the name signed purports to be that of a receiver or trustee in bankruptcy of the shareholder, and evidence of this status acceptable to the corporation has been presented with respect to the vote, consent waiver, or proxy appointment;

 (iv) the name signed purports to be that of a pledge, beneficial owner, or attorney-in-fact of the shareholder and evidence acceptable to the corporation of the signatory's authority to sign for the shareholder has been presented with respect to the vote, consent, waiver, or proxy appointment; or

 (v) two or more persons are the shareholder as co-tenants or fiduciaries, the name signed purports to be the name of at least one of the co-owners, and the person signing appears to be acting on behalf of all the co-owners.

5.14.3. Rejection of Vote. The corporation may reject a vote, consent, waiver, or proxy appointment if the secretary has reasonable basis for doubt about the validity of the signature or about the signatory's authority to sign for the shareholder.

ARTICLE VI. BOARD OF DIRECTORS

Section 6.1 General Powers. The business and affairs of the corporation shall be managed by its board of directors.

Section 6.2 Number, Tenure, and Qualification. The number of directors set forth in Article III of these bylaws may be increased or decreased from time to time by amendment to or in the manner provided in these bylaws. No decrease, however, shall have the effect of shortening the term of any incumbent director unless such director resigns or is removed in accordance with the provisions of these bylaws. Except as classification of directors may be specified by the articles of incorporation and unless removed in accordance with these bylaws, each director shall hold office until the next annual meeting of the shareholders and until a successor shall have been elected and qualified. Directors need not be residents of the state of Washington or shareholders of the corporation.

Section 6.3 Annual and Other Regular Meetings. An annual meeting of the board of directors shall be held without other notice than this bylaw, immediately after and at the same place as the annual meeting of shareholders. The board of directors may specify by resolution the time and place, either within or without the state of Washington, for holding any other regular meetings of the board of directors.

Section 6.4 Special Meetings. Special meetings of the board of directors may be called by the board of directors, the chairman of the board, the president, the secretary, or any director. Notice of special meetings of the board of directors stating the date, time, and place thereof shall be given in the manner described in Article IV or by oral notice (communicated in person or by telephone, wire or wireless equipment, which does not transmit a facsimile of the notice or by any electronic means that does not create a Record) at least two (2) days prior to the date set for such meeting by the person or persons authorized to call such meeting, or by the secretary at the direction of the person or persons authorized to call such meeting. If oral notice is given, it shall be effective when received by the director. Notice given by wire or wireless equipment that does not transmit a facsimile of the notice or by any electronic means that does not create a Record is effective when communicated to the director. If no place for such meeting is designated in the notice thereof, the meeting shall be held at the principal office of the corporation. Unless otherwise required by law, neither the business to be transacted at, nor the purpose of, any regular or special meeting of the board of directors need be specified in the notice of the meeting.

Section 6.5 Waiver of Notice.

6.5.1. By Delivery of a Record. Any director may waive notice of any meeting at any time. Whenever any notice is required to be given to any director of the corporation pursuant to applicable law, a waiver thereof executed by the director entitled to notice shall be equivalent to the giving of notice. The waiver must be delivered by the director entitled to the notice to the corporation for inclusion in the minutes for filing with the corporate records. The waiver shall be set forth either in an executed written Record or, if the corporation has designated an address, location or system to which the waiver may be electronically transmitted and the waiver has been electronically transmitted to the designated address, location or system, in an executed electronically transmitted Record. Neither the business to be transacted at nor the purpose of any regular or special meeting of the Board need be specified in the waiver of notice of the meeting.

6.5.2. By Attendance. A director's attendance at or participation in a board of directors meeting shall constitute a waiver of notice of the meeting, unless the director at the beginning of the meeting, or promptly upon his or her arrival, objects to holding the meeting or transacting business at the meeting and does not vote for or assent to action taken at the meeting.

Section 6.6 Quorum. A majority of the directors in office, but no less than one-third of the total number of directors specified in or fixed in accordance with these bylaws, shall constitute a quorum for the transaction of any business at any meeting of directors. If less than a majority shall attend a meeting, a majority of the directors present may adjourn the meeting from time to time without further notice, and a quorum present at such adjourned meeting may transact business.

Section 6.7 Manner of Acting. If a quorum is present when a vote is taken, the affirmative vote of a majority of directors present is the act of the board of directors.

Section 6.8 Participation by Communications Equipment. Directors may participate in a regular or special meeting of the board by, or conduct the meeting through the use of, any means of communication by which all directors participating can hear each other during the meeting and participation by such means shall constitute presence in person at the meeting.

Section 6.9 Presumption of Assent. A director who is present at a meeting of the board of directors at which action is taken shall be presumed to have assented to the action taken unless (a) such director's dissent or abstention from the action taken is entered in the minutes of the meeting, (b) such director delivers notice of dissent or abstention from such action to the presiding officer of the meeting before the adjournment of the meeting or to the corporation immediately after adjournment of the meeting or (c) the director objects at the meeting, or promptly upon his arrival, to holding the meeting or transacting any business at the meeting. Such right to dissent or abstention from the action taken shall not apply to a director who voted in favor of such action.

Section 6.10 Action by Board Without a Meeting. Any action permitted or required to be taken at a meeting of the board of directors may be taken without a meeting if one or more consents setting forth the action so taken, shall be executed by all the directors, either before or after the action taken, and delivered to the corporation, each of which shall be set forth in an executed written Record or, if the corporation has designated an address, location or system to which the consent may be electronically transmitted and the consent is electronically transmitted to the designated address, location or system, in an executed electronically transmitted Record. Action taken by consent is effective when the last director executes the consent, unless the consent specifies a later effective date.

Section 6.11 Board Committees.   The board of directors may by resolution designate from among its members an executive committee and one or more other committees, each of which must have two (2) or more members and shall be governed by the same rules regarding meetings, action without meetings, notice, waiver of notice, and quorum and voting requirements as applied to the board of directors.   To the extent provided in such resolutions, each such committee shall have and may exercise the authority of the board of directors, except as limited by applicable law.   The designation of any such committee and the delegation thereto of authority shall not relieve the board of directors, or any members thereof, of any responsibility imposed by law.

Section 6.12 Resignation.   Any director may resign at any time by delivering an executed notice to the chairman of the board, the president, the secretary, or the registered office of the corporation, or by giving oral notice at any meeting of the directors or shareholders.   Any such resignation shall take effect at any subsequent time specified therein, or if the time is not specified, upon delivery thereof and, unless otherwise specified therein, the acceptance of such resignation shall not be necessary to make it effective.

Section 6.13 Removal. At a meeting of the shareholders called expressly for that purpose, any director or the entire board of directors may be removed from office, with or without cause (unless the articles of incorporation provide that directors may be removed only for cause) by a vote of the shares then entitled to vote at an election of the director or directors whose removal is sought if the number of votes cast to remove the director or directors exceeds the number of votes cast not to remove the director or directors. If shareholders have the right to cumulate votes in the election of directors and if less than the entire board of directors is to be removed, not one of the directors may be removed if the votes cast against his removal would be sufficient to elect him if then cumulatively voted at an election of the entire board or the class of directors of which he is a part. If the board of directors or any one or more directors is so removed, new directors may be elected at this same meeting.

Section 6.14 Vacancies. A vacancy on the board of directors may occur by the resignation, removal, or death of an existing director, or by reason of increasing the number of directors on the board of directors as provided in these bylaws. Except as may be limited by the articles of incorporation, any vacancy occurring in the board of directors may be filled by the affirmative vote of a majority of the remaining directors though less than a quorum. The term of a director elected to fill a vacancy expires at the next election of directors by the shareholders.

If the vacant office was held by a director elected by holders of one or more authorized classes or series of shares, only the holders of those classes or series of shares are entitled to vote to fill the vacancy.

Section 6.15 Compensation. By resolution of the board of directors, the directors may be paid a fixed sum plus their expenses, if any, for attendance at meetings of the board of directors or committee thereof, or a stated salary as director. No such payment shall preclude any director from serving the corporation in any other capacity and receiving compensation therefor.

ARTICLE VII. OFFICERS

Section 7.1 Number. The corporation shall have a president, and may have one or more vice presidents, a secretary, and a treasurer, each of whom shall be appointed by the board of directors. Such other officers and assistant officers, including a chairman of the board, as may be deemed necessary or appropriate may be appointed by the board of directors. By resolution, the board of directors may designate any officer as chief executive officer, chief operating officer, chief financial officer, or any similar designation. Any two or more offices may be held by the same person.

Section 7.2 Appointment and Term of Office. The officers of the corporation shall be appointed by the board of directors for such term as the board may deem advisable or may be appointed to serve for an indefinite term at the pleasure of the board. Each officer shall hold office until a successor shall have been appointed regardless of such officer's term of office, except in the event of such officer's termination of an indefinite term at the pleasure of the board or such officer's removal in the manner herein provided.

Section 7.3 Resignation. Any officer may resign at any time by delivering written notice to the chairman of the board, the president, a vice president, the secretary, or the board of directors, or by giving oral notice at any meeting of the board. Any such resignation shall take effect at any subsequent time specified therein, or if the time is not specified, upon delivery thereof and, unless otherwise specified therein, the acceptance of such resignation shall not be necessary to make it effective.

Section 7.4 Removal. Any officer appointed by the board of directors may be removed by the board of directors with or without cause. The removal shall be without prejudice to the contract rights, if any, of the person so removed. Appointment of an officer or agent shall not of itself create contract rights.

Section 7.5 Chairman and Vice Chairmen of the Board. The chairman of the board, if there be such an office, shall, if present, preside at all meetings of the board of directors, and exercise and perform such other powers and duties as may be determined from time to time by resolution of the board of directors. The vice chairman of the board, if there be such an office, or in the event there shall be more than one vice chairman, the one designated most senior at the time of election, shall perform the duties of the chairman of the board in the chairman's absence, or in the event of the chairman's death, disability or refusal to act. The vice chairman of the board shall exercise and perform such other powers and duties as may be determined from time to time by resolution of the board of directors.

Section 7.6 President. The president shall be the principal executive officer of the corporation and, subject to the control of the board of directors, shall generally supervise and control the business and affairs of the corporation.

When present, the president shall preside at all meetings of the shareholders and in the absence of the chairman of the board, or if there be none, at all meetings of the board of directors. The president may sign with the secretary or any other proper officer of the corporation thereunto authorized by law, certificates for shares of the corporation, and may sign deeds, mortgages, bonds, contracts, or other instruments that the board of directors has authorized to be executed, except in cases where the signing and execution thereof shall be expressly delegated by the board of directors or by these bylaws to some other officer or agent of the corporation or shall be required by law to be otherwise signed or executed. In general, the president shall perform all duties incident to the office of president and such other duties as may be prescribed by resolution of the board of directors from time to time.

Section 7.7 Vice Presidents. In the absence of the president or in the event of his death, disability, or refusal to act, the vice president, or in the event there shall be more than one vice president, the vice presidents, in the order designated at the time of their election, or in the absence of any designation then in the order of their election, if any, shall perform the duties of the president. When so acting the vice president shall have all the powers of and be subject to all the restrictions upon the president and shall perform such other duties as from time to time may be assigned to the vice president by resolution of the board of directors.

Section 7.8 Secretary. The secretary shall keep the minutes of the proceedings of the shareholders and board of directors, shall give notices in accordance with the provisions of these bylaws and as required by law, shall be custodian of the corporate records of the corporation, shall keep a Record of the names and addresses of all shareholders and the number and class of shares held by each, have general charge of the stock transfer books of the corporation, may sign with the president, or a vice president, certificates for shares of the corporation, deeds, mortgages, bonds, contracts, or other instruments that shall have been authorized by resolution of the board of directors, and in general shall perform all duties incident to the office of secretary and such other duties as from time to time may be assigned to the secretary by resolution of the board of directors.

Section 7.9 Treasurer. If required by the board of directors, the treasurer shall give a bond for the faithful discharge of his duties, in such sum and with such surety or sureties as the board of directors shall determine. The treasurer shall have charge and custody of and be responsible for keeping correct and complete books and records of account, for all funds and securities of the corporation, receive and give receipts for moneys due and payable to the corporation from any source whatsoever, deposit all such moneys in the name of the corporation in the banks, trust companies, or other depositories as shall be selected in accordance with the provisions of these bylaws, and in general perform all of the duties incident to the office of treasurer and such other duties as from time to time may be assigned to the treasurer by resolution of the board of directors.

Section 7.10 Assistant Officers. The assistant officers in general shall perform such duties as are customary or as shall be assigned to them by resolution of the board of directors. If required by the board of directors, the assistant treasurers shall respectively give bonds for the faithful discharge of their duties in such sums and with such sureties as the board of directors shall determine.

Section 7.11 Compensation of Officers and Employees. The board of directors shall fix compensation of officers and may fix compensation of other employees from time to time. No officer shall be prevented from receiving a salary by reason of the fact that such officer is also a director of the corporation. In the event any salary payment, or portion thereof, to an officer or other employee is not allowable as a deduction for employee compensation under Section 162(a)(1) of the Internal Revenue Code of 1986, as may be amended from time to time, on the grounds such payment was unreasonable in amount, then such officer or employee shall promptly repay the amount disallowed as a deduction to the corporation.

ARTICLE VIII. CONTRACTS, LOANS, CHECKS, DEPOSITS

Section 8.1 Contracts. The board of directors may authorize any officer or officers, agent or agents, to enter into any contract or execute and deliver any instrument in the name of and on behalf of the corporation, and that authority may be general or confined to specific instances.

Section 8.2 Loans. No loans shall be contracted on behalf of the corporation and no evidences of indebtedness shall be issued in its name unless authorized by a resolution of the board of directors, which authority may be general.

Section 8.3 Checks, Drafts, Etc. All checks, drafts, or other orders for the payment of money, notes, or other evidences of indebtedness issued in the name of the corporation shall be signed by the officer or officers, or agent or agents, of the corporation and in the manner as shall from time to time be prescribed by resolution of the board of directors.

Section 8.4 Deposits. All funds of the corporation not otherwise employed shall be deposited from time to time to the credit of the corporation in the banks, trust companies, or other depositories as the board of directors may select.

Section 8.5 Contracts With or Loans to Directors and Officers. As permitted by RCW 23B.08, the corporation may enter into contracts and otherwise transact business as vendor, purchaser, or otherwise, with its directors, officers, and shareholders and with corporations, associations, firms, and entities in which they are or may become interested as directors, officers, shareholders, members, or otherwise, as freely as though such interest did not exist.

ARTICLE IX. SHARES

Section 9.1 Certificates for Shares. The shares of the corporation may be represented by certificates in such form as prescribed by the board of directors. Signatures of the corporate officers on the certificate may be facsimiles if the certificate is manually signed on behalf of a transfer agent, or registered by a registrar, other than the corporation itself or an employee of the corporation. All certificates shall be consecutively numbered or otherwise identified. All certificates shall bear such legend or legends as prescribed by the board of directors or these bylaws.

Section 9.2 Issuance of Shares. Shares of the corporation shall be issued only when authorized by the board of directors, which authorization shall include the consideration to be received for each share.

Section 9.3 Beneficial Ownership. Except as otherwise permitted by these bylaws, the person in whose name shares stand on the books of the corporation shall be deemed by the corporation to be the owner thereof for all purposes. The board of directors may adopt by resolution a procedure whereby a shareholder of the corporation may certify in writing to the corporation that all or a portion of the shares registered in the name of such shareholder are held for the account of a specified person or persons. Upon receipt by the corporation of a certification complying with such procedure, the persons specified in the certification shall be deemed, for the purpose or purposes set forth in the certification, to be the holders of record of the number of shares specified in place of the shareholder making the certification.

Section 9.4 Transfer of Shares. Transfer of shares of the corporation shall be made only on the stock transfer books of the corporation by the holder of record thereof or by his legal representative who shall furnish proper evidence of authority to transfer, or by his attorney thereunto authorized by power of attorney duly executed and filed with the secretary of the corporation, on surrender for cancellation of the certificate for the shares. All certificates surrendered to the corporation for transfer shall be cancelled and no new certificate shall be issued until the former certificate for a like number of shares shall have been surrendered and cancelled.

Section 9.5 Lost or Destroyed Certificates. In the case of a lost, destroyed, or mutilated certificate, a new certificate may be issued therefor upon such terms and indemnity to the corporation as the board of directors may prescribe.

Section 9.6 Restrictions on Transfer. Except to the extent that the corporation has obtained an opinion of counsel acceptable to the corporation that transfer restrictions are not required under applicable securities laws, all certificates representing shares of the corporation shall bear a legend on the face of the certificate or on the reverse of the certificate if a reference to the legend is contained on the face, to the effect as follows:

> These securities are not registered under state or federal securities laws and may not be offered, sold, pledged, or

otherwise transferred, nor may these securities be transferred on the books of the company, without an opinion of counsel or other assurance satisfactory to the company that no violation of such registration provisions would result therefrom.

Section 9.7 Stock Transfer Records. The stock transfer books shall be kept at the principal office of the corporation or at the office of the corporation's transfer agent or registrar. The name and address of the person to whom the shares represented by any certificate, together with the class, number of shares, and date of issue, shall be entered on the stock transfer books of the corporation. Except as provided in these bylaws, the person in whose name shares stand on the books of the corporation shall be deemed by the corporation to be the owner thereof for all purposes.

ARTICLE X. SEAL

This corporation need not have a corporate seal. If the directors adopt a corporate seal, the seal of the corporation shall be circular in form and consist of the name of the corporation, the state and year of incorporation, and the words "Corporate Seal."

ARTICLE XI. INDEMNIFICATION OF DIRECTORS, OFFICERS, EMPLOYEES, AND AGENTS

Section 11.1 Power to Indemnify. The corporation shall have the following powers:

11.1.1. Power to Indemnify. The corporation may indemnify and hold harmless to the full extent permitted by applicable law each person who was or is made a party to or is threatened to be made a party to or is involved (including, without limitation, as a witness) in any actual or threatened action, suit or other proceeding, whether civil, criminal, administrative, or investigative, by reason of that fact that he or she is or was a director, officer, employee, or agent of the corporation or, being or having been such a director, officer, employee, or agent, he or she is or was serving at the request of the corporation as a director, officer, employee, agent, trustee, or in any other capacity of another corporation or of a partnership, joint venture, trust or other enterprise, including service with respect to employee benefit plans, whether the basis of such proceeding is alleged action or omission in an official capacity or in any other capacity while serving as a director, officer, employee, agent, trustee, or in any other capacity, against all expense, liability and loss (including, without limitation, attorneys' fees, judgments, fines, ERISA excise taxes, or penalties and amounts to be paid in settlement) actually or reasonably incurred or suffered by such person in connection therewith. Such indemnification may continue as to a person who has ceased to be a director, officer, employee or agent of the corporation and shall inure to the benefit of his or her heirs and personal representatives.

11.1.2. Power to Pay Expenses in Advance of Final Disposition. The corporation may pay expenses incurred in defending any such proceeding in advance of the final disposition of any such proceeding, provided, however, that the payment of such expenses in advance of the final disposition of a proceeding shall be made to or on behalf of a director, officer, employee, or agent only upon delivery to the corporation of an undertaking, by or on behalf of such director, officer, employee, or agent, to repay all amounts so advanced if it shall ultimately be determined that such director, officer, employee, or agent is not entitled to be indemnified under this Article or otherwise, which undertaking may be unsecured and may be accepted without reference to financial ability to make repayment.

11.1.3. Power to Enter Into Contracts. The corporation may enter into contracts with any person who is or was a director, officer, employee, and agent of the corporation in furtherance of the provisions of this Article and may create a trust fund, grant a security interest in property of the corporation, or use other means (including, without limitation, a letter of credit) to ensure the payment of such amounts as may be necessary to effect indemnification as provided in this Article.

11.1.4. Expansion of Powers. If the Washington Business Corporation Act is amended in the future to expand or increase the power of the corporation to indemnify, to pay expenses in advance of final disposition, to enter into contracts, or to expand or increase any similar or related power, then, without any further requirement of action by the shareholders or directors of this corporation, the powers described in this Article shall be expanded and increased to the fullest extent permitted by the Washington Business Corporation Act, as so amended.

11.1.5. Limitation on Powers. No indemnification shall be provided under this Article to any such person if the corporation is prohibited by the nonexclusive provisions of the Washington Business Corporation Act or other applicable law as then in effect from paying such indemnification. For example, no indemnification shall be provided to any director in respect of any proceeding, whether or not involving action in his or her official capacity, in which he or she shall have been finally adjudged to be liable on the basis of intentional misconduct or knowing violation of law by the director, or from conduct of the director in violation of RCW 23B.08.310, or that the director personally received a benefit in money, property, or services to which the director was not legally entitled.

Section 11.2 Indemnification of Directors, Officers, Employees, and Agents.

11.2.1. Directors. The corporation shall indemnify and hold harmless any person who is or was a director of this corporation, and pay expenses in advance of final disposition of a proceeding, to the full extent to which the corporation is empowered.

11.2.2. Officers, Employees, and Agents. The corporation may, by action of its Board of Directors from time to time, indemnify and hold harmless any person who is or was an officer, employee, or agent of the corporation, and pay expenses in advance of final disposition of a proceeding, to the full extent to which the corporation is empowered, or to any lesser extent which the Board of Directors may determine.

11.2.3. Character of Rights. The rights to indemnification and payment of expenses in advance of final disposition of a proceeding conferred by or pursuant to this Article shall be contract rights.

11.2.4. Enforcement. A director, officer, employee, or agent ("claimant") shall be presumed to be entitled to indemnification and/or payment of expenses under this Article upon submission of a written claim (and, in an action brought to enforce a claim for expenses incurred in defending any proceeding in advance of its final disposition, where the undertaking in subsection 11.1.2 above has been delivered to the corporation) and thereafter the corporation shall have the burden of proof to overcome the presumption that the claimant is so entitled.

If a claim under this Article is not paid in full by the corporation within sixty (60) days after a written claim has been received by the corporation, except in the case of a claim for expenses incurred in defending a proceeding in advance of its final disposition, in which case the applicable period shall be twenty (20) days, the claimant may at any time thereafter bring suit against the corporation to recover the unpaid amount of the claim and, to the extent successful in whole or in part, the claimant shall be entitled to be paid also the expense of prosecuting such claim. Neither the failure of the corporation (including its board of directors, its shareholders, or independent legal counsel) to have made a determination prior to the commencement of such action that indemnification of or reimbursement or advancement of expenses to the claimant is proper in the circumstances nor an actual determination by the corporation (including its board of directors, its shareholders, or independent legal counsel) that the claimant is not entitled to indemnification or to the reimbursement or advancement of expenses shall be a defense to the action or create a presumption that the claimant is not so entitled.

11.2.5. Rights Not Exclusive. The right to indemnification and payment of expenses in advance of final disposition of a proceeding conferred in this Article shall not be exclusive of any other right that any person may have or hereafter acquire under any statute, provision of the articles of incorporation, bylaws, agreement, vote of shareholders, or disinterested directors or otherwise.

Section 11.3 Insurance. The corporation may purchase and maintain insurance, at its expense, to protect itself and any director, officer, employee, agent, or trustee of the corporation or another corporation, partnership, joint venture, trust, or other enterprise against any expense, liability or loss, whether or not the corporation would have the power to indemnify such person against such expense, liability or loss under the Washington Business Corporation Act or other law.

Section 11.4 Survival of Benefits. Any repeal or modification of this Article shall not adversely affect any right of any person existing at the time of such repeal or modification.

Section 11.5 Severability. If any provision of this Article or any application thereof shall be invalid, unenforceable, or contrary to applicable law, the remainder of this Article, or the application of such provision to persons or circumstances other than those as to which it is held invalid, unenforceable, or contrary to applicable law, shall not be affected thereby and shall continue in full force and effect.

Section 11.6 Applicable Law. For purposes of this Article, "applicable law" shall at all times be construed as the applicable law in effect at the date indemnification may be sought, or the law in effect at the date of the action, omission, or other event giving rise to the situation for which indemnification may be sought, whichever is selected by the person seeking indemnification. As of the date hereof, applicable law shall include RCW 23B.08.500 through .600, as amended.

ARTICLE XII. BOOKS AND RECORDS

The corporation shall:

(a) Keep as permanent records minutes of all meetings of its shareholders and the board of directors, a record of all actions taken by the shareholders or the board of directors without a meeting, and a record of all actions taken by a committee of the board of directors exercising the authority of the board of directors on behalf of the corporation.

(b) Maintain appropriate accounting records.

(c) Maintain or hire an agent to maintain a record of its shareholders, in a form that permits preparation of a list of the names and addresses of all shareholders, in alphabetical order by class of shares showing the number and class of shares held by each.

(d) Maintain its records in written form or in another form capable of conversion into written form within a reasonable time.

(e) Keep a copy of the following records at its principal office; (1) the articles of incorporation and all amendments thereto as currently in effect; (2) these bylaws and all amendments thereto as currently in effect; (3) the minutes of all meetings of shareholders and records of all action taken by shareholders without a meeting, for the past three years; (4) the financial statements described in RCW 23B.16.200(1), for the past three years; (5) all communications in the form of a record to shareholders generally within the past three years; (6) a list of the names and business addresses of the current directors and officers; and (7) the most recent annual report delivered to the Washington Secretary of State.

(f) Maintain any other records as required by applicable law.

ARTICLE XIII. FISCAL YEAR

The fiscal year of the corporation shall be determined by resolution adopted by the board of directors. In the absence of such a resolution, the fiscal year shall be the calendar year.

ARTICLE XIV. VOTING OF SHARES OF ANOTHER CORPORATION

Shares of another corporation held by this corporation may be voted by the president or vice president, or by proxy appointment form executed by either of them, unless the directors by resolution shall designate some other person to vote the shares.

ARTICLE XV. AMENDMENTS TO BYLAWS

These bylaws may be altered, amended, or repealed, and new bylaws may be adopted by the board of directors or by the shareholders.

The undersigned, being the secretary of the corporation, hereby certifies that these bylaws are the bylaws of **Error! Reference source not found.**, adopted by resolution of the directors on _____,
_____.

DATED   this   _____   day   of
_____,_____.

_____, Secretary

SPECIAL NOTES

[OPTIONAL replacement paragraphs for Article II. NUMBER OF DIRECTORS:

The board of directors of this corporation shall consist of a number of directors between _____ and _____, as set from time to time by the board of directors.

[or]

The board of directors of this corporation shall consist of between _____ and _____ directors as may be determined from time to time by the board of directors or the shareholders.

[OPTIONAL Section 3.2. Special Meetings. If the corporation is not a public company (as contemplated by the Washington Business Corporation Act) the articles or bylaws may require a maximum of twenty five percent (25%) of all votes entitled to be cast on any issue proposed to be considered at the proposed special meeting.]

[OPTIONAL Section 4.5. Quorum. The articles or bylaws may authorize a quorum of the board of directors to consist of no fewer than one third of the fixed or specified number of directors.]

F. FORM: CORPORATE SHAREHOLDER AGREEMENT

SHAREHOLDERS AGREEMENT of

_____

This Agreement dated as of _____, _____, is made by and among _____, a corporation (the "Company"), and the shareholders set forth on attached Exhibit A (the "Shareholders").

RECITALS

This Agreement is intended to set forth the restrictions to which any transfer of any or all of the shares of the Company's capital stock now or hereafter outstanding ("Shares") will be subject. The Shareholders together own all the currently outstanding Shares as set forth in attached Exhibit A.

AGREEMENT

1. RESTRICTIONS ON TRANSFER

1.1 Transfers by Shareholders. No Shareholder may transfer any Shares except as expressly permitted by this Agreement. For purposes of this Agreement, "transfer" is intended to be construed as broadly as the law allows and to include any change of legal or beneficial ownership with respect to the Shares or the creation of a security interest by any means. Any transfer made in connection with the foreclosure of a security interest will constitute a separate transfer.

1.2 New Stock Issues. The Company may not transfer Shares by new issue to anyone (including a Shareholder or an outside party) or permit anyone (including a Shareholder or an outside party) to subscribe to a new issue of Shares without the prior written consent of all Shareholders [or, if that consent cannot be obtained, without first offering to the Shareholders the right for a period of _____ days to subscribe to the proposed issue in proportion to the Shareholder's respective interest at the time of issue].

2. PERMITTED TRANSFERS

2.1 With Consent. A Shareholder may transfer Shares at any time with the written consent of [all] the other Shareholders [who hold at least _____ percent (_____) of the Shares of the Company at the time of the proposed transfer].

2.2 Without Consent. A Shareholder may transfer Shares to trusts created by the Shareholder for the Shareholder's benefit or for the benefit of family members of the Shareholder. For purposes of this Agreement, "family members" means lineal descendants of the Shareholder.

2.3 Binding on Transferees. No permitted transfer may be made unless the transferee (and, if applicable, the transferee's spouse) executes a document substantially in the form of attached Exhibit B evidencing the transferee's agreement to be bound by the provisions of this Agreement, as amended.

3. PERMITTED LIFETIME TRANSFERS. Any Shareholder desiring to transfer Shares in a bona fide voluntary transfer not permitted by Section 2 must first give written notice to the Company and the remaining Shareholders of the Shareholder's intention to do so. The notice ("Transfer Notice") must name the proposed transferee and the number of Shares to be transferred and, if the transfer constitutes a sale, must specify the terms of a bona fide offer, including the price per Share, and the terms of payment.

3.1 Company Option. The Company will have the option, exercisable within _____ days after receiving the Transfer Notice, to purchase the Shares. To exercise the option, the Company must give written notice to the offering Shareholder. Subject to Section 3.4, the Company must pay the purchase price on the same terms and conditions set forth in the Transfer Notice.

3.2 Option of Remaining Shareholders. If the Company does not exercise its option as to all or any of the Shares set forth in the Transfer Notice, then the Company must so notify the remaining Shareholders.

(a) The remaining Shareholders will each have the option, exercisable within _____ days after receiving notice from the Company, to purchase any Shares not purchased by the Company. To exercise the option, a Shareholder must give written notice to the Company and to the offering Shareholder specifying the number of shares the Shareholder wishes to purchase.

(b) If the total number of Shares specified in the notices of election exceeds the number of offered Shares, each Shareholder will have priority, up to the number of Shares specified in the notice of election, to purchase the Shareholder's Proportionate Share of the available Shares. Proportionate Share means that proportion determined by dividing the number of the Company's Shares that the electing Shareholder holds by the total number of the Company's Shares held by all Shareholders electing to purchase as of the date the offer was made.

(c) The Shares not purchased on a priority basis will be allocated to those Shareholders that elect to purchase more than the number of Shares to which they have a priority right, up to the number of Shares specified in their respective notices of election to purchase, in the proportion that the number of Shares held by each of them bears to the number of Shares held by all of them as of the date the offer was made.

(d) Promptly after receiving the written notices of election of the remaining Shareholders, the Company must notify each Shareholder of the number of Shares as to which the Shareholder's election was effective and must provide to the offering Shareholder a notice summarizing these elections. Subject to Section 3.4, each Shareholder must pay the purchase price on the same terms and conditions set forth in the Transfer Notice.

3.3 Conditions of Transfer. If the Company and the Shareholders elect not to purchase all the Shares set forth in the Transfer Notice, then all those Shares may be transferred subject to the satisfaction of all the following conditions:

(a) Within thirty (30) days after receiving notice from the Company, the offering Shareholder must transfer the Shares to the transferee identified in the Transfer Notice at the price and on the same terms stated in the Transfer Notice; and

(b) The transferee (and, if applicable, the transferee's spouse) must execute a document substantially in the form of attached Exhibit B evidencing the transferee's agreement to be bound by the provisions of this Agreement, as amended.

(c) If all of the above-conditions are not satisfied, the offering Shareholder may not transfer the Shares under this Section 3 without giving a new written notice of intention to transfer and complying with this Section 3.

3.4 Right to Purchase Pursuant to Agreement. Notwithstanding any other provision to the contrary, the Company or the remaining Shareholders, or both, will be entitled to purchase all the Shares specified in the Transfer Notice at the price and on the terms set forth in this Agreement (and not at the price and on the terms set forth in the Transfer Notice), if any of the following occur:

(a) The price stated in the Transfer Notice is greater than the price set forth in this Agreement;

(b) The offering Shareholder has included in the Transfer Notice the terms of a gift, pledge, or other transfer not constituting a sale; or

(c) The terms of a bona fide offer in the Transfer Notice provide for the payment of nonmonetary consideration, in whole or in part, and the offering Shareholder and the Company or remaining Shareholders, or both (as applicable), are not able to agree on the equivalent cash value of that consideration.

(d) If appraisal is required to determine the value of the Shares under Section 8, the Transfer Notice will be deemed to be given on the date that the Company receives notice of the appraisal determination.

4. OBLIGATIONS OF TRANSFEREES. Unless this Agreement expressly provides otherwise, each transferee or subsequent transferee of Shares, or any interest in those Shares, will hold those Shares or interest subject to all the provisions of this Agreement and may make no further transfers except as provided in this Agreement.

5. PURCHASE ON DEATH

5.1 Mandatory Purchase on Death by Company or Shareholders

(a) Upon the death of a Shareholder, the Company must purchase all the decedent's Shares and all Shares that have been transferred to third parties under Section 2.2, and the decedent Shareholder's estate and any such third parties must sell those Shares, at the price and on the terms provided in this Agreement. Subject to Section 9.1, the purchase must be completed within a period commencing with the death of the Shareholder and ending sixty (60) days following the qualification of the Shareholder's personal representative.

(b) If the Company is not legally able to purchase all of the decedent's Shares and all Shares that have been transferred to third parties under Section 2.2

under applicable law, the remaining Shareholders must purchase all of the decedent's Shares and all Shares that have been transferred to third parties under Section 2.2 that the Company is legally unable to purchase at the price and on the terms provided in this Agreement.

(c) The obligation of the remaining Shareholders to purchase those Shares will be [joint and several] [several and not joint and will be prorated based on their respective shareholdings in the Company].

5.2 Insurance: Corporate Buyout. The Company [may] [must] apply for a policy of insurance on the life of each Shareholder to enable the Company to purchase the Shares of that Shareholder. Each Shareholder agrees to do everything necessary to cause a policy of life insurance to be issued pursuant to that application. The Company must be the owner of any policy or policies of life insurance acquired pursuant to the terms of this Agreement. Each policy, and any policies hereafter acquired for the same purpose, will be listed on attached Exhibit C.

6. DISABILITY

6.1 Optional Purchase on Disability. If any Shareholder who is then an employee of the Company becomes disabled, the Company and the remaining Shareholders will have the option, for the periods set forth below, to purchase all or any part of the Shares owned by the Shareholder and all or any part of the Shareholder's Shares that have been transferred to third parties under Section 2.2.

6.2 Exercise of Option

(a) To exercise its option, the Company must give written notice to the disabled Shareholder within _____ days after receiving notice of the determination of disability under Section 6.3.

(b) If the option is not exercised within that _____ -day period as to all Shares owned by the disabled Shareholder, the remaining Shareholders will have the option, for a period of _____ days commencing with the end of that _____ -day period, to purchase all or any part of the remaining Shares owned by the disabled Shareholder, at the price and on the terms provided in this Agreement. To exercise the option, a Shareholder must give to the disabled Shareholder written notice of election to purchase a specified number of the Shares.

(c) If the notices of election from the other Shareholders specify in the aggregate more Shares than are available for purchase by the other Shareholders, each Shareholder will have priority, up to the number of Shares specified in the notice of election, to purchase the Shareholder's Proportionate Share of the Shares. Proportionate Share means that proportion determined by dividing the number of the Company's Shares that the electing Shareholder holds by the total number of the Company's Shares held by all Shareholders electing to purchase as of the date the offer was made.

(d) The Shares not purchased on a priority basis will be allocated to those Shareholders electing to purchase more than the number of Shares to which they have a priority right, up to the number of Shares specified in their respective notices of election to purchase, in the proportion that the number of Shares held by each of them bears to the number of Shares held by all of them as of the date the offer was made.

(e) If this option is not exercised as to all the Shares owned by the disabled Shareholder, the disabled Shareholder will hold the remaining Shares [subject to] [free and clear of] the provisions of this Agreement.

(f) For purposes of this Agreement a Shareholder will be deemed to be "disabled" if one of the following conditions is satisfied:

(i) Under the terms of a bona fide disability income insurance policy that insures the Shareholder, the insurance company that underwrites the insurance policy determines that the Shareholder is totally disabled for purposes of the insurance policy.

(ii) A physician licensed to practice medicine in the state _____ of or _____, who has been selected by the Shareholder (or agent) and the board of directors of the Company, certifies that the Shareholder is partially or totally disabled so that the Shareholder will be unable to be employed gainfully on a full-time basis by the Company for a _____ -month period or more in the position that the Shareholder occupied before the disability. If the board of directors of the Company and the Shareholder (or agent) do not agree on the choice of a physician, these parties must each choose a physician who must in turn select a third physician. The third physician will have the authority to determine the Shareholder's disability. If the Shareholder refuses to choose a physician, the determination made by the physician selected by the Company will be conclusive. The Company must pay for the costs and expenses of the physician. As used in this Section 6.3(b), "agent" means, if applicable, the conservator of the Shareholder's estate or a person duly granted power-of-attorney to act on behalf of the Shareholder.

(iii) The Shareholder and the board of directors of the Company agree in writing that the Shareholder is partially or totally disabled so that the Shareholder will be unable to be employed gainfully on a full-time basis by the Company for a _____ -month period in the position that the Shareholder occupied before the disability.

7. TERMINATION OF EMPLOYMENT

7.1 Option to Purchase on Termination of Employment. If any Shareholder who is an employee of the Company [and who has not attained age _____] voluntarily terminates employment with the Company [or is discharged for cause], the Company and the remaining Shareholders will have the option to purchase all or any part of the Shares owned by the Shareholder and all Shares transferred to third parties pursuant to Section 2.2. The option will be exercisable first by the Company and thereafter by the remaining Shareholders, and the price, terms of purchase, and method of exercise of the option will be the same as are provided in Section 6.2. If this option is not exercised as to all of the Shares, the Shareholder and any third party to whom Shares were transferred under Section 2.2 will hold the Shares [subject to] [free and clear of] the provisions of this

Agreement].

8. VALUATION

8.1 Agreed Price With Arbitration. The purchase price to be paid for each of the Shares subject to this Agreement will be equal to the agreed value of the Company divided by the total number of Shares outstanding as of the date the price is to be determined.

(a) The initial agreed value of the Company is $ _____, and, at regular intervals hereafter, but no more often than quarterly and no less often than annually, the Shareholders to this Agreement will review the Company's financial condition. The Shareholders will at that time determine, by a vote of two-thirds of [the outstanding shares held by the Shareholders] [Shareholders (each Shareholder having one vote)], the Company's fair market value, which, if so voted, will be the Company's value until a different value is so determined or otherwise established under the provisions of this Agreement.

(b) If the parties are able to determine the value by that vote, they will evidence it by placing their written and executed agreement in the minute book of the Company. However, if the Shareholders have been unable to establish a value by that method within _____ years after the date on which the Shareholders last agreed on the value of the Company, the purchase price for each of the offering Shareholder's Shares will be determined by appraisal, in accordance with Section 8.2.

8.2 Appraisal. If required under Section 8.1(b), promptly after the occurrence of the event requiring the determination of the purchase price under this Agreement, the Company will appoint an appraiser to determine the fair market value of the Shares.

(a) If the Company and the offering Shareholder fail to agree on the identity of the appraiser, they will each appoint an appraiser to determine the fair market value of the Shares. If the appointed appraisers are not able to agree on the fair market value of the Shares, the appraisers will appoint a third appraiser, and the decision of a majority of the three appraisers will be binding on all interested parties.

(b) If a party fails to designate an appraiser within fifteen (15) days after receiving written notice from the other designating an appraiser and demanding appointment of the second appraiser, the first appraiser appointed may determine the fair market value of the Shares.

(c) The appraisal must be completed and communicated to the relevant parties not later than sixty (60) days after appointment of the first appraiser. [The appraisal fees must be paid by the Company.]

(d) Among other things, in making the appraisal, the appraiser must value real estate at fair market value; machinery and equipment at replacement cost or fair market value, whichever is lower; goods in process at cost, using the cost accounting procedures customarily employed by the Company in preparing its financial statements; receivables at their face amount, minus an allowance for uncollectible items that is reasonable in view of the past experience of the

Company and a recent review of their collectibility; all liabilities at their face value; [bank orders]; good will based on probable future work; and must establish a reserve for contingent liabilities, if appropriate. The appraiser must also consider the value of other comparable companies, if known.

9. PAYMENT TERMS

9.1 Terms. Unless otherwise agreed, the purchase price for Shares purchased under this Agreement must be paid as follows:

(a) If the purchase price is $ _____ or less, the purchase price must be paid in full within ninety (90) days after the offering Shareholder receives notice of the mandatory or optional purchase of the offering Shareholder's Shares.

(b) Subject to Section 9.2, if the purchase price is greater than $ _____, a down payment of _____ percent (_____) of the purchase price must be paid within ninety (90) days after the offering Shareholder receives notice of the mandatory or optional purchase of the offering Shareholder's Shares.

(c) Subject to Section 9.2, the balance of the purchase price must be paid in _____ equal monthly installments, including interest at the prime rate announced from time to time in the Wall Street Journal, plus two percent. The installment payments must commence on the first day of the month next following the date on which the Company or the remaining Shareholders or both purchase the Shares, and like payments must be made on the first day of each month thereafter until the purchase price is paid in full. All or any part of the unpaid balance of the purchase price may be prepaid without penalty at any time. The purchase price for the Shares must be paid to the offering Shareholder or the offering Shareholder's estate, as the case may be.

9.2 Insurance. The purchase price for the Shares must be paid as follows if the Company has insurance under Section 5.2 on the life of a deceased Shareholder whose Shares are purchased in accordance with Section 5.1.

(a) If the purchase price for the Shares is less than or equal to the amount of the proceeds received by the Company or the remaining Shareholders or both from the insurance on the life of the deceased Shareholder, the purchase price for the Shares must be paid in cash on the date of the purchase of the Shares.

(b) If the purchase price for the Shares of the deceased Shareholder exceeds the amount of the insurance proceeds, an amount equal to the proceeds of the insurance on the life of the deceased Shareholder must be paid in cash on the date of the purchase of the Shares, and the balance of the purchase price must be paid in accordance with Section 9.1(b).

(c) The Company must file the necessary proofs of death and collect the proceeds of any policies of insurance described in Section 5.2 outstanding on the life of the deceased Shareholder. The decedent's personal representative must apply for and obtain any necessary court approval or confirmation of the sale of the decedent's shares under this Agreement.

9.3 Documentation

(a) The deferred portion of the purchase price for any Shares purchased under this Agreement must be evidenced by a promissory note executed by the Company or all the purchasing Shareholders or both (as applicable) substantially in the form of attached Exhibit D. Except to the extent otherwise provided under Section 5.1(c) (but in that event only with respect to purchases under Section 5.1), the obligations of the Company or the Shareholders or both (as applicable) under the note will be [joint and several] [several and not joint prorated based on the number of Shares that each purchaser is purchasing]. If the obligation is several and not joint, each purchaser must sign a separate promissory note substantially in the form of attached Exhibit D. If the obligation is joint and several, all purchasers must sign the same promissory note, substantially in the form of attached Exhibit D but appropriately modified to reflect the joint and several obligations of each.

(b) The note or notes must be secured by a pledge of all the Shares being purchased in the transaction to which the note or notes relate [and of all other shares owned by the purchasing Shareholders], as set forth in the promissory note attached in Exhibit D and must contain such other provisions as set forth therein.

9.4 Payment of Consideration; Procedures for Transfer. Upon the exercise of any option under this Agreement and in all other events, consideration for the Shares must be delivered as soon as practicable to the person entitled to it. The Company must have the certificates representing the purchased Shares properly endorsed and, on compliance with Section 11, must issue a new certificate in the name of each purchasing Shareholder.

10. ADMINISTRATIVE REQUIREMENTS

The Company agrees to apply for and use its best efforts to obtain all governmental and administrative approvals required in connection with the purchase and sale of Shares under this Agreement. The Shareholders agree to cooperate in obtaining the approvals and to execute any and all documents that may be required to be executed by them in connection with the approvals. The Company must pay all costs and filing fees in connection with obtaining the approvals.

11. SHARE CERTIFICATES

On execution of this Agreement, the Company must place the legend set forth in Section 12 on the certificates representing the Shareholder's Shares. None of the Shares may be transferred, encumbered, or in any way alienated except under the terms of this Agreement. Each Shareholder will have the right to vote that Shareholder's Shares and receive the dividends paid on them until the Shares are sold or transferred as provided in this Agreement.

12. LEGENDS ON SHARE CERTIFICATES

Each share certificate, when issued, must have conspicuously endorsed on its face the following legend:

SALE, TRANSFER, PLEDGE, OR ANY OTHER DISPOSITION OF THE SHARES REPRESENTED BY THIS CERTIFICATE IS SUBJECT TO AND RESTRICTED BY THE TERMS OF A SHAREHOLDERS AGREEMENT DATED _____, _____,

BETWEEN THE COMPANY AND ITS SHAREHOLDERS. A COPY OF THE SHAREHOLDERS AGREEMENT IS AVAILABLE AT THE OFFICE OF THE COMPANY. THE SHARES REPRESENTED BY THIS CERTIFICATE MAY BE SOLD, TRANSFERRED, PLEDGED, OR OTHERWISE DISPOSED OF ONLY UPON COMPLIANCE WITH THE SHAREHOLDERS AGREEMENT.

On the request of a Shareholder, the secretary of the Company must show a copy of this Agreement to any person making inquiry about it.

13. TERMINATION OF AGREEMENT. This Agreement will terminate upon the occurrence of any of the following:

(a) As to each Shareholder only, the transfer of all Shares held by that Shareholder pursuant to the provisions of this Agreement;

(b) The written agreement of all parties who are then bound by the terms of this Agreement;

c) The dissolution [,or] bankruptcy, [or insolvency] of the Company; or

(d) At that time, if ever, that only one Shareholder or other transferee who is subject to the terms of this Agreement remains.

14. SHAREHOLDER WILLS

Each Shareholder agrees to include in his or her will a direction and authorization to the Shareholder's personal representative to comply with the provisions of this Agreement and to sell the Shareholder's Shares in accordance with this Agreement. However, the failure of any Shareholder to do so will not affect the validity or enforceability of this Agreement.

15. EQUITABLE RELIEF IN THE EVENT OF BREACH

The Shares of the Company subject to this Agreement are unique and cannot be readily purchased or sold because of the lack of a market. For these reasons, among others, the parties will be irreparably damaged if this Agreement is breached. Any party aggrieved by a breach of the provisions of this Agreement may bring an action at law or a suit in equity to obtain redress, including specific performance, injunctive relief, or any other available equitable remedy. Time and strict performance are of the essence of this Agreement. These remedies are cumulative and not exclusive and are in addition to any other remedy that the parties may have.

16. SUBCHAPTER S ELECTION AND STATUS

If all the Shareholders elect (or have elected) for the Company to be taxed as an "S Corporation" pursuant to Code Section 1362, then the Shareholders and the Company and will maintain that status until the Shares representing percent (_____ %) [NOTE TO DRAFTER: more than fifty percent (50%)] of the outstanding shares of Company are voted to terminate this election. Any provision of this Agreement is void that would prevent the Company from being able to make an effective election to be classified as an S Corporation once the decision has been made to elect S corporation status or that, once the Company becomes an S Corporation, would cause that status to be involuntarily terminated.

17. LEGAL LIMITATIONS

The obligation of the Company to purchase Shares under this Agreement is in all respects limited and by the ability of the Company to draw upon a legal source of funds from which to pay the purchase price. If the Company is legally unable to purchase and pay for any Shares that it is required to purchase under this Agreement, the Shareholders must promptly vote their respective Shares to take whatever steps may be appropriate or necessary to enable the Company to lawfully purchase and pay for all of the Shares.

18. MISCELLANEOUS PROVISIONS

18.1 Deletion and Addition of Parties. The secretary of the Company may add as a party to this Agreement any transferee of Shares or delete as a party any Shareholder who transfers all of the Shareholder's Shares. The secretary may take this action without the need for any further action by the board of directors of the Company or the consent of any party to this Agreement or of their respective heirs, personal representatives, successors, or assigns and regardless of whether or not a counterpart of this Agreement has been executed by that party. The Secretary may do so by amending the Shareholder list attached as Exhibit A.

18.2 Extension of Time for Closing. If in the opinion of legal counsel, additional time is needed in order to comply with applicable securities laws, the time of the closing of any sale or other transfer hereunder may be extended for a reasonable period not to exceed sixty (60) days.

18.3 Authorization. The Company is authorized to enter into this Agreement by virtue of a resolution duly adopted at a meeting of its Board of Directors dated effective _____ .

18.4 Employment Not Guaranteed. Nothing contained in this Agreement nor any action taken hereunder is intended to be construed as a contract of employment or to give a Shareholder any right to be retained in the employ of the Company in any capacity, or to be a director or officer of the Company, or to be retained by the Company as any type of independent contractor.

18.5 Notices. Any notice or other communication required or permitted to be given under this Agreement must be in writing and must be mailed by certified mail, return receipt requested, postage prepaid, addressed to the appropriate party or parties at the address(es) set forth in attached Exhibit A. Any notice or other communication will be deemed to be given at the expiration of the _____ day after the date of deposit in the United States Mail. The addresses to which notices or other communications are to be mailed may be changed from time to time by giving written notice to the other parties as provided in this Section.

18.6 Attorney Fees. If any suit or arbitration is filed by any party to enforce this Agreement or proceedings are commenced in bankruptcy or otherwise with respect to the subject matter of this Agreement, the prevailing party will be entitled to recover reasonable attorney fees incurred in preparation or in prosecution or defense of that suit or arbitration as fixed by the court or arbitrator, and if any appeal is taken from the decision of the court or arbitrator, reasonable attorney fees as fixed by the appellate court.

18.7 Amendments. This Agreement may be amended only by an instrument in writing executed [by all the parties] [by the Company and by Shareholders holding at least _____ (_____ %) of the Shares as of the date of the Amendment, except that, if another provision of this Agreement specifically requires the consent or vote of a lesser or greater percentage with respect to a particular action, that provision will control as to that action].

18.8 Headings. The headings used in this Agreement are solely for convenience of reference, are not part of this Agreement, and are not to be considered in construing or interpreting this Agreement.

18.9 Entire Agreement. This Agreement (including the exhibits) sets forth the entire understanding of the parties with respect to the subject matter of this Agreement and supersedes any and all prior understandings and agreements, whether written or oral, between the parties with respect to that subject matter.

18.10 Counterparts. This Agreement may be executed by the parties in separate counterparts, each of which when executed and delivered will be an original, but all of which together will constitute one and the same instrument. Signature pages may be detached from the counterparts and attached to a single copy of this Agreement to form an original document.

18.11 Severability. If any provision of this Agreement is held to be invalid or unenforceable in any respect for any reason, the validity and enforceability of that provision in any other respect and of the remaining provisions of this Agreement will not be in any way impaired.

18.12 Waiver. A provision of this Agreement may be waived only by a written instrument executed by the party waiving compliance. No waiver of any provision of this Agreement will constitute a waiver of any other provision, whether or not similar, nor will any waiver constitute a continuing waiver. Failure to enforce any provision of this Agreement will not operate as a waiver of that provision or any other provision.

18.13 Further Assurances. From time to time, each of the parties agrees to execute, acknowledge, and deliver any instruments or documents necessary to carry out the purposes of this Agreement.

18.14 Time Is of the Essence. Time is of the essence for each and every provision of this Agreement.

18.15 No Third–Party Beneficiaries. Except as may be expressly stated herein, nothing in this Agreement is intended to confer on any person, other than the parties to this Agreement, any right or remedy of any nature whatsoever.

18.16 Expenses. Each party agrees to bear its own expenses in connection with this Agreement and the transactions contemplated by this Agreement.

18.17 Exhibits. The exhibits referenced in this Agreement are a part of this Agreement as if fully set forth in this Agreement.

18.18 Governing Law. This Agreement will be governed by and construed in accordance with the laws of the state of _____.

18.19 Venue. This Agreement has been made entirely within the state of . If any suit or action is filed by any party to enforce this Agreement or otherwise with respect to the subject matter of this Agreement, venue will be in the federal or state courts in _____, _____.

18.20 Arbitration

(a) Any claim between the parties, under this Agreement or otherwise, must be determined by arbitration in _____, _____ commenced in accordance with applicable law. All statutes of limitations that would otherwise be applicable will apply to the arbitration proceeding. There will be one arbitrator agreed upon by the parties within ten (10) days before the arbitration or, if not, selected by the administrator of the American Arbitration Association ("AAA") office in _____, or failing that, the nearest AAA office. The arbitrator must be an attorney with at least fifteen (15) years' experience in commercial law and must reside in the _____ area. Whether a claim is covered by this agreement will be determined by the arbitrator. At the request of either party made not later than seventy-five (75) days after the arbitration demand, the parties agree to attempt to resolve the dispute by nonbinding mediation or evaluation or both (but without delaying the arbitration hearing date).

(b) The arbitration must be conducted in accordance with the AAA Commercial Arbitration Rules in effect on the date hereof, as modified by this Agreement. There will be no substantive motions or discovery except that the arbitrator may authorize such discovery as may be necessary to ensure a fair hearing, and discovery may not extend the time limits set forth in this Section. The arbitrator will not be bound by the rules of evidence or civil procedure.

(c) The arbitrator must hold a private hearing within one hundred twenty (120) days after the arbitration demand, conclude the hearing within three (3) days, and render a written decision within fourteen (14) calendar days after the hearing. These time limits are not jurisdictional. In making the decision and award, the arbitrator must apply applicable substantive law and must make a brief statement of the claims determined and the award made on each claim.

(d) Absent fraud, collusion, or willful misconduct by the arbitrator, the award will be final, and judgment may be entered in any court having jurisdiction thereof. The arbitrator may award injunctive relief or any other remedy available from a judge, including the joinder of parties or consolidation of this arbitration with any other involving common issues of law or fact or which may promote judicial economy, and may award attorney fees and costs to the prevailing party but will not have the power to award punitive or exemplary damages.

18.21 Legal Representation. Each of the undersigned recognizes and acknowledges that the law firm of _____("Counsel") has represented _____ with respect to this Agreement and no other party and that Counsel has advised each of the undersigned to obtain independent legal counsel.

DATED this ___ day of _____, _____.

COMPANY: _____

By: _____

Its: _____

SHAREHOLDERS:

_____

_____

SPOUSES:

1. I acknowledge that I have read the foregoing Agreement and that I know its contents.

2. I am aware that by its provisions my spouse agrees to sell all of my spouse's Shares of the Company (including, if applicable, my community interest in them) on the occurrence of certain events.

3. I hereby consent to the sale, approve the provisions of the Agreement, and agree that those Shares and my interest in them are subject to the provisions of the Agreement and that I will take no action at any time to hinder operation of the Agreement on those Shares or any interest in them.

4. In the event of a dissolution, divorce, annulment, or other termination of marriage of my spouse's and my marriage other than by reason of death, I hereby agree to release or transfer (or both) whatever interest I may have in the Company (including, but not limited to, any interest as a Shareholder or creditor, or interest in the Stock or debt of Company) to my spouse on the termination of our marriage.

5. As part of any property settlement of our marital assets, my spouse must compensate me for my interest. In the event the parties cannot agree as to the value of my interest or upon terms of payment, the value of any Shares in which I have an interest will be determined and will be paid to me in accordance with the terms and conditions of the Agreement.

6. If my interest in Company is in the nature of debt, the value of that debt will be deemed to be its outstanding principal balance plus any accrued and unpaid interest thereon and compensation therefore will be provided as agreed by the parties.

7. I acknowledge that I have been advised to consult with independent legal counsel regarding this Agreement and this provision and, further, expressly acknowledge the provisions of Section [18.21] regarding legal counsel and conflicts of interest.

_____

_____

_____

_____

EXHIBIT A

LIST OF SHAREHOLDERS SUBJECT TO SHAREHOLDERS AGREEMENT

Dated _____

[Company name and address]

Shareholder Name	Address	Number of Shares Held

EXHIBIT B

LIFE INSURANCE SCHEDULE

Name of Insured	Insurance Company	Policy Number	Type pf Policy	Initial Cash Benefit	Death Benefit

EXHIBIT C

PROMISSORY NOTE

$_____

1. For good and valuable consideration, the undersigned promises to pay to the order of _____ ("Holder") the sum of _____ ($ _____), together with interest thereon, in monthly installments of not less than $ _____. The first installment is due on _____, _____, and a like installment is due on the same date of each successive month thereafter until _____, at which time the entire unpaid balance of this Note, any accrued but unpaid interest, and any other amounts payable under this Note, must be paid in full. The unpaid balance of this Note will bear interest at the rate of _____ percent (_____ %) per annum.

2. The undersigned may prepay a portion or all of the balance at any time without penalty.

3. With respect to any payment not made within ten (10) days after it is due

and without waiving any other remedy the Holder may have under this Note or otherwise, the Holder may charge the undersigned a late payment charge of five percent (5%) of the unpaid amount.

4. If any payment required by this Note is not paid within fifteen (15) days after receipt by the undersigned of notice of nonpayment from the Holder ("Event of Default"), at Holder's option, the unpaid balance will bear interest at a default rate of fifteen percent (15%) per annum from the date the payment was due until paid in full.

5. As security for the obligations of the undersigned evidenced by this Note, the undersigned hereby grants to Holder a security interest in _____ shares of the common stock of _____, (the "Shares") issued under certificate number _____ (the "Certificate"). The undersigned has delivered to the Holder the Certificate, together with a stock power endorsed in blank, to hold subject to the terms of this Agreement. Holder agrees to take reasonable care in the custody and the preservation of the Certificate. On payment in full of the principal and interest on the Note, Holder must deliver the Certificate to the undersigned, together with the stock power endorsed by the undersigned in blank.

6. The undersigned irrevocably appoints Holder as attorney-in-fact and grants Holder a proxy to do (but Holder shall not be obligated and shall incur no liability to the undersigned or any third party for failure to do so), after and during the continuance of an Event of Default, any act that the undersigned is obligated by this Note to do and to exercise such rights and powers as undersigned might exercise with respect to the Shares. With respect to voting the Shares, this Section 6 constitutes an irrevocable appointment of a proxy, coupled with an interest, which shall continue until the Note is paid in full.

7. Upon the occurrence of an Event of Default under this Note, the Holder may, in the Holder's sole discretion and with or without further notice to the undersigned and in addition to all rights and remedies at law or in equity or otherwise (a) declare the entire balance of the Note immediately due and payable, (b) register in Holder's name any or all of the Shares, (c) sell or otherwise dispose of the Shares, or (d) exercise Holder's proxy rights with respect to all or a portion of the Shares. In such event, the undersigned agrees to deliver promptly to Holder further evidence of the grant of such proxy in any form requested by Holder.

8. The undersigned hereby waives demand, notice of default, and notice of sale, and consents to public or private sale of the Shares upon the occurrence of an Event of Default, and the Holder will have the right to purchase at the sale.

9. If any action, suit, or other proceeding is instituted concerning or arising out of this Note, the prevailing party will be entitled to recover all costs and attorney fees reasonably incurred by such party in such action, suit, or other proceeding (including all bankruptcy courts), including any and all appeals or petitions therefrom.

_____

Signature

G. FORM: ASSET PURCHASE AGREEMENT

ASSET PURCHASE AGREEMENT

The parties to this Agreement are:

(i)_____, a_____("Seller");

(ii)_____,and_____(collectively Shareholders"); and

(iii)_____, a_____("Purchaser").

RECITALS

A. Seller desires to sell to Purchaser and Purchaser desires to acquire upon the terms and conditions set forth in this Agreement substantially all of the property, assets and business of Seller.

B. Shareholders own all the issued and outstanding shares of stock of Seller.

In consideration of the mutual agreements set forth below, the parties agree:

1. SALE AND PURCHASE OF ASSETS. On the terms and subject to the conditions of this Agreement, at Closing Seller will sell, assign and convey to Purchaser and Purchaser will purchase from Seller, all of Seller's right, title and interest in and to the "Assets," as defined below, free and clear of all liens, claims and encumbrances except as otherwise provided in this Agreement.

1.1 Description of Assets. The "Assets" are all of the assets and properties of Seller, except as specifically excluded below, existing as of Closing.

(a) Assets Included. The Assets include, without limitation, all of the following:

(i) Operating assets, furniture, fixtures, machinery, equipment, vehicles, computers (and related peripherals and software), including but not limited to the specific items listed in Exhibit 1.1.1(a) attached to this Agreement;

(ii) Inventories of raw materials, work in process, finished goods and supplies, all subject to the Closing audit described below;

(iii) Leasehold improvements at all leased premises occupied by Seller;

(iv) Accounts receivable;

(v) Trademarks, trade names (including the name _____ and any variation thereof), trade secrets, proprietary information, copyrights, patents, and other intellectual property rights of any and every nature, including but not limited to the specific items listed in Exhibit 1.1.1(e) attached to this Agreement;

(vi) Goodwill;

(vii) Business and accounting records, including product formulae, customer lists and supplier lists (including all such records and lists stored on computer disks and other similar media);

(viii) Telephone and fax numbers and post office boxes (effective as of Closing, Seller grants Purchaser the right to open all mail delivered to such post office boxes);

(ix) Credits and deposits with suppliers, utilities, taxing authorities and all other persons and entities including but not limited to the specific items listed in Exhibit 1.1.1(i) attached to this Agreement;

(x) Product warranties from Seller's suppliers;

(xi) The contracts and leases to which Seller is a party and which are listed in Exhibit 1.1.1(k) to this Agreement

(xii) Assignable permits, licenses and governmental approvals including but not limited to the specific items listed in Exhibit 1.1.1(*l*) attached to this Agreement; and

(xiii) Stationery, forms, publications, office supplies, reference materials and other miscellaneous assets.

(b) Assets Excluded. Except as provided elsewhere herein, the Assets do not include the following:

(i) Corporate minute books, stock books and corporate seal;

(ii) Cash, bonds, savings certificates and other cash equivalents not included in the Assets;

(iii) Those specific items described in Exhibit 1.1.2 attached to this Agreement;

(iv) All Seller's rights under this Agreement and related documents; and

(v) All Seller's rights under any insurance policies in effect at or prior to Closing.

1.2 Liabilities and Obligations. Except for those liabilities, debts or obligations listed on Exhibit 1.2 to this Agreement, which Purchaser shall assume at Closing, Purchaser assumes no liabilities, debts or obligations of Seller of any nature whatsoever, whether absolute, accrued, contingent or otherwise, or whether due or to become due, including without limitation any liability for taxes or any liability under any lease, purchase agreement or other contract of Seller.

2. PURCHASE PRICE.

2.1 Amount and Payment. Subject to adjustment as provided below, the purchase price ("Purchase Price") for the Assets and for the covenant not to compete contained in section _____ of this Agreement (the "Covenant Not to Compete") is _____ _____ Dollars ($_____) payable as follows:

$_____ by cashier's check or wire transfer at Closing;

$_____ by assumption of those liabilities and in those amounts described in paragraph 1.2 above; and

The balance payable in accordance with the terms of a promissory note (the "Note") in the form of Exhibit 2.1 attached to this Agreement.

2.2 Security. As security for the Note, Purchaser will deliver to Seller at Closing a security agreement in the form of Exhibit 2.2 attached to this Agreement (the "Security Agreement"), granting to Seller a first-lien security interest in the Assets, together with appropriate financing statements and other documents necessary or appropriate to perfect the security interests granted in the Security Agreement.

2.3 Adjustment to Purchase Price. Immediately [prior to/following] Closing, an audit of the inventory and accounts receivable included in the Assets ("Closing Audit") shall be performed by _____, an independent certified public accountant ("Auditor"). The Closing Audit shall include a review of the relevant books and records and a physical inventory, using such procedures and to such extent as deemed necessary or appropriate by the Auditor to enable the Auditor to give an unqualified opinion to Purchaser. Inventory will be valued at the lower of actual cost or market value, reduced by a reasonable reserve for returned merchandise. Accounts receivable shall be valued by excluding those more than ____ days past due and shall be adjusted by a reasonable allowance for uncollectible accounts. The results of the Closing Audit shall be conclusive. Representatives of Purchaser and Seller may participate in the physical inventory. The cost of the Closing Audit shall be paid by _____, _____. In the event the Closing Audit indicates an adjusted book value for Seller's inventory and/or accounts receivable which is greater than or less than the amount of the Purchase Price allocated to inventory and/or accounts receivable below, then the Purchase Price shall be adjusted dollar-for-dollar for any such variance ("Purchase Price Adjustment"). The amount of the Purchase Price Adjustment shall be paid by, or credited to, Purchaser as follows: _____.

2.4 Allocation of Purchase Price. The Purchase Price, as adjusted, shall be allocated to the Assets as follows:

(a) Inventory (subject to the Price Adjustment) $_____

(b) Accounts receivable(subject to the Price Adjustment) $_____

(c) Fixed Assets $_____

(d) Intangible Assets and Goodwill $_____

(e) Covenant Not to Compete $_____

The parties shall report consistently with the above schedule for all tax purposes.

2.5 Escrow. At Closing, Purchaser shall pay $_____ of the Purchase Price into escrow pursuant to the terms of the escrow agreement attached as Exhibit 2.5 to this Agreement (the "Escrow Agreement"). Purchaser and Seller shall sign and deliver the Escrow Agreement at Closing.

3. CLOSING. The Closing of the transactions contemplated by this

Agreement (the "Closing") shall take place at the offices of _____ in Seattle, Washington, at __:_____ a.m., local time, on _____, 199__, or at such other date, time and place as Purchaser and Seller shall mutually agree in writing ("Closing Date"). Conveyance, transfer, assignment and delivery of the Assets shall be by bills of sale, certificates of transfer, endorsements, assignments and other instruments of transfer and conveyance in such form as Purchaser may request. Seller and Shareholders will from time to time after the Closing make such further conveyances, transfers, assignments and deliveries, and execute such further instruments and documents, as Purchaser deems reasonably necessary in order to effectuate and confirm the sale of Assets and other transactions contemplated by this Agreement.

3.1 Possession. Purchaser shall take possession of the Assets immediately following Closing.

3.2 Taxes and Fees.

(a) Any transfer, sales, use or other tax payable as a result of the sale of the Assets pursuant to this Agreement shall be paid by Purchaser and Purchaser shall timely remit such taxes to the applicable taxing authorities; provided, however, that Purchaser may withhold the amount of any such taxes from the Purchase Price and pay them itself.

(b) All real and personal property taxes attributable to any of the Assets and payable in the year in which Closing occurs shall be apportioned and prorated as of Closing. The proration of such taxes shall be made on the basis of the tax rate for the most recent tax year available applied to the latest assessed valuation of the Assets, and when the tax rate and assessed valuation are fixed for the tax year in which Closing occurs, Seller and Purchaser shall adjust such proration and, if necessary, to refund or pay such sums to the other party as necessary to effect such readjustment.

(c) Except as provided above, all Seller's taxes which are not yet due and payable and which relate to periods prior to Closing shall be paid by Seller no later than the date such payments are due.

3.3 Deliveries by Seller and Shareholders at Closing. At or before Closing, Seller and Shareholders shall deliver to Purchaser the following instruments, documents and agreements duly executed by the appropriate persons and entities:

(a) Warranty bills of sale, certificates of transfer, certificates of title, endorsements, assignments and other instruments of transfer and conveyance in such form as Purchaser may request;

(b) A certificate of Seller's president and each Shareholder certifying that all representations and warranties made by Seller and Shareholders in this Agreement are true and correct as of the Closing Date;

(c) An opinion of Seller's counsel in the form attached as Exhibit 3.3(d) to this Agreement;

(d) The Escrow Agreement;

(e) _____; and

(f) Such other documents, instruments and agreements as are necessary or appropriate to carry out the provisions of this Agreement.

3.4 Deliveries by Purchaser at Closing. At or before Closing, Purchaser shall deliver to Seller the following instruments, documents and agreements duly executed by the appropriate persons and entities:

(a) A cashier's check, wire transfer or other immediately available funds in the amount of $_____;

(b) An assumption of the liabilities and obligations that Purchaser is to assume pursuant to section 1.2 of this Agreement;

(c) The Note;

(d) The Security Agreement and associated financing statements and other documents of perfection described in section 2.2 of this Agreement;

(e) The Escrow Agreement;

(f) A certificate of Purchaser's president certifying that all representations and warranties made by Purchaser in this Agreement are true and correct as of the Closing Date;

(g) An opinion of Purchaser's counsel in the form attached as Exhibit 3.4(g) to this Agreement;

(h) _____; and

(i) Such other documents, instruments and agreements as are necessary or appropriate to carry out the provisions of this Agreement.

3.5 Covenant to Change Name. On or before the Closing Date, Seller shall change its name to a name wholly dissimilar to _____ and shall take such other and further actions as are necessary or appropriate to transfer that name to Purchaser.

3.6 Covenant Not to Compete.

(a) Seller and Shareholders agree that for the period of five (5) years following Closing, they will not, without the prior written consent of the Purchaser, directly or indirectly, whether as principal or as agent, officer, director, employee, salesman, consultant, independent contractor or otherwise, alone or in association with one another or with any other person, firm, corporation or other business organization:

(i) Enter into, participate in, engage in or own any interest in the business of any person, firm, corporation or other business organization which is engaged in or proposes to become engaged in any business which is in substantial competition with any part of the business now or hereafter engaged in by Purchaser in the state of Washington; or

(ii) Solicit any business of any type now or hereafter engaged in by Purchaser from any clients, customers, former customers or clients, or prospects of Purchaser; or

(iii) Solicit any employee, consultant or independent contractor of Purchaser to terminate his or her relationship with Purchaser.

(b) The period of time during which Seller and Shareholders are prohibited from engaging in certain activities pursuant to the terms of this section shall be extended by the length of time during which Seller or any Shareholder is in breach of the terms of this section.

(c) Seller and Shareholders acknowledge and agree that, in the event of any violation of this section 3.6, money damages will not provide Purchaser with a fully adequate remedy for such violation and Purchaser shall, therefore, be entitled to an injunction prohibiting any further violation. Seller, Shareholders and Purchaser agree that, any bond posted in connection with obtaining such an injunction shall not exceed ten thousand dollars ($10,000) in amount.

3.7 [If Accounts Receivable Not Purchased]. Accounts Receivable. After the Closing Date, Purchaser promptly will pay to Seller any amounts received by Purchaser on account of Seller's accounts receivable which Purchaser is not purchasing under this Agreement ("Accounts"). Seller and Shareholders agree to: (a) act in a business-like manner in the collection of Accounts; (b) consult with Purchaser regarding any collection problems; and (c) use reasonable efforts to retain for Purchaser the good will of all customers. In the absence of a designation by the customer of the invoices to which a payment is to be applied, payments shall be applied to the oldest invoices first.

4. REPRESENTATIONS AND WARRANTIES OF SELLER AND SHAREHOLDERS. The "Disclosure Schedules" shall mean all of the disclosure schedules required by this Agreement, which are simultaneously delivered to Purchaser and initialed by all of the parties to this Agreement for identification. As of the date of this Agreement and as of Closing, Seller and Shareholders, jointly and severally, represent and warrant to the Purchaser:

4.1 Organization, Good Standing, Power. Seller (a) is a corporation duly organized, validly existing and in good standing under the laws of the state of _____; and (b) has the requisite power and authority to own, lease and operate its properties and to carry on its business as currently conducted.

4.2 Authorization. Shareholders and Seller have taken all necessary and proper corporate action, including approval by Shareholders' and Seller's boards of directors, to authorize and approve this Agreement, its consummation and the performance by Seller and Shareholders of all terms and conditions of this Agreement.

4.3 Property. Seller has good and marketable title to all of the Assets, free and clear of all liens, security interests, mortgages, conditional sale agreements, encumbrances or other charges whatsoever, except as set forth on the schedule of liabilities attached to this Agreement as Disclosure Schedule 4.3 and at Closing Purchaser will obtain good and marketable title to the Assets, free and clear of all liens, security interests, mortgages, conditional sale agreements, encumbrances or other charges whatsoever, except as set forth on Disclosure Schedule 4.3.

4.4 Leases. All leases under which Seller leases real or personal property are described in the schedule of leases attached to this Agreement as Disclosure Schedule 4.4. All such leases are valid and subsisting and no default exists under any of them and no event exists which, with the giving of notice or the passage of time, or both, will be a default. Except as otherwise noted on such schedule of leases, Seller does not occupy and is not dependent on the right to use any property of others.

4.5 Contracts. Except for this Agreement and the contracts and agreements set forth in the Schedule of Contracts attached to this Agreement as Disclosure Schedule 4.5, Seller is not a party to or subject to any agreements, contracts or other commitments (written or oral).

4.6 Taxes, Etc. Seller has filed all tax returns and paid all taxes or installments thereof, and all employment security premiums, workers compensation premiums and other governmental charges, required under applicable federal, state and other laws and regulations and will timely pay all such taxes and other items not yet due and payable which are owing with respect to any period before Closing.

4.7 Effect of Agreement. The execution, delivery and performance of this Agreement by Seller and Shareholders and the consummation of the transactions contemplated by it will not: (a) violate any provision of law, statute, rule or regulation to which Seller or Shareholders are subject; (b) violate any judgment, order, writ or decree of any court, arbitrator or governmental agency applicable to Seller or Shareholders; (c) have any effect on any of the permits, licenses, orders or approvals of Seller or Shareholders or the ability of Seller or Shareholders to make use of such permits, licenses, orders or approvals; or (d) result in the breach of or conflict with any term, covenant, condition or provision of, or result in the modification or termination of, any charter, bylaw, commitment, contract or other agreement or instrument, to which Seller or any Shareholder is a party.

4.8 Financial Statements; Absence of Undisclosed Liabilities.

(a) The financial statements of Seller (the "Financial Statements") including but not limited to the unaudited balance sheet dated as of _____, ____ (the "Balance Sheet") as set forth on Disclosure Schedule 4.8 are correct and complete and fairly present the financial position of Seller as of the date thereof in accordance with generally accepted accounting principles consistently applied, and no event has occurred since the date of the Financial Statements which would render them misleading or inaccurate or incomplete in any material respect.

(b) Except to the extent reflected or reserved against or otherwise disclosed on the Financial Statements, as of the date of the Financial Statements, Seller had no liabilities, debts or obligations of any nature, whether absolute, accrued, contingent or otherwise, or whether due or to become due including, without limitation, liabilities for taxes. Subsequent to the date of the Financial Statements Seller has not incurred or become subject to any liabilities, debts or obligations other than in the ordinary course of business or otherwise disclosed in the Disclosure Schedules, and Seller has properly recorded in its books of account all items of income and expense and all other proper charges and accruals required to be made in accordance with generally accepted accounting principles and practice consistently applied. Since the date of the Financial Statements, no debts or liabilities of or to Seller have been forgiven, settled or compromised except for full consideration or except in the ordinary course of business, the aggregate amount of which has not had a material adverse effect of Seller's financial condition.

4.9 Litigation. Except as set forth on Disclosure Schedule 4.9, there is no claim, action, suit, proceeding, arbitration, investigation or inquiry pending before any federal, state, municipal, foreign or other court or any governmental, administrative or self-regulatory body or agency, or any private arbitration tribunal, or threatened against, relating to or affecting Seller or any of the assets, properties, employees or businesses of Seller, nor is there any basis for any such claim, action, suit, proceeding, arbitration, investigation or inquiry which may have a material adverse effect upon the assets, properties or business of Seller or the transactions contemplated by this Agreement.

4.10 Inventories. The inventories reflected on the Balance Sheet or thereafter acquired consist of items of a quality and quantity which are usable and salable at regular prices in the normal and ordinary course of business of Seller and the values at which such inventories are carried on the Balance Sheet are stated at the lesser of cost or market value. None of the Assets are held on consignment.

4.11 Purchase and Sale Obligations. All unfilled purchase and sales orders and all other commitments for purchases and sales made by Seller were made in the usual and ordinary course of its business in accordance with normal industry practice and Seller's normal practice.

4.12 Powers of Attorney. No person has any power of attorney to act on behalf of Seller in connection with any of Seller's properties or business affairs.

4.13 No Broker. Neither Seller nor Shareholders have taken any action which would give to any firm, corporation, agency or other person a right to a consultant's or finder's fee or any type of brokerage commission in connection with the transactions contemplated by this Agreement as a result of any agreement with, or action by, Seller or Shareholders.

4.14 Absence of Certain Changes or Events. Except as set forth in Disclosure Schedule 4.14, since the date of the Balance Sheet, Seller has not:

(a) Incurred any obligation or liability (of fixed or variable amount, absolute or contingent) except trade or business obligations incurred in the ordinary course of business;

(b) Suffered the occurrence of any events or gained the knowledge of the possibility of any events occurring (including, without limitation, events concerning customers, suppliers, equipment, employees, facilities, environmental issues or any other matter that is material to Seller's business) which, individually or in the aggregate, have had, or might reasonably be expected to have, an adverse effect on Seller's financial condition, results of operations, properties, business or prospects;

(c) Incurred damage to or destruction or other loss of any of its assets, in any material amount;

(d) Discharged or satisfied any lien or encumbrance or incurred or paid any obligation or liability (fixed or variable in amount, absolute or contingent), except (i) current obligations and liabilities included in the Balance Sheet and (ii) current obligations and liabilities incurred since the date of the Balance Sheet, in the ordinary course of business;

(e) Mortgaged, pledged or subjected to lien or any other encumbrance any of its assets or properties;

(f) Sold, transferred or leased any of its assets or properties, except for the sale of inventory in the ordinary course of business;

(g) Cancelled or compromised any debt or claim, except for adjustments made with respect to contracts for the sale of products or services in the ordinary course of business which in the aggregate are not material;

(h) Waived or released any rights of any material value;

(i) Transferred or granted any rights under any licenses, agreements, patents, inventions, trademarks, trade names, service marks, copyrights or other intellectual property rights;

(j) Made or entered into any contract or commitment to make any material expenditures;

(k) Declared or paid any distribution, whether in the nature of dividends or otherwise or purchased or redeemed any of its outstanding shares of capital stock; or

(*l*) Made any commitments to any employees, sales representatives, dealers, sales agents, suppliers or customers, except in the ordinary course of business, consistent with part practices of Seller.

4.15 Trade Names and Trademarks. Seller has the right to use the following trade names and trademarks in its business: _____.

4.16 Environmental Matters.

(a) Except as set forth in Disclosure Schedule 4.16, Seller has obtained all permits, licenses and other authorizations which are required in connection with the conduct of its business under any and all laws, statutes, regulations, ordinances, zoning and land use requirements, directives, rules, and other governmental requirements, orders, decrees, judgments, injunctions, notices and demands relating to pollution or protection of the environment (collectively "Regulations"), including Regulations relating to emissions, discharges, releases or threatened releases of pollutants, contaminants, chemicals, or industrial, toxic or hazardous substances or wastes into the environment (including without limitation ambient air, surface water, groundwater, or land), or otherwise relating to the manufacture, processing, distribution, use, treatment, storage, disposal, transport, or handling of pollutants, contaminants, chemicals, or industrial, toxic or hazardous substances or wastes.

(b) Except as set forth in Disclosure Schedule 4.16, Seller is in full compliance in the conduct of its business with all terms and conditions of all required permits, licenses and authorizations, and is also in full compliance with all other limitations, restrictions, conditions, standards, prohibitions, requirements, obligations, schedules and timetables contained in any Regulations.

(c) Except as set forth in Disclosure Schedule 4.16, there are no (nor has Seller received any notice or claim of any) events, conditions, circumstances, activities, practices, incidents, actions or plans which may interfere with or prevent compliance or continued compliance with any Regulations, or which may give rise to any liability, or otherwise form the basis of any claim, action, demand, suit, proceeding, hearing, study or investigation, based on or related to the manufacture, processing, distribution, use, treatment, storage, disposal, transport, or handling, or the emission, discharge, release or threatened release into the environment, of any pollutant, contaminant, chemical, or industrial, toxic or hazardous substance or waste.

(d) Except as set forth in Disclosure Schedule 4.16, there is no civil, criminal or administrative action, suit, demand, claim, hearing, notice or demand letter, notice of violation, investigation, or proceeding pending or threatened against Seller in connection with the conduct of its business or any real property occupied by Seller relating in any way to any Regulation.

(e) Seller and Shareholders agree to cooperate with Purchaser in connection with Purchaser's application for the transfer, renewal or issuance of any permits, license, approvals or other authorizations or to satisfy any regulatory requirements involving Seller's business.

4.17 Insurance. Disclosure Schedule 4.17 contains a complete list of all insurance policies maintained by Seller. Seller shall keep all such insurance policies in full force and effect through the Closing Date.

4.18 Employment Agreements and Benefits. Disclosure Schedule 4.18 is a correct and complete list of every employment agreement, collective bargaining agreement, stock option, stock purchase, stock appreciation right, bonus, deferred compensation, excess benefits, profit sharing, thrift, savings, retirement, major medical, long-term disability, hospitalization, insurance or other plan, arrangement, commitment or practice of Seller providing employee or executive benefits or benefits to any person, including, but not limited to, plans administered by trade associations, area wide plans, plans resulting from collective bargaining and plans covering foreign employees. All reasonably anticipated obligations of Seller, whether arising by operation of law, by contract, by past custom or practice or otherwise, for salaries, vacation and holiday pay, bonuses and other forms of compensation which were payable to its officers, directors or other employees have been paid or adequate accruals therefor have been made in the Financial Statements.

4.19 Assets. Seller owns all the tangible assets used in the operation of its business or located on its premises except those listed in Disclosure Schedule

4.19 to this Agreement.

4.20 Compliance with Laws. Seller is not in violation of any law, ordinance or governmental or regulatory rule or regulation of any federal, state, local or foreign government to which Seller or its assets are subject. Seller has all governmental permits, licenses and authorizations necessary or appropriate for it to carry on its business as presently conducted.

4.21 Interests in Other Entities. Seller holds no shares, partnership interests or other investments or ownership interests in any other corporation, partnership, joint venture or other entity.

4.22 Corporate Matters.

(a) Shareholders own all the issued and outstanding capital stock of all classes in Seller and there are no other holders of shares in Seller.

(b) The following are all the directors of Seller: _____ .

(c) The following are all the officers of Seller:

_____President

_____   _____

_____   _____

_____   _____

5. REPRESENTATIONS AND WARRANTIES OF PURCHASER. Purchaser represents and warrants to Seller and Shareholders:

5.1 Organization, Good Standing, Power. Purchaser (a) is a corporation duly organized, validly existing and in good standing under the laws of the state of _____; and (b) has all requisite corporate power and authority to execute, deliver and perform this Agreement and consummate the transactions contemplated by this Agreement.

5.2 Authorization. Purchaser has taken all necessary and proper corporate action, including approval by its board of directors to authorize and approve this Agreement, its consummation and the performance by Purchaser of all terms and conditions hereof and this Agreement constitutes the valid and binding obligation of the Purchaser fully enforceable in accordance with its terms.

5.3 Effect of Agreement, Consents, Etc. No consent, authorization or approval or exemption by, or filing with, any governmental or public body or authority is required in connection with the execution, delivery and performance by the Purchaser of this Agreement or the taking of any action hereby contemplated by this Agreement.

5.4 No Broker. There is no firm, corporation, agency or other person that is entitled to a consultant's or finder's fee or any type of brokerage commission in connection with the transactions contemplated by this Agreement as a result of any agreement with, or action by, Purchaser.

5.5 Effect of Agreement. The execution, delivery and performance of this

Agreement by Purchaser and the consummation of the transactions contemplated by this Agreement will not: (a) violate any provision of law, statute, rule or regulation to which Purchaser is subject; (b) violate any judgment, order, writ or decree of any court, arbitrator or governmental agency applicable to Purchaser; (c) have any effect on any of the permits, licenses, orders or approvals of Purchaser or the ability of Purchaser to make use of such permits, licenses, orders or approvals; or (d) result in the breach of or conflict with any term, covenant, condition or provision of, or result in the modification or termination of, any charter, bylaw, commitment, contract or other agreement or instrument, to which Purchaser is a party.

6. INDEMNIFICATION.

6.1 Seller and Shareholders Indemnification. Shareholders and Seller will, jointly and severally, defend, indemnify and hold harmless Purchaser and any person claiming by or through either Purchaser or its respective successors and assigns (individually, an "Indemnified Party") from and against any and all costs, losses, claims, liabilities, fines, penalties, damages and expenses (including, without limitation, all legal expenses and reasonable fees and disbursements of attorneys and expert witnesses, with or without suit, on appeal and in bankruptcy or other insolvency proceedings) arising in connection with:

(a) Any breach of (i) any of the representations and warranties of Shareholders or Seller or (ii) any covenant or agreement made by Shareholders or Seller in this Agreement; and/or

(b) Any liability or obligation of Seller or Shareholders, whether known or unknown, absolute or contingent, except as specifically assumed by Purchaser under this Agreement.

6.2 Purchaser Indemnification. Purchaser will defend, indemnify and hold harmless Seller and Shareholders and any person or entity claiming by or through either Seller, Shareholders or their respective successors and assigns from and against any and all costs, losses, claims, liabilities, fines, penalties, damages and expenses (including without limitation, all legal expenses and fees and disbursements of attorneys and expert witnesses, with or without suit, on appeal and in bankruptcy or other insolvency proceedings) which arise in connection with:

(a) Any breach of (i) any of the representations and warranties of Purchaser or (ii) any covenant or agreement made by Purchaser in this Agreement; and/or

(b) Any liability or obligation relating to Purchaser's ownership or use of the Assets after Closing.

7. EMPLOYEES.

7.1 Immediately prior to Closing and effective no later than Closing, Seller will discharge and terminate the employment of each of its employees, contractors and others working in its business in compliance with any employment agreements or collective bargaining agreements then in effect and with applicable laws and regulations in a manner such as to ensure that those persons cannot and will not make any claim against Purchaser for reemployment, back pay, vacation or sick leave, vacation pay, expense reimbursements, benefits or any other obligations of Seller, whether arising under any such employment agreement, collective bargaining agreement or otherwise imposed by statute or common law, or otherwise. Upon such termination, Purchaser will have no obligation to any such persons (except as created by or at the direction of Purchaser) under any pension, profit-sharing, other benefit plans for Seller's employees or otherwise.

7.2 At its discretion, Purchaser may offer employment to any former employee of Seller on such terms and conditions as Purchaser shall determine.

7.3 The parties understand that Purchaser's ability to retain the good will of its employees through the transition from Seller to Purchaser is critical to Purchaser's future success. Seller agrees to coordinate its termination actions with the reasonable requirements of Purchaser and to consult with Purchaser on all matters affecting that process. Purchaser has the right to be present at, and to participate in, both the notification to Seller's employees that they are being terminated and the announcement of the sale to Purchaser.

7.4 Seller shall give all notices of the sale of the Assets required by any statute, regulation or contract, including but not limited to any notices required under the Worker Adjustment and Retraining Notification Act and any collective bargaining agreements.

8. CONDITIONS TO SELLER'S OBLIGATIONS. The obligations of Seller under this Agreement are subject to the fulfillment, at or prior to the Closing, of each of the following conditions, any or all of which may be waived in writing by Seller, in its sole discretion.

8.1 Accuracy of Representations and Warranties. Each of the representations and warranties of the Purchaser contained in this Agreement shall be true in all material respects on and as of Closing with the same force and effect as though made on and as of Closing, except as affected by transactions contemplated by this Agreement.

8.2 Performance of Covenants. Purchaser shall have performed and complied in all material respects with all covenants, obligations and agreements to be performed or complied with by it on or before Closing pursuant to this Agreement.

8.3 Litigation. No claim, action, suit, proceeding, arbitration, investigation or hearing or notice of hearing shall be pending or threatened against or affecting Purchaser which might result, or has resulted, either in an action to enjoin or prevent or delay the consummation of the transactions contemplated by this Agreement or in such an injunction.

9. CONDITIONS TO PURCHASER'S OBLIGATIONS. The obligations of Purchaser under this Agreement are subject to the fulfillment, at or prior to Closing, of each of the following conditions, any or all of which may be waived in writing by Purchaser, in its sole discretion:

9.1 Accuracy of Representations and Warranties. Each of the representations and warranties of Seller and/or Shareholders contained in this Agreement shall be true in all material respects on and as of Closing with the same force and effect as though made on and as of Closing, except as affected by transactions contemplated by this Agreement.

9.2 Performance of Covenants. Seller and Shareholders shall have performed and complied in all material respects with all covenants, obligations and agreements to be performed or complied with by them on or before Closing pursuant to this Agreement.

9.3 Litigation. No claim, action, suit, proceeding, arbitration, investigation or hearing or notice of hearing shall be pending or threatened against or affecting Seller or Shareholders which: (a) might result, or has resulted, either in an action to enjoin or prevent or delay the consummation of the transactions contemplated by this Agreement or in an injunction; and (b) could have a material adverse effect on the Assets or the business of the Purchaser to be carried on following Closing and has not been disclosed in this Agreement.

9.4 Lease Negotiation. Purchaser shall have entered into an agreement, satisfactory to Purchaser in its sole discretion, regarding Purchaser's right to lease the premises at _____ currently occupied by Seller. If Purchaser has not entered into such an agreement by the date three (3) days prior to the Closing Date, Purchaser may terminate this Agreement by written notice to Seller, which notice shall be delivered by the date three (3) days prior to the Closing Date. If Purchaser has not terminated this Agreement pursuant to this Section, Purchaser shall be deemed to have waived this condition to Closing.

9.5 Due Diligence Investigation. Purchaser shall have completed, to its sole satisfaction, a due diligence investigation of Seller, the Assets and Seller's operations. If Purchaser is not satisfied with such investigation, Purchaser may terminate this Agreement by notice to Seller. If Purchaser has not terminated this Agreement pursuant to this Section by the date three (3) days prior to the Closing Date, Purchaser shall be deemed to have waived this condition to Closing.

9.6 Documents. Prior to Closing, Seller shall have delivered to Purchaser the following documents:

(a) Certified copies of Seller's articles of incorporation and bylaws;

(b) Certified copies of resolutions of Seller's board of directors and shareholders authorizing the execution, delivery and performance of this Agreement and the consummation of the transactions provided for in this Agreement;

(c) Certified copies of all documents evidencing any consents, permits or governmental approvals necessary or appropriate to the consummation of the transactions provided for in this Agreement; and

(d) An incumbency certificate of Seller's secretary certifying the names of the officer or officers of Seller authorized to sign this Agreement and the documents, instruments and agreements to be executed by Seller pursuant to this Agreement, together with a sample of the signature of each such officer.

10. TERMINATION. This Agreement may be terminated prior to Closing

by either party:

10.1 No Closing. If the Closing has not taken place on or before _____ _____, _____; provided, however, that such termination shall not relieve any party from liability if such party, as of the termination date, is in breach of any of the provisions of this Agreement; and provided, further, that if the delay is caused by the act or omission of a particular party, such party shall not have the right to terminate this Agreement; or

10.2 Failure of Conditions. If on the Closing Date, any of the conditions set forth in Sections 8 or 9 have not been satisfied, or waived by the Purchaser or Seller, as applicable.

11. GENERAL.

11.1 Survival. The representations, warranties, covenants and agreements set forth in this Agreement shall survive Closing.

11.2 Expenses. Except as otherwise provided herein, whether or not the transactions contemplated by this Agreement are consummated, each party shall pay its own expenses and the fees and expenses of its counsel and accountants and other experts.

11.3 Assignment. Purchaser may assign its rights under this Agreement to a wholly-owned subsidiary, provided that such assignment shall not relieve Purchaser of its obligations under this Agreement.

11.4 Announcements. At Closing the parties will make a mutually agreeable joint press release announcing the consummation of the transactions contemplated in this Agreement. Other than the above press release, each party agrees that for the period commencing on the date of this Agreement and concluding forty-five (45) days after Closing, it shall not, except as otherwise required by applicable law or regulations, make or release any statement, announcement or publicity with respect to this Agreement or the transactions contemplated in this Agreement or permit any of its officers, directors or employees to do so unless the form and content of any such statement, announcement or publicity and the time of its release shall have been approved by the other party.

11.5 Waivers. No action taken pursuant to this Agreement, nor any investigation by or on behalf of any party, shall be deemed to constitute a waiver by the party taking such action of compliance with any representation, warranty, covenant or agreement contained in this Agreement. The waiver by any party of a breach of any provision of this Agreement shall not operate or be construed as a waiver of any subsequent breach.

11.6 Binding Effect; Benefits. This Agreement shall inure to the benefit of the parties and shall be binding upon the parties and their respective heirs, personal representatives, successors and permitted assigns.

11.7 Notices. All notices, requests, demands and other communications which are required or permitted under this Agreement shall be in writing and shall be deemed to have been given when delivered in person or three (3) days after deposit in the United States mail, certified postage prepaid, return receipt requested, addressed as follows:

> If to Seller or Shareholders, to:
>
> _____
>
> _____
>
> _____
>
> Attn: _____
>
> with a copy to:
>
> _____
>
> _____
>
> _____
>
> Attn: _____
>
>
> If to Purchaser, to:
>
> _____
>
> _____
>
> _____
>
> Attn: _____
>
> with a copy to:
>
> _____
>
> Attn: _____

or to such other address as any party may designate by written notice to the other parties.

11.8 Further Assurances. Seller shall, from time to time, at the request of the Purchaser, and without further consideration, execute and deliver such other instruments and take such other actions as may be required to confer to the Purchaser and its assignees the benefits contemplated by this Agreement.

11.9 Entire Agreement. This Agreement (including its Exhibits and Disclosure Schedules) contains the complete and final expression of the entire agreement of the parties with respect to the subject matter of this Agreement and, except as otherwise expressly stated in this Agreement, supersedes and replaces any and all agreements, representations and understandings with respect to the subject matter of this Agreement. This Agreement may not be amended, modified, revoked, interpreted or waived orally, but only by means of a written document executed by the party against whom the amendment, modification or revocation is sought to be enforced. No party is entering into this Agreement in reliance on any oral or written promises, inducements, representations, understandings, interpretations or agreements other than those contained in this Agreement.

11.10 Headings. The section and other headings contained in this Agreement are for reference purposes only and shall not be deemed to be a part of this Agreement or to affect the meaning or interpretation of this Agreement.

11.11 Severability. The invalidity of all or any part of any section of this Agreement shall not render invalid the remainder of this Agreement or the remainder of such section, If any provision of this Agreement is so broad as to be unenforceable, such provision shall be interpreted to be only so broad as is enforceable.

11.12 Counterparts. This Agreement may be executed in any number of counterparts, each of which, when executed, shall be deemed to be an original and all of which together shall be deemed to be one and the same instrument.

11.13 Third Parties. Nothing in this Agreement, whether expressed or implied, is intended to confer any rights or remedies on any person other than the parties to this Agreement, nor is anything in this Agreement intended to relieve or discharge the obligation or liability of any third party, nor shall any provision give any third party any right of subrogation or action against any party to this Agreement.

11.14 Governing Law. This Agreement is made in and shall be governed and interpreted in accordance with the laws of the State of Washington without giving effect to their principles or provisions regarding choice of law or conflict of laws.

11.15 Jurisdiction and Venue. In the event of any litigation to enforce the provisions of this Agreement or recover damages for the breach of any provision of this Agreement, such litigation may be brought only in the Superior Court of Washington for _____ County or the United States District Court for the _____ District of Washington.

11.16 Gender and Number. Whenever appropriate to the meaning of this Agreement, use of the singular shall be deemed to refer to the plural and use of the plural to the singular, and pronouns of certain gender shall be deemed to comprehend either or both of the other genders.

11.17 Time of Essence. Time is of the essence of this Agreement.

DATED this _____ day of _____, _____.

SELLER: _____

By _____

Its _____

SHAREHOLDERS:

_____

_____

_____

PURCHASER: _____

By _____

Its _____

LIST OF EXHIBITS

1.1.1(a)   List of operating assets, furniture, fixtures, machinery, equipment, vehicles, computers, etc.

1.1.1(e)   List of trademarks, trade names, patents, copyrights and other intellectual property rights

1.1.1(i)   List of credits and deposits

1.1.1(k)   List of contracts and leases transferred to Purchaser

1.1.1(*l*)   List of permits, licenses and governmental approvals

1.1.2   List of Excluded Assets

1.2   List of assumed liabilities

2.1   Form of Note

2.2   Form of Security Agreement

2.5   Form of Escrow Agreement

DISCLOSURE SCHEDULES

4.3   Liens, encumbrances and charges

4.4   Real and personal property leases

4.5   Contracts, agreements and commitments

4.8   Financial Statements

4.9   Litigation

4.14   Certain changes or events

4.16   Environmental matters

4.17   Insurance policies

4.18   Employee benefits

4.19   Non-owned assets

Index

References are to Pages

S-T-U

†